THE
WINNING TRAINER
FOURTH EDITION

JULIUS E. EITINGTON

THE

WINNING TRAINER

FOURTH EDITION

WINNING

WAYS

TO

INVOLVE

PEOPLE

IN

LEARNING

An Imprint of Elsevier

Boston   Oxford   Auckland   Johannesburg   Melbourne   New Delhi

An Imprint of Elsevier

ℛ   A member of the Reed Elsevier group

Library of Congress Cataloging-in-Publication Data
Eitington, Julius E.
   The winning trainer: winning ways to involve people in learning /
Julius E. Eitington.—4th ed.
   p.   cm.
   Includes bibliographical references (p.) and index.
   ISBN 0-7506-7423-7
   1. Employees—Training of. 2. Problem solving—Study and teaching.
3. Organizational behavior. 4. Training. I. Title.

HF5549.5. T7 E38 2001
658.3'124--dc21   2001052433

British Library Cataloguing-in-Publication Data
A catalogue record for this book is available from the British Library.

The publisher offers special discounts on bulk orders of this book.
For information, please contact:

Manager of Special Sales
Butterworth–Heinemann
225 Wildwood Avenue
Woburn, MA 01801-2041
Tel: 781-904-2500
Fax: 781-904-2620

For information on all Butterworth-Heinemann publications available, contact our World Wide Web home page at: http://www.bh.com

10 9 8 7 6 5 4 3 2

Printed in the United States of America

Contents

Whatever you can do, or dream you can, begin it. Boldness has genius, power and magic in it.

—Johann Wolfgang von Goethe (1749–1832),
German poet and dramatist

work Effectively. Co-training: Some ABC's. Broadening the Trainer Base for Management Training. Vertical Training. How to Upgrade Your CQ (Credibility Quotient). Terminology for the Training Effort. Key Points. References. Recommended Reading.

22

Intelligence and Learning; Principles of Adult, Experiential, and Accelerated Learning   530

Intelligence and Learning—How Our Learners Process Information. Principles of Adult Learning. Principles of Experiential Learning. Principles of Accelerated Learning. References. Recommended Reading.

23

Distance Learning: Boon or Bane?   554

Distance Learning—Its Advantages and Forces Propelling It. What Distance Learning Looks Like (Formats). Web-Based Training—Four Major Formats. If You Embark on E-learning, Some Vital Issues to Consider. How to Maximize Your Use of Online Learning. Online Learning—Problems and Challenges. Limitations of E-learning. Key Points. References. Recommended Reading.

Preface to the Fourth Edition

EVERY trainer knows that the training field is a highly dynamic one. New ideas, new materials, and new techniques continually enrich the training function. I thus have attempted to capture in this new edition a good number of new concepts and techniques which should prove valuable to the trainer who is interested in involving his/her learners experientially.

As in the prior three editions, the new materials presented in this book have been gleaned from training literature and workshops, the experience and suggestions of various trainers, and my own continuing learning as a trainer/facilitator. The result is a work that is updated, enriched, and enlarged.

Significant new additions to the book include materials on these topics: new, easier-to-accomplish approaches to evaluation—ROE (Return on Expectations) and Customer Satisfaction as a business indicator; a methodology to secure group feedback at program's end concerning the trainer/facilitator's role/participation in the course; an instrument for early screening of likely obstacles to transfer of training; added techniques to ensure that our training "sticks" (transfers to the job); how to conduct a quick needs assessment when under pressure to do so; keys to successful training in other cultures; several new instruments, including how to assess one's prowess as a facilitator, how to assess trust in a team, and how to measure one's CQ (creativity quotient).

Two chapters have been added to treat new material on intelligence and learning, principles of adult learning, and distance learning. In addition, numerous new group-in-action techniques and conceptual materials have been added to the existing chapters.

I believe this fourth edition will be a worthwhile tool for the trainer/facilitator interested in new, dynamic concepts and techniques to assist in the delivery of high-quality, participative-type training. As for previous editions, your reactions to and suggestions for improvement of this work are very welcome.

Julius E. Eitington

Introduction

Learning is not a spectator sport.

—Anonymous
(The author wishes he
had said it.)

WINNING trainers are not only "on the ball," "they get it rolling." Winning trainers get results in the form of measurable learning achievements among the individuals and groups with whom they work—greater retention, better on-the-job application, and increased learner interest. They also have this in common: They have mastered the use, and they know the importance of, *participative training methods.*

The reasons trainers* should be concerned with participative training methods are compelling:

☐ *Our understanding of the adult as a learner.* Authorities like Malcolm Knowles, Gordon Lippitt, Leonard Nadler, and many others have been telling us for years that the adult learner wants to be involved, wants to participate, wants to be treated with respect and dignity, and wants to be challenged. Conversely, he or she does not want merely to sit and listen, to take notes, to struggle with exams, to be talked down to, to be bored, or to be bombarded with theory without opportunities for practical application.

☐ *Trends in society at large.* There is a significant and unwavering trend in society of people making demands for "a piece of the action." This is true of minorities, women, students, voters, consumers, parents, taxpayers, and other identifiable groups. Certainly today's higher educational levels and a stronger sense of independence among employees are triggering these demands.

Underpinning these requirements for participation, too, is an evolving humanistic philosophy, worldwide, which sees human beings as uniquely capable of personal and collective growth, self-determination, and transformation.

☐ *Trends in organizations.* Organizations of all sorts—business, industry, government, the military, volunteer organizations—have been moving gradually toward various forms of participative management. Indications of this trend include the Scanlon Plan, human relations training, management-by-objectives systems, job enrichment plans, suggestion plans, organization development programs, quality-of-worklife programs, and quality circles. These activities reflect a recognition that employees have needs and values that relate to self-control, self-determination, self-development, meaningful work, and other, related forms of self-actualization.

Trainer is used throughout the book to cover instructors, facilitators, teachers, conference leaders, etc., in all kinds of training/class/discussion room settings where participative methods are employed.

☐ *Training trends.* Although the use of participative methods in training was becoming noticeable in World War II and certainly existed to some degree before that time, this kind of training emphasis really reached a high point with the birth of the T-group (sensitivity training) in 1947. The T-group, of course, is dedicated totally to learner participation. In addition to laboratory education, many new participative training techniques were being invented in the 1940's and 1950's and thereafter, including brainstorming and other forms of group problem-solving and group decision-making techniques. Also, a whole host of training programs that involved participants to very high degrees via group-in-action methods, including the Managerial Grid®, creative thinking, transactional analysis, assertiveness training, stress management, conflict resolution, and the human potential movement, were being developed.

☐ *Brain research.* Recent research about the right and left brain has revealed that people are not only logical and rational (left-brain thinking) but also have the capacity to be spontaneous and creative (right-brain thinking). Certainly, participation provides one with the opportunity to use the right hemisphere of the brain to a significant degree.

WHY THIS BOOK?

This is a book about how to make things happen in your training activity; how to make training come alive for your participants; how to involve your learners fully and actively in the *learning process.* So while this book presents many dynamic and involving methods and techniques for the trainer to use, its purpose is to help learners learn with greater depth and retention and with less pain and more fun.

Methods are what make the training activity hum (as opposed to a response of "ho-hum"). Methods are akin to the engine in the Mercedes, the sparkle in the champagne, the pitching in a baseball game, and the characters in a novel. But this book is not merely about participative training methods. Although it does catalog and describe many of them, it goes much far-

ther. That is to say, it endeavors to be practical in these ways:

1. It presents numerous thought-stimulating examples of what the trainer might do in using participative training methods.

2. It shows how to *use*—and use effectively—the techniques presented, be they in-baskets, role plays, case studies, games, brainstorming, or other methods.

3. It shows how to *design* or construct various training activities, such as instruments, games, role plays, diaries, and application-type exercises.

This book is a veritable "how-to" in the realm of participative training methods. Books on training typically do not provide this type of aid to the trainer, since they cover the total spectrum of the training function. Methods and techniques thus tend to receive relatively short shrift, being sandwiched in with many other training topics.

A second way to use this book is to treat it as a reference work or source book. Thus, when designing a training program, the trainer might refer to it to be certain that a good range of participative methods is being employed. As trainers, we tend to develop fairly constant approaches to training design. Hence our methodologies may reflect the tried-and-true more than the exciting and the new. This approach obviously entails a certain amount of risk-taking. But if we've never used a fishbowl, fantasy, or metaphor, these methods may merit a try. For how else can we broaden our repertoire and thus enliven our training offerings?

Those who are conducting "train the trainer" courses for instructors, discussion leaders, teachers, facilitators, trainers, curriculum designers, and others will certainly find this work useful in acquainting them with the wide variety of participative techniques available.

Our emphasis is on participative, involving, dynamic methods. That is to say, we approach methods primarily from the standpoint of experiential, interactive, discovery, or action learning. This is not to say that classroom methods of a one-way communication sort—lectures, films, slide talks, panel presentation—do not have value. In fact, imaginative ways to use lectures and films so that participation is enhanced and learning is more likely to take place are suggested in the book. But the bias of the book is that a tremendous amount of worthwhile learning can take place without reliance on traditional, one-way communication approaches. Thus, no attempt is made to provide instruction on how to give better talks or how to use the overhead projector properly, so that one becomes a better platform person. Also, since the book is group-in-action oriented, it does not concern itself with self-instruction methods such as programmed learning, interactive video (tape or disc), or computer-assisted instruction (CAI). These methods obviously have their place when very practical skill development and/or knowledge acquisition is desired.

METHODS AND THE TRAINING CYCLE

The classic four-step model of the training cycle can help put the book into proper perspective. I have used four "D's" for mnemonic purposes, but the ideas are standard.

Diagnose or determine need. Here we are looking for difficulties (problems), deficiencies, or new developments that indicate that a training effort is in order.

Design or develop the program. Based on the identified needs, we plan and design a course or program to meet that need.

Deliver or present the training in the most effective way possible. Training methods are the most important aspect of this part of the cycle.

Discern differences or measure results of the training. Our question is this: Has the training made a difference in

☐ Knowledge
☐ Skill (behavior, performance)
☐ Attitude

Performance may relate to individual, group, intergroup, or organizational accomplishment. The term most commonly used to describe this step is "evaluation."

This book primarily covers methods that relate to the delivery of the training. However, the other three steps—diagnose, design, and discern differences (evaluation)—have also been treated, though in much lesser detail, to point out that participative techniques can and should be used in these steps as well.

We should also make it clear that the book deals solely with methods used in the formal training situation (classroom). Obviously, certain training needs may be met more properly with informal methods such as on-the-job training, performance aids, or self-development (for example, membership in a Toastmaster's Club). This book does not treat the area of informal training methods.

HOW TO USE THIS BOOK

The book's organization reflects my group-in-action bias—thus the more participative, experiential methods appear in the chapters at the beginning of the book, and the less involving methods (case study, film, and lecture) appear at the end. Chapter 21 is concerned with various participative training issues rather than with techniques or methods per se.

The Training Cycle

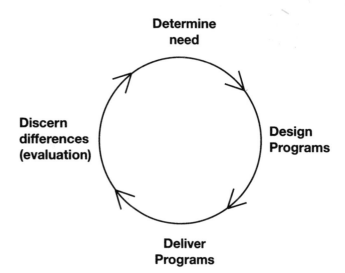

The obvious way to benefit from this book is to read it through carefully to learn of the great potential for the application of participative training methods. However, if you are already familiar with brainstorming, small group work, icebreakers, or other material covered here, there is no reason why you should not skim those particular pages and move ahead to less familiar material.

SOURCES

The idea for this book came from my experiences as a training director in government (the National Park Service, Washington, D.C.) and private industry (BNA Communications, Inc., Rockville, Maryland); as the conductor of workshops on management development for the graduate school of the U.S. Department of Agriculture; as a T-group trainer working closely with highly skilled trainers from the National Training Laboratories Institute of the Behavioral Sciences, Arlington, Virginia; and as a conductor of the course on public administration for the George Washington University and of a special management course for Indonesian students sponsored by Indiana University. In addition, my wife, Norma Jo Eitington—a teacher, educator, and counselor with teaching and training experience at elementary, high school, college, and graduate school levels—was a major influence on this book.

The material for this volume came from various sources: conferences, workshops, meetings of professional societies, periodicals, books, colleagues, and personal experience. To the extent that it has been practicable, credit has been given to the sources of particular techniques, methods, and concepts. Obviously, some material has crept into my repertoire over the years for which credit to the originator cannot be given. This I regret; I can only hope that the creator of a particular technique or concept will feel pleased that his or her idea is being shared further with other training practitioners.

AND FINALLY . . .

My goal or hope for this book is best expressed by the following Zen parable:

It seems that two Zen monks were having a heated discussion, which produced these statements:

"No, it is the *flag* that is moving."

"No, it is the *wind* that is moving."

A third monk came on to the scene and, hearing the debate, intervened with these statements:

"Brothers, listen to me. *No*, it is not the banner that is moving. *No*, it is not the wind that is moving. Yes, it is your *minds* that are moving."

So my hope for this book is that you will not merely page through the scores of techniques that are presented. Rather, I hope that the ideas that are treated will stimulate your mind to think constantly in terms of techniques and methods. You will thereby be alerted to look for other ones and to create many new ones yourself!

Acknowledgments

AUTHORS typically receive the kudos for the final version of a book. But others, behind the scenes, quietly transform a raw manuscript into the finished product. The author thus wishes to acknowledge the assistance of the following individuals who aided immeasurably in getting the manuscript into its finished form:

Dr. Leonard Nadler, Professor Emeritus, Human Resource Development and Adult Education, George Washington University, who patiently reviewed and critiqued the entire manuscript for the first edition from a professional standpoint. His constant review made for a significantly better final product.

Dr. Norma Jo Eitington, formerly Director of Learning Services, Georgetown University, and the author's spouse, who provided invaluable critique and general assistance for the four editions. She merits a good deal of credit for making the initial work and the three revisions possible.

How to Start Things Off

When we give our creative being its proper place in our lives, we have a sense of meaningfulness and purposefulness. The moment we touch upon this wellspring of life a change takes place in our personality. That is the moment of breakthrough.

—Pir Vilayat Inayat Khan, head of the
Sufi Order in the West, speaker and author on
science, mysticism, and holistic health

Only that day dawns to which we are awake.

—Henry David Thoreau
(1817–1862), U.S. naturalist,
philosopher, and writer

SUPPOSE you could, through some magical gift, tune in on the thoughts and shared conversations of the participants who are about to enter one of your training programs. Intriguing? Or frightening, perhaps?

Assuming you could tune in on their wavelengths, you might hear thoughts and statements such as these:

"I wonder if I made the right decision in coming here."
"I bet it's the same old stuff."
"It looks like I don't know any one here at all."
"I hope I can pick up all this stuff they'll probably throw at me."
"I wonder what these other people are like."
"If my boss hadn't insisted I come, I sure wouldn't be here. No way."
"I hope the lectures won't be too dull."
"I'm sure they'll tell us they want questions. I wonder if they mean it? How candid can I really be here?"
"Will I look good in this group?"
"Will the trainers be nice or just the usual smart alecs? I certainly hope they don't treat us like we're still in the fourth grade."

If these thoughts are realistic, may we, then, pose the following questions to you: How do you start your training programs? Do you begin conventionally by getting all the announcements out of the way? ("I have been asked to announce that the painters will be moving their equipment into the training room at 3:45 P.M.") Do you button down the usual "administrivia" concerning coffee breaks, starting and quitting time, the location of the rest rooms, and the nature of the luncheon menu? Do you launch things with an account of the history of this program? Do you crisply list (or worse, read) the program objectives? Do you zip into Session One in high gear so everyone knows you mean business? Do you introduce people to one another? Do you distinguish between icebreakers and openers? Do you use more than one icebreaker or opener? If you use one of these or another procedure, what is your training rationale for it? Have you reflected on that at all? Have you discussed it with a colleague or subordinate? Or have you merely acted out of habit?

Both icebreakers and openers are start-up activities that help participants ease into the program. Icebreakers are relatively subject-matter free, whereas openers relate directly to the content (subject matter) of the session, course, or program. Thus, if everyone knows one another, icebreakers may not be necessary. But regardless of the participants' prior acquaintances with one another, an opener would seem to be quite desirable in any program.

Basically you can start a training program in only one of two ways:

1. By introducing the participant group to the content at the outset.
2. By easing the group into things before directly involving them in the subject matter.

Regardless of which start-up procedure you use, you should recognize that your approach to the opening of the program communicates the following loud and clear:

☐ Your philosophy of learning
☐ Your style of training
☐ Your attitudes toward the participants as learners
☐ Your anxiety level

In other words, your first communication effort, whether you have reflected on it or are conscious of it, is immediately creating attitudes toward you and your program. Why? Because a basic principle of communication is that all behavior with others is perceived (subject to the perception of others). Behavior does not take place in a vacuum. Rather, it is observed, sifted, weighed, interpreted, and given meaning by those who experience it. The meaning may not be the one we intend, but it registers its impact, nevertheless.

Hence the need to make certain that the opening of your program communicates what you really want it to. I think it is far more important to provide the right communication about ourselves and our program in the first hour than it is to bombard participants immediately with the course material per se.

A well-thought-out, professional training effort should give full attention to icebreaking and/or opening activities because they

☐ Warm up (energize) the participants and thus put them at ease; learning proceeds best when the learners are ready to learn.
☐ Set the tone for the program and indicate whether the program will be participative, sit-and-listen, or some mixture of these approaches to learning.
☐ Indicate who has responsibility for learning. You want to communicate that the trainer is a facilitator and that only the participant can assume responsibility for what is learned.
☐ Communicate immediately the kind of trainer you are—relaxed or compulsive, friendly or distant, super-sober or fun to be with, subject matter or participant oriented.
☐ May provide later linkage with a particular topic or session; for example, an icebreaker that deals with values can serve as a bridge to such topics as motivation, career planning, management philosophy, and leadership style.

PLANNING THE USE OF ICEBREAKERS AND OPENERS

If you are convinced that icebreakers and openers have real merit, you will undoubtedly want to plan them properly. This means you should select ones based on such factors as

- ☐ Composition of the group
- ☐ Expectations of the group
- ☐ Nature of the program
- ☐ Length of the program
- ☐ Culture of the sponsoring organization
- ☐ Style and personality of the trainer(s)

The nature or composition of the group will obviously influence your choice of start-up activities. For example, if your participants are mental health professionals, they will probably be comfortable with activities that stress movement, fantasy, sharing of personal information, etc. Conversely, if your learners are blue-collar foremen with strong rural roots and limited communication skills, you would be well advised to avoid novel and threatening icebreakers, which might have boomerang effects.

Group expectations of their role in the learning process will also influence how active and involving your icebreakers or openers will be.

Program content will determine what icebreakers or openers will be used; for example, in a free-wheeling, experiential management development program in a cultural island setting, novel warmer-uppers would be quite appropriate. But a sales program, particularly one conducted in corporate headquarters, would probably put a damper on anything that might be perceived as "too far out."

Program length should be considered, too. A program that runs a full week could easily absorb 30–60 minutes of icebreaking and/or opening activity. The three-hour program, in contrast, may only be able to spare five or ten minutes for warm-up time.

The culture of the organization is another factor influencing the choice of icebreakers and openers. Attempts at innovation, fun, and excitement have to be tempered with what the culture will bear. As one trainer who experienced a trust walk (see page 5) for the first time in a workshop I conducted said, "I like this technique, but I'm not sure I could explain it to my boss's satisfaction should he happen to walk into the classroom while the activity was in progress."

The style and personality of the trainer will (and should) influence the choice of icebreakers and openers.

If you are comfortable with start-up activities that involve the group in novel, experiential ways, though they may take time from the formal program and reduce your control over the group or the subject matter, then you should explore the wide variety of such activities that are available. But if you are concerned about matters of control, getting started, relevance, and so on, the choice of icebreakers and openers had best be limited to conventional, very brief devices.

One trainer offers a checklist to test the appropriateness of your proposed icebreaker [1]:

- ☐ Is there a possibility the activity could build barriers rather than create rapport?
- ☐ Is there a possibility that the participants might experience failure in involving themselves in the task?
- ☐ Could it provoke embarrassment, especially for those who are introverted to varying degrees?
- ☐ Would it be desirable to build more trust before asking for this type of participation?
- ☐ Could the end result be accomplished with less threatening procedures?
- ☐ Is this icebreaker one that I like to do, but one that is not appropriate for other learning styles or personality types?
- ☐ Would it make sense to query a more conservative associate to assess the activity, so as to check his/her reaction?

The following pages present a range of icebreakers and openers. Regard them as one would food in a cafeteria—select only those items that make sense to you, fit into your overall program, and present no threat to those exposed to your fare.

WORKING WITH ICEBREAKERS

Although a training group composed of participants who know one another quite well may not require icebreaking activities, groups of strangers can certainly profit from them. Trainers, all too typically, merely warm up their groups via various introduction-type procedures. For example: "Let's go around the room and tell our name, job title, organization, and why we're here." This ritual may have some value, but it all too often becomes meaningless because the required responses are inaudible and group members do not listen to or are bored by the routine involved. This is particularly true if the introductions are offered by 12 or more people.

Another problem is that participants may have needs more significant than merely learning other participants' names and job titles. Since the odds are that the usual introductions won't do much for the participants, it is essential to use more dynamic, experiential activities (icebreakers) for warm-up purposes. The group will benefit for several reasons:

☐ Icebreakers allow participants to become acquainted with one another in a more meaningful way; that is, glimpses into attitudes, values, aspects of personality, and concerns become possible.

☐ A start can be made on overcoming possible feelings of loneliness, and icebreakers certainly help to involve shy people.

☐ They help to relax the group and make people more spontaneous. By engaging in meaningful, often fun-type activities, participants can feel reduced anxieties and tensions.

☐ They set a climate, tone, and pace for the program, particularly if it is to be a participative one.

☐ They help to build momentum for the next phase of the program.

☐ They achieve the instant involvement of everyone.

☐ They help to build group identity and group cohesiveness.

☐ They assist in developing trust among participants and with the trainer as well.

☐ They help participants learn about the resources of the group.

☐ They help energize the group. To the extent that participants are permitted to engage early on in activities that are marked by movement, standing up, meaningful sharing, fun, novelty, and the like, they are put into an alert, stimulated, and motivated state.

☐ They help to develop the credibility of the trainer as a facilitator, not a leader or a lecturer.

☐ They give the trainer a feel for the group—are the members open to new experiences, fun-loving,

nondefensive or cautious, super-sober, rigid? These data can provide indicators as to how active and free-wheeling your later exercises and games should be.

☐ Finally, icebreakers can help to reduce the anxieties of the trainer, who is a human being, too! Since the interaction puts the participants more at ease, in a circular and contagious way it reaches the trainer as well.

Examples of Icebreakers

The following icebreakers are simple to understand and easy to administer. They can be used singly, or several may be used depending upon course objectives, the nature of the group, available time, etc. Additional icebreakers are described in Chapter 15 under "Movement."

Interviews for Creative Introductions

When participants are strangers, have them:

1. Meet in pairs.
2. Interview one another for five minutes or so.
3. Introduce each other, stating to the group at large: the partner's job, something interesting or different about the person, and the partner's expectations from the course. (A variation of this step is to have each pair join another pair and make introductions in and from the quartets.)

Note: If the total group is large (20–30 persons), there is little point in feeding back the data from the pairs to everyone else since it is time-consuming and little will be remembered anyway. In such a case, limiting the introductions internally to the quartets is much more practicable.

My Personal Shield [2]

In a shield segmented into six boxes, have participants respond to the following list:

1. The best time I ever had
2. My greatest accomplishment
3. My most prized possession

4. What I would do if I had one year to live
5. The two descriptive words I would most want on my tombstone
6. The two descriptive words I would least want on my tombstone

Participants then stand and meet in pairs to discuss their shields for about five minutes. The procedure may be repeated with a new partner.

Trust (Blind) Walk

In pairs, one person whose eyes are closed is led by the other. The leaders are instructed to make the trip as interesting as possible and to ensure no harm befalls the followers.

Note: I usually introduce this icebreaker by relating it to the importance of participation: "We want active participation and questioning of what is said or done, but willingness to participate depends upon trust. So to symbolize the importance of trust, let's hold a trust walk." The trust walk is then explained and the participants are encouraged to participate in this activity, but their participation is totally voluntary.

For specific instructions to participants concerning the administration of the trust walk, see the section "Movement" in Chapter 15.

Values Assessment—Consensus

A good way to achieve instant interaction is to provide participants with a list of ten values, such as the following:

☐ A satisfying family life
☐ Job success
☐ Having fun, excitement, adventure
☐ Satisfying friendships
☐ Personal growth
☐ Being a good neighbor
☐ Financial achievement
☐ Community contribution
☐ Health
☐ Professional achievement

Then give the participants five minutes by themselves to drop three of the values. Participants then meet in small groups for about ten minutes to agree on the seven most significant values.

Note: It may be anticipated that some groups will have difficulty agreeing. This is not of great consequence. What is important is that the participants have an opportunity to get to know one another on more than a surface basis.

Values Billboard

Give participants a list of values (on flipchart) that are to be prioritized by them. Participants then mill around, find a partner, and discuss their lists. The list can be written on letter-size paper or, preferably, on newsprint (flipcharts) with felt-tip pens. Typical values include: good citizenship, financial success, a good reputation, professional recognition, new experiences, good friends.

Cardswap

In advance of the opening session, prepare numerous 3" × 5" slips or cards (four or five per person) with terse statements relating to a given topic such as communication, leadership, values, personality characteristics, or management philosophy. Advise each participant to pick four cards randomly and then try to exchange their cards with other participants. The idea is to end up with four cards, if possible, that one finds totally acceptable.

Note:

1. Inevitably, some participants will have cards they can't trade off.
2. In preparing the cards, try to develop statements that have a range of opinions on a given topic. For example, if the topic you select relates to personality, you may have statements such as these:

☐ I like everyone I meet.
☐ Integrity is paramount in a friend.
☐ New experiences are what I need most.
☐ I have a high tolerance for ambiguity.
☐ I am too creative to be a team member.
☐ I admire people who have self-discipline.

Know Your Sign

Post signs around the room bearing opposite personality traits, for example, adventuresome vs. cautious, theatrical vs. practical, industrious vs. fun-loving. Have participants select a sign with which they can identify and then discuss with others why they chose that particular sign.

Note: If some participants select a sign without any one else being there, they can elect to join another group with which adequate identification is possible.

Art Mart

Have each participant draw on a flipchart an illustration that describes a current problem he/she is having. The problem may be job, career, personal (family), or community related. The drawing may be either symbolic or directly representational. Then have participants find partners to get help on "improving" the art work.

Puzzle Fun

Present participants with a puzzle, which they are to solve in small groups of three to five persons. The following is an example of such a puzzle:

> A farmer, on his death, left his three sons a herd of 17 cows with instructions that the oldest was to get one-half of them, the middle son one-third, and the youngest one-ninth. (Solution: Since 17 is not divisible by those fractions, they decided to seek out a wise old woman on the mountain top. She quickly solved their problem by giving them one of *her* cows. They then made the division of the herd into groups of nine, six, and two, respectively. They were very pleased. After the division, she took her cow back, since they no longer needed it!)

Nicknames

Have participants in small groups discuss their nicknames considering: where they were acquired, when they were acquired, when and if they were lost, and one's feelings (like or dislike) about them. If time allows, select new partners to discuss sources for nick names. Some sources that might be considered include diminutives from regular names (Jimmy, Fran); physical appearance (Shorty, Red); personality (Smiley, Grump); last name influence (Mac from McDonald, Rusty—last name Irons); geography (Tex, Klondike); parental influence (Sis, Buster); occupation (Doc, Prof); and self-adopted nicknames.

Note:

1. In lieu of sharing feelings about nicknames, participants may discuss their given names. Do you like it? Why or why not? Is it a family tradition? Would you like to trade it for another one? Did your name influence your choice of names for your children?

2. The sharing may take place in a pair rather than in a group.

3. Alter the sharing of data about nicknames/first names, participants may report back to the total group something they learned about their partner(s).

Hobby Hunt

Provide each participant with a list of 15–20 popular hobbies (for example, gardening, movies, jogging, crocheting, golf). (See Appendix 1.) Then give participants seven minutes or so to locate other participants who have these hobbies, writing their name and organizational affiliation on the worksheet.

Early Grades

In small groups, ask each participant to think about and report on an experience they recall in grades 1 through 5. Conclude the activity by asking for volunteers to share their experiences with the group at large.

Shoe In

Ask participants to identify themselves with a shoe: "If I were a shoe I would be a _____." Possible answers are soft shoe (a gentleperson), boot (a tough person), sneaker, gym shoe (for a highly active person), football shoe (or any shoe with cleats or spikes, symbolizing a person who may run rough-shod over others).

Note: This activity should be reserved for an experiential training program where less conventional, more personalized activities are expected.

Preferences

Pass out a worksheet listing categories that participants may have preferences in, such as a favorite food, color, movie actor, sport, or world city. (See Appendix 2.) After participants have written a preference for each listing, have them share their preferences with another person or small group. The sharing may be repeated with a new person or small group.

Self-Descriptors

To help participants get acquainted in an active and novel way, have them stand, move around the room, and introduce themselves, giving first name, two adjectives about themselves, and a quick handshake. *Examples:* "Hi, I'm Fran, and I'm fun-loving and sensitive." "Hello, I'm Pat, and I'm helpful and courteous." *Note:* Suggest that the participants use different adjectives with each new introduction.

Me: Yesterday, Today, and Tomorrow

Have participants draw a figure with three segments, such as a coat of arms or a geometric design, as in Figure 1-1. Then have them label the segments "Yesterday," "Today," and "Tomorrow," or "Past," "Present," and "Future." The participants then enter the appropriate data for each segment and process the data in pairs.

Note: To process data means to share/exchange one's completed work, to comment on or possibly critique one another's work, and to provide support/positive reinforcement to the extent possible about the other's work.

Team Icebreaker

Assign participants randomly to groups of four or five. Provide them with a list of everyday sayings or cliches in the workplace and ask them to convert them into more sophisticated language. Tell them to be as creative as possible. *Examples:*

Usual Statements	Revised, fun-type, "fancy" statements
☐ Get on the ball	☐ Climb aboard the spheroid
☐ Play it by ear	☐ Execute via the aural cavity
☐ Work as a team	☐ Perform as an amalgamated entity
☐ Put the shoulder to the wheel	
☐ Call him/her on the carpet	
☐ No sweat	
☐ Let's not pour oil on troubled waters	
☐ He/she can't cut the mustard	
☐ Let's put no one on the spot	
☐ Sweep it under the rug	

Then ask for "solutions" from the teams. (Anticipate friendly vying as to which team was more creative.)

Group Creation

In small groups, participants design a worthwhile icebreaker activity. The total group then selects one

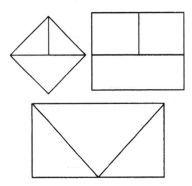

Figure 1-1. Examples of geometric designs participants might draw for use in the icebreaker *Me: Yesterday, Today, and Tomorrow.*

approach from all the ideas and uses it as their next activity.

Note: It may be desirable to provide a warm-up activity to stimulate creativity as a prelude to this exercise, particularly for groups not oriented along these lines.

Distraction Banishment

On the assumption that participants often bring various outside concerns to the training situation, this activity may help eliminate the participants' awareness of them. Pass out the worksheet in Appendix 3, which explains to participants what they should do.

Note: Participants generally discard the envelopes when they are returned to them, for they have no meaning at program's end.

Name Cards

Have participants write their first name or nickname at the top of a name card. They should then write descriptive terms beginning with each letter of their name as in Figure 1-2.

Note: A dictionary will quite readily trigger ideas if participants are having trouble.

As an icebreaking activity, have participants form pairs or triads to share their data about themselves.

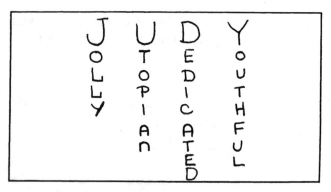

Figure 1-2. An example of a name card used as an icebreaker.

Wallet Waggery

Working in a small group, have each participant take three things from his/her wallet or purse. The others then try to decide what they tell about the person.

The following four added icebreakers are offered by training consultant Bart A. Berry [3]:

"One Thing About Me . . ."

Ask your people to stand up and form a circle, each person standing shoulder to shoulder. Explain that the purpose of this strange formation is to help us learn who is who, "who we're dealing with today." Ask one person to "start us off" by giving his/her name, nickname or name he/she wants to be called while in this session, and where he/she is from. Have each participant complete this sentence: "One thing about me that makes me a (good manager, good engineer, effective team player) is . . ."

Added ground rules:

1. The speaker must maintain good eye contact with the others while speaking.
2. The group renders applause to each presenter when he/she finishes.

The Gordian Knot

This is a somewhat physical activity. Again, in a circle, have each person grab the hands of two others not standing next to him/her. The result: an awkward, hilarious tangle.

Then have the participants try to untangle themselves without breaking the connections between hands. (Anticipate one large circle or two or three interconnected ones.) A guarantee: certain to bring most groups together.

Make a List

Have participants interview one another to learn of their favorite sports, vacation spots, books, sports teams. The data is then reported back to the total group.

A variation: "Two Truths and a Lie." Each person lists aloud three significant accomplishments in his/her life that the group is unfamiliar with, including a fictitious one. The group then tries to guess which one is false.

Two Truths and a Lie

Procedure: Ask your participants to stand up and form a circle.

Task:

1. Ask participants to think of "two truths and a lie" about themselves.

2. Select one participant to share that personal data.

3. Ask the participant to the right of the data presenter to guess "the truth."

4. If the truth is not revealed about the first respondent, let the participant to the presenter's right offer his/her personal data—two truths and a lie, again.

5. Continue around the circle until all have offered their data and the truth is uncovered about everyone.

Note: Keep the group small, maximum of 12 participants. If you have a larger group, divide participants into two or three standing groups, all operating in their circle simultaneously. (The "buzz" from the extra group(s) will add to the liveliness of the activity.)

Out of Sight

An experiential, problem-solving activity is as follows: Blindfold a group of 15 people maximum and then have them work to build something, for example, the firm's logo out of blocks or rope, or a special geometrical figure such as a square, triangle, or parallelogram. Anticipate behavior relating to leadership, communication, roles taken, etc. Within the time available, let the group process (discuss) these behaviors.

Test for Traits

Present each member of your group of strangers with the following list of nonsignificant characteristics or traits. Their task is to find someone who has that particular trait. The first one who does receives a prize of some sort, possibly a three-dollar bill or a year's supply of white eggplant.

Note: If someone should actually locate a person with a particular trait as listed below, in just a short time, you may wish to provide another icebreaker.

The Trivial Traits

- ☐ A person who drinks spinach juice.
- ☐ One who owns a 16-year-old car.
- ☐ A vegetarian who makes his/her own veggie burgers.

- ☐ Someone who pulls the labels out of his new shirts or her blouses.
- ☐ A person who has three dogs (for an Arctic three-dog night).
- ☐ An individual who has been on flex-time for five years or more.
- ☐ A person who has 60,000 miles or more on his/her current set of tires.
- ☐ An individual who drinks the recommended eight glasses of water per day.
- ☐ An individual who commutes to and from work, 37 miles or more each way.
- ☐ A person who prepares his/her own fish burgers for barbecuing.
- ☐ A chairperson of his/her church's membership committee.
- ☐ A person who does not own a color TV.
- ☐ A person who has a foot control for the garbage can in his/her kitchen.
- ☐ A person who has a home office and regularly receives a tax deduction for it.
- ☐ A person who teaches Saturday A.M. courses at his/her local college or university.
- ☐ A person who is a fancier of green bananas.

Card Circle

With a group of 10–12 participants, form a stand-up circle and give each person a 5" × 8" card that asks the participant to

1. "Introduce yourself"
2. "Respond to the question on your card"

For instruction 1, the trainer may wish to set the guidelines on the card as to the nature and extent of the introduction (for example, name, job title, organization, expectations from the course, any prior similar training).

For instruction 2, to heighten interest, each card should have a different question. Typical questions follow:

- ☐ What educational experience was most influential (helpful) in getting you into your current job?
- ☐ What is your organization's greatest challenge today?

☐ What is the most significant quality (skill, trait) for a . . . (manager, engineer, financial person, etc.)?

☐ What is your greatest job accomplishment to date?

☐ How important are athletics/sports in your life?

☐ How do you feel about vegetarianism?

☐ If you could change your work team back home, in what area or in what respect would it be?

☐ What is the best vacation you've ever had?

☐ What is the most important ingredient in team effectiveness?

☐ When buying a new car, to what extent do you investigate its safety features?

☐ How important is fruit in your daily diet?

☐ Assuming you encounter a stressful condition/event now and then, how do you cope with it?

☐ What is your boss's best skill? Why do you regard it as "best"?

☐ How important are pets in your life? Explain your response whether or not you are a pet owner.

Note: The above 14 questions may be used as is, amended in any way you deem appropriate, or replaced by others that may be more appropriate.

Nuts and Bolts

Assume that you have a large group of 100 participants. Assume further that you want to split the participants into ten groups of ten in a fun sort of way. A good way to do this is to buy in advance ten pairs each of five *differently sized* pairs of nuts and bolts so that you have one matching pair for each two participants. (*Note:* 10 × 5 = 50 matched pairs or 100 individual pieces.) Give everyone a nut or a bolt upon his/her entry into your training or meeting room. When everyone is seated, ask them to rise and find a match to their nut or bolt. This produces a lot of hilarity, movement, and touching. In about 15 minutes, everyone has mated his/her piece of hardware and ten groups of ten persons each are readily formed [4].

Shyness Counteractant

If you have a shy or reluctant participant group, e.g., a class of welfare recipients being taught how to enter the world of work, loosen them up at the outset in this manner: Pass around a big bowl of M&Ms with this advisory: "Take as many as you want." Anticipate your trainees will help themselves to handfuls.

Now "drop the other shoe" and say: "For each M&M you took, please tell the class something about yourself."

Anticipate chuckles, groans, etc., but also a willingness to respond to the reward.

Significance: The activity underscores the principle that everyone has to become committed and involved [5].

The "No-Brainer"

For an icebreaker that's simple, easy, and nonthreatening, and certain to loosen people up, go around the circle or table and ask everyone to respond to the following everyday questions, or supply similar ones of your own:

Non–Work-Related Questions

☐ What is the most important thing to think about when you plan a vacation?

☐ What makes for an ideal weekend?

☐ What is your favorite spectator sport? Why?

☐ What is your best advice to anyone considering the purchase of a home?

☐ What was your greatest learning from your academic work (high school, college)?

Work-Related Questions

☐ What was your first paid job, and did it bear on your career in any way?

☐ Think of the best boss you ever had. What made him/her "the best"?

☐ What gives you the most satisfaction from your current job?

☐ What one quality is most important in being a "good" subordinate?

Suggestion: You may wish to ask a question or two from the first grouping and then select one or two from the second grouping. Or, depending on the nature of your participant group, use all questions of one grouping rather than the other one.

Significant Sharing

Form a circle, everyone standing; now ask participants to share with the total group three significant things about themselves. Say: "The idea is to provide a meaningful portrait of yourself that tells everyone the meaning of you. Not that you have a BMW, a dog, and three children. But that you are a person who is concerned, is goal oriented, has real values, has real likes and dislikes, is attractive to others because of certain attributes, attitudes, or behaviors, O.K.? We'll give you ten minutes for this." Ask for comments from the group after activity's end.

Trust Stroke

This activity is designed for use in an experiential program where participants are strangers to one another.

Procedure:

1. Ask participants to form pairs. If you have mixed group as to gender, team participants on a male-female basis.
2. Ask participants, now partners, to designate themselves a No. 1 and No. 2.
3. Ask partner No. 2 to close his/her eyes.
4. Ask partner No. 1 to stroke the face of partner No. 2 for about three minutes.
5. Reverse the procedure, with partner No. 2 now stroking No. 1, again for about three minutes.
6. Call time after three minutes.
7. Process the activity with questions such as these: How did it feel at the outset? Later, at the end of the three minutes, did trust develop? Why or why not?

Note: Other icebreakers appear under "Movement," in Chapter 15.

Evaluating Icebreakers

The checklist shown in Figure 1-3 may be helpful in evaluating the suitability of an icebreaker. You may want to add to the checklist other elements that you find important.

Element	Low	Moderate	High
1. Time consumption			
2. Threat potential			
3. Possible group dissatisfaction (boomerang effect)			
4. Novelty			
5. Fun, excitement			
6. Creative quality			
7. Data Producing (learn about people)			
8. Relaxes people			

Figure 1-3. A checklist for evaluating icebreakers.

WORKING WITH OPENERS

Openers are tools to help participants ease into the subject matter of the course. They are intended to set the stage, to avoid abrupt starts, and generally to make participants comfortable with the formal program that they are about to experience. Unlike icebreakers, they are essentially subject-matter-related, work-oriented "preludes."

Openers may also provide the participants with the opportunity to express their reasons for coming and their goals and expectations about learning from the course or program [6]. If some of those objectives are quite different from yours and you proceed, unaware of that circumstance, you may encounter considerable difficulty—boredom, limited cooperation, argumentation, and possibly post-session complaints from the participants' bosses. Conversely, if you learn of this variance in goals/expectations early on, you can do one of several things:

1. State candidly (and regretfully) that a particular goal is outside the purview of this course.
2. Advise the participant that his/her special interest is covered in another (later) course.
3. Adjust the program to the extent possible.
4. If someone is really in the wrong ball park, ask if he/she wishes to leave. Why waste his/her time and have a disgruntled participant on your hands?

Note: At times your quest for participant expectations may unearth this added bit of useful datum: One or more participants may have been sent by their bosses and may not have any real interest in what you and the course are offering. If so, you may wish to make this type of statement to them: "I'm sorry that you were sent and you don't really want to be here. But perhaps we can make a contract that will be beneficial to all of us here. If you will try to be as patient and cooperative as you can, I will do my utmost to make this as worthwhile a training experience for you as I possibly can."

Some examples of activities that can set the stage in a substantive sense and give you ideas for creating your own openers follow:

Goal Analysis

Participants form small groups and tell the trainer their goals for the course. These goals are posted on a flipchart, and the trainer categorizes them as "R" (Realistic) or "U" (Unrealistic or Unattainable). After adding the trainer's own goals, all the posted goals are discussed. This is a means of involving both participants and trainers in planning the course and opening the communication process.

Individual Goals

In small groups, the participants declare their goals for the course or program and enter them on a flipchart. The individual goals are discussed in the small group for five to ten minutes; then the flipchart is posted on the wall. The trainer comments supportively on all goals as to relevancy, practicality, etc. The flipcharts can and should be referred to at various stages in the program.

A variation of this procedure is to have pairs discuss their goals for two minutes; the pairs merge with another pair to form quartets and buzz for four minutes; the quartets merge with another quartet (now octets) and buzz for eight minutes. The octets record their goals on flipcharts, the flipcharts are posted on the wall, and a recorder from each octet explains its goals. The trainer points out the similarities and divergencies of the stated goals.

Another variation of the goal-setting opener is to have each goal identified with its owner; for example, in a power negotiation session we may get a T-column on a flipchart such as this:

Participant Learning Goals	
Participant	**My Learning Goal**
Jo	Negotiate cutbacks
May	Get a raise
Hank	To learn the skill for everyday life
Edna	Get what I want from the boss
Frank	Do better in negotiations with a client
Bill	Selling change

Fears and Fantasies (Hopes and Fears)

Gather from the total group their fears of and hopes for the course and write them on the flipchart, using a T-column.

Note: This activity is particularly helpful if you sense that the participants have some concerns about the course or program.

Commitment Continuum

If you sense that several participants in your program are there reluctantly or have negative attitudes for other reasons (the boss sent them), a good way to deal directly and constructively with this circumstance is to use a 10-point continuum. Draw a horizontal line on the flipchart and number a scale on it from one to ten. Label one end "Dull, Terrible, Threatening" and label the other end "Great, Exciting." Then ask the group such questions as: Why are you here? Are you here voluntarily? Were you sent by your boss?

You can gather data for the continuum in one of two ways:

1. With your back to the participants (for anonymity) have them call out a number on the scale, which you then mark with a check.

2. Have participants enter their numbers on slips of paper, which another participant can collect and post on the scale.

If the data indicates a certain amount of disinterest, anxiety, etc., make this point: "Those of you who have doubts about or disinterest in the program because you were sent here or for other reasons, may I suggest you approach the session with this attitude:

'O.K., I'm not excited about being here, but now that I am here, what can I do to make it pay off? It just may be that by entering wholeheartedly into things, I may find the course worthwhile.' I'll do what I can, as a trainer, to help. But I can only be responsible for the general conduct of the program, not for your expectations or blocks. Incidentally, I'm more concerned about those 9's and 10's [assuming there are a few] than the 1's and 2's because the program may not come up to those high expectations."

Common Concerns Checklist

To provide your participants with the opportunity to express their feelings about the forthcoming course, trainer Cynthia H. Merman suggests the use of a checklist along the following lines [7]:

You are about to begin a course on ... Some thoughts may have occurred to you, such as those listed below. Please check those about which you have been thinking. You may wish to add other concerns not on the list below. We will hold a general discussion concerning participant responses to the checklist.

—Lectures will be boring.
—Discussions will ramble and drag on.
—Some people will monopolize the available airtime.
—Some material won't be covered.
—Breaks will be too short.
—Breaks will be too far apart.
—Too many overhead projector slides will be used.
—I don't expect anything new.
—I doubt if I'll fit into this group.
—We could cover this topic in less time.

Note to trainer:

1. You can use dyads, small groups, or the group-at-large for discussion of participant reactions.
2. You may wish to customize the introduction or the checklist itself in any way you deem beneficial.
3. You may wish to ask the trainees to number their choices in order of importance.
4. The discussion time may range from 5 to 20 minutes, depending on group size and the participants' need to express their concerns.

Inspiring the Uninspired

If your participants are highly timid and reluctant to open up, you can change the situation pretty quickly by having *each* participant answer four pointed questions. The queries, used by trainers/consultants Lawrence Myers and Yvonne Grewe of Team Associates, Inc., Tulsa, Oklahoma, are [8]:

1. How would you estimate the degree to which your fellow participants want to be here?
2. To what degree will they be willing to be candid about their concerns and feelings in this workshop?
3. How would you describe their willingness to adopt and be committed to the proposed changes?
4. To what degree are you confident that real change will result from our sessions?

The trainers then draw up a profile of the responses and try to deal with them. They feel very strongly that it is very important to work on resistance points and barriers to change at the very outset of the workshop.

Praise Parade

People thrive on praise and recognition because they are signs of caring by the grantor. Generally speaking, managers treat others as they themselves are treated. This exercise is designed to provide insight into the importance of receiving praise by letting managers become the recipients of it. Procedure [9]:

1. On Day One in a session on "The Power of Praise and Recognition," ask participants to jot down on paper two or three things they are proud of. Be sure they add their names to their papers.
2. Collect papers.
3. On Day Two, read the achievements aloud, by name, encouraging group applause after each reading.
4. After all papers have been read, ask participants how they felt about receiving the applause.
5. Ask people to talk about times they received public recognition for their work successes. (Note whether any recollections relate to

long-past incidents. People are likely to remember public praise even when it occurred five or ten years earlier.)

6. Ask: "Why are we so insane about not praising, when we know how motivating it is to be appreciated?"

Ventilating Feelings

Again, if you sense that participants may resent attendance or be reluctant to attend, you may ask them to do the following:

"In teams of two, talk for five minutes about (1) how you feel about attending this course: enthusiastic? confused? anxious? punished? resentful? neutral? and (2) why you feel this way." (The pairs generate their data as requested.)

"Now, please introduce your fellow team member, using the data he or she provided to you."

As a final step, you should summarize the attitudes expressed and indicate how they relate to the program. For example, a feeling that "there's little to learn about supervision after 22 years doing of it" may be countered with: "That's certainly a lot of experience. Perhaps you can help the rest of us profit from that rich experience. I'm sure, too, that in those 22 years you've learned that sometimes a new idea does come along the pike unexpectedly and maybe—just maybe—there may be one here for you. So why not give it a whirl? O.K.?"

Resentment Reducer

If you have a mandatory training course or program and you know your very reluctant attendees are seething with resentment about it, you may find it helpful to use the following tension-relieving energizer per trainer Allison Blankenship [10]:

1. Before your participants arrive, tape a seven- to nine-inch balloon (deflated) on each chair.

2. Begin your opening session with this question: "Is anyone here who doesn't want to be here or who feels stressed today?" (Anticipate a lot of smiles in response.)

3. Now state, "Please blow away all that stress or tension into your balloon. Keep blowing until all that nasty stress is exhaled." (As some balloons pop, anticipate some helpful laughter.)

4. Now say, "Please pinch the neck of your balloon with your fingers without tying a knot. Place the balloon over your head."

5. Announce, "I'm going to walk around the room now to check who has the most stress."

6. Final instruction to the group: "On the count of three, let go of your balloons." Anticipate much hilarity, which should help you to create the desired positive learning environment.

Pre-work

Assign a pertinent reading in advance of the first session. Have participants meet in groups of four or five for 15 minutes to discuss the reading. Each group then selects a spokesperson who reports back to the total group the reactions to the reading.

Hopes and Change

To elicit feelings about hopes for the program and attitudes toward personal change, have participants complete a form such as the ones in Appendices 4, 5, and 6. The completed form may be shared in a dyad (pair) or simply retained in the participant's notebook for a second completion and review on an individual basis at the end of the program.

Fishbowls

Using the group-on-group observation technique (see Chapter 4), have the group in the inner circle work on this task for 10–15 minutes: What do we hope to get out of this course (program, conference, session)? Then reverse the groups, the outer group responding to the same question and commenting on the comments of the first group. (Limit groups to six or eight participants. Two or three fishbowls can meet simultaneously, preferably in separate rooms.)

Geometrics

The following two exercises allow participants to express themselves graphically:

1. Have participants complete the worksheet in Appendix 7 in illustrative or graphic form.

Then have them share the worksheet with a partner.

2. Have participants draw a box with four quadrants and have them enter data about their job concerns and career aspirations as indicated. (See Appendix 8.) The graphic data should then be processed in small groups with everyone having a chance to play both the presenter and the helper role.

The rationale for the geometric framework is as follows:

- ☐ It aids in focusing upon specific areas which should be subject to introspection. Some people have difficulty entering into or concentrating on a given task.
- ☐ It is *a finite* request, which gives it an aura of reasonableness and manageability. (Contrast this procedure to a totally open-ended set of questions about one's career.)
- ☐ By juxtaposing the several queries in adjacent quadrants, their relatedness is highlighted.
- ☐ The novelty of the structured approach heightens interest in the task.
- ☐ For many participants, the desire to fill or complete all the boxes is a motivational force.

Tinker Toys

Using Tinker Toys (or other construction toys or materials), have participants (in small groups) construct something which symbolizes leadership, communication, organization, time management, expectations for this program, etc. (For example, to symbolize good or effective communication, a group might decide to construct a bridge.)

Quiz

Start things off with a pertinent, thought-provoking quiz on leadership, communication, safety, selling style, customer service attitudes, etc.

Think Sheets

An effective and provocative way to kick things off is to provide participants with a think sheet, which can later be discussed in small groups. (See Appendix 9 for an example of such a sheet.)

Dyadic Analysis

This is an opener to check listening skills prior to the start of the session that treats that subject.
Procedures:

1. Assign participants to dyads. Provide everyone with two profound questions:
   a. The U.S. government is preparing a time capsule for the nation's 300th birthday (2076). Which three of your personal possessions will you give them to include in it?
   b. As a child you probably had many toys. Which one is so vivid in your mind that you can describe it today?
2. Ask dyads to discuss and share the two questions (ten minutes).
3. Ask participants to examine and report to the total group who spoke first, how time was allotted, what was done when one was not speaking, and any noticeable nonverbal interaction.

Problem Census

Encourage the group to think about their problems as salespersons, managers, or whatever position they hold by conducting a problem census. The worksheet found in Appendix 10 instructs participants in the procedure for conducting the census.

The values of this procedure:

- ☐ You can learn of actual problems bugging your participants.
- ☐ You can work problems into the agenda as practicable.
- ☐ The census serves as a basis for program evaluation: Does the program actually provide help in resolving the participants' concerns?
- ☐ The census provides catharsis—a chance for the participants to get their concerns off their chest.
- ☐ It brings people together, and they get to know one another better at the outset.

Starting with a Game

An effective way of opening is to start with a subject-matter-relevant game. The advantages are that it can introduce pertinent ideas and concepts or stimulate thinking about them; it initiates lively discussion, which helps immediately set the desired atmosphere of intimacy and inquiry; and it provides early on a common fund of experience for everyone. It does all this in a novel, lively, and fun way, which helps to set a relaxed, friendly, and enthusiastic atmosphere.

Note: See Chapter 6 for ideas concerning the use of games.

Garnering Goodies

To start things off on a positive note, tell the participants: "We're going to spend seven to eight hours together today. What are the 'goodies' or rewards you might get out of this course?" Then ask them to draw a T-column on a sheet of paper and list on an individual basis personal goals and organizational goals.

Note: The idea is to emphasize that there are dual benefits, including personal ones. Many courses have dual benefits. For example, learning about safety, time management, communication, and problem solving can be used both on and off the job.

Have participants meet in small groups to discuss their T-columns, and then secure ideas from the small groups, posting them to a T-column on the flipchart. A long list of benefits of both types should encourage participant interest in the course.

Note: A variation is to team up participants on a special interest group basis; for example, in a time management course, small groups may be formed to discuss planning, delegation, telephone use, or use of secretary.

Learning Contracts

Have participants develop in writing one or more learning objectives that they pledge to work on in the course and thereafter. Process these learning contracts in small groups to add outside support for the commitment.

Introducing the Program

One way to help launch a program is to draw the diagram or model on a flipchart, as shown in Figure 1-4. Use this model to point out that

☐ The participants are a vital part of the learning
☐ The trainer is only one of four elements basic to goal accomplishment.

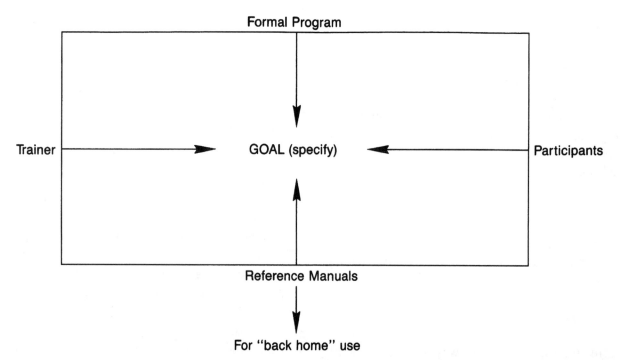

Figure 1-4. A model that may be used to explain the nature of the training program.

☐ The reference manuals are a tool for making learning a continuing process rather than a one-shot classroom event.

Note: After presenting this diagram, kick things off immediately with a participative opener.

Climate Setting

Malcolm Knowles, internationally recognized authority on training, uses this procedure to help establish a climate conducive to learning [11]:

1. Organize participants into groups of five or six. (You can use tables if you have them.) Allow 30 minutes for the procedure.

2. Have participants share their current work roles and how they got there.

3. Have them share one thing about themselves—a human interest story—which will set them off as unique individuals.

4. Have them indicate any relevant resources that they bring with them (from training or the job) that they are willing to share to help others learn better.

5. Have them develop a list of questions, problems, concerns, or issues they hope the workshop will cover.

6. Secure feedback on steps 2 through 5. Note:

    a. Anticipate that some of the data generated by this training procedure may raise expectations which the course cannot meet. If so, candidly acknowledge that that is the case and compliment the participants for their contributions. Of course, participant suggestions which can be integrated into the course should be accepted to the degree practicable.

    b. With a small participant group of some 15 to 25 people, reports can readily be secured from all the groups. With a larger group, time constraints may require that you secure feedback on a sample basis only. You may thus wish to state at the outset of the feedback phase of the activity: "We have a large group and we will only be able to secure reports from a limited number of the teams. Who wants to start us off?" After securing several reports, you may wish to state: "O.K., that gives us a good idea of your main concerns. Does anyone in a group that has not reported have a really 'hot' item they wish to share?" Accept one or two of the added ideas, if forthcoming, and then advise the group that "We have to move on to stay with our very full program."

7. Ask for adjectives that describe the climate as they now experience it. You will probably get terms like "warm," "informal," "safe," etc. If so, tell them that these are the characteristics of a climate that facilitates learning.

Change Challenge

Assign participants to dyads (pairs) and ask them to discuss any changes they may be undergoing in their personal and/or professional lives: Are they planned or unplanned? Major or minor? Anxiety/stress producing? Enriching or challenging?

Then canvass the group via a show of hands to help complete the table presented on a flipchart:

Changes in Our Lives

Type	Number
Planned	
Unplanned	
Major	
Minor	
Anxiety- or stress-producing	
Enriching or challenging	

Aerial Animation

I. Flying Airplanes

1. Ask each participant to respond in writing to an assigned task, for example, "Develop a list of traits of a leader vs. a manager." Suggest the use of a T-column to help contrast the ideas.

2. Have the participants form small groups and pool their ideas on a sheet of paper (letter or legal size). Also ask them to make a second copy since they will be exchanging their copy with another group and will need their own for reference purposes.

3. Ask each group to fold its sheet of paper into an airplane.
4. Ask all the groups to toss their airplanes across the room.
5. Ask several participants to read the statements on the newly acquired sheet of paper, comparing them to their own.

II. Flying Paper Balls

Optionally, at another point in the session or presentation, use the same procedure as above but with another topic, for example, "What one action would you advise a manager to take to ensure effective communication?" This time, however, have them crumple their sheet of paper into a paper ball which, again, is tossed across the room for exchange purposes.

Note: Either one or both of these activities may be used in a single session. If both are used, it may be desirable to use the airplane activity first since tossing paper airplanes may be perceived as a more conventional task than tossing paper balls.

These paper tosses work particularly well with a fair-sized group, for it produces a wild, fun-type atmosphere—the room becomes filled with flying objects. Management consultant Geoffrey Bellman used both activities in a session on leadership at the 1987 ASTD Conference in Atlanta.

ICEBREAKERS AND OPENERS: CLASSIFICATIONS AND CAUTIONS

If we can more fully understand the nature of icebreakers and openers, we can more properly use them. We should thus recognize that *icebreakers* can be divided into these two categories [12]:

☐ *The personality report—directly* asks participants to provide information about themselves: needs, hopes, fears, goals, details about one's background. Examples: "Value Assessment" (page 5) and "Art Mart" (page 6) enable participants to present data about themselves readily.
☐ *The personality clue*—provides *indicators* about one's personality. Examples: how one performs in "The Ball Toss" (see "Movement" in Chapter 15)

and "Nicknames" (page 6) affords a few glimpses into people's personalities.

Similarly, *openers* can be divided into these two categories:

☐ *The attitude report*—asks participants in a *direct* way to verbalize their attitudes toward the topic or subject that they will be entering. Examples: "Ventilating Feeling" and "Fishbowls" (page 14).
☐ *The attitude clue*—provides indirect data or indicators about a person's feelings toward the subject at hand. Examples: "Goal Analysis" (page 12) and "Pre-Work" (page 14).

As was indicated in "Planning the Use of Icebreakers and Openers" (page 2) and in "Evaluating Icebreakers" (page 11), warm-up activities require care in their selection and implementation. Additionally, one trainer offers the following added cautions [13]:

☐ Don't get cute. Only use openers that relate to the learning goal.
☐ Don't use icebreakers or openers that may embarrass people or cause them to fail. Everyone should succeed and, depending on the task assigned, everyone should have fun.

Another trainer gives the following advice [14]:

☐ Be *authoritative*. Provide direct commands as opposed to asking for permission. New participants expect leadership rather than indecision on your part. Assume everyone will participate rather than seek consensus about it. Give a direct command: "Let's all stand up. Let's form two circles. Those in the first two rows meet by the windows. Those in the last two rows form your circle by the wall."
☐ Be *prepared*. Know your procedural instructions completely. Communicate instructions clearly. Anticipate contingencies—things don't always pan out as expected.
☐ Be *sensitive*. Be certain that people can physically do what you expect and that they are properly dressed for their assignment. Don't force people to engage in self-disclosure that may go beyond their expectations and value systems.

It's also a good idea for you, as trainer, to enter into the fun and games, if at all possible. In fact, if the activity calls for pairs, quartets, or an even number of players, be sure to join in if there is an odd number of participants. Simply say, "I'll play, too."

Frames of Reference

Another approach to using openers is to begin with what trainer Susan L. Michel calls "frames of reference," tools to create meaning. She cites these three techniques in particular: *structured overviews*, *effective graphics*, and *conceptual maps* [15]. Each of them can be posted on the wall for constant reference, to help people keep their bearings.

Structured overviews. This is essentially a road map or, more familiarly, a course outline. It serves as a "prompt," a device to guide or spark thinking. It tells participants where you, as the trainer, are going to take them. It helps to frame the learning for participants and tells them what will and won't be covered. They can readily see items they are familiar with and those they are not. Suggestions for group involvement/interaction with this tool are given below. An example of a structured overview is given in Figure 1-5. Note that the usual words in an outline such as "introduction" and "conclusion" are not used because they are not directly related to session content.

Graphic display. Graphics can also provide a framework for learning. Typically, graphs come in circles, overlapping circles, wheels, gears, squares, rect-angles, triangles, steps, and other shapes. Geometrical figures such as squares, rectangles, and triangles are segmented in various ways to illustrate and elucidate particular concepts more precisely. An example of a graphic display appears in Figure 1-6. Suggestions for participant involvement are given below.

Conceptual map. Our third type of framework combines the characteristics of an outline with the appeal of a graphic display. Its purpose is to show significant relationships between concepts and to provide visual help for the trainer and the participants. By "chunking" horizontally, the participant can more readily see key relationships. An example of a conceptual map is given in Figure 1-7.

In general, these three tools help learners to learn more easily and to recall better. Why? Because the material is framed in ways that help link the new course material to knowledge already possessed. These learning aids can also provide a schematic summary of what was learned.

Involvement of participants in using tools for frames of reference. As indicated above, we want to ease our learners into the course/session/program. Openers are an ideal way to do this. In respect to the three tools or frames discussed above, we can involve our participants via small group work by asking them to focus on questions such as these:

- ☐ What do you like most in the frame of reference provided?
- ☐ Are there any illogical elements included?
- ☐ What seems to be missing?
- ☐ What should be more detailed?
- ☐ What is ambiguous (needs clarification)?
- ☐ What would improve the frames of reference presented?
- ☐ Would another type of presentation be more helpful to aid your understanding?
- ☐ Is this frame of reference really necessary to aid your understanding?

Note: We can anticipate that people will perceive a given frame of reference differently. Their varying backgrounds will ensure that this will happen. To tap these varied responses, we suggest using groups (four to six participants), as opposed to dyads or triads.

The Manager as a Communicator

- ☐ How to listen effectively
- ☐ How to manage one-way vs. two-way communication
- ☐ How to manage gender differences in communication
- ☐ How to prevent the defensive response
- ☐ How to recognize and use nonverbal communication
- ☐ How to provide negative feedback
- ☐ How to deal with the angry person
- ☐ How to deliver bad news
- ☐ How to engage in creative contact
- ☐ How to ask questions
- ☐ How to increase upward communication
- ☐ How to communicate new policies and procedures
- ☐ How to manage the grapevine

Figure 1-5. Example of a structural overview (presented on flipchart).

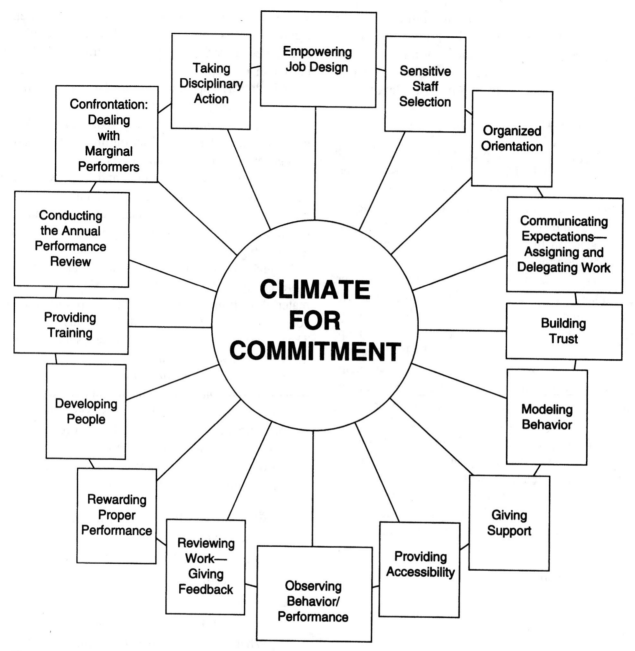

Figure 1-6. The coaching skills sequence.

Dynamic Opening Strategies

Icebreakers and openers are great ways to kick things off. However, there are some other strategies to consider and use to ensure a powerful opening. Training consultant Dorothy Leeds asserts that "powerful trainers start powerfully" and advises us to "be creative from the start." She believes that "openings have more crucial responsibilities than almost any other part of your training. They're not only for gaining attention: openings contain many subtle nuances. One well-crafted opening can combine many tasks into just a few minutes."

Ms. Leeds offers trainers these ten strategies for a powerful opening [16]:

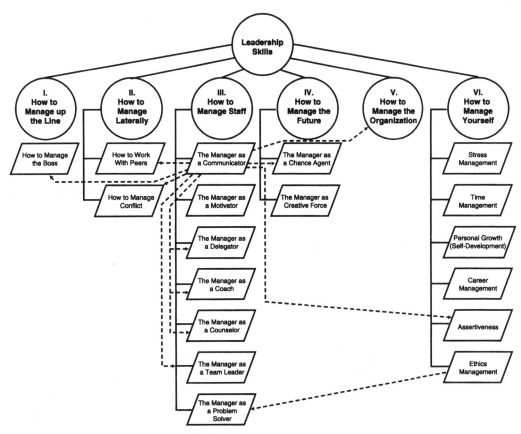

Figure 1-7. Example of conceptual map.

1. *Get participants' attention and interest.* Recognize that people may be nervous about dealing with new learning, or they may resent having been sent to training. It's your job to create an atmosphere that's user-friendly and stimulating. Leeds offers this example:

   Assume you're doing a program on body language. You stride into the room with vigor; you stop, stare at the group for a few seconds, move to the flipchart, pick up a large felt-tip pen, and silently print on the flipchart, "Take out a pen and paper and write down everything you know about me already."

What does this strategy accomplish? Several things:

   ☐ You get attention.
   ☐ You certainly excite curiosity.
   ☐ You indicate that the program will be participative.

   ☐ Your trainees have already learned something about nonverbal communication, which is your topic, of course.

   Key point: Use your imagination/creativity to construct a lively learning atmosphere.

2. *Construct a bridge* between prior learning and what is about to come. For example, you can simply ask which concepts/skills/techniques presented yesterday were most helpful, or you can tie what is coming to a current event. For example, if you're teaching time management, you can discuss how the A.M. traffic affected the day's plans.

3. *Communicate your purposes precisely.* Avoid weak statements about objectives, for example, "We're going to learn something about delegation today." Better: "I'm going to give you seven skill pointers that can make you more effective as a

delegator." People need to know what you intend to accomplish at session's end.

4. *Provide for involvement.* Ensure that the experience is an active rather than a passive one. Provide participative tasks (in dyads, triads, quartets) and have people move around if at all possible.

5. *Build realistic expectations.* Do this with a friendly greeting when people enter the training room, a neatly arranged room, and an exciting icebreaker or opener to kick things off.

6. *Warm up your participants.* Show them that your session will not be a session in catching up on one's sleep. Rather, they will have fun while they are learning. Use icebreakers and/or openers for this purpose.

7. *WIIFM.* People want to know "What's In It For Me?" No one wants to be trained for the sake of training. So if your topic relates to motivation, you might ask, "What's in it for you if you can become a better motivator?" or "How would it help you if you were to pick up new techniques on communication?"

8. *Communicate that you're on top of things for their advantage.* Examples: Advise how you'll deal with questions ("at any time" and "there are no stupid questions"); provide a properly set up room; ensure easy visibility for everyone.

9. *Disclose something about yourself personally.* People want to know who you are as a person, not just as a trainer or instructor. So share personal incidents/anecdotes that reveal some aspects of yourself, your personality, your trainer style, and/or your family life.

10. *Communicate that you're glad to be here.* You do this not by saying so, but by your enthusiasm, good cheer, good humor, smiles, revealing some thing about yourself, etc.

Note: The section on "Climate" (Chapter 21) has a number of useful pointers to help create the "right" climate/atmosphere, including pre-arrival activities, greeting participants, the learning environment, and the trainer's style and behavior.

Starting Right

1. Post these three flipchart sheets on the wall or blackboard.

What must this session (course, program) do to best meet my needs?	What must I, as a participant, do to make this program fully meaningful to me?	What must the total group do to ensure our program's success?
-1-	-2-	-3-

2. Form pairs, two or three pairs to tackle one of the questions on the flipcharts. To be certain all three questions will be dealt with by the pairs, assign pairs a numbered sheet.

3. Call time after the allotted 10 or 15 minutes and have the two-person teams post their ideas on the flipchart sheets.

4. Lead a general discussion, including facilitator comments regarding how the participants and the program itself can assist to implement the group-generated ideas on the sheets.

5. Compliment the group on their good ideas.

Note:

1. The activity creates participation immediately and sets a climate for it. It signals that participation is wanted and expected throughout the program.

2. It provides guidelines for participant responsibility to produce a truly worthwhile training effort.

Now or Later?

Tape two flipchart sheets to the wall or blackboard. On one sheet provide this heading: "Learnings I want for immediate use." On the other sheet add this heading: "Learnings for later use." Provide Post-it Notes (or use 3" × 5" cards with sticky tape) for posting to the flipcharts.

Objectives:

1. To stimulate participants to think about their needs for specific ideas/skills/techniques which the course or program may provide.
2. To show your interest in their needs.
3. To indicate the degree to which the program will be helpful.

Note:

1. Anticipate that most participants will post their slips or cards on the sheet for immediate use of learnings.
2. Respond to posted comments. Be candid—indicate where the course will respond positively to their expressed needs and where it can't. Where the course won't help, suggest, if you can, how and where a particular need can be met.

Find the "f's"

Using an overhead projector, flash the following statement on a white screen or wall for a minute or so:

> Finished files are the result of years of scientific study combined with the experience of many years of experiments.

Then turn off the projector.

Ask: How many "f's" do you see?

(Anticipate that one or more f's will probably be overlooked by most participants. Turn on the projector again to give participants another viewing of the f-laden sentence).

The correct answer: 7. The seven f's are as follows: four appear in the word "of"; the other three are in "finished files" and "scientific." What is typically overlooked is the "f" in "of," because of its "v" sound.

Significance:

1. To point up how our perception is influenced (distorted) by our presumed familiarity with what we observe. In perception much can be lost because we don't really take the time or make the effort to see what is really out there.
2. A possible learning for managers: If you can overlook something you are looking for *con-*

sciously (the above letter in the sentence containing the f's), is it not likely that you can miss discriminatory management practices (or other undesirable practices) taking place in your organization?

Fun with Nursery Rhymes and Children's Stories

A fun way to involve and ignite your participant group is to have them work briefly with children's rhymes and stories. The idea is to get them to ideate creatively in a fun way on a given rhyme or story, possibly pointing up the implications of a management skill area—problem solving, decision making, communication, planning, delegation, person-power utilization, etc.

Some examples of commonly known rhymes and stories:

Little Miss Muffet. Assigned task: What actions might Miss Muffet have taken to avoid and/or cope with the calamity (problem) she encountered?

Jack and Jill: Use questions as above.

Humpty Dumpty: Use questions as above.

Little Red Riding Hood: Assigned task: What are the communication, decision-making, or other management implications in (or learnings from) this story?

Other stories: *The Tortoise and the Hare, The Fox and the Grapes, Cinderella.*

Suggestion: Start your group off with this encouraging instruction: "Be as creative and as 'far out' as you can—think outside the box! This is a fun-type activity, so have a ball with it."

KEY POINTS

1. Training groups can typically profit from some kind of warm-up activity.
2. Icebreakers, which are usually not course related, can help reduce tensions, anxieties, and loneliness; energize the group; set a tone for the program; and certainly involve everyone.
3. Icebreakers are particularly useful for the stranger or cousin group.
4. In choosing an icebreaker, the trainer should pay attention to the organization's culture; the

participant group and its tolerance for novelty, fun, and excitement; the available time; the nature of the course itself; etc.

5. If a group is well acquainted, icebreakers may not be essential. However, even such a group can profit from an opener, that is, the use of a subject-matter-oriented device to ease into the course or program.

6. In general, icebreakers and openers are training devices that recognize the importance of establishing a proper climate for learning.

REFERENCES

1. Dahmer, Bart, "Kinder, Gentler Icebreakers," *Training and Development* (August 1992), pp. 47–49.

2. Baron, A. S., "How to Start a Seminar," *Training and Development Journal* (December 1979), p. 24.

3. Berry, Bart A., "Getting Training Started on the Right Foot," in "Training 101," *Training and Development* (February 1994), pp. 19–22.

4. Benini, Carla, "In-Room Interaction," *Meetings and Conventions* (May 1995), pp. 125–129.

5. Hammonds, Keith H., "Hard Lives, Low Pay, Big Stakes," *Fast Company* (November 1999), p. 94.

6. Pearlstein, G., "Participant Objectives: Advice You Can Take to the Bank," *Training* (September 1983), p. 106. Also see in this same issue of *Training:* "First Find Out What They Want," pp. 60, 64.

7. Merman, Cynthia H., "Common Concerns Checklist," in "Training 101," *Training and Development* (February 1992), pp. 22–23.

8. "Trainees Uninspired? Try These Tested Tips to Boost Production," *Training/HRD* (November 1982), p. 9.

9. Ludeman, Kate, "Instilling the Worth Ethic," *Training and Development Journal* (May 1990), pp. 53–59.

10. Blankenship, Allison, "Get Your Course Going with a Bang," *Creative Training Techniques* (August 1999), p. 94.

11. Knowles, M. S., "Some Thoughts About Environment and Learning-Educational Ecology, If You Like," *Training and Development Journal* (February 1980), pp. 34–36.

12. Brue, C., "Breaking the Ice," *Training and Development Journal* (June 1985), pp. 26–27.

13. *Ibid.*

14. Berry, Bart A., "Getting Training Started on the Right Foot," in "Training 101," *Training and Development* (February 1994), pp. 19–22.

15. Michel, Susan L., "Three Tools to Help Learners Learn," in "Training 101," *Training and Development* (June 1992), pp. 17–19.

16. Leeds, Dorothy, "Ten Powerful Opening Strategies," *Training and Development* (July 1991), pp. 26–27.

RECOMMENDED READING

Jones, Ken, *Icebreakers: A Sourcebook of Games, Exercises, and Simulations*, 2nd edition, Gulf Publishing Co., Houston, Texas, 1997, 284 pages.

Provides 66 training activities. Useful whenever an icebreaker is desired. Also contains considerable textual information concerning the rationale for icebreakers, how to choose them, how to conduct them, and how to adapt them into another type of activity.

Laus, Michael D. and Champagne, David W., "Ghosts in the Training Room," in "Training 101," *Training and Development,* March 1993, pp. 21–23.

Training programs are often visited and possibly disrupted by "ghosts" of participants' past classroom experiences, work histories, time and life demands, and personal needs. The authors offer clues to identify these ghosts and advise exorcising them at the outset. In effect, an excellent rationale for use of icebreakers and/or openers.

Using Small Groups Effectively

2

For learning to take place with any kind of efficiency students must be motivated. To be motivated, they must become interested. And they become interested when they are actively working on projects which they can relate to their values and goals in life.

—Gus Tuberville, President,
William Penn College, Oskaloosa, Iowa
(quoted in *The Washington Post,*
March 7, 1981)

THE small group is the basic unit for participative training. By small group we mean a subdivision of a larger group that may range in size from three to eight people. I prefer to keep such groups quite small, about three to five participants.

The small group, also known as a buzz group because of its noise production, has a number of unique advantages:

☐ It provides for the relatively easy and certain involvement of everyone.

☐ It permits and encourages meaningful participation in a low-risk, threat-free way. Contrast the perceived risk of having to stand up in a large group to make a statement or ask a question as opposed to engaging in actual give-and-take discussion with a small number of peers.

☐ It provides for the opportunity to learn from one's peers and to test out the validity of one's own ideas.

☐ It is a flexible tool that allows restructuring ("O.K., let's form some new groups so we can meet and work with some new people") and size expansion and contraction.

☐ Individual needs and differences can be recognized by assigning individuals to groups on the basis of interest, experience level (all new supervisors may meet together), management level (place supervisors and managers in their own small groups), job background (all sales people may be placed together), etc.

☐ It can provide the diversity of views essential for good problem solving.

☐ It can provide a sense of rapport, a source for support and recognition, and an opportunity to become acquainted with others. (The level or depth of the acquaintanceship will obviously vary, depending on the nature of the tasks, exposure time, personality differences and needs, etc.)

Just as small groups are advantageous in the previous ways, large-group situations have these disadvantages:

☐ The learning situation encourages passivity.

☐ It is much more difficult for participants to develop trust, rapport, mutual support, and intimacy—all of which are important to learning.

☐ Participants are kept out of touch with other participants and the trainer. People prefer, of course, more individualized attention.

☐ It may become even more difficult to read flipcharts or the blackboard.

☐ From a trainer standpoint, there may be a loss of control of the group, indicated by such things as subgrouping, side conversations, late returns from breaks and lunch, passivity (some just sit and observe), and running behind schedule (more people produce more questions and comments; however, this additional input is usually from a minority of highly active and verbal personalities).

Note: Though small groups are the basic unit for participative training, there are obviously times when the small groups function collectively as a total group. This may be at the outset of a session before the small groups are formed or when the small groups are brought back in the total group situation to discuss their learning experience. Also, in opting for small group work we should not overlook the need to keep the *total* group relatively small and thus workable. A total group should contain from 12 to 25 participants.

The techniques described in this book are intended for use in the training situation. Though some of these techniques could be used in group therapy, our purpose is to give you techniques that will provide participants with the best possible learning experience. In general, our assumption is that we are dealing with normal people who function appropriately in organizations, rather than with those who have deep-seated emotional problems and require help thereon.

Throughout the book you will encounter terminology that is more or less standard in the training field. You should carefully consider whether certain terms will be readily accepted by the participants. It may be desirable to use "pair" rather than "dyad" or "trio" rather than "triad." (Interestingly, in Hong Kong the Triad is the Mafia!) Other terms that may frustrate or irritate participants include "fishbowl," "lecturette," and "role playing." This book, of course, suggests alternative words.

SMALL GROUP COMPOSITION

It is better to change the membership in the small group frequently because doing so:

☐ Energizes people by keeping them from getting too comfortable with the familiar.

☐ Provides for the opportunity to meet new faces, personalities, viewpoints, and talents. This is especially desirable when two or three people come from the same work unit (or the same organization in the case of a public seminar). I candidly tell cliquish participants: "We'd like to move you to another group so you can get exposed to new people, new views, etc. You won't learn anything new if you only confer with people you already know pretty well."

☐ Automatically provides you with the opportunity to restructure group membership if things are not going well in a particular group.

An easy way to gather small groups at random is simply to have people count off and have all the ones meet together, all the twos meet together, etc. Other ways are to restructure group formations arbitrarily by pointing to several somewhat adjacent people to form a group, by asking people to turn around, or by having the participants move around themselves to locate new team members.

If tables are used, set a ground rule at the outset that everyone is to seek a new table location each day. Explain the reason for this procedure, of course.

When considering the formation of groups, take into account that at times it may be desirable to balance the small groups, for example, headquarters and field, line and staff, newcomers and seniors, men and women, functional combinations (such as sales and production).

SEATING

Use flexible seating (light, comfortable chairs) so that participants can readily rearrange themselves for dyads, triads, buzz groups, and role playing teams. Try to avoid the use of tables and desks—much too classroom-like—unless there is a real need for them, for example, considerable writing or note taking. I prefer a free-flowing room that allows for informality, ready movement into new small group configurations, and easy circulation.

The initial configuration can be lecture hall fashion or even a circle (with a total group of about ten participants). However, the starting arrangement doesn't really matter too much. For if you use group-in-action methods, as I advocate, the furniture will soon be in friendly disarray.

Note: Participants new to small group techniques often are reluctant to form an actual circle with their chairs. The trainer should clearly establish, the first time around, that a buzz group is a truly circular arrangement, and that for the best communication and rapport to take place, they need full eye-to-eye contact.

SHOULD WE USE THE OUTDOORS?

The author strongly favors holding one or more sessions outdoors, either for the total group or for small group work. Its advantages:

☐ A change of location can have an invigorating effect. Being confined to a single room, possibly

without a window, for six hours or more can become a bit debilitating, particularly if you have participants whose jobs allow them to be outdoors much of the time.

☐ Participants whose images of a school room are the usual one of tight indoor quarters are likely to be surprised and pleased by a bold venture to the outdoors.

☐ After a particularly heavy session, it can have a relaxing effect.

☐ To the extent that we can provide variety, change of pace, and the freedom of a classroom without walls, we can stimulate the creative juices to flow.

Of course, there may be some negatives to the outdoor venture. For example, some people may not be comfortable seated on the grass; it may be noisy outside (cars, airplanes, lawn mowers); it may be hot and sticky in the summer months; people (nonparticipants) may be walking by and cause distractions; time may be lost going to and from the outdoor location. *Note:* If sitting on the grass is a problem, arrangements may be made in advance to set up chairs in a circle under a large shade tree.

ASSIGNING TASKS

The key to effective group action is the nature of the task given to the small groups. Groups thrive on assignments that entail challenge, novelty, some element of controversy, and certainly relevance to their job situation. Cited in Figure 2-1 are some typical thought questions to which most groups should be able to respond with vigor. You may not care to use these questions, but they merit study as to their general thrust or tenor.

Assignments in the form of questions may be given orally to small groups, written on the flipchart, or presented in handout fashion. Questions which are relatively easy to understand may be assigned orally. However, it is probably wise to repeat the question and then check for understanding by everyone. People absorb (listen, understand) at different rates of speed and with different degrees of comprehension.

If a question (or set of questions) is of some complexity and likely to be misunderstood, it's a good idea

---

Thought Questions

1. If I were the head of the organization I would _____.
2. How could this situation have been prevented?
3. Now that this incident has taken place, what should _____ do?
4. If I had unlimited funds (or staff) I would _____
5. If we were organized along these lines (centralization, or decentralization, or flat organization, etc.), we would be able to_____.
6. Would you work for (this company, this boss, etc.)? Why or why not?
7. Would you invest in this company? Why or why not?
8. At this stage in the organization's history, it should _____.
9. Assume it is the year 2025. What should our program for_____ be?
10. Assume that the life span of the average American is 110 in the year 2025 (or that unlimited energy is available, etc.). What implications would this have for our products (or our recruitment program, etc.)?
11. Pareto's Law tells us that 80% of the results are a result of 20% of the activity; e.g., 80% of the revenue comes from 20% of the product line or 20% of the sales force; or 80% of the accidents comes from 20% of the work force; etc. How does this "principle" apply to our results (in marketing, research, management of time, etc.)?_____.
12. What would make this work team effective is (are)_____.
13. The current (or future) trends affecting our activity in a significant way are (or will be)_____
14. Based upon what you have read in the case (or seen in the film or in the role play), what assumptions have you made about the boss (or the subordinate or the colleague, etc.)?
15. Has our organization experienced any major environmental or internal changes that affect careers (marketing strategies, product lines, personnel policies, etc.)?
16. Look back 10 years (or 20 years). What changes have occurred in government policy (technology, overseas marketing, etc.)?
17. Is this act (behavior, policy, program) a broad-gauged or narrow one? If it is narrow what would it take to make it broad-gauged?
18. Is this behavior (plan, program) a short or long-range view?
19. What criteria would you use to decide whether the organization has a "good" marketing program (communications program, pay plan, safety program)?
20. If you could be "Dutch Uncle" to the comptroller (personnel director, production manager, sales manager), what advice would you give?
21. If we were to select only people who could _____(or had certain qualifications), would that solve these kinds of problems?
22. Suppose you were asked to resolve a problem like that. What would you do? How would you go about doing it?
23. What values seem to underlie his (the organization's, work team's) decision?
24. What does the situation tell us about creativity (delegation, career development, motivation, sales success)?
25. If we could come up with a machine to _____,what effect would it have on_____?
26. How can we tell that the plan (project, program, policy) has succeeded?
27. Is _____ in touch with reality? Explain your answer.

Figure 2-1. Examples of questions designed to stimulate discussion in groups.

---

to present it in handout fashion. This procedure will ensure that everyone can digest it at an individual pace and have the chance to reread it if necessary. Questions reduced to writing also force the trainer to think through more carefully what he/she actually has in mind and can serve as a permanent record for future use (or revision, if necessary).

In making assignments to small groups, set a definite time limit for completing the task. Use a timer or a digital watch as a monitoring aid for this. Provide the groups with a warning when their time is almost up. If time is not a big factor, just tell participants: "Take a few minutes to discuss _____."

Consider giving the groups assignments that have some element of controversy, and advise them that they must agree in ten minutes on a particular point. The need for a group decision coupled with time constraints provides an up-beat tempo for motivated, energized performance.

To ensure clarity in giving task instructions to small groups, trainer/consultants Chip R. Bell and Fredrick H. Margolis have developed a helpful four-step guide [1]:

1. State the *rationale* for the assignment from the *learner's* view. People are entitled to know not only what they will do, but *why* they are to do it. As the learner might well phrase it: "What's in it for me?"

2. Explain the *nature* of the task. Step 1 responds to the *why* question. Step 2 answers the *what* question, that is, what is to be done. It describes a *product* to be produced: develop a list, answer a question, solve a problem, take a position on an issue. The quality or quantity of the product should also be spelled out.

3. Specify the *context* or setting of the task, that is, *how* the task is to be done. This instruction specifies: (a) whether the task is individual, small group, or both; (b) group composition (homogeneous or heterogeneous); and (c) time allotted.

4. Describe the feedback report to be provided. This request for reporting is also known as "processing" or "sharing." Participants must know precisely what they are going to have to communicate to the total group about their learning.

Viewing-Listening Teams

Consider using listening-viewing teams when your program calls for inputs of a one-way communication nature, that is, talks, lectures, films, slide shows, or panel presentations. These teams are small groups that have been given an assignment to look/listen for something in particular while the talk or film is in progress.

Note: If the input is a film/video, the small group is a *viewing-listening team;* if the input is a talk, the small group is a *listening team.*

The rationale for this procedure is that it gives the participants something specific to do while the one-way input is in process. This encourages tune-in, commitment, and responsibility as opposed to a possible tune-out or drift effect.

Procedurally, the trainer gives a listening and/or viewing assignment to each small group in advance of the presentation. After the presentation, the small groups meet to discuss their assignments and then report back on them to the group at large.

The assignments to the teams may be specific or more general. An example of specific assignments in the case of a talk on communication might be the following:

"Group 1, pay attention to and be prepared to report back on the role of feedback in the communication process.

"Group 2, pay attention to the relationship of communication and decision making.

"Group 3, you will be asked to respond to this question: What are the relative merits of two-way vs. one-way communication?"

The more general assignments can be treated in this manner:

"Group 1, you are *the questioners*. Listen (or look) for anything which triggers a question in your mind.

"Group 2, you are *the clarifiers*. Listen for anything that comes across in a muddy or obscure way.

"Group 3, you are *the agreers*. Listen for anything that you can most readily accept or 'buy.'

"Group 4, you are *the disagreers* (not the 'disagreeables'). Listen for anything that doesn't make sense and which you can't 'buy' or accept.

"Group 5, you are *the implementors* or *the appliers*. Listen for something so practical that you can pick it up and run with it starting Monday morning."

The T-Column

Groups can see dichotomized or polarized issues in better perspective if you

1. Assign the two different sides of an issue to different groups.
2. Elicit data from the groups and post the data in a T-column. An example follows:

Reporting Requirements As Seen By

Headquarters	Field
Basic to policy development	Too many reports
Needed for control and supervision	Too short deadlines
Frequently late	Instructions not clear
Data often obscure or missing	Looks like data is collected for data's sake
	Not staffed to do reports right

In general, the T-column is useful in highlighting comparisons and contrasts, pros and cons, risks vs. ways of overcoming them, our views—their views, past-present, benefits-losses, headquarters-field, reports on a single issue from two groups (Group A—Group B), hopes and fears (as an anxiety-reducing program opener), etc.

Risk Analysis

Issues often arise in groups that relate to the taking of risks, for example, the risks supervisors run if they delegate, hire minorities, allow subordinates to rate their effectiveness as a coach, and let work teams make group decisions.

A good way to resolve the risk-laden issue is to

1. Ask the small groups to enumerate all the risks they can think of. This helps participants reveal their concerns so that these concerns can be analyzed, and it allows the participants to vent their feelings.
2. Rank the lists in priority order (the most serious is number one). This shows that not all risks are equal in gravity.
3. Develop procedures to overcome the risks. This encourages a great deal of positive thinking about what are often only presumed or minor fears.

A T-column can be used to help sharpen the issue. An example follows:

Risk Analysis: Letting Work Groups Make Their Own Decisions

Risks	Overcoming the Risk
1. Decisions made without all the facts	Provide written background Encourage group members to visit units that have pertinent data Only allow them to work on problems where they readily have the facts Meet with the group, but only at the outset
2. Decisions made that ignore cost factors	
3. Loss of management authority	
4. Too much time spent away from the job	

Risk Zapping

Risk-taking concerns also arise in training programs concerned with assertiveness, career planning, and other personal growth areas. Educator Merrill Harmin, Southern Illinois University, suggests posing these two questions to low risk takers [2]:

1. Are there steps ahead that I *know* would be good for me and that would serve me *now,* but which I feel are too risky to take?

2. What can I do to "zap" that risk so I *can* take those steps to get myself moving the way I want to move?

If these questions are recognized as realistic means to reach personal goals, participants can be presented with these options:

☐ *Worst scenario.* What's the worst that could happen? *Note:* Asking this question, identifying the most frightful situation or event and talking about it often helps one to decide that the worst is not all that bad—nothing really to run from.

☐ *Comfort-zone action plan.* Assume a participant has expressed a fear of some sort—embarking on a new career, transferring to another location, confronting the boss about a vexing issue, etc. Use the following procedure:

1. Ask him/her to auto-brainstorm a long list of things (6 to 12 items) he/she could do to resolve the problem and to overcome the fear or reluctance. The list should include both easy, small steps and large, frightening ones.

2. Mark the items on the list A, B, or C—A for frightening steps, actions that are "impossible" to take; B for in-between acts, neither easy nor frightening; C for easy actions.

3. Then ask the participant to begin with a step within his/her comfort zone, no matter how tiny or insignificant. Once started with C steps, one's comfort zone can be expanded to include B steps.

☐ *Taking the fear and going anyhow.* Assume that someone is generally afraid to give a talk to a group or to ask the boss for a raise. We know that king-sized butterflies will invade the tummy. But self-talk can help: "O.K., it's scary. I've got the butterflies, but I have to do it. And once I start, my fears will dissolve in the energy of the action." In effect, we accept the existence and scary reality of the fear, but stride ahead

nevertheless. We can also be comforted by the memories of other past actions where we rose above a big fear.

☐ *Living a purpose.* Another good way to dissolve a fear is to have participants get in touch with their larger purposes. What are my goals? What are my values? What is really best or right? Am I living my life as fully as I should? Once we can act on our persisting inner wisdom, as opposed to transient superficial impulses, we can become satisfied and powerful. Fears will fade when we recognize that we are using our life in ways that it was meant to be used.

Note:

1. The options just listed are for possible integration into an established program in the areas suggested, such as assertiveness training. They are intended to serve as an adjunct to such programs.

2. Procedurally, one or more of these four options may be assigned by the trainer to the participants in the small groups. Your decision as to which one to assign would be based on how well participants seem to be progressing, residual needs, and the like. Also, any one of the options may be presented to an individual participant in a group-at-large discussion for his/her processing and further general discussion.

3. Also consider securing feedback from the small groups as to how helpful any one option may have been: "Group 1, can you share with us your experience with the 'Worst Scenario' technique? Was it easy or hard to use? How was it helpful? Would anyone care to share their experience with the technique?"

THE SPOKESPERSON AND THE RECORDER

If a spokesperson is necessary for reporting back on small-group-generated data, have the group designate one person using objective selection criteria. (See discussion on "Leadership in the Small Group.")

If a recorder is needed, you should advise the group of that, too. As to selection, the group often gives the task to a low-status person. Conversely, someone may simply grab the ball and run with it. Again, see the discussion on "Leadership in the Small Group" for ways to make this appointment more objective and thus less traumatic to participants.

USING OBSERVERS

Observers are a helpful adjunct to small group work. Using them is a valuable technique for reporting what went on in the group, in a role play, in an exercise, etc. This may relate to leadership, to such processes as communication, goal setting, and decision making, to group morale (via giving support, encouragement, recognition), to planning, to creativity, and to participation.

The observer also learns by seeing group activities from a detached perspective, an opportunity that one does not ordinarily have in organizational life.

To ensure that the observation process produces meaningful results

1. Provide guide sheets to the observers so they will know precisely what to look for. The alternative: floundering and frustration.

2. Provide enough time for the observers to familiarize themselves with the guide sheets.

3. Meet with the observers (perhaps while the role players are reading their instructions) to be sure that they understand their responsibilities. Sometimes it helps to tell the observer that: "You have the most important job. If you don't pick up the needed data, the whole exercise will fall flat on its face and no one will learn a thing from it." The reassurance about job importance is often necessary since the observers may feel left out or that they are just unnecessary extras.

4. Consider using a team of two observers if the data to be garnered is adequately complex. A pair of observers may also have greater credibility with the observed.

One valuable and well-established form of observation is the use of a "sociogram," which reports on the nature (who speaks to whom) and frequency of group member contribution. For example, let's assume we have six participants in a group. We give each person a number, as in Figure 2-2.

The observer is instructed to make two kinds of diagrammed entries:

1. Hook up appropriate numbers with lines when one participant speaks to another participant, for example, 3 to 5, 2 to 4. Use arrows to indicate recipients of the communication.

2. When a participant speaks to the group at large, direct the line to the center (designated by a square).

An example of a completed sociogram is given in Figure 2-3. In this diagram person 2 has received most of the communication, and person 5 is the heaviest contributor in the group.

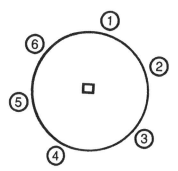

Figure 2-2. Diagram showing how members of a small group are assigned numbers for the purposes of a sociometric analysis.

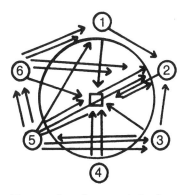

Figure 2-3. Example of completed sociogram.

The data should be fully processed by the group.

In connection with the observer role, we might mention that sometimes visitors come to the training room and take an observational role. They may be members of management, invited colleagues of the trainer, etc. Naturally group members are curious about these "interlopers." Why are they here? Who are they? What is their role? Are they spying? The best procedure is to nip any suspicions and anxieties in the bud by promptly introducing the observers to the group.

MONITORING

While the small groups are working on their tasks, it may be desirable to look in or listen in on their discussions so you can

- ☐ Answer possible questions about the assignment. By circulating around the room, as opposed to standing aloofly up front, you are more likely to get questions and various requests for help.
- ☐ Ascertain progress on the assigned task. Teams that finish too soon are suspect—check to see if they were on track.
- ☐ Pick up at first hand some ideas that may be useful in the general or summary session following the small group work ("I heard Group 2 make the point that . . .").
- ☐ Show that you are interested in their work.

These listening visits should be accomplished as unobtrusively as possible and be conducted only long enough to get an idea of where the discussions are trending. Visits should be made to all or most of the teams so that there is no feeling that only one group is being "picked on."

In more specific terms, the roles of the trainer in these visits are

- ☐ *Sensing:* interest-disinterest, anxiety, frustration, teamness, conflict, incompatibility, participation.
- ☐ *Listening:* for methods of attack, attitudes, reactions, learnings, "being with it," key ideas expressed, progress, creativity, winding down.

Note: Sensing relates to the affective or emotional side of the group's work; listening relates to the subject matter or task aspects of the work.

- ☐ *Intervening:* this should be done only if the group is floundering or if instructions were poorly delivered or simply misunderstood. If a group asks for help, you should respond enthusiastically to the request, of course.

QUESTIONS AND ANSWERS

Small groups function as a total group for such purposes as processing (discussing) the data they have generated and listening to a lecturette (short, concise lecture). In the course of such total group activity, you may, at times, pose questions to the participants. What if no one responds? Here are some suggestions for coping with this problem:

- ☐ Wait a little longer. Place the pressure on the group. The odds are that someone will break the hard-to-bear silence and respond to your query.
- ☐ Rephrase the question: "I guess I didn't state that very well. Let me restate the question. What if . . ."
- ☐ Introduce a bit of humor into the situation: "Gee, I didn't realize I came up with such a profound question."
- ☐ You may wish to call on someone. "Mary, could you help us on that one?" Or, "George, could you give us the benefit of your experience?" Consider this as an opportunity to involve the hesitant contributor.

As to questions from the group, try to be the good facilitator and let other group members answer as many of them as possible. Remember, this is *their* program and *their* opportunity for growth. One workable response technique for this is: "I could answer this, but I think we ought to get some input from a few other people."

Note: See "Using the Question-and-Answer Period Effectively" (Chapter 18), for more detail on the use of the question and answer technique. The "Thought Questions," Figure 2-1, may also be helpful.

REPORTING

The formal and most important opportunity to learn from small group work takes place when each team reports back its conclusions—essentially, *what was learned.* This phase of small group work is also termed "processing," "debriefing," and "sharing." For added guidance in this area, see "Skill Pointers on Processing," Chapter 22.

Small groups may present their reports via a single spokesperson, a pair of reporters, or even the whole group on a division-of-labor basis. Observers may also provide reports, either totally or as supplements to the key team reporters.

As to methods of communication, reports may be made verbally, nonverbally, via flipchart, or with the aid of overhead transparency slides. If the reports are delivered orally for recording on the flipchart, you must be certain that you are capturing the participants' ideas faithfully. Recognize that since you are trying to pick up key words and phrases from possibly windy speeches, you must tune in very carefully. And even if you don't like or agree with what you hear, record it as presented, nevertheless. You can discuss the "disturbing" point later. It is a good idea to check with the reporter from time to time to see whether you have extracted the essence of what was said. Participants will appreciate your concern for careful recording of their ideas. (See Chapter 15, "Flipcharting," for pointers on this process.)

Note: Although the reporting process is essentially designed for learning from the ideas of others, it also serves another vital function. Namely, it gives each team, through its spokesperson, a chance to strut its stuff. It is a form of show and tell wherein the teams have a chance to say to everyone else: "We have a good group. We're proud of it. And here's what *we* came up with!" Anticipate reactions such as "Hey, we already said that," or "Group B always has the best list."

Regarding actual reporting procedures, Margolis and Bell suggest that reports from the small groups be secured in one of the following ways [3]:

1. *Cream off the top.* This procedure entails securing *key* data from all group reporters on a rotational basis. It is used when all groups have had the *same* assignment. In this way, all groups have the chance to contribute equitably, as opposed to one team sharing all the items on their list and thereby leaving the others with little more to add. A typical query to the reporters is, "What is your *best* reason for your decision?" or "Give us the *one* approach of which your group is particularly proud."

2. *Report plus add-ons.* Use this procedure when all the teams have been given totally *different* assignments. (See examples under "Viewing-Listening Teams," in this chapter.) Elicit information from Group 1, then Group 2, and so on. Each group learns by doing its own work and from the contributions of the other small groups as well.

3. *Formal presentations.* When all small groups have been working on a total problem/issue/question, they may be asked to report back on *one* aspect of it. Again, people learn from their own work and that of others.

4. *Polling.* This entails securing a quick response (answer/solution) to a problem. Example: "How would you deal with Manager Pat White?" (*Note:* This procedure is akin to the "Circular Whip" described in Chapter 3.)

LEADERSHIP IN THE SMALL GROUP

When a small group works on an assigned task, from a leadership standpoint it can proceed in one of three ways:

1. Operate without a designated leader.
2. Operate with a leader of its own choice, using its own criteria as a basis for selection.
3. Operate with a leader of its own choice, using criteria for selection provided by the trainer.

Let's examine the learning implications of each of these three approaches.

☐ *A leader is not designated.* In most cases a formal leader need not be designated. This is particularly true if the task is not too complex and is to be accomplished in relatively short order, say 5–30 minutes. The leaderless group may learn from this situation:

　a. In problem solving, brainpower and insight are more important then the status of leadership.

b. Leadership roles (for example, summarizing, supporting) can be assumed by any and all group members.

c. A single leader, if really necessary, will emerge in an informal way. Sometimes, of course, the leader who emerges does so simply by taking over. The learning, then, for most participants, is that no one appreciates a power-hungry autocrat.

☐ *The group chooses its own leader based on its own criteria.* This procedure is often not too effective because no one (or most participants) wants to be perceived as pushy. Hence, someone may say: "George, why don't you be the leader?" And since ordinarily no one will contest this quick act of coronation, the "winner" is actually the one who made the uncontested designation of leadership. In reality, the leadership role is merely that of recorder, spokesperson, or a combination of the two roles. Consequently, no one really objects too much to the railroading procedure used to select the leader. Group members may learn that some people are dominators (like the one who selected the leader), others have strong power needs and thus may be very willing to be designated as leader, and most participants have the insight to avoid involvement in any power making or receiving ploys. They may also observe that the one selected may be a high-status person and that the sponsor or king-maker was deferring to that fact.

☐ *The group chooses its own leader based on trainer supplied criteria.* If you sense that a high-status or dominant person is likely to be given the leadership job, or you have seen it occur previously in a small group, you may provide selection criteria that will ensure more rotation of the leadership role. Thus, the small groups can be instructed to select a leader using very arbitrary but impartial and fun-type criteria; for example, the person with the least seniority, the youngest person in the group, the one with the brightest or lightest colors (this may produce a female leader), the one who had to travel the farthest to this session, the one who was born farthest from this locale, the one whose birth date is closest to

today. Fun-type instructions of this sort will prevent power ploys, deflate the importance of the formal leadership role, and help to spread the leadership job around. The learnings for the group may be that leadership may well merit rotation as opposed to being doled out on the basis of such traditional factors as status, seniority, power needs, and bartering, and that the leadership function, in the absence of a strong or autocratic leader, can be shared with no adverse (and indeed with possibly salutary) effects on productivity.

ASSESSING GROUP FUNCTIONING

Training groups, like work groups, are typically so involved in their tasks that they are not likely to stop the clock, step back, and assess how well they are functioning. They often do not stop to examine important skill elements such as communication, interpersonal relations, listening, participation, leadership, or working under pressure.

Obviously, the group must generate enough data about itself before it can assess its effectiveness. Also, group members have to become comfortable enough with one another before they are ready to give or receive any critique of their own behavior or their prowess as a team. In any case, the data is there. It definitely (and inevitably) has been produced. The only question is the group's readiness to examine it candidly and carefully and to try to learn from it. Interestingly enough, the group may find a review of its own dynamics to be more interesting and valuable than the formal agenda.

The trainer/facilitator's role, then, is to raise pertinent questions about group functioning and interaction. Trainer/consultant Steve De Valk offers several areas that merit group exploration [4]:

☐ *Seating arrangements.* Note who consistently chooses to sit next to whom. Do they opt to sit next to someone like themselves—someone of their own gender, age, race, and/or ethnic background? Or did they choose to be near someone of their own work unit, job interest, or geographic location? *Significance:* It is very natural (comfortable) to surround ourselves with people like ourselves. But does this obvious team member selection (in and out) possibly affect team unity, cohesion, and productivity?

☐ *Who contributes.* Observe which of your participants are the prompt answer givers. For example, in defining the problem, are the experienced people likely to rush to judgment with tried-and-true solutions before adequately exploring the problem? Does this not imply that those with less experience have little to contribute? Does this also imply that a fresh perspective is not really wanted? Are we content to opt for pat answers rather than true solution development?

☐ *Gender issues.* What roles do men and women take in our group discussions? Are they different? Do women do more supporting, encouraging, active listening, and reflecting than their male counterparts? Do men do more solution seeking and challenging than women? Who is more competitive? Who is more collaborative? How do men and women relate to one another? Would there be any advantage in seeking a female perspective or a male perspective when making decisions back home?

☐ *Listening.* Have people really been listening to one another? Do group members' responses reflect actual listening or possibly an eagerness to get one's own ideas into the hopper? Is listening impacted by differences in communication styles, gender, level of experience, race, ethnicity, age, or expertise? How does listening affect group productivity, here and on the job?

☐ *Working under pressure.* When we have been working under a time constraint and time is about over, what happens to group interactions? Are there interruptions, attempts to bulldoze one's input through to the exclusion of others' ideas? Can we develop strategies to include and value everyone's input despite working under time pressures?

☐ *Leadership roles.* How have leadership roles been assumed? By default? By self-anointment? By rotation? By group choice? Why was a particular leader chosen? What implications does this have for back-home behavior?

☐ *Trainer/facilitator role.* Don't hesitate to subject yourself to feedback. *Ask:* What could you

have done to make things go more effectively? Which behaviors helped group process and which behaviors hindered it? *Significance:* You want to provide a model as a leader who is open to critique (feedback) from others. You may also enhance your personal growth as a person and a trainer.

Note: An assessment of the above type is a good way to heighten awareness of diversity issues back home, on the job. Your training group can serve as a resource for this purpose.

BREAKS—HOW TO GET THEM BACK TO CLASS

Getting participants back on time from the usual A.M. and P.M. breaks is hardly a sure-fire operation. Participants simply enjoy chatting with their colleagues and thus tend to resist the trainer's need to get them back to work. And the trainer certainly doesn't want to make too big an issue of this lest he/she be perceived as a hard-nosed, Simon Legree type of trainer.

So what can be done? Consider these possible courses of action:

1. The trainer can learn to live with the tardy, reluctant returns to class.
2. He/she can experiment with various forms of reward (not punishment). For example, you may wish to experiment with a system of points to each table (group) for prompt return and then award a prize at program's end to the team that amasses the greatest number of points.
3. He/she can organize in one way or another to hasten the return to class.

Obviously, course #1 above is hardly a practical solution. After all, a schedule must be met in order to cover essential course content.

Course #2 will provide you with an opportunity to test your creativity, but don't count on its efficacy.

Course #3—taking certain concrete actions—has the greatest potential to produce adequately acceptable results. Here are some possibilities:

☐ *Participant assignment:* On a rotational basis, ask designated participants to perform the task of bringing the class back to work when break time is over. Consider giving these aides a large school bell to assist in their communication to their chit-chatting colleagues. *Note:* All of these assignments might be made at the time of the first break. Post names and break times on a permanently displayed flipchart sheet.

☐ *Audio signals.* You can use any one of a number of noise makers to communicate that it's time to get back to work, for example, train whistles, cow bells, referee's whistles, electronic noise makers, drums. Or if you begin the break with music, you can signal break's end by abruptly stopping the music. Or abruptly start a tape or CD with loud marching music.

☐ *Visual signals:* Dim the lights or blink them on and off.

☐ *Tie into small group work.* If you are assigning groups/teams to execute a lengthy assignment, for example, 45 to 60 minutes, add (integrate) the break time to the work time. This puts the responsibility on the trainees to monitor their time rationally. You might provide this type of instruction: "It's now 9:30 A.M. We'll expect you back here at 10:30 A.M. So take 45 minutes to execute your assignment and work your break into that one-hour time frame."

☐ *In-class break.* In some rare instances, where time is extremely important, ask participants to break but to return with their beverages to class.

☐ *Trainer timing.* If you ordinarily take a break with the participants and mingle and chat with them, you can serve as the timekeeper for the group.

☐ *Two-minute warning.* Signal return time via a bell, whistle, or music just before the break is to end.

COPING WITH PROBLEM PARTICIPANTS

While most participants are cooperative and quite manageable, at times you will encounter a few problem types. Some of the more common ones are The Hesitant One, The Monopolizer, The Voice of Experience, The Arguer, The Clown, The Show Off, and The Tangent Taker.

While there are no easy answers for dealing with these difficult personalities, here are a few pointers that may be of help, at least some of the time.

The Hesitant One

This kind of person—shy, reluctant, silent much of the time—is found in almost every group. Hesitant Hanna is easy to overlook since she melts into the background so successfully and is certainly not annoying anyone. In fact, some might say: "Why worry? Hanna will participate when ready." However, if we look at a training program as a vehicle to help people grow, and if growth is dependent on one's opportunity to contribute (analyze ideas, present ideas, defend them), then we must figure out ways to "draw out" and thus to draw in Hesitant Hanna. Some suggestions: Use a lot of dyads and triads, for participation is certain in the very small group. Also, politely call on the silent one from time to time ("I don't think we've heard from Hanna yet on this issue.") Ask the shy person easy questions, particularly those that relate to everyday or back-home experiences. Some trainers make it a point to socialize with the shy participant at the break. It gives such a person an ego boost and often has an encouraging impact thereafter.

Other techniques are to smile at Hanna and offer encouraging statements like: "You look like you were about to add something to that" or "You've had a lot of work with . . . May we have the benefit of your experience?" (Hanna is probably saying to herself: "I was afraid you wouldn't ask.") Also, you can use the "chained" or "relay" technique, that is, ask the same question in sequence of several participants, which would automatically include Hanna. The latter device avoids putting Hanna on the spot; others are also being asked to contribute. And if she is a bit slow to assemble her ideas, she won't be called on first.

You can also assign participants to work in pairs. Specify that their report to the total group is to be in two parts, each partner to give one portion of it. Finally, be sure to give Hesitant Hanna a lot of praise for her contributions. Positive reinforcement will encourage added responses.

The Monopolizer

This participant is the "big talker" and will gobble up all the available air time if permitted. In a polite but firm way, ask Monopolizing Mike: "Would you mind if we got another opinion on this one? Several haven't had a chance to respond yet." Or "Could we talk about that at the break?" The message to Monopolizing Mike is that "we play fair here, so let's please share the available air time." However, as with any of the other difficult participants, we can't afford to put Mike down. Why? Because, as a participant, the group may well rally to *his* side. In sum, we want Mike to know we appreciate his help, but on a more selective basis.

At times, peer pressure may also be relied on. You may hear comments such as "What, you again?" or "Hey, knock it off Mike. Give someone else a chance."

The Voice of Experience

Like the Monopolizer, Victor, the Voice of Experience, seems to have a tremendous need to be heard. Victor is probably not currently getting adequate job satisfaction, hence the need to bring in incidents and anecdotes from more halcyon days. Treatment of The Voice's malady is not easy because the inputs are not necessarily offensive, just somewhat tedious and unnecessary. The best advice is to treat Victor politely but endeavor at times to communicate that "This is very interesting, but we do have to move on." Or, better still, "We do have to get to our main issue, which is . . ."

The Arguer

Arguing Arthur is a tough kind with whom to deal. He constantly looks for opportunities to disagree or to show up the other participants and the trainer. While healthy disagreement is great, incessant quibbling is annoying and disruptive. One approach to coping with Arthur is to let the group deal with him: "Anyone want to respond to that?" Also, avoid getting trapped or baited into a debate with him. If, after an exchange of views, Arthur persists, simply say: "I understand your position. You believe that . . . Can we agree to disagree on this one?" Or, "We've given this issue considerable attention. We really should move on to something else. See me at the break and we'll talk some more about it."

Another technique is to look for a chance to defuse Arthur's disagreements by stating promptly whenever you can: "I agree with you and I think the group does, too. Any comment, anyone?"

The cardinal rule to remember: No trainer ever won an argument with a participant. For as we said before, participants are quite likely to identify with problem participants, because they are one of their group. They also expect finesse and patience from the trainer.

The Nonlistener

Nonlistening Norma presents a unique challenge to the group and its leader. Norma tends to interrupt, cut others off, and leap into the fray before others have had their say. Her eagerness to get in keeps her from listening. On the one hand, Norma's nonlistening may simply be due to a desire to be heard, to best others in the discussion. But it may also be due to her keen interest in the subject; hence her strong desire to advance her ideas. Regardless of Norma's motivation, though, her harassing behavior hardly facilitates group satisfaction and progress. Hence the need to cope with Norma's listening peccadillos. Some tactics to deal with Norma are these:

☐ Insist on sharing the available air time: "I know you have a worthwhile observation, but we haven't let Hank have his full say yet, have we?"

☐ Ask for a restatement: "Norma, just to be sure we're all in the same ballpark, could you restate for us what Tom just said?" If Norma has not heard Tom properly, ask Tom to repeat his statement and then go back to Norma: "O.K., Norma. You heard Tom. Can you tell us what he said before you give us your view?"

☐ Ask for a comparative analysis: "How does your idea/viewpoint stack up with Ann's?"

Tactics such as these will help Norma to see that she must try to incorporate other's views—which requires listening—before she unleashes her own opinions.

The Idea Zapper

Idea Zapping Ida is a master at putting down other people's ideas. She predictably offers an endless barrage of suggestion squelchers to anything new or different: "It'll never work." "We've tried that before." "Too early." "Too late." "Top management will never go for that." "Good theory, but not usable in the real world." Often her negatives come forth with a "Yes, but . . ." If we could crawl into Ida's head, we would probably find that her motivation is envy of the ability of others to ideate. So she uses what creativity she has to deflate everyone else.

Ida is particularly dangerous because her tendency to toss buckets of cold water on new approaches may inhibit creative suggestions from others.

Some possible ways of coping with Idea Zapping Ida are these:

☐ Promptly rescue the idea from Ida's trash bin by asking the group: "How do the rest of you see this? Is there another side to it?"

☐ Ask Ida if she can use her creativity to come up with an idea of her own, in lieu of the one she just zapped. If she doesn't, you may wish to say: "Well, if we don't have a better idea than Kim's, maybe we ought to look at that one a little bit."

☐ If you happen to like the idea that was zapped on arrival, don't hesitate to agree with it and say to the group: "I think there may be some possibilities here. Can anyone provide any arguments for it?"

The Complainer

Complaining Chester is a specialist in blaming, fault-finding, griping, and sharing his endless pet peeves. Chester not only finds life and the world unfair, but he insists on foisting his jaundiced view of things on any audience he can get. His ploys are easy to spot, for he is likely to begin his gloomy observations with such statements as: "Ain't it awful that . . ." or "If it weren't for . . ." He tends to sprinkle his laments with the all-encompassing "never" and "always." Chester is not a problem solver, but a problem magnifier. He's unhappy with top management, other departments ("those clods in shipping . . ."), his boss, his staff, the suppliers, the union, the local sports team, the press, etc.

To cope with Complaining Chester try these approaches:

☐ Ask him: "Do you have any ideas to cope with Department X?" or "Would you want the group

to suggest some ways of dealing with . . . ?" or "Have you leveled with . . . and told . . . how you feel about it?" The approach is to force Chester into a problem-solving mode, something from which he typically shies away.

☐ Encourage a search for the other side of things: "O.K., you've told us how terrible they are in Department X. But you're a fair person. Can you think of anything good about them at all? Just one thing?" If he begrudgingly admits to that one thing, ask "Anything else?" If you can squeeze two or three admissions out of him about another or opposite point of view, and possibly a few positives from the rest of the group, you may elevate Chester to a more positive level for a little while. A T-column, to show contrasting views, should help him put things in balance.

☐ Switch him to the high ground by stating early on: "Yes, there may be a problem with Department X. And the reason we're here is to find some answers (or better ways of cooperating). So if you and I and all the rest of us can keep thinking about ways to cope with this kind of issue, we'll have a truly profitable experience this morning (or this week). How can we accomplish that?"

The Rigid One

Rigid Roberta is a tough cookie, indeed. Roberta is not obnoxious in the sense that she argues, disagrees, pontificates, or quibbles, but in that she staunchly takes a position on an issue and will rarely, if at all, move from it. Since Rigid Roberta is so unyielding and so positive that she has a monopoly on *The Truth,* she makes it difficult for the group to make any progress. One way to deal with Roberta is to try to get her to admit that there *is* another side to the issue. Thus, the trainer might say: "Roberta, we're pretty clear about your position since you have stated it so well. But there is some other thinking on it. Can you cite any evidence at all, as an objective person, that would indicate that the problem can be seen in different terms?"

If Roberta does supply some data or opinion contrary to her own, follow this up by saying: "Yes, that is an argument on the other side. Can you cite one more view (or piece of data) that the other side considers important?" If Roberta supplies two opposing arguments, they should be put on the flipchart and the other participants asked for added evidence which is contrary to Roberta's position. In effect, Roberta is being asked to verbalize some opposing views, kick off the development of a "laundry list" of such views, and visually inspect the posted opposition views. No guarantees here to reduce Roberta's rigidities, but at least it forces her to recognize more directly that other views *do* exist.

The Hostile One

Hostile Harry is even more annoying than Arguing Arthur. Harry has a need to zero in on a defenseless target, and the trainer, as he sees it, is as good a victim as any. He thus presents highly hostile questions designed to embarrass or inflame. The best response to Harry's hostility is to keep your cool and simply rephrase the question in milder, more objective terms. Or, you may respond in this fashion: "I see that you have some strong feelings on this issue. Would you care for my opinion? (Or the group's opinion?)" It may also help if the answer is given to the group at large rather than to Harry. These procedures should "defang" Harry a bit, at least for the time being.

The Angry One

While Hostile Harry is antagonistic, aggressive, and unfriendly, Angry Arnie is a much more complex personality. His behavior may range intermittently from total silence and withdrawal to constant complaining—hard seats, lousy coffee, cold room—and the posing of harassing, negative questions. His forte is finding loop holes in your ideas and/or presenting impossible "what if" scenarios. The interesting thing about Arnie is that he is not mad at you, the trainer. Rather, he is mad at the world, including his boss, who had the gall to send him off to training.

Obviously, few trainers have the therapeutic skills to deal with an intimidating, somewhat paranoid trainee who is probably having serious problems at home, on the job, or both. Dr. Sandra Weintraub [5], a management trainer and psychotherapist, suggests that when you encounter Angry Arnie, deal with him by asking yourself these questions:

- ☐ Am I regarding the situation as a professional challenge and acting accordingly?
- ☐ Have I done everything I can to eliminate possible threats from the training?
- ☐ Have I created a climate/atmosphere where all participants can freely share possible frustrations about all aspects of the training?
- ☐ Have I considered the use of activities (exercises, role plays) to allow venting of frustration in a positive manner? Feedback to Arnie resulting from a role play may be a helpful shock to him.
- ☐ Have I considered openly addressing the problem with the group? It may be helpful to Arnie to find out how people feel about his behavior. Arnie may not be aware that his behavior is affecting others or making them feel uncomfortable until he receives some candid feedback from them.
- ☐ As a last resort, should I approach his organization about his possible need for outside professional help?

The Negative One

Negative Nellie can be counted on to find the gloomy side of things: nothing will work, people are impossible, the world has long gone to the dogs. Nellie is a specialist in dredging up gripes, past grievances, cantankerous complaints. She is a tough cookie to deal with, indeed. The best approaches with Negative Nellie are to ask her if she can find anything positive in the situation (also ask the group the same question) and suggest that she may have a point, but that we're all here to find constructive answers to these difficulties. Sometimes it helps to respond merely by saying: "I understand" or "Uh-huh."

The Dominator

In general terms, and each in his/her own disruptive way, The Monopolizer, The Voice of Experience and The Arguer are all dominators. However, the full-fledged Dominator is totally interested in controlling whatever is taking place. He wants to ensure that he has the floor, that he always has *the* answer, that his views are always on target and those of others much less so, that his views are superior to those espoused by the course and the trainer, that debating becomes more important than learning, and that the trainer is hardly worthy of being in charge. He also has an irritating tendency to interrupt others.

So what can be done? Here are some practical pointers to keep The Dominator in check [6]:

☐ When your session/course starts, establish this ground rule: All participants are to receive equal "air time" throughout the program.

☐ To help reinforce the above point, give each attendee six poker chips or other tokens, each worth two minutes of air time. When all of one's chips have been put in play, the participant has to observe silence.

☐ An allied device to the poker chip approach is to employ the "talking stick" This means that one may speak only when one has the stick. Participants receive the stick on a rotational basis. In effect, that means taking turns. (For a fuller explanation of the talking stick approach, see Chapter 11.)

☐ The facilitator can interrupt The Dominator with a question directed to another participant, possibly one who has been less active. ("I'd like to bring Pat in on this point.")

☐ The Dominator's comment can be acknowledged and another participant can be asked to respond to it. But don't let The Dominator rebut the response. Instead, seek an observation from another person.

☐ State clearly and forcibly that it is highly important to get inputs/observations/comments from everyone else. ("Let's get some added inputs and we'll come back to you.")

Other possibilities are to use dyads, triads, and small groups, where there is less opportunity for showmanship before the whole class. Also consider rotating group leadership. The Dominator and everyone else thus will be placed in a role where they have to facilitate, that is, encourage others to contribute, rather than selfishly corral all the available air time. And in particularly egregious cases, treat it as a team problem. Hold a team critique of the team's performance thus far, with particular emphasis on dominating behavior and its impact on group progress.

Sometimes a professional chat with the egregious one during the coffee break may rein him in. Compliment him on his knowledgeability, but point out that in the interests of fairness to his fellow participants he should let them into the discussion. Also suggest, "You know your views. But as a knowledge-seeking person wouldn't you like to learn how others see things?"

The Clown

Clowns come in all shapes and sizes, but their main characteristic is an abundance of ill-fitting, sometimes irritating humor. Some trainers may say: "I'd rather have a little humor than no participation at all." Possibly. But the effective discussion leader's job is to keep things moving in an orderly, productive way. And if Charlie the Clown is hindering group progress or annoying participants, he should certainly be dealt with. Some suggestions: Call on Charlie on occasion for serious dialogue. Show him that he can be heard (his real objective, of course), but at a more sophisticated and adult level. Compliment him (positive reinforcement) when he makes a worthwhile, serious contribution. Conversely, don't reward his attempts at humor. In some cases you may ask Charlie for a restatement of the joke: "I guess I missed the point of your quip. Could you give me your idea straight?"

Sometimes the problem is compounded by Charlie's clique who continually reinforce his behavior by exchanging banter and assorted putdowns. It is not an easy problem, of course. Again, the best strategy is to try to tap and reward his serious side.

The Show Off

Show-off Sandra likes to parade her knowledge before everyone—big words, fancy phrases, lots of statistics, name dropping, describing her long-time or unique experiences, etc. If Show-off Sandra contributes with the frequency of Monopolizing Mike, she can be treated in somewhat the same way. If the contributions are not as frequent, but merely pompous, the problem, although annoying, is probably one the group can live with. The odds are that some group members will kid her quite clearly about the big words and her other ploys. In effect, let the group deal with this type of problem participant.

The Tangent Taker

Tangent Tanya is the kind of person who has interesting inputs that typically belong in some other "ball park." One suggestion is to state politely to her: "This is an interesting experience, but could we try to bring it in a bit closer to home? You see our issue is . . ." Or, "Any one want to comment on Tanya's experience as it relates to our concern here?" Group silence may reduce her meandering inputs. Some of Tanya's tangents may, of course, have to be lived with. But it's still worth a try or two to plead for relevance from her.

When dealing with the Tanyas of the group, it is also important to remember that a tangent can be a *positive* contribution. Training consultant Robert A. Luke, Jr., suggests that a diversion may lead to important new directions and cover new ground. Of course, if it is truly a "side trip," it is important to get back on track. How can you tell the difference? Use these criteria [7]:

- ☐ Observe your group closely. If only one or two participants are involved, it is probably an unneeded diversion.
- ☐ Negative, highly heated feedback, particularly from those who do the same work and know their jobs well, should merit your serious attention. They may well be on to something worthwhile which suggests a program modification.
- ☐ Monitor your own reactions. If you suddenly ask yourself, "Where are we going?" it may be a self-message that you can't afford to ignore.

Luke advises that diversion-makers may be further classified as one of these four participant types:

- ☐ *The Attention Seeker.* His/her verbal trademarks include "Have you thought of doing it this way?" and "Let me play the devil's advocate."
- ☐ *The Advocate.* This diverter speaks with equal facility to support or to oppose ideas, depending on whether they conform to his/her own ideas.
- ☐ *The Converser.* He/she suddenly gets a brainstorm and immediately starts to share it with his/her immediate seatmates, whether or not they are interested.

- ☐ *The Homer.* (This is a baseball term for the radio/TV announcer who pulls for the home team.) He/she can't resist telling "how we do it."

So, once you've decided the diversion is unnecessary, how do you get back on the main track? Luke offers these possible strategies:

- ☐ *Laissez-faire:* Ignore the side-tracking and hope the speaker will simply run out of gas.
- ☐ *Plea for deferral:* State, "You have a good point, but can you hold it until the next unit (or Friday), when we'll deal with that issue?"
- ☐ *Group canvas:* Ask, "Anyone else see it that way? Could I see a show of hands?" (The odds are that the bulk of the group is no more favorable to a diversion than you are.)
- ☐ *Counseling:* Talk personally to the errant ones. Explain why it's important to stick to the course program or outline presented at the program's onset.

The Unwilling Participant

Some participants are neither volunteers nor willing attendees. In fact, some may be in your group because their bosses want you to "fix" them, to correct their deviant ways. Some suggestions for coping with "drafted" participants follow [8]:

- ☐ Acknowledge at the outset that some people are in attendance mandatorily, for example, at their bosses' insistence. Indicate that you can empathize with anyone who has come reluctantly, but advise that "You do have a choice. You can stonewall the program and refuse to enter into things, or you can decide to get the most out of the course while you're here. The mindset you want to employ is up to you."
- ☐ If the situation is quite serious—for example, there are a fair to large number of "reluctant dragons"—take a somewhat therapeutic approach and spend an hour or so dealing with the emotion. Let people talk out their resentment (or even talk out their anger) freely. This may be a sound procedure as opposed to going through eight hours of training with those who don't want it.

□ *Step One.* Draw out the issues and feelings of the group. Ask what is happening on the job that relates to the subject matter of your seminar. Collect comments (post to the flipchart) without passing judgment on them. Ask if the participants agree with those statements. Then ask if they are ready to move on to the planned course/ seminar. *Note:* If you are asked, "What do you intend to do with those statements?" ask them, "What would you like me to do with them?"

□ *Step Two.* Take a break. This will give you and your group a breather. If an appropriate authority is available, the break may give you time to discuss with him/her the resistance that has emerged. In some cases, you may wish to bring in a credible top manager to talk to the group about the value of the course to the organization.

□ *Step Three.* Divide participants into teams to develop solutions for the issues raised in Step One. Indicate that their ideas will be presented to management and followed up on. This may be a more productive approach than offering training that attracts little or no participant interest.

Management writer Margaret Kaeter suggests that trainers approach the resistance problem on a prevention-first basis. Prevention may entail the following [9]:

□ Make certain that the training addresses clear-cut, crucial organization goals. People are more likely to salute what the organization deems vital than what the training department deems so.

□ Involve line managers as trainers. This will clearly communicate management support for the training; it will also allow training to be delivered by those who have direct experience of the subject matter rather than mere theoretical knowledge. Furthermore, managers are unlikely to resist training that they themselves deliver.

□ Involve participants in the decision to attend. If employees have the opportunity to assess the value of the course and to see how it ties into corporate goals, there is less likely to be resistance.

□ To the extent practical, provide "just-in-time" training, that is, training that can be used right away rather than on a deferred basis.

□ If certain employees are being sent to training to acquire or upgrade a particular skill, they should be assured that this is in no way a critique of their personal worth. Rather, they are to attend because they, like everyone else, require periodic updating and/or broadening of skills, particularly in today's complex, competitive world.

□ If the attendees might feel that they have been singled out to attend, for example, to acquire or upgrade their skill in interpersonal relations, make certain that they are included as part of a more diverse group—those with different occupational backgrounds, tenure, gender, or unit affiliation.

□ Break the training into short modules, deliverable in two or three hours. This is particularly helpful for team training. The module can be taken when the team has integrated the prior work and can readily perceive the value of more training input.

□ Make certain that the training is not dull or boring. Even a technical subject like accounting can come alive if the trainer uses games, exercises, art, music, and/or puzzles. Word will spread that the training is fun and lively.

□ Be certain that management supports the training. For example, there's little point in stressing participative management, diversity, or group decision making if management doesn't "walk the talk." Support through positive role modeling, as opposed to mere lip service, is essential.

□ Finally, research the situation early on. Talk to the course sponsor to find out what support there is for the training and what problems might be anticipated.

Resisters, passive or angry, may still come to the classroom despite all your careful planning. Here are some techniques to deal with them, says Margaret Kaeter:

□ Advise participants at the outset that you've done your homework, that is, that you've researched the environment and you plan to make the training relevant to their work. If you have encountered any problems, for example, reorganizations, downsizing, or new leadership, tell them that you're aware of those new situations and possible impacts resulting from them.

☐ Introduce job-relevant situations and problems into classwork. For example, if the topic is communication, introduce back-home circumstances and events into classwork.

☐ Function as a facilitator rather than as a lecturer. You don't want to create resistance by communicating that you know it all.

☐ Stress the "WIIFM" ("What's in it for me?") factor. People want to see the benefits that the training will provide them. This emphasis should begin at the outset and be repeated at various times later on in order to reinforce the message.

☐ Don't hesitate to place on the table obvious resistance problems. Ignoring them only allows them to fester. Since problems won't go away by themselves, it's much wiser to let people discuss their feelings openly.

☐ If you are attacked by a participant via a hostile comment or question, deflect it by involving the total class. This approach should help to defuse the anger and reinforce the idea that you're facilitating the class rather than running it in an arbitrary way.

☐ Indicate and act on your availability for post-training counsel and assistance. People are likely to feel better about the training if they know that the trainer sees the training as more than just a formal presentation. Provide participants with reference materials and your phone number.

Summary

Problem participants are a fact of training work. We have tried to suggest some ways of coping with them. Basically, you will be ahead of the game if you regard the problem participant as a challenge rather than as a headache. This means that you must show patience and avoid arguments and putdowns. Endeavor to deal politely with the problem participant's peccadillos, using some of the suggestions made above. Also, wherever possible, let the group try to deal with such participants. They will probably do it more effectively than you can, most likely in a kidding way. For example, I recall one participant who employed "two-dollar" words and thus was soon referred to by several group members as "Parameters," a favorite word of his. Needless to say, "Old Parameters" began to get the message before too long.

Of course, in extreme situations you can exercise other options such as:

☐ *Group critique.* Take time to process group behavior. Zero in on the trouble maker, if no one else does.

☐ *Confrontation.* At the break, you might speak candidly to the obstructionist: "I think we have a good group and it has potential for a lot of progress. It would be helpful to the group and myself if you tried to involve others in the discussions and soft-pedaled some of your own inputs. Can I secure your help on this?"

☐ *Expulsion.* "May I be open with you? You have disrupted several sessions and no one here knows what to do about it. I don't either, but I do not intend to have you interfere with group accomplishment. If you cannot avoid arguing, disagreeing, and monopolizing our limited time, I shall have to ask you to leave."

There are also a number of other techniques which may prove applicable to several of the above problem-type participants. *Examples:*

☐ In anticipation of the presence of difficult, disruptive, or dominating participants, ask the group before the program starts to create a set of formal ground rules for the management of unwanted behavior, for example, arriving late, departing early, leaving frequently to take phone calls, conducting private discussions. Post the rules on a prominently displayed flipchart. The idea is for the rules of behavior to become *team-created* rather than facilitator-created, thereby making the group the rules enforcer.

☐ In connection with the above group rules input, you may wish to state, "I think those are very good guidelines. Why don't we take time out from time to time, stop the action and, as a group, check to see how well we are functioning as a problem-solving unit?"

☐ Give a difficult person a special (but legitimate) assignment, for example, recording minutes, timing the length of a group member's speeches (to aid in keeping the windy session dominator in check), summarizing at various points in the meeting, taking over the chairperson role for a short time period for discussion of a particular topic. *Rationale:* Since difficult participants are often attention seekers, providing them with a special task may help to meet that need.

One approach that is *not* recommended is that of manipulation, for example, special seating for purposes of better control, asking the difficult person to serve as an observer, ignoring the person by devices such as turning your back to him/her, etc. Being up front about the problem will retain the respect of the group and possibly the irritating one, too.

ADDED WAYS TO MOTIVATE LEARNERS

Training consultant Dean R. Spitzer, author of *Super Motivation: A Blueprint for Energizing Your Organization from Top to Bottom* (New York: AMA-COM Books, 1995), offers these approaches to trainee motivation [10]:

1. *Highlight training's value.* The organization must communicate that it feels strongly about the worth of training. Some visible ways to do this: require training for everyone from the CEO to the custodial force; have the CEO sit in classes to show his/her personal commitment; reward top employees with additional education and training of their choice.

2. *Provide enough time to do the training job properly.* Training that is rushed or squeezed into other activities is demotivational. So build training time into people's schedules.

3. *Train people when they are motivated to learn.* This means just-in-time rather than just-in-case training.

4. *Zero in on core competencies.* Provide training that is critical to on-the-job success; avoid information dumping.

5. *Seek learner input into training design.* Since people support what they create, invite interested

employees to become involved in training-design teams. Also, use interviews or focus groups to invite suggestions from employees for future training.

6. *Let people choose their own training.* This can be realized via employee self-assessment procedures which result in an employee's annual training plan. Another term for this is the Individual Development Plan.

7. *Provide financial incentives to learn.* This means paying for knowledge. Base pay rates might reflect various levels of job knowledge and skills. However, this device must be managed properly lest people are rewarded for acquiring useless credentials and unnecessary skills.

Note: The above ideas relate to what to do *before* the training takes place. The following of Dean Spitzer's ideas relate to what to do *during* the training.

8. *Provide active training.* You don't want your learners to sit passively as they might in their Sunday morning pews. Employ devices that display your recognition that the mind can only absorb what the seat can endure. (*The Winning Trainer* is dedicated to this concept.)

9. *Include fun in your training.* Interactive devices such as games, exercises, puzzles, and the use of art and music are keys to this end.

10. *Opt for variety.* Vary your training activities as opposed to punishing people with tedious lectures.

11. *Don't overlook the social side of training.* Plan for social interaction via small group work, simulations, collaborative problem solving, and cooperative learning.

12. *Allow for expertise sharing.* That is, let your participants share their secrets of success. People like to be recognized for their special skills and knowledge. Peer tutoring and mentoring opportunities can turn people on.

13. *Ensure a safe environment for learning.* Fear has no place in today's classroom. A good practice to follow is to ask trainees at the outset to come up with the rules they feel their training group should live by. Anticipate norms like "Don't be late to class," "Don't interrupt any-

one," "Keep what is said here confidential," and so on. Also, communicate that there are no mistakes in the classroom, nor are there stupid questions. We only have learning opportunities.

14. *Build positive measurement into the design.* Seek out ways to utilize self-measurement. Let trainees track their own progress. Self-graded quizzes are one device for this purpose.

15. *Build in early success.* This means letting your trainees master the easier tasks before they tackle the more complex ones. All of us need the benefit of confidence builders to ensure that our self-esteem is maintained and even augmented.

16. *Don't overlook adequate practice.* It's all too easy to underestimate actual proficiency. Sending people out to perform before they're truly ready is a certain demotivator. (Management guru Peter Drucker once observed that we know a lot about *demotivation* but very little about motivation!)

Note: The above points relate to what to do motivationally before and during the training. Here are Dean Spitzer's pointers on what to do, motivation-wise, *after* training's end.

17. *Ensure prompt application of newer skills.* The phrase "use it or lose it" sums up the need to implement the new learning immediately rather than at some time in the uncertain future. ("Sure, they showed me how to use that fancy computer, but that was four months ago.")

18. *Ensure performance assistance.* On the assumption that classroom learning can fade quickly unless supported by actual performance opportunities, it's a good idea to create support for the training by training intact work groups. If employees are trained together, *they* can help each other when they return to their jobs. Also consider the use of memory-free job aids and follow-up meetings.

19. *Encourage supervisor support.* The supervisor is often the key link between what is and is not implemented after training's end. The idea is for the boss to discuss with the trainee on his/her return what was learned, how it can be applied in the office, what added support may be needed, any added training that may be needed, and so on.

20. *Employ a new approach to the training certificate.* Traditionally, we give our trainees certificates after they have completed training. Spitzer suggests a more meaningful approach: Why not pass out the certificates *after* employees have demonstrated increased competence in their jobs? This will elevate the routine certificate-awards ceremony to a truly significant high-level plane.

KEY POINTS

1. Small group work is a basic tool for high participant involvement and learning. It entails limited risk for the participant and provides significant opportunities for peer learning, support, recognition, and camaraderie.

2. Effective use of small group techniques requires attention to such issues as getting started (icebreakers/openers); use of outdoors; group composition; seating arrangements; task assignments; leadership; monitoring group work; using spokespersons, recorders, and observers; and dealing with unwilling and problem participants.

3. When participants work in small groups for considerable time periods, group composition should be changed. This will energize participants and allow them to work with and learn from new people.

4. Participant seating should be planned and organized so that movement into small group configurations is quick and painless. Desks and tables, which add to formality, should only be used when considerable writing takes place.

5. Effective small group task assignment procedures entail concern with clarity of instruction, thought provocation, time limits, and as appropriate, requiring group decision or agreement on the task. The use of viewing-listening team assignments can enrich the discussion process.

6. The effective trainer endeavors to stay on top of things via monitoring small group proceedings. Key skills are sensing, listening, and intervening if necessary.

7. Leaders, recorders, and spokespersons should ordinarily be permitted to emerge naturally. If the small groups are having problems in deciding on who executes such roles, the trainer may introduce random methods of selection.

8. Problem participants should be looked at as a challenge rather than a headache. While many strategies are available to deal with such people, quite often the group itself can best decide how to deal with them.

REFERENCES

1. Margolis, Frederick H., and Bell, Chip R., *Managing the Learning Process,* Lakewood Publications, Minneapolis (1984), pp. 53–63.

2. Harmin, Merrill, "Zap the Risks from the Steps Ahead," *AHP Perspective,* Newsletter of the Association for Humanistic Psychology (November 1987), p. 17.

3. Margolis, Frederick H., and Bell, Chip R., *Managing the Learning Process,* Lakewood Publications, Minneapolis (1984), pp. 69–79.

4. DeValk, Steve, "Holding up a Mirror to Diversity Issues," *Training and Development* (July 1993), pp. 11–12.

5. Weintraub, Sandra, "Defusing Anger in the Training Room," *Training News* (July 1986), pp. 13–14.

6. Thiagarajan, Sivasailam, "Real Interactivity: Connecting People with People," *Performance Improvement* (March 2000), pp.47–52.

7. Luke, Robert A., Jr., "Managing Bunny Trails," in "Training 101," *Training and Development* (January 1994), pp. 19–21.

8. Beary, Rodney P., "When They're Sent to Be Fixed," in "Training 101," *Training and Development* (January 1995), pp. 13–14.

9. Kaeter, Margaret, "Coping with Resistant Trainees," *Training* (May 1994), pp. 110–114.

10. Spitzer, Dean R., "20 Ways to Motivate Trainees," *Training* (December 1995), pp. 52–55.

RECOMMENDED READINGS

Grote, Dick, "Dealing with Miscreants, Snivelers, and Adversaries," *Training and Development*, October 1998, pp. 19–20.

    A long-time trainer provides practical tips on how to disarm disruptive participants.

Huitman, Kenneth E., "The Trainer as 'Scapegoat,'" *Training and Development Journal,* July 1982, pp. 44–53.

    Participants who attend workshops may engage in "dysfunctional" behaviors such as arriving late, arguing, dominating, withdrawing, and embarrassing others including the trainer. The article presents causes for and strategies to deal with disruptive behavior.

Jensen, Melinda, "Perilous Personalities," *Successful Meetings,* November 1995, pp. 80–88.

    The author lists a number of unpleasant personalities that plague meetings and offers solutions to deal with them. Types discussed include The Prima Donna, The Blabber-mouth, The Me-First Participant, The Shrinking Violet, The Doubting Tom (or Tammy), Teeny Boppers, and the Space Cadets.

Jones, John E. "Dealing with Disruptive Individuals in Meetings," in *The 1980 Annual Handbook for Group Facilitators,* San Diego, University Associates, 1980, pp. 161–165.

    This article provides a repertoire of responses to deal with difficult participants more effectively, including pre-session and in-session approaches.

Pickhardt, Carl E. "Participant Hostility: Why It Comes with the Territory," *Training/HRD,* September 1980, pp. 16, 18–20.

    This article offers a psychological explanation for trainer-directed hostility as well as five strategies to cope with difficult individuals.

Suessmuth, Patrick, "Handling Classroom Problems," *Canadian Training Methods,* October 1975, pp. 26–27.

    Based on his personal experience, the author provides suggestions to deal with the big talker, the silent person/group, the person who starts to cry, the late-comers, the excessively polite group, undesired conflict in the group, an attack on one person, etc.

Thiagarajan, Sivasailam, "Participants from Hell: Checklists for Handling Disruptive Behaviors in Meetings," *Performance and Instruction,* August 1993, pp. 25–28.

    The author identifies 29 disruptive, negative behaviors of some participants at team meetings and offers a number of practical suggestions to deal with each of these behaviors. The author groups these unwanted behaviors into four major categories: disruptive talking behavior, disruptive behaviors related to preparation (homework problems), disruptive behaviors related to time, and disruptive interpersonal clashes.

Zander, Alvin, *Making Groups Effective,* Jossey-Bass Publishers, San Francisco, 1982.

    This work presents practical advice on making groups stronger and more cohesive, on setting realistic goals and standards, on overcoming obstacles to group decision making, on improving member communication, on coping with conflict and power.

Basic Techniques for Small Group Training

Many ideas grow better when transplanted into another mind than in the one where they sprang up.

Oliver Wendell Holmes, Jr. (1841–1935),
Associate Justice, U.S. Supreme Court

IN the prior chapter we discussed in a general way the use of small groups to enhance participant learning. In this chapter we shall present a number of specific small-group training techniques that are considered "basic," or relatively easy for the trainer to use. In the following chapter we shall present additional small-group techniques, which require more skill and experience on the part of the trainer.

USING DYADS AND TRIADS

The Dyad

The dyad, or pair, is a sure-fire participative technique. Every trainer or discussion leader can readily use it to involve the total group—and with remarkable quickness and efficiency. For example, all the trainer need do is to tell the group: "Turn to the person on your right (or your left, or your neighbor behind you) and discuss for five minutes the implications of _____." And presto! The training room is filled with the enthusiastic sound of all the participants partaking of a piece of the action. A skill point: The "turn around" procedure is a good way to meet a new person as opposed to conversing with a pal from the shop or office with whom one is buddied up.

Why does the dyad work practically all the time? Because it places two persons in a no-threat, eyeball-to-eyeball, head-to-head relationship where rapport is easy to achieve (just like starting a conversation with a passenger on a plane) and neither party can readily escape from it. Rare, indeed, is the participant who can block out the intimacy that the dyadic encounter provides.

Management professor Dr. Susan T. Kinney identifies five differences in the dynamics of dyads versus large units [1]:

☐ *Attention span.* The attention span on a topic is longer in a dyad than in a group because the partners can present only two viewpoints.

☐ *Influence on outcome.* Again, given the smaller unit (the pair), each party has greater influence on outcomes and decisions than the average group member is likely to have.

☐ *Influence on one another.* Dyadic participants are more readily able to influence one another than group participants are.

☐ *Presence.* With only two people involved, there is great pressure to be there; for example, one can't mentally wander off and thus abandon one's partner.

The dyad can be employed in many ways such as to:

☐ Serve as an icebreaker: "Find someone you don't know (at all or very well), introduce yourself, and talk about why you are here and what you hope to accomplish in this program."

☐ Encourage thought and discussion about a topic *prior* to its presentation.

☐ Discuss an assigned topic and have a spokesperson report back on it. "What do you think should be done about this issue (or problem, event, situation, development, influence, difficulty, shortcoming, result, conflict)?"

☐ Serve as a team of two observers who are to give feedback about an ongoing training activity (for example, an exercise, a role play).

☐ Give feedback on an exchange basis concerning one's behavior (participation, etc.) in a fishbowl activity. This private approach to feedback would be in lieu of the more usual public feedback. A procedure of this sort would be followed when it is evident that fishbowl participants are not ready for public feedback. (Of course, private feedback, since it is not subject to public scrutiny, may be watered down or not given at all.)

☐ Give support (encouragement, ego building) to another group member.

☐ Serve as a two-person training team, where the task is facilitated by working in pairs (for example, how to lift properly, how to listen).

☐ Orient and/or break in a new employee (the buddy system).

☐ Critique one another's plans or targets (contracting) for back-home improvement.

Note: One way to heighten interest in the assigned task is to suggest the following procedure to the pairs: "In your pair, have one person (Dyad Member A) present his/her plan as the client and the other person (Dyad Member B) serve as a consultant. As a consultant you ask for clarification if necessary, point up possible inconsistencies, encourage reality testing (will this really fly?), possibly suggest an alternate procedure, etc. Then reverse, Dyad Member A now becomes the consultant and Dyad Member B becomes the client." By calling the non-presenter a consultant we highlight the importance of that role. This ensures greater seriousness and active involvement plus a heightened analytical effort. Also, one may acquire new insights into the task by virtue of critiquing someone else's finished product.

☐ Resolve a conflict between two group members. For example, in an experiential training program such as team building, the trainer may use role negotiation to resolve the interpersonal block; that is, the trainer may start a rational dialogue by asking each party to the conflict to respond to this question: "What do I (John) want (or expect) from Mary (the other party to the conflict)?" And, in reverse: "What do I (Mary) expect from John?"

☐ Confer with another participant concerning the nature of an assignment in order to ensure full understanding of the ramifications of the assigned task.

☐ Share information about oneself (for example, regarding management style: whether one feels it is important to be close to subordinates, and if it is, how one goes about it).

☐ Serve as the basis for the formation of a larger group: a dyad, after discussion of a topic, may be asked to merge with another pair and continue to discuss the topic. Another pair may be added a bit later until six participants are discussing the topic. The added participants should serve to provide more "windows" on the topic and to energize the group.

☐ Use in first aid training, especially in such activities as examining patients, finding the pulse in one another's neck and wrist, executing the Heimlich maneuver (when food is stuck in the windpipe), bleeding control, and treating the injured for shock.

In some training programs dyads have been used in more intensive fashion:

☐ In a Consolidated Edison Co. of New York, Inc. "Communication Flow" seminar, 234 first- and second-level supervisors were brought together from all over the company. The objective was to improve horizontal communications in this large organization. Since this very large group was intimidating, the trainer had the managers pair off, after an icebreaker task, with a person they didn't know. The members of the dyads then interviewed one another to learn about work location, area of specialization, length of service, career history, and job performance areas most praised and criticized. Other small group activities followed the dyadic work. The training program, overall, was intended to establish a horizontal peer network across functional areas. Communication and social support were deemed to be more attainable in this fashion than by relying on those

above or below the level of the program participants [2].

☐ In a leadership or human relations program that runs a week or more, two participants can be assigned to meet each day for 30 minutes. They can discuss topics such as learnings from the course, relationships back on the job, or career objectives.

Note:

1. If the dyads are scheduled for 30 minutes before lunch, the pair can then go on to lunch together.

2. In a nonurban setting, a dyadic walk and talk through the countryside will provide an added dimension to the experience.

☐ Participants in a management training program can be assigned a different (or possibly the same) luncheon partner each day. At lunch they can build on the discussion that the formal program has initiated.

☐ In a leadership laboratory (sensitivity training or the T-group) pairs can be formed the first morning for an in-depth (one hour) get-acquainted session. Weather and other conditions permitting, this can, again, be a walk-and-talk activity.

☐ *Personality perceptions.* In a training program where participants are adequately well-acquainted and it is desirable to provide feedback to one another as to how one is perceived, for example, in training programs concerned with leadership, team building, assertiveness, or other personal growth areas, the following procedures may be used:

1. Team up participants in pairs.

2. Provide them with a list of personality characteristics, such as the one below.

3. Have each person in the dyad write his/her partner's first name (use initial only) after the five or six characteristics which are most descriptive of him/her. Characteristics not on the list may be added in the blank spaces.

4. Repeat step 3. This time each partner selects characteristics most applicable to himself/herself.

5. Ask dyad members to share perceptions of other and self, noting areas of agreement/disagreement. Explanations are to be provided as to why a particular trait was assigned to one's partner. (Total time: 15–20 minutes.)

6. If time allows, repeat the activity with a new partner.

7. Wind up the exercise by securing comments from the pairs. Some questions: Any learning about self? Was there a lot of agreement? Disagreement? Was there candor? Any surprises? How do you feel about your partner?

Note: If the program is designed for confidence building, instruct the participants to select *positive* traits only.

Figure 3-1 lists some personality characteristics that participants might attribute to one another.

Personality Characteristics				
Flexible	Aggressive	Earnest	Feminine	Stubborn
Playful	Docile	Cheerful	Masculine	Suspicious
Lively	Thoughtful	Self-confident	Calm	Hostile
Social	Receptive	Energetic	Sexy	Angry
Creative	Kind	Practical	Stable	Negative
Optimistic	Cooperative	Conforming	Persuasive	Impatient
Cautious	Pleasant	Submissive	Assertive	Pessimistic
Reserved	Dominating	Organized	Impulsive	Opinionated
Enthusiastic	Timid	Warm	Vigorous	Argumentative
Affable	Humorous	Determined	Open	Competitive

Figure 3-1. A list of personality characteristics participants in "Personality Perceptions" might draw ideas from.

These more intensive dyads provide an opportunity to build a deeper relationship with one or more participants, something that the formal program does not generally provide. (I remember one participant, who when asked how her 11:00 A.M. dyad was working out after two attempts at it, replied facetiously: "I'm not sure, but it does give me someone to go to lunch with every day!")

As to possible limitations of the dyad, it can obviously generate only a lesser amount of data about or insight into an assignment, compared to a larger group (triads or quartets). Also, on rare occasions the dyad may not work well because of bad chemistry between the two participants (for example, one person may be timid, hostile, uninformed, extremely nonverbal, not into the program, physically ill).

Note: If you have an odd number of participants and thus need an extra person to form a pair, you, as trainer, can join in and fill that gap.

As indicated in the prior chapter, our preference is to "mix up" group/team composition from one activity to another to allow participants to work with different people and to avoid getting too comfortable. Thus, in selecting partners for the dyad, the selections can be made at random by assigning numbers (e.g., 1 through 12) and then let your participants team up as follows "If you have an odd number, select someone with another odd number, preferably someone you don't know very well. Similarly, if you have an even number join up with someone who also has an even number, again with someone you don't ordinarily work with or know well."

The Triad

Triads or trios are an important configuration in small group work. They are small enough to provide privacy and intimacy, and at the same time they are large enough to bring a multiple viewpoint to bear on a problem or training assignment. They also provide for variety in small group work.

They are particularly useful in certain training situations, such as:

☐ In forming three-person role playing teams—two role players and an observer. For example, the three roles—boss, subordinate, and observer—may be rotated, allowing one triad to participate in all three roles.

☐ In providing help on the completion of an in-depth training assignment. For example, in working on a project for back-home application, the trio operates in this fashion: one person presents his/her project and the other two participants react to it in the form of feedback, critique, help, reality testing. Each person has an opportunity to present his/her project for analysis by the other two members of the trio.

☐ In a stress management workshop. One person can present a stress-laden situation (the participant's or the trainer's) to the other two, for example, a strong belief that he/she should have gotten a promotion awarded to someone else. One team member presents the irrational or emotional beliefs and attitudes that might be adopted by the non-promotee ("The best qualified person should always be promoted" or "Hard work should be rewarded"). The other team member presents the rational or logical position for the non-promotion-action ("In the real world many factors other than merit are at work"). Both team members, in essence, are trying to point out that in any stress situation, the irrational factors in our heads—our perceptions—may be as significant to that stress as the external event itself [3].

☐ Trios may be used as project teams or small task forces to work on an assigned problem. For example, if the program calls for field trips, plant visits, and the like, triads could be formed for such purposes.

☐ To improve communication, interaction, and relationships among key operating officials in an organization, a team of three managers may be sent to an outside facility for special training. For example, the prestigious Center for Creative Leadership, Greensboro, North Carolina, conducts a workshop designed to encourage and facilitate the management of innovation in an organization. Participants attend in triads, teams representing three pertinent functions, such as manufacturing, R&D, and marketing. The course works to develop each triad's ability to communicate and coordinate across organizational lines. Through such cross-functional team building, and with an awareness of the organization as a whole, the team will return prepared to help their organization put innovation into practice.

Note: Selection of those to attend the external facility on a joint basis would be based on *need,* for example, a possible history of less-than-cooperative relationships, mission changes which now require a very high level of cooperation, or the impact each manager's function has on the other. The training experience would not in itself be a substitute for a true team building effort. However, it may lead to better working relationships, greater coordination and communication, and possibly a start toward a more profound effort at team building.

☐ Triads may be formed early in the program to work intermittently (small group work) and to serve as a support system. If a participant group has not previously worked in triads, you may wish to point out that the best position for the triad is one that ensures that participants are connected via a very tight circular arrangement. Figure 3-2 illustrates seating arrangements that diminish productivity because eye contact is very difficult. (Since people are not fish, they don't have eyes on the sides of their heads.) Figure 3-3 shows the most effective arrangement.

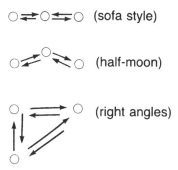

Figure 3-2. Examples of ineffective seating of triad members.

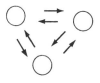

Figure 3-3. Example of effective seating of triad members.

Note: In most training situations, participants are sitting on standard rather than swivel chairs. Hence, unless the chairs are properly positioned by the participants, the furniture may get in the way of their learning.

The communication dynamics among a triad are quite different from those in a dyad [4]. In a conversation among a trio, any exchange between two of the parties is automatically subject to observation by the third person. Since the pair in communication is aware that there is an observer, they become more self-conscious, more aware of their own behavior, and thus more likely to behave with reasonableness and courtesy. This subtle social control serves to make the threesome more relaxed than a duo.

Other advantages of a triad: if a conflict arises or seems to erupt, the third person may serve as a mediator (voice of reason) between the two disagreeing parties. In addition, unlike in the dyad, one member can intermittently reduce his/her involvement/interaction and can take a breather, that is, become a listener, only offering a comment now and then. Finally, it is easy for a party to disengage totally. He/she simply picks an opportune time to leave, for example, when the pair is so engrossed in conversation that one can leave with the clear implication that one's presence is no longer needed. The departure may be accomplished without an oral comment, since the conversing dyad recognizes that the third person is out of the conversation.

You should also be aware that the dynamics of a triad can make for a certain amount of conflict. Why? Because one member may team up with another, producing an "odd person out" situation. This phenomenon of rejection is particularly likely to occur if the triad is composed of two men and one woman. One man may hit it off with the woman, leaving the other man in a rejected state. Of course, the pairing off problem can also occur in a triad of two women and one man in which one woman is left out. An answer to the possible pairing-off/rejection problem is to have the three participants collectively and candidly explore their feelings about their interpersonal relationships.

Skill pointer: If a dyad is struggling because of differences in personality, capability, interest, or enthusiasm level, consider adding a third party to alter the interaction/communication pattern. Also, replacing a member of a struggling triad may revitalize the unit.

PRODUCING DEFINITIONS

At one or more points in a training program, terms must be defined: motivation, time, discipline, coaching, counseling, manager, sexual harassment, women's

liberation. Although the trainer can readily provide a definition, it is frequently more thought-provoking to participants if they, individually and/or in small groups, create one of their own. You can anticipate, of course, that different individuals and small groups will produce different definitions. Thus, the learning, at a minimum, is that you cannot take for granted essentially complex terms—there are varying perceptions about them.

Sometimes a certain definition of a term or the term itself may not be acceptable to participants; for example, discipline may be considered too harsh a concept. Thus, you may ask the group for other more acceptable terms. You might use a flipchart for this procedure.

DISCIPLINE (put an X through it and ask for more acceptable terms)

CORRECTING (more acceptable)

TRAINING (more acceptable)

If a term or concept is quite complex and defies ready agreement as to its definition, you can use this divergence of opinion to construct an exercise or activity along the following lines:

☐ Ask each person in a mixed group (men and women) to define first a woman and then a man. A T-Column on a flipchart or a previously prepared sheet of paper can be used as a guide by the participants as shown:

Adjectives and Roles that Describe or Define

A Man	A Woman

Have participants meet in small groups (quartets or quintets) to compare definitions. Instruct them to look for stereotypes as to role (for example, the woman must take care of the children) and traits (for example, men are more creative or more artistic or more athletic). Then secure feedback from the small groups as to principal learnings from the exercise.

Note: A variation is to put all the completed T-columns in a box and have participants select on a random basis new sheets for analysis.

☐ Assign a definition to several small groups. Tell them that their definition will be judged by an impartial panel which will select a winner. The criteria for the decision will be based on:

a. Quality (maximum 15 points)

b. Creativity (maximum 10 points)

c. Language or phraseology (maximum 10 points) Select the judges either from outside the class, if practicable, or from the group at large. You may wish to provide a small prize to the winning team.

☐ In the selling area, it may be essential to introduce (or reacquaint) sales personnel with the "feature-benefit" concept. A good way to do this is to begin with a definition of the product or service concerned. To illustrate, let's assume our product is a toaster.

Definition: A toaster is an electrically powered appliance used primarily in the kitchen to produce dry bread quickly. Since everyone knows that much about a toaster, it is hardly a reason why a customer should be interested in our product as opposed to the dozen or more that our competitors make. Hence we need to provide additional information about our product that will make the prospect take real notice. We do this by moving from definition to features and benefits: This toaster has an electronic sensor, an expandable receptacle or well, an insulated plastic cover, push-button tray removal, and extended warranty. But your customer wants to know: "What's in it for me?" A T-column can help here, as in Figure 3-4.

Product: Toaster

Features	Benefits
1. Electronic sensor	No need to adjust control for dryness for it is done automatically and thus can never burn the bread. It also saves energy.
2. Expandable receptacle	Permits toasting thick slices of bread, muffins, rolls, biscuits, etc., and even handles irregular shapes and sizes.
3. Plastic cover, insulated	It doesn't heat up like metal so there is no danger of hand burns.
4. Push-button tray removal	Simplifies removal of tray which captures crumbs.
5. Extended warranty (10-year period) because of its advanced precision engineering	High quality all-around permits you to buy it and forget about replacements or annoying minor repairs.

Figure 3-4. Example of using a T-column to distinguish between features and benefits.

DEVELOPING AND WORKING WITH LISTS

A thought-provoking and easy-to-administer task for small groups is to have the participants develop a list and then have them process it in some fashion. The simplest format is for the trainer to state: "Come up with a list on _____ (problems, goals, challenges, reinforcers, characteristics of something, concerns, satisfactions, worries, strengths, needs, causes)."

Other formats follow:

Priority Development

The task is to develop a list and then prioritize all the items on it. The criterion for prioritizing may be creative value, criticalness or urgency, cost, feasibility, etc. Two possible lists are a list of stressors on the job and a list of needs retirees will have in the post-retirement period.

Weight and Rank

Another form of prioritizing is to have participants develop a list—each item on the list subject to a weight of ten votes (maximum). All members of the group vote 1–10 on each item, thereby producing a ranked preferences list. For example, members of the ORI (Organization Renewal, Inc., Washington, D.C.), a sophisticated, highly professional trainer-consultant network, produced a weighted list (in April 1980) on "What Are We Pleased to See in the Field of Human Resource Development in 1982?" (See Figure 3-5.)

Enrich the List

Give the participants a "starter" list of three to four items and ask them to expand on it.

Complementary Pairs

The task is to develop data in list form on complementary pairs such as parent-child, teacher-student, doctor-patient, husband-wife, male-female, boss-employee, consultant-client, coach-trainee, performer-audience.

ORI NETWORK MEETING
April 9, 1980
"WHAT ARE WE PLEASED TO SEE IN THE FIELD OF HRD IN 1982?"

	Number of Votes	Element
1.	17	Career and life planning systems are installed within the new educational system, organizations, and corporations.
2.	15	The public school system is organized for the benefit of each individual child.
3.	12	We have standards of certification for trainers and consultants.
4.	12	The American Management Association and National Institutes of Health have declared a requirement for meditation and reflection periods to improve quality of worklife.
5.	11	More follow-through on recommendations has been developed with the help of consultants.
6.	10	We have a free and functioning clearing house for consultants and trainers.
7.	10	There is greater concern with values and purpose (organizational and individual).
8.	9	Organizations realize the value of and support training at all levels.
9.	9	Many members of the Third World emerging governments are involved in our training workshops and are inviting us to theirs.
10.	7	There are more academic training courses on consulting.
11.	7	There are better systems for predicting and producing future outcomes.
12.	7	There are closer links to organization goals and the activities of trainers.
13.	7	There is more EEO development and involvement.
14.	6	There is an increased commitment to stress management.
15.	6	Greater line involvement in HRD.
16.	5	There is greater emphasis on development of in-house staff competencies.
17.	5	There is more scientific rigor in consulting.
18.	5	There are more in-house consultants and trainers.

Figure 3-5. Example of ranked preference list. (Reproduced by permission of Organization Renewal, Inc., Washington, D.C.)

Opposing Pairs

A list is developed on contrasting elements such as cause-effect, cost-benefit, most-least, newest-oldest, or the practical–the impractical. (Data on the complementary and opposing pairs can be collected via a T-column or posted on separate flipcharts.)

We Need to Know

Ask participants to provide must-have type of data. For example, in a time management course the task may be as follows: "We need to know what time it is to _____ (keep appointments, eat our meals, watch our favorite TV program)."

Question List

Participants are asked to develop a list of questions rather than statements, such as: What questions would you use to interview a prospective secretary (or director of marketing, or personnel manager, etc.) properly? What questions should a manager use to conduct a good career development interview?

Making Decisions

Ask participants to come up with as many options or courses of action as they can regarding a possible decision on a problem (for example, handling a marginal employee, conducting supervisory training). Then for each option have participants list its pros and cons, thereby ensuring a carefully thought-out decision,

Causes/Reasons

Have participants individually develop a list of ten reasons or causes for problem areas, such as failure to sell successfully, failure to delegate properly, failure to communicate properly, high accident rates, or lack of cooperation in an organization.

Ask a participant to read aloud the most important reason from his/her list, and then ask the group for solutions to the reason given. Then have another participant offer his/her most significant reason and, again, secure group solutions. Continue the process until everyone has had a chance to present a cause or reason for group resolution.

Criteria Development

Ask participants to develop a list of criteria for such matters as evaluating communication effectiveness in an organization, resolving conflicts between offices, giving feedback, conducting a coaching (or any other kind of) interview, making a sound decision, or administering an effective safety program. (One way to introduce this assignment is to say: "If you had to measure or assess the effectiveness of your promotion plan, what would you look at?")

After the participants have developed their lists, they may be asked to prioritize them, share them in small groups, develop a master list for each group on a flipchart, and post the flipcharts on the wall for total group review and discussion.

Bug List

Ask participants to develop a list of the things that are "bugging" the operation, the team, or the organization.

Wish List

Have participants imagine or brainstorm as many wishes as they can concerning something. This is done without concern for feasibility since the idea is to trigger insights.

Advice Giving

Have participants describe the advice they would give to another on a particular concern (for example, "My advice to the manager who wishes to manage his boss properly is to _____").

Expanding the List

At times it may be desirable to have participants develop a list that can be continuously expanded upon or added to *after* the training. For example, in an assertiveness training program, participants may be asked to develop a list of needs they feel they have a right to have met, such as to return an item to a store or to ask one's boss for feedback about one's performance. Group members are then told to keep this list and add to it frequently as their personal growth continues.

Quantity Considerations

From a quantity standpoint, you can present the task of developing a list as:

Unlimited. Ask for as many items as possible. This is the old "laundry list" idea. (In fact, the task can be introduced as follows: "Come up with a 'laundry list' regarding the skills an effective supervisor must have.") The aim of this approach is to stimulate broad thinking on a given topic.

Limited. Here we are seeking a well-screened list pertaining to something. For example: "Agree upon the three most significant characteristics of an effective leader." Note that we are asking the small groups to *agree* upon something, which gives them an added challenge to perform well.

In both the limited and the unlimited requests, we can build competition (added motivation to perform) into the task if we wish. An example is: "We have four small groups. Let's see which group can come up with the most suggestions or ideas on how to use secretaries effectively. You have 15 minutes to do this." In some instances a prize may be offered to augment interest.

Task Assignment Considerations

From a task assignment standpoint, the request to develop a list can also be presented differently:

- ☐ *Oral vs. written.* You have the option of giving your instructions verbally, putting them on the chalkboard or flipchart, or providing them on an instruction sheet. The written instructions are preferred if you need to ensure clarity of the assigned task or if you desire to operate more formally, for example, in respect to a course or program which is to be presented uniformly by different trainers.

- ☐ *Structured vs. unstructured.* When using a worksheet we can choose a relatively unstructured style by simply stating the task on the top of the paper. The remaining white space is the area to be filled in. Conversely, we can add motivation by giving participants a structured worksheet, which in effect sets up numerical targets for them. An example of a structured worksheet is given in Appendix 11.

- ☐ *Public vs. anonymous.* Although lists are ordinarily developed for publicly posting the items, there may be instances when participants wish to treat their data more privately. For example, in an in-house stress management workshop, public listing of one's sources of stress may be perceived by some participants as too threatening. In such circumstances, each participant may develop a separate or private list. The trainer would then collect the lists and randomly post the stressors on the flipchart for further action or discussion.

□ *Individual vs. group.* Assignments can be made directly to individuals, directly to groups, or both to individuals and then to groups. In the latter instance, we use a two-stage process:

1. Individual work for ideation.
2. Small group work to consolidate (combine, screen) the individual lists.

The final steps in list development, regardless of our approach to generating quantity or quality, are to:

1. Post them (preferably on flipcharts) for public display.
2. Hold a group-at-large discussion about them.
3. Process the data in other ways; for example, a list of problems on employee discipline (violation of safety rules, lateness, insubordination, etc.) may form the basis for role plays wherein the supervisor has to coach, counsel, or reprimand the offender in some way.

Trainer-Developed Lists

The previous paragraphs have been devoted to the development of lists by participants. It is also possible for the trainer to provide participants with lists from which they can work. For example, in a stress management program participants may be given the two lists in Figure 3-6 and asked to circle those items in each list which relate to their current circumstances. The selected items are then shared and discussed in pairs or triads.

Note: The same format used in Figure 3-6 could be used for other topics. Some examples: What I would like my work to be/What I would not like my work to be; What I would like my career to be/What I would not like my career to be; What I would like my work group to be like/What I would not like my work group to be like.

SHARING PERSONAL INCIDENTS

Group members can be quickly and significantly involved by asking them to draw on their past experiences for incidents or events which relate to or exemplify course concepts. Some examples of tasks which might be assigned:

Payoff Discussion

Where did careful listening (or planning, customer relations, or reinforcing desirable behavior) pay off? Have participants discuss their incidents in small groups, and then secure reports from the small groups on the importance of these events.

Helped-Hindered Approach

Divide the total group into buzz groups with one set of groups to come up with personal experiences wherein their boss either failed to (or was reluctant to) delegate or hindered delegation. The other set of groups reports on the opposite—where delegation was accomplished and how it affected them favorably.

I see work as	I see my lifestyle/situation as
a challenge	adventuresome
opportunity	confining
pleasure	draining
a chore	exhilarating
tedious	buoyant
travel/field trips	affluent
new experiences	neutral
repetitious	care-free
wearing	over-extended
all pay	balanced
new contacts	harried
reports	worrisome
in-basket	successful
growth-oriented	pleasing
a hassle	growth-inducing
endless	oppressive
energizing	rapid-paced
professional	relaxed
tops	fulfilling
enervating	anxiety-laden
dull	joyful
stimulating	questionable
rewarding	superficial
stifling	casual
delightful	meaningless
treadmill	zestful

Figure 3-6. Example of a trainer-provided list for participant response.

An alternate topic relates to incidents when the supervisor was a coach who encouraged personal growth vs. instances where the supervisor's poor coaching was detrimental to growth.

Note: Collecting small group data on a T-column on a flipchart can help sharpen the issue.

A variation on these procedures is to have the participants respond to the assignment on an individual basis before the small group work. The individual work can be facilitated via a worksheet such as the one in Appendix 12. Reducing the incidents to writing aids participants to think through the ramifications of the event in more precise and meaningful detail.

Influence vs. Authority

Have participants in small groups share instances where they, as supervisors, accomplished something important with subordinates by virtue of the influence they had as opposed to the authority they had and could have used. Then show a film/video (or give a lecturette) on informal authority or leadership. Discuss the film (or talk) in relation to the previously discussed personal experiences with influence.

New Worker Orientation

To start a supervisory training session on the orientation of the new worker, assign participants to small groups. One set of groups is to cite personal experiences they recall when their orientation was very effective; the other set of groups produces examples of orientations they experienced which were not effective. Post examples to a flipchart, using the T-column again; compare the two sets of examples and develop principles of orientation from them.

Card Draw

Using a set of topics on cards that you have previously developed, have each participant draw a card and cite a personal experience pertinent to the card. For example, in a supervisory (or sales) training course the cards might read as follows:

- ☐ The best boss I ever had _____.
- ☐ As a supervisor (or salesperson) the most important thing I've learned is _____.

- ☐ An employee I almost gave up on but didn't was _____.
- ☐ My most successful case of delegation (or selling) was _____.
- ☐ The most important thing I ever did for my self-development was _____.
- ☐ An experience I had which really made me feel good as a supervisor (or salesperson) was _____.

Note:

1. Each card should be written so that practically everyone can come up with a personal incident relating to it. If not, have the participant put the card back in the deck and allow the drawing of another card.
2. This activity should make for a good opener in a supervisory (or sales) training course.

Goal Setting

In an MBO (Management by Objectives) or goal setting training program, have participants:

1. Individually select a key task (major responsibility) in one's job and come up with the "indicators" or control data governing it. (For example, indicators concerning the success or failure of an executive recruitment program, in the case of a personnel director's job, would be: the number recruited, the quality of the recruits as measured by annual performance data, meeting of deadlines, adherence to budget.)
2. Meet in pairs or trios to discuss the validity of their selected indicators.
3. Hold a general discussion regarding the value of indicators, the difficulty, if any, in identifying them, problems of validity (are they measuring what they are supposed to?), etc.

Best-Worst Approach

Ask participants to think of incidents in best-worst terms:

- ☐ The best boss I ever had did _____.
- ☐ The worst boss I ever had did _____.

☐ The best communicator I ever knew did _____
_____.

☐ The worst communicator I ever knew did _____
_____.

☐ My most successful sales experience occurred when _____.

☐ My least successful sales experience occurred when _____.

Note: The individually developed data can be processed in either small groups or the total group.

Near-Miss Analysis

In a safety program ask participants to recall near-miss accidents they have seen or personally experienced. Then record them on a flipchart. Use a tri-column to aid the group to understand better the causative factors involved and how to minimize or remove them:

Near-Miss Analysis Chart

Near-miss Incidents	Causes	Preventive Measures

To conclude the near-miss analysis activity, give participants a blank copy of the preceding worksheet. Encourage them to use it wherever accidents may occur—on the job, at home, on vacations, on the highway, etc. Point out, too, that near-miss accidents cannot be dismissed lightly, for they are indicators, or even warning signs, of hazards to guard against.

PREDICTION

A means of introducing a topic in an interest-generating and involving way is to use the technique of prediction. For example, assume you are introducing brainstorming to a group that is not familiar with it in the full sense of the term. You might start out in this fashion: "We're going to have some skill practice in working with the technique of brainstorming. But before we have our brainstorm-

ing session, let's go around the room and get some words, phrases, characteristics, or qualities that describe brainstorming as you understand it."

The elicited ideas or adjectives are then posted to the flipchart. You then say: "O.K., this describes brainstorming as you see it. Let's run this set of slides and see what they tell us about brainstorming. We'll then compare our ideas—essentially a prediction—with those on the slides."

After the slide presentation the ideas presented by the group can be compared and checked off as to their appropriateness. *Note:* Be complimentary concerning the predicted items which were on target. (For the use of prediction in working with film/video, see Chapter 16.)

GROUP DEBATES

Debates are a helpful way of exploring opposing sides of an issue. If done on a team basis rather than on the more typical individual basis, everyone can "play." Suggested procedures follow:

Formal Debate

The following is a step-by-step procedure for organizing a debate:

1. Assume the total group size is 19. Set up four debating teams of four each, with two teams taking the pro side of the issue and two the negative side. Advise the teams that their positions can be presented by one or more members.

2. Appoint as judges the remaining three members. Give them criteria to judge the debate: force (logic, powerfulness) of argument (10 points maximum); creative ideas produced (20 points maximum); etc.

3. Provide for adequate preparation time (20–30 minutes).

4. Set time limits for the presentations (5–7 minutes).

5. Have one quartet present the affirmative position and another the negative.

6. Have another quartet present a rebuttal to the negative view and have the last team of four rebut the affirmative position.

7. Have the judges retreat for their deliberations.

8. Conduct a group-at-large discussion as a wrap-up to the debate.

9. Have the judges announce the results of the debate. *Note:* It is desirable to have the judges' decision come after all discussion has been completed. This procedure will avoid an over-emphasis on who "won" and who "lost."

Informal Debate

A less-formal way of debating is as follows:

1. Announce a topic that has a potential for differences of view.

2. Ask participants to select the pro or con side of the issue.

3. Ask the "pros" to move to one side of the room, the "cons" to the other. (Try to have the two sides be roughly equal in number.)

4. Ask each group to muster all the arguments it can for its position.

5. With the groups in their different locations, informally secure affirmative and negative arguments. Continue the debate until the topic is adequately discussed.

Note: This highly participative procedure is particularly useful to introduce a session or a topic. It may also be used on an *ad hoc* basis when opinions differ in the course of a discussion.

Facing Chairs

Another way to deal with a controversial issue is to place the chairs in two lines so that participants can face one another. Then use these procedures:

1. Seat everyone, for example, seven participants (the pros) in one row and seven participants (the cons) in the other.

2. Let the pros state their arguments to the cons.

3. Now let the cons state their arguments to the pros.

4. Shift participants to the opposite chairs so that the pros are now the cons and vice versa.

5. Have all the new pros state arguments for the pro side.

6. Have the new cons state arguments for the con side.

7. Hold a general discussion, noting if there is a shift away from the earlier polarized views.

Note: In contrast to the fishbowl (see Chapter 4) where one group is active and the other is silent, in this technique *both* groups are interacting with each other.

Seeking Consensus

A variation on the typical "win-lose" debating procedure, such as the ones just described, is to have the teams strive for consensus. Here are the procedures:

1. Divide the full group into two teams, one taking the positive view and the other the negative side of a controversial issue.

2. Have each team discuss its position in private (20–30 minutes).

3. Have each team appoint a spokesperson to articulate its position. Allow five minutes for each presentation.

4. Have each team present a rebuttal to the initially stated position of the opposing team (three minutes). Have the teams select another spokesperson for the rebuttal.

5. Now ask each team member to contribute $1.00 (or more) to a kitty. Tell them it will go to "a worthy cause," which will be explained shortly.

6. Tell the participants that they are now to start a second phase of the debate. This phase requires the *total* group to reach a consensus on the issue. (Allow 30–45 minutes for this.) Advise participants that if they reach a consensus, you will add 50% of the amount already contributed to the kitty, to be spent by the group in any way it wishes. But if they do *not* agree in the time allotted, you will pocket all the money.

7. After the time is elapsed, discuss with the total group such issues as the ease or difficulty of achieving consensus on a controversial issue, the importance of money as a motivator, how they felt about the trainer arbitrarily setting

ground rules involving money, and the application of this debating procedure to the back-home situation.

Research on Controversy

How well do participants learn from debates, controversy, etc.? An experiment involving 84 sixth graders in a Minnesota school indicated that controversy may be a valuable learning device [5]. Three student groups were set up along these lines:

- ☐ *Controversy group.* Half the group were told to defend strip mining, the other half to oppose it. But the group as a whole had to reach a consensus on the issue.
- ☐ *Concurrence seeking group.* Their instructions were to decide whether to strip mine coal, but to avoid arguments, stress agreement, and compromise quickly.
- ☐ *Individual work.* Each student in this group worked on the issue without talking to others about it.

The results were these:

Those in the *controversy group* saw the others reach an opposite conclusion and thus felt their own new point challenged. Since no one could be sure that he/she was right, additional information had to be secured. This meant everyone was forced to articulate their positions and to try to understand those of the others, too. After arguing each view, a joint conclusion was reached, and the study concluded that this group had a better grasp of the material.

Those in the *concurrence seeking* group suppressed differences to achieve a compromise, became fixed in their positions, were reluctant to explore options, and failed to see validity in different perspectives. They later expressed dislike of the other students and the subject matter!

Those *working alone* did not need to elaborate their position. Since they were unaware of other alternatives, they closed their options prematurely.

The conclusions of the study: Openness to alternative views means better communication and problem solving; clearer thinking results in better management of conflict and ethical reasoning.

TRIAL FOR ERROR (MOCK TRIAL)

This group-in-action technique is an old standby, entailing a "trial by jury" for some "egregious" behavior. Examples of "crimes" for which its perpetrators could be "prosecuted" are

- ☐ A lost sale
- ☐ A lost customer
- ☐ Failure to delegate
- ☐ Failure to develop an able subordinate who, as a consequence, leaves the organization
- ☐ Failure to conduct an appraisal interview
- ☐ Failure to level in the appraisal interview
- ☐ Failure to face up to widespread bad morale caused by an overbearing key assistant who reports to you
- ☐ Reluctance to develop a needed policy
- ☐ Toleration of unsafe work practices or conditions

Unless the group is unusually large, the jury trial provides the opportunity to establish roles for everyone:

- ☐ The defendant
- ☐ Attorney for the defense (this may be a single participant or a team of two or three)
- ☐ Witnesses for the defense (optional; useful if more roles are needed to involve everyone)
- ☐ The prosecuting attorney
- ☐ Witnesses for the prosecution (optional)
- ☐ Judge
- ☐ Jury (12 participants including a foreperson)
- ☐ Bailiff (very optional, for this is only a nonsubstantive role)

To give the "courtroom" adequate atmosphere, try to have the judge seated at a higher level complete with black robe and gavel.

Remember, the secrets to a good jury trial are

- ☐ Careful casting of the key characters.
- ☐ Adequate preparation by the key participants—attorneys, witnesses, defendant.
- ☐ Allowing enough time for the case to be developed in the court.

☐ Allowing enough time for the jury to weigh the evidence before it reaches a decision. Have these deliberations take place publicly so everyone in the group can listen to the issues again and in another, possibly more objective, setting.

CIRCULAR WHIP

With everyone (maximum of 10–15) seated in a circle, "whip" around it and allow everyone to make a *single,* brief contribution on an assigned topic. As illustrations, this may be on:

☐ My major goal in this program

☐ The most important trait of an effective leader

☐ What really counts in customer relations

☐ The way I see motivation

☐ A key to accident prevention

☐ My most important learning in this program

The whip, as a round robin device, adds elements of novelty, energy, and involvement to a session or program.

The circular whip is effective only in a relatively small total group. This follows, since it would be extremely awkward, for example, to seat 30–50 participants in a circle and then solicit their opinions. In a large participant group, two or more such whips may be conducted simultaneously.

LEARNING FROM FIELD TRIPS

Visits to points of interest away from the training room, wherever practicable, are advantageous because they

☐ Are a means of enriching the training experience.

☐ Are particularly essential if much of the training is theoretical and conceptual.

☐ Provide a desirable change of pace.

☐ Provide an opportunity for participants to get to know one another in a more in-depth way.

☐ May provide fun, excitement, novelty, new motivation to learn, and so on.

☐ Provide a chance to develop oral and/or written communication skills in respect to the reporting phase of the trip.

To maximize results from field trips, these guidelines should be considered:

1. Be certain that the objectives of the trip are well defined and related to the central purposes of a given training unit and/or the total training program. Literally ask yourself: Is this trip really necessary?

2. Plan logistics properly: who to contact, how to reach the visitation point, when to arrive, when to depart.

3. Provide written instructions to the participants concerning what to look for at the point of visitation. Also provide appropriate background materials.

4. Indicate whether the work is done individually, in pairs, in small groups, etc.

5. Indicate what kind of tasks participants are responsible for upon return to class: a report (written or oral), a case study, a completed survey, summaries of interviews, certain documentation such as photographs, collection of materials.

6. Schedule enough time for the processing of the learnings from the field trip.

7. Secure feedback (evaluation) from the group concerning the trip. This will enable you to strengthen your programming for future trips.

Field trips obviously may be organized as a total group activity, with each member being *individually* responsible for observing and reporting on his/her experience. However, our concern is with the use of small groups or teams of two to five who engage in the field trip.

MASTERING REFERENCE MATERIAL

At times it is desirable to have participants become familiar with various resources or reference material. This may be textual material in a notebook, a set of handouts, policies/procedures in a manual, etc. One way to do this is to:

1. Establish teams of two to four participants.

2. Assign the teams several problems which can be answered by checking the reference work. This is essentially the "open book" method used frequently in college courses.

3. Secure reports from the teams concerning their findings.

Note: The research may be done in class or treated as a homework assignment.

ENDINGS: WRAPPING UP AND SAYING GOODBYE

Every training course or program has to come to an end. For participants, this ending may provoke a sense of relief. ("I'm sure glad that's over. Now I can get back to what I'm paid for.") Or it may cause no particular concern—courses start and courses end. ("I'm glad they spelled my name correctly on that Certificate of Course Completion.") Or it may entail a touch of sadness. After all, participants may have spent long, intense and possibly intimate blocks of time together. They have certainly gotten to know one another and have probably developed respect and appreciation for one another, too. These feelings have grown because of much discussing, debating, supporting, cooperating, and sharing of ideas and emotions, some of which may have been quite personal.

So if at program's close there is a feeling of intimacy and camaraderie and a degree of regret that the experience must now end, you, as the trainer/facilitator, certainly don't want people to leave with a sense of confusion and incompleteness. It thus behooves you to give serious thought to the close out, just as you did at the beginning of the course when you concerned yourself with establishing a proper atmosphere and kicked things off with one or more icebreakers or openers. You should try to end things with something of a meaningful bang, rather than with an unsatisfying whimper.

Trainer Pamela E. Burns asserts that the trainer must do much more at course end than simply restate course objectives. She believes that a good conclusion [6]:

☐ Provides an opportunity for group members to assess their own learning/progress/accomplishment.

☐ Offers trainees reassurance that they've met their goals and thus highlights course achievements.

☐ Stresses that learning is not a one-shot accomplishment but rather a continuing process.

☐ Recognizes each participant as a unique and special person.

A trainer who pays attention to the above concerns can help instill program participants with the confidence they need to turn course learnings into new, on-the-job action. Specific approaches the trainer can use to address these concerns are as follows:

1. *Be certain to allow enough time for a meaningful ending.* Don't breathlessly run activities right up to quitting time. The precise amount of time dedicated for this purpose will vary with the length of your program, its nature (for example, lecture-oriented vs. experiential), the personality of your group (warm, friendly, fun-oriented vs. cold, distant, withdrawn), and the degree of rapport and intimacy achieved among group members and with the trainer.

2. *Plan for some "thank you" time.* If you've been primarily a lecturer ("the sage on the stage"), thank people for listening. If participants have worked on tough projects, compliment them or their hard work. If the program has been highly interactive and participative (small group work, role playing exercises, etc.), provide an experiential activity that allows participants to say thanks to one another.

3. *Provide a course-end opportunity for measurement of one's learning.* People have a need to assess their progress before they depart, so include an activity that serves as a helpful barometer of accomplishment. This can be a self-evaluation, feedback from others, or some combination of these two procedures.

4. *Provide activities which highlight each person's unique individuality.* While your overall program had goals for the group to accomplish, everyone is a unique personality and thus has his/her own objectives to be met. A helpful procedure is to encourage each learner to identify the one or more phases of the course that were most helpful/significant/

relevant to him/her. You might ask each person to make a public statement about his/her learnings or accomplishments. Or if part of your program has included journal-keeping, people might be asked to make a private entry into their diaries.

5. *Build in action plans.* Hopefully, you indicated at the course's onset that participants would have the opportunity to develop plans to implement their new learning back-home. Your program, then, should be structured so that time is available to develop and share action plans with fellow participants.

Feedback and Personal Learning

In the following paragraphs, a number of exercises are presented to help close out one's training course/program.

Circular Whip

With everyone seated in a circle, the trainer "whips" around the circle and lets each participant respond to one or more of these statements:

- ☐ The most important thing I have learned from this program is _____.
- ☐ What I intend to use more of when I get back to my job is _____.
- ☐ What I learned about myself in this experience is _____.
- ☐ My feeling about this group is that _____.
- ☐ My feelings now that we are breaking up and going home are _____.

Opportunities for Growth

Standing in a tight circle with the group, the trainer tosses a catchable object (an orange, bean bag, softball, football, tennis ball, or small pillow) to one participant, who will now receive feedback from the other group members concerning any one or more of these topics: performance in the group; apparent personal strengths; possibilities/opportunities/potential for personal growth/development/improvement.

Card Statements [7]

Pass out 5" × 8" cards and ask group members to enter on one side "My *thoughts* now are . . ." and on the other side "My *feelings* now are . . ." Then ask all participants to read aloud their thoughts. As a second round of readings, ask participants to read aloud their feelings: "My feeling about this group is that . . ."

Round of Appreciation [8]

Have participants stand and form a circle. Give each person a glass or paper cup. The idea is to have each participant "capture" from his/her fellow group members one significant quality—his/her essence—and put these qualities in the glass or cup. Each participant then addresses all the others, one at a time, in this fashion: "Betty, I want to take back with me your cheerfulness (or your good humor, support giving, concern for others, etc.). I will now place it in this cup." Be sure that each person is addressed by his/her name and that eye contact is maintained as the statement is made.

Note: If you have a large group, divide it into smaller groups of 6–10 participants so that everyone can participate.

Group Mural

One way to set a happy tone for departure is to have the group develop a mural depicting the group's "history"—beginnings, significant events (high and low), learnings, strong personalities who emerged, fun-type views of the trainer, predictions about the future, feelings about the ending.

Procedurally, all that is needed are several flipcharts posted *laterally* on a wall, large felt-tip pens for all, and contributions by everyone. This activity is more workable with a fairly small group—8–12 participants. The mural might be photographed and copies made to be forwarded to group members as a keepsake of the event.

The Same, More of, Less of

In an experiential training program where people have had considerable time to observe one another's behavior, ask all participants to provide feedback to all the other group members on a one-at-a-time basis. For example, if there are 12 group members, 11 of them would give their feedback (impressions) to the 12th group member. This is done rotationally until all 12 per sons have received feedback from the other 11.

The format in presenting feedback is as follows: "Pat, what I liked about your performance/contribution here is . . . What I would like to see you do more of is . . . And what I would like to see you do less of is . . ."

Note:

1. It is suggested that the one receiving the feedback from his/her fellow participants take notes on a *three-column basis*—the same, more of, less of—so that the feedback is readily captured. By using the columnar format, the feedback recipient can easily see which suggestions are most common. Obviously, if six of the twelve participants comment on one behavior, it is more meaningful than if only one or two do.

2. The trainer may wish to pass out previously prepared sheets with spaces for the three categories of feedback.

3. Writing the feedback down is very important because memory is a fickle thing.

4. To ensure that the feedback recipient actually hears what is said, he/she might be asked to summarize it to the group.

Circular Close

In an experiential training program, another way to close things out is to have participants stand and form a tight circle, arms firmly around one another's shoulders. Then ask for a volunteer first to say something positive or complimentary about the person on his/her immediate right and then to indicate his/her primary learning from the program. Repeat the process until everyone has participated. As a final (optional) step, participants may say goodbye through a hug with the person next to him/her.

Anticipate that each participant will wish to hug all the others before the final goodbye is said.

Initial and Final Feelings

Ask each participant to complete these two sentences and express them out loud to the group: "When the course began I felt that . . ." and "Now that the course is over I feel . . ."

Post-Course Contact

Typically, courses or programs end with the trainer and the participants saying goodbye to one another, and for all practical purposes, all meaningful contacts are ended. Of course, on occasion a participant may drop the trainer a note of appreciation or may even telephone to ask for some help. Formal follow-ups by the trainer, either in the form of post-course sessions or some type of contracting (action plans), may also prolong the contact for a month or two.

One way you can continue the relationship is to offer continuing assistance to the departing participants. A sample form for participants to use in seeking post-program assistance is found in Appendix 13. Thus, you may say: "Now that we've met and worked together, I would like very much to remain in touch with you even though the program has ended. So when you turn in your evaluation form, please pick up two or three of those forms on the table. I have also provided envelopes addressed to me. The envelopes will make it easy for you to contact me for any help you may think I can offer."

Note: While techniques for saying goodbye may also apply to large training groups, the request to "keep in touch" takes on special and significant meaning with a relatively small total group (10–20). Why? Because the trainer has been in a position to establish rapport with all or nearly all group members, something which cannot happen with a larger group.

KEY POINTS

1. Small group work, by definition, includes dyads and triads as well as buzz groups. Dyads provide intimacy and thus instant interaction. Triads have the advantage of offering multiple views on the problem being discussed.

2. Assignments to small groups typically assume the form of a question or problem. Other ways

to challenge small groups are to ask them to produce a definition, develop a list, share personal incidents, or make a prediction.

3. Producing a definition requires group members to engage in focused rather than generalized thinking. The pressure of agreeing on a definition intensifies the learning experience.

4. Producing a "laundry list" on a subject challenges participants to tap the resources of the group fully.

5. Sharing of personal incidents has the merit of introducing "live" data into the discussion. Realism is thus substituted for someone else's experience and problems; that is, from an outside source.

6. Additional ways to involve participants are via group debate, field trips, "trial by jury," the circular whip, and mastering reference material.

7. In closing out a training program, attention should be given to procedures for saying goodbye.

REFERENCES

1. Johnson, Virginia, "Two-person Interactions: Trifle or Treasure?" *Successful Meetings* (December 1992), pp. 128–129.

2. *Training/HRD* (December 1981), pp. 16–17.

3. This example is adapted from "A Cognitive Approach to Stress Management," *Behavior Today* (March 2, 1981), p. 7.

4. "Conversation In Two's or Three's?" *The Pryor Report* (September 1987), p. 5 (from the book by Emile Pin, *The Pleasure of Your Company: A Socio-Psychological Analysis of Modern Society,* Praeger, New York (1985)).

5. "Minnesota Experiment Shows Controversy May Be Teaching Aid," *Leading Edge Bulletin* (February 1, 1982), pp. 1, 3.

6. Burns, Pamela E., "Endings: Bridges to the Future," in "Training 101," *Training and Development Journal* (October 1988), pp. 19–29.

7. Adapted from "114. Closure: Variations on a Theme," in Pfeiffer, J. William, and Jones, John E. (Eds.), *A Handbook of Structured Experiences for Human Relations Training,* Vol. 4, University Associates, Inc., San Diego (1973).

8. Adapted from "176. Symbolic Toast: A Closure Experience," in Pfeiffer, William, and Jones, John E. (Eds.), *The 1976 Annual Handbook for Group Facilitators,* University Associates, Inc., San Diego (1976).

RECOMMENDED READING

Davis, Lany N., and McCallon, E., *Planning, Conducting and Evaluating Workshops,* Learning Concepts, Austin, Texas, 1974.

This presents an overview of workshop planning and management from the standpoint of adult education. A section on methods is included.

McLagan, Patricia A., *Helping Others Learn: Designing Programs for Adults,* Addison-Wesley Publishing Company, Reading, Massachusetts, 1978.

This approaches the training function from the standpoint of the learner and focuses on these components of the learning process: motivation, information processing (using appropriate methods and strategies to facilitate learning), learning results, and learning application and transfer.

Walter, Kate, "Bring on the Entertainment," *Personnel Journal,* July 1995, pp. 84–90.

Today's training is "audience friendly" (participative, interactive), using games, exercises, props, music, song, magic, dramatics, theater, comedy, and videos. This approach increases attention levels while boosting learning and retention.

4 Additional Techniques for Small Group Training

The only kind of learning which significantly influences behavior is self-discovered or self-appropriated learning—truth that has been assimilated in experience.

—Carl R. Rogers, U.S. humanistic psychologist, founder of client-centered or nondirective counseling/therapy

THE prior chapter discussed a number of basic training techniques for small group work. In this chapter we will present a number of added small group training techniques, all of which require more skill and experience on the part of the trainer. They are

☐ The fishbowl
☐ Working with "mind pictures"—fantasy, guided imagery, etc.
☐ Working with pictures
☐ Using art
☐ Using music
☐ The journal or diary
☐ Working with models

Other chapters will deal with additional methods wherein groups are put to work very actively, particularly role playing (Chapter 5), games and simulations (Chapter 6), exercises (Chapter 7), puzzles (Chapter 8), and instrument-data analysis (Chapter 9). The chapters on problem solving (Chapters 10, 11, and 12) treat other group-in-action methods such as brainstorming and working with metaphor and analogy.

THE FISHBOWL

Also known as clusters or the group-on-group technique, the fishbowl is a highly worthwhile tool for the trainer who is interested in dynamic group involvement methods.

The fishbowl can assume several configurations. Its most common form is simply an inner ring (Group A), which is the discussion group, surrounded by an outer ring (Group B), which is the observation group, as shown in Figure 4-1.

The inner group can be given an assignment based on content, processing, or content and processing. If the assignment is one of content, you ask the inner circle (Group A) to address itself for 10–30 minutes to a given subject such as production problems, scouting the competition, the sales program, how to improve communications (or safety, or employee morale, or field relations, or supplier relations). The outer group (Group B) observes silently.

After the inner circle's time is up, the outer circle can be asked to respond to the same assignment Group A had, to comment on Group A's deliberations, or to do both. It is also beneficial at times to repeat the

entire process a second time. Each group thus engages in discussion and observation twice.

If anxiety exists in the inner circle because of the presence of the observers in the outer cluster, it (the anxiety) should be processed. By talking about it, the imagined fear can readily be allayed. Conversely, until the anxiety has been orally acknowledged, the inner group is likely to be inhibited in its discussion.

In discussing process as opposed to content, the inner group focuses on the behavior of the other group as a functioning unit. In effect, one small group is giving the other small group feedback about its performance or behavior. The feedback may relate to individual or group functioning, or both.

Note: An alternative to public discussion of individual behavior is to process such data privately in dyads (pairs). This more private procedure may be essential if one senses that participants are not ready for the more usual public feedback. But a possible shortcoming of this procedure is that in the absence of group surveillance, the feedback may be toned down or not given at all.

Guide sheets for observation of both group behavior and individual functioning are given in Appendices 14 and 15.

Fishbowls work best when the inner and outer groups are small in number—not more than ten persons. The smaller group ensures more air time for everyone and encourages greater willingness to contribute.

If the total training group is fairly large, for example, 20–30 participants, there is no reason why two to four fishbowls cannot operate simultaneously. A good-sized room or separate rooms will facilitate this operation. You should try to monitor all fishbowls a bit to get a feel for what is being said. Data that are picked up in this way can be used as feedback in the summary session.

Additional Configurations

Fishbowl configurations other than the basic type just described are these:

☐ Place an empty chair in the center of the discussion group, or in the ring itself as in Figure 4-2. Then allow anyone from the outer circle to take the empty chair at any time for one minute and

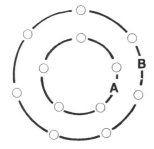

Figure 4-1. Diagram of a typical fishbowl.

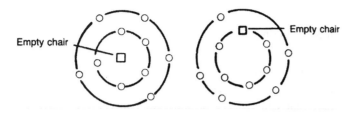

Figure 4-2. Diagram showing two options for placing the empty chair in a fishbowl configuration.

to use it as a springboard to interject his/her comment or viewpoint.

Another way for a member of the outer circle to get into the act is to allow, every three minutes, someone in the outer circle to tap the shoulder of someone in the inner circle and take the inner member's place. The new fishbowl member may then amplify, clarify, disagree, call attention to silent participants, etc.

Each of the two empty chair techniques has a specific purpose. If the participant sits on the empty chair inside the circle, the purpose is to engage in an interaction with everyone in the inner ring. If the participant sits on the empty chair within the ring, he/she is merely trying to enter the discussion as an added fishbowl participant.

Added involvement of the observers is possible through this procedure:

1. Let the inner circle (Group A) discuss the assigned topic or problem (15–20 minutes).
2. Then have those in Group A turn around and secure feedback from those in the outer circle (Group B) on a one-on-one basis, recalling what was heard and the related feelings.
3. Group A returns to its prior discussion mode, integrating the comments of Group B into the new round of discussion (10–15 minutes).
4. Groups A and B switch places, and Group B is now the discussion group (15–25 minutes).

☐ Assume you have three or four fishbowls going simultaneously. Upon completion of these data-generating discussions, have one or two representatives from each cluster join with their colleagues to form a new fishbowl. In effect, we have in action a new set of A and B groups of four to eight members each. The objective is to augment or enrich total input on a given problem, but one drawback is that not everyone can participate, for the rest of the groups' participants are only observers. To overcome this problem, allow the observers to interject at five- or ten-minute intervals.

☐ A variation of the preceding procedure is to have several clusters work on a problem and then have each small group select a representative to present its views in the center cluster [1]. The four representatives would discuss the problem for 10–20 minutes and then return to their respective small groups for further discussion. Again, a representative (preferably another person) from each small group would join the cluster. You might elicit specific proposals for action and post them on a flipchart. This procedure is particularly useful in conflict management.

☐ A novel way to improve interaction and possibly understanding of the view of others is to mix up the groups after one or two usual rounds of fishbowl activity. Thus, if you began with six participants from sales and six from production, you might set up a fishbowl with a new mix: two clusters, each having three members from sales and three members from production.

☐ It is also possible to use the same cluster groups but to have them switch their positions or arguments. Thus, in your Sales-Production fishbowl situation, after one or two usual fishbowl encounters, you might ask each side to argue the other's position. This would force verbalization of the other viewpoint and thus promote understanding of the position taken by the other group.

Fishbowl Uses and Limitations

The fishbowl has a number of highly worthwhile, dynamic uses:

As a problem solving tool. By having one cluster listen to and critique the other, and vice versa, a great deal of interaction and stimulation is engendered. In essence, this puts sparks into the communication and problem-solving process.

As a tool to generate divergent views. The fishbowl can be particularly helpful when it is essential to learn of perceptions from groups having divergent viewpoints, such as headquarters and field, line and staff, sales and production, "old line" people and minorities, parents and teenagers, or men and women.

For team building. The fishbowl is a long-time tool of many trainers who work in the area of team building. It is so widely used because it is a powerful tool to get people to open up, to generate divergent views, and to hold these views up for analysis.

For improvement of intergroup communication and relations. By bringing divergent groups together, conflict can be worked through. The dynamics involved are these: possibly for the first time, "warring" groups are given the opportunity to listen seriously to one another. In time, both groups learn that neither group is totally on the side of the angels.

As an icebreaker. In experiential training programs, the fishbowl is very useful to get people into action quickly. This approach is not recommended for more conventional, didactic training programs, particularly those having very cautious participants.

To learn of group behavior. As has already been indicated, this is a good way to study the dynamics of groups—leadership, membership, decision making, communication processes—and to give feedback on them.

As an agenda setting device. Some groups can work well with the fishbowl to establish an agenda for a conference, to use it as a problem solving device, etc.

To identify objectives. In either training or problem-solving situations, it may be necessary, at times, to clarify objectives: Why are we here? What are our goals? What does headquarters (or the chief executive) expect? The fishbowl can aid immeasurably in clarifying possible confusion and misconceptions about program purposes.

To resolve conflict. if there is conflict or controversy concerning a substantive issue, the trainer may introduce the fishbowl as an *ad hoc* device to help resolve it. Talking through issues, as opposed to letting the controversy smolder, is certainly preferred.

To resolve a training issue. On occasion, participants may be in conflict with some aspect of the training endeavor. For example, participants may resent being forced to attend the program. Or participation may be inhibited because bosses are in attendance with their subordinates. In such circumstances, the trainer may suggest that the participants "fishbowl" the difficulty.

For mid-program assessment. One way to find out how well the training is going is to use the fishbowl. To the extent practicable, mid-program corrections may thus be accomplished early on rather than at program's end, at which time it may be too late. Typical issues that may emerge are clarity of objectives, the degree to which objectives are being met, pace (too fast or too slow), and possible problems in applying the new learning.

For evaluation of training. The fishbowl can be used to assess how well a training effort went. In fact, this is one use that all kinds of training groups—technical, professional, management, sales, safety—can use to equal advantage. The evaluation may take place at one or more points in the on-going program or, more typically, at program's end.

As a tool to engender fun and novelty. Too many training programs suffer from a surplus of the conventional, the expected, the tried and true. The fishbowl reverses this deadly process by injecting, instead, a great deal of spark, excitement, novelty, fun, and change of pace. Participants are thus energized instead of bored.

One limitation of the fishbowl is that it is not likely to be productive in technical or skills training where the overall training format is heavily didactic instead of experiential. However, even in these situations, it can be used:

1. To have participants talk about applications of their new learning to the back-home situation—will it be easy? Difficult? What are the problems (concerns, anxieties) in application or implementation?

2. To evaluate the training effort—what went well? What went less than well? What do we recommend for program improvement?

The fishbowl may also present problems if participants are highly self-conscious, not open to new experiences, not very verbal, or not accustomed to the give and take of a vigorous problem-solving encounter. A word to the wise: Trainer, know thy participant group.

WORKING WITH "MIND PICTURES"— FANTASY, GUIDED IMAGERY, ETC.

To imagine is everything.

—Albert Einstein, physicist (1879–1955)

When I train the biceps, I picture huge mountains. You do something to the mind. The mind is the limit. It's all mind over matter.

—Arnold Schwarzenegger,
body building authority, actor,
and TV personality

The ability to fantasize is the ability to survive.

—Ray Bradbury, science fiction writer

Participants can often be involved and reached with mind pictures, which they create and use when other more conventional training approaches may not be productive. These techniques bear such diverse names as fantasy, guided fantasy, group fantasy, mental imagery, guided imagery, visual imagery, visualization, and symbolic visualization. Regardless of the terminology, however, we are talking about processes that use and develop the intuitive, creative part of our brain (right brain thinking). These processes relate to our ability to think in *images* as well as in words.

In respect to the terminology just cited, we should point out that in the area of fantasy the nomenclature is not used by writers in any consistent way. However, for our purposes we will group these devices into several rather precise categories, using titles and definitions which seem to be most descriptive and helpful. Here, then, are several key definitions:

Fantasy entails the creation of a mind picture by the participant in response to a *general* idea or topic provided by the trainer. (The terms "imagining," "imaging," or "imagistic thinking" are adequately synonymous with fantasy.) For example: "Imagine that you are on a flight in outer space . . ." or "Project yourself into the year 2100. You are alive and well. You see the world as . . ." or "Fantasize that you are the president of this company . . . ."

Guided fantasy entails the joint development of a scenario by the facilitator and a participant as fantasizer. The former guides the latter with such techniques as questioning, channeling, overcoming obstacles, encouraging, and supporting. Used primarily in human potential development programs, it may entail entering one's own body, becoming someone else, etc. [2].

Group fantasy entails the development of a story through contributions of the total group. After one member kicks things off ("We are on a large ship at sea. The waves are very tall . . ."), the other participants may build on the fantasy in sequence or on an *ad hoc* or random basis. This device may be used in highly experiential, personal growth programs rather than in more conventional training activities.

Mental imagery involves the creation of images or mind pictures via one's own command, such as when a tired jogger might create an image of a cold beer in an over-sized, icy glass which is available at the end of the run and is thus revitalizing. Other examples of self-imaging are given later. However, our concern is with the creation of images guided by the trainer, hence our use of the term "guided imagery." (See definition which follows.)

Guided imagery entails the provision of a *specific or detailed picture or image* by the trainer, which participants react to and build on with their own mind pictures.

Visualization, as we will use it, entails the recall and interpretation of images of actual situations, events, persons, and relationships, both past and present.

In general, these approaches to the augmentation of our intuitive capacity are a recognition that most of us use no more than ten percent of our creative potential. Hence the need to tap the wisdom buried below our normal level of awareness.

Using Fantasy

Fantasy is an "auto-process" of creating mind pictures on demand. A general suggestion by the trainer triggers the image. It is used in various training situations to stimulate creativity, tap potential, improve problem solving capability, make participants more aware of their feelings, aid in overcoming ungrounded fears, reduce stress, introduce an element of fun or play, energize the group, and generally aid in personal growth. It is a process of tapping and developing the intuitive, creative, and spontaneous part of the brain. In current psychological language, it is a form of "right brain" (or creative) thinking.

Its rationale is that by engaging in creative daydreaming, we can imagine the impossible, which can provide us with insights into the possible. Several uses follow:

Management training. In management training, fantasy can be helpful in expanding the imagination of managers and thus opening up new, unthought-of possibilities of accomplishment. Too often managers limit their capabilities for dynamic action because of overconcern with barriers—actual and presumed. Some examples of the use of fantasy in management training are as follows:

What If (Let's Pretend) Technique

Ask the group to fantasize various management issues such as:

☐ What if I had all the time in the world? What would I do that is worth doing that I'm not doing now?

☐ If I were to delegate to my staff as much as I wanted to, my operation would _____.

☐ If we had the perfect management team, we would _____.

☐ If I could design the truly effective performance appraisal system (or pay plan, or marketing plans, or product line), it would _____.

☐ If I could build the ideal organization it would be able to _____.

In-House Prophet Technique

"Fantasize that you get a call at home at 9:30 P.M. on Saturday night. It is the big boss. This person wants very much your advice on _____. You are elated. This is your big chance! What do you say?"

Worst Case Scenario Technique

"What are the worst results that could happen if you asked for a raise (or quit, or transferred, or disagreed with your boss, or expressed your feelings about an issue candidly)?" The objective is to get all the fears, anxieties, and negatives out and hold them up to the light of day for reality testing. Verbalized fears, as opposed to unexpressed ones, tend to lose their intensity.

Worst Case Scenario Follow-up

Ask the participants to fantasize: "What are the benefits that might accrue if you did A rather than B?" (With the fears out in the open and discussed, the gains will look more attractive.)

Top Dog Technique

"Fantasize that you are the plant manager (or district manager, or company president) for the month. What would your goals or methods be to improve productivity (union relations, quality of work life, employee enthusiasm, etc.)?"

The Magic Wand Technique

"Plop! A magic wand has been dropped in front of you. Oh, how it sparkles. You hear a voice somewhere above which tells you encouragingly: 'You can change anything you like with the wand. Just hold it with both of your hands and decide to change that which needs to be changed.' How would you change yourself (your job, your priorities, your boss, your staff, your organization)?"

Sudden Enrichment

It is the day before Christmas. Your boss has been chatting with you at your desk. As he gets up to leave, he says: "Oh, by the way, here's $250,000 you can use to help your unit in any way you deem best." How would you use this windfall?

Note: The above devices, such as "What If," "The Magic Wand," and "Sudden Enrichment" can be used in other areas as well, such as career planning, personal growth, or stress management.

Career Development. In career development workshops there are numerous opportunities to use fantasy. Some examples follow:

As a confidence-building vehicle: "You are about to enter an office for a job interview. You stride in alertly and energetically, displaying a big smile of pleasure and confidence. You are asked to be seated. You explain with enthusiasm why you are interested in the job . . . ." (The participant, in fantasy, begins a monologue.)

In an in-house career development workshop, participants were asked to describe the images that career development brought to mind in their organization. Some responses were: "A farce." "A P.R. gimmick." The participants were then asked to fantasize what a real or ideal career development program would be like (ideal images). Some responses were: "Learn about all vacancies so we can apply for self-development interests and efforts." "Establishment of career ladders." "Accomplishment rather than seniority as a criterion for advancement." The data were then forwarded to management for their consideration.

In another in-house career development workshop participants were asked to fantasize a real (ideal) career development program if they were first: management; second: employees; third: the personnel office; fourth: the training department. By using fantasy, specific goals were developed expending a minimum amount of energy and time.

Personal Growth. Fantasy is extremely well suited to training activities that encourage personal growth—building greater self-confidence, increasing assertive behavior, reducing weight, being more friendly at meetings, getting rid of anger, facing up to unpleasant tasks such as making tough decisions affecting people, etc. As the trainer, you can direct fantasy experiences (guided fantasy) about some of these problems in a "two-stage scenario" fashion:

Trainer: Think of a problem you have with yourself or with others. Pause for a minute or two. O.K., who has a problem that they will share with us, one that we can use as a demo?

Participant: I would like to be more friendly, more congenial, and more supportive at meetings.

Trainer: That's a good one; very much worth working on. O.K., close your eyes; lean back in your chair; relax; relax some more; make yourself comfortable, very, very comfortable; very loose. (Pause.) Now visualize yourself at a recent meeting. Can you do this?

Participant: (Nods head.)

Trainer (Starts Scenario I): O.K., visualize your behavior. (Pause.) Can you tell us what you are doing, how are you "coming on"?

Participant: I am glum, unsmiling; at times I make negative comments.

Trainer: O.K., visualize the people at the meeting. Can you do that? (Pause.)

Participant: (Nods head.)

Trainer: How are people reacting to you? (Pause.)

Participant: Several are throwing unfriendly glances at me. Others don't pay any attention to me at all.

Trainer: And how do you feel about that?

Participant: Not too good.

Trainer (Starts Scenario II): O.K., let's see if you can change things a bit. Fantasize, imagine, that you come on as a very warm and friendly person. You are really smiling; you have a big, easy smile and your eyes sparkle; you give people encouragement, praise for their ideas. You are enjoying yourself. (Pause.) Can you do this?

Participant: I think so; yes.

Trainer: Good. Can you see the others at the meeting? (Pause.)

Participant: Yes, I can.

Trainer: And how are they reacting to you?

Participant: It's different; very different. They seem to like me. Yes, they like me. They're smiling back at me.

Trainer: How do you feel as a member of this group?

Participant: I feel as if I'm now part of the group. Yes, I'm really part of the group.

Similar fantasies can be encouraged on other problems such as being overweight. The participant can be asked to fantasize a significant weight loss (pause after each question for a response): What if you were to lose 40 pounds? What would you look like? How would people you know react to you? Your spouse? Your boss? Your associates at work? Your children? Your neighbors?

Or take a situation where a participant would like to be more confident or more assertive. Again, the first, unsatisfactory scenario is visually reproduced by the participant. Then the second, more satisfying scenario is fantasized. The aim is to give the participant opportunities (in fantasy) to be successful in situations that are normally not very satisfying or successful.

Other fantasy-type situations to encourage introspection for personal growth purposes are as follows:

☐ Imagine that you have been given all the resources and skills to make a movie of yourself. What would be its major theme? What major areas would you try to cover? What would you call it? Why? Who would you cast as you?

☐ Pretend that you can live anywhere in the world that you wish. Where would you go? What would it be like? How would you feel?

☐ You have been given a magic wand. See how it sparkles. You can instantly tell that it has great powers. Suddenly a voice tells you that you can use it to choose the kind of work that you always wanted to engage in. What would you decide to do? What satisfaction would it bring?

☐ Imagine that you have befriended an older person. That person passes on and, to your great surprise and satisfaction, leaves you with $500,000. What would you do with this sudden enrichment?

Note: After the participant fantasizes wishes in the examples of relocation and job change, the trainer would then ask the fantasizer to visualize the plans that should be taken to reach those desirable ends.

It should be stressed that fantasy is only one technique to aid participants to resolve personal growth-type problems; it would not necessarily be used in isolation from other devices. For example, in a workshop concerned with career burnout, you might utilize talks along with small group discussion, group or individual tasks, role plays, and fantasy.

Stress Management. You can encourage your participants to use fantasy to deal with everyday stressful situations. Eleanor Rowe, a physical and mental fitness philosopher and professor of comparative literature at The George Washington University, offers these examples [3]:

☐ You are in a bad traffic jam. You transport yourself to a far-off mountaintop, observing the tangled mess from on high. Simultaneously, you imagine a pleasant rain pouring over you, washing away the stock market, irritated customers, and all your problems at home.

☐ You are very tense, filled with negative thoughts. Imagine that you are walking in a large field filled with spring flowers. You encounter a wooden stand which has attached to it balloons in gay colors. Each one has one of your problems/worries written on it. Slowly, you release the balloons, one by one, and watch your cares gently float far away. You lie down on the spring grass, close your eyes, relax, and smile.

☐ You have a lot of concerns and negative thoughts. Fortunately, you have an extra-large garbage bag. You recap all your gloomy thoughts, load the bag with them, and watch yourself dropping them off at the local garbage dump (or throw the bag off a high cliff, or let it float out to sea).

Similarly, group members might be asked to fantasize ways of discharging anger. Some responses to this fantasy are: Pour several tons of concrete on X's front lawn, which spell out a four-letter word. Hit a baseball (really a head) on top of Y's shoulders. Beat Z's new car with a heavy six-foot chain. Stick an 18-inch pin into A's bottom. Treat B's charcoal with a skunk potion so that when the barbecue fire starts, it promptly breaks up the party and enrages the neighbors. The idea, of course, is to get the hostility out in a harmless, make-believe way, as opposed to acting it out in a confrontation-type situation. After the fantasizing, group members can be asked to brainstorm other ways of dealing with anger, such as writing (and then discarding) a nasty letter; talking to a friend about it; yelling out the negative feeling through the car window when going to or returning from work; jogging or other strenuous exercise; beating on a mattress with a canoe paddle; adopting a resolution that I—and only I—will decide when to become angry, that is, I won't let any one else determine (influence or produce) my anger.

Retirement Planning. In a pre-retirement seminar it may be desirable to stimulate participant thinking about such key post-retirement concerns as retirement location, possible job activity, and investment planning (possibly reshuffling one's portfolio of assets). Thus, you may say: "Let's pretend that you could live anywhere" or "You could work at what you always wanted to do" or "Someone gave you $500,000 to invest."

Fantasy as Play. Fantasy can be used as a fun thing. One can exhilarate and enliven the group by giving them a play-type task. For example, in a session on motivation you may ask the group to fantasize doing their jobs in a fun way, free from the usual restraints, protocol, and decorum of the organization. A group of radio newscasters was asked to engage in this fantasy: How would you deliver the news if you could really be yourself? Some responses were

☐ Do it in a hot tub.

☐ Sing it instead of speak it.

☐ In shorts and my running shoes.

☐ In the nude(!).

☐ With a swinging musical band.

☐ Like a sports announcer I know with a lot of "You know's," "Hey man's," etc.

☐ Spoof the commercials.

Using Guided Imagery

This is designed to tap a person's inner world. It entails using and developing the intuitive, creative hemisphere of the brain (right brain). It can be used for career planning, life planning, creative writing, exam preparation, stress reduction, building the confidence of public speakers, general problem solving, and improving interpersonal relations and communication.

Procedurally, it is generally begun by introducing a relaxation exercise. ("Remove your shoes, loosen your tie and belt, lie down, close your eyes, be real loose and comfortable . . . breathe in slowly . . . slowly, exhale slowly . . . slowly, etc.") The idea is to inhibit somatic muscle activity and verbal thoughts, thereby permitting mental images to come alive and supersede conventional brain action. In effect, by quieting the left hemisphere of the brain (the logical, rational side), you allow the right brain to take over with all its potential for spontaneity, creativity, and imagination.

When participants are relaxed, provide an image for everyone to visualize and build upon:

"You are walking on the bottom of the sea . . . you come to a coral-coated cave you enter it . . .

"You are walking down a winding road . . . now there's a fork in it . . . which do you take? You follow it and you see . . ."

"You go into a cave . . . it is dark . . . you walk along the wall, feeling your way . . . Now there's a light . . . on

a ledge is a large treasure box . . . you open it up . . . there is a book in it . . . you look at the title . . ."

"You are on a desert island . . . it is sunny and warm."

Note: The creation of an image by participants need not only be visual. Participants thus may be asked to feel the wind on their faces, imagine the smells and sounds on the beach, sense the texture of objects at hand, etc.

After participants have developed images in their minds, ask the participants to share them with the small group. The group helps individual participants to interpret the image and gives support about it. A further sharing may entail the presentation of experiences from participants to the total group.

You may also present an image with enough detail so that it stimulates a specific form of problem solving. For example, after a brief relaxing exercise, including closing of the eyes, you may say:

"Imagine you are near a waterfall . . . experience it . . . what do you see . . . what do you feel . . . what do you smell . . .

"You now see two people standing near the waterfall. They are observing you enjoying yourself. One person is someone you relate to very well. The other person is someone you don't relate to well at all. Think about both relationships. Now open your eyes.

"Share in your small group your feelings about the two persons, indicating who they are and why you feel about them as you do."

Sharing takes place in the small group for 10–20 minutes. Then continue the imagery.

"You are near a stream. The person with whom you have the conflict is on the other side. The stream can be a slow moving stream or a raging river. You decide that. What do you do? What does the other person do? Do either of you communicate with the other person? If so, what do you say?" (Deciding upon a roaring river obviously will prevent or impede communication.)

"Open your eyes. Share your experience along the side of the river with the members of your group."

After the small group work, you may ask: "How many improved relationships? How many did not? Any comments, observations?"

Another way of using guided imagery is to ask participants to tap their Inner Advisor. The Inner Advisor is part of one's own deeper wisdom, that is, below the level of our usual awareness.

1. Explain the Inner Advisor concept.
2. Assign a topic about which participants are to seek wisdom or advice, for example, health, careers, relationships.
3. Provide the usual instructions for a relaxation activity.
4. Provide an image to facilitate the use of the Inner Advisor, for example, "Imagine a lake and an animal comes out and talks to you. You decide on the animal, one that you like."
5. The experience is shared in the small group, both as to the advice received and the animal selected.

One way to close a session concerned with personal growth, communication, or interpersonal relations is to conduct this nonverbal exercise: Have participants get comfortable again, take a deep breath and relax, then tell them:

"Imagine you're at a remote beach. There is no one there. It is very quiet. Take in the sights, smells, sounds. Now, you are to cast something away: an undesirable attitude, behavior, habit, something you have wanted to rid yourself of for a long time. Cast it far out on the water—the tide will carry it away.

"Now move to a new spot on the beach. You are still very relaxed. The tide is now coming in. Try to take something in: a new attitude, behavior, etc." [4].

One organization development (OD) consultant used the following guided imagery in an MBO workshop [5]:

"Imagine that this company is a very old and beautiful Victorian house and that each department in the company is a room in the house. How would your room look? What would be in it? To illustrate, as the OD consultant, I really don't see myself right now as a permanent part of the house. I feel more like a temporary addition that was recently built. So, I'm the newest part of the house, and I'm on the second floor, over the garage. My decor is mixed, because everyone else has donated some of their own furniture to the addition. I have a water bed, a lovely old oak bureau with a mirror, a large closet, an oriental rug, a small bathroom with a cast-iron tub, a 19th-century roll-top desk, and lots of green plants. I'd like to hear what the rest of the house looks like."

He then asked participants to share their fantasy or imagery by describing their own "rooms." He then asked if this would be a desirable place to reside, who else would be living there, etc. The objective was to help participants gain insight into the nature of the organization—perceived hierarchy, authority structure, communication patterns, climate. The concept of the organization as an interdependent system is more easily understood when everyone sees everyone else as residents of the same house.

Another practical use of guided imagery is to help people imagine desired changes in their workplace. By picturing such changes in their minds, they can more readily believe that they can overcome the status quo and commit themselves to taking appropriate steps. Example: A managerial group wishes to streamline/improve operations. After the usual breathing and relaxing procedures, ask them to paint a word picture of the hoped-for changes. Knowing these specifics, you can then ask general questions that will help them to picture the hoped-for changes: "The time is 30 days from today—July 1. How does the office look? What things look different? Who is in the office? Where are they? What are they doing? What are the signs/indicators that the change has really worked?" These images of change can be captured on paper, for example—who will do what after the change has taken place [6].

Using Mental Imagery for Learning

One way to enhance learning is to have participants form mind pictures, or mental images, related to the task to be mastered. For example, elementary school students (fifth and sixth grade) who formed pictures in their minds concerning complex textbook material they had read—about fictitious people living on a remote Pacific island—performed better on both immediate- and delayed-recall tests than control group students [7].

Similarly, mental imagery aided flight attendant trainees at one airline. They had to memorize for an FAA examination the location of some 50 pieces of emergency equipment (masks, flashlights, fire extinguisher, etc.) on five different planes, but they were flunking out at a 30% rate—obviously an expensive cost to the airline. However, with the aid of relaxation and visualization techniques, the trainees enjoyed a

100% pass rate. The specific procedures used were these:

1. Test anxiety was reduced through relaxation techniques.
2. A tour was made of the five planes to see the location of the equipment. Equipment was also touched, lifted, etc., which stimulated the other senses.
3. After leaving the plane they filled in equipment locations on cabin diagrams.
4. The next day they were again relaxed and taken on a guided imagery journey through the five aircraft.
5. Again, the cabin diagrams were completed.
6. The above procedure was repeated for five days before the exam.
7. On the morning of the exam the trainees were told to use the relaxation-mental image walk before and during the exam, as needed [8]. As indicated above, the exam was a tremendous success experience.

Some added uses follow [9]: Memory can be aided if connections are made by developing a mind picture with the items to be remembered, such as people's names, a grocery list, new vocabulary, new spelling words, and lists of numbers. Weight control can be aided through imagery ("imagine your slim self"). Stress can be reduced by developing mini-vacations in one's head. Sales personnel can overcome "phono-phobia" (call reluctance) by creating success images. High school students improved their free-throw shooting ability by practicing this skill in their heads; they actually outperformed a conventional practice group as well as another group that didn't practice at all. Confidence in public speaking and being more assertive can also be aided in this manner.

One writer suggests using mental imagery to improve trainee study skills, particularly insulating oneself against irrelevant thoughts and problems and thus improving needed concentration. His procedure is to teach trainees to begin a study session by picturing themselves studying and learning successfully while resisting distractions. The mental imaging gets them psyched up for study/learning; that is, it creates a proper study mood and centers all thoughts to relevant issues. He also encourages trainees to form mental images or to draw diagrams or flow charts about the study material. In this way, what is real is reinforced by a picture, doubling the chance of recall [10].

Gerry Reid, an authority on "accelerated learning," states that many mnemonics (memory devices) depend on the use of imagery. For example, learners can use their imaginations to create far-out, silly, humorous, out-of-proportion, illegal, immoral, or impossible images to provide an interesting diversion to the assigned task. The diversions themselves provide the mechanism to associate the new information, thereby accelerating the learning process.

Reid also points out that the learners' imaginations allow them to experience situations and events not in the training room. They can go anywhere, anytime, and observe anything under any condition. Learners can see, hear, feel, smell, taste, and experience any subject through their imaginations. They can watch themselves perform numerous tasks or skills related to their learning, everything from organizing their approach and using reference materials to seeing the success of proper application of the information being learned. Once a task has been performed in the mind, the learner need only recall what was imagined to perform it.

As Reid phrases it, "The physical performance becomes a repeat performance rather than an attempt to do the unknown. The brain, of course, can't distinguish between the real and the imagined, since it undergoes the same electrochemical processes when something is done in actuality or is imagined [11]."

The challenge for the trainer, obviously, is to encourage participants to seek out situations where learning and performance can be improved through their creation of mind pictures or images.

Using Visualization

As is apparent from the previous paragraphs, when using fantasy, guided imagery, and mental imagery, we are *imagining, creating,* or *manufacturing* an event or situation. In visualization, however, we draw upon or recall an actual experience, particularly one where strong feelings emerged or were involved. The recalled event is then subject to one or more forms of analysis. Here are some examples:

☐ In a session on interpersonal relations, you may wish to have your group experience the following:

"Think of an experience you had some years ago with another person. This was a hurtful experience: You were embarrassed, humiliated, put down, pained in some way.

"Close your eyes. Bring to mind the details of the experience. How old were you? Why did it take place? Where? What was said to you? What did you say, if anything, in reply? What were your feelings at the time?

"Open your eyes. How do you feel about that experience now?

"Close your eyes again. Restructure the incident in light of all the experience you have had, and everything you have learned since that event. Give yourself a second chance. What would you say to the other person now? (Most should now approach the problem more constructively. But some participants may say: "No change; I was trapped," or "I really told her off this time.")

"Close your eyes again. Now visualize the incident from the other person's point of view. (Possible responses might be: "It throws a new light on it." "Maybe I took it too hard.")

This visualization activity is useful in helping participants to get in touch with their feelings, to become more sensitive to the feelings of others, etc.

☐ In a sales training situation, have the participants visualize a success experience such as the best sale they ever made. Ask them questions such as these: What made it successful? What did you do? How did you feel? Was it a learning experience, that is, have you been able to apply the learnings to other sales situations? Have you ever shared this experience with anyone else? Why or why not? If you did share it, to whom and how often? How did the other person react to your experience? Ask several participants to share their visualizations.

☐ In an assertiveness training situation have participants visualize an actual unsatisfying experience (for example, an attempt to return a dress to a store in which one was "browbeaten"

by the salesperson). Then have participants fantasize how they might have handled the same situation with greater effectiveness.

Using Fantasy Outside the Classroom

Our discussion so far has related to invigorating and liberating the participant group via fantasy and related techniques *in the training room*. It may also be desirable to give them added pointers regarding the continuing use of fantasy and imagery in their everyday situations: at work, at play, in the home. Some examples of opportunities to use fantasy and mental imagery on one's own follow:

Imagined Behavior or Action. The idea is to develop a picture in one's mind about the accomplishment of a difficult event or activity, for example: "I am jogging and am feeling tired. But do I have to feel tired? No! I imagine a giant hand lifting me up and propelling me forward, and I easily move with it, the tiredness having vanished."

That positive mind pictures, at least in athletics, are more than a pipe dream is illustrated by research on "imaging" of free-throw shooting. In one controlled study, three groups of students practiced throwing basketball free throws. Group 1 practiced for 20 days. Group 2 didn't practice at all. Group 3 spent 20 minutes each day imaging or visualizing the taking of free throws. The results: Group 1 improved 24%; Group 2 showed zero improvement; Group 3 improved by 23% [12].

There are many opportunities for imaging or imagining success in on- and off-the-job situations—for example, successfully confronting a "hard-to-reach" peer or subordinate; confidently delivering a speech before a large group; asking the boss for a raise; securing one's rights on a warranty problem; discharging anger by fantasizing the causing of discomfort to someone (far better than acting it out!); preparing for a tough exam.

Industrial psychologist Dr. Harry Levinson advises enlisting the aid of fantasy and imagination when major life changes are coming—the death of a parent, the birth of the first child, marriage, divorce, promotion, retirement, etc. In respect to personal acceptance of and planning for retirement, he suggests: "It takes time to get past the glib characterizations ('Oh boy, I'll never get out of bed!' or 'My husband and I will drive each other nuts!') and start imagining how you'll really feel. This sort of mental rehearsing is very important. Of course things won't be exactly as you imagined them, but you'd be surprised what insights will come if you let your imagination go. One of the reasons widows do better than widowers is that they rehearse this way for the probable loss of their husbands. Men rarely do. The more different situations you daydream yourself into, and the more different reactions you can imagine having, the more complete a picture will emerge of what retirement will mean to you. And the meaning *will* be complex, with conflicting aspects and alternating feelings [13]."

Self-reinforcement of One's Behavior. The procedure is to create an image of an event with highly favorable consequences. These consequences will obviously be reinforcing for the desired behavior, for example: "I give the boss a new proposal on the restructuring of the marketing organization. He really eats it up and tells me so repeatedly! Wow! Since my boss is so receptive and complimentary, I intend to submit the proposal immediately. And I *know* I'll pull it off and feel great about it!"

Fantasy—Using It Wisely

To maximize results from the use of fantasy in its various forms, the following skill pointers should be considered:

☐ Have a specific learning objective in mind. Is it to loosen people up? To encourage creativity? To build confidence? To have fun?

☐ Know your group. Will they enter into the spirit of the thing with enthusiasm, or will they hold back?

☐ Watch your timing. Use fantasy, guided fantasy, etc., when it fits best into the training program. For example, you probably wouldn't start most programs with a fantasy experience. Also, fantasy works best when the group is free and easy with one another, something that is not likely to develop until later in the program.

☐ Consider both structured (planned) and unstructured *(ad hoc)* fantasy. The latter may be more effective if it meets a real need, for example, at a point when the group is stuck on an issue or needs a lift. To illustrate: I recall a situation in a management training course,

which I was conducting, wherein the group was polarized over the issue of leveling with subordinates about an instruction or policy from the boss with which one didn't agree. Some felt vigorously that one must be a good soldier and support the boss regardless of one's own feelings about the issue. Others felt strongly that it was dishonest not to reveal one's true feelings about the policy or instruction and, besides, the subordinates would probably sense the lie anyhow. I resolved the impasse by asking the group to fantasize the worst—what if you were to actually level with the staff about one's own true attitude toward the policy? What might happen to you? Then, what would be the best payoffs if one leveled?

☐ Introduce the fantasy in an exhilarating, challenging way: "Close your eyes. Let's fantasize that _____. Let your imaginations soar! Be creative! Pull out all the stops! You have the power to do this!"

☐ A good way to process the fantasy is by having participants share their images/ideas in small groups. Then hold a general group-at-large discussion about the results/effects of the fantasizing.

☐ Don't expect everyone to enter into the process with the same degree of enthusiasm, spontaneity, or success. One or more may not wish to play at all. Individual differences are certainly to be expected and respected.

☐ Obviously, this kind of activity is best done in an experiential training program by a trained facilitator.

WORKING WITH PICTURES

Pictures (photos, drawings, advertisements) can be used to involve participants in meaningful and novel ways. A focus on photos/pictures can encourage introspection, induce attitude change, tap creativity, liberate/loosen up the ideation process, provide fun and novelty, and stimulate communication and interaction in the group. Pictures and/or photos can be used in a variety of ways for different end results, as indicated by the suggested group activities that follow.

Quiz

Give participants a 10–20-item safety quiz. Working from photographs showing hazardous situations (some obvious, others less so) in the shop, plant, laboratory, etc., have participants identify as many unsafe working conditions as they can in each photograph. Then have the participants meet in small groups to compare and discuss their responses to the quiz. At the end of the small-group discussion period, pass out the answer sheet for self-checking purposes. Wind things up with a general discussion about hazards in the workplace.

Developing Nonverbal Communication Skills

Show participants various photos, drawings, etc., and have them describe the nonverbal communication that is taking place. Some examples: a group is sitting lethargically around a conference table looking pained or bored; a prospect is showing signs of impatience as the sales person makes a presentation; a subordinate has just had an idea turned down by the boss. Then, in small groups, have participants discuss ways of dealing with the exhibited behavior.

Photographs that require interpretation of emotional states, relationships (boss-subordinate, married-unmarried), group behavior, etc., can also be subject to a multiple choice or true and false quiz and subsequent group discussion.

Icebreaker

Divide the group into triads and instruct each participant to come up with five or more interesting things about the other two members. The data are written on 3" × 5" cards which are then hooked up vertically with tape. Photos (self-developing) are taken of each participant and attached appropriately to the card chains; the completed displays are posted to the wall for "permanent" exhibit [14].

Adding Captions

Provide participants with cartoons, novel photos, etc., and ask them to supply the captions. The captions can be analyzed in various ways; for example, in relation to basic Transactional Analysis concepts of parent, adult and child; in respect to motivations or needs people may have.

Using Projective Techniques

Participants can be involved in a meaningful way by the use of pictures, drawings, and ads from magazines or newspapers. The idea is to ask participants to select those subjects (people, situations, objects) with which they can identify or which they can accept. Examples follow:

☐ Working from a folder containing many (one hundred or more) photos culled from magazines, a participant (particularly one who is shy or reluctant to communicate for various reasons) is asked to group the pictures into three piles: those that elicit positive feelings, those that elicit negative feelings, and those that elicit only neutral affect (emotion). The sorting out process will "smoke out" feelings or attitudes that the participant may not be able to present verbally. I have used this device in leadership laboratories to help participants indicate who they really are, where they are coming from, what their preferences and prejudices are, etc. The group may then query the participant about the overall patterns produced by the selections, why a particular photo was preferred or rejected, etc.

☐ Participants may be given a group of old magazines and asked to cut out quickly those items which show the career or lifestyle they favor. These may be put in a folder or mounted on the wall or on a poster board in collage fashion. Again, the pictorial selections are subject to group questioning and analysis and serve as a form of feedback to aid participants to reality test their career decisions better. A good training design is to have the participants share their data about the selected pictures in trios or quartets.

A variation on this technique is to have participants identify both their current career or life style and the preferred career or life style, assuming they see a need for a change.

☐ Show participants a picture (ad, photo, drawing) and have them write a short story or account of its significance for them. Possible subjects are an intensely involved group at a meeting; a harried executive with an overflowing in-box reaching for the phone; a foreman with an angry look on his face pointing with his finger as a worker looks on; two people conversing at the water cooler. Then have participants discuss their stories in pairs or trios. Complete the activity by a group-at-large sharing of what was learned.

☐ Show participants a somewhat ambiguous photo of a boss-subordinate interaction; for example, going over a work plan, an interview situation, a discussion in an office or on the shop floor. Then ask them to rate the subordinate on various aspects of personality, performance, and attitude, using the rating scale shown in Figure 4-3. Have participants discuss their ratings in small groups and then discuss the results with the group at large.

The objective is to ascertain to what extent we project our feelings about subordinates (and others) into an essentially neutral situation. Halo effects or hypercriticalness are cues to lack of objectivity in judging others.

☐ In training managers to hire and work with handicapped workers, pictures may be used to reveal hidden attitudes about such persons. Two examples:

1. Pictures are distributed of people observing handicapped individuals in a variety of situations. The trainer then asks the participants how they would react to seeing a disabled person. This activity generally reveals a whole gamut of attitudes and feelings: guilt feelings that they themselves aren't handicapped, a belief that the disability is "contagious" (!), that the disabled are bitter or feel sorry for themselves, etc.

Subordinate's Traits	Low	Moderate	High	Don't Know
Cooperativeness				
Enthusiasm				
Creativity				
Initiative				
Dependability				
Listening Skills				
Other				

Figure 4-3. Example of a rating sheet used by participants to evaluate an ambiguous photo.

2. Similarly, when asked to choose a prospective employee from four handicapped applicants, a subjective decision typically results—the one chosen is usually one disabled in later life or one who is least threatening to them personally. The rationale for picking the one disabled later in life is that people can identify more readily with one recently disabled. The latter exercise shows managers that people may *think* they can make objective decisions in such cases, but in actuality they don't [15].

Note: The first example of projective techniques would be best used on an *ad hoc* basis with only two or three group members. Otherwise, its novelty and thus its effectiveness would be lost. Conversely, the other activities could be used readily by and with the *total* group. The second, fourth, and fifth examples are essentially "projective devices," for they ask the participants to project themselves as individuals into the picture to the degree they are able to, thereby revealing or explaining a certain aspect of their personality, value system, or attitudinal system.

Using Participant Photos

In the previous examples, the photos used for analysis were not personally related to the participants. However, it may be desirable in highly experiential training programs to use photographic material that relates directly to the participants. Some examples include [16]:

☐ In weight-reduction groups, photograph the participants intermittently, for example, monthly. Paste the photos on large sheets of paper and have participants describe themselves below the photos. The objective of these self-image descriptions, according to Dr. David Krauss, a visual therapist, is to give participants "reinforcing feedback about their weight and looks which is generalized into other areas, such as grooming, attitudes and self-esteem."

☐ In leadership laboratories (the T-group), encounter groups, stress management courses, etc., it may be desirable to have participants bring photos of themselves in to the program. The instructions about the types of photos to be selected should be quite general:

"Bring in photos of yourself, as many as you wish, in any period of your life, alone or with others, in any situations you prefer." Obviously, the photos will serve as a rich personal resource for the exploration of one's feelings, attitudes, and values about self, family, early history, career, etc. One of the specific ways Dr. Krauss uses these kinds of photos is to have participants project themselves into the photo. For example, a photo may show a person, a car, a tree, or a house. Dr. Krauss then asks the participant to speak about these objects in the present tense: ". . . tell me what it is like to be the person, house, tree, car, driveway and so forth." The metaphoric content of the discourse, as disclosed by the participant, serves as a rich source of data about the participant and may provide him/her with self-insight as well.

☐ Take photos of group members, then discuss their degrees of relaxation, attentiveness, etc. The photographic data could be used by the participants to attempt to change their behavior, as appropriate.

☐ You may also photograph one or more participants and use the photos as a basis for their reaction to and critique of themselves. Thus, Dr. Krauss may ask participants questions such as: Who is this person? What do you like about this photograph? Is there a part you dislike? If we take another photo of you in six months, what do you think we will see that may be different? How would you title this picture?

Note: These examples reported by Dr. David Krauss are used by him in therapeutic situations. Obviously, the trainer's skill and the type of training involved would determine whether similar photographic approaches would be appropriate in nontherapeutic training situations.

How to Select and Organize Photos/Pictures for Your Training Activities

Careful trainer selection of picture/photo materials is essential. Here are several suggestions regarding this selection:

1. Decide on a theme(s) or topic(s) for the training activities, for example, leadership, EEO, customer relations, safety, communication, stress management, motivation, or team work.

2. Use a variety of magazines as your source of materials. Different magazines have different subjects, emphases, styles, and tones. For example, compare *Business Week, Forbes,* and magazines concerned with current affairs to those magazines relating to travel or home and garden. Advertisements in all these magazines provide interesting materials. If you don't have ready access to a good stock of magazines, don't hesitate to request them from colleagues, relatives, friends, and neighbors. Many of them would like to clean house anyhow, and your request is the nudge they probably need to do so.

3. Select a large number of photos/pictures. They should be a mix of the conventional and novel, heavy and light, happy and sad, representational and even surrealistic; in their totality, they should create an emotional impact. Also, round out your packet of materials with a number of possible discards—images that are ambiguous, neutral, "far-out," or fun-type items.

4. Winnow down your materials to those which have high interest, communicate a mood, provoke, disturb, stimulate, challenge, and/or inspire.

5. Mount your selections on 8½" × 11" white bond (or cardboard if you have it) to increase ease of handling and to reduce the wear and tear on them.

6. Group your materials into three to six packets of about 15–25 items each. Try to have enough photos so several small groups can "play" simultaneously. The packets' contents should be generally similar in topic coverage, number, and variety. However, the photos in all the packets need not be identical.

The materials in the packets are now ready to be used by your participants to execute the assignments you choose to give them.

USING ART

The arts are a way to bring order out of chaos—the chaotic feelings and impulses within and the bewildering mass of impressions from without. The arts are a means to discover both the self and the world—and to establish a relationship between the two.

—Dr. Elinor Ulman, authority on art therapy,
The George Washington University

Participants can be involved in the learning process dynamically via tasks that require some form of artistic expression. The art forms may be representational, symbolic, abstract, or some combination of these forms. The emphasis, of course, is not on perfected productions, but on free expression of feelings: "Try to draw the emotions you're now feeling. Just let yourself go!"

Why would we want our participants to engage in an activity which requires them to respond in a graphic, pictorial, illustrative or artistic way? The best response might be: "Why not?" But some specific reasons are:

☐ It taps our creativity. If you will recall the findings of recent brain research, our brain has two hemispheres, known as the left brain and the right brain. The left brain's functions control our thought processes, the cognitive-analytical realm. Its proper functioning assures that we engage in logic, reason, caution, rationality, analysis, evaluation (seeking and weighing evidence), assessment of consequences, and sequential thinking. Conversely, the right brain governs our intuitive-feeling processes, the side of ourselves that is curious, impetuous, emotional, speculative, creative, open to new experiences, and playful. In other words, the two hemispheres produce control and spontaneity, respectively.

Most of our work and training activities ask (or insist) that we think and be logical. Only infrequently are we challenged to tune in to our feelings and emotions that can unleash our playful, intuitive, and creative self. Art is a medium to encourage spontaneity and creativity. Since it can help us to think in images as well as in words, it can capture the potential of the total brain.

☐ Since art expression reaches the affective or emotional side of ourselves, it can generate and communicate data about feelings, values, and attitudes, something that conventional written or verbal approaches may not be able to do. In other words, art can get at thoughts and feelings more readily because it works in a less direct way.

It can lower defenses—both psychological and perceptual—of our participants since they are "approaching themselves" through a new perspective and an unfamiliar medium [17].

(*Note:* Psychological defenses relate to such mechanisms as denial, repression and projection; perceptual defense relates to our tendencies to select data with which we are comfortable and reject data with which we are not.)

☐ It can improve communication among participants. To the extent that our participants are encouraged to express what they really think and feel, understanding of one another is simplified and accelerated.

☐ It can help to reduce status differences. When participants engage in activities that create a relaxed, playful atmosphere, one's job title, rank, and grade are of much lesser significance. Camaraderie and openness are thus more easily developed.

☐ It can highlight individual differences of the participants—values, emotions, life goals, stresses, and coping strategies.

☐ The images which our participants create tell us a lot about them. In fact, the bit of art work may tell us more about the artist than about the item being imagined or described. In essence, the artistic renderings about a person, problem, event, or interaction express the participants' own methods/styles of seeing reality. So we are getting an authentic piece of information about each of the participants [18].

☐ It can help to discover and develop hidden resources in the participants; for example, the imaging/visualizing technique—an important component of drawing—is a device for understanding and remembering complex information; the use of art allows the addition of intuition to one's usual rational mode of problem solving; art is a means of seeing various phenomena from different perspectives.

☐ It gives participants an opportunity to achieve a special focus and to perceive from a different standpoint, often from a part of the mind that is deeper and uncluttered from the details of day-to-day living and working [19].

☐ It is interest-arousing because of its novelty and lesser structure. Typical participant expectations are that their training will be patterned, structured, predictable, uneventful, and generally pretty dull.

☐ It is fun to do. Engaging in the creation of art forms provokes the child in us, that is, those aspects of our personality that are curious, spontaneous, intuitive, alive, bold, carefree, imaginative, and idealistic. In other words, it loosens us up.

☐ To the extent that we are encouraged to be playful and imaginative, we are more likely to be motivated to learn. It gives us a mindset that seeks out the new rather than the tried and true.

☐ Finally, our artistic constructions let us take pride in our accomplishments and let us feel good about ourselves. As one participant said, "It's not Rembrandt, but *I* made this."

Some examples of the use of art in the training situation follow.

☐ In a career-planning activity, participants can be asked to draw their career progress to date. The career "lifeline" should depict successes, plateaus, setbacks, etc., using illustrations, symbols, and graphics.

☐ In a personal growth program, participants can be asked to draw their *personal* lifeline, complete with such symbols as mountain peaks, valleys, plateaus, clouds, sun, and other appropriate drawings to highlight major events.

☐ In a management development seminar, have participants draw a segmented geometrical form on a flipchart or sheet of paper. Then

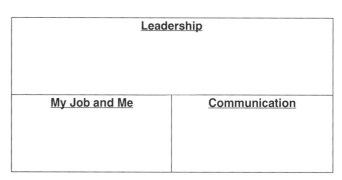

Figure 4-4. Example of a geometrical figure labeled and ready for artistic completion.

have them label each segment (usually three or four) to encourage reflection on particular issues, for example, leadership, communication, my career, my job, the organization, my staff. See Figure 4-4 for an example. Finally, each labeled segment is to be responded to in an artistic, graphic, or symbolic way.

☐ As an opener, have participants describe a current problem they are facing, using artistic, graphic, or symbolic expression. The problem may be work-related, career-related, personal (for example, stress), in the community, etc., depending on the nature of the course.

☐ In a supervisory training course, have participants draw a symbol(s) which represents a strong or attractive attribute of a boss, or a characteristic which depicts the negative or undesirable side. Examples: an ear might symbolize that the boss listens; a group of people in a circle might indicate that a team has been developed and that the boss operates as a team manager; an open door would show good communications and interpersonal relationships; dull meetings conducted by the boss might be depicted by an assembled group with "Z's" over their heads; a boss who does not delegate might be shown at a desk overflowing with paper or overloaded in-baskets.

☐ Have participants draw their "support system." Our support system enables us to cope with vexations, frustrations, and disappointments, and may include people (friends, carpool, colleagues, the boss, mentors, relatives, family), resources (our bank account, home, car, pension plan, other assets), off-the-job activities (hobbies, vacations), our ego strength or resources within ourselves, or organizations (church, professional associations, social and fraternal groups) [20].

Note:

1. A variation of the preceding activity is to divide the flipchart sheet in half, one side showing negative sources of support and the other side positive sources of support. Bosses, colleagues, subordinates, family may be either a negative or a positive source. Some negatives are debts, travel, long hours. Some positives are praise, recognition, successes.
2. This activity can be used in many training situations: leadership, human relations, sales, assertiveness, sensitivity and encounter groups, or stress management.

☐ As a getting-acquainted activity, participants can be asked to complete the diagram entitled "Getting Acquainted—A Patchwork Quilt" (Figure 4-5) [21] and then share the data.

☐ To facilitate communication between two persons, use the "Your Space Together" activity designed by psychologist Natalie Rogers, founder of the Person-Centered Therapy Institute [22]. *Procedure:* Put a large sheet of paper

between two persons (a whole or one-half of a flipchart sheet will do) and ask them to use crayons or felt-tipped markers to "explore that space simultaneously." Give them these instructions: "This is your shared space. In the next 15 minutes, use the pens to explore it. The rules are simple: Keep it non-verbal, and be as true to yourself and your feelings as you possibly can."

☐ After the drawings are made, these discussion questions might be used: Did I tend to lead or follow? Was I self-protective? Adventurous? Did I respect my partner's boundaries? Did I enjoy this relationship on paper? If so, why? if not, why? Were we really communicating? Did I favor communication or prefer to be with myself?

Note: This exercise can be used for those from other cultures, couples, business partners, etc.

☐ In a course on strategic or corporate planning, participants may be asked to "Take a metaphorical leap. Imagine your company as a vehicle. Any kind of vehicle. Now draw it on a piece of paper and describe it in a few words." This was the assignment given in a seminar on strategic management to a group of senior executives at the Wharton Applied Research Center, University of Pennsylvania. The seminar director says that the exercise forces the executives to think of their company as a whole, where the company is, and where it is going (or not going). Some examples of the art work: one participant portrayed his company as a bike with *two* sets of handlebars—one in front and one in the rear—to show movement in opposite directions. Another executive drew a car which was ancient in its front half and super-modern in the other section. The idea was to show that the company was struggling to get into another field, but the old phase of the business was a drag on the new side. A third executive drew a solid, fully-tracked vehicle, the idea being that the firm was hard-charging and steady, but certainly not built for speed [23].

In another Wharton seminar, which tackled problems of family-owned companies, one

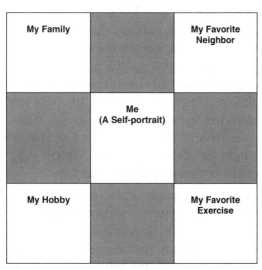

Figure 4-5. Getting Acquainted—A Patchwork Quilt

drawing showed a car with three people in it—all driving. A father who had grave doubts about his children's ability to run the business drew a truck speeding into a brick wall. Other drawings revealed generational conflict, sibling rivalry for control of the firm, and resentment toward non-working relatives living off the business [24].

☐ A problem with another unit can be worked on by drawing the roles of the various individuals involved and then using the pictures as references in an actual meeting with the other group [25].

☐ In a session or program concerned with confidence building, ask the participants to draw their most positive attribute of self and then to discuss it in pairs or trios.

☐ Cited previously under "Icebreakers" in Chapter 1 as a paper and pencil or flipchart task, the six items in *My Personal Shield* could also be presented in a graphic or illustrative way in a highly experiential program.

After the individual completion of the art work in each of the above activities, participants can be placed in dyads or triads to share the significance of their work. The intimate nature of these small groups should encourage full communication about the meaning of their graphic work. It should also provide added insight into it.

☐ In a public speaking training course, participants may be given colored felt tip pens and flipchart sheets and asked to draw "ideographs" (symbolic pictures) to pictorialize the points of a speech. The ideographs are used in lieu of notes or outlines. The rationale for this is that the bulk (85%) of what we retain is learned visually. So if speakers can translate an idea into an easy-to-comprehend picture, they can clarify their own thinking and better imbed the idea in the minds of their listeners.

Participants were advised to have their idea graphs follow the usual speech outline: (a) statement of the problem; (b) solution; (c) positive results from the solution; (d) evidence for the solution—a personal incident, an analogy, the judgment of an expert, an example, and

statistics/facts; (e) summary (restatement of a, b, and c). This added up to nine ideographs.

An example of a convincing but simple presentation: a personnel administrator drew a large table, with a missing leg, about to fall. This symbolized a warning to the branch personnel directors that if information was missing from their budget presentations, their budgets could not be approved [26].

Group Art Activities

Group Identity

To aid in the development of group identity, ask each group to draw a picture on a flipchart that describes the group.

Note: It may be anticipated that less cohesive groups will draw something about *individual* group members. Conversely, a more cohesive group will produce something that symbolizes the nature of the total group.

Group-at-Large Mural

☐ In an experiential training activity, post five or more flipchart sheets (or brown wrapping paper) on a wall. Advise participants that each day they can enter reactions to or feelings about any aspect of the course in artistic form. The art work will give the group a running account of course progress, movement, impact, learnings, and feelings about the course.

☐ A group of participants may be given an assignment of drawing a mural with the objective of studying their interaction while at work. The observers, one or two participants, or the group-at-large may focus on decision making, communication patterns (including possible breakdowns), formation of alliances, willingness to assume responsibility, planning approaches and skills, and so on. Start the assignment by giving each participant a different color marker; then ask them to draw a picture of themselves at work, or assign any other task which is of group concern. The purpose of the differently colored pens is to track the nature and amount of each person's participation clearly [26].

Small Group Mural

Participants, in small groups, may construct a group mural in response to an assigned subject. For example, in an intercultural training program, women from particular developing countries could be asked to depict (draw) the status of women—past, present, and future—in their country.

Group-at-Large Collage

You may wish to ask your total group to construct a collage which represents their image, spirit, mission, nature of their learning, feelings about the course, and/or communication prowess. Provide colored construction paper, old magazines which have photos and ads in them, 5" × 8" cards, felt-tipped marking pens and/or crayons, tape, cord, paper clips, stapler, paste or glue. Depending on course objectives, this activity, using observers, could be processed or critiqued upon completion in terms of leadership, decision making, participation, cooperation, planning, intimacy and rapport, member satisfaction, and the like [27].

Problem Perception

A group of five to ten participants collectively describe (in art form), on three adjacent flipchart sheets (1) how they see the nature of a given problem (problem definition or description), (2) how they feel about it, and (3) what should be done about it.

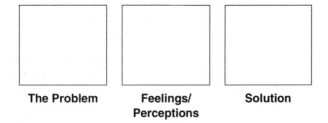

| The Problem | Feelings/ Perceptions | Solution |

Group Guess

Have one or more teams draw a picture to demonstrate a point graphically. Have another team guess what point has been made.

Note: Advise the graphic communicators that they are to strive for clarity. If the other team has difficulty interpreting the drawing, the communication is not effective.

Terrific/Horrific Depiction

Working in teams, participants draw on a flipchart the ideal/extraordinary/stellar manager or team leader, the perfect planner, or the consummate communicator. Alternately, ask them to draw the deplorable delegator, the manipulative motivator, or the nefarious negotiator.

Post drawings on the walls of the room for interpretation and discussion.

Geometrical Forms

Most of the examples of art assignments we have presented are drawn without any prescribed boundaries. However, at times it may be advantageous to provide such structure. The rationale for the use of "geometrics"—squares, triangles, rectangles, a segmented shield—is given fully on page 15. (We have provided such art assignments on pages 7, 15, 83, 84.)

Another thought-provoking geometric form is the circle. Participants can draw several circles to provide highly significant meaning about self and/or various interpersonal relationships. It is to be noted that the circle is the easiest form to draw. Examples:

☐ Organization development specialists Fordyce and Weil [27] have their participants draw circles in team building sessions to describe influence and communication relationships. More specifically, participants draw a circle for each team member, including the boss and his/her boss. Team member names are entered in the circles. The circles are drawn "to scale"—larger circles for those who have greater influence over the way the group operates. The circles are placed near or far apart from one another to show how closely team members must work together for proper results. Blue lines are then drawn to connect those who are personally close to one another. Red lines are drawn to depict relationships in difficulty—those with either little communication or the existence of friction. The highly revealing data are then processed.

☐ A three-circle test can be used to communicate attitudes toward life, per Tulane University social psychologist Frederick Koenig [28]. The test is quickly done, and its nature is such that it always works. Try it yourself now by simply drawing three circles, one representing the past, one for the present, and the third signifying the future. Then label the circles. The circles may be of any size, and arranged in any way.

The psychological principles at work are circle *size* and their *relationship* (distance) to one another. if things are in close relationship, we tend to draw our circles close together; if they are not, we draw them somewhat apart.

Circles which are drawn separately indicate that one's life periods (past, present, future) are perceived as being separate and unrelated. Overlapping circles show life as being continuous and related. This means that past and present actions impact what we will do in the future. People who view life as a continuous process typically are those who have control over their destiny.

A large circle about the past indicates that family and background are very important. A large present circle indicates the leading of a very busy life, a lot of living for today. A large future circle is equated with optimism, a good future is ahead.

In Dr. Koenig's tests, very few people are past oriented.

Possible uses: In workshops concerned with personal growth, stress management, assertiveness training, career planning, or management development.

Note: As in any other art assignment, it is desirable to ask the participant to verbalize why he/she drew his/her circles as he/she did. The trainer may draw on the above analysis to help explain individual drawings; however, the trainer's attempts at processing past actions and insights should be governed by the limits of his/her psychological background.

Combining Guided Imagery and Art

Present a guided image to the group in sufficient detail so that they are led to the point where it is possible for them to complete the imagery; develop a *symbol* of their experience, thoughts, and feelings; and draw the symbol on paper. The symbol may be very simple or quite complex, just so it interprets what was experienced.

Typical scenes or situations for the guided imagery: at the bottom of the sea, in a shaded wood, on a space ship. Present imaginative imagery by building sound, smell, color, flowers, animals, etc., into it. Develop the imagery to a point where the participants can take it over: "You enter the farm house. There is a long, circular mahogany staircase in it. Sunlight is shining on the staircase. You mount the staircase. You have the feeling that . . ."

Be certain to have the participants close their eyes when the activity begins.

Allow several minutes to reflect on the experience. Instruct participants to select a symbol that summarizes it. Then have them draw their symbols as described below.

Individual approach. Provide each participant with several crayons and a sheet of sketching paper which has a large circle on it, lightly drawn in pencil. The circle is a focusing element. Have them enter their symbolic representation in or outside the circle. Then have each participant share the drawing with a partner.

Small group approach. Divide the total group into two or three sub-groups. Place a large (six to eight feet in diameter) circle, constructed out of brown wrapping paper, on the floor, one paper circle for each small group. Provide each participant with a box of pastel-colored chalk. Have participants sit on the floor around the paper circle and enter their symbol on it. If participants wish, they may merge their drawing with the work of others. Have the participants share their drawing with the small group.

Note: As an optional feature of this activity, you may wish to point out that the circle has special significance in early cultures. The late Swiss psychologist Carl A. Jung used the Hindu word *mandala* (or magic circle) as a symbolic representation of the "nuclear atom" of the human psyche, the essence of which we don't know. In Eastern cultures the mandala is contemplated to bring about an inner peace, a feeling that life has again found its meaning and order [29]. The circle is, of course, found in nature in the form of the sun, moon, certain flowers and fruits, etc.

Guided Visualization

The above activity is obviously highly general and open-ended, designed to encourage free expression of feelings and also to create a mood. The exercise which follows is totally management-focused. It employs art as a form of communication (through use of visual, pictorial or graphic representations) to stimulate creativity.

Participants use crayons or large felt-tipped pens to draw pictures on large flipchart sheets. The drawings represent ideas about the themes raised by the session leader. Possible topics include descriptions of what the firm is like, where it is now, and where it is going (visualization of the future), in order to solve current problems or to clarify a long-term plan.

Procedure:

1. After the individual drawings are completed, participants team up in pairs to explain their illustrations to each other. Their joint task is to create a *new* picture that embraces the most significant aspects of the two original pictures.
2. Next, each pair joins another pair to create a new group (quartet) picture.
3. Each quartet then joins another quartet to form an eight-person drawn graphic or picture.

Two rules govern the guided visualization activity:

1. Talking is allowed only when someone (individuals, pairs, groups) explains what has been drawn. The actual art work is created silently.
2. Everyone must be involved in the drawing of the shared picture. Each person must ensure that what matters most to him/her gets carried over from his/her original picture to the new group picture.

Rationale: Very few of us have used drawing as a means of analyzing problems. By creating art work, however, the right brain is engaged for greater creative output than is ordinarily the case in written creation. Drawings help to show relationships between things much more readily than words do. The process is also a good consensus builder. Similarities emerge, overcoming the usual squabbling over details.

The process was developed by management consultants Chris Musselwhite and Cheryl De Ciantis [30].

Skill Pointers

To ensure that your use of art in the training situation is accomplished in an effective and professional way, these guidelines should prove helpful:

1. Have a clear-cut training objective, for example, to use art as an icebreaker, as a means of generating more profound and/or personal data, to develop intimacy and rapport, to get the creative juices flowing.
2. Limit the subject matter of a drawing to avoid confusion and possible resistance to the total assignment.
3. Introduce the assignment in an up-beat way, as a fun thing. For example, say, "We're going to do something a bit different this afternoon and have some fun doing it. Any great artists here? None? Good. Then we're all on an equal footing, skill-wise. Now here's the task. I'm going to ask you to do some thing in a graphic, illustrative, or artistic way."
4. Present clear instructions. Remember, drawing something in a training situation is a new experience for most adults. You may thus wish to present the assignment in writing as well as orally. (See Figure 4-6 for a sample task assignment sheet.)
5. Anticipate that some participants may have difficulty expressing themselves in artistic fashion. Actually, *everyone* can draw. The "I can't draw

---

Task Assignment Sheet: Visualizing Your Work Team

Procedures:

1. Think a moment about your back-home situation. Now identify the work team of which you are a member; e.g., if you are a trainer in a training department, that is your work team; if you are the trainer in the personnel office, that is your work team. If you are a manager, you are part of two work teams: your own and that of your supervisor.

2. Reflect on *your* work team in terms of these two dimensions:
   a. What is it like?
   b. What *should* it be like?

3. Now draw a picture of your work team, both *present* and *ideal*, in a graphic or illustrative way. Use as your artistic concept a vehicle, animal, bird, fish, plant, or whatever else comes to mind.

4. Use the reverse side of this paper for your work. Turn the sheet horizontally; segment it into two parts by drawing a vertical line down the middle. Label the left segment "My team—what it's like." Label the right segment "My team—what it should be like."

5. Now let yourself go! Be as creative and imaginative as you can in depicting your team. You have 10 minutes for this task.

6. Share your drawings in a trio (10 minutes).

7. Processing—group-at-large discussion (15 minutes).

Figure 4-6. Example of a Task Assignment Sheet entailing the use of art in a team-building session.

anything" complaint is essentially a fear of expressing one's self in a new manner. Ask the "reluctant dragon" to "give it a whirl and do the best you can."

6. Monitor (walk around) the group and offer suggestions as may be appropriate; for example, suggest use of stick figures, symbols, or simple graphics. Also, don't be too concerned if someone does only partial work or totally "goofs up" the task.

7. As in any experiential activity (exercise, game, role play), processing or debriefing is a must. Dyadic and small group work should be supplemented by total group discussion.

8. The group-at-large phase of the work typically entails a sharing of the meaning of the drawings. As facilitator, set the right tone by encouraging the group to ask clarifying questions and by providing praise for creative work. ("I particularly liked the motorcycle you drew to show your need to go into the country after work to get away from it all.") Discourage negative comments, argumentation, and psychoanalyzing of drawn objects and persons.

9. In vertically structured training, such as in team building, let the boss present (explain) his/her drawing last to avoid possible influence on the other presentations.

Added Skill Points

It is a good idea to post completed art work to the walls for purpose of later reference, to help create an atmosphere, and for recognition of accomplishment.

A word about the use of art materials: Flipcharts are preferred to the usual 8½" × 11" writing paper because their larger size permits greater freedom of expression. As to drawing implements, large felt tip pens are easier to use than are crayons, charcoal, or pens.

The previous examples, as has been indicated, relate to activities in the training situation. If these activities produce insight and learning in the classroom, that in itself is worthwhile. However, with proper emphasis by the trainer on the potential (transfer) of these activities for on-the-job use, there is no reason why at least some participants should not use art in their work. For example, at Weyerhaeuser Company, Tacoma, Wash-

ington (manufacturers of wood and paper products), members of three departments—information systems, engineering, and research and development—hold weekly problem-solving meetings. In groups of 15, in three-hour sessions, the reps set up a problem to solve. They then share free-flowing images about the problem on a large drawing board. The process at work is this: As the symbols and their possible meanings emerge, new solutions often arise.

Participants in these sessions also learn

- ☐ To be more flexible, more open to change and risk.
- ☐ To look at work in new ways—reps find that the group problem-solving effort is fun as well as productive.
- ☐ To strengthen intuition via the freer imagery; intuition serves as a complement to traditional left-brain thinking about problems [31].

USING MUSIC

Music can enhance many types of learning experiences. Trainer/consultant Gregory J. Trulson (president, Training Solutions, Boca Raton, Florida) believes that: "Music has magic. You can't see it or taste it, but it can arouse emotions, create moods" [32]. Gerry Reid, consultant and engineer with IT Services, Kasson, Minnesota, and a proponent of "accelerated learning," sees music as a tremendous way of accelerating and intensifying the learning experience. He points out these worthwhile benefits [33]:

- ☐ Reduces anxiety in the classroom and builds a team feeling.
- ☐ Builds a "whistle while you work" environment.
- ☐ Challenges and inspires participants.
- ☐ Provides an atmosphere of relaxation and achievement.

Other worthwhile uses, according to Dr. Joel Zamkoff, a practitioner of accelerated learning at General Physics Corporation, Columbus, Maryland, are these [34]:

- ☐ *Relaxation.* Baroque music aids relaxation, which makes learning easier.

☐ *Information retrieval.* The rhythm of music impacts/engages the right brain, thereby furnishing a method to retrieve what has been learned.

☐ *Environmental change.* Music creates a learning atmosphere that is very different from our usual or traditional learning environments.

☐ *Communication complexity.* Music is a form of communication, but a highly complex one. For example, songs have the potential to activate both the left and right hemispheres of our brains. The result: The message is embedded into memory.

☐ *Mood creation.* Music can be employed to stimulate a variety of moods from relaxed to energetic, depending on the appropriate classroom activity.

Specific Uses

Music may be used to advantage in these situations:

☐ *Prior to the start of a session.* Typically, people are sitting around awkwardly and uncomfortably, possibly in silence, waiting for things to start. Why not turn those painful moments into a pleasant and relaxing experience? Canadian trainer/consultant John Spencer (president, Universal Training, Inc., St. Catherine, Ontario) suggests filling the void with a good quality table-top radio [35]. Locate a tasteful radio station and you should be able to provide music which most people will find pleasant, easy-to-take, and enjoyable; it should help to put them into a relaxed mood. (*Note:* If you prefer to play your own tapes on your cassette player, that's O.K., too.)

☐ *During breaks.* The break can begin with music. The cessation of music can serve as a signal to return to work. Upbeat music is appropriate.

☐ *At close out.* The musical selection should relate to the nature of the course, the nature of the group, overall program accomplishment/success, etc. An upbeat, inspiring piece should work in many situations.

☐ *For motivational purposes.* Gerry Reid favors motivational theme music and popular light

classics for they imply that, "This is a challenge, but you can do it and enjoy it."

☐ *For background/atmosphere while people work* Gerry Reid uses very soft baroque music, environmental sounds or relaxation compositions during formal sessions—lecture and individual and small group activities—to keep the atmosphere of relaxing and achieving alive.

☐ *For guided imagery, meditation, and fantasy.* Use soft, gentle music to serve as a soothing, relaxing background. Music that suggests outdoor sounds (wind, streams, brooks, birds, etc.) is appropriate. Trainer Judith Simpson finds that music is useful to stimulate the imagination in guided imagery. Of course, one must know something about participant tastes lest one choose something with negative associations. Music should be inviting, not intrusive. Simpson states that in working with guided imagery, she has used baroque music, harp music and some New Age music. A final caution: The music should inspire variety and shouldn't be repetitive or boring [36].

☐ *For training in nonverbal communication.* Varying, contrasting styles of music may be played—romantic, hard rock, folk, etc.—with the participants (in a personal growth program) acting out their feelings in dance [37].

Gregory J. Trulson suggests the use of music in these varied situations:

☐ *To represent a decade:* The Vietnam era, the era of the Big Depression, World War II, the Eighties. The Vietnam era had numerous anti-war pieces; the Thirties had "Brother Can You Spare a Dime?" and so on.

☐ *Women's workshops:* For example, points about the mores and folkways of days gone by can be made with such pieces as "The Girl That I'll Marry" vs. "Anything You Can Do I Can Do Better."

☐ *Personal growth workshops:* Uplifting music such as "The Impossible Dream," particularly at program's end, can be impacting. Theme music from such films as *Rocky* and *Chariots of Fire* may be appropriate.

☐ *Creativity enhancement:* The goal is to evoke innovative imagery, facilitate self-expression, and dislodge surface material which impedes creative flow. Thoughtful, relaxing, and impressive symphonic music should help.

☐ *Marriage retreats ("couples labs"):* Members of each sex group may be given the opportunity to pick a musical piece from a large collection of cassette tapes. After listening to several, they select one that they want to play to their partner to communicate how they feel. Some people can't verbally express their feelings and the music can serve as a helpful substitute. Each partner plays his/her tape to the other. (*Note:* With the popularity and ready availability of cassette players, the logistical problems involved, if any, are insignificant.)

☐ *Stress management workshops:* Music that helps people to relax, to improve their state of mind, and to create pleasant and positive images is helpful. Music can be played in the workshop while conducting relaxation exercises. Also, you can pass along these pointers to your participants for their post-workshop use:

1. Since all of us give our own meaning to music, select pieces that you like and find peaceful, restful, and soothing.
2. Make a 30-minute tape of that music.
3. Play it each day in a period that you have set aside for relaxation. *Note:* Repeated use of music that has helped relaxation in the past provides a positive association that is likely to be beneficial thereafter.
4. While the music plays, assume a comfortable position and close your eyes. Concentrate on the music and your relaxed state. Check your body mentally. Are there areas of pain, tension, or relaxation? What is your mood? If unrelated thoughts invade your relaxed state, discard them, and focus on the music and on relaxing.
5. When the music ends, scan your body again. How does it feel? Any difference now compared to the start of your relaxation period? Any change in your mood?

☐ *Career development workshops:* Consider a courage-building tune like "Take This Job and Shove It" for those who are enmeshed in no-win job situations. "Rocky" and similar inspirational musical pieces may be helpful, too, at appropriate points in the program.

Career planning workshops lend themselves well to the use of music. Training specialist Mitch Mitchell of Hewlett-Packard, San Diego, recommends the following musical pieces (presented at the Annual Conference of the National Society for Performance and Instruction, April 8, 1988, Washington, D.C.):

> *Keep On Working,* Peter Townsend
> *Working Man,* Creedence Clearwater Revival
> *Work to Do,* Average White Band
> *Working 9 to 5,* Dolly Parton
> *New Attitude,* Patty LaBelle
> Theme from *Rocky*
> Theme from *Chariots of Fire*
> *It's My Job,* Jimmy Buffett

Song

When considering music, we should not overlook song. Singing is a dynamic way to accelerate learning. Why? Because tunes and lyrics are stored and processed in the right hemisphere of the brain, areas which relate to imagination, spontaneity, and emotion. Song can aid learning and recall tremendously since it utilizes powerful mental circuitry.

Old, well-recognized tunes can be given new lyrics. This makes recall of the new information easy and fun. Or the trainees, in small groups, can write their own subject-related lyrics to a tune you select. Pride in creation and ownership can further aid the long-time storing of the new material.

Songs which lend themselves to new lyric development are "Three Blind Mice" and "The Mexican Hat Dance" [38].

Music and song can be powerful aids to memorization. For example, at Eastman Kodak Co., Rochester, New York, a memory problem was solved with music [39]: In electronics, resistors carry color codes to indicate numeric resistance values, tolerance, and reliability. But the trainees frequently find it hard to remember that "green" is 5 and "violet" is 7. The solution? The instructor cleverly tied the colors and the numbers together with a song based on "The 12 Days of Christmas."

Key point on music as an aid to memorization: We can remember songs for years, but the same lyrics (words) without the music are soon forgotten, even in a few days.

Sources

Long-time trainer Robert W. Pike in his *Creative Training Techniques Handbook* cites a three-audio-tape set of diverse music for trainer use with all royalties paid. The uses of the music: for Upbeat Introductions (walk-in), Celebratory Exits, Energized Breaks, Meditative Reflections, Flowing Discussion, and Fun Games Background. The six types of music are presented in 30-minute blocks. *Source:* Resources for Organizations, Inc., 7620 N. 78th St., Edina, MN 55439; (612) 829-1954, Price: $59.00 [40].

Another source for well-chosen music is the San Francisco–based LIND Institute (Learning in New Dimensions). They offer CDs with both calm and upbeat selections designed to optimize learning [41].

The Trainer's Warehouse offers these musical items for trainer use:

☐ *Jazzy Tunes for Trainers.* Bright, cheerful, royalty-free jazzy tunes provide lively background music for breaks, games, or energizers. Format: a 70-minute CD, $32.00.

☐ *Tunes for Trainers.* Royalty-free humorous selections to announce coffee, lunch, and evening breaks and selections to accompany more serious work sessions. Format: 2 cassettes, 60 minutes each, $26.00, or CD, 72 minutes, $32.00. Phone: 1-800-299-3770 or 508-653-3770.

If you prefer music and video, playable via a VCR and TV, consider these VCR tapes recommended by performance consultant Theresa Calabrese, Allstate Corp., Northbrook, Illinois [42]:

Nature Serenade: Vivaldi's *Four Seasons,* which gives footage of the four seasons.
Nature's Symphony: Has works by Tchaikovsky, Strauss, Mozart, Puccini, Grieg, and Mussorgsky.

The tapes are provided by Readers Digest, 800-234-9000 for $29.95 each.

Skill Pointers

Gregory J. Trulson offers these suggestions and cautions regarding the use of music:

1. If you have not used music before, ease into it. Use it initially as a pre-session relaxer and at breaks. As you get more comfortable with it, expand your use to serve as an adjunct to specific subject matter areas.

2. Don't force your musical preferences (biases) on people. It has been said "that one person's tune is another person's tomb." Try to hit a common denominator and use musical pieces most people will relate to. Take into account a possible generation-gap factor if you have a mixed participant age group.

3. Try to provide music with simple equipment. Hauling expensive, bulky stereo equipment to the training room is overkill.

4. If you are conducting training programs commercially, that is, receiving some sort of fee or honorarium, be aware of copyright laws. You may be able to get permission from the publisher for only occasional and minor use. Some publishers may appreciate that you wish to tout their music.

CREATING POETRY

Another way to involve and energize your participants is to have your teams or small groups report back in rhyme their conclusions on an assigned topic, issue, or problem. This technique will not only provide a sense of fun, but it will also get everyone's creative juices flowing.

Note:

1. Introduce your instruction to the teams in this manner: "We're going to ask you to give your reports in a fun kind of way—that is, to develop your report as a poem, in any form of rhyme that you wish—couplets, limericks, etc. This will give you a chance to unleash your creativity."

2. Since some participants may feel overwhelmed by this type of off-beat assignment, remain silent for a minute to let the shock wear off. Then you

may wish to pass out a sample poem, one that a prior group produced. Here is an example:

Time Out

The phone calls are lean
My desk is clean
That time management credo's a sensation.
The only problem is that
I have naught to do
Thanks to that last delegation.

3. Allow more time for this activity than the usual time allotment to develop a small group report.
4. To heighten interest, you may wish to set up a competition. Offer a prize for the most original and expressive poem. Select two participants to serve as judges of the competition.

THE JOURNAL OR DIARY

. . . no feeling fully experienced is inappropriate; that its expression, whether within the privacy of the journal or among trusted intimates, may well be a matter of mental health, an important tool of adjustment or a creative solution to the difficulties of any life. To restrain or deny feelings limits our depth of perception, loses empathy for other people and leads to an inner disunity. And for us men, especially, to become a man of more conscious feeling is to become more fully human.

—Michael Rubin in *Men Without Masks,*
Addison-Wesley, Reading, Mass., 1980.

More and more, the personal journal or diary, as a supplement to the group experience, is becoming recognized as an invaluable tool to help participants acquire insight about their behavior, motivations, values, attitudes, and feelings. The twin acts of introspection and recording one's thoughts and feelings help considerably to produce something none of us can get enough of—self-awareness. Some recent and varied examples of where and how journals have been used follow:

☐ In the CBS, Inc. five-day Professional Management Program, students are asked to keep daily diaries and to discuss their experiences at the end of the week [43].

☐ Trainer-consultant Patricia McLagen, president of McLagen & Associates, St. Paul, instituted two different training activities at NASA on the premise that people, as learners, learn in different ways. One was group-oriented: group discussion; the other was solitary for "stop-and-think" purposes: the activity journal. McLagen recommended the journal as a tool to apply the classroom learning to the on-the-job environment [44].

☐ In an experimental New York City program for the elderly, 300 recruits from the welfare and unemployment rolls attended an Intensive Journal Workshop. This was a part of their on-the-job training for such jobs as nurse's aids, housekeepers, dietary workers, guards, and maintenance men. Surprisingly, 90% of them kept their journals over a six-month period (they met weekly), finished their training, and stuck with these low-status hospital jobs. After a year, 80% were still on the job or had moved on to better ones. Also, one in three secured better housing, and one in four started night school or community college. The journal method was credited with much of the program's success by program officials. Ira Progoff, founder of the Intensive Journal Method, said this of the trainees and their initially impoverished condition: "Poverty is not simply the lack of money. Ultimately, it is a person's lack of feeling for the reality of his own inner being [45]."

☐ In a stress management program, participants identify sources of stress they encounter on the job; they then select a target problem that they wish to manage; and, as a third step, they keep a record for a week about what happens when the problem occurs. The rationale for the diary approach is that a basic step in changing behavior patterns is the observation and recording of cues that trigger a particular behavior. The recording of the behavior helps participants to learn how their thoughts and actions, as well as the influences (actions or stimuli) of others, may be inducing the stress. In effect, the recorded data are feedback basic to managing the unwanted stress.

As an aid to keeping their week-long record, participants are given these kinds of questions to respond to when the problem arises: What precipitated the problem? What were you doing at the time? What were you thinking about? What was the nature of the tension that was experienced? What was your response to the stressor [46]?

☐ Roger W. Axford of the Department of Higher and Adult Education, Arizona State University, Tempe, asks participants in his management seminars to keep a weekly journal to record learnings of the week. He finds that the insight it provides managers tends, among other things, to reduce stress on the job. He also reports that having a week's record of insights and ideas provides "a sourcebook for program planning, administrative revisions, and possible career changes or development" [47].

☐ In the area of creativity, writer and teacher of writing Nancy Kuriloff advises her clients to keep a "process log" as a way of unleashing one's creativity. She recommends these steps [48]:

1. When the ideas won't come, write down all your feelings and frustrations.
2. Focus on your creative periods. What circumstances seem to help the ideas flow?
3. Jot down, brainstorming style, whatever comes to mind. Polish the material later.

Industrial psychologist Harry Levinson, commenting on Kuriloff's journal technique, points out that the creative process is the same whether it's writing or engineering design [49].

☐ Eugene Raudsepp, a psychologist and president of Princeton Creative Research, a consulting firm that specializes in creative problem solving for industry, states that diary-keeping is the best way to check whether one has genuine intuitive hunches or mainly wishful projections. He suggests that if your record shows that your hunches are mostly inaccurate, make a serious self-appraisal to ascertain how personal interests or anxieties might be distorting your perceptions. Committing your insights to writing as they arise also aids in retaining ideas

that all too readily evaporate due to an interruption or distraction [50].

☐ Charles M. Vance, Syracuse University, recommends that you, as a trainer in human relations or management, mention the journal idea as the program starts. Point out to participants that it is a good tool to record insights about themselves and about the relationships with others that they reach during the training. Then distribute a mini-journal for recording these insights in relation to the back-home situation. Schedule time at the end of each day to share one's personal journal with a fellow participant. At program's end allow enough time for each participant to prepare and leave with you a summary of the insights gained during the week. Also advise participants to keep their journals alive by constantly recording successes, failures, and insights. Finally, tell them you will follow up in six months to assess their progress with the insights recorded in their journals [51].

☐ Management trainers Michael J. Kruger and Kay H. Smith used the journal approach as a means of post-training reminder following a two-week management training course. Specifically, they secured agreement from the managers to take their journals home, review and revise them, and return them to the course coordinator within 30 days. The latter then forwarded a complete set of *one* manager's weekly journal entries to all 24 course attendees for 24 consecutive weeks. This procedure provided each manager with the opportunity to relive the learning experience via peer writings and insights for a six-month period after course's end [52].

Reference was made earlier to the need to transfer classroom learning to the job. Although contracting (self-contracts for action plans) is one way to do this, we know from experience that not everyone is willing or able to develop an action plan easily. The diary is a good way to help participants develop the mind-set basic to the preparation of their action plans. A tool for this purpose is a journal-type worksheet given in Appendix 16. It starts the proper thought processes at the program's outset, so that participants can ease into the preparation of their contracts and action plans at program's end. Advise participants on Day 1 that they should complete their diary as the program goes along and review it regularly to update, revise, complete, and refine their statements. Completion of the last column—Possible Action Plan—may be deferred until the end of the program. The important thing is that a lot of the thinking basic to the action plan will already have been completed on a regular and continuing basis.

Another example of a structured form of journal or diary is given in Figure 4-7. It is an aid to resolving a problem in interpersonal relations, communication, etc. A separate page, such as in a notebook, should be used to record the daily reactions to one's new behavior.

Sharing Data Developed by Journaling

A final step in the journaling process is sharing what one has recorded. Of course, not all recorded data need be shared. In fact, if it is very personal, it may not be desirable to do so. In such a circumstance, the task of the journal keepers may be to share what was learned from the experience, as opposed to sharing the details of the journal.

In general, whether participants share data from their journals will depend on such factors as:

☐ *Nature of data.* If the recorded material relates to, say, delegation problems, this would probably be easy to share. Conversely, if the data relates to personal stressors, there may be an understandable reluctance to share them.

☐ *Nature of program.* In a management development seminar containing limited experiential activities, sharing may seem inappropriate and threatening. Conversely, in a highly experiential leadership laboratory, full sharing may be a very natural thing to do.

☐ *Recording time.* If the journaling has proceeded for a very short time, sharing may be premature.

☐ *Nature of participant group.* A group of blue-collar foremen, law enforcement supervisors, or upper level business executives may be less likely to share their journal data than mental health workers at a "burnout"

Resolving a Problem with Another Person

<u>Here's where I am now:</u>
I'm a negative person.

<u>People react to me in this way:</u>
They avoid me; they seem to be startled by some of the things I say.

<u>I will try the following new behavior:</u>
I will say nice things; give praise; be patient.

<u>Reactions from others on Day 1:</u>
I haven't noted any changes by others toward me yet; I'll keep trying tomorrow, however.

Figure 4-7. Example of a structured form of journaling.

conference or participants at a career planning workshop.

Keeping a journal of events, thoughts, and perceptions enables us to capture them before they become hazy or disappear entirely. By reducing them to writing, they also serve as building blocks for the development of new (future) observations/perceptions. The more complete and candid the journal becomes, the greater the self-insight one can garner from it.

Post-Training Use

Attention should be given in the classroom to the use of the journal *after* the training experience. The operative concept is that journaling is a form of both personal stress management and personal growth. It thus should not die at training's end.

When should a diarist do his/her recording? One longtime diarist suggests doing it "when the spirit moves rather than to force it. It might be easier to find things to write about in the evening, when the chaos of the day can be sorted." Since we are creatures of habit, some journal writers will ritualize the time, place, chair, lighting, beverage. All of which is O.K. if it establishes the mood for writing. And if one can't evoke a thought, reference can be entered in the journal to the effect that one "didn't feel like writing" [53].

WORKING WITH MODELS

A model is a conceptualization. It gives us a way of looking at a lot of information quickly and with greater overall understanding. In short, it gives us something we all want and need—the big picture.

Typically (but not universally), the model is presented in a diagrammatic or graphic form.

In the training situation, models provide a framework against which individuals and/or groups can test the validity of their attitudes, values, assumptions, and behavior.

Several examples of ways trainers can work with models follow.

Working with the Hierarchy of Needs

The late Abraham H. Maslow, a creative clinical psychologist and the founder of humanistic psychology, postulated the most widely quoted theory of motivation called "The Hierarchy of Needs." His theory or model identified the five different levels of human motivation. It also asserted that one could move up to a higher level only if the prior level was satisfied. The model is often presented diagramatically, as in Figure 4-8.

Four ways of involving participants with the Maslowian model are given below:

1. Have participants complete the form given in Appendix 17 and then share it in small groups.
    Note: The objective of this activity is to encourage introspection or soul-searching in

Figure 4-8. Diagrammatic presentation of Maslow's "The Hierarchy of Needs."

respect to one's job satisfaction, values, career aspirations, etc.

2. In a time management course, draw the Hierarchy of Needs on a flipchart, explain it briefly, and then pose this question for general discussion or small group work: Assuming that managers are often reluctant to manage their time better, can the Hierarchy explain their possible motivations for such behavior?
    Example answers include

    Safety/Security: The workaholic can be explained, in part, by anxieties and insecurities which drive him/her to constant effort.

    Social: If a need to socialize (to be loved) with others is very strong, socializing will be done even if it results in wasted time. Thus, time-consuming interruptions by phone, drop-ins, etc., will be tolerated.

    Ego: The dirty or cluttered desk syndrome, a real time-waster, may be explained by the desire to look busy and important. (Any rational observer would assert that a dirty desk, often accompanied by one or two other cluttered tables, hardly makes for efficiency.)

    Self-actualization: If one has a strong need for self-fulfillment, to be creative, to plan ahead, one will seek ways to find the time to so function. Conversely, if one is stuck at a lower level of motivation, there is no real need to move up to the apex of the Hierarchy.

3. Working with five small groups (or five sets of small groups if there is a large participant group), have each come up with practical motivators in relation to one level of the Hierarchy. (This means assigning one of the five levels to each small group.)
    Note: This assignment can be varied by letting each group decide for itself which level it wants to treat.

    Some examples of what may be produced by the groups:

    Physiological level: pay, fringes, good working conditions.

    Security level: share information to reduce anxieties about what is going on, manage consistently (don't upset people by sudden changes), don't shake people up by "big bear" behavior, provide a safe place to work.

Social level: encourage recreational activities, car pools, picnics, Christmas parties, informal groups, etc.

Ego level: provide opportunity to do one's job well, delegate, use job enrichment approaches, give praise and recognition, use participative methods such as the Quality Circle.

4. A Maslowian concept, at the self-fulfillment or self-actualization level, is that of the "peak experience." It is a "high" from an event or accomplishment where one goes beyond the normal or everyday expectation. It is a state of becoming, not just being (the Ego level). Examples include: climbing a mountain, natural childbirth (or any birth), being elected to an office one prizes, writing a book, conducting a unique piece of research, overhauling an engine for the first time, shooting a hole in one. Have individuals reflect on and share such experiences in small groups.

Note: This exercise might be used in a course on career development, in a session on self-development, in a session on motivation, in self-assertiveness training. (What are you doing to move up the Hierarchy? Are you letting others keep you down? What is keeping you from being a self-actualizing person?)

Choosing a Leadership Pattern

Robert Tannenbaum and Warren H. Schmidt, in the now-classic "How to Choose a Leadership Pattern," *Harvard Business Review,* March–April 1958, presented an array or continuum of leadership styles ranging from "boss-centered" to "subordinate-centered." The styles in their leadership model are these:

☐ The manager decides alone and simply announces it.

☐ The manager makes the decision alone, but tries to *sell* it to subordinates.

☐ The manager presents an idea (or decision) and *tests* subordinates by asking them: "What do you think?"

☐ The manager presents a decision tentatively, subject to possible change after the discussion. (There is no commitment, of course, to accept the advice, no matter how sound.)

☐ The manager presents *the problem* and consults with subordinates who are asked for suggestions *before* the decision is given to them.

☐ The manager asks the *group to make the decision* subject to the manager's boundaries or limits.

☐ The manager joins with the group in problem identification, diagnosis, consideration of alternatives, and making of the decision (team management).

The model avoids value judgments concerning the wisdom or the correctness of decision-making along any point on the continuum. Rather, such a decision may be made depending on the situation, that is, the need for telling, selling, testing, consulting, or joining. In addition to the forces in the situation, the manager also considers the forces in himself/herself and in the subordinates.

Have participants draw the continuum, as just described, then have them locate the point at which they, as managers, typically operate. Assign participants to small groups, and have them address themselves to these questions:

☐ Does my leadership style vary at all? If so, when? Why? Do I choose or merely use a style?

☐ Does my style match my boss's style? If it varies, why does it? Is it desirable or undesirable for the styles to match?

☐ What about my style in relation to my subordinates? What do they prefer? If I vary it, do they understand why I do so? (This is a consistency-logic-perception issue.) Or do the changes, if any, confuse them?

☐ Have I always had the same style? Do I anticipate any change in the future? Why or why not?

☐ How does one's personality affect or influence the style one employs?

Note: Since there are many profound questions here, allow enough time (30–45 minutes) to deal with them.

Secure reports from the small groups regarding learnings from the exercise.

A Model of Personal Power and Influence

To understand the "influence process," Roger Harrison and Jim Konzes have presented a model comprising four ways we use our psychological energy to bring about change [54]:

☐ *Pushing:* Here we direct our energy toward others in an aggressive way to bring about what we consider to be a desired change. When we are pushing we engage in direct attempts to move; to induce; to teach; and to control through orders, information, arguments, criticism, pressure, and threats.

☐ *Attracting:* We behave in ways that draw others to us based on our attractiveness, magnetism, excitement, and the like. We may also appeal to common values, ideals, goals. This, obviously, is more of an inspirational approach than a frontal attack.

☐ *Joining:* The change effort entails adding our energy to, and thereby increasing, the energy of others. We do this by encouraging, empathizing, summarizing, reflecting feelings, and seeking cooperation. Trust, support, and concern are key elements in this mode.

☐ *Disengaging:* We avoid or deflect the other's energy. This entails withdrawal, failing to respond, changing the subject, postponing, reducing (needed) conflict and interchange.

Using a 10-point scale, rank each mode of influence as to the frequency that you use it in your work (home, community, etc.) Then discuss your rankings with a partner.

A Model Regarding Burnout

Dr. Paul O. Radde, president and founder of Thrival Systems, has presented a model regarding the Burnout Syndrome [55]. Participants were given this definition of burnout (by R. Kundel): "a progressive cycle which depletes one's energy, results in loss of vitality, and progresses to more serious stages that affect the body, emotions, and spirit. The end result of burnout is dysfunctional behavior and low productivity." Dr. Radde

then asked the participants, in small groups, to check their own experiences of burnout against a five-stage progression of the syndrome: physiological, social, intellectual, psycho-emotional, and spiritual. The groups then developed strategies, both organizational and individual, to counter burnout.

Working with Transactional Analysis

The TA model covers three "ego states"—Parent, Adult, and Child. The model may take the following diagrammatical form when two people are in communication:

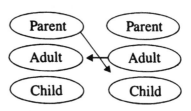

To chart the nature of a given transaction or communication event between two persons, draw an arrow from one circle to another as shown. The charting process is done for all transactions.

Two examples of the use of the TA model in the training situation follow:

☐ To help participants better understand their organization's culture, ask them to think of the organization as a person. A good way to do this, per TA authority Dorothy Jongeward, is to have participants draw the organization's three ego states, a basic TA concept. The idea is to see how large its Parent (both nurturing and critical sides), Adult (rational side), and Child (both creative and rebellious sides) would be. In effect, the TA model is used to help analyze and explain organizational culture [56].

☐ Explain this problem to participants: "Allied Widgets is facing severe financial problems. Management appeals to employees for help have been ineffective thus far. The reason: A total reliance on Parent to Child appeals. Thus, people feel that they are being talked down to. Can you provide examples of such appeals?"

"One example of a Parent to Child appeal is: 'Everyone will have to watch their arrival and quitting times and the length of their coffee breaks. Five minutes here and there multiplied by the total work force can add up to many lost dollars.' Can you provide examples of more *effective* appeals, that is, Adult to Adult? An example of this kind of appeal is 'We need your ideas to help turn things around.' Exercise your creativity. Every idea for improvement, big or small, is wanted and may well prove helpful."

WRITING TO LEARN (WTL) METHOD

The WTL method is a device that gets participants to think creatively by requesting that they do something that everyone (or at least most everyone) does naturally and frequently—namely, writing things down. Here's the procedure from training consultant Julie S. Hile [57]:

1. As trainer/facilitator you say to your group: "Take three minutes to jot down everything that pops into your head when you think of the word 'quality' (or customer service, effective communication, cost control). Don't worry about spelling or sentence structure. Just write the way you talk."
2. People pause to think for a few seconds and then begin to jot down their ideas. They pause and write some more. A lot of ideation takes place in the three-minute time allotment.
3. The timer soon beeps, signaling that the three minutes are up.
4. The trainer now says, "Finish that last sentence you wrote. Quickly review what you jotted down and check the two responses you'd like the group to know about."
5. The trainer then records participants' contributions on a flipchart.

Note:

1. In the course of the writing, no one reviewed anybody's work, nor was anyone's spelling, grammar, or handwriting criticized.
2. To convince the participants that you, as facilitator, are learning too, you should write along with the group.

3. The three-minute time limit shows that you are managing the training environment. It also shows that you think that the participants have a lot of ideas and that they can rise to the three-minute challenge.
4. By collecting two ideas from each person, you make everyone an active contributor.

Ms. Hile offers ten brief workshop exercises that use the WTL concept and technique. Use the ones that can benefit your training programs.

Participant Goals

Have participants read workshop objectives and list on paper what they themselves expect to accomplish. Goals are to be prioritized in order of importance—this shows where one will put most of one's energy. During the work shop people check to see how close they are to achieving their goals. At workshop's end, participants measure accomplishments against initial goals/expectations.

Written Brainstorming

Ask participants to brainstorm (in writing) for one minute on an assigned topic. Then ask them to draw circles around their written ideas and to write for another minute on the same topic. Call time and ask people to take a deep breath, circle the second set of ideas, and, for a final minute, brainstorm the third time.

Why the circles? They provide visual cues to encourage participants to keep reflecting more deeply about the assigned topic.

Miscellaneous Notes and Questions

Participants often have thoughts and ideas that are not quite in sync with the discussion underway at the moment. To recognize this and to help participants get these somewhat tangential ideas out of their system, do the following:

1. Tape a flipchart sheet titled "Miscellaneous Notes and Questions" (or possibly "Back Burner Agenda") to the wall.
2. Ask participants to enter their random thoughts on the flipchart.

3. Advise that session-related ideas will be brought up for discussion later on. Or, if not in line with the current workshop's goals, they will be communicated to the appropriate people in the organization for action or response.

Key point: Posting deferrable ideas to the flipchart assures participants that these ideas won't be forgotten or ignored. It allows people to focus fully on the topic under discussion.

Definitions

Early in a session/program, ask the participants to jot down their definitions of particular terms. Several hours later ask them to reread and revise their definitions in light of what they have learned in class.

Key points:

1. People are more likely to understand the definitions they created than those which emanated from a textbook.
2. Revision of definitions evidences to participants that their thinking has changed, that there is a "then and now" in their learning.

Dialoging

Assign people to dyads (pairs) and then proceed as follows:

1. Each team draws a vertical line down the middle of a sheet of paper.
2. One partner then writes something about the assigned topic or discussion on one side of the sheet of paper.
3. The other party responds on the other side of the page.
4. They continue the back-and-forth, written interchange until they are finished.

Key points: Sharing thoughts with a partner stimulates people to state something significant. The procedure also helps to overcome anxiety about sharing ideas. It also encourages minority view points to emerge.

Silent Discussion

Procedure:

1. The facilitator writes on a flipchart several words that are very likely to elicit responses.
2. The participants write their responses on the flipchart.

Key points: The silence and the writing tend to provoke more intense thinking. Note that the act of writing causes more considered responses, something which verbal opportunities may not do. "Blurting out" often produces less valuable thoughts. As participants fill up the flipchart space, they become eager to talk. The result: a lively discussion.

Time Out

Sometimes discussions may bog down, become hard to follow, or become really tense. If so, have your participants jot down their views on possible disagreements and then share them.

Key points: The silence and writing slow the pace and reduce tension. When written ideas are shared, people begin to see common areas, and disagreements get clarified. In fact, they may find there is more agreement than disagreement.

Directions

Ask participants to write down directions for completion of a task they have just mastered. The directions are to be written for six audiences: a child, a colleague, their mothers, their supervisors, an expert in this field, and a beginner in this field.

Key points: To teach a subject well, you must learn it well. Each special audience needs its own special directions. Also, by writing directions, one clarifies one's knowledge about how to perform the task.

Participant Menu

Have participants develop a written list of questions about the application of newly learned skills and about possible snags that may arise. Then set up a troubleshooting session to share written ideas.

Key points: The menu helps everyone—trainer and trainees alike—to recognize what people know and don't know about the topic/task. Also, it encourages participants to fill in the voids in their learning, instead of hoping the trainer will read their minds to discover their gaps.

Graffiti

Ask participants to write graffiti on certain workshop materials, to cut through "the sterile factual facade of black-on-white print." They are to mark margins and text with underlines, circles, highlighting marks, written questions, and/or memories.

Why the graffiti attack? It neutralizes the authority behind the sanctioned structure. Once that authority is powerless, people are free to ask real questions and to assert real objections. As Ms. Hile put it, "They begin personally negotiating with the ideas in the text."

These advantages accrue: The trainer can learn what people know or think about the topic, what interests they have for more learning, and what their attitudes are toward the topic. This should permit the facilitator to tailor/adjust the workshop to meet the needs of the class better.

Hile summarizes WTL benefits thusly:

☐ No special equipment or facilities are required.

☐ Writing is a time saver because it makes people choose their words carefully and get to the point. (In brainstorming and group discussions there is typically a lot of repetition and unneeded elaboration.)

☐ Writing moves people's ideas from inside their heads to the outside, where they can be reality tested and improved upon.

☐ Energy saved by not having to memorize ideas can be channeled into generating more ideas.

☐ Once ideas are written, people are less protective of them. Why is this so? Because the ideas no longer seem to be a part of them.

☐ Writing provides people with a record of their thinking processes and what they've learned.

☐ The whole thrust of this technique is to keep learning participant-centered rather than facilitator-dominated. When the trainer sees that people have worthy ideas of their own and are willing to share

them, he/she can readily avoid dominating the session. He/she can also see that people's learning from one another is as least as powerful as their learning from him/her.

☐ The thinking required back on the job is activated by WTL.

KEY POINTS

1. A variety of more specialized techniques may be used to secure high involvement. These include fishbowls, fantasy, guided imagery, mental imagery, working with pictures, using art, keeping journals, creating poetry, and using models.

2. Fishbowls can provide added means of increasing interaction and ideation as well as novelty. The technique is useful for analysis of a given problem and/or group functioning.

3. Fantasy, guided imagery, and mental imagery are tools to augment creativity by having participants produce mind pictures. The stimuli may be provided by the trainer (in fantasy and guided imagery), by the participant (in mental imagery and visualization), or by both parties (in guided fantasy).

4. Pictures can provide added opportunities for participant involvement and learning. Their use may range from the conventional (for example, to identify parts of a piece of equipment) to the more advanced (for example, as a projective technique in an experiential training program).

5. Art is another way to tap participant emotions, creativity, and the "child" within us. Art activities may be individual, small group, or total group.

6. As part of your overall training design, consider the use of music for fun, mood-setting, invigoration, and inspiration.

7. Keeping a journal is a relatively new training tool designed to help participants develop insight into their needs, motivations, emotions, attitudes, and behaviors.

8. Models are a useful tool to help participants better visualize major ideas, concepts, theories.

Working participants with insight into the model's ideas and possibly into themselves.

9. Regardless of the kind of technique in which small groups engage, the activity must close with a complete analysis (processing) of it. If adequate time is not allowed for such closure, learning will be minimal and participants may experience a sense of frustration.

REFERENCES

1. Based on a format presented in Hart, L. B., *Learning from Conflict: A Handbook for Trainers and Group Leaders,* Addison-Wesley Publishing Company, Reading, Massachusetts (1981), pp. 189–90.

2. Banet, A. G., Jr., and Jones, J. E., "Fantasy: Theory and Technique," in *The 1978 Annual Handbook for Group Facilitators,* University Associates, San Diego, California (1978), p. 198.

3. Smart, William, "Diversions: The Waiting Game," *The Washington Post* (December 9, 1983), p. D5, which draws on the book by Eleanor Rowe, *Waiting Games: How to Get Rich, Powerful, Sexy, and Healthy While You're Killing Time,* Facts On File, New York (1983), 126 pages.

4. The examples of training exercises in guided imagery are based on a presentation by Dr. Marilyn Saunders, a specialist in guided imagery, to the Washington, D.C., Chapter of the Association for Humanistic Psychology (January 10, 1982).

5. Larquit, L., "Work in the Fast Lane," *Northeast Training News* (June 1980), p. 18.

6. Pearlstein, Gloria, "Guided Visualization Fact Sheet," *Performance and Instruction Journal* (September 1987), p. 22.

7. *Training/HRD* (July 1976), p. 7.

8. "Right-Brain Training Helps Flight Attendants Pass FAA Exams," *Training/HRD* (June 1981), pp. 17–18.

9. Zemke, R., "Picture This: Using Mental Imagery to Enhance Learning," *Training/HRD* (January 1981), pp. 79–81.

10. Diekhoff, G.M., "How to Teach How to Learn," *Training/HRD* (September 1982), pp. 36–40.

11. Reid, Gerry, "Accelerated Learning: Technical Training Can Be Fun," *Training and Development Journal* (September 1985), pp. 24–27.

12. *Newsletter,* Association for Humanistic Psychology (December 1979), p. 27.

13. *The Levinson Letter* (October 15, 1981), p. 2.

14. Per Lee Beckner, Sales Training Manager, Coca Cola Foods Division, reported in *Meeting News* (May 1980), p. 98.

15. "Seminar Enlightens Managers on Best Ways to Hire and Handle Disabled Employees," *Wall Street Journal* (May 27, 1981).

16. "Phototherapy Enhances Therapeutic Process—Start to Termination," *Behavior Today* (February 15, 1982), pp. 4–5.

17. Culbert, Samuel A., and Fisher, Jerry, "The Medium of Art as an Adjunct to Learning in Sensitivity Training," *The Journal of Creative Behavior* (Winter 1969), pp. 26–40.

18. Garanzini, Michael J., "What We Learn Through Children's Art," *Today's Catholic Teacher* (March 1984), pp. 53–55.

19. Goldstein, Marilyn, Scholthauer, David, and Kleiner, Brian H., "Management on the Right Side of the Brain," *Personnel Journal* (November 1985), pp. 40–45.

20. Connelly, S., *Participant's Manual to Accompany Self-Motivation in Selling—A Sales Training Program,* BNA Communications Inc., Rockville, Maryland (1979).

21. Javernick, Ellen, "Off to an Art Start," *Today's Catholic Teacher* (September 1984), pp. 50–51.

22. Rogers, Natalie, "Using Expressive Arts to Communicate Across Boundaries," *Perspective,* Newsletter of the Association for Humanistic Psychology, San Francisco (July 1992), p. 16.

23. Jacobs, Sanford L., "Wharton Course Teaches Planning Using Managers' Drawings of Firms," *Wall Street Journal* (October 31, 1984), second section, first page.

24. Jacobs, Sanford S., "Problems of Family Companies Tackled at Wharton Seminar," *Wall Street Journal* (July 9, 1984), second section, first page.

25. Ault, Robert E., "Draw on New Lines of Communication," *Personnel Journal* (September 1986), pp. 72–77.

26. Haight, G. G., "Fear of Speaking," *Across The Board* (March 1980), pp. 44–45.

27. Fordyce, Jack K., and Weil, Raymond, *Managing with People: A Manager's Handbook of Organization Development Methods,* Addison-Wesley, Reading, Massachusetts (1971), pp. 152–155.

28. Dworken, Art, "The Three Circle Test," *The Washington Post,* Health Section (February 6, 1985).

29. Jung, C. G., *Man and His Symbols,* Doubleday and Company, New York (1964), p. 213. Also see "How

to Use the Mandala," *Newsletter,* Association for Humanistic Psychology, Washington, D.C. Chapter (July 1983), reprinted from *Expansion Magazine,* undated.

30. Barker, Julie, "Get Outta Line," *Successful Meetings* (October 1994), pp. 45–53.

31. "Weyerhaeuser Groups Tune Intuition, Imagination," *Leading Edge Bulletin* (October 19, 1981), p. 2.

32. Trulson, Gregory J., "The Sounds of Music," presentation at the National Conference of the American Society for Training and Development (June 22, 1987), Atlanta, Georgia.

33. Reid, Gerry, "Accelerated Learning: Technical Training Can Be Fun," *Training and Development Journal* (September 1985), pp. 24–27.

34. Zamkoff, Joel, "Accelerating Learning," *Report,* General Physics Corp. (March 1994), pp. 1, 2.

35. Spencer, John D., "How to Provide a Sensational Environment," *CTM (Canadian Training Methods): The Human Element* (December 1982), pp. 16–17.

36. Simpson, Judith, "Visionary: More Than Meets the Eye," *Training and Development Journal* (September 1990), pp. 70–72.

37. Pfeiffer, William I., and Jones, John B., *A Handbook of Structured Experiences for Human Relation's Training,* Vol. 1, activity #22, Nonverbal Communication, item 19, University Associates, Inc., San Diego (1970).

38. Reid, Gerry, "Accelerated Learning: Technical Training Can Be Fun," *Training and Development Journal* (September 1985), pp. 24–27.

39. Cournoyer, Robert, "Integrative Learning Speeds Team work," *Management Review* (December 1991), pp. 43–44.

40. Pike, Robert W., *Creative Training Techniques Handbook,* 2nd Edition, Lakewood Books, Minneapolis, MN (1994), p. 189.

41. Braley, Sarah J. F., "Music for the Brain" in "Short Cuts," edited by Loren G. Edelstein, *Meetings and Conventions* (November 1997), p. 13.

42. Calabrese, Theresa, "Will Classical Music Videos Soothe Your Trainees' Savage Evaluations?," *Creative Training Techniques* (June 1997), p. 6.

43. *Business Week* (October 20, 1980), p. 125.

44. *Training World* (September–October, 1979), p. 29.

45. Kaider, R. B., "The Way of the Journal," *Psychology Today* (March 1981), p. 67.

46. Weigel, R., and Pinsky, S., "Managing Stress: A Model for the Human Resource Staff," *The Personnel Administrator* (February 1982), p. 57.

47. Axford, R. W., "A Journal: Management and Development Tool," *Training and Development Journal* (September 1980), p. 8.

48. *Time* (July 14, 1980). Cited in *The Levinson Letter* (September 15, 1980), p. 2.

49. *The Levinson Letter* (September 15, 1980), p. 2.

50. Raudsepp, B., "You Can Trust Your Hunches," *Inc.* (July 1981), p. 89.

51. Vance, C. M., "Personal Journals in Training: Get More Mileage Out of Your Training Programs," *Training and Development Journal* (August 1979), pp. 54–55.

52. Kruger, Michael J., and Smith, Kay H., "Evaluating Management Training," *Performance and Instruction* (November and December 1987), p. 23.

53. O'Neil, L. Peat, "For Write Minded People: The Journal," *The Washington Post* (April 3, 1987), p. B5.

54. Harrison, R., and Konzes, J., "The Power Potential of Organization Development," *Training and Development Journal* (April 1980), pp. 44–47.

55. The presentation was made to the Washington, D.C. Chapter of the American Society for Training and Development (April 1980).

56. Caplin, D., "Corporate Culture: Training Problems and Prospects," *Northeast Training News* (August 1981), p. 10.

57. Hile, Julie S., "Getting the Lead Out," *Training and Development* (April 1992), pp. 55–58.

RECOMMENDED READING

Barnet, Anthony G., Jr., and Jones, John E., "Fantasy: Theory and Technique," in *The 1976 Annual Handbook for Group Facilitators,* University Associates, Inc., San Diego (1976), pp. 191–201.

    The authors provide a discussion of psychological underpinnings for fantasy and describe its types, techniques for structuring it, training considerations, and precautions.

Casewit, Curtis W., *The Diary: A Complete Guide to Journal Writing,* Argus Communications, Allen, Texas (1982).

    This book contains advice to the diarist including benefits, how to get started, how to keep it going, diary style, and formats.

Galyean, Beverly-Colleene, "Guided Imagery in Education," *Journal of Humanistic Psychology* (Fall 1981), Vol. 21, No. 4, pp. 57–72.

    Galyean describes how educators use imagery processes for higher consciousness, relaxation, receptivity to learning, and increased mastery of information.

Jaffee, Dennis T., and Bresler, David E., "The Use of Guided Imagery as an Adjunct to Medical Diagnosis and Treatment," *Journal of Humanistic Psychology* (Fall 1980), Vol. 20, No. 4, pp. 45–59.

This article offers examples of the use of imagery to obtain diagnostic information, for relaxation, to make positive suggestions to alter physical processes, and in the discovery of "an inner adviser."

Long, Donna M., and Lucia, Al, "A Little Bit o' Soul," *Training and Development* (July 2000), pp. 16–17.

The authors, co-owners of Juke Box Learning based in Kissimmee, Florida, and Lewisville, Texas, suggest attaching learning concepts to classic rock'n'roll songs as memory anchors and for inspiration of baby boomers,

Oldenburg, Don, "Creativity from Chaos: A Free-Form Theory for Transforming the Common Meeting," *The Washington Post,* Style Plus section (February 20), 1992, p. C5.

An account of Harrison Owen's "Open Space Technology" meeting conducted with 50 senior administrators of the U.S. Forest Service. After 32 minutes of the open-ended conference, the managers created and scheduled 13 workshops.

Pfeiffer, J. William, and Jones, John B., "Fantasies," in *A Handbook of Structured Experiences for Human Relations Training* Vol. 1., University Associates, Inc., San Diego (1969), pp. 77–80.

The authors present fantasy exercises including 15 individual fantasies, 5 guided fantasies, and 3 group fantasies. They cite professional standards for their use.

Simmons, Annette, "Using Art in Training," *Training and Development* (June 1999), pp. 32–36.

The author shares her experience with corporate clients on how to break through barriers of skepticism and mistrust using art in working with teams and other groups. Her thesis: art can help create a safe place to discuss dangerous truths—issues/conflicts people are afraid to discuss publicly. She offers tips on how to overcome participants' reluctance/resistance to engage in the art task. The article has several actual participant drawings from her work. A "must read" article.

Role Playing

5

You cannot teach a man anything. You can only help him discover it within himself.

—Galileo Galilei (1564–1642),
Italian astronomer and physicist

ROLE playing is one of the trainer's primary techniques to provide participation, involvement, and action learning. It allows the acting out (experiencing) of real-life situations in a protected or risk-free locale. That is to say, it is far safer and wiser to make mistakes as a role player in the training situation than it is to make them in work or other social environments.

Role playing in the training situation allows the receipt of adequately objective feedback about one's performance so that one can learn from what others (peers, the trainer) see, hear, and feel. Conversely, in the actual life situation we perform and behave, but rarely does anyone share their reactions about what we've done and how we can improve upon it.

We should also note that in role-playing activities participants are learning "full time." This occurs because they are either experiencing (acting out the role play), introspecting, engaging in self-critique, or critiquing others.

PURPOSES AND BENEFITS

In a more specific sense, role playing has these purposes and benefits:

☐ *To present information* to participants; for example, a top management official and the personnel manager assume the roles of a manager and an accountant, the latter learning that there are now legal taboos on sexual harassment.

☐ *To learn certain principles,* such as in coaching, counseling, customer relations, conflict management, and interviewing for fair employment.

☐ *To change attitudes,* for example, to become less prejudiced toward another department, a minority group, the opposite sex, foreign persons/those of another culture, or handicapped persons. (In respect to the latter group, student attitudes toward the disabled were altered in a positive direction after students sat in a wheelchair for an hour.)

☐ *To develop practical skills,* such as how to close a sale, how to handle customer objections, how to handle a disciplinary interview or a grievance, how to apply for a job, how to "upgrade" a sale.

☐ *To reality test* or check out the effectiveness of one's approaches or techniques; for example, in sales training one can try out one's ability to anticipate problems, to make timing more effective, or to employ sound reasoning. *Note:* Role playing provides for practice without penalty.

☐ *To disclose one's attitudes* towards others, a given subject, or a problem, so that one may receive related feedback.

☐ *To provide a "mirror"* (via feedback) so that participants can see themselves as others do, a basic step toward fostering insight (about self) and sensitivity (toward others).

☐ *To identify with others.* By acting out the role of another person, one can understand better "where the other is coming from." For example, a student having problems in school can achieve new insights into his/her behavior by assuming the roles of parent, teacher, and principal.

☐ *To learn how others think and feel* (empathy), such as customers, prospects, subordinates, members of the opposite sex, minority group members, persons of other ages, employees of other departments, persons of another organizational level (for example, headquarters vs. staff, line vs. staff).

☐ *To change behavior* such as to become more assertive, to become more spontaneous, to learn how to listen actively, to learn how to counsel nondirectively, to learn how to coach subordinates so they feel psychologically rewarded when the interview is over.

☐ *To prepare employees realistically* for some of the discouraging experiences they may encounter on the job. Thus, several major real estate firms have used role-playing courses to prepare their rookie sales personnel for encounters with difficult customers. For example, in one scenario, a trainee vendor was constantly interrupted by the seller's mother. Finally, he told the old woman: "Why don't you take a walk in the garden?" and literally threw her out, obviously a "no-no" in conducting proper customer relations. Other specialists have to learn how to deal with a lot of unpleasantness; for example, police officers who have to mediate nasty family disputes, park rangers who have to calm would-be campers who are squabbling over the last space in a campground, foreign service officers who have to deal with troubled Americans and anxious foreigners [1].

In the U S. Border Patrol Academy, law enforcement trainees are unwittingly enrolled in "Pepper Spray 101." A physically threatening experience, it entails these procedures: while trainees are engaging in the jumping jack exercise, without warning an "assailant" hits the trainees in the face with pepper spray. The trainee must draw a service weapon (a Beretta modified to shoot plastic dye-filled bullets) to shoot at a Border Patrol instructor who role-plays the attacker. The latter is shielded by a visored helmet and black, full-body armor. The trainees are unprotected and fight as in a real life-threatening situation. Why the realism of pepper spray? Says one instructor, "I wouldn't want to be exposed out in the field and not know what to expect" [2].

Another interesting example of role plays which are marked by high realism is that of training bus operators to drive the disabled properly, For example, Fort Worth, Texas, bus operators receive two days of study for disabled services. This includes operating lifts that bring wheelchairs onto buses. In Seattle, trainees must board and exit buses in wheelchairs to understand better the problems involved. The importance of this training, as seen by a Federal Transit Administration official, is expressed thusly "If you don't train the drivers and tell them that picking up the disabled is as important as picking up their paychecks, it doesn't work" [3].

ROLE-PLAYING DESIGNS

The following sections will show the considerable variety role-playing formats may take and will give you, as a trainer, practical role-playing models, all of which have been tested in the training situation. These explanations will also challenge you to use your own ingenuity to create new formats or to adapt the ones provided based on your study of them.

Informal Role Playing

Informal role playing [4] develops from the needs and special circumstances in the training situation. It is thus unplanned, unstructured, unwritten, and unrehearsed (compared to the structured or more formal role play, in which the role players are given a fairly good set of role instructions plus time to think about them).

It may arise in one of two ways:

☐ *From a participant problem.* A participant may say: "I have this problem at home (in the office, in the community) . . ."

Trainer: O.K., Doris, tell us a little bit more about your subordinate—name, age, personality, skill level, etc.

Doris: (provides added detail)

Trainer: O.K., let's see if we can develop any strategies to deal with Mary and her tendency to deliver putdowns, sarcastic and negative comments, etc. Fran, would you like to be Mary? (Fran agrees.) You (Mary) and your boss, Doris, have just completed a review of a project of yours. Doris has complimented you on it and now she's about to bring up some other business—the putdown problem.

(The role play is conducted.)

Trainer: That was quite good. But let's see if you can deal with this problem in any other way. Let's try this with another role playing team. Who wants to be Doris? Good. Who wants to be Mary? Great. O.K., here's the office. Doris is seated and Mary walks in . . .

☐ *From the need to sharpen issues.* In the discussion of a case or problem, a participant might say: "If I were the field rep, I would tell the inspector . . ."

Trainer: O.K., Pat, you be the field rep; Kim, you be the inspector. Here's your office, Pat. The inspector has just brought up the matter of which you are quite irritated about.

The rationale for this procedure is that it is one thing to say: "If I were the boss . . ." It may be something entirely different to have to actually handle that situation. Hence the need to reality-test what can or can't be done in a given interpersonal situation, as well as the more effective ways of accomplishing it.

In some cases you may decide to assume one of the two roles should you feel that the desired behavior or skill can be better portrayed by the trainer. Or the person who brought up the problem with another person may be asked to assume the role of the other person (role reversal) to develop insight concerning how the other person feels.

In general, the alert trainer will be on the lookout for situations where role play opportunities arise naturally in discussion. They give the training effort an extra, vivid dimension, something which participants will appreciate and from which they will learn.

Spontaneous Role Playing

Spontaneous role playing [5], also known as "live" or "hot" role playing, deals with real people (the participants) and their actual problems with others—on the job, at home, in the community, elsewhere in the everyday world.

Typically, the trainer asks the participants to cite the problems they have on a given subject. For example, in a course on interviewing techniques, you may say: "What are your most perplexing or difficult problems in your interviews?" You then post them on the flip-chart and the group prioritizes them. The top problems (for example, how to conduct a firing interview or how to listen more effectively) on the list are selected for the role play.

Then ask for volunteers to do the first role play. You may advise the group: "Here's a great opportunity to try out some things, to take some risks, for that's how we'll learn and grow. Also, it's not too serious if we come up with a mistake or two here. The idea is to get rid of the mistakes in the training situation so we won't make them where they really count—back on the job."

The first role play is subject to group critique and may be conducted again if it is inconclusive or if another approach is desired. Principles and skill pointers are developed by the group for the conduct of a particular type of interview, such as coaching. The group then moves on to another problem in interviewing.

Using live cases has real appeal to participants. In fact, it would be hard to imagine a course in, say, assertiveness training, where the participants were not allowed to work through some of their own problems—for example, communicating directly to the boss that one cannot work overtime due to other commitments, returning a dress to a small specialty shop, complaining about a bad steak in a first-class restaurant, or being given a hard time at work by another department.

In processing (critiquing) the action, you may explore the role players' feelings—tensions, frustrations, satisfactions, dissatisfactions, inhibitions, etc. The group should be encouraged to engage in the same kind of exploration of emotion, plus an analysis of what was learned, what behavior was predominant, what behavior was lacking or in need of improvement, etc.

In general, spontaneous role play works well because participants are utilizing their own experiences rather than trainer-assigned roles. This tends to heighten their emotional involvement in the training being provided, which in turn, augments learning and facilitates on-the-job application.

The Demonstration-Type Role Play

Demonstration-type role plays are acted out before the rest of the participant group. Typically, they are of two types: the dramatic skit and the personal growth enactment.

The dramatic skit. A skit is presented to the total group by two or more role players. The objective is to illustrate a problem or skill approach and to generate total group discussion about it. The enactment is based on role instructions provided by the trainer. The instructions may be given orally in either a general or a specific manner. Sometimes a written script may be given to the role players to ensure that they present the problem accurately or that a particular point is made. The script may also help to speed things up. For some role players, reliance on the script may also be tension reducing. Since the role players are only presenting a problem, their behavior itself is not subject to critique. In consequence, there is no expectation that greater personal growth will accrue for the role players, as opposed to the group at large, from the enactment of the skit.

A variation of the dramatic skit format is the "Wrong Way, Right Way" technique. The enactment follows the trainer's general instructions. Participants observe the "improper" procedure demonstrated by the role players (for example, how to orient a new worker, how to close a sale) and critique it. Then the second role play follows, which depicts the "proper" way to carry out the orientation, or closing of the sale, etc. Another discussion ensues.

An added variation entails the use of small group planning for the enactment before it is given to the total group. This procedure helps to involve all participants more fully than in the typical dramatic skit. The procedures are as follows:

1. Disseminate general background data about the role-playing case, if any, to all participants.
2. Divide the group at large into two smaller groups (A and B). Give all the A's one set of role playing instructions and the B's the other.
3. Ask each group (A and B) to discuss and agree on the purposes (goals, end results) of the interview and, as appropriate, the specific strategy to be followed in the role play.
4. Ask for a volunteer from the A and B groups to role play the case. Give them enough prep time to internalize their respective roles.
5. Simultaneously with step 4, brief the rest of the group, who are to be observers, concerning what to look for in the role plays. (It's a good idea to give the observers a written question or guide sheet.)
6. Run the role play (about 20–25 minutes).
7. Hold a general discussion after the role play. Start things off by comparing each group's planned strategy and expectations about results with what actually transpired. If there was a difference, try to learn why. Use the observer's question sheet to guide the discussion.
8. Summarize learnings from the role play.

Still another variation of the dramatic skit is for one role player (for example, an employee in a disciplinary interview) to choose at random a role from an envelope or box having five or six different role-playing instructions. Neither the other role player (the boss), the observer group, nor the trainer knows which role has been selected. They, therefore, do not know the attitudes, values, emotional state, etc. of the employee. Their task is to be sensitive to the employee, to pick up or read the cues and clues which the employee communicates. In effect, this is an exercise designed to test and develop awareness to feedback. The participant playing the role of the supervisor has the task of assessing the employee's current attitudinal state and making adjustments in strategy as it comes into focus.

Note: Since there are a half-dozen or so different employee roles available, the enactment, using different role players, can be repeated several times, if desired.

An effective way to involve the total group in the role plays, and to avoid participant embarrassment about demonstrating weaknesses, is to use what trainer Ted Voelker calls the "tag out" procedure. Here's how it works [6]:

☐ Divide the participants into two or more groups.

☐ Provide one group with a brief description of a situation, presented from the viewpoint of the manager or sales representative.

☐ Provide the other half of the total class with the same scenario, but presented from the perspective of the employee or potential customer.

☐ Allow enough time for everyone to read the assigned scenario.

☐ Ask for a volunteer from each group to role play the scenario. Advise that within three to five minutes each role player must raise a hand to signal another team member to "tag into" the role play (to replace the first role player).

 Note: Any participant can raise his/her hand at any time as the role play ensues. The trainer must call for a tag if someone exceeds time limits. The tag-out procedure need not occur by both groups simultaneously.

☐ When everyone has played, ask the participants these questions:

 Did you tag out because you felt the issue was fully resolved?

 Did some tension or fear cause you to tag out?

 Would you care to work on that difficulty further?

 If you were back home, on the job, what preparations could you have made so you wouldn't have needed to tag out?

Key points about the tag-out procedure:

☐ People tag out for different reasons. Since they know they can quit whenever they are ready to do so, they become more comfortable in the enactment. They needn't worry about embar-

rassment resulting from publicly showing their weaknesses.

☐ Since everyone plays, and thus numerous enactments occur, there are more opportunities to observe both good techniques and undesirable ones. The idea, of course, is to learn from favorable styles and techniques and to resolve not to use the less effective ones.

☐ There is a physical "lift" when participants rise, move, and stand in the tag lines with their teams.

Trainer/consultant David F. Swink offers these added skill factors to observe when conducting a dramatic skit or role play [7]:

☐ Provide opportunities for warm-up to reduce participants' sense of risk (looking silly or inept before their fellow participants). One technique for this is to divide the total group into pairs or small groups to discuss the topic at hand. Another is to place people into a *spectrogram* (or continuum). This measures literally (and physically) where people stand on an issue. *Example:* In a stress management course, ask people to line themselves up according to the amount of change (or stress) they are now experiencing in their daily lives: "If you have no change (or stress) stand by the far right chair; if you are experiencing total change, stand by the far left chair. Or place yourself at a point between the two chairs." The trainer then interviews several of those on the continuum to ascertain the reasons for their self-positioning.

☐ Praise the forthcoming role play as a great opportunity to try out new things. State that there is always an element of perceived risk when some thing new is undertaken.

☐ Advise that there is more than one way to enact any situation and that it is O.K. to make mistakes. State: "If you err, we'll have more data from which to learn."

☐ Point out that acting out the situation is the only way to make learning come alive, to make it relevant and practical.

☐ Stress that in the role plays all of us become teachers—we teach one another by using our job and life experiences to help others learn.

☐ Choose a *protagonist,* the person refining old roles or learning new roles, as the main or leading character in a role play. This role is the group's learning vehicle, so pick this person carefully, favoring participants with top communication skills. *Examples of a protagonist:* a customer service rep trying to improve skill in dealing with an irate customer; a supervisor trying to increase her delegation to a reluctant, less-than-confident subordinate.

☐ Choose an *auxiliary,* the person with whom the protagonist is learning to interact more effectively. It is a good idea to use the total class to help develop the nature of the auxiliary's role.

☐ Ask the class to help establish the setting in which the interaction takes place. Use props appropriately (and if available) for added realism (desk, phone, chair, file folders on desk, etc.).

☐ Start the action. The protagonist tries out the more effective skills (for example, communication approaches) previously learned in class.

☐ At strategic, timely moments, stop the action. Ask the protagonist to critique his/her own behavior and to suggest other strategies to try out. Input from the class is wanted, too. *Note:* This self-critique precedes class critique, making it easier for the protagonist to receive feedback from the group.

☐ In this feedback phase, limit the group's usual tendency to unload negative feedback on the protagonist. Do this by using a question of this sort: "What behaviors/skills has Pat used *effectively?*" Then ask for added/alternate approaches: "Assume you are Pat. Could you try another procedure?" *Note:* The trainer is eliciting feedback from the group to avoid being the oracle with all the "right" answers, and thus inhibiting group ideation. So the trainer makes his/her suggestions *after* the group has had its say and even then only if really necessary.

☐ Consider rotating protagonists, selecting participants with different styles and approaches.

☐ To close things out, review what the protagonist and the group learned.

☐ Also check with the auxiliary how it felt to be in that role. He/she may directly tell the protag-

onist about certain feelings he/she experienced as the role play developed.

☐ Lead the group in applause for the role players.

☐ Form small groups to discuss (a) how the role play relates to actual job life and (b) how to apply what was learned. Secure feedback from the teams for a general discussion and wrap-up.

These procedures should also help your participants to learn from the demonstration-type role play [8]:

1. *Prepare the participant group.* The idea is to reduce possible anxieties about performing before others and to create an atmosphere of warmth and inclusion/acceptance. *Some pointers:* Before the break, mention that several issues have surfaced and "we will explore them by acting them out." Also state that "we want to include everyone in the activity, so some of you may wish to be part of the actual demonstration, while others may wish to be involved as observers."

2. *Select and prepare the role players.* Set the stage by citing the specific situation to be acted out. Provide some structure by offering a simple line of action, but don't over-engineer it. Ask the total group to describe the roles to be played—what they're like, what they might do, and how they might feel.

   Then ask for volunteers to play the actual roles as described by the group. Write short character descriptions on a flipchart while the participants are considering volunteering. Check to ensure that the focus of the enactment is clear, for example, solving a problem, handling a situation, or developing a skill.

3. *Brief the observers.* Stress the importance of their task. Advise them to take notes to help their reporting back to the total group. Assign specific tasks to the various observers: some to assess the effectiveness of the behavior enacted; others to evaluate the enactment's reality; others to report on behaviors that helped or hindered the situation being enacted; others to suggest alternate ways of enacting the situation.

4. *Enact the stipulated situation.* Keep the role play short. Continue it only until a skill has been practiced, an idea expressed, a character developed,

or an impasse reached. Express your appreciation for the enactment to the role players.

5. *Discuss the completed role play.* Secure feedback from the observers. Refer to the stipulated focus repeatedly to prevent "drift." Allow the various sides of an issue to be fully explored and exposed. Recognize opposing views. Summarize key ideas on a flipchart.

The personal growth enactment. In this type of demonstration role play, any number of role players enact an interpersonal situation of some complexity. The role players are challenged to deal with a situation that has no single or best solution. In the course of their enactment, they exhibit or demonstrate their actual feelings, attitudes, and skill approaches. In effect, they play the role as they see it. The learning for the role players ensues from the opportunity for skill practice, self-critique, and the critique of the total group. The learning for the group is presumed to come from observing, analyzing, and giving feedback rather than from doing.

Note: The personal growth enactment is discussed as a demonstration-type role play because it is demonstrated before the total group. The other types described hereafter are accomplished on a more private basis.

Advantages and limitations. The advantages of the two demonstration-type enactments are several:

☐ Since the total group observes the same role play, and thus acquires the same data (at least in a general sense, for obviously perceptions will vary), they can analyze and critique it collectively.

☐ The group can bring multiple judgments or perceptions to bear on the role play.

☐ As a limited participation device—few do the role playing—it gets reluctant or anxious players off the hook. They observe and engage in critique rather than act out a given situation before their colleagues. (Of course, the program may call for every one in the group to "have their turn in the barrel." In fact, some participants may welcome it.)

On the other hand, the demonstration-type role play has certain serious disadvantages:

☐ Since the bulk of the group merely observes, most participants do not have the opportunity to engage in the actual development of appropriate skills, empathy, sensitivity, etc.

☐ In fact, some (or even many) may not be very active observers and may engage in a rather mild and passive critique.

☐ The role players may feel anxious or embarrassed because they are acting out the problem before the total group.

☐ The trainer can control the enactments to highlight certain principles, skills, or problem areas for the group. This may be done by explicit instructions to the role players or by structuring the situation so that certain desired behaviors are quite likely to ensue. Of course, while the control is quite certain to produce the desired results if the dramatic skit is used, if the personal growth enactment is employed the outcomes are less predictable or not predictable at all.

Reducing role player anxiety. To overcome feelings of anxiety about role playing before the full group you can

☐ Conduct such an activity late in the program, when people feel comfortable with one another and are more willing to take some risks.

☐ Utilize volunteers only.

☐ Provide a full orientation as to purposes; values; methods; how feedback will be given; if all participants will, in time, appear before the group in role-playing situations; etc. The fact that "we're all doing it" should reduce some of the anxiety.

☐ Start off with volunteers, if all are to play in time.

☐ Set a model for the group by playing in the first role play with a volunteer.

☐ Ensure that feedback to the role players is gentle, with heavy emphasis on positive reinforcement for the things done well in the role play(s).

☐ Use role plays judiciously, even sparingly.

☐ Select role play situations that have little or no threat potential. Or, putting it in the positive, select role plays which participants will readily recognize as having worthwhile learning benefits.

☐ Select role plays which are easy enough to produce a success experience, particularly in the first try.

☐ Select role players who are strongly extroverted rather than shy.

☐ Let the participants develop or present their own cases for enactment and the criteria for critique as well.

☐ Avoid role plays in vertically structured training (where the participant and his/her boss are being trained together). No one wants to risk looking silly in front of the boss!

☐ Explain to the participant group that here's a chance to get some worthwhile skill practice in a risk-free atmosphere and that it's far wiser to make a mistake or two here than in real life.

☐ Introduce structure into the role plays in the form of prerole-play planning sheets and post role-play self-critique sheets. (See "Using Structure.")

☐ If practicable, select, in advance, the role players who are to engage in the demonstration role play. Rehearse it once or twice so the acting is appropriate and natural.

Low- and high-threat role plays. Descriptions of several demonstration-type role plays follow. They are given in the order of their threat potential. (The first ones are low-threat; the latter ones are more threatening.)

Low-threat Situations

☐ A single participant, as a near graduate of a training program, gives a three minute talk before a group back home, describing what was learned, endeavoring to sell them on the desirability of their attending the program, or attempting to persuade management that the total organization should adopt such training (for example, time management, team building). *Note:* This is a low-threat role-playing assignment since (a) it is one-way communication

and thus is interaction-free; (b) depending on group size, either all of the group or at least a significant number of them would ordinarily make this presentation; (c) participants are presenting their own material to the group; and (d) the situation is not one involving work with feelings, attitudes, conflict, or sensitivity. Of course, not everyone is comfortable in giving a talk to a group, even a very short one; in fact, one or two participants may even decline the opportunity.

☐ Four to seven participants engage in a group role play, acting out situations such as a work group holding a staff meeting, a new committee or task force holding its opening session, or a problem-solving group having to deal with an obstreperous group member. The low-threat, obviously, results from being in a small group rather than in the usual one-on-one role play.

☐ A history professor, seated in his office, receives three visitors in succession: a student who lost his book and wants to borrow one in preparation for an exam; a fellow instructor who wishes to borrow a book; the university president who wishes help in the preparation of a talk before a community group. The group at large has the task of observing how status influences the communication process in the three situations. This is a low-threat situation: the enactments are typically very short, the role assignments are clear-cut and thus easy to execute, and the role players' performances are not subject to critique.

☐ Two role players present a situation of an interpersonal sort. The presentation, however, only entails reading an assigned script. There is no interaction between the participants. The role play sets the stage for analysis by the participant group.

Moderate-threat Situations

☐ An employee has violated a clear-cut disciplinary standard—disregard of a no-smoking rule, a parking violation, a failure to safeguard classified documents, etc. Cases of this type are relatively easy to handle because the rules are clear.

Thus, the threat in role playing a case of this sort is reduced considerably.

☐ In a role play concerned with listening, one role player is instructed to communicate nonverbally that he/she is not tuned in (by yawning, looking away, fidgeting). Or both role players may be instructed to utilize nonverbal behavior to demonstrate "active listening" (engaging in restatement, nodding one's head actively, maintaining eye contact, smiling). Since the assigned tasks are clear-cut, the threat potential is not too great.

High-threat Situations

☐ In a two-person role play, a young manager has the task of bringing about a change in attitude/behavior on the part of a 55-year old supervisor with 30 years of supervisory experience and a top-notch production record. It seems that the "old timer" harasses new hires, especially college graduates, as part of the breaking-in process. The young manager is concerned about possible turnover, community image, etc. This is a tough case to resolve. Why? Because the old timer is hard to reach—not motivated by threats of firing, or denial of advancement (the old timer isn't going anywhere anymore, no matter what). The protagonist may well anticipate resistance, too, from the long-tenured manager.

☐ A salesperson has the task of closing a sale with a tough, somewhat combative prospect.

☐ The role players are concerned with other tough human relations situations, such as counseling an employee who is depressed, alcoholic, highly suspicious, or in some way troubled; conducting an appraisal interview; counseling a male subordinate accused of sexual harassment; or informing the boss that a favorite program simply isn't working.

While there are ways to reduce the possible threat inherent in the demonstration-type role plays, to the extent possible you should utilize mass role playing—either multiple role playing or multiple group role playing—where the role players perform more privately in small groups such as triads or quartets. And, of course, in such a situation everyone gets to play and can learn from doing rather than from observing.

One way to make the personal growth enactment or interview less threatening, and thus more effective, is to use the Advisory Role Play (ARP) advocated by William Cooper, Queen's University, Ontario, Canada [9]. In the ARP the trainer capitalizes on the possible "sensitization" participants may have already developed after experience with a standard role play. The idea is to have fellow participants (possibly managers) give advice to the interviewer about how to conduct an inter view (possibly a performance appraisal). The procedures are these:

1. Everyone is given background information on the case to read.
2. Both parties to the interview read their role instructions.
3. The interviewee is sent out of the training room.
4. The group advises the interviewer how to conduct the interview. Typically, the initial advice is general, but soon gets into more helpful particulars.
5. The interviewee is called back into the training room, and the interview begins.
6. The interviewer then evaluates his/her own performance.
7. The interviewee evaluates the interview.
8. The group critiques the interview.

According to Dr. Cooper, the interview works well when the interviewer is able to apply at least some of the group's advice, thus giving the coaching/observer group a chance to assess the effect of their advice-giving. The ARP obviously has the merit of involving the non-role players to a greater degree than is the case with the more standard personal-growth role play.

A final note on reluctance to role play before others: The greatest reluctance to participate in a demonstration-type role play comes from those who may not have experienced it before, those who are not very verbal, and those who are shy. On the other hand, those who are highly motivated to improve their interpersonal skills, such as management trainees, graduate students majoring in counseling, and disadvantaged persons who are very much in need of a job, are quite likely to welcome it. In fact, in one training group the trainers gave the participants (cosmetic sales clerks) a choice of either role playing fairly privately in a triad (cosmetician, customer, and observer, with a chance to rotate in all three roles) or appearing before and receiving feedback from the total group [10]. The choice was given to ten different classes. The result: All classes chose to do the role plays "up front" rather than in the small groups. Because the cases and resulting role-plays were seen as real, that is, job related, and there was a desire to learn how to do the job well, they realized group feedback was superior to that of a single observer.

Multiple Role Playing

Multiple role playing entails formats that allow all participants to "play" simultaneously. The following are advantages of this type of design:

☐ It is a low-threat procedure since no one is asked to appear on center stage. Rather, the action takes place privately in small role-playing teams. Also, "since everyone is doing it, it can't be too bad."

☐ It embodies the principle of learning by doing, as opposed to merely observing. The opportunity to try out a particular behavior is essential for skill development and personal growth.

☐ Since a number of teams experience the role play, more ideas can be generated for comparative analysis as to how to tackle a given interpersonal situation.

Two forms of the multiple role play are the triad and the quartet.

The triad. The procedures for forming triads and using them in role playing follow:

1. Divide the participants into groups of three. You can have them count off with the "ones" being the salespersons or bosses, the "twos" the prospects or subordinates, and the "threes" the observers. Extra participants can be paired and work without an observer, or they can be added observers in other groups.

2. Give the observers their guide sheets, and give the role players their respective role assignment sheets. Copies may also be given to the observers for background purposes. Advise the role players to read only their own sheet and not to discuss it with anyone, since in a real-life interview they would only know their side of the issue. A major purpose of the interview, obviously, is to exchange views about the problem or difficulty as the first step in resolving it.

    Note: Every role play requires instructions, either oral or written, for the role players. Trainers should provide complete instructions to ensure full understanding of the assigned roles.

3. Give the role players their guide sheets, as explained in the section "Using Structure," to prepare for the interview properly. (The observers may also be given the guide sheets for general background purposes.) Allow 10–15 minutes for Steps 2 and 3.

4. Privately explain to the observers their observational role and its importance and answer any questions they may have. Also briefly explain the nature of the problem the role players will be tackling. Advise the observers to observe and take notes, but not to interfere in any way.

    Note: While the observers are being briefed, the role players are reading their role-play instruction sheets silently and privately.

5. Assign the role-playing teams to different corners of the room and/or other break-out rooms. This will enable the role plays to proceed without distracting noise from other role players. Instruct them to role play for about 20–30 minutes. This should allow enough time to reach an agreement of some sort.

    Note: Role plays will end at different times despite set maximum time limits. In fact, some of the role-playing teams may finish prematurely and some may not finish in the allotted time. (Keep the finished role players in their respective locations so that they do not disturb the others who may still be at work.) Of course, different data may emerge because of varying use of the available time. But that is to be expected. Actually, we should expect different data from the various role players due to a host of factors, namely, the time invested by them, energy invested, pre role-play preparation including development of a strategy for the role play, and personality factors and the resultant compatibility/incompatibility mix. In sum, we can only set the same time for all (a goal, in effect), but we can hardly expect that time to be used up equally by all or used in the same way.

6. While the role players are interacting, monitor each team briefly and unobtrusively to get a sense of how the role plays are trending.

7. Tell them when time is up.

8. Pass out post interview self-critique guide sheets to the role players. (Again, a copy may be given to the observers.) Allow about 10–15 minutes for the self-appraisal aspect of the role plays. Ask the trios to stay together since in the feedback session there will be a cross-checking of observer data with the role players and between role players as well.

9. Secure observer reports (see "Processing Role Play Data"), discuss results of the role play, and extrapolate general principles from the data.

To secure maximum benefits from this design, it is desirable to

☐ Conduct *three* role plays so that all members of the triad can perform in all three roles (for example, salesperson, customer, and observer; boss, subordinate, and observer). This rotational procedure will provide maximum insight into the problem involved since the problem will be experienced and thus viewed from more than one perspective.

☐ Start the first role play, if three cases are used, with an easy-to-resolve case. This will give the role players a success experience and confidence and encouragement for the next two role plays.

☐ Allow enough time for each role-play experience. Preparation time, the enactment, and the feedback phase should take about an hour, possibly a bit more. Don't give the processing time short shrift, for this is where the payoffs from the role plays will come. If at all possible, keep the schedule loose so that a lively discussion about the role plays doesn't have to be cut off. A possible minimum time schedule for a single role play is as follows:

Instructions by trainer	5 minutes
Preparation time by role players	10 minutes
Role play	20 minutes
Self-critique (Post role play)	5 minutes
Feedback/discussion phase	20 minutes
Total	60 minutes

In general, if three role plays are conducted, as recommended, allow about three to three and one half hours. (The extra 30 minutes will allow for longer feedback periods.)

☐ If the group is new to role playing and there is reason to believe that several or even more group members may be reluctant, it may be desirable to begin with a demonstration-type role play. The role-playing pair may comprise the trainer and another participant or two volunteers from the participant group.

The quartet. Sales trainer William H. Cover has developed a role playing procedure to improve the coaching skill of sales managers [11]. Teams of four are set up, with each participant rotationally taking the roles of salesperson, customer, coach, and observer. The coach leads the critique for the group using these steps:

1. Observe the role play, noting things done well and aspects needing priority improvement.

2. Ask "customer" for reactions to the interview, considering commitment to agreements reached, feelings, what helped and hindered progress, what could have been done differently, etc.

3. Ask sales representative for a self-critique—what helped, what hindered, what could have been done differently.

4. Check for similar data with observer.

5. Secure reaction of sales representative to the feedback, and check for understanding and agreement on added or alternative skills proposed by the others.

6. Summarize, pointing out both things that went well and possible desired improvements; check for group agreement.

To wrap things up, each team reports back to the total group the things that helped or hindered the coaching process, such as concentrating on only a few important points, enhancing the representative's self-esteem and confidence, involving the rep in problem solving, being specific about behaviors requiring improvement, and not playing "parent" with a lot of lecturing or quizzing.

The multiple role play can be used with small or very large participant groups. For example, I attended a session on "The Changing Roles of Men and Women in the '80's" at the 1980 conference of the American Society for Training and Development. The presenters had a large audience role play a manager interviewing a secretarial job applicant. Information sheets were provided for both role players. I played the role of the secretary (a form of role reversal indeed!) and acquired some extremely worthwhile insight into that particular role. An observer helped each team to process the action. A role-play-process questions sheet was also given to each team. It contained questions such as:

☐ What is there about the manager/secretary position that implies power or powerlessness?

☐ What factors seem to influence the amount of power an individual has within your organization?

☐ What are the implications for male or female training professionals?

A variation on the above multiple role playing designs is to use the "wrong way—right way" approach. Assume our training objective is to develop skill in dealing with a difficult customer, that is, one who is angry, unreasonable, possibly even aggressive/attacking. Consider using these procedures [12].

1. Assign participants to teams of two, one to assume the role of the harried customer service representative, the other to act as the "tough" customer. Let the trainees flip a coin as to who makes the choice of roles.

2. In the first role play, the customer service rep models the enactment as it should not be con-

ducted. (The rational participants may see some of their own behavior and thus recognize that it can irritate/alienate an already unhappy customer.)

3. In the second role play, the rep conducts the role play in the most helpful, positive way he/she can.

4. *Debriefing:* Ask the role players these questions: Did the second role play work better and, if so, why? What was the customer's response? What was your stress level during each of the role plays? Does the principle of "I'm not going to let anyone else determine my behavior" apply here? Ask for additional comments to close the activity.

Using Structure

Informal and spontaneous role plays are invaluable means to enrich the participant learning experience. But if we are planning a training program and have specific learning goals, we can't rely on the *ad hoc*, serendipitous event; we must instead depend upon planning and considerable structure. Structure, as used in role playing, may range from brief instruction sheets for the role players to complete scripts which are to be read before the group, with pre- and post role-play guide sheets for the participants and detailed check sheets for the observers.

Structure obviously directs or channels the learning experience so that participants are given the opportunity to assimilate what they are supposed to. Structure can also ensure that the role-play experience is a meaningful, easy-to-take learning activity rather than a source of frustration, anxiety, or embarrassment.

One of the main causes for role-play failure is that participants are rushed into the role play without being given a chance to internalize their roles and reflect on the possible course of action they will take in the role play. Thus, when the trainer says: "O.K., read your role play sheets for a couple of minutes and we'll begin our role plays," visualize the confusion and anxiety the participant is certain to experience.

To overcome this shortcoming, I advocate using a role-play-planning work sheet. Certainly, one of the learnings from the training experience should be that an effective interview, whether it be for selling, counseling, performance appraisal, employment, or termination, takes adequate planning time. A suggested "Guide Sheet to Plan for the Interview" is given in Appendix 18.

If the guide sheet is completed with adequate thought by the role players (allow 10–15 minutes for this), we can expect a role play that is

☐ Well-conceived rather than hastily contrived

☐ Calmly executed rather than anxiety-laden

☐ A pleasurable and natural experience, and thus more likely to be replicated on the job

The observer, too, needs a guide sheet in order to know precisely what to look for in the role play and thus to have specific data to provide feedback about it. The observer sheet may be general or specific. Samples of both types are given in Appendices 19, 20, and 21.

Using Observers

A highly participative role-playing design is to set up teams for three participants—two role players plus an observer. Rotating roles will ensure that all members of the triad will function in the observer role one time.

The observer is a vital adjunct to full learning from the role play. Since the observers are a "neutral," detached party, they are in a position to see and hear things that the engrossed role players may not, for example, whether and how rapport is established, whether a role player interrupts, and whether there is two-way communication. The presence of the observer will also help the role players to take their roles more seriously.

You should communicate to the observers that they have a very important function to perform lest they assume that observing is a secondary chore. I assemble all observers outside the training room, while the role players are studying and internalizing their roles, and explain to them their tasks and how important they are. At this time the observer sheets are reviewed to ensure full understanding of them. The observers are also told in specific terms what feedback they will be asked to report on to the total group.

Note that I said "to the total group." This public procedure, rather than private feedback to the role players, is recommended for these reasons:

1. A more formal report will ensure that the job is done more thoroughly, both in collecting data and in reporting back on it.

2. It establishes the norm that "We're here to learn and feedback is a vital way to do this."

3. Greater learning is made possible when one hears the reports of all the observers.

There is no reason why the observers should not be given the total set of materials—role playing instruction sheets, role players' guide sheets (pre-role and post-role play), etc. It will help to give them a better overview of the total case.

Although I indicated that the structured role plays included previously prepared guide sheets for the observers, it may be desirable, at times, to have the group develop its own criteria for the observers to use as they observe the role plays. This procedure should give the observational criteria greater understanding, credibility, and acceptance. You can, of course, add items that you feel the group overlooked.

Although I stated that all observers receive the same guide sheets, you may want to vary the observational role; for example, one set of observers may be instructed to observe specifically nonverbal communication, another set to observe how a decision was reached, another set to look for dependency needs and relationships. These special assignments would be in addition to their regular one.

Incidentally, if the total group does not break down neatly into triads, assign the extra person to another triad as a second observer. Or if there are two extras, they may role play the situation without an observer. In the latter instance, the trainer may assume the observer role.

In advance of the interview you should emphasize that the observer role is a critical one, for it is their feedback that will provide the basis for a significant portion of the participant learning from the interview. Obviously, few of us can see ourselves as well as a neutral observer. Point out, too, that the "Guide Sheet for the Observer" (Appendix 19) encourages a search for strong points in the interview so that at least some feedback can be supportive (positive reinforcement). Also, the guide sheet asks for behaviors in the interview that could be strengthened, not for those that are poor, ineffective, weak, or "lousy." The final item asks for a forecast of the relationships that will exist now that the interview is over. The rationale for this item is that an effective interview should result in improved relationships. In fact, everyone embarking on an interview should ask themselves: "What impact will my behavior have on the relationship?"

A guide sheet that helps the role players assess their own behavior in the interview is useful because

☐ Introspection is basic to meaningful learning. Behaviors or skills in need of strengthening, which are self-perceived, are easier to internalize than those which are pointed out by others.

☐ Since the role players are encouraged to engage in self-critique, they are more likely to be receptive to observer feedback. In other words, we wish to establish an atmosphere wherein critique becomes an understandable and welcome norm rather than an extraneous and threatening element that might produce defensiveness.

The "Guide Sheet for Self-Critique of the Interview" is given in Appendix 22.

A good use of observers to critique the action takes place in the State Department's training program, which readies its foreign service officers for overseas work. A mock consulate office is set up in "Land Z," a nation "a bit west of the continent of South America," discovered in 1508 by Zenry the navigator and famous for the Zramp Mountains and the cities of Zruch, Ziff, Zeel, Zorrest, and Zug. Much of the role playing involves handling troublesome issues, with the trainees impersonating people who pop in with demands for help from their government. The consulate officers in Z have to deal with haughty opera stars, the student arrested for drugs, a psychotic, etc. After every session students critique each other on why they approved or denied requests for aid. They learn pretty quickly from their role play work that there usually are no "right" or "wrong" answers, as will be the case on the job [13].

Group Role Playing

As mentioned before, a role play need not be limited to two participants. An example of a group role play follows:

A group of six managers is listening and responding to a proposal from the personnel officer for a dynamic

supervisory training program. The role players have been given different instruction sheets, including favorable, neutral, and negative positions. Two observers note and record the interaction, one being concerned with "task" roles (initiator, summarizer, etc.) and the other with "group maintenance" roles (morale, support, encouragement, etc.). After the observer reports are given, the total group discusses the interaction and its implications for group problem solving.

Multiple Group Role Playing

In this design the total participant group is broken down into role-playing groups or teams so everyone gets to play. The procedure can be followed with a small or large (several hundred participants) group.

Another advantage of MGRP is that, to the extent that all play, no one feels singled out or embarrassed. Also, it enriches the feedback process—data can be collected from a number of role-playing teams and critically compared.

In the case of the large group, feedback is elicited from the role-playing teams on a sample basis only.

An example of a role play enacted by several groups is one role played in the week-long "family awareness" workshops held by General Motors's Hydra-Matic Division. The objective of the role plays is to learn consensus decision making. Procedurally, eight hourly and salaried workers are randomly assigned headbands with various labels, such as "boss" or "expert." Their task is to plan a picnic. Typically, things go wrong. The meetings degenerate into a scrapping match. They are then asked to doff their headbands and try again for agreement. Success comes easier on the second try. People learn, in the words of one union official, "that if we all take off our headbands, we can work together to get the job done [14]."

For a now-classic book containing numerous multiple group role-playing situations and detailed instructions for the trainer to conduct such activities properly, see N. R. F. Maier, A. R. Solem, and A. A. Maier, *The Role Play Technique: A Handbook for Management and Leadership Practice,* University Associates, Inc., San Diego, 1975 [15]. This volume contains the well-known "New Truck Dilemma" wherein each group has to decide how to distribute a new truck among six members of a telephone repair crew. Since the various groups generally come up with different solutions based on the varying values of the groups, the learning is that the foreman is better off opting for a decision made by the group and with which it is satisfied. The alternative is for the fore man to impose his values on the group, with the very likely risk of producing dissatisfaction with the decision.

Total Group Role Playing

It is also possible to design and conduct a role play that involves the total group simultaneously. As an example, let's take a situation involving conflict management. The activity may be planned in advance, or it may be used as a "live experience" when the group is divided on an issue. Here are the procedures:

1. Select a topic which divides the group. This may be an in-house issue or an external one, such as gun control, legalizing marijuana, or outlawing abortion.

2. Divide the total group (14–20) into two smaller groups (7–10), each of which takes a pro or con position on the issue in question. (Try to form groups of equal size.)

3. Send one small group to another room for their discussion; the other group remains in the training room. By physically separating the two groups, we are polarizing them further. We are establishing a strong "we vs. them" and a "win-lose" outlook.

4. Give both groups the following instructions. (This may be in writing if this is a planned rather than an extemporaneous activity.)

   a. Develop as strong a case as you can for your position.

   b. What arguments do you believe the other group will use? List them. (Allow 30 minutes for Steps a and b.)

   c. Select a representative or spokesperson who will best present your group's position to the other group.

5. After the 30 minutes is up, give both groups a short attitude questionnaire to measure their strength or intensity of feeling about the issue. Keep the forms for the two groups separate.

6. Seat both representatives at opposite ends of a *long* table. (Two or three tables may be used for

length.) This will further emphasize the strong cleavage between the two groups.

Note: You may wish to label the groups "Pro" and "Con" or simply "A" and "B."

7. For five minutes, let both representatives take turns presenting their group's position to the other group.

8. Let a cross-dialogue ensue between the two representatives for about five minutes.

9. As a form of role reversal, select a member of Group A to join Group B to help the Group B representative strengthen their case.

10. Continuing the role reversal procedure, select a member from Group B to help the Group A representative.

11. About five minutes later, send two members of Group A to help Group B and two members of Group B to help Group A. Continue the discussion for another five to seven minutes.

12. Repeat Step 11 at about five minute intervals, until there has been a complete turnover in both groups' memberships.

13. As a final switch, have the two leaders change places. We now have the A group arguing for B's position and vice versa. Continue this discussion for seven to ten minutes.

14. Administer the attitude questionnaire again to both groups, keeping their forms separate. Tally results to check whether the role reversal procedure tended to reduce the intensity with which attitudes were held.

15. Hold a general discussion about attitude rigidity and its implications for intergroup conflict. Point up the need to shift groups from "we vs. them" and "win-lose" positions to a more open dialogue and "win-win" possibilities. This role-play procedure is one way to start the dialogue.

Note: In both MGRP and TGRP everyone is involved. However, in MGRP the action takes place in small groups or teams. This procedure permits comparative analysis of data generated by the teams. Conversely, in TGRP the learning comes essentially from what is experienced without the opportunity—or possibly the need—to learn from such comparative analysis.

For example, see the role play "Trial for Error" described in Chapter 3.

Write Your Own Role Play

Participants in role-play situations often feel a lack of realism in their assigned roles. Why? Because they have to work with (enact) a contrived scenario based entirely on trainer-supplied information. One way to give "canned" role plays a real-world flavor is to allow role players to modify the role play. They do this by supplementing the trainer-furnished information with their own. They thus may be given questions which ask for details relevant to their own work situations; the trainer then adapts the conduct of the role play accordingly.

For example, assume the participants have to make a persuasive presentation. They could be asked to enact it as if they were making it to a particular official in their organization whom they know. They would be asked to take into account prior contacts with that manager, his/her personality, major organizational issues, and preferences for how the material is to be presented to the decision maker. For greater authenticity, also encourage participants to brief the other role players on how to personalize the enactment before conducting it.

If you decide to take this modified real-world approach to role playing, you may have to contact your participants in advance (a pre-work assignment) to develop requisite information pertaining to the forthcoming enactment in class [16].

PROCESSING ROLE PLAY DATA

Participants learn from a role play they have enacted in one of the following ways, or in some combination of them:

- ☐ By reflecting upon and talking about one's assigned role, one may develop insight into the concerns, problems, and outlooks of the role portrayed.

- ☐ By practicing new interpersonal behavior (for example, being more assertive, exhibiting more concern for the customer or subordinates, listening actively), one may acquire new, worthwhile behavioral skills.

- ☐ By receiving feedback from the observers after the role enactment, one may be helped still further to improve one's skill or behavior.

- ☐ By observing others, one may improve one's skill or acquire self-insight.

- ☐ By discussing in depth all that we have seen and done, we can round out and button down our pertinent learnings.

In short, in role playing one learns by doing, by introspecting, by observing, by giving feedback, by receiving feedback, and by engaging in an overall analysis of the total activity. And since changing attitudes and behavior are not easy things to accomplish for most of us, being involved in all of these operations is the way we are most likely to really learn.

So for more complete learning, to ensure that it actually "glues in" and will be carried over to the real-life situation, the trainer must give ample time to processing the data generated by the role plays. Processing means giving and receiving feedback about the behavior exhibited in the role plays and critiquing (discussing, extrapolating general principles) the enactments.

Trainer-consultants John E. Jones and J. William Pfeiffer of University Associates distinguish between "processing" and "generalizing" as follows [17]: Processing is "sharing one's reactions . . . The dynamics that emerged in the activity are explored, discussed, and evaluated (processed) with other participants." Generalizing, the next logical step, "is the need to develop principles or extract generalizations from the experience. Stating learnings in this way can help participants further define, clarify, and elaborate them."

Feedback, as a device to help us see ourselves as others do, can be given to the role players in several ways:

- ☐ If the enactment takes place publicly before the total group, the feedback is necessarily given to the role players on a public basis by the group and the trainer.

- ☐ It can be given quite privately after the role play by the observers and/or the coaches in three- or four-person role-playing teams. In a team of four, there are the two role players, an observer, and a coach who coordinates the feedback and analysis of the role play.

□ It can be given publicly by the observers after the role-playing teams have privately completed their enactments. In this circumstance you control the feedback with these objectives in mind:

1. To ensure that feedback by the observers is balanced rather than one-sided; minimal or moderate rather than overwhelming (the instruction to the observers might be to report on two things they liked in the interview and one thing that could have been improved upon); easy rather than hard-to-take (internalize); cross-checked with participants for reality testing.

2. To extrapolate from the feedback general principles applicable to all of the group.

Two procedures, the T-column and the spread sheet, may be used to give public feedback after private role playing. These procedures may be used singly or in combination.

The T-Column

This device can be used in various ways to elicit from the observers, subject to a cross-check with the participants, data about the role play. For example, if the behavior of both parties to the role play is to be critiqued, a double T-column may be used. See Figure 5-1.

Team	Pat		Kim	
	Did well.	Could be strengthened	Did well	Could be strengthened
1.	Used active listening	Lacked specifics re nature of problem	Tried to define problem	Tendency to sit back
2.	Opened in a friendly manner	Never got to closing the sale		

Figure 5-1. Example of a double T-column.

If only one role play is to be subject to critique, a single T-column will suffice.

The Spread Sheet

In various role plays, both parties are often in a conflict situation. Hence their meeting or interview is intended to bring about some reconciliation, some plan of action to reduce their interpersonal differences.

Typically, then, we wish for data from the various observers to tell the group at large the following things: What was the strategy of the protagonist (the one who initiated the action, such as a supervisor or a salesperson)? Was the strategy followed (good intentions often go awry)? Was the strategy successful? If so, what was the motivator that reached the other party? What agreement, if any, was reached? Will their future relations be stronger, weaker, or unchanged?

A sample spread sheet covering these points, designed to secure on a flipchart data from all teams' role-playing activity, is given in Figure 5-2.

In respect to the timing of feedback, it's a good idea to let the role players engage in self-critique before the group prior to their receiving feedback from the observers. This will help to defuse possible defensiveness from observer feedback since the idea of critique—from self and others—is introduced on a gradual basis.

VIDEO PLAYBACK AND FEEDBACK

Participant learning from a role play experience ordinarily depends upon one's recollection and impression of what one did in the role play, as well as upon feed sack from the observer, the other role player, and possibly the trainer. These multiple sources, although certainly helpful, have limitations: recollection is obviously dependent on memory, one's impressions may be marked by self-deception, the observer may not have captured pertinent behaviors or may be reluctant to state them, and the other role player may be limited by individual biases.

Videotaping can overcome the problems cited above. It can accurately capture what was said and done and present it for analysis by the role players, the observing participants, and the trainer. Videotape, then, makes possible the rendering of multiple-source feedback based on objective data the total group can observe and critique simultaneously.

Videotaping role plays has another advantage—it can capture the highly significant nonverbal behavior that ensues between two parties in an interview. We have reference to facial expressions of all sorts; hand gestures; body positions; the distance between the role players; touch, if any; eye contact; movement; etc. By studying nonverbal behavior (their own and that of others), participants can be made aware of the

Team No.	Planned strategy of boss	Was it followed?	If strategy was used, was it effective?	What "motivator" was used?	Nature of Agreement Reached	Future Relations (+, −, 0)
1	Persuasion	Became hard sell	No, produced resistance	Pressure	None	− (weaker)
2	Mutual problem solving	Yes	Yes	Chance for larger travel budget	Expanded Program	+ (stronger)
3	etc.					

Figure 5-2. Example of a spread sheet.

nonverbal behavior they exhibit and its importance on others. They can also learn to assess how effective they are in transmitting and receiving nonverbal cues [18].

Several examples of the use of videotape with role plays in vastly different settings follow.

Counseling the Disadvantaged

In a program designed to teach disadvantaged youths and adults how to find a job, these videotape procedures (along with other training techniques) are used:

☐ *Stimulus:* A five-minute videotaped vignette presents a problem; for example, a job applicant flounders in an employment interview.

☐ *Evocation:* A small group (15 or less) analyzes the problem presented.

☐ *Objective:* inquiry: The trainer introduces the group to new information, concepts, and behavioral models; for example, how employment agencies work or where to find training programs.

☐ *Application:* Each member of the group tries out the new learning, for example, how to be effective in a job interview. A videotape is made of the interview, which is then subject to group critique.

The ten-week Employability Skills Series was developed by the Research and Development Center for Life Skills and Human Resource Development, Teachers College, Columbia University, and is used nationwide [19].

Teaching Counseling Skills

Dr. Diana Teta, a clinical psychologist at the Capital District Psychiatric Center, Albany, New York, uses videotape and role playing to teach counseling. She uses video 90% of the time in her counseling classes, for it enables the student to go beyond textbook knowledge and theory. Some of her skill pointers in working with video are these:

☐ Many criticisms don't even require mention; for example, video clearly shows excesses in hand movement or head nodding or deficits such as lack of eye contact with the client.

☐ The students who operate the camera are instructed to zero in on significant nonverbal behavior, thereby stressing the importance of body language; for example, the counselor can give support through body posture as well as verbally, hand movement should be congruent with verbal messages, leaning forward or looking attentive can show an understanding.

☐ Verbal interventions can be reinforced or critiqued; for example, reflecting back (restating) feelings or clarifying a client's statement. Dr. Teta believes that the correct intervention at the right time enhances client progress.

☐ The before-and-after method is used by Dr. Teta in teaching assertiveness training by videotape. The class comes up with a problem, such as a dissatisfied customer who seeks redress from a service manager at a department store. A video enactment then takes place subject to critique by Dr. Teta and the class. The aim is to try to "shape in" a better performance for the role player. The same role players then act out the problem again, and the two tapes are compared. Says Dr. Teta: "There's really a big difference between the two videotapes, and since the improvements are so apparent, the play back is intrinsically rewarding" [20].

Communication Skills for Judges

Many judges communicate poorly. They may mumble, murder grammar, talk in a monotone, cover their mouths while talking, ramble on in legal jargon, and maintain poor eye contact. Dr. Jack Barwind, head of Syracuse University's speech department, was therefore hired by New York state to train 600 judges in a mock courtroom where they could be taped, say, imposing a sentence, and then critiqued.

The need for better communication skills by judges arises from the fact that they are "on stage." They are communicating nonverbally as well as verbally. The way a judge addresses a defendant may influence whether the latter complies with probation or a conditional discharge. Also, judges, once they assume a power position, tend to accept less responsibility for their message getting through. All in all, the judges readily provide much grist for the videotape mill [21].

Developing Skills in Conflict Resolution

Jerome Barrett, formerly Associate Director, Office of Mediation Services, Federal Mediation and Conciliation Service, Washington, D.C., teaches specialized skills essential to settling disputes. He uses short and long role-play scenarios that simulate conflict resolution situations. The short ones are for warm-up purposes. The longer ones require study and consultation with team members. The trainees, in a group of six to ten participants, play a lead role in a short scenario and participate in the long one. All sessions are videotaped for playback and feedback by the trainer. Barrett's suggestions for best results are as follows:

☐ Advise trainees that the tapes will be erased and reused; this reduces a lot of unnecessary anxiety.

☐ The critique made of the trainees playing the lead roles includes trainer comments and group discussion.

☐ Very sensitive feedback, such as on personal mannerisms, is given privately.

☐ Tapes may be reviewed alone during the breaks.

☐ Feedback should cover all the skills treated in prior sessions. The aim is to encourage reflection on one's skill inventory and to develop action plans for further skill development [22].

Question-Asking Role Playing for Sales Managers

At a brokerage firm, sales managers are taught how to question salespersons after a sales call so as to secure valid, informative answers for managerial decision making. The procedures involve the use of a videotaped sales call. The manager watches the tape and is asked to assume he/she is accompanying the salesperson. As the tape is watched, the manager should be thinking about the questions to be presented when they're both "back in the car." The questions are then posed live to the same salesperson who appeared in the tape.

Three managers are selected for the questioning process. They do their role plays one at a time; the second and third role players do not get to observe the ones who precede them. Having three role players assures two things: a presentation of different ways of conducting the questioning and an assurance that at least one of the role plays will work.

The training is designed to learn how to ask open-end rather than directive, manipulative or answer-laden questions; to listen; to focus on the concerns and feelings of subordinates; to deal with salespersons who may exhibit frustration and rancor; to avoid backing off from a problem; to respond to body language (for example, signs of frustration, boredom, or astonishment).

In general, the technique is designed to help the managers to see themselves as they interact with sales personnel and to learn new ways of managing and working with subordinates [23].

Sales Training

In a well-thought-out training program for salespersons of the American Porcelain Corporation, sales people learn both people skills and product information. The course's procedures are these [24]:

1. The selling skills required for an effective sales call are shown on videotape.

2. The salesperson prepares for a series of sales calls, each dealing with a specific selling problem.

3. A group discussion is held about the calls.

4. Three salespersons are selected to show their selling skills in a simulated customer's office. While the sales calls are taped, the other sales

personnel work on other selling situations. The role plays on the various skill areas are done in separate rooms. To ensure that no one is influenced by the others' actions, one salesperson role plays the problem, and the other two wait their turn outside the "customer's" office.

5. The full group reassembles to critique all video-taped role plays. Typically, they learn about personality effects, the impact of suggestions and persuasion, the value of structuring ideas for clarity, the role of nonverbal communication, the gap between self-perception (deception?) and what is shown on the monitor about one's performance.

The playback reveals weaknesses in both selling skills and product knowledge. From this may develop new ideas to improve the next role plays. The role plays, as might be expected, increase in difficulty. This tends to encourage a pooling of techniques and approaches.

The distinguishing feature of this course, compared to others that use videotape, is that each role play is preceded by a taped presentation illustrating different selling techniques and also updating product knowledge.

The participants receive a broad perspective of their selling roles by being first observer, then role player, and then self-appraiser.

It is apparent from the previous discussion that a vital key to learning from videotaped role playing is the quality of the feedback the role players receive after the enactment. Recognizing that feedback may often be either hard-hitting (punitive and threatening) criticism or vacuous statements of support, rather than the hoped for helpful critiques, two trainers report on their model for feedback that overcomes such shortcomings. Briefly, their procedures are these [25]:

1. In a supervisor-employee role play before the total group, feedback is given only to the "boss." Why? To prevent those who volunteered for the subordinate role from feeling that their material will be subject to analysis by the group. In other words, the "employee" serves only in a data-generating or facilitating capacity, so that the supervisor can receive the feedback about his/her performance.

2. Feedback must be phrased only in terms of what was observed. Thus, participant-observer statements assume these forms: "I saw . . . ," or "I heard . . . ," or "I felt that . . . ." The objective is to reduce defensiveness. If one is busy defending oneself, the feedback will most likely proceed unheard.

3. Feedback is received silently. The role player thus can accept or reject whatever is presented without having to justify or defend such a posture.

4. The cameraperson also provides comments about the role play.

5. The trainer is the last to give feedback. The objective is to tie up loose ends, bring up unexplored issues, etc. Feedback, again, is based on observable behavior.

6. The videotape is then reviewed, the principal role player critiquing his/her own role play. The tape can be stopped for analysis only by the trainer and the principal role player, although others may make comments or ask questions once the tape is stopped.

7. In the feedback process, it is the trainer's job to allow all who wish to be heard to comment and at the same time to prevent the role player from being overwhelmed by data overload.

Another issue of concern in video-based role playing is how to process "image shock" for participants new to the process. Dorothy Bolton [26], Ridge Consultants, Rochester, New York, has pointed out that viewing oneself on video can be a painful experience because of the gap between a long-standing self-perception and what is seen on the screen. The specific elements of concern are body image, voice image, and personal/social image. One way to deal empathically with the concerns is for the trainer to relate to the group his/her personal experience (reactions) when viewing a videotape of self for the first time.

Note: Dorothy Bolton advises how to intervene in an ongoing role play without disrupting the training:

☐ Don't let a poorly performed role play continue; stop it immediately and correct it.

☐ Set key phrases such as "reflect" ahead of time in the minds of the role players.

☐ Whisper the word "reflect" as the role play progresses to keep the role players on track.

How to Write a Role Play

While published role plays may ordinarily be quite satisfactory, at times you may need to develop your own role plays for a particular subject. To do so, decide on the problem to be presented, write the role play, and then field test it.

Deciding on the Problem

The best way to select a problem for the role play is to draw on your own experience or that of others:

☐ If you wish to develop a role play for sales personnel dealing with overcoming customer objections, you might jot down typical objections you know about such as price, color, certain convenience features not available, delivery date, and warranty.

☐ If you wish to develop a role play on discipline for supervisory training, you might consider topics such as tardiness, absenteeism, insubordination, safety rule violation, drinking on the job, gambling on premises, and failure to secure classified documents.

☐ If your concern is with delegation problems, you might brainstorm alone or with others problems such as the subordinate who won't take on added responsibility, the boss who doesn't really "let go," or the boss who abdicates rather than delegates.

Once you have your problems identified, all you need do is select those that seem most relevant, practical, and credible. If time will allow and several problems will be used, try to develop role plays that vary in difficulty and complexity. In this way the group can begin with an easy situation and move up to more involved ones.

Writing the Role Play

In our second stage we take the topic and make it come alive using the following steps:

1. Look for a point of conflict or difference, an area where both parties view the problem or situation from a different perspective, such as:

   ☐ The employee who feels she was unfairly denied a promotion.

   ☐ The colleague who won't cooperate with his peers.

   ☐ The employee who sees little point in observing certain safety rules.

   ☐ The executive who "nitpicks to death" everyone's letters.

   ☐ The young supervisor who is hurting his career by antagonizing others.

2. Decide on the characters to be involved in the role play. If they are a customer prospect and a salesperson, or a manager and a subordinate, give the characters a set of characteristics that clearly define them: age, sex, status, reputation, personality, job title and responsibilities, strengths, weaknesses, family ties, job history, seniority. These characteristics, along with the view of the problem, give the role player the basis for the enactment of the role.

3. Give the characters names. We suggest using sexually neutral names to avoid the problem of a female participant trying to assume the role of the supervisor John Hanks. Some common across-gender names are given in Table 5-1. You could also use nicknames, initials, or last names. Sometimes "fun" names like R. U. Eager, O. Gurr, Kerr Les or T. D. Umm may be used.

4. Use these guidelines in writing the role play:

   ☐ Keep it short—the role players have only a limited time to read and think about their roles.

   ☐ Keep it readable—use short sentences, simple words, very short paragraphs, and job-related vocabulary.

   ☐ Keep it credible and realistic.

   ☐ Keep it adequately flexible. While each character has to be defined to give the exercise clarity, strength (or weakness), credibility, identifiability, etc., it should not be so overdrawn that the role player has no discretion whatsoever to depart from the prescribed

Table 5-1
Examples of Sexually Neutral Names

Sexually Neutral Names	Derived from the Name of	
	Male	Female
Jerry	Gerald	Geraldine
Bobby	Robert	Roberta
Les	Lester	Leslie
Robin	Robin	Robin
Sal	Sal	Sally
Sam	Samuel	Samantha
Joyce	Joyce	Joyce
Sandy	Sander	Sandra
Win	Winston	Winifred
Kim	Kim	Kimberly
Lee	Leland	Leona
Fran	Francis	Frances
Ross	Ross	Ross
Val	Val	Valerie
Shirley	Shirley	Shirley
Kyle	Kyle	Kyle
Gene	Eugene	Jean
Marion	Marion	Marian
Carol	Carrol	Carol
Pat	Patrick	Patricia
Charlie	Charles	Charlotte
Terry	Terrance	Theresa
Chris	Christopher	Christine
Alex	Alexander	Alexandra
Sherry	Sheridan	Sharon
Vern	Vernon	Verna

role. In other words, the best role play occurs when the role player recognizes weaknesses in the assigned role prescription and, given a chance or reason to change, will do so.

☐ Keep it general enough to avoid possible nit-picking. Avoid inclusion of data in the role prescriptions which may be attacked as out of date, inapplicable, or rarely occurring.

5. Complete your write-up by giving the case a title that will excite interest in it, such as

☐ The Case of the "Retired" Supervisor
☐ Role Play: Allen and Gibbs in Conflict
☐ The Reluctant Prospect
☐ The Case of the Over-supervised Employee
☐ Chris Confronts the Boss—A Role Play
☐ Application Session: Morale and Motivation at the Maintenance Shop

Field Testing the Role Play

If possible, try out the role play in a "mini" situation, rather than a full-blown one. As a minimum, check it out with colleagues, line officials, one's boss, or subordinates for readability and realism.

Revise the role play, as indicated, after the session is over. Participant feedback should indicate possible ambiguities, inaccuracies, omissions, etc.

SPECIAL TECHNIQUES

While role players can acquire considerable skill, self-insight, and sensitivity to others in the usual two-person role enactments, greater impact can be felt by experiencing a number of special role-playing techniques.

Note: Most of these techniques depend upon a high degree of trainer intervention. They would thus be more applicable to single rather than multiple role playing. Also, they would be used in more in-depth, spontaneous, and highly experiential training programs.

Role Reversal

This is the device most commonly used as an adjunct to the conventional role play. By taking the role of the other person, one can now see the world from that person's perspective, though in real life we are too preoccupied with self (our own problems, needs, anxieties) to do so. Through the magic of role reversal, we can look through a new set of lenses and learn of the other's values, attitudes, concerns, and needs. Some examples are:

Police officer ⟶ Citizen
Sales rep ⟶ Prospect or customer
Teacher ⟶ Student
Nurse ⟶ Patient
Boss ⟶ Employee

The role reversal can be accomplished by:

☐ *The training design.* For example. working in teams of three, each person can rotationally experience the roles of supervisor, subordinate, and observer. Three role plays are necessary, of course, to accomplish this.

☐ *The situation.* For example, a role play before the group may result in a block or conflict between the two role players. No one is willing to give. The trainer may intervene as follows: "Jan, why don't we switch roles here. You take Ann's role as the employee. Pick up your line where your boss, Jan, says . . ."

The trainer may ask both participants to switch roles more than once in an attempt to give greater insight into the other's feelings and world view and thus loosen up the players' rigidities.

Empty Chair Technique

In this role-playing procedure, one talks to the (imaginary) person in the other chair. One says everything to the other person that one would like to if that person were really there. The emotionality can be heightened and insight augmented by switching chairs (roles) and attempting to say the things the other would be very likely to say. The chair switches should be repeated as many times as may be necessary to complete a meaningful dialogue between the two parties in question. Some examples of where this technique might be used are a husband and wife in a dual-career conflict; an employee asking the boss for a raise; a mixed performance appraisal by the boss; or a lost sale.

A variation of this technique is to have another participant sit in the empty chair to help explore and develop the role relationships more fully.

The Soliloquy

In this technique the role player talks alone before the audience. Some uses are

☐ To define and explain one's role before the total group as an introduction to the actual enactment. For example: "I'm Pat. I've been around 30 years. I'm a good producer and I know the ropes. No one shoves me around because I'm pretty good at shoving right back. Now, lately . . ."

☐ To heighten one's awareness of who one really is and how one sees the world—others, the situation, a given problem, one's concerns, needs. The trainer may intervene and ask a role player to describe his/her feelings, perceptions, etc. at this point in the role play. By talking aloud about these circumstances, one can develop greater insight into what one really feels and

believes. It may also serve to elicit feedback from others about that view of self and the world.

The Double

While the enactment is taking place, the trainer may assign a participant to verbalize one of the role player's unstated feelings and thoughts. Physically, the double (also known as the "auxiliary ego") sits behind the role player and, as "the inner voice" or conscience, expresses feelings whenever it seems the role player is unable or unwilling to do so.

One way to introduce this technique to the group is for the trainer to model the double before asking anyone else to do it. The modeling not only shows how it's done but, in addition, "legitimizes" it. Of course, the trainer may assume the role of the double at any stage of the role play at which a role player's blocked feelings or thoughts need to come out.

The doubling process, it should be noted, is a form of soliloquizing, for in it one is expressing feeling out loud. The double, of course, is expressing a role player's feelings rather than his/her own.

Mirror Technique

At times a group member may have a block or impasse that prevents him/her from achieving the necessary involvement to share a meaningful element in his/her experience. In this circumstance, the trainer may ask another participant to assume the reticent role player's entire role. This is done by "mirroring" the feelings that the participant is having difficulty expressing. In effect, the other participant is saying: "This is the way I feel you coming across. This is what I see." The trainer encourages the inhibited person to correct or amplify upon the mirrored statements. With successful mirroring, the reticent role player may be able to return to the role and continue the role play.

Some typical mirroring dialogue:

Mirror: attempting to express the other's feelings strongly) I *resent* the way she conducts our staff meetings. It *really* upsets me.
Role player: (playing the statement down) I guess it does make me a bit irritated. But not always.
Mirror: (still with feeling) It *really* ticks me off, makes me feel *very, very* angry.

Role player: (hitchhiking on the mirroring) Yes, angry.

Mirror: (developing the problem further) It makes me so angry I tune out the *whole* thing.

Role player: (agreeing) I just retreat. It's too much.

Mirror: So I don't contribute. I clam up.

Role player: (now more fully in the role) Sometimes the boss asks if I have anything to offer. I just sit there and shake my head.

Mirror: (developing the role further) I wish I had the guts to tell the boss what I really think.

Role player: Yes, I would really like to speak up. I really would. In fact, I came close two meetings ago . . ."

Multiple Role Taking

Two or more persons can perform a given role; two supervisors and three subordinates may each enact a given two-person role play. The objective is to explore more facets of the role relationships. The generation of more data helps to produce a richer post-enactment critique and thus greater insight into the roles for the role player.

An example of how the multiple role-playing process takes place may be illustrated by the following diagram.

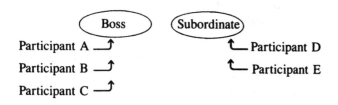

The trainer may also assign a given role to a number of participants, each of whom makes a short statement about how he/she sees an aspect of the role or role relationship. For example, in a session concerned with male-female relationships, several women may quickly move through one of the roles to express their feelings about a particular attitude or relationship.

Behind-the-Back Technique

With an inhibited group, the trainer may ask the role player to turn his back to the group while they discuss his performance in the role play. This procedure makes it easier for the group to discuss the role play since they have to neither look directly at the "absent" role player nor interact with him. Similarly, the one receiving the feedback can listen more objectively since he is not in a face-to-face situation with the group.

After receiving the feedback, the role player may turn his chair around, in effect rejoining the group, and give his own feelings about the role play and comments on the group's feedback.

EVALUATING RESULTS

Role playing is a dynamic means of developing skill and changing attitudes and behavior. Role playing works because it gives participants "real life" skill practice, it provides a rare opportunity to experience the roles others assume but which one ordinarily does not in real life, and it affords opportunities to critique one's performance and to receive feedback from others as to how one did.

Some examples of payoffs from role playing follow:

☐ One study analyzed short- and long-term effects of six methods used to get English workers to use safety gear: a poster campaign, films, fear techniques, discussion groups, role playing, and discipline. Most of these approaches produced an immediate effect, but only role playing resulted in a long-term increase in the use of helmets, shoes, glasses, and gloves. The training procedure involved was to have employees play the roles of managerial personnel, safety officials, and people who failed to get compensation due to their own negligence. Assuming these new roles produced these impressive results: In the experimental group, the wearing of hard hats went up from 27% to 68% immediately and only dropped to 62% four months later. Those not wearing hard hats dropped from 32% to 5% in the long run [27].

☐ In a two-day sales training course using role plays and videotape, the American Poclain Corp., Fredericksburg, Virginia, produced very satisfactory results. One distributor who attended the course marveled at how hard the sales personnel worked at improving their techniques. He thus decided to send his 30 sales-people to the course, even though their product line was broader than that of Poclain. One of his salesmen reported after the training: "Thanks to the new insights I got concerning the customer/salesman relationship, I feel I now have better tools to solve these problems I have been avoiding in the past."

A Poclain salesman stated: "I sold two $200,000 machines only one week after I attended the course. During the final negotiations with the customer, I had to handle the same objections I had been faced with in the video role play. Since I had a better insight into the customer's problems, I was able to handle the situation easily and made a sale I did not really expect to make [28]."

☐ New York City police officers learned how to negotiate with a hostage taker. "Through simulations and role playing, police officers were taught to depersonalize situations, to withdraw their own egos, to make it possible for concessions to be made to a hostage taker without a cop fearing a loss of his own status. Officers were instructed in the interpretation—and communication—of body language nuances, as well as verbal strategies that might reinforce or stabilize a gunman's mood" [29].

ROLE PLAYING: SOME QUESTIONS AND ANSWERS

☐ *What is the best response to the participant's question "How do I play this role?"* As a trainer I usually say: "I guess you have three choices: One, you can play the role literally per the instruction sheet; two, you can be yourself and just do what comes naturally, so if you're a nice guy, be a nice guy; if you're an s.o.b., be that; or three, you can strive for the execution of an 'ideal' set of behaviors."

☐ While offering choices may confuse or overwhelm some participants, it's still a better procedure than telling people how to behave.

The simplest procedure, of course, is to say: "Just be yourself; act it out as you see it."

☐ *Is it desirable to use the term "role playing" if participants might react negatively to it?* If you have concerns about the language, exercise caution. Talk about an "application session," "skill practice," "skill building session," "tryout phase of our work," "practical work," "problem solving session," "we'll act out some situations," etc.

☐ *What is the best physical set-up for role playing?* Any size room will do if the enactments take place on a one-at-a-time basis. If multiple role playing is used and everyone plays, a good-sized room is essential so that the role plays can take place with out too much competitive noise. Some buzzing from the other role-playing teams is helpful—it literally sets the tone for the work, communicating that "we're all involved in this." Adjacent breakout rooms may be used, too, of course. If plants, partitions, or a large blackboard are available, use them for added privacy.

☐ *What are the relative merits of written vs. oral instructions to the role players?* Written instructions about roles eliminate fuzziness and aid absorption (people do receive at different rates). They are particularly helpful if the roles have some element of complexity to them. They also avoid arguments with the trainer about your poor communicating ability: "I thought you told us that . . ." On the other hand, a short role instruction may be given orally. Its merit lies in its spontaneity. Example: "Georgie, you be the secretary. Alice, you be the salesperson. You've tried to see Mr. Frank, Georgie's boss, three times. This time you're determined to see him and not let Georgie sweet talk you out of it."

☐ *To what extent are role players permitted to add their own facts to the situation?* No set of instructions is intended to button down every detail for the role players. A certain amount of improvisation is almost inevitable. The role players can then introduce added facts, just so they're in sync with the basic thrust of the role.

☐ *How many role-playing enactments should be used in a single multiple role-playing session?* It all depends on course objectives, available time, etc. The trainer can assume that the first one is an opener and that at least two or three added situations of greater complexity are essential for adequate skill practice.

☐ *What is the best use of volunteers in role playing?* In enactments before the total group, volunteers can help break the ice and set a norm that role playing is worth doing and not too scary. Of course, by using multiple role playing, where everyone plays, volunteers are unnecessary.

☐ *Should the trainer intervene in a role play that is proceeding poorly?* If the role plays are being conducted privately (in pairs, trios, quartets), the answer is no. The odds are that the trainer does not have enough data about what took place to correct things. The observers and/or the role players will probably report back to the total group on their less-than-successful experience. If such a role play is subject to group analysis and discussion, learning from it should take place. On the other hand, if a role play *before the total group* is developing poorly, it should be stopped and corrected at once. Obviously, no learning for anyone—the role player or observer—will accrue if appropriate skill elements are not being applied.

☐ *Is it desirable to have the role players engage in public self-critique before the observers give their feedback?* Very much so. This approach encourages introspection—a basic tool for learning in role playing—and also defuses a possible negative reaction (defensiveness) to observer feedback. Self-critique is a good way to help the role players save face, should that be necessary.

☐ *What is the best type of feedback for the role player?* Keep it low-key and supportive, and stress the positive reinforcement approach. Negatives may be introduced, but in a gentle way—not "This was lousy," but "The interview could have been strengthened by . . ." Also, don't clobber anyone with a ton of negative feedback.

☐ *What is the best source of critique for the role players?* There is no single best source; rather,

multiple source critique is more effective. The pros and cons of each source are included in Table 5-2.

☐ *What are the skill factors in making role playing succeed?* It takes quite a few, actually. Adherence to some of the major ones, listed below, should help.

1. Have clear-cut learning objectives lest the role playing be perceived as an add-on. Be sure to provide participants with a clear understanding of what they are to do and why.

2. Try to involve everyone. Do this by paired enactments before the total group for everyone, on a one-at-a-time basis; or, better still, by multiple role playing.

3. Use group-developed situations or members' problems.

4. Consider using group-developed criteria for the observers.

5. Make certain the observers know what to look for and understand the importance of their job.

6. "Field test" your cases, especially the instructions to role players and observers.

7. Allow the role players enough time to internalize their assigned roles (in structured role playing) and to develop a strategy for dealing with the other person.

8. Provide enough try-out experiences so real learning is possible. Since role playing is designed to teach skills, the concept of "repractice" is basic.

9. If the cases are yours rather that those of the participants, make certain they are marked by a high degree of realism; for example, in sales training the problems and type of customers should obviously be those that the participants will actually encounter.

10. Allow enough time for the processing (critiquing) of the action. This will be the source of payoffs.

11. Include a summary of group learnings at session's end. Let the group tell you what they learned or, possibly, what they still need to learn.

Table 5-2
Sources of Critique—Advantages and Limitations

Sources	Advantages	Limitations
Self-critique	Basic to development of insight; also, aids to defuse negative feedback	No one can see themselves as others can; hence the need for other sources of feedback
Critique from one's partner	Provides another desirable perspective	But this is only one person's opinion, and it may not be objective because of involvement in the role play or may be cautious to avoid hurting other's feelings
Single observer	An added worthwhile source due to the detachment of the observer role	One person's opinion; may be reluctant to level; may lack skill and be too hard-hitting in giving feedback
Two or several observers	Multiple judgment is desirable	Ineffective only if observers are inexperienced, biased or reluctant to level
Trainer	Can provide his/her experienced view including being supportive (positive reinforcement)	One person's view; not too helpful in multiple role plays
Coach (used in multiple role plays in addition to observer	Adds an element of experience to the critique; objective, since not involved in the role plays; assumes worthwhile roles of coordinator and summarizer	Depends on high skill and personal qualities (patient, empathetic, candid supportive, enthusiastic, all of which establishes good rapport with role players)

BEHAVIOR MODELING

The latest innovation in role playing is known as "behavior modeling [30]." It is a reaction to some of the weaknesses or limitations of role playing as it is typically used to develop interpersonal skills. Specifically, critics of role playing assert that role-play exercises only provide general guides for the trying out of new behavior, thus allowing the role players latitude to improvise within that framework. Also, on repeating a role play of the same role, players may act differently and thus fail to button down the skill to be learned [31].

Role playing authority Malcolm E. Shaw cites these flaws in role playing used to teach selling skills [32]:

☐ Participants are allowed to do the wrong things, a trial-and-error learning approach.

☐ Participants are often "set up" to receive negative reinforcement.

Workshop Phases

To overcome these deficiencies, behavior-modeling workshops proceed along these six very specific phases [33]:

☐ *A conceptual presentation is made.* This entails an explanation of the concepts basic to the skill to be mastered. Each step in the skill is described in detail along with the uses of it.

☐ *A modeled, videotaped demonstration of the skill is provided.* A company supervisor (not an outsider), with whom the group can identify, shows the right way to apply the skill. (The skill can relate to performance appraisal, a disciplinary interview, a selling skill, etc.) Key actions are performed on the videotape on a step-by-step basis. Participants are required to identify each action step, record them in their notebooks, and then discuss them.

The modeled behavior takes place within the company (not in a "foreign" location) and is introduced by an executive of the firm whom the super visor knows. This shows that management supports the program. Using an in-house model allows participants to identify with the company person and thus perceive that person and the program as credible. They also gain confidence that the behavior modeled is one that they, too, can perform.

Another view on the customizing of models is held by Donald T. Tosti. He states that customizing "to produce effective skill learning has not been supported. In fact, there is some evidence that model demonstrations that match the work environment too closely, or use familiar settings and co-workers as actors, may be distracting" [34].

☐ *A rehearsal period is provided to practice the behaviors.* Following the viewing of the videotape, the demonstrated skill is rehearsed, one pair at a time. The trainer guides the role-playing supervisor's attempts at skill replication, one step at a time. The rehearsal is videotaped for feedback and reinforcement, stage four in the process.

Note: The videotape is not used as a "trigger film" to provoke discussion. Thus, the trainer would never say to the observer group: "What did you like, what did you not like?" Instead, a skill-oriented question such as this would be posed: "How did the sales manager use active listening with the subordinate?"

Active listening entails acceptance of what is said without engaging in value judgments, as well as clarification of expressed feelings and restatement (reflecting back) of what is said.

Note, too, that the enactment is not an open-ended role play—"do it as you see (or feel) it"—which often produces a lot of anxiety. Also, the approach is trainer-intensive.

☐ *Feedback and reinforcement are provided to fine-tune the behavior.* Using the action steps shown in the videotape as their criteria, the observers provide the role player with supportive feedback. Successes rather than miscues are stressed. Action steps improperly performed or skipped are reenacted, at the request of the trainer, until properly executed. So every role play becomes a success story.

Besides trainer and observer feedback, the role players also engage in self-critique.

The most significant skill for the trainer is to emulate what is taught; for example, the trainer can't teach the value of self-esteem and then erode it.

☐ *Commitments are made by participants to apply the learned skills to their on-the-job problems.* Written contracts are secured from the trainees to use the new learning.

☐ *Follow-up discussions are provided.* Each session begins with a review of the contracts developed in the prior session—what worked well on the job and what didn't. If a problem or block is encountered, the trainer calls for another rehearsal to ensure that the pertinent skills are learned.

Several features of the program design, which ensure a "gluing in" of the classroom learning, are these:

☐ The training is spaced out over a six-week period. This allows for on-the-job practice after each full day's session.

☐ The trainees' supervisors, who have had the training, provide added reinforcement upon their return to the job.

☐ Line managers, who have been properly trained, are used as trainers in the workshops.

☐ A reinforcement day is provided every four to six months. This prevents erosion of the classroom learning.

The supervisors who have been trained by behavior modeling are expected to use several general principles of motivation [35]:

☐ It is essential to maintain and enhance the employee's self-esteem along with a concern for productivity. Candor, rather than manipulation, is to be employed.

☐ The focus is on behavior, performance, results (for example, errors, absenteeism), not on changing anyone's personality. This approach avoids defensive reactions.

☐ Individual differences of subordinates are to be recognized.

☐ Positive reinforcement is the key to shaping behavior. This procedure avoids possible negative side effects from other kinds of reinforcement.

☐ Active listening is to be used to demonstrate understanding of the other's feelings, attitudes, etc.

□ Reasonable goals and follow-up dates are therefore the "contracts" to get the specified changes in behavior.

Starting a Program

If you or your organization are considering embarking on a behavior-modeling training program, you should ask these key questions [36]:

□ Is the performance deficiency due to a clear-cut lack of skill and knowledge, or are there other factors at work (for example, lack of motivation)?

□ Is it a skill or a knowledge deficiency? Actually, most skill training also requires attention to an accompanying cognitive component, so both elements typically have to be attended to. However, one must be able to distinguish between the two deficiencies to be able to provide the proper training for them.

□ Are the behaviors that are needed to overcome the deficiency identifiable? Often, one set of learned behavior is inadequate since different situations, requiring different behaviors, may be encountered.

□ Will there be an opportunity for *all* learners to practice the desired skills? A small group (about 8–12) makes for a manageable training operation.

□ Will there be adequate reinforcement for the new skills that are learned? This should take place in class *and* on the job. Sources of reinforcement: peers, workers, managers, and the total organization.

□ Is the training cost effective? Quantitative data must be gathered before (an estimate) and after (an evaluation) the training to demonstrate actual payoffs.

Uses and Results

Behavior modeling has been used to train supervisors in skills relating to performance review, to improve poor work habits and/or performance, to discipline effectively, to reduce conflict between two subordinates, to introduce a new procedure or policy, to reduce turnover of new hires, and to maintain a supportive and open climate. It has also been used in sales training, in training newly promoted scientists in people-handling skills, and in training inner-city minority youth in interpersonal skills to avoid possible failure on the job.

A growing number of research studies have reported favorable outcomes as a result of training in behavior modeling. One sophisticated study, using before and after measures plus comparison or control groups, merits citation. The study took place in a manufacturing operation (700 unionized employees) of a major forest products company. The key findings were as follows [37]:

□ Supervisors who received training in supervisory skills via behavior modeling were perceived by their employees to be using these skills at levels significantly superior to supervisors in the control groups (untrained supervisors).

□ Over a six-month period, the running average of total monthly production per direct worker-hour improved 17% compared to a control (or untrained) plant.

□ Average daily production, again compared to the control group, was up 25% in the fifth month.

□ Significant waste reduction, over a six-month period, was also accomplished compared to the controls. Raw material converted to end product increased at a rate equal to a reduction in cost from $40,000–$50,000 monthly. This meant a $250,000 cumulative saving for the six-month research period.

In another evaluation study, employees of supervisors who had undergone behavior-modeling training anonymously completed a "Supervisor Interaction Behavior Profile" to rate their bosses on their progress in resolving work problems. The ratings took place six months after the training was completed. Sixty-five supervisors had been trained, and 19 volunteered to receive the feedback from their subordinates. The results: Each profile served to motivate and maintain job use of learned interaction skills. Action plans were developed by the supervisors to overcome highlighted deficiencies. Also, the assessments improved communications and awareness among all concerned [38].

Overcoming Shortcomings

Despite the wide use of behavior modeling and its numerous successes, many users have encountered shortcomings with it. For example, Scott Parry and Leah R. Reich, president and vice president, respectively, of Training House, Inc., Princeton, New Jersey, see these kinds of lingering issues [39]:

☐ *Simplistic models.* Trainees typically learn to handle all situations in a given way—"one size fits all." In reality, a single model cannot accommodate all situations in varying work environments. *The solution:* Regard the model as a starting point, not the end-all. The trainees should be taught to discriminate between situations where the model is and is not appropriate. Trainers (and the pro grams) must be flexible enough to accept alternatives and to apply some models (and modules) and reject others that don't fit the organization's norms and culture.

☐ *Absence of theory.* Employees today want to know the "why" as well as the "how." As has been said, "There is nothing as practical as good theory." *The solution:* Trainers should know and share behavioral science concepts and data underlying each model before participants are given the model and asked to enact it. Other responses (behavioral options) which derive from these theories should be elicited and enacted.

☐ *Boredom.* The above two problems create boredom, as does the fact that all classes follow the same format. Also, all participants reenact the same basic role play. Finally, behavior modeling puts the trainer in a parental role; there is total reliance on the "show-and-tell" *inductive* method. Trainees' experiences are not tapped. They learn to do as instructed without opportunity to contribute or question. *The solution:* Use more *deductive* methods, that is, draw their experiences from the participants to vitalize and enrich concepts and skills.

Note: Another view on the inductive vs. deductive issue is held by Kenneth E. Hultman,

a director of ministerial counseling services [40]. He does not believe that inductive learning has to be parent-child in nature. He asserts that an effective trainer can make most points in a module by asking the learners questions and allowing them opportunities to discover the answers for themselves. He would have them respond to questions and draw on their experience at several points in the training: in the module introduction, following the video model, prior to skill practice exercises, and after those exercises.

☐ *Wrong examples are not used.* Trainees are given only "perfect" models to study. But other experts in this field believe that people also learn by seeing negatives and nonideals, and learning to distinguish between effective and ineffective behavior patterns. *The solution:* Expose the learners to weak/ineffective models, too. When they understand the difference between the desirable and the less so, they should then practice in their role plays the appropriate concepts and skills.

Note: In respect to the issue of positive vs. negative models, Darlene Russ-Eft and Linda Zucchelli, of Zenger Miller, Inc., Cupertino, California, a firm with extensive experience in behavior modeling, have researched this area. Their study provides these implications for training [41]:

1. Showing two *positive* models (positive/positive) results in improved learning. But using a negative model with a positive one produces similar effective results.

2. When employing a negative model, use the "negative/positive ordering." This format is most effective if you are training people in subtle, ambiguous behaviors. Why? Because it provides more contrast, improved retention, and heightened trainee satisfaction.

3. Using more than one model improves learning, probably due to repetition and generalization. One of these models must be positive.

4. Two negative models produce ineffective learning. People learn best from a correct

model. So if you only use one model, be certain it is a positive one.

☐ *Weak transfer to the job.* Actual application on the job may not occur for these reasons:

1. Learners are not motivated by the satisfaction of measuring their own improved performance. Why not? Because on entry into class they did not assess their own strong points and weak points. Consequently, they can't share with their bosses and/or subordinates any real basis for change or improvement.

2. Since the program is essentially a "canned" rather than a tailor-made one, the training may not be seen as relevant.

3. Positive reinforcement to support the new behavior may be absent.

   The solution: Participants' bosses should be trained in coaching and mentoring to support the new learning. Also, action plans should be prepared and reviewed with the boss after the training, in order to review successes and failures in applying the new behaviors.

Another criticism of behavior modeling as it is taught comes from Dr. Melvin Sorcher [42], who developed it in 1969–70 when he was Manager of Personnel Research at General Electric. (He co-authored *Changing Supervisory Behavior,* the pioneering work in this field, with A. P. Goldstein, Pergamon Press Inc., New York, 1974. He is currently Director of Management Development at Richardson-Vicks Inc.). He states that he got better results than current practitioners because he carefully trained *employees* how to react to these kinds of situations: how to react to constructive criticism, how to ask for help or information, how to ask for performance feedback, and how to cooperate with change. In his training classes at GE he used different behavior modeling video tapes for supervisors and employees and trained them separately. He found that training both parties on how to interact with one another made for effective responding.

KEY POINTS

1. Role playing is a technique basic to every trainer's repertoire. It is a skill-oriented form of experiential training.

2. It is a versatile training tool, taking such forms as the informal (*ad hoc*, unplanned); the spontaneous (using participants' live cases); the demonstration type (includes dramatic skits and personal growth enactments); multiple role playing (teams of three or four, including observers); group role playing (a group assumes roles and works on a problem subject to total group critique); multiple group role playing (several or more groups or teams work on the same problem producing comparative data); total group role playing (for example, in a simulation).

3. The trainer must be aware that role playing and the feedback received from it may produce anxiety and should take appropriate steps to reduce the threat involved.

4. Structure (using worksheets, instruments) is a tool to direct learning and reduce possible anxiety or embarrassment.

5. Observers are useful for collecting data for feedback purposes. They should be fully oriented as to the nature and importance of their task.

6. Processing the role play properly is basic to participant learning from it.

7. Video feedback is a means of capturing the full dimensions of a role play in an objective way.

8. Trainers should acquire skill in developing their own role-playing situations. A good role play is short, is easy to understand, has believable characters, contains enough conflict to be realistic, and relates directly to learning goals.

9. The role-playing experience can be enhanced by special or advanced techniques such as role reversal, empty chair, the soliloquy, the mirror technique, multiple role taking, and the "behind the back" technique.

10. Behavior modeling is a powerful tool—and a system—to ensure that role playing produces real learning and is transferred to the job.

REFERENCES

1. "Role Playing Polishes New Sales People," *Wall Street Journal* (September 30, 1987).

2. Branigin, William, "Border Patrol Being Pushed to Continue Fast Growth," *The Washington Post* (May 13, 1999), pp. A3 and 10.

3. Rose, Frederic, "Driving the Disabled Means More Training for Bus Operators," in "Work Week," *The Wall Street Journal* (June 9, 1998), p.1.

4. Broadwell, M. M., "Rediscover Role Playing," *Training, The Magazine of Human Resources Development* (July 1977), p. 19.

5. Wohlking, W., and Weiner, H., "Structured and Spontaneous Role Playing: Contrast and Comparison," *Training and Development Journal* (January 1971), pp. 8–14.

6. Voelker, Ted, "Tag, You're It," in "In Practice," *Training and Development*, (March 1993), p. 11.

7. Swink, David F., "Role-Play Your Way to Learning," *Training and Development* (May 1993), pp. 91–97.

8. Balli, Sandra J., "Oh, No . . . Not Role Play Again!," in "Training 101," *Training and Development* (February 1995), pp. 14–15.

9. Cooper, W. H., "Play Well Thy Part," *Training and Development Journal* (August 1980), pp. 64–68.

10. Bub, J., and Suessmuth, P., "Lesson Design: Predicting Student Choice," *Canadian Training Methods— The Human Element* (June 1980), pp. 35–36, 38.

11. Cover, W. H., "Curbstone Coaching," *Training and Development Journal* (November 1980), pp. 33–37.

12. Caulton, Kathy R., "How to Prepare Your Staff to Deal with 'The Customer from Hell,'" in "Best Practices in Customer Services," *Business and Legal Reports, Inc.*, Madison, CT (May 15, 1998), p. 7.

13. McAlister, Bill, "Service In A Foreign Fantasy Land," *The Washington Post* (March 6, 1987), p. 21.

14. Schlesinger, Jacob M., "Auto Firms and UAW Find That Cooperation Can Get Complicated," *Wall Street Journal* (August 25, 1987), p. 20.

15. Maier, N. R. F., Solem, A. R., and Maier, A. A., *The Role Play Technique: A Handbook for Management and Leadership Practice*, University Associates, Inc., San Diego (1975).

16. "Training Away Work Place Problems," *Training and Development Journal* (Nov. 1987), pp. 18–19, which provides suggestions by Michael Shahnasarian, ISFA Corporation, Tampa, Florida.

17. Jones, J. B., and Pfeiffer, J. W., "Role Playing," *The 1979 Annual Handbook for Group Facilitators,* University Associates, Inc., San Diego (1979), pp. 182–193.

18. Millington, W. G., and Gross, L. S., "Video for Teaching the Non-Verbal Language," *Educational and Industrial Television* (August 1976), pp. 20–22.

19. *TC Today, The Newsletter of Teachers College/ Columbia University* (Spring 1981), p. 4.

20. Goldfaden, B., and Teta, D., "Video for Psychology Instruction and Practice," *Educational and Instructional TV* (December 1980), pp. 43–45.

21. Power, William, "With Any Luck Soon All Judges Will Be Like Joseph Wapner," *Wall Street Journal* (August 12, 1984).

22. Barrett, J., "Skilled Are the Peacemakers," *Northeast Training News* (June 1980), p. 19.

23. Whyte, R., "How to Role-Play Your Way to Better Management/Salesman Communications," *Sales Management* (May 1, 1972), pp. 29, 31, 86, 88.

24. Gschwandtner, G., "A New Approach to Videotaped Role Plays," *Educational and Industrial Television* (March 1978), pp. 66–69.

25. Klein, R., and Smith, F., "Supervisory Feedback in Training," *Training and Development Journal* (September 1981), pp. 106–110.

26. At the September 1981 ASTD Region II Conference in Rochester, N.Y.

27. *Personnel Journal* (June 1976), p. 270.

28. Gschwandtner, G., *op. cit.,* pp. 66–69.

29. Horne, J., "Cops to the Rescue," *Quest* (July–August 1981), pp. 32–36, 85, 88–89.

30. Goldstein, A. P., and Sorcher, M., *Changing Supervisory Behavior,* Pergamon Press, New York (1974). (The technique was originated at General Electric in 1970.)

31. Porras, J. I., and Anderson, B., "Improving Managerial Effectiveness Through Modeling-Based Training," *Organizational Dynamics* (Spring 1981), p. 66.

32. Shaw, M. E., "Sales Training in Transition," *Training and Development Journal* (February 1981), p. 81.

33. Porras, J. I., and Anderson, B., "Improving Managerial Effectiveness Through Modeling-Based Training," *Organizational Dynamics* (Spring 1981), pp. 64–67.

34. Tosti, D. T., "Behavior Modeling: A Process," *Training and Development Journal* (August 1980), p. 73.

35. Rosenbaum, B. L., "Common Misconceptions About Behavior Modeling and Supervisory Skill Training (SST)," *Training and Development Journal* (August 1979), pp. 40–44.

36. Robinson, J. C., and Gaines, D. L., "Seven Questions to Ask Yourself Before Using Behavior Modeling," *Training, The Magazine of Human Resources Development* (December 1980), pp. 60–69.

37. Porras, J. I., and Anderson, B., "Improving Managerial Effectiveness Through Modeling-Based Training," *Organizational Dynamics* (Spring 1981), pp. 70–76.

38. "Low-Threat Truth-Telling Aids Supervisor Assessment," Training (August 1983), pp. 69–70.

39. Parry, Scott B., and Reich, Leah R., "An Uneasy Look At Behavior Modeling," *Training and Development Journal* (March 1984), pp. 57–62.

40. Hultman, Kenneth E., "Behavior Modeling for Results," *Training and Development Journal* (December 1986), pp. 60–63.

41. Russ-Eft, Darlene, and Zuchelli, Linda, "When Wrong Is Alright," *Training and Development Journal* (November 1987), pp. 78–79.

42. Sorcher, Melvin, "Developer of Behavior Modeling Shows How to Make It More Effective," *BNAC Communicator*, BNAC Communications Inc., Rockville, Maryland (Summer 1987), p. 2.

RECOMMENDED READING

General

"Bosses, Cops, G-Men Prepare for Crises by Acting Them Out," *Wall Street Journal*, November 25, 1981.

This is an account for the lay person concerning current uses of role playing in business and government.

Callahan, Madelyn R., "Art Imitates Work Life: The World According To PACT," *Training and Development Journal*, December 1986, pp. 56–59.

This article describes the work of the Manhattan-based Performing Arts For Crisis Training (PACT), an actor-trainer group that recreates actual scenes of crisis used to teach handling situations "in reality": rape victims, angry customers, problem employees, hijackers, alcoholics, abused wives, suicidal teenagers, etc. PACT calls its work "structured improvisations," presenting the realities of office, plant, school, police precinct, emergency room, and the like.

Harmon, Paul, and Evans, Kay, "When to Use Cognitive Modeling," *Training and Development Journal*, March 1984, pp. 67–68.

Behavior modeling works for overt, observable activities, but to teach covert cognitive skills—for example, teaching a loan officer to make correct loans—a sequential cognitive procedure must be identified. Job aids are used for this such as a worksheet, decision chart, checklist, flow chart.

Hosbrink-Engels, Geralien A., "Designing Role Plays for Interpersonal Skills Training," *Performance Improvement,* October 2000, pp. 32-39.

The article presents ten steps to provide a structure in which designing role plays can be a successful venture.

Jones, John E., and Pfeiffer, J. William. "Role Playing," in *The 1979 Annual Handbook for Group Facilitators*, University Associates Inc., San Diego, California, 1979, pp. 182–193.

Topics covered include the context of role playing, its use in human relations training, advantages and disadvantages, designing role plays, role playing in the experiential learning cycle, and conducting role plays.

Maier, Norman R. F., Solem, Allen R., and Maier, Ayesha. *The Role-Play Technique: A Handbook for Management and Leadership Practice*, University Associates Inc., San Diego, California, 1975.

This unique role-playing case book contains role plays for both multiple-group and single-group situations. Instructions for the trainer are provided for each case so that the activities can be conducted successfully.

Shaw, Malcolm E., Corsini, Raymond J., Blake, Robert, and Mouton, Jane S., *Role Playing: A Practical Manual for Group Facilitators*, University Associates Inc., San Diego, California, 1980.

This is an updated version of a classic work on the role play method. It describes why and how it is useful, as well as how it can be applied to meet problems of information dissemination, individual assessment, and training.

Behavior Modeling

"Behavior Modeling Trains Underprivileged Youths for Jobs," *Behavior Today*, November 17, 1980.

Learning interpersonal skills through observing role models on videotape, role playing, and group feedback helps underprivileged youths prepare for retail sales jobs in Philadelphia.

O'Connor, Terence, "How to Set Up, Run and Evaluate a Training Program Based on Behavior Modeling Principles," *Training/HRD*, January 1979, pp. 64–67.

At St. Luke's Hospital, New York City, supervisors learn through behavior "rehearsal" these seven skills: greeting the new employee, introducing a new policy or procedure, improving poor work habits, improving poor performance, the discipline interview, performance appraisal, and reducing conflict between two subordinates.

Validation studies indicate that problems are solved by the program.

Porras, Jerry I., and Anderson, Brad, "Improving Managerial Effectiveness Through Modeling-Based Training," *Organizational Dynamics*, Spring 1981, pp. 60–67.

Tangible payoffs from a behavior-modeling program in a major forest products company are reported. An outside team of investigators conducted the research.

"Retailers Discover An Old Tool: Sales Training," *Business Week*, December 22, 1980, pp. 81–82.

Using behavior-modeling principles and techniques, a training/consulting firm teaches retail clerks these selling points: greeting, ascertaining what the customer wants, benefit to the customer, overcoming objections, closing the sale, selling extra items, and enhancing buyer self-esteem.

Robinson, James C. and Linda E., "How to Make Sure Your Supervisors Do On-The-Job What You Taught Them in the Classroom," *Training/HRD*, September 1979, pp. 21–22, 24–25.

This article asserts that for actual transfer of the new behavior to the job, two conditions must be met: determination of needs of supervisors who are to be trained, and management support of the new skills that are learned.

Robinson, James C., and Gaines, Dana L., "Seven Questions To Ask Yourself Before Using Behavior Modeling," *Training/HRD*, December 1980, pp. 60–65, 67–69.

Behavior-modeling training, to be successful, requires decisions in respect to these seven questions: (1) Could he/she do it if his/her life depended on it? (2) Is it a skill deficiency? (3) Can you identify behavior needed to overcome the skill deficiency? (4) Can a positive, credible model be demonstrated? (5) Can each learner practice the skill? (6) Will the new skills be reinforced? (7) Is it cost beneficial? These principles were applied to a training program for the Homespun Insurance Company with financial benefits to the company.

Robinson, James C. and Linda E., "Modeling Techniques Applied to Performance Feedback and Appraisal," *Training and Development Journal*, January 1978, pp. 48–53.

Describes a system wherein supervisors can deal more effectively with employee performance in today's work environment. The system overcomes these shortcomings in supervision: (1) lack of specific goals/standards, (2) lack of immediate feedback, (3) lack of planning for discussions about performance, (4) lack of future orientation, (5) lack of supervisory skills, and (6) lack of management support.

Rosenbaum, Bernard L., "Common Misconceptions About Behavior Modeling and Supervisory Skill Training," *Training and Development Journal*, August 1979, pp. 40–44.

If behavior-modeling training for supervisors is to be successful, they must follow these principles: (1) maintain and enhance self-esteem of the employee, (2) focus on behavior, not personality, (3) use reinforcement techniques to shape desired behavior, (4) use active listening to show understanding, (5) set goals, follow up dates and maintain communications.

Rosenbaum, Bernard, "New Uses For Behavior Modeling," *The Personnel Administrator* July 1978, pp. 27–28.

Besides training of supervisors, behavior modeling can be applied to blue-collar workers to improve peer relations; to reduce conflict among professionals and managers; to improve security guards' skills in dealing with executives and employees; etc.

Shaw, Malcolm E., "Sales Training in Transition," *Training and Development Journal*, February 1981, pp. 74–76, 78–83.

Answers these two related questions: (1) What are the desirable sales behaviors which should be supported and enhanced in sales training? and (2) what are the methodologies, structures, and design elements that will develop and sustain those desired behaviors?

Tosti, Donald T., "Behavior Modeling: A Process," *Training and Development Journal*, August 1980, pp. 70–71, 73–74.

This article points out shortcomings in application of behavior-modeling training, such as use of poor models, ineffective practice situations, ineffective feedback. ("Poor" models relate to a confusing or distracting situation, unconvincing actors, demonstration of inappropriate verbal and nonverbal behavior along with appropriate actions. Ineffective feedback entails more criticism than encouragement, failure to focus on critical behaviors, poor timing, or sequence.)

Wehrenberg, Stephen, and Kuhnie, Robert, "How Training Through Behavior Modeling Works," *Personnel Journal*, July 1980, pp. 576–80, 593.

This article is a well-rounded treatment of the subject, including the motivational/learning theories at work, history, steps in a model program, and a summary of several evaluation studies.

Zemke, Ronald, "Building Behavior Models That Work—The Way You Want Them To," *Training*, January 1982, pp. 22–27.

This article discusses various issues in behavior modeling that may facilitate or inhibit trainee identification with the model: the "dressiness" of the set; perfect vs. coping performance; real company problems or neutral issues; negative vs. positive examples.

Using Games and Simulations

*The teacher if he is indeed wise does not bid you to enter
the house of his wisdom but leads you to the threshold of
your own mind.*

—Kahlil Gibran (1883–1931),
Syrian symbolist poet and painter

GAMES, simulations, exercises, and puzzles, also known as structured experiences, provide participants with significant opportunities to experience learning. By "experience" we mean to learn from one's personal involvement with the structured event or incident, as opposed to being told by the trainer what should be learned from it. Thus, in the classic "NASA (Lost on the Moon)" exercise [1], participants learn *experientially* of the power and value of group decision making. Or participants may be assigned the task of constructing a tower out of construction paper, cardboard, newspapers, magazines, and tape, and learn from this the importance of and approaches to planning, organization, leadership, utilization of member skills, participation, communication, creativity, teamwork, decision making, and pride in accomplishment.

Note that although the trainer provides the vehicle for the learning—the exercise—the learning comes about by actually undergoing the experience. The point we are making, then, is that although the structured event itself is not reality, the learning from it, coming as it does from one's experience, is very real indeed.

To put this type of learning into proper perspective, we should recognize that other—and possibly more powerful—learning ensues when you learn primarily or even totally from your experience. Such experience-based activities include laboratory learning (the T-Group, or sensitivity training; encounter groups; the Managerial Grid®); team building; keeping a diary or journal or completing various instruments as tools for introspection; participating in a simulation; and role playing a live or real job-oriented case. An overview and summary of experiential learning is provided in Chapter 22. Several brief definitions of games and simulations as forms of experiential learning follow:

Simulation—Any training activity designed to reflect reality. This may include a role play, an in-basket exercise, or any other learning experience that has real-life aspects integrated into it. The learning comes from the participant's own experience in the activity.

Game—A learning activity governed by rules, entailing a competitive situation, having winners and losers. Although games do *not* reflect reality, there is (and must be) learning. The learning typically comes from experiencing the game, including the interaction of the participants, but not from the subject matter or content of the game per se.

Simulation-game—A reality-based game wherein the participants experience what people do in the real world. The learning comes from the real-life content of the game. The game is played competitively and, of course, has outcomes (including scores, winners, losers).

Exercise—A structured experiential activity. The learning comes from participant input, participant interaction, and participant analysis of the attitudes and/or behaviors generated by the activity. Competition is *not* an element of the exercise.

The common denominators of all of these learning tools are

- ☐ Concrete learning objectives
- ☐ Structure provided by the trainer
- ☐ High participant involvement
- ☐ Generation of data
- ☐ Participant/trainer analysis of completed results (data)

Note that competition and reality are *not* the distinguishing features of *all* of these experiential forms of learning.

In this chapter we shall discuss games and simulations. In Chapter 7 we shall introduce the reader to exercises. In Chapter 8 we will show how puzzles can be used in the training situation. To integrate the key ideas of Chapters 6, 7, and 8, we shall provide some key concepts about experiential learning at the close of Chapter 22.

WORKING WITH GAMES

A simulation game is like a kiss, interesting to read about but much more interesting to participate in. And those that do tend to repeat the experience.

—From a promotional brochure of the Institute of Higher Education Research and Services, The University of Alabama

Games set up a "free space" which participants can use to experiment with new roles or variations of their present roles. . . . It is a space where norms of validity are suspended and totally new approaches to the real world can be formulated.

—Burkhart Holzner, Department of Sociology, University of Pittsburgh

A good game will drive itself. In some exercises, the facilitator is constantly saying, "Now this is the next step." But a good game takes on a life of its own.

—Barbara Steinwachs, training consultant and authority on games

What is a game, insofar as the training situation is concerned? One group of trainers endeavored to respond to this question by brainstorming the characteristics of a game [2]. Here's what they came up with:

Rules	Action learning
Competition	Processing of data
Skill	Imagination
Win/lose aspect	Fantasy
Threatening	Discipline
Beginning/end	Options
Focus	Strategy
Self/others	Luck
Brings out child	Problem solving
Fun	Motivational
Noisy	Team spirit
Scoring	Applications (cognitive/
Chance/skill	affective/psychomotor)
Roles	Communication
Goal	Skills
Betting (sometimes)	Chance to try out
Spectators	new ideas, roles, skills,
Rewards	behaviors, simulation
Risk (low/high)	of real world
Experimental	

This list is interesting in that it shows the multifaceted character of a game. However, it does not provide us with a clear-cut definition of a game; rather it combines purposes, major and minor attributes, and end results. Actually, a game is marked by the presence of these principal elements:

- ☐ Learning goals
- ☐ Rules (which are clearly defined)

☐ Competition

☐ Player interaction/participation

☐ Termination point or closure (time, points, most money earned, etc.)

☐ Outcomes (winners and losers are determined)

Current language used to describe many games is "simulation-game." The term "simulation" is intended to point out that there is also present a representation of reality, a "slice of life." The simulation-game could be diagrammed as in Figure 6-1. The simulation-game then is a combination of the game and the simulation.

Of course, not all games are a slice of life. For example, several groups may compete in placing 30 pegs in a peg board. This is what might be termed a "pure game." The learning comes from analyzing participant behavior exhibited in the course of the game—leadership, communication, planning, organizing—rather than the intrinsic components of the game.

Other games may involve competition in constructing a bridge out of Tinker Toys or a tower out of newspaper, magazines, and construction paper. Again, the learning typically comes from the interaction of the participants and the data generated by them rather than from the subject matter or content of the game.

Sometimes games are referred to by trainers as exercises, learning exercises, activities, application sessions, etc. to defuse a possible negative reaction by some participants to "playing a game."

Simulation-games, including war games and business games, have been used for many purposes: decision making, negotiation, sales, communication, planning, problem solving, delegation, time management, equal employment, urban affairs, transactional analysis, goal setting, career planning, safety, performance appraisal, and communication.

In the balance of this section we will use the term "game" to include games and simulation-games as well.

Why Use Games?

A game has these purposes and advantages:

It is an experiential form of learning. Participants learn from what they do, as opposed to what the trainer tells them they should know. It is active rather than passive learning.

It heightens participants' awareness, interest and curiosity, thus making them more receptive to learning.

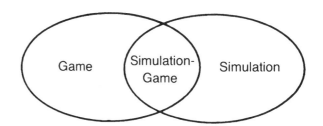

Figure 6-1. Diagram illustrating the concept of a simulation-game.

It helps participants drop their possible resistance to new learning by fully immersing them in an active task.

It may provide a degree of reality that other learning devices cannot. For example, compare learning about how a decision was made in a case study situation vs. reaching a decision required by a game.

It has high motivational value. Learners respond to a game because they are actively involved, and it is a fun way to learn. Competition—beating the other teams—is also an incentive to "dig in."

It provides participation for everyone. All learners—fast, medium, slow, or ostentatious—have the same opportunities for involvement. (Of course, prior familiarity with the subject, possession of certain skills, etc., may determine the nature and degree of the involvement.)

It emphasizes the role of the participants. The participants are the active ones, and the role of the trainer is deemphasized. The trainer is removed from the usual roles of knowledge-disseminator, expert, authority figure, and evaluator. Typically, the trainer need only help participants to get started and to assess learning progress and outcomes.

It emphasizes peer/collaborative learning. Participants learn from their interaction with one another. It recognizes that the participant group is a splendid learning resource. To the extent that this is true, it reduces the usual dependency on the trainer.

Learning is rapid. Since a game compresses considerable experience into a short time frame, learning is accelerated.

The game only produces winners. A game produces winners and losers insofar as the rules of the game are concerned. But, in fact, everyone is a "winner" since everyone learns (or at least has the opportunity to learn) from the experience.

It allows for risk-taking in a safe atmosphere. It is far better to err in the training situation than in real life. Games reward (learning or experience is the reward) rather than penalize the learner.

It serves as a projective device. To the extent that participants are caught up in the spirit of the game and become themselves, their behavior is displayed for the others to see. The behavior can be critiqued and thus becomes the basis for learning about one's own behavior in relation to others within the rules of the game.

It can aid skill development. Since the game requires active participation, there are typically opportunities to develop such skills as planning, conferring, negotiating, analyzing, prioritizing, decision making, and giving and receiving feedback.

It helps to "glue in" the training. Participants are much more likely to remember the game experience than they are something they were told by the trainer. It is not unusual for a trainer to encounter a participant who experienced a game several or more years back who says: "Remember when we played the game of . . ."

It reinforces principles, concepts, and techniques previously taught.

It taps the right brain, thereby stimulating the intuitive, creative, emotional, spontaneous side of the participants.

It permits learning the costs, benefits, and effects (results, impacts) of decisions without risking the costly resources (money, material, manpower machinery, minutes) of the real world. People can safely learn the tradeoffs and pros and cons of different strategies and alternatives.

Despite their many advantages, games may not work well if the game is not in sync with learning objectives, if participants have difficulty getting caught up in the spirit of the game (a rare event), if the trainer is not familiar with the game or is not prepared to administer it, or if time runs out before the game is fully processed (discussed and analyzed).

One writer suggests other limitations: some participants get hooked on winning and may thus overlook training goals, others may not take the game seriously enough to garner any learning, and learning may dissipate at game's end unless there is reinforcement back on the job. (I would point out that reinforcement is always a problem regardless of the training technique employed [3].)

When to Use Games

From the standpoint of course design, games are indeed versatile learning tools that can be used in several ways.

☐ Games may be used to open an activity or program. They are an effective way to secure participant attention, heighten interest, set the tone of the program (high participation, an atmosphere of inquiry), and set the stage for the next activity. Games can also get participants to interact with one another very quickly, and they give everyone a common experience at the outset.

☐ Games may be used at many points in the ongoing course or program. They are particularly helpful to provide a change of pace and/or to introduce variety into the learning experience. Should interest begin to lag in the middle of a course, a game can help rekindle interest. Of course, the trainer should have prepared an appropriate game for that part of the course.

☐ Games may be used to conclude (possibly summarize) a session or program. The impact of the game should serve to provide participants with an enthusiastic, close, and durable reminder of course learning.

☐ Games are a highly effective experiential learning tool for teams. Three conditions significantly increase the likelihood that a learning game will have lasting influence in the back-home situation [4]:

1. *Learnings from the game pertain to a clearly defined context.* Maximum effect ensues when the game is used in relation to the work or a problem basic to the group's needs/concerns. Learnings "glue in" with participants when their application to the work can be seen clearly.

2. *Learnings are reinforced.* Heightened, sensitive on-the-job communication, when applied in day-to-day activities, is a potent reinforcer of the new lessons learned.

3. *The game experience is shared.* The common experience—new learnings, possibly new language, new perspectives, and new perceptions—which the team can recall later (a new group memory) will have an enduring influence on group strivings and accomplishments.

Administering the Game

Good "game management" requires concern with issues and procedures such as the following:

☐ Have I made certain that the game I have selected is truly relevant to the topic being discussed as well as to the back-home environments of the trainees?

☐ Have I considered carefully the size of each group at play and recognize that a group that is too large may affect its functioning negatively?

☐ Have I considered the use of a "dry run" (rehearsal) with colleagues so that possible "bugs" are eliminated before we conduct the game?

☐ Is the game being played at the most appropriate time in the session or program?

☐ Have I familiarized myself with the game— objectives, procedures, materials—so I can properly introduce it, conduct it, and process it?

☐ Have I allowed enough time for the game, particularly for processing it? (With good planning, you can avoid participant reactions such as this one: "Imagine, we worked two and one-half hours on the game and now the trainer tells us we only have 11 minutes left to 'summarize learning.'")

☐ Have I planned for all pre-game preliminaries, such as game materials, instruction sheets, instructor's manual, seating arrangements, flip-charts, and pens? Do I have extra items likely to get lost, such as dice, chips, markers, and cards?

☐ How will I introduce the game? What should I say? Will I be sure to keep the introduction brief?

☐ Are my written instructions, if any, clear?

☐ Will I allow enough time to let participants ease into the game before they start, or will I rush them into it? Will I remember to ask for questions before the signal to start is given? ("Does this make sense?" "Are we on the same wavelength?" Have I rushed the explanation?")

☐ Will I remember that a game is a form of experiential learning and that one must avoid taking away the participants' experiences by over-communicating about it before the game starts or while it is underway?

☐ How do I form small groups? On the basis of propinquity of participants? Randomly (count-off method)? Self-selection? Does it matter?

☐ Will I remember to advise participants of time limits? Should I warn of the approaching deadline (five or ten minutes) before it arrives?

☐ When I give participants the time warning ("Three more minutes, please"), do I adhere to that time limit strictly, or do I use it just as a reminder that things have to be wrapped up very soon?

☐ Will I remember to instruct observers and/or judges, if any, about their roles?

☐ Will I need a co-trainer? Is the role of the co-trainer or assistant clear?

☐ Will I strive to keep the atmosphere informal, fun-filled, remembering that this *is* a game?

☐ What is my role during the game? Do I move around to clarify procedures and rules? Do I "tune in" a bit to get a sense of participants being with it, questions or issues arising, team feeling, etc.? Do I avoid intervening, remembering that this is *their* game?

☐ Do I know quite well what is to be accomplished in the processing or debriefing period and how it is to be done?

☐ Do I recognize that debriefing should proceed at two levels: game analysis *and* its application to the real world?

☐ In the processing, do I recognize that although everyone has had the same experience, they may still perceive it differently?

☐ Have I considered asking game participants for feedback about the administration of the game, ways to make it more effective?

☐ Have I planned to record group feedback and my own observations to ensure an improved activity in a future presentation?

Designing Your Own Games

Although a great number and variety of games are available from publishers, at times it may be desirable to design your own game. This may be to meet the needs of the course or program better, for economy or cost reduction, to exercise or test one's creativity, or to ensure that participants have a fun as well as a learning experience.

Keep in mind the following suggestions when designing a game:

1. Develop a good feel for games in general. Do this by participating in or administering a number of them. Try to experience a variety of games: pure games, paper and pencil games, board games, card games, and construction-type games.

2. Work with one or more colleagues on the project. A well-thought-out game has many nuances to it, and two or three heads can zero in on them more readily than one.

3. Use the checklist in Figure 6-2 as a guide to meaningful game design.

Descriptions of games you can probably design follow:

Board Game

This game is fairly easy to create. As in board games such as Monopoly, the players have money ("funny bucks" or poker chips will do), roll dice, and move their counters around the board. The play objective is to win the most money or points possible. This is done by answering questions, typed on cards. The questions could relate to any subject desired: product knowledge, customer service, safety, or management topics such as communication and effective supervision.

Let's say you wanted to create a game dealing with delegation. You would first brainstorm data for the cards, such as the advantages of delegation, problems in delegation, techniques to make delegation work (the control side of delegation), why managers may be reluctant to delegate, and why employees may be reluctant to assume greater responsibility. This data could be used to form questions, which, if answered correctly, earn points.

Checklist For Design of a Game

	NO	YES	NOT SURE
1. Terminal objectives (attitudes, skills, behavior) are fully thought out and reduced to writing.	☐	☐	☐
2. There is a high probability that the game will actually provide the desired learning outcomes.	☐	☐	☐
3. There is a logical relationship between the length of the game session and participant learning (cost effectiveness).	☐	☐	☐
4. The game is the best training method to achieve the terminal objectives.	☐	☐	☐
5. The game has been constructed so that winners and losers will learn equally.	☐	☐	☐
6. Observers have been included to facilitate the post-game analysis.	☐	☐	☐
7. Provisions have been made, either orally or in writing, to instruct the observers properly in their roles.	☐	☐	☐
8. Judges have been included since the end-result requires an "objective" appraisal (such as in the construction of a tower).	☐	☐	☐
9. A prize will be awarded to stimulate interest.	☐	☐	☐
10. If a prize is awarded, money will be collected from all participants.	☐	☐	☐
11. If a prize is awarded, it will be awarded by the trainer or an impartial judge or referee.	☐	☐	☐
12. Total time of the game has been carefully measured.	☐	☐	☐
13. Time for processing (analysis) of the game is planned for.	☐	☐	☐
14. The game has been subject to a "dry run" before it is used in class.	☐	☐	☐

If any of these critical questions do not have a clear-cut response, one is well-advised to "go back to the drawing board." Remember, a game should produce an "ah ha" rather than a "ho hum" response.

Figure 6-2. A guide for designing a game.

You could also introduce positive (rewarding) and negative (punishing) experiences as a result of delegation practices, for example:

"You have been recognized as 'The Delegator of the Year.' Go to the next green square and collect two hundred fifty dollars."

"One of your more promising employees has resigned because she felt she was not growing in the job. Pay three hundred fifty dollars to the United Community Fund and fifty dollars to each player."

"You introduce a weekly meeting with the Manager of Task Force Z-Four to ensure that the project is on target. Add thirty points to your total."

The end result should be the acquisition of new insights about delegation, and unlike with the lecture method, they will be acquired in a fun way.

Board games that deal with diversity issues can help trainers to present these subjects to managers and employees in a non-threatening environment and to stimulate lively discussions about these issues. Games can be used as icebreakers/openers or as follow-ups to reinforce the subject [5].

If you are interested in constructing your own board games, you will want to review the many helpful details provided by trainer Stephen E. Sugar [6].

Board games to provide business-literary and financial education are available from commercial organizations. Says Cathy Rezak, president of Paradigm Learning, Tampa, Florida, "Board games are a fun way to teach a fairly dry subject and the story line helps bring the participants along" [7].

Frame Games

The idea is to give you, the game designer, a structure (the frame) and then let you "plug in" the content you wish. For example, let's say you want to create a game on leadership. You follow these procedures [8]:

1. Prepare in advance of the game five cards (3" × 5" or 5" × 8") for each participant. Each card should have statements about leadership typed on it. Include statements that participants will be likely to accept ("I want to employ Theory Y management techniques"), statements participants will readily reject ("Leadership is keeping everyone happy"), and statements participants may feel ambiguous about ("Group decision is a useful technique for developing standards").

2. Prepare a similar batch of cards (the same number) for the table, mixing the positive, negative, and ambiguous cards.

3. Give each participant five cards.

4. Tell participants to read their cards and group them into two piles: likes (agrees with) and dislikes (disagrees with).

5. Have participants find a partner and endeavor to trade off their worst cards and garner better ones from one another. Tell them an explanation must be offered for surrendering or taking a particular card.

6. Participants are free to secure a "fresh" card from those on the table after every two or more exchanges, but may only take the top card, putting discards on the bottom of the stack.

7. Allow exchanges to take place for 30 minutes or until the "decibel count" seems to be decreasing.

8. Ask participants to form trios or quartets and to agree on the five "best" cards. The discards are to be put on the table.

9. Secure reports from several groups concerning the cards they retained. Secure comments from the other groups concerning the cards that were not retained.

Note: A variation on Step 1 is to have the participants rather than the trainer prepare the cards. This step will add more time to the game, but it will produce added involvement. You, as trainer, may have to edit the cards a bit for clarity.

Tic-Tac-Toe

Remember Tic-Tac-Toe, which has nine boxes that are to be completed with X's and O's? Well, the Tic-Tac-Toe frame can serve as the basis for another frame game, letting you provide whatever content you wish. As an example, in a management development/career development workshop for trainers, we might have the participants label the vertical cells "first line supervision," "middle management," and "top management" and the horizontal boxes "early-career," "mid-career,"

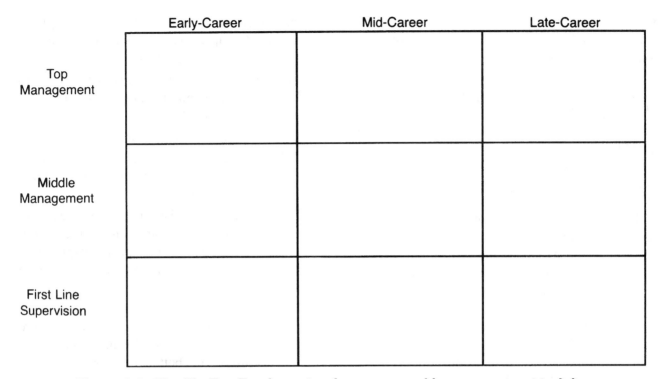

Figure 6-3. The Tic-Tac-Toe format or frame as used in management training.

and "late-career," as in Figure 6-3. Procedurally, we might then do the following:

1. Split the group into two smaller groups, "A" and "B."

2. Toss a coin for the first play. The starting team picks any cell it wishes and tries to fill it in (answer it). The trainer should be prepared with answers on all cells to approve or disapprove the participants' answers. Since opinion is involved in these career-oriented decisions, the trainer should be liberal in approving subgroup data. Each subgroup may challenge the other group's answers; the trainer again arbitrates the decision.

3. Play continues until one subgroup completes a line of three cells in a row in any direction.

Note: A variation of the game is to let each team fill up all nine boxes, with the winner being decided on the basis of who completes the whole matrix first. Factual data will be less controversial and will thus allow the game to proceed more smoothly. For example in a game involving determining accidents, the vertical axis could be labeled "day shift," "evening shift," and "night shift." The horizontal axis could be labeled "plant," "warehouse," and "loading docks." Then the accident type could be inserted in appropriate boxes [9].

Construction Games

Groups can be given materials, such as blocks, Tinker Toys, newspapers and magazines, to produce a physical structure such as a tower. The purpose of the construction activity is to allow the small groups to generate behavior for analysis, such as planning, leadership, communication, cooperation, participation, decision making, manpower utilization, and teamness. Observers can report on the data generated by the participants as they perform their tasks. Judges may be used to evaluate the completed work; for example, construction of a free-standing tower may be awarded points on the basis of height, stability, aesthetic design, creativity, etc.

Production Games

Instead of constructing physical objects, as above, participants in teams may produce greeting card verses, political or advertising slogans, management sayings, and laws and proverbs (such as Murphy's laws). Again, the behavior generated in team production is subject to observation, feedback, and analysis.

Maximum Numbers Games

A sure-fire way to produce competition between or among small groups is to assign them a task wherein they are required to produce a maximum number of something. Two examples of such games, using this approach, follow.

Archeological Game

The objective is to reveal how our screening filters out unwanted data, detail, and minutiae. This is important to us so that we can get through the day and get our tasks accomplished without being sidetracked by trivia bombardment.

Note: This objective is *not* given to participants; this perceptual phenomenon is what they will learn from the game.

Give participants the following instructions:

1. "You are to function as archeologists. This means that you are interested in reconstructing a given culture based on artifacts you discover."

2. "The culture you are concerned with is the United States in the year 7,000—5,000 years or so past today."

3. "You are in a dig and come up with a small, flat, round object. It has a man's face on it; the man has a beard. The object is a U.S. penny and has this year's date on it."

4. *"Without* reaching for a penny from your pocket or purse, come up with as many characteristics of U.S. culture at that time as you can. This is what archeologists do all the time. You will have to rely on your memory to recall the data on the penny. You are in competition with the other teams. You have five minutes for the task."

At the five-minute mark, call time and ask participants to total their cultural characteristics. (The totals typically run in the "teens.")

Secure a verbal report from the highest team and list its data on a flipchart. Anticipate items such as these:

Bi-lingual (English and Latin)	System of writing
Architecture (if Lincoln Memorial is on rear)	Appearance conscious (Lincoln's beard)
Metallurgy	Liberty-loving (liberty)
Calendar	Sewing skills or tailoring (Lincoln's shirt and coat)
Coinage system	Cloth production
Hero worship (Lincoln)	Dress conscious (coat, tie)
A federal government ("E Pluribus Unum")	System of numbers
Religion ("In God We Trust")	Agriculture (if a "wheat penny")
Mining	Patriarchal society

Also anticipate friendly rivalry—the losing team will deny the validity of certain cultural traits listed by the winning team. Secure added (new) items from the other team.

To process the game, ask participants what was learned. Some possible responses from the groups, which are put on a flipchart: Importance of teamwork (several heads are better than one); a leader in group is not necessary; importance of background or perception (different groups see different things). At this point add: "I'd like to pick up on the perception aspect. Was the task difficult to do, relying solely on memory?" (Participants respond affirmatively.) "Why was it difficult to remember what is on an object that you handle *daily?*" (Pause at this point, for this is *the* profound question of the game.) Some possible participant answers are: "We don't pay attention to it." "It's not important information." "We take it for granted."

At this point say: "Yes, we overlook the detail, the trivial because we have a mechanism in our heads (phenomenon of perceptual choice or selective attention) that screens out the unimportant. This is a tremendously helpful device because it allows us to get through the day without getting bogged down by the innumerable stimuli that constantly bombard us—trees, signs, houses, stores, cars, ladies' dresses, colors. But at the same time our screening mechanism may work the other way. It may screen out data we *should be cognizant of,* for example, the need to call old Harry to our meeting. We forget him and he gets mad at us. So our screening device works for good and for less than good. So we must be aware of this perceptual process and try to keep it from overlooking the important stimuli, which are also out there.

25 Object Game

The objective is to demonstrate that creativity is more likely to flourish under unstructured than under structured supervision. (But don't tell the group this in introducing the game.) Before introducing the game, assemble 25 objects and place them in a 8½" × 11" envelope, one envelope per team. Each envelope should contain an identical 25 objects. The objects should cover a wide variety of materials and may include the following:

Commemorative postage stamp	Key Piece of wire
Plastic spoon	Screw or nail
Highway map	Hair pin
Ketchup (in small plastic bag)	Pencil
Sugar packet	Telephone memo slip
Coin	Needles or pins
Stone	Button
Small pine cone	Piece of cloth
Aspirin	Matches
Candle	Beer can opener
Piece of plastic (apparently functionless)	Coping saw blade

To play the game:

1. Divide the group into teams of five to nine persons.
2. Appoint a leader for each group. The leaders are to function differently—some will be relaxed, encouraging, unstructured leaders (Supervisors A); the others will be more structured (Supervisors B). Each leader receives only his/her instructions in writing and does not see the other instructions.

The instructions to be given to the unstructured leader, Supervisor A, follow:

Instructions for Supervisor A

Your group has the task of grouping (classifying) a number of miscellaneous objects. Your group's creativity will be measured by its ability to come up with as many groupings as it can in the *ten minutes* available.

Your job is to unleash the creativity that resides in the group. Since the task is clear-cut, just start them off with an encouraging sentence or two.

Then give them their instruction sheets, dump the 25 objects on the table, and begin to work for the ten minutes.

The instructions for the structured supervisor follow:

Instructions for Supervisor B

Your group has the task of grouping (classifying) a number of miscellaneous objects. Your group's creativity will be measured by its ability to come up with as many groupings as it can in the *ten minutes* available.

Prior experience with this game indicates that your group will perform well if it receives a helpful "pep talk" preliminary to their actual work on the task. It is thus essential that you talk to them for four or five minutes on the importance of putting things into groups or categories. Use examples from

☐ Everyday experience—for example, a supermarket couldn't function if it didn't group its products properly (apples, oranges, cookies, cereals, meats, frozen foods, etc.); the auto industry couldn't serve its clients if it didn't carefully group its replacement parts using various lists and catalogs; imagine a library without a system of classifying its books, or stamp collectors who didn't group their stamps by country, or zoologists and botanists who failed to classify fauna and flora.

☐ Company experience—for example, the personnel office groups jobs in classes for recruitment and pay purposes; secretaries maintain groupings of letters (files) for easy reference.

After your introduction, *don't* pause for questions. Just pass out the instruction sheets, dump the 25 objects on the table, and begin to work for the ten minutes.

3. The best physical arrangement for the game is to have each group work in a separate room. A large room may also allow for privacy and noninterference from the other group(s). If a private room is not available, let the teams work one at a time, with

the nonplayers staying outside the game room. Instruct each group to stay together and not to talk to each other, or it will spoil the game.

4. Each team should have a table to work on, a flipchart sheet or two to record their categories, and a felt-tip pen.

5. Have the team leaders hand out the following instructions to each member of their team when the task begins, but not before that time:

Group Instructions

This game is designed to ascertain the creative power of your group. Your task is to

☐ Come up with as many different groupings (categories or classifications) as you can of the 25 objects that you have been given; for example, your ball point pen can be put into such groupings as plastic, metal, etc.

☐ List the groupings on the newsprint sheet.

☐ Perform the task in ten minutes.

---

6. If manpower allows, appoint observers, one for each team. Instruct them to look for factors which influence—help or hinder—creativity. Also pay particular attention to items in their instruction sheet, which follows:

Instructions for Observer

As observer you observe the action silently. Do not intervene, except to call time after ten minutes of work.

Note: The team leader begins the assigned task after he/she has made his/her introductory remarks. He/she is not to allow for a question period since the participants have instruction sheets.

Pay particular attention to

☐ Factors or influences which encourage group creativity.

☐ Factors or influences which inhibit creativity.

☐ The role of the leader: Is he/she encouraging, friendly, supportive, dominating, discouraging, argumentative, neutral, passive?

☐ Climate: What is the group atmosphere and is it conducive to creativity?

☐ Participation: Is it widespread, or do one or two people take over? Does this help or hurt creativity?

☐ If there were any real breakthroughs, what were they and what produced them?

---

7. Divide the total group into subgroups and position them at different points in the room.

Introduce the game as follows: "We are about to engage in a game which will test the creative power of your group. I will now appoint team leaders and give them their instructions. Will the team leaders please step forward and read your instructions privately?" After they have read their instructions, give them each the big envelope of objects and a group of participant instruction sheets.

Call *each* group of leaders (A vs. B) aside separately to check if they have questions. Tell them that their sequence of operations is as follows:

1. "Have everyone find a seat around the table."

2. "Deliver your introductory remarks and get going. Do *not* pause for questions since the participants are being given an instruction sheet."

3. "Pass out the participant instruction sheets and dump the 25 objects on the table. This is the signal to begin work."

4. "Conduct the task for ten minutes."

After all teams have done their work, either simultaneously or in sequence as privacy conditions may allow, have the team leaders post their flipcharts to the wall and count the number of categories their groups produced.

Note: Every entry is a category since the instructions said nothing about general categories, subcategories, etc. Anticipate some argument on this point, but hold firm to your position.

Experience with this game indicates that these results will typically ensue:

1. The structured team(s) will perform less well than the unstructured ones. Why? Because structure inhibits creativity: "If you give Johnny a paint brush and ask him to paint a horse, you'll only get a horse. But if you say: 'Johnny, draw whatever you like,' you may get the Mona Lisa."

2. Sometimes both kinds of teams have a tie, or nearly so. If so, the question is: "If lectures don't make a difference, why give them? Why run the risk of smothering creativity with a lot of patter? If you over-communicate, the group has *two* problems: the assigned task *and* how to cope with the leader's input about the task."

3. If, as a less likely possibility, the structured team wins by a large margin, ask the observer what produced the creativity. Also, tell them that this result is unusual, for typically the added structure tends to confuse people, slow down the group, and inhibit its creativity.

Conclude the discussion by asking participants to draw on their own experience concerning the impact of high/unnecessary structure on creativity.

Converting an Exercise into a Game

Sometimes an exercise can be converted into a game by introducing a competitive element into it. For example, take an exercise that is concerned with getting participants to become more aware of feelings or emotions. The participants act out an emotion, such as disgust, affection, fear, anxiety, embarrassment, anger, or determination, and the total group tries to guess what the emotion is. To convert this exercise into a game, follow these procedures:

1. Divide the group into two teams.
2. Place on a table (or put in a box) a packet of cards, each of which has a particular emotion typed on it.
3. Have a participant from Group A take the top card from the table and act out (pantomime) the emotion for his/her group. This is to be done in a fixed time limit (such as a minute or two).
4. If the emotion is guessed correctly by Group A, they receive ten points.
5. Now have a participant from Group B act out an emotion; award points as appropriate.
6. Rotate the acting opportunities between the two groups.
7. After 20–30 minutes, call time and announce the winning team based on its point total.

Note: A prize will heighten the competition.

WORKING WITH SIMULATIONS

A simulation is a training device designed to give the participants an experience comparable to what they would experience in real life. Training systems analyst Bruce Lierman states that there are four kinds of simulations [10]:

1. *Psychomotor and perceptual simulations. Example:* In a flight simulation, trainee pilots practice visual and motor coordination and task sequences. Cues are taken from the simulator.

2. *Cognitive-task simulations.* Here participants learn the concepts and abstractions underlying the rules and principles governing their work environment. *Example:* a stock-market game. Note that since the focus is on thinking processes, these simulations don't mirror real-world situations as precisely as psychomotor and perceptual simulations do.

3. *Systems simulations.* This simulation is for tasks involving communication and coordination. Several trainees can function simultaneously in different roles as part of a total work system. *Examples:* tasks ranging from planning and marketing strategies to managing nuclear power plants. We can anticipate that, in the future, these simulations may train personnel in understanding the implications of their behaviors/actions on colleagues. This procedure may also show them how to work effectively in firms with widely dispersed operations.

4. *Virtual-reality systems simulations.* This is an emerging tool, still in its infancy. In this approach, an attempt is made to achieve total-sensory stimulation through the use of special headgear and electronic gloves. Goggles, fitted with small computer screens, are used to view the target environment in three-dimensional images. As one looks or moves in different directions, the simulation mirrors one's moves on the goggle screens. The simulation allows trainees to reach into, interact with, and manipulate the environment electronically.

Here are some examples of the use of simulations:

☐ Company officials participate in mock disasters to provide experience in dealing with corporate crises such as possible product tampering, the burning or explosion of a plant, a power outage in a utility, or the kidnapping of the company president. Part of the simulation may include "confrontational training" wherein some managers play the role of tough reporters who vigorously try to obtain information about the crisis from the company president or a designated spokesperson [11].

☐ Commercial pilots receive special training, on the ground, to simulate the take-off and landing of planes under severe winter conditions.

☐ Office workers undergo a "dry run" evacuation due to fire in a high-rise building (or a bomb threat or an approaching tornado).

☐ Hotel workers receive training in how to calm concerned guests in case of a fire alarm; they also learn how the fire detection and alarm systems operate in case of emergency.

☐ A group of public sector managers experiences the operation of a hypothetical federal field agency; the simulation runs for two full days.

☐ New fast-food store managers operate a "mock" restaurant. They experience many problems of dealing with young workers, a wide range of customers, food preparation, cash control, and contingencies.

☐ A community undertakes an elaborate civil defense exercise, simulating evacuation, rescue work, medical treatment of the injured, etc.

☐ New auditors are given a full range of financial statements to "audit" a fictitious company. Interviews with operating officials are also conducted to ferret out discrepancies in data.

☐ New meter readers read residential, commercial, and industrial meters in a simulated urban area. Special problems such as discrepancies in meter figures and tampering with meters are included in the training.

☐ A special U.S. military helicopter unit rehearses a rescue of Americans in the Iranian Embassy. The embassy and its grounds have been re-created in complete detail to facilitate the operation.

☐ An electric power company trains its nuclear power plant operators how to react to a variety of emergency situations. A replica of a plant's control room is used to help the operators think through accidents and perform the proper functions to resolve the simulated crises.

☐ A bank instructs its new clerical hires in a simulated banking center, including a staged drive-in window, to learn prescribed procedures to open accounts and process the full range of daily transactions.

☐ A local fire department burns an abandoned house to provide paid and volunteer firefighters with a live fire-fighting experience. A blaze is set on the contents of the rear bedroom. The participants learn to locate a fire they can't see by feeling for a hot spot, such as a door, or by sound. Team coordination is part of the training. Other fires are also experienced in the attic and another bedroom [12].

☐ A group of 40 business owners and community leaders in Fairfax County, Virginia, one of the nation's wealthiest counties, meet on a Saturday morning to experience first hand the horrific life of a family struggling to make ends meet. In this poverty simulation one businesswoman became a young single mom barely able to assemble enough money to keep her house lights on. Also, adding to the mom's frustrations, the bank refused to cash her welfare check in the absence of an account there. The pawnshop clerk refused to buy an old chair from her. One "son" kept insisting on "Cocoa Puffs." Another child of hers disappeared from the grocery store.

In general, the simulation produced these by-products for the participants: creation of a program to provide refurbished computers and training for underprivileged families; a landscaping firm offered to collect food donations from their clients and deliver them to a soup kitchen; a sign maker decided to print bold fliers for food banks to be displayed throughout the county [13].

Note: A distinction should be made between "content-free" and "content-full" to describe the nature of simulations [14]. The simulations described above are *content-full* for they mimic trainees' actual job situations, for example, managing an auto dealership. Other simulations deliberately put participants in situations that are free of specific work or job content, for example, various exercises concerned with "survival" in deserts, jungles, sub-arctic environments, on the high seas, on the moon, etc. In the latter simulations there is *no formal job content;* instead, the total emphasis is on providing opportunities to work on the development of such leadership skills as teamwork, listening, decision making, diversity, planning, etc, through experiential learning. Of course, the content-full simulation may also help to develop some of the "soft skills" the content free simulations are concerned with, such as communication skills.

In recent years there have been a spate of content-free, outdoor, physical, risk-oriented, experiential simulations for team-building purposes. Examples:

☐ Negotiating a high ropes course that is 30 feet above the ground, plus challenges such as rope walking over a 150-foot river gorge. There is also rock climbing, whitewater rafting, and, yes, race car driving. These activities require a group to combine their physical and mental resources to meet a goal. In the course of these simulations, people are communicating and learning of their fellow participants' strengths and shortcomings [15].

☐ The Disney Institute, Orlando, Florida, provides team building through active learning activities to enhance participants' perspectives. For example, a group may plan and prepare a gourmet meal in its Culinary Challenge program. Or it may produce a TV news broadcast under deadline pressure, developing skills having professional application for those who function in professional settings. These activities provide intellectual stimulation and team bonding at the same time. Larry Lynch, director of business development at the Disney Institute, says of the Culinary Challenge, "The cooking is, after all, just a vehicle to achieve the result of team bonding among a group" [16].

Reducing Fear/Anxiety of Self-Directed Teams by Simulation

A management consultant who works with organizations in the implementation of self-directed teams finds fault with the technique of gradually teaching workers essential skills by creating problem-solving teams or task forces for them to work on. This gradual method doesn't ease anxiety when it comes time to move into the real thing. Resistance remains because the usual management control structures are still in place. Specifically,

☐ Managers select the problem for the teams to analyze.

☐ Managers require the teams to submit possible solutions to them for approval.

☐ Managers attend to the implementation of the solution.

☐ Employees participate, but their bosses are accountable.

☐ The managers' role has not fundamentally changed, for they still supervise their teams, assign work, solve problems, and make decisions—basically, they are in full control.

Conversely, true self-directed teams manage their own work processes to achieve results. They are expected to identify and solve their own problems. With maturation, the teams select the best solution, act on it (implement it) and monitor results. Managers appropriately avoid detailed direction of team activities.

So if real self-directed team management is to take place, roles must change for both parties—managers and team members. How can people learn about self-directed team management? Management consultant Drew Lathin states that sending employees to other firms to "see how they work" is not adequate. He says, "Understanding without experience is extremely difficult to achieve when the paradigm is being changed."

Lathin's answer? He suggests using simulations to give team members genuine team experience. This may be in four-hour, full-day, or even three-day simulations, depending on the needs of the particular team. His procedure: He creates a self-directed team by assigning specific roles to team participants, support staff, and management team members; he assigns these people to work on a team, create a product, and then discuss their experiences. He may also create a second simulation, using traditional roles. He then compares the results of the two simulations.

How do team members feel about the two simulations? In the former situation they feel better utilized and more in control. And with the "test drive"—the simulation—workers and managers are less fearful about true, on-the-job tryouts [17].

Situation Simulations

"Situation simulations" differ from large-scale behavioral simulations, which tend to focus on a broad range of issues facing a firm. They focus, instead, on a specifically designed situation challenging one person, typically a new manager. Their approach is to pose issues explicitly as opposed to challenging participants to both identify and solve them [18].

The training strategy involved is to combine the analytical learning given by a comprehensive case study with the experiential learning of a powerful role play. This is done within a brief time frame in a quick-moving program. Thus the simulation confronts participants with specific situations reflecting ambivalent managerial feelings. *Examples:*

- ☐ *Responsibility overload simulation.* The manager seems to have more on his/her plate than one can cope with.

- ☐ *Loss of control simulation.* The simulation focuses on a manager's annual objectives becoming at risk because of inadequate/indifferent performance by two staffers.

- ☐ *Loss of work satisfaction simulation.* The manager's financial duties compete against more abstract responsibilities, for example, resolving a work group conflict or coaching a staffer on a critical next day's sales call.

- ☐ *Ambiguous authority simulation.* A subordinate, a former colleague before the manager's promotion, requests special considerations/privileges from the new manager.

Participants are presented with an array of challenges for each issue. For example, they may be required to analyze the issue and develop a strategy to deal with it. Or they may assume the manager's role and make a presentation to his boss or hold a delicate meeting with a subordinate.

Where does the design's power come from? It comes from the simulation's ability to create a strong reality so that participants are apt to say "Yes, that's how I feel too." For the new manager, this is the first step toward learning how to rise above the very likely frustration and disillusionment of the new post.

Advantages of Using Simulations

Simulation is beneficial for many of the following reasons:

- ☐ Participants are involved in a real-life rather than a theoretical situation. This training facilitates entry on the job, or readiness for "the real thing."

- ☐ Learning is active rather than passive; everyone "plays."

- ☐ The learning process relies on the best approach to adult learning, namely, experiential or discovery learning.

- ☐ Mistakes can be made in a risk-free atmosphere. The boss is not there to grimace, raise eyebrows, "chew out," or punish in other ways for a miscue. Also, mistakes can be made without cost—not always the case in real-life decisions.

- ☐ Participants can function in a low-stress environment and learn how to deal with a high-stress situation.

- ☐ Time spans can be compressed; for example, key problems likely to be encountered in the next two months or more may be presented in the simulation in a few days.

- ☐ The learning situation provides the opportunity for immediate feedback concerning proper and improper actions or decisions. Thus, participants can correct their behavior promptly rather than continuing to err, and they can be psychologically rewarded for proper performance.

- ☐ The trainer's role can shift from a didactic one to that of learning facilitator.

Possible drawbacks of the simulation include the following:

- ☐ A simulation, while very real, may still not be able to replicate all situations or complexities that may arise. (For example, a new hotel, which was just about to open, operated a mock registration desk to provide experience with the myriad of expected problems. But a power failure, which was not expected, caused havoc on opening day.)

- ☐ Participants may tend to generalize (or overgeneralize) from what is only a slice of life, but not life itself. They may also develop a false sense of confidence concerning their ability to cope with reality on the job.

- ☐ A simulation must be carefully constructed to ensure that the desired learning outcomes are certain to be reached.

- ☐ Simulation facilitators need to be ready and able to handle unpredictable, ambiguous, even emotional outcomes. If the trainer has a low tolerance for ambiguity, he/she is not likely to "pull it off" successfully.

☐ This is a time-consuming training method, more so than most other methods. (Most simulations run one to four days.)

Should You Use a Simulation?

Bruce Lierman advises consideration of these criteria before embarking on a simulation [19]:

1. *Cost factors.* Short-term use is expensive because of development costs, so figure the return on your investment—this is the product of the size of the training audience and its training effectiveness divided by the total cost. Cost is based on requirements for fidelity/accuracy.

2. *Size of trainee group.* The greater the number of users, the more likely you will get a measurable return on your simulation investment. Large employee turnover in the job(s) to be simulated signals possible appropriateness. Conversely, a stable occupational group makes the investment very questionable.

   Consider, too, whether others—supervisors, support and maintenance workers—might profit from the training. And if you have a dispersed target group, is it worth duplicating the simulator in each of those locations to train more people?

3. *Effectiveness.* You should compare effectiveness of a proposed simulation to other training approaches. Cost-effective simulations are more appropriate when the training relates to skill development and attitude changes, as opposed to possible knowledge gains. For example, in skills training, five minutes in a real work environment can teach more than trainees would absorb in an hour of lecture. Depending on the task, simulations can reduce training time by up to 85%. Simulations are also effective when the ability to obtain feedback from environmental cues is basic to success.

   Refer back to the examples of actual simulations cited above. Note that simulations have been used to teach soft skills (for example, how to calm hotel guests in case of a fire alarm; how to deal with corporate crises such as product tampering), as well as hard skills (such as fire-fighting in a high-rise building and safety training of all sorts).

Note, too, that a simulation may be the only way to assess a worker's readiness for on-the-job training (OJT).

4. *Fidelity.* This relates to the degree to which a simulation represents the actual work environment. In the military, simulations (for example, war games) are a vital, high-fidelity training tool since a war can't be started to provide real-life experience. A common, well-tested example of a high-fidelity simulation is the flight simulator.

Note: After you have worked through the above steps, you should define and document on paper the level of interactivity required to meet training needs. Be certain that all who are involved in developing the simulation understand its complexity.

Trainer/Facilitator Skills Required

Top-flight facilitation skills are mandatory. Recognize that you are not delivering information, but instead eliciting it from the participants by setting the right climate for learning and by posing the right questions.

The key skills are [20]:

☐ Matching participant needs and skill/background levels in the initial design of the simulation.
☐ Setting the stage properly before the simulation starts.
☐ Helping participants confront tough issues without become a lightning rod for their anxieties.
☐ Delivering straight feedback in a sensitive, caring way.
☐ Assisting participants to focus on a broad range of inter-group and/or organizational issues.
☐ Debriefing participants after what is typically an intense, action-packed experience.

Implementing the Simulation

Attention to these skill pointers will help participants maximize their learning from the simulation:

1. Introduce the simulation to the participants so that objectives, roles, rules, procedures, and time frames are clear.

2. Monitor the simulation in a facilitating way. That is to say, recognize it is *the participants'* learning opportunity and don't intervene unnecessarily. Provide help as requested or as seems indicated by events. "Tune in" to group work to get a feel for progress, possible resistance points, team cohesion, etc.

3. Assess performance in the simulation: What areas have Helen and George mastered or assimilated in which they were previously deficient? How do we find out what Helen and George have learned?

4. Allow for enough processing time so that loose ends, in the form of principles and key skill points, are firmly buttoned down.

5. Provide for other kinds of training activities that may be needed in support of the simulation. Relate those activities to the simulation ("You will recall that in the simulation we . . .").

Designing a Simulation

The best way for the trainer to design a simulation based on the organization's activities is to work with a group of operating officials on the project. First, explain the nature of simulation and provide them with several examples. Then have them draw on their practical experience to develop situations and problems they want the participants to experience.

Hindy Lauer Schachter of the New Jersey Institute of Technology, Newark, provides these ten guidelines to construct a meaningful simulation, using a "pilot run" approach [21].

1. Determine its purpose, listing each ability you wish to develop.

2. Design activities that develop the stated abilities; for example, if the group is to learn how to negotiate with an outside group, create such a learning situation.

3. Outline the scenario, deciding on the purpose and name of the organization involved, nature and number of roles, and so on.

4. Use a plotline and props (for example, manuals and contracts if a union negotiation is involved) that are logical, believable, and consistent.

5. Assign participants appropriate roles; realism, in relation to objectives, is essential, of course.

6. As the simulation develops, ask participants to generate alternatives and to choose a solution or course of action therefrom.

7. Make certain all activities have been assigned enough time for their completion.

8. Provide opportunities for giving participants oral feedback, with particular emphasis on the giving of praise for good performance. (Positive strokes will encourage greater participation.)

9. Conduct a dry run to "debug" the simulation.

10. Arrange for participants to critique the simulation; use the data to make it more realistic, relevant, and exciting. The feedback may also improve the clarity of participant instructions and eliminate unnecessary detail and dull spots.

Trainer/consultant Beth A. Loewendick, Corporate Response Group, provides several guidelines for the creation of simulations (she terms them "table top exercises") for various corporate crises or emergencies such as explosions, fires, product tampering/contamination, and oil spills. She suggests the use of these four steps to prepare for effective crisis management [22]:

1. *Design the simulation.* As the simulation developer, you should respond to these key questions:

   ☐ What are your *objectives?* What do you want to define, explore, test, verify, or solve?

   ☐ What aspects/phases of your *response capabilities* do you wish to test, examine, or verify?

   ☐ What are the potential *risks* and *vulnerabilities* your organization (or even industry) faces?

   ☐ Who should be involved as *participants* in the simulation?

   ☐ Have you identified/appointed a *professional evaluator* to observe and document group discussions?

2. *Develop the simulation.* At this stage you need to create *specific scenarios* to provide the basis for discussion during the simulation. Consider these issues, then, says Lowendick:

☐ What real-world events could occur that would cause significant effects, both short and long term?

☐ What type of events/incidents/happenings will best allow those involved to meet simulation goals?

☐ Which persons, internal or external, would be expected to respond to the unwanted situation?

☐ Does the event or crisis have observable features, such as fires, explosions, natural catastrophes, injuries, fatalities, ransom notes, or steep stock-market declines?

☐ What information is likely to be available about the catastrophic incident? Anticipating the sequence of events, when (at what stage) is it likely to be available?

Note: You want to ensure a realistic simulation that provides a challenge in its execution. This entails the identification of crucial issues and the assumption of roles (both individual and team) as responses to realistic events and situations. It also requires the provision of appropriate support materials to prompt discussion, to record lessons learned, and to follow up on action plans.

3. *Conduct the simulation.* Anticipate that meaningful learning will necessitate two to eight hours of training time. The scenarios can be introduced by written materials or video clips. Information can be given to participants in time-based pieces or "moves," a technique which requires them to react to the event as it evolves. As in a real crisis, information might be delivered to participants on a limited or fragmented basis.

A key assessment for the participants is whether they have the needed resources to support their response activities/recommended actions.

4. *Evaluate the outcome.* The professional evaluator, having observed the performance/discussions of the participants in the simulation, will report back on group abilities to respond to key issues, to reach decisions, and to meet objectives. He/she will offer specific recommendations for maintenance and improvement of plans, procedures, skills, and capabilities.

Note: The rationale for the above activities is for the key players to be fully capable of moving into action if and when the disaster eventuates. This ensures that there will be no panic, wheel-spinning, blaming, or other non-productive behaviors. Instead, a plan of action will be confidently launched.

The Right Ways to Create a Successful Simulation

Dr. R. Garry Shirts, chief designer for Simulation Training Systems, Del Mar, California, a publishing firm which creates and markets top-flight experiential simulations, draws on his 30-plus years of simulation design experience to offer ten secrets of creating successful training simulations [23]:

1. *Watch the "replication" trap.* Replication is not to be confused with simulation. To the uninitiated, there is often a temptation to design "a small-scale replica of some full-blown reality." The logic involved is that the closer the simulation relates to reality, the more valid and unforgettable the experience is likely to be. This may be true with a flight simulator, but in a "soft skills" simulation, the designer must "look past the details to the *essence* of a reality," says Dr. Shirts.

2. *Not all subjects can "survive" a simulation.* That is to say, some subjects are more appropriate for a simulation than are others. According to Dr. Shirts, these characteristics (use one or more of them) will serve as clues to possible suitability:

☐ Does the simulation have the necessary impact to help participants really see the world as others do? Shocking people into action, rather than stimulating mere intellectual learning, is paramount.

☐ Will the simulation create an environment in which people learn to perform *multiple skills* under pressure? In our regular training work, we help people to learn skills one at a time, that is, to learn in linear fashion. But in the real world, people often need to perform a number of skills simultaneously. *Example:* A manager may be dealing with a tough vendor and an unhappy customer, while working on a memo from a demanding boss.

☐ Will the simulation help participants to grasp *systems thinking?* The integration of relationships is a tough concept to assimilate. The simulation should therefore put participants on the inside of the system so they can fully comprehend how altering one component inevitably influences everything else.

☐ Will the simulation help participants recognize the contradictions entailed in *cognitive dissonance?* Many of us often hold values, attitudes, and beliefs which are contradictory with our behavior, but we are not likely to be aware of that inconsistency. Learning about it produces what psychologists call *cognitive dissonance. Example:* A manager may believe that he/she is prejudice-free. But his/her behavior evidences otherwise; for example, he/she automatically recruits people of his/her own skin color for immediate staff positions. An effective simulation will shock (confront) the manager into recognizing the inconsistency in his/her behavior.

3. *Prepare a comprehensive design plan.* Two planning decisions must be made:

    a. Will your design be totally your own, or will you employ a design team?

    b. Will you use a structured creative process, or will the process be on an *ad hoc* or informal basis?

    Regardless of your answer to Question A, you will need people to fill these key roles: a principal expert simulation designer, a subject matter expert, an overall administrator for the project, and a client or representative who provides a "reality check" as the project proceeds.

    For the most creative simulation, follow these guidelines, says Dr. Sheets:

    a. Don't settle on the first idea that appears. Keep digging to ensure that you uncover the best possibility.

    b. Look at a problem from multiple perspectives. This will ensure maximum realism.

    c. Use your unconscious mind to think through the problem. A great idea can appear regardless of where you are or the time of day.

4. *Plan/design the simulation so that participants face up to their responsibilities in the simulation.* You don't want anyone to duck responsibility for an action or decision driving the simulation by asserting that they did what they did because the simulation suggested/encouraged it. In other words, you want people to learn from the simulation without rationalizing their way out of it. So in your design, look out for these certain "responsibility avoiders."

    ☐ *Pretending.* Don't introduce rules which allow trainees to pretend to be someone else. You don't want "actors." Rather, you want people to assume full authority and responsibility for their assigned roles. In other words, the roles in the simulation should be so designed (full realism) that participants cannot explain their decisions with rationales such as "That's how I thought a plant manager would behave."

    ☐ *Using competition for its own sake.* Only use competition if it is basic to the reality you are trying to simulate. You don't want participants to rationalize inappropriate behavior in order to win.

    ☐ *Giving inappropriate behavioral choices.* Outcome-altering instructions like "the labor force is on a prolonged strike" or "the company has just had a catastrophic product recall" invite participants to escape responsibility. How? They can later claim that "Our decisions were sound, but luck was against us." *Key point:* Says Dr. Shirts, "Limit chance. to events that actually occur randomly in the real world."

5. *If your simulation has emotionally charged ideas, use symbols.* This is essential to avoid the likelihood that participants will assume stereotypical roles. If trainees can hide behind stereotypes (for instance, "black," "white," "race riot"), they take advantage of a convenient "escape hatch," says Dr. Shirts. In designing a simulation to teach campus conflict resolutions, Shirts found that his initial use of emotionally charged and guilt-laden themes threatened the participants to the point that they were almost incapable of authentic responses. In effect, he made it impossible to get

at the essence of racism: power or the lack of it. He overcame these blocks by changing both the name of the simulation (from "The Race Game" to "Star Power") and the names of the groups (from blacks and whites to Circles, Squares, and Triangles).

6. *Avoid game playing with your participants.* Don't use rules which are intended to manipulate the trainees. If certain behaviors are likely to influence outcomes, be up front about them. Participants who are deceived are likely to be so angry that the vital post-simulation critique will be derailed.

   Also, don't trivialize the experience by using cutesy proper names, for example, "Fly by Night Airlines," or "Marion Haste, Marriage Counselor," or "The Any Body Mattress Company—We stand behind every bed we sell." The names may be clever, but they run the risk of undermining the authority and effectiveness of the simulation by sending the message that the activity is not to be taken very seriously.

7. *Employ nontrainee participants for added realism.* Nontrainees (strangers) can serve to bring the simulation alive. For example, in a simulation designed to train sales managers, Dr. Shirts hired ten people from a temporary agency to function as prospective job applicants. The simulation participants interviewed them, selected some as sales staff, trained them to sell a product, organized them into efficient organizational units, and coached them to success.

   Note: The outsiders have no stake in the outcome, so they perform without preconceptions about proper behavior.

8. *Develop an appropriate performance model.* Assessing trainee performance via math-based scoring systems may be effective for simulations in finance or other highly precise fields, but such techniques don't work well for qualitative simulations such as in the areas of teamwork, diversity, or ethics. The mathematical approach is usually either too limited and inflexible to assess the myriad variables involved or too complicated to generate meaningful results. Then, too, participants may figure out quantitative models and slant results inappropriately.

9. *Don't include in the early tests of your design those who have a high stake in the simulation.* People who have an investment in the success of the simulation will panic if they see problems early on; however, problems in the preliminary stages are to be expected. So watch carefully whom you invite to the early (alpha) tests.

   Note: Dr. Shirts distinguishes between *alpha* and *beta* tests as follows:

   ☐ An *alpha* test occurs early in the simulation design process. It is intended to assess the simulation's basic assumptions, overall structure, and logic of progression. Anticipate problems in the early stages.

   ☐ A *beta* tests is a real test, a "shake down" of the final product or design now at least provisionally set.

10. *Maintain your objectivity in evaluating the success of your simulation.* As you receive feedback from those who take part in your tests, anticipate that the trainees may overvalue or undervalue its participative aspects or that they may exaggerate results (learning) if they get emotionally involved in the simulation. So stick to your initial standards for success, and don't let yourself be seduced by enthusiasm or destroyed by negative criticism.

Criteria for Vendor Selection

If you have a complex simulation in mind and need an outside contractor, consider the following criteria [24]:

☐ Credibility. You need to select a vendor who can gain full credibility with senior management. Says Robert Brodo, V.P. of Strategic Management Group, Philadelphia, "Interviewing senior managers and probing the business issues are skills that are very important to the process. The ability to ask the right questions and to know what to do with the answers is the difference between toys like Nintendo games and tools for sophisticated business planning and education."

☐ *Experience.* The unexpected is certain to occur—business changes, staff changes, delays, getting wrong information, etc. Warns Brodo, "If the vendor doesn't have the experience to plan for the unexpected and be flexible, the project will be late, of poor quality, and won't achieve the desired results."

☐ *Content expertise.* The supplier should be very familiar with the subject matter for the simulation. "If not," says Brodo, "there will be mistakes that are apparent and, worse, not apparent until a participant challenges a result."

☐ *Instructional design.* Obviously, simulations are intended to teach participants to do something. Says Brodo, "If you don't craft the simulation around achieving learning results, then you are simply playing a game." So the instructional design must blend content and learning into the simulation product.

☐ *Technology.* You must use the technology that best produces the desired learning results.

☐ *Team effort.* Constructing a simulation is a team enterprise including the supplier and the client. The client must work closely with the vendor and expect to devote adequate time to the project.

SUMMARY GUIDES TO MANAGE GAMES AND SIMULATIONS

Trainer Kuon C. Hunt provides the following pointers when using games and simulations [25]:

1. *On quantity:* Use fewer and shorter games. Too much of a good thing is less effective.

2. *On start-up:* Get into your activity quickly. Don't over-introduce it. Allow people to be surprised by what they learn. Tell them as little as possible about your objectives or how they will be achieved.

3. *On logistics:* Keep them simple and handle them impeccably, well in advance.

4. *On the instructions:* Don't count on people to read them. Provide a backup activity to ensure that critical information is assimilated.

5. *On learning goals:* Use games and simulations for *affective* (emotional) emphasis and to create experiential "hooks" on which to hang *cognitive* material. Include opportunities for more subtle, gentle learning—as well as the big "aha!"

6. *On participant pace:* Accept that people must start where they are and move only as far as they can go.

7. *On participant comfort:* Be willing to have participants feel uncomfortable at points during the activity. Anticipate that participants may look to factors inside or outside the activity (like the facilitator) to blame for their discomfort. Graciously encourage them to take responsibility for their own learning experience.

8. *On the debriefing:* Be open and provocative. Elicit responses; do not instruct.

   ☐ Respect all participants' points of view, even if some voice perspectives precisely counter to what they were supposed to learn. If your activity was effective, others will naturally rise to articulate your intended objectives in response. Relax, it works.

   ☐ Allow participants to influence the direction of the debriefing. They don't have to get every point embedded in your activity.

   ☐ Be adequately directive in your debriefing to ensure that your client's objectives are met.

9. *On client briefing:* Clarify the differences between simulations/games and other training/learning modes with new clients beforehand. This precludes their attempting to "fix" things, should they walk in during an uncomfortable segment of a powerful activity.

KEY POINTS

1. Structured experiences, in the form of games, simulations, simulation-games, exercises, and puzzles, are ways for participants to learn experientially; that is, they learn from what they do rather than what they are told, observe, or read.

2. All of these training devices are marked by flexibility and may be used at various stages in a course or program.

3. Games, simulations, and exercises may be designed by the trainer. This may be accomplished by studying such activities developed by others and paying attention to certain design principles.

4. Although games, simulations, and exercises have specific learning goals, it is not always practicable to share such information with the participants at the start. The reason for this is that the learning comes only from experiencing the activity; stating the goal in specific terms may unnecessarily "spill the beans."

5. Since a key characteristic of a game is competition, an exercise may often be converted into a game by introducing a competitive element into it.

6. Games provide learning by doing, realism, motivation, peer learning, intense learning in short time frames, a participant rather than a trainer-centered learning experience, fun, and novelty.

7. Design of a game requires general familiarity with games as training tools, setting specific learning objectives, selecting a game format, developing written instructions for participants and observers, deciding upon time frames, developing a scoring system, and planning for a debriefing or processing session at game's end.

8. Simulations, which can provide experiences resembling real life, should be designed in conjunction with operating officials. This ensures that the fullest possible realism will be cranked into them.

REFERENCES

1. Pfeiffer, J. W., and Jones, J. E., *A Handbook of Structured Experiences for Human Relations Training*, Vol. 1, University Associates Inc., San Diego, (1969), p. 52.

2. At the monthly meeting of the American Society for Performance Improvement, Potomac Washington, D.C. Chapter (October 14), 1981.

3. Broadwell, Laura, "Business Games: They're More Than Child's Play," *Successful Meetings* (June 1987), pp. 36–39.

4. Gardner, Bette, "This Is No Time to Play Games . . . or Is It?" *Catalink*, The Resources Connection, North Towanda, New York (Fall 1997), p. 4.

5. Gunsch, Dawn, "Games Augment Diversity Training," *Personnel Journal* (June 1993), pp. 78–83.

6. Sugar, Stephen, "Training's the Name of the Game," *Training and Development Journal* (December 1987), pp. 67–73.

7. Krell, Eric, "Learning to Love the P & L," *Training* (September 1999), p. 70.

8. Hutson, H., and Dormant, D., "The Name of the Game Is Frame, *Training/HRD* (April 1981), pp. 54–56.

9. Stolovich, H. D., "Frame Games," *National Society for Performance Improvement (NSPI) Journal* (December 1978), pp. 8–10.

10. Lierman, Bruce, "How to Develop a Training Simulation," *Training and Development* (February 1994), pp. 50–52.

11. Jeffrey, Nancy, "Preparing for the Worst: Firms Set up Plans to Help Deal with Corporate Crises," *Wall Street Journal* (December 7, 1987).

12. Hall, Charles, "Training with Fire," *The Washington Post* (May 21, 1987).

13. Glod, Maria, "Spending a Saturday Morning Being Poor," *The Washington Post* (October 15, 2000), p. A6.

14. "In Simulations, Reality Is Optional," in "Training Today," *Training* (July 1999), pp. 18–19.

15. Doser, Mike, "Reality and 'Risk' Enter Team-Building Programs," *Meeting News* (March 19, 2001), pp. 57–58.

16. Stiteler, Rowland, "Disney Institute to Take Its Learning Programs Off Site," *MeetingNews* (March 19, 2001), pp. 57–58.

17. "Easing the Fear of Self-Directed Teams," in "Training Today," *Training* (August 1993), pp. 14, 55–56.

18. Cole, James M., "Situation Simulations," *Performance in Practice*, Newsletter of the American Society for Training and Development (ASTD) (Fall 1999), pp. 12–13.

19. Lierman, Bruce, *op. cit.,* pp. 50–52.

20. Slack, Kim, "Training for the Real Thing," *Training and Development* (May 1993), pp. 79–89.

21. Schachter, H. L., "Role Plays: 10 Rules for Development," *Training and Development Journal* (February 1982), pp. 9–10

22. Loewendick, Beth A., "Laying Your Crisis on the Table," in "In Practice," *Training and Development* (November 1993), pp. 15–17.

23. Shirts, R. Gary, "10 Secrets of Successful Simulations," *Training* (October 1992), pp. 79–83.

24. Salopek, Jennifer J., "Work Station Meets Play Station," *Training and Development* (August 1998), pp. 33–34.

25. Hunt, Kuon C., "How to Use Games and Simulations," *News and Notes*, newsletter of the National Society for Performance and Instruction, Washington, D.C. (October 1992), p. 2.

RECOMMENDED READING

Games

Doyle, Eva C., "Games 101," *Training and Development* February 2001, pp. 16–17.

To energize participants when things seem to lag, use familiar games, e.g., Tic Tac Toe, Bingo, Jeopardy. The article tells how to implement these games.

Ellington, Henry, Addinall, Eric, and Percival, Fred, *A Handbook of Game Design*, Nichols Publishing Company, New York, 1982.

This is a practical introduction to designing games, including manual, cardboard, and computer games.

Ellington, Henry, Addinall, Eric, and Percival, Fred, *Case Studies in Game Design*, Nichols Publishing Company, New York, 1983.

This is a companion volume to the preceding *A Handbook of Game Design*. In 12 case studies, it examines in depth the detailed design of the many types of games.

Gunsch, Dawn, "Games Augment Diversity Training," *Personnel Journal*, June 1993, pp. 78–83.

Presents extensive background data on the use of board games in diversity training. Cites specific games available from commercial suppliers for this purpose. The games serve as lively teaching tools to raise awareness and under standing of many diversity issues among workers.

Hequet, Marc, "Games That Teach," *Training*, July 1995, pp. 53–58.

The author points out that games and simulations, which are finding more use in the workplace, can help people learn better and faster. Cites certain problems in and limitation of games/simulations.

Hitchcock, Darcy B., "Building Instructional Games," *Training*, March 1988, pp. 33–39.

The author presents a step-by-step process to aid in developing your games.

Olivas, Louis, and Newstrom, John W., "Learning Through the Use of Simulation Games," *Training and Development Journal*, September 1981, pp. 64–66.

The article presents a rationale for games, guidelines for their use, and an explanation of how learning is facilitated by their use.

Perry, Scott B., "The Name of the Game Is Simulation," *Training and Development Journal,* February 1971, pp. 28–32.

This discusses why games and simulations should be used, distinguishes between those that aid application of prior learning and those that aid discovery of one's own behavior and that of others, and describes several games and how participants learn from them.

Rausch, Erwin, "30,000 Ways to Invent Your Own Group Games," *Successful Meetings,* March 1976, pp. 50–51, 178–179.

By using the author's matrix, literally thousands of different types of games may be constructed. (Note: The article does not advise how to construct a game, but indicates what one's choices are.)

Stolovich, Harold D., "Technology of Simulation Gaming for Education and Training," *National Society for Performance Improvement Journal,* December 1981, pp. 24–28.

This is an overview, providing definitions, uses, and examples.

Stolovitch, Harold D., and Vanasse, Sylvia, "FlexGames: Flexible Game Formats for Improving Learning and Performance," *Performance Improvement*, February 1998, pp. 40–45.

The authors present a detailed explanation of the FlexGame and point up the differences among Flex-Games, FlexSims and Frame Games.

Thiagarajan, Sivasailam, "Take Five for Better Brainstorming," *Training and Development Journal,* February 1991, pages 37–42.

Describes in detail a flexible, practical "frame game." Complete instructions are provided to lead your own game of "Take Five" and to customize the activity to your group and objectives.

"Game-Playing to Help Managers Communicate," *Business Week,* April 9, 1979, pp. 76–78.

The article describes the use of games in the business world.

Simulations

Barbian, Jeff, "Get Simulated," *Training,* February 2001, pp. 66–70.

Provides an update on the state of simulations and games, including computer-based simulations. The author quotes a professor as follows: "Board games don't expand whereas a computer-based game will expand, react and change to market conditions. The payoff is simultaneous, concrete feedback."

Mallory, W. J., "Simulation for Task Practice in Technical Training," *Training and Development Journal*, September 1981, pp. 13–20.

Although we ordinarily think of games as part of management or other "higher-level" training, they can also be used at the skilled trades level.

Salopek, Jennifer J., "Work Station Meets Play Station,' *Training*, August 1998, pp. 26–35.

A comprehensive update on the realm of simulation. Discusses elements of simulation, how to maximize return on investment, use of PC/CD-ROM–based simulations, guidelines for implementation, choosing a vendor, and trainer role.

Slack, Kim, "Training for the Real Thing," *Training and Development*, May 1993, pp. 79–89.

Discusses various types of simulations with particular emphasis on organizational simulations. Provides tips and resources for getting started and describes facilitation skills needed to conduct a simulation.

Waddell, Geneva, "Simulation: Balancing the Pros and Cons," *Training and Development Journal*, January 1982, pp. 80–83.

This cites key concepts and the advantages and limitations of simulations.

Whitcomb, Chris, "Scenario-Based Training at the FBI," *Training and Development,* June 1999, pp. 42–53.

A detailed account of the revamping of the FBI's training program for new agents into a single, comprehensive scenario (14 weeks) so that when they arrive for their first assignment they will have a clear understanding of how to conduct a full investigation from start to finish. In effect, the new session offers training as an integrated simulation of the agent's actual job,

Games and Simulations

Chartier, Myron R., "Facilitating Simulation Games," in Jones, John E., and Pfeiffer, J. William, editors, *The 1981 Annual Handbook for Group Facilitators,* University Associates, Inc., San Diego, 1981, pp. 247–257.

This is a comprehensive presentation of simulation games, covering games as simulated social systems, designing games, and facilitating games.

Gray, Lynton, and Waitt, Ian, *Perspectives on Academic Gaming and Simulation 7—Simulation in Management and Business Education,* Nichols Publishing Company, New York, 1982.

The book contains proceedings of the 1981 Conference of the Society for Academic Gaming and Simulation in Education and Training, covering experience-based and theoretical material.

Sugar, Stephen E., "The Teaching Game—Curing the Night Student Blahs," *Training News,* May 1984, pp. 15–16.

The author advocates the use of games to provoke student interest. The article covers the essential features of a simulation game (flexibility, adaptability, cost, playability, proper instructions), how to use it (introduction, briefing, actual playing, debriefing) and costs and payoffs.

Sussman, Vic, "What's in a Game? Often Not Enough," *The Washington Post Magazine,* November 8, 1987, pp. 39–41.

Discusses the role of the computer in games and simulations, particularly its ability to provide interaction and thus "intellectually stimulating and substantial experience." Also states that the interaction between people is more important than the game per se.

"A Shopping Guide to Training Games and Simulations," *Training/HRD,* February 1982, p. 31.

The article lists the major categories (25) in which games may be found commercially (for example, time management, values clarification, productivity improvement) and the suppliers (some 55) of them.

Using Exercises

7

*I never teach my pupils; I only attempt to provide the
conditions in which they can learn.*

—Albert Einstein (1879–1955),
German/U.S. physicist

IN the prior chapter we were introduced to two forms of experiential learning: games and simulations. In this chapter we will treat the exercise as another form of experiential learning.

Exercises are easier to describe than they are to define. This is so because they come in such a great variety of shapes and sizes. Exercises may be

- ☐ Simple or multifaceted
- ☐ Short or long in duration, ranging from a few minutes to one or more hours, or even all day
- ☐ Job-related or non–job-related
- ☐ Personal-learning based or with a more general learning outcome
- ☐ Physically active (for example, the trust walk or trust fall) or fairly passive (for example, a paper and pencil activity plus discussion)
- ☐ Accomplished with or without observers
- ☐ Trainer guided, totally group conducted, or some mix of the two
- ☐ Individual participant or group oriented
- ☐ Accomplished in small groups, in the total group, or on an intergroup basis
- ☐ Restricted to group member input or including inputs of participants' bosses
- ☐ Instrument or non–instrument oriented
- ☐ "Homemade" or publisher supplied

Because of the great diversity in formats and purposes, some trainers prefer to use more general terminology in describing exercises: namely, "experiential learning," "structured experiences," or simply "activities" or "application activities." In any case, an exercise may be distinguished by these characteristics:

- ☐ Direction toward specific learning goals.
- ☐ Structure, that is, guidelines/instructions as to procedures, individual/group roles, time limits.
- ☐ High participant involvement.
- ☐ Generation of data for participant analysis.
- ☐ Debriefing: Processing or analysis of data by participants/observers/trainers to make the experience meaningful. The learning from the exercise may be general, consisting of the acquisition of principles and concepts; it may be personal, resulting in the acquisition of new skills, attitudes, and insights; or it may be *both*.

Note: If an activity involves competition between individuals or groups, it becomes a game rather than an exercise.

SOURCES OF EXERCISES

Exercises may be obtained from publishers; from colleagues; from participation in training programs, professional conferences and institutes, and occasionally in university courses; and from professional training/ personnel journals. However, professional trainers would agree that the best trainers are those who can create their own exercises. This is an essential trainer skill, since quite often an outside source may not be able to meet your need for an exercise. Of course, not all exercises need be as "profound" as, say, Jay Hall's NASA Exercise ("Lost on the Moon"). The important thing is that they meet participant needs, have predictable outcomes (meet learning goals), and have high learner involvement.

In the pages that follow, a number of easy-to-use exercises are given. These models may be administered "as is" or adapted to varying degrees to meet the needs of your participant group better. By studying them carefully, you should gain a good feel for ways to put your groups into action productively.

EXERCISES THAT YOU CAN CONSTRUCT YOURSELF

Laundry Lists

Have participants develop individually, in pairs, or in small groups, a "laundry list" on a given subject; for example, principles of good listening, how to give feedback, principles/techniques of delegation, customer objections we encounter, or hazards in our unit. Then post data and discuss.

Checklists

Have participants develop a checklist for back-home use—for example, procedures to develop a follow-up call on a prospect who responded to some advertising; how to orient a new worker; how to check a work area for unsafe situations; how to plan an effective meeting; how to investigate an accident.

Sharing a Personal Experience

Have participants describe and share a personal experience concerning, for example, a boss who showed interest in one and encouraged growth, delegation to a secretary to make a boss-secretary team, enriching a routine job, or saving time at a meeting.

Brainstorming and Solution Selection

Have participants brainstorm the solution to a problem and then select the top three solutions via a simple voting procedure, such as a show of hands.

Feedbacking

Design activities which provide for giving and/or receiving feedback based on data developed from instruments. Use dyads or triads for sharing data. For example, in an experiential training program participants may rate the effectiveness of their own listening skill and that of their colleagues on a 10-point scale and then share these ratings.

For a more formal and complete rating scale–type instrument on listening, see Appendix 33, "My Skill as a Listener—A Self-Test." This quiz may be used to give and receive feedback, as described above.

Giving Constructive Feedback via "When-I-Because" Technique

Provide practice in giving others feedback that entails describing the offending behavior and then expressing how one feels about it, as opposed to blaming, yelling, scolding, responding with anger, name calling, or putting others down. The three-step technique is as follows [1]:

Component One: "When . . ."—Describe the irksome behavior in a purely descriptive, non-judgmental way. *Example:* "When you turn in your report two or three days after the established deadline . . ."

Component Two: "I feel . . ."—Describe your feeling about the unwanted, possibly disruptive behavior. *Example:* "I feel frustrated . . ."

Component Three: "Because . . ."—*Example:* "Because we cannot consolidate our report for submission to the national office. The headquarters people depend on prompt data from all the regional offices, including ours, so that they can . . ."

Use these procedures for the following exercise:

1. Explain the "When-I-Because" approach to giving feedback.
2. Assign various interpersonal problem situations to pairs for application of the three-step technique. Or, better still, ask participants to suggest the topics. (Typical situation where the technique might be used advantageously: A staffer confronts his boss who teases him at staff meetings. A supervisor provides feedback to a subordinate about the impact of his/her frequent tardiness in reporting to work. A manager challenges a peer who is not cooperating in respect to the provision of data needed for the office's annual budget.)
3. Secure reports from the pairs.
4. Discuss the applicability and values of the technique.

Note: This technique is also referred to as the "I Message" technique, wherein one delivers the message and highlights how one feels about the unwanted behavior. It is also possible to begin the message with "I," as in "I feel embarrassed when you tease me at staff meetings because everyone then laughs at me."

Sharing a Contract

Participants may be asked to develop and then share a personal contract concerning the performance of a new behavior, for example, greater delegation to staff. A form may be designed for this purpose: the far left vertical column should list one's responsibilities; several other columns list staff members' names, which are to be checked off wherever delegation is deemed possible; and a final column (far right side of sheet) should have room for comments such as whether the delegation can proceed fully or whether some training may be required. (See Appendix 23.)

Developing a "Behavior Mod" Plan

After indoctrinating participants in behavior modification principles and procedures, have them develop a behavior modification plan to control absenteeism, to reduce accidents, to increase production, to reduce customer complaints, etc.

Group Instrument Design

Have participants design an instrument, such as a quiz on leadership, communication, or coaching, complete the instrument individually, and discuss their answers in small groups.

Situational Problem Solving

Provide participants with concepts pertaining to situational problem solving, and then give them one or more problems to resolve using that approach. (Situational problem solving refers to bringing about a change in behavior by working on or changing the situation, as opposed to working on the employee via lectures, counseling, discipline, threats, training, or transfer. An everyday example: We influence driver behavior by placing a white line down the middle of the road, as opposed to using signs which say "Keep to the right." Similarly, we can reduce complaints about slow elevator service by placing large mirrors on the wall near the elevator, or we can reduce complaints about waiting in line by having two parallel lines so that people can talk to one another while they wait. The latter approach—encouraging conversation—can also be used to reduce boredom in routine assembly-type jobs.) Some possible problems for resolution: floors are messy (use more wastebaskets in the area); theft of materials at night from outdoor storage area (use lights); people are tripping over a pipe protruding above ground (cover it with a wooden ramp).

Dynamic Use of Film/Video

Use films/videos dynamically via pre-film, stop-film, and post-film assignments; also use other devices such as question lists, nonverbal or silent (no sound) viewing, and predictions.

Using a Model

Develop an activity around a model; for example, after having explained a particular model, have participants develop data to support it. Or have small groups discuss the model: Is it valid in all respects? What are its limitations or weaknesses? Would you amend it in any way? Does it have relevance to your work situation?

Group Self-Evaluation

Provide opportunities for the group to assess its own functioning. Give them criteria to do this or let them develop their own. You can provide guides, such as task and maintenance roles used as observation/check sheets, or a sociometric diagram plotted by an observer to note who speaks to whom and the frequency of contributions by participants.

Dealing with Risk

1. Use *ad hoc* exercises such as a risk analysis if there is reluctance to "buy" a concept because of its perceived risk. Participants in small groups use a T-column to identify risks and to list solutions—ways of overcoming the risks.
2. Another way to deal with risk or fear of dire consequences is to have participants use mental imagery or fantasy to build positive images of accomplishment—for example, making that tough sale, or asking the boss for a raise and succeeding at it.

For details on this Chapter 2 exercise, see "Risk Analysis," pages 29–30.

Using Fantasy

Don't hesitate to use fantasy to solve other problems, too: "What if we were to . . ." (See Chapter 4.)

3-C Analysis

Have participants use a 3-C Analysis Chart to solve problems they have identified, as shown in Figure 7-1.

Resolving Problems

Concern (Problem Difficulty)	Cause (Source)	Cure (Solution)

Figure 7-1. Example of a 3-C Analysis Chart.

Group Construction

Provide activities involving the physical construction of an object such as a bridge or tower, using construction paper, newspaper, magazines, blocks, etc.

Use observers to study and report back on group planning, interaction, creativity, communication, participation, decision making, and leadership.

Tapping Group Creativity

Provide activities that involve group creation of greeting card verses, pithy management sayings, "Confucius Says" (He who delegate in depth/Will surely have little to regret), limericks, etc. Process the work as in the group construction exercise.

Best-Worst Assignment

Assign a "best-worst" task; for example, the attributes of the best/worst boss I ever had; the characteristics of the best/worst communicator; the qualities of the best/worst salesperson; the nature of the best/worst delegator.

Resolving a Perplexing Situation

Present a perplexing situation, for example, sexual harassment on the job, denial of a promotion, or multiple (and ambiguous) responsibilities for an accident. Pose these questions to small groups: How would you handle this situation? How would your boss handle it? How could this problem have been prevented from occurring?

Stress Management—"Easy as 1, 2, 3"

In a stress management program or session, introduce participants to an easy-to-implement and easy-to-remember stress management procedure involving these three logical steps, "easy as 1, 2, 3":

In reacting to a stressful situation, ask yourself:

1. What can I *control?* If nothing, ask:
2. What can I *predict* will occur to ease matters? If nothing helpful comes to mind, ask:
3. What can I *do* based on my prior handling of stressful situations? (Some answers: take a long walk; hook up with people who can provide support and satisfaction, such as family, significant others, co-workers, friends; engage in meditation and relaxing exercises.)

Note: All three steps could be processed (discussed) in dyads or triads, with each person presenting his/her three steps and the other person(s) serving as "consultants."

Designing a Plan

Have participants in small groups design a model performance appraisal plan, a fool-proof promotion posting plan, a policy on sexual harassment, etc.

Preparing Concrete Goals

Present the group with vague, overgeneralized goals or objectives. Request them to convert these statements into specific targets, preferably quantitative ones so that they are measurable.

Developing Terminal Objectives

Present the group with general statements concerning training to be accomplished. Have them convert these fuzzy statements to behavioral objectives (specific end results or terminal behaviors).

Ego Bombardment

Have group members form a circle, standing up. On a rotational basis, have group members give each other positive feedback. A variation is to form two lines, so that each person has a partner. Have participants in Line A give those in Line B positive feedback on dress, appearance, performance in this class, etc., for three minutes. Those in Line B only listen and do not respond. Then process the action by discussing such issues as: Is it easy or hard to give praise? How does it feel to receive praise? Do we tend to discount praise?

Value System Origins

To demonstrate the importance (possible influence) of one's family on one's value system, provide the group with one or more of these activities:

1. Have group members recall and report on family sayings, for example, "If you always do the right thing, you won't have to worry about explaining why you did it." "What will the neighbors think?" "It's important to save for a rainy day."
2. Have group members report on "shoulds" which were emphasized at home, for example, "You should always be on time for work." "You should

get good grades in school." "You should dress so you make a nice impression." "You should lock the door at night." "You should introduce your date to the family."

3. Have participants develop a "values list" which represents family influences, for example, party affiliation, role of government, sexual attitudes, charity, school attitudes, work attitudes.

Each activity may be conducted in sequence. An alternate design is to assign all three tasks to three separate small groups and secure reports from each for total group discussion. A worksheet as in Figure 7-2 may be prepared, incorporating these ideas.

Family Influences

Family Sayings	Family "Shoulds"	Family "Should Nots"	Family Values

Figure 7-2. Example of a worksheet to help participants recall and record family influences and values.

Sharing "Peak Experiences"

In a session devoted to Maslow and his "Hierarchy of Needs," have participants share "peak experiences." (This could be a great personal or professional achievement, a marriage, the birth of a child, an athletic accomplishment, a super vacation or trip.) Have participants describe how they felt at the time.

Strength Billboard

Have each person draw a T-column as follows and provide the data as requested:

Strengths

As a Man/Woman	As a Manager (or Teacher, Engineer, Salesperson)

Then have participants find partners and present and discuss their billboards.

Note: The "billboard" display idea can also be used to share values as an icebreaker, to share objectives or goals in an experiential course, or to present and share a personal or job problem in a graphic or illustrative way.

Self-Concept Reality Check

In this experiential exercise, which might be used in assertiveness training, you encourage your participants to focus on themselves (self-concept) and to secure feedback from others to check its "validity." Procedures:

1. Ask your participants to draw a large circle on a flipchart sheet.
2. Have them enter into the circle the characteristics or traits, positive or less than positive, that they know or believe about themselves.
3. Working in triads, each person gets feedback about those traits/characteristics. Are they valid? Invalid?
4. The feedback givers should provide data about what may have been left out. *Note:* In a non-assertive person, strong, important qualities may well be omitted, for example, verbal skills, alertness, listening ability, or attractive smile. By pointing out these added characteristics, feedback givers can strengthen the self-concept of the recipient.

Enriching a Job

Ask participants (supervisors or managers) to select a subordinate's job, preferably a routine one, and then come up with several ways it could be enriched (not just enlarged). Process the data in dyads. You may want to provide a worksheet with a T-column for this activity, including a column for subordinates' names and a column for enrichment suggestions.

Tips from the Expert

Ask participants to assume the role of expert and list on a worksheet their tips on a particular subject, such as how to deal with the angry customer, how to deal with an upset employee, or how to provide motivation to people in dead-end jobs. Entitle the worksheet "My Tips on _____ Are." The sheet may be completed on a pre-work or in-class basis. The ideas may be collected and fed back to the other participants by posting them on flipcharts and discussing them or by producing a member-prepared handout.

Achieving Consensus

1. To give small groups practice in achieving consensus, give them five or ten problems of an interpersonal sort. Advise them that they must agree on the answer or solution to the problems. Observers may be used to analyze how the groups make their decisions or what hinders the making of such decisions. Sample problems:

   ☐ A colleague engages in hard-hitting humor (putdowns) at other people's expense, including yours.

   ☐ A very able computer specialist who reports to you is frequently late to work.

   ☐ Your boss's staff meetings are boring, drawn out, and generally nonproductive.

   ☐ Petty stealing has reached a noticeable point in the office—staplers, scissors, and cellophane tape are disappearing, and several employees have reported losses of coins and postage stamps from their desks.

   Note: The problems may be presented on an open-ended, answer-free basis, or you may offer several solutions (in writing) from which the participants choose one. For example, the person who overdoes the "putdown bit" may be dealt with in these ways:

   ☐ Ignore the comments; just live with them. Look at it as *her* problem.

   ☐ Confront her about her behavior by telling the putdown artist how the putdowns make you feel. ("When you talk to me in this way, I feel less good about myself.")

   ☐ Respond in kind; "fight fire with fire," which should cause her to cool it.

   ☐ Combine with other colleagues to deal with the putdown giver on a team basis.

   ☐ Ask your boss for help on this problem.

   ☐ Assume an "educator" role. Suggest to the person who engages in putdowns to consider using a new and more effective behavior. Thus, she should ask herself this question: How many times today have I made those with whom I have interacted feel better about themselves? By consistently posing this question to oneself, one will look for ways to be supportive, considerate, encouraging, and praise-giving rather than cutting.

2. Another way to give small groups practice in achieving consensus is to give them a list of ten statements on a given subject. Give them about five minutes to indicate individually whether they agree or disagree with the statements. They then meet in small groups for about 15 minutes to seek agreement or consensus.

Finding Problems and Solutions

Provide participants with a worksheet such as in Figure 7-3, and have them add to it. The example worksheet lists two common problems in performance review, but any problem area could be used. Participants should add three more problems and then meet in small groups to agree on solutions to all the problems identified.

Analysis

Have participants select a problem they are currently facing and enumerate in force-field-analysis fashion (see Chapter 10) the favorable and unfavorable forces that exist in the situation. A T-column can help the diagnosis, and the data can be processed in dyads or triads.

Identifying Motivators

To set the scene for a presentation on motivation, ask participants to approach motivation from a retrospective, current, and prospective viewpoint. A tricolumn as shown may be given to participants for them to complete.

My Motivators

As a Teenager	Today	At Retirement

Another way of focusing attention on motivators is to encourage reflection on them throughout one's career or to have participants think about them from the three different standpoints shown in the following tricolumn.

My Career Motivators

Early Period	Mid-Career	Late Career

Problems in Performance Appraisal

Problem	Solution
1. Manager tries to avoid conducting annual performance review sessions.	1. Appropriate modeling by his/her supervisor, i.e., the manager's boss conducts an in-depth appraisal. 2. The reward system should be changed to recognize the importance of the annual performance review system. 3. Institute an MBO system. 4. Training.
2. Manager conducts an annual review session that deals with traits rather than accomplishments.	1. Change the system, e.g., introduce an MBO system. 2. Training.

Figure 7-3. Example of a worksheet that focuses on problems and solutions.

Another way of differentiating motivators is to encourage reflection from the standpoints of my boss, my subordinates, and myself. Provide a worksheet with a tricolumn, as in the preceding examples. The data can be shared in small groups. Learnings from the exercise should be reported to the full group.

Tapping the Motivation of Others

Another motivational exercise is to have participants list the names of their employees in one column of a tricolumn, and the employees' principal motivators in the next column. After participants have discussed their data in small groups, have them complete the third column—"How to Tap the Motivation." Share Column 3 results in the same small group, then hold a general discussion about what was learned in this exercise.

Using an Opener

As an opener to reduce anxieties and to get participants into the swing of things, have participants form a double line with everyone standing and facing another person. In the paired situation, have them discuss for ten minutes questions such as: "Why am I here? How can I best help others in this program? How can others best help me?" A variation is to have the participants present data about their partner to the total group based on the preceding questions.

Converting Negatives to Positives

As a fun-type, small group activity, have participants come up with as many negative approaches as they can to such problem areas as giving feedback, orienting a new worker, developing employees, and conducting an annual performance review. Then in the discussion, convert the negatives to positives.

Evaluation Activities

In the evaluation phase of the course, use novel approaches such as the fishbowl, the human continuum, and the whip. (See Chapter 19.)

Working with Principles

Have participants in small groups come up with ten principles concerning a given topic, and then have them cite an example to illustrate each principle. Figure 7-4 gives an example list on the topic of conflict. The small groups' ideas should be written on flipcharts, posted, compared, and discussed.

Conflict—Some Principles

Principle	Example
1. Conflict provides a test of power.	1. A strike.
2. When a group is subject to conflict with an external force or source, cohesion is likely to increase.	1. Attack by another nation. 2. A disaster, either natural or man-made.
3.	
4.	

Figure 7-4. Example of a T-column that elicits principles and examples of those principles.

Working with Theory X and Y

Participants can work through Theory X and Y concepts via activities such as the following:

1. To determine leadership styles, have participants complete and process in small groups a forced choice instrument on Theory X and Y. Appendix 24 presents such an instrument.

2. Present a problem for discussion, such as the following: One of your subordinates expects guidance all along the way on a given project, is reluctant to make decisions on her own, and seems content with low-risk or even no-risk approaches. You decide to use Theory Y principles to meet this problem head-on. How would you do this? What specific *actions* would you take?

3. *Have small groups discuss the following question:* Which leadership styles—Theory X or Theory Y—would you apply in these situations:

   ☐ A city police force
   ☐ A correctional institution
   ☐ An R & D laboratory
   ☐ A steel mill
   ☐ A national chain of fast-food restaurants
   ☐ Harvard University
   ☐ A major state university system

Career Counseling

Have participants, in small groups, come up with solutions to these typical career counseling situations:

☐ The young and able engineer who has a great future except for his tendency to irritate those with whom he interacts.

☐ A very capable senior professional has reached a plateau career-wise, and should be "kept alive" via imaginative motivation techniques.

☐ A middle-aged manager has grown roots in the community and has turned down two cross-country promotions.

☐ Your secretary, aged 29, has been talking about getting out of the "dead end" job in which secretaries often find themselves. Your practice of "raises and roses" no longer seems to be working. There is no evidence of any serious self-development activities on your secretary's part.

Note:

1. In addition to the small group work, role plays may be used to "reality test" proposed solutions.

2. The wrap-up discussion should include an identification of career divergencies and career commonalities revealed by the several situations.

Planning for Goal Accomplishment

Have participants develop two allied lists: one for goals, the other for specific action plans or steps for goal accomplishment.

The Boss as a Communicator

Provide participants with several boss-subordinate communication (or other type) problems and have them exchange solutions in trios or quartets. Some typical problems follow:

☐ Your boss communicates in three ways: face-to-face; via notes and memos (or notes on your memos); through someone else.

☐ You find that the face-to-face contacts are relatively pleasant. The memos are often negative, even nasty, sort of "hit and run." The communication with others at times relates to you and may be negative in character. In effect, he talks behind your back.

Some questions to answer are: What is going on? Is it a problem? Do you do anything about it? if so, what action(s) do you take?

☐ Your boss frequently closes the door of his office, which bothers some employees. Why should it bother them? Should you take any action about this?

☐ Your boss's staff meetings are not very productive. No one really "levels" on important subjects.

☐ At times you receive instructions, policy statements, etc., from your boss with which you do not agree. You would like to be loyal and support your boss by stating to your subordinates that you agree with these policies. On the other hand, you hate to be dishonest with your staff, and besides, they will probably know you're being less than truthful when you say you support poor policies.

Studying Nonverbal Behavior

To study nonverbal behavior in a group at work, use the following procedures:

Select a problem of enough complexity and controversy for a group to tackle. This may be an in-house issue or a social issue, such as prayer in the public schools, abortion, or gun control. Or a management problem may be used, with roles assigned to the discussion group (in writing). The roles should be designed to engender a fair degree of conflict.

Select a discussion group of about eight participants. The balance of the group is to function as observers. Assign an observer to a designated discussant.

While the discussion group is thinking about the assigned topic or problem, or reading its instructions as to role, instruct the role players to observe nonverbal behavior exhibited by the discussants. Give them a list of such behaviors as eye contact or the reverse, winks, smiles, scowls, hair twirling, nail biting, yawning, chair moving, shrugs, tenseness, hand use, leaning forward or the reverse, fidgeting, head nods, head shakes, ear pulling or scratching, and doodling.

Hold the discussion for 20–30 minutes, then secure reports from observers. Hold a general discussion of the significance of nonverbal behavior in the communication process.

Success Analysis

One way to augment participant understanding, insight, skill, etc., is to have participants analyze experiences which have been marked by success (meaning a real "payoff" occurred) and something less than success (note that we avoid the negative term "failure"). The topic may relate to introducing a change, enriching a job, motivating, delegating, selling, listening, communicating, or confronting a peer on an undesirable behavior.

Break the total group into two or more small groups. Give the first subgroup's members a worksheet entitled "Describing a Less-Than-Successful Experience" (see Figure 7-5). Give the other subgroup a similar work sheet entitled "Describing a Successful Experience," with the column headings changed accordingly. Have participants complete the worksheets on an individual basis and then share their experiences described in the worksheet in small groups.

Describing a Less-Than-Successful Experience

Incident Experience	Factors Which Made for Non-Success
	1. 2. 3. 4. 5. 6.

Figure 7-5. Example of a worksheet used in the Success Analysis Exercise.

Secure reports from the small groups and post on flip-charts factors contributing to successful and unsuccessful experiences. Ask the group at large to note differences and commonalities between the positive and negative lists.

Constructing an Attitude Survey Form

Have the group construct an attitude or "climate" questionnaire for possible use in their departments.

Explain to participants the purpose of the climate survey, then pass out sample questionnaire items which allow for either a "Yes–No–Not Sure" response or for ratings on, say, a 7-point scale.

Once the format is understood and agreed upon, divide the item construction task among the several small groups; for example, one group might develop survey items on working conditions, another on adequacy of communication, another on team feeling, another on motivation/job interest, etc.

Have participants read aloud completed survey items for review by the total group. This checks for adequate coverage of the topic, clarity of survey items, and possible overlappings or duplications.

Coping with "Sticky" Situations

Divide the total group into small groups, each of which addresses itself to and reports back on how a supervisor should cope with such sticky situations as

- ☐ Delegating deeply but not losing control of the situation.
- ☐ Intervening when a delegation is not working out, yet not actually nullifying the delegation.
- ☐ How to draw the line between desired intimacy with subordinates and undesired fraternization.
- ☐ Deciding when a group decision is and is not proper.
- ☐ Deciding when to share and when to withhold information from subordinates.
- ☐ Deciding how to communicate to subordinates a decision of one's boss with which one does not agree.

Criteria Development

1. Give the group a problem or organizational concern such as:

   - ☐ Is communication in our organization good or bad?
   - ☐ Is our work team effective?
   - ☐ Is our office work force productive?

2. Ask the group to develop criteria as to what to look for in assessing the problem area. For example, if we are trying to determine whether our work team is effective, we would look at the nature of our goals, the communication process, the decision making process, member satisfaction, leadership, etc.

Note: Once we know which areas to investigate, then the group might go further and actually develop specific standards for analysis. For example, if we are studying communication in the team, we might examine how open people are, how effective staff meetings are, how willing people are to share information. But as far as this activity is concerned, we are only asking the group to work on Step 2, not any added steps.

How People Make Meaning

Recent thinking (neurolinguistics) about communication, particularly about how we transmit and receive messages, indicates that we may be classified as one of the following types of communicators:

- ☐ Kinesthetic (touch)
- ☐ Visualizing
- ☐ Auditory

That is to say, we tend to *use* to a greater degree—and *receive* better—words which fall into one of the above three groupings. An exercise on this concept may take this format: Explain the preceding three-style communications concept to participants. Then ask them to offer words or phrases which fall into each category. Anticipate responses such as the following, which are then to be posted on the flipchart:

Kinesthetic	Visualizing	Auditory
I'm beaten	like a fish	noisy type
latch on to	see	hear this
get a feel of	perceive	rings a bell
handle	imagine	listen
grasp	focus	sounds good
grab	clarity	tuned in
I can't budge him	the big picture	bend an ear
break bread	open door	roar of the crowd
pushing 40	in a nut shell	windy
butt in	hazy	buzz group
hot stuff	crystal clear	makes a big splash

Assign participants to pairs. Have both members of the dyad talk for five minutes to the partner on any subject desired. While one person is talking, the other listens silently and takes notes about the type of words or phrases which are used, that is, kinesthetic, visual, or auditory. The note taking should produce a pattern to identify the speaker's communication style.

Summarize by pointing out that if we know another person's style we can reach that person better by using words or phrases more likely to bring response. The same approach may also apply to communicating with a group.

Dice Toss

You can easily design an activity using a pair of dice. One helpful use: for review and reinforcement of prior learnings. Procedures [2]:

1. Develop a group of questions on your topic of interest. Prepare as many questions as you have participants.
2. Write each question on an individual card and give each card a number (2 through 12).
3. When starting the game, explain the ground rules (see the following).
4. Let each player roll the dice. The number on the dice determines the question to be answered. If a number has been rolled, have the player roll the dice for a new number.
5. Participants should be encouraged to add to the responses of the one initially responding to the question.

Variations of the above activity are as follows:

1. Use a roulette wheel or playing cards to select questions.
2. Prepare a circular board, having alternating colors, with numbers on the colored spaces. Add a needle or indicator which can be spun to select a number.
3. With group members in a circle, spin a beer or soft drink bottle (on the floor or on a table) to select participants to respond to prepared questions which are on cards.

Headliners

Have participants describe who they are in "headline" style, that is, using only two or three highly descriptive words. Examples: Support Giver, Big Talker, Computer Memory, Constant Debater, Most Friendly Fellow, Dedicated Dieter, Free Spirit, Constant Worrier.

Note:

1. The exercise may be used both early and late in a course to note if there is any change in participants' self-perceptions.
2. The headliners may also be used as a form of feedback, with participants giving the descriptors to one another.
3. More authentic descriptors are likely to be forthcoming later in the course when participants are more relaxed and candid with one another. Hence, consider using this device at course's end if it is only done once.

Bucolic Break

Provide a short relaxation break via a reference to pleasant natural scenes such as

- ☐ A peaceful, sweet-scented gurgling brook.
- ☐ In a rain forest: rain falls in the lush forest to the sounds of tropical birds.
- ☐ On the California coast: seagulls sail above white-capped incoming ocean waves.
- ☐ In the north woods: the calls of loons blend with summer night sounds.
- ☐ The gentle soothing pattern of early spring rain.
- ☐ Sweet-smelling, multi-colored flowers on a sun-lit mountain meadow, swaying gently in the mountain breeze.
- ☐ Water from a gently falling waterfall, spraying mist alongside the stream.

To start the relaxation response, provide the usual instructions of "make yourself comfortable in your chair, loosen your clothing, and close your eyes." Then select one of the above natural scenes and develop it in imaginary detail for three or four minutes. *Example:* "You are lying in the warm sun in a mountain meadow. Through your half-closed eyes, you can see an ocean of lush flowers: yellows and reds and oranges and blues. The wind blows them ever so gently, so that they resemble a group of young ballerinas swaying to and fro. The warm sun feels good so you close your eyes more firmly and you relax more fully. You . . ."

Present your description of the natural scene in a soft, slow voice. Use silent pauses to facilitate the relaxation response.

When time is up, ask your participants to gently open their eyes and remain silent for 20 seconds or so; then ask them for comments.

Cartoon Captioning

Working in small groups, participants provide captions to cartoons, for example, on leadership, communication, safety, sales, productivity, or creativity. Delete the captions already provided. Depending on your course objectives, the nature of the cartoon, and the nature of the group, you may wish to instruct the teams to provide humorous captions or any which they deem appropriate.

The Desirable and the Undesirable

Select any topic which can generate data along *opposite* lines. *Examples:* listening skills; delegation practices; leadership attributes; communication practices in organizations; unleashing creativity.

Procedures:

1. Ask participants individually to come up with three ways to encourage creativity. After a few minutes, ask them to do the opposite: come up with three devices/approaches to discourage/devastate creativity.
2. Ask each participant to team up with another person to form a pair.
3. Ask the paired participants to exchange/discuss their data.
4. Optionally, the pair may be asked to agree on the three most desirable and the three least desirable (undesirable) ways to stimulate creativity. (*Note:* The pair now has six desirable and six undesirable items to choose from.)
5. Optionally, a pair may join another pair. The new quartet can repeat the selection procedure to agree on the three most desirable and the three least desirable approaches to creativity. (*Note:* The foursome has 12 items to choose from.)
6. Secure data from pairs or quartets and post on a flipchart sheet for discussion.

Note: This activity has been titled "The Desirable and the Undesirable." Other, allied titles might be used, such as "The Positive and the Negative," "The Successful and the Unsuccessful," "The Best and the Worst," "The Helpful and the Hurtful." Use the title which best relates to your situation.

Race Awareness

To introduce a discussion of ethnic/racial differences in a Managing Diversity workshop, follow these procedures:

1. Form a stand-up circle of all participants (10–15).
2. *Task:* Reflect on and report to the group on your first exposure or awareness of race. What were the circumstances? Your reaction? Your age at the time? What is your current reaction to that earlier introduction to race?
3. Secure verbal reports from all participants.
4. Hold a general discussion regarding how we may have learned about race and its meaning to us over the long haul.

Stopping Stereotyping

In a session/course on diversity awareness, present the group with stereotypical statements such as these:

☐ Politicians are out for themselves and only care about being reelected.

☐ Athletes are a bunch of dumb jocks.

☐ You can't trust people in the Mideast.

☐ Mexicans are highly emotional people.

☐ The Irish are heavy drinkers.

☐ Latins are loud.

☐ People in Division X are empire builders.

☐ People in the ghetto could do better for themselves if they just tried.

Task: Discuss in small groups questions such as these: How valid are these cited generalizations? Is the "disease of allness" at work here? Do you ever catch yourself making such all-inclusive statements? How do you feel when you hear others making these kinds of generalizations? What do you say, if anything, to a person who employs such stereotypes? How does stereotypical thinking affect our ability to work well with groups or individuals we may generalize/stereotype about?

Secure reports from the small groups and lead a discussion on the significance/impacts of stereotypical thinking.

Stress Management—Self-Talk: Looking Forward

In a stress management/life vitality course or session.

1. Assign participants to small groups.
2. *Task:* What common expressions (self-talk) are possible aids for good mental health? Enter them on a flipchart sheet and post to the wall. Let me give you an example or two to get you started: "One step at a time." "Go with the flow." "Take the cards life dealt you." Advise (optional): "We have a prize for the group that comes up with the most ideas." (Other possible expressions: "Haste makes waste." "Plan ahead." "S--t happens." "Don't cry over spilt milk." "Life's what you make it." "I'm not going to let anyone control my behavior" (in regard to returning an angry, nasty response to someone who gives you one).
3. After 15 minutes call time and secure reports from the small groups.
4. Hold a general discussion (group-at-large) regarding the value/significance of such self-talk to preserve good mental health.

Encouraging Future Thinking

1. *State objective:* "We have a brief exercise to encourage future thinking."
2. *Procedure:* Assign tasks such as the following:
   - ☐ To what degree, if any, do you think and act in the future tense?
   - ☐ What do you want to be doing five to seven years from now and how might you go about getting there?
   - ☐ What procedures/techniques do you apply to learn from less-than-successful experiences?
3. Have participants meet in pairs to share their individual reports.
4. *Debriefing:* Hold a general discussion concerning possible learnings from the activity.

Narratives of Our Life History

Instructions to participants:

1. Compose (write) two narratives of your life history on the following assigned topics:

   Narrative #1: "Everything I have ever done has been leading me to where I am today."

   Narrative #2: "It's only after many surprises and choices, interruptions and disappointments that I have arrived somewhere I could never have anticipated."

2. Assign participants to pairs to discuss their respective narratives.
3. Secure reports from several of the pairs regarding possible learnings from the exercise.

Significance of the exercise: Our lives are seldom a straight line. There are ups, downs, detours, successes and less-than-successes. Life is continually evolving; we rarely can "arrive" and hold it firm.

(Anthropologist Mary Catherine Bateson gives this exercise to adults. It was cited by syndicated columnist Ellen Goodman, "The Commencement I'll Never Forget," *The Washington Post,* June 10, 2000.)

Who Am I and Who Do I Want to Be?

Task:

1. Prepare (write) a statement relating to the person you want to be. There are no limits, no guidelines. Think broadly and creatively. Explore yourself in all possible dimensions—vocation, family, community, neighborhood, relationships with others, your goals, your values.
2. Meet in small groups to discuss your write-ups.
3. Now rewrite your statement.
4. Return to your small group to discuss your possible revision.
5. Hold a general debriefing on what was learned from the activity.

List Exchange/Comparison

1. Assign participants to teams.
2. *Task:* Develop a list on—(select your topic for the group.) Reduce it to writing. Make a second copy of your list for exchange purposes.

3. Exchange your team's written list with another team.

4. Compare/discuss the content of the other team's list in relation to your own.

5. Select a team spokesperson and report to the group at large what may have been learned from the exchange of lists. (A possible learning: Input from another source may enrich our understanding of or approach to a given problem, topic, etc.)

Added Exercises

Note: For added exercise approaches/techniques see:

- [ ] Chapter 3, "Basic Techniques for Small Group Training," particularly using dyads and triads; producing definitions; working with lists; ending the course/program.
- [ ] Chapter 4, "Additional Techniques for Small Group Training," particularly using fishbowls, fantasy, guided images and visualization; working with pictures; using art; working with models; writing to learn (WTL) method.
- [ ] Chapter 10, "Defining a Problem and Generating Data About It," especially group-in-action techniques such as force field analysis and brainstorming; working with analogy and metaphor; imaging.
- [ ] Chapter 11, "Generating Solutions to a Problem," particularly brainstorming, slip method, card posting techniques, mind mapping, story boarding, analogy.
- [ ] Chapter 15, "Other Group-in-Action Tools," under "Movement."
- [ ] Chapter 20, "How to Overcome the Transfer Problem," under "Application Activities" and "Contracting at Program's End."

PLANNING THE CONDUCT OF AN EXERCISE

To ensure that a given exercise works, that is, provides participants with a high-quality learning experience, the following questions can serve as a guide to the trainer:

- [ ] Why am I doing this? Is this the best vehicle to achieve the learning outcome?
- [ ] Is the exercise realistic and relevant? Or is it too theoretical?
- [ ] Are the procedures fully developed and likely to be clear to the participants? Should the instructions be reduced to writing to ensure participant understanding?
- [ ] Will the trainer's role in the exercise be clearly understood?
- [ ] Should a lecturette or talk be used to set the stage for the exercise?
- [ ] Are the time frames for each phase of the exercise realistic? Have I allowed enough time, in particular, for the all-important processing (analysis) phase?
- [ ] Is the exercise being introduced at the proper stage of the program? Might learning be aided by programming it at an alternate time?
- [ ] Have I planned for necessary supplies, materials, equipment?
- [ ] Have I considered the use of observers? If observers are being used, have they been properly briefed?
- [ ] Have I considered the use of a summary sheet (handout) at exercise's end to help participants "button down" learnings?
- [ ] When the exercise is completed, how will I know that participants have learned what they were supposed to? What are my procedures for assessing results?

BOOKS CONTAINING EXERCISES

Exercises are available from publishers in several formats:

1. Books devoted exclusively to exercises and covering a variety of topics on management and human relations.

2. Books that have textual material for the trainer, but also contain exercises on a variety of management and interpersonal subjects. The exercises are presented independently of the text.

3. Books on a single subject containing many exercises and a minimum of text.

4. Books that treat a single subject (for example, assertiveness, time management, supervision) in traditional textual fashion but also contain exercises throughout the books. These exercises are an integral part of the books, intended to aid in "gluing in" key ideas. These skill practice or application materials may be used individually (self-instruction) or on a group basis.

EXERCISES FROM PUBLISHERS

Listed below are the names of several publishers that offer numerous experiential activities for trainers—exercises, games, instruments. Each firm publishes a catalog describing training materials. It will be helpful to you to secure a copy of each of these catalogs. The catalogs, typically, are updated quarterly.

Jossey-Bass/Pfeiffer
350 Sansome St.
San Francisco, CA 94104-1342
1-800-274-4434

(This firm provides the broadest range of training materials, drawing on a wide variety of other publishers' offerings as well as their own. Particularly useful are the *Annual,* Volume 1, *Training,* and Volume 2, *Consulting.* The *Training* volumes, which are devoted to many experiential activities and instruments, were first published in 1969. Earlier *Annual*s are still available in a complete set as well as in single-volume format.)

HRD Press (Human Resource Development Press)
22 Amherst Road
Amherst, MA 01002-9709
1-800-822-2801

HRDQ
2002 Renaissance Blvd. #100
King of Prussia, PA 19406-2756
1-800-633-4533

Talico Inc.
4375-4 Southside Blvd. Suite 157
Jacksonville, FL 32216
904-642-0300

Creative Training Techniques: A monthly newsletter devoted to highly participative training activities such as icebreakers, exercises, openers, energizers, closers, etc. Publisher: Lakewood Publications, 50 S. Ninth St., Minneapolis, MN 55402. Phone: 1-800-707-7749.

KEY POINTS

1. Exercises take many forms. They may be borrowed from printed sources and from colleagues, adapted from games, or created anew by the trainer.

2. The exercise will produce a worthwhile learning experience if the trainer pays attention to such skill elements as setting learning objectives, developing and/or providing clear-cut procedures and instructions for participants and observers, setting realistic time frames for the elements of the exercise, conducting it at an appropriate stage in the training program, and planning and conducting the vital processing (debriefing) session to wrap up the exercise.

3. The exercises suggested in this chapter may be used "as is" or adapted to meet participant needs better. A study of these exercises, plus those in exercise books, should help the reader to develop a "mindset" or orientation toward exercises. Of course, the best way to learn about exercises is to use them in the training situation and constantly critique such experiences (what went well, what did not).

REFERENCES

1. Raelin, Joseph A., "Making Feedback Work," in "Training 101," *Training and Development Journal* (July 1989), pp. 25–27.

2. McLaughlin, Ian, "Why Not Play Games?" *Successful Meetings* (March 1983), pp. 51–53.

RECOMMENDED READING

Thiagarajan, Sivasailan, "Real Interactivity: Connecting People With People," *Performance Improvement*, March 2000, pp. 47–52.

A long-time experiential trainer provides a template for structured sharing that facilitates mutual learning and teaching among participants. With the author's template (framework/mold/pattern), one's own topic or problem area can be used by group members to generate data for analysis and discussion. The article provides the necessary procedures to conduct several structured sharing activities. *Examples:* The Best and the Worst, Shouting Match, Comparison Table, Brainstorm, Concept Analysis, Top/Tips.

8 Using Puzzles

People who have learned to organize their ideas into sequences or chains of logic can usually reason their way effectively through confused or complicated situations in the business of living.

—IFTDO NEWS, newsletter of the
International Federation of Training and
Development Organizations, July 1983

IN Chapter 6 we learned how to work with games and simulations. In Chapter 7 we studied the exercise and how to work with it. In this chapter we shall explore puzzles and how to work with them in the training situation.

Puzzles, another useful tool for the trainer, may be used for various purposes, such as to

- ☐ Stimulate curiosity and creativity.
- ☐ Encourage a broad-gauged, free-flowing approach to problem solving (right-brain thinking).
- ☐ Encourage a logical approach to problem solving (left-brain thinking), whenever appropriate.
- ☐ Serve as an icebreaker, that is, to loosen up participants.
- ☐ Serve as an opener, to introduce subjects such as career planning, assertiveness, risk-taking, perception, and following instructions properly.
- ☐ Provide fun, excitement, a change of pace, and new experiences.
- ☐ Prove that learning need not be dull, dreary, totally didactic.
- ☐ Provide for participant involvement (with puzzles everyone "plays").

We will first present a number of puzzles, indicate how to introduce them to a group, and examine the purposes of each of them in the training situation.

Secondly, we will take a global view of puzzles, relating them to current ideas about left/right brain thinking.

AN ASSORTMENT OF PUZZLES

These puzzles serve various substantive purposes, and they come in various formats—they may be presented visually (via a handout or a flipchart or a blackboard), orally, or physically (via toothpicks, matchsticks, coins).

Nine-Dot Puzzle

This is probably the oldest and most widely used puzzle in training.

Presentation format: The figure may be posted on a flipchart/blackboard with oral instructions, or it may be given to participants as a handout, complete with written instructions, as in Figure 8-1. Since it is an old puzzle, ask those who have seen it before to disqualify themselves. Quite often, however, even those who have previously experienced the puzzle have since forgotten its solution.

After several minutes, ask if anyone has the solution. If someone has it, have that person come forward and provide the answer to the group. (A large display copy of the puzzle should have been drawn on the flipchart/blackboard by the trainer as the group worked on the puzzle.) If no one has the answer, provide it yourself. The correct answer is given in Figure 8-2.

Processing: Now ask: "What does this solution tell us?" Some answers are that it teaches us the need to go beyond the boundaries when solving a problem, the need to overcome tunnel vision, and the need to take some new approaches or risks.

Instructions: Place the pencil on one of the dots and draw *four* straight lines through all of the remaining dots, without lifting your pencil from the paper or retracing any of the lines you have drawn.

Figure 8-1. The classic Nine-Dot Puzzle as presented to the participants.

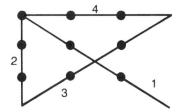

Figure 8-2. Solution to the Nine-Dot Puzzle.

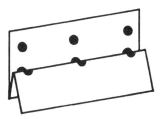

Figure 8-3A. Fold the bottom part of the paper so that the bottom line of dots half covers the middle line of dots.

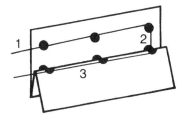

Figure 8-3B. One solution to the Nine-Dot Puzzle using three lines.

Now ask: "Can anyone do it with *three* lines?" This is a request for a still more novel solution and few participants if any, will figure it out. In any case, here are *two* three-line solutions.

1. Fold the bottom part of the paper so that the bottom line of dots half covers the middle line of dots. The *overlap* will produce the result shown in Figure 8-3A. Now connect the dots or circles with the three lines as shown in Figure 8-3B.

2. Draw the lines vertically so they slant a bit. Somewhere "out in infinity" they should meet and (hypothetically) permit the three-line result shown in Figure 8-4.

Now ask: "Can anyone do it with *one* line?" Here we are encouraging the group to use its creativity, which we hope has been stimulated by the prior challenges. At this point the group may come up with solutions such as the following (if necessary provide one or two possibilities yourself to stimulate their thinking):

1. Just use a paint roller or wide paint brush and make a single, fast downward sweep. (Whoosh!)

2. Connect the lines as in Figure 8-5. (No one said the line had to be straight!)

3. Move the nine dots very close together as in Figure 8-6 so that they can be covered in one downward sweep with a felt-tip pen. (No one said the dots were stationary and could not be moved.)

4. Stack the nine dots, one on top of the other, and draw a line through them as in Figure 8-7 (!).

5. Make a *double* fold of the paper, and then draw a line through the overlapping lines of dots with a felt-tip pen, as in Figure 8-8.

6. Move the last line of dots into the middle line and move both of those lines into the first line. Then draw a line through the nine dots, as in Figure 8-9.

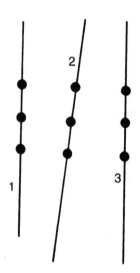

Figure 8-4. One way to solve the Nine-Dot Puzzle with three lines: The lines meet "in infinity."

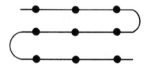

Figure 8-5. A one-line solution to the Nine-Dot Puzzle: The dots are connected with a curved line.

Figure 8-6. A second one-line solution to the Nine-Dot Puzzle; the dots are moved close together so they can be covered by one stroke of a felt-tip pen.

Figure 8-7. Another one-line solution to the Nine-Dot Puzzle. The dots are stacked vertically and one line is drawn through them.

Figure 8-8. A one-line solution to the Nine-Dot Puzzle: If the paper is folded twice, the nine dots overlap and one line can be drawn though them with a felt-tip pen.

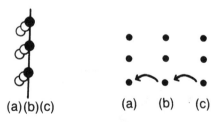

Figure 8-9. By moving the dots in vertical line C to line B, and by moving lines B and C to A, we can then cover the nine dots with a single line drawn vertically.

7. Draw a line through three dots and then move the other two rows of dots *onto* the drawn line as in Figure 8-10.

8. Write "one line" through each dot as in Figure 8-11. (The question was "Can you do it with one line?")

There are several practical applications of the nine-dot puzzle, such as to:

☐ Expose the need for a broad "free-form" approach to problem solving. Don't hem yourself in by imagined restrictions, regulations, "can't do's," or "should not's."

☐ Unleash one's creativity by stretching the imagination.

☐ Overcome tendencies to limit oneself in career planning: "I'll never pass the math test." "I'll never pass the graduate school entrance exam." "They'll never take a woman (or a black person or a 50-year-old person) for the job."

☐ Overcome prejudices and stereotyping: Just as we screen out other possibilities in problem solving by making faulty assumptions (that we can't go beyond the boundaries), so, too, in assessing people we may prejudge/misjudge them. In other words, let's not limit our poten-

tial to understand what they are really like and what they might do.

☐ To demonstrate in assertiveness training that there are often other options besides the usual timid nonproductive approach of "backing off."

☐ To encourage risk-taking: "Why stick with the tried and true?" "Why not break out?" "Who is the loser if I always do the conventional thing?"

Cake Cutting Puzzle

Presentation format: Draw an aerial view of a cake on the flipchart, as shown in Figure 8-12. Tell the group: "A woman had baked a cake for her party to be attended by eight guests. Her (and your) task is to produce eight pieces of cake with only three cuts of the knife."

Possible solutions:

1. The Lateral Cut Method: First make two cuts as in Figure 8-13A, which will produce four pieces. Now cut the cake laterally as in Figure 8-13B to give eight pieces, all of equal size.

Figure 8-12. Can you produce eight pieces of cake with only three cuts of the knife?

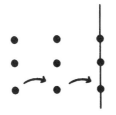

Figure 8-10. A one-line solution to the Nine-Dot Puzzle: A line is drawn through one row of dots, and the other two rows are moved onto the line.

one line   one line   one line

one line   one line   one line

one line   one line   one line

Figure 8-11. The words "one line" are superimposed on each of the nine dots.

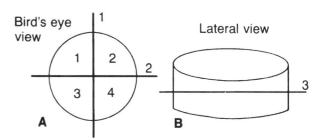

Figure 8-13. The Cake Cutting Puzzle lateral cut solution: (A) Right angle intersecting cuts produce four pieces. (B) A lateral cut produces eight pieces.

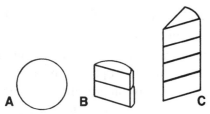

Figure 8-14. The Cake Cutting Puzzle stacking method solution: (A) a vertical cut down the middle produces two pieces, (B) stacking the two pieces and cutting them vertically produces four pieces, (C) a final stacking and cutting of the pieces produces eight pieces.

2. The Stacking Method: Start with one cut across the center and stack the two pieces. Make a vertical cut, producing four pieces, and stack them. Make a final vertical cut, and you have eight pieces, all equal at that. (See Figure 8-14.)

3. Center Cut Method: Make two vertical cuts at perpendicular angles, and then a circular cut as in Figure 8-15.

    Note: No one said that the pieces had to be equal or the cuts made via a straight line. Remember this is *her* party with *her* guests, and she can cut the cake any way she wishes!

4. The Disgustingly Sneaky Method: Make one straight cut and two curved ones as shown in Figure 8-16 to produce eight unequal pieces.

Processing: Ask "What does the puzzle tell us?" Some answers are: "There may be more options than we think; let's stretch our imaginations and then we can produce solutions that are varied and unique."

The puzzle may be used to stimulate thinking about problem solving, creative approaches, alternative seeking, etc.

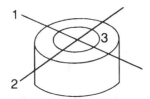

Figure 8-15. The Cake Cutting Puzzle circular cut solution: Two vertical cuts and then a center circular cut are made to produce eight pieces.

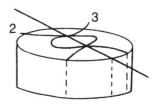

Figure 8-16. A solution to the Cake Cutting Puzzle that uses two curved lines and a center straight cut to produce eight, albeit unequal, pieces.

The Garage Window Puzzle

Presentation format: Instructions are given orally since the group has to visualize a garage window. Tell them: "A homeowner had a single garage window which only let in a limited amount of light. He decided to double the amount of light that came in and to do this without changing the height or width of the window. So he measured the window, up and across, as a good carpenter should. It measured 15 inches by 15 inches. He now made four cuts around the window. He had succeeded—twice as much light now came in. He took new measurements, and the window was still 15 inches high and 15 inches wide! How come?"

Solution: The window took the form shown in Figure 8-17.

Processing: Ask: "What does this tell us about communication/perception?" Then provide this answer: "You had a picture in your head of a conventional square window; the picture I had was the same square window, but 'tilted' to stand on one point. We had different pictures of windows because our experiences, our worlds, are different. Hence our perceptions are different. So if we try to communicate without 'matching

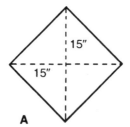 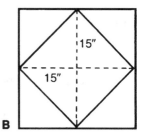

Figure 8-17. The Garage Window Puzzle solution: (A) The window before the cuts are made; (B) the window after the cuts are made.

up' or exchanging perceptions, we'll be in deep trouble. Remember, meanings are in people and people are different, so meanings must be shared to ensure understanding of one another's meanings."

The Dollar Bill Quiz

Presentation format: Ask orally: "Can you tell me how many 'ones' there are printed on a dollar bill? No, not counting the serial number. This should be easy since all of us use it every day."

Solution: There are 8 "ones" in numbered fashion and 8 more spelled out for a *total* of 16.

Processing: Ask: "Why should it be hard to know the answer when we use and glance at a one dollar bill almost daily?" Answer: "We have a screening mechanism in our heads (selective attention or perceptual choice) that helps us screen out the unnecessary, the unimportant, the details, the trivia. This allows us to get our jobs done properly. If we had to pay attention to all the stimuli that comes at us all of the time, we'd never get through the day. Imagine driving to work and noting precisely each tree, each person and his/her clothing, each house, each store, etc. Of course, this screening device can work the other way, too. It may cause us to overlook pertinent, vital details. For example, we may forget to call George and Mary to our meeting, and they may get pretty mad at us. So we have to be on guard to avoid screening out necessary detail. We can do this via checklists, memos or notes to self, calendar notations, reminders from our secretaries, and so on."

Geometric Figures

Various puzzles challenge us to design geometrical figures such as squares or triangles by using toothpicks or matches.

Presentation format: Pass out a bundle of 24 toothpicks (matches or nails would do, too). Draw on the flipchart the figure illustrated in Figure 8-18; it represents 12 toothpicks down and 12 toothpicks across. The toothpicks are touching each other. Assign this task orally: "Can you make two squares by removing (not moving) eight toothpicks?"

The answer is shown in Figure 8-19.

Presentation format: Pass out a bundle of nine toothpicks. Draw on a flipchart three triangles as

shown in Figure 8-20. Now ask participants to move three toothpicks and come up with five triangles.

Solution:

1. The right triangle is broken up and the three toothpicks are placed as shown by the dotted lines in Figure 8-21.

2. In the second solution (Figure 8-22), the right triangle is moved to the top of the other two

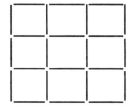

Figure 8-18. A diagram of the figure made of 24 toothpicks used in a geometric puzzle.

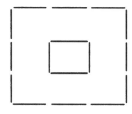

Figure 8-19. Eight toothpicks are removed from the figure, leaving two squares. The solution to the geometric puzzle.

Figure 8-20. A diagram of the arrangement of the three triangles for the geometric puzzle.

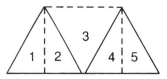

Figure 8-21. A solution to the geometric puzzle involving the three triangles: Five triangles are created by placing the toothpicks from the right triangle in the positions shown.

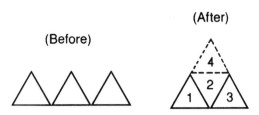

Figure 8-22. A second solution to the triangle puzzle: The right triangle is placed on top of the other two triangles.

triangles as shown. The fifth triangle is the entire configuration.

Processing: Both of these toothpick problems are typical of many puzzles. We know there is a generally simple solution, but yet it is elusive. Why? Some might say because it takes a kind of imaginative approach, which is hard to achieve in a "strange" field. After all, how much time do we ordinarily spend moving matchsticks or toothpicks around? But there still is a principle for us which applies to our own fields: To be creative, or at least to create new applications, does not mean we have to be an Edison, a Kittering, or a Bill Lear. It *does* mean that we have to reassess and reprogram our modes of attack, back off and start again, search for another alternative, explore many possible avenues, be patient, and, most important, we must ask ourselves: "Are we going at this conventionally, or are we rising above our conventional approach? Are we settling for a conventional, 'tried and true' solution when what we may really need is a bold, new one (right-brain thinking)?"

How Many Squares?

Presentation format: Make reference to your subject matter (typically a problem of some sort) and say: "Here's a fun task related to it. Total the number of squares that you see and we'll compare scores." Pass out the sheets with the squares, as shown in Figure 8-23. Allow several minutes for the

How many squares do you see?

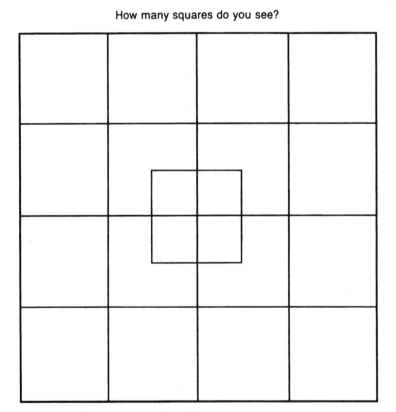

Figure 8-23. Multiple square puzzle.

task, and then post scores to the flipchart as you receive them. Sample:

Solution: The correct answer is 35 squares. See Figure 8-24.

No. of Squares	Frequency
16	IIII
17	III
18	IIII I
20	IIII
24	II

Uses of the puzzle: This puzzle has several uses or learnings. (You may think of some other than those we provide):

1. *Be tolerant of different opinions.* Every answer is O.K. No one is really wrong, for one's answer is what one happens to see. So if in the course of everyday events people come up with different answers, it's not because they're ignorant, malicious, or stubborn. Rather, they see what they are able (programmed) to see.

2. *Creativity.* In problem solving we should not be content with the obvious answer. Typically, we need to keep digging and probing lest we only come up with minimum possibilities.

3. *Planning and problem solving.* Any problem is a puzzle with overlapping pieces. Some parts (squares) are portions of other parts, which creates difficulties in sorting out the pieces. Planning is analogous to problem solving in that it is a matter of recognizing how all the (apparently unrelated) parts fit together.

Everyday Things

Presentation format: Pass out the sheet "Everyday Things," shown in Figure 8-25. Ask your participants to decode these abbreviations of very familiar things. Allow about five minutes for the task.

Uses of the puzzle: It can be used as a fun way to start any session or, possibly, to provide some fun and stimulation if people seem to be showing signs of fatigue. It

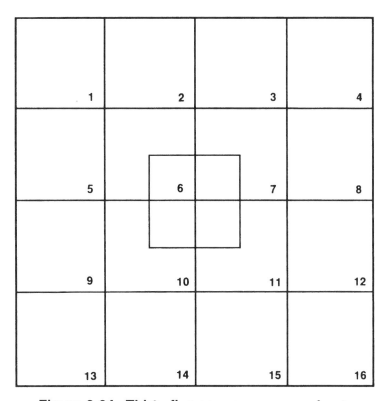

Figure 8-24. Thirty-five squares answer sheet.

```
┌─────────────────────────────────────┐
│     Everyday Things—What are they?   │
│                                      │
│      7 = D. in the W.                │
│     32 = D.F. at which W.F.          │
│     26 = L. of the A.                │
│     54 = P.C. in a D. plus J.        │
│     11 = P. on a F.T.                │
│      8 = H. in a W.D.                │
│      3 = B.M.—S.H.T.R.               │
│     64 = S. on a C.B.                │
│      3 = L. on a T.L.                │
│    100 = S. in the U.S.S.            │
│      8 = S. on a S.S.                │
│      6 = N. on a D.                  │
│      7 = C. in the S.                │
│     16 = P. in a C.G.                │
│     18 = H. on a G.C.                │
│      4 = B. on a B.D.                │
│                                      │
│     76 = T. led the B.P.             │
│    110 = C. close B.                 │
│                                      │
│     Source: Unknown                  │
└─────────────────────────────────────┘
```

Figure 8-25. Abbreviations for *Everyday Things.*

```
┌─────────────────────────────────────────┐
│      Everyday Things—Answer Sheet        │
│                                          │
│      7 = days in the week                │
│     32 = degrees Fahrenheit at which     │
│          water freezes                   │
│     26 = letters of the alphabet         │
│     54 = playing cards in a deck plus    │
│          jokers                          │
│     11 = players on a football team      │
│      8 = hours in a work day             │
│      3 = blind mice—see how they run     │
│     64 = squares on a chess board        │
│      3 = lights (or lamps) on a traffic  │
│          light                           │
│    100 = senators in the U.S. Senate     │
│      8 = sides on a stop sign            │
│      6 = numbers on a die (as in dice)   │
│      7 = colors in the spectrum          │
│     16 = pawns in a chess game           │
│     18 = holes on a golf course          │
│      4 = bases on a ball diamond         │
│                                          │
│     76 = trombones led the big parade    │
│    110 = clarinets close behind          │
│                                          │
│     Source: Unknown                      │
└─────────────────────────────────────────┘
```

Figure 8-26. Answer Sheet for *Everyday Things— What Are They?*

can also be used in a more profound way. Point out that in problem solving/creative thinking we may get hemmed in by overlooking the obvious or commonplace when it appears in another form. *Question:* Are we over-programmed with the "tried and true" so that we can't strike out in a new direction? *Note:* In football the mark of an effective quarterback is his ability to "read" new defensive formations and adjust his lines of attack accordingly. Similarly, in product development or marketing, if conditions have changed, adjustments and new approaches are necessary. A principle worth remembering is this: If you're not getting what you want, quit doing what you're doing! The answers to the puzzle are given in Figure 8-26.

Pun Fun

Presentation format: Pass out the sheet "Check Your I.Q. (Imagination Quotient)" found in Appendix 25. Read off each item on the sheet and secure group responses. Pass out the answer sheet after completing the 22 items.

Use of the puzzle: To warm up a participant group about to begin a brainstorming or other problem solv-ing activity, that is, to get them in a play-orientated, creative mood.

The Encyclopedia Attack

Presentation format: Pass out an instruction sheet with the data and drawing, as shown in Figure 8-27.

Solution: Eleven inches. Note that the beetle began his journey on page 1 of the *first* book, which is on the *right* side of the book as it rests on the shelf. He finished eating on the *last* page of the last book, which is on the *left* side of the book. So he ate through *all* of the pages of the *middle four* books, which totals ten inches (4 × 2½" = 10"). The beetle also ate through *all* the covers of the *middle four* books (eight covers), the *right* cover of the *first* book (one cover), and the *left* cover of the *last* book (one cover)—or a total of ten covers, equal to ten tenths or one inch. Ten inches of pages plus one inch of covers equals eleven inches in all.

Processing: Ask: "What is significant about this puzzle? What can we learn from it?" Some answers: It shows the need for carefulness in interpreting instruc-tions; sometimes one has to look at the instruction

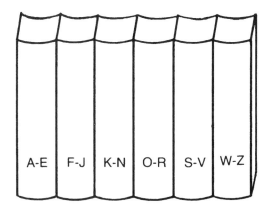

A six-volume encyclopedia set, which belonged to entymologist Gwen Brown, was attacked by a voracious beetle. The beetle's trip/feast began on page I of the first book (A-E) and continued through the last page of the last volume (W-Z).

When Gwen discovered the damage the beetle (bookworm?) had accomplished, she was dismayed. At the same time she, as a scientist, was curious to know how many inches the bug had traversed from the starting to the finishing point. She made her measurements quickly, since all six volumes were of the same dimensions:

Thickness of total pages in each book—2½ inches

Thickness of each cover—$^1/_{10}$ inch

Question: What was the length of the journey of our book-biting bug, measured in inches?

Figure 8-27. Instruction sheet for The Encyclopedia Attack Puzzle.

from more than one angle to really understand it; also, one must avoid "traps" such as oversimplification (assuming that all there is to the problem is to add a few figures together).

I have told groups who worked on this puzzle that it is a hard puzzle for today's culture; no one reads books anymore because of television, so how should one know where page 1 of a book is?

The Farmer's Will

Presentation format: Give the group the following problem, either orally or in writing:

A farmer, who had three sons, died. His will stipulated that his 17 cows be divided as follows: one-half to the oldest son, one-third to the middle son, and one-ninth to the youngest. Since the sons knew enough about arithmetic to recognize that the 17 cows could not be divided as stipulated, they discussed the problem and finally hit on the idea of seeking help from the Wise Old Man on the Mountain.

So they presented the old man with their dilemma. He listened carefully, was silent a long time, and then said, "Come back in 17 days and I will have a solution for you." They returned at the designated time and the Wise Old Man on the Mountain gave them this solution: "I will lend you one of my cows. Now make your division of your cows." They did, and they found that 18 broke down readily into 9 (one-half), 6 (one-third), and 2 (one-ninth), as the will had required.

The Wise Old Man asked, "Are you satisfied?"

They replied, "Oh, yes. You are very wise."

So the Wise Old Man said: "Since you are satisfied, you don't need my cow any more. I, therefore, will take it back. Please note that 9 plus 6 plus 2 equals 17." They left pleased, but a little perplexed as to the arcane arithmetic the Wise Old Man had employed.

Processing: Ask: "What is going on here? What does the story tell us?" Answer: The three sons thought they had an insoluble problem. Using their conventional problem-solving approaches, they were correct in that assessment. But what was needed was an *unconventional* approach. This was provided by the Wise Old Man, who stepped back, looked at the problem in new, more creative and more global terms, and gave it a new framework (the eighteenth cow). So there's nothing really arcane about the arithmetic. Just good right-brain (creative) thinking. Could it be that the farmer expected his sons to do some right-brain thinking?

The Hotel Refund

Presentation format: Present the following data orally or in writing:

Three itinerant farmers bedded down for the night in a motel in a small town, all three in the same room. The desk clerk, a part-time worker, asked for $30, which they paid without question. Later that evening, the regular desk clerk discovered that the three farmers had been overcharged. He called his teen-age son over and said, "Our day clerk made a mistake on the rate for Room 42. He overcharged them five bucks. Here's five singles. Split it among those three travelers."

This, understandably, was a tough arithmetic problem for the teenager. But being a sharp kid, he simply gave them each a dollar and pocketed the other two dollar bills. As the boy walked back to the motel office, he thought about the new rate the men had received. It was now $9 each ($30 divided by 3 = $10, and $10 − $1 = $9). But he thought to himself: "Three times nine dollars equals twenty-seven dollars, and I've got two bucks, which only totals twenty-nine dollars. Where is the other buck?"

Processing: Ask: "What's going on here?" Answer: The teenager is simply trying to resolve too much at once. He is simultaneously (and unnecessarily) looking at the problem from *two* standpoints: what the farmers paid for their motel room and what monies are circulating outside their room. What our teenager should do is to engage in very logical left-brain thinking; that is, just deal with three clear-cut realities: The three farmers paid $27, the hotel collected or netted $25 ($30 less the returned five singles), and the teenager now has two unexpected bucks in his pocket. In these terms, there is no problem at all for the boy. But if he persists on focusing on and intermingling two unrelated issues, one of which is really irrelevant, he will be eternally confused. Moral: Try to define a problem in its simplest, most coherent, and uncluttered terms; don't use right-brain thinking (creative approaches) on a left-brain (logical) problem.

Bookkeepers, who necessarily engage in a lot of left brain thinking, would immediately see that there is no missing dollar. They would simply look at the *expenditures* involved: the $27 ($25 in the hotel till and $2 in the boy's pocket). And the initial outlay—$30—of the lodgers now looks like this: the hotel racked up $25, the farmers had the rebate of $3 and the teenager had a self administered tip of $2. Why the confusion? Our bookkeepers would point out that the trouble arose because the lad added an *asset* ($2) to an *expense* ($27) instead of the other asset ($25)!

Both of these problems, the division of the 17 cows and the $5 refund, have appeared in many formats and in many places. They are classic cases of good puzzles. In fact, they are so good that in one sense they can't be answered: Where is the missing dollar? Were the 17 cows divided fairly?

One writer, Robert H. Long, director, Advanced Studies, Bank Administration Institute, Park Ridge, Illinois, has analyzed these two stories in terms of problem-solving principles and left-brain, right-brain

thinking [1]. He asserts that poor problem solving is often a result of "one-sided" thinking, whereas coordinated, two-hemisphere (left and right brain) thinking could easily resolve difficulties. He sees both puzzles as illustrations of how problem formulation, language, and logic can cause problems rather than generate solutions. Long's analysis of the puzzles is this: "Combining these parts of different situational viewpoints creates a verbal illusion—and an unresolvable problem—as long as these two viewpoints remain in the same problem statement."

Here is a final personal incident to illustrate the power of creative, right-brain thinking in a simple problem in the office. I asked the office typist to provide "bullets" to a manuscript. Bullets are black dots placed before key words or sentences to highlight them:

- Communication
- Motivation
- Innovation

The typist said this was difficult to do with her word processor. She asked if "dashes" would do. I said O.K.

Several days later a manuscript appeared in the office, from an outside author, with nice big, round, black bullets. They were used in several places. I happened to notice, however, that one set of bullets had not been filled in and was just a set of o's:

o Communication

o Motivation

o Innovation

The author had come up with a creative solution to the bullet-typing problem: regular "o's" were typed and then filled in with a thick-pointed black-ink pen!

I then asked several other expert typists if they could make nice, large bullets if they had to. None could. (They could, of course, use periods to form small bullets.) In each case I showed them the manuscript with the black o's and then the "plain" o's. Their jaws dropped.

Question: Are we doing enough to train people to use right-brain thinking?

Summary Chart. Table 8-1 sums up the significance and uses of the previously presented puzzles.

Table 8-1
A Summary of Puzzle Uses

Puzzle	Uses in The Training Situation	Puzzle	Uses in The Training Situation

Nine Dots
Cutting the Cake
	Learnings:
	  In problem solving:
	  □ Go outside the boundaries
	  □ Take some risks
	  □ Take new approaches
	  □ Avoid "tunnel vision"
	  □ Avoid setting artificial limits
	  In creative thinking:
	  □ Stretch the imagination
	  □ Use the right brain
	  In career planning:
	  □ Overcome tendencies to set up unrealistic limits, restraints, barriers
	  In dealing with prejudice:
	  □ Overcome tendencies to stereotype, limit, or narrowly define others
	  In assertiveness training:
	  □ Look for new options as opposed to staying "frozen" in a given nonproductive position
		How Many Squares?	Learnings:
			  □ Respect the opinions of others
			  □ Planning entails understanding many overlapping parts
			  □ Problem solving requires persistence, looking beyond the obvious

		Pun Fun
		("Check Your I.Q.")
			Uses:
			  □ To warm up the group
			  □ To provoke curiosity

		The Encyclopedia Attack	Learnings:
			  □ Follow instructions carefully
			  □ Avoid making faulty assumptions or oversimplifying

		The Farmer's Will	Learning: Creative, right-brain approaches to a problem are important

The Garage Window	Perception: When we are not "on the same wavelength" with others, we make assumptions that are not likely to be valid, hence the need to share perceptions for effective communication	The Hotel Refund	Learnings:
			  □ There are times when logical, left-brain thinking is appropriate
			  □ Define a problem clearly simply, and avoid extraneous considerations

Dollar Bill Quiz	Perception: The screening mechanism in our heads can eliminate unnecessary detail; it may also screen out important information		

Geometric Puzzles (Using toothpicks or matches)	Learnings:
	  □ Look for new approaches
	  □ Use the right brain to solve problems creatively rather than conventionally
		Everyday Things	Learnings:
			  □ Shows need to overcome tendencies to be limited by our "programming"
			  □ Demonstrates the need to adjust to new conditions

INNOVATION INVOLVES THE OBVIOUS

Ernie J. Zelinski, a management consultant and university lecturer who specializes in creativity and innovation, suggests that the best solutions to difficult problems are often right before our eyes, yet most of us may not see them. He presents four brief problems which test our ability to see the obvious [2].

We describe the problems first and then the solutions.

Problems

Problem 1: What Is Going On Here?

Six-year-old Milisa received a new bike on her birthday from her mother, a school teacher, age 42. The next day she rode the bicycle in front of an office building and, unfortunately, was hit by a car and injured. The police and an ambulance appeared shortly.

Milisa's injury was not serious, but the ambulance personnel made her lie down on a stretcher to take her to the hospital for observation. As she was being placed in the ambulance, a 28-year old typist hastened out of the office building and cried, "That's Milisa! What happened to my daughter?"

Question: Whose daughter is the six-year-old, the school teacher's or the typist's?

Problem 2: Dressing for Success

A U.S. bank wanted to improve its image. One possible approach was to get the employees to dress better, but the bank officials feared that a dress code imposed by top management wouldn't go over very well. After much discussion, they hit on a solution which permitted resolution of the problem without significant employee resistance. What innovative approach was used?

Problem 3: Winning by Being Slowest

An eccentric, highly successful businessman wanted to will his riches to one of his two sons. His bizarre approach: Let them run a horse race; the one who owns the *slower* horse inherits the total financial empire.

The sons' reaction? Each feared the other would cheat by forcing his horse to go slower than his actual capability. Faced with this unwanted possibility, they sought out a wise old philosopher for guidance as to how to make the race fair. The old man's advice was given in two words. What were they?

Problem 4: Finding the Fastest Way

You are the president of Fly-By-Nite Airlines, which flies to some 20% of U.S. and Canadian cities. You have had a rough week trying to complete various projects. One project entails a new Charter Holiday Service, designed to serve all of North America. You have printed some 15,000 brochures to go to travel agencies in all the major North American cities. You have to find the fastest way to distribute them, but peak holiday season is about to start and every minute counts.

So, as a creative manager, how do you get the brochures to their intended destinations in the shortest possible time?

Solutions

Problem 1. Milisa is the daughter of both the school teacher and the typist. They are married to one another, the school teacher being female and the typist male!

Problem 2. Top management "gave the problem away" to the work force. How was this done? They appointed a committee of employees to produce a workable policy. *The result:* The problem was researched by the committee, who proposed an acceptable change.

Problem 3. Change horses (!)

Problem 4. As president, stay out of details and delegate the problem to the head of the mail room. The way you get innovation is to provide people with opportunities to succeed (or fail) at critical tasks.

PUZZLES FOR FUN

The previous paragraphs have discussed the use of puzzles in relation to the subject matter being

treated. It may also be desirable, at times, to introduce puzzles as a change of pace, a relaxer, or an attention stimulator, without any direct integration with a topic at all. Thus the puzzles need not be learning tools, but rather "fun things." Some puzzles of the fun type follow.

Bowling Pin Puzzle

Tell participants: "Ten bowling pins are set up in conventional bowling array." (Post the configuration shown in Figure 8-28A on the flipchart.) "Your task is to move three pins and thereby produce a totally reverse effect, that is, the first pin should be on top and the four pins on the bottom."

The answer may be given out later in the day if no one comes up with the solution immediately.

Solution: Draw a ring hooking up or enclosing the seven pins, as shown in Figure 8-28B. Then move pin number one to the line immediately above and place it on the left; move another pin from the top line to

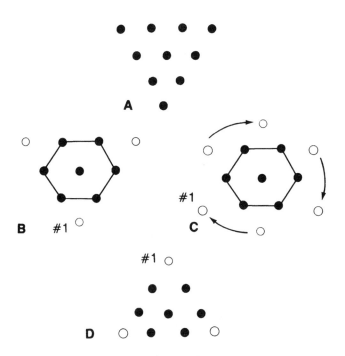

Figure 8-28. The Bowling Pin Puzzle: (A) This diagram of the configuration is drawn for the participants; (B) a line enclosing or linking seven of the pins is drawn; (C) the three pins are rearranged; (D) the final solution—the configuration is reversed.

form a new row of four as shown in 8-28C. Finally, move the far-lefpin in the original row of the four to the number one position, as shown in 8-28C. (The line of three pins was not touched.)

This is a very straightforward puzzle that only requires the use of logical thinking and spatial visualization to achieve the correct solution.

Six-Figure Puzzle

If you wish to provide a more "sneaky" puzzle, draw the following figure and tell participants: "Make this figure into a six by adding one line."

IX

Solution:

1. Add an "S" as shown:

    SIX

    Note: No one said the line had to be a straight one or that only Roman numerals were involved. (Why limit yourself by setting up a particular frame of reference?)

2. In this approach add the line as shown:

    IXI

    Then count all the lines and *segments* thereof. The left line equals one line; the X, counting its segments equals four lines (!); and the line on the right is one line, again. So we have made the figure "IX" into six.

Dilemma in a Small Town

You are visiting in a small town to make an important presentation to the town's key figures in business, education, and government. You are badly in need of a haircut. You check around and note that there are two barbers in town. One barber (Barber A) has a meticulous, very up-to-date shop and sports a neat, professionally delivered haircut. Barber B has a poor haircut which, you think, could only have been performed by a novice in barber college. His shop is a real disaster area: old magazines scattered around,

clumps of hair all over, walls in need of paint, antique-looking chairs.

Your dilemma: Which barber should you visit?

Solution: Since there are only two barbers in town, it's quite likely that the barbers cut one another's hair. So you should go to Barber B for he performed the great job on Barber A Key Points

1. Puzzles can provide interest, novelty, and fun; encourage a mindset oriented toward problem solving and creativity; and involve all participants to a high degree.

2. Puzzles have considerable flexibility as to their use. They can serve as an icebreaker, an opener to a topic or course, a relaxer, an energizer, a thought stimulator, an imagination stretcher, a mood changer, a learning reinforcer, a mindset jogger, and even a session or course closer.

REFERENCES

1. Long, R. H., "Avoiding One-Sided Thinking through the Other Brain Hemisphere," *The Magazine of Bank Administration* (August 1980), pp. 8, 10.

2. Zelinski, Ernie J., "In the Land of the Blind, One Eye Is King," in "Training 101," *Training and Development* (September 1991), pp. 30–34.

RECOMMENDED READING

Sternberg, Robert J., and Davidson, Janet E., "The Mind of the Puzzler," *Psychology Today,* June 1982, pp. 37–44.

Based on research, the authors suggest that insight alone is not enough to solve problems. Rather, a composite of elements is essential: prior knowledge related to the problem; certain "executive processes" such as how one plans or approaches the problem, how one monitors one's solution process, tendencies to switch strategies; motivation/perserverance; style—a combination of impulsive and reflective styles works best.

9 Instrumentation: A Tool for Self-Discovery Learning

In the outskirts of Dubuque, on the farm, when I was growing up—back there, back then—I learned, with all the pigs and chickens and the endless sameness everywhere you looked, or thought, back there I learned—though I doubt I knew I was learning it—that all of the values were relative save one . . . "Who am I?" All the rest is semantics—liberty, dignity, possession. There's only one that matters: "Who am I?"

—Elizabeth, in *The Lady from Dubuque,* a play by Edward Albee, American playwright

To know one's self is, above all, to know what one lacks. It is to measure one's self against truth, and not the other way around.

—Flannery O'Connor (1925–1964), American novelist and short story writer

I have to live with myself and so I want to be fit for myself to know.

—a couplet taught to Dan Rather, CBS newsman, by his mother (quoted in *The Wall Street Journal,* November 19, 1981)

INSTRUMENTATION is a technique to facilitate learning via the gathering of data in a systematic or structured way. The learning may relate to individuals, groups, or the total organization (organization development). The data may come from oneself or from others.

Robert R. Blake and Jane S. Mouton, famous for the Managerial Grid® and pioneering work in the field of instrumentation, state that a learning instrument "may be the most important discovery in education since programmed learning or even the podium. Certainly, it differs fundamentally from either" [1].

As every trainer who has worked with instruments knows, they are dynamic tools for live, action learning. Their key characteristics are

- ☐ *Involvement:* When instruments are used in the training situation, everyone "plays." There are no passive bystanders. Participants are either giving data (feedback) to others or generating data about themselves, or both. If high (or full) participation is desired, instruments are indeed one of the best ways to go.

- ☐ *Realism.* Since the data generated by instrumentation is derived from and concerned with live people in the ongoing training situation, there is nothing remote, second-hand, contrived, or artificial about it. The data is "here and now," live, personal, pertinent, (often) observable, and thus highly believable.

- ☐ *Introspection.* Instrumented data are designed to make one think about oneself—one's values, attitudes, practices, behavior. In the real world most of us are too busy to "stop the clock" and say: "Hey, am I doing this the best way?" But in the training situation the rules are reversed. The norm becomes one of stopping the action for the express purpose of learning about oneself. This situation is akin to the athletic world—in the heat of the game one cannot stop to process the action. But in practice (the training situation), stepping back and looking at one's performance is what it's all about.

- ☐ *Attitude and behavior change.* The purpose of instruments is to bring about a change in attitude and/or behavior. One's outlooks, habits, and performance are the grist for the mill. Since the data is our own (a credible source!) and/or from peers

with no special ax to grind, why shouldn't we take the data to heart? At least the data is believable enough so that we have the basis for making appropriate changes.

I recall conducting a management seminar that used a "coaching practices survey." This entailed securing live data from the subordinates of those attending the program and feeding it back to the participants in the session entitled "The Manager as a Coach." Several participants, months later, told me this was the most meaningful part of the (two-week) program for them.

Are there any disadvantages to instrumentation? Pfeiffer and Jones cite several [2]. Some participants may feel threatened by the information it reveals. (One predictable reaction is nitpicking the instrument.) Others may be overly impressed by the "numbers" involved. Still others may feel that they are back in school, conjuring up unpleasant memories of test taking, grading, and the like. Data overload may also be a problem. However, in my experience (and that of many other trainers as well), if the instruments are related to worthwhile learning objectives, administered in a professional and low-key way, used sparingly, and placed in a supportive rather than threatening group climate, there is really no problem.

A final general point about instruments: In the training situation they typically are *not*—and need not be—validated psychological instruments complete with norms or validity/reliability data. Rather, they are stimuli for:

- ☐ Self-assessment of one's behavior, and thus self-help.
- ☐ Assessment of others' behavior—individual or group—so that those assessed may use the data (feedback) for examination (introspection, discussion, analysis) and possibly a change in behavior.

INSTRUMENT FORMATS

Behavioral scientists use many types of instruments. Undoubtedly, you have heard of such devices as the semantic-differential rating instrument, the Likert scale for attitude measurement, the forced-choice technique, and sociometric ratings, plus many other inventories, questionnaires (sometimes called opinionnaires), opinion-rating scales, reaction forms, surveys, tests, quizzes, and checklists. But regardless of the precise nomenclature of a particular instrument, our interest in them, as trainers, is simply to generate data for assessment (diagnosis) of individual, group, or organizational attitudes or behavior.

In a more specific sense the instruments—let's call them *learning instruments*—most helpful to trainers fall into two categories: feedback devices and self-report inventories.

Feedback devices are tools which are used by participants to collect data about the attitudes or behavior of other participants. The data collectors are typically called observers. Their job is to report back to the "learners" information which can help them to identify strong points (positive feedback) or shortcomings (negative feedback). The learners, armed with data that they would not ordinarily be aware of, are now in a position to alter their attitudes or behavior. Any such modification assumes, of course, that (1) the data is acceptable ("makes sense") to the learner and (2) the data is something that is under the learner's control so that change *is* possible. For example, if the learner is a rather serious person, there is little point in feedback which suggests the greater use of humor in group work. Conversely, the person who monopolizes the available air time at group sessions or who regularly "holds back" (the low participator) may find observer data about such behavior quite helpful.

Feedback devices are discussed in more detail in Chapter 13, which is about team building.

Self-report inventories (also called self-description and self-assessment inventories) are tools that produce structured data about an individual's on-the-job behavior and attitudes, values, traits, perceptions, and the like. Typical inventories used in the training situation relate to how one sees one's leadership style; or one's skill as a delegator, time manager, communicator, motivator, coach, planner, risk-taker, or salesperson; or if one sees oneself as a safety-oriented person; or as a customer service person; etc.

Although these self-report devices may obviously be used to measure and evaluate results of training on a "before and after" basis, we are primarily concerned with these devices as tools during the training situation. In short, they are designed to encourage introspection about one's attitudes and/or behavior in the work environment so that one can bring about changes that seem appropriate.

WHEN TO USE INSTRUMENTS

Instruments can be used at various points in the training situation. For example, they can be used as:

Pre-work. Instruments are a good way to involve participants very early in the training process. To the degree that group members work on a task before they even come to class, they are clearly involved in the course or program. Additionally, they are motivated by it, made aware that they are in an active program, and alerted to the fact that the trainer is trying to maximize everyone's return from the training experience.

An icebreaker. An instrument may be used to warm up the group. A simple, fun-type one to use is the sentence completion instrument in Appendix 26.

A session opener. A formal session, such as one that ordinarily opens with a formal presentation—a talk, panel discussion, or film—can be made participative and thought-stimulating by starting things off with an instrument. In some cases data may be collected from the group and used as "live" input to make certain points.

A mid-session stimulator. The instrument may be used strategically at various stages in the ongoing program. In some cases it can be used as part of a group exercise.

A program wrap-up. The instrument can also be used as a practical way to end a session or a total program. Assuming the participants have been exposed to a certain amount of theory and practice, the instrument can be used as a means of applying what was learned to one's personal situation.

Note: The best use of instruments takes place when the data is thoroughly processed by the group. So be certain to allow enough time—30 to 60 minutes—for working it through.

A back-home thought-stimulator. Training programs dealing with leadership, human relations, assertiveness, personal growth, team building, time management, communications, etc. are often concerned with the encouragement of introspection after participants return to their jobs. One or more instruments may be given to participants for such a purpose.

Note: Most instruments may be used at various points in the program, as suggested, but certain instruments, because of their possible frustration or stress potential for some participants, should be used late in the course or program. This thought is developed in more detail in the chapter summary.

HOW TO USE INSTRUMENTS

These guides should help to maximize the use of instruments.

1. Before using an instrument in the training situation, you should ask yourself: Why am I doing this? Will it fit into and further the overall training design? Am I relating it to a specific theory, a model, a film, or an exercise? How does the quiz relate to participant expectations? Am I allowing enough time for processing by participants? Will the instrument create anxiety for the participants?

2. The first step in the use of an instrument is for the trainer to explain to the participants that it is not a test in the traditional classroom sense; no one is going to be graded on it. Rather, it is a tool to encourage an inward look (introspection) about one's practices (or beliefs) about the subject under discussion; the forms will be discussed in small groups after they are completed.

3. When everyone has completed the questionnaires, have them score the forms if a scoring key is provided. Alternatively, it may be desirable to score the instruments *after* the small-group work. The latter procedure will avoid a focus on the scores.

4. Assign participants to small groups for discussion of the quiz. Trios work out well for this since they permit both diverse thought and intimacy for candid sharing of results. Typical questions for the groups to discuss are: "Which items gave us the most trouble? Was there a pattern in our responses and, if there was, do we agree with it? Was the quiz helpful, overall? What was our major learning?" Give the groups 30 or 40 minutes for discussion.

5. Wrap up the activity by holding a group-at-large discussion of the learnings in the small groups. A sure-fire starter for this is: "Who would like to share what went on in their trio?" Be prepared for one or two participants to challenge the clarity or even the validity of certain quiz items. A good way to avoid unnecessary confrontation is to turn the (possibly hostile) question back to the group and ask: "Does anyone else also feel that way? Yes, two or three others do. You may have a point." In some instances it may be desirable to respond to a persistent challenger in this fashion: "Do you feel that those two questionable items destroy the overall value of the quiz?" A "no" response to this question will be an admission that the experience, overall, was helpful.

Action Planning

A good way to maximize results from the individual, small group, and group-at-large work is to take an additional 10–15 minutes for Action Planning (self-contracting for change). A sample form for this purpose is given in Appendix 97.

To reinforce the pledges for change made on the form, you may wish to have your participants meet in pairs or trios to discuss their self-contracts. Advise the participants that the purpose of the small-group work is to give and receive feedback about the realism of the self-contracts, to secure any other help about the contracts that may be needed, and generally to give help, support, and encouragement to one another.

As a final step to minimize slippage, the action plans could be discussed again—a progress check—in a follow-up session (see page 472).

INSTRUMENTS YOU CAN MAKE

Instruments can be obtained, ready-made, from certain publishers of training materials, management and training books, articles in periodicals, consulting firms, training programs you attend, colleagues, and so on. A list of publishers who supply instruments for training is given in Chapter 7, "Using Exercises."

However, if you cannot readily locate an instrument on a particular subject or if you feel purchasing instruments in quantity is too costly, there is no reason why you can't design many of them yourself. If you have any doubts about your capability to do so, let me assure you that you don't need to have a Ph.D. in tests and measurements to design worthwhile instruments for training purposes. We say for *training* purposes because we are not talking about tests that have to be marked by a high degree of validity and reliability. Rather, we are talking about instruments or quizzes whose aim is essentially to irritate, provoke, unsettle, stimulate, excite, and challenge rather than to measure in the psychometric sense. In short, we are talking about training tools to encourage introspection.

To appreciate how this might be done, let's take a look at five commonly used instruments:

- ☐ The yes-no type
- ☐ The sentence-completion type
- ☐ The rating scale
- ☐ The forced-choice technique
- ☐ The multiple-choice type

The Yes-No Type

Several forms of the yes-no type are given in Appendices 27–30. It is suggested you take these quizzes yourself to get a good feel for them. After you have done this, you will note these patterns in them:

1. The quiz quite clearly tries to elicit all "yes" answers ("Selling an Idea to the Boss," Appendix 27).

2. The quiz clearly tries to elicit all "no" answers ("Giving Employees Feedback," Appendix 28).

3. The desired responses in the quiz may be both "yes" and "no," with the first half of the questions calling for one response and the last half calling for the other response ("My Time Management Practices," Appendix 29).

4. The preferred responses to the quiz do not fit a predictable pattern.

5. The quiz is designed to elicit a "yes," "no," or "sometimes" response to give the participant more leeway than is possible in the yes-no format.

It doesn't really matter what form the quizzes take, because the instruments are designed to encourage introspection, much of which comes from the discussion of the quizzes in small groups. Of course, some instrument designers would argue that the mixed or nonpatterned yes-no type forces more careful concentration by the respondent.

Further variations in the format of the yes-no type instrument include:

1. The quiz items themselves can be presented either as statements ("My Time Management Practices") or as questions ("Giving Employees Feedback"). Some instrument designers would argue that the question style is more challenging, more stimulating, and more encouraging. This is possible, but I feel that the real learning takes place when the data is processed via small-group work.

2. Responses may be placed in a box or on a short horizontal line, or the boxes and lines may be completely omitted. This is a minor matter and only reflects designer preference. (I like the "professional" look of the boxes, as in the instrument "Selling an Idea to the Boss.")

3. Questions may be phrased in one of two ways: "Do *you* believe . . ."("Giving Employees Feedback," Appendix 28) or "Do *I* favor . . ." ("My Capabilities as a Delegator," Appendix 30). The latter is certainly more personal, possibly more inviting. But whether one style encourages more introspection, and thus more learning, than the other is doubtful.

4. Questions may be phrased to elicit yes-no responses in relation to time—now and in three months (90 days)—as a means of gauging possible improvement after the participant leaves the training program (Appendix 29a). The idea, of course, is to learn if there has been a change or improvement in one's behaviors/practices.

Note: The trainer may wish to send a follow-up note, possibly with another copy of the form, to remind program graduates to take a new look at themselves.

All of these variations are of minor importance. The content of the quiz items and the opportunities to process one's answers are the major keys to learning from instruments.

The Rating Scale

In the yes-no type instrument, the respondent is asked to reply to questions or statements that require only a positive or negative answer. In other circumstances it may be more realistic to ask the participants to indicate the degree to which they hold a certain attitude or the frequency with which they behave or perform in a certain way. Hence the need for a rating scale.

Examples of two rating scales are given in Appendices 31 and 32. Note that they differ both as to format and as to scoring:

1. "My Skill as a Listener" uses the words *Never, Seldom, Occasionally, Frequently,* and *Always,* rather than numerical weights to express degree. It also uses questions rather than statements to present the 15 elements to be rated. The data is summed up by the participant in the form of a profile as in Figure 9-1.

2. "My C.S.Q.," conversely, uses a four-factor numerical scale to express degree. It employs statements rather than questions in presenting the 15 elements, and the data is summed up via a single score.

In respect to the five rating words we used in "My Skill as a Listener," we could have retained the basic format and made these variations in that rating scheme: We could have replaced the words with a simple numerical rating scheme, which would also express degree, or we could have combined the word and numerical rating scales, as in the following:

My Skill As a Listener

Element	Never	Seldom	Sometimes	Frequently	Always
	1	2	3	4	5

We could also have reversed the sequence of the words, putting *Always* first and *Never* last.

Note: I do not ordinarily favor the reversed format, because I want the respondent to read all the words carefully before considering checking one of higher frequency.

We could also have altered the format along this line:

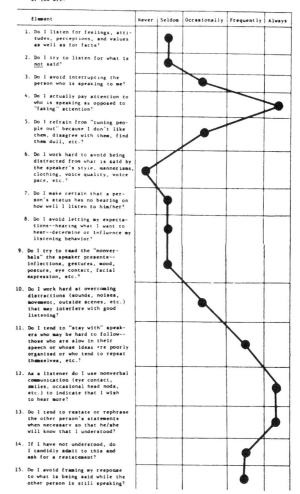

Figure 9-1. Example of a rating worksheet that uses a rating scale with a sample profile drawn in.

Do I listen for feelings, attitudes, perceptions, values as well as for facts?

Never (1). . . . . Always (10)

Another way to score the quiz "My Skill as a Listener," besides using a profile, is to assign points to each rating such as:

Never	2 points
Seldom	4 points
Sometimes	6 points
Frequently	8 points
Always	10 points

On this scale a large score is best. The points could also be assigned conversely so that a low score would be desirable. However, a profile seems to be more helpful to the participant than this scoring procedure. The point of all this is that there are many ways to present rating scales. We have presented some of the more common variations.

Another way to use the profile is to have the participants complete the form twice—at the outset of the program and at its end. They would use separate forms for each rating and enter the second set of data on the first form. This would give two profiles on one form for comparison.

The profile technique as just described is designed for self-evaluation. It may also be used to allow participants to evaluate each other. For example, in a program concerned with learning counseling skills, participants could compare their actual performance as perceived by their peers with their original self-evaluation. The two profiles would dramatically show the difference in self and peer perceptions.

A commonly used scale is one which presents a number of statements, each of which is followed by a 5-point rating scale, for example:

1. I listen for the actual message, not just the words presented to me.   1 2 3 4 5
2. I avoid interrupting a speaker at all costs.
                                                        1 2 3 4 5

A simple form of weighted scoring may be used with the 1 response (or rating) receiving 1 point, the 2 response (or rating) receiving 2 points, etc. A complete copy of this instrument, with scoring instructions, is given in Appendix 33, "My Skill as a Listener—A Self-Quiz."

Another form of the rating scale follows:

1	2	3	4	5	6	7	8	9
(LO)								(HI)

It is essentially a continuum with a high and low range. It could be used, for example, to rate oneself, one's boss, one's subordinates, one's peers, and other group members in the training situation. A specific example of its use is given in Figure 9-2.

Trust Exercise

Many authorities on leadership, communication, and management assert that a trusting relationship is basic to leadership effectiveness. On the scale below enter data at three points to indicate the degree to which:

1. You trust your subordinates (S)
2. You trust your boss (B)
3. You believe your subordinates trust you (S-I)

Here is a sample of a complete rating on the scale:

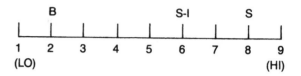

Here is the scale *you* are to use:

After you have made your entries on the scale, you will meet with two fellow participants to discuss your ratings. We will conclude this exercise by a general discussion of (1) the importance of trust as a factor in successful leadership and (2) how it can be further developed if we are so inclined.

Figure 9-2. Examples of an exercise containing a continuum-type rating scale.

In respect to the continuum approach, such rating procedures could be used to assess assertiveness, intimacy (getting close to others for more authentic communication), delegation prowess, skill and/or interest in developing subordinates, creativity, etc.

Another way to use the continuum is on an *ad hoc* or informal basis—that is, when a situation arises in which it is desirable to help an individual or the total group better think through a problem, concept, feeling, or decision by applying a measurement ("quantitative thinking") to it.

For example, here is a dialogue between a participant and the trainer.

Participant: I'm not sure I could succeed in that kind of job situation.
Trainer: Not sure?
Participant: No, not really sure.
Trainer: Let's see if you can be more specific about your feeling. Here's a 10-point scale (draws scale on flipchart); could you express your feeling for us on this scale?

Another participant-trainer exchange that could precipitate using a continuum follows:

Participant: I just can't count on my staff.

Trainer: They're not a dependable group?

Participant: Overall, I'd say not really.

Trainer: Let's see if we can make this more specific. Here's a scale of 1–100. If you had to rate them on "dependability," where would you put them on this scale?

Participant: OK, about a 20. (Trainer enters 20 on scale.)

Trainer: That's pretty low.

Participant: Right.

Trainer: And how would you rate them on creativity, risk taking, and cost consciousness?

Or, in a race-relations-improvement program, the trainer may begin a discussion:

Trainer: Minorities often make references to a lack of concern by the majority of society at large. "Betty, where would you see yourself on this concern continuum?"

Betty: I'd say about 85.

Trainer: (Enters Betty's score on continuum) Emma, do you agree with Betty's self-rating?

Emma: Definitely not. I'd say she's at about 30. (Trainer enters score.)

Or, the trainer may present a scale dealing with confronting conflict—the willingness to face up to and work through differences candidly and constructively. The trainer would then ask each person to rate themselves, entering each rating on the continuum.

Another informal use of the rating scale is to secure ratings on *two* scales simultaneously. For example, in a session concerned with change, quality improvement, productivity, and team effectiveness, the trainer might ask the group to provide comparative data on a "before and after" basis, or "past and present" basis, or "present and future (hoped for)" basis. The latter two scales might be presented to the group for rating in the following manner.

The trainer would then secure ratings on each scale from the individual group members, tally them, and develop a group average. The data could be collected by oral statements on a "round robin" basis, by show of hands, or by entering ratings on small pieces of paper if participants wish to "vote" (rate) anonymously.

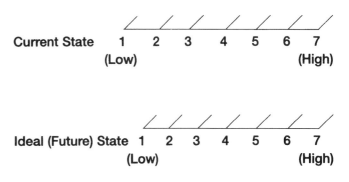

The Sentence-Completion Type

One of the easiest instruments to develop, assuming one has the content well in hand, is one which asks participants to complete a group of open-ended statements. The objective is to have the participant react to the incomplete sentence and thereby disclose information on attitudes and perceptions about self, job, career, and working with and supervising others. The rationale for this procedure is that the best way to achieve personal growth is to hold up to the light of day one's attitudes, values, and practices. In the absence of such self-disclosure and subsequent self-examination, growth or change is not very likely.

Parenthetically, it may be observed that other instruments—for example, the yes-no type—could do a good job of encouraging disclosure and introspection about self. But the point is that the sentence-completion type is particularly well suited for this purpose. Why? Because it necessitates deeper *reflection* and actual *verbalization* about the data being elicited, as opposed to requiring a response to a complete statement previously prepared by someone else.

In any case, we can readily identify four typical uses to which we can apply the sentence-completion instrument:

As an icebreaker. One simple use of this type of instrument is for social or fun purposes—more specifically, to loosen up group members and acquaint them with one another. It merely asks participants to disclose everyday favorites or preferences among a variety of things. See Appendix 26 for an example of this type of instrument.

A more profound form of this instrument, "As I See Myself" in Appendix 34, may also be used as an icebreaker. However, because of its personal character, it would be used only in a training program that is highly experiential and personal-growth oriented.

As a program opener. Another type of sentence-completion instrument takes a different tack. For example, at the very outset of the program it may ask for disclosure concerning one's career, leadership beliefs, job satisfaction, and relations with bosses, subordinates, peers, and the organization. Aside from the usual objective of instruments—to encourage introspection—an added value is that it alerts the participant at the outset that the program is for deeper, personal development, not merely for teaching abstractly "about management." For an illustration of this type of instrument, see "Management Development—Openers," in Appendix 35.

For mid-program use. Completion-type instruments, like other instruments, can be used at various points in the program. The instrument "As I See the Coaching Process," in Appendix 36, would be useful before, during, or after a session concerned with "the manager as a coach." It might be used early in the program to help set the stage for things to come, or at the close of the program as a wrap-up activity. Although our sample instrument would stimulate the participant's thinking to a fair degree, it would not be as challenging as "Management Development—Openers" since it is less personal.

As a personal awareness stimulator. In an experiential training program, that is, where one learns primarily from one's experience, the encouragement of introspection is very much the norm. Such programs include assertiveness training, T-groups, encounter groups, and diversity training. The sentence-completion instrument might be used as an opener (see "As I See Myself," Appendix 34) or at other stages in the program (see "As I See You," Appendix 37).

A question might be raised whether the statements presented in "As I See Myself" and "As I See You" ask participants to engage in considerable self-disclosure and thus might be stressful to some people. It should be remembered that in the context of the goals and norms of the aforementioned experiential training programs (assertiveness training, etc.), few, if any, participants would be subject to undue anxiety by completing the statements as requested.

The processing of the data generated by the sentence-completion instruments is typically shared in pairs or trios. The small group procedure allows for intimacy, privacy, and support, as may be needed. In less experiential (more conventional or intellectual) programs, the instrument can be processed instead on a solo basis. More specifically, the participant could

1. Privately complete the instrument at the start of the program. (See "Management Development—Openers," Appendix 35.)
2. File it in a notebook as opposed to discussing it with anyone.
3. Complete it again, using a second copy, at program's end. Different responses on any of the items represent the "net gain" of the program.
4. Optionally, the participants could (at program's end) meet in pairs to share their reactions to both forms, discussing their "before" and "after" responses.

Here are a few sample open-ended statements in areas where sentence-completion-type instruments could be used.

☐ Communication
  I am at my communication best when I _____.
  I am at my communication worst when I _____.
  In communicating with peers or colleagues I find that _____.

☐ *Group functioning*
  I see this group as _____.
  What bothers me about this group is _____.
  What I like about this group is _____.

☐ *Development of intimacy*
  My pet peeve is _____.
  I see money as _____.
  My hobby is _____.
  If I were to change my name (first, last, or both), I would _____.

☐ *Giving feedback*
  My feeling about giving praise is _____.
  My feeling about giving criticism is _____.

☐ *Careers*
  Five years from now I hope to _____.
  The biggest obstacle to attaining my career goals is _____.
  As I see my boss in relation to my career _____.

Remember, the trick in developing open-ended statements is simply to "auto-brainstorm" ideas and concepts in relation to a given theme or topic, select the best ones, and write them out, as in the preceding examples.

The Forced-Choice Technique

In the forced-choice technique, participants are given an inventory form (see "My Style as a Manager" in Appendix 24) that asks them to choose between two items or statements. The preferred item may be hard to decide upon, since both statements may be ones that the respondent can readily "buy." However, by being constantly forced to choose between the two more or less acceptable statements, the participant creates a pattern of responses.

As is explained under "Scoring of Instruments," a numerical score on the forced-choice quiz is useful primarily as an indicator of a tendency toward a point of view or set of behaviors. It is *not* intended to measure the general "correctness" of one's responses.

Note: Anticipate complaints about the difficulty of making a hard choice. You can only agree with the complainants and simply advise them to do the best they can under the circumstances. (Life frequently offers us difficult choices!)

The Multiple-Choice Type

The multiple-choice technique is particularly useful when you want to help participants see their pattern or style when a number of patterns or styles may exist—for example, a style of leadership, a communication pattern, a consulting style, a training style, a selling style, a style in "managing" one's boss, or a problem-solving style. An example of a problem-solving style quiz, in multiple-choice format, is given in Appendix 38, "My Approach to Problem Solving."

As you have probably surmised, this type of quiz is more difficult to construct than the yes-no type, the rating scale, or the forced-choice type. This follows since several well-thought-out and well-stated choices have to be developed for each quiz item, and all quiz items have to be logical and consistent with one another. We built seven problem-solving styles into the quiz on problem solving. Of all the sample instruments we have provided, this was the most complex to construct.

GUIDELINES FOR CONSTRUCTING INSTRUMENTS

If you should find it necessary to develop your own instruments, here are some suggestions that should help you accomplish this task.

1. Build a reference file of instruments of *varying formats.* Don't worry too much about the content. As we indicated above, they can be found in books, magazines, and newspapers, or purchased from instrument publishers.

2. Study the formats which have been used by others—yes-no, multiple-choice, rating scales, etc.

3. As you analyze them, try to acquire a feel for their rhythm, style, tone. Note the way the authors of particular instruments have chosen word patterns to stimulate thought. Also note the length and variety of the quiz items.

4. Collect data about the content of the area you wish to instrumentalize. For example, if you decide to construct an instrument on delegation, check out five or ten meaty articles on that subject. Extract the key points from those articles and add them to what you already know about the subject. You are now ready to go to work!

5. Put each major idea on a separate note card. Then rank (arrange) them in order of importance. The odds are that you'll have more ideas than you need.

6. Select the most important ideas to constitute the quiz. You may have as many as 20, possibly a few more. Remember that a "fancy" questionnaire that seeks opinions on trivial or irrelevant questions is really no instrument at all.

7. Arrange your quiz ideas in the sequence that makes the most sense. For example, in a quiz on one's skill as a communicator, you would probably group together all ideas that pertain to listening, all that pertain to perception, all that pertain to feedback, etc.

8. Decide on the format you wish to use. The yes-no, the sentence-completion, and the rating-scale formats are the easiest to construct.

9. Develop your instrument by writing the necessary quiz items. Review them several times for clarity, logic, coverage, etc.

10. Decide whether you wish to provide a scoring system. If you do decide to have one, select a simple one.

11. Check out your handiwork further on one or more colleagues. They may note some things you missed—ambiguities, inconsistencies, or even omissions.

12. "De-bug" the instrument further by informally trying it out on a small group of participants. Try to ascertain which items, if any, they disliked. Correct or drop such items.

13. After your first use of the instrument in the training situation, revise it and keep revising it, as indicated, based on feedback from the participants.

SCORING OF INSTRUMENTS

If you have taken the quizzes cited in this chapter, or at least studied them, you will have noticed that the scoring procedures vary quite a bit. In fact, if you begin to collect instruments, as we suggest you do, you will find a great variety of such procedures. Regardless of the variations, though, we can say that in the training situation an instrument may be scored in either one of two ways: generally or precisely.

If the scoring is intended to call attention to "tendencies," only general scores are necessary. For example, the forced-choice instrument "My Style as a Manager" in Appendix 24 asks participants only to identify and tally their Theory X and Y items. It does not ask them to compute percentages or to total points to ascertain "how much" of a Theory X or Y leader one is. Such precise computation would not be very meaningful.

Conversely, a number of our sample instruments provide scoring instructions so that participants can assess quite precisely *the degree* to which they are effective delegators, effective givers of feedback, effective introducers of change, effective "promoters" of an idea to one's boss, etc. For some participants numbers can have worthwhile catalytic value.

How general or how precise you decide the scoring of your quizzes should be will depend, of course, on such factors as the composition of your group, your course objectives, and your own pedagogical philosophy. In fact, you may wish to try out different procedures from time to time. But regardless of the

approach you take to scoring, here are some suggestions regarding the use of scoring systems:

Keep them simple and logical. Avoid complex scoring systems which are likely to produce confusion, frustration, or defensiveness. For example, a scoring system that gives a 3 for the desirable responses and a 1 for the undesirable ones, or one that *subtracts* points for undesirable responses, may be questioned vigorously by at least some participants.

Emphasize to participants that the scores are hardly final, iron-clad, scientific judgments. Rather, they are merely general guides as to patterns or tendencies.

Stress to the group that discussion of the quiz items is what it's all about. The quiz is intended to encourage one to focus on one's behavior, attitudes, values, and perceptions, not on the numbers which accompany it. *Introspection* is the name of the game.

THE PARTICIPANT-PREPARED INSTRUMENT

Participants may be utilized to construct their own instruments. This makes for a novel, fun-type activity. It is also a good way to defuse hostility toward or questioning about an instrument, inasmuch as the participants have developed it themselves. This follows since all of us are more likely to accept what we create, even though someone else's product may be superior in certain ways.

A procedure for developing the participant-prepared instrument is as follows:

1. Have the total group develop a list of the points to be covered. This may relate to the qualities of an effective leader, an effective team, or an effective communicator. This may be done via brainstorming, the slip method, small-group work, or contributions by the group at large. I prefer to have this work performed on a small-group basis to ensure maximum participation.

2. If it is done by small groups, have them put their data on flipcharts. Then post the completed charts on the wall for a brief discussion about them.

3. Have the participants return to their small groups to prepare a master list, selecting the best ideas from all the flipcharts. Have the small groups limit their lists to a certain number of items, possibly 15 or 20.

4. Post the lists again, noting similarities and differences. Then working from one flipchart, have the total group agree on the best 10 to 20 items. This can be done by a voice vote or a show of hands: "How many want to include this item? Sixteen. This one? Ten." Then go to the other flipcharts and repeat the process. The items which have the most votes become the quiz items.

5. Let the group add a numerical rating scale to the quiz items, such as 1–5, 1–7, or 1–10.

6. The instrument, in final form, can be typed and reproduced (assuming clerical help and equipment are available) for all participants, or it can be written on flipcharts.

7. Have the participants complete the new form and then discuss their self-ratings in trios, as described in the prior section.

A SUMMARY

The following paragraphs and Table 9-1 summarize the nature and use of the five types of instruments previously presented.

Ease of construction. The sentence-completion type is the easiest instrument to construct (just come up with pertinent ideas you want participants to "spell out"), and the forced-choice type is the hardest. Forced choice is difficult because *two* statements have to be created for a given concept, both of which are plausible and acceptable enough to present the respondent with a dilemma as to choice. But despite the apparent plausibility of the two statements, they must be, in fact, different enough to help consistently set off one set of beliefs or behaviors from another.

The multiple-choice type of instrument is also fairly complex to construct since it entails working with a large amount of data essential to differentiating a variety of patterns and styles (for example, of leadership, communication, assertiveness). Our example, "My Approach to Problem Solving," Appendix 38, is very complex since this instrument delineates seven problem solving styles.

Structure. By "structure" we mean a set of completed statements or questions, a scoring procedure, etc. All but the sentence-completion type of instrument are high in structure. The sentence-completion type is "free-form" and permits no scoring.

Ease of responding. The sentence-completion type, if it probes fairly deeply into feelings, attitudes, and beliefs, may be the most difficult instrument to complete. This follows since the participant is "forced" to use his/her own thoughts and words to complete the sentence. Obviously, some participants may find this hard to do. The forced-choice type, while not a strain on one's verbal ability as is sentence completion, often presents a problem to the participant because of the *apparent* acceptability of the paired statements. Not everyone enjoys wrestling with alternatives.

To put the "ease of responding" issue into proper perspective, we should recognize that *any* instrument which encourages introspection about one's style, attitudes, beliefs, values, and practices may be difficult for participants who are not comfortable with self-disclosure

Table 9-1
Evaluation of the Five Types of Instruments

Evaluation Factor	Yes-No	Rating Scale	Sentence Completion	Forced Choice	Multiple Choice
Ease of construction	Easy	Easy	Very Easy	Very Difficult	Fairly Complex
Degree of structure in format	High	High	Low	Very High	Very High
Ease of responding	Easy	Easy	May be difficult, depending on quiz	Often difficult	Not too difficult
Possible stress on respondent	Little	Little	May be high, depending on quiz	A fair degree	Moderate
Discussion stimulator	Good	Good	Good (or better)	Good (or better)	Good
Data collector and organizer	Very effective	Very effective	Poor	Very effective	Very effective
Time required by group to process data	Variable, depending on number and complexity of items, group motivation	Variable	Variable	Variable	Variable
Effectiveness in relation to nature of group	No special problem	No special problem	With an "uptight" group, use later or not at all	With an "uptight" group, use later on	No special problem
Face validity	Fairly high	Excellent	Low	Fair to good	Fairly high

(talking freely about themselves). Fortunately, this is not a problem for most adults in training programs that match participants and course content properly.

Stress. In light of the previous considerations, stress on certain respondents may be highest for the sentence completion and forced-choice types of instruments. The best training procedure, therefore, is to know one's group well, and, if a negative reaction is expected, either use the more challenging instrument late in the program or possibly not at all. Stress may also be related to participant expectations of the program. For example, participants may expect somewhat "stressful" activities at an experiential learning program but not at all at an "intellectual" management development program relying primarily on case study, films, and lectures. Feelings of stress may be based, too, on whether attendance in the program is voluntary or required.

Discussion stimulator. All instruments, given the right content and training environment, are good discussion stimulators. Experience with instrumentation indicates that it is highly natural for participants to respond to statements or questions that either inquire about or challenge their beliefs and practices.

Introspection stimulator. Again, all instruments, if properly constructed, possessed of the right content, and used in the right training situation, will encourage participants to look inward.

Data collection. As to the feasibility of collecting data for individual or group scoring, all but the sentence-completion type work well. The latter type obviously cannot be scored or tallied.

Processing time. All instrumented work in the training situation takes time. There are no shortcuts to a (desired) profound discussion. Depending on the number and complexity of the items in a quiz, 30–45 minutes is a minimum time period; 60–90 minutes may be more desirable. Processing the data in pairs or trios, rather than in larger groups, does help to move the discussion along. The two- or three-person teams also provide the desired privacy and intimacy.

Group factors. What about effectiveness in relation to the nature of the group? As mentioned before, the only possibility of a negative reaction is from a group that has several "uptight" members who are asked to deal with a highly *unstructured* instrument such as the sentence-completion type. (Of course, some respondents may be uncomfortable with any instrument that they perceive as too personal in its probing.) The resis-

tance may come because of the requirement of verbalizing and declaring oneself on issues that may be regarded as too close to home. On the other hand, most participants should respond favorably to sentence completion, given the psychological need for closure, that is, to complete the sentences on the form.

Stage of program. Most instruments may be used at any point in the program. Some groups, however, may not be ready for the sentence-completion and forced-choice types until later on in the program. Of course, *any* instrument that asks for considerable self-disclosure of attitudes and feelings has to be employed judiciously.

Face validity. Finally, all instruments by virtue of their formal structure, except possibly for the sentence-completion type, should be well received by participants. The scoring, development of one or more profiles, etc., all help in this regard. Actually, since the material generated by the quizzes relates to oneself (as opposed to, say, a case or an abstract game) acceptance is typically high. Most participants find instruments to be fun, even fascinating. Learning about oneself, even if somewhat discomforting, is ordinarily perceived as being very much worthwhile.

Note: The intent of the evaluative comment "No special problem" in Table 9-1 is to encourage the trainer to use all the types of instruments. Most groups, if they are "with the program" and properly indoctrinated, should not resist the assignment. Certainly any instrument may provoke a negative reaction from *some* participants, at times. But the instruments basically work, with the caution that the sentence-completion type requires a bit more sophisticated (and verbal) group.

KEY POINTS

1. Instruments are basic tools for experiential learning.
2. Instruments are useful for generating data that individuals, groups, and the total organization can look at to augment their effectiveness.
3. In the training situation, instruments are a tool for introspection and discussion. Accordingly, it is not essential that they be subject to validation, norming, etc., as are instruments used in psychological assessment, counseling, therapy, and attitude measurement.

4. Instrument data is generated via self-report and/or feedback from others. Although self-assessment is not necessarily an objective source of data, it nevertheless serves as a basis for discussion with others.

5. Instruments may be used at various stages in a training program—as pre-work, as icebreakers and/or openers, in mid-session, to close things out, or as a back-home follow-up.

6. Instruments may be purchased, found in professional journals and books, or designed by the trainer.

7. Instruments that are fairly easy to make are the yes-no, sentence-completion, and rating-scale types. Of greater complexity are the forced-choice and multiple-choice types.

8. Rating scales can assume many formats. Certain ones lend themselves readily to the construction of *profiles*. Profiles may also be used for self-comparison and comparison with scores given by others.

9. To construct an instrument, one should collect data on the subject it is to treat; select a format and scoring system; develop 10–20 statements/ideas; prioritize the ideas; check out the instrument with colleagues for logic, readability, and the like; and "field test" it if possible.

10. Instruments also may be developed by participants. It is fun to do and gives the device ready acceptance by participants.

11. A key factor for maximizing results from instrumentation is to allow adequate time for processing.

REFERENCES

1. Blake, R. R., and Mouton, J. S., "Instruments to Create Involvement," *Sales Meetings* (October 1971), p. 62.

2. Pfeiffer, J. W., and Jones, J. E. (Eds.), *The 1976 Annual Handbook for Group Facilitators,* University Associates, San Diego (1976), p. 65.

RECOMMENDED READING

Blake, R. R., and Mouton, J. S., "Instruments to Create Involvement," *Sales Meetings,* October 1971, pp. 62–68.
This article discusses theory and advantages of instrumented learning. It also describes various types of instruments, including ratings, forced-choice, and multiple choice.

Bumstead, R., "Delicate Measures," *Northeast Training News,* July 1980, pp. 10, 12.
This article treats various issues in instrumentation such as overcoming resistance by participants, keeping data private, and do's and don'ts in instrument use.

Buzzota, V. R., Lefton, R. E., and Sherberg, M., "Instruments," *Sales Meetings,* October 1971, pp. 77–87.
This describes various instruments which can be used in training, including feedback instruments, questionnaires and surveys, tests, and problem-solving instruments.

Lomac, J., "On Tests and Behavior Change: Individualizing Feedback," *Northeast Training News,* December 1981, pp. 19–20.
This describes how to individualize the feedback that develops from a well-constructed diagnostic assessment instrument.

Pfeiffer, W. J., and Hestin, R., *Instrumentation in Human Relations Training: A Guide to 75 Instruments with Wide Application to the Behavioral Sciences,* University Associates, San Diego, 1973.
The book is designed to introduce group facilitators from a variety of orientations to the use of instruments in human relations training.

Pfeiffer, J., and Jones, J. E., *Annual Handbook for Group Facilitators,* University Associates, San Diego, 1972 and each following year.
Each *Annual* contains a section on instruments, comprising (1) summary statements about instrument theory and use as well as (2) a number of actual instruments authored by various trainers.

Van Velsor, Ellen, and Wall, Stephen J., "How to Choose a Feedback Instrument," *Training,* March 1992, pp. 46–52.
If you wish to use commercially prepared instruments, you can make an informed choice by considering these elements: objectives, how the instrument was developed, its soundness in terms of validity and reliability, the feedback it delivers to the manager who is rated (for example, how much feedback and in what form), and whether the feedback format helps the participating manager interpret the data.

Zemke, R., "Using Testing Instruments in Your Training Effort," *Training/HRD,* November 1982, pp. 30–32, 36–38, 40–44.
An overview of instrumentation in training, including its impact on the training function, how to use instruments properly, vendors, and a survey of its intended usage (for example, in communication, personal growth).

10 Defining a Problem and Generating Data About It

No problem is so large or complex that it can't be run away from.

> —Charlie Brown, character in *Peanuts*
> cartoon strip

Creative thinking may mean simply the realization that there's no particular virtue in doing things the way they have always been done.

> —Rudolph Flesch, U.S. author and
> popularizer of communication skills

To an ever-increasing degree, organizations are insisting on payoffs from all training activities. As a consequence, more and more training programs are becoming job-oriented, either in whole or in part. This is true whether we are talking about management development, supervisory training, team building, quality circles, or sales and customer service training.

Trainers, then, are expected to utilize their skills to help participants generate new ideas rather than just to have them listen to old ones. The concern is to increase productivity/quality by helping people to work smarter, rather than just harder [1].

One way to ensure that training is organization- and job-related is to introduce into the training endeavor opportunities for identifying and solving real problems. Consequently, the lines between what is termed a conference or a sales or management meeting and what is termed a training program are often quite blurred.

The value of working on live problems is well stated by one writer: "When participants use the training session to solve their own problems, they do not experience 'training shock' from returning to their jobs and not knowing how to apply their new-found knowledge and skills. The reason: they brought chunks of their jobs into the classroom" [2].

On the assumption, then, that organizational personnel should be encouraged to solve their own problems effectively, the trainer must be well equipped to provide such guidance as may be necessary. This means providing problem-solving instruction to participants for

☐ Use in the training situation.

☐ Use back home on a continuing basis after the training is over.

PROBLEM SOLVING—SUGGESTED CONTENT

What kind of problem-solving skills should the trainer be able to develop among those who solve problems? The skills, which relate to the classic model of problem solving and decision making, are how to

☐ Define the problem.

☐ Generate data about the problem.

☐ Generate ideas or alternative courses of action for problem resolution.

☐ Choose among the alternative solutions.

☐ Implement the solution or decision.

The pages that follow develop these skill areas in more detail. This chapter will treat the first two steps in the problem-solving process: "How to define the problem" and "How to generate data about the problem."

Chapter 11 will treat the third step: "How to generate ideas (solutions) about the problem for its resolution."

Chapter 12 will discuss our final two steps (or skill areas) in the problem-solving process: "How to choose among alternatives" and "How to plan and implement the solution." The chapter will also discuss a number of additional approaches to problem solving.

The whole thrust of this and the following two chapters is this: problem solvers and decision makers should be equipped with a *broad* repertoire of techniques/approaches to augment their potential for developing strategies to resolve difficulties and capitalize on opportunities. As the late, great humanistic psychologist Dr. Abraham Maslow stated, "If the only tool you have is a hammer, you tend to see every problem as a nail."

LAUNCHING PROBLEM-SOLVING TRAINING

Before beginning a problem-solving session, consider these warm-up activities (openers):

☐ Help participants get into a problem-solving mood by walking them through the exercise sheet entitled "Check Your I.Q. (Imagination Quotient)," in Appendix 25. This is a fun activity that will experientially make the point that problem solving requires nonconventional, even bizarre thinking.

☐ Puzzles may also be used for this purpose.

☐ Conduct a dry run of the particular technique to be used. For example, if the group is new to brainstorming, conduct a mini-brainstorming session to give them a feel for the process.

HOW TO DEFINE THE PROBLEM

Said management authority Peter Drucker: "The most common source of mistakes in management decisions is the emphasis on finding the right answer rather than the right question." Scientist Albert Einstein put it this way: "The formulation of a problem is far more often essential than its solution, which may be merely a matter of mathematical or experimental skill."

Unquestionably, groups (and individuals) often handicap themselves by failing to define a problem properly. For example, a school superintendent was advised he had two choices to resolve a temporary classroom shortage: he must either add more mobile classrooms to the already crowded playground or bus students to other schools, which would then become crowded in turn. Instead of choosing either of these two solutions, however, he redefined the problem. This approach indicated that more space was needed, not just more units or busing. He thus recommended the purchase of an adjacent vacant lot, which the school district agreed to buy and construct a building on. It was later sold off as commercial property [3].

In a similar vein, a languishing firm producing audiovisual materials for the industrial market had difficulty solving its problem as long as it saw it simply as a "poor selling effort." It was not until it defined the problem as vending dull and dated materials ("yesterday's bread winners," as Peter Drucker calls them) that it was able to make any real headway in resolving its difficulties.

Clinical psychologists have long observed that people often formulate their problems in ways which actually prevent them from solving them. Some examples, both organizational and individual, are these: "Our problem is that the field is too competitive." "Our problem is that the market is too fluid." "Our problem is that we just don't understand *that* market." "Our problem is that we just don't have the trained personnel." "My problem is that I can never get the boss to listen to any of my ideas." "My problem is that I don't have the . . . (time, energy, connections, education, track record, 'smarts') to pull it off." In other words, problems which are defined in terms of resignation, blame of others, self-blame, insurmountable barriers, and the like are certain routes to non-resolution.

This concept is illustrated by the story of the boy who showed his father a book containing only blank pages. This brief dialogue ensued:

Dad (discarding book in dismay): "This book says nothing!"

Son (retrieving book respectfully): "This book says anything!"

Moral: You can't find new ways of doing things if you only look at them harder in the usual way.

Besides working on the wrong problem, problem solvers may be grappling with a problem that suffers from vagueness. The symptoms of a vague problem, according to David Murphy, are these [4]:

Buzz words. Reliance on generalized buzz words such as "communication," "morale," "marketing," and "productivity," terms which no one really understands.

Many versions/answers. Due to the vagueness of the problem, people are certain to define it differently and come up with many different answers. Guideline: When there are many answers, all dissimilar, look for a vaguely stated problem.

Murphy's answer to the vague problem dilemma is to ask people what the buzz words mean *to them.* Also, ask them to assume they have a magic wand. If the wand is waved, what will people stop doing or begin doing? A third alternative is to ask people to assume that they are movie directors, directing Tom Hanks or Emma Thompson. "How would you tell them to act? What would you have them say or do?"

The trainer or moderator can help a group look at its problem more realistically by posting the following criteria on a flipchart and asking them to respond "yes" or "no" to each of the five items [5]: Is the problem as now stated . . .

- ☐ Clear?
- ☐ Concise?
- ☐ Realistic?
- ☐ Achievable?
- ☐ Measurable (as practicable)?

If there are one or more "no" responses to these criteria, the problem must be restated or rephrased.

Brain Chain Reaction

To identify opportunities, often disguised as problems, use a savvy group to identify and define them. Consider the following procedures, offered by creativity authority Floyd Hurt, author of *Rousing Creativity: Think New Now!* (CRISP Publications, 1999) [6].

Problem Listing

1. Bring six knowledgeable people together, those who have a real insight into day-to-day operations. Have each team member list three problems he/she believes exist in the outfit. This will add up to 18 possible opportunities/problems.

2. Have each group member show his/her list to another person. Their task is to narrow their six identified problems to three.

3. Now have each of these pairs prioritize their three problems in descending order of importance. So now a total of nine problem statements or session objectives (three sets of three) are highlighted. The most important problem/opportunity is now No. 1 on each team member's list.

Problem/Opportunity Clarification

To be certain that each identified problem/opportunity truly merits the time, energy, and effort needed to work it through to completion, the group must clarify them. *Rationale:* There's no point developing a super plan only to learn later that the wrong problem or the wrong aspect of the problem was fixed. To get to the correct solution, then, use these three techniques, says Floyd Hurt:

a. *What then?* Once the problem focus is clear, group members should ask enough tough questions to be certain they are zeroing in on the heart of it. This will throw light on what the real problem is and also suggest the best course of action.

b. *Attack and defend the problem as stated.* Have two group members defend the statement of their problem as they have presented it. The rest of the team attacks the statement to be certain it is clear and concise in all respects. If a change is offered and accepted, those defending the change must assume the role of defender of the new statement/objective. At the end of the attack-and-defend phase, the group should have a statement objective on all identified problems that everyone can support, for they are now very clear, all of them having been subjected to maximum scrutiny.

c. *Redefine and review.* Now the group has its problem statements/session objectives presented to it for a creative look. Each team member jots down at least two diverse ways of presenting it. The idea is to see if these new statements/objectives trigger new thinking or amendments. A redefinition is not necessarily required. But we want to be certain that the statement/objective is fully ready for movement to the next step in the problem-solving process.

Are the above procedures too elaborate? Not if we want to be certain that we are totally clear about what we are ready to solve.

Other ways to zero in on the real problem include the use of techniques such as Pareto's analysis, brainstorming, statistical procedures, the check sheet, a checklist, and problem identification—ABC approach. Descriptions of these techniques follow.

Pareto's Analysis

Vilfredo Pareto (1848–1923), an Italian mathematician and economist, is famous for his "Law of Disproportionate Distribution." His "law" was based on an economic finding: 80% of Italy's wealth was subject to control by 20% of the total population. This finding has been applied by management writers to a variety of management circumstances:

- ☐ 80% of a budget may be allotted to 20% of the budgeted items.
- ☐ On the average, 80% of a firm's sales may be accomplished by 20% of the sales staff.
- ☐ 80% of sales may come from 20% of the customers.
- ☐ 80% of the company's gross profit may be produced by 20% of the product line.
- ☐ 80% of a productivity effort may come from 20% of the total input or effort.
- ☐ 80% of the complaints may come from 20% of the customers.
- ☐ 80% of the grievances may arise from 20% of the workforce.
- ☐ 80% of the downtime may derive from 20% of the equipment or machines.
- ☐ A political candidate, who analyzed his schedule, found that 80% of his exposure came from 20% of his speeches.

☐ Time management authority Alan Lakein advises that 80% of one's success comes from 20% of one's activities. Hence the need to avoid getting bogged down in low-value activities.

Extrapolating Pareto's rule to the safety area, it is not unusual to find that the preponderance of accidents are caused by relatively few personnel, or occur in a few specialized situations.

In general, the "maldistribution rule," or the "law of 20/80," while hardly an accurate predictor of results in all organizational situations, is useful as a way of getting managers (and others)

☐ To think in terms of inputs and outputs.

☐ To recognize that there is *not* an automatic relationship—one to one—between input (effort) and output (results).

☐ To realize that inefficiencies arise from failure to concentrate on the results-producing inputs, be it financial controls, personnel, products, daily activities, or training courses. (In respect to the latter item, you might carefully assess your training program offerings lest a mere 20% of them are producing 80% of the benefits to the organization!)

Pareto's analysis, then, is a useful tool for looking at problems and what seems to affect them. It tells us that although many factors may be present or at work in a problem situation, quite often only a vital few may have payoff possibilities. The technique could be used to advantage in team building sessions, quality circles, management and sales training courses, etc.

As an illustration of how we can apply Pareto's analysis to a specific problem, let's assume we operate a lawn mower plant. Our franchised dealers have given us data concerning customer complaints for the past one-year warranty period. Their defect data is shown in Table 10-1. We then group and tally all the defects, which gives us the data shown in Table 10-2.

The data are then put in a bar chart—the Pareto diagram—which takes the form shown in Figure 10-1.

Note that the chart shows each category of defect on *both* a numerical and a percentage basis. The 100% figure relates to the numerical total of defects (400); by segmenting or scaling the percentage line downward (from 100 to 0), we can see at a glance how the percentages relate to the numerical data. That is, we can

Table 10-1
Customer Complaints Concerning Lawn Mowers

Defect	Number of Complaints
Handle assembly fell apart (at welds)	120
Bolts on handle snapped	53
Controls defective	32
Tire fell off wheels	26
Tire fell apart	5
Height adjusters inoperative (when new)	9
Height adjusters snapped	15
Wheel bolts snapped	14
Wobbly wheels	36
Oil leak	14
Air filter fell apart	6
Engine block cracked	4
Carburetor not functioning (when new)	7
Idling screw could not be turned	19
Tear in grass catching bag (when new)	11
Zipper in grass catching bag inoperative (when new)	19
Blade fell off chassis	7
Safety device in rear fell off	3

Table 10-2
Grouping of Customer Complaints

Defect	Number
Handle and controls	205
Tires, wheels, height adjusters	105
Engine problems	50
Bag problems	30
Miscellaneous problems	10
Total	400

readily identify the percentage of each category of defects. Note, too, that the line going from 0% to 100% is a cumulative line (also known as the "cum line") and shows us the accumulated numerical total of defects as we go from the far left bar to those on the right.

In our chart, then, we can see that the first two bars represent the bulk of our problem—310 defects, or over 75% of the cases. This sets our priorities for us.

Brainstorming

Problems can also be identified via brainstorming. This technique may be used in such areas as

☐ Team building sessions
☐ Quality circles

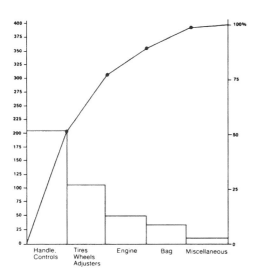

Figure 10-1. A Pareto diagram that shows the number and corresponding percentage of defects in each category of lawn mower component.

☐ Meetings with employees, such as "gripe" sessions

☐ Determining training needs

☐ Determining hazards in the workplace

☐ Generating topics for conference agendas

Since brainstorming typically generates a long list of ideas, the list, obviously, must be whittled down to a workable number. This can be done quite easily by having the group vote on the importance of the identified problems. Those problems with the most votes become the ones that will receive priority attention.

Brainstorming, a multipurpose technique, can also be used to generate (1) data about a problem, such as causes and defects (Step 2 in our five-step problem solving model) and (2) solutions to resolve the problem (Step 3). Details concerning the conduct of a brainstorming session are included in Chapter 11, on generating ideas about the problem for its resolution.

Statistical Procedures

Various statistical procedures can help us to focus on the problem. They entail collecting data so that we are operating from fact rather than conjecture. Two simple examples follow:

Scatter diagram. This procedure is designed to ferret out and graphically depict a relationship between two sets of data presumed to be related. Some examples are relationships between test scores and I.Q., grades and I.Q., salary and college major, salary and sex, weight and age, heart disease and smoking. In the workplace some examples are absenteeism and seniority (or absenteeism and age, sex, or type of work); accidents and seniority, age, sex, or type of work; and factory defects and day of the week. An example of a scatter diagram is given in Figure 10-2. It plots the relationship between accidents and time of day. In this hypothetical instance, the relationship is a very strong one.

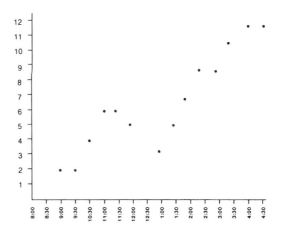

Figure 10-2. A scatter diagram showing the number of accidents in January by time of day.

Ordinarily we use the horizontal axis for the variable impacting the other one and the vertical axis for the variable subject to or influenced by that change. Thus, in our diagram, we have placed time of day on the horizontal axis and number of accidents on the vertical axis.

A check sheet. This is a device to aid in collecting data about a problem. After data is fully collected, a pattern emerges that highlights the problem or difficulty. For example, a supervisor may keep records for a month of all employees' arrival times; a shop foreman may keep a daily record of defects of particular parts for a five-day period; to analyze workload, a customer relations supervisor may keep a weekly record of orders and inquiries processed by the staff. The latter check sheet is given in Figure 10-3.

Note that by glancing across the columns from left to right, the supervisor can quickly learn that Jo

Weekly Orders and Inquiries Processed

Name	Week	1	2	3	4	5	6	7	8
Fred		26	25	28	30	29	30	28	31
Alma		22	25	24	26	30	28	26	27
Jo		12	14	12	14	15	on leave	12	11
Jean		29	26	28	36	28	34	30	33
John		32	24	32	26	22	26	33	32
Will		24	20	36	26	14	20	14	19
Chris		15	26	13	14	22	12	12	15
Ed		35	31	30	35	34	30	37	33
Total		195	191	203	207	194	180	192	201

Figure 10-3. Example of check sheet.

and Chris are the weakest producers and Fred and Ed the strongest. Also, Will seems to have "tapered off" during the last four weeks. Note, too, that we could add three more vertical columns: one to sum up individual production for the eight weeks and two others for average individual *and* group weekly production.

Checklist

A checklist has two functions:

Preventive—To ensure that a mistake does not occur or that quality is maintained; for example, a supervisor may develop and use a checklist in orienting a new worker to the job.

Diagnostic—To locate a trouble spot, error, or malfunction; for example, auditors may examine the internal operations of an office with a checklist; an engineer may try to isolate a mechanical or electrical problem on an automotive engine.

Checklists provide a system, particularly if a sequence of events is involved. By using a checklist as opposed to relying on memory, you ensure that all items are checked out or covered. Checklists thus save time in locating the shortcoming or problem.

Problem Identification—ABC Approach

On the assumption that if we sincerely want to identify problems it's "as easy as A B C," a comprehensive question list that should aid groups in locating their problems is given in Figure 10-4.

Groups working with this list have several options:

1. They can define or redefine any item in the list.
2. They can add new items, using the ones provided to trigger other, more pertinent ones.

A—Attitudes? Antagonisms? Apathy? Adaptability? Aesthetics? Automation?

B—Behaviors? Bottlenecks? Bargaining? Bureaucracy? Budgets?

C—Communication? Climate? Change? Crises? Complaints? Careers? Conflict?

D—Delegation? Decentralization? Defects? Danger? Difficulties? Deviations? Durability? Deadlines?

E—Environment (situation)? Economy? Errors? Ethics (morality)? Experimentation?

F—Frustration? Fear? Fantasies? Fun? Failure? Forecasting?

G—Garbage (as in computer inputs–outputs)? Goals? Group (processes)?

H—Hazards? Half-measures? Hierarchy?

I—Indecision? Interaction (inadequate, inappropriate)? Intentions? Insensitivities? Ideas? Ideals?

J—Job (design, enrichment, cycle, rotation, security)?

K—Knowledge?

L—Listening? Loyalty? Leadership? Lemons? Laziness?

M—Motivation? Money? Manpower? Material? Methods? Mixups? Meetings?

N—Negativism? Nitpicking? Negotiation? Needs?

O—Organization? Objectives? Operations? Opportunities? Obstructions?

P—Pressures? Performance? Policies? Plans? Personnel? Procedures? Pay? Pessimism? Production?

Q—Quality? Quantity?

R—Resistance (to change)? Rejects? Reward System? Relationships? Responsibility?

S—Safety? Standards? Seasonal set-ups? Scheduling? Sales? Secretaries? Staff?

T—Training? Turnover? Time Management? Timing? Team (building, management)?

U—Utilization? Urban (aspects)? Union? Unity? Unification?

V—Vendettas? Venom? Variables? Visibility?

W—Waste? Workweek? Workday? Warehousing?

X—eXpense?

Y—Yesterday's breadwinners? You–I?

Z—Zero defects? Zig zags?

Figure 10-4. An alphabetically arranged question list to aid in problem identification.

3. They can respond directly to what they see: "Yes, our problem is the 'half-measures' we take."

HOW TO GENERATE DATA ABOUT THE PROBLEM

Once we have properly defined our problem, we are ready to collect data (causes, effects) about it. Several methods are described below, including:

☐ Force field analysis
☐ Value analysis
☐ Structured analysis

- 5-M analysis
- 7-S analysis
- T-column

☐ Analogy

☐ Working with metaphors

☐ Analogies vs. metaphors

☐ Imaging

☐ Brainstorming

☐ Other idea-producing techniques

Force Field Analysis—A Tool for Problem Diagnosis

According to the late Kurt Lewin, a renowned social psychologist and father of the group dynamics movement, any problem situation can be understood better if we use this metaphor: "a sea of forces in motion." Some of these forces, as we may perceive them, are favorable (positive) and some are unfavorable (negative or undesirable). Although these forces are in constant motion, their pressures and counterpressures produce a situation of stability at any one point in time. In other words, we have movement yet stability. Lewin described this situation as one of "quasi-stationary equilibrium."

As problem solvers, then, we can look at (diagnose) any problem situation and understand it more properly by identifying the forces at work and their relative influence on the situation. This is true whether our problem is the current level of production, the sales picture, the accident rate, the state of employee morale, the amount of participation in the classroom, or the degree of support for a public policy.

Force field analysis is an extremely useful concept and technique since it says to us: "Hey, don't try to come up with a solution to the problem or change a situation before you know what forces at work underlie it. Be an expert diagnostician first, and then you'll be a much better problem solver or change agent. Discern carefully the forces that are favorable to your desired goal (the driving forces) and those which are unfavorable (the restraining forces)."

We can diagram a typical problem situation as shown in Figure 10-5. Note that while each force may have a different intensity, in concert they exert an impact of a particular degree. As an example, take the

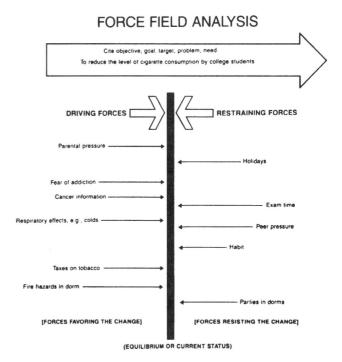

Figure 10-5. An example of a force field analysis showing the forces at work that increase or reduce cigarette smoking by college students.

number of cigarettes consumed by young people in the United States per year. There may be forces such as holidays, exams, and parties which increase consumption at certain times of the year. But basically, despite ups and downs in consumption, we can plot a trend line (our point of stability or equilibrium) that reflects the interaction of the driving and restraining forces.

Thus, if we wish to change the status of a current phenomenon (problem, difficulty, area of concern), we have to diagnose the forces at work and then change (influence) certain of those forces. To illustrate, let's take the state of participation in our classroom. Let's assume it is at a particular level (low) and we would like to raise that level. Our diagnosis of the forces at work gives us the following data as displayed in a T-column.

Present Level of Participation

Driving Forces	Restraining Forces
Student complaints about dull classes	Too much lecture Nonverbal participants
New progressive director of Training Center	Formal classroom atmosphere (desks, lectern, etc.)
Training Department at corporate level concerned	Instructors not trained in participative methods
Many new participative techniques are now available	Tradition, inertia Indifference

How might we alter this situation? Our change strategy can consist of (1) adding to or strengthening the driving forces, (2) removing or weakening the restraining forces, or (3) doing both (1) and (2) in some combination.

Note: While increasing or strengthening the driving forces may work, one runs a big risk—that is, by applying pressure, the response may be a natural one of resistance to that pressure. Hence, a more effective (less chancy) strategy is to eliminate or weaken the restraining forces and let the driving forces take over. In our participation in the classroom example, we might remove a restraining force—too much lecture—via instruction in participative (group-in-action) training methods. This would be preferable to adding more driving forces such as pep talks, memos, and more (negative) participant feedback data.

To allow your participants to try diagnosing an existing force field of their own, a set of instructions and a diagram are provided in Appendix 39, "Force Field Analysis." It may be used on problems of the participants' choice (this is the recommended option) or on one provided by the trainer.

Value Analysis

Value analysis (or value engineering) applies principles of group problem solving to reduce costs or to increase value. Its basic assumption is that any product or service can be refined, reengineered, or replanned to cut the costs of producing it.

Credit for the term is given to H. A. Winne, vice-president of engineering, General Electric Company. Under his direction GE began an intensive effort (in 1947) to identify the essential functions of consumer products as a means of lowering component costs. In the 1950s the Navy Department's Bureau of Ships launched a major value engineering program [7].

The procedure for working on a value engineering problem is as follows:

1. Analyze the item in question as to function and cost. As an example, let's take a power lawn mower and describe its hypothetical functions and costs:

Function	Cost
Power	$ 50.00
Cut	7.00
Control	10.00
Movement	10.00
Safety	25.00
Total	$100.00

Each of the above functions is then broken down further; for example,

Movement Function	Cost
Wheels	$ 5.00
Tires	3.00
Bearings	1.50
Bolts	.50
Total	$10.00

2. Ask cost improvement questions such as these:

☐ Can a smaller part be used?

☐ Can another (less expensive) type of material be used?

☐ Can a weight reduction in any part be accomplished?

☐ Can a part be bought more cheaply "on the outside"?

☐ Can any part be eliminated?

☐ Are all features necessary?

Another approach to value management/engineering is the "FAST" method, or Function Analysis System Technique. Here are its six steps [8].

1. *Information.* A function is reduced to a two-word definition, for example, "kill mice," "remove staple," or "ripen melon." The value management task force team (people from different departments) gathers all the data on the item: specs, cost, etc. These questions are used:

☐ What is the item?

☐ What does it do?

☐ What must it do?

☐ What must it cost?

☐ What else will do the job?

☐ What does that cost?

2. *Speculation.* Alternatives are brainstormed that fulfill or exceed the basic function of the service or product. Outside vendors may also be contacted for ideas. Negative thinking (which serves as a roadblock to creativity) is to be avoided. In the "kill mice" problem, alternatives to the standard mousetrap might be a cat or a poison.

3. *Planning.* Ideas are ranked in terms of effectiveness, and the "how" (ways and means) of implementation is developed. The major focus is on ideas which have greatest cost-benefit potential. In the "kill mice" problem,

it develops that an improved mousetrap, using lighter-weight wood, is Number 1 and poison the alternative.

4. *Execution.* Unit and volume costs are figured along with a discussion of alternatives. Plans with proofs and models are forwarded to management. In our "kill mice" mission, proposals for both methods of eliminating mice are drawn up. Costs of mousetrap materials (spring and wood) and alternative materials are calculated. Measurements of effectiveness for both alternatives are presented, too.

5. *Reporting.* Oral and written reports are presented to sell management on the proposal. The task force uses sketches, outlines alternatives, and highlights cost and performance gains.

6. *Implementation.* If management accepts the proposal, people are assigned specific implementation tasks, information is provided to all those who are involved/concerned, schedules are set, and follow-up reports to management are prepared. A responsible value engineer is assigned to monitor the project and to answer questions from plant personnel.

Similar approaches can be taken in respect to office activities, programs, or projects. Again, the functions of each operation must be identified, cost factors assigned, and an analysis undertaken to reduce costs.

Note that in conventional cost-reduction programs the goal is to produce the same item at reduced cost, whereas in value analysis, which approaches the problem from *a functional* standpoint, a totally fresh, global, and open-ended attack is undertaken.

Also, while in the fullest sense of the term value engineering is a technical and professional function (for example, its practitioners may belong to the Society of American Value Engineers, founded in 1959), the principles nevertheless can be used by non-professional personnel on many in-house projects where cost should (and can) be reduced.

Structured Analysis

The trainer can aid group problem solving by providing "structure"—worksheets, guide sheets, T-columns, etc. Structure serves these purposes:

□ It provides a framework so participants know with certainty how to attack the problem. In the absence of such structure, feelings of "wheel spinning" and frustration are likely to develop.

□ It provides a basis for self-checking: "Have we covered all bases?"

□ It serves as a motivator by meeting the needs participants may have for completion. In effect, people are saying to themselves: "Hey, we have to fill up those empty columns."

Several examples of structured formats follow:

5-M Analysis. The traditional "M's," or resources, of management—manpower, machinery, methods, materials, and money—can be used as a guide to diagnose what affects (hinders) a given operation or causes a problem. A sample worksheet for this purpose appears in Appendix 40.

Note:

1. Some groups may wish to add a sixth "M": *minutes,* reflecting a recognition that time is also a resource that may be poorly managed. Other groups, such as quality circles, typically drop "money" since it is not a factor in determining causes for defects in a product or the malfunctioning of a system or a procedure.

2. Causative data about the "M's" can be collected via individual ideation such as the slip method, group methods such as brainstorming and buzz groups, and/or general discussion by the group at large.

3. Structured analysis can be used to learn why an operation, activity, or project has been successful, as well as why it has been problem laden.

7-S Analysis. A more up-to-date method of management problem solving is the 7-S approach developed by two business school professors—Richard Pascale of Stanford and Anthony Athos of Harvard. In their book *The Art of Japanese Management* (Simon and Schuster, 1981), they contrast Japanese and Western approaches to management. They refer to the three "hard S's" of Western management—

structure, strategy, and *systems*—and the four "soft S's" of the Japanese—*superordinate goals, skills, style,* and *staff.* The latter "S's" relate to people: their values, uniqueness, talents, and processes. Shared values are considered to be most central and the "secret weapon" of the Japanese.

The "7 S's," in combination, could be used by groups at various levels in the organization to assess their functioning. A chart, such as used in the 5-M Analysis, could be employed for this purpose.

T-column analysis. Groups can put their problems into better focus by framing (highlighting) them via the T-column. Dichotomizing and thus sharpening the issue challenges the group to a greater degree. The T-columns might address the advantages of an in-house program vs. using an outside consultant, the concerns of employees vs. management, or short-term gains vs. long-term gains.

Analogy

An analogy is a direct comparison of similar things or concepts; for example, a heart and a pump have similar actions. It is useful both as a data-generating device (Step 2 in the problem-solving process) and as a tool to produce ideas or solutions about a problem (Step 3). The latter use is developed in more detail in Chapter 11.

Experiential training programs, having a heavy concern with personal growth, team building, etc., typically utilize such involving techniques as introspection, self-disclosure, and feedback. However, at times, depending on the participant group, disclosure and feedback may not provide the hoped-for involvement and learning. Consequently, other, less direct techniques, such as analogy, may be more appropriate. Examples of the use of analogy as a data-generating tool are cited by two experiential trainers [9].

☐ A personnel unit in a team building session would not acknowledge its problems. The trainers, therefore, introduced an exercise based on a fictitious company that required the participants to create an ideal personnel system. The result was that in the simulation the personnel managers gradually began to focus on (rather than deny) their own problems!

☐ A professional group was reluctant to be candid about its needs for professional growth, so another analogy-type exercise was employed. The trainers gave each of the participants a hypothetical budget for their professional development. It consisted of the usual budgetary items such as an allotment of days, travel costs, tuition charges. The ground rule was that one's budget could be expended as one saw fit. As might be expected, the exercise "smoked out" honest disclosure about growth needs and real development opportunities.

In essence, the same learning goal may be achieved via alternate and sometimes less direct methods, as in the preceding instances. Hence the need for analogy.

Working with Metaphors

A metaphor is "a figure of speech in which a word or phrase literally denoting one kind of object or idea is used in place of another to suggest a likeness or analogy between them" (per Webster's *New Collegiate Dictionary*). In effect, it is a reference to one thing to suggest a resemblance to something else. When used in everyday speech or writing, metaphors help us to view a situation, concept, or behavior in ways which may be new, more concrete, or more vivid. In short, they create images. Some everyday examples:

"Gofers"	Voodoo	High and dry
Stonewalling	economics	Wallflower
Horseplay	Pig-in-a-poke	No shrinking
Brainstorming	Trojan horse	violet
Cogs in a wheel	Montezuma's	A real prima
(or in a	revenge	donna
machine)	Sacred cows	Gone
Bearhug	Saturday Night	Hollywood
Ivory tower	Special	Grapevine
Basket case	Paint yourself	Protecting one's
Star gazing	into a corner	turf
The ship of	Cold turkey	Paper shuffler
state	Trickle-down	Wool gathering
	theory	

Note that these metaphors are brief, using only a single word or a phrase. Metaphors may also be more lengthy and involved, their impact depending on the way the metaphor is developed in its many facets. In effect, the metaphor user, having stated the metaphor, then talks about the subject in metaphorical terms. Several examples of such metaphors follow.

The Boston Globe, in discussing roles of female entrepreneurs, said "the metaphor of bearing a child and watching it grow was repeated constantly by the women entrepreneurs to describe their feelings about their ventures. One of the great joys, they say, is creating something where there had been nothing" [10].

Industrial psychologist Harry Levinson uses the metaphor of the spider's web to help us better understand the importance of interpersonal communication [11]. He asks us to visualize the spider positioned at the web's center, listening for vibrations to alert it to other life at the web's periphery—its mate, possible prey, and/or enemies. In other words, the spider is constantly sensing, seeking out information which is basic to its survival.

We, too, says Levinson, occupy a central point in relation to others. Some people are close at hand, others farther off. But the closeness-distance dimension is *not* only a physical concept; it also has emotional significance. That is to say, some people are close to us emotionally, some are distant; some send strong and clear signals to us, regardless of their physical distance; some can only send weak or unclear signals. Of course, some of us may be more tuned in to these signals, whether strong or weak, than are others.

But regardless of our perception or awareness of these signals, they represent "connections" with others, hookups which all of us require to the fullest extent. Why? Because they can provide affection and support as well as sheer information. They keep us from being isolated and from having to sort out these signals without the aid of others. Man, as a social being, can hardly function without full interchange with others. Sometimes isolation can, of course, produce creativity; more typically, it produces distress. In sum, the images, thoughts, and fantasies that we constantly create in our heads can only be understood and thus managed by interaction with others.

Dr. Levinson asks us, then, to study the vibes in our own web. How strong and clear are the signals? Who sends them to us? From what (emotional) distance? What is the content of the signals? Do they give us information, support, approval, intimacy? What happens if a signal fades due to death or other separations? Do we lose support? Do we replace the signal? With whom? Some people only give us information; others a lot of emotional richness. Levinson concludes his metaphor by saying: "But perhaps the most important thing is the knowledge that the web exists—that we will pick up whatever vibrations are sent out, because we are connected."

A metaphor that highlights man's tendency to resist change is the "Wallenda complex." It relates to the late Karl Wallenda of the famous Wallenda family of high-wire circus performers. Karl Wallenda, a performer until his death in his seventies, had learned early in his childhood to use his 16-foot pole for balance. He was told repeatedly that he would always be safe and balanced if he used his pole.

Wallenda accepted a challenge of walking a high wire between two buildings, ten stories above ground level. It was a windy day and Wallenda nearly lost his balance, but he regained it with the aid of his pole. As he continued across the wire, a sudden strong gust hit him hard, and he began to fall. He could have caught hold of the wire as he went down, but he did not. Why not? Because he did what he had been taught to do—to hold tightly to the pole. The unfortunate result: Wallenda hit a taxi on the city street below, still holding on to his pole.

Rick Thyne, an international peace advocate, used the tragic Wallenda experience as a metaphor to describe the current arms race. He said: "We, too, are on a high wire . . . we're determined to hold on to our pole—our weapons—as we have been taught. We think that in them lies our only safety. And we may die believing that.

"We can let go of our old learning. We can still try to catch the wire. That doesn't mean we'll be safe, but at least we'll have a chance to struggle back to the window" [12].

Trainers will be interested in a metaphor used to describe "quiet leadership" of the training department, that is, doing the job but giving the line departments credit for effective training results. The metaphor: not leaving any fingerprints which permit the tracking of a project to the training department. It was cited at an 1980 A.S.T.D. conference in an awards presentation to a corporate trainer at Ford Motor Co.: "When Duke Schmidt left corporate training at Ford . . . his staff gave him a framed picture with five fingerprints in it, because Duke's management philosophy was that the training department never took credit for anything—never left its fingerprints on any project. They put out a brochure at the end of the year and all the brochure contained was examples of the divisions in Ford solving performance problems" [13].

Examples in the training situation. In the training situation, too, we can help participants generate data about problems and see problems, concepts, and behaviors in new lights or more concretely, by having them work with or construct metaphors. Several examples follow.

☐ In a leadership session or course, give participants the worksheet in Appendix 41, "Some Ways of Looking at Leaders and Leadership," to complete individually; then have them discuss it in small groups. Conclude the activity by securing comments from each small group.

☐ Have participants individually analyze their leadership or management styles by drawing on an analysis and description of the three major U.S. sports. How coordination is achieved by the manager or coach is the major differentiating factor among the three games.

1. *Baseball:* Highly independent player action, with necessary but highly general coordination achieved by the manager. For example, a baseball manager can hardly predict a double play or direct its execution should the opportunity arise. At the most, he can advise his players to try to make one, if possible, because there are less than two outs and there are one or more players on base. Of course, this is hardly unexpected advice to his professional infielders who have handled double plays innumerable times in their careers. Baseball is essentially a game of *autonomy.*

2. *Football:* Coordination comes from above, top-down direction from the head coach. Visualize him constantly signaling in each play from the sidelines. He even has observers in the stands to provide him with intelligence to sharpen his many decisions. His assistant coaches on defense, offense, and special teams constantly provide further inputs to ensure that everyone stays with the

game plan. The result: each player has a minute piece of the action. Football represents *control.*

3. *Basketball:* The coach is the catalyst who provides coordination to the spontaneous interaction of the players themselves. The game is so fast paced and interdependent that the coach can hardly orchestrate in detail the many moves and plays the players make on a minute-to-minute basis. Basketball represents *voluntary cooperation,* free-form teamwork [14].

After everyone has decided on his/her current managerial style, have participants meet in small groups to discuss (1) the adequacy of one's current style to meet the unit's needs; (2) the nature of the boss' style; (3) if one wishes to change one's style, which one would be most appropriate, given one's personality, management philosophy, the nature of the work itself, and the nature of the group being supervised; and (4) if a change is to be accomplished, how would one go about it?

☐ In a supervisory or management training program you may want the participants to reflect on how employees really see their organization. You thus might ask them to

1. Take a sheet of paper and jot down some answers to the following question: "If we were to ask our employees to imagine our company *as a person,* what kind of person might they describe?" (Some possible answers: An energetic youth; an old man with a pot belly; an erect, sturdy middle-aged person; a happy giant; a relaxed, carefree person; a cold, insensitive miser.) Allow five minutes or so for this.

2. Meet in small groups (three to five persons) and discuss their metaphors. "See if you can agree on the kind of person that best describes our organization, as our employees are likely to see it. You have 15 minutes for this."

3. Share their metaphors with the group at large.

☐ In a session concerned with problem solving, creativity, imagineering, etc., give the participants the following task to point out how rigid attitudes and conventional thinking may hinder our creativity or originality.

1. In small groups have participants come up with metaphors—descriptive words or phrases— they use regularly to connote such concepts as "flight from reality," "ignoring the real world," and "narrowmindedness." To start them off, say: "'Head in the sand' would be an example of flight from reality; 'tunnel vision' would be an example of narrowmindedness. You have 20 minutes for this."

2. Tell them: "O.K., let's get some data from each group." Process the data with a T-column, as in the following example.

Metaphors Indicating

Flight from Reality	Narrowmindedness
Living in a cocoon	Wearing blinders
Ostrich mentality	Blind side
Head in the clouds	Can't see beyond one's nose
Blue sky thinking	Going by the book
No man is an island	Throwing out the baby with the bath water
Maginot Line psychology	Penny wise and pound foolish
Dream world	
Ivory Tower	

☐ In a leadership program or management retreat, it may be desirable to encourage participants to think about the nature (character) of organizations in general and possibly their organization in particular. If so, the task in the worksheet in Appendix 42, "Organizations—An Analysis with the Aid of Metaphor," may stimulate such thinking [15].

Complete the exercise by securing group reports, posting their data on flipcharts, and discussing the implications of the data for organizations (or your organization).

☐ In a human relations/communications program, metaphor as a data-generating device may be used to develop closer relationships among participants. For example, participants in a dyad may be assigned this task: "Write a metaphor to describe your partner."

The metaphors are written as instructed, then shared with one's partner; on a volunteer basis, several may be read to the total group. Two examples of metaphors developed by dyadic partners in response to the preceding task follow. Note that the first one deals quite directly with the person and her work, whereas the second one is written as a fairy tale. (The latter metaphor was based on the fact that Kim had indicated earlier to Joyce that he engaged in vegetable gardening as a hobby.)

1. "My partner, Joyce, is the prototype of the good baseball coach. She is concerned about uncovering developmental needs, has patience to work on those needs, and uses empathy plus her professional skills to bring about the needed change. She is on the lookout for new techniques, recognizes individual differences, is content to settle for small changes in difficult cases. She relates well to the trainees/pupils/students/clients and has a knack of gaining their confidence so they will trust her. Her skills and attitudes should make for a lot of home runs and a winning team."

2. "Kim was the best gardener in the village of 'Plenty.' No one in the kingdom grew bigger, better, or more squash.

    "One day he said: 'Oh, if only these squash would turn to gold how rich I would be'.

    "Lo and behold the next morning he found several squash had turned to gold! He was astonished and wondered why *this* wish had been granted, when so many others had never been answered.

    "What he didn't realize was that it happened because his heart had also 'turned to gold.' He now had the ability to turn all he touched to gold if he desired."

In general, metaphors permit us to go beyond standard thinking, thus allowing us to see a bigger picture. *Example:* If we are into team development or team management, we can draw on sports metaphors to give our team a better focus. We can thus talk about "team players," "not dropping the ball," "beating the competition," "hitting a home run," "grandstanding," "practice run," "full court press," "coming from behind," "let's not move the goal posts," "too much coaching from the sidelines," "out of bounds," and so on.

Here are two examples of changing our patterned or basic thinking by changing our metaphors: (1) The firm is not being sold off, but is "up for adoption." (2) People constantly complain that the elevator in our office building is too slow. So do we spend a half million dollars or more to get a new one, or do we simply add mirrors on each floor so people can kill time by primping rather than griping? *Significance:* We change the complaining-type metaphor "slower than molasses in January" to a happier one: "Here's a chance to sharpen up a bit."

Analogies vs. Metaphors

An analogy is a direct comparison with a similar thing, object, or idea. For example, we may compare the manager to the nurturing parent, for both are concerned with the growth of those for whom they have responsibility.

In contrast to the analogy, a metaphor is a reference to one thing, object, idea, or person, to suggest a reference to something else, for example, "The Ship of State" in relation to government, or the batter drove a *clothesline* to right field.

Although metaphors are more potent than analogies because they encourage (demand) a greater change of perspective, both help participants to see new principles, relationships, and possibilities [16]. As figurative tools, they are useful to both Steps 2 and 3 of the problem-solving process, that is, to generate data and to produce ideas or solutions about a problem.

Imaging

According to management psychologist Dr. Warren H. Schmidt of U.C.L.A., groups can significantly improve their problem-solving capacity by assuming or thinking of a problem as already solved! The first procedure involved, then, is to visualize or imagine (engage in "imaging") what the situation would be like with a solution in effect.

Second, have participants imagine the conditions that existed just *before* the solution was produced; also, visualize the changes that might have influenced that final increment of improvement. Now have the group work backward, step by step, until it reaches the current (unsolved) status.

In general, the idea is that we can understand much better the first steps—identified last in the imaging process—because we have shifted from the confines of our usual and ordinary forward-looking ways of attacking a problem to a novel, idea-provoking, rear-ended approach. The imaging process lets us create our own panoramic view of the situation, with the helpful option of tracing causes/events backward and thus understanding more objectively the forces and factors at work [17].

Another form of imaging or visualizing is to have the group reduce to writing the conditions that will exist once the problem or difficulty is resolved. The next step is to have participants think positively and creatively about how to ensure that those conditions will reach fruition.

Brainstorming

Brainstorming is a versatile problem-solving tool. It is extremely useful in the first three stages of the problem-solving process:

1. Identify problems for resolution.
2. Generate ideas (about causes, about the problem).
3. Generate solutions to resolve an identified problem.

Brainstorming is described in detail in Chapter 11 under Step 3—how to generate ideas (solutions) about the problem for its resolution.

Some common examples of the use of brainstorming to generate data about a problem (causes, effects, etc.) are these:

☐ A group of factory workers in a quality circle identifies the causes for a high reject rate on products produced in their department.

☐ A sales/marketing group identifies the reasons why a new product is not moving.

☐ A personnel office group develops a "bug list" concerning the ineffective operation of the company's suggestion plan.

Focus Groups

A focus group is an information-gathering technique to amass *qualitative* data. It seeks to elicit detailed insights into people's understandings, motivations, needs, competencies, and attitudes—likes, dislikes, biases, and a broad array of other possible emotional responses. In the commercial world, marketers wish to assess feelings toward particular products or services, either new or well established. In the organizational world, organizational development (OD) specialists and personnel people may wish to learn how people feel about organizational function in respect to the adequacy of communication, opportunities for innovation/creativity, involvement in problem solving and decision making, identification with the outfit (pride, loyalty), career opportunities, job satisfaction, and so on.

Trainers typically use focus groups to assess training needs, to evaluate completed training, and to learn generally how well their services are received and understood. Trainers may also work with individuals who are knowledgeable about certain job roles to identify critical competencies they believe are required for success. In the latter instance the focus group may comprise incumbents of the target job roles, their managers, and possibly customers, too.

An organization which conducts surveys via questionnaires to learn of employee attitudes on particular subjects, or on the organization in general, may also use focus groups to learn the "why" (feelings, attitudes) behind the numerical responses given on the survey forms. Following up with focus groups helps to bring the quantitative data of attitude/climate surveys into more understandable perspective.

To use focus groups to maximum advantage, consider the following steps:

1. *Question preparation.* Using your own expertise or drawing on knowledgeable people from your own or other units, develop a list of pertinent questions which require answers. For example, it may be desirable to get a good look behind a statistic which a climate survey may have produced—that 40% of the workforce thought opportunities for training were not clear, or that their productivity could be helped greatly by additional training.

2. *Focus group selection.* Select a group of people who can provide answers to your predetermined questions. The group may be comprised of people with special insight or expertise if your concerns require tapping the wisdom of "experts." Or it may be a group of run-of-the-mill employees who are certain to have attitudes/feelings concerning the issues you have identified, such as training needs or the value of particular training they may have experienced. In general, the focus group should comprise people who have common knowledge, interests, or concerns. It also may be desirable to select people from different segments of the organization to capture a broader view of the issues.

3. *Memo to participants.* Limit your focus group to a workable number (e.g., 6 to 10 or 12). Send your selectees a memo in advance of your focus group meeting so they know why they're coming, what will take place (format), how long the session will last (two hours maximum), who will be the facilitator, location, date, and time. Also, it's a good idea to phone people on the day of the session to prevent "no-shows," although if one or two invitees don't make it you should still have enough people to ideate satisfactorily.

4. *Atmosphere.* Provide a participant-friendly atmosphere. Greet invitees warmly and provide beverages and fruit or cookies. Ideally, comfortable chairs should be available, for the activity may go on for two hours. A circle without a table will help to create a less-structured environment.

5. *Starting off.* Have your participants introduce themselves—their jobs, where they work, and how long they've been with their outfit. Explain the purpose of your study, why your attendees were chosen, and how the data will be utilized. Be sure to ask for questions to clarify possible misunderstandings about your focus group's objectives and procedures,

6. *Facilitation.* As facilitator your role is to encourage participant contributions. You may ask for expansion on or clarification of ideas presented. But you should avoid evaluating (commenting on) the worth of the ideas. You job is to generate responses to your questions, not to get mired down in a debate about their value. Think of an open-ended, free-flowing brainstorming session as the kind of meeting you wish to conduct. If there are one or two dominators in the group,

make a point of "going around the circle" to ensure that you have secured broad participation.

7. *Winding up.* Bring things to a close by asking if there are other comments that should be made that weren't expressed. Tell the group how the data will be used. Thank everyone for their contributions and for taking the time to participate.

8. *Number of groups.* If essential to secure a more representative and possibly a more objective set of data, consider meeting with more than one group. Of course, your informational needs and available resources and time will guide you to that determination.

9. *Data interpretation.* Analyze the data you've garnered, possibly using a diverse group to do so. Some of the information you've collected may be interpreted in more than one way. If a written report is to go to your superiors, be certain to think in terms of highlights. Keep it brief and crisp rather than encyclopedic. If your focus group was used to follow up on survey questionnaires, tie your new findings to the survey.

10. It's a good idea to send group members a thank you note for their participation.

Note: Additional material concerning how to use focus groups to maximize results from them appears in Chapter 19, "Using Participative Methods to Evaluate Training."

Other Idea-Producing Techniques

Another technique to help generate data about a problem is "the journalist's six questions"—who? what? when? where? why? and how? This technique is described in more detail in Chapter 12 in the section on additional approaches to problem solving.

Various techniques are useful for *both* Steps 2 and 3 in the problem solving process. These techniques—brainstorming, the slip method, card posting techniques, etc.—are discussed in detail in Chapter 11 under Step 3.

KEY POINTS

1. Training programs that teach managers and others to solve their problems are being demanded more and more by organizations.

2. Training in problem solving should begin with a workable model. A five-step model for this is one that involves defining the problem, generating data (causes, effects) about it, generating various courses of action (solutions), choosing (deciding) among the alternatives, and implementing the decision.

3. Problem definition (Step 1 in the model) may be accomplished via Brain Chain Reaction, Pareto's analysis, brainstorming, statistical approaches, checklists, and problem identification—ABC approach.

4. Brainstorming may be used to identify (define) the problem, determine its causes, and produce solutions about it. Key principles in brainstorming are quantity in ideation and deferred judgment.

5. To generate data about a problem (Step 2 in the model), including cause and effect factors, these techniques are useful: force field analysis, value analysis, structured analysis, analogy, metaphor, imaging, brainstorming, the journalist's six questions, the slip method, focus groups, and card posting techniques.

REFERENCES

1. Stredl, Henry J., and Rothwell, William J., *The ASTD Reference Guide To Professional Training Roles and Competencies,* ASTD Press and HRD Press, 1987.
2. Yates, L., "Wrestling the Alligators," *Northeast Training News* (September 1980), p. 12.
3. "Creativity: Looking for the Right Questions," *Leading Edge Bulletin* (September 28, 1981), pp. 1–2.
4. Murphy, D., "When a Problem Is Not a Problem," *Northeast Training News* (December 1979), p. 12.
5. Hurt, Floyd, "Brain Chain Reaction," *Successful Meetings* (August 1999), pp. 93–95.
6. *Bulletin on Training* (November–December 1978), p. 7.
7. Tocco, A. R., "Value Engineering (Value Analysis)," *The Encyclopedia of Management,* 3rd edition, Van Nostrand Reinhold Company, New York, 1982, pp. 1277–1283.
8. "Value Management—What Comes After Quality," *Productivity* (December 1983), pp. 8–11.
9. Margolis, F., and Bell, C., "Making Organization Development Work at the Department Level," *Training/HRD* (September 1981), pp. 116–119.
10. Quoted in *The Levinson Letter* (October 1, 1981), p. 3.

11. *The Levinson Letter* (December 1981), p. 2.

12. *Leading Edge Bulletin* (November 30, 1981), p. 2.

13. Cited by McCampbell, J. F., "Six Guiding Images to Measure Training Results," *Training/HRD* (September 1981), p. 38.

14. Game Plans and Sports Strategies," *Training News* (January 1986), p. 4 (based on an interview of Robert Keidel of the Wharton Applied Research Center, University of Pennsylvania, as reported initially in *Inc.,* November 1985).

15. The entire task, slightly modified, is borrowed liberally from a presentation made by Dr. Warren H. Schmidt, a leading trainer and educator at U.C.L.A., at the 1980 Annual Conference of the American Society for Training and Development, Anaheim, California.

16. Yates, L., "Wrestling the Alligators," *Northeast Training News* (September 1980), pp. 12–13, 19.

17. Giegold, W. C., *Objective Setting and the MBO Process,* Vol. II, McGraw-Hill Publishing Company, New York (1978), p. 183.

RECOMMENDED READING

Bial, Boris, "Eight Steps to Successful Problem Solving," *Supervisory Management,* January 1986, pp. 7–9.

The author presents an eight-step problem-solving model, the last step being one not found in most models: know what alternative action can be taken if the original decision fails.

Dahle, Cheryl, "He Knows How to Be Diligent About Due Diligence," *Fast Company,* September 2000, pp. 66–68.

In data-gathering situations such as sizing up a new investment or evaluating a new hire, you have to dig deeper than studying the financials or the references. Keys to desired diligence include probing to go behind rehearsed pat answers; be curious and don't just accept yes/no answers; skip assumptions and find out what people really mean; take time to get real answers; ask open-ended questions; secure permission to call back later for more information; learn from your interviews by taping and transcribing them.

Goddard, Robert W., "The Vital Few and the Trivial Many," *Personnel Journal,* July 1987, pp. 30–34.

The article presents a solid overview of Pareto's Law and provides guidelines to apply it to one's own job. The bottom line: spend most of your effort on the critically few but vital tasks.

Phillips, Steven R., and Bergquist, William H., "Focusing Problem Management," *Training and Development Journal,* March 1987, pp. 87–89.

The writer advocates a three-step problem-solving model called "STP," for situation (what is the current state?), target (what is the desired state or goal?), and proposal (identifies the path from situation to target and defines the strategy/plan to make the change).

"Involve Your People in Organizational Problem Solving," in "Training 101," *Training and Development Journal,* July 1987, pp.73–74.

A three-step problem-solving model is presented: *data gathering,* which includes problem definition; *problem solving,* which encompasses finding alternatives and choosing among them; and *action planning.* Stress is placed on the need for consensus at all stages of the process in order to secure *commitment.*

11 Generating Solutions to a Problem

If you continue to think the way You always thought You will continue to get What you always got Is it enough?

—Anon.

There is always an easy solution to every human problem—neat, plausible and wrong.

—H. L. Mencken (1880–1956), American journalist, essayist, critic, and lexicographer

In the prior chapter we learned about the first two steps (skilling areas) in the problem-solving process: "How to define the problem" and "How to generate data about the problem." We are now ready to learn about Step 3: "How to generate solutions or ideas for resolving the problem."

Devices for generating ideas or solutions to a problem are abundant. Described below are a number of these techniques:

- ☐ Brainstorming
- ☐ The slip method
- ☐ Nominal group technique
- ☐ The Delphi technique
- ☐ Ideawriting
- ☐ Card posting techniques
- ☐ Client-centered approach to problem solving
- ☐ Upside-down problem solving

☐ Action learning (action-reflection learning)
☐ Checklists, attribute listing, morphological analysis, and forced relationships
☐ Using analogy
☐ PCT approach and analogy
☐ The Gordon technique
☐ Dialogue via the "talking stick"

BRAINSTORMING

One of the oldest forms of systematic group problem solving (introduced in the 1950's) is brainstorming. Originally developed in the U.S. advertising industry, it has been used in all kinds of organizations, worldwide. Its basic tenet is to separate idea creation from idea evaluation. Why? Because if the two processes are combined, ideation is likely to suffer. Visualize these typical reactions anyone of us might have to a new idea:

"Good theory, but it'll never work."
"We've tried that one before."
"It conflicts with current policies."
"The boss (or headquarters, or the field) won't go for it."
"Sounds expensive."
"It might set a precedent."
"Not in the budget."
"Is this the time for it?"
"Let's not rush into *that*."
"But our people (or customers) are different."
"What about the extra people to implement it?"

Many more of these "killer phrases" could be added. The point is that if you or I come up with an idea and someone reacts negatively to it, it isn't very likely to encourage further ideation on our part. Conversely, if all of our ideas are accepted (recorded) without evaluation, we'll keep contributing.

Brainstorming works best with a group of 6–12 people, a recorder, and a moderator who encourages ideation: "We've produced 28 ideas in four minutes; let's see if we can get another dozen more." The moderator may ring a bell (a cowbell would work well) if someone expresses a negative reaction to an idea in the idea-generating phase.

Brainstorming in the training situation may be programmed, or it may be used informally, that is, as the need arises. By programming, we mean including brainstorming in the training design on a planned basis. For example, in a customer relations course, participants may be asked to brainstorm the benefits or characteristics of a particular product; in a supervisory training course, participants may be asked to brainstorm key points for developing a checklist to ensure that new employee orientation is conducted properly.

Informal or *ad hoc* brainstorming may occur in a variety of ways; for example, the trainer may hit a dull or dead spot in a session and thus ask the group to brainstorm ways to teach this topic more creatively or imaginatively; in a management development seminar, should a discussion arise about the ineffective nature of staff meetings, the trainer may suggest brainstorming to come up with ways to pep up such meetings. In general, the trainer should be alert for opportunities to say: "Why don't we brainstorm it?"

Encourage participants to use brainstorming back on the job by showing its versatility in different settings and situations. Typical examples of brainstorming topics in different locales are the following:

☐ In advertising: How to sell a video recorder to all households.
☐ In the community: How to improve the local transportation system. How to make our home town more beautiful. How to collect taxes more effectively.
☐ At home: How to cut down on expenditures. How to improve the garden. What shall we take along on a motor trip to Canada? What do we give Aunt Nellie for Christmas?
☐ On the job: How do we deal with litterbugging in this park? What shall we do with employees who are passed over for promotion? How can we reduce motor vehicle accidents by our drivers? How do we make this year's Christmas party different or more successful?

The rules for brainstorming are these:
No critical remarks are allowed. If the bell rings while you're speaking, it means you're breaking this rule. Remember, the basic principle of brainstorming is *deferred judgment*.

"Hitchhiking" is O.K. If you can improve on some one else's idea, or combine two or more fragments of ideas that others have offered, so much the better!

"Free-wheeling" is welcomed. The "wilder" the ideas, the better; it's easier to tame them down than pump them up. Free-wheeling also helps to keep the group pepped up.

Quantity is wanted. The percentage of usable ideas that comes out of the average brainstorming session is typically quite small. Obviously, the more ideas, the more winners! Out of quantity will come quality.

Evaluation comes later. Hold a screening and evaluation session *after* the idea-generating session.

To conduct a brainstorming session properly, these procedures *will* help:

1. Narrow or limit the problem. People need a finite problem they can tackle.

2. Limit the group to 6–12 persons.

3. Work in a circle.

4. Keep it informal; refreshments may help.

5. Each person gives only *one* idea at a time.

6. A chairperson (moderator, trainer) is necessary to lead and encourage "ideation," especially when it lags.

7. A recorder (two are even better) is necessary to record ideas. This is best done on a flipchart because visibility of the ideas is a stimulus to added ideation.

8. Keep the tempo quick-paced to keep everyone alert and the ideas flowing.

9. Use praise concerning volume, not individual ideas, to keep the ideas flowing: "That's great, group; let's see if we can get another dozen." We avoid saying a *particular* idea is "great" or "terrific," for it may imply the others are not.

10. If the group is new to brainstorming, use a warm-up topic before the real effort; for example, "What uses can we make of a ball of cord (or a brick)?"

Newer Approaches

A number of variations developed in recent years to update brainstorming merit citation.

Brainstorming Deluxe

This approach to brainstorming may be termed "value-added brainstorming." Trainer/consultant Greg

Bachman groups generated ideas into *five* segments of a *compounding* process. It provides structure so that each segment of ideas *adds value to the next one.* The five segments in the order of attack are Demand, Objectives, Resources, Processes, and Communication. Since ideas which materialize don't always fit neatly, stepwise, into the desired segment, it's a good idea to have five flipchart sheets on the wall, each labeled with one of the five steps. In this way an "out-of-order" idea can be captured when given. Here are the five steps [1]:

1. *Demand.* What that needs a "fix" is demanding your attention? To answer this question have the brainstormers list ideas about what's triggering (causing) the problem, difficulty, or unwanted situation. This first step is basic to good problem solving, since if you don't know the causes/reasons for why the problem has arisen, your group will be off to a false start. The reasons for the problem demanding your attention must be fully exposed or the group can't analyze it realistically. A big value of this step is that it can uncover causes that haven't been identified as driving the problem. As the medicos will tell us, "Let's treat causes, not symptoms."

2. *Objectives.* Now have your group list what they want their ideas to accomplish. They do this by describing the outputs that meet the demand previously determined. Here we're talking about objectives or outcomes—the end/finished process and the products. For a major payoff, opt for multiple objectives, So in Step 1 the group catalogs all the conditions that control the problem. Here, in Step 2, the group catalogs all the ways it can profit by finding a solution. Identifying many likely solutions will add to the value-added brainstorming process.

3. *Resources.* The group is now on its way. Their task is to list all possible places to go to find solutions. For example, it could be other offices or even in other companies. Here we try to plumb participants' imaginations for idea sources, "from science fiction to gourmet cooking," says the article's author. By asking for solutions outside the conventional procedures, the team may well get more than the expected stack of ideas. *Example:* If you're a wholesaler, could you tap retailers for ideas? Or, if you're in the federal government, could you look for solutions at state or municipal levels?

4. *Process.* At this stage have your group enumerate ways to convert the previous ideas into solutions—specifically, methods, plans, products, and services targeted to meet your stated objectives. The idea is to expand possibilities—add value to the brainstorming process—by listing all the ways they (the group) can apply the resources to meet objectives. This is done by listing "process ideas." What are processes? They are concepts that take resources and mold them into reality-based measures that allow implementation. "Processes," says Bachman, "build on and link the resource ideas that responded to the objectives that dealt with the demands that caused the problem."

5. *Communication.* The group's final step is to list possible ways to transfer its ideas to those who might profit from them. Remember, communication transfers the value of the solutions (processes) to the total outfit, including pertinent stakeholders.

The bottom line: By the session's end, the group will have considered more causes (multiple causation), more objectives, more possible solutions, and more ways to communicate the value of their ideas than they might have imagined at the very beginning. And very significantly, they may have learned that the problem is actually more complex, more multi-faceted than they had imagined at the session's onset.

Reverse Approach

In our usual brainstorming sessions we want positive thinking—new ideas, new solutions, new procedures, new uses. Using the reverse procedure, we approach our problem or concern in a negative way; that is, we assume that the way to make things "right" is to identify first the things that are "wrong." So we list all the deficiencies we can of a policy, procedure, or product, and then brainstorm ways to correct these faults. For example, assume our problem is to reduce crime in our city. We can stimulate new thinking about this concern by asking: How can we *increase* crime in city X? Some possible answers are to give guns away, leave doors unlocked, reduce lights on the street, reduce the size of police force, disarm the police, increase heroin usage, reduce punishment, increase the time it takes to get the accused to court.

Rotational Ideation

Ideas can be presented in the brainstorming circle in sequence on a one person-at-a-time basis. The trainer or moderator obviously has to exercise more control over member contributions than in conventional, free-flowing, contagion-oriented brainstorming. The advantage of this orderly procedure is that it encourages everyone to get into the act. The disadvantage is that the spontaneity, the stimulating disorder of everyone shouting out ideas, almost at once, is lost.

Note: This technique is similar to "the whip," wherein the trainer whips around the circle in a rotational way to elicit ideas from everyone.

If a participant does not have an idea to offer, he/she states "pass." The procedure continues until *everyone* says "pass."

SIL Method

SIL, a German acronym for "Successive Integration of Problem Elements," entails these procedures [2]:

1. Ideas about a problem are generated in writing on an individual basis.
2. The written ideas are read aloud by two group participants.
3. The other group members try to integrate those two ideas into *one* solution.
4. A third participant reads his/her idea.
5. The group integrates the third idea with the solution obtained in Step 3.
6. The integration process proceeds until all ideas are tapped.

Note: Not all ideas may be used, but all are heard and given a try in the integration process.

Developing Creative Alternatives

Trainer/consultant Harold Scharlatt builds on the brainstorming technique in order to enhance creativity in this manner [3]:

1. Present the usual objections/misgivings managers (and others) may have about creative thinking approaches, for example, "I'm not the creative

type," "That's impossible," "They'll never go for it," "I might appear foolish," "It's not logical (or practical)," "We're making assumptions."

2. Ask for ways to overcome each of these objections, doubts or fears. For example: "It's not logical" can be countered with "No, it's *creative,*" or "It's not exactly right" can be responded to with: "We don't want perfection—yet."

Note: Steps 1 and 2 are designed to confront people's doubts and fears gently and thus break down some of their self-imposed barriers to creativity.

3. *Clarify the mission/goal/problem.* What decision on our part requires fresh, new possibilities?

4. *To secure alternatives,* brainstorm the problem or concern in two or more subgroups: How can we accomplish our goals?

5. Have each buzz group expand its list based on a review of the other list(s).

6. *Choose the most outlandish ideas.* Have each participant write down three of the most preposterous/weird/impractical ideas which are in this (or another) list: Which ones look crazy?

7. Record all the wild ideas on a flipchart.

8. As a group, list all the *positive attributes* of each wild idea. Search for the positive attributes, the good points, in each.

9. Divide participants into small groups. Their task is to *combine* two or more of the ideas to create a new alternative: How can we merge two or more ideas into one idea which maximizes the positive characteristics of the original components?

10. Secure participants' *concerns* (lack of practicality) about each alternative.

11. In small groups or as a total group discuss this concern: Why is the idea not perfect?

12. In the same group configuration, discuss *ways to overcome* these concerns: What can we do to overcome these anxieties or fears?

13. *Identify acceptable attributes:* Which of these ideas have enough positive attributes, balanced with manageable concerns, to be considered alternates for evaluation?

The theory behind these sequential procedures is that it disrupts neither the logic behind sound deci-

sion making nor people's needs to move ahead comfortably in developing and selecting unique, creative alternatives.

Rolestorming

In traditional brainstorming some participants may be reluctant or even afraid to offer their wildest ideas, something which brainstorming typically seeks. One way to secure wacky ideas is to allow participants to attribute them to someone else, for example, the boss, a peer, or a subordinate. Procedurally, after each brainstormer has given his/her ideas, have him/her adopt a new identity and then toss out ideas as he/she believes the absent person would conceive them. Sample statement: "The person I've identified would favor a *daily* newspaper to all employees" (as a response to improvement of organizational communication).

According to Richard E. Griggs of Management Fitness Systems, Inc., Mountain View, California, the added process of rolestorming—so named because it combines features of role playing and brainstorming—can increase a group's idea production by 60%–70% and significantly better their quality, too [4].

Pause That Refreshes

As has been indicated, brainstorming typically involves a rapid-fire burst of ideation, a count of the quantity of ideas produced, praise by the trainer for the idea generation, and a return to ideation with encouragement to produce more ideas. A variation of this basic procedure is to begin with ideation, follow this with a silent period for "renewal" of group energy and creativity, and return to the ideation phase again. Ideation and pauses may be "programmed," too; for example, a three-to-four-minute burst of ideas is encouraged, an equal period of silence is introduced, and then ideation proceeds again for three to four minutes. The pause may be longer, too—a few hours or a day or two.

Overcoming Boredom and Frustration

Even highly imaginative groups may find that, on occasion, "the well has run dry." When that occurs, creative thinking authority T. Rickards recommends these measures to get the group back into its creative mode [5]:

Recorded round robin. Everyone is given a card bearing the problem and instructions to add a new idea thereon. The card is then passed on to a fellow participant, who adds an idea that has been triggered by the prior idea. Cards are passed around several times.

Wildest idea. Each participant is asked for the most "far-out" ideas imaginable. The others use this stimulus to produce as many new ideas as possible.

Trigger Method

This interactive technique was invented by Ford Motor Company; it uses this six-step procedure [6]:

1. The facilitator reads the problem to the team/group.
2. Each team member/participant jots down (for five minutes) his/her immediate reactions to achieving a solution.
3. After this silent idea-generation period, one member reads one of his/her ideas to the group.
4. The group discusses—but does not evaluate—the idea for ten minutes. The aim is to use the idea as a springboard for variations and other ideas.
5. This procedure continues until all ideas have been read aloud and "batted about."
6. The new ideas and variations can be used for another session, or the evaluation/recommendation stage can start.

A variation. A large group can be divided in half, with one segment conducting the trigger session as outlined above and the other half silently surrounding and observing the proceedings. (This is basically a form of "fishbowl" arrangement, although in this case the outer group does not critique or question the inner circle.) The observers (in the outer circle) write down any ideas which are triggered by the discussion of the inner group. These new ideas are added to the discussion once the group exhausts the ideas from their original silent-generation round.

Wildest Idea

This technique (mentioned briefly above) is used by the facilitator or team leader when the brainstorming group is "running out of steam" or isn't ideating very creatively. The facilitator interrupts the group and throws in a far-out, totally wild or far-fetched idea; alternatively, he/she may ask the group to do so.

A variation is to alter the current stimulus field. The facilitator does this by giving each brainstormer a folder of assorted photos clipped randomly from magazines and newspapers. They are asked to examine the diverse illustrations and to write down any ideas the photos may stimulate. The photo review runs for 15–20 minutes; then the discussion begins again.

Note: Since the above jump-starting techniques depend on the element of surprise to be successful, they can be used only once [7].

Creativity via Environmental Changes

To increase ideation after an initial start, try changing the environment. For example, close (or open) the blinds; open (or close) the door; turn on the lights; replace the recorder and/or the moderator with another person; switch to a new color of felt-tip pens; move the flipchart easel to a new position in the room; rearrange participants so they are in different chairs; have everyone stand up and either stretch or yell aloud, "Creativity!"; execute the task standing up in a circle.

Experimental Approach

To prove the efficacy of brainstorming, give a trained group (that is, one familiar with or instructed in brainstorming) and an untrained group the same problem in the same time frame (about five minutes). The problem should be one that is likely to generate a lot of ideas, for example, how to manage time or how to use a secretary most effectively. Appoint an observer to note what helped/hindered the group's ideation.

Let the two groups brainstorm in separate rooms. Then compare their results. Ordinarily, the trained group should be much more effective (that is, having a greater pool of ideas) than the untrained one. If not, the observer may shed some light on the atypical difference in results.

Evaluation Aid

A power of brainstorming lies in *deferred judgment.* Thus, ideation always proceeds independently from the possible onslaught of evaluation. One way to make the evaluation process more challenging and objective is to have the group select two ideas from the total list: the most bizarre and the most appealing. Then ask the group: What conditions would have to be met to make each idea—the bizarre one and the appealing one—work?

The rationale for this procedure: Something that looks ludicrous on the surface may not be that at all when the group gives it a fair trial.

Disadvantages of Brainstorming

Generation of many ideas in a short time frame and in a fun way are the main reasons for the popularity of brainstorming. However, it also has several limitations [8]:

- ☐ It is not useful as a problem-solving tool where trial and error, as opposed to judgment, is vital.
- ☐ It often produces only superficial (low-quality) ideas.
- ☐ It works best when the problem is simple, specific, or limited.
- ☐ Recognition for one's ideas is not possible (all ideas go on the flipchart anonymously); on the other hand, most people seem to respond favorably to the procedure of having their ideas posted publicly.

Hence the need for other techniques to help solve problems. A number of these are given in the following paragraphs.

THE SLIP METHOD

A productive, rapid, and highly participative means of identifying problems and solving them is to use the "slip method" [9]. This entails writing ideas on slips of paper on an individual basis. The completed slips are grouped into logical categories and then analyzed. Procedurally, the method requires these steps:

1. State the problem or difficulty being faced, using "how to" language, since people respond well to a challenge and such language encourages them to think in action terms. Some examples are: How can we reduce litterbugging in this park? How can we improve relations with our customers? How can we save energy in this plant? How can we ensure a safe working environment? How can we raise morale?

   Note: These questions are designed to elicit solutions to known problems. A prior step may be to identify problems, for example: What are the things which keep us from being fully effective (or more competitive or more profitable)? What needs changing in our organization?

2. Pass out a large quantity of 3" × 5" slips to each participant. Slips should be purchased (preferred procedure) or cut up from full-size sheets of bond paper in advance of the problem-solving session. Don't use cards since they look expensive and may inhibit some people from writing on many of them. The whole idea, as in brainstorming, is that many ideas are wanted. Basically, this is a "brainpicking" process. Instruct participants to put only one idea, tersely stated, on a slip. Tell them not to worry about economizing on paper, that they should use a lot of slips.

   Visualize a small group of ten people engaged in this process. if each participant averaged only ten ideas, we would have 100 of them in short order. With 15 participants, possibly 150 ideas could be generated.

3. Provide participants with these specific instructions:

   a. Organizing the slips will be easier if everyone writes the same way on the slips, so turn the slips so that the long sides are on the top and bottom.

   b. Write at the *top* of the slip. (This will help you, as trainer, to arrange the slips, one under the other.)

   c. Write only one idea per slip.

   Note: It is a good idea to collect a handful of slips from a few writers to ensure that your instructions are being followed.

4. Keep the writers at work, since the first few ideas may be the more common or obvious ones. More ideation, "going deeper in the well," should produce more novelty and quality.

5. After the group has been "drained dry," collect the slips and group them into appropriate categories. Discard duplicates, ambiguous and illegible items, etc.

6. If the first round of activity entails identification of problems or difficulties, use the second round to garner solutions. Each problem, stated in "how to" fashion, is treated procedurally as in Step 3. Each participant is given another batch of slips to produce solutions to the problems that were identified. If problems are specialized in character, subgrouping with "specialists" may be in order.

The slip method is particularly useful to accomplish the following:

☐ Ensure full participation

☐ Generate a large number of ideas quickly

☐ Guarantee privacy or anonymity to contributors

☐ Aid those who are more skilled with the written (rather than the oral) medium

☐ Generate ideas on an individual rather than on a group (interactive) basis

The major shortcoming of this method is that the contagion of the group, unlike in brainstorming and other group methods, is not utilized. Some trainers or discussion leaders may also feel that the procurement and handling of slips is a burdensome procedure.

If it is desired to make the method more "groupy," a procedure such as the one in Appendix 10, "Problem Census," may be used.

Another important use of the slip method, in addition to problem solving as discussed, is to create a manual, guidebook, or text. The procedures follow:

1. Round up a group of experts on the subject of concern.

2. Give them a batch of slips and instruct them on slip-method procedures.

3. Have them list on slips the major chapters for the book (in "how to" fashion); then collect them.

4. Have a panel review the slips and decide on the chapter headings.

5. Working with one chapter at a time, have participants list subheads (subtopics) for the chapter. Collect slips.

6. Have the panel screen slips to decide on the subtopics.

7. Have the group develop answers or solutions, on slips, to each subtopic.

The end-result is a detailed outline, complete with answers to topical areas. The text itself can be developed from the material garnered on the slips.

NOMINAL GROUP TECHNIQUE

The NGT, developed by Andre Delbecq and Andrew Van de Ven at the University of Wisconsin in 1968, is a relatively new technique [10]. It brings people together for problem solving, but limits their interaction so that ideation will not suffer due to premature evaluation, social pressures, etc. The term "nominal" is used because true or full verbal group communication is not employed.

NGT employs the following procedures:

1. A group of five to nine problem solvers are assembled at a table. They are given a written question and asked to "ideate" *individually* and *silently* on that sheet of paper for five to ten minutes. (A more complex problem may take more time.)

2. Going around the table, each participant presents *one* idea at a time from his/her list.

3. The moderator records these ideas on a flip-chart.

4. After posting all ideas, the group discusses them, providing clarification, support, or non-support for the posted ideas. Hitchhiking on others' ideas is encouraged.

5. Participants vote individually (rank-ordering) on the ideas. This statistical procedure produces a group decision, either on the first or a later ballot.

Note that unlike other group problem-solving techniques, consensus through discussion is subordinated to simple mathematical pooling of individual judgments. Whether this is a plus or a minus will depend upon how one feels about the importance of "working through" (full and open group discussion) a problem for a group decision.

As to its advantages, NGT does separate the fact-finding and ideating activities from the evaluation phase of the problem-solving process. It also balances participation, avoiding the not-unusual problem of the eager beavers taking things over. Good results can be produced in a short 60–90 minutes, and it is easily learned by participants.

The nature of the NGT is such that it does have some limitations: A very able and objective trainer is needed, that is, one who enforces the rules (especially the non-verbal aspects) and refrains from amplifying the stated question or endeavoring to influence group thinking; the question to the group must be very precisely stated or the results will be less than expected; since group interaction is limited, it may not produce a true consensus.

NGT Rating Procedures

In Step 5, the participants rank the ideas in their small groups. A sample rating procedure follows.

1. Assume there are five or six groups of five participants each (part of a larger group of 25–30 people). The small groups are asked to come up with one powerful solution to a problem presented to them.

2. In each small group the participants present their ideas to the group. The individual ideas are *not* evaluated, although they may be discussed to ensure understanding.

3. Each idea in the small group is rated by the other participants on a 5-point scale. This produces a set of scores for a given group, as given in Figure 11-1.

The best idea from each small group might be subject to another round of ratings, as in the preceding Step 3, or a panel of judges might do the rating. In either case, the best idea will receive the highest point score.

Participant	Idea A	Idea B	Idea C	Idea D	Idea E
A	X	3	2	3	1
B	4	X	3	3	3
C	2	2	X	4	4
D	2	1	3	X	4
E	2	1	2	5	X
Total Points	10	7	10	15	12

Note: *Participants rate only their colleagues' ideas, not their own.*

Figure 11-1. A record of NGT scores for a hypothetical group.

Note: The NGT, like brainstorming, is useful for identifying problems (Step 1 of the problem-solving process) and determining causes (Step 2) as well as generating ideas for solutions to the identified problem (Step 3).

THE DELPHI TECHNIQUE

The Delphi technique (named after the "Delphic Oracle") is a consensus-seeking device wherein anonymous ideas are generated and then run through a filter, but without any group interaction or discussion. (The technique has been referred to as "absentee brainstorming.") Initially developed to elicit individual ideas solely through the mail, it has more recently been adapted to group use. Both formats are described below to ensure full understanding of their procedures and potentialities. Trainers can use the Delphi to forecast training needs.

Original Format

The Delphi technique was originally developed as a forecasting tool by the RAND Corporation (credited to Norman Dalkey and colleagues) in the early 1950's. It is now used for problem solving as well as forecasting. Its key tenet is to seek consensus from experts while avoiding confrontation. Procedurally, it operates as follows:

1. Experts are selected by a decision-making team to work on a given problem, policy, or issue.

2. Questionnaires are developed by a staff unit and mailed to the participants in the study.

3. The respondents complete the questionnaires individually and mail them back to the staff unit.

4. The staff unit summarizes all responses from the experts, develops a second questionnaire, and mails it back to the respondents with a request to reconsider their ideas in light of the new or composite opinions.

5. The experts vote on or rank ideas as to priority and return their responses to the staff team.

6. The staff team prepares a final summary and feed back report, which is sent to both the respondent and decision-making groups.

Three to five rounds of questionnaires and rankings may be necessary to secure consensus. The decision makers then take it from there [11].

Advantages

The Delphi technique works best under these conditions:

- ☐ Participants can't be brought together for group discussion purposes because of geographical or scheduling problems.
- ☐ Participants are strong individual thinkers, working better without group interaction.
- ☐ Since the experts involved engage in what is essentially an anonymous debate, with opinions being exchanged through a removed neutral party, problems of over-protecting one's ideas, domination of group discussions by high-status or highly verbal types, and acquiescence to group think need not arise.
- ☐ Since there is no cost entailed in convening the experts, large numbers of respondents may be used, if desired. (Of course, too large a group may have other cost implications. A minimum of seven experts and a maximum of 100 is a general guideline.)

Other advantages follow [12]:

- ☐ Generation of ideas in isolation produces high quality ideas.
- ☐ The writing process forces a careful thinking through of the complexity of the problem.
- ☐ The respondents' behavior is proactive since they can't react to anyone else's ideas.
- ☐ Since all ideas submitted are pooled, the Delphi participants are treated on an equal basis.
- ☐ The process concludes with a moderate perceived sense of closure and accomplishment.

Limitations

The method also has several drawbacks:

- ☐ The considerable time involved in the process—sending opinions back and forth several times and awaiting responses—hardly creates a rapid sequence of events.

- ☐ The lack of personal interaction (and healthy conflict resulting therefrom) may limit the quality of ideas or solutions garnered.
- ☐ Participants must be highly motivated to spend the required time on the series of questionnaires forwarded to them.

The Delphi Technique—Group Approach

Although the original Delphi technique operated solely on a "mail-order" basis, it has since been modified to permit use with a group. Its procedures are these:

1. Participants are given a problem and are asked to generate on an individual basis as many ideas as they can about the problem. They are to record their ideas on a sheet of paper. (If the participant group numbers ten and each member produces ten ideas, 100 ideas may be collected.)
2. The moderator consolidates the batch of ideas, eliminating duplicates. Let's assume this procedure produces a total of 75 ideas.
3. The new list of 75 ideas is given to group members, and each is requested to select and circle the five most important ideas. This step should produce some 50 "screened" ideas.
4. Working from the list of 50 ideas, everyone is asked to pick three of the most important ideas. The moderator now has 30 ideas, some 70 having been dropped or consolidated.
5. The 30 ideas go back to the participants with a request to pick one or two of the best ones. This procedure produces 10–20 ideas.

In essence, this filtering process produces, say, five to seven worthwhile solutions or ideas. It does not, of course, rank or prioritize them.

Note, too, that while the assembled group is polled for ideas, *all* the ideation is actually individual and discussion-free. The whole idea is to avoid discussion because it is assumed that "the strong" will attempt to beat "the weak" [13].

IDEA WRITING

With a group of participants who can easily express themselves in writing, worthwhile ideas to solve problems can be generated quite simply and rapidly.

Idea writing—also known as "brain writing"—entails individual ideation which is reduced to writing and followed by written comments about those ideas by colleagues or fellow participants. More specifically, here's how it works [14]:

1. Break the total group into small groups (four to six persons). Seat them at tables.

2. Provide all participants with full-size writing pads.

3. Assign a task for idea production. This may be a single topic (problem, question, issue) to all groups, or the small groups may select a topic from several provided.

    Note: If groups select their own topics, duplication may occur; but the trade-off is high topic interest.

4. Have all groups count off 1 through 6; the "ones" become the leaders. The leaders' role is to keep operations on track.

5. Ask participants to write their names on the top sheet of their pads (upper right corner) and the assigned "trigger" question at the top. The top sheet is *not* to be removed from the pad.

6. Participants respond in writing to the question in any form they wish (20–30 minutes).

7. Pads are then exchanged; each small group member comments on the ideas of *all* other colleagues.

8. Pads are returned to their owners. Each now has his/her original comments plus four or five added comments on those ideas.

    Note: Steps 1–8 have been accomplished silently.

9. Each participant orally summarizes the ideas on his/her pad for the small group. (An alternative is to turn the pads in to a monitoring team for a later reporting.) A discussion is held on the ideas generated within the small group.

10. The ideas of each small group are summarized on a flipchart sheet and reported back by the group leader to the total group.

11. The session concludes with a group-at-large discussion of all ideas or solutions recorded on the flipchart.

Brainwriting works best when there is a large group, limited time, and minimal participant need for the give-and-take of group interaction. It can also be used to avoid the possibility of the influence of status smothering creativity.

Other Formats

Another term for ideawriting is brain writing. Here are several variations on this technique [15]:

☐ *Brainwriting Pool.* Its procedures are as follows:

1. Five to eight participants are seated around a table.

2. The facilitator gives a problem to the group.

3. Team members write their ideas on a sheet of paper or a large note card.

4. When a participant has produced and written four ideas, he/she puts his/her idea sheet (or card) in the center of the table (this is the pool), in exchange for someone else's idea sheet or card.

5. Each person reads the ideas on the new sheet or card and adds ideas of his/her own. If more inspiration is needed, another idea sheet or card can be picked up.

6. After 30–40 minutes, the above process ends. The idea sheets/cards are collected and evaluation now begins.

☐ *Method 6-3-5.* As a variation on the Brainwriting Pool, six participants take five minutes to write down three ideas apiece on sheets of paper. (Hence, 6-3-5.) After the five minutes, the sheets are passed clockwise around the table, with each participant adding his/her own ideas to the sheet he/she receives. Passing continues until the original sheet owners get their sheets back. Participants now take a break, after which the evaluation process begins.

☐ *Pin-Cards.* In this variation, each person receives a stack of note cards, each of a different color. The problem is presented and people write down their ideas—limited to one per card—and then pass their cards to the participants on their immediate right. When a participant needs added stimulation for ideas, a card is picked up and read, and any new ideas stimulated by that card are added to it. This process goes on for 20–30 minutes. Then all cards are collected, scanned, grouped by topic, and pinned to a large board. Duplications are discarded and evaluation starts.

☐ *Gallery Method.* Flipchart sheets are taped to the walls. Each person writes his/her ideas on a single sheet. After 20–30 minutes, a 15-minute break is taken, with everyone walking around the room to scan the others' sheets. They then return to their chairs to engage in another round of ideawriting. This second round of writing is followed by a consolidation of ideas, and evaluation commences.

CARD-POSTING TECHNIQUES

A useful way to generate ideas is via the "pin cards" technique developed by the Battele Institute, Frankfurt, Germany. Its procedures are these [16]:

1. Inform participants that the initial ideation phase of the problem-solving activity is done individually and nonverbally.

2. Present the group with a problem.

3. Provide participants with a stack of cards.

4. Instruct participants to enter only one idea on each card (as in the slip method).

5. Instruct participants to pass their completed cards (on a one-at-a-time basis) to the person on their right.

6. Ask each person to quickly study the card he/she has received and to utilize it as a stimulus to create new ideas.

The cards are moved on to the other participants for about 20–30 minutes. Upon completion of the written work, the cards are collected by the trainer, screened for overlaps or repeats, grouped into major subjects, and pinned to a pin board. A title card heads up each group of cards.

The group peruses all pinned or posted cards. Participants may ask for clarifications and add new ideas as well.

Another ideation approach, using card-posting procedures, is as follows:

1. Provide participants with a stack of 5" × 8" cards.

2. Instruct them to enter only one idea on a single card. Ideas are to be printed in large letters, using a felt-tip pen.

3. Advise group members that they can post their cards to the wall (via masking tape) as soon as they have completed several of them. (The movement of people to the wall for posting encourages the others to keep producing ideas.)

4. When the individual ideation phase is over, have participants collectively group (categorize) the cards. (*Note:* The large print facilitates this procedure.) Possible categories in a team-building session are people problems, policies, procedures, and equipment needs.

5. On the basis of the card array, encourage another round of individual ideation.

What function do the posted cards serve? Several, as a matter of fact:

☐ Everyone's ideas are considered. As in a good brainstorming session, no one's idea is criticized, argued with, or minimized. Instead, all ideas are accorded equal recognition via the posting procedure.

☐ It forces people to give the essence of an idea without unnecessary elaboration, exemplification, justification, or pontification.

☐ It encourages added ideation.

☐ It permits the easy "patterning" of concepts (or problems), as previously described.

☐ It facilitates the prioritizing of ideas (or problems).

☐ It provides a written record for later use.

Both card-posting techniques produce the same result: a set of posted cards, which are then rearranged into logical groupings for further ideation, discussion, etc. The first technique emphasizes moving the cards to fellow participants to stimulate added ideas. The second procedure uses the visual display and movement of people to stimulate ideas. This latter procedure is more group-oriented since the participants rather than the trainer (or leader) do the card grouping.

THE CLIENT-CENTERED APPROACH TO PROBLEM SOLVING

A unique problem-solving firm, Synectics, Inc., Cambridge, Massachusetts, has been researching the process of innovation, creative problem solving, and meeting effectiveness since 1960. (*Synectics* is a Greek word that means joining together different and apparently irrelevant elements.) The firm finds that although the quality of group thinking—*content*—is generally adequate, groups run into difficulty in the *process.* Content relates to the *what* of the problem-solving process; process relates to the *how.* In other words, how groups go about their business of problem solving is the core source of their difficulties. Process troubles include unclear problem definition, groups too large to function, status, nitpicking, judgmental attitudes, hidden agendas, information being hoarded rather than shared, negativism and putdowns, sloppy time management, and poor listening.

Synectics' solution to the process difficulty is to recognize that one person—usually designated as chairperson—cannot effectively monitor both the content and the process roles. Synectics splits the chairperson role into two parts or two chairs: one for content and one for process. The former is designated the "client," that is, the one who has the problem. The latter is designated "traffic cop" or facilitator.

The client, the problem owner, has these responsibilities: calling the meeting, directing the discussion to be sure people stay on track, making decisions, and evaluating. The facilitator assumes the responsibilities of scribe (records ideas on a flipchart), time keeper, protector of idea presenters from attack or criticism, and idea catalyst (peps up group when they go flat).

Both the client and the facilitator respect the other's responsibilities and avoid crossing over. (In rare instances, a highly sensitive and participation-oriented manager can assume both roles.)

In the Synectics approach, then, we have three roles:

- ☐ Client
- ☐ Facilitator
- ☐ Resources (participant group of five or six)

In planning for the most effective functioning of those who perform in these roles, the journalist's six questions merit consideration as follows:

- ☐ Who—The client plus a divergent group including a "novice."
- ☐ What—What is the objective?
- ☐ Where—Away from phones, interruptions.
- ☐ When—Ask: are you an A.M. or a P.M. person?

- ☐ Why—Why is it a problem? Why am I calling this meeting? Do I need a group?
- ☐ How—The process issue.

The Synectics approach also stresses the importance of the "mental dynamics" of problem solving. It hypothecates two selves: the "safe-keeping" self and the "experimental" self. The former evaluates, reassures, supports, is realistic and logical, avoids surprises and risks, and punishes mistakes. The latter takes risks, breaks rules, is intuitive, speculates, sees fun in change, and takes chances. Ideally, participants in problem-solving activities need to work on expanding their experimental selves, something which has been inhibited in many of us during the transition from childhood to adulthood [17].

UPSIDE-DOWN PROBLEM SOLVING

Typically, when we are confronted with a problem, we tend to think of the approaches we've used before or have heard about, all of which are based on common sense and logical thinking. But what if we were to tackle the problem by approaching it in less conventional terms—more particularly, in opposite terms—and forgot about common sense? For example, assume we have the classic supervisory problem of the habitually tardy employee. What have we done before about this kind of problem? We give the usual lectures and warnings, circulate memos to *everyone* concerning the need to report to work promptly, possibly count the lateness as time to be reduced from annual leave, etc. But what if we were to turn things around and consider strategies which would make it *easier* rather than harder for the employee? If so, we might conceive of new strategies (bizarre ones are fine) such as these: changing (delaying) the starting time, putting the employee on another shift, introducing flextime, ignoring the problem for several weeks, asking the employee when he/she would *like* to start(!), having everyone wait until the employee arrives before beginning the day's work, starting the employee's work yourself or assigning someone else to do it, giving the late employee the key to open the door in the morning for everyone, putting the employee on a committee that is to develop a new lateness policy [18].

This approach, known as "second order" thinking, is a means of achieving some new breakthroughs on our problem. This is not to say that the preceding ideas are necessarily worthy of adoption, but they do encourage participants to think in nonconventional terms. The alternative is to continue to treat the ailment with the same "tried and true" remedies.

ACTION LEARNING/ACTION-REFLECTION LEARNING (ARL)

ARL is a group-in-action training device used to solve real business/organization problems under actual work conditions. An ARL program has these key characteristics [19]:

☐ Using teams to solve complex problems.

☐ Teaching participants how to learn and think creatively.

☐ Building skills for training needs which arise as the team project proceeds.

☐ Developing a team member's own conceptualization/theory of management, leadership, or employee empowerment. This theory will be tested against real business experiences as well as against established principles.

Team members engaged in ARL use the "laboratory" of the project in order to garner insight into similar problems back on the job. They receive feedback and experiment with new behaviors.

ARL makes these assumptions:

☐ Learning increases when we reflect on our performance in the training.

☐ We should focus on independent, precedent-free solutions, as opposed to relying on experts who offer their solutions and thus may smother our creative thinking.

☐ New perspectives are likely to emerge since the ARL teams are cross-functional and non-hierarchical.

☐ Facilitators help to accelerate learning and to develop and unleash critical thinking.

☐ Learning should encompass and challenge many diverse learning-style preferences.

☐ The organizational system as a whole is subject to individual and team learning.

To design an ARL program, which may take three to six months of planning, these steps are key:

1. Educate line managers as to ARL's philosophy and procedure. They should understand that they are the final decision makers and that they provide the projects (problems) for the ARL teams to tackle. They also identify a given problem's stakeholders and use that data as a basis for selection of project team members. The ideal team composition is one with diverse personalities with different educational and functional backgrounds. This diverse team member mix permits the project teams to assess problems from new, bold, and different viewpoints.

   Note: A wise tactic for anyone launching an ARL program is to soft-pedal the use of the term "action-reflection learning." It may produce red flags and skepticism among managers. *Suggestion:* Talk, instead, about using diverse groups to help solve current business problems.

1. Develop learning activities around the various projects. *Example:* Facilitators observe team interaction and provide feedback thereon. This is followed by training on giving and receiving feedback, conducting meetings, or any other needs which emerged during project work.

2. Plan informal team meetings and structured sessions for all team members. The informal activities cover actual project work; the structured meetings discuss subjects pertinent to total group development, for example, leadership roles or communication.

3. Assign a new facilitator, one the team doesn't know, to the team. This facilitator can act independently of the firm's culture. When the team project is completed, he/she helps team members reflect on their work to augment their learning about how they identify, assess, and solve problems. Members also evaluate how they think and learn as a group. The facilitator's function is to help team members assess their listening, their style of giving feedback, how they and conduct meetings, how they work with others, and the assumptions which shape their beliefs and actions.

The facilitator, as an outsider, is free to ask questions which the team may prefer to avoid. His/her concern is that the team focuses on learning, not just on task completion.

Note: The R ("reflection") in ARL means thinking about project content *and* the processes by which participants and project teams develop and learn.

The facilitator helps team participants continually redefine the stated problem. This process continues until it's certain that team members are asking themselves the questions necessary to arrive at a proper solution.

ARL is used appropriately in these circumstances:

- [ ] For complex problems which have no obvious solution
- [ ] When there is a need to develop a cross-functional overview
- [ ] When learning is closely allied to a cultural change
- [ ] When judgment and strategic thinking need to be developed
- [ ] When team members wish to learn by doing and simultaneously to zero in on the task

The bottom line of ARL: People not only learn problem-solving skills, but they also solve actual, complex organizational problems. As Noel Tichy, of the University of Michigan's Business School and one of the foremost proponents of action learning, said [20]:

"The problem with management is that we treat it as a quasi-scientific thing. Management is a clinical practice. You don't train heart surgeons by having them read Harvard cases. Management development has to get much closer to the real world. How do you train people in the crafts? That's all we're talking about. The basic principles apply all the way to the shop floor."

Note: General Electric has been using this type of training for its executives since 1986. They call it "action learning," a learning-by-doing approach in which the training addresses actual business problems. In 1988 G.E. began to apply action learning with a global perspective. Currently, all of G.E.'s executive education and training programs are international in scope. There is also a heavy emphasis on "team dynamics," that is, discussing such issues as team output and team process, including each team member's involvement and contributions. So building and managing project teams becomes a key source of learning for the participants [21].

Keys to Program Success

If the above paragraphs have stimulated your interest in launching an action learning/ARL program in your organization, be guided by these 12 key elements essential to the action learning process [22]:

Sponsorship: To start the ball rolling, to give the program continuing life, and to ensure that recommendations of the problem-solving team will be seriously considered and fully implemented, a sponsoring steering committee is essential. For example, American Home Products (AHP), Madison, New Jersey, which finds that the action learning/ARL device transforms senior managers into leaders as well as solves real problems, uses a steering committee of senior-level executives (leaders of key business units), all deeply committed to the activity.

A Strategic mandate: A major business issue must be defined, one that affects the organization's future. AHP considers becoming an integrated global company basic to its survival and success.

A Learning process: Potential sponsors expect a full road map that defines how the action learning program will proceed. For example, AHP action learning participants devote eight full days in their action learning teams, which includes one day in a "team immersion" activity. This information is essential for the sponsors before they give it their all-out support.

A Selection process: In selecting participants for the teams, diversity is a key; people from different functions with different backgrounds are essential. This mix provides the creative tension that contributes to real learning. At AHP an annual talent review seeks out potential leaders from all segments of the firm and from all parts of the globe.

Learning teams: Team members are selected for their differences, not their similarities, This approach builds in the conflict vital for the creative thinking and action. At AHP the participants are divided into four learning teams, representing both U.S. and international members from a mix of job levels.

Coaching: Each team has two coaches to help develop skills in group problem solving and conflict resolution. Thus, in AHP's Global Leadership program the teams are aided by an outside consultant plus an in-house executive who acts as the team mentor throughout the action learning process.

Orientation to the issues: Participants receive background from a group comprising company execs, global business thinkers, professors and consultants in interpersonal skills. As an added aspect of this educational component, team members receive pre-learning material about individual team objectives. They also are encouraged to brainstorm solutions before their team activities start.

Data gathering: This is a live exercise, going beyond the perusing of available reports. The teams collect data from all possible sources—from in-house staffers; interviews with customers, suppliers, and industry leaders; as well as long-untouched computer files.

Data analysis: The teams are vastly more than data collectors. Their task is to evaluate their data for relevance, relating it to their assigned business issue. The outside consultant provides techniques to assess data and to keep teams on target.

Presentation drafting: The aim of the action learning process is to force participants to think systematically, politically and realistically. The teams now have to create recommendations from their data that are relevant and actionable. The team's executive mentor provides a big assist toward this end.

Presentation: This is the payoff step. The teams are now ready to sell their proposals to the organization. Each team provides as many as three recommendations to a panel of senior officials who probe and comment on what they hear. At presentation's end, the panel decides immediately whether to act on the proposals or not to, So the teams learn promptly whether their hard work struck a resounding note with top management.

Debriefing: Now a process of "facilitated self-reflection," basic to the action learning process, takes place. With assistance from the consultant, team members reflect and give one another feedback on their functioning. At HP, participants are also asked to give the CEO a letter outlining the value of the experience and indicating how their new learnings may be applied in the months and years ahead.

DEVICES TO UNLEASH IDEA DEVELOPMENT

Although many of us have considerable potential to produce new and different ideas for purposes of problem solving, all too often that capacity remains untapped. Hence the need for trainers to employ devices that stimulate idea production.

Sidney J. Parnes, former president of the Creative Education Foundation, State University College at Buffalo, New York, distinguishes between techniques that encourage the free flow of ideas, like brainstorming, and devices that initiate idea development, such as checklists, forced relationships, attribute listing, and morphological analysis [23].

Using Checklists

A checklist is a tool that helps participants focus on a list of categories to which the problem under review might relate. The checklist, consisting of a series of verbs (also known as "trigger words"), is used to change one's conventional approach or mindset to a problem. Three potent verbs for this purpose, per Alex F. Osborn, brainstorming inventor and author of the now classic work *Applied Imagination:*

- ☐ Magnify
- ☐ Minify
- ☐ Rearrange

As a simple illustration of the way these verbs might be used to stimulate ideas, take the problem of space utilization in a shop, lab, office, or store. We can take the three verbs and expand them into questions relating to our problem.

Question 1. How can we increase (magnify) our space? Some answers: knock down unnecessary walls and partitions; eliminate minimally used storage areas and closets; negotiate for more space with Divisions X and Y; rehabilitate the attic and the basement; close in the porch; since we have high ceilings, make two-story levels out of one level wherever practical.

Question 2. How can we shrink (minify) our need for space? We could eliminate bulky furniture and unneeded file cabinets; use microfilm for files; reduce staff; drop unnecessary activities and operations.

Question 3. How can we rearrange our space more effectively? Some answers: start with a floor plan; use wall space more imaginatively; reduce size of reception area; use modular furniture; stack file cabinets from floor to ceiling; use an open plan instead of partitions, and use potted palms for privacy; put all heavy phone users (such as our customer service reps) in one section of our large room behind noise-proof walls.

Note: These three verbs represent only a partial list of those used by Alex F. Osborn. Others are modify, manipulate, substitute, combine, adapt, and reverse, with each category having several subquestions under it.

Two other types of checklists are *area thinking* and *word stimulation* [24]. Area thinking is the opposite of attribute listing. With this procedure we start with several major aspects of a problem and then work toward details and specifics. In word stimulation, we use word lists to trigger creative ideas and solutions.

Note that these checklists, as well as attribute listing, discussed later, are designed to unleash creativity. They are not to be confused with checklists that auditors, managers, and others might use to be certain that the right procedures are being followed in a given situation, such as in responding to a bomb threat in an office building, inspecting the effectiveness of a decentralized operation, or orienting a new worker.

Random Word Stimulation Technique

Much of our thinking is logical; that is, we are concerned only with what is fully relevant, and we systematically discard elements not related to a subject. According to management professor Dr. Thomas S. Isaack, though, striving to free-associate *unrelated* concepts can jump start the intuition (our right brain) to spot reasonable relationships among unrelated ideas.

How to do this? Simply randomly select a word from the dictionary and play with uncovering relationships between the random word and the topic/subject on which you are working. *Example:* Dr.

Isaack says that the title for his article—"Intuition: A Treasury of Knowledge"—was produced by trying to connect intuition with the random word "bullion." By thinking about riches, gold, silver, pirates, and buried treasure, Isaack ultimately tied together *intuition* and *treasure* [25].

In another example, a group of product developers at Campbell Soup Company randomly selected from the dictionary the word "handle." Via free word association, one member suggested the word "utensil," which led to "fork." One group member joked about a soup that could be eaten with a fork. The group reasoned that you could eat soup only with a fork it were thick with vegetables and meat. Presto! Campbell's Chunky Soups line, a big seller for that firm, was created.

James Higgins, management professor and author of *Creative Problem Solving Techniques: The Handbook of New Ideas for Business* (New Management Publishing Co., Winter Park, Florida, 1944), suggests the following procedures, which he calls "Free Association: By the Numbers," to produce ideas that might trigger solutions to a problem [26]:

1. Start with a random word; enter it in Line 1 of a 10-line worksheet.
2. On Line 2 enter the first word triggered by Line 1.
3. On Line 3, enter a word stimulated by Line 2.
4. On Lines 4–10: Continue the above procedure until you have ten words. Higgins suggests that 20 or 30 words are better.
5. Now assess your word list. See if any of them provide insight into your problem.
6. If you find one or more "hot" words, work with them: brainstorm solutions, form new associations, or draw analogies.
7. Write your new ideas on ten more lines.

Note that the stimulus (the random word) must be truly irrelevant and unrelated to the problem. If you or I were to select the stimulus, it would most likely be logically associated with the problem. This would defeat the intent of a random word, which is to depart totally from the problem situation. In sum, the idea is to disengage our thinking from logical patterns in order to open up new routes for exploration and to encourage full use of intuition to achieve break-through thinking.

Mindmapping (Ideamapping)

This technique was developed by Tony Buzan of the Learning Methods Group, England [27], and based on the idea that many (though not all) people find it helpful to dump out a lot of ideas in very short order. We simply start with a key concept in the center of a page (or flipchart), circle it (the catalytic word), and then branch out from the trigger word in all directions. Creating a free-flowing web of ideas, as opposed to stacking them in the usual columns and rows, can be a great idea stimulator. The technique is useful for both groups and individuals.

The ideas may be related to causes, effects, solutions, lists of things to do or remember, etc. The important thing is to branch out from the core idea. The branches are typically areas to consider, with sub-branches flowing from the major branches.

As an example, why don't we plan Jane Jones' wedding? We'll start by putting "Jane's wedding" in the center of a flipchart sheet. We'll then randomly enter, as branches, the major areas of concern that have to be considered—announcement, invitation list, church service, reception, and so on. For each of these branches, we can then add the specific tasks (sub-branches) that have to be performed. (See Figure 11-2.)

So what we have, essentially, is an elaborate, king-size doodle with words. It represents a nonlinear, right-brain way of visually organizing thoughts, associations, and/or relationships. Once a branch or two is identified as pertinent, it quickly triggers other related branches.

Story Boarding

Like brainstorming, this creative problem-solving device elicits ideas from a group very rapidly, but it does so along somewhat structured lines. A major theme or problem area, possibly with several sub-themes, is used to spark ideas. Here's how it works [28]:

1. Set up a large (4' × 4') story board (usually a black or green felt board) in the front of the room.

2. State the purpose of the meeting and the ground rules; for example, no blaming or finger pointing is allowed, just generating ideas on the topics/problem areas at hand. It's a good idea to loosen up the group with fun warm-up exercises.

3. Post pink cards (4" × 6"), each bearing a key question, on the board. For example, Diane Elko, director of Quality for American Capital Management and Research Inc., brought together 13 senior executives of a mutual bond firm. Their goal: to enhance the firm's quality improvement process. The pink cards bore these four questions: How can we turn managers into quality leaders? How can we keep employees excited about quality? What quality improvements will grab the attention of every customer? What can we do to make us feel terrific about measuring quality?

4. The participants then shout suggestions, which two participants write on index cards. These cards are then pinned beneath the larger pink cards. All ideas must be specific rather than vague.

5. The participants vote on the best and most actionable suggestions. *Note:* In story boarding, meetings must end with a commitment to action.

This particular meeting delivered these results: 80 ideas were generated, 20 were put into action. The visual information, posted up front, encouraged active responding. *Note:* The group was able to compress into one hour what could have been a day-long strategy session.

The McNellis Co., New Brighton, Pennsylvania, which provides seminars on story boarding, adds another procedure to aid in prioritizing the ideas for action. Using adhesive colored dots, each participant marks ideas which merit "floating to the top." The advantage of this procedure: It avoids both politicking and time-consuming efforts at persuasion; ideas stand or fall on their own, separated from the egos of the contributors. The ideas with the most dots win a place on the story board [29].

Outcome Objective

Creativity consultant/author Bryan W. Mattimore stresses that creative, free-wheeling problem-solving

Figure 11-2. Illustration of a mindmapping diagram.

sessions will benefit from clearly defined goals [30]. An effective way to create such goals is via "time-track visualization."

Procedure: Simply tell your participants to pretend that their session has just ended and everything went off terrifically. Then ask them what turned them on and what ideas were generated. Post the ideas to a flipchart. In effect, you are asking them to visualize "the future," that is, the end of the session and what was accomplished. The result is to establish clear-cut goals (results, outcomes) for the meeting/session.

Then, when your session ends, use the visualized goals as a basis for assessing what was accomplished. Mattimore states that most groups are able to accomplish all the results they visualized.

Attribute Listing

This technique is intended to generate ideas about a product, service, or situation. After the list is developed, the various attributes, traits, or characteristics listed are analyzed for means of improving the product, service, or situation. Thus, each item may be subject to a special focus using the techniques of

checklists (described previously) and forced relationships (described later).

Example: We may wish to improve the landscaping around our plant or office. We thus develop a list of its features or attributes, such as the following:

Lawn

Beds, flower

Beds, nonflowering (for example, ivy)

Fences

Flowering trees

Other shade trees

Shrubs

Hedges

Walks

Stone walls

Picnic/luncheon areas

Signing

Hazards

We may then develop checklists concerning these items; for example, in considering the picnic/luncheon areas, we may highlight benches, tables, trash cans, shade, shrubbery, flagstone, etc.

Morphological Analysis

This is a problem-generating and problem-solving approach that relates (or interrelates) all elements (independent variables) of a problem to aid in discovering fresh solutions. As will be apparent from the following discussion, it entails combining attribute listing with forced relationship in a matrix approach. The steps for conducting the analysis include

1. Identifying the major elements (variables, parameters) of a problem.
2. Further identifying the subelements or factors that relate to the major variables.
3. Establishing a matrix to highlight the several variables and their subelements.
4. Choosing, generally on a random basis, the subelements in the matrix. One subelement from each of the major variables is selected and combined with the others.
5. Analyzing the feasibility of combining the elements.
6. Selecting and analyzing the practicality of added combinations of elements.

In general, the whole process is designed to generate ideas. The combining and recombining of subelements provides numerous opportunities to look at a problem and to come up with fresh, novel solutions, and our natural tendencies to ideate along habitual lines are upset.

To illustrate the process, let's assume we have developed a morphological matrix such as the one in Figure 11-3 relating to slow-moving products in a retail department store. Our objective is to design a program or campaign to help move these ten "slow-movers": men's hats, toasters, suede jackets, half-inch garden hoses, portable first-aid kits, small electric fans, ladies' garter belts, porch paint, rolltop desks, and classical records. Our three key variables to accomplish this are internal management activities or programs, promotional approaches, and employee incentives.

Going to our three-columned matrix, we might consider as our program the use of special sales or campaigns (column 1), via radio (column 2), coupled

with special time off to employees who are the best performers (column 3) [31]. This tripartite program, along with others similarly selected, would be evaluated as to possible payoffs.

Internal Management Activities	Promotional Methods	Employee Incentives
Notices on bulletin boards Memos to employees with tips on selling the "dogs" Boxed items in company news letter Encouragement of brainstorming sessions with employees Pep talks at supervisors' meetings Review of pricing practices Study of competitors' practices Special campaigns as "Discard Sale," "Overstock Sale," "Three-for-Two" pricing, etc.	TV spots, radio spots Newspaper ads School newspaper ads Suburban newspaper ads Leaflets with customers' bills Small catalog featuring "dogs" Mail flyers to homes Leaflets on individual items at various points in store Ads on store delivery trucks	Contests with prizes ("Dog Mover of the Week") Special commissions Supervisory praise Letters of commendation from top management Special time off Extra employee discounts on these items Give some items away as prizes for perfect attendance Suggest these items for early Christmas gift buying (get your shopping done early)

Figure 11-3. Example of a morphological matrix.

Forced Relationships Technique

To develop new combinations of ideas, participants may be given a new word, concept, phrase, or object and asked to relate it to the problem being studied. All senses may be tapped; attention may be called to a sound or odor as well as to items in view. Or the group may be asked to take an imaginary trip somewhere. In general, the idea is to find new stimuli to force creativity.

Example: Assume the group is working on a problem of tardiness. The moderator or supervisor introduces a bag of lemons (!) and asks participants to use it to help solve the problem. Some possible solutions: Using behavior modification principles, give the latecomer a glass of lemonade whenever arrival is prompt; add oranges to the lemons and set up a "data" display (visual feedback) for two weeks: give a lemon for tardiness, an orange for promptness; promise a cake (a lemon cake) and coffee party for the whole group if arrival time has improved materially at week's end; put a lemon on the employee's desk whenever he/she is late; add to the lemons a case of cokes as a reward for improved arrival time.

Another way to apply the forced relationship technique is to follow these procedures:

1. Cite your concern, problem or difficulty, for example, customer complaints.

2. Enter "customer complaints" in the T-column below.

3. Brainstorm or list by free association the possible causes for the problem. Enter them in the T-column.

4. Select an activity totally unrelated to customer complaints. Let's take "baseball."

5. Brainstorm or free associate a list of attributes of the game of baseball. Enter them in the T-column.

Customer Complaints, causes for	Baseball, attributes of
Poor selection of sales personnel	Hot dogs
Lousy products	Scoreboard
Policies not clear	Vendors
Lack of training	Bats
Ineffective reward system	Gloves
Lack of time to spend	Stadium
with customers	Home run
Lack of feedback to reps	Coaches
Nasty customers	Diamond
	Tickets
	Players

6. Try to tie together individual items in the two columns.

7. List on a flipchart the related ideas which have been generated. Possible examples: Hooking together "lack of feedback" and "scoreboard," we might have a daily display board on the number of complaints received; tying together "reward systems" and "tickets," we might provide sales reps with tickets to the game for a complaint-free week or month; "lack of training" and "coaches" might signify to us that we should start doing a better job of coaching.

Dyads/Triads Analysis

Working in dyads (pairs) or triads (trios), one participant offers ideas about the assigned problem, issue, topic, or question. The other partner(s) uses the Journalist's Six Questions to elicit more information from the idea presenter. Roles are reversed so that all members of the pair or trio get a chance to be an idea-offerer/generator.

After the work in pairs or trios, a general, class-at-large discussion is held as to what about the issue in question was learned or agreed upon in the small group meetings.

Movement—Talk While You Walk

Have pairs or trios take a 15–30-minute walk—down a shady path, across a meadow, or around the block—to talk about an issue or problem. *Purpose:* to change perspectives. Most of us do a lot of sitting in a room devoid of fresh air, with a resultant quieting down (stagnation) of our creative juices. An outdoors "walking meeting" has the potential to stir us up and provide a fresh, possibly more imaginative view about the question at hand.

USING ANALOGY

One effective way to augment problem-solving capacity is to work with the principle of "making the strange familiar." This is an approach developed by William Gordon of Synectics, Inc., Cambridge, Massachusetts [32]. It is a recognition that people, as problem solvers, are basically conservative. New concepts or ideas are perceived as threatening; hence, there is the need for many of us to dredge up or draw upon the familiar in order to accommodate the new or strange idea.

To facilitate the familiarity process, Gordon encourages the use of *analogy,* or model or comparison seeking. He has his problem solvers use these three types of analogies:

☐ Direct analogy
☐ Personal analogy
☐ Symbolic analogy

Direct Analogy

Also called example seeking, this entails the comparison of one thing with another. Two historical examples:

The telephone is based on the human ear; Darwin's theory of evolution resulted from comparing the natural state with controlled breeding on stock farms [23].

Even those fields unrelated to the field one is working on can provide the problem solver with a viable analogy. An engineer, for example, might study human systems to gain insight about a mechanical problem. In general, the process calls for drawing upon one's experience and knowledge to locate examples similar (analogous) to the subject being studied.

To "tease out" an analogy, it helps to use this sentence: "This situation (or thing) is comparable to ____" or "This situation reminds me of ____."

An example of the use of *direct* analogy in the training situation is the training used by the airlines to teach flight attendants to smile continually, despite various job pressures and irritations from customers. (One West Coast airline's jingle is "On PSA our smiles are not just painted on, so smile your way from L.A. to San Francisco.") A Delta Airlines trainer advised a group of trainees to: "Think of the airplane cabin as your own living room. Now, if you invited some people into your own home, wouldn't you want them to think you had gone to some trouble for them? Wouldn't you want to put them at ease? It's exactly the same thing in the cabin. These people are your guests."

Further, the flight attendants are told to think of demanding passengers "as if" (analogy again) the passengers were their own children, seeking attention. One trainer advised the use of this "as if" principle: "It can help to think of rude passengers as having had some terrible tragedy in the past."

In general, by using these analogies in flight, the attendant is better equipped to handle stressful situations as well as to maintain a continuing appearance of pleasantness [33].

Personal Analogy

This is a form of creative problem solving wherein one takes on the identity of something else or somebody else. In respect to the "something else," the idea is to look from "the inside" at an object subject to change or improvement. By being in and part of it, one can better understand the thing and its "feelings," and thus be in a superior position to improve on it [34]. For example, small groups may be asked to brainstorm improvements in a toaster, a woman's purse, a man's shirt, or a power drill, using the personal analogy approach to unleash their creativity.

In human potential programs, where group members are trying to achieve greater sensory awareness, a greater ability to express feelings, and greater personal insight, the participants may be asked to take on

the identity of a flower, a cloud, the sun, a brook, etc. The data (feelings) produced individually may then be subject to pairing and sharing plus later general discussion with the total group [35].

People problems as well as technical and marketing problems can also be subject to personal analogy. This is essentially a form of role playing (minus the enactment): "If I were the sales manager..." In this process one hypothecates or imagines how the other person would think, feel, behave, react.

Obviously, the identification with an object rather than a person is much more difficult to do. Why? Because in everyday life we (at least some of us) do, at times, try to empathize with another person—namely, "I know what she is going through," "I know how he feels." But how many of us have had an experience trying to think and feel like, say, a kitchen sink?

Symbolic Analogy

Also called compressed conflict, this analogy uses a "close-coupled" phrase in which the words engage in "combat" with one another. For example, Pasteur's antitoxin research was based on the expression "safe attack"; Nobel Prize-winning Spanish neurologist Ramon Y. Cajal was stimulated in his accomplishment by the phrase "protoplasmic kiss" [36].

Creating symbolic analogies can aid materially in creative problem solving. Procedurally, we do the following [37]:

1. Select a key word or ask participants to select a key word from the problem statement.

2. Ask participants for its meaning to *them*, empathizing or feeling for its most important significance.

3. Ask participants to put the feeling into one or two words to form a symbolic analogy.

Some examples:

Key Word	Symbolic Analogy
Ratchet	Dependable intermittency
Solidity	Enforced togetherness
Mixture	Balanced confusion
Receptivity	Involuntary willingness

Productivity Teams Aided by Analogy

To illustrate more fully how analogy works in problem solving, the experience of a consulting firm concerned with productivity improvement merits citation [38].

A Pittsburgh-based consulting firm, the Advanced Manufacturing Cost Reduction and Productivity Service Group, PROFITCO, forms two-day productivity improvement teams in manufacturing plants to work on problems that

☐ Have been studied extensively by staff experts without success.

☐ Have *not* been attacked at all because everyone "knows" they are "impossible" to solve.

☐ Persist due to lack of time to work on them or because necessary technical personnel resources are limited.

In sum, the teams work on the kinds of problems that typically tend to remain untackled in manufacturing plants.

The teams are formed from internal supervisory and managerial personnel drawn from various units of the plant. The team members' main qualification is an ability to approach a "strange" problem in a fresh, inventive, and creative way. They are successful because they avoid thinking like experts. These teams help one "key man," the supervisor who has been living with the problem. The latter explains the problem, answers questions of team members and converts the team's semi-useful ideas into practical reality.

The teams are successful on one out of every four problems tackled. Savings typically range from $100,000 to $1,000,000 or more.

The "targets of opportunity," as the problems are called, are subject to "invention-thinking." This means defining the problem differently and looking at the problem differently than the technical experts in quality control, R & D, value engineering, and human resources. The techniques the productivity teams use are direct analogy, projection (or personal analogy), and fantasy (described elsewhere).

Let's take a look, then, to see how a productivity team employed direct analogy to solve a perplexing productivity problem. The problem was as follows: There were delays in completing metallurgical test reports, which prevented the timely release of ore shipments via railroad cars. The team defined the problem as "overcoming delays" and "speeding up" testing. Accordingly, comparisons (analogies in other contexts such as sports or music) were utilized. Some examples:

☐ How runners manage to have a speed-up kick left for the finish

☐ How harmonica players manage to play the melody at the same time they produce a rhythmic accompaniment

☐ How traffic moves at a complex intersection with and without a police officer

☐ How pass receivers in football speed up and vary their running patterns to outwit the defense

☐ How power failures are circumvented in electrical distribution systems

☐ How leap-frogging and flanking are used in military operations

☐ How credit collection agencies speed up collections on seriously delinquent accounts

☐ How artillery units get on target faster via bracketing versus creeping fire

☐ How flywheels continue to operate long after being speeded up

☐ How hang gliders can accelerate upward

☐ How sailboats accelerate going into the wind at an angle

☐ How the old Western stage coach managed to race across great distances in just a few days

The productivity team studied these analogies to resolve the railroad car delay problem. The key man saw the stage coach practice (last item in the list of analogies) as being pertinent, because it entailed replacing fatigued horses with fresh ones at regular intervals. Also, not all horses ran simultaneously. The logical solution, then, was this: Transfer a staffer of the metallurgical test lab to a special one-person late shift (3 P.M. to 11 P.M.) to continue conducting critical tests on steel specimens on loaded railroad cars awaiting release. The shift in thinking to "not running all horses at the same time" allowed test reports to be accomplished and forwarded to the production departments in time to release the railroad cars before the 7 A.M. deadline the next morning.

(The lab, of course, was closed from 5 P.M. to 8 A.M. daily.) Net savings for a half-day of this team study was a whopping $181,000!

The PROFITCO consultants point out that analogy-type thinking works because it puts the problem in a remote and strange context. This allows for the discovery of a much-needed, productive new viewpoint.

Another steel manufacturing problem, one of quality control, was solved via *projection* or *personal analogy,* that is, the team becomes part of the problem. This solution produced an annual cost reduction of $540,000. The problem was the following: Unwanted black streaks (snakes) formed on the surfaces of steel strips rolled into coils. These snakes came from strip surface oil not completely removed by the internal environment of the box annealing heat treatment furnaces. Not all coils were bad, but some were. Though some of the bad coils could be cleaned up, some could not and had to be junked. The oil treatment was required in making the strip and in preventing rusting during storage before heat treating.

The team examined the defective coils carefully and noted their thickness (they were thinner than the good ones) and their length (usually longer when uncoiled). Size and weight were the same for both good and bad coils.

After the study of the defective coils, the team projected themselves momentarily as oil drops. From this they concluded that they had all started to move toward the edges and out of the coils while in the heat treating furnace, but had stopped short for some reason.

The team then made a further projection (personal analogy): they became the steel strip, all coiled up, with a need to shed the oil completely "like good coils should." In this projection or personal analogy mode, these preferences (personal analogies) were stated by the various team members:

- [ ] It would be nice to be a bit more slippery so I could shed the oil and not feel gunky.
- [ ] I'd like to stay longer in this nice hot furnace because it feels so good.
- [ ] I feel superior to all the good coils because I'm so much longer and I have these pretty black lace decorations that they don't!
- [ ] I hate this greasy stuff on me—I wish I had a million tiny blow torches to burn each drop away.

- [ ] I'm so skinny and weak that I get exhausted pushing the entire oil film to my edges.
- [ ] I detest crowds and there're so many oil drops on me that I feel like I'm at Times Square on New Year's Eve.
- [ ] I'm suffocating, wrapped up so tight in this coil; I'm drowning in oil, and it tastes, ugh, awful.
- [ ] I'm disgusted, getting bad-mouthed because I can't shed five times as much oil from my surfaces as the good coils have to unload. Why can't I get credit for trying?

The productivity team studied these personal analogies and saw the problem as "too-much-oil-on-too-much-surface" of these coils coming out of the furnace with "snakes." (This was inspired by the last-cited personal analogy.) But how to reduce the amount of oil film remaining on the strip surfaces, and yet leave enough to prevent unwanted rust formation while being stored before the heat treatment?

Quick agreement was reached that the oil film on the steel strip coming into the final series of roll stands could be reduced. An oil (or other substance) that would self-destruct under high temperature would also be helpful. Other ideas included the realization that nearly all the oil on either the top or the bottom of the strip at the end of the rolling sequence could be removed via steam blast or air knife; oil remaining on the other side should spread out on the "dry" side as the strip was coiled and compacted—this could cut to one-half the total volume of oil on the coils sent to storage awaiting heat treating.

Why does this approach to problem solving work so well on such tough problems? PROFITCO provides these skill points:

- [ ] Total top management support, including tolerance for "nonsuccesses."
- [ ] A team approach to problem solving, with members being drawn from different parts of the plant.
- [ ] Use of the key man (the one having the problem) as part of the team. He helps the team by explaining the problem and answering questions about it. He zeroes in on and adapts the pertinent idea and follows up on it or gets authorization to act on it.

☐ The teams define the problem differently than the staff experts and often find it to be something other than as stated. Their thinking about the value of negative information—where and when the problem is and is not occurring—is often more important to this kind of problem-solving group than to more conventional groups.

☐ The team assumes that any problem can be solved and that the experts are wedded to obsolete approaches.

☐ Team members are results-oriented. Their only interest is to see the creation of low-cost solutions that get tried out and implemented when effective.

☐ The team thinks laterally, not vertically; for example, a chemical problem might be solved via a mechanical or biological approach.

☐ The teams carefully separate idea generating from idea evaluating (as in brainstorming).

☐ The two-day work period is long enough to sustain interest and short enough to avoid "burnout."

☐ The use of the highly imaginative techniques of analogy (direct and personal) and fantasy are basic to the way the teams go about their business of problem solving.

PCT Approach and Analogy

"Purposeful Creative Thinking" (PCT) is another way to solve problems via analogy or comparison. It encourages us to tap or draw upon the vast storehouse of information all of us have. It entails a six-step process as follows [39]:

1. Describe the problem or difficulty.
2. Identify the paradox that underlies the problem. That is, what *conflict* is basic to the problem?
3. Identify or locate an analogy to the paradox. This is the crucial step, for it forces novel or creative thinking.
4. Describe the "unique activity" or characteristic of the analogous circumstance (event, situation) as it relates to the paradox.
5. Equate the unique activity of the analogy to the problem or concern.

6. Produce a new solution or idea based on this equivalent.

To illustrate: The administrators of a once-small hospital wished its personnel to meet informally to discuss and share ideas as they once did. This was difficult to do because the hospital was no longer a small one. The price of growth and success was the loss of the highly desirable informal lines of communication.

So Step 1, problem definition, tells us that there is a lack of informal meetings. Step 2 cites the paradox: Unless employee gatherings are "unorganized," they won't be effective. (Formal meetings are not very useful for authentic communication.) Step 3 entails the search for an analogy to the paradox. In this case, one of gulls surrounding a fishing boat in a highly unorganized manner was produced. Step 4, the unique activity of the analogy, is identified as it relates to the paradox—the gulls are attracted to the herring boat by the accidental presence of good food tossed overboard by the boatmen. Step 5 requires finding an equivalent, in terms of the problem, to the gulls at the boat (the analogy). This equivalent was perceived as offering food at reasonable prices to the employees. Gourmet food was offered weekly in the hospital cafeteria (Step 6), which drew employees together again.

The PCT procedure can be made more vivid to those participants applying it by setting up a worksheet as lows: Allow space at the top for the entering of "Problem Description"; this is followed by four boxes, each large enough to write in, labeled: "Paradox" (Step 1), "Analogue" (Step 2), "Unique Activity" (Step 3), and "Equivalent" (Step 4); below the boxes provide a space for describing the "New Idea."

THE GORDON TECHNIQUE

In the "Gordon Technique" (named after its developer, William J. Gordon, Arthur D. Little, Inc., Massachusetts) the leader alone knows the exact nature of the problem to be solved [40]. The leader utilizes six to eight experts, drawn from different fields, to bring their specialized knowledge (sales, personnel, finance) to bear on the problem. Why is the problem presented to the group not defined more precisely? To avoid premature judgments as to what the solution might be.

Expert leadership is critical since the group leader must stimulate creativity, give encouragement to the specialists, and lead them along a predetermined path.

This technique is hardly a fast process—a session may last as long as three hours, and several sessions may be essential. A second disadvantage is that there are problems in assembling all of the desired specialists since they typically have full schedules of their own.

DIALOGUE VIA THE "TALKING STICK"

To understand *dialogue* and to use it properly, we should compare it with *discussion,* which is what usually takes place in meetings of various sorts. In discussion we typically try to tell, sell, or persuade. We become advocates of our position, and we try to convince the other parties of its total correctness. We defend our assumptions and are more interested in debating ("How right I am") than in learning.

In dialogue, conversely, our concern is to inquire so as to understand and to learn. We listen rather than advocate, and we speak without judgment. We respect differences and try to uncover and examine assumptions. We try to create a fuller picture of reality rather than breaking it down into parts. In sum, there is no stress on making points or winning. Instead, we emphasize learning, collaboration and the melding of points of view [41].

To understand how dialogue works in a group setting, consider (and visualize) these procedures:

1. Group members/participants sit in a circle. (This should be a workable number, somewhere from 8 to 12.)

2. The American Indian device of the "talking stick" is used. The person who receives the stick receives permission to speak. It is passed around the circle from one speaker to the participant on that person's right (or left). *Note:* The Indians typically use a short branch of a tree for their talking stick. A flower or a feather might also be used. In our office situations, a pen or pencil is used to symbolize the talking stick.

3. One participant receives the talking stick and then makes a statement about the topic or issue. He/she then asks a question of the person on his/her right, giving him/her the talking stick.

4. The recipient of the talking stick responds to the question and poses a question of his/her own to the person on his/her right. This procedure is followed until everyone has responded to a question and has posed a question of his/her own.

The author participated in a group dialogue, as described above, and came away with these impressions:

☐ The technique forced us to suspend both judgment and our assumptions.

☐ We stayed on the topic (!)

☐ We listened more, as opposed to rushing to share our own thoughts.

☐ Everyone had a chance to speak.

☐ We became quiet, calm, and relaxed, and no one interrupted anyone.

☐ There was more sensitivity to language; for example, a participant from Denmark asked, "What is 'walk the talk'?"

☐ We lost track of time due to our involvement.

☐ There seemed to be a great deal of honesty, intimacy, and respect for each other.

☐ We built an alignment (or common understanding) around the topic.

☐ The talking stick helped to give a ceremonial, as opposed to an adversarial, air to our proceedings. (Moviegoers may recall the Kevin Costner film *Dances with Wolves* (1990), which featured a respectful meeting among the Indians.)

KEY POINTS

1. To obtain solutions (Step 3 in our problem-solving model) to a problem, these techniques are useful: brainstorming, the slip method, the nominal group technique, the Delphi technique, ideawriting, card-posting techniques, the client-centered approach, the upside-down

method, action-reflection learning, checklists, attribute listing, morphological analysis, forced relationships, analogy, the Gordon technique, and use of the "talking stick."

2. Brainstorming, a now "classic" problem-solving tool, has been updated via such variations as brainstorming deluxe, reverse approach, rotational ideation, SIL method, developing creative alternatives, pauses, wildest idea, trigger sessions, eliciting far-out ideas, rolestorming, and altering the environment.

3. Whereas brainstorming depends upon group action and interaction, other techniques primarily tap individual creativity, for example, the slip method, the nominal group technique, the Delphi technique, ideawriting.

4. In the client-centered approach to problem solving, problem-solving responsibilities in a group are divided between the "owner" of the problem and the facilitator. The assumption is that very few problem owners can handle the many diverse tasks of problem solving.

5. In upside-down problem solving, a problem is worked on by approaching it in opposite, nonconventional ways.

6. Certain techniques—checklists, attribute listening, morphological analysis—initiate *idea development*. These are in contrast to devices like brainstorming that encourage the free flow of ideas.

REFERENCES

1. Bachman, Greg, "Brainstorming Deluxe," *Training and Development* (January 2000), pp. 15–17.

2. Van Gundy, A., "Try These Problem Solving Techniques in the Classroom," *Training/HRD* (December 1980), pp. 32–35.

3. Scharlatt, Harold, "Beyond Brainstorming," *Training and Development Journal* (August 1984), pp. 8–9.

4. "A Storm Of Ideas," *Training* (November 1985), p. 66.

5. Rickards, T., *Problem Solving Through Creative Analysis,* Gower Press, New York (1975).

6. Zemke, Ron, "In Search of . . . Good Ideas," *Training* (January 1993), pp. 46–52.

7. Ibid.

8. "Group Techniques: Part 2, Alternatives to Brainstorming," *Small Business Report* (October 1981), pp. 15–17.

9. Crawford, C. C., *How to Make Training Surveys,* published by the author, Los Angeles (1954).

10. Murnighan, J. K., "Group Decision Making: What Strategies Should You Use?" *Management Review* (February 1981), pp. 59–62, and Messer, L. A., III, "Management Circles—An Idea Whose Time Has Come," *The Quality Circles Journal* (November 1981), pp. 35–36, describe the NGT.

11. For an account of the use of the Delphi technique to predict developments in the video field, see Vermilyea, D., "New Technical Developments in Video—A Symposium," *Educational and Industrial TV* (July 1980), pp. 23–24. For an account on the deliberations of a Delphi panel of 65 experts in the field of organization development, who were asked to forecast the impact of world and U.S. trends on the demand for OD in the coming 20 years, see Shephard, K. O., and Raia, A. P., "The OD Training Challenge," *Training and Development Journal* (April 1981), pp. 90–96.

12. Somers, Ken, Baker, Gus, and Isbell, Clint, "How to Use the Delphi Technique to Forecast Training Needs," *Performance and Instruction Journal* (May 1984), pp. 26–28.

13. The modified or group Delphi technique was presented to the Montgomery County, Maryland, group of the American Society for Training and Development, by Joseph Greenberg of George Washington University, (July 25, 1981).

14. Moore, C. M., and Coke, J. G., *Guide for Leaders Using Ideawriting,* pamphlet, National Training and Development Service for State and Local Government, Washing ton, D.C. (September 1979).

15. Zemke, Ron, "In Search of . . . Good Ideas," *Training* (January 1993), pp. 46–52.

16. Van Gundy, A., "Try These Creative Problem-Solving Techniques in the Classroom," *Training/HRD* (December 1980), p. 33.

17. These ideas were presented by Eric Baron of Synectics, Inc., at the 1981 Annual Conference of the American Society for Training and Development, Boston. For an overall summary of Synectics' ideas, see Prince, G., "Creativity and Learning as Skills, Not Talents," *Phillips Exeter Bulletin* (June–July 1980), pp. 1–12; this article is by the founder of Synectics, Inc. A detailed account of the Synectics process is given in (a) Prince, George, M., "The Operational Mechanism of Synectics," in Parnes, Sidney I., Noiler, Ruth B., and Biondi, Angelo M., *Guide to Creative Action,* Charles Scribner's Sons, New York,

1977, pp. 155–160 and (b) Ulschak, Francis L., Nathanson, Leslie; and Gillian, Peter, G., *Problem Solving: An Aid to Organizational Effectiveness,* Addison-Wesley Publishing Co., Reading, Mass. (1981), pp. 67–83. For a journalist's breezy account of her participation in a Madison Avenue Synectics session, see Kanner, Bernice, "Birth of A Nation: Brainstorming For Avon," *New York* (June 18, 1984).

18. The ideas were brainstormed by a group that was using "second order" strategies, per Kim Barnes of Lawrence Livermore Laboratory, California, in a presentation given at the American Society for Training and Development Annual Conference (1979), St. Louis.

19. Marsick, Victoria, J., et al., "Action-Reflection Learning," *Training and Development* (August 1992), pp. 63–66.

20. Froiland, Paul, "Action Learning: Taming Real Problems in Real Time," *Training* (January 1994), pp. 27–34.

21. Noel, James J., and Charan, Ram, "GE Brings Global Thinking to Light," *Training and Development* (July 1992), pp. 29–33.

22. Goidwasser, Donna, "Reinventing the Wheel—How American Home Products Transforms Senior Managers into Leaders," *Training and Development* (February 2001), pp. 54-55.

23. Parnes, S. J., "Idea-Simulation Techniques," in *Guide to Creative Action,* Charles Scribner's Sons, New York (1977), pp. 193–200. (This article appeared originally in the *Journal of Creative Behavior* (1976) Vol. 10, No. 2.)

24. Mariotti, J. J., "Checklists in Problem Solving," *Management Review* (August 1971), pp. 52–54. The article appeared originally in *Management Advisor* (May–June 1971).

25. Isaack, Thomas S., "Intuition: A Treasury of Knowledge," *Personnel Administrator* (July 1980), pp. 74–78.

26. Higgins, James M., "Creating Creativity," *Training and Development* (November 1994), pp. 11–15.

27. Buzan, Tony, *Use Both Sides of Your Brain,* Revised Edition, E. P. Dutton, New York (1983).

28. Eyes on Quality," *Performance* (March 1995), p. 53.

29. Barker, Julie, "Get Outta Line," *Successful Meetings* (October 1994), pp. 44–53.

30. Mattimore, Bryon W., "Imagine That!", *Training and Development* (July 1994), pp. 29–32.

31. For a four-column matrix, dealing with the generation of ideas about ways to reduce serious accidents, see Tagliaferri, L., *Creative Cost Improvement for Managers—A Self-Teaching Guide,* Wiley and Sons, Inc., New York (1981), p. 114.

32. Gordon, W. J. I., "On Being Explicit About Creative Process," in Parnes, S. J., Noller, R. B., and Biondi, A. M., *Guide to Creative Action,* Charles Scribner's Sons, New York (1977), pp. 172–174. The article originally appeared in *The Journal of Creative Behavior* (1972), Vol. 6, No. 4.

33. Hochschild, A., "Emotional Labor in the Friendly Skies," *Psychology Today* (June 1982), p. 14.

34. Parnes, S. J., Noller, R. B., and Biondi, A. M., "Personal Analogy," in *Guide to Creative Action,* Charles Scribner's Sons, New York (1977), p. 103.

35. Parnes, S. J., Noller, R. B., and Biondi, A. M., "Creativity Through Personal Analogy," in *Guide to Creative Action,* Charles Scribner's Sons, New York (1977), p. 123.

36. Gordon, W. J. J., "On Being Explicit About Creative Process," in Parnes, S. J., Noller, R. B., and Biondi, A. M., *Guide to Creative Action,* Charles Scribner's Sons, New York (1977), p. 173.

37. Prince, G. M., "The Operational Mechanism of Synectics," in Parnes, S. J., Noller, R. B., and Biondi, A. M., *Guide to Creative Action,* Charles Scribner's Sons, New York (1977), p. 158.

38. The material herein is drawn from "The Hidden Productivity Improvement Weapon for Manufacturing Management," a report (undated) on the use of special productivity improvement teams, prepared by PROFITCO, the Advanced Cost Reduction and Productivity Service Group, Pittsburgh. PROFITCO president Jerry D. Brooks also described the work of the productivity teams in "Pretend You're a Drop of Oil . . . Don't Laugh Until You Look At The Results," *33 Metal Producing* (March 1982), pp. 60–63.

39. Cookman, G., "The Trainer's Guide to Problem Solving," *Northeast Training News* (June 1981), pp. 8, 9, 16.

40. "Group Techniques: Part 2, Alternatives to Brainstorming," *Small Business Report* (October 1981), pp. 15–17.

41. Gerard, Glenna, and Teurfs, Linda, "Dialogue and the Learning Organization," a handout used in conjunction with a presentation at the annual national conference of the American Society for Training and Development, Dallas (June 1995).

RECOMMENDED READING

Dotlick, David and Noel, James, *Action Learning: How the World's Top Companies Are Recreating Their Leaders and Themselves,* Jossey–Bass, San Francisco, 1998.
    The authors view action learning as a dynamic leadership process essential for today's rapidly changing

technology-driven business environment, The work details the experience of the authors with action learning sessions they've conducted at Shell, Ameritech, Citibank, and other leading corporations to quickly and successfully implement a variety of change initiatives. Provides a clearly defined framework readers can use to create an action learning program of their own.

Ewing, Jack, "Siemens: Building a 'B-School' in Its Own Backyard," *Business Week,* November 15, 1999, pp. 281–282.

Describes how Siemens, the German conglomerate, uses company engineers and analysts from different divisions to solve problems which would have required high-priced consultants. Linking theory and practice in its in-house corporate management training program, millions of dollars are saved and the training pays for itself.

Froiland, Paul, "Action Learning: Taming Real Problems in Real Time," *Training,* (January 1994), pp. 27–34.

An overview of action learning, presenting the varying formats of it as used by different companies.

Hammer, Michael, and Champy, James, *Reengineering the Corporation: A Manifesto for Business Revolution,* Harper-Collins, New York, 1993.

The authors' thesis is that corporations must engage in a radical reinvention of how their work is done, to create a new kind of company for the new world of business. This means the radical redesign of a firm's processes, organization and culture. Old management ideas—division of labor, elaborate controls, managerial hierarchy—must be abandoned for they no longer work in a world of global competition and unrelenting change. In their stead, the authors introduce the notion of process orientation, of concentrating on and rethinking end-to-end activities that create value for customers. Adam Smith's 18th-century idea of simplification of tasks should give way to reunifying these tasks into coherent business processes. Business reengineering isn't about fixing anything. It means starting all over, starting from scratch, (*Note:* "Process" simply means a set of activities that, taken together, produces a result of value to a customer')

Lawrie, John, "Take Action to Change Performance," *Personnel Journal,* January 1989, pp. 59–69.

The article defines action learning and highlights the characteristics which differentiate it from conventional, classroom-type management development—such as, it is solving here-and-now management problems. The bulk of the article is concerned with the use of action learning in an organization which had just undergone a merger between a large successful utility company, managed in a traditional way, and a smaller, younger, reactive, entrepreneurial, participative-management cable company.

Marquardt, Michael J., *Action Learning in Action: Transformation Problems and People for World-Class Organizational Learning,* Davis-Black Publishers, Palo Alto, Calif., 1999.

A how-to guide, bringing together step-by-step guidance and the personal experiences of front-line managers from around the world to show how to create and implement action learning programs in any organization. Offers lessons from worldwide leaders such as GE, Bristol-Myers Squibb, and Arthur Anderson. These examples show how to leverage the benefits of action learning to solve problems, develop people, and create organizational learning and success.

Noel, James L., and Charan, Ram, "GE Brings Global Thinking to Light," *Training and Development,* July 1992, pp. 29–33.

Action learning helps GE's executives and managers to think globally so they can compete globally. Simultaneously, the training helps them solve internal problems and become more adept at team and project management.

Thompson, Charles, *What a Great Idea! The Key Steps Creative People Take,* Harper-Collins, New York, 1992.

A very readable, practical work to get one's creative juices flowing. Contains numerous application-type worksheets, principles/guides to unleashing creativity, and a host of very usable techniques for ideation such as idea mapping, using metaphors, thinking in opposites, overcoming mental blocks, free association, idea generation, reframing, trigger words, and exercises to change perspectives and envision the future.

Selecting and Implementing a Solution

To put one's thoughts into action is the most difficult thing in the world.

> —Johann Wolfgang von Goethe (1740–1832), German poet, dramatist, novelist, and philosopher

Plans are only good intentions unless they immediately degenerate into hard work.

> —Peter Drucker, management authority, consultant, writer, and educator

IN the prior two chapters we learned about the first three steps (skill areas) in the problem-solving process: "How to define the problem," "How to generate data about the problem," and "How to generate solutions or ideas for resolving the problem." In our final chapter on problem solving we will learn "How to choose among alternative solutions" (Step 4) and "How to plan and implement the solution" (Step 5). We will also be introduced to a number of additional approaches to problem solving.

HOW TO CHOOSE AMONG ALTERNATIVES (STEP 4 IN THE PROBLEM-SOLVING PROCESS)

Quite often participants in the training/problem-solving situation need to decide among a variety of possible courses of action. Typical situations in which the need for choice might arise are these:

☐ In an in-house management development seminar there may be a need to rank, on a priority basis, the importance of management problems that have been identified.

☐ In a team-building session the group may wish to select a solution to a problem from several available alternatives.

☐ In a time management workshop participants may be asked to rank in order of their severity the "time wasters" they encounter. (Action plans are then developed to deal with them.)

☐ In a career planning workshop participants may wish to choose among career alternatives, job opportunities, etc.

☐ It may be desirable to sort out (prioritize) ideas which were produced in a brainstorming session.

Of course, a simple way for the group to make choices is through voting. Let's take our brainstorming situation for example. The participants may be asked to indicate by a show of hands which of the brainstormed items, posted on the flipchart, they favor. The idea receiving the most votes is "Number One," meaning it is the number one problem to be tackled or the best solution among the many offered.

But voting, unfortunately, may not produce the best answer if there is a need to make more careful distinctions among the alternatives. If finer discrimination is appropriate, the group can be aided by the use of various ranking and rating procedures, either with or without criteria, to facilitate the process. It should be stressed that the purpose of the numbers which are generated and displayed is not to decide things quickly or arbitrarily, but to encourage thought and discussion of the available options.

Ranking Procedures Without the Aid of Criteria

At times a group may wish to rank certain items *in order of their importance,* for example, sources of time wasting identified in a time management course, ideas that came out of a brainstorming session, or the value of various employee motivators. The ranking can be aided by a system of point assignments.

A simple procedure to rank needs, problems, or other data is as follows:

1. Provide group members with an individual worksheet, such as the one shown in Figure 12-1.

2. Instruct each participant to enter from the flipchart onto the worksheet the problems that have been identified by the group. Since this is a priority ranking, the most serious problem is entered on the top of the worksheet and is thus given a ranking of 10; the least serious problem is entered on the bottom of the worksheet and is given a ranking of 1; all other items are ranked in accordance with this system, that is, from 10 to 1.

3. Assume our group (of seven participants) has been actively engaged in a team building session. They have individually ranked their problems, as previously described. They are now ready to enter and consolidate their individual rankings onto a group worksheet. Their worksheet might look like the one shown in Figure 12-2.

Ranking Procedures Using Criteria

Note that in the previous ranking process, criteria are not provided to the participants. Rather, their judgments are based on individual and consolidated group perceptions of the importance or priority of the problems under review. To sharpen the decision-making process, criteria

Individual Ranking Sheet	
Problem Area	**Values for Ranking**
	10
	9
	8
	7
	6
	5
	4
	3
	2
	1

Figure 12-1. Example of a ranking sheet for use by individual participants.

Group Ranking Sheet

Problem Area	Individual Member Rankings	Total Value of Rankings	Group Ranking
Policies unclear	9-7-3-5-7-5-7	43	3
Policies absent	5-4-10-9-4-2-1	35	5
Gaps in product line	8-10-9-4-3-1-9	44	2
Staffing	4-6-7-3-2-8-10	40	4
Relations with field	7-5-2-2-9-4-2	31	7
P.R.	6-2-4-1-8-3-8	32	6
Slippage in MBO program	10-9-8-10-10-3-10	60	1
Staff meetings	2-3-1-7-5-9-4	31	7
Teamwork	3-1-5-8-1-6-5	29	8
"Meetingitus"	1-8-6-6-6-7-6	40	4

Note:

1. The MBO program was deemed to be the most important problem, receiving a 60-point total and thus a number 1 ranking; team work received a total of 29 points and the lowest ranking—number 8.
2. While this weighting system uses a maximum of 10 points, we could also have used a ranking of 7 through 1 or 5 through 1.
3. There are two ties in the rankings, 7 and 4.

Figure 12-2. Example of a completed group ranking sheet rating the importance of previously identified problems.

for ranking identified problems may be provided. For example, these three criteria may be used:

1. Predominance, prevalence, or frequency of problem (widespread character)
2. Criticalness, seriousness, or severity of problem (impact)
3. Amenability or vulnerability of problem to resolution (success likelihood)

Note: Some groups may wish to add other criteria such as cost.

The identified problems can be evaluated using these criteria on a five-point scale shown in Figure 12-3.

In the preceding example we used specific criteria to help us *prioritize* our problems. In the following example we use criteria *to choose among several possible courses of action.* For example, let's assume a decision has to be made concerning the launching of a supervisory training program. The possible courses of action are home study, attendance on an individual basis at various outside (external) courses, conduct of a course by a consultant, and an in-house conducted program. Criteria to evaluate these four approaches, according to the group, are

1. Cost
2. Rapidity of completion time for the participants
3. Impact (learning level)
4. Basic learnings for everyone

Problem	Frequency	Severity	Solvability	Total Weight
1. Tardiness by clerical staff	2	3	3	18
2. Absence of policy on over-time	2	4	5	40
3. Customer complaints	5	4	3	60
4. Breakdowns of office copier	3	4	2	24

Note:

1. The process entails multiplying the numbers from left to right, thereby providing a heavier weighting factor. If the numbers were merely added, the differences among the four totals would not receive the same importance and prominence.
2. At this point we are choosing our problems for resolution, but we are not solving them as yet.

Figure 12-3. Example of a ranking sheet using a weighting system to prioritize significant problems.

Decision-Making Matrix

Alternative	Cost	Completion Time	Impact	Basic Learning	Total Points
Home study	5	2	1	5	13
One-at-a-time attendance	1	1	4	2	8
Consultant-developed course	2	5	5	5	17
In-house course	5	5	4	5	19

Note: Weights have been added rather than multiplied across the columns. Accordingly, point totals are fairly close to one another. A multiplication of the four factors would produce much more varying point totals: home study, 50; one-at-a-time attendance, 8; consultant, 250; in-house, 500.

Figure 12-4. Example of a decision-making matrix.

A grid or matrix, as in Figure 12-4, can be readily constructed, using a 5-point rating system to assess each possibility. A rating of 1 is low or unfavorable; 5 is high or very favorable.

In passing, we might mention that the procedure shown in Figure 12-4 was used by an insurance company to select a producer to make a training film. Five possible producers were evaluated (via a 10-point scale) on the basis of these criteria: estimated production costs, professional efficiency in film production, and overall film-making quality (creativity, visual and sound elements). Each alternative is subject to what a member of this company calls "test of preferredness in grids" [1].

Another way of systematically assessing options or alternatives is to compare each one against the others. That is to say, solution A can be compared to solutions B, C, and D; then solution B can be compared to solutions A, C, and D; and so on. A grid or matrix, as in Figure 12-5, can facilitate the comparison process.

Cross-Comparison of Solutions

Solution	A	B	C	D	E	F	Totals
A	X	B	A	D	A	A	3
B	B	X	B	B	B	B	5
C	A	B	X	D	E	C	1
D	D	B	D	X	D	F	3
E	A	B	E	D	X	F	1
F	A	B	C	F	F	X	2
Totals	3	5	1	3	1	2	15

Note:
1. *When an item is compared with itself in the grid an X is put in the space.*
2. *The process entails judgment but not criteria to facilitate those judgments.*

Figure 12-5. Example of a matrix for comparing solutions or alternatives with one another.

Predicting Success

Decision making, as opposed to problem solving, is typically concerned with future consequences or, putting it another way, the probability of success. To quote management authority Peter Drucker on the distinction between problem solving and decision making [2]:

> Well, you solve a problem so that you don't have to make a decision. Every time you solve a problem you try to "restore" the process to where you know it should be so that you don't have to make a decision. You make a decision when you want a change, and a decision therefore creates a new set of circumstances. It is focused on the future. Solving a problem is almost, really, looking back. This is the way it should be and it no longer is. So let's go back to it. In fact, problem solving can be greatly overdone because it creates a fear of change. Managers have to learn to see in change an opportunity; and not to ask how do we get back to where we were, but what is the new optimal stage. And so a decision has consequences; it changes the environment and the situation. It focuses on making things happen in the future. You do that when you make the most critical of all decisions, the people decisions—how to promote somebody, to move somebody, to let somebody go. You do it when you make a decision to buy a house and move out of the one you're in. And a decision therefore has a risk and an uncertainty, but it also creates an opportunity.

In respect to on-the-job decisions, we know that investing in a new product line, buying new equipment, selecting an executive for a key post, or embarking on a particular employee-management relations policy all have important consequences for the future. Therefore, these decisions must have a high likelihood (probability) of succeeding.

To aid in measuring success probability, one prominent management consultant and author, Edward Roseman, uses this formula [3]:

Desirability (of alternative) × Probability (of success) = Expected value (of the decision).

As an example of how the formula works, let's assume we are conducting a career planning workshop and our participants have to choose a wise course of action among several career alternatives. One participant is a young woman with a newly earned Ph.D. in industrial psychology. Her career options are these: teaching in the business school of a small college in the midwest, a personnel research job with IBM, a consulting position with a newly formed consulting firm, establishing herself as an independent consultant, and a training job with a multinational firm.

The young woman sets up a weighted decision-making matrix along the lines shown in Figure 12-6, using a modified version of the Edward Roseman model. Note that the weights shown are percentages of 1.00. A weight of 1.00 would be a maximum weighting, indicating an extremely strong feeling concerning "desirability" or "success probability." In general, by quantifying the alternatives and success data, one can put the possible decision in better perspective.

Prediction of success can also be aided by using a number of nonquantitative approaches including:

Success-failure analysis. With this technique participants brainstorm conditions for both success and failure. A T-column, with the headings "What Will Guarantee Success" and "What Will Guarantee Failure," can help sharpen the issues.

Devil's advocate technique. Participants are asked to focus on failure: In what ways can this solution (decision, idea, course of action, alternative) be less than successful?

Success Prediction Matrix

Option	Desirability of Option	× Success Probability	= Expected Value of Option
1. Teaching	.25	.75	.188
2. Research	.50	.75	.375
3. Trainer	.70	.75	.525
4. Consultant with firm	.65	.50	.325
5. Independant consultant	.75	.25	.188

Figure 12-6. Example of a weighted matrix for predicting success, based on the Edward Roseman formula.

If there is a possibility a higher body—board of directors, a legislative group, a higher echelon—may ask this question before it approves the decision, it may be desirable to role play this eventuality. Several participants may assume the role of board members who ask searching, "negative" questions about the proposal.

Reality testing. Here we are concerned about success in the real world—"Will it really fly?" A T-column, with the headings "Our Expectations" and "Our Concerns" can facilitate the analysis.

Risk analysis. The analysis of possible risks to be encountered and means to meet them can be helped with a T-column with headings "Anticipated Risks" and "Ways of Overcoming the Risks."

Premortems: Fix problems before they happen. A highly useful form of problem solving is to imagine/evaluate/predict how a course of action may unfold and ultimately play out. By using this technique a group can unearth a new project's likely hidden defects/flaws/imperfections—in other words, prevent possible unwanted costly, embarrassing time bombs [4].

Here's how the premortem works. When a team assembles to launch a new project, the meeting is ended by everyone imagining themselves looking into a crystal ball. They gaze six months into the uncertain future. What do they see? Bad news! They had high hopes but the project became a cropper. So the team runs a mental image (simulation) for three minutes. They jot down all the possible reasons they believe their project flopped. Many causes are highlighted. *Note:* Because the team engages in a *future* look, people may feel adequately secure to engage in actual truth telling, to express what they really think and feel.

Causes for failure may be legion. They may range from the project being overly ambitious to project leaders being so saddled with other responsibilities that blowing the deadline was inevitable. So now that all involved have been alerted to the potential snags ahead, they can now proceed with confidence that the likely disasters can be prevented. Says cognitive psychologist Gary Klein, "With a postmortem everything you learn is after the fact. With a premortem, we give ourselves a chance to uncover problems and then fix them in real time as the project unfolds."

In general, since a decision is concerned with future consequences, it is essential to give thought to negative eventualities that may arise once the deci-sion is implemented. To do otherwise is to ignore the real world. The trainer who raises such questions is providing extremely worthwhile assistance to the participant group. For more details on this procedure, see "Risk Analysis," Chapter 2.

HOW TO PLAN AND IMPLEMENT THE SOLUTION (STEP 5 IN THE PROBLEM-SOLVING PROCESS)

After a problem is "solved," that is, a course of action is decided upon, the problem-solving process is hardly over. Why not? Because steps must be taken to *implement* or *activate* the solution. In effect, the group is concerned with questions such as these: How will we implement the decision? Who will be responsible for which aspect of the implementation plan? Will we need outside resources? When are the various phases of implementation to be completed? Is there a sequence for these phases? What conditions will exist so we will know when "we are there"? Who is to be informed of the decision and the implementation plans?

The reader will note that these questions are merely an expansion of the journalist's six questions: Who? What? Why? When? Where? How? Responses to the six questions may provide the data needed for good plan implementation. The six questions may also stimulate other questions.

To ensure that planning proceeds in an orderly way, a control sheet or chart for time and another one for responsibility (who is responsible for what) are very useful. Sample charts relating to a marketing plan are depicted in Figures 12-7 and 12-8.

Activities	Jan. 15	Jan. 31	Feb. 15	Feb. 28	March 15	March 31
1. Hiring						
2. Training						
3. Promotion						
4. Trade shows						
5. Press releases						
6. Budget						
7.						
8.						

Figure 12-7. Example of a planning chart for ensuring proper scheduling.

Activity	Joan	Pat	Kim	B.J.	Chris
Hiring					
Training					
Promotion					
Trade Shows					
Press releases					
Budget					

Figure 12-8. Example of a planning chart for ensuring that project assignments are clearly specified.

Another procedure is to brainstorm the concerns entailed in implementation, write each idea on a 5" × 8" card with a felt-tip pen, and post the cards on the wall with masking tape. Then rearrange the cards for chronological implementation.

Card-posting procedures, previously discussed under Step 3 of the problem-solving process, may also be used in the implementation phase (planning for action) of the process. For example, it may be desired to work through each step of how a particular action plan is to be carried out. A procedure for this is to have participants (via brainstorming) list on large cards the steps to be considered in such planning. For example, if the action plan relates to the launching of a new sales campaign, steps such as space (magazine) advertising, direct mail efforts, exhibits at trade shows, TV and radio ads, press releases, hiring of new personnel, and training of new sales personnel have to be considered. The cards can be posted on the wall and repositioned in relation to desired time frames. The names of those responsible for each step can also be entered on the cards. In effect, the posted cards would provide a PERT (Program Evaluation and Review Technique) chart depicting a complete action plan. The chart could be photographed with a camera using a self-developing film and copies made on a photocopier and distributed to all concerned.

ADDITIONAL APPROACHES TO PROBLEM SOLVING

Several added approaches to problem solving follow. They have not been included in the prior material because they cut across or overlap our five-step problem-solving model. These techniques are

- ☐ Rotational problem solving
- ☐ Past/present/future approach
- ☐ Using the journalist's six questions
- ☐ Personal needs analysis
- ☐ Problem solving for quality control
- ☐ Quality circles
- ☐ Maximizing idea power at meetings

Rotational Problem Solving (PSR)

Problem Solving Rotation (PSR) is a highly participative and original problem-solving device involving movement, ideation, individual and team effort, and recognition. It works as follows [5]:

1. With a normal-size group of about 20–25 participants, appoint four "problem solvers." (A smaller group may require only three problem solvers.)

2. The four problem solvers are each given a short, written statement about a problem in need of resolution. The problems are different, meaning there are four problems.

3. The other group members become "advisors" and are teamed up into four advisory groups—A, B, C, D. They are positioned at four different points in the training room.

4. Problem Solver 1 goes to Advisory Group A for ideas, guidance, and advice about the assigned problem. Simultaneously, Problem Solver 2 goes to Advisory Group B about the problem, and so on, until each problem solver has contacted the four advisory groups for inputs. (Visits to the four advisory groups should take about 30 minutes in total. In this time frame, visits have been made to all four advisory groups and the latter have worked on, or advised on, four problems.)

5. The four problem solvers are given several minutes to summarize and digest the inputs they have garnered.

6. The four problem solvers form a panel and each gives a five-minute report on his/her solutions, recommendations, conclusions, etc.

7. The advisors interact with the problem solvers, quizzing them about their reports.

8. The advisors vote (secret ballot) on the "best" solution.

9. The problem solvers vote on the most helpful advisory group.

Steps 8 and 9 are designed to provide recognition for quality accomplishment.

Past/Present/Future Approach

Problem solving can be aided if groups can agree on these key issues:

- ☐ Where we are (current status of events)
- ☐ What happened (causes) to get us there
- ☐ Where we go from here (establish new goals)
- ☐ How we can get there

Note: No mention is made of *who* did what to get us there. Avoidance of blaming people is essential to prevent defensive behavior from arising. When people are preoccupied with defending themselves, they can hardly engage in constructive problem-solving behavior.

Using the Journalist's Six Questions

The journalist's five W's and H—who, what, when, where, why, and how—can be used as a framework to analyze a problem and then to resolve it. The procedure calls for problem analysis via the journalist's six questions and then a reworking of the situation via a new set of responses to the six questions. An example follows:

Problem Analysis

Who: Safety personnel in Region 3 office.

What: Late (two weeks) submission of monthly safety reports; also, data often incomplete and hard to interpret.

When: Due tenth of each month.

Where: Due at corporate level.

Why: Data basic to overall coordination of safety program. Region 3 not aware of how data is used at corporate level; also absence of positive reinforcement for prompt, accurate submissions; deadline not realistic for Region 3.

How: Problem has become aggravated because we, at corporate level, have tolerated incomplete submissions.

Problem Resolution

Who: Safety personnel in Region 3 office and at corporate level.

What: Need to shift to new behavior: timely submission of safety reports.

When: Change reporting date to twentieth of month since other activities at Region 3 office make it difficult to meet our deadline of the tenth.

Where: Initiated in Region 3 office; submitted to corporate level.

Why: Data are basic for continuing program review.

How: The change can be facilitated by having two key Region 3 staffers work in corporate office for four weeks to get corporate viewpoint as to importance of report; the change in behavior can be maintained via positive reinforcement, that is, provide praise for timely reports and for work done well as reported in those reports.

To generate data about each of the six questions, these techniques may be used:

- ☐ Brainstorming by the total group
- ☐ Small group work (buzz groups)
- ☐ Assignments to individual participants, such as in a quality circle that may have six members
- ☐ Assignments to dyads or triads

Investigating a problem situation. The journalist's six questions can also be used to form a checklist to use in investigations—for example, to investigate an accident, a theft, an employee fight, an incident of employee insubordination. Thus, the six questions are used as a guide to systematically ferret out vital information as follows:

Who: The name(s), job title(s), branch or department, etc., of the person(s) involved in the incident. Similar data on witnesses, those reporting the incident, etc., should be collected.

What: Description of incident, event, accident, loss, injury. Photos may be used for added detail.

When: Time of event or incident (date, time of day).

Where: The scene of the event should be clearly described: in or outside of the building; on what street; on what floor; in an office, shop, lab, cafeteria, hallway, stairwell, restroom.

How: What took place; what was the beginning event(s) and the conclusion.

Why: Causative factors—why did the event take place?

Problem Solving for Quality Control

A particular system in an organization—a bank, a warehouse, a customer service office—may be established with great care and cost. Yet, all too often one or more of its basic procedures may be ignored in whole or in part. The result: The intended payoff from the system is not realized. This undesirable result occurs despite the fact that everyone knows that a system is no better than the degree of "respect" it receives. One bank (Irving Trust Company, New York) was concerned about the lack of quality in its telecommunication operations due to the failure to observe the procedures required by its system. It thus set up a study group on quality measurement. These procedures were used by the facilitator:

1. At the first meeting, a description of the system's boundary and its workflow was provided. These questions were raised and answered:

   □ At what point are inputs received?

   □ When is it finished with outputs?

   □ What major charges (unit operations) occur from input to output?

   □ How are these unit operations divided into subtasks?

2. After the description of the workflow, all possible deviations in quality were listed on a sheet of paper by group members on an "auto-brainstorming" basis.

3. Each person then stated aloud a deviation from his/her list.

4. The process was repeated until all deviations were reported and recorded on the flipchart. This listing was done without comment to save time.

5. Those deviations that were not clear were clarified.

6. Participants were given a packet of 3" × 5" cards and asked to select the eight most important deviations and to mark them on a priority basis. Of the 122 deviations identified, 22 were deemed to be the most significant.

7. The session coordinator then led a discussion on the deviations. Numerous improvements came out of the discussion. Seventeen measures were proposed; top management later reduced that number to 11 measures. Actions to produce improvement included more training for some operators, rescheduling working hours, reducing the action time on a cable from three to two hours, and rearrangement of the workflow.

It is to be noted that measuring the quality of the system's operations took place over a four-week period. But it only took about 12 hours of management time [6].

Quality Circles

Using ideas developed in the United States about participative management, the Japanese (since 1962) have made significant industrial strides with the aid of the quality circle. We now have the interesting phenomenon of American business executives going to Japan to see how an *American* idea can be implemented successfully. In any case, many quality circles have been introduced into U.S. plants, offices, hospitals, and other organizations.

Basically, a quality circle is a problem-solving unit composed of 8–12 employees who volunteer to do the job. They concern themselves with quality, safety, maintenance, cost, waste, faulty equipment, poor procedures, and the like. They meet one hour per week to work on problems that they have identified themselves. When they have solved their problem, they formally present their solution to top management officials for review and possible approval.

Quality circles not only can save organizations money and aid efficiency and profitability, but they can also augment employee morale and self-esteem and provide a worthwhile social experience.

To be effective, the quality circle should operate in a company that already has a participative climate. In the absence of appropriate understanding and support by management, quality circles can hardly be anything but short-lived.

Another must for the success of the quality circle is training:

☐ Training of circle leaders in group dynamics, team leadership, communication, and motivation, as well as in using problem-solving tools.

☐ Training of circle members in the purpose and functioning of the circle plus such practical problem-solving tools as brainstorming, Pareto diagrams, cause-and-effect analysis, Four-M approach (manpower, materials, machinery, method), check sheets, checklists, histograms (vertical bar chart showing frequency of occurrence), and graphs. They also learn how to make presentations to management on their recommendations.

Another form of the quality circle is the "pyramid" developed by the U.S. Air Force. It is designed to permit the solving of problems that are broader in scope than those which are undertaken by the typical quality circle. It is a "super-circle," drawing on members in two other circles. Thus, if there are work problems such as distribution between two units or shops, the pyramid works on them [7].

Note: In Japan quality circles may be composed of outside suppliers and company personnel. This is the model for the quality circle which goes beyond the one-shop level.

How big an impact can a quality circle make in an organization? One quality circle practitioner, E. J. Metz of General Telephone and Electronics, Stamford, Connecticut, responds to this question by pointing out that a quality circle can only hope to solve a small proportion of an organization's problems [8]. His reasoning is based on the fact that problems are of three types:

☐ Type I problems are appropriate for quality circles to solve since they have fairly complete "control" over them.

☐ Type II problems are influenced by quality circles only in part, because control rests with others elsewhere in the organization. As a circle matures, it can take on Type II problems, working cooperatively with outside line and staff people who can aid in solving the problem.

☐ Type III problems are those over which the circle has neither control nor influence.

Metz asserts that 80% of an organization's productivity-quality problems are not Type I and must be solved by management action. In effect, these higher-level problems result from coordination matters, management policies, product design, vendor-relation practices, etc.

Metz thus proposes the "verteam" circle to work on the broad, Type III problems. What is a verteam circle? It is a vertically structured problem-solving unit. It is a heterogeneous rather than a homogeneous work group and may meet for extended periods rather than for only one hour per week. Its problems come from top management rather than from the circle, and in general it is more closely allied to upper levels of management and may be integrated into and reinforce other improvement efforts such as organization development and quality of work life.

How successful the basic quality circle and the verteam will be in the United States remains to be seen. In fact, Robert E. Cole, an expert at the University of Michigan on Japan and quality circles, asserts that only about one-third of Japanese circles have been effective. Given the less-than-participative nature of most American organizations, a wait-and-see posture would seem to be very appropriate [9].

A recent general review of the status of quality circles indicates that not all companies have been able to sustain their interest in them. Causes for their demise range from lack of management understanding and support to lack of demonstrable cost savings. In some cases the name has been changed to employee involvement team, worker participation group, continuous improvement process, and quality communication circles. Membership in the International Association for Quality and Participation Circles (formerly the Association for Quality Circles) totals over 6,000, a fairly stable figure [10].

Since quality circles and similar productivity teams don't succeed (or even survive) merely because they have been established, team leaders should maintain/invigorate their teams with the following kinds of approaches [11]:

☐ *Secure management recognition.* The use of these techniques can show achievement: show before-and-after results of a project; ask line managers to attend team sessions on occasion; publicize results via newsletters and graphic displays in work areas; seek out commendation memos and other praise from top management.

☐ *Emphasize ongoing individual development.* To perk up member interest over time, devices of this sort merit use: evaluate the team's strong points and areas in need of improvement; invite other team leaders and specialists from various parts of the organization to input new ideas; work on new problems in excess of current capabilities ("stretch"); develop new projects around new member skills; spot check other teams to broaden perspectives; tap the skills of experts and specialists to stimulate interest.

☐ *Share leadership.* The team leader should rotate leadership roles among the team; let the team set its own goals and select its own problems; share information fully.

☐ *Provide rewards and recognition.* Since the organization rather than the team leader controls the formal reward system, the leader should rely on nonfinancial incentives such as praise, certificates and letters of commendation, and pins; show how the team's efforts impact on organizational productivity and/or quality; stress value of team cooperation with the organization; point out value of the team experience to future job/career possibilities.

Study Groups

One of the devices used in Japan for greater productivity is the study group [12]. It has been transplanted to the United States in a growing number of companies. This technique entails the meeting of managers from different functional areas one to three hours per week to define and resolve productivity problems. Examples of such problems are: how to install the "Just-In-Time" inventory system, quality improvement, participative management, waste reduction, and how to install a new technology. Typically, managers read a book on a topic of concern and collectively bring to the study group a shared level of understanding of the theoretical material of the text. The meetings are results-oriented, and are not bull sessions of griping and blaming others for creating problems.

The key to the success of these learning experiences is that they comprise observation/problem definition, theoretical learning (the book discussion), and *action.* Unlike the usual office meeting, where there is a presenter who has information which others don't have, here all have a common fund of knowledge since they all have read the assigned book. This

increases the vitality and pace of the discussion and raises the potential for locating a workable solution.

To set up a study group, these steps should be followed:

1. Define the problem.
2. Secure *volunteers* from the affected departments (engineering, finance, marketing, R&D, production, possibly personnel). Obviously, it helps considerably if the plant manager attends, too.
3. Recommend a book (or let the group select one) relating to the problem.
4. Select a group leader/facilitator or let the group select its own.
5. Schedule a suitable time for the weekly meetings, which may continue for two to five months to resolve the problem.
6. Discuss the book and apply its ideas to the identified problem.
7. Secure several solutions to the problem.
8. Select the best solution.
9. Plan implementation of the solution. Consider the use of spin-off groups to study specific applications of the new concepts.
10. Take corrective action.
11. Evaluate results upon the agreed-upon date of project completion.

Another, allied reading and discussion technique is used by The Woodlands Group, a group of trainer/consultants and other high-level trainers who meet quarterly for networking purposes. Their procedure is as follows [13]:

☐ *Individual reading.* Articles (one or more), a book, or a report are assigned for reading. Enough time is allowed in advance to permit preparation for the discussion. Reading is not done at the session. Particular assignments are given arbitrarily, randomly, or voluntarily. A ground rule is that at least three people should have accomplished the reading. Several discussion questions are provided: "What are the major trends?" or "What are the key leadership characteristics, according to the author?" These questions are merely devices to focus attention and to stimulate thinking.

☐ *Small group analysis.* Groups are formed of those who have read the same article or book.

They are given a task which will require a more comprehensive analysis of the material.

☐ *Reporting.* Each group sums up the main points of its discussion on a flipchart. Members of all groups study these reports.

☐ *Major point examination.* New groups are formed of individuals who have read different assignments. They receive an assignment which focuses more on what the materials mean to the participants, for example, "What leadership characteristics are critical for success in our company?"

☐ *Reporting.* Again, each group records its key points on a flipchart.

☐ *Personal application.* Each person develops action plans to meet his/her personal needs best.

The plus factors of The Woodlands approach are group pressure to read; learning becomes fun; it has great flexibility in terms of subject matter; learning can occur at several levels—informational, analytical, interpersonal, and group process. The major disadvantage: people may not carry through on their reading assignments, which dooms the session, of course.

SEA formula. In any reading and discussion program some members will profit from guidelines of a general sort to assist them in "wrestling" with the assigned reading. If so, a practical and logical way to attack the book is to use the SEA approach: Significance, Evaluation, and Application. More specifically, these are

☐ *Significance:* What is the author saying? His/her main thesis? Main arguments for his/her position? Is there a "call for action"? Why? *Note:* At this stage the goal is to grasp fully and objectively what is said or advocated, not to accept or reject ideas or proposals.

☐ *Evaluation:* How do I find the major thesis and the arguments which are presented for it? Do I agree or disagree? Why? Did the author overlook anything? Where did he/she go "wrong," if he/she did? How does the material relate specifically to my experience?

☐ *Application:* Based on what I read, what should I (or the team or organization) do to capitalize on the author's ideas?

Note: An ideal arrangement, insofar as guidance to the reader is concerned, is to (a) encourage participants

to use the SEA formula and (b) provide them with questions which focus more specifically on the content, for their use when they reach the evaluation step.

Knowledge Circles [14]

To help people work smarter, the knowledge circle is a useful device. As a complement to more formal classroom training, it provides a system to share one's knowledge with others. At these meetings short presentations—one to ten minutes long—are used to pass along tips, shortcuts, new ideas, and new approaches. Presenters of ideas may come from the immediate unit, other parts of the organization, or the outside. People who have just returned from training programs are good idea sources. For maximum learning, the short presentation should be followed by group discussion. Handouts should be provided, as appropriate.

Certain administrative/organizational/procedural details require attention for maximum success of the circle:

☐ Provide a leader who assumes responsibility for scheduling speakers, setting up meetings, documenting activities, and evaluating results. A volunteer leader works best since he/she will bring his/her enthusiasm to the operation.

☐ Although the knowledge circle can take place during the regular staff meeting, a special meeting time will demonstrate management commitment to the idea.

☐ Schedule meetings frequently enough to establish the concept in everyone's mind. Anticipate that the frequency will probably taper off as the volume of available ideas decreases.

☐ Circle size will depend on the number of people who have a need to know, to learn, and to share information. Thus meetings will vary in size. It is the leader's job to invite the appropriate audience.

☐ Activities should be documented. Keep summaries of the meetings in a binder to serve as a permanent record and to orient new workers.

Ongoing evaluation is essential to determine circle usefulness, that is, whether job performance has improved or cost reduction has occurred. Calculate dollar savings whenever possible. Other, less tangible benefits, such as improved communication, better inter-group problem solving, improved teamwork, and greater job involvement, may also accrue.

How to Maximize Idea Power at Meetings

In the pages that follow, several techniques are provided to maximize efficiency at meetings. By "efficiency" we mean tapping participants' ideas and converting them into specific solutions and/or action plans. The "jury technique" is particularly useful for a small group of about 12 in-house participants. The other three techniques—idea reinforcement teams, small group psychological reinforcement, and the Phillips 66 method—can be used with both small and large audiences at conferences, meetings, conventions, etc.

Problem solving via the jury technique. Problems that require quick action can be properly resolved via the jury technique. By focusing on the "evidence," the technique can overcome tendencies toward "search-and-destroy" or "judgment-at-Nuremberg" strategies and proceedings, as well as other blocks to effective problem solving such as personality conflicts, status, domination (intended or otherwise) by "experts," and the heavy influence of the crisis situation resulting in too quick a decision. Here are its procedures [15]:

1. The top executive who will ultimately decide on a solution states the nature of the problem.
2. The top executive decides who can best contribute to the resolution of the problem and the implementation of a solution.
3. The top executive calls the problem-solving meeting, limited to 12 participants. They are encouraged to bring all necessary background material (memos, notes, statistics, reports).
4. The trainer provides the guidelines for an effective problem-solving effort:
   a. Each person states what he/she knows about the problem (the evidence).
   b. Each presenter is quizzed by the group about his/her ideas.
   c. The problem is redefined, as may be indicated.
   d. Small work units are formed to develop solutions. A recorder in each small group is designated to identify incomplete information and necessary follow-up action to secure missing data.
   e. The recorder consolidates all data to produce a problem definition and to identify subproblems and an appropriate action plan.
   f. Assignments are made to team members for the various agreed-upon action steps and for reporting on progress at the next meeting.

The principles of problem-solving underlying this technique are these:

☐ Initial statements of problems tend to be improperly phrased due to a tendency to describe situations or symptoms.

☐ Freedom of inquiry by all participants is basic to effective problem solving.

☐ A friendly, supportive climate is also vital.

☐ All participants are of equal importance; everyone who has evidence to submit is an important person.

Idea reinforcement teams. On the assumption that far too many meetings and conferences produce much talk but little commitment to action thereafter, the idea reinforcement team technique merits consideration. Here are its procedures [16]:

1. Divide the total group into trios.
2. Provide each team of three with a packet of materials that, when divided, gives each participant two 5" × 10" note cards, one sheet of graph paper, and one sealed envelope. (The envelopes remain sealed until instructions to open them are given by the trainer or moderator.)
3. Ask each person to write on the note cards five or six points he/she got from the session.
4. Instruct each participant to create a visual on the graph paper that explains one of his/her learning points. Advise that stick figures, graphs, flow charts, or anything of an illustrative sort may be used.
5. Assign these roles to each team: presenter, prober, and observer. (The latter silently observes the effectiveness of the communication process.)
6. Tell the prober to open his/her envelope. The message therein advises on the attitude to assume, for example, "Be hard to convince. Ask

tough questions: 'Why do you think that?' 'How can that be used?' 'Why?'"

7. Have the presenter tell the prober what he/she has learned. (Allow five to nine minutes for this.)

8. Have the prober respond according to his/her written instructions in the envelope.

9. Call time and have the observer report (feedback) to the presenter and the prober the effectiveness of the communication process between them.

10. Encourage all team members to discuss the data generated therein.

11. Give a signal to the probers to interrupt the presenters and ask: "What *two* things do you plan to do about this?"

12. Have team members switch roles and repeat the above process two more times. In this way, all team members will have had a chance to function in all three roles.

The advantages of this procedure are these:

☐ Instant and total participation.

☐ Each team member is encouraged not only to think about his/her learning and plans for action, but also to listen to the ideas of his/her colleagues.

☐ Each presenter is challenged to sharpen up his/her plans for action.

☐ As a team effort, each member helps the others in their action planning.

☐ The team discussions become a form of peer pressure, augmenting the possibility that personal commitments will be acted on upon return to the job.

Small group psychological reinforcement. Two major barriers to meeting effectiveness are

☐ Lack of full and meaningful participation

☐ A reluctance to nail down answers to specific questions and problems

To overcome these two problems, the small group psychological reinforcement technique merits consideration. Its procedures are these [17]:

1. Seat participants (six to eight) at round tables.

2. Provide each table with easel, pad, and felt-tip pen.

3. Instruct each group to select a recorder-reporter.

4. The chairperson announces the problem in concise terms and requests suggestions thereon.

5. At each table ideas are collected and put on the easel pad. *Key point:* The name of each contributor is added to his/her idea. This provides motivation to the others, including shy persons, to contribute too. People *do* like to see their names on the pad!

6. The chairman calls on several of the RR's to report their groups' ideas in full. Ideas may thus be seen as repetitive, but this is O.K. because, by repetition, ideas become imprinted in participants' minds. They psychologically reinforce their importance and adaptability.

7. The chairperson then calls on other RR's to add ideas not already reported on.

In general, the technique stimulates ideation at each table, it sets up a competition among the groups to produce ideas, and it elicits specific solutions to problems.

Phillips 66 method. A classic, easy-to-implement idea-collection device is the Phillips 66 method, named after J. Donald Phillips of Michigan State University. Originated in the 1950's, it works well with groups of 36, 66, or 666. Use these procedures:

1. Arrange chairs so that participants can readily form groups of six.

2. Ask three people to turn around so that they are in eye contact with three other participants.

3. Ask them to select a recorder.

4. Assign (or state) the problem.

5. Provide these instructions: "In the next six minutes come up with as many ideas as you can on the problem under discussion. The recorder is to write all of them down. In the last minute of your six minutes, you are to select the better ideas. I will ask you to prioritize them at the five-minute mark. O.K., go to it."

6. Call time after five minutes and ask the group to rank their ideas in order of their importance.

7. Collect the lists of ideas at the six-minute mark.

8. Depending on the nature of the meeting and time constraints, ideas may be posted on a flipchart, discussed orally, or simply collected for later screening and analysis.

Note: Step 1 may be varied by having participants seated at tables or by counting off 1 through 6. The latter procedure may be used if it is desirable to have people form new groups. The new teams can provide some invigoration and break up cliques. The technique can be used to respond to a speaker or presentation; to obtain data from the participant group concerning needs, preferences, interests, problems, suggestions, or attitudes; to explore various facets of a fairly complex problem by letting one or more groups discuss and analyze segments or phases of it; to react to a short handout.

The Open Space Meeting

With this technique, meetings of any size (from 5 to 750 participants) can be used to identify problems and/or to generate solutions to known problems. Designed by Harrison Owen, an Episcopal priest and management consultant, it has tremendous potential to transform an ordinary group of people into a dynamic, powerful problem-solving force.

Here's how facilitator Owen conducted a blockbuster meeting for the Rockport Company, a shoe manufacturer in Marlboro, Massachusetts [18]:

The meeting was attended by the entire work force—350 people in all, comprising people at all organizational levels (managers and rank-and-file workers)—with only a skeleton crew left behind. The meeting took place in a company warehouse and was planned for two days, but no agenda was announced, there were no planned sessions, and no speakers were scheduled. The attendees at the Open Space meeting obviously felt that chaos was about to ensue.

Owen then stepped into the center of the audience, which was positioned in a loosely formed circle, and spelled out the nature of the Open Space meeting:

- ☐ "It is your meeting and your time."
- ☐ "What you do with it is entirely up to you."
- ☐ He would not "conduct" anything, but would be available.
- ☐ Anyone who wished could step forward into the circle, give his/her name, and announce a topic about which he/she felt passionate enough to take responsibility to convene a "break-out" session.
- ☐ The ones who stepped forward should write a topic on a flipchart sheet and post it to the wall

with masking tape. They should also indicate the time and place of their break-out group meeting.
- ☐ This procedure would be continued until all topics were posted.
- ☐ Everyone could then examine the posted topics and sign up for as many topics as desired.
- ☐ The meeting leaders were responsible for convening groups, facilitating discussions, and recording minutes of the meeting on computers set up for that purpose.
- ☐ Owen pointed to four "principles" to guide this unique event:
  1. Whoever comes are the right people.
  2. Whatever happens is the only thing that could happen.
  3. Whenever it starts is the right time.
  4. When it's over, it's over.
- ☐ Owen then pointed to a poster with two footprints and a caption beneath them that said "The Law of Two Feet." This, explained Owen, meant that participation was voluntary. If anyone was bored or not learning anything, or had nothing to contribute, he/she could use his/her feet to exit.

When all these instructions had ended, there was a mammoth silence. But gradually people rose, and everyone went to a stipulated meeting location.

The result at the end of the two-day meeting: 66 sessions were conducted, and brisk ideation took place at all of them. Issues which had not previously been faced up to were now addressed. Also developed, besides ideas about the issues, was a sense of camaraderie and purpose.

Note:

1. The Open Space technique has now been used all over the world in all kinds of organizations, independently of Owen.
2. The size of the group doesn't matter.
3. The technique works best in situations of uncertainty, ambiguity, and recognition that new ideas are needed. It is a great tool to release the company's potential, which was the Rockport Company president's aim.
4. Open Space meetings create expectations that afterward things will be different—more empowerment, less bureaucracy, greater cooperation, and so on.

Participant	Major Concern (growth need)	General Course of Action	Specific Activities to Be Undertaken
Al	Dead end job; losing motivation	Seek out opportunities to secure new challenges, on and off the job	1. Ask boss for added responsibility 2. Seek transfer within organization 3. Start an advanced degree program
Amy	Dull existence; all work, no play	Seek out situations and activities which provide new stimulation	1. Join two or three groups 2. Take exciting vacations
Betty	Facing retirement; fear of future	Begin realistic planning now	Consider: 1. Second career 2. Academic work 3. Volunteer work

Figure 12-9. Example of a completed worksheet for helping participants plan for personal growth.

5. The technique is thus not recommended if management prefers the usual control of things and favors predictable outcomes.

Personal Needs Analysis

In various personal growth programs such as career development workshops, retirement planning sessions, assertiveness training, T-groups, and encounter groups, it is desirable to help participants focus on their needs for growth and learn how to take some action to meet their needs. The worksheet given in Figure 12-9 may be helpful for this purpose. It can be completed and processed in small groups [19].

The worksheet obviously provides structure or a framework for the endeavor so participants can think things through. It also emphasizes that as members of the small group, "we're all in this together." By "together" we mean that group members provide help, counsel, support, feedback, and critique to one another, so that the end result is realistic and better than if one worked on one's problem alone.

SOME PROBLEM-SOLVING PRINCIPLES

We have identified and discussed numerous techniques for and approaches to problem solving. We would be remiss, however, if we ignored the *importance* of certain principles/strategies basic to effective problem solving.

"Swiss cheese" principle. At times it may make more sense to work on *part* of a problem than to tackle the whole thing. Backing off a bit from a "monster" problem, that is, one having many aspects or ramifications, may be the acme of practicality.

"Bleed-off" principle. When working on a long-term problem, it is helpful to point to short-term or more immediate gains or benefits. This will reassure those who authorized the project that their judgment was correct, for payoffs are already apparent. The alternative—not being able to demonstrate any success—may very likely cause doubts and anxieties in the minds of the project's sponsors.

Success principle. A new group, for example, a quality circle, should tackle a relatively easy ("low-hanging fruit") or sure-fire problem at the outset. This approach will establish the group's credibility with management and give group members confidence in their ability to succeed.

Studying the winners. Problem solving is more likely to succeed if we assess our successes as opposed to probing our defeats. To quote Robert L. Woodson, president of the Center for Neighborhood Enterprise, Washington, D.C.: "The only reason to spend your time studying failure is if you want to produce more failure. You cannot learn to produce success by studying failure. Every school, every neighborhood, no matter how dismal its circumstances, has successes. It's a mystery to me why we spend so much time crying over our failures and so little time trying to learn from our successes" [20].

Illogical thinking. Although much of problem solving depends upon thinking that is logical, orderly, sequential, and objective, many of the techniques presented in this book, such as brainstorming and imaging, help to encourage thinking which is non-conventional and fanciful. The ultimate horror of totally logical, left-brain thinking is epitomized by the incident involving the individual who, upon learning that most auto accidents happen within ten miles of home, immediately decided to move to a new, far-away location!

Pilot runs. When conducting demos or pilot runs, it is wise to begin with two or more such projects. Why? Because if only one is started and some special circumstance beyond our control affects it adversely, we're out of business. Conversely, if two out of three pilots do work, we now have a successful track record and "are in."

Sampling. When collecting data about a problem, there's little point in engaging in overkill—as the saying goes, "drowning in data, but starved for information." Sensible data collection techniques will always consider the possibility of using simple sampling procedures. Depending on the problem, the sample can be random or systematic (for example, every fifth or tenth item).

Causes vs. solutions. We have stressed in these pages the importance of gathering all the data we can about a problem, particularly its causes. However, in certain situations we may find that the continuing search for and assessment of causes may be nonproductive. To illustrate: Let's assume you or I find that our morning newspaper is frequently not at the front door as it should be. We want to learn the causes for this inconvenience. One training group brainstormed this problem and came up with 35 (!) possible causes—everything from theft by a dog, excess wind, dishonest/hostile neighbors, and shortages in delivery, to the newsboy donating the paper to the home for the aged, keeping samples to secure new customers, and selling "leftovers." However, since the causes for the missing newspaper are purely speculative, it is apparent that prolonged discussion of them is not very productive. It is thus essential to concentrate, instead, on *solutions.* The situation is akin to treating phobias—the causes, if not readily known, can be readily dispensed with. What is more important is to work out a program to teach the phobic new behaviors, such as by desensitizing the person gradually to his/her nonproductive fear.

Flipcharting. Flipcharts are a basic tool in problem solving. They encourage objectivity—data are collected and posted as opposed to possible finger-pointing or blaming others. Also, a visual display stimulates added ideas. Unlike the blackboard, the group can never run out of space to capture ideas, even if such ideas are numerous, as in a brainstorming procedure. Finally, the flipchart enables the group to store its ideas easily for use in later sessions.

Tangible results. The best measurements of successful problem solving are those that show tangible results: quality improvement; cost savings; reductions in waste, scrap, rejects, customer complaints, employee grievances, accidents, absenteeism; etc. Conversely, "soft" indicators of improvement such as changes in attitudes, while interesting and useful, are not likely to receive the same degree of acceptance by upper-level management.

SOME DO'S AND DON'TS

Groups can solve problems effectively if they avoid these six pitfalls [21]:

Failure to identify the real problem. Often groups reduce their problem-solving capability by working on *symptoms* instead of the problem. Dealing with a symptom will, at best, provide short-term results. Remember, symptoms tend to recur; problems which are solved ordinarily do not.

Failure to identify problem ownership. In other words, whose problem is it? Sales? Production? Service? Personnel? "Solving" the wrong group's problem only produces resentments, non-cooperation, charges of meddling, etc. Once we know who assumes responsibility for the problem, we can work with that person or unit in resolving the difficulty.

Failure to identify all possible alternatives. This may be due to sloppy thinking, impatience, bias (predisposition toward a solution), or other factors. But regardless of the cause, high-quality decisions require a good look at the choices.

Failure to create a written plan for implementation. No solution is better than the plan developed to activate it. This means attention (getting agreement) on who does what, how, and when. Use the flipchart to record group members' responsibilities for their piece of the action plan. Visibility helps to avoid misunderstandings about responsibility.

Failing to monitor the implementation. The best laid plans of groups often go awry due to various factors—illness, pressure of new events, unanticipated delays, unforeseen "bugs" that arise, etc. The solution: Appoint a monitor, coordinator, or trouble-shooter to stay on top of things. The alternative is slippages, bottlenecks, disappointments, frustrations, finger-pointing, and defensiveness ("that wasn't my job").

Failure to use a trained resource person or catalyst. As is apparent from everything that has been presented in this chapter, effective problem solving is dependent on the intelligent (appropriate) use of a good variety of techniques and procedures. The properly trained facilitator can help a group immeasurably, whether we are talking about ensuring that the problem is defined at the outset, that it is subject to force field analysis (or other cause-effect analysis), that it is brainstormed (or "ideated" in some way), that all alternatives are really considered, or that a plan for implementation is developed and monitored.

So much for pitfalls. The other and more positive side of the problem-solving coin is what we can do in the training situation to ensure that we train our participants well. Here are some pointers [22]:

Use a problem-solving model. Participants need to work from a model, a conceptualization, or a process so that they can check themselves at the various stages in the problem-solving process. We have suggested a five-step model, but yours can have as many steps as needed. The Problem Solving Center in New York uses four steps: understanding the problem, devising a plan, carrying out the plan, and evaluating the results.

Solve participants' problems. This approach ensures full participant involvement, provides participants with something they can use immediately, and acquaints participants with one another's work.

Build upon problem presentations. Using live, challenging (unsolved) problems, the trainer can help participants zero in on each aspect (stage) of the problem-solving process. The idea is to slow down the action and make them do the job on a step-by-step basis, rather then permitting replication of the hurried, global approaches ordinarily used on the job.

Encourage sequential questioning. Have participants ask questions of one another on each step of the problem-solving process. This will make for increased participation plus an internalization of the notion that solutions must await exploration of the earlier stages.

Assign written exercises about participants' problems. This procedure will aid in consolidating participant knowledge and skill about problem-solving techniques.

Encourage the use of "figurative" techniques. Introduce participants to analogy and metaphor. For the analogy, start them off with phrases like: "This thing reminds me of _____." or "This thing can be compared to _____." For the metaphor, use this starting phrase: "The (key person or object) is (another person or object)." Example: "The inventory system is a vehicular fuel system." The analysis picks up easily enough from the fuel system metaphor.

KEY POINTS

1. To decide among alternatives (Step 4 in the model), ranking procedures are helpful. The rank-

ing may be done with criteria developed by the group or without any criteria.

2. Procedures may also be used to predict the success of one option (decision) over another.

3. The last step in the model—planning and implementation—may be aided by time and staffing assignment charts.

4. Other, more general approaches to problem solving are these: rotational problem solving, past/present/future approach, the journalist's six questions, personal needs analysis, quality circles, study groups, knowledge circles, ways to maximize idea power at meetings, and Open Space meetings.

5. The best problem solving follows principles and procedures such as these: use of pilot runs, sampling, flipcharting, "Swiss cheese" and "bleed-off" principles, tackling easy problems first, moving appropriately from causes to solutions.

REFERENCES

1. Carspecken, P., "How to Pick a Producer for Your Training Film," *Training and Development Journal* (December 1977), pp. 28–29.

2. "Peter Drucker on the Manager and the Organization," *Bulletin on Training* (March–April 1977), p. 4.

3. Roseman, E., *Confronting Non-promotability: How to Manage a Stalled Career*, American Management Associations, New York (1977), pp. 234–235.

4. Breen, Bill, "What's Your Intuition?," *Fast Company* (September 2000), p. 296.

5. Developed by Weiss, K. D., Laredo State University, and reported in *Training and Development Journal* (September 1978), p. 27.

6. Latzko, W. J., "Quality Circles Won't Work Without Quality Control," *Bank Administration* (December 1981), pp. 23–26.

7. *Productivity* (March 1982), p. 10.

8. Metz, E. J., "The Verteam," *Training and Development Journal* (December 1981), pp. 78–85.

9. Dr. Cole's views on the problems of transplanting the quality circle to the United States are given in "QC Warning Voiced by U.S. Expert on Japanese Circles," *World of Work Report* (July 1981), pp. 49–51.

10. Geber, Beverly, "Quality Circles: The Second Generation," *Training* (December 1986), pp. 54–61.

11. Miskin, Val, and Gmelch, Walter H., "Quality Leadership for Quality Teams," *Training and Development Journal* (May 1985), pp. 122–129.

12. "Middle Management: Making the Grade Through Study Groups," *Productivity* (July 1984), pp. 1–3.

13. Belcher, Forrest R., "About This 'Cognet' Business," *Training* (May 1985), p. 94.

14. James, Randolph, "'Working Smarter' Through Knowledge Circles," *Performance and Instruction Journal* (July 1986), pp. 7–11.

15. Devine, D. W., "The Jury Technique: Will the Real Problem Stand Up?" *Personnel* (September–October 1976), pp. 25–30.

16. Clark, C. H., "Teams Reinforce Ideas," *Successful Meetings* (June 1973), pp. 122–123.

17. Jones, J. E., "Structure Your Meeting for Success," *Meetings and Conventions* (January 1976), pp. 44, 57.

18. Rao, Srikumar S., "Welcome to Open Space," *Training* (April 1994), pp. 52–56.

19. For ideas on how to "pep up" one's life, see Carlisle, M. W., "Is Your Fun Too Much Work?" *Parade* (October 11, 1981), pp. 26–27. The worksheet is adapted from a chart in the article.

20. Quoted in the column by William Raspberry, "Studying Success," *The Washington Post* (March 10, 1986).

21. Bledsoe, J., "When Solving Your Problems Here Are Six Pitfalls to Avoid," *Training/HRD* (May 1977), p. 86.

22. "Six Tips to Help Improve Your Problem-Solving Training," *Training/HRD* (October 1979), pp. 10, 16.

RECOMMENDED READING

Ackoff, Russel L., *The Art of Problem Solving,* John Wiley and Sons, New York, 1978.

In an anecdotal, humorous way, Ackoff explores problem solving and creativity and explains why many of our attempts at problem solving go awry.

Breen, Bill, "What's Your Intuition?" *Fast Company*, September 2000, pp. 290–300.

Based on his research among firefighters, a cognitive psychologist advises that in decision making, even if you don't have all the information you need or all the time you'd like, you still must decide. How to do this? Forget analysis paralysis and trust your instincts instead.

Dyer, William G., "When Is a Problem a Problem?" *The Personnel Administrator*, June 1978, pp. 66–71.

Dyer distinguishes between problems and "felt needs," the former being a condition below standard and the latter being a situation where one or more people "hurt" enough to take some action on it.

Gryna, Frank M., Jr., *Quality Circles: A Team Approach to Problem Solving,* AMACOM, American Management Associations, New York, 1981.

This research study examines the status of the Quality Circle in the United States. Covers history, benefits, determining feasibility in an organization, design, training, implementation, and evaluation.

Ingle, Sud, *Quality Circles Master Guide,* Prentice Hall, Englewood Cliffs, New Jersey, 1982.

This is a comprehensive treatment of the subject by an early practitioner in the field.

Ingle, Sud, and Eitington, Julius E., *Implementing Quality Circles: Trainer's Manual and Leader's Handbook,* BNA Communications, Rockville, Maryland, 1985, looseleaf, 179 pages.

These materials serve as a guidebook for Quality Circle leaders who need to know how to train QC members and conduct QC meetings. *Note:* A QC member's workbook of 107 pages is also available.

Maier, Norman R. E., "Leadership Principles for Problem Solving Conferences," *Michigan Business Review,* May 1962.

This article presents ten principles for problem solving, including admonitions to direct effort toward solving surmountable problems, use *available* facts even when inadequate, recognize that the starting point of a problem is richest in solution possibilities, increase problem-mindedness and delay solution-mindedness, learn that disagreement can lead to hard feelings or to innovation, diagnose for facts vs. feelings, and recognize that solutions suggested by the leader tend to be improperly evaluated.

Murnighan, J. Keith, "Group Decision Making: What Strategies Should You Use?" *Management Review*, February 1981, pp. 55–62.

This discusses and critically compares various group decision-making methods including the unstructured group meeting, brainstorming, statistical aggregation, the Delphi technique, and the nominal group technique.

Osborn, Alex, *Applied Imagination,* Charles Scribner's Sons, New York, 1960.

This is a classic work on problem solving, particularly on the technique of brainstorming.

Parnes, Sidney J., Noller, Ruth B., and Biondi, Angelo M., *Guide to Creative Action,* Charles Scribner's Sons, New York, 1977.

A rich source book of short readings and practical exercises, this covers the vast field of problem solving and creativity.

Parnes, Sidney J., Noller, Ruth B., and Biondi, Angelo M., *Creative Actionbook,* Charles Scribner's Sons, New York, 1976.

This is an exercise book to accompany *Guide to Creative Action.*

Rawlinson, J. Geoffrey, *Creative Thinking and Brainstorming*, John Wiley and Sons, New York, 1981.

This treats (1) barriers to creative thinking and how they can be removed, (2) how to organize and eval uate brainstorming sessions, and (3) the do's and don'ts of brainstorming.

Ulschak, Francis L., Nathanson, Leslie, and Gillan, Peter G., *Small Group Problem Solving: An Aid to Organizational Effectiveness,* Addison-Wesley Publishing Company, Reading, Mass., 1981.

This presents an overall problem-solving model that considers both technical and human factors in small group problem solving. It also treats in individual chapters these specific problem-solving techniques: synectics, nominal group techniques, systems analysis, force field analysis, and brainstorming.

13 Team Building: Overcoming the "Lone Ranger" Syndrome

Coming together is a beginning; keeping together is progress; working together is success.

—Henry Ford (1863–1947),
American industrialist

People acting together as a group can accomplish things which no individual acting alone could ever hope to bring about.

—Franklin Delano Roosevelt (1882–1945),
thirty-second U.S. President

There is nothing good or bad per se about a group. A group can be a roadblock to progress, enforcing 'group think' and conformity upon its members, paralyzing decision-making processes, and smothering individual initiative. Under other conditions, a group can be a powerful synergism of talents, strengthening its members, speeding up the decision-making process, and enhancing individual and personal growth.

—Rensis Likert (1903–1981),
director of the Institute of Social Research,
University of Michigan

TRAINERS who have been delivering management training for some time may find that it is essential to move into team building. This is a logical development since conventional management training is concerned only with the dissemination of management concepts and with individual skill development. Conventional training does nothing to resolve the real problems of work teams or to help managers who interact on the job communicate and relate better to one another. And if the trainers don't move in this desirable direction, management may nudge them into it. Hence trainers should prepare themselves to become team builders or facilitators.

Team building is an organized effort to improve team effectiveness. It may relate to defining and clarifying policies/goals; to reviewing and refining procedures; to eking out ways to be more innovative and creative; to improving management practices in such areas as communication, decision making, delegation, planning, coaching, career development, and incentives; to improving relationships between team members; to improving external relations (with customers, suppliers); to improving relations with other work teams; and/or to improving products and/or services.

In a sense, team building draws upon the athletic model for its basic concepts. These concepts include the assumptions that performance must be continually critiqued, that the team can't rest on past accomplishments, that a team must constantly strive for greater teamness, that a team must be willing to engage in introspection and feedback (receiving as well as giving), and that such values as openness, trust, spontaneity, mutuality, sharing, caring, risk taking, and experimentation are paramount.

Team building typically begins when the team leader realizes that there are blocks to team effectiveness, that the team is not hitting on all cylinders, that improvement or change is desirable, and that help along those lines *is* wanted. Note that this is not the same as the team leader wanting team development so that the team leader's will can be imposed more fully on the group. In the latter case team building would be wasted effort, for such a leader's concept of a team would be one where members were subservient rather than creative, independent, or questioning.

Team building is also not likely to succeed if it is instigated because another department is doing it or because someone at a higher level directs that it be undertaken.

A very useful form of team building is the "transition team build" [1]. Its purpose is to facilitate the entry of a new manager into an ongoing operation. Each manager has a lot to learn about the new team, and vice versa, and, obviously, the sooner the better.

The manager wishes to learn of member strengths and weaknesses, their temperaments, possible interpersonal issues, the degree of teamness which exists, the team's history, current operating goals, priorities, problems, etc.

Similarly, team members want to remove uncertainties concerning their new leader's management philosophy and style, personality, expectations, "hot buttons," and the like.

Some organizations regard the transition team build as so important that they require it to take place whenever a manager is assigned to a new post.

Team building may also take place following a major reorganization, a merger or an acquisition, or staff cutbacks. It may also be triggered by new organizational requirements such as significantly added responsibility, a change in mission, or new programs such as cost reduction or quality improvement. A highly critical report resulting from a communications, climate, or morale survey may also indicate the need for team building.

A new plant, office, or special team project can also profit from team building before actual start-up. Objectives are to clarify mission, policies, priorities, and expectations generally, as well as to get employees acquainted more meaningfully and to make a good start on the development of authentic relations among team members.

One way to understand team building better is to consider what it is *not:*

☐ It is not something that can be successfully accomplished by every manager or team leader. Sharing the leadership and decision-making roles, listening, displaying a willingness to receive as well as to give feedback, supporting and praising others as opposed to blaming people, and creating a climate for openness are skills and attitudes not all managers possess. In other words, leader readiness is a key concept for successful team building.

☐ It is not likely to be effective if all members of the group are not committed to the idea. Lip service to team building by one or more members will vitiate the effort.

☐ It is not only for the work team "in trouble." All work groups can improve their effectiveness.

☐ It is not a one-shot affair. Initial sessions must be supported by continuing follow-up meetings. It is a long-term investment for unit or group health.

☐ It is not a T-group (sensitivity training). Although the facilitator may draw upon certain techniques and activities that are used in such training, the basic thrust is toward work improvement rather than improvement in interpersonal competence [2].

☐ It is not a panacea. It cannot overcome problems that relate to the larger system, such as insufficient resources, an ineffective reward system, poor leadership at the level above the work team, an ineffective organizational communication system, or lack of cooperation by other work units.

☐ It is not an easy thing to accomplish. Hard work, patience, a willingness to invest the necessary time, risk taking, and experimentation are some of the ingredients of successful team building.

☐ It is typically not something that can be done well without a trained facilitator. Some managers may be able to accomplish it on their own, but they are few in number. In essence, a neutral observer of the group—the facilitator—is an indispensable adjunct to the total process. The facilitator's role as a catalyst, standard-setter, challenger, issue-raiser, processor, and arbitrator is what makes things happen meaningfully.

☐ It is not a process that is intended to create dependence on the facilitator. In fact, the proof of a facilitator's effectiveness comes when the group no longer needs the facilitator.

It is to be noted, too, that there are times in the life of an organization when team building may not be appropriate. For example, management consultant Price Pritchett cautions against its use during heavy downsizing. He feels that when turmoil hits an outfit, teams revert to primitive forms of group development. He states, "This is when people are trying to get a reading on their own roles in the organization. They need to find out what the group is going to be like, what's accepted and what isn't accepted."

Conventional team-building techniques won't help much in this atmosphere—these methodologies require the ability to build trust, but at this point the trust level is low. Says Pritchett, "People are preoccupied with self-preservation issues. They look to the person in charge to point the group in the direction it's supposed to go. It's a leader-dependent outfit" [3].

As a final observation, what distinguishes team building from more conventional group efforts in the work place is that it has a *dual* concern:

1. The work per se (goals, policies, priorities, procedures, problems, products, services).

2. An appraisal of the group itself as it functions to do that work (group process). Although the emphasis on work vs. the emphasis on process will vary with (a) the needs of each group, (b) the group's ability and willingness to receive feedback about itself, and (c) the facilitator's style, the primary emphasis, typically, is on work improvement.

Regarding item 2, there are three member-related issues that determine whether a group striving to become a team will actually become one. They are [4]:

☐ *Membership:* Am I in or out? (The more "in" we feel, the greater our cooperation and zeal, and vice versa.)

☐ *Influence:* Do I have any power and control? (This relates to maintenance vs. loss of self-esteem.)

☐ *Personal growth:* Will there be opportunities to use, develop, and expand my needed skills and resources?

IS TEAM BUILDING REALLY NEEDED?

Before you gather data about the work team and generally prepare for a team-building effort, you should be certain that (a) team building is the answer to the problems of the requesting outfit and (b) you can determine the most appropriate team-building approach for the task. Trainer/consultant Robert W. Barner suggests that you address the following six questions before you go ahead [5]:

1. *What performance concerns do you hope to resolve through team building?* You want to be certain that the training effort has the potential for real payoffs. For example, if there are only isolated performance problems, or if the outfit's problems relate to broader organizational issues which lie outside the team's control, or if the team leader is a totally authoritarian personality who browbeats everyone in and outside the organization with whom he has contact, team building is hardly the remedy. In other words, the issues of concern must be those that affect the entire team and are clearly within team control.

2. *Is the team building concerned with an intra-team or an inter-team building focus?* In *intra-team building* we are concerned with such issues as:

   □ *Decision making:* How are team decisions made, who makes them, and what degree of opportunity exists for them?

   □ *Role clarity:* Who is responsible for what, and are team members' contributions fully appreciated?

   □ *Leader-member communication:* Are people getting enough direction and input from the boss to perform properly?

   In *inter-team building* we are concerned with group-to-group interaction. If work is interdependent, what are the blocks to cooperation and how can they be overcome? Typical interface issues follow:

   □ *Alignment:* To what degree do the teams understand and respect one another's goals, priorities, and deadlines?

   □ *Responsiveness:* Do the groups provide one another with the service and support they need to perform properly?

   □ *Customer/supplier interface:* Do the teams work well together to deal effectively with outside suppliers and customers?

   □ *Work procedures:* Is there full cooperation so that typical inter-departmental conflicts (for example, between engineering and marketing) do not arise? Role clarity is necessary, and the type of assistance each department must provide the other for effective performance must be delineated.

3. *Are team members part-time or full-time?* If team members are working on a special task force or a cross-functional quality improvement team, there will be problems of dual loyalty. That is to say, participants may well encounter conflicting performance demands from their part-time leader and from their permanent functional leader. An added problem is that the heads of the part-time teams may feel they have insufficient authority to conduct their team's activities. So if team building is conducted for the part-time team, the focus should be on capturing full commitment to team success and on encouraging a feeling of accountability/ownership for hoped-for outcomes.

4. *Are there different levels of power/authority among team members?* If there are several levels of management in a team, the facilitator in the team building effort has to work toward reducing/de-emphasizing the distinctions that inevitably arise from disparities in the team power structure. Why? Because the lower-level managers are very likely to withhold information or to be reluctant to level with their more powerful bosses. Barner advises facilitators to look for the "weather vane" phenomenon, which occurs when lower-level managers look carefully to see which way the wind is blowing before they come forth with their own opinions.

   One way to deal with the status and power problem is to use "break out" sessions. In this technique, the facilitator divides a team into two or more teams; managers and their subordinates are assigned to different groups. This procedure will de-emphasize status and authority problems and will meet the "safety needs" of everyone on the team(s).

5. *What is the experience level of the teams—are they recently created or of long standing?* Different experience levels will require different

learning approaches and different consulting roles by the facilitator.

□ *Newly formed teams:* Since there is little history of work experience as a team, structured team simulations should be used to develop team rapport and management skills. In essence, this means taking a "preventive-maintenance" approach.

□ *Established teams:* Since these teams have a lot of history to work from, training is oriented toward "renovation and repair" rather then preventive maintenance. Also, the facilitator can use the team-building session to observe team member interaction on real-life problems and decisions.

Note, too, that the novice team will lean more on the facilitator, whereas the experience-based team will look to the facilitator primarily to guide it through the resolution of critical issues.

Another difference: The well-established team will not require an introduction to *all* team management skills, so the facilitator should focus on the less effective aspects of their team functioning.

6. *What is the role of the facilitator?* How much direction and control should he/she exercise? Barner points out that depending on the needs of the team, team-building programs will fall into two categories: facilitator-directed programs and facilitator-coached programs.

□ *Facilitator-directed programs:* Here the facilitator's methods are structured and each stage of the program is tightly controlled.

□ *Facilitator-coached programs:* This role entails a less directive approach. The facilitator is there to give coaching and advice. The regular team leader and the team members conduct each phase of the team-building process very much on their own.

The advantage of the facilitator-directed approach is that it can give the newly formed team an accelerated, low-risk method to treat tough team-building issues. In contrast, the facilitator-coached sessions give teams more opportunities to develop the particular manage-

ment skills needed to run their own sessions later on.

When should teams adopt facilitator-directed programs? Under these circumstances, says Barner:

□ The team has a limited life span. In this case, they need help to move into action quickly. They certainly don't need a lengthy, drawn-out team-building process.

□ There is the threat of an imminent breakdown. The team needs help now to keep things from deteriorating beyond recall.

□ There are high-risk performance challenges being faced; unless corrected, there may be major adverse impacts throughout the organization.

□ There is a high likelihood of explosive contact between team members in the team-building session. The facilitator will need to exercise his good conflict resolution skills.

□ There is limited time to treat performance challenges.

In summation, it is apparent that there are a good number of serious issues which must be addressed by the facilitator before he/she "signs on" to do the team-building job. To plan ahead without adequate pre-session deliberation is to encourage a quite certain boomerang effect.

PRELIMINARY WORK

Prior to the first session, it is essential for the facilitator to gather data about the work team. This can be done via

□ Interviews with team members (for one to one and one-half hours).

□ Questionnaires.

□ Questionnaires supplemented by interviews (preferred over method 2).

The gathering of such data will serve these purposes:

□ Provide some "feel" for the group—their personalities, problems, needs, hurts, reservations, hopes, and dreams.

☐ Provide the facilitator with a chance to meet the team members, and vice versa (if interviews are conducted).

☐ Make team members aware that this is a serious, databased training effort.

☐ Provide data that can be introduced into the group for analysis.

The best way to begin an interview is to state clearly who you are, your relationship with the boss, why you're doing this, and what ground you hope to cover.

Data to be collected in the interview can fall logically into these broad categories:

☐ General questions
☐ Task (work) elements
☐ Interpersonal factors
☐ Process factors
☐ Systems influences

General questions may follow these lines: What are the group's key problems? What are the group's major strengths? Its major weaknesses? Its opportunities? What one thing would make the group more effective than it is? How do you feel about being a member of this group? What, if anything, would make you more effective? What are your major satisfactions/dissatisfactions on the job? What would you like to see happen in the team building session that would make it a worthwhile venture for you?

Task or work-related questions may assume these forms: What are the goals of the team? Are they clear? Logical? Current? Attainable? Are any goals absent, as you see it? Are there any policies, either current or absent, that affect team effectiveness? Is the team planning minded? Are priorities clear? Are there any procedures that are hindering effectiveness? Is your own job clearly defined? How do you know when you've done a good job?

Interpersonal factors may be probed with questions like these: How do you relate to the team? Do you feel you are part of it? How would you describe each team member? Who is most influential? Are there any members who produce conflicts? If so, how do they get resolved? Who do you work with the most? How sound is this relation-

ship? How is your relationship with your superior? What one thing would strengthen it (or make it even stronger)? How would you describe your boss as leader? What is your boss's influence up the line?

Process factors relate to how the group goes about doing its work. These kinds of questions should illuminate this area: How are decisions made? What is the nature of your input in decisions? Are problems faced up to? How would you characterize communication in our team? Do people level with one another? Do people trust one another? Is this a creative or a conforming group? How effective are staff meetings? How effective are other problem-solving meetings? How is conflict handled? Is it welcomed or smothered? In what kind of climate does the team operate?

Systems influences relate to broader aspects of the group's culture that influence behavior. Questions worth asking are these: How effective/adequate is the information system? What is the nature of the reward system? Does real accomplishment get rewarded? What could you say about the nature/adequacy of the pay system? The training system (growth opportunities)? The career development/promotion system?

A problem that is likely to arise in the interviews is the offering of data with constraints. That is to say, the interviewee may offer data "just so it is kept in confidence." In this circumstance the trainer has the obligation to make it very clear that while a request to treat the *data source* as confidential is fine, the issues presented cannot be treated that way. In other words, there is little point in listening to team problems that cannot be reported back to the team.

Once all the data has been collected, what do you, as facilitator, do with it? You organize it so it can be presented logically and meaningfully to the group. You do not try to interpret it; this task is left to the group. Why? Because it is *their* data and it is thus *their* responsibility to deal with it. They may elect to use it or to ignore it, but that's the team's prerogative.

Also, the data is not to be shared with anyone before the team building effort begins. The data is *group* property and must be treated as such. So questions from the team leader or anyone else to the facilitator, such as: "What have you been finding so far?" or "What did George have to say?" must be politely turned away on the grounds of confidentiality and/or incompleteness.

Pre-work

Another aspect of preliminary work is to consider activities—"pre-work"—which team members might undertake in advance of the formal team building sessions. This assignment is to accomplish these three objectives:

1. To provide team members with a task which provides a rationale for why we'll be leaving the very important and familiar work site for two or three days, for the novel and vague team building retreat. ("Team building? What's that?")

2. To indicate that team building is serious business, totally integrated into the productivity of the team.

3. To help team members ease into the team-building session, moving from the day-to-day, hurly-burly operational world to a new locale where broader, calmer, longer-range thinking will be sought.

A suggested pre-work task is to have all participants do a SWOT analysis. SWOT stands for strength, weakness, opportunity, and threat. The analysis relates to what we're doing well and what we're doing less well, how we stand in the marketplace vis-à-vis ourselves and our competitors, what negative factors might loom on the horizon, and what are the possibilities for growth and innovation that we should be cognizant of.

All of the above would be part of the agenda for the team-building session. The SWOT assignment might be included in a memo to the staff providing details concerning the team-building session—why, when, where, the name of the facilitator, and that the latter will be coming around to interview all attendees in advance of the retreat.

STARTING THE FIRST SESSION

Team building is both difficult and important. It thus merits the best possible atmosphere/location for its proceedings. A motel/hotel or conference center away from town is extremely helpful. This "cultural island" retreat is essential for getting away from the usual job/family pressures and distractions and for permitting total concentration on the team-building task.

The core or initial effort should be planned to last two or three days. It is a good idea to begin things with a social or cocktail party the first evening. This should be followed by dinner and the opening session of two hours or so.

The first session is a crucial one, for at this time team members are eager to learn answers to questions such as these:

☐ Is this going to be a serious effort, or are we just going to go through the motions?

☐ Will I be put on the spot in any way?

☐ How candid can I be? Or should I just "play it safe?"

☐ What is the facilitator like? Is he/she the boss's stooge? Will he/she take sides?

☐ How eager are the boss and others to learn about their own shortcomings?

☐ Can *this* group really be helped?

Recognizing, then, that participants do have concerns, anxieties, and misconceptions, one way to start is with an opener such as "Hopes and Fears." Using a T-column, ask the group to list candidly its greatest hopes for and worst fears about this training effort.

Going to the right column first—the worst fears—we may expect responses such as "go over same old stuff," "reinvent the wheel," "waste time," "make an ass of myself," "be put on the spot," "open up 'wounds' (old and new) unnecessarily."

By getting the fears out at the outset, we are candidly recognizing that it is legitimate and logical to have some doubts about the program. The fears need not be processed. Recognizing that they exist is a step forward.

If it is desired to process this material, a good way to do this is to establish subgroups—assign one or more this task: "How to make those hopes realized"; assign the other subgroups: "How to overcome these fears."

One of the fears that is certain to be expressed is that of being too frank or too open. A question may also arise about the impartiality of the facilitator—is he/she a stooge or spy for the boss, top management, or the personnel office? Since these questions are trust issues, experienced facilitators try to meet them head on. You may thus say: "I can't tell you how much you should level and express your feelings. It's your decision to decide how much to say. But based on my experience with these kinds of training programs, I must say to you that whether we succeed or fail depends on what each of you does here—how willing you are to say what you think."

As to the positive side—the hopes or possibly "fondest fantasies"—we may get responses such as: "solve all of our tough problems," "improve cooperation," "remove blocks to communication," "set realistic goals," "improve profitability," "strengthen our product line."

Another safe way to start is to approach things on a highly positive note. Thus, an assignment to several subgroups, or possibly to a fishbowl group, is to respond to this question: "What is our team particularly good at? What are our strengths?"

The data may be posted on a flipchart and "reality tested." A second, logical task might then be to ask the reverse of the above question: "O.K., we know now what we're good at. What aspects of our team functioning could be improved upon?"

An obvious alternative to the prior approach is to have subgroups develop a T-column on both effective and less-than-effective capabilities (The Things We Do Well vs. The Things We Do Less Than Well). The data is posted and then discussed and critiqued in the total group.

Another easy, low-key way to start is to have subgroups develop data that responds to these questions: What behaviors should team members engage in to produce teamness (build the team)? What behaviors should team members avoid lest they hurt teamness?

Note: The data requested is adequately general in character and not pinpointed at any one member of the team. The data may be posted on a T-column (Behaviors That Help vs. Behaviors That Hinder).

Yet another way to start is to break the group down into subgroups, each of which develops a list of problems facing the team. Some facilitators term this a "bug" list. The data that emerge—essentially a problem census—is then prioritized and becomes the team's agenda.

Things can begin, too, by taking an MBO (management by objectives) approach; that is, current overall goals can be posted and discussed as to their relevancy, adequacy or comprehensiveness, clarity, reachability, tie-in to those of horizontal units, etc.

Another safe way to start is to have the team experience a training program together, for example, on time management. A number of the topics that are treated in such a course relate to all team members as a working unit, for example, defining key results areas (major responsibilities), conduct of meetings, the interruptions problem, delegation by the boss, the possible establishment of a quiet period. Stress management is another training activity that may have team development implications.

Another low-key, low-threat way to start is with an exercise that relates to teamwork, group decision making, etc. The NASA Exercise is useful for this purpose because it shows how group judgment is superior to individual decision making; the Broken Squares exercise may also be used as a learning experience concerning cooperation [6].

Of course you may provide your own small group exercises on subjects such as:

☐ Trust—What behaviors by the team (members and leader) build trust; what behaviors reduce trust.

☐ Cooperation—What behaviors increase cooperation; what behaviors reduce it.

☐ Team building—risks vs. benefits.

Or the group may be asked to fantasize: What would things be like if we could all work well together? Or they may be asked to respond to a question such as this: What do you want for *you* as a result of our work here?

Still another way to start is with the completion of an instrument which tells the group how its members feel about current "teamness." The data is quickly tallied and can serve as the basis for much of the agenda for the day. This approach is recommended only for an advanced group, that is, one that is really ready to move into an analysis of sensitive but basic team issues. The data that was gathered via questionnaires in advance of the program may also serve as a starting point for a team that is "ready to move."

Data can also be generated via "fun-type" activities such as using Tinker Toys. Thus the total group may be divided into two or three small groups and given this task: "Build a representation of what the team is really like." In one program the small groups constructed the following: two forts with big cannons; a large tower with an object pointed out the window upward, to symbolize that "decisions are made in space"; a boat in disarray.

The point of suggesting alternate approaches is to indicate that there is no "best way" to start. What is best for one group may not be suitable at all for another; what is meat and potatoes for one group may be high threat for another. Hence the need to know the group, its leader, and its problems quite well. Sizing up both the group and member tolerance for approaches and data that confront them with their own functioning is a major art of team building.

A key rule: Wait for team readiness to introspect. Rushing or forcing such analysis will only blow it. Timing is basic to interventions that confront the group with its own behavior.

It is also a good idea to propose a set of ground rules early on for the proceedings. These may include the following:

1. No blaming. Instead, talk about opportunities, challenges, problems, difficulties, bottlenecks, restraints, etc.

2. Don't talk about people who are not in the room.

3. When questioning or speaking to a team member, make comments directly to the person. For example, in lieu of saying "But she is always late with her reports" or "I have this problem with her," state "I have this problem with you, June . . ." [7].

You may also wish to ask if other ground rules should be added to this list. This may produce suggestions such as responding to phone calls only during breaks or lunch, no smoking at sessions, full-time attendance by everyone (assuming this

ground rule has not been clearly stated before the retreat). Other possibilities, which may emanate from the trainer, are to avoid interrupting a speaker, to resolve issues by consensus rather than voting, and to avoid "plops." (A plop occurs when someone makes a statement and no one responds to it: the comment, then, simply plops to the floor, totally unrecognized. A likely reaction to the plop: "They don't seem to want my ideas. So I won't give them any.")

One way to emphasize teamness, with particular emphasis on shared leadership, is to suggest a procedure of rotating the chairperson role on a two-hour or half-day basis.

CORE ACTIVITIES IN THE TEAM BUILDING SESSION

Day One

The first day of the team-building session is designed to develop a collaborative/supportive climate and tone for the total program. Hence the need to use openers to help team members ease into things (see "Starting the First Session"). The learning at this early stage is concerned with what an effective team is like; openness (leveling) and trust; feedback, both giving and receiving; assessing team functioning; and identifying problems and developing an agenda therefrom.

Note: In a certain sense the nature of the tasks the team works on in the morning of Day One is not too significant. What *is* significant is that the team is doing the tasks together—developing rapport, respect for one another, supportiveness, trust, intimacy, cooperation, warmth, etc.

In Day One a great deal of introspection is going on: "Who are we? What kind of place (organization) are we working in? What is our mission? What philosophy underlies our mission? What kind of collaboration do we need and what kind do we have? What are our strengths and weaknesses?"

For a team that has been experiencing confusion over responsibilities, the management responsibility/accountability guide is useful [8]. It takes the form shown in Figure 13-1.

ACCOUNTABILITY CHART

Job Duties	President	Marketing Vice Pres.	Financial Vice Pres.	Managing Vice Pres.	Field Sales Manager
1. Manages corporation to achieve corporate goals.	P				
2. Establishes and estimates overall operating policies.	P	C	C	C	
3. Establishes overall company financial, sales & production goals.	P	C	C	C	N
4. Prepares quarterly operating statements.	N		A		
5. Maximizes sales volume.	S	P			C
6. Supervises field salespeople.		S			P
7. Operates plant to produce quality product at minimum costs.	S	N		P	
8. Determines inventory levels.	N		C	C	
9. Purchases capital equipment.	A		A	C	
10. Administers employee benefit program.	D	C		C	

Key to Chart

S = must *supervise* (but not perform) the work, including planning, organizing, and coordinating it; maintaining contact with workers; training and instructing employees.

P = must *perform* the work, including making decisions related to getting the work done.

N = must be *notified* of actions and decisions of the person who performs the work.

A = must *approve* of actions and decisions.

D = must *decide* on any matter when an internal conflict arises.

C = must be *consulted* on an advisory, non-binding basis prior to actions and decisions.

Figure 13-1. Example of an accountability chart. Source: "Accountability Charting Using Job Descriptions," *Small Business Report* **(June 1979), p. 17. Reproduced with the permission of the publisher of** *Small Business Report,* **Monterey, California.**

The chart may reveal a lack of delegated authority, overlapping responsibility, failure to assign responsibility for an activity, failure to appreciate one another's roles, etc. Obviously, these problems must be resolved on a team basis, and the results should be ones that team members find logical, equitable, and generally worth supporting.

The chart may be begun on Day One and possibly refined the next day or back on the job.

Closing Day One. In the course of the first day's work (including the prior evening's post-dinner, two-hour opener), considerable progress should have been experienced by the team. Members should be speaking more freely, a number of real issues should have been identified, the team should have a sense of where it is going, and the group may even begin feeling a degree of teamness.

One way to wrap things up is to have the group complete and process (tally, analyze, discuss) the instrument "My Assessment of Group Functioning," Appendix 43. Another way of finishing the day is to have every one jot down responses to the two questions on the worksheet given in Appendix 44, "Questionnaire—End of Day One." The data should be posted on flipcharts; the data may either be processed that night after dinner or carried forward as the agenda item for the start of Day Two.

Another exercise that might be used is called "Catastrophe, anyone?" [9]. It entails the anonymous writing by each group member of sensitive topics that others (not themselves) would be too reluctant or embarrassed to discuss publicly. The lists are then posted on newsprint, ranked according to payoff if discussed openly, and the top four or five items are subject to this prediction and discussion by the group: What "catastrophes" are averted by avoiding these issues? The exercise tends to help allay fears about discussing these *assumed* sensitive issues.

In general, by the end of Day One the group should have reached the stage where it is willing to take some risk in analyzing and discussing its problems as well as its own functioning. If the group is not ready for self-appraisal, it obviously cannot be performed and should be deferred. Its desirability, however, should be explored by the facilitator with the group.

Day Two

A good way to start the second day is to "reality test" feelings about the all-significant first day, for Day One is the stage setter, the climate establisher, the communication channels opener. If progress in these areas has not been made, the team is not really ready to move into its main tasks.

Tests of readiness for "movement" may be accomplished via various activities: a fishbowl exercise; completion and analysis of an instrument about teamness; asking people to move to one of three positions in the room (a "human continuum") representing their feelings of minor, moderate, or considerable progress. These feelings about progress or movement should be subject to team processing if the "reading" is low or only moderate. Also, additional work to improve climate and trust may be essential. If the trust problem revolves around the leader, this issue has to be resolved or there is little point in continuing the team development process.

If the group is "with it" on Day Two, they will dig in and identify problems realistically, establish goals and priorities, review and alter policies as necessary, and develop action plans to meet goals. They will also begin work on relationships (see the discussion of role negotiation in the section that follows). Decisions may also be made concerning time frames for future meetings. At these later dates, action plans would be reviewed for progress/completion and any additional input as deemed necessary would be given.

Depending on the "contract" as to time, an evening session may be held on Day Two. Additional business may also be conducted on Day Three, for either a half or full day.

Note: The above description of team building is based on the assumption that the entire team has "closed shop" and taken off for a two- to three-day retreat in a cultural island setting. However, a team may also work on its problems on a less intensive basis. For example, the U.S. Public Health Service uses the Rubin, Plovnick, and Fry model and has the team meet once a week (for two hours) for eight sessions [10]. It covers these topics in that time period:

☐ Mission/priorities
☐ Roles and responsibilities
☐ Decision-making process
☐ Staff meetings
☐ Rewards and recognition
☐ Interpersonal relations
☐ Performance standards (includes "where do we go from here")

The spread-out approach helps the team to digest and use what it has learned and thus make connections with the real world. It also overcomes such problems as reentry and exhaustion which may accrue over the long weekend at the cultural island.

TOOLS FOR TEAM BUILDING

Icebreaker

Assign group members to trios or quartets. Give them this task:

You are marooned on a Pacific island. Select the five most significant/useful items you would have taken along had you known in advance you would be stranded. Be prepared to defend your choices. (The idea is to loosen people up and given them an appreciation of others' values, problem-solving styles, etc.)

Have the teams enter their lists on a flipchart and post them to the wall, then secure reports from a team spokesperson. *Note:* To minimize possible influences of seniority, status, and/or gender in team selection of a spokesperson, request the teams to select a spokesperson on the basis of who joined the outfit most recently. This procedure may help to nurture the idea that it is legitimate for a "junior" member to serve in a leadership role.

Lecturettes

At early stages in the team-building program, short talks may be given on topics basic to the team-building process, such as the feedback process, including descriptive vs. evaluative feedback; the Johari window [6]; and consensus for group decision making. Or various models relating to management may be introduced, such as Herzberg's Motivation-Hygiene Theory, McGregor's Theory X and Y, Likert's Systems 4, the parent-adult-child model of Transactional Analysis, and Maslow's Hierarchy of Needs.

Consensual Problem Solving

While all work units solve problems using one technique/approach or another, the team-oriented unit accomplishes this *consensually.* That is to say, the work on resolving problems is done on a mutual consent basis. This process is illustrated in Figure 13-2. *Note:* Consensus means the fullest possible opportunity for each team member to contribute his/her ideas. Agreement comes about by "talking things through," not by voting. The latter process tends to create winners and losers and thus detracts from the development of teamness. Also, voting is all too often done prematurely, before everyone is fully clued in to the alternatives, including the pros and cons of each.

Let's use the three-step problem-solving model by Dave Quinlivan, Solution Finders, Inc., Vancouver, British Columbia, to develop this concept more fully [11]. The steps are data gathering, problem solving, and action planning.

1. *Data gathering.* The group collectively attempts to define its problems. Obviously, agreement in problem definition is basic to moving on to the next two stages. In fact, a common cause for difficulty in agreeing on a solution (stage 2) and on an action plan (stage 3) is that real consensus was not established in respect to problem definition.

2. *Problem solving.* At this stage alternatives are developed and explored, and a solution is chosen. The selection is accomplished not via bargaining, compromising, accommodating, acquiescing, or fiat, but on a "win-win" basis—for example, what is best from a team standpoint.

3. *Action planning.* Here the group looks at the potential impact of the implementation of their agreed-upon solution. They consider obstacles and opportunities offered by an action plan. If consensus is reached at all of the above stages, *commitment* for implementation of an action plan is very certain. Conversely, if there has been limited participation/involvement/discussion, commitment will have to depend on the leader's authority.

If the model is introduced to the group early on by the trainer, he/she can make reference to it as the group works on its problems. The trainer's role is not to become involved in the content of a particular problem, but to provide guidance on the *process* that is used in problem solving. The trainer's monitoring should be concerned with (1) adherence to the model

in sequential fashion—for example, action plans are not to be developed before the problem is defined—and (2) encouragement of the fullest possible participation at all three stages of the process.

Subgroups

These are useful for generating considerable amounts of data, which can then be critically compared. The smaller group size not only aids participation because of its more intimate and thus open character, but also, in a low-key way, creates a friendly competition.

Instrumentation

To enable the group to look at itself and its functioning, various instruments may be used. A number of them are given later.

Fishbowl

At times, various issues can be discussed advantageously by dividing the total group into two smaller groups. One group serves as the discussant group, the other group functions as observers. The discussion phase may last 20 minutes or so and then roles are reversed. At this point the ideas of the first group are discussed and enlarged upon. The fishbowl, as a small group device, provides greater participation, novelty, a change of pace, and a chance to build on and/or critique the ideas (content) of others. It may also be used for purposes of group process; that is, the observers (outer ring) may give the discussants (inner group) feedback about their behavior, both as individual participants and as a group.

Role Negotiation

This is a technique to clarify and improve *work* relations between two team members so that they can do their jobs better. At times, however, it may result in or relate to the improvement of *interpersonal* relations as well. Typical work-related problem areas are the need for added or more timely information, meeting deadlines, coordination matters, scheduling concerns, and

A Saga of Support and Cooperation

A group of five hunters and their guide, while walking in the woods, fell into a deep pit.

At first they wept and bemoaned their fate.

Then they blamed themselves . . .

. . . and blamed one another . . .

. . . and then their guide.

Then they tried prayer . . .

. . . and climbing the wall . . .

. . . and jumping off the ground.

Days passed; gloom settled on the group and none tried anything anymore . . .

. . . until one day, a farmer came by, peered into the pit, saw their plight and said, "Why don't you help one another out?"

So they discussed this suggestion and decided to try it out. And, lo and behold, it worked. And they went on their way.

> *Moral:*
> If your group finds itself in a hole, try cooperating.

Figure 13-2. Example of team problem solving. (*Source:* Julius E. Eitington, *The Winning Manager: Leadership Skills for Greater Innovation, Quality and Employee Commitment,* Gulf Publishing, Houston, Texas, 1997, p. 392.)

eliminating actions or behaviors that produce bottle-necks, tie-ups, delays, and uncertainty.

The following dialogue is an example of negotiating changes in interpersonal behavior between a boss and a subordinate:

Subordinate: *I wish you would listen to me more when I'm in your office, instead of shuffling your papers.*

Boss: *I wish you would come to the point more directly when you present me with a proposal.*

In general, the idea is to talk through expectations so that misunderstandings are removed and mutual cooperation is secured.

The procedures for conducting a role negotiation follow:

1. Pass out "Form for Role Clarification/Negotiation," Appendix 45, to each member in quantity so that everyone can prepare a form on everyone else, or have members copy the three statements in the worksheet off a flipchart.

2. Members complete their forms on all the other team members, including the boss.

3. The facilitator asks for a volunteer "to start us off."

4. The volunteer then teams up with another team member and discusses his/her form.

5. After the negotiation is worked through, the same two negotiators reverse roles.

Note: Although the negotiations can be done privately in dyads, it is more effective if the negotiations are conducted publicly. The reason for the public sharing is that it allows everyone to know what is going on, for everyone else may be involved in the problem, too.

A caution about role negotiation: It is not recommended for use with a team that has a lot of conflicts. In this circumstance it will only produce a great deal of wrangling and little forward movement.

NERV Model [12]

Developed by a Canadian R&D company, this model is used to improve communication. NERV stands for *needs, expectations, rights,* and *values.* In the model, a matrix is set up with these four components. Participants enter in the component blocks what they deem essential to convey what they need, expect, have a right to, and value from the other parties. It is a highly effective tool to ensure that team members understand their roles, to set goals, and to resolve conflicts. It can be used one-on-one, in groups, and in inter-group situations. Externally, it can be used to firm up commitments and relationships with suppliers or to identify customer needs better.

Needs: These are the bottom-line requirements that people must have to do their jobs properly. Needs may range from physical items such as equipment or supplies to personal requirements such as training.

Expectations: These are often equal to unarticulated needs. *Examples:* notifications from another unit as to possible material shortages; securing clarification as to the format, content, and length of required reports.

Rights: These are typically spelled out by company policies and procedures. There is usually little flexibility to negotiate on rights. However, it's important to distinguish between a right and an expectation. Where company policies don't exist and certain expectations may consequently arise, it is essential to clarify the reasonableness of expectations.

Values: These are the hardest to articulate since they are often ambiguous and subject to individual interpretation.

When completing one's matrix, individuals answer these questions:

☐ What should parties B, C, and D do to respond appropriately to my needs?

☐ What should B, C, and D do to meet my expectations of them?

☐ What rights do I have which B, C, and D should recognize?

☐ What do I value from B, C, and D?

The data in the matrices are then discussed candidly, ambiguities are clarified, new understandings are developed, and appropriate actions are taken (for example, training, third party intervention to resolve conflicts).

Relationship Recourse

Another way to encourage exploration of member relationships is to use the following procedure:

1. Have each member draw on a flipchart a circle, segment it, and then label each segment with the name of one of the other team members, including the boss.

2. Enter in each segment a percentage representing the strength of one's relationship with the other member. A perfect relationship rates 100%. (See Figure 13-3.)

3. Explain the basis for the assigned percentages and what behaviors on the part of the other parties would permit raising them to 100%.

4. Encourage team members to really level with one another. You may wish to say something like this: "You may feel that it is wiser and safer to give everyone a rating of 100%. But if you do, you may be losing out on a real opportunity to make things more satisfying for you over the long haul. And glossing over less than solid relationships certainly won't build a strong and open team. There may be some risks here, but in my experience the benefits far exceed the risks." *Note:* Some groups may find it helpful to work through their concerns by using the Risk Analysis procedure given in Chapter 2.

Brainstorming

The group may be asked to brainstorm ways it can improve its communication effectiveness, improve the product line, make regularly scheduled staff meetings more useful, or improve cooperation. One group brainstormed "Obstacles to Team Effectiveness" and came up with 78 items! The team then spent six two-hour sessions explaining and clarifying the items [13].

The staff meeting improvement problem is often fertile ground for group ideation. One managerial team that I worked with brainstormed it and produced this batch of ideas in a short seven minutes:

- ☐ Invite secretary to attend regularly
- ☐ Rotate minutes-taking chore
- ☐ Limit time to one hour
- ☐ Meet twice weekly for 45 minutes
- ☐ Make them luncheon meetings
- ☐ Meet in a nearby restaurant
- ☐ Meet in a bar
- ☐ Use an observer to monitor how we do
- ☐ Distribute minutes next day
- ☐ Rotate chairmanship as we've been doing here
- ☐ Invite Mr. Williams to attend occasionally (the boss's boss)
- ☐ Invite experts from other departments to talk to us
- ☐ Use a flipchart as we've learned here
- ☐ Meet in a conference room (rather than in Chris's office)
- ☐ Serve coffee and cake
- ☐ Serve fruit juice
- ☐ Invite an employee to attend each time
- ☐ Use meetings to solve problems as well as to give information
- ☐ Prepare an agenda in advance (secretary to coordinate)
- ☐ Ban smoking

Figure 13-3. Example of a circle representing relationships.

☐ Get more comfortable chairs

☐ Invite our consultant to attend to see how we're doing

☐ Ban telephone interruptions

☐ Latecomers pay $1.00 fine to go into coffee fund

☐ Introduce short cases for added management training

☐ Fine anyone $2.00 who gives a "putdown" to someone

☐ Assign someone to call attention to "plops"

Using Metaphors

As an activity to facilitate climate building, the group may be asked how it sees its functioning, using such metaphoric images as:

☐ A car—for example: "a Mercedes without a motor"; or "a Ford Escort—small, but up-to-date, perky, and efficient"; or "a very old Oldsmobile—we always seem to be running out of gas."

☐ An animal—for example: "We're an ostrich, not seeing what's going on around us"; or "We're an old pussy cat when we should be a tiger"; or "We're a bear in the spring, living on previously accumulated fat."

Force Field Analysis

This tool involves an enumeration (identification) and analysis of forces—favorable and unfavorable—at work in any problem-solving situation. Analysis of the forces will make for a more sophisticated resolution of the problem.

Note: For additional information on these topics, see the chapter as indicated: instrumentation, Chapter 9; fishbowl, Chapter 4; brainstorming, Chapter 11; metaphors, Chapter 10; force field analysis, Chapter 10.

Conflict Management

Groups that are active, energetic, and concerned will inevitably have differences among their members. But disagreement can lead to creativity—watch the sparks fly!—or to hard feelings. The trick in team management is to encourage the former and to soft-pedal the latter.

Management consultant Robert Lynch of L. M. Miller & Company, Atlanta, Georgia, believes that groups should learn about and post on their meeting wall this three-step procedure to manage conflict:

1. *State your case.* Each party to the conflict states his/her side of the issue objectively. Inflammatory words like "always" and "each time" are taboo.

2. *Investigate the other's case.* This is the critical step. People tend to misuse their time allotments: much of it goes into defending positions and all too little of it into listening.

3. *Shift the focus to identify other options.* A good statement for this is: "I have heard you; I know where you are coming from. You have heard my position/preferences. Why don't we collectively see if there are other options which merit our consideration?"

These steps set a new tone, unfreeze people from the rigid positions which they have already stated over 20 times, and permit new ideation and consideration of alternatives [14].

In sum, disagreement should be accepted as normal and useful rather than being smothered. It should be brought out into the open and managed for innovation/creativity. Controversy can unleash high interest, stimulation, excitement, enthusiasm, challenge, exploration, participation/involvement, and ultimately, new, worthwhile directions. Candid airing of differences can also lead to greater respect for others and stronger team cohesion.

Team Member Continuum (Spectogram)

As the team-building activity proceeds past the early "let's-play-it-safe" stage, it may be helpful to secure a quick public reading from all team members on how they see key issues facing the group (examples: how powerful and influential one feels in the group; the degree of openness in the group; the extent of team member cooperation).

If so, ask team members to stand and position themselves against a fairly long wall. Then provide this instruction: "Let's create a continuum concerning how we feel about our power and influence in the group. If you feel you have very little power and influence, position yourself to my far left. If you feel you have a lot of power and influence, position yourself to my far right. If you feel you have a moderate amount of power and influence, position yourself somewhere between the two ends of the continuum. You might consider the continuum as a 1–7 rating scale, 1 being low and 7 very high."

After the self-rankings, hold a discussion concerning the reasons for team member feelings.

Personality Preference Indicator

To help team members understand themselves and their colleagues better, and thus to value more varied views, a personality indicator, such as the Myers-Briggs Type Indicator, may be used. The MBTI can provide data to enable each person to look at the styles team members use to take in and process information, communicate, solve problems, and make decisions. Style indicators can help members (1) to learn of their own style and how they personally interact with others having the same and different styles, (2) to value the unique attributes of different styles, and (3) to understand the total group better [15].

Start with Art

As an opener to team-building sessions, Marty Jordan, a senior consultant with Amoco Oil, sets a tone of openness and fun with an art-oriented task for team members. His procedures [16]:

☐ Provide each trainee with a flipchart sheet and a batch of colored marking pens.
☐ Ask them to divide the big sheet into four quadrants.
☐ Have them label each segment as follows:

—Upper left: Strengths I bring to the class
—Upper right: Ways I might hinder the team

—Lower left: What I need from others to do my best
—Lower right: Hobbies, interests, and outside activities

☐ Task: Using drawings only—no words at all—respond to the title of each quarter. *Note:* The trainer models the task by also completing a flipchart.
☐ Time: 20–30 minutes to accomplish the requested art work.
☐ Sheets are then posted on the wall, and each participant shares his/her data with the total team.
☐ Drawings are left on the wall as conversation-starters during breaks and lunch.

Rationale: The art exercise stimulates participants' creative juices. It encourages more ready sharing about themselves by overcoming the self-consciousness which words might produce.

Play Time

Opportunities should be found for play, fun, and relaxation. The purpose of the recreating is not only to provide a change of pace and to loosen people up, which in themselves are highly desirable goals, but, more importantly, to afford team members the opportunity to experience one another in another setting and thus appreciate their own attributes and dimensions. ("She's really a smashing tennis player.")

Play time may be scheduled between 4:30 and 6:00 P.M., with a possible evening session following dinner. Or, if the group works the full day and doesn't opt for an evening session, the recreation can take place before a later dinner. Some activities can take place after dinner, too.

Outdoor activities—tennis, softball, running, hiking, swimming—are best, weather permitting. Indoor activities may encompass ping pong and billiards. Watching Monday night football and beer/soft drink drinking on a group basis also has cohesion-building potential. If dinner at the motel is not a must (that is, there are no contractual arrangements for it), a small motorcade to a more distant and desirable restaurant would also be a fun thing.

Note: The trainer should anticipate assuming the role of "recreation director," or participants may simply drift off to watch TV in their rooms on an individual basis. This means learning about available recreational facilities and announcing up front the desirability of having some play time together as an added but vital part of the team-building process. Also the trainer should be careful in the planning, organizing, and implementation of play activities to ensure that competition does not get carried back into the learning situation.

INSTRUMENTATION

At various points in a team-building training program, the facilitator can help the group look at its own functioning via instruments covering:

☐ "Teamness" (Appendix 46)

☐ The communication process (Appendix 47)

☐ The decision-making process

☐ Group creativity/innovation (Appendix 48)

☐ Leadership (Appendix 49)

☐ Cooperation (Appendix 51)

☐ Trust (Appendix 49a)

☐ Goals and policies (Appendix 50)

☐ Team membership (Appendix 51)

Other, more specialized instruments may also be used relating to

☐ Conduct of meetings (Appendix 52)

☐ Time management (Appendices 29, 76)

☐ Individual growth and development

The facilitator may also wish to use a simple rating scale to assess satisfaction with the proceedings, particularly that of Day One. The procedure for this is as follows:

1. Just before the morning break, say to participants: "It might be helpful to us if we took the temperature of the group—a reading concerning our satisfaction with our proceedings up to this point."

2. Then draw a scale on the flipchart, as follows:

1	2	3	4	5	6	7
Lo						Hi

3. Tell participants: "Jot down your rating on a piece of paper, fold it, and pass it forward. O.K., I'll read the scores aloud and, Pat, will you average them, please?"

4. Pat gives the group an average score of 3.5, the facilitator marking the scale appropriately.

5. Then say: "We'll be taking these readings as we go along and I'll post them on the flipchart on this wall." You point to a flipchart sheet that has either of the formats given in Figures 13-4 and 13-5.

SATISFACTION RATING CHART

Time	Average Score
Day 1 Break A.M.	3.5
Lunch	**4.0**
Break P.M.	**3.8**
End of day	**3.5**
Day 2 Break A.M.	**5.0**
Lunch	**5.0**
Break P.M.	**4.0**
End of day	**5.5**

Figure 13-4. Example of a chart that indicates group satisfaction by using team averages.

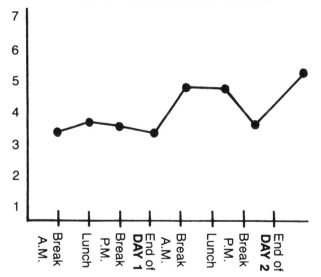

Figure 13-5. Example of a graph using team averages to show team satisfaction.

Depending on how things seem to be going, you may ask the group if they wish to talk about their average score. This may be the first score or a later one. In effect, this intervention is an attempt to secure candid comments about how the group is progressing.

A group that is quite open may raise this question itself. Also, it may prefer to do the rating publicly rather than anonymously. The anonymous procedure obviously is "safer" for a group that has not yet developed a high degree of openness and trust.

Incidentally, the term "satisfaction" may be questioned by one or more participants, either when asked to give a rating or if a discussion is made of the rating. You may turn the question back to the group and ask them to define it, or simply say it relates to how we feel about "progress" so far.

In general, the rating of satisfaction is significant not for its accuracy, but for the idea that the group has been challenged, possibly for the first time in its history, to assess its own functioning.

The group may also be given a more elaborate rating form to complete at noon or towards the end of the first day. This form would help to assess the group feelings about team work from a number of standpoints. The data would be tallied and averaged and fed back to the group. A sample form is given in "My Perceptions About My Boss," Appendix 49.

As a practical device to assist the team in its assignment and discussion of trust, consideration might be given to use of the instrument "The Trusting Relationship—How I See It in Our Team," Appendix 49a. Team members could be asked to provide their perceptions of trust on the instrument's 15 elements. The results should then be tallied (group average per element) and discussed as to (a) accuracy (consensual feeling) of a given rating and, hopefully, (b) how mediocre or low ratings could be elevated.

GIVING FEEDBACK

It is (or should be) obvious from what has been said in the prior pages that a key to success in team building is the ability to give feedback effectively. The instrument "Feedback—My Skill/Attitude Pro-file," Appendix 53, might be used to appraise one's prowess as a giver of feedback. While the use of the form may be beneficial if used totally on a "self-help" basis, much more significant results will ensue if it is processed in, say, trios. The triad will provide the intimacy and safety needed for sharing as well as external motivation (via two other team members) to stay with the task fully.

The instrument should be used at a stage in the program—midway or later—when participants realize clearly why they are here and the importance of giving feedback properly.

EVALUATION OF THE TEAM-BUILDING EFFORT

As every trainer knows, management training is far easier to deliver than it is to evaluate. This follows since after a management development seminar or workshop, all return to their original environment where the pressures to perform in the old way tend to undo the new learning and the best of participant intentions.

Team building, on the other hand, is a lot harder to pull off successfully than it is to evaluate. For if the team development has succeeded, the results will be quite apparent in terms of both "soft" (attitudinal) and "hard" (quantitative) data.

Let's consider, then, soft data or indicators of how people feel about team work one to six months after the training is completed. We can use various attitude survey instruments to measure change and current satisfaction with the new way of doing things. We can ask team members how they feel about teamness in general or various aspects of it, such as cooperation, communication, climate, creativity, problem solving, decision making, leadership, trust, and clarity of goals.

We can also secure harder data in terms of specific and measurable end results. Here are some indicators:

☐ Roles are clearly defined.
☐ Goals are established by the team and are clear to everyone.
☐ Policies have been established or revised.

☐ Procedures/systems have been set up to make operations efficient.

☐ Study groups/task forces are established and are readying action plans to implement decisions agreed to in the team-building sessions.

☐ A schedule is set up for continuing team-building sessions.

☐ When the team meets, quite often process matters (how we operate as a group and interpersonally) are examined rather than ignored or taken for granted.

☐ Relations with external groups are improved.

☐ There is less dependence on the trainer, who may not be brought in very much or at all.

☐ Delegation is greater (deeper and more authentic).

☐ Greater opportunities for training (professional growth) are taking place.

☐ Group decision making is a norm.

☐ Costs have been reduced.

☐ Turnover may be reduced.

☐ Budgets are adhered to.

☐ Service to customers is better.

☐ Profitability (if a profit center) is improved.

☐ New and better products/services are being introduced.

FACILITATOR TRAINING FOR LEADERS OF SELF-DIRECTED TEAMS (SDTS)

A growing number of organizations have been creating self-directed teams (also known as self-directed work teams and high-performance teams). A 1995 study by the University of Southern California's Center for Effective Organizations indicated that about two-thirds of U.S. companies are experimenting with self-managed teams, up from only about one-fourth of all firms in 1987 [17].

SDTs are an outgrowth of the Quality Circle movement of the 1970's and early 1980's. The driving force of SDTs has been the need to compete more effectively in a highly competitive global market. More effective competition requires constant improvement in quality of products and customer service, which must be accomplished at lower cost and in speedier fashion.

By way of definition, Bob and Ann Harper define the SDT as a work group of 5–15 employees

> . . . who are responsible for a whole product or process. The team plans the work and performs it, managing many of the things supervision or management used to do.
>
> The team meets regularly (once a week or every day) to identify, analyze, and solve problems. They may schedule, set goals, give performance feedback, hire, fire, etc. The team's duties grow with their skills. They aren't expected to do all these things at the beginning; their responsibilities are increased as their new skills are mastered and the team grows and develops [18].

SDTs may have a leader chosen for them, or the team may select one. In either case, a trained facilitator is essential to help the team get started and stay on track thereafter. As the team learns to work together effectively, its dependence on the facilitator decreases.

What does a facilitator do? An erroneous assumption is that he/she is just a good meeting leader. Another misconception is that he/she functions as a judge, teacher, or leader. In reality, the facilitator is a motivator/encourager, helping people to discover themselves. In more specific terms, the facilitator assumes these distinct roles [19]:

☐ *Role model.* Facilitators are carefully chosen people from line management who are then trained in facilitation skills, process improvement, and problem-solving methods. These individuals have high credibility; employees on the SDTs can thus readily identify with them and strive to emulate their behavior.

☐ *Catalyst.* The role here is to be a driving force for critical thinking, to attack the "tried and true" way of doing things in order to promote forward movement. The facilitator's role, then, is to get people excited about constant improvement.

☐ *Meeting manager.* Note that many SDT members never attended meetings. So the facilitator, trained in group dynamics and possessed of group process skills, uses his/her skills to draw people out, to keep discussions on track, and to assist people in reaching consensus. He/she also has to be able to diagnose issues and to know if the team is staying on (or straying from) the objective. Allied to these skills is the ability to create a "safe" atmosphere so that people won't be afraid to open up and to say what they think and feel.

Note, too, that because of downsizing there are fewer people to do the work. So poor, rambling meetings can't be tolerated.

☐ *Trainer/consultant.* The role here is to function as an internal consultant and trainer. Facilitators use these skills to start new teams; to mentor; to support people; to maintain team momentum; to give process management advice; to trouble shoot; to provide needed "just-in-time" training as opposed to waiting for classroom training opportunities.

☐ *Guide and goad.* New groups typically work their way through four stages before they become a true team: *forming, storming, norming,* and *performing.* Each stage permits new accomplishments until the last stage is reached. It's the facilitator's job to make certain that the team doesn't get "stuck" on any one of the earlier stages and that it moves through the stages very rapidly.

In *forming,* Stage One, the goal is to overcome the early limited focus and the presence of many competing hidden agendas. During Stage Two, *storming,* team members challenge each other because of these hidden agendas. In *norming,* roles are now clarified and established, and operating rules and standards are developed. Having worked its way through the first three stages, the team is now ready to begin *performing.*

☐ *Peacemaker.* Conflict management skills are another asset of the facilitator. Managing conflict extends not only to within-the-group disagreements, but also to conflict with other groups and the total organization. Typical issues to resolve relate to subgrouping, hidden agendas, and unwillingness of individuals to compromise.

☐ *Coach/mentor.* A key task of the facilitator is to win the confidence of the team leader so that he/she sees the former as his/her personal coach. The facilitator works toward the goal of having the team leader become the team facilitator. In effect, he/she works himself/herself out of a job.

To ensure that the facilitators in the organization can execute the above roles well, these areas must be considered:

1. *Define the overall facilitator job.* If the task is to help teams get started, full-time consultants who move from one team to another are best. If the purpose is to help meetings proceed well, it is essential to give facilitator training to everyone who runs meetings. Or the organization can establish a facilitator pool and employees can choose the facilitator they'd like for each meeting.

   If the goal is long-term guidance of the SDTs, team leaders should be trained as facilitators. One way to do this involves the mentor approach—the facilitator stays with the teams in one function (division) for about two years and then moves on to another division to help it organize around teams. Another approach is to have no managers, only facilitators, people who help employees as opposed to telling them what to do.

2. *Provide training in leadership skills.* Typical skills include total quality management concepts and techniques; introducing and guiding change; leading and facilitating teams; group development and group dynamics; conflict resolution; assessment of individual styles; problem-solving and decision-making skills; facilitator interventions—when and how to do it; stimulating creativity; managing meetings; listening skills; dealing with dysfunctional behaviors.

   Obviously, the above skills cannot all be learned quickly. So management has to temper its desire for quick, visible results in order to accept the realistic time interval it takes to develop cooperative teams and to get facilitators up to full speed.

3. *Provide facilitator training in a safe environment.* The candidates selected for this training

may not have previously been in a leadership role, so they need a chance to experience mistakes in a non-punitive atmosphere. To grow and succeed, heavy repeated practice is paramount.

4. *Allow enough time for skill development.* A facilitator who functions well will require about a year of training. He/she will need to observe and then to take over at meetings in order to learn when to intervene and how to adapt each skill to varying circumstances. Facilitators should be debriefed after each tryout.

As is apparent from the above discussion, the facilitator's job encompasses much more than ensuring that meetings go well. It also entails furthering team cohesion between meetings. As one training director terms it, it means a lot of "schmoozing" and "butterflying" [20].

"Schmoozing" involves checking with team members to learn how things are going and whether help is needed. It also entails generally "hanging out" and building good will.

"Butterflying" means bringing team members together to help one another. (Visualize butterflies helping flowers spread their pollen.) This role is also essential when anger and/or heavy disagreement arise. The trick is to restore peace and to exit promptly.

KEY POINTS

1. Supervisory and management development, however effective, can only deliver improvement in individual skills. If the broader management concern of effective work group functioning is to be addressed, team building has to be undertaken.

2. Team building must start with full understanding and support by the team leader. This means a candid facing up to key problems, a true desire for participative management, and a willingness to receive feedback about one's own functioning as a leader.

3. Team building has to proceed with careful groundwork in the form of interviews/questionnaires by the trainer to secure data about the team's functioning. Data collection relates to work problems, process factors, interpersonal relationships, and system impacts.

4. Typically, the initial team-building effort takes place for two to three days, away from the demands and routines of the office.

5. Early team-building activities are designed to establish rapport, mutuality, trust, open lines of communication, and so on.

6. As the team-building program develops, the group begins to look at its own functioning, goals, policies, relationships, and barriers to effectiveness.

7. Typical training tools that are used include small group work, fishbowls, dyads, triads, instrumentation, role negotiation, brainstorming, and feedback (giving and receiving).

8. A successful team-building effort results in a positive resolve to "do better." This takes the form of concrete action plans to meet key problems head on.

9. Follow-up sessions are generally necessary to keep the resolve alive.

10. The best team-building effort is one wherein the work team is able (learns) to function effectively with little or no dependence on the trainer.

REFERENCES

1. Looran, James, "The Transition Meeting: Taking Over a New Management Team," *Supervisory Management* (September 1985), pp. 29–36.

2. Woodman, Richard W., "Team Development versus T Group Training," *Group and Organization Studies* (June 1980), pp. 135–143.

3. Quoted in Solomon, Charlene M., "Simulation Training Builds Teams Through Experience," *Personnel Journal* (June 1993), pp. 100–108.

4. Weisbord, Marvin R., "Team Effectiveness Theory," *Training and Development Journal* (January 1985), pp. 27–29.

5. Barner, Robert W., "The Right Tool for the Job," *Training and Development Journal* (July 1989), pp. 46–51.

6. The NASA and Broken Squares exercises are in Pfeiffer, J. W., and Jones, J. E., *A Handbook of Structured Experiences for Human Relations Training,* Vol. I, University Associates Publishers, San Diego (1969). For a vivid description of how the Broken Squares worked in one team-building session, see Hines, W. W., "Increasing Team Effectiveness," *Training and Development Journal* (February 1980), pp. 80–82.

7. Johnson, Cynthia R., "An Outline for Team Building," *Training* (January 1986), pp. 48–52.

8. For a detailed discussion of this tool, see Miller, N., "The Accountability Chart—A Tool for Team Building," *Personnel* (November–December 1977), pp. 51–56.

9. Steel, F., and Jenks, S., *The Feel of the Work Place: Understanding and Improving Organization Climate,* Addison-Wesley, Reading, Mass. (1977), p. 163.

10. Rubin, I. M., Plovnick, M. S., and Fry, R. E., *Task Oriented Team Development,* McGraw-Hill, New York (1978).

11. "Involve Your People in Organizational Team Building," *Training and Development Journal* (July 1987), pp. 73–74.

12. MacLaurin, Sue, "A Real-Life Communications Model," *Training and Development Journal* (March 1991), pp. 79–80.

13. Hines, W. W., "Increasing Team Effectiveness," *Training and Development Journal* (February 1980), p. 79.

14. Lynch, Robert, "The Shout Out Among Non Team Players," *Training* (January 1986), pp. 48–52.

15. Cooper, Colleen R., and Ploor, Mary L., "The Challenges That Make or Break a Group," *Training and Development Journal* (April 1986), pp. 31–33.

16. "Non-verbal Introductions Can Get Self-conscious Trainees to Open Up," *Creative Training Techniques Newsletter,* Lakewood Publications Inc. (June 1994), p. 6.

17. "Teams Are the Management Fad, but Do They Work?" *Washington Post* (October 22, 1995).

18. Harper, Bob and Ann, *Succeeding as A Self-directed Work Team,* MW Corporation, Croton-on-the-Hudson, New York (1991).

19. Kaeter, Margaret, "Facilitators: More Than Meeting Leaders," *Training* (July 1995), pp. 60–64.

20. Sisco, Rebecca, "What to Teach Team Leaders," *Training* (February 1993), pp. 63–67.

RECOMMENDED READING

Cooper, Colleen R., and Ploor, Mary L., "The Challenges That Make or Break a Group," *Training and Development Journal,* April 1986, pp. 31–33.

The writers discuss procedures to help groups accomplish their work effectively: introductions, agendas, ground rules, voting vs. consensus in decision making, the use of personality preference indicators such as the MBTI. Of particular interest from a team-building standpoint is dealing with two prime issues: (1) Purpose ("What business are we in, anyway?") and (2) SWOT Analysis ("What are our strengths, weaknesses, opportunities, and threats?").

Goodale, James G., "Employee Involvement Sparks Diagnostic Conferences," *Personnel Journal,* February 1987, pp. 79–87.

The article presents an account of a team-building effort entailing diagnostic analysis by *employees.* The employees discussed problems in their departments, and causes of poor communication and teamwork, and recommended changes and improvements.

Dyer, William G., *Team Building: Issues and Alternatives,* 2nd edition, Addison-Wesley, Reading, Mass., 1987.

This is a comprehensive treatment of the subject covering rationale, methods, implementation, design options, special situations such as the new team and the complacent team, and interteam conflict.

Fordyce, J., and Weil, R., *Managing with People: A Manager's Handbook of Organization Development Methods,* Addison-Wesley, Reading, Mass., 1971.

The book treats in detail the many technologies for developing teams and bringing about change. Coverage extends from methods of data collection to methods for the conduct of team-building sessions.

Laabs, Jennifer J., "Team Training Goes Outdoors," *Personnel Journal,* June 1991, pp. 56–63.

The article discusses the objectives, nature, and values of team building involving various outdoor, physical activities. Examples of such activities include rock and mountain climbing, hiking through the desert with temperatures in the 90's, deep water rafting, and engaging in outdoor exercises such as confronting an eight-foot wall or crossing a stream via an overhead rope.

Margerison, Charles, Davies, Rod, and McCain, Dick, "High-Flying Management Development," *Training and Development Journal,* February 1987, pp. 38–41.

The article describes how an Australian airline developed crew members (generally regarded as technicians rather than managers) by sharpening their *management* skills. The reason? Team management in the cockpit is essential to flying a modern jet airliner. Joint training in decision making, communication, conflict management, etc., is a must, particularly if the crew is to cope effectively in pressure situations.

Miller, Barry W., and Phillips, Ronald C., "Team Building on a Deadline," *Training and Development Journal,* March 1986, pp. 54–57.

The article discusses a successful team-building effort among warring project managers in an Ohio electric utility company.

"Nurses Build a Multi-Shift Team," *Training and Development Journal,* October 1984, pp. 14–15.

This brief article describes how nurses on a 24-hour, three-shift schedule developed an effective work team. One interesting end-product: a statement of agreement about what the manager will do (for example, give more positive feedback) and what the manager will ask the staff to do (for example, "remind me that you need more information," "remind me when I'm being abrupt").

Reilly, Anthony I., and Jones, John E., "Team Building," in Pfeiffer, J. William, and Jones, John E., *The 1974 Annual Handbook for Group Facilitators,* University Associates Publishers, San Diego, 1974, pp. 227–237.

This covers the whole sequence of team building, including its goals, consultant's role, role of games and simulations, issues, effective problem solving, planning the team-building session, coaching the team leader, conducting the session.

Thiagarajan, Sivasailam, and Parker, Glenn, "Teamness and Teamplay: Games and Activities for Building and Training Teams," Jossey-Bass Pfeiffer, San Francisco, 1999.

Two long-time trainers provide insights on effective teamwork and facilitation and provide over 35 team-orientated activities: games, exercises, and simulations. These activities are designed to develop skills in idea generation, self-directed training, consensus building, problem solving, and conflict resolution.

Weisbord, Marvin R., "Team Effectiveness Theory," *Training and Development Journal,* January 1985, pp. 27–29.

A long-time management consultant and team builder presents an insightful overview of team-building concepts and procedures.

Woodcock, Mike, *Team Development Manual,* John Wiley and Sons, New York, 1979.

In addition to general background about how to improve team performance, this provides 45 activities (exercises) and nine lecturettes for facilitator use in the training situation.

Woodcock, Mike, and Francis, Dave, *Organization Development Through Team Building: Planning a Cost Effective Strategy,* John Wiley and Sons, New York, 1981.

This is not a how-to-do-it book, but rather a tool to think through whether you should attempt team building. Some factors the book suggests you consider are whether poor teamwork is a significant problem, whether the organization's culture supports team operations, team readiness, and skills available to do the job.

Woodcock, Mike, and Francis, Dave, *Unblocking Your Organization,* University Associates Publishers, San Diego, 1978.

This contains numerous activities (exercises, instruments, etc.) useful for the team-building facilitator.

14 The In-Basket Exercise—How to Conduct and Design It

Many persons might have achieved wisdom had they not supposed that they already possessed it.

—Seneca, Roman philosopher and author (B.C. 4?–65 A.D.)

THE in-basket exercise is a management simulation designed to provide skill practice in problem solving and decision making. It is composed of a set of 15–20 items, more or less interrelated, which have to be acted upon in a relatively short time frame under considerable pressure.

The completed in-basket is subsequently analyzed and discussed by the group, thereby giving the participants an opportunity to receive feedback about their prowess as decision makers. The feedback may also reveal strengths and weaknesses in other leadership/managerial skills such as communication, motivation, delegation, planning, and time management.

What might participants derive from an in-basket activity in the way of specific learning or benefits? The following are typical end results:

1. Skill in problem solving and decision making should be strengthened. More specifically, participants are challenged to note the interrelatedness of items awaiting action, to respect the importance and urgency of problems (prioritizing), and to take appropriate (logical) action in a short time period.

2. They may also learn that it is all too easy to over-emphasize, under-emphasize, or overlook various elements which relate to the decision-making process.

3. Conceptually, participants should learn that there is no "best" way to handle (decide upon) a managerial problem. This learning comes about through exchange and discussion of the actions taken.

4. The importance of utilizing staff in working on day-to-day problems also comes through quite clearly.

5. Participants can possibly learn to coordinate matters with colleagues and superiors.

6. Effective time management skills are usually developed.

7. New managers may be expected to learn about the kinds of problems they are quite certain to encounter, as well as how to go about resolving them.

WORKING WITH THE IN-BASKET

To appreciate more fully how participants operate in relation to the in-basket, let's examine the situation that exists when the in-basket is first encountered in the exercise.

Typically, the participant, in the role of manager, is about to report for duty on a new job. The new assignment has come up suddenly. He/she is to succeed someone who has just transferred, retired, died of a heart attack, etc. The visit to his/her new office is very brief—60–90 minutes, sometimes 2 hours. Why the short visit? Because he/she has to catch a plane to go to headquarters to work on a special project, or attend an important conference, or take a field trip, or attend a three-to-four-day management seminar.

What is the purpose of the visit to the new office? To check the in-basket to see if there is anything which may require attention (must be "handled") before going off on the required trip.

When does the visit to the office take place? Unfortunately, at a time when no staff members are available—Sunday evening, Saturday afternoon, possibly a weekday morning at 7:00 A.M., Friday evening at 5:30 P.M., or the like. (As we said, this is just before flight time, so one cannot dally.)

And what are the conditions under which one attacks the in-basket? Not only are there no staff members present because of the time of day, but typically the secretary has just gone on annual leave or is hospitalized ("I'll be back in a week. Sorry I wasn't there to help you."). Also, the manager's immediate assistant has just been killed in a private plane crash; the telephone switchboard is unmanned and inoperative or is simply out of order; the file cabinets are locked; the photocopier is in a locked office, which means that one cannot make copies of any items to take along for further study, but must act now.

So what do all these harrowing circumstances add up to for our manager, as decision maker?

1. The pressure is on!

2. The in-box must be examined in a short time frame (one to two hours).

3. No one can be reached now for advice or to give oral instructions.

4. Instructions to staff, if any, can only be given in the form of short notes, either scribbled on the in-basket item or written on slips which are clipped or stapled to it.

5. All action is taken solely on the basis of the information in the in-basket, even though there may be information voids, irrelevant facts, or conflicting information.

Are the limitations and pressures contained in this simulation likely to produce a feeling that this is not a very realistic situation? Not at all, for managers typically work with the in-basket and often find themselves in pressure-laden situations. Also, the problems themselves are plausible.

THE IN-BASKET EXERCISE— ADVANTAGES AND LIMITATIONS

An in-basket has a number of advantages:

1. It can provide participants with materials for analysis which are marked by a high degree of realism. What is more natural than for a manager to "attack" an in-basket?

2. It is a truly inexpensive form of training for managers. Most trainers should be able to study the guidelines for the construction of an in-basket exercise described herein, plus the models provided here and elsewhere, and create an engrossing and high-impact learning tool. (Of course, the trainer should have experienced the in-basket activity, too.)

3. It is a flexible tool and thus can be used in a variety of ways: as the basis for a rather comprehensive management training program or as an adjunct to such a course; for general and/or more specialized managers; with or without small group work in the evaluation phase of the activity. Also, the content (examples) may be closely work-related or more general in character; the individual analysis and group evaluation phases may be separated timewise by several days if necessary.

4. Since the basic work-analysis of the in-basket is done on an individual basis, there is no problem of self-consciousness arising among participants. Other management training techniques, such as role playing, and certain exercises may present this problem for some managers.

5. It helps to "pep up" the training program.

Some limitations of the in-basket are these:

1. The total time of the in-basket activity is fairly extensive. While the individual processing of the in-basket is ordinarily limited to one hour or so, the subsequent group-in-action work (analysis phase) takes two or three hours. (On the other hand, the time investment is worthwhile if real learning ensues. In fact, some trainers may argue that the long time element is what gives the activity its impact.)

2. For the trainer, considerable detail is involved in preparing and reproducing letters, memos, etc., to give them an authentic look. Also, large amounts of materials have to be carefully assembled; for example, visualize an in-basket of 15–20 items for 15–20 participants. Obviously each packet of items must be complete and assembled in its appropriate order. Duplicates must be avoided.

3. The moderator/facilitator must both be skilled in working with groups and possess the creativity, logic, perseverance, and management (or other) knowledge to develop an interesting, challenging, and technically sound in-basket. Not all trainers might meet these multi-faceted qualifications. (Of course, in-basket materials can be purchased from publishers of training materials. They may also be found in books.)

HOW TO DESIGN YOUR OWN IN-BASKET

While in-baskets may be obtained from various publishers, you may wish to tailor-make your own. This procedure will allow you to include problems typical of your own organization. The greater realism of and interest in such materials should help to augment participant learning. Also, by avoiding the off-the-shelf product, you may keep your costs down. Of course, a printed in-basket from a publisher may look more polished than your own.

In any case, here are the steps you should follow if you wish to design your own in-basket.

Step 1: Study Several In-Baskets

This procedure will give you a feel for their general thrust, style, format, tempo, etc. These materials are available in books and from publishers of such materials. Colleagues may also be helpful in this regard.

Step 2: Selection of Subject Matter

In designing an in-basket for managers, you have these choices as to subject matter:

☐ *General character.* The items in the in-basket can be *general* in nature, that is, applicable and of interest to *all* managers, regardless of their organizational affiliation. Our goal in this situation is, of course, to provide practice in analyzing and resolving management problems. In other words, just so there is a good mix of problems, with enough elements of complexity, challenge, pressure, realism, and interrelatedness, the precise nature of the items in the in-basket matters very little, if at all. Our assumption here is that all managers, whether general or more specialized (for example, finance, engineering), regardless of who their employees may be, will identify with and learn from the problems presented in our in-box.

Thus we could have items related to personnel management, budgets, public relations, customer relations, communication, production, safety, marketing, etc., all of them relating to a fictitious organization. This type of in-basket would fit in well in a general management seminar or a leadership program, either in-house or one available to the general public.

☐ *Specialized character.* We could also design our in-basket to have these special appeals:

1. To managers in particular organizations such as banks; hospitals; various state, federal, or city government agencies; schools; manufacturing plants; or retail enterprises.

2. To managers engaged in particular job specializations such as engineering personnel, finance, manufacturing, or R&D.

☐ *In-house character.* In this type of in-basket we select the items carefully by subject, because our goal is to present opportunities to deal with and thus learn about typical in-house problems, for example, our marketing matters, our personnel concerns, our budgeting problems, our customer complaints, our vendor relations, and other problems peculiar to the operations of our enterprise or organization.

Step 3: Selection of In-Basket Topics

Now that we know the general character and direction of our in-basket, we are ready to select specific in-basket topics. A good way to do this is to meet with a committee composed of several knowledgeable, training-oriented management officials. They can give us guidance concerning the emphasis our in-basket should take—problems relating to finance, production, human relations and communication, marketing, customer and vendor relations, community relations, etc.

Specific items for the in-basket may be drawn from actual problems encountered in dealing with other managers, employees, suppliers, or customers. Or they may be invented, drawing on our general familiarity with the problems involved. The in-baskets of colleagues may also provide us with models for adaptation.

Step 4: Guidelines for a Quality In-Basket

Our in-basket can be provocative of thought, challenging, and realistic, or it can be received with a "so what?" reaction. To ensure the former response, attention to these skill pointers should be given.

☐ Strive for a good mix of items; have an in-basket containing the following:

1. Crisis-type items (one or two); these are items which give the in-basket interest, challenge, excitement. (Position-wise, they could be placed at the middle or near the end of the in-basket and suddenly loom very significantly.)

2. Other substantive items, that is, real problems of considerable magnitude or complexity. Examples: budget matters, complaints, personnel concerns.

3. Interrelated items, those which affect or are affected by items 1 and 2 above.

4. Distractors or chaff, items which in themselves are minor and can be handled fairly easily. Of course, the chaff may be indicative or symptomatic of poor organizational functioning; for example, Why is the secretary not handling routine items? Why are anonymous complaints on personnel matters, in sealed envelopes, coming here? Why are subordinate managers dodging run-of-the-mill decisions or engaging in incomplete staff work?

☐ Strive for realism. This should be done not only with the selection of high-interest, relevant topics, but in the use of language and style contained in the items. Variety in written style will aid realism.

☐ Try to avoid repetitious items. They provide little added challenge and are likely to turn the participants off. If there is a fair amount of chaff in the in-basket, at least vary such materials.

☐ Use a mix of formats for the items: memos, letters, informal notes, reports, telephone slips, possibly e-mail and faxes.

☐ The use of humorous names on the in-basket items should help to keep participants chuckling and loose. Some examples are Edward Euphoria, Miles A. Way, I. M. Vigilant, Gordon Knott, John Nagg, John Sharp Quill, Otis B. Joiner, Y. B. Close, R. U. Meek, E. Z. Mark, John A. Quickwit, Rise N. Fast.

Fun-type names should be related to the role or character of the particular person. For example, an overly ambitious management trainee might be called E. Gore Beevore. Or an autocratic manager might be called Tigh Wrant.

☐ For added realism and help to the participant, include such aids as an organization chart and a calendar.

☐ The in-basket should be self-contained. That is, the problems being presented in all the items should be workable, to varying degrees, based on the information provided. Of course, relevant information concerning a problem may often be contained in two or three interrelated items rather than in just one. Or the nature of the item may be such that the participant may also have to "invent" information (make his/her own assumption about the facts).

☐ A workable in-basket may have 15–25 items, depending on (1) the time available for the analysis and (2) the complexity of the items themselves. An in-basket having considerable chaff would obviously have more items than one containing mostly relevant items.

☐ The traditional practice of creating a situation where there is no staff available for help, no telephones, no photocopier, etc., is essential. It ensures that decisions are made on all items. "Cop outs" such as "I'll check this out with personnel before I do anything at all" are thus avoided.

Step 5: Sequencing the In-Basket Items

Part of the challenge for our participants in attacking their in-basket is to be able to separate the wheat from the chaff; the urgent and demanding items from the inconsequential; the interrelated items from the independent ones; the old from the new (are we watching our dates?); the significant and symptomatic from the commonplace (are there bottlenecks, delays, crises, poor team relations, timidity-prone individuals, etc., possibly indicative of a less-than-well organization?).

Hence, a well-constructed in-basket will not only have items such as the above in it, but the items themselves will be arranged carefully to give the *appearance of randomness*. In this way, the manager's skill in winnowing out, prioritizing, and "inter-relating" is tested and hopefully developed.

Randomizing the in-basket items also provides for realism and a change of pace as well. An in-basket of serious items without a break would be a bit much.

Step 6: Try to Experience an In-Basket Yourself as a Learner

The wise trainer will try to become acquainted with the in-basket via a personal experience before he/she attempts to construct one. Why? Simply because there are considerable nuances and complexities built into a good in-basket. The personal experience will help you to appreciate those elements fully so that your in-basket will "hang together."

A Sample In-Basket

To explain the anatomy of the in-basket exercise better, we have provided an example.*

Provide each participant with the following:

☐ Twenty-five sheets from a notepad similar to that shown in Figure 14-1.

☐ Ten blank memos as shown in Figure 14-2.

☐ The instructions shown in Figure 14-3.

☐ The organizational chart in Figure 14-4.

---

*All memos, letters, and other handouts for the in-basket exercise may be copied directly or retyped to fit on regular 8½″ × 11″ paper.

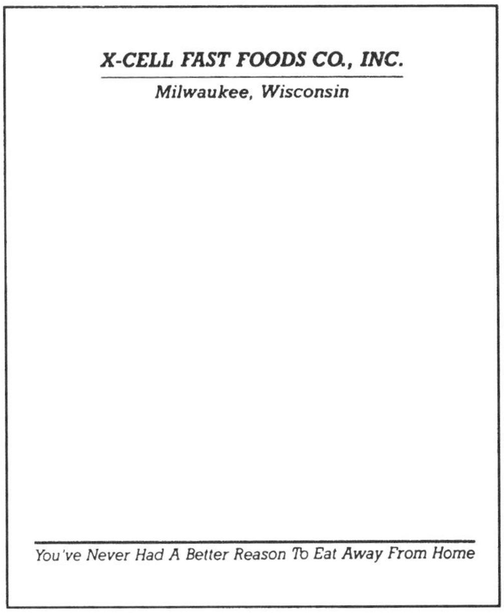

Figure 14-1. Sample of a sheet of a notepad to be provided to in-basket exercise participants.

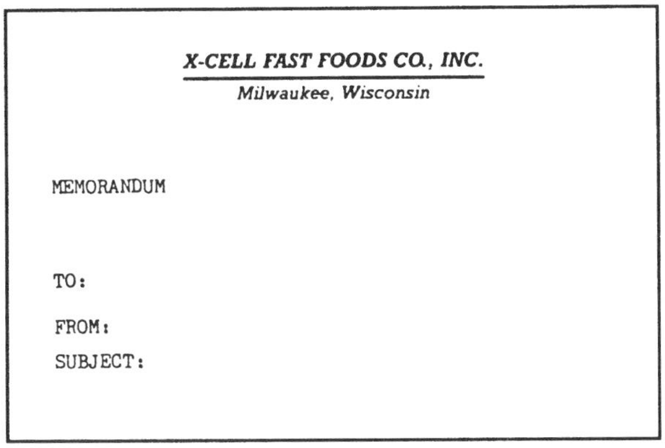

Figure 14-2. Sample memo to be used in in-basket exercise.

☐ The calendar shown in Figure 14-5.

☐ The memos found in Figure 14-6.

COMMENTS ON THE IN-BASKET PROBLEMS

In the paragraphs that follow, we offer an analysis of the various items in the in-basket. The comments should not be regarded as perfect solutions. Rather,

they present ideas on how these cases or incidents might be handled. It may be anticipated that group members will come up with other approaches, many being very innovative and highly workable as well.

It is suggested that the trainer carefully record participant solutions to the various problems for use with other groups at a later date. In this manner, one can amass a good set of management knowledge which can be shared with other participants.

Note: The best procedure is to go through the whole box to spot "must do" items and to bring related items together, *before* acting on anything.

☐ *August 13 Memo*—Give secretary a note to send condolences to Fran Beck's spouse. Secretary won't be back until August 23, but this is not a rush item.

☐ *Fax*—Some options: (1) Ask your subordinates via notes to them to work as a team and quickly check out other possible equipment deliveries. Put the same note on all staffers' desks and tell each to join with the others to work on this. (2) Cancel the equipment conference. This can be done via a note to a subordinate—put it on his/her desk and ask that action be taken to notify all regions of this.

Note: That a staff exists, and thus is available to provide help, is indicated by memo of July 5th from the personnel officer, which summarizes leave taken by all employees of the Branch of Operations.

Note that you cannot use your secretary to relay this message, for she won't be back until Monday, August 23, at the earliest. An interesting question: Could the boss's (the company president's) secretary be used to help out on this and other urgent matters?

☐ *August 8 Letter*—Routine—Tell secretary via note to respond with a letter of appreciation, for your signature. Also give secretary a note to send a copy of letter to the regional director for transmission to the restaurant manager concerned. *Note:* No hurry; this can await your secretary's return.

☐ *August 11 Memo*—Prepare note to secretary: "Sorry you're out, I'll see you when you return. Please keep in touch so we'll know when to expect you back." *Note:* Secretary will not be

(text continued on page 315)

Instructions to Participants

You are about to participate in an in-basket training experience. You have a packet of materials which simulates those found in the in-box of Ken Fixx.

You are Ken Fixx. You have just been promoted from the field to the position of Chief of Operations, X-Cell Fast Foods Co., Inc. (Congratulations!) X-Cell is a nation-wide chain of fast food restaurants, headquartered in Milwaukee, Wisconsin.

You were initially told to report for duty in Milwaukee on Monday, August 16. However, on Friday, August 13, you were told, instead, to report to a team-building session in Wild Woods Conference Center, near Houston, Texas, on Sunday evening, August 15.

You decided to visit your new office in Milwaukee before going on to Houston. Although you have only an hour and one-half before you catch your plane to Houston, you thought you might at least check out the in-basket. In this way you might be able to get on top of a few things, maybe make some photocopies of items worth taking along for further study on the plane. (By copying items, rather than taking originals, you leave the in-basket intact for others, such as your assistant, the boss' secretary, and/or your own, who may have need for certain items.)

You also hope to phone your secretary and assistant chief at their homes to let them know you've arrived and to say hello, and possibly to get background on some of the in-basket items. Also, you would like to let them know you won't be back until Thursday (August 19) due to the Houston team building session.

As you check things out in the office, you quickly learn that the switchboard is unmanned and calls can be neither made nor received, that the two file cabinets which might have provided you with background about some of the in-basket items are locked, and the photocopy machine is also locked. (You probably wouldn't know how to start this model even if it weren't locked.)

Given these circumstances, here are your instructions:

You are to examine the in-basket items and decide how to deal with all of them.

All the actions you take are to be written out. You have a memo pad, a notepad, paper clips and a stapler to help you on this. You can draft memos to your secretary or anyone else or give yourself notes. If you wish, you may write notes on any of the in-basket items themselves.

To sum up:

- You are Ken Fixx.
- This is Sunday, August 15, 12 P.M.
- You have 1 hour to act on the total in-basket. (The plane leaves in 1½ hours.)
- You must write down every action you take.
- Assistance from anyone is not available at all; you're entirely on your own.
- You can only work with the materials on hand. (A calendar and an organization chart are included as your aids.)
- No materials are to be taken to Houston.
- You will be back in the office on Thursday noon.
- If you're thinking that this is a heck of a way to start a new job, well, you may be right! But, then, as a former U.S. President once said: "Life is unfair."

Figure 14-3. These instructions should be distributed to all participants.

X-CELL FAST FOODS CO., INC.
Milwaukee, Wisconsin

```
                    ┌──────────────┐
         ┌──────────│  President   │──────────┐
┌────────────┐      └──────────────┘      ┌────────────┐
│ Comptroller│                            │    Legal   │
│            │                            │   Advisor  │
└────────────┘                            └────────────┘
```

| Real Estate | Operations | Management Information Systems | Personnel and Training | Administrative Services | Planning | Marketing |

| Region 1 (Philadelphia) | Region 2 (Atlanta) | Region 3 (Chicago) | Region 4 (Houston) | Region 5 (Los Angeles) |

Figure 14-4. The organization chart for the in-basket exercise.

July

S	M	T	W	T	F	S
				1	2	3
4	5	6	7	8	9	10
11	12	13	14	15	16	17
18	19	20	21	22	23	24
25	26	27	28	29	30	31

August

S	M	T	W	T	F	S
1	2	3	4	5	6	7
8	9	10	11	12	13	14
15	16	17	18	19	20	21
22	23	24	25	26	27	28
29	30	31				

September

S	M	T	W	T	F	S
			1	2	3	4
5	6	7	8	9	10	11
12	13	14	15	16	17	18
19	20	21	22	23	24	25
26	27	28	29	30		

Figure 14-5. The calendar needed by in-basket exercise participants.

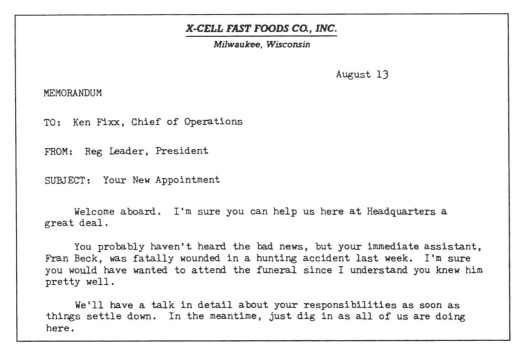

X-CELL FAST FOODS CO., INC.
Milwaukee, Wisconsin

                                                    August 13

MEMORANDUM

TO: Ken Fixx, Chief of Operations

FROM: Reg Leader, President

SUBJECT: Your New Appointment

    Welcome aboard. I'm sure you can help us here at Headquarters a great deal.

    You probably haven't heard the bad news, but your immediate assistant, Fran Beck, was fatally wounded in a hunting accident last week. I'm sure you would have wanted to attend the funeral since I understand you knew him pretty well.

    We'll have a talk in detail about your responsibilities as soon as things settle down. In the meantime, just dig in as all of us are doing here.

Figure 14-6A. This and the following figures show the material to be used for the in-basket exercise.

```
                              FAX

                                                   August 13

TO:  CHIEF, BRANCH OF OPERATIONS

RESTAURANT EQUIPMENT TRAILER IN ACCIDENT YESTERDAY.  DOUBTFUL IT WILL

ARRIVE IN TIME FOR DEMONSTRATION AT NEW EQUIPMENT CONFERENCE, THIS WEDNES-

DAY.  CAN YOU MAKE OTHER ARRANGEMENTS FOR THIS EQUIPMENT WITH APPROPRIATE

MANUFACTURERS?  TWENTY-FIVE PEOPLE DUE TO ATTEND.



                                        LEE GOODE

                                        REGIONAL DIRECTOR
                                        REGION #4

                                        HOUSTON
```

Figure 14-6B.

```
                                        1800 Dill Street
                                        Los Angeles, California
                                        August 8


President
X-CELL FAST FOODS CO., INC.
Milwaukee, Wisconsin



Dear Sir:

      My wife and I arrived at your Los Angeles restaurant #7 on July 20
near closing time.  We ate our meal and in our hurry to leave, I left my
briefcase which had some very important business papers.

      I needed those papers for a meeting early the next day.  To our sur-
prise, one of your employees, who lived near our neighborhood, delivered
the briefcase to our home the next morning at 7:45 A.M.

      We thought this was a very considerate act and felt compelled to
write to you about it.  We can assure you that your employee has made us
a friend of your restaurant chain for life.

                                   Sincerely,

                                   Mr. and Mrs. B.N. True
```

Figure 14-6C.

FROM THE DESK OF
Kim Rogers, Secretary/Operations

August 11

Dear Mr. Fixx:

I am very glad to learn that you will be heading up Operations.
We have a lot of problems, as you may know. But with your reputation
as a trouble-shooter, we should be in great shape shortly.

I have been called away to Orlando, Florida. My mother has just
been hospitalized with a bad back. I have to make arrangements to take
care of my younger brother and sister (ages 6 and 9) and help out at
home until mother can come home.

I would say I should be back by Monday, August 23, assuming all
goes well.

I hope I am not inconveniencing you too much.

Kim Rogers
Kim Rogers

Figure 14-6D.

X-CELL FAST FOODS CO., INC.
Milwaukee, Wisconsin

August 10

MEMORANDUM

TO: Burton Quagmeyer, Chief, Operations Branch

FROM: Win Learnwell, Corporate Training Officer

SUBJECT: Coaching and Counseling Course

Our plans are firming up for the Coaching and Counseling Course.
All we need to do to get moving on this is your appointment of two
trainers from each of our five regions. They will be responsible for
training supervisors in their respective regions.

The training is set for the last two days of this month. We have
three University resource people lined up to train the trainers at that
time. The trainer course will take place in Chicago.

Do you see any problems with any of this?

Figure 14-6E.

X-CELL FAST FOODS CO., INC.
Milwaukee, Wisconsin

August 9

MEMORANDUM

TO: Burton Quagmire, Chief, Operations Branch

FROM: Bobby McGee, Assistant Manager, Restaurant #4, Boston

SUBJECT: Management at Restaurant #4

    I don't know how much you know about management at Restaurant #4 here in Boston, but things are really bad. Morale is low; turnover is high; the boss plays favorites; costs are up because of wasted food and failure to observe energy regulations.

    I know I'm out of channels in writing to you, but the regional office doesn't seem to know what's going on. The Regional Director visits here fairly often, but the boss wines and dines him and generally snows him. The only reason we're making a profit is because we're near the two schools (public and private high schools). With half-way decent management we could do a lot better.

Sorry to have to bring this up in this way, but in view of the circumstances, I didn't feel I could go directly to anyone in Region 1.

Figure 14-6F. This item came in a sealed envelope marked "Personal and Confidential," addressed to the Chief, Branch of Operations. The trainer should provide an envelope for this item. Place the memo in it and seal it.

SOUTHERN WISCONSIN DIABETES ASSOCIATION
Madison, Wisconsin

August 6

Burton Quagmeyer
Chief, Operations Branch
X-CELL FAST FOODS CO., INC
1219 Glendon Dr.
Milwaukee, Wisconsin

Dear Mr. Quagmeyer:

    Just a note to indicate that we are glad that you will represent your organization at our planning meeting here in Madison on August 20.

    Nationally, some 600,000 people will be told this year that they have diabetes. We have our share of that number in Southern Wisconsin. So I know you will want to attend the meeting to help our campaign get launched well.

    We shall look forward to seeing you at the kickoff meeting.

Sincerely,

R.W. Felton

R.W. Felton
President

Figure 14-6G.

X-CELL FAST FOODS CO., INC.

Region #4 Office
Houston, Texas

August 2

MEMORANDUM

TO: Burton Quagmeyer, Chief, Branch of Operations

FROM: Lee Goode, Regional Director

SUBJECT: New Equipment Demonstration and Conference

    As the host for the New Equipment Demonstration and Conference, I wish to tell you we're all set to go.

    As I've been telling anyone who will listen, this conference is a darn good thing. We need to update our kitchen ranges, dishwashers and other small equipment items as well.

    I expect the demonstration restaurant equipment trailer to arrive here August 11 or 12. We can check everything out with plenty of time to spare for the August 18 Conference.

    I have lined up two reps from each of the five regional offices plus several restaurant facility managers in each region. This should be a total group of about 25 keenly interested people.

    We'll keep you posted on the results of all this.

    Sorry you couldn't make it to Houston.

Figure 14-6H.

X-CELL FAST FOODS CO., INC.

Region #2 Office
Atlanta, Georgia

July 26

MEMORANDUM

TO: Burton Quagmeyer, Chief, Branch of Operations

FROM: Val Sanders, Regional Officer, Region 2

SUBJECT: Proposal for Conference of Regional Officers

    It's been over two years since we last had a Regional Officers' Conference. Problems are piling up and a good week-long discussion on these matters should help us a lot.

    We'll be glad to host the conference here in Atlanta. Just give us enough lead time so we can do the job properly.

Figure 14-6I.

X-CELL FAST FOODS CO., INC.
Milwaukee, Wisconsin

July 23

MEMORANDUM

TO: Burton Quagmeyer, Chief, Operations Branch

FROM: R.V. Reddy, Chief, Administrative Services Branch

SUBJECT: Security in Urban Restaurant Facilities

    I think we have to take another look at the security problem in
our big city facilities. Our break-ins are running well ahead of last
year and the year is only about half up.

    Since we purchased the heavy safes, on our recommendation, we haven't
been losing any money between 11 P.M. and 7:00 A.M. But there have been
break-ins for food after we close up at 11 P.M., and hold ups at night
(9:00 to 11 P.M.) are increasing.

    We can plug most of these leaks, but cost will be a big factor to
consider.

    How about exploring this further at lunch soon?

Figure 14-6J.

X-CELL FAST FOODS CO., INC.
Milwaukee, Wisconsin

July 20

MEMORANDUM

TO: Chief, Branch of Operations

FROM: Comptroller

SUBJECT: 5-Year Plan

    At our next meeting of our planning group, August 23, 9:00 A.M.,
we will get into the actual numbers - revenue projections, expenditures,
the whole bit.

    You should be prepared to give the other budget team members your
data for their review.

Figure 14-6K.

X-CELL FAST FOODS CO., INC.

Milwaukee, Wisconsin

July 14

MEMORANDUM

TO: Burton Quagmeyer, Chief, Operations Branch

FROM: Kyle Pyle, Chief, Planning Branch

SUBJECT: Food Industry Conference

    I intend to take in the fast food industry conference in September. The agenda features several sessions dealing with economic and social trends affecting our functions. I would be delighted to have you join me.

        Place: New York City
        Dates: September 20-22

    Let me know and I'll have my secretary register and hotel both of us at the same time.

    While we're in the East we might also visit the Philadelphia Regional Office. Is this O.K.?

Figure 14-6L.

CITY MANAGEMENT ASSOCIATION
MILWAUKEE, WISCONSIN

July 12

Burton Quagmeyer
Chief, Branch of Operations
X-Cell Fast Foods Co., Inc.
1219 Glendon Dr.
Milwaukee, Wisconsin

Dear Burton:

    Since your organization has been going ahead full blast on Quality Circles (at least two of your regions are gung-ho on this), I thought you might want to share your Q.C. experience with our group.

    Could we "sign you up" to handle the September meeting? This would be a good start for our fall programming.

    Let me know of your acceptance so I can get notices out. (We meet the fourth Thursday of the month.) We may invite the Madison Chapter to attend and make this a joint meeting.
    Regards.

                    Cordially,

                    Dee Scission

Figure 14-6M.

X-CELL FAST FOODS CO., INC.
Milwaukee, Wisconsin

July 9

MEMORANDUM

TO: Burton Quagmeyer, Chief, Operations Branch

FROM: Mann Powers, Chief, Personnel and Training Branch

SUBJECT: Turnover and Absenteeism at Restaurant Facilities in Major Cities

I thought you would be interested in personnel turnover and absentee rates in our big city operations. They are about twice the rates of our other operations. The figures are for the first 6 months of this year.

	Turnover	Absenteeism
Atlanta	15%	10%
Chicago	18%	12%
Philadelphia	20%	11%
Los Angeles	22%	13%
Pittsburgh	19%	15%
Boston	24%	10%

May we discuss this? The figures are disappointing considering that we pay well and all our supervisors have had that one week course in supervision.

Figure 14-6N.

X-CELL FAST FOODS CO., INC.
Milwaukee, Wisconsin

July 5

MEMORANDUM

TO: Burton Quagmeyer, Chief, Branch of Operations

FROM: Mann Power, Chief, Branch of Personnel

SUBJECT: Leave Summary, Branch of Operations

The data below summarizes annual and sick leave taken (full days only), January 1 - June 30, by staff members of the Operations Branch, corporate headquarters:

	Annual	Sick
Burton Quagmeyer, Chief	10	1
Fran Beck, Assistant Chief	6	2
Jacques Frost, Operations Specialist	12	1
Wilde Oates, Operations Specialist	15	4
Sarah Chance, Operations Specialist	5	0
Kim Rogers, Secretary	10*	7
V.R. Tell, Clerk-Typist	3	3

* Plus 4 days LWOP

Figure 14-6O.

July 1

Burton Quagmeyer
Chief, Operations Branch
X-CELL FAST FOODS CO., INC.
1219 Glendale Dr.
Milwaukee, Wisconsin

Dear Mr. Quagmeyer:

  I am writing to you for the last time. And if I don't get an
appropriate cash settlement I shall have to bring suit about this.

  Your waitress in the Newark restaurant, No. 7, dropped that tray
of dishes on my neck last March and I haven't been able to move it
properly since.

  If you are a reliable company at all, you will see to it that my
claim is taken care of without further delay.

  I assure you that my next letter will be from my lawyer's office.

          Very truly yours,

          Les Payne

Figure 14-6P.

X-CELL FAST FOODS CO., INC.
Milwaukee, Wisconsin

July 1

MEMORANDUM

TO: Burton Quagmeyer, Chief, Operations Branch

FROM: Lotta Land, Chief Real Estate Branch

SUBJECT: Disposal of Urban Properties

 This memorandum is to encourage further thinking on the problem of
our big city restaurants. (See my memoranda of March 6th, May 12th
and June 15 on the same subject). These operations have good volume
but, as you know, they suffer from high turnover of personnel, vandalism,
break-ins, high waste ratios, and huge property taxes and so on. Their
annual net profit is always marginal compared to our other operations.

  But the big thing is that the properties could be sold at a very
handsome price and we could use that money to relocate elsewhere in
those metropolitan areas. We could go to locations where customer
parking is available, labor is more dependable, and have facilities
which are up to the standard of most of our other successful operations.

  I have asked your support before (see prior memos) to set up a
task force to really study this problem. I believe strongly that we should
move on this now.

Figure 14-6Q.

X-CELL FAST FOODS CO., INC.
Milwaukee, Wisconsin

June 30

MEMORANDUM

TO: Burton Quagmeyer, Chief, Operations Branch

FROM: Mann Power, Personnel Officer

SUBJECT: Employee Orientation

    I am setting up a special team to study employee orientation at all our facilities and in the regions and to make recommendations thereon.

    Could we have one of your staffers serve with us for 3 or 4 days, starting August 23?

    We'll be meeting in the Region 5 office for this.

    Thank you.

Figure 14-6R.

X-CELL FAST FOODS CO., INC.
Milwaukee, Wisconsin

June 15

MEMORANDUM

TO: Burton Quagmeyer, Chief, Operations Branch

FROM: Robin Well, Chief, Marketing Branch

SUBJECT: New Product Line

    Our consultant group is about ready to bring in its report. They seem to be ready to propose some serious changes in our evening menu.

    I don't think our equipment at the facilities could do the job.

    You may want to check this out with Operations Specialist Wilde Oates who has been keeping up on this possible development.

    Glad to discuss further.

Figure 14-6S.

X-CELL FAST FOODS CO., INC.
Milwaukee, Wisconsin

June 5

MEMORANDUM

TO: Burton Quagmeyer, Chief, Branch of Operations

FROM: Reg Leader, President

    I don't know whether or not you are thinking about another Regional Officers' meeting. I don't believe we've had one for three years now.

    We do have the funds to handle the travel, pay for outside speakers, etc.

    If you were to hold it early in November my schedule would permit my attendance for practically all of the first day.

Figure 14-6T.

X-CELL FAST FOODS CO., INC.
Milwaukee, Wisconsin

May 22

MEMORANDUM

TO: Burton Quagmeyer, Chief, Operations Branch

FROM: Win Learnwell, Corporate Training Officer

    Evidence is accumulating that MBO (Management by Objectives) is really working well in only one region - Region 2. I think the training we did on it two years ago got things off to a good start. But, somehow, the enthusiasm seems to be waning.

    We could do the training bit again, but I think the problem is deeper that that.

    Can we discuss soon ?

Figure 14-6U.

X-CELL FAST FOODS CO., INC.
Milwaukee, Wisconsin

March 29

MEMORANDUM

TO: Burton Quagmeyer, Chief, Operations Branch

FROM: Sandy Mandee, Comptroller

We have just completed a study of costs of restaurant operations by region. While one might expect some differences to exist, there really are some astounding differences in the operational figures among the five regions. Region # 1 is particularly bad in almost all the indicators we use.

We have the printouts, any time you want to go over them with me.

Some of this data might be worth discussing at a future Regional Officers' Conference.

Figure 14-6V.

X-CELL FAST FOODS CO., INC.
Milwaukee, Wisconsin

January 15

MEMORANDUM

TO: Burton Quagmeyer, Chief, Branch of Operations

FROM: Reg Leader, President

SUBJECT: Regional Operations Programming

My recent trip around the regions produced these items of interest for the Operations function:

1. There's some question whether our management development program for restaurant managers is doing what it was set up to do - namely, better human relations.

2. Equipment breakdowns and equipment obsolescence seem to be on everyone's mind.

3. A meeting of the Regional Officers seems to be overdue. Wasn't the last one held some $2\frac{1}{2}$ years ago ? If so, you may wish to look into this.

Figure 14-6W.

615 Smallwood Dr.
Boston, Mass.

January 5

President
X-CELL FAST FOODS CO., INC.
Milwaukee, Wisconsin

Dear Sir or Madam:

This letter is to let you know that I was never so shocked and insulted in a restaurant in my life. Several of your employees were openly soliciting tips on December 24. They had a soup bowl on the counter with quarters in it and a sign near it which said: "FOR OUR XMAS CHEER. THANK YOU." I passed by the bowl without tipping, however, and really received some dirty looks.

I thought you should know about this, which is why I am taking the trouble to write to you.

Sincerely,

J.M. Straight
J.M. Straight

P.S. This incident occurred in Restaurant #4 in Boston.

X-CELL FAST FOODS CO., INC.
Milwaukee, Wisconsin

Burton Quagmeyer:

Please look into this.

Thanks.

Reg Leader

2/15

You've Never Had A Better Reason To Eat Away From Home

Figure 14-6X.

there when you come back on Thursday, August 19; she hopes to be back on August 23, however.

☐ *August 10 Memo*—Give note directly to all your staff members to meet as a team and to select the trainers. (*Note:* Action is needed now since the training is coming up quickly, August 30 and 31. Also, as headquarters staff members, they should know how to work this out with the regional offices quite well.)

☐ *August 9 Memo in Sealed Envelope*—A serious item. Since you'll be going to Region 1 soon, you can save it for that time. Give yourself a note to do that. You may also wish to meet with your staff about this. (*Note:* Visit to Region 1 office is likely, per item of July 14. Also, an old

memo—March 29—reports on high operational costs in Region 1.)

☐ *August 6 Letter* (Diabetes Letter)—Options: (1) Give a staffer a note with instructions to attend for you. (2) Give a staffer a note to call R. W. Felton and express regrets, that you're brand new on the job and will be out of town until Thursday afternoon, so August 20 can't be handled.

☐ *August 2 Memo*—Just put with fax on the disabled truck problem. No action to take on this, if fax is being acted on.

☐ *July 26 Memo from Atlanta, Re: Need for Regional Conference*—There are two other items on this from the president. Put on agenda for your next staff meeting. Advise staff to be thinking about this.

☐ *July 23 Memo*—Give secretary note to (1) set up a meeting at an appropriate date and (2) give you pertinent back-up material.

☐ *July 20 Memo*—Give your staffers a note to do preliminary work on this, if nothing has been done as yet. Tell them you'll meet with them to discuss this on your return. (*Note:* The meeting is on Monday, August 23, and Ken Fixx comes back on Thursday, August 19.)

☐ *July 14 Memo*—Have secretary, via a note, indicate to Pyle that you'll attend. Also, ask secretary to have Pyle arrange for the visit to Philadelphia Regional Office. (*Note:* The personal item in the sealed envelope talked of trouble in a Boston restaurant and said that the Region couldn't be counted on to correct a bad situation.) You may also ask secretary to learn whether other staff members may wish to attend the New York City conference. Tell secretary to tell them that you will discuss their recommendations on this with them.

☐ *July 12 Letter*—You can attend or have a staffer do it, depending on (1) your interest in this topic and (2) your anticipated workload. (*Note:* Have you committed yourself to go to the Philadelphia Regional Office, after the September 20–22 conference in New York? See letter of July 14 in this regard.)

☐ *July 9 Memo*—Ask secretary to arrange for an early meeting with Personnel Officer Powers. *Note:* There are interrelationships with other items: (1) Memo of July 1 from Chief of Real Estate branch re: urban facilities and (2) a supervisory training program is also present here. There is also a training program in the memo on May 22 from the training officer. The president's memo of January 15 talks about ineffective results of prior human relations training.

☐ *July 5 Memo*—*Note:* This is the first written indication that there is a staff to aid the Chief, Branch of Operations. No action required; this is just informational, although the secretary seems to be using all types of leave to the fullest.

☐ *July 1* (Complaint Letter)—Route to legal advisor for review and recommendation.

☐ *July 1 Memo from Chief of Real Estate Branch*—Have secretary arrange for meeting with staff to discuss the task force idea. (*Note:*

Other items related to urban facilities are (1) Memo of July 9 on turnover and absenteeism and (2) Memo of July 23 on security matters.)

☐ *June 30 Memo*—Give staff a note to meet with you the first thing, on your return, to discuss this. You want to cooperate, but you don't know who is the best person to serve on the task force, who is free to serve, etc. (*Note:* You return on Thursday, August 19, and the task force begins its work on Monday, August 23 in Los Angeles.)

☐ *June 15 Memo*—Give to your staffer, Wilde Oates, with a note to discuss when you return. *Note:* This may be a team matter, but you probably should discuss with Oates first.

☐ *June 5 Memo*—The big boss is pushing for a regional meeting in November. He had mentioned it earlier, too, in the memo of January 15. The Atlanta Regional Office is also interested in such a meeting, per memo of July 26. Memo of March 29 also suggests such a meeting. Action: Ask boss's secretary, via a note, to meet with him on this at his convenience.

☐ *May 22 Memo*—This may be an agenda item for the November Regional Officers' meeting. You may wish to discuss this first with your boss and then with the personnel officer and the training officer.

☐ *March 29 Memo*—A complex problem. First action: Have staff join you to study printouts. Second: Establish as an agenda item for the November Regional Officers' meeting.

☐ *January 15 Memo*—In view of date, probably no need to respond on this memo. The training item should be picked up for action along with other training items. The equipment item should be resolved by the August 18 equipment conference, and you are working on the Regional Officers' conference.

☐ *February 15 Note from President Forwarding Complaint Letter of January 5*—Since nothing was done on this January letter, it may be that it is too late to reply since an investigation would have to be made first. This would take more time. Perhaps the letter should be carried along to the Philadelphia Regional meeting for discussion. Certainly the regional director should advise the restaurant manager, facility #4, to "watch it" this coming Christmas. But recall, too, in enveloped, personal memo of August 9th from Boston restaurant facility #4, that the asst. manager thought things were poorly managed at the facility and the Regional Office in Philadelphia wasn't doing any thing about it.

GROUP PROCESSING OF COMPLETED WORK

Participants typically experience learnings by taking action on the 15–25 in-basket items. They may become more aware of communication, staff utilization, public relations, managing in a crisis, prioritizing, etc. But the more profound learning eventuates from the exchange of views with fellow participants in a permissive atmosphere, concerning the best way to handle a given item. One's reasoning for a given action taken may frequently be challenged by the group. One may find that the thrust of an item may have been missed in whole or in part, or that one worked too rapidly or too carelessly. Of course, as in case study, there is typically no "best way" to treat an item. This, in itself, is a significant learning. Yet, one can learn that there are better ways of getting the job done (or solving a problem) than one may have initially imagined.

Nature of Responses

One of the purposes of the in-basket activity is to gauge the extent to which the participants, as managers or would-be managers, are acting appropriately. As an obvious example, a routine personnel matter hardly calls for a group meeting; similarly, an instruction from one's boss to "look in on this personally" is certainly not a delegatable item.

In other words, for the manager the learning is that there are a *range* of possible responses to each action item in his/her in-basket. These include, in addition to making a decision:

1. Taking no action at all—the timing may be wrong, there may not be enough information upon which to act, there may be no urgency involved, the problem may cure itself in time, etc. But one must have a reason for inaction.
2. Instructing one's secretary to act.
3. Asking the secretary for additional information.

4. Instructing a staff member to act on the item.
5. Instructing a staff member to see you about the matter.
6. Calling a group meeting, at a later date, to work on the problem.
7. Asking the group to work it out among themselves (group decision).
8. Contacting a peer for advice, information, to resolve a conflict, etc.
9. Asking one's boss for guidance or advice.
10. Contacting someone on "the outside" for information and clarification.
11. Returning the item to the originator for his/her action ("Do what you deem appropriate").

As to choice of media of communication in acting upon the items in the in-basket, the manager has various options:

The manager can write instructions in the form of notes, write/dictate memoranda, arrange for one-on-one meetings, call for a group meeting, etc. These meetings are not conducted immediately since typically the manager is alone in the office (Friday at 5 P.M., Sunday after 6 P.M., a weekday at 7:30 A.M., etc.). Rather, they are designed to take place when the manager returns from the "trip."

In respect to the calling of meetings, we might suggest that the effective team manager may also encourage the staff to meet on a problem alone as a group. They can study the problem and then recommend, as a group, the best course of action. In some cases, they may act collectively without the boss, the latter agreeing in advance to abide by their decision.

Group Analysis

The total group may analyze participants' in-basket decisions or actions in various ways. A common procedure is simply to begin with the first action item and discuss it collectively. This approach works out fairly well in a small group, say, 8–12 members.

In a larger group, the use of small group methods is preferable. Let's assume that we have 16 participants in our in-basket activity. We can assign them to four groups of four members each. The teams are asked to swap completed in-baskets for analysis, as follows:

Each team is given either the rating schedule in Figure 14-7 or the rating form in Figure 14-8 to

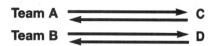

In-Basket Rating Schedule

As a team, you are to review each completed in-basket action. You are to agree on points to be assigned to each action taken, as follows:

5 Points—The action taken is logical/rational/reasonable in all significant respects. *Note:* It may not be the action you would take, but it is a very appropriate solution, one which you can respect fully. The odds are very high that it should succeed.

4 Points—The action taken is quite effective. It is not as persuasive/logical/appropriate an action as might have been taken, but it is certainly a workable one. The odds are in its favor for success.

3 Points—The action taken is acceptable; hardly creative and may have some questionable or risky aspects to it. But it is one that merits a try.

2 Points—The action taken is very marginal or questionable. The odds against its success are considerable. One or more key elements have been overlooked or not considered appropriately.

1 Point—This appears to be an inappropriate response. The proposed action has little chance of succeeding and is very wide of the mark.

Figure 14-7. The in-basket rating schedule for reviewing in-basket solutions.

appraise and rate all the items in the in-basket. Be certain to advise the participants that the point scores are a tool to aid in the analysis; they are not the analyses themselves.

The teams are also given the In-Basket Item Comment Sheet shown in Figure 14-9. It calls for the making of entries, for reference and discussion purposes, about each item. Writing statements concerning the analysis of the items in the in-basket will help to sharpen the thinking involved.

SUMMARIZING THE EXPERIENCE

After all in-basket items have been analyzed and discussed, the trainer should extract from the group what they learned. One way to do this is to use the "circular whip" technique—that is, whip around the

In-Basket Rating Form						
Elements in Decision Making	N/A	1 (LO)	2	3	4	5 (HI)
1. Pertinent facts were fully considered						
2. Timing was considered						
3. The problem rather than the symptom(s) was treated						
4. The decision considered the context which underlies it (climate, interrelationships, etc.)						
5. Future consequences of the decision were considered						
6. Interpersonal factors (human impacts) were considered						
7. Resources of others (boss, staff, peers, etc.) were utilized						
8. Implementation aspects of the decision were considered						
9. Inaction rather than action was taken appropriately						

Using a 5-point scale (1 is low and 5 is high), analyze and discuss each action taken on all in-basket items. Use the nine-factor criteria for effective decisions in rating the actions taken. Agree, as a team, on the point scores you assign to the factors relating to each completed action. As an illustration of how the scoring might go, let's assume you were totally impressed with the logic/reasoning/appropriateness of all actions taken on, say, 20 items. If each action taken were deemed "perfect," it would receive 45 points (9 elements @ 5 points = 45). And if all 20 in-basket items received 45 points, the total in-basket score would be 900 points (45 × 20 items = 900).

Figure 14-8. The in-basket rating form used to assess the decisions made on an in-basket item.

room and secure one statement of learning from each participant, and post the responses on the flipchart.

The process may be repeated two or three times until all significant points have been recorded. Typically, we may anticipate responses such as the following:

☐ Delegation (details were coming to the top)

☐ Time management

☐ Communication

☐ Peer relations

☐ Importance of indicators of malfunctioning in the organization

	In-Basket Item Comment Sheet
Item #1	
Item #2	
Item #3	
Item #4	
Item #5	
Item #6	

Figure 14-9. An In-Basket Item Comment Sheet to explain actions taken.

☐ Importance of setting priorities (was the in-basket to be "attacked" as the items appeared, grouped, or handled in some other manner?)

☐ Need to avoid handling problems piecemeal (interrelationship of items)

☐ Importance of observing dates

☐ Pressure of the in-box or in-basket

☐ The nature of the managerial job (for a new or future manager)

☐ Managing in a crisis

The above learnings may be referred to or commented upon, in summary fashion, to wrap up the exercise.

SUMMARY

The in-basket exercise is a simulation of the kinds of activities which managers, and possibly others, face (or are likely to face) on the job. It is designed to improve their capability to solve problems and make decisions, particularly where problems are quite interrelated and have significant time implications.

In-baskets work well because they provide realism, challenge, fun, and significant learning. A possible disadvantage is that they do take considerable time.

Although the in-basket typically has followed a single format, there is no reason why one cannot be creative and develop new approaches to and uses of the in-basket exercise. Also, while the in-basket is ordinarily used for management training, it would seem that the technique could be adapted to non-managerial training as well. For example, after basic or "theoretical" training, a bank clerk could engage in an application activity using the in-basket approach. It could provide exposure to the varied transactions likely to be encountered in a typical banking day. This type of activity could be conducted on either an individual or a group basis.

KEY POINTS

1. The in-basket exercise is a simulation to which, because of its very nature, managers (and others) can readily relate.

2. Managers can develop a variety of skills from the in-basket activity, including problem solving and decision making, time management, utilization of staff members, coordination with other units, and crisis management.

3. The in-basket exercise is a flexible tool and can be used in a variety of ways to develop managers and others.

4. Although in-basket exercises may be purchased or found in books, the trainer may wish to design his/her own to meet the needs of the participant group better.

5. While the initial analysis of an in-basket is accomplished on an individual basis, that analysis should be subject to further small-group analysis. This procedure allows for learning from the approaches to in-basket problems taken by one's peers.

6. In-basket analysis can be aided via rating forms and rating schedules.

7. Although the "best" in-basket entails the use of "real" memos, letters, reports, etc., an alternate format is to present incidents, events, and problems in summary form.

8. In addition to management training, an in-basket can be used to provide training in report writing, training of tellers in a bank, etc.

RECOMMENDED READING

Burchett, Tern, "In-Basket Cases Keep Policies In Line," *Personnel Journal*, May 1987, pp. 61–65.

This article describes the use of the in-basket technique to orient/train managers in personnel policies, for example, regarding overtime, disciplinary action, sexual harassment, vacation policy, reference requests on former employees.

Daly, Andrew A., "In-Basket Business Game," *Training Directors Journal*, August 1960, pp. 8–15.

Presents an in-basket of 11 items, including instructions to the participants.

Engle, Herbert M., *Handbook of Creative Learning Exercises,* Gulf Publishing, Houston, 1973.

Chapter 9 describes the in-basket in detail and tells how to develop such materials. Chapter 10 presents two complete in-baskets, one of interest to business managers, and the other to professional managers in the public and nonprofit sector.

Ferner, Jack D., *Successful Time Management: A Self Teaching Guide,* John Wiley and Sons, New York, 1980.

The appendix contains a 20-item In-Basket exercise concerned with daily planning. Chapter 12 discusses the in-basket in general and specific terms. Skill practice relates to setting priorities, organizing time in a weekly planning guide, delegating, planning a meeting, accumulating similar tasks.

Gilson, Thomas Q., "A Look at the In-Basket—A Realistic Technique for Selection and Training," *Management of Personnel Quarterly,* Autumn–Winter 1962.

Provides an overview of the in-basket technique, shows sample memoranda, provides a system of scoring responses, and discusses its use in selection as well as development.

Joyce, Robert D., "In-Basket Training for Engineering Managers," *Educational Technology,* January 1970, supplement, pp. 20–26.

Describes an in-basket exercise to broaden engineering managers. Topics covered by the 40 incidents (memoranda): promotion policies, performance evaluation, project assignments, employee sharing on projects, interdepartmental conflicts, interpersonal rivalries, design problems, customer and vendor relationships, turnover, morale, communications.

Joyce, Robert D., "In-Basket Programs—How to Make Them, How to Use Them," *Training in Business and Industry,* February 1971, pp. 40–44.

Provides guides to the creation of one's own in-basket and procedures to conduct the program.

Kemerer, Richard, and Wahlstrom, Merlin, "How to Develop and Use In-Basket Simulations—A Case Study in the Selection of Bank Managers," *Performance and Instruction Journal,* May 1984, pp. 6–8.

While in-baskets are typically used for training managers and others, they may also be used for personnel appraisal and selection purposes. This article describes the latter use in a Canadian bank.

Nylen, Donald, Mitchell, J. Rubert, and Stout, Anthony (Eds.), "Decision Making Under Pressure in the In Tray," in *Handbook of Staff Development and Human Relations Training: Materials Developed For Use in Africa,* NTL Institute For Applied Behavioral Science, Washington, D.C., 1967, pp. 153–170.

Provides a 16-item in-basket including general instructions to conduct the activity.

Other Key Group-in-Action Tools

15

Retention is best when the learner is involved.

> —Edward Scannell, director, University
> Conference Bureau, Arizona State
> (quoted in *Meeting News,* January 1980)

IN the prior pages we presented a variety of issues, techniques, and methods that relate to working with small groups. In the following pages we will discuss several additional areas of concern that are significant to effective group training, both small group and total group. They are

- ☐ Pre-work
- ☐ Seating
- ☐ Movement
- ☐ Flipcharting
- ☐ Humor and fun
- ☐ Props for empathy
- ☐ Handouts
- ☐ Using silence
- ☐ Telling stories

PRE-WORK

At times it is desirable to provide participants with an assignment in advance of the first session of a training program. The basic principle behind the pre-work concept is that the more the participants bring to the training situation the more they will carry away from it. Thus, the more participants can prepare themselves for the learning experience ("early entry"), the more effective—easier, quicker, more profound—it is likely to be.

Pre-work also has these advantages:

- ☐ It alerts participants early on that the forthcoming learning is a two-way street—that participants and the trainer have joint responsibilities for the success of the training effort.
- ☐ It indicates that the learning experience will be an active, involving one, rather than just another passive training exposure.
- ☐ It provides an early opportunity to understand the nature of the course or program.
- ☐ It sets a professional tone for the course: "Hey, these people really mean business. Why they're putting us to work before we even get to class. Maybe this _will_ be worth coming to."
- ☐ It stimulates interest, provokes curiosity, provides involvement, and thus encourages motivation.

In general, pre-work helps establish the right kind of expectations by participants.

When to Assign Pre-work

Pre-work, as a training tool, is most effective when it is fully integrated into the overall learning design. It should therefore be used if the following guidelines apply to your pre-work assignment:

It is basic (relevant) to the course, that is, it is something that must be done on the job before attendance at the training session. For example, you might have participants

- ☐ Keep a time log as a prelude to analysis and discussion in a time management workshop.
- ☐ Complete an instrument to produce data for subsequent analysis in a leadership training course.
- ☐ Identify work problems related to the forthcoming training.
- ☐ Read a rather complex case that will be discussed in class.

It is essential to assemble on-the-job materials or acquire other data to be used in the course. For example:

- ☐ In a course on effective writing, the participants select and bring to class copies of letters, memos, and reports of a type specified by the trainer.
- ☐ Participants visit a plant, office, gallery, school, museum, or store prior to attending a course that treats a topic related to those locales. (Be sure to provide guidelines so the trainees know what to look for.)
- ☐ In preparation for a management development seminar, participants prepare a "minicase" on an assigned aspect of leadership or a current management problem.
- ☐ Participants bring in pertinent "live data" and added perspectives about the subject by interviewing their bosses or peers.
- ☐ Participants bring to class items culled from the media relevant to the topics to be discussed, for example, newspaper or magazine articles, editorials, photos, book reviews, ads.

It is desirable to provide participants with subject-matter background prior to class attendance. For example, have participants

- ☐ Read one or two articles that explore nuances of the MBO (Management by Objectives) process prior to attending the MBO course.
- ☐ View a film or videotape or listen to an audio-cassette that sets the stage for the course. (This presumes appropriate equipment is readily available.)

It is considered worthwhile to motivate (excite, interest) participants about the course in general or the first session in particular. For example:

- ☐ In advance of a public speaking course, provide participants with an article that challenges them to become better formal presenters.
- ☐ In advance of a course on communication, present participants with one or more models and accompanying text which highlight complexities of the communication process.
- ☐ In advance of a course on improving one's dictation skills, provide participants with (a) data concerning the economics (potential dollar savings) of good dictation, plus other benefits (for

example, making life easier for one's secretary) and (b) a short exercise or two to check out certain principles of good dictation.

When *Not* to Assign Pre-work

Although the preceding paragraphs reveal the value of pre-work, it is nevertheless a tool that should be used only with considerable forethought. In the absence of such care, one may anticipate negative effects on the training effort. More specifically, pre-work is not recommended when

☐ The participant group is an extremely busy one (for example, upper-level managers, those who are subject to considerable travel) and thus not likely to cooperate. Of course, insistence by the head of the organization that all participants are to do the pre-work may prove to be a helpful motivator.

☐ The participant group possesses limited educational background and is uncomfortable with the somewhat "academic" course requirements that may be entailed in pre-work.

☐ There is insufficient time to get the materials to the participants to complete the assigned tasks.

☐ The tasks can more properly be completed in class (for example, due to the complexity of the instructions or the initial need to involve the group).

☐ The benefits of pre-work are only marginally advantageous to a particular training effort. As one anonymous sage put it: "If it ain't broke, don't fix it."

☐ Past experience with a particular participant group indicates that pre-work is quite certain to provide a negative reaction.

☐ Top management may not be sympathetic to activities which connote "training overload."

Some Skill Pointers in Assigning Pre-work

Successfully completed pre-work is likely if attention is paid to these skill factors:

☐ Provide an explanation in writing concerning the reason for the assignment. Remember that participants, especially busy ones, may resent the idea of doing tasks outside the training situation. In fact, some may even object to attending the training program in the first instance.

☐ If practicable, meet with the group to explain the pre-work assignment. This procedure is essential to secure cooperation from the participants in a "must do" situation, for example, keeping a time log in preparation for an intensive time management course.

☐ Keep assignments simple and brief. One easy-to-do task is clearly preferable to two or three assignments that may take considerable time to complete.

☐ Provide clear-cut written instructions concerning the conduct of the assignment. Conduct a "field-test" to ensure that your meaning is being communicated clearly.

☐ As applicable, facilitate the execution of the assignment by providing simple forms or work sheets. For example, see the worksheets on delegation in Appendix 54.

Despite your best efforts to plan and organize your pre-work activity, one or more participants may not have completed the requested assignment. So what do you do? Some possible answers:

☐ If the assignment is not too complex and thus not time-consuming, one possibility is simply to take time for it to be done as the first order of business. The assumption here is that the completion of the assigned work is basic to the learning from the course.

☐ Another possibility is to have the "delinquent" ones try to participate as well as they can; for example, in the case of an uncompleted time log, the participants may attempt to reconstruct the work week or at least a work day on a memory basis (admittedly a poor procedure) or at least make an effort to recall some of their daily problems in managing their time.

A final caution regarding pre-work: Be sure that you process any pre-work you assign. Pre-work that is not actively used in class will have only limited value. Maximum benefit accrues from sharing and discussing the assigned work.

SEATING TO FACILITATE PARTICIPATION

Seating of participants is important for these reasons:

☐ It can facilitate participation.
☐ It can energize the group.
☐ It communicates the trainer's philosophy of adult learning and training style.

A meaningful approach to seating is to think in these terms: How much involvement of participants do I want? How much movement should take place to facilitate that involvement? Let's discuss, then, three situations: *low* participant involvement, *moderate* participant involvement, and *high* participant involvement.

Low Involvement

Seating configurations for low participant involvement are given in Figure 15-1. The physical setup is obviously very formal. The tables themselves (sometimes desks are used) contribute to a stilted, highly traditional classroom atmosphere.

Note that the course conductor is in a position of authority, seated behind a table or standing behind a lec-

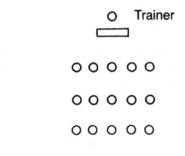

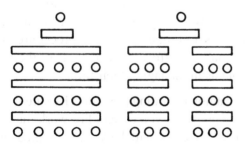

Figure 15-1. Seating configurations for low participant involvement.

tern. Communication is intended to flow primarily from the front of the room to the rear—one-way communication. Lateral communication, that is, inter-participant communication, is not deemed to be important. In effect, the trainer is in complete control of the instructional process. The trainer is active, and the participants, if we can use that term, are passive. All (or nearly all) the knowledge or wisdom is presumed to reside with the trainer.

If we could secure comments from our participants they might say to us: "Looks like we're back in that old high school/college lecture hall." "I hope the trainer doesn't forget the break."

In short, what we have operating in this situation is an instructional effort underpinned by the "funnel theory" of learning—"just pour it in and they'll get it." Probable impact/retention is limited or low.

Moderate Involvement

Seating of participants for medium or moderate involvement is given in Figure 15-2. In the U, V, or I setup, the instructor is, again, very much in control. However, these configurations are designed to have some participant interchange. Also, with movable chairs "buzz grouping" should be possible, even if only done occasionally. In general, there is an assumption that participants can learn from one another, at least in part. Much of the learning still depends upon one-way communication devices: lectures, slide talks, films, and handouts.

If participants have been exposed entirely to lecture-hall learning atmospheres, these configurations will probably be regarded by them as "a step forward." Their observation might be: "The trainer is in charge, but we do have the opportunity to have some exchange." Probable impact/retention is fair to good, depending on opportunities for participant interaction provided by the instructor.

High Involvement

Seating configurations for high participant involvement may assume these forms:

Use of several square, rectangular or round tables. In these configurations, shown in Figure 15-3, the trainer serves primarily as a resource person or facilitator. He/she does not work directly with the group, and the

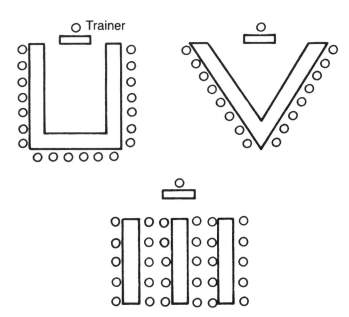

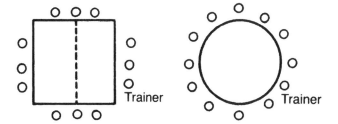

Figure 15-4. Other seating arrangements for high participant involvement in which the trainer joins the group.

Figure 15-2. Seating configurations for moderate participant involvement.

emphasis is on small group work. In fact, the major resource in this learning experience is the small group. Note that the trainer has a work table to his/her right; merely having a chair in the front of the room reduces the social distance between the trainer and the participants. The trainer also has a flipchart, a symbol of informal learning, to his/her left. The trainer is in a position to

move around the room, auditing and helping the teams at the tables as may be necessary. Short talks, rather than lectures, stimulate/generate the small group work.

Use of a single square or round table. In this configuration, shown in Figure 15-4, the trainer joins the group and assumes the role of catalyst/facilitator/resource person. The trainer deliberately reduces his/her status to encourage full and free interaction among participants and between participants and the trainer. The atmosphere is informal, relaxed, participant-centered. Everyone is concerned with exploration, problem solving, critique, discussion, etc.

Flexible, no-desk/table seating. In this approach, the trainer may start the group off in lecture array, as in Figure 15-5. However, this apparently neat and tidy arrangement is short-lived. After a few short comments, or none at all, the group is put into action via dyads, triads, buzz groups, fishbowls, stand-up activities, or movement. And the neat configuration with which things began hardly, if at all, returns. In fact, the room typically remains in informal, relaxed disarray, with the participants at times communicating from buzz group positions or even an informal U-shaped circle, as in Figure 15-6.

The use of many participant configurations—dyads, triads, buzz groups, etc.—is facilitated by

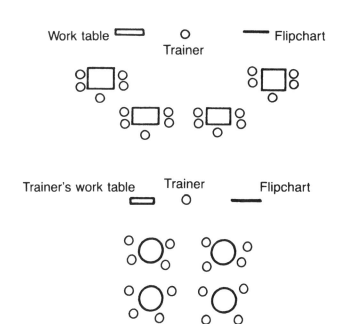

Figure 15-3. Seating configurations for high participant involvement.

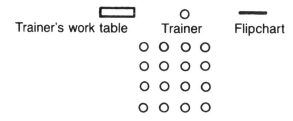

Figure 15-5. Diagram of a lecture hall arrangement as a prelude to a highly informal seating configuration.

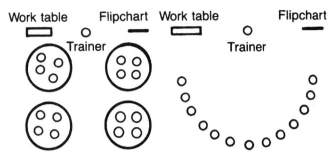

Figure 15-6. Diagrams of seating arrangements for high involvement that can flow from the lecture hall arrangement.

movable chairs and the absence of desks or tables (inhibitors of ready participant movement). If notebooks have been distributed, they are used for occasional writing tasks.

The trainer's role, obviously, is to set the stage for a variety of activities; to get the group into action; to secure data from the small groups, role players, etc.; to record the data on flipcharts, as necessary; and to work with the group to interpret (analyze, summarize) its experience.

Use of a circle without the tables. In this configuration—Figure 15-7—the trainer joins with the group on a more-or-less peer basis. The assumption is that "we're all here to learn together." This is the hallmark of advanced forms of experiential learning (T-group, encounter group, team building). The atmosphere is totally informal, and as the group matures, it becomes warm, egalitarian, supportive, caring, spontaneous, and highly trusting. Thus, the trainer's highest skill is to create an environment where everyone can work/learn well together. Note that tables—the trainer's and the participants'—are discarded to accent informality, to eliminate the traditional classroom atmosphere, and to stimulate the freest possible flow of communication.

The probable impact/retention of learning in these four configurations is high, at least for most participants. Satisfaction with the trainer and the training process should also be high.

Seating for Larger Groups

Various meetings, conferences, or symposia may be attended by fairly large groups. "Large" may be defined as a group of more than 25 participants and can range up to audiences of several hundred people.

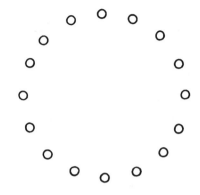

Figure 15-7. Diagram of the circular, table-free arrangement, which, by also involving the trainer, is designed for maximum informality and high involvement.

Despite this size, certain kinds of participation are still possible. Proper seating can contribute to such participation. Several examples follow to trigger your own thinking about appropriate seating configurations for at least some participation and involvement.

Panel discussion for an audience of 50–75 people. A helpful arrangement—Figure 15-8—is to use a "theater in the round" approach. Assume, then, that we have four panelists and a moderator. We can place them in the center ring, with two or three added rings or clusters around them for the audience. Two empty chairs can be added to the center ring for use by audience members who wish to ask a question of a panel member. The ground rules: participants may pose a question to one or more panelists by taking an empty chair, a follow-up question or two is also permitted, and then the questioner relinquishes the chair to another audience member. The use of the second chair for another audience participant expedites the movement of the questioners in and out of the inner ring. *Note:* An aisle should be provided for easy entry into the inner ring.

The use of this configuration gives everyone a sense of being near the action—no one is in a rear row. While the number of questioners is limited, as in any large audience, it is still possible for audience members to identify with the questioners and thus feel a certain degree of involvement in the proceedings.

Lecture for an audience of several hundred. An audience of 100–500 people can be involved to a degree despite a lecture-type situation. One way to do this is to use large round tables which seat 8–10 peo-

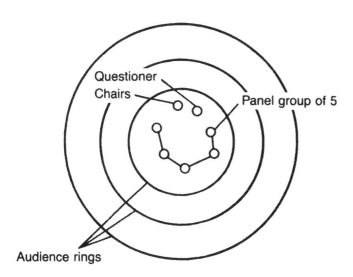

Figure 15-8. Diagram of "theater in the round" seating for a large group.

ple. For example, a group of ten (or two groups of five) can "buzz" on an assigned topic or question and report back its conclusions to the total audience. Not all groups may be able to report back, but a small number, selected randomly, can. It is also possible, with proper instructions, to have several team role plays at each round table—two role players and one or two observers per team. *All* at the round table participate in the role plays.

In the traditional lecture hall set-up, small group work is possible if the chairs are movable. Participants simply turn their chairs around to form groups of four or six.

Round tables are preferred to lecture-hall style since they allow for the development of much more rapport. In fact, by reducing the number of participants at the round tables from ten to say, seven or eight, even greater intimacy is possible.

Use of an Outside Facility

If you are using an "outside" facility such as a hotel, motel, conference center, school, or other public building, some suggestions are offered to help you cope with Murphy's Law: if anything can go wrong, it will. (Seasoned trainers will say that Murphy was essentially an optimist!)

☐ Inspect the facility in advance, if at all possible. It may be too small to move chairs and people

around once you have your work table, a registration table, a coffee table, a motion picture screen, a movie projector, one or two flipcharts on easels, and a coat rack in the room. There may also be posts to limit your usable space. Remember that when you ask a nontrainer if the space is "large enough," his/her perception of "large" is quite different from yours. Hotel/ motel sales personnel particularly are accustomed to fitting 50 people, lecture hall style, into a small room. They may also wish to save the bigger rooms for other clients in case such requests should arise.

☐ Arrive early on the morning of the training. It is a good bet that no one has communicated to the setup crew what your needs and expectations really are. For example, they may have set up the room with tables which you did not request. Or they have a mammoth blackboard instead of a compact easel and flipchart. By arriving early, you may be able to rearrange the room as you wish, get rid of unwanted items such as lecterns and tables, accomplish your other preliminary tasks, keep your frustrations down, and be able to greet your early arrivers in good humor.

☐ A possible way to secure compliance with your requests is to provide the hotel's coordinator with a diagram of your proposed room setup.

Seating Management

In addition to displaying concern with seating configurations, the trainer opting for high participation will give attention to these issues:

Seat "ownership." Since a body at rest literally tends to stay at rest, we may anticipate that participants will try to acquire "vested rights" in the seats that they take at the outset of the course. It is your job to overcome this "squatter's rights" tendency. Why? Two reasons: We don't want people getting too comfortable and routinized; rather, we want to keep them in a free-flowing, more active, energized, and motivated state. New seating locations provide an opportunity to work with and get to know other participants, to learn how they see things.

Seating changes can be brought about via:

☐ The "count-off" approach. In this way the ones, twos, threes, etc. will team up.

☐ A statement at the end of the first day to this effect: "Tomorrow we'll be working with new partners. So when you come in in the morning, please take a chair at another table."

The buddy relationship. Participants often tend to gravitate toward and team up with someone they know. Or they may ally themselves with the person with whom they came to the course. Sitting next to a buddy is undoubtedly comfortable and anxiety reducing. But the purpose of the training program is, again, to meet new faces, to encounter new views, to attempt to enter into the world of someone one knows less well or not at all, to develop a relationship with a stranger. Again, it is your job to undo the buddy seating relationship.

Chair count. If the program calls for 15 people to attend, don't set up seating for 20 to 30 people. Instead, limit the number of chairs to the number expected. In this fashion, when participants sit down they will be certain to acquire a neighbor, either immediately or shortly thereafter. And if a coat rack is provided, no one will "neutralize" a chair by draping his/her coat over it.

Flexible seating. Try to have a training room with comfortable but lightweight chairs. Chairs should be light enough so that anyone can push or carry a chair to a new location for role plays, fishbowls, and small group work.

Seating instructions. All too often, participants assigned to dyads, triads, or buzz groups will assume seating configurations that ignore the need to be on an eyeball-to-eyeball basis with fellow participants. Face-to-face contact is essential, of course, for good communication. Hence, the trainer must politely insist that dyadic partners "eyeball" it and that buzz groups sit in a true, tight circle rather than in a half-moon or even an elliptical configuration. One way to do this is to ensure proper seating before assigning the task. To the reluctant ones, simply say: "Would you please try to eyeball it? I assure you that you'll be able to communicate a lot more effectively if you can look at one another."

Seating position by the trainer. Whenever possible, the trainer should operate informally by using a chair as opposed to standing up before the group. By being seated, and drawing your chair close to the group,

you will reduce your status and help yourself to become a member of the group.

The table issue. Trainers of the nonexperiential, low-participation bent are inclined to place chairs around tables. Their rationale is that it provides a writing aid, it gives participants a storage area for notebooks, and it provides a comfortable resting place for arms, elbows, and tired heads. However, the experiential trainer sees tables only as providing added clutter and formality to the training room. The extra impediments certainly don't help to form fishbowls and small groups or to allow participants to move their chairs to corners or other locations for role plays.

Certainly if writing is minimal, it can be accomplished readily enough on a notebook. If it is a heavy part of the course, tables are indeed warranted. Notebooks can be placed easily enough underneath one's chair on the floor, and as for resting one's elbows and head on the table, comfort of that sort is hardly the energizing we wish in the dynamic training room.

In general, tables add to formality; they give the training room more of a traditional classroom flavor. Do we really want that?

The auditorium problem. Sometimes you may find yourself in an auditorium setting, complete with chairs bolted to the floor and a stage with lectern. Obviously, an informal atmosphere and small group work are not easy in this situation. What to do? First, you should learn of the nature of the facility before the actual training day and consider whether it is worth doing the training there. Second, if small group work is desired, it can still be done in one of two ways:

☐ Have participants stand and have every other row turn around to face those behind them. Groups of four to six are then possible. (Participants will find it very difficult to work in small groups while seated.)

☐ Use adjacent break-out rooms, if available.

The smoking problem. In recent years it has become customary to divide the seating opportunities into smoking and nonsmoking categories. This is certainly a considerate way of doing things. However, it cannot be done in the type of seating I advocate. For with movement and the changing composition and size of small groups, the smokers and nonsmokers typically become intermingled. One trainer deals with the problem by announcing at the outset of the workshop various ground rules, including a ban on smoking. As to his rationale for such action, he advises the participants that he cannot provide them with excellence for the three days involved if he is subjected to smoke. However, he makes the rule more palatable to the smokers by scheduling frequent, short breaks. Also, he advises the smokers that they may leave the room at any time if they find they must smoke.

MOVEMENT

This is a training device to keep participants alert and energized. In general you should opt for those techniques that require participants to "rearrange" themselves, for example, fishbowls, role plays, certain exercises, field trips, and in-plant visits. Some other forms of movement that can be used follow.

Icebreakers

Depending on the group, course objectives, and so on, it may be desirable to start things off by getting participants into motion. This approach will communicate at the outset that your program is indeed going to be a "live one." Here are some examples:

Envelope Enigma

Simply put all participants' name cards or tent cards (folded cards that once set up look like tents) in a box. Let the participant select a card randomly from the box. Instruct the participant to move around and locate the person whose name is on the card. Then the participant exchanges personal data with the other participant: name, goal for the course, etc.

Values Billboard

The procedures for this are as follows:

1. The trainer posts on a flipchart (or provides a handout of) a list of values such as the following:

☐ To be a good citizen
☐ To achieve above-average financial success
☐ To help mankind
☐ To develop a reputation in my field
☐ To help my family grow and be happy
☐ To have worthwhile friends
☐ To have the opportunity to apply my creativity
☐ To be a physically able person
☐ To be a good neighbor

Note: The trainer may substitute other values. Limit the number posted to seven or eight.

2. On a sheet of paper, or preferably a flipchart sheet (with felt-tip pen), have the participants rearrange (prioritize) the values as they see them. (A variation is to let participants drop two values and prioritize the others, if nine or ten are given.)

3. Then have everyone stand up, mill around, display their "billboard," find a partner, and discuss the values.

4. The partners share (discuss) their values with one another for several minutes.

5. The trainer calls "time" and asks everyone to find a new partner. Finding a new partner is accomplished two or three times.

6. Wind up the activity by processing the action: What did you learn? Anything about anyone? About yourself?

Trust Walk or Blind Walk

Begin by pointing out: "The success of our program depends on participant participation. But participation depends upon *trust*. To symbolize the importance of trust, let's conduct a trust walk. Is there anyone who doesn't want to participate? O.K., here are our procedures:

"Find a partner, preferably someone you don't know at all or don't know very well. In your pair, decide who will be the leader and who will be the follower." (This step can also be performed randomly by having everyone call out "one" and "two," with the "ones" automatically becoming the leaders and the "twos" the followers.)

"The followers are to close their eyes. The trust walk is executed silently—nonverbally.

"When I give the signal, the leader will steer the follower around the designated area. The leaders should try to make the trip as interesting as possible and should do so safely. Remember eyes closed, followers, since you trust your leader to ensure that no harm befalls you. Let's walk around, then, for five minutes or so." (The time period can be 15–20 minutes in an experiential program that emphasizes sensory awareness and where the outdoors is available to feel trees and rocks, smell flowers, etc.)

"O.K., let's stop our walks and process the action. Followers: How did you feel? Anxious? Fearful? Dependent? Trusting?" (Secure several responses.)

"Leaders: How did you feel about your role and responsibility? Concerned? Silly? Responsible?" (Secure several responses.)

"Was a system of communication established? Was trust accomplished to any degree? Any general comments or reactions from anyone?"

Several key or skill points to make the trust walk an effective experience:

- ☐ Keep it voluntary. Don't put pressure on anyone to participate. This would defeat the whole purpose of the exercise—building trust.
- ☐ Limit the use of this activity to groups oriented toward experiential training.
- ☐ Stress the nonverbal or silent aspects of it. This behavior is typically hard for participants to grasp. (I sometimes facetiously tell the group, "I generally say that nonverbal means no talking, and I always have difficulty communicating this idea.")
- ☐ To make the experience worthwhile, the walk should take at least five minutes. Tell them that you will signal them when the five minutes are up, and that if they quit sooner they won't get much out of the experience.
- ☐ Be certain to provide time to process the action. People *do* want to talk about this unique experience.

The trainer should be ready to adapt the trust walk experience to the needs of the group; for example, with a sales training group, the processing of feelings can be shifted to a discussion of how the *customer* feels in a selling transaction. Or are we only concerned with our feelings as salespeople? Also, how do we develop trust with a prospect or customer?

I Am

On a sheet of paper or, preferably, using felt-tip pens on a flipchart sheet, have participants develop a comprehensive list of nouns that describe themselves. Stimulate their thinking by giving them a partial list about yourself: I am a

- ☐ Father/Mother
- ☐ Husband/Wife
- ☐ Neighbor
- ☐ Beer drinker
- ☐ Lover
- ☐ Trainer
- ☐ Moviegoer

Then have each participant find a partner and exchange data. The process may be repeated once or twice with a new partner.

Hum Fun

To get acquainted, participants are given the opportunity to team up in trios or quartets via the humming of well-known songs.

1. Type or write the names of three or four well-known songs on 3" × 5" cards. The number of cards and participants should be limited to 12–16. The songs may be drawn from such categories as Irish songs, folk songs, popular oldies. For example, with 12 participants, four cards might have typed on them "When Irish Eyes Are Smiling," four others might have typed on them "Let Me Call You Sweetheart," and four others "I've Been Working on the Railroad."

2. Distribute the 12 cards randomly.

3. Instruct participants to *hum* their song, mill around, and try to team up with others who are also humming their song.

4. When the trios or quartets are formed, have them exchange data about themselves. It is

essential to limit the number of participants to 12–16 since, with a larger number, teaming up would become too difficult in a hum-filled room.

Name Game

When participants are assembled, give them blank name cards and ask them to write their names in bold, capital letters, but *spelled backwards.* (If they already have name cards which they received on their arrival, have them put these cards away temporarily.) Then ask people to stand, mill around, seek out as many partners as they can in five minutes or so, and introduce themselves with their newly spelled name. *Examples:* Greta now becomes Aterg, Kim becomes Mik and Fran becomes Narf.

As an added fun-type introductory instructional comment, advise that if anyone is named Otto or Hannah (write the names on the board or flipchart), they can either (a) function as observers or (b) spell it "inside out"—for example, Otto becomes Toot and Hannah becomes Nahnah.

Also advise that if anyone has a multi-syllabic name like Montgomery, Millicent, Bernadine, or Christopher, they should use a shortened version of the name.

After the exchange of their new names, ask how they felt performing the activity and whether the exercise had a helpful icebreaker effect.

Find Someone Who . . . [1]

This icebreaker is particularly useful for people in a stranger group. Provide participants with a sheet of paper which contains 10–15 items relating to their work (see the following). Allow two lines per item so that entries can readily be made for all items. On the top of the sheet write in large letters with a felt-tipped pen: "Find Someone Who . . ." Immediately below, provide these instructions:

Directions: Find someone who can sign one of the lines on this form, with name, company, and phone number. Each person can sign your form up to two times only. You cannot sign your own form. Once your entire sheet is completed, jump up and down and shout: "I win!"

Here are the items which may appear on your form:

- ☐ Forms a one-person department
- ☐ Lives at the shore
- ☐ Is a first-timer at this conference
- ☐ Really understands quality circles
- ☐ Knows a lot about management development programs
- ☐ Teaches time management
- ☐ Has a great idea for avoiding burnout
- ☐ Knows all about career ladders
- ☐ Has a great idea for motivating employees

Note: Anticipate a lot of noise because of the many simultaneous conversations of the total group. Also, the preceding questions were used with a trainer group. Other groups would require other items on their forms.

Note: For additional icebreakers, but not necessarily ones entailing movement, see Chapter 1.

Stand-ups

It is very desirable to get people to stand in place and engage in some type of physical movement or activity. Several examples of such activities follow.

Sign-ups

Post to the wall several (five to seven) signs. Ask participants to "sign up" with the sign that relates most closely to themselves. Sample topics:

- ☐ Leadership styles (for example, team management; totally participative; moderately participative; somewhat participative; happy ship; strictly business; management by objectives)
- ☐ Off-the-job interests (for example, totally outdoors; totally indoors; mostly outdoors; mostly indoors; equally indoors and outdoors)

Then have participants, on a stand-up basis, introduce themselves and talk about the sign they selected and how they relate to it.

Value Clarification Activity in Leadership [2]

An opener, designed to clarify values in a leadership session, can help people to feel comfortable by having them get up and move around. It utilizes these procedures:

1. Take four large index cards; number them 1, 2, 3, and 4; and post them in the four corners of the room.

2. Write these (or other appropriate) questions on the flipchart:

   ☐ Who would you prefer to be your leader?
      1. One who has vision
      2. One who has compassion
      3. One who communicates well
      4. One who is judicious
   ☐ Where would you like to work?
      1. Disneyland
      2. IBM
      3. Your own organization
      4. American Red Cross
   ☐ What do you most value in an employee?
      1. Loyalty
      2. Creativity
      3. Thoroughness
      4. Interpersonal skill

   Note: The above questions used by the trainer reflected the spirit of the class she was conducting.

3. Cover up the four sets of questions and unveil them, one set at a time.

4. As you uncover each set of questions, ask participants to walk to the number representing their choice. When everyone is at a corner, ask them to discuss, standing up, why they made their choice and to share their values with the class. (Anticipate that the involvement and sharing of insights and perspectives will generate a lot of enthusiasm and a deeper understanding and interest in the leadership area.)

Armfold

To make the point that habits are hard to break (overcoming resistance to change), give your group this assignment while they are standing:

"Fold your arms.

"Raise your head and glance at the ceiling.

"Make a mental note concerning how your arms are folded, such as the right arm is placed over the left.

"Now reverse the position of your arms." (Most people find this awkward to accomplish.)

Ask: "Was this hard to do? Why?" (Answer: strength of habit. Say: "If we can't break a *physical* habit very easily, we can hardly expect to break one that is of an ingrained intellectual or emotional sort. So in trying to change habits (or a learned behavior) of others, be prepared for resistance. People are obviously now doing something which is satisfying to them, so why should they change?")

Note: The activity may also be accomplished via clasping and unclasping of hands.

Break

To introduce the coffee break in an active and fun way, give your participants these instructions:

"Stand up.

"Extend your arms forward, the palms facing one another.

"Clap your hands together, separate them, and everyone yell: 'Break!'"

This procedure may be used again from time to time.

Instant Interaction

Start the first session (possibly a formal one) with instant interaction by everyone. Say to participants: "Is everyone comfortable? Good.

"O.K. Stand up, please.

"Turn to your neighbor and talk for three to four minutes about _____.

"O.K., what did you come up with?" (Secure a few comments.)

"Good. Let's take our seats again."

Power Play

In a session concerned with power, open things up by asking for several volunteers to come forward. Have the volunteers introduce themselves to one another, if they are strangers, and talk briefly about possible program (course, session) benefits. Then ask the volunteers how they felt about coming to the front of the room. Also, ask: "Why did you do it? To make an impression? To cooperate? Or what? Did you consider that you ran the risk of looking foolish?"

Then turn to the audience: *"All* of you participated in this activity. How? Because you made a decision *not* to volunteer. Are you glad or sorry about your decision?" (Secure feedback from nonvolunteers.) "To sum up: This activity relates to two important dimensions of power: *visibility* and *risk-taking.* If you participated, you acquired power; if you did not participate, you didn't acquire it."

Meditation in Motion

Meditation in the training situation is intended to relax participants and/or to establish a quiet, pensive mood. A helpful way to look at meditation is to regard it not as a means of *leaving* where we are but, rather, as a technique to become *aware* of where we are (taking our environment inward). Two exercises for meditation follow.

Have participants

1. Form a circle (8 to 20 participants are a workable group) away from the chairs, with everyone standing.
2. Put their left foot forward.
3. Close their eyes.
4. Sway their body gently back and forth (20–30 seconds).
5. Halt the motion (eyes still closed), and return their left leg to its original position.
6. Put their right foot forward.
7. Sway their body back and forth (20–30 seconds).
8. Return their right leg to its original position.
9. Keep their eyes closed for another 10–20 seconds, palms facing the floor, head slightly bowed.
10. Open their eyes and return to their chairs.

Another format for a stand-up meditation is to have participants:

1. Form a circle, everyone standing.
2. Put their left foot forward and close their eyes.
3. Extend their arms to the left.
4. Gently move their arms and develop a gentle, rhythmic, circular motion (30 seconds).

5. Return their left leg to its original position, cease the arm motion, and put their arms down.
6. Extend their arms to the right (their eyes are still closed).
7. Gently move their arms to form a circular motion again (30 seconds).
8. Return their right leg to its original position, cease the arm motion, and put their arms down.
9. Bow their head, their eyes still closed, with palms now at the side and facing downward (10–20 seconds).
10. Open their eyes and return to their chairs.

Energy Check

At various stages in the program day you may want to check the energy level of the group. If so, ask participants:

"Will you stand up, please?

"Let's see how energetic/vigorous we are at this point. Let's sing out 'E' in an increasing crescendo.

"Let's sing out 'I,' and louder this time.

"Let's sing out 'O', really loud now.

"Was it fun? Yes? Let's hear it?" (Applause) *Note:* The larger the group, the more the impact, of course.

Stretch Break

If the group has been sitting for an extended period of time and/or appears to be in need of invigoration, have them stand up and do these simple exercises.

☐ Extend arms to side and shake vigorously for five to seven seconds.

☐ Extend arms overhead and shake vigorously for five to seven seconds.

☐ Shake shoulders up and down ten times.

☐ Shake shoulders sideways (left to right and reverse) ten times.

☐ Move head from left to right and reverse ten times.

☐ Move head in a circular movement clockwise (ten times).

☐ Move head in a circular movement counter-clockwise (ten times).

Note:

1. As each exercise proceeds, make encouraging statements such as "That's the way. Get those kinks out of your neck. You're doing great."
2. When the exercises are completed, ask:
   a. How many feel more invigorated?
   b. How many feel more fatigued?
   c. How many don't feel?

Group Hum

In an experiential training program, the following icebreaker may be useful to relax participants as well as to set a desirable tone or mood. Procedures are as follows:

1. Ask everyone to stand up and form a circle. This may be a single circle or several circles, depending on group size.
2. Instruct them to close their eyes, take their partners' hands, and exercise a firm, friendly grip.
3. Have everyone take a deep breath and then exhale out loud with an "ommm."
4. Then ask everyone to take *three* deep breaths and exhale each time with a loud "ommm."
5. Ask participants to please be seated.

Note: If this icebreaker is used with a fairly large audience, the "ommm" is quite impressive and will probably be rendered more loudly each time.

Ball Toss

This is an active, fun-type icebreaker; it also encourages creativity. Procedures:

1. Form a circle of five to eight participants, everyone standing.
2. One person tosses an imaginary ball to another participant, calling out that person's name prior to making the "toss."
3. Repeat the process until everyone's name has been called out.
4. When the last person in the circle has "received" the ball, he/she may transform the ball into another object (for example, a wallet of $100 bills, an egg, a TV set).

Note:

1. One should toss the "ball" or other object with gestures, vigor, and verbal comments. ("Dotty, here's that ball. Look out. Here it comes!")
2. Two or three tosses of different objects are adequate to familiarize everyone with participants' names.
3. This activity may be done with one or more groups operating simultaneously.
4. If several groups are playing, anticipate that your training room will be filled with totally loud and friendly responses.

Mobile Continuum

Participants can be asked to position themselves at various points in the training room to indicate their attitudes/feelings on various issues. For example, in a session concerned with the explanation and exploration of assertive behavior, provide a continuum for participants to assess their degree of assertiveness.

Procedures:

1. Post on opposite walls of the training room two flipcharts as shown in Figure 15-9.

Very willing to execute this task, I'm very comfortable with it.	I'm highly reluctant: makes me very uncomfortable

Figure 15-9. Examples of flipcharts for use in a "mobile continuum."

2. Ask participants to stand up and position themselves mid-way between the two walls bearing the flipcharts.
3. Read aloud the statements such as the following, one at a time.

   ☐ Ask the boss for a raise above the average being doled out.

☐ Attend an office party in our building where I know several people but don't have a specific invitation.

☐ Confront a tough colleague about his/her continuing lack of cooperation.

☐ Ask the boss for the day off after Thanksgiving, knowing that the office will be understaffed and the boss has already expressed oral disapproval of such requests.

☐ Speak frankly to a colleague who annoys me with his/her putdowns and other assorted hard-hitting humor.

☐ Remind a very capable staff member, who doesn't like feedback, that his/her reports are often late and that this behavior will have to stop.

☐ Return to the hardware store an inexpensive electrical switch that isn't functioning well, although you probably abused it on installation.

☐ Tell a colleague that you don't really care to listen to the gossip he/she regularly provides.

☐ Tell a subordinate who likes to take up your time with trivia that you don't have that kind of time.

☐ Tell your boss that the proposed new office arrangement, which he/she personally designed, will cause many new problems.

☐ Inform a peer that he/she has a personal hygiene problem on hot summer days.

4. After each statement has been read, ask participants to position themselves at an appropriate point between the two signs, regarding the signs as a five-point continuum. (Give them these instructions: "If reluctant, go to or near the appropriate sign; if willing, go to or near the other sign; if undecided, take a mid-room position between the two signs.")

5. After all the statements have been read, process the activity. Ask participants what they noticed about their behavior. Anticipate answers such as: "I was timid in a fair number of situations," "I was surprised at the variety of positions everyone took, some like mine, some quite different."

Note: The stand-up continuum can also be used to indicate the degree of stress or change one is experiencing ("nothing is changing in my life now" vs.

"everything is changing now"); the extent of learning one acquired from the course (little, moderate amount, a great deal); one's attitude about a (possibly controversial) subject (unfavorable, neutral, favorable).

Ballistic Break

At break time put everyone into a circular congo line; have everyone put their hands on the hips of the person in front of them. To the accompaniment of an appropriate musical tape, have people go into motion. The idea is to get the hips moving and the "juices" flowing.

Causing Change Creatively

Position your participants in two lines so that each person faces a partner. Instruct participants to look their partner over carefully and try to remember everything they observed.

Now ask people to turn their backs on one another and to change seven things about their appearances. Explain that it's natural to feel awkward when changes are made. (Anticipate laughter when changes are made.)

Ask participants to turn around, again facing the same partner. People notice that jewelry and clothing have been moved around or removed entirely.

Repeat the prior instructions two more times, each time asking for seven more changes. People now find that it is getting harder to take off or change anything else.

At this point people are puzzled as to the purpose of the exercise. The trainer (Kenneth Blanchard, author of *The One-Minute Manager*) explains: "Be careful how much you ask in change. You thought first of what you could get rid of—how to do more with less. Next time you are faced with change, think instead of how to better use your resources" [3].

Tag Out

In a role-play activity, set up a group of role players who stand in line and wait for an opportunity to join the activity when someone currently playing "wants out" and signals that by raising his/her hand. (See the "tag-out" role-play procedure described in Chapter 5).

Energizers

At certain points in your training activities it may be highly desirable to re-invigorate your participant group. This may occur because of a lengthy formal presentation, a heavy lunch, or a long day. Participants who are ordinarily active back on the job particularly need recharging. Brief "pick-me-ups" can make a real difference between participant liveliness and lethargy, which in turn bear on interest, enthusiasm, and creativity.

If you require an energizer to relieve tension, particularly if your participants at the outset are filled with resentment or stress, here's one suggested by Allison Blankenship, a training manager for Uniscribe Professional Services, Boston [4]:

1. Before your trainees arrive, place a nine-inch deflated balloon on all chairs.

2. When everyone is seated, start by asking: "Anyone here who doesn't want to be?" or "Who feels stressed today?" (Anticipate a lot of quick smiles.)

3. Ask group members to blow out all the stress in their systems into the balloons. Advise: "Keep blowing until you've exhaled all your stress" (Anticipate laughter as some balloons exceed capacity and explode.)

4. With balloons blown up, ask the group participants to pinch the neck of the balloon in their fingers rather than tying a knot,

5. Ask everyone to hold the balloons over their heads.

6. Now tell the group: "I am going to check to see who has the most stress." (You walk around the room to make your inspection,)

7. Advise your trainees at your count of 3, to release their hold on the balloons. Anticipate hilarious responses, which will ease the tension at once and help to create a positive learning environment.

In addition to the fatigue factor, dissension/conflict among group members may also be a threat to group cohesion and thus group progress. If so, an energizer may be very much in order.

Several activities discussed in this section on movement can be used as energizers, for example, "Ballistic Break," "Ball Toss," "Energy Check," "Group Gibberish," and "Trust Fall." For an exercise-in-place activity, use "Stretch Break."

Added energizers are given in Chapter 1, under "Icebreakers," for example, "The Gordian Knot" and "Out of Sight."

Relaxers

If at certain stages in your program you wish to relax participants or to establish a quiet, thoughtful mood, consider the use of guided imagery, music, and meditation. For activities involving the use of guided imagery and music, see Chapter 4. Also see the activities given in this chapter under "Movement" ("Meditation in Motion," "Group Hum," and "Guided Imagery").

Shifting to Right Brain Thinking

Formal inputs, if abundant or prolonged, are quite likely to put participants into a highly intellectual or left brain frame of mind. If you would like participants to shift gears, that is, move from left-brain (logical, rational) thinking to right-brain (spontaneous, creative) thinking, the following fun-type activities, in succession, can contribute positively to such a goal.

Start things off by telling participants: "We've had a lot of heavy intellectual stuff. We now want to get into a fun, creative mood. So let's do some things that will help us accomplish that."

Group Gibberish

Have participants move all chairs to the walls and take standing positions. Then instruct them to mill around the room, talking loudly at their colleagues in gibberish. Stop the activity after three or four minutes.

Guided Imagery

Have participants stand in a circle, close their eyes, and reflect on a highly imaginative bit of imagery such as the following: "You are on a space ship. You are enjoying a voyage into outer space. You pass breath-taking galaxies; you can almost reach out and touch the moon. Suddenly you see another space ship. It is larger than yours, emitting bright, colorful lights. It is trying to hook up with your ship. You now see . . ." (Have participants continue the imagery, going around the circle until everyone has contributed to it.)

Exercises

Be on the lookout for and utilize exercises that require some movement or physical activity. Several examples follow.

Praise Bombardment

1. Have participants move the furniture to the walls. Then ask your participants to form two lines, everyone facing someone in particular. (The double line may have as many as 10–15 pairs. In a small room, two sets of double lines may be more appropriate.)

2. Designate the two lines "A" and "B." Tell the participants that: "We are going to conduct an experiment in giving and receiving praise. Those in line A will give their partner praise for five minutes—this can be on anything: appearance, dress, smile, performance in the program so far, performance on the job (if one knows of it), etc. Those in line B are to listen, 'drink it in,' but not to respond orally."

3. Process the experience. Ask questions such as these: How did you feel about receiving praise? (Secure several responses.) How did you feel about giving praise? (Secure several responses.) Any other observations? Conclude the exercise by pointing out that in our culture it's very difficult for many people (supervisors, parents) to give praise (positive reinforcement). Also, some people have difficulty receiving praise. They may discount it by saying things like: "Oh, it wasn't much," or "Oh, I've had this dress a long time," or "Aw, shucks, anybody could have done it."

4. In some situations it may be desirable to reverse the roles and let those in line B become the praise givers. In this case, have people acquire a new partner. Another variation, which should be used carefully, is to reverse the procedure and let those in line B give negative feedback to their new partners. This will make the receivers uncomfortable, emphasizing the destructive effects of negative reinforcement, even in an exercise situation.

Trust Fall

This is an exercise involving physical activity and contact as well as movement. Here are the procedures:

1. Have participants form a very tight circle of about eight participants.

2. Ask for a volunteer to enter the inside of the circle.

3. The volunteer is to stand in a stiff, erect way, eyes closed, and to fall back on a signal from the trainer.

4. The participants in the circle then gently move the volunteer around the circle.

5. Ask for other volunteers to enter the circle and engage in the trust fall.

6. Process the action: Did you trust the group to catch you? How did it feel to be moved about? Did the activity affect or improve group cohesion?

Note: Pairs (one on one) may also conduct the trust fall, but the receivers must be physically able to cope with a falling, inert body.

Frame Game

1. Select a topic you wish your participant group to focus upon, for example, leadership, values, praise, delegation.

2. Develop a set of statements, about four or five per participant, and type them on 3" × 5" cards. The statements should be written so that participants will find some statements philosophically acceptable and some not.

3. Give each person a set of cards (four or five).

4. Instruct participants to review their cards, stand up, find a partner, and exchange their cards. The

exchange is designed to "perfect" one's set of cards, that is, to get rid of those which are undesirable or even repugnant.

5. Have each participant repeat the process of exchange with a new partner some five or six times.

6. Have participants meet in small groups to discuss their cards—the ones they like and the ones they don't.

7. Process the activity after the small group work.

Note:

1. A variation of this activity is to let the participants develop the statements and print them on blank cards. A possible topic is ideas about motivation.

2. "Frame" simply refers to the concept of a frame, vehicle, or format, which you use to "plug in" any topic you wish, as illustrated in Figure 15-10.

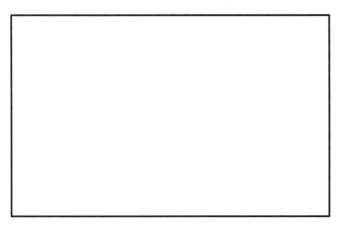

Figure 15-10. Graphic presentation of the "frame" concept.

Role Play

Have participants, in pairs, role play a supervisor who approaches a subordinate who is on a scaffold. (Use a chair to simulate the condition of height.) The problem: The subordinate has failed to use the heavy safety belt required by safety regulations.

Networking

If one of your goals in a supervisory (or other) training program is to encourage post-program support (networking), have participants do the following:

1. Provide data along the lines suggested in the work sheet in Appendix 55, that is, help wanted/ help offered. The data may be written on a flip-chart for easy reading.

2. Post the flipchart sheets to the wall.

3. Move around the room to inspect the posted sheets, entering their name and phone number to offer and/or request help.

Note:

1. This exercise may be presented as an icebreaker or at other stages in the program.

2. The large sheets may be retained on the wall so that data may be entered throughout the program. At program's end, the participants may retrieve their sheets from the wall.

Resource Rotation

If you have five or ten resource people—experts on a particular subject—and you want your total audience (25–50) to sip at the learned cup of all or most of them, you can accomplish your goal via this procedure:

1. Set up five to ten "stations"—round tables are best if you have them. Post a large card on a two- or three-foot post which labels the name of the resource person and his/her specialty.

2. Ask your participants to go to the expert of their choice. Let them know, of course, that they will have a chance to visit with the other experts, too.

3. Let each expert interact (talk, advise, answer questions) with his/her group for some 15–20 minutes, depending on the number of stations and available time.

4. When the allotted time is up, blow the whistle and ask people to move to another location.

Note: The ratio of stations to participants should be based on the size of the participant group. Ideally, each expert should have the opportunity to communicate with five to ten participants at any one time. Of course, the actual number of people who visit a particular station or table will depend upon participant needs and interests and possibly on the prestige of the resource persons as well. To prevent an overflow at one table and limited visitation at another, set up a ground rule that no more than *x* number of participants may visit a table at any one time.

Other Opportunities for Movement

Be on the alert for various ways to secure movement of participants. Some examples:

☐ Although it may not always be possible, it is helpful to have lunch at a "removed" location. Similarly, coffee should be served outside or away from the training room so that at least some movement is required. (Of course, many trainers will prefer to have the coffee close at hand to conserve time.) In passing, we should note that there is nothing sacred about the twice-a-day coffee break. Why not, then, consider shorter, more frequent breaks, say, five for the training day? Remember, it is highly unusual for people in their normal situation to sit in one place for considerable periods of time without some movement. So why should we make training a less-than-normal experience for our participants?

Also, in a "cultural island" setting, consider arranging the schedule so that free time for recreation is available between 3:30 P.M. and 5:30 P.M. Then hold an evening session after dinner. Try to limit the pre-dinner cocktails so that everyone is able to come back for work after dinner!

☐ Encourage participants to take different seats each day. Although this is not movement in the physical sense such as the activities just described, this procedure will help to break up the comfort of the routine. Explain to the participants why you are asking them to do this, of course: "You'll learn more if you interact with someone you don't already know. It may not be as comfortable, but it may help your learning."

On the subject of seating, it should be apparent that activities involving movement can best be engineered if (1) chairs are movable (avoid the heavy executive-type chair or the fixed seating of auditoriums), (2) desks or tables are not used unless essential for considerable writing (most people can do their minor writing chores on a notebook), and (3) the room is adequately large and "loose." If projectors are in use, be certain that their electrical wires are not likely to be tripped over.

☐ Allow participants to leave their locations to enter data on flipcharts and to post flipcharts on the walls.

☐ In problem-solving sessions where participants enter ideas on cards which are then posted (pinned) to a wall or special board, participants should be encouraged to walk up front to do the posting, as opposed to having the trainer/facilitator do it for them.

☐ Pairs (dyads) can have a "walking meeting" to discuss a problem. In warm weather this can be in a park, in a meadow, on a shady path, or if the training is in town, around the block. The movement should help to provide both a change of pace and a change in perspective.

☐ Consider permitting participants to refill their cups or glasses at any time, rather than insisting that they wait until the break. This freedom to move about will help to provide an informal atmosphere. Inform them at the outset that such movement is O.K., unless, of course, you find it too distracting. (*Note:* Some of the distraction can be reduced by having the beverage table *inside* the classroom, thereby eliminating the opening and closing of doors.)

☐ Use one wall for a "running" mural for participants to record in an illustrative or graphic way their initial reactions to the program, learnings during the day, and final reactions.

☐ In the evaluation of completed training, have participants position themselves with a group with which they identify; for example, with those who learned a lot, with those who learned to a moderate degree, or with those who feel they learned minimally. Briefly process the feelings of those in each group about their degree of learning.

A final, "contemporaneous" aspect of participant movement: The trainer and the group needn't worry about establishing smoking and nonsmoking sections in the training room if participants are continually rearranging themselves in small groups, pairs, trios, and role playing teams. The movement makes such segregation impractical.

You, as trainer, should use movement in as many ways as possible:

- ☐ You should move among the small groups (discussion groups, role playing teams) to garner impressions, reactions, live data, etc., as opposed to standing "above and beyond" the action. This movement will also help to show that you want to be one of the group, not the traditional pedagogue.
- ☐ You can position yourself at *different* points in the room when exercises, games, and fishbowls are processed. The discussion can be led from the *new* position in the room.
- ☐ You can work with two sets of flipcharts set 15–20 feet apart, thereby creating movement for yourself.
- ☐ You can post flipchart sheets on the wall.

FLIPCHARTING

Flipcharts, also called newsprint, are indispensable tools for the trainer and the participant group. (In fact, some would say that the three main tools of a trainer/facilitator are flipcharts, felt-tip pens, and masking tape!) Flipcharts can be used to advantage in several ways:

- ☐ For inputs from (or by) the trainer, prepared on a pre-session basis. (These should be few in number lest one take the program away from the participants.)
- ☐ For inputs from the group at large. The data may be obtained by the trainer from various participants or from spokespersons representing small groups.
- ☐ For inputs (or reports) from small groups that have been entered on the flipchart by either group members or a recorder appointed by the small group.
- ☐ For inputs by a dyad or triad who are working on an assigned project, such as steps to implement a plan or project back on the job (for example, a new quality circle program).

Obviously, our major concern is with the last three procedures, since they actively involve individuals and the group by securing and posting their ideas. Trainer-

prepared flipcharts, conversely, are *didactic* rather than participative tools.

Purposes

The use of flipcharts—which I call "flipcharting"— is best accomplished when all the big sheets produced by the group with the aid of the trainer are posted to the walls for the full life of the course, space permitting. (I recall a workshop that I conducted for new trainers wherein the group was asked late in the day the following question: "I've been posting these flipcharts on the wall all day. Why have I been doing this?" Came a reply from one participant: "You're doing this because all facilitators like to do this!" In another program a participant advanced this reason: "Because you don't have a wastebasket!") Flipcharting, then, is designed to accomplish the following purposes:

- ☐ To provide reinforcement to what is said by the trainer and the participants.
- ☐ As a visual aid, it can significantly augment retention.
- ☐ To serve as a ready and indisputable source of reference to what was said previously.
- ☐ To aid in note taking.
- ☐ To help the latecomer or absentee to catch up with things.
- ☐ To encourage participation. It provides an opportunity to get one's ideas displayed before the entire group.
- ☐ To provide participants with pride in accomplishment (recognition, reward) relative to their contributions. After all, the *participants* made the flipcharts. In a sense the trainer only served as a "scribe" for the group. (Of course, the trainer may also have posed the "right" questions, sharpened the issues, encouraged participation, and condensed the verbiage, besides doing the actual writing.)
- ☐ To create a sense of atmosphere. ("This is not just a classroom or a training room. It is a workroom, *our* workroom; for it is our work that is on the walls.")
- ☐ To record progress. By posting the flipcharts in sequence, the trainer provides everyone with a running record of what has been accomplished.

In some cases a pattern of results may be evidenced. (Depending on the need, it may help to date the sheets.)

☐ As an aid or control for the trainer so that he/she can see that his/her coverage is on the right track, that is, reaching the goals.

☐ To aid in a reviewing session of course activities that have been completed.

☐ To serve as a role model for all those in attendance, especially managers. It is hoped that some day all managers will have a flipchart in their offices (and regard it as their key problem-solving tool) instead of the usual fancy desks, chairs, sofas, and other assorted status symbols.

☐ For the trainer, who can take the sheets back to the office, the flipchart can serve as notes for future sessions or as a basis for reviewing and redesigning the program, either in whole or in part.

Skill Points

To help you do a good job of flipcharting, here are some skill points:

☐ Use the largest size paper to provide maximum visibility and clarity.

☐ Start with a new pad of paper to avoid the nuisance of having to install a new pad midway in a presentation or while recording group data. (Or have a second easel handy.)

☐ Use the broad-tipped marking pens to ensure maximum clarity.

☐ To ensure visibility, avoid writing on the bottom of the flipchart sheet. This caution is particularly important if you are using a lecture hall seating arrangement.

☐ Pen a welcoming statement ("Welcome to ____" or simply "Good Morning") and/or graphic (for example, a round, happy face) on the visible flipchart pad. Why should people have to stare at an empty flipchart pad for 15–20 minutes while they wait for things to get started?

☐ As recorder for the group, be sure that you are capturing participants' ideas as opposed to replacing them with your own. Check with the idea presenter whenever you are in doubt.

☐ Share the recording chore with a participant from time to time. (*Note:* If you are perceived as *the* leader, it may be desirable to share the leadership role to help set a more democratic learning atmosphere.)

☐ Consider using two flipcharts. This will provide you with the opportunity to move around and, as may be helpful in some cases, will allow you to compare the data on the two flipchart sheets.

☐ Another use of two flipcharts is as a time saver: use one for previously prepared material; use the other for fresh data generated by the group.

☐ Make liberal use of the T-column. It is an invaluable tool for displaying comparative and contrasting data and has considerable value whenever two columns are required (for example, in risk analysis).

☐ Use a flipchart sheet as a visual reminder to respond to questions or issues that were deferred. The "back burner" flipchart will "keep the trainer honest" and assure participants that their postponed points will be addressed.

☐ The flipchart can serve as a basis for post-session or post-course participant-prepared handouts. (Remember, the data belongs to the participants.) This can be done in one of two ways:

1. Have your secretary type up the flipchart ideas from the big sheets for next-day or post-course distribution.

2. Take a self-developing picture of flipcharts you want participants to retain. Four such photos can be posted on a single sheet of paper and run through a copying machine to produce multiple copies. (You may wish to follow the camera procedure for your own use; it will eliminate the need to carry back to your office the large and clumsy newsprint sheets.)

☐ Try to conduct your training in rooms that have a lot of usable wall space. Rooms with a wall of windows, drapes, or paintings are poor training rooms, for they frustrate attempts at flipcharting.

☐ Post flipcharts with masking tape. Unlike cellophane tape, it will not remove paint.

☐ Try to secure a large enough training room so that you can post the completed flipcharts without climbing over people. As an alternative, post the sheets during breaks, lunch, or role plays—times when participants will not be near the walls.

☐ Try to print or write legibly, that is, in large size with bold letters.

☐ When posting the flipchart to the wall, fold over the end of the tape toward yourself. This simple procedure will make it easy to remove the flipchart sheet without picking at the end.

☐ To facilitate locating and picking up the tape end from your masking tape roll, place the small plastic tab from a bread wrapper or a paper clip on the end of the tape.

☐ As a back-up, should you run out of tape or forget to take it along, wrap some masking tape around two or three magic markers.

☐ If your participants (in teams) will have to post several flipchart sheets to the wall in the course of their training, give each team a magic marker with masking tape already rolled around it. In this way, you eliminate the chore of personally providing tape pieces to each team for each posting. (Or, if the budget allows, provide each team with a roll of masking tape.)

☐ Use multicolored markers. They heighten interest and aid retention. Be certain to avoid weak colors such as yellow, light orange, or pale red.

☐ If possible, use water-based, nontoxic markers. This type does not bleed through the paper onto other sheets.

☐ Don't let a flipchart remain on the easel, for it serves as a distractor. Either flip the sheet over, post it on the wall, or discard it.

☐ If a fair number of flipcharts have to be distributed for participant use, you can "economize" by cutting the large sheet vertically in two halves. Also, rather than providing each group or team with a full roll of masking tape, consider wrapping some around the large section of the felt-tip pens.

☐ One way to provide small groups with flipcharts is simply to hand them several sheets. Another way is to post on the wall two or three blank sheets, with masking tape, at several points in the room. These points would be the areas where the small groups would meet and write on the flipcharts. Felt-tip pens may be distributed to the participants or affixed to the wall in advance (next to the flipcharts) with masking tape.

☐ Use a single color of pen for each major topic, theme, or unit. Thus, if four main subjects are covered, the flipcharts would be written in four colors. Color coding is designed to facilitate the search for particular references. Another use of color is to indicate data gathered *before* the course, such as information from customers, from employees, from the participants themselves, or from superiors. As appropriate you can use green to highlight money-making approaches, skills, and scenarios, and red for money-losing ones.

☐ Consider posting a flipchart on the wall labeled "Unfinished Business." Advise participants to enter items on it at any time when it is apparent that some need is not being met. The flipchart may have subcategories on it such as "More of," "Additions," and "Needs Clarification" to help participants better describe their needs vis-à-vis themselves and the course. You may wish to tape a pen to the wall for convenient use.

☐ At various points in the program (session, course), ask participants to walk around the room to review the flipcharts. This procedure may be particularly helpful if a detailed or comprehensive evaluation form is to be completed at program's end and a reminder about course coverage would be useful.

☐ If your writing is a bit hard to read, you may wish to consider one or more of these approaches: Let an associate or participant write for you; print rather than write; use lined flipcharts if there is a problem in writing in a straight line; use larger-size flipcharts with king-size, felt-tip pens.

☐ If you have a flipchart pad, but no easel, you can use the wall as a writing and display board. The procedure is to tear off a batch of sheets from the big pad and tape the sheets to the wall. Each flipchart sheet is placed just above the one underneath it. The tape is placed on the two sides (horizontally) of the sheet, at or near the top, rather than on the top of the sheet (vertically), as is normally done to post the big sheets to a wall.

☐ At times an exercise, game, or other activity may have the participants in small groups in different parts of the training room. In processing (analyzing) the completed action, it may be desirable to have the participants stay with their small groups rather than returning to their more conventional group-at-large configuration. If so, move the flipchart pad and easel to an adequately central point in the room and lead the discussion from that new, more visible location.

☐ Try to talk to the audience rather than to the flipchart. If, while entering data, you have a comment for the group, simply stop writing, turn completely around, and make your statement.

While flipcharts are standard equipment in most organizations, some still shy away from them. Trainer/consultant Patricia A. McLagan cites an incident involving an organization which told her prior to the training that "the group won't go for it." She replied that she would not use them throughout the process. But she insisted on using them to document participant input and as a tool to help the group reach decisions. The result: What the group "wouldn't stand for" turned out to be one of the most successful sessions they ever had [5]. *Moral:* Stand for your principles concerning the use of flipcharts, but modify them to avoid alienating the sponsor or client.

HUMOR AND FUN

Learning that is enjoyable, fun-filled, and humor-based is always easier to take than that which is super-serious, deadly, and dull. If we, as trainers, can put our participants in a relaxed, receptive, childlike mood via laughter and fun, the training experience will be a joy for everyone concerned. Humor, enjoyment, and learning are not antithetical to one another.

By humor we don't merely mean dusting off a lot of old jokes and projecting them intermittently and mercilessly on your participants, or trying to entertain them in other ways. The trainer is neither a stand-up comic nor a supper club M.C. Rather, we have in mind the use of the sophisticated techniques advocated and employed by educator/trainer and humor

authority Dr. Joel Goodman. He favors the use of the following eight "E-lettered" devices [6]:

☐ *Environment.* First, build a humor-laden atmosphere via a bulletin board that has cartoons, funny quotations, poems, and/or photos. Your participants can check these out before the start-up, at breaks, and after lunch; garner a few chuckles from them; and interact a bit more easily with fellow participants.

☐ *Enter.* You may wish to start a session by sharing a personal, humorous anecdote or a funny incident illustrating the program's theme. (At one time I conducted EEO workshops. I began things by recalling an incident that had occurred at a large EEO conference that I had attended. The speaker made the point that treating all racial and ethnic groups with dignity and respect was not a new concept. To buttress his observation, he asked the audience if anyone knew who had said: "I never met a man I didn't like." As if on cue, a guy in the back of the room yelled out: "Elizabeth Taylor." The crowd roared. The speaker, of course, was quoting American humorist Will Rogers. This true incident always got a big laugh from my workshop groups.)

One trainer finds that her use of humor is the best way to relieve tension—the group's and her own. She thus may start out by saying something like this: "We've got eight hours worth of training to squeeze into two, but with a group that learns as fast as this one, we should still have time for a ten-minute break and a chess game. Well . . . perhaps not chess, but maybe checkers." She garners a lot of laughs thereby and simultaneously communicates some key information: There's a lot to cover, they're smart, the class will run two hours, and there will be a break. She may also use other humorous devices, such as showing a cartoon on an overhead transparency or posting a trivia question to be answered at session's end.

In the warm-up phase of the first session you may wish to make a point about the need for participation by everyone. I often pass out the following statement as an encourager and chuckle producer:

NXXDXD VXRY MUCH!

Xvxn though my typxwritxr is an old modxl, it works quitx wxll xxcxpt for onx kxy. Thxrx arx 46 kxys that function wxll xnough, but just onx not working makxs thx diffxrxncx.

Somxtimxs it sxxms that our group is somxwhat likx my typxwritxr, not all thx kxys arx functioning propxrly. You may say: "Wxll, I am only onx pxrson. It won't makx much diffxrxncx." But, you sxx, thx group to bx xffxctivx nxxds thx activx participation of xvxry pxrson.

So thx nxxt timx you think you arx only onx pxrson and that your xffort is not nxxdxd, rxmxmbxr my old typxwritxr and say to yoursxlf, "I am a kxy pxrson and am nxxdxd vxry much."

☐ *Ear Ye, Ear Ye.* Use the "circular whip" (whip around the room) and let each participant share a funny joke, quotation, or perspective on the work at hand. Not everyone may have something to contribute, but all will have the opportunity to do so. (In one workshop that I ran on delegation, one of my participants defined it as "deliriously dodging the drudgery which you can unload or dump on someone else.") This device, obviously, encourages listening to one another as opposed to focusing on the trainer alone; it also loosens people up.

☐ *Exercise.* Look for ways to introduce humor into training exercises. For example, when I introduce brainstorming to a group, I have them practice it by listing uses of a somewhat ridiculous object, for example, a pair of mixed socks, an old tennis ball, or a live elephant; or listing causes of particular phenomena, for example, fleas on my dog or my frequently missing A.M. newspaper. Humor, in these instances, is also mind-stretching, a means of encouraging creativity.

A fun thing to do when participants seem to be suffering from the "blahs," discontent, or disappointment, is to engender some robust laughter via this simple procedure:

1. Ask everyone to stand up.

2. Have everyone stare straight ahead and say: "Hee, hee, hee." Start low and repeat it several times, each time increasing the volume until a loud roar is produced.

3. Then turning heads to the right, have everyone say: "Ho, ho, ho." Repeat, this time turning to the left side. With each "Ho, ho, ho," start low and finish robustly.

4. Ask: "How are you feeling now? Good? Let's hear it. Let's hear it again."

You can have a lot of fun by doing two things: (1) provide humorous tasks/activities and (2) convert the activity or exercise into a competitive event or game. For example, I may have two or more groups compete in the identification and listing on a flipchart of certain metaphors. The team which has the greatest number of metaphors is the winner. A small prize will add energy and fun. Allow 10–15 minutes for the small group work. Two possible topics are metaphors using body parts or animal references. You can start the groups off by providing these examples:

1. *Body Parts Metaphors:* "I can't stomach that"; "I'm all ears"; "foot in the mouth"; "pain in the neck"; "get off my back"; "he's a headache"; "they're dragging their feet."

2. *Animal Metaphors:* "It's a dog's life"; "dog eat dog"; "clever as a fox"; "bull in the china shop"; "quiet as a mouse."

The "archeological game" will also create a lot of fun-filled rivalry (see Chapter 6).

When small groups have to select a leader and you wish them to do this randomly, rather than having them assign the task to the same person, you can provide some fun criteria for the selection. For example, the one who has the most $10 bills in his/her wallet or purse; the one who was most recently promoted; the one who has the brightest colored ballpoint pen; the one who came here from the farthest distance.

☐ *Exaggerate.* By stretching examples and demonstrations to the point of hilarity, you can make your point well. For example, I have trained managers in how to conduct the annual performance review. I had two of my participants act out (a demonstration role play) all the horrors of a really third-rate appraisal interview. They used a script I provided. I also selected role players whom I thought could really ham it up and get a big kick doing so.

☐ *Engage.* Provide activities which involve movement and fun. For example, I have found that the icebreaker "the Ball Toss" (page 334) raises the decibel level considerably and loosens people up with laughter. The University Associates' *Handbook of Structured Experiences for Human Relations Training,* Vol. 5, No. 149, describes a number of "Energizers: Group Starters."

☐ *Enhance.* The key to good humor is that which enhances participants' readiness to learn. In other words, you want humor that encourages laughter with people, not at them. This means avoiding putdowns, stereotyping, ridiculing, demeaning, playing practical jokes.

☐ *Extend.* As trainers we want to transfer or extend the new learning to the back-home situation. Dr. Goodman offers several suggestions. One is to use a humorous "chain." After the workshop ends, the person on the top of the group's roster sends a humorous item (cartoon, quotation, joke) to the next one on the list and so on. Another is to develop a "jargon dictionary," for example, "It's under consideration," "I agree with you, but . . ." Third, during the workshop, appoint on a rotating basis a "court jester" who is responsible for providing a fun thing (a humorous skit which serves as a lampoon of the course, some art work which has some fun with certain course concepts, etc.).

Dr. Goodman's eight "E" concepts should also trigger interest in looking for devices which:

☐ Kid the instructor (yourself).

☐ Kid the subject matter.

☐ Kid about the facility or food being provided, especially if it is high-calorie or monotonous. (This may be a sensitive area, however.)

But one "no-no" is to kid the organization and/or its hallowed traditions, or the professions or specializations in which your participants work. These are cultural taboos and, if violated, they may backfire badly. If the participants do this on their own, that's O.K., of course.

PROPS FOR EMPATHY

When developing interactive, experiential activities—games, exercises, role plays, etc.—try to think in terms of heightening or intensifying the experience with the aid of real-life, everyday objects. Typically, cost is minimal or even nonexistent, but these objects can produce a great impact on participant learning and retention.

The trick is to ask yourself questions concerning the proposed simulation. The following are some example situations that lend themselves to the use of props:

☐ *In an activity on eye safety, how can we vivify the effect of the loss of sight?* Have participants put a cotton ball over one eye and tape it in place with masking tape, or have them wear a pair of glasses with one lens masked over.

☐ *How can we demonstrate the effect of carelessness around fast-moving machines?* Allow participants to run a weiner through a machine to show what machinery can do to a finger.

☐ *How can we show the great value of wearing the hard hat?* Use the before-and-after method in a demonstration that is not likely to be forgotten. First, drop a heavy object such as a bowling ball or an item in the workplace on a round watermelon. Let your participants observe the ensuing crunch, squish, and squirt. Then repeat the drop on a new melon, this time placing a hard hat on it.

☐ *How can we simulate an injury to an arm?* Have everyone bandage his/her arm and wear a sling.

☐ *How can we drive home the importance of the tactile sense in performing certain tasks requiring acute finger dexterity, such as threading a needle?* Provide participants with surgical gloves.

☐ *How can we give added empathy to the execution of a given role, for example, in black-white communication?* Provide black and white masks to the role players and use the role reversal technique.

☐ *How can we augment identification with a given occupation in an exercise or role play?* Provide appropriate costumes, for example, a doctor's smock, a laborer's hard hat, a police officer's badge, or a truck driver's cap.

☐ *How can we sensitize customer contact personnel to the concerns of older customers?* Have the employee/trainee don eyeglasses smeared with Vaseline to limit vision, stuff cotton in his/her ears to reduce hearing, and have him/her wear rubber gloves to impede writing ability. These procedures were used by the American Bankers Association (ABA) in its member banks [7] and by the Florida Power and Light Company [8].

Note: According to the ABA, older people hold 68% of all bank deposits, and their checking account balances average 25%–50% higher than the other age groups.

☐ *In a role play (or other activity), how can we increase empathy for the handicapped?* Have role players use a wheelchair.

☐ *How can we dramatically introduce the topic of "control" in a management training course?* Provide three to five participants with yo-yos; ask them to come to the front of the class and play with their toys. Anticipate that several players will experience some difficulty in operating their yo-yos. Ask: "What is significant here? Why are we doing this demo?" If class members don't provide the proper answer, do so yourself. *The answer:* "The reason the yo-yos didn't operate smoothly was *lack of control.* So control, as a management tool, is very important. And that's what we're going to deal with in this session—problems of control."

Note: As an alternative, you could pass out several different metal handles, purchasable in your local hardware store. Then ask: "What is significant about these handles?" Again, as above, explain that handles are tools for control, and control is the topic for discussion.

☐ *How can we simulate a telephone pole on which a maintenance person is working?* Use a chair to stand on. (In a group exercise all who are linemen would stand on a chair.)

☐ *How can we show the "connectedness" of the self to all its components, such as:*
1. *The physical self*
2. *The intellectual self*
3. *The emotional self*

4. *The sensual self (includes all the "holes" in the body—eyes, ears, nose, mouth, navel, genitals, nipples, skin)*
5. *The international self (the way one reacts with others)*
6. *The nutritional self (relates to solids and liquids for physical growth)*
7. *The contextual self (sound, light, air, color movement, space, time influences, our being)*
8. *The spiritual self (which may or may not be related to religion)*

After a short talk on this topic, ask a participant to come to the front of the room. The participant is the "I" or "the self." Tie a rope around that person's waist. Then call up eight participants, one at a time, each representing the various parts of the self. As each "part" comes up front, tie the rope around that person's waist. Have all of them mill around to demonstrate how the self is pulled in various directions by its component parts. Then instruct the self to "get control"—not let each part lead a life of its own—and to tell each part what it must do to help connect or integrate self [9].

☐ *How can we help customer service personnel to visualize what they look like if they lose their cool and "unload" on an upset customer?*

Customer service authority Dr. Scott J. Simmerman (in a handout prepared in conjunction with a presentation at an annual national conference of the American Society for Training and Development) describes the "Grumpy and the Mirror" role-playing exercise, which is designed to show customer service people what they look like when they overreact to (or become upset with) an angry customer. Here are Dr. Simmermann's role-playing procedures [10]:

1. Ask for two volunteers, one to be an angry customer and the other a customer-service person.
2. Ask one volunteer to act as would a totally obnoxious and upset customer; tell the other to react to this customer as he/she would like, so as to really "unload" and "get even."
3. Run the role play for a minute or two before the total group.

4. Lead the audience in applause for the demonstration role players. Point out how easy it is to fall into the trap of behaving like the customer does. Dr. Simmerman calls that behavior "mirroring."

5. Provide both role players with a hand-held mirror and ask them to repeat their prior enactment with the same intensity, this time looking in their mirrors as they talk. The result: The role players can't perform with the same energy. In fact, they begin to laugh.

6. Point out the significance of this result for on-the-job performance: Have a mirror handy at the work site. Look at it before answering an angry telephone caller or trying to interact with an angry or upset customer on a face-to-face basis. Most of us have difficulty acting mad when we have to see ourselves behaving in that unattractive manner. Also, by placing a large mirror in a position where the irate customer can see himself/herself, we may calm the angry demeanor of the customer.

☐ *How can we "dramatize" the concept of the manager as a coach?* If the budget can handle it, provide your participants with a baseball cap emblazoned with the word "Coach." Add company colors and initials to the caps. *Key concept:* Managers wear many hats, and that of coach is a significant one.

☐ *After our diversity seminars are over, what reminders can we provide the participant managers to be sensitive to the diversity of subordinates, fellow team members, and co-workers?* One answer is to pass out the "diversity sensitivity kit" developed by the Fargo, North Dakota, chapter of the Society of Human Resources Management (SHRM). The kit contains items such as the following [11]:

Button: A reminder to "button your lips" to keep from uttering hurtful comments or jokes about people; avoid insensitive statements that are racist, sexist, or homophobic.

Life Saver: A reminder to be a "life saver" to others by courageously standing up to negative/punishing comments that can diminish a person's self-esteem.

Toothpick: A reminder to pick out the best qualities/ characteristics of all persons irrespective of their race, gender, age, physical limitations, height, weight, or other superficial characteristics.

Golden thread: A reminder that friendship and kindness serve as the "golden thread" that binds together the hearts of all of us.

Mint: A reminder that you're worth a "mint" to your outfit by eradicating insensitive discrimination and harassment.

Eraser: A reminder that mistakes on our part will occur. So we need to ease our embarrassment by offering regrets/apologies when we "blow it."

Magnifying glass: A reminder to observe more closely how you and your organization react/respond to acts of racism, agism, sexism, and other types of hurtful discrimination.

Marker: A reminder to make your mark as a leader, to have fun and always work at making those you work with feel special. (A specific question to ask yourself: How many times today did I act to help others feel better about themselves?)

Some added examples of the use of props are:

☐ To introduce the topic of creativity, show your group a steel stapler, preferably an older one if you have it. Ask: How can this product be made more useful? Secure answers.

Provide an answer of your own. Show a modern stapler (e.g., a Stanley Bostich) which has on both sides of the shaft (which holds the staples) an open slot showing a red metal piece *behind* the staples. This makes visible the small quantity of staples still available. So the red marker in the open slot serves as an advisory to refill the stapler.

☐ To make the point of "cutting ties with the past," pass out small pocket knives.

☐ To point up an overall (or umbrella) concept which encompasses a number of subordinate concepts, flash an umbrella! (Similarly, in an English or writing course, the umbrella can equate the main idea in relation to supporting ones.)

☐ In a vocabulary building activity, either for non–English speakers or for remedial native readers, show a paper clip and ask: "How can this paper clip help to build your vocabulary?" If no one has an answer, provide this one: "Each time you look up a word in your dictionary, put a clip on that page. The next time you add a clip to highlight a new word, check to see if you remember the previous word(s). Remove a clip only when you feel you have achieved full mastery of that word."

Now pass out a large paper clip to all of your students. (Alternatively, the clips could have been passed out when the question of the clip's use was presented.)

☐ Fresh produce—a banana, a carrot, or a green or yellow zucchini—can be used as a substitute for:

　a. A mike (microphone) to let paired participants introduce one another after they have interviewed one another to get job or personal data.

　b. A "talking stick" (see Chapter 11). Use: To rotate discussion in a group. One speaks only when one has the stick and then passes it on. Purpose: To have an orderly, low-key dialogue wherein one speaks and everyone else has to listen without interruption.

☐ To make the point of "helping to find your way in a competitive world," pass out small, inexpensive compasses.

Trainer Janet T. Cherry uses props (tools and toys) to bring visual communication into the training room and training session [12]. She finds that they give participants an immediate "hook" to connect session *objectives* with session *content*. By visually or graphically illustrating key learning points, the trainer can assist interpretation, enhance total learning, stimulate the natural creative process (for facilitator/trainer and participants alike), build stronger alliances for common goals, and bring mutual understanding among diverse groups.

The first step in finding a hook, says Cherry, is to ask and answer these questions:

☐ What's the most unique (unusual, special) part of your topic?

☐ What's the most interesting/exciting segment?

☐ What's the most dramatic aspect?

☐ What's the most humorous part?

☐ What do you want people to remember?

☐ What will help cement learning for real transfer to the job?

To be certain that you have selected the proper hook, ask these questions, says Cherry:

☐ Does my hook lead to the session objective?

☐ Will the audience relate to it? (For example, heavy hardware may not impress female participants.)

☐ Is it in sync with my style?

☐ Will it draw the attention I seek?

☐ Will it connect to and provide a transition into my session subject matter?

USING HANDOUTS

Handouts are vital training aids. Their proper selection and use can enrich a program and thereby enhance the learning experience. The checklist in Figure 15-11 is designed to assist you, as a trainer, to rethink your use of handout materials and thereby augment your instructional effectiveness.

One trainer suggests that handouts passed out in class may become a distraction and consume time unreasonably [13]. He thus suggests alternate procedures: pass them out when participants arrive, or just before a break, or, in some cases, use overhead transparencies instead. To simplify their distribution, he places them on a rear table with a sign that reads: "Take one from each pile."

I would suggest that a good guideline to follow in distributing handouts is to only pass out in mid-session those items which are to be used immediately, for example, worksheets, checklists, instruments, quizzes, and cases.

USING SILENCE

As trainers, we typically expect our participants to be active and energized and to engage in all kinds of verbal activity—interviewing, conferring, discussing,

---

Handouts—Help, Hindrance, or Happenstance?

General — No — Yes

1. Do I regard handouts as aids or tools rather than just "throw aways?" — —
2. Do I choose handouts carefully and opt for quality rather than quantity? — —
3. Do I constantly update and enrich my handout files? — —
4. Do I think in terms of *variety* of formats and uses: outlines, charts, graphs, models, cartoons, poems, quotes, cases, articles, question sheets for films, instruction sheets for exercises, editorials, self-quizzes, topic summaries, etc.? — —
5. Do I plan their use carefully? — —
6. Have I secured permission to reproduce copyrighted materials? — —
7. Do I use handouts at *all* stages of the course: 1. *Pre-Session;* 2. *In-Session;* 3. *End-of-Session;* 4. *Post-Session?* — —

A. Pre-Session — No — Yes

1. Do I utilize pre-work materials for one or more of these reasons: — —
   a. To establish early contact with the participants — —
   b. As a "motivator" — —
   c. As a topic introducer — —
   d. To bring everyone up to a common level of understanding of a topic — —
   e. To facilitate entry from the job to the classroom — —
   f. To save time — —
2. Is there a *plan* to tie advance work to *specific* class activities? — —
3. Do advance readings, exercises, etc. consider carefully trainee interests and needs? — —
4. Are instructions re advance work clear and goal-oriented? — —
5. Time factors:
   a. Will the materials be received early enough to work on them? — —
   b. Will the participants' schedules allow for pre-work? — —

B. In-Session — No — Yes

1. Do I provide participants with a bulky notebook of materials "for effect" rather than for actual class use and benefit? — —
2. Are all or most sessions supported by handout materials? — —

3. Do I provide *outlines* so participants can have an *overview* of an activity or the total course? — —
4. Do I hand out materials to advance the session rather than to compete with it (e.g., extensive in-class reading of handouts is to be avoided)? — —
5. Do I pass out more items at any one time than people can digest? — —
6. Do I tap participant motivation via:
   a. Participant-prepared handouts (i.e., assembly and reproduction of ideas developed by participants in their small groups or general sessions)? — —
   b. Encouraging trainees to bring in pertinent materials which can be reproduced for the total group? — —
7. Do I provide in writing key points or summary statements of talks, learnings from exercises, complex ideas, etc.? — —
8. Do I "imagineer" handout distribution (e.g., put an item on everyone's chair during the break)? — —
9. If I use handouts extensively do I try to evaluate their effectiveness? — —

C. End-of-Session — No — Yes

1. Have I provided any materials for backhome reading? — —
2. Have I pointed up the importance of take-home materials so they are seen as reference items rather than "throw aways?" — —
3. Have I allowed enough class time for distribution of final take home materials? — —
4. Should all take-home materials be distributed to everyone or, alternately, might they be placed on a table for optional selection? — —
5. Have I facilitated storage (via notebook, folder or envelope) and retrieval (via dividers) of handouts? — —

D. Post-Session — No — Yes

1. Do I think in terms of *follow-up,* of stimulating participants via handouts provided 1, 3 or 6 months *after* training's end? — —
2. Have I considered contacting course "graduates" re additional materials they might wish to receive? — —
3. Can handouts developed in class by participants be made available to other segments of the organization? — —

Figure 15-11. Use this checklist to rethink your use of handout materials. (Prepared by J. E. Eitington, *Bulletin on Training,* July/August 1977, page 6. Used with special permission from the copyright holder, BNA Communications Inc., 9439 Key West Avenue, Rockville, MD 20850. Further printing or reproduction without specific permission of the publisher is prohibited.)

challenging, critiquing, questioning, responding, initiating, interpreting, summarizing, reporting, and so on. There are numerous instances, however, when the training situation is better served by silence. Here are several such examples:

☐ Role players are given instructions about their roles and asked to enact them. It will be helpful to the role players if they are given several minutes to reflect silently about the nature of their role assignments and how they propose to execute them (their strategy). Certainly, as a minimum, silent reflection will aid in reducing possible anxieties and thus will strengthen the enactments.

☐ Small groups are given an assignment. Again, the opportunity to think through its significance on a quiet basis will be helpful to the participants. They can ask themselves: Do I understand the instructions? How should our group proceed? What outcomes should we strive for?

☐ Individual participants are asked to complete an instrument. The basic work, of course, is done silently. Silence aids the twin processes of *introspection* (how do I see my attitudes, beliefs, values, perceptions, behavior) and *reflection* (making meaning out of the material I have developed/discovered in introspection). The silence inevitably triggers the desire to share verbally what was learned or to seek out the learning from one's colleagues.

☐ Meditation, performed silently, provides participants with an opportunity to experience a change of pace so as to regroup psychologically. It can help one renew one's energies and get in touch with feelings that may be hard to reach while one is in an active, verbal state.

☐ Nonverbal exercises can aid participants to achieve a new awareness based on the use of the other senses, they can help to set a particular mood, and they can produce a change of pace and encourage a deeper contemplation.

☐ In a group discussion or team building session that is marked by an impasse (creative block), fatigue, or possibly conflict accompanied by the expression of unusually strong feelings, the trainer may ask the group to disengage

from the task by taking a silent "time out" for two or three minutes. These moments of silence should help to restore energy, good humor, and creativity, and to chart a new course.

☐ After a profound, highly impacting film, allow participants to reflect quietly for a minute or two on what they have experienced, rather than disrupting the mood by immediately embarking on its discussion.

Long-time trainer/consultant Dugan Laird also suggests that trainees need "silent, introspective time . . . time to put a new information into perspective . . . time to contract with themselves about how they will apply their new skills . . . how they will measure their effectiveness in doing so . . . how they will overcome the inevitable obstacles to change. Such commitment requires an unpressured environment of which silence is one key ingredient" [14].

The trainer can also use silence constructively in other ways; for example, after posing a question to a group, one should wait patiently for a response. The silence may be "painful," but if the group understands that you intend to wait them out, someone in the group will break the silence.

In a T-group, which is a special training situation, of course, participants may lapse into silence for various reasons ranging from extreme caution about revealing feelings to fear of embarrassment from saying something inappropriate or "stupid." The skilled trainer accepts the silence and waits until someone says something. Not everyone can endure silence for any length of time. (Actually, the silent periods seem longer than they really are.) If the group seems completely bent on "clamming up," the trainer may break the silence with a comment of this sort: "We seem to be in a silent mood, which is fine if you find it helpful. I have the feeling, however, that there are many things which could be said, that we have many feelings which are going unexpressed. For starters, would anyone care to explain this silence? Why are we doing it? What does it mean? Is it helpful to group progress? How are we feeling about it?" Questions of this sort are certain to get the group going again.

And in management development programs, particularly in time management, managers (and others) should be encouraged to adopt the practice on the job of having a "quiet period" each day. An hour of silent contemplation for planning and considering major issues, as opposed to dealing continually with the demands of the telephone, the in-box, visitors, meetings, and assorted conflicts and crises, can only make one more calm and thus more effective.

Other opportunities back home to use silence are while engaging in the communication process, particularly in the all-important act of listening, and while coaching and counseling.

All in all, silence is a potent and valuable tool. The effective trainer should understand its potentialities and utilize it appropriately along with the many other techniques available.

TELLING STORIES

Well-thought-out, well-developed stories can capture the imagination and can even reach resistant learners. Stories can entertain, inspire, and instruct. They can fit in anywhere—as introductions, in mid-session, or as conclusions. They can even provide "breathers," welcome respites when training material becomes "heavy" (complex or abstract) or when emotionally charged discussions should be alleviated.

You may not be Garrison Keillor, the raconteur extraordinaire, but by following these suggestions, you can reach your group and augment their insight and learning.

Trainer/consultant Chip R. Bell suggests that the trainer conduct this self-check at the outset to clarify a story's purpose [15]:

☐ My key learning point—what do I hope to communicate?

☐ Is the story, as an analogy, the best way to communicate this point?

☐ Is telling the story the best use of session time?

☐ Are my listeners likely to identify with the story and appreciate the point being made? Or will literal-minded people regard it as "very small potatoes"?

☐ Do I have the skills to tell a story properly?

One way to increase the likelihood of group acceptance/appreciation of your story is to structure it via these elements: *context, challenge,* and *climax.*

Context. Your story must be germane to the training; your listeners must readily recognize its appropriateness. Bell suggests you consider these questions when creating context.

☐ What do I hope my listeners will feel?

☐ How can I develop a sense of adventure, mystery, suspense, or joy?

☐ How can I paint a word picture so that my listeners will readily visualize the scene I am picturing in my own mind?

☐ Will my group, as listeners, readily relate to the story/picture I've painted?

Challenge. An on-target story should contain a challenge, or "dissonance." To communicate dissonance you must create a dilemma with which the listeners can identify. *Example:* A required cutback forces you to fire a long-time employee, who is nearing retirement, but is only an average performer.

Once you've developed the dilemma, describe the challenge for each key character: "Pat's challenge is . . ." "Kim's challenge is . . ."

Use these questions to create the needed dissonance:

☐ What feeling do I want listeners to experience?

☐ What device can I use to build a sense of concern, conflict, or suspense?

☐ Is the dilemma one with which listeners can readily identify?

☐ Will listeners perceive the challenge(s) as I do?

☐ Will my dilemma trigger enough dissonance so that those on the receiving end favor a resolution?

Climax. This is the learning vehicle—it educates the listener. A surprising, unexpected twist at story's end is most likely to impact the listening group. The climax must be realistic, not far-fetched. When creating the climax, ask yourself these questions:

☐ Will the story's ending meet learning goals and thus provide learning? Is a story the best vehicle to produce this effect, considering my particular group of listeners?

☐ Will this ending challenge, amuse, or even amaze listeners?

☐ Will the ending be seen as relevant and realistic?

☐ Will listeners visualize several possible endings before I reveal the climax?

☐ Will new understanding, insight, and/or attitudes result from the story's resolution?

In sum, viewer response to the story's ending should be: "I wasn't expecting that kind of result."

To ensure top-notch storytelling, do the following:

☐ *Dramatize.* "Get into it"; and "ham it up" to a degree that promotes high realism.

☐ *Describe.* Start with full detail at the outset (in the context) and then reduce the detail as you get into the challenge and climax.

☐ *Shift.* Move between past and present, in and out of the action. There is no one prescribed way to carry the story to a logical, interesting end.

☐ *Pause.* Using "pregnant pauses" for effect is a key to good storytelling.

☐ *Gestures.* Add varied facial expressions, body movement, and gestures to enliven your story.

Also keep your story free of biting sarcasm and satire. A story with too sharp an edge will be resisted.

Final point: Your story can become a vehicle to trigger a lively discussion. Use it for that purpose.

Storytelling—An Innovative Way to Communicate Memorable Messages

Stories, when told with adequate forethought and flair, can educate, inform, motivate, and inspire people. They have high value in an increasingly technological and impersonal world. We may have a lot of communication hardware at our disposal, but whether we can communicate ideas with others as well as in decades past is an open question.

Telling stories to heighten people's interest is as old a communication device as man ever invented. Visualize early man, huddled around a fire in a cave, absorbing the nuanced wisdom from a story-telling leader.

So how do you make a good story? Management professor John O'Neill, Johnson and Wales University, Providence, Rhode Island, asserts that we have to combine two elements to make storytelling a high-impact mode of communication and thus promote change. The two elements are *color* and *repetition* [16].

Color involves presenting elements that have the potential to grip the listeners fully. Colorful stories conjure up images that are vivid, believable, unique, possibly exciting and humorous, and certainly meaningful to the particular audience involved.

Repetition makes certain that a useful message will be disseminated throughout the organization unbound by time. Since the story readily captures the imagination of the first group of receivers, second and third tiers of receivers will propel the mighty message forward again and again.

Here's how color and repetition can be combined to make four kinds of stories:

1. High color plus low repetition produces the *Anecdote Story. Characteristics:* amusing, entertaining, possibly timely, but not really memorable. *Example:* A simple joke such as managers in the firm who get three weeks' vacation but never have the chance to take it.

2. Low color and low repetition create the *Descriptive Story. Characteristics:* Detailed, accurate, possibly timely and helpful, it's more a narrative than an actual story. *Example:* The firm's top information officer renders a verbal report on a new computer installation.

3. Low color and high repetition equal the *Script Story. Characteristics:* Provides a specific purpose, but doesn't aim to amuse or entertain. *Example:* A supervisor who praises a staffer's hard work on a project that was ultimately canceled, pointing up that real effort doesn't go unrewarded.

4. High color combined with high repetition creates the *Epic Story. Characteristics:* Rich in comedy, tragedy, or hero elements told repeatedly. It may evolve a bit, but the basic lessons remain fully intact. *Example:* The story of a top exec who had to overcome gigantic personal difficulties to achieve.

What Stories Can Do—The Power of a Story

Stories can serve as powerful communication devices. Here's what they can do [17]:

☐ *Impart corporate culture and values.* It's a great way to show new hires in particular what ensues if we do something right or, conversely, if we do it wrong. Didactic stories tend to stick in people's heads.

☐ *Help employees accept a new initiative.* Vivid stories can help people to imagine what the workplace will look like after the planned change effort. Exhortations, oral or written, can hardly compete with a powerful, on-target story.

☐ *Create a shared vision of the organization's future.* People will more likely rally to the described future if it is presented in exciting story terms rather than in a dry lecture.

☐ *Convey a meaningful message.* A well-told, significant story can be readily converted into a memorable lesson. *Example*: Here's a short, somewhat facetious story new park rangers will never forget: A gushing park visitor approached the park ranger and excitedly asked, "Ranger, what kind of flower is this?" His very serious reply: "Madam that's a *picked* flower." (The story may or may not be apocryphal, but it makes the telling point, nevertheless.)

Story Structure

The traditional framework for a high-impact story unfolds via these five steps [18]:

1. *Establish the setting.* Here we describe time, locale, the players, and the context, Our descriptive, active words bring the listeners to the scene, ready for the action to start.

2. *Build the plot.* We then present a sequence of events which warns the audience that some kind of trouble is ahead.

3. *Resolve the crisis.* We present the story's climax, the primary event that the plot leads up to.

4. *Describe the lessons learned.* We now imply or state explicitly what the episode taught the protagonist (the leading character).

5. *Explain how the characters changed.* We now have the moral of the story. Our focus is on retained learning or how the action will result in new behavior/attitude/awareness by the main character. The audience understands that new

learning takes root, that the experienced trauma is certainly not in vain.

Note: For high storytelling skill, listen to and watch others tell their stories. Pay attention to how the narrative is structured, how it's colored with the right amount of detail, the pacing employed, and the proper voice tone used for the particular situation. Pay attention, too, to eye contact and body language. People to observe are stand-up comics, TV reporters, and top lecturers of all sorts And like any other skill, you must practice. Don't overlook opportunities to develop your skills, which may involve relating stories to your spouse about unusual happenings during your work day.

How to Find Your Own Stories

Organizational consultant Beverly Kaye provides seven techniques to locate stories which can impact those in the workplace. She advises looking for [19]:

1. *Patterns.* These are the plots and themes of our lives. *Possible topics:* Dealing with adversity, securing hard-to-get resources, and prevailing over obstacles and challenges.

2. *Consequences.* These are the cause and effect of our choices. Here we communicate meaning out of a series of our experiences.

3. *Lessons.* We report on the development and change from our experiences. For example, listeners are more likely to internalize advice about patience/persistence when it's packaged in a memorable story.

4. *Utility.* Here we convey the application and reapplication of our successes. The elements that get us to our success–for example, timing, people, financial resources, vision—are the attributes that can apply to other circumstances and situations.

5. *Vulnerability.* All of us have imperfections, shortcomings, problems. So our failures, booboos, sidetracks make for high-interest stories. They add to our credibility as narrators.

6. *Future experience.* Look for the thoughts and ideas residing in the innovative side of oneself. Our learning may be enhanced by insightful

assessment of experiences that are yet to come, imagining our possible new behavior if we had those experiences.

7. *Story reflections.* Engage in introspection. Search out the story meanings and memories of our past. If we can access and assess these events as surprises, lessons, and inspirational examples, we can locate our story within ourselves.

Why Storytelling Works [20]

Is it because people learn from the story itself? Possibly. But more realistically, it's because your listeners can relate it to their own stories (incidents, events, experiences). They thus personalize the message and internalize its significance. Your aim, then, is to help your listeners to reflect on and apply meaning to their own life events working from your life experience.

Remember that when you tell your own stories, those you know so well, you can tell them with integrity, authenticity, and passion. You thus capture your listeners' attention, you establish rapport with them, you build credibility, and you provide a message people will readily remember.

The Trainer's Instructional Role

As a trainer, your role in respect to the technique of storytelling is to

1. Demonstrate and explain the storytelling technique, possibly drawing on some of the above points. Your aim is to make the technique so intriguing that your participants (most likely those in leadership positions) will most certainly want to use it back on the job. They now should be well equipped to tell a story so that it has a clear-cut message, has high impact, and will be taken seriously and long remembered.

2. Tell a story and put your participant group in action to assess it for possible learnings, One possible approach is to divide your total group into several types of subgroups:

   a. Subgroup(s) A extracts as many learnings as possible from the story. Let's call these "the Extractors."

   b. Subgroup(s) B assesses the story in terms of enriching/strengthening the story so that it will be more powerful and memorable. These are "the Strengtheners."

   c. Subgroup(s) C are "the Critiquers." Advise that these participants are "the Critiquers," not "the Critics." Their task is to look for areas that are weak, are less than credible, are too hypothetical, or contain any other elements or aspects that have the potential to undermine the story's desired credibility or potency.

Then secure reports from the small groups and follow with a general discussion as to what was learned from the exercise.

Another group-in-action approach is to break your total group down into teams of four or five. *Their task:* Locate a powerful story from within your team (for presentation to the total group) and then assess it in these terms: How can we help the storyteller to tell his/her story so that it will make a profound impact on the listeners? Each team will have a team member to present a story to the total group. *An option:* Offer a prize to the team that produces the best story. Appoint a panel of three judges to assess the quality/power of the stories presented.

KEY POINTS

1. Pre-work is a useful device for involving participants "early on," that is, before the formal training program begins.

2. While pre-work has a number of advantages from a learning standpoint, it should be used judiciously. Time constraints and reluctance by the participant group should be carefully considered.

3. Keys to the effective use of pre-work are course relevance; a pre-session meeting to explain purposes and procedures; avoidance of pre-work overload; and the use of forms, instruments, etc. to facilitate assigned tasks.

4. Seating is a vital factor to consider if you want to facilitate your approach to participative training.

5. The key element in effective seating is to avoid formal, classroom configurations in favor of flexible, free-flowing seating.

6. Desks and tables should be used only if considerable writing is to take place.

7. Movement is helpful in keeping participants alert, alive, active, and energized.

8. Movement may accrue from training activities per se as well as from program management, for example, walking in a dyad to lunch.

9. Flipcharting is useful for capturing participant inputs, as an aid for reinforcement of what was said, for giving participants recognition for their contributions and accomplishments, for giving the training room a working look or atmosphere.

10. As part of the overall training design, include experiences which provide fun and humor. A light, relaxed classroom climate is a positive aid to learning.

11. Physical objects (props) can be used to heighten the learning experience. By engaging in physical contact with objects that relate to the subject matter, the participants can be made more fully aware of the learning to which they are being exposed.

12. Handouts are much more than materials which participants can cart home in their heavy notebooks. Look at them as learning tools and consider their use on a pre-session and post-session basis as well as during sessions.

13. Use silence to heighten training experiences such as role play, fantasy, guided imagery, or viewing of a profound film, and to overcome impasses in problem solving or conflict situations.

14. Telling a well-crafted, interesting, believable story can provide new or added insight, understanding, and appreciation of a particular point or topic. Use it as a discussion generator.

REFERENCES

1. Askins, Nancy, Director of Educational Development, Shore Memorial Hospital, Somers Point, New Jersey, used this icebreaker at the 1986 National Conference of the American Society for Training and Development with a group of 75–100 people.

2. Wangler, Joan S., "What Do Leaders Value?" *The Torch,* Newsletter of the Washington, D.C., Metropolitan Area Chapter of the American Society for Training and Development (November 1986), p. 11.

3. Reported in "Departures: Facing Changes," *Meeting News* (July 1993), p. 52.

4. Blankenship, Allison, "Get Your Course Going with a Bang," *Creative Training Techniques*, Bill Communications (August 1999), p. 8.

5. "What Do We Need to Know About a Group Before Designing Training for It?" *Training and Development Journal* (September 1984), p. 19.

6. Goodman, Joel, "Using Humor in Workshops," in Pfeiffer, J. William, and Goldstein, Leonard E. (Eds.), *The 1983 Annual for Facilitators, Trainers, and Consultants*, University Associates, San Diego, 1983, pp. 137–141.

7. Reported in *Modern Maturity* (October–November 1986), p. 16.

8. Reported in *The Wall Street Journal* (August 12, 1986), p. 1.

9. The last example, concerned with connectedness of self, is based on a presentation by Dr. Virginia Satir at the Annual Conference of the Association of Humanistic Psychology, Washington, D.C. (July 23, 1982).

10. Simmerman, Scott J., "Empowering Service and Sales Personnel by Building Their Personal Resources: Experiential Exercises and Activities," handout accompanying a presentation at the annual conference of the American Society for Training and Development, San Francisco (1991).

11. "'Diversity Kit' Keeps Managers Sensitive to Employee Differences," *Creative Training Techniques Newsletter,* Lakewood Publications, sample issue (1995), pp. 6–7.

12. Cherry, Janet T., handout used in conjunction with a presentation at the Annual National Conference of the American Society for Training and Development (ASTD), Atlanta (May 1993).

13. Dunnit, Ben N., "To Pass Around or Not to Pass Around—Is It Worth the Distraction?" *Training News* (October 1983).

14. Laird, D., "Uses of Silence," *Training News* (September 1982), pp. 5–6.

15. Bell, Chip R., "The Trainer as Storyteller," *Training and Development* (September 1992), pp. 53–56.

16. Dennehy, Robert F., "The Executive as Storyteller," *Management Review* (March 1999), pp. 41–42.

17. Breuer, Nancy L., "The Power of Storytelling," *Workforce* (December 1998), pp. 36–41.

18. Dennehy, Robert F., *op. cit.,* p. 43.

19. Breuer, Nancy L., *op. cit.,* p. 40.

20. Hicks, Sabrina, "Leadership Through Storytelling," *Training and Development* (November 2000), p. 63.

RECOMMENDED READING

Broadwell, Martin M., "Seating Arrangements," *Training,* July 1975, pp. 18–19.

This article discusses the best way to arrange a room, the effect of crowding, student preferences, whether to assign seats.

Crocker, Marilee, "The Art of Seating," *Meetings and Conventions,* October 1993, pp. 53–59.

Discusses different types of seating arrangements at meetings. Points out that they rank among the critical details that can make or break a meeting. The right arrangement guarantees personal comfort and effective communication.

Edelstein, Loren G., "Taking Shape," *Meetings and Conventions,* August 2000, pp. 87–90.

On the very valid assumption that the placement of tables, chairs, speakers, and A/V can support or undermine a meeting's objectives, the writer presents seven room setups, along with the pros and cons of each configuration.

Eitington, Julius E., "Seating Arrangements and Participant Learning," *Bulletin on Training,* March/April 1978, pp. 4–5.

This relates various forms of seating arrangements to trainer style, trainer philosophy, classroom atmosphere, possible trainee attitudes, and impact on the learning process.

Facilitator, G. F., "Dead Men Don't Use Flip Charts," *Training,* February 1984, pp. 35–40.

A tongue-in-cheek article discussing the many advantages of the flipchart over the highly sophisticated electric and electronic A/V devices.

Greenberg, Jerald, "The Role of Seating Position in Group Interaction: A Review, with Applications for Group Trainers," *Group and Organization Studies,* September 1976, pp. 310–327.

This summarizes experimental research on seating positions and relates it to advice for the trainer, for example, how physical layout influences participation, how different group activities are facilitated by different seating arrangements, why tables should be avoided.

Kaye, Beverly, "Up Is Not the Only Way," Consulting Press, 1997.

An organizational consultant relates her experience working with numerous Fortune 500 companies using stories to convey a firm's corporate culture. Stories are something anyone can tell based on their experiences. She believes the telling is as worthwhile for the narrator as it is for the listeners. She also describes the techniques to mine (find) your own stories.

Kaye, Beverly, and Jacobson, Betsy, "True Tales and Tall Tales—The Power of Organizational Storytelling," *Training and Development*, March 1999, pp. 45—50.

The authors see storytelling as a vivid, memorable way to pass on an organization's history, values, and vision. They believe everyone has a story to tell and the capacity to become a great storyteller. The article describes different types of stories and provides pointers on how to create a repertoire. Includes tips for the facilitator to lead a discussion by posing incisive questions.

Koneya, Mele, "Privacy Regulation in Small and Large Groups," *Groups and Organization Studies,* September 1977, pp. 324–335.

Research is reviewed to show that seat location is associated with verbal interaction rates and visual accessibility among and between group members and leaders.

Mclaughlin, Kathleen, "The Lighter Side of Learning," *Training,* February 2001, pp. 48–52.

Cites examples of trainers' use of humor to diffuse stress and stimulate creativity.

Smith, Homer, "Communicating with a Flip of the Chart," *Sales and Meeting Management,* July 2, 1984, pp. 90–98.

The article discusses advantages of flipchart work, what to put on a pad, and techniques for best use.

Stone, Donald, and Stone, Alice, "The Administration of Chairs," *Public Administration Review,* January–February 1974, pp. 13–25.

The authors' thesis, presented with humor, is that "not the persons or subject, but the arrangement of chairs determines the success of a meeting."

Suessmuth, Patrick, "The Psychology of Classroom Seating," *Canadian Training Methods (CTM): The Human Element,* August 1980, pp. 63–64, 66.

This uses questions and puzzles (problems) to help the reader develop new ideas about seating.

Involving Participants in Film/Video

16

If you see in any given situation only what everybody else can see, you can be said to be so much a representative of your culture that you are a victim of it.

—S. I. Hayakawa, general semanticist and
former U.S. senator from California

FILM VERSUS VIDEO

IN our discussion we will use the word "film" to include video as well. The rationale for using film and video interchangeably is that both media are forms of one-way communication; both impart ideas to a passive learner. As will be indicated, the real learning occurs via the group-in-action devices that the trainer employs to involve the learner fully.

Of course, there are certain technical (nonsubstantive) differences between the two media:

☐ A film has the advantage of impacting a high-quality picture every time it is shown. Unlike videos, it is not subject to loss in color fidelity due to electrical interference or improper set adjustment. Also, it can be shown with no loss of fidelity to large audiences (although a special lens is required in a very large room). However, new, large TV screens of good quality are now overtaking this advantage of film.

☐ Video, on the other hand, has a number of advantages. For one thing, there is no need for the careful threading of a projector—just insert the video cassette, and you're off and running. For another, there is no projector noise. Also, rewind and reverse actions can be executed simply and rapidly. Finally, the room need not be darkened, thereby permitting note taking or using handout material. And if you have a video camera, you can make your own videotapes for playback.

Film captures large scenes—the outdoors, crowds, panoramic views—better than video. Conversely, video can provide a feeling of greater intimacy for one-on-one interactions and small group scenes.

USES OF FILMS/VIDEOS

The film/video is a valuable training tool. It is widely used by trainers and universally expected by participants. However, we should recognize that the film, despite its popularity, is essentially a form of one-way communication. It is a carrier of information, like the lecture or the panel discussion. Hence the need for the trainer to exploit a visual presentation properly so that participants have opportunity for full involvement in the learning process. In the pages that follow, we shall present a variety of techniques that the trainer can use to secure such active participation.

Before we do so, however, it might be helpful to ask ourselves this basic question: Why do we, as trainers, use film? Or, putting it another way, what specific values or benefits do films actually have? They are beneficial in many ways in that they

- ☐ Can hold attention easily, far more effectively than a book or a speaker.
- ☐ Provide a quick way to get a story across. Because of a film's careful planning and organization, a lot of learning can be packed into a 20–30-minute film (or even into a minute or two if the trainer uses a vignette from the film).
- ☐ Offer a great deal of realism. Filmed incidents, events, situations, and interactions bring the viewer as close to real life as is possible.
- ☐ Tap the visual sense so vital in much of our learning. The visual material is supported or reinforced by the sound, of course.
- ☐ Provide a high-impact, high-interest learning experience. Participants can readily be emotionally involved in many dynamic situations: conflict, cooperation, missed signals, vexing problems, unresolved relationships, misunderstandings, frustrations, aspirations, successes, and failures.

- ☐ Allow the case or problem to be presented in all its dimensions, something that the lecture or printed page cannot do.
- ☐ Allow for identification (or nonidentification) with characters in the film who serve as role models.
- ☐ Provide an immediate group experience, since all participants see the film at the same time. The story becomes "group property." That is not to say that everyone sees (perceives) the film's events and characters in the same way. In fact the opposite—varying perceptions—is more likely. But it is a *common* experience, unlike a previously assigned case or article, which may or may not be read by everyone who comes to class, and which, if read, may be hazily remembered or even forgotten.
- ☐ Provide an opportunity for discussing perceptions. As people project themselves into the film, they read different meanings into it, all of which is grist for the "discussion mill" and a basis for real learning.
- ☐ Allow for standardization; that is, repeated presentations by the trainer—to the immediate group or to other groups—are always the same in all vital particulars. And, of course, the message is the same even if the film is shown by different trainers.
- ☐ Are expected by participants in our visually oriented culture. Consequently, people readily relate to them.
- ☐ Vary the pace of the training day, particularly if it is a "heavy" one.
- ☐ Illustrate concepts and situations that can't very readily be observed or appreciated, for example, how to deal with an angry customer.
- ☐ Provide an opportunity to "meet" and learn from an expert or authority in a given field.
- ☐ Can humanize an expert who may appear in them.
- ☐ Provide a worthwhile training experience at a relatively low cost per participant. Most films have a relatively long shelf-life, which helps to keep costs down.
- ☐ Are extremely versatile; that is, they can be used as a program opener to provoke thinking about the topic about to begin; to reinforce a given topic

or presentation; to set the stage for other training activities (exercises, games, role plays); to demonstrate a skill (how to lift properly or conduct a meeting); to alter attitudes (on controversial subjects such as sexual harassment); and to help summarize a session or program.

☐ Are a uniquely flexible and versatile tool for the trainer. That is, various training activities may be conducted *before* the film/video showing, *after* its showing, and even *midway* or at other points in the course of its presentation. These strategies are developed in more detail later.

To put the use of films into proper perspective, we should add that films should *not* be used to fill in a "blank spot" in the program, to offset the effect of a weak or marginal instructor, because it is the "prestigious" thing to do, to provide entertainment, to fill in for a resource person who didn't show, or to give the trainer some free time. A film is a training tool; it should thus be used appropriately.

Also, while films have many advantages, they also have some decided limitations [1]. These include an emphasis on passive rather than active learning (unless the trainer does something about this); realism may be lacking, with artificial and exaggerated situations being presented to make the major points; individual differences may be ignored, for not everyone will perceive the content with the same relevancy; too many examples of inappropriate or undesirable behavior may be shown.

Other disadvantages/limitations are that they can't readily transfer somewhat idealized materials (in the film) to the participant's here-and-now world; they also cannot lead a group discussion, that is, serve as a substitute for an insightful, provocative, and enthusiastic trainer [2].

PREVIEWING

A fundamental rule in using films/videos is to always review a film before you present it. This vital procedure will avoid unwanted surprises to you and your participant group as to film relevancy and quality. Additionally, part of your planning for a given session entails designing activities that will actively involve your participants in the film's content. (See "Post-Film/Video Activities.") You can only design relevant activities if you have seen and reflected on the film. In sum, a film isn't merely something you show. Rather, it is a tool which you use with purpose and care.

It is a good idea to involve several people in the previewing process—a colleague(s), your boss, two or three supervisors or managers, or possibly several people who are representative of your client/participant group. (If you are showing a film on customer relations, invite several customer relations personnel to your preview.) Your objective is to garner multiple reactions about the film's pertinency, quality, and overall suitability. Multiple judgments should provide adequate assurance that your participants will find the film a helpful learning tool in relation to course objectives.

In your preview session you will want to

☐ Note parallels and contrasts to the real (work) world and your own in-house situation as well.

☐ Note major questions/issues which the film *raises*.

☐ Note questions/issues which the film *answers*.

☐ Note significant incidents, events, or situations which you will wish to emphasize.

☐ Look for opportunities to exploit the film properly. (See "Post-Film/Video Activities.")

It is also a good idea to preview the film twice. You are very likely to observe certain things which were not evident on the first viewing [3].

A systematic, quantitative approach to evaluation of training videos has been developed by Laura Winig, publisher of *Training Media Review*. She suggests the use of 12 categories (criteria) for evaluation purposes. They are as follows [4]:

☐ Degree of support for training goals
☐ Ability to hold viewer attention
☐ Presentation
☐ Pacing
☐ Instructional value
☐ Content accuracy
☐ Production quality
☐ Information value
☐ Casting of women and minorities
☐ Portrayal of women and minorities

☐ Supplementary materials

☐ Value for the money

Procedures:

1. In the Winig system you assign points—*category values*—to the above categories (criteria) *before* you see the video, as follows: 3 for very important; 2 for somewhat important; and 1 for not important. Here you decide the value of the criteria most important to you. *Note:* You may not wish to use all 12 categories, for not all may be important or pertinent to you.

2. Next, you play the tape, take notes, and then assign a *category (criterion) rating* of 0 to 3 points to the categories (criteria) you chose, using these quantitative ratings: outstanding, 3 points; above average, 2 points; average, 1 point; poor, 0 points. You have now assigned numerical values to the criteria you have deemed important.

3. You then multiply each of the category's values by its category rating. This provides a weighted score for a single category (criterion). *Example:* Portrayal of women and minorities—3 (category value) × 2 (category rating) = 6 (category score). *Note:* Each category (criterion) can achieve a maximum of 9 points (3 × 3 = 9).

4. Your final step is to add all scores (12 or less), divide that total by the number of categories you considered, and obtain an average score for the video. This will allow you to compare average scores between/among various videos you may be considering for purchase or use.

    Note: In using a quantitative system of evaluation, you should consider it as a guide, not as a system which precludes the use of judgment and intuition as well.

INTRODUCING A FILM/VIDEO

In today's complex and demanding training world, you can't simply load your projector or VCR, tell the group that a film/video is coming, and "let'er roll." Your participants will expect and need much more. Your job, then, as an introducer of the film/video is to

☐ Provide an opening statement which will challenge and excite your participants. ("You are about to see a film/video about a manager who came into a plant besieged by numerous production and morale problems, and how he gradually turned things around so that his plant became the best-producing plant in his company.")

☐ Tell them what to look for in both a general and particular way so that they can transfer the incidents observed in the film/video to their own job situations.

☐ Discuss areas that may be outside the group's experience or possibly have an element of controversy or ambiguity.

☐ Anticipate and defuse possible negative reactions by candidly stating at the outset that they will see something which they may not like or with which they may not agree.

☐ Overcome almost certain complaints about the film's age. Be candid about it being an older film/video. Ask them to zero in on the key learning points and not to get too hung up on the older cars, dated dress and hairdos, and so on. Assure them that other groups have found the film/video helpful despite its production date.

All in all, your objective in your introduction is to set positive expectations and encourage the rendering of full attention.

POST-FILM/VIDEO ACTIVITIES

An effective way to exploit a film is to put a group into action following their viewing of it. Some ways of doing so follow:

Dyads

The simplest, quickest, and most effective way to involve participants with one another (and the subject) is to ask them to join with someone else to form a pair. The "someone else" may be on one's right or left, or in front or behind, or elsewhere in the room if a "new" partner is to be secured. The pairs may then be asked to respond to a general, open-ended question for five to ten minutes. The result is instant interaction and conversation. Some examples of easy-to-respond-to, open-ended questions that permit the participants full leeway to discuss the film/video on their own are these:

- [ ] What was the most significant learning in the film/video for you? *or* What are the lessons to be learned?

- [ ] Why do you suppose the film/video maker produced this kind of film/video? What was he/she trying to accomplish?

- [ ] What did you like or not like (agree/disagree with)?

- [ ] What did the film/video omit or overlook, if anything?

- [ ] Was the film/video a balanced presentation of the problem?

- [ ] If you were to redo the film/video, what approach would you take?

- [ ] How do the film/video's ideas square with your own experience? *or* What is significant to you from the standpoint of your current job?

Specific questions, rather than general ones, may also be used. Some examples:

- [ ] With what characters could you identify in the film/video?

- [ ] With what character could you *not* identify?

- [ ] Do you feel the policy regarding promotion is a sound one?

- [ ] Comment on the company president as a decision maker (or as a delegator, communicator, planner, time manager).

- [ ] What are the implications of the film/video for team management (or for customer relations, intercultural awareness, problem solving, creative selling)?

- [ ] What are the risks in taking the course of action the police officer did?

Triads

When a somewhat greater variety of inputs than is possible in the dyad is needed, the trio works well. While the trio is less intimate than the pair, it is still conducive to a high degree of interaction. The assign-

ments can take the same form as those just suggested for the team of two.

Buzz Groups

Groups of four to six can be asked to "buzz" on any question or issue that the film/video raises. Or the groups may be asked to frame a question to which another small group or the total group can respond. Buzz groups typically provide a good diversity of viewpoints. Hence a good technique is to ask them to *agree* on some aspect of the film/video's content—for example, the three main learning points, the wisdom of the sales manager's course of action, the nature of the communication process at work, the correctness of the salesperson's approach to closing the sale, the role of the secretary.

Note: In "putting the group to work" following the showing of the film/video, you have two options. You can start the pairs, triads, or small groups "to buzz" immediately, or a more reflective approach to the assignment of tasks may be taken. In the latter instance, you may say: "O.K., you've seen the film/video. Let's take two minutes to sit back and reflect on what we've experienced."

The rationale for the second approach is that, at times, participants are prodded into verbally reacting before the full impact of the film/video's message has actually settled in. The two-minute reflection period makes sense particularly when a group has seen a film/video with a great deal of impact, such as when considerable emotionality has been presented or a theme such as prejudice has been treated.

Brainstorming

Groups of six to ten can be used to generate multiple ideas about or solutions to a problem raised in a film/video, for example, how to make our promotion plan (or career development plan, performance review plan, compensation plan) more effective; how to motivate persons who have reached a plateau in their career; how to improve communication in an organization (or *our* organization). Two or three groups can brainstorm the assignment simultaneously. Each group must have a recorder (scribe) to capture the ideas on a flipchart.

Role Play

If a film/video explores a problem of an interpersonal sort, you may ask for two (or more) volunteers to explain how they would handle the problem. This may relate to coaching, counseling, performance review, discipline, employment interviewing, a sales interview, etc. The purpose of the role play enactment is to explore alternative, more effective ways of resolving the one-on-one difficulty that the film highlighted.

Using a Fishbowl

The fishbowl, or group-on-group observation technique, is a means of involving participants in a novel, high-interest way. Procedure:

1. Assign participants to two clusters, an inner one (Group A) and outer one (Group B). Five to eight participants in each group are workable groups.
2. Give Group A a discussion assignment (10–20 minutes) based on the film/video. Group B observes and listens silently.
3. After time is up, switch the groups so that Group B is now in the fishbowl. Have Group B develop the topic further, including an analysis of Group A's conclusion and observations.
4. Reverse groups again, if appropriate. A shorter time-frame may be used on the second go-around.
5. Sum up conclusions of the total activity.

Contracts for Reentry

If a film/video is used at program's end to solidify or reinforce learnings, you can then plan for back-home activity. For example, if the closing film/video stresses the importance of team action or team development, participants may be asked to develop an action plan (or contract) to improve the functioning of their team.

PRE-FILM/VIDEO ACTIVITIES

Whereas the post-film/video assignment is designed to exploit the film/video after it is seen, the pre-film/video assignment or activity is designed to set the stage for the visual presentation.

Group-at-Large Participation

Various tasks can be given to the total group for individual completion prior to the film/video viewing. The data generated by these tasks can be discussed as a prelude to seeing it. Begin by giving everyone small cards or a sheet of paper to record their responses on. Some example tasks:

☐ Ask participants to enter on a 3" × 5" card some quantitative data, using a 100-point scale, such as a percentage estimate of one's listening efficiency, or the amount of discretionary time (as opposed to reaction time) one has at one's disposal, or how good a delegator one is. Collect the cards, have someone quickly tally the results, and discuss their implications. Then run the film/video. The "live" data can be referred to again in the post-film/video discussion session.

☐ Have everyone jot down a definition pertinent to the subject, such as job enrichment, coaching, counseling, innovative marketing, or support systems. Record a number of the definitions on a flipchart, discuss them briefly, run the film/video, then refer back to definitions after the film. Check to see if anyone wants to alter their definition.

☐ Have everyone come up with one basic principle or technique to aid in closing the sale; then collect the cards, post ideas to a flipchart sheet, comment on the ideas, and run the film/video. Afterwards refer back to the flipchart, comparing participant ideas to those in the film/video.

Small Group Work

In a unit on the role of the supervisor in the orientation process, kick things off by having small groups develop two kinds of laundry lists. You might say some thing like:

"Groups One and Two, come up with things an effective supervisor should do to make a new employee's first day a rewarding one. You have ten minutes for this."

"Groups Three and Four, come up with the things you as a supervisor might do, if you were so inclined, to really 'louse up' the orientation process for that new worker. Do this in ten minutes."

Post group reports to a flipchart. Then tell the group: "We will now see a film/video which shows a supervisor orienting a new worker. Let's see how well we predicted what our supervisor might do."

After running the film/video, check off the things done by the orienting supervisor on both the positive and negative lists.

In effect, the small group work, the list development, and the effort at prediction were interest generating or attention-getters. They involved the participants in *advance* of the film/video by exciting them or raising their anticipation level.

Role Playing

If a one-on-one problem-solving situation or interview is to appear in the film/video, it may be desirable to let two participants role play that interaction. The enactment can then be compared with the one seen in the film/video.

The role-playing activity can also be organized along more formal lines, that is, giving it a good deal of structure. The advantage to this approach is that learning points are "buttoned down" more tightly.

1. In a session on interviewing (coaching, counseling, discipline, employment, discharge, performance appraisal) conduct a role play.

2. Have the role players provide a self-critique of their interview. Have them list on a flipchart the things they felt went well and those that could have been strengthened. (A group critique may also be employed if the participants want the added feedback.)

3. Show a film/video that presents an interview of the same type as was role played.

4. Have the role-playing participants review their lists in relation to the film/video and report to the total group on them.

5. Secure group critique as may be helpful.

Using Viewing/Listening Teams

The trainer can heighten interest in a film/video by giving small groups or teams an assignment *in advance* of seeing it. The rationale for this procedure is that by giving participants responsibility for a task in conjunction with the forthcoming film/video, you ensure that they are "tuned in" rather than "tuned out." Viewing becomes purposeful rather than "loose." These assignments may be specific or general.

Specific assignments: The viewing/listening teams may be asked to look for such elements in the film/video as

☐ Leadership styles

☐ Decision-making procedures

☐ Communication processes

☐ Techniques used to close a sale

☐ Handling of customer complaints

☐ Climate of the organization

After the film/video has been shown, the teams meet to discuss their assignment and then have a spokesperson report back on group findings.

The assignments may be treated in various ways: all teams may be given the same assignment; each team may be given a different assignment; one-half the teams may receive one assignment and the other half another one; etc.

General assignments. Teams may be asked to function in these capacities:

☐ *Question-raisers.* "Look for something that raises or stimulates a question in your mind."

☐ *Clarifiers.* "Look for something that is presented in a hazy way and requires clarification or amplification."

☐ *Agreers.* "Look for something you really agree with, identify with, or like."

☐ *Disagreers.* "Look for something that you can't buy, possibly something that even turns you off."

☐ *Appliers.* "Look for principles or techniques that you can readily implement on Monday morning when you return to your jobs."

After seeing the film/video, the teams meet to discuss their assignments and report back their conclusions or recommendations.

Point-of-View Teams

Another technique based on the viewing/listening team is to have teams observe/listen from a given frame of reference (for example, top management, first-line supervision, employees, the personnel office, the comptroller) or from the views of production vs. sales; headquarters vs. field, line vs. staff, senior personnel vs. newcomers, men vs. women; or adults vs. teenagers.

Committee Work

In advance of the film/video showing, assign teams pertinent readings or discussion topics. This may be done on a pre-work (or homework) basis. Discuss the pre-work assignment in class *prior* to showing the film/video. The pre-work and in-class discussion, in effect, set the stage for the film and the post-film/video discussion.

Incident Application

In advance of the film/video showing, have participants jot down on a sheet of paper an incident, event, or situation pertinent to the forthcoming film/video's content. Some examples participants might include are

- ☐ An incident where they helped a customer with a problem and really got turned on because of it.
- ☐ An incident where they got something important done, not because of authority but because of the ability to influence the situation.
- ☐ An event or situation involving delegation which really paid off.
- ☐ An instance where persistence in follow-up produced a big or otherwise important sale.

Then run the film/video and have participants form small groups to share and compare the significance of the recorded incidents in relation to the film/video's message. Secure reports from the small groups concerning what was discussed and learned.

Another way of treating incidents is as follows:

- ☐ Have everyone describe on a card an incident, event, or happening related to the subject matter of the session (for example, one-half of the group may be asked to describe an incident in

their career wherein their growth was encouraged and one-half of the group can describe an incident where growth was discouraged); collect incidents and randomly select and read aloud several of the positive and negative incidents; draw some tentative generalizations and then run the film; refer back to the incidents in the post-film discussion.

Note: In the previous examples, specific training techniques were suggested, either on a pre-film/video or post-film/video basis. It should be obvious that the same techniques—fishbowls, brainstorming, role plays—if used one way (pre-film/video) could be used the other way (post-film/video) too.

STOP-FILM/VIDEO TECHNIQUE

We have indicated previously that proper exploitation of a film/video calls for a group involvement either before or after a film/video viewing, or possibly at both times. Added involvement is also possible via the "stop-film" technique. This simply entails stopping the film/video at one or more appropriate points and putting the group to work discussing the film/video up to that point.

Some films/videos have the stop-film technique (also known as "viewer participations") built into them by the producer. But there's no reason why you can't stop a film/video at logical points without such guidance.

Some examples of stop-film use are as follows:

- ☐ In the film *Twelve Angry Men* the film/video may be stopped by the trainer at various points to allow participants to predict which person will now shift his position from "guilty" to "not guilty."
- ☐ In the film *The Eye of the Beholder* the film/video may be stopped at midpoint and the group asked: "What is your impression of Michael Gerard based on what you now know about him?" This film/video has a stop-film point provided by the producer.
- ☐ A film/video may be stopped to allow participants to discuss the action (or decision) a manager should take in light of the facts presented up to this point.

☐ In a film/video having separate wrong-way/right-way sequences, the film/video may be stopped after the wrong-way presentation to allow participants to propose the right-way course of action. Their solutions can then be compared with the film/video's solution.

In summation, be on the lookout for stop-film opportunities that relate to the following:

☐ *Prediction:* What is likely to happen? Who will do _____?

☐ *Decision:* What would you do? What decision will _____ make?

☐ *Perception:* How do you see the sales manager (or the organization, or the situation, or _____'s prospects) at this point?

The rationale for the stop-film technique is as follows:

☐ It allows for discussion when the issue is "hot"—that is, before the group "here and now," rather than sometime later.

☐ It prevents information overload, particularly if a film/video is fairly long and meaty.

☐ It gets attention. ("Hey, she stopped the film/video!")

☐ It creates suspense. ("I wonder what the rest of the film/video is like.")

☐ Most important, it converts a one-way communication device into a participant-involving medium.

OTHER AIDS AND APPROACHES

There are a variety of other aids that can ensure participant involvement with film/video presentations. The following paragraphs mention some of these other approaches.

The Vignette

Ordinarily we take a film/video as the producer prepares it and show it in its entirety. There is no reason, however, why we cannot merely show a perti-

nent segment of it—a vignette or film/video clip. By isolating a particular vignette, we may actually achieve a greater participant impact than by showing the full 20 or 30 minutes of film/video. Vignettes which run for only one and a half to three minutes can be quite powerful. They can present an incident, a problem, a case, or an interview, all of which require participant reaction, analysis, or problem resolution. The vignettes can be exploited via pre-film/video or post-film/video devices as previously described.

Of course, a short case or problem can also be prepared on videotape on a "tailor-made" basis to meet the needs of a particular group. Thus, one writer cites the use of "trigger tapes" to train student teachers to handle discipline problems, an area of special concern to a new teacher. The procedure used was to query experienced teachers concerning typical classroom discipline problems. Nine problems were chosen (note passing, tardiness, drugs, falling asleep, rebellious attitude, etc.) for preparation of tape simulations. Cards were also developed containing background data concerning the children shown in the taped situations. The two-minute tapes present a role-played incident on an open-ended basis. At the conclusion, the teacher must make a decision.

Trigger tapes can also be used for in-service training of experienced teachers and for discussions of classroom management [5].

Prediction

A helpful way to involve participants is through the device of prediction. Three examples of the use of prediction in working with films/videos are as follows:

☐ A new employee is being pressured by two senior workers to join with them in holding down production. The new worker seems to favor "rate busting" because of his economic needs and because he feels that hard work will be noticed. The vignette presents the forces pressuring the new worker to "join with the boys" and the forces pushing him to join up with management. At this point the trainer may stop the projector and ask: "Which way will the new worker go? How many think 'with management'? How many 'with the boys'? O.K. let's watch the rest of the film/video and see what happens." Another vote may be taken after more footage is observed, to see if there is a shift in participant opinion.

☐ In the film classic *The Eye of the Beholder,* the trainer may stop the film after several film characters have met Michael Gerard and have commented upon him. The trainer then asks: "How do you see Michael now?" Adjectives are supplied by the group and put on a flipchart. "O.K., we're going to learn now how Michael sees himself. How do you predict Mike will present himself? Let's get some other adjectives."

☐ The group may be shown a scene involving a fall from a ladder resulting in a serious injury. The trainer may ask the group for possible causative factors. Responses by group members—leaning too far, insecure feet of the ladder—become predictions. These are "checked out" with the next film/video sequence, which reports on the actual investigation of the accident. The trainer may then ask for suggestions concerning how to prevent this kind of accident. Ideas may be offered (such as tying the ladder to increase stability), which, again, are predictions. The trainer returns to the film/video to see how the problem is actually handled, thereby validating the accuracy of the predictions [6].

Prediction, at times, may pose a threat to some participants. Consider the following set of circumstances: After viewing a filmed sequence presenting an unresolved problem, the trainer may ask a participant: "What would you do in this situation?" For some participants this may present them with a threatening situation. Why? Because not everyone wishes to display his/her "ignorance" before the total group. One way to get the participant "off the hot seat," so to speak, is to phrase the question in less personal terms, for example: "What will the person in the film do next?" In essence, by asking for a prediction of *someone else's* behavior, the trainer can turn a high-threat situation into one provoking little or no anxiety [7].

Threat can also be minimized or eliminated by having predictions made in (and by) small groups or by several individuals in the total group. No particular attempt need be made to identify the predictors. Con-

sequently, the concern of threat is not present as may be the case in the one-on-one situation.

Note: Reference has been made to having participants predict the action that will take place in a film/video. The prediction may relate to the film/video, in general, *before* it begins as well as to sequences in it *as the film/video progresses.* For example: A film/video may show the orientation of a new worker. As a means of stimulating interest, the trainer may ask one small group to list the elements that make for effective orientation and another group to list the things that a supervisor might do if he/she wished to really mess up the orientation process. Both sets of data are posted to a T-column on a flipchart, the data serving as a prediction of the behavior to be observed in the film/video. After the film has been seen, the group checks off the items on the flipchart in relation to the observed behaviors.

Film/Video Discussion Aids

If the film/video displays a form such as a sales call form, a model, an instrument, a diagram, or a chart with key points, the trainer should reproduce these aids, if possible, and distribute them to participants. (This is subject to copyright restrictions, of course.) These aids present pertinent ideas, which on film/video pass by all too quickly. Also consider distributing other aids, such as an organization chart that may be in the film/video's leader's guide.

Whenever practicable, the participants should be given the opportunity to work with these materials. For example, a film/video on team management may show the characters in it discussing an instrument that facilitates the rating of team effectiveness. Why not let the participants rate their own work teams and discuss the results with their colleagues in the training group?

Nonverbal Approach

At times it may be worthwhile to have participants analyze the nonverbal communication in which characters in the film/video engage. If so, simply turn off the sound and have the group analyze the silent interaction.

Another approach, allied to the above, is to show certain vignettes in the film/video in two ways: first, *without* the audio portion, the audience hypothesizing or predicting what was said; second, presenting the vignette with both sound and picture, and then discussing why the predictions were or were not "sound."

Of course, the trainer can also do the reverse—that is, turn off the picture and just present the sound track. This might be done with very powerful dialogue, the participants creating their own images of the interaction taking place.

Using Viewing Worksheets

Participant involvement with films/videos can be augmented by using viewing worksheets. They are passed out to participants *before* the film/video begins. The structure of the worksheets helps to stimulate and channel observation and thinking about the film/video. Three such worksheets are presented in Appendices 56, 57, and 58. The first is essentially an open-ended aid to note taking; the second two direct the participant to specific elements in the film. Allow time after the viewing to complete the form (five to ten minutes). Data entered on the worksheets can be shared in small groups after the film/video viewing.

Using Question Sheets

Questions to the small groups for pre-film/video or post-film/video discussion may be reduced to writing. The advantages of the written format are these:

☐ Written instructions are more likely to be easily understood than an orally presented question is. Why? Because they can be read at one's own reading pace and even reread, if necessary. Also, since the trainer has taken the pains to write them out, the odds are that they will be carefully phrased and concisely written.

☐ They may be taken home as a post-course reference.

Advantages also accrue to the trainer. They are these:

☐ The writing process encourages more careful thought as to what should be asked.

☐ Instructions to the small groups are simplified and systematized. Thus, the trainer need merely say: "Group One take question one; Group Two take question two."

Understanding Our Relationships
Questions for Discussion

1. What is the role of *feedback* in a healthy relationship?

2. What place does *support* have in a successful relationship?

3. How is *conflict* handled in a relationship that works well?

4. Comment on the importance of *trust* in a successful relationship. How can it be developed if it is weak or lacking?

5. Is *openness* an element in a good relationship? Are there any limits to it? If so, what might they be?

Figure 16-1. Example of a question sheet for stimulating pre-film/video or post-film/video discussion.

☐ Instructions are available for future reference in the course of program planning or revision.

An example of a question sheet is given in Figure 16-1.

Another form of the question sheet is one that asks participants to respond in writing to certain questions. Two forms of the question sheet are as follows:

1. *Post-film/video.* Participants are given the question sheet, post-film/video, and are asked to complete it and then meet in small groups to discuss their answers.

2. *Pre-film/video.* Participants are given a question sheet in *advance* of the film/video showing, and are asked to read the questions and to focus on them as they view the film/video. They are encouraged to make entries on the question sheet as the film/video evolves and to complete their answers to the questions at the film/video's end. Again, they would meet in small groups to discuss their answers.

Examples of two question sheets are given in Appendices 59 and 60.

Developing Question Sheets

Questions given to participants should be challenging in nature. They should provoke significant thought, adding a worthwhile dimension to the film/video viewing and analyzing process. You can prepare "good" questions if you recognize that

1. Questions can serve different functions and thus take different forms.
2. Questions can assume a hierarchy of complexity; that is, we can rank questions as to how simple or involved they are.

Questions, then, may take these forms or levels [8]:

Factual level. Some examples:

☐ Who were the main characters in the film?

☐ Why did Alexandra refuse the promotion?

☐ What guidelines did the expert in the film/video offer for effective communication?

☐ How did the general manager's and the president's views on discipline differ?

☐ What causes burnout in a customer relations job, according to the film/video?

General level. Some examples of questions that are general and thought-stimulating and take an open-ended form follow:

☐ What does the film/video seem to be telling us?

☐ Is there more than one theme in it?

☐ What's the most significant point made in the film/video?

☐ How does this film/video relate to our own experience?

☐ Would you like to work for the comptroller?

☐ Would you like to supervise Allen and Jean?

Analytical level. Here we involve the group in an analysis of, for example:

1. What is going on—the characters' reactions, motivations, feelings, attitudes, values, support systems, conflicts, frictions, rivalries, dependency tendencies, defenses, styles of leadership (communication, delegation, selling).
2. Processes and systems in the organization, such as the communication system, the reward system, authority vs. the power of the informal organization, the decision-making processes, teamwork, innovation, creativity, leadership, setting objectives. Typical questions relative to this are

   ☐ Who seems to have the power in Division X?

   ☐ How would you describe McBride as a leader?

☐ Is the company subject to the problem of "yesterday's bread-winners"?

☐ What does the corporate level seem to expect of its divisions?

☐ Can you describe and evaluate the organization's system for self-appraisal?

☐ What kind of stress factors seem to be at work in Division X?

☐ What is the real source of conflict between the two branch chiefs?

Application level. At this level we move beyond an attempt to analyze or interpret the action and interaction pertaining to the individuals, the groups, and the total organization depicted in the film/video. We now wish to see if we can *apply* our learnings from the film/video and its subsequent discussion to a higher level—prevention of undesirable situations, improvement of our own policies and practices, etc. Sample questions include the following:

☐ What significance does the film/video have for our job situations?

☐ What are the implications for our long-range planning system?

☐ How would we go about utilizing these principles with our customers?

☐ How would organization renewal or organization development aid the company in the film/video and our own organization as well?

☐ How does an MBO program relate to all the problems we saw?

☐ How important is openness and trust? Do we have it? To what degree? How can we increase it?

☐ Is our organization vulnerable to the same set of external forces we saw in the film/video?

☐ Do we have (or need) an early warning system to avoid these and other oversights?

☐ Do these ethical factors relate to us at all?

☐ What do you think the business environment will be like in the next five to eight years? What problems will this pose for us?

☐ How could we go about changing the attitudes of *our* employees?

☐ Should we be working on team building in the same way as the group in the film/video did?

☐ How can we apply these concepts of discipline to our kinds of workers and situations?

Participant-Prepared Questions

Although the trainer ordinarily presents questions to the group after a film/video viewing, at times it may be desirable to reverse this responsibility. The task, then, for the participants working in small groups, is to frame several questions to which the other teams or the total group are to respond.

Summary Sheets

One way to "button down" learnings from the film/video is to provide participants with a handout that lists the key ideas or learnings that emerged from it. It's a good idea to go over these pointers or principles with the participants to ensure understanding. Also, you should take notes about the reactions to the discussion so that you can revise and enrich the sheet for use with future participant groups.

Adjectival Description

1. After showing the film/video, have each participant jot down on a sheet of paper two or three adjectives that describe *all* the main characters in the film/video.
2. Then have participants meet in small groups to develop composite descriptions that are to be written on a flipchart and posted on the wall.
3. Test the "validity" of the descriptions via total group review and discussion.

Note: A variation is to ask each small group to develop a composite description of only *one* character.

PLANNING FOR MULTIPLE FILM/VIDEO USE

At times the training design may call for the use of several films/videos. Or an off-the-shelf audio-visual program may be built around a group of films/videos. In such cases it is desirable to vary the techniques

used to "exploit" the film/videos. This approach will augment participant interest in both the films/videos and the training.

Let's assume, then, that we are working with a six-film/video series. As part of our plan to "kick off" and generally work with each film/video, we might use the ideas suggested in the following list. The list will encourage us to think systematically about diverse ways to enrich each film/video presentation.

1. *Post-film/video, dyadic discussion:* "Turn to your neighbor and discuss and agree on the most significant learning for you from the film/video."
2. *Post-film/video, small group assignment:* Ask each group a different question, such as: "What turned you on; what did you really like?" "What raised a question in your mind about what you saw?" "Was there something in the film/video you are somewhat reluctant to accept?"
3. *Post-film/video fishbowl:* Have the participants discuss what was learned or the implications of the problem under review.
4. *Pre-film/video, small group assignment:* Relate the tasks to the film/video's subject matter. "Group One, look for and report back on the most significant ideas on planning. Group Two, look for and report back on the most significant ideas on decision making."
5. *Post-film/video, group-at-large discussion:* Use general questions such as: "Any reaction?" "Significance?" "Do you agree?" "Disagree?" "Do you buy it all?" "Any omissions?"
6. *Post-film/video, group-at-large discussion:* Use specific questions such as: "What did the expert in the film/video say about product liability?"

PARTICIPANT REACTIONS TO FILM/VIDEO CONTENT

In various workshops for trainers and in other contacts, I have been asked how to deal with or respond to troublesome or "negative" reactions that participants may have to certain films/videos or portions thereof. Some of the trainers' most common questions, along with my answers to those concerns, follow:

☐ *"But we work in a hospital."* How do you as a trainer respond to trainees who work in a given occupational setting (for example, an office) and thus assert they can't identify with an unrelated setting (a factory)?

This is a classic problem, but one principally aired by inexperienced trainers. These suggestions generally help: First, you should use your introduction to the film/video to defuse in advance such possible objections. Specifically, you should point out that the setting the participants will see is different from theirs, but that "this shouldn't matter too much because our goal is to study managerial behavior to better understand management principles and processes (or sales techniques, or communication processes, or leadership styles), not the nuts and bolts of the industry depicted in the film/video. So as you watch the film, relate the incidents in it to your own job situation."

Ordinarily, these introductory comments should quiet such criticism. If complaints persist, you can also point out that "just as a student in a Michigan law school may study a California case to extract the legal principle involved, so, too, managers study management cases regardless of their source. In any case, other management (or supervisory) groups have used this film/video without difficulty, so I don't think this will cause any problem at all for you." You can point out, too, that if a case is "organization- (or industry-) specific," all too often participants get distracted by the minutiae (technology, policies, regulations) of the job or industry portrayed, hence "outside" filmed cases are desirable. Finally, it's simply too expensive to try to produce a film/video for every job or industrial situation. In general, the alert, interested, and flexible participant will successfully transfer the learning from the "abstract" film/video to his/her job situation. Conversely, and at a deeper level, the inability to make the transfer may indicate resistance to the training. If participants find the message unsettling, they may understandably discount it by quibbling over the setting or the occupations presented in the film/video.

☐ *"This is a 'racist' (or 'sexist') film/video."* How do you deal with a trainee who complains that a film/video is "racist" or "sexist"?

1. Listen carefully to the participant's complaint as to its logic or validity. If it is an older production and there are no women, blacks, or other minorities in managerial or professional roles, obviously the complaint is based on fact. All you can say to the participant is something along this line: "You are quite right. But you have to consider when the film/video was made."

2. If the complaint is somewhat less than "logical," for example, "In the opening stage-setting shots, there are no women operating the big cranes in the pipe yard," it is your job to try to elevate the conversation to a more logical plane. You thus might say: "What you say is correct. But there is a woman in a key managerial role throughout the film/video (or film/video series). There are blacks in important roles in the film/video, too. I believe that showing women and minorities in important roles, such as in managerial positions, is more significant than showing them in traditional blue-collar roles, don't you?"

3. It is also possible, at times, to turn a complaint into a plus element. For example, in the British film *Blowing Hot and Cold,* the production manager uses the term "Jap." Use this incident as an opportunity for the participant group to discuss the implication of the comment in relation to prejudice. In effect, the racial slur can become grist for the discussion mill.

☐ *"Hey, this film/video is a dozen years old."* What is the best way to handle complaints about an old or older film/video? The message may be lost on participants because of the age of the film/video and the fact that styles of clothing, hair, and cars are "dated."

You might respond to a complaining participant by saying: "Yes, there's no question that it is an older film/video. But the message is still worthwhile." You can use the film successfully by introducing it carefully. That is to say, point out to the group *at the outset* that the film/video is an older one, that the costuming and cars are a bit "dated," but that the content, nevertheless, is still highly valid. Advise the participants: "Don't get too concerned about such details, but concentrate on the principles and techniques the film/video is pointing out." This candid type of introduction should defuse in advance possible non–content-type objections. Some older films are classics and should be so designated along with a statement such as "Thousands of participants have seen this film since 1980 (or 1990) and have found it quite helpful."

In most cases, a challenging film/video-related assignment will stimulate participant thinking about content as opposed to peripheral items in the film/video.

☐ *"This film/video runs too long."* If you are concerned that participants will like the content of a film/video, but will be turned off by the film's length, you could use some of the following suggestions to overcome this problem.

1. Use certain (not all) of the vignettes in the film/video.

2. Stop the film/video midway (or at any other logical break point) and introduce a group-in-action activity.

3. In some instances the lecture portions, if any, can be dropped.

Another possibility, of course, is to try to locate another film on the same subject that is somewhat shorter.

☐ *"This film/video is hardly realistic" (or "too far out" or "too idealistic").* What is the best way to deal with extremely negative comments about a film made by a participant?

It is to be expected that some participants may overreact to a film/video or some portion of it. But is this a disaster—something to be feared? Will these negative comments frighten off the positive thinkers? Hardly.

An *extreme* comment is actually grist for the discussion mill. An effective way to deal with the negative thinker (probably one who is merely engaging in attention-seeking behavior) is to turn the comment back to the group in this fashion: "Does anyone else have any other thoughts on this point?" The odds are that the extreme comment will draw the opposite (more favorable) reaction. Why? Simply because fair-minded people find it hard to sit idly by when far-out, unfair over-reactions are expressed.

Remember, too, that diversity of opinion indicates that the film/video is live, provocative, disturbing, and thought-provoking—something every alert trainer is always seeking.

☐ *"The film/video failed to discuss . . ."* What do you do or say when participants point out gaps or omissions in the film/video?

You should realize that no film will discuss every conceivable aspect of a subject. If another substantive point should be made, there's no reason why a participant or the trainer can't make it. That is part of the trainer's job. The film/video is designed to present certain issues, to get some thinking in motion, to spark discussion. It can only set a groundwork for exploration of other, related issues; it cannot serve as a substitute for such exploration.

Thus you might say to the participant: "You are quite correct. The film/video does not delve into that aspect of the problem. I'm glad *you're* making that point."

Remember the film/video is essentially a springboard for group discussion, so there's no reason why participants or the trainer cannot bring up added points. By so doing, all parties can expand upon the significant points already contained in (or made by) the film/video.

☐ *"Too much lecture in the film/video."* Ideally, films/videos should use the medium properly and be highly dramatic. However, at times a worthwhile film/video may have one or more somewhat lengthy "talking-heads" scenes in it.

So when trainers tell me: "The concepts are excellent, but our audience will be turned off by the excessive lecture," I offer this response: "I'm glad you feel your participant group will profit from the ideas in the film/video. However, even if the formal inputs are long, your skill as a trainer can help to make the film/video a valuable learning vehicle. By using the problems, questions, and exercises in the leader's guide (or workbooks), or some of your own, you can provide the participants with a change of pace—a break from the lecture aspects of the film/video."

Other possibilities are:

1. To use the vignettes, if any, and omit or reduce the film/video's lecture portions.

2. To break up the film/video, rather than running it straight through, and provide practical work or discussion at strategic stop-film points.

3. To use an alternate film/video on the same topic.

USEFUL SCENES FROM POPULAR MOVIES [9]

Movie: Monty Python and the Search for the Holy Grail
Scene: Captain giving instructions to nincompoop guards
Use: Active listening (clarifying and confirming)

Movie: Monty Python and the Search for the Holy Grail
Scene: Knight asking peasants to figure out if a woman is a witch
Use: Problem solving

Movie: Lost in America
Scene: Albert Brooks in boss's office, thinking that he's getting promoted
Use: Transactional analysis (from adult mode to child mode)

Movie: Lost in America
Scene: [same scene]
Use: Career management (making assumptions about getting a promotion)

Movie: Modern Times
Scene: Company president turns on spy-screen and shouts out orders
Use: Management style

Movie: Airplane
Scene: Two black guys talking jive, subtitled
Use: Cultural and language barriers in communications

Movie: The Karate Kid
Scene: Coaching boy by having him wax car, paint fence, etc.
Use: Coaching techniques

Movie: The Caine Mutiny
Scene: Queeg stating how he solved the stolen strawberries mystery
Use: Problem solving—using same old methods to solve all problems

Movie: Take the Money and Run
Scene: Virgil Starkweather applying for a job and getting interviewed
Use: Interviewing and selection skills

Movie: The Great Dictator
Scene: (Hitler) and (Mussolini) racheting up their chairs
Use: Communications skills—positioning, territory

Movie: 12 O'Clock High
Scene: [the whole movie]
Use: Situational leadership

Movie: Five Easy Pieces
Scene: Jack Nicholson ordering breakfast in the diner
Use: Communication skills; transactional analysis

Movie: Teachers
Scene: [the whole movie]
Use: Train-the-trainer (commitment to performance improvement)

Movie: Patton
Scene: Opening speech
Use: Leadership style

Movie: Patton
Scene: [same scene]
Use: Making effective presentations

Movie: Pee-Wee's Big Adventure
Scene: Pee-Wee calls a meeting to discuss his stolen bike
Use: Managing meetings/agendas

Movie: 2001: A Space Odyssey
Scene: Dave lobotomizes HAL; HAL apologizes for being bad
Use: Recognizing the feelings of others

KEY POINTS

1. Films/videos have many virtues—everything from providing realism and a great deal of information in a short time frame to the fact that they are very much in tune with our film/video culture.

2. Nevertheless, films/videos are a form of one-way communication. The trainer, therefore, must exploit them properly to ensure participant involvement.

3. Films/videos can be made participative via pre-film/video, stop-film/video, and post-film/video activities. Numerous techniques in each category are available to the trainer.

4. Added approaches to dynamic film/video use include the vignette approach, trigger tapes, prediction, film/video discussion aids, the non-verbal approach, worksheets, question sheets, summary sheets, and adjectival description.

5. If more than one film/video is used in a program, it's a good idea to vary the techniques that are used.

6. Films/videos, as a training tool, must relate to learning objectives. They should not be used as "filler," to entertain, or for other non-germane reasons.

7. Be sure to preview the film/video while planning and again just before using. The first screening is to make sure it is appropriate and that you have the necessary materials to supplement the film/video. The second review is to be sure it is the correct print (if rented) and is in good shape.

8. Consider carefully how you introduce a film/video. Use your introduction as a means of providing interest and motivation and to defuse in advance possible negative reactions and comments.

REFERENCES

1. Nolan, J., "The Use and Misuse of Films in Management Training," *Training and Development Journal* (March 1980), pp. 84–86.

2. Faris, John P., "How to Use Films in Training," *Training and Development Journal* (May 1984), pp. 108–110.

3. Eitington, J., "How to Preview a Film," *SM (Sales Meeting Magazine)* (January 1972), pp. 41, 99, 101–102.

4. Winig, Laura, "Evaluating Training Videos," in "In Practice," *Training and Development* (January 1994), pp. 14–15.

5. Zeimet, E. J., Miller, K., and Turner, P., "Trigger Tapes—A Tool for Teacher Education," *Educational and Industrial Television* (March 1975), pp. 43–44.

6. Lowry, C. R., "Sensitivity to Safety Taught by Videotape," *Educational and Industrial Television* (July 1977), p. 22.

7. Levine, S. J., "Prediction—New Tool for Videotape Involvement," *Training* (April 1974), pp. 25–26.

8. Based on material developed by Eitington, J. E. (Ed.), *Bulletin on Training* (September–October 1979), p. 8.

9. This list was distributed by Mitch Mitchell, Training Specialist, Training Department, Hewlett Packard, San Diego Division, San Diego, California 92127-1899, at the 1988 Annual Conference, National Society for Performance and Instruction, Washington, D.C., April 8, 1988. The list was part of a presentation paper for his session entitled "Dagwood, Penthouse, and Patton: Using Offbeat Resources to Spice Up Your Seminars and Workshops."

RECOMMENDED READING

Carley, Mark, "Training Goes to the Movies," in "Training 101," *Training and Development,* July 1999, pp. 15–18.

Recommends 12 Hollywood films useful for training in such subject-matter areas as change management, team building, management and leadership, creativity and problem solving, and diversity. For each film listed, the author provides a description of its content and suggested questions for discussion plus exercises for trainer use. If you don't have time to show the whole feature, you can select relevant scenes.

17

Maximizing Participation and Learning in the Case Method

The real voyage of discovery consists not in seeking new lands, but in seeing with new eyes.

—Marcel Proust (1871–1922), French novelist

IN a day when the industrial training world employs so many involving (experiential) and exciting training methods (role plays, dyads, buzz groups, fishbowls, in-baskets, exercises, games, simulations) the case method (also called the case study method and the case discussion), at least in its classic form, is hardly the most glamorous of training methods. Nevertheless, it *is* a student- or learner-centered method and has many advantages over such one-way communication devices as lectures, films, and panel discussions.

The case method is an age-old teaching device, having taken through the ages such familiar forms as fables and parables. In more modern times, the case method was developed and used at Harvard University in the 1880's. First used in the business school, it spread to other schools of the university and to other universities. In time it entered the industrial training scene, where it was used extensively in management training in conjunction with the traditional lecture method.

ADVANTAGES AND DISADVANTAGES

The *Management Development Casebook*, prepared by the Veterans Administration, cites 12 advantages in using the case method [1]. The method is advantageous in that it

1. Is personal. It puts the burden of thinking on the members and arouses their interest by making them active rather than passive participants.

2. Is real. The members examine situations that have actually occurred.

3. Is specific. The members deal with specific facts and events rather than with generalities. The method brings about the recognition that formulas and principles are of little value in specific situations and that each situation requires its own understanding and reaction.

4. Places the members in a group situation. It provides opportunities to work cooperatively and with satisfaction within the group, and gives some feeling for the importance of the group.

5. Establishes a strong give-and-take. Members must justify and defend their own views and, at the same time, must try to comprehend and use the contributions of others.

6. Brings about a recognition by the members that other people look at situations in different ways, that other people have problems similar to their own, and that other people have difficulty in solving these problems.

7. Produces a realization that the types of problems discussed do not have a single subject or a single answer.

8. Develops judgment and ability to think independently and more maturely.

9. Provides experience for performing essential parts of the supervisory or administrative task. It enables members to develop the habits of analyzing a situation, using factual knowledge, formulating a program of action, and making decisions. And it provides this experience without risk to the members or to the organization of which they are a part.

10. Brings about a better understanding of human behavior, an increased sensitivity to causes behind behavior, and an awareness of the necessity for seeking these real causes. The members realize that people tend to have feelings, sentiments, and beliefs which are not logical, which are important to them, and which have to be considered. They also see more clearly how their actions affect the behavior of others.

11. Increases skill in communication. Members learn how to listen better. They also improve their ability to convey ideas.

12. Reduces fixed attitudes, such as "all redheads are hotheads" and "fear makes people work harder." It produces changes in attitudes and outlook and develops a willingness to see problems from all points of view.

The *Casebook* also listed these disadvantages: The case method

1. Does not actually provide *real* experience. While the case method uses real situations, there are a number of aspects in which it lacks realism. Participants do not have actual responsibility for the decisions they make. The facts are presented; the members get little practice in seeking and recognizing facts and relationships. Because it may not be feasible to present all of the available facts, the situation may be oversimplified. The printed case doesn't convey many subtle but important overtones of human personality and conduct. The members don't experience the successive interactions which are a part of real experience.

2. Is incomplete. It does not include the process of carrying out the decisions and checking on the results.

3. Sometimes overemphasizes the making of decisions. In real life action may not be justified, or a particular solution may not be feasible.

4. Takes a more skilled discussion leader than do other methods. It is easier to "tell" than it is to phrase questions which will stimulate discussion and keep the discussion on track. It takes great self-control for a leader to refrain from giving his/her own views. A lecturer can select the questions which he/she will discuss; in the case method the leader cannot anticipate all the questions which may be raised.

5. Is different. Not only that, but it is radically different. Participants usually feel frustrated at first when they find there are no specific conclusions, answers, or recipes. Some may find the idea of thinking for themselves to be new and even terrifying.

6. Is slow. The discussion and deliberation which this method requires naturally take more time than do the methods which pass on "the word." Usually it takes some time to get past the frustration period mentioned in point 5.

7. Is not adaptable to all employees.

8. Presents greater opportunities for the "eager beavers" to monopolize the discussion.

9. Does not create results which can be easily integrated with specific operating practices.

10. Is not useful when the primary purpose is the transmission of facts.

11. Can be a waste of time and effort, if not used properly.

In *executive* development programs the case method has these special benefits [2]:

□ Participants (executives) can assume the position of and identify with the real-world manager; they are challenged to make decisions and action plans.

□ Retention of concepts used to solve real-world problems is increased.

□ Skills in appraising situations and applying concepts are developed, as opposed to theoretical, textbook ideas being emphasized.

Special disadvantages accrue in using cases in executive development programs [2]:

□ The written case does not fully convey the complexity of a management situation.

□ The participants don't have the opportunity to collect and sift the data which aid in identifying significant trends and organizational climate. (The case writer does this.)

□ The case lacks immediacy. It is essentially a historical document.

□ Since the participants are not involved in the actual decisions, they will not experience the uncertainty of decision making or the risks associated with it.

Assessing the pluses and minuses just cited, one can safely say that case study is a useful training method, a *participative* method, but hardly the most exciting and profound training method available today. However, maximum return from its use can be achieved by (1) varying the format of the cases and (2) providing supplementary training devices to exploit a given case more fully. The bulk of this chapter will be concerned, then, with these two "enriching" approaches to case study.

THE CASE STUDY—A POTPOURRI OF FORMATS

In the pages that follow we will present the case study in many forms. In doing so, we offer selections which are essentially representative rather than exhaustive. All of the formats, however, have the same purpose—to get the participants to *think*.

The Classic Harvard Case

In a classic case study, participants are given a comprehensive case. It is drawn from a real situation and is very well researched. While no case writer can capture all of the facts, there is generally enough data for analysis. In fact, the discussion leader may ask in response to participant requests for more facts: "But are you using the facts you already have?"

Because of the length of the Harvard case, participants must spend considerable time (two or three hours) in preparation for the case discussion session. The discussion itself is very nondirective, the trainer's role being that of catalyst, encourager, climate-setter, devil's advocate, issue-sharpener, "referee," etc., rather than that of expert, lecturer, or authority figure. The trainer's technique to start the discussion is a simple question: "What seems to be going on here?"

The group will typically identify a good many issues in the case since it is so comprehensive and ramified. A major goal is for participants to see the "big picture," the interrelatedness of events, the internal and external forces at work, and the role of personality in decision making. Learning takes place in large part by listening to the divergent views of the group. A major learning is that there is no single or best solution to a case, and indeed, sometimes there may be no answer at all.

Due to the length of the Harvard-type case, industry tends to use much shorter cases. Few managers have the time or motivation to engage in the preparation required by such cases. This chapter presents examples of the kinds of cases used in industrial training.

The Short Case

A case need not be long to excite participant interest and encourage creative efforts at problem resolution. This is exemplified by the following case and the many creative, high-quality solutions regarding it that were developed by participants in several separate sessions.

The Case of the Undesirable Job

A meat-packing plant has a job that is marked by extremely high turnover. Employees rarely stay more than three or four months. Some workers leave after only two weeks. Absenteeism and tardiness are also high. The reason? The duties are repetitive, tedious, dirty, smelly, and generally low status. Typical tasks include readying the garbage for removal, sweeping and mopping floors, scrubbing walls, cleaning several restrooms, and hosing down garbage cans. The volume of the work is such that "free time" is generally available, ranging from 45 minutes to nearly 2 hours daily depending on the workload as well as the pace of the worker.

Assume you are the personnel officer of this plant. What might you do to extend in a fairly significant way the period of time in which the employee stays with the company?

Some solutions:

☐ Job-design-type approaches

1. Mechanize the job to remove as much of the "dirty work," monotony, and fatigue as possible.
2. Ensure the availability of high-quality materials and equipment that will minimize job irritations.
3. Enrich the job with higher-level duties and responsibilities, if at all possible, either on the job or elsewhere in the organization. *Note:* Free time is available for this.
4. Another approach, taking into consideration normal turnover, would be to utilize that employee's time with training for higher-level positions. He could be a "spell" man, as they call them in industry (replacing regular employees who must take a short personal break during group operations).
5. Distribute or rotate tasks so the same person doesn't have to perform this job all the time.

☐ Recruitment-type approaches

1. Spend as much or more time interviewing for these positions as you do for others. Don't hurry through this interview just because it is a low-paying job. The rule here is, if you don't interview properly the first time, you'll have to the second time or the third time . . .
2. Selectively interview only those people who may find this type of job rewarding and interesting; that is, someone who will regard the job as a promotion.
3. When you find a likely candidate, completely explain to (and, if possible, show) the prospect what the job entails. Be candid about job drawbacks.
4. If the candidate is still with you at this time, explain in a very honest, truthful way the importance of the job as it relates to what your organization does.
5. Selectively hire a person who is psychologically more able to take the unpleasantness of the work. (This is the only approach that will work in some situations.)
6. Be certain to hire someone who has all the physical characteristics needed for the job.
7. Hire a retarded individual who is able to function in a regular job environment. You may consider that people are leaving because the job is beneath their capabilities and insults their personal senses. They may be overly qualified for that type of work.
8. Recruit a college student who would relish the free time for study.

☐ Motivational approaches

1. Treat the position as an "entry job" and move the employee to other work as soon as possible.

2. Add incentive by allowing the person to leave when the job is done and still get paid for the full shift.

3. Have constant contact and communication with that particular person. Help make the job important by checking often as to the employee's progress or problems. (Most often these jobs are relatively low paying and easy to forget, except every several weeks, when you are hiring a new "body.")

4. Ask the employee from time to time what could be done to make the job less unpleasant or more rewarding. Don't hesitate to repeat the question even if you don't strike "paydirt" the first time or two. Certainly some employees will appreciate the fact that you asked!

5. Don't hesitate to give sincere praise for tasks well done.

Note: I developed this tripartite classification of the solutions on a post-discussion basis. However, it would be a good training technique for the trainer to have the participant group classify their suggested solutions, posted on the flipchart, as to JD (job design), R (recruitment), or M (motivational) approaches. This would allow the group to see its tendency to propose "across-the-board" or one- or two-category solutions.

The Incident Process

The incident process, like the short case, was a reaction to the lengthy Harvard-type case with all its complexities, long advance preparation time, and long discussion periods. Developed by Dr. Paul Pigors, a retired professor of industrial relations at M.I.T., and Faith Pigors, the incident process is used to teach managers to collect a full set of facts before making a decision.

In this method the participant group receives a short account of an incident, which can be read and digested quickly. The incident typically involves the need for the manager concerned (meaning the participants) to make a decision. However, before the man-

ager decides, it is essential that one have as full a set of facts as possible. And how does one get these added facts? One must ask you, the trainer, for them. Thus, group members, in the role of the decision maker, must raise questions of a fact-seeking nature such as:

☐ What is the organization like? (The trainer will then distribute organization charts to everyone, assuming the trainer has them stockpiled.)

☐ What is the company's financial condition? (The trainer will likely provide a statement containing financial data.)

☐ Is there additional information on the performance record of the senior engineer? (Again, such data may be forthcoming.)

☐ Is there a policy concerning promotion in the company? (If available, this too, will be provided.)

If the trainer cannot answer a question with a data sheet, he/she will simply indicate that: "We don't have any information on that point."

To illustrate how the process works, let's work through the following real-life incident.

Observing the Lennon Vigil [3]

You are Mary Ames, manager of a variety store. It is Sunday, 2 P.M., December 14, 1980. Betty Carnes, one of your cashiers, decides to bow her head and stop work. She does this to observe the ten-minute silent memorial to the late rock star John Lennon. The vigil has been requested by the former Beatle's widow upon Lennon's murder. In explaining her behavior, Betty simply says that: "John Lennon stood for peace and love, and that's what's important." As a consequence, some customers waiting in a long Christmas-time line stalk out.

Assume you are Mary Ames. What action do you take, if any, respecting Betty?

As indicated, the group will need to garner more facts before a decision is reached regarding Betty. Presumably they would raise questions such as the following:

☐ What is the performance record of Betty Carnes, and what is her tenure at the store? (Betty, a high school senior, is a part-time worker. Presumably she would not have a great deal of seniority.)

☐ Did any other clerks also engage in the silent vigil? (Another cashier and a stock clerk did, but only for a couple of minutes, according to management. Betty stated that they also observed the ten-minute work stoppage.)

☐ How many customers out of what total left the store because of Betty's action? (Some left; we don't know how many were in the store at the time.)

☐ Did Ms. Ames order Betty to return to work? (Yes, but Betty did not.)

☐ What is company policy regarding insubordination? (Any action, including discharge, is acceptable.)

☐ What disciplinary action was taken regarding the other two clerks? (They were reprimanded.)

Thus far we have dealt with the first two steps of the incident process, namely,

Step 1: The incident (available to participants in writing).

Step 2: The fact-finding process. Assuming the available facts have been obtained, the participants are now ready for the third step, namely,

Step 3: The issue. Here the trainer tries to get the group to define the major issues and sub-issues, if the latter exist.

Step 4: The decision by the manager. The trainer asks participants to write their decision and give reasons for it. The statement is turned in and those with like decisions form discussion groups. In our case on the Lennon vigil, possible decisions by the manager could be these:

1. Fire Betty Carnes (which is what happened, and thus the case hit the newspaper).

2. Reprimand or possibly suspend Betty. (Two other employees were merely reprimanded since they only took a couple of minutes out.)

3. Explain the situation to the customers, request their cooperation, and ask them to wait the ten minutes.

4. Pass out fruit juice to the waiting customers.

5. Ask the customers to join in the silent vigil.

6. Take over for Betty for the ten minutes involved.

Note: What might appear to be a simple case, could, nevertheless, have at least six solutions. The reader may think of others, too.

When the discussion groups are formed, they choose a chairperson who will also be their spokesperson. The spokespersons briefly debate their positions. The group at large then critically compares the reasoning of the several groups. This phase of the process is completed by the discussion leader telling the group what the actual or real-life decision was. (Betty was fired.)

Step 5: Evaluation. In the final step, the broader issues of the incident are examined in depth. This is the payoff point, that is, where the real learning takes place. Questions such as these are considered: How could this incident have been prevented? What might the long-range effects of the firing decision be on customer relations and relations with the rest of the workforce? Would Ms. Ames' superiors feel the incident was handled properly?

The incident process has several benefits, including:

☐ The short case gets the group into action quickly.

☐ It obviously teaches the manager to respect facts and to seek them out in full before making a decision.

☐ It involves the participants to a high degree. The debate aspect is generally a fun thing, and the question-posing aspect of the process is usually a fast-moving activity.

☐ It sharpens up one's skill in decision making. Note the emphasis on reaching a sound decision.

On the other hand, we should recognize these limitations or disadvantages, too:

☐ It is a highly trainer-oriented activity. In fact, some critics say it unwittingly teaches dependence on the leader or trainer. Certainly much of management training today endeavors to de-emphasize the importance of the leader's role and to discourage adulation of the all-powerful, all-knowing, authoritarian leader. This is done to provide a democratic-participative role model for the participants.

□ The process is more suited for low- to mid-level managers than for executives because of its emphasis on fact gathering. In the real world top officials rely on subordinate managers for fact collection, concerning themselves with the broader, strategic aspects of the decision-making process.

□ The process also lends itself best to short cases of limited complexity, again making it less suitable for executive groups.

□ In the questioning process the more bright and verbal participants take over, leaving others in the group to serve as spectators.

□ The questioning process may fail to elicit certain elements or issues. Thus, vital factors in the case may be overlooked.

□ The debate on particular points in the case may become so lively that the groups become polarized around their positions.

Action Maze [4]

An action maze is a highly structured group activity relating to problem solving and decision making. It is a form of case study, but goes beyond it in its complexity, that is, it is highly programmed. Here's how it works:

The trainer gives the participants a written case. It not only states the problem, but also provides options in respect to possible solutions. The group discusses these alternatives and then agrees on a solution. They then ask the trainer for another "frame" which explains the *consequences* of the decision they chose. They receive more alternatives, and the process goes on.

To illustrate, let's take this problem which requires resolution:

You have a secretary—Kim Biles—who has been taking advantage of her position and has been abusing leave privileges: frequent late arrivals, long lunch periods about once per week, and use of sick leave in excess of others in like jobs. The problem is complicated by the fact that Kim has been around over three years, knows the job very well, and is an unusually fast, helpful, cheerful, and competent worker. You have received several complaints from staff to the effect that Kim "seems to be getting

away with murder." Your action is (select one alternative):

C—*Counsel* Kim on the abuse of the leave regulations.

S—Invite Kim to your *staff* meeting, where a general discussion will be held on leave abuse. Hopefully, Kim will get the message.

L—Lay it on the *line*. Tell Kim in no uncertain terms that things have gone far enough.

N—Do *nothing*. Kim will probably come around in time. Kim is too valuable an employee to risk "turning off."

The group selects one of the options, for example, "N." They are told what happens (consequences) as a result of their decision: "Kim doesn't 'shape up' as you had hoped. In fact, two months later you can see that things have gotten worse. So you must now make one of the following decisions . . . ," etc.

Each decision the participants make produces particular consequences. If high-quality decisions are made, the group receives sets of more desirable choices. Bad choices garner less desirable alternatives. In the latter case, there is always one good choice in the new set so that the group can still work its way out of the maze.

A variation on the above procedure is to let small groups form on the basis of their preference for a particular alternative in the first round. Each buzz group then has to work its own way out of the maze.

The strong points of the action maze are that the participants have to debate their choices (as in case study), they get to learn the consequences of their decisions (unlike case study), and they have a lively time working their way out of the maze. On the down side are the difficulty of developing well-thought-out sets of decisions for each step of the maze and the time consumed in class to advance through all the frames or steps. Also, some small groups may get "lost" in the maze and, if time runs out, be frustrated due to lack of closure.

Note:

1. The action maze requires a more comprehensive file of materials than any other case study approach.

2. It may begin with an incident rather than a case. This is particularly helpful when one of the learning objectives is for the participants to learn how to ask the right questions to get the kinds of information they are usually given in a case.

The Mousetrap Technique

The mousetrap technique is designed to show participants that their thinking about organizational problems and issues may be marked by various forms of faulty reasoning—engaging in rationalizations, tolerating double standards, ignoring inconsistent enforcement of rules, overlooking the significance of the leader as a role model, confusing personal and societal values, and arguing for standards to follow practice rather than vice versa.

"The Gambling Case," which follows, is adapted from a case used some years back by the Navy Department's Civilian Personnel Division in Washington, D.C., in its leadership training program. This program was concerned with leadership and such issues as ethics, values, authority, discipline, and standards.

As will be apparent from the three situations presented below as part of "The Gambling Case," the learning objective is to sharpen thinking concerning leadership by example, toleration of double standards, and inconsistent rule enforcement. The case raises the question of whether standards should follow actual practice or vice versa, and challenges the all-too-easy rationalization that a practice may be acceptable simply because "everybody does it" or "it's done all the time."

To overcome these usual rationalizations, the mousetrap technique is used in this case. Three quite different situations are presented, but each calls for acceptance or denial of the same set of standards. Participants readily commit themselves to Situation 1, unaware of Situation 2; they further commit themselves to Situation 2, unaware of Situation 3. Each commitment makes it extremely difficult to avoid enforcing the next situation without being patently inconsistent.

All three situations should be discussed in one session, lest the impact of the participants' inconsistencies become lost. Situation 1 (but not the other two situations) may be given to participants for advance reading or pre-work.

The Gambling Case

Situation 1

You are Fred Blair, chief of administration in Big City Hospital. This morning you are faced with a perplexing situation. It seems that last evening four hospital attendants were caught playing cards for money. Their excuse was that they were playing on their supper period, as they often do. Ordinarily no money is wagered, but since it was payday they decided to set up some small stakes. They were playing just ten minutes past their supper period when they were spotted by a patient who promptly reported their gambling activity to the shift supervisor.

The four men have been with the hospital for periods ranging from five to eight years. Three have above-average performance records; the fourth has a history of intermittent absenteeism and was involved in a gambling incident several years ago and received a reprimand as a first-time offender. One of the three good performers admits to having urged the others to play for money.

The hospital has a clear-cut schedule for all disciplinary offenses. The section on gambling specifies the following penalties:

1. *Gambling*
   a. First offense
      Minimum: Written reprimand
      Maximum: Suspension for ten days
   b. Second offense
      Minimum: Suspension for ten days
      Maximum: Discharge
2. *Promotion of gambling*
   a. First offense
      Minimum: Suspension for ten days
      Maximum: Discharge
   b. Second offense: Discharge

As Fred Blair you have to decide:

1. Do you enforce the no-gambling rule?
2. If so, do you treat all four men alike?

Situation 2

A week after the problem with the four card players, Fred Blair had an irate visitor in his office—Vina Dixon, chief dietician of the hospital. This dialogue ensued:

Ms. Dixon: I'm here to find out who's running my department.
Fred Blair: What?
Ms. Dixon: I'm tired of people coming into my department and hassling my employees to buy raffle tickets.
Fred Blair: Hassling?
Ms. Dixon: Oh, sure, they say it's voluntary and it's always for a worthy cause—underprivileged kids, volunteer firemen, church groups, and so on. But that isn't the point.
Fred Blair: The point is . . .
Ms. Dixon: That people are promoting gambling on official time and on city property, too.
Fred Blair: Which has been going on since year one . . .
Ms. Dixon: Exactly. And I'm here to put a stop to it.
Fred Blair: How will you do that?
Ms. Dixon: By calling a spade a spade rather than a shovel, Mr. Blair. This is *gambling*, not charitable soliciting, and I hereby bring formal charges of promoting gambling against Supervisory Nurse Betty Burns.
Fred Blair: You mean official charges . . .
Ms. Dixon: Exactly. Here's my memorandum which has all the details. Now what are you going to do about it?

You are Fred Blair. What should you do about the charges presented?

Situation 3

A month later Fred Blair has another visitor. It is Tommy Edmonds, a branch chief who reports to Blair.

Tommy: You'll want to get in on this one.
Fred: What one?
Tommy: You know, the Super Bowl is on next week and we've got our usual pool on. Only this time the ante is higher and we got twice as many "investors." A big pot is really shaping up.
Fred: Uh, I'm not sure . . .
Tommy: Come on, you've always played and have hit more winners than the rest of us. Give us a chance to get some of that green back. How about it?

You are Fred Blair. How do you respond?

Wrong Way–Right Way

Fran's Request of Pat

Fran is administrative officer in the Information Division with a responsibility for, among other things, renewing subscriptions to magazines, newspapers, and newsletters. Although subscription items number about two dozen, some 50–60 other items are regularly received on a complimentary basis. These "freebies" come from two sources: (1) various publishers who wish to secure ads for their publications and (2) as a result of subscription exchange arrangements made by Pat, editor of a management newsletter. All freebies are routed directly to Pat by the mail room.

As Fran sees it, it is not always clear when an invoice to renew a subscription should be honored since there are so many freebies coming in. Fran decides to talk to Pat about the problem. Pat is not always the easiest person to deal with.

Sequence A—The Wrong Approach

Fran: Pat, I'd like to talk to you about that subscription problem again.
Pat: What subscription problem?
Fran: The one I mentioned last summer—this business of the renewal notices.
Pat: Don't know anything about it.
Fran: But I asked you to give me a list of all freebies.
Pat: You did?
Fran: Yes, I did.
Pat: Well, maybe you did. But what do you need the list for anyway?
Fran: You get all the freebie magazines and papers, don't you?
Pat: Sure. So what?

Fran: Well, sometimes I get a bill for a renewal of a subscription when we've never subscribed to it. That's why.

Pat: Well, if you have a question about paying the bill, why don't you just look in your file?

Fran: I do. But sometimes a receipt for a subscription gets misplaced and I don't know whether we actually subscribed or not.

Pat: Why not ask the person who's interested in the publication, they'll know whether they actually ordered it or not.

Fran: That's just what I want to avoid. I don't want to heckle people about something that I ought to have information on.

Pat: Or you could ask me. I know the ones we get free on an exchange basis and most of the others, too.

Fran: Most?

Pat: Yeah, most. I'm not a computer.

Fran: Well, how about giving me a list of all the free ones so there's no slip-up.

Pat: Seems like a lot of coolie labor to me. Can't you just keep a good file on your subscriptions? What you bought you bought. If you have no record of it, it's a freebie. Simple.

Fran: You're giving me a hard time.

Pat: Look. You're trying to get me to prepare a report for you on something that's totally your problem.

Fran: You're not willing to cooperate . . .

Pat: Why not ask the mail room to compile a list for you? They know what comes in.

Fran: This is ridiculous. I'm going to see the boss about this.

Pat: You're making an issue out of very little.

Fran: I need this information, and you're not cooperating.

Pat: O.K., I'll get that list for you. But I'm not guaranteeing it's going to be one hundred percent accurate.

Fran: When will you have it?

Pat: Come on. I said I'll get it, so I'll get it. As soon as I can.

Fran: O.K., but if I have to remind you again I'm going to the boss instead.

Discussion question: What did Fran do improperly?

Sequence B—The Right Approach

Fran: Hi, Pat. How are things?

Pat: Good, but busy. Real busy.

Fran: Well, then I won't take much of your time.

Pat: Be sure you don't.

Fran: I'd like your help on a little problem, Pat.

Pat: I'm good at the *little* ones. Shoot. What is it?

Fran: Well, as administrative officer they expect me to pay the bills.

Pat: Yeah, I know that.

Fran: But sometimes I get a bill that I shouldn't pay, or at least I'm not certain if we should honor the invoice.

Pat: So?

Fran: So I don't want to authorize payment on something that is doubtful or at least should be checked into before it's okayed. Why waste the company's money?

Pat: Makes sense.

Fran: I was hoping you'd agree.

Pat: So where do I fit into this?

Fran: Glad you asked. Here's the way you can help. What if—I'm only asking "if"—starting tomorrow you kept a running list of every freebie publication you get?

Pat: Wait a minute. We get a lot of them here. I don't want to do a lot of research.

Fran: I'm with you on that. *No* research. Just jot down the name of each publication *as it comes in.* No checking back into history.

Pat: I guess I could do that. But you're sure your own file of paid invoices won't give you the dope you need?

Fran: Good question. Most of the time it's O.K. But other people use the file and sometimes invoices get borrowed or misplaced or something. In any case my file isn't one hundred percent accurate.

Pat: Well, if all I'm to do is record the titles of the publications as they come in . . . You don't need all the other stuff like addresses, and frequency, and rates . . .

Fran: Heck, no. Just the titles. Simple as that.

Pat: Well, they won't be in any special order, then, so the list won't be the easiest to use.

Fran: Good point. What if—another "if"—you jotted down each title on a three by five card, just dumped 'em in a box or brown envelope and eventually let me have them. I'll sort'em out alphabetically, and the list will be perfect to match against any invoice I'm not sure about. If you get the magazine free, I don't pay the invoice.

Pat: When do you want the list?

Fran: Whenever you feel you've captured all the titles.

Pat: A two-month cycle should give me a chance to record every title we get.

Fran: Good. Today's the 12th of May. What if I checked back with you on, say, July 20th?

Pat: Fair enough.

Fran: And one more thing.

Pat: Yeah?

Fran: You're an easy person to get cooperation from.

Pat: (smiling and obviously pleased) I guess you caught me in a weak moment.

Discussion question: What did Fran do that made for success?

The Multiple-Case Technique

An interesting and worthwhile variation on case study is to present for analysis three or four cases on a given problem area. This affords participants the opportunity to compare critically the events of and principles in the several cases. A variety of cases can help to ferret out and firm up a set of allied concepts, which a single case may not be able to do as well.

The four short cases that follow are designed to stimulate thinking concerning proper managerial outlooks toward appraisal and development of their employees.

Case 1: The Day and Night Scholar

Mary Evans, a young professional worker in the Management Analysis office, presented her boss, Tom Tuff, with a proposal to take two management courses at the university, located in walking distance of the office. One course would be taken during the day on company time (an hour on Monday, Wednesday, and Friday) and the other evenings on her own time. (Cost was not particularly an issue, since the company paid in full for job-related university courses if the employee received a grade of "C" or better.)

Tom's immediate response to the request was this: "If you've got that kind of time, maybe there's a lot of other things you ought to be doing around here."

Case 2: The Toastmaster Membership Case

You are Bill Brown, operations manager. You have five supervisors who report to you. One of them, young Hank Peters, approaches you about his possible regular attendance at a Toastmasters Club meeting during working hours. You have no objection to the toastmaster idea, but the club meets for its luncheon meeting every other Friday at noon and Hank has to leave early (around 11:15 A.M.) to get to his meeting. Hank has been very active in the Toastmasters Club and is now its president. Hence his need to arrive early to be sure everything is set up and in order, to greet arriving members, and to greet guests from other clubs.

The difficulty that arises for you is this: Your weekly staff meeting takes place from 10:00 to about noon. You like this period because you generally have lunch with your staff right after the meeting. You have found that going to lunch with the group on a once-a-week basis helps to maintain rapport and good communication with all concerned. These Friday meetings fit into your schedule very well and, besides, they enable you and your team to plan and coordinate certain things for the following week.

Case 3: Appraisal by Surprise

Bill Arndt is a member of a personnel management evaluation team that visits military installations to assess the effectiveness of their civilian personnel management programs. At large installations, the total team of five evaluators conducts the analysis; at smaller units, two or three team members may do the assessment job. The team chief, Frank Nels, does not always join the team, particularly at the smaller civilian personnel offices.

It is performance review time and Frank is completing his discussion with Bill about Bill's performance for the year.

Frank: Something that I would like to bring up is your interpersonal relations with the personnel people with whom you interact.

Bill: Oh, something wrong?

Frank: Well, not exactly. But I thought I'd bring it up and see what your reaction is.

Case 4: Appraisal by Default

Arch Bricker is a young foreman in the maintenance yard. He recently attended a supervisory training course. One of the topics discussed in depth was performance review. He thus expected his supervisor, Superintendent Dan Oakes, to call him into his office at the end of the year to review the year's work, discuss strengths and weaknesses in performance, discuss development needs, etc. However, several months went by after year's end, and Arch was not called in for the annual performance review discussion.

Arch decided to bring the issue up informally with Dan. So one evening he approached Dan in the parking lot and said, "Boss, I'm ready for my annual appraisal whenever you are." Dan looked at Arch in wonderment: "How's that? Appraisal? You're putting me on! The fact that you're still here at the end of the shift means that you've gotten your appraisal."

The Filmed Case

A worthwhile variation on the written case is the case presented on film or videotape. Its advantages follow:

☐ It can present the problem with a realism that the written case can rarely equal. Seeing and hearing "live" characters present their personalities and problems is an extremely helpful way for the participant to get "cued in" as to what is really going on.

☐ It can encapsulate and simplify ideas and events so that participants get the message with relative ease.

☐ It enables participants to identify (or dis-identify) more readily with the characters and events presented in the film/video because of its live, dramatic character.

☐ It is particularly helpful to those who have difficulty gaining ideas from a printed page.

☐ Reading of the case in advance of the session or in class is, of course, made unnecessary. It thus enables the group to get into action quickly, thereby saving preparation time. Also, typical problems such as not having read the case, having read it too quickly, or not remembering it too well are eliminated.

Using Audiotape

A case may also be presented on audiotape. This may be desirable in order to

☐ Vary the format.

☐ Highlight the dialogue of the case's characters.

☐ Present participants with more of the feelings of the principals in the case, something that the conventional written case may not communicate as well.

☐ Provide added realism via the spoken language, for example, to communicate a regional accent, a halting manner of speaking, a commanding (or indecisive) tone of voice, male vs. female voices, sarcasm, possibly certain sound effects (cars, clocks, typewriters, machinery).

As a cautionary note, the audio case should be relatively brief, for most of us have a limited aural attention span—too much input and our minds will wander. A case length of about ten minutes or less is adequately listenable. In some cases it may be desirable to play the tape a second time.

A limitation of the case on tape is that it cannot present non–dialogue-type material very well. A solution to this problem, of course, is to draw on the best of the two worlds—use the written word for background material and the tape for dialogue.

The Live Case

An interesting variation on traditional case study is the live case. This entails bringing into the training room a top-level personage (a company president, a bureau chief of a government department, a key university official) who presents a live case or problem to the participant group. By "live" we mean a problem currently being worked on, possibly one that is really "bugging" the organization.

The case can be presented to the group at large by the outside executive for immediate response and interaction, or preferably, small groups can be formed for initial framing of questions and subsequent attempts at solving the problem.

The live case has considerable appeal to participants since they are dealing with a current, unresolved problem rather than a "stale" one from a casebook; the case is presented in person by a key (often prestigious) official and, in some cases, he/she may bring along other company representatives to provide added insights about the problem; they have the opportunity to develop case data further by live interaction with the official, thereby overcoming the frequent complaint in case study work that "we don't have all the facts"; and they can reality-test their solutions with the authoritative "on-the-spot" case presenter. In essence, it provides splendid opportunities for the dynamic and more satisfying aspects of two-way (rather than one-way) communication.

It is also possible to have the official present the case from his/her office via an audio (or even video) teleconference hook-up if a personal appearance is not practical. Procedurally, this would (should) entail two separate interactions—the first for the presentation of the problem and possibly a question period immediately thereafter to establish a fuller understanding of it, and the second (possibly the next day or at a later date) to present participant solutions to the official and to secure reactions (feedback) thereon from the official. Typically, participants work in small groups to develop solutions or decisions.

If the participant group is a knowledgeable and sophisticated one, the presenting official is quite likely to be surprised at the creative solutions presented. If this positive reaction (praise) is communicated to the participants, they would be psychologically reinforced (rewarded) for their "digging in" to the case so well. Of course, the participants do not expect that their suggestions will necessarily be adopted. Nor is the official obligated to implement them.

General Electric, at its Management Development Center, Crotonville, New York, has developed another format for what they call the "living case." Their idea is to have participants work on a major, unresolved challenge facing the company, instead of focusing on something that happened in the past.

Their case is not a single document, but a collection of data—similar to what managers have for their regular analysis—for sorting through and organizing.

To illustrate, a live case was developed by a University of Pennsylvania business school professor and the Crotonville staffers. They interviewed key individuals and assembled significant documents. Their "big picture" topic concerned magnetic research to advance medical technology via better images than X-rays and CT scanners. This tool can also be used to study basic inside body cells, a means of signaling diseases like cancer well before symptoms appear.

At the center the participants were divided into four groups—two to develop a marketing strategy based on the introduction of a high-end medical product (just described) and the other two to work with a low-end product. After presenting their preliminary recommendations, the four groups discussed them with their colleagues and executives from the center and the GE Medical Systems Business Group. They used these discussions as a basis for development of final recommendations that went to top management.

As GE sees the value of live case study, it familiarizes participants with the kinds of decisions they will actually make, as well as introducing them to the risks, ambiguities, and pressures facing managers who have to introduce a new technology [2].

Note:

1. The GE approach is also known as action learning or action-reflection learning (ARL). For a more detailed discussion of ARL, see Chapter 11.
2. For a fuller account of the GE experience with action learning, see James J. Noel and Ram Charan, "GE Brings Global Thinking to Light," *Training and Development* (July 1992), pp. 29–33.

Citing a Personal Case

The Case of the Partying Conferees

A group of school officials from Mid-Area School District annually attends a professional conference for one week at an out-of-state location. Jane R., one of the group, finds that her fellow participants (three males and two females) seem to be more interested in partying than in attending conference sessions. She has the feeling, too, that although several of her colleagues have spouses back home, there seems to be an interest in "pairing off." Also, much of the group's conversations and jokes are very suggestive and off-color. Jane R. doesn't want to be a "wet blanket" and wants to be part of what is, of course, her professional group. But at the same time she is here for the conference and, besides, has a loving husband back home.

What would you do if you were Jane R.?

Note:

1. After the case has been thoroughly discussed by the group, move into a more personal level by asking participants to relate similar pertinent incidents from their own experience.

2. This particular case relates to problems of assertiveness, possibly sexual harassment, peer pressure, and self development.

3. Since the technique asks for personal incidents, one has to know the nature of the group. That is, are they willing to share personal incidents? Also, the sharing is obviously more likely to be acceptable to the participants at a later rather than at an earlier stage of the program.

Citing an Allied Case

The Case of the Simple Cover-up

A corridor in the basement of a large office building led to the company cafeteria. Unfortunately, at one point in the concrete corridor, a four-inch pipe protruded just above ground level. The pipe was large enough to be visible, but inevitably employees who were distracted by conversation, preoccupied, or simply in a hurry tripped over it. New employees were almost certain to stumble over the pipe at least once. Employees in wheelchairs and those with visual problems also had a hard time with the pipe.

Management tried many remedies to cut down on the tripping-type accidents: posting a notice on the wall near the pipe, issuing warning memoranda (generally after a mishap), painting the protruding pipe a bright color (different colors were tried), rerouting traffic (quickly abandoned because this proved to be a nuisance), and encouraging supervisors to remind employees from time to time about the hazard. The problem was finally solved when a legally blind employee who stumbled over the pipe suggested putting a gently sloping wooden ramp over it.

The case illustrates how a rather simple *change in the situation*—as opposed to more complex attempts to *change people's behavior* via signs, memos, and lectures—solved the problem instantly and for everyone and for all time.

Task assignment: Have participants relate an incident from their own experience where a change in behavior was accomplished by working on the situation (as in this case) as opposed to working on the person via the usual lectures, signs, warnings, reprimands, memos, and bulletin board notices.

Using Participant Cases

A worthwhile variation on the conventional case study method is to introduce several participant-developed cases for group analysis. The advantages of this approach are these:

☐ Greater participant involvement and interest in a truly live case.

☐ The cases are quite certain to be complex and thus challenging. Why bring in a case that lends itself to ready resolution?

☐ Increased responsibility by participants to contribute materials for the learning experience, with a corresponding reduction in dependency on the trainer who ordinarily "does it all."

Training-wise, a good design is to ask the participants who bring in their cases to identify people who can best help them to analyze and resolve the problem presented. In this way, they are being encouraged to seek out (assess) the most knowledgeable resources in the group, a concept they should carry back to their jobs. Those who are not chosen by the case presenter to work in a small group should form other small groups. Solutions then can be compared—the "expert" small group vs. the others.

If a format has been provided to analyze problems, such as a multistep problem-solving model, cases may be analyzed along those lines.

The Participant-Modified Case

Another way to overcome the problem of trainer-prepared or trainer-selected cases that typically lack immediate relevance is to allow the participants to *modify* the "canned" case. They can supplement or substitute the usual trainer-supplied information with data specific to the challenges and problems they now face. In essence, they direct their own learning and problem solving by drawing on their experience and applying their knowledge to current situations and actual personalities.

If you take this real-world application to case study, you may have to notify your participants in advance (a pre-work assignment) with instructions concerning the information they need to gather. For example, in a case involving selling a boss on a radical idea, the participants will have to gather data on their bosses' leadership styles—communication patterns, tendencies toward (or against) innovativeness, and problem-solving and decision-making approaches [5].

The Rating Approach

Another way to vary the case method and to stimulate discussion considerably is to provide specific statements regarding the significance of the case and have participants express their agreement/disagreement with the statements using a prescribed rating scale, as given in Appendix 61.

Advice from the President

The Key Brands Chain Store has its headquarters in Philadelphia. Each year six to eight promising young supervisors are brought into headquarters from the field for six months of management training. The purpose: "broadening." While at headquarters these "management interns" are subject to rotational assignments, take one or two university courses on management, attend various institutes or workshops that relate to their career objectives, attend the president's weekly staff meeting, attend other "big picture" meetings, work on a group project, meet regularly as a group with the trainer to discuss problems of the organization, and periodically write reports on their training experiences.

When the six months of training are over, the trainees typically return to their original assignments in the field. However, one or two of them may be assigned to headquarters or to a regional office upon completion of the training. The training seems to do what the organization expects in terms of broadening, but new assignments for everyone do not materialize immediately. In fact, the trainees may return to their old jobs for two to two and a half years before they receive a new assignment. In effect, most graduates of the program are "stockpiled" for future upward assignment.

Because of the delay in capitalizing on their training, the trainees typically feel "lost and abandoned" after returning from Philadelphia. In fact, recently a number of the graduates of the program felt strongly enough about the problem to write the following letter to the company president:

> Dear Mr. Rogers:
>
> We greatly appreciate the training we received at headquarters some two years ago. It was a fine program and hardly a week goes by that we don't apply something of what we learned in Philadelphia.
> We do feel, however, that as time goes by we are getting out of touch with things and are losing some of the "big picture" we received. We thus thought it would be helpful to us if we could be assigned to our respective regional offices for two weeks for special assignment, once or twice a year. This procedure, if adopted, would not only help us, but would protect the company's large investment in our training.
>
> Sincerely yours,
>
> Matt Thomas (6th Mgt. Intern Program)
> Henry Briggs (6th Mgt. Intern Program)
> Elaine Woods (7th Mgt. Intern Program)
> Nat Spencer (7th Mgt. Intern Program)
> Al Knowles (7th Mgt. Intern Program)

Upon receipt of the letter, the president entered this notation on it: "Why can't the training department work up a good distance-learning (e-learning) course on management for these trainees?" The letter was then routed to the chief administrative officer and the personnel director, both of whom added to the president's note: "I concur." The letter then went on to the training department. The director of training, on receipt of the letter, had a strong, negative reaction to it.

Memo from the Boss

A memorandum from the boss that demands, complains, or criticizes unfairly is always a headache for the receiver. If used as a case, it can challenge participants to take notice and to react in one form or another. A healthy form of reaction is to develop and consider one's options, as opposed to acting precipitously and possibly aggravating matters. Possible options are these: do nothing, grin and bear it, and engage in soothing self-talk: "This, too, shall pass"; respond with a memo to defend one's actions or position; visit the boss in his/her office to explain things or to confess error and assure the boss it won't happen again; and so on. Obviously the actual action taken will depend on the nature and gravity of the "offense" as well as the personalities of the two parties involved.

A sample "Memo from the Boss" case follows. Note the case is very brief and contains background about the circumstances relating to the memo as well as the memo itself. Questions to the participants follow the case.

Memo from the Boss: "Quality Circle Overtime"

You are the facilitator for a group of quality circles in your company. You recently worked with one group that got so engrossed in their problem solving that they ran over the allotted time by some 30 minutes. (Meetings run for one hour per week, one-half of it on company time and the other half on the QC member's lunch time.) Your boss, who is not really sold on quality circles, sent you this scorching note:

> The Quality Circle time has gotten completely out of hand. These meetings are for *one hour* only. Today we lost the production time of eight workers.
>
> This abuse will lead to disqualifying a circle. You are responsible for keeping it on track and observing the rules.
>
> *Jim*

Questions: What is the likely impact on the receiver? If you were the facilitator, what would you do? What are your options? Which would you select? Why? Would you show the letter to your participants? Why or why not?

The Ranking Approach

A good way to involve and excite participants is to have them rank possible solutions to a case on an individual basis and then let them discuss their rankings in small groups. They should be asked to agree, as a team, on their rankings. After the small-group work, secure feedback from the teams concerning their key rankings—that is, which were first, second, and last. Secure the teams' reasonings for their rankings.

A sample case follows.

The Case of the Successful Training Director

Pat Teal, training director for High-Tech Diversified Products, Inc., has been on the job some 18 months. The training program, as Pat found it, consisted of employee orientation and an occasional skills-training course. At the outset, Pat identified a strong need for management training and promptly planned, organized, and implemented a series of highly successful management training workshops. The workshops of 18–20 managers were conducted in out-of-city locations, ran for five full days, relied heavily on group-in-action methods, and achieved rave notices from the participants and the regional directors who had sent their managers to the training.

The company president was informed of Pat's successful work and now wants to "ride" on Pat's success. Specifically, he wants Pat to provide the same kind of training to some 150–175 managers and others who will be attending the company's biannual, three-day management conference in Las Vegas this coming summer. The big boss has also invited various outsiders to attend, such as suppliers, trade association officials, and business journalists. Several new products are to be unveiled at the meeting. In other words, the president sees this conference as a big sales-motivation–PR opportunity rather than intensive management training as Pat has been providing. Pat appreciates the president's enthusiasm and praise for her work, but knows that one can't replicate the workshops' success under the extravaganza-type conditions which will prevail at the national conference.

You are a close colleague of Pat, doing similar work in another company. Pat has contacted you for advice in respect to the alternative strategies that might be considered in coping with the company president's request. These strategies are listed below. Rank them in the order in which you would recommend them to Pat. (No. 1 is most recommended; No. 10 is least recommended.)

Possible approaches for Pat Teal:

1. Why argue with your own success? Just try your best to give the big boss what he wants.

2. A key department head, who has an "in" with the president, is aware of the problem and sees it as Pat does. In fact, he said: "What's the use of providing the training if it won't be any good?" This official would probably intercede for Pat, if asked. Why not arrange a meeting with the big boss, your ally, and yourself; explain the facts to the president; and ask him to "cool it"?

3. Confront the president on a one-to-one basis and candidly explain to him that a large, PR-type conference in Las Vegas will not accomplish what your small-group training programs can do in a cultural-island setting.

4. Secure advice and assistance from a consultant who specializes in making large-group meetings and conferences effective, and go ahead and participate in the big bash.

5. Call a special meeting of the Training Advisory Committee to explain the problem and try to get their support for a strong negative recommendation on the president's idea.

6. Ask your boss, the VP for Human Resource Management, to run interference for you. (*Note:* The VP's major strengths are in the areas of recruitment and benefits, rather than training.)

7. Write a detailed memo to the president. Explain the basis for your reservations and suggest alternatives such as having two or three nationally known speakers talk to this rather large audience, rather than trying to conduct genuine management training.

8. Since you are on excellent terms with several regional directors as a result of your training, ask one or more of them to intercede for you.

9. On the assumption that this is the kind of "support" a training program hardly needs, start looking for another job.

10. Get off the hook by suggesting that the management training to be provided at the conference be turned over to the Management Department at Local University for their execution. Let them get the credit or the brickbats.

Using a Letter

The following two cases use a letter to stimulate discussion. The first case, "Shopping for an Ice Chest," is a rather simple one, dealing with the very common problem of sales clerks in a department who are weak in both product knowledge and customer relations.

The second case, "The Case of the Bureaucratic Manager," is more complex. It asks the participants to identify and deal with problems of bureaucracy in an academic setting. This letter writer (or complainant) raises two issues: refund policy and the provision of "perishable" information on a promotional brochure that is made available to prospective enrollees in a non-credit course in a community college. Both issues have public relations implications. These complaints were actually handled via a letter of apology to the complainant (see a third letter) plus an invitation from the president to the complainant to accompany him to a Rotary Club luncheon, a unique public relations gesture. In addition, management at the college presumably had to deal with a somewhat arrogant, inflexible bureaucrat in its ranks.

Shopping for an Ice Chest

> John L. Quinn
> President
> Lincoln-United Stores, Inc.
>
> Dear Mr. Quinn:
>
> My wife and I had the misfortune to shop in the River Oaks suburban store last Friday night. We were in the camping department and saw two clerks there, but apparently they couldn't see us. Or at least so it seemed after a 15-minute wait.
>
> We finally approached one clerk and he said to us: "Sorry, but I'm still on my supper hour. You'll have to talk to someone else." So we approached another clerk and asked her if she was familiar with the ice chests. She replied: "Oh, sure. What do you want to know?" We asked: "What is the difference between

these two ice chests? They look the same, but this one costs $7.50 more." She replied: "Well, if it costs more it *must* be the better one." Not being satisfied with her answer, we asked her if anyone else might know more about the chests. She said: "Oh, yes, my supervisor." So we asked her if we could talk to him. She replied: "Sorry, but he's not on the floor right now." And when would he be back? "Gee, I don't know."

At this point another clerk came to us and said: "May I help?" Relieved, we said: "By all means." Again, we went through our questioning about the relative merits of the two ice chests. Would you believe that all he could tell us was that *both* chests were very good. Why? Because he owned *both* of them *himself!*

So we went across the street to Kelly's and were waited on promptly, got decent answers to our questions and bought a moderately priced ice chest of high quality having all the features we required.

Do you think we should return to Lincoln-United Stores? We have some big doubts.

Sincerely,

Mr. and Mrs. Ben Grayson

Small group assignment: Assume you are the company president, Mr. Quinn. What action do you take, if any?

Bureaucratic Manager

Dr. Herman Peters
President
Central Community College

Dear Dr. Peters:

Since you are the top-level administrator of your organization, I am certain that you are acutely concerned with both high-level instruction by your faculty and sensitive, flexible administration by your subordinate managers. I thus wish to call your attention to what I consider to be an instance of inflexible, arrogant, and bureaucratic management by one of your management officials. The facts, as I perceive them, are as follows:

1. I enrolled in a Central College Community Services course entitled "Independent Consulting: Is It for You?" The course was scheduled to meet on Saturday, February 13.

2. The announcement on the yellow brochure said the class was to be held at "Wiley Square." When I arrived at the college campus I asked several students where I could find Wiley Square. No one knew. I went to the guard's office and made the same inquiry. None of the three guards knew, although one of them thought it might be "somewhere in Hinton." One guard made several phone calls to secure the needed information, but this was Saturday and no one was available.

3. I decided to return to my home. My wife decided to call the instructor at his home; possibly his wife or a family member might know where the course was being given. She actually reached the instructor at his home (someone else was pinch-hitting for him), but he couldn't provide specific information either.

4. On the following Monday I called Mrs. Watt, the Registration Supervisor of Community Services. I told her the brochure did not indicate where Wiley Square was. She agreed with me and readily admitted that they had goofed in their placement of the information. It seems that the brochure *did* have the requisite information, but on the *reverse* side of the registration form!! Hence, once the form was sent in to the college, the student no longer had this vital information in his/her possession.

5. I asked Mrs. Watt for a refund of my $17.00. But apparently life is not that simple. I had to write a letter to her to justify the refund! O.K., this is a small bit of bureaucracy, certainly not Mrs. Watt's fault, so I wrote her a detailed letter. She was quite certain that I'd get the refund since the college had goofed.

6. I received a letter dated February 26, from Mr. John May, assistant dean for management services, who denied my request!

7. I called Mr. May (on Tuesday, March 2), who turned out to be as arrogant, inflexible, and supercilious a bureaucrat as one might find. He told me in no uncertain terms that the student is expected to be "responsible" and "adult" in preparing to arrive for his class. He also told me that since the information *was* on the form, I should have read it early on instead of waiting until the class morning to find out where the class was. He even gave me a far-fetched analogy about

preparing *in advance* to locate a theatre which one might attend. Question: Do all your bureaucrats tell your student/citizen/customers *when* to prepare for their arrival, *when* to read the announcement? A bit much, I'd say. Mr. May also implied that since only $27.00 was involved, this was really a minor matter. I told him it was a matter of principle and that I could get along O.K. without the $27.00. In general, Mr. May would not concede any possible error on the college's part, despite the obvious careless placement of the school location on the registration form.

To sum up:

1. Location information on a brochure must be placed in a *permanent* position. Perishable information is equal to none at all. I happen to be in the training business; our company conducts various public seminars. We learned a long time ago about proper, helpful placement of the location data. It should *never, never* be put on the back of a registration form which has vital information on the reverse.
2. Even if the customer were only half right, a helpful and sensitive firm provides a refund for purposes of good will and good customer relations. My company provides refunds if a customer has any reasonable complaint. If we didn't, we wouldn't be able to continue to serve the public. Is a public bureaucracy above a reasonable (and logical) request of a citizen/customer?

I don't wish to make a federal case out of this, although I am tempted to write the local newspapers and/or my representative about this. Before I do so, however, I shall await your considered reply.

Thank you for your interest in dealing with bureaucracy in your organization.

Sincerely,

I. Rayte

Dear Mr. Rayte:

Your letter of March 8 has been received by the college president, who is concerned about the issues you have raised and has asked me to respond. We are indeed interested in dealing with behavior such as you experienced. I enclose your refund check and apologize.

Your approach to the question of brochure design and placement of critical information is correct in my view; your comments on the issue of refunds are also well taken. Be assured that the dean of community services will be following through on these matters.

Although I am sorry it has been necessary for you to write the president, I appreciate your taking the time to do so.

Sincerely,

Rhee Lee Syncere
Academic Vice-President

Using an Editorial

Beef over the Deli

The *Daily Blade* carried the following editorial:

If you've been reading our news columns of late, you know that city officials are blocking a liquor license sought by a delicatessen in the New Square Shopping Plaza. Their rationale: Sale of wine and beer in community shopping centers inevitably attracts young loiterers, hot rodders, unruly partyers, and other assorted nuisance makers, causing annoyance to merchants and shoppers alike. In fact, the granting of such a license to a pizza parlor recently in the Elmark Shopping Center has already netted fourteen disorderly conduct complaints to the police.

City Councilperson R. U. Stern has been quoted as saying: "We don't want to hurt a legitimate, hardworking businessman, and we know the present owners are good citizens and responsible business people. But the ready availability of beer and wine just creates headaches we'd as soon do without."

As for the deli owners, they say their small carryout will "go under" if the Board of License Commissioners denies them the license. Says co-owner Bill Wines: "Beer and wine are economic necessities. If we don't get the license, we'll just have to give up the store. All we're trying to do is to earn a fair living and give the people in this area a chance to shop for our kind of foods without driving six and one-half miles to get it."

To complicate matters a bit more, Mayor Edgar Bruntovitall cites a state law which bans the granting of liquor licenses to a store within 700 feet of a school, church, or government-sponsored youth center. The deli is opposite such a youth center. However, the Board of License Commissioners can (but by unanimous decision only) grant the license up to within 300 feet. The mayor hopes the board will follow the intent of the state law to the letter.

As for us, we see this as a "damned if you do, damned if you don't" kind of case—the kind of decision Solomon would have relished (no pun intended) and our elected officials sink their teeth into all the time. Our only thought at the moment is that before the decision makers decide, they should stop for a thick corned beef on rye at the deli in dispute, savor each warm morsel, and contemplate its potential added goodness if it could be washed down with a cold beer or two.

Questions for discussion:

1. What is the main issue or problem here?
2. How would you decide the case so that the community is well served?
3. What is the role of city management in a case of this sort?

Dialogue

Improving the Weekly Staff Meeting

Pat Cane, department chief, has asked his assistant, Melissa Blunt, to discuss ways of improving the weekly staff meeting that is attended by eight branch chiefs. This dialogue ensues:

Pat: Melissa, you've got a lot of good ideas about management. What do you think we should do to improve our staff meetings?

Melissa: Hey, wait, boss. I'm not that much of an expert on that.

Pat: Well, we keep getting little digs about how dull they are and how much time they take. And you know as well as I do that some of the branch chiefs keep looking for excuses to skip'em whenever they can.

Melissa: I suppose there is a problem . . .

Pat: Sure there is. So let's be frank. What would you do if you were me?

Melissa: Umm. Umm. I might turn the problem over to the group. In a sense it's their meeting, you know. Why not let them . . .

Pat: Whoa, wait a minute. We don't want to stir up all the animals over this, do we? Can't we just make some simple changes without getting everybody all riled up?

Melissa: I suppose that's true. How about rotating the chairmanship among everyone? This would get them all in the act and . . .

Pat: Hey, wait a minute. Why half of'em couldn't run a meeting properly. Why we'd be running those meetings even longer than we do now.

Melissa: I just thought . . .

Pat: Besides we got enough trouble already with some of them acting as if they're ready to take the place over. Naw, that'd never work.

Melissa: Yeah, I guess that's a little far out.

Pat: Glad you see it that way. Anything else?

Melissa: As I said, I'm not an expert on this stuff. But what if we could cut down on everyone reporting what they've been doing all week and use the time instead to work on some of our problems . . .

Pat: Oh, we couldn't do that. People want to know what's going on. That would cause more of a problem than we have now.

Melissa: I suppose you're right. But what if everyone just prepared a short written statement about the events of the week and we passed them around? Then we could use the time for some real problem solving.

Pat: You mean we're not solving our problems now?

Melissa: Oh, no, I didn't mean that . . . It's just that . . .

Pat: Sure. Well, it's nearly lunchtime and I've got that meeting downtown and I'm running late already. Why don't you give it some more thought and we'll talk some more about it another time. And keep the ideas as practical as you can . . .

Melissa: Sure thing, boss—real practical.

Questions for discussion:

1. What is (are) the real issue(s) here?
2. Does Pat really want help on the problem?
3. How well did Melissa read Pat's attitudes about staff meetings?
4. If you were Melissa, how would you have responded to Pat's request?
5. If you were Melissa, how would you respond should Pat bring it up again?

6. How open is Pat to feedback?

7. How would you characterize the climate in this department?

8. Would Pat and the department be just as well off if they eliminated staff meetings? If you were Melissa, would you consider recommending this course of action?

9. What can managers do to "pep up" staff meetings?

10. What are the implications of this case for participative management?

Monologue

Jeffery Bates Returns from the General Management Course

"Man, these management training courses are really something. I've been to three of them now and they all tell you the same thing—delegate more, communicate more, listen more, involve people in decisions more, develop subordinates more, and on and on.

"Who doesn't know all that? As if a manager doesn't do all that anyhow!

"Boy, if I followed all the behavioral science stuff these bushy-eyed trainers teach, I'd never get the work out. If they knew of the pressures for production and control of costs I get from the bosses, all the paperwork I have to do, my having to deal with other managers who want everything their own way, my supervising employees who complain about the work and the pay and everything else, and my working for a boss who's never got time to listen to some of your problems . . .

"Yeah, I wonder how many years of management experience these trainers have. Probably nowhere near my 22, if they have any at all.

"And the worst part of it is these younger managers. They keep buttering up these trainers by picking up all their jargon about motivation and group decision making, and beating that drum about hiring more women and minorities . . . Gad, what a farce . . . They're not doing any more of this newer stuff than I am, and they know it. They just want to look smart in class. Well, they can put on that up-to-date act all they want to. I've been managing a lot longer than they have, and neither they nor these trainers are going to get old Jeff to change anything that he's been doing."

Questions for discussion:

1. Is Jeff consistent in his statements?

2. How do you see Jeff as a manager? Is he strong, weak, effective?

3. Is Jeff typical of most managers you know?

4. What is Jeff's major problem, if any? What are his strengths, if any?

5. Does Jeff have a good fix on his own motivations, needs, values? The needs or values of others with whom he regularly deals?

6. Should people like Jeff be sent to management training courses? Why or why not?

7. Would you be willing to work for a man like Jeff? Why or why not?

8. If you were Jeff's boss and wanted to "upgrade" and "update" him, how would you go about it?

9. What kind of future, career-wise, do you see for Jeff?

10. Are behavioral science ideas compatible with "getting the work out"?

Note: The monologue is a variation of the case study format. It creates or communicates a certain mood, a depth of feeling, which the usual form of case study does not. It gives the participants a chance to get inside the head of the principal character in the case.

The Decision Analysis Approach

Depending on the group's and your training goals, it may be desirable, at times, to present participants with a case and several possible solutions to it. This would entail asking the participants to do either one or both of the following:

1. Analyze the pros and cons of *each* given decision, including its possible future consequences if implemented.

2. Come up with *another* decision that would be *superior* to those suggested at the end of the case.

The rationale for this approach is that there is

☐ A need to concentrate on the decision-making process as opposed to other aspects of case study, such as agreeing on facts and identifying the issues involved.

☐ A need to teach the manager, as a decision maker, to be deliberate rather than precipitate. The best way to overcome tendencies to make snap judgments is to slow the manager down by insisting that he/she weigh the pros and cons of all possible decisions.

☐ A desire to challenge the participant to be creative, to break new ground. This is done by asking participants to come up with a solution superior to those already presented.

To illustrate the nature of this variation of the case study method, here is a short case accompanied by several solutions to it.

The Request for a Salary Increase

You are Lance Adams, controller for the Blue Bag Independent Food Stores. Your firm operates six supermarkets in a large metropolitan area. You are 52 years old and a professionally trained accountant, and you have been with the firm 8 years now. You report to a vice-president and realize that in a relatively small firm a promotion to other or "better" work is not very likely. So you expect worthwhile pay raises to be forthcoming each year. However, the raises that have come have been token, nowhere near actual cost-of-living increases. In fact, you wonder if any raises would be forthcoming at all if the nonmanagerial employees, who are subject to a collective bargaining agreement, were not getting annual increases. As a result, you see yourself falling behind, each year, in terms of real income. Also, it seems unfair that you have not been rewarded for the experience you have gained on the job. Certainly you are more valuable to the company now than you were when you started eight years ago.

The company has an annual performance review system, but it is largely a "paper" plan. There is no job evaluation or salary standardization plan for managers. Information about managerial salaries is kept very secret—so it is hard to know what others are earning.

You have brought up this matter of a worthwhile raise twice with your boss—once at a staff meeting and once at performance review time. In response to the first request, the boss said: "We'll have to talk about it." But he never did. When you brought it up at performance review time the next year, he "finessed it" by telling you he was giving you an increase that seemed surprisingly good; but when you got back to your desk he called you on the intercom to tell you he had made a mistake in his figures, and the actual increase turned out to be the usual minor one. You are pretty well convinced that there is going to be a tough stand by your boss on this pay issue.

As you now see it, you have these options:

1. Try to "fight fire with fire"—try to out-maneuver the boss with a strategy superior to his.
2. Try to present an ironclad case for a real raise.
3. Make an "end run"—go to the company president with your problem, bypassing your boss entirely.
4. Look around quietly for another job.
5. Drop hints that you have been approached for employment by a couple of other companies in recent months.
6. Team up with two other managers who have the same problem and try a "united front" approach.
7. Grin and bear it and take early retirement at age 62, per company policy.

Analyze and reduce to writing each of these solutions as to strengths, weaknesses, and possible future consequences. Then, either select one of these decisions or arrive at one of your own. In either case, give a full justification for the course of action you propose to take.

Benefits-Risk Approach

The Children at Work Case

Management in a large publishing firm has called this problem to the attention of its employees:

"Increasingly, employees have been bringing small children to work with them for a day or a part of a day. In most instances the reason is the unexpected nonappearance of a baby-sitter. Management is impressed by the determination of the employees to come to work in such cases. But the distraction caused by the presence of small children—and it's usually more than their parents realize—is neither fair to other employees nor conducive to a good work environment. There have been many complaints from employees and supervisors alike on this matter. This practice has never been approved in a formal way.

"Accordingly, we are issuing this policy: Any employee who comes to work with a child (for more than a brief visit) should be sent home, using personal leave or leave without pay."

Assignment to trainer: Have participants use a T-column to list the risks and benefits of management's decision. After they have completed the T-column, have them answer the questions presented in the worksheet in Appendix 62.

Using Judicial Cases

In case study work our cases are typically drawn from problems encountered in organizational life: marketing, production, finance, interpersonal relations, safety, organization, general management, and so on. And these cases are ordinarily presented with all of their many ramifications, with neither organizational identification nor any indication as to their actual resolution.

At times, however, the need for greater credibility may necessitate the use of cases drawn from court actions. This is particularly true in the area of sexual harassment, where it is essential to demonstrate the serious nature of potential liability for both the organization and employees [6]. In such cases the actual organization involved, the decision, and the liability assessed, if any, would be presented.

Similarly, in training salespersons to understand and respect the potential legal implications of their actions, actual court cases may be used. We have reference to such potentially troublesome areas as the delivered product being below agreed-upon quality standards, misrepresentation (for example, regarding use of the product), extra charges added without the purchaser's knowledge, kickbacks, delivering a brand other than the one agreed upon, giving favorite customers price concessions, violating the contracted-for delivery date, slandering a competitor, and failure to warn a buyer of potential hazards in using a product [7].

A Case for Self-Review Purposes

This case is designed to provide an opportunity for self-evaluation and review of material that has been previously discussed in class or has been read on an individual basis. The technique is designed to help participants "button down" pertinent details about a problem situation. Unlike our other cases, it is not intended to broaden outlooks, encourage exploration of alternate courses of action, or call attention to management implications.

The County-Wide Illness

You are the county health officer. Several adults and children have requested treatment at various hospitals in the county for an illness marked by these *initial* symptoms: listlessness, a slight fever, and influenza-type aches and pains. Typically, by the third or fourth day an eruption appears on the wrists and ankles.

Assignment to trainer: Have participants answer the questions in Appendix 63. After the pairs have discussed and compared their answers, pass out the answer sheet for total group discussion.

HOW TO DEVELOP CASE MATERIAL

Cases and material to prepare cases may be obtained from many sources. These include

- ☐ Case books
- ☐ Articles in training, personnel, and management journals
- ☐ Articles in newspapers and magazines
- ☐ The experiences of colleagues
- ☐ Problems presented by lecturers at conferences, workshops, and training sessions
- ☐ Organizational events
- ☐ Personal experiences

However, quite often the trainer requires a case that must be integrated with a specific learning objective and is not readily available from these sources. Under these circumstances, you must develop your own case. Bradford B. Boyd offers these six steps as guides to developing the tailor-made case [8]:

1. *Decide on the principle(s)* you wish to have the case emphasize. This first step is obviously the most critical one. *Example:* Delegation may not be viable because of forces at work among subordinates, and not necessarily because of problems with the boss.
2. *Establish a situation* that demonstrates the principle. This requires us to draw upon our experience with typical problems and problem individuals. *Example:* Delegation goes awry because subordinates fail to keep the boss posted as they are getting into "deep water."
3. *Develop appropriate symptoms.* These may be positive or negative or both types of symptoms, whichever best illustrates the principle we plan to teach. Here we seek out incidents and situations which are symptomatic of the attitude expressed in Step 2. *Example:* "The boss might punish me if I give him the bad news." "He'll learn about it in time." "Maybe the situation will get better." These attitudes are rationalizations to avoid having to share with the boss one's inability to carry out the assigned delegation.
4. *Develop the characters.* They can be those who are doing things right or doing them improperly. Characters, of course, are plentiful. We need only bring them to life by giving them names, titles, responsibilities, attitudes, values, perceptions. *Example:* Jennifer Bayliss is a section chief in the Operations Department. She has a tendency to procrastinate about things and blame others for her problems.
5. *Write the case.* Here we fully develop the pertinent details surrounding events, problems, and personalities, all of which are the specific building blocks for the case.
6. *Provide questions.* This is to guide participants' thinking about the problem presented; it is the vehicle to reach the principle involved.

Robert J. Inguagiato presents added helpful pointers for case development [9]:

1. *Identify a case goal.* This is the foundation for case development. Doing this will guide you toward the information you must collect. Some typical case goals are

   ☐ To resolve a problem/event/situation.
   ☐ To persuade/influence a person or group to act in a particular way.
   ☐ To establish causative factors for the problem you have identified.
   ☐ To gather support/commitment to resolve the problem.

A clear focus will prevent wandering randomly to gather the needed data.

2. *Establish a case objective.* This creates the "playing field" on which the case will be executed by your participants. The case objective has these components:

   ☐ Identification of the sector of the firm in which the case will occur, for example, marketing, R&D, human resources, or information systems.
   ☐ Identification of the "cast of characters" *by title.* This will provide the necessary realism as to who is involved in the case.
   ☐ Explanation of why the characters are meeting or conversing. This answers the question of what caused the encounter to take place. *Example:* "A new systems analyst (nine months on the job), who is a recent Harvard MBA, confronts her boss, the chief of Information Systems, about the 'Mickey Mouse' assignments which keep coming her way. She feels her major skills, which could help the company in significant ways, are not being utilized."

   When all three of the above components are tied together, a case objective is established. *Example:* "A meeting between a young, bright MBA (a Harvard grad) and her boss, head of the Information Systems branch, is about to take place. The issue, as the subordinate sees it, is the fact that her assignments are limited in challenge and are not improving after nine months on the job."

3. *Collect general background information.* To collect pertinent information on all the characters involved in the case, use these elements as a guide:

☐ Education

☐ Age

☐ Tenure (time on the job)

☐ Prior work history

☐ Current duties and responsibilities

☐ Number of persons supervised

☐ Person to whom he/she reports

☐ Job objective

☐ Next job aspired to

Note: Not all elements need be used.

4. *Depict (characterize) the case study figures.* The above information relates only to bare-bones demographics. You now want to add descriptive information which will give life to your characters. Consider the following:

☐ *The job pressures* of each person in the case, for example, demands for increased production or cost reduction, budget restrictions, peer pressure.

☐ *Personal pressures,* for example, an ailing spouse, financial concerns, conflicts between personal and career goals.

☐ *Historical relationships* between the parties involved: good, bad, strained? Why? Length of the relationship? What information has the rumor mill provided each about the other?

☐ *Hidden agendas* for the meeting, for example, to look good to the boss, to improve career possibilities.

☐ *Outcome:* What does each person hope to gain from the meeting?

☐ *Possibilities for cooperation*—consider personal motivations, lack of trust between characters, widely differing leadership styles, etc., to highlight tension points between/among participants.

☐ *Personal values,* for example, one person favors candor whereas the other holds back on giving feedback, or one stresses team development at the expense of production.

Again, not all of the above elements need be included in character descriptions. But include enough of them so that your discussants will tackle the case with enthusiasm.

5. *Describe the organization's culture.* As an added element of realism, the organization's dynamics must be presented. Include such elements as values; sources of external pressures, such as competition; time perspectives (recurring nature of the problem over time).

The bottom line: Cases which are true to life, using the pointers suggested above, will elicit high interest instead of a reaction that "This situation doesn't apply to us at all."

Trainer/consultant Phillip H. Owenby offers these added pointers for the actual writing of a "good" case—a case that involves learners and increases their interest in the course material [10]:

1. *Use a "story" format.* By presenting your case as a story, you ensure universal appeal. Everybody likes a good story, one having a "gossipy" quality to it, whether it's in a novel, in a play, on TV, in the movies, or anywhere else. You want to grab and hold your participants' attention. Stories with real people will do that for you.

2. *Give the characters in your case fun-type names.* A little humor will help to make the characters and the case itself come alive to the learner. *Examples:* Penny Wise, chief accountant; Marion Haste, marriage counselor; Rusty Gates, maintenance supervisor.

3. *Add dialogue to your story.* Your case has characters, and people do talk. So why not let them speak up? Keep your dialogue authentic, though. You don't want your learners to say (or feel) that "people don't talk like that."

4. *Provide realistic details for authenticity.* Slang, shop expressions, and nicknames are all great grist for your case study mill. Realistic detail gives your story credibility and high interest.

5. *Write descriptively.* Appeal to people's senses—eyes, ears, touch, and smell. This will really put the learner into the situation. Consider statements like these: "Terry sank into his office chair. It was new and still smelled of fine leather." "Marion entered the shop floor. She

saw a large, pool of thick, dark liquid. It couldn't be oil because . . ."

6. *Present a logical flow.* People can't follow a story if the sequence is disjointed, so keep things in chronological order. Flashbacks might work well on the movie screen, but in a short story they will only produce confusion and frustration.

7. *Provide both completeness and a bit of mystery.* Your story should provide enough information so that your trainees can get a ready handle on what is going on and have a basis for analysis. You don't want to provide a "tricky" case. ("But the case never said or even inferred that Alma was upset because she wasn't promoted.") On the other hand, you don't want to provide ready solutions either. That is your group's task. So leave a thread or two hanging to arouse interest and mystery, but don't overdo it. (Your case study isn't akin to a typical TV detective story where only "the Inspector"—never the audience—can make sense of what has ensued and neatly tie it all together.)

It may be desirable, in writing the case, to think of situations where a role play could develop from the case discussion. This will provide added interest in and insight about the problem presented. It should also be remembered that the best case is one that is marked by realism, a certain amount of conflict, somewhat strong personalities, and avoidance of unnecessary detail.

In developing a case, use this checklist to ensure that it will be of high quality to be effective as a learning tool:

_____ 1. Subject matter is realistic; it contains believable situations, events, circumstances, difficulties.

_____ 2. Facts are presented sequentially, clearly, and briefly

_____ 3. Facts are adequate to resolve the case.

_____ 4. Characters are believable and interesting; the case avoids "Attila the Hun" and "Robin Hood" types, which are extreme and thus unrealistic.

_____ 5. The case includes conflict or friction points among the characters.

_____ 6. Unnecessary detail is avoided.

_____ 7. The case is open-ended; solutions are neither given nor implied.

_____ 8. Multiple solutions are quite possible (no one best answer).

_____ 9. The case is short enough so that it can be read quickly in class.

_____ 10. The case is very likely to provoke a lively discussion or debate.

LEARNING FROM CASES

Although a case is a learning device designed to display certain principles to participants, it is not unusual for the trainer to receive a complaint such as this: "Why don't we discuss cases drawn from our own organizational or industry setting?" You can respond in a number of ways to this classic complaint.

First, you should point out that the case is a tool for learning, and its origin or location is really not too pertinent. What *is* pertinent is the learning we can extract from it in terms of principles, concepts, processes, and forces at work. This is similar to the law student who uses legal cases to develop legal reasoning ability and who could not care less whether the cases used come from Maine, Maryland, Texas, or Oregon. So whether the managers are wearing hospital smocks, three-piece suits, or fire chief's uniforms is really of no great importance. A meaty case is still the main thing!

Secondly, using a case that is "organization specific" may actually produce boomerang effects—participants may get hung up on particular details of organizational structure, organizational policy, various in-house rules, regulations, and procedures. By using a "culture-free" case, you allow participants to concentrate on the case per se and not be detoured by incidental elements in it.

Thirdly, quite often an outside case may be richer in learning potential because of its superb context (realism, conflict), the way it is written, and the personalities portrayed in it.

Finally, if the case is in a film/video format, it is obviously too costly to produce your own case.

All in all, most participants accept the case for what it is—a tool for learning. They thus are able to internalize the learning despite its being somewhat abstract in relation to their particular job situations. Persistent inability to transfer classroom learning to the job may well indicate resistance to what is being taught; for example, the staunch nondelegator may endeavor to "pick the case apart" rather than state publicly that he/she disagrees with the delegation concepts that the case advocates.

Using the In-House Case

In the preceding paragraphs we presented a number of reasons why the outside case is preferable to the in-house one. However, there may be special circumstances where the in-house case would be preferred, such as in the issue of sexual harassment.

According to EEOC (Equal Employment Opportunity Commission) guidelines, an organization can limit its liability when it is involved in sexual harassment cases by demonstrating that it did take "immediate and corrective action." Thus, if cases have occurred and the organization has already taken appropriate disciplinary action on them, such cases merit introduction into the sexual harassment training program. The cases should be presented anonymously, of course. The use of these cases would show the company's concern for a harassment-free work environment plus the fact that disciplinary action is taken promptly and appropriately.

In a sensitive area such as sexual harassment, the in-house cases will have high impact since the participants are learning about situations involving some of their fellow workers.

The best in-house cases on sexual harassment are those marked by [6]:

☐ Across-the-board fairness—discipline was extended to both managerial and nonmanagerial employees.

☐ Pocketbook impacts, that is, demonstrating how paychecks are affected (via discharge, demotion, or suspension).

☐ Broad subject-matter coverage—cases that deal with employees relating to an "intolerable working environment" as well as dealing with demands for sexual favors in relation to employment and promotion.

Note: If an organization has not had any disciplinary cases in this area, it may have to draw on the experiences of other companies. If so, the cases would again be presented as "live" ones, albeit less indigenous.

TECHNIQUES TO MAXIMIZE LEARNING FROM CASES

Using Small Groups

In the lecture method, participant learning comes from the "wisdom" that is heard (and presumably absorbed) from "on high," from the expert. In case study, conversely, learning comes from what one analyzes, discusses, advocates, defends, and listens to; in short, learning (or wisdom) accrues from interaction with peers.

In traditional case study, participants and the trainer often arrayed themselves around a table for good eye contact and generally better communication. They also assumed this configuration to emphasize that all concerned were equals. All of which was true enough, except that the more verbal and aggressive participants became "more equal" than their fellow discussants. This competition for "air time" obviously became most acute when the group was quite large. If the group were composed of 25 participants and the session ran 2 hours (120 minutes) and everyone actually had equal opportunities to participate, per-person participation time would be less than 5 minutes. This figure is exclusive of added time consumed by trainer inputs.

Because of this participation problem, trainers in time began to employ small group methods as a major means of attacking the case. This can be done in one of several ways:

☐ Hold a group-at-large discussion to be certain that everyone agrees on the facts and issues involved. Then have the participants break into small groups of four to six persons to come up with a solution to the problem. Solutions or decisions are then reported back to the total group for further discussion.

☐ Alternatively, the total group could be immediately divided into small groups with instructions to respond to the trainer's usual opening query of "What seems to be going on here?" Then the groups could report their conclusions on that question to the large group, endeavoring to secure agreement on the facts and issues, and then return to the small groups for the problem-resolution phase of the work (as in the preceding procedure).

☐ If the case has specific questions for discussion (see the following discussion on "Focused Analysis"), specific questions could be assigned to various small groups for discussion and feedback to the total group. A variation on this technique would be to have individual participants develop their responses to the questions in writing prior to entry into their small discussion groups (see the discussion on "Using a Worksheet" later). More specifically, the procedures are as follows:

1. Have participants read the case in class.
2. Have each person jot down his/her responses to the assigned (focused) questions.
3. Form small groups to discuss and agree on responses to the assigned questions. (Answers may be written on a flipchart.)
4. Ask each team to select a spokesperson/responder to answer questions from the other teams. *Note:* Keep the groups intact while the discussion is going on to establish clearly the group for whom the responder is responding.
5. As trainer, wrap up the discussion by highlighting responses to the questions which were assigned. Alternately, you may ask for volunteers to provide such summary responses.

Note: Twenty-seven "Thought Questions" are given in Chapter 2, Figure 2-1. They may help you to stimulate discussion, either total or small group.

Focused Analysis

In classic case study, participants are put into action via such general questions as: What seems to be going on here? Is there a problem here? If so, what is it? What are the issues of which we should be

cognizant? The theory here, of course, is that providing specific questions encourages too much dependency on the trainer; what is preferred is that participants attack the case on a totally open-ended basis.

Alternatively, and depending on the learning objectives and the group's needs, it may be quite desirable to provide participants with more structure in the form of specific questions on which they should focus. For example, the following short case on delegation may take this focused format.

Rationalizations About Delegation

In a management seminar a participant told the group about his attempts to get his dad, who ran a small metal fabricating plant, to "loosen up" and delegate more. He cited these conversations with his dad.

Son: Dad, why don't you make it easier on yourself and let someone else do the maintenance on those machines?
Dad: No one has had the experience I've had taking care of them.
Son: Are you saying you're the only one who can maintain them?
Dad: Oh, sure, there are others who can do the job, too.
Son: Then why not let them do it?
Dad: They *could* do it. But how do I know they'd do it *right*?

Another conversation went as follows:

Son: You took the *full* two weeks vacation and the plant is still there.
Dad: I really missed the plant.
Son: I can understand that. But you've got to get away now and then.
Dad: But what if something comes up while I'm away?
Son: Did anyone call you while you were away?
Dad: No.
Son: So they didn't *need* to call.
Dad: Since they didn't have my number, how do I know they didn't *try* to call me?

Questions for discussion:

1. Why may managers be reluctant to delegate?
2. Assume you had a subordinate manager working for you who was "weak" at delegating. How might you change his approach to delegation?
3. One way to encourage delegation by managers is to acquaint them with proper control procedures? What might some of these be?

Note that the preceding questions took a specific focus—they dealt with reluctance to delegate. It is also possible, however, to provide a broader or multifocus. We thus could explore this case in respect to other dimensions of the management job:

☐ *Communication:* Would you say it is hard or easy to communicate with Dad? Does the son seem to have the kind of relationship with Dad that makes authentic communication possible? Was Dad interested in feedback about his prowess as a manager?

☐ *Motivation:* Assume everyone has a "need" system. What is Dad's? Is it possible to bring about a change in Dad's (or anyone's) need system? If so, how might this be done?

☐ *Managerial Grid®:* Using Grid concepts, what are the leadership styles of Dad? His son?

☐ *Johari Window:* How do people in the plant see Dad? Does Dad see himself as others do? Or does Dad have serious "blind spots"?

☐ *Coaching:* How would you see Dad as a developer of people? If you were working for Dad, what problems would you see arising between you?

Another form of focus is to learn from failure. Thus, participants zero in on the mistakes or failures contained in a given case. The written case may be followed by questions such as these:

☐ What went wrong?
☐ How or why did Marie fail?
☐ What were Marie's principal mistakes?
☐ Was the series of errors inevitable?
☐ How could the failure (crisis, emergency) have been prevented?
☐ How could Andy have avoided getting into this jam?

☐ What are the company's chances for survival?
☐ How can Miss Benedict establish a plan or procedure to deal with future emergencies (contingencies, disruptions, crises)?
☐ Was there any learning in the organization as a result of these unsuccessful events?
☐ Is it possible to learn from failure? If so, how?

Still another focused approach is that of *empathic analysis.* Here we ask the participants to put their feet in the shoes of the case's characters and respond to questions such as these:

☐ How would you have handled this incident (situation, problem, crisis, event) if you were the district manager?
☐ Assuming you were the head of the company, _____ ?
☐ Could this situation have been prevented? If so, what would *you* have done?

It would also be useful to the group to analyze a case in terms of the *forces* at work that produced the problem:

☐ Those in the persons, including leaders, peers, and/or subordinates
☐ Those in the group
☐ Those in the organization (its structure, values, policies)
☐ Those in the world at large (if applicable)

As a final example of focused analysis, the psychological/psychoanalytical model developed by industrial psychologist Harry Levinson merits consideration. Dr. Levinson provides these key questions for case analyses [11]:

☐ Where is the pain? (That is, who is most upset by the behavior?)
☐ When did it begin? (Cases with a long history are less amenable to managerial intervention.)
☐ What is happening to affection?
☐ What is happening to aggression?
☐ What is happening to dependency?
☐ What is the nature of the ego ideal? (This relates to self-appreciation, self-perception, self-aspirations and their realizability.)

☐ Is the problem solvable? (Some problems have to be lived with.)

☐ If so, how?

Introducing a Role Play

Management cases typically present situations involving poor communication, conflict, resistance to change, role confusion, unrealistic values, and fuzzy goal setting. Added insight into these interpersonal dynamics may be secured by acting out the roles of the personalities presented in the case. This may be planned in advance by the trainer, or it may be structured on an *ad hoc* basis. In the latter instance a participant may trigger the role play by saying: "If I were the manager and Terry were working for me, I would _____." At this point the trainer interrupts and says: "Fine. Rod, you be the manager. Fred, you be Terry. Fred is in your office and _____ ."

Introducing Brainstorming

Brainstorming, like role playing, can be planned in advance or introduced as the situation seems to call for it. For example, in the prior delegation case, you could have the group brainstorm control procedures a manager could use to ensure that delegation is proceeding as intended. Typical controls might be periodic written reports, computer printouts, briefs at staff meetings, planned inspections, spot checks, informal chats.

Personalization

After discussing the formal case, greater insight into the issues raised might be obtained by asking participants to volunteer data or examples drawn from their personal experience. Thus, in the delegation case, participants could be encouraged to share instances, past or preferably present, of their own reluctance to delegate.

Using a Worksheet

A case may be presented in worksheet format. This entails providing the particulars of the case as usual plus an opportunity for the individual participants and possibly the small groups to reduce their conclusions to writing. The advantages of this more structured approach are as follows:

☐ Offering conclusions in writing requires more careful thought.

☐ Everyone is more certain to participate. (People can "cop out" even in a small group.)

An example of a case presented in this format appears in Figure 17-1.

The Case of the Non-Team-Playing Peer

Len Thompson is a relatively new member of the personnel office. He was recently brought in to head up all matters pertaining to recruitment and placement. In a meeting with his boss, Rex Ross, the personnel officer, Len dropped a comment to the effect that Arch White, the training officer, did not seem very interested in the new career management program he (Len) was developing.

Several days later you (Arch White) are in your boss's office on some business, and Rex unloads this bombshell:

Rex Ross: Len tells me that you don't seem to be interested in the new career management plan he's working on.
Arch White: What?
Rex Ross: That's what he implied.
Arch White: Where did he get that idea? I've always said we needed that program to complement our overall training and development program.
Rex Ross: Um . . .
Arch White: This really beats anything.
Rex Ross: Well, I thought you'd want to know how he feels.

You leave the boss's office, both stunned and puzzled. The next day you return to your boss's office to try to button down Len Thompson's statement to the boss. You also let your boss know that Len's statement really irritated you. Rex Ross, however, doesn't provide you with any more specific information, merely repeating what he said yesterday. You leave your boss's office wondering what kind of a team player Len Thompson is.

Figure 17-1. Example of a case presented in a worksheet format.

Case Study Assignment Sheet

1. You are Training Officer Arch White
    a. What action, if any, do you propose to take?

    _____
    _____
    _____
    _____
    _____
    _____

    b. What are the reasons for your action?

    _____
    _____
    _____
    _____
    _____
    _____

2. Small group assignment: Agree, as a group, on the best course of action Arch White should take.

    _____
    _____
    _____
    _____
    _____

Figure 17-1. Example of a case presented in a worksheet format. (*Continued*)

Using Fishbowls

The fishbowl, or group-on-group observation, can be used to increase both involvement and excitement in the group. At any of the various stages of the case study discussion, the trainer can divide the total group into two smaller groups—one to discuss the case and the other to observe and listen to the discussants. After 20–30 minutes the roles can be reversed, with the outer group becoming the discussants and the inner group the observers. On the second go-around the discussion can cover both the group's own ideas about the case and its reactions to the comments of the first group.

For best results, the discussion group should have no more than eight people.

Added Skill Pointers

The following guidelines and cautions will help to ensure a high-quality learning experience for your participants [13]:

1. Choose cases carefully to meet course objectives.
2. Allow sufficient time for your group to read the case thoroughly before you start the discussion. Skip lengthy cases unless they can be read on a pre-work basis.
3. One practical way to begin is to have a group member summarize the facts and main issues in the case. Check to see if there is agreement with this presentation.
4. Anticipate resistance to the case method by some participants who are more comfortable

with *the* answer. Part of the learning, of course, is that in management there is typically no one "best" or "right" answer. Also, managers must learn to become comfortable with ambiguity.

5. Avoid taking away the participants' opportunity to think by providing answers, or worse, "*the* answer."

Summary of Techniques to Facilitate Case Discussions

Instructional designer Darryl Ann Lavitt suggests that the facilitator/trainer can use these techniques to keep case discussions on track [12]:

Clarify issues. Pose questions and at times restate them; summarize responses; tie case material to overall course/program material.

Guide discussion. Pose new questions to redirect/refocus the discussion; encourage more profound thought and broader perspectives by asking "what if" type questions; organize and consolidate issues which have emerged.

Challenge participants. Be certain everyone has had a chance to have his/her say; use debates on controversial or unresolved issues; encourage deeper thought by asking "Can you develop that thought further?"; pose hypotheticals: "What action would you take in this kind of situation?" (or "given these circumstances?"); assume the role of "devil's advocate"; query participants about their assumptions (what they are and their bases).

Explain. Cite incidents from your own experience; present a model or conceptualization to systematize and deepen thinking about an issue; generalize case issues and learnings to back-home situations.

Close. Review and summarize key points/issues which have emerged; discuss alternative courses of action; check to see if consensus is possible; cite paradoxes, dilemmas, unresolved issues.

Evaluation of Participants

If the group wishes to evaluate its behavior as a group, it can employ various devices for this. These include the use of a sociogram to diagram participation, a role observation chart to record assumption of task and maintenance roles, and a check sheet to assess problem solving behavior.

KEY POINTS

1. The case study method is our oldest training technique for achieving trainee participation.

2. Its major limitation is that it is somewhat intellectual and academic in its approach; that is, it merely involves an analysis and discussion of someone else's problem—and often in a large group setting at that.

3. Also, it is not as involving as newer participative training devices such as exercises, games, simulations, role plays, or instruments.

4. In using case study the trainer should seek out formats that make for greater participant interest, such as using letters and editorials, dialogue, filmed cases, the live case, personal cases, and the rating approach.

5. The filmed case has greater realism than the printed case. It is more interesting and eliminates the need for prior preparation (pre-work).

6. Although cases may be acquired from outside sources such as books and magazines, the alert trainer will be on the lookout for incidents, events, and problems that can be converted to case materials of a particular interest to the participant groups.

7. In writing cases, structure them so that they have the potential to accent principles/issues you deem pertinent. Develop "strong" characters and include adequate conflict in their interactions to ensure interest and realism.

8. Since the traditional group-at-large approach to case study allows for only limited participation and has an "academic" cast to it, use other devices with it to ensure greater involvement—small group work, role plays, fishbowls, brainstorming, or focused analysis.

REFERENCES

1. *Management Development Casebook,* Training Guide TG 5–16, Office of Personnel, Veterans Administration, Washington, D.C. (1958).

2. Andrews, Eugene S., and Noel, James, L., "Adding Life to the Case Study Method," *Training and Development Journal* (February 1986), pp. 28–29.

3. Based on an Associated Press news item which appeared in *The Washington Post* (December 17, 1980) with a Lake Ronkonkoma, New York, dateline. The names of the persons in the case have been changed.

4. This description is based on the author's experience with the Action Maze technique plus the incisive observations contained in (a) Broadwell, Martin M., *The Supervisor as an Instructor*, 3rd edition, Addison-Wesley, Reading, Mass. (1978), p. 194; and (b) Laird, Dugan L., *Approaches to Training and Development*, Addison-Wesley, Reading, Mass. (1978), pp. 143–144.

5. "Training Away Work Place Problems," *Training and Development Journal* (November 1987), pp. 18–19, which describes suggestions submitted by Michael Shahnasarian, ISFA Corporation, Tampa, Florida.

6. Kronenberger, G. K., and Bourke, D. L., "Effective Training and Elimination of Sexual Harassment," *Personnel Journal* (November 1981), pp. 879–883.

7. "Selling and the Law," *Industrial Distribution* (October 1981), pp. 38–41.

8. Boyd, B. B., "Developing Case Studies," *Training and Development Journal* (June 1980).

9. Inguagiato, Robert J., "Case Studies: Let's Get Real," in "Training 101," *Training and Development* (October 1993), pp. 20–23.

10. Owenby, Phillip H., "Making Case Studies Come Alive," *Training* (January 1992), pp. 43–46.

11. Levinson, H., *Psychological Man,* The Levinson Institute, Cambridge, Mass. (1976), pp. 135–138.

12. Lavitt, Darryl Ann, "A Case for Training," in "Training 101," *Training and Development* (June 1992), pp. 19–22.

13. "Case Method: Tips," *Government Training News* (August 1984), p. 8.

RECOMMENDED READING

Amistead, Colin, "How Helpful Are Case Studies?" *Training and Development Journal*, February 1984, pp. 75–77.

The article covers types of case study, criteria of a good case, pros and cons, learning objectives, and writing cases.

Andrews, Kenneth R. (Ed.), *The Case Method of Teaching Human Relations and Administration*, Harvard University Press, Cambridge, Mass., 1953.

A now classic reference work on the case study, the book features a collection of papers by those who taught and conducted research in human relations at the Harvard Business School.

Boyd, Bradford B., "Developing Case Studies," *Training and Development Journal*, June 1980.

This presents a six-step method for writing cases to fit the special needs of one's course or program.

Glover, John D., et al., *The Administrator: Cases on Human Aspects in Management*, 5th edition, Richard D. Irwin, Inc., Homewood, Ill., 1973.

This is the "granddaddy" of case books that emanated from the Harvard Business School. The book was originally published in 1949 by two Harvard Business School professors, John D. Glover and Ralph M. However. It was titled *The Administrator: Cases on Human Relations in Business* and went through several revisions under that title.

Green, Thad B., and Cotlar, Morton, "Do Filmed Cases Improve the Case Method?" *Training and Development Journal*, May 1973, pp. 28–31.

This is a research report that concluded that "presenting case materials on film does improve the case method. Although the film did not promote greater transferability, those students using film-based simulation demonstrated a superior performance in comprehension of management principles and concepts, and a more realistic understanding of the environment in which the manager interacts."

Hennecke, Matthew J., "Case Studies: A New Approach," *Training and Development Journal*, March 1983, pp. 70–71.

The author shows how to overcome a problem of case study—namely, its remoteness from the participants' real world. The answer? Use individualized case studies which include the participants' own staff, peers, and bosses.

McCarthy, John J., "The Case Method," *Sales Training*, January 1977, and "A Case Handling Technique," *Sales Training*, March 1977.

A long-time sales trainer shows how case study can be effectively applied to sales training.

McNair, Malcolm P. (Ed.), *The Case Method at the Harvard Business School: Papers by Present and Past Members of the Faculty and Staff,* McGraw-Hill Book Co., New York, 1954.

This is a work devoted to the broad application of case study, for example, marketing, production, control, economic aspects of business, and advertising. (*Note:* The book by Andrews, cited earlier, was concerned solely with teaching human relations via the case method.)

Pigors, Paul, and Pigors, Faith, "Learning Through Experience in Leadership Training," *Office Executive*, October 1955, pp. 1–3.

This is a description of the incident process by its founders.

Pigors, Paul, and Pigors, Faith, "Case Method," in R. Craig (Ed.), *Training and Development Handbook,* 3rd edition, McGraw-Hill Book Co. New York, 1987, pp. 414–429.

Contains a description of the incident process.

Stringer, David, "Case Writing 101," *Training and Development*, September 1999, pp. 53–57.

A professional case writer for a management consulting firm presents his many helpful tips to write a realistic case study.

Wilterding, Jim, Baughn, C. Christopher, and Wanek, James E., "The Inquiry Process: Another Way of Facilitating Problem Solving Through Training," *Performance Improvement*, October 2000, pp. 27–31.

A streamlined, updated version of the incident process. The authors find a significant increase in participant questioning skills after several sessions.

18 "If You Must Lecture . . ."

The biggest enemy to learning is the talking teacher.

—John Holt, educator and author

A prominent newspaper columnist—Colman McCarthy of The Washington Post—*was invited to speak to a journalism class while he was visiting the University of Iowa. He noted very quickly that many of the 40 students were taking notes, obviously responding to the usual professorial imperative of "covering ground." So he asked them if they would join him in an experiment. He gave them these instructions: "Stand up. Leave the building. Stand on the curb for 15 minutes and count all the red and green cars that pass. Then come back to answer questions."*

When the students were halfway down the hall, he called them back. He then posed these questions: Didn't anyone think it was stupid to count red and green cars? Why didn't anyone ask the objective of the "experiment"? Do you let your profs push you around this way? Since it was raining, why didn't someone say he/she didn't want to get wet?

Of course, the aim of the experiment was not merely to down-grade note taking. It was about passivity and coercion, the long time enemies of learning and the permanent assailants of students. He wished to show the students that they were in school to learn by questioning and to get their questions answered. Also, they should question oppressive authority and ask whether the university was giving them their money's worth. If not, said Mr. McCarthy, let the professors count red and green cars in the rain. And let them take notes, too, for "there's ground to be covered" [1].

THE LECTURE—A PROBLEM-LADEN TECHNIQUE

More than any other training method, the lecture has been continually cussed and discussed. Newer, more involving methods have certainly moved the lecture off "center stage." Here are some of the many charges levied against it:

- ☐ It is dull, boring, and thus a waste of time.
- ☐ It makes the learner passive.
- ☐ It causes a loss of motivation, curiosity, and creativity.
- ☐ Since it is a one-way communication device, the presenter can hardly tell whether the message is coming through.

- ☐ It has a high "tune out" and "turn off" potential.
- ☐ Participants may not be able to seek a necessary clarification because of the size of the group, time constraints, the lecturer's "flow," and the presumed embarrassment of interrupting.
- ☐ It ignores varying listening rates of participants.
- ☐ It ignores varying learning styles of participants.
- ☐ The formal presentation may be poorly planned and organized.
- ☐ The delivery itself may be poor.
- ☐ The speaker may "talk down" to the audience.
- ☐ It endorses the authority figure concept, something that is not appreciated in a democratic culture.
- ☐ Retention is very low—much is lost in 24 hours, most of the rest is lost thereafter.
- ☐ It is archaic as a teaching device. Socrates, who lived around 450 B.C., sensed this. Hence his development of the Socratic method, which entailed asking a series of well-planned questions to lead his learners to the "ultimate truth."
- ☐ It ignores the old adage, "The mind can absorb only as much as the seat can endure."

Lecturing, of course, is the way professors teach in the colleges and universities. But this approach is hardly a model for the alert and sophisticated trainer. In fact, a former academic teacher, now a professional trainer, Don M. Ricks, president of Industrial Writing and Communications Consultants Ltd. of Calgary, Canada, candidly stated why he wouldn't hire "academics" as instructors in his company. Here are his well-articulated objections [2]:

- ☐ They know little about how adults learn. They even pride themselves "in *not* knowing how people learn."
- ☐ They have a limited range of instructional skills, knowing little of modern audio-visual and group-in-action devices as discussed in the preceding pages. Also, their instruction is often mind-bending (manipulation) rather than mind-liberating.
- ☐ They teach the wrong people, that is, they "play" to the bright students, the ones who need help the least.
- ☐ They teach the wrong things; the students are overburdened with detailed content as if they

were to become instructors in the field. Most academics have limited experience in these vital roles: setting directions, answering questions, providing feedback, and helping the learner define objectives and solve problems.

- ☐ As "experts" they are reluctant to surrender "ownership" of learning, thus shortchanging students by withholding vital content from them.
- ☐ They have too much confidence in words, despite the well-known fact that listeners have short attention spans and poor retention rates. Academic teachers often get trapped by the beauty of their own voices and drone on and on.
- ☐ They hesitate to trust learners, preferring to control them rather than to provide general guidance and direction.
- ☐ They have a limited understanding of the effects of their own behavior. They thus overlook the need to display such desirable qualities as openness, receptivity, confidence, and interest, all key elements in establishing a sound instructor-student relationship.
- ☐ Finally, they simply misunderstand their primary function—to induce change. They ignore the fact that learning is intended to bring about a change in knowledge, perception, or behavior, not to "expose" people to information or to "cover" a subject.

Regardless of whether one accepts this indictment of those who live (and die?) totally by the lecture method, Ricks' statements do reveal that one can all too readily become enamored with communicating from "on-high" to the detriment of participant learning.

Not all observers, certainly, see the lecture as evil or even as a necessary evil. For example, Donald B. Miller, program manager of human resources for IBM in San Jose, California, sees it quite positively [3]:

The growth activity to which we have been most exposed is the lecture. We sometimes wonder about its effectiveness; however, when it works we can grow as a result of the exposure. A good lecture is one which engages our attention, sharpens the differentiation between alternative actions, and motivates us to new experience, or aids us in internalizing the information. A good lecture gets us emotionally involved. A good lecture presents material in a way which captures our involvement and interest. A good lecture disciplines our use of time and our actions in a way we cannot or have not done for ourselves.

WHEN TO USE THE LECTURE

The issue, of course, is not whether the lecture is totally bad or is, on occasion, helpful. Rather, our concern, as trainers, is: When does its use make sense? When is it most appropriate? The late Donald Bullock, who was responsible for marketing training development with the C & P Telephone Company, Silver Spring, Maryland, offers these guidelines to help trainers decide when "lecture-driven instruction" may be adequately useful [4]:

☐ The instructor has the need to present his/her ideas to the group. (Not a trivial consideration, says Bullock.)

☐ The lecture is the most convenient and cost-effective means to disseminate material.

☐ Concepts are to be given inductively and the expected varied responses of the group can only be responded to by the instructor.

☐ In a non–lecture-type program occasional lecturettes (short talks) may provide a worthwhile change of pace, reduce boredom, etc.

☐ Participants' needs to ask questions or to comment can best be met in a typical lecture-type format. (Conversely, the need may not be met well in a non–lecture or participative mode.)

☐ A demonstration of equipment or a job aid may require a lecture-type explanation so that key points or features are highlighted.

☐ A high-status person or skill in delivery is deemed essential to ensure the credibility of the information or instruction.

☐ The content or material changes so frequently that an "update" can only be handled via formal input by a lecturer.

CONSIDER A PANEL PRESENTATION

One way to avoid the limitations of the lecture is to use a three- to six- person panel instead. The panel can provide variety in presentation and permit interchange among the panelists, all of which should add interest to your proceedings. The panel presentations and interchanges should be followed by an opportunity for the audience to ask questions. The facilitator/trainer serves as moderator or moderator/panelist.

To ensure that the panel doesn't merely become a form of multiple lectures that puts the audience to sleep, you should consider these procedures [5]:

1. *Ascertain specific audience interest in advance of the presentation.* Use questionnaires or interviews, face-to-face or via telephone, to learn of participant problems, concerns, and interests. Then provide feedback on these issues to your panelists so that they can respond helpfully.

2. *Select panel members with care.* Choose them for their expertise, possibly divergent viewpoints, and skill in articulating their ideas.

3. *Define your own role.* Don't compete with the panelists. Let the panel answer audience questions. Coach the panelists as to their role; for example, if one doesn't have an answer to a question, he/she should simply pass on the question. Also, panel members should be brief in their responses to questions as well as in their initial remarks.

4. *Highlight panel members' qualifications.* Introduce each panelist and explain why he/she was selected to serve on the panel.

5. *Pay attention to the physical setup.* For example, if panelists are at floor level, seat them informally in a semicircle. If there is a large audience, the panelists might stand up when they talk so that they will be heard more easily.

6. *Decide on Q&A procedures.* Do you want questions to come directly to the panel from the floor, or do you want questions to come to you on cards? In the latter case you can screen the questions for relevance and general merit. If questions come from the audience directly, be certain that they are true questions rather than mini-lectures. Windy questioners can be controlled with a brief "And what is the question?" You may also ask the questioners to address their questions to a particular panelist.

In summary, a panel is one way to vary the lecture method. Also, the Q&A period can prevent it from becoming a total one-way communication event.

"TUNE-OUT"—COPING WITH LEARNER LISTENING LAPSES

Remember the old saying, "You can lead a horse to water but you can't make him drink"? Similarly, you can seat participants in the lecture hall (or training room), but you can't make them listen. Why not? Two reasons: They may not be highly motivated to tune in, and/or they may not have well-developed listening skills.

For the trainer, then, the challenge is to get through to the participants despite these listening problems. One way to meet this challenge is to recognize at the outset that there are various dangerous assumptions that we may make about our listeners that will bedevil us in our training effort. Communication/training specialists Kittie W. Watson and Larry L. Barker advise us to consider these eight faulty assumptions about trainee listening and to adopt the following ways of coping with them [6]:

1. *Looking at the trainer equates with actual listening.* The reality is that people have learned since early childhood how to fake attention. ("Look at me when I talk to you!") So what to do? Check for understanding by looking for nonverbal cues and listening for verbal cues. Nonverbal attentiveness is evidenced by facial expressions, head nods, and forward leans. Verbally, listeners may repeat key phrases, ask on-target questions, and request clarification.

   If active listening is indeed absent, pose questions and use small-group work and/or role plays.

2. *When the talk begins, trainees start listening.* Actually, participants don't focus on the speaker immediately. Why not? Because it takes several seconds, possibly minutes, for people to orient themselves to the message. Prior thoughts, worries, diverse distractions, and competing messages in the environment can prevent listening from shifting into the desired high gear. So the trainer's first point or fact may well be lost.

   How can we facilitate prompt tune-in? Use a warm-up activity or opener to help participants align themselves with your message. Also use attention-getting illustrations, and emphasize the value of the course.

3. *Participants will remember the key points that the trainer wishes to convey.* The sad news is that after a ten-minute talk, listeners can recall half or less of what was presented. Without any precise cues from the trainer, people will remember only the first and last ideas, regardless of their importance.

   What might be remembered? Certain facts, numbers, vivid examples. Unless your key points fall into those categories, expect high loss rather than high retention. But you can raise the odds in your favor if you (a) preview major points in your introduction, (b) summarize at various times in the talk, and (c) highlight key ideas at presentation's end.

   It also helps to reinforce key ideas with strong, vivid examples and to state the most important points at the beginning and end of the presentation. Another good idea is to have participants review major points from exercises, films, and discussions. Don't forget to emphasize key points via verbal and nonverbal cues such as increases in vocal variety and volume and changes in gestures and facial expression.

4. *Participants cease listening only when the trainer stops talking.* The reality: Trainees may tune out whenever they wish. If their energy runs low, listening will stop at any time. Also, the longer the talk, the less likely they will stay tuned to the end.

   The answer? Keep talks short. Seek out ways to dump any irrelevant or unimportant information. Use variety in your presentation to wake up those who have departed mentally. Ask questions; suggest ways to visualize your ideas; use exercises; plan breaks strategically (for example, in lieu of the usual long A.M. and P.M. breaks, provide two short ones in both the morning and afternoon). Also, encourage questions at any time in your presentation.

5. *Trainees can accurately repeat what they're told.* This should certainly be recognized as a wish by the trainer. Memory, language interpretation, personal interests, priorities, perceptions, and values dim and distort the message.

To help "glue in" the message, provide written reinforcement for key ideas. Use visual aids, repeat key ideas three or more times, increase vividness by sharing personal examples, and use role plays and case studies. And, of course, anything that you can do to make the new learning applicable to the job situation will help.

6. *Trainees and trainers process information alike.* Not so. Trainers with technical/professional backgrounds may use statistics, equations, and professional terms. Conversely, the non-technical trainer is likely to draw on personal examples, illustrations, and everyday language. Unfortunately, trainers may assume (erroneously, of course) that trainees are interested in the same facts and examples that they are.

   Compounding the problem is the fact that people are different. Some trainees want facts alone; others want to see the big picture. So if you have a mixed group, you have to vary the information you provide in order to hook all segments of your audience. It's a good idea, too, to let the participants provide their own examples.

   As to the pace of the training, vary it; people learn at different rates and in different ways. Humor may also help to reach participants.

7. *Trainees can live with (ignore) distractions.* The idea that trainees can "roll with the punches" (distractions, that is) is a dubious one. The trainer's appearance (clothing, jewelry, mannerisms, body language), room appearance, lighting, and temperature can create unwanted distractions. In fact, certain mannerisms may become more intriguing than the course content.

   Fortunately, most of these elements are remediable. For example, if people have trouble staying awake after lunch, consider lowering the room temperature a bit. If people are used to being active, have more frequent breaks. At least provide in-place, stretch breaks.

8. *If the new information is understood and agreed with, it is likely to be applied on the job.* Oh, that it were that simple. The actuality is that implementation of the new learning is dependent on trainee motivation. If motivation exists,

this assumption is O.K. But this may well be a hoped for, but highly erroneous and dangerous, assumption.

You have to work to unleash the desired motivation in participants. For example, point out the value of the new learning to their work, or have those who work together commit both to helping one another apply the new learning and to supporting new behaviors. Use follow-up methods to ensure that in-class-developed action plans do indeed take root back home.

READ THE AUDIENCE'S RECEPTIVITY

Anticipate that your audience will be adequately diverse, which means that their interest and attention levels will differ. If you can recognize the different listener types, you may be able to make some adjustments to capture their attention more fully. Consultant/speaker Dorrine Turecamo offers these seven basic listener profiles [7]:

1. *"Just the facts ma'am."* This is the no-nonsense, get-to-it listener. He/she won't tolerate long, rambling wind-ups. This listener expects specifics, such as "What's the problem and how can it be fixed?" Anticipate this person will pepper you with tough questions and will be persistent at it.

2. *"Please like me."* This is the type very much concerned with "warm, fuzzy feelings." He/she is very anxious with the impression he/she (rather than you) is making, so he/she won't retain much of what is heard.

   Women will be more courteous listeners in a diverse audience, especially if they're exposed to a female lecturer. Men will put on a polite listening front to a woman speaker. So if you're a woman speaker, you have to provide a special wrinkle to keep their attention. If you don't do this, anticipate body language which communicates "Oh, I knew that."

3. *"Mr. or Ms. Universe."* The "talk-is-power" listener is a power worshipper. He/she looks for "power symbols" to determine how much respect/attention to bestow the presenter. Of

significance to him/her are paper credentials, status, voice tone, body language. The assumption is that "if you look good and sound good, you are good; so I'll listen in."

4. *"Don't overload me."* Anticipate that some of your listeners have intake valves which overload easily. They shrink from what they perceive as information (new, unfamiliar) designed to overwhelm them. To prevent tune out, give these people a break now and again so they can stretch and move around.

5. *"Can you top this?"* This is the competitive type who can't wait until you finish so that he/she can top your renderings. He/she has his/her own agenda and thus listens only to learn how the message may impact him/her. So, if practical, learn in advance all you can about your listeners so you can respond to their "WIIFM" question (What's in it for me?).

6. *"The Yawner."* A single yawn or two is to be expected. Some people may not have had their eight hours last night. But if you observe a lot of yawns and fidgetings, you're in real trouble. So be prepared to shift gears to recapture your audience: tell a funny story; provide an in-place, stand-up, stretch break; put them to work in buzz groups with a pertinent question or a problem of yours.

7. *"The Police."* Some of your listeners may be of the "now I've gotcha" type. They're looking for something which is offensive, biased, inconsistent, or factually incorrect. They want to prove that you're simply wrong. So if forewarned is forearmed, carefully think through what you might say that could inadvertently provide raw, red meat to the hungry ones, the fault-finders extraordinaire.

GIVING THE LECTURE POLISH

Since the lecture is so problem-laden, a lot of advice is constantly being doled out to lecturers in hopes that they will give a "good" talk or a "stimulating" lecture. Some of this advice includes the following:

- ☐ Know your subject.
- ☐ Prepare well—use a tape (audio) recorder for practice.
- ☐ Study yourself "in action" via videotape.
- ☐ Over-prepare.
- ☐ State your objectives at the outset. Remember, participants are eager to learn very early on the answer to this question: "What's in it for me?"
- ☐ Use visual aids, but make certain they can be read easily.
- ☐ Watch your techniques of delivery; use voice variation, gestures, movement, and pauses; vary the tempo; abandon the lectern or podium.
- ☐ Maintain eye contact.
- ☐ Use humor, anecdotes, examples, analogies.
- ☐ Use handouts.
- ☐ Breathe properly.
- ☐ Don't read from a manuscript; use general notes only.
- ☐ Introduce surprise.
- ☐ Enunciate carefully.
- ☐ Exude confidence, sincerity, conviction.
- ☐ Exude energy, enthusiasm.
- ☐ Don't turn down an opportunity to speak before a group; practice is invaluable.
- ☐ Watch your beginnings—get interest at the onset.
- ☐ Watch your closes—give them a message they'll remember.
- ☐ Try to get feedback about your performance.
- ☐ Join a speaking-improvement group, such as a Toastmaster's Club, to upgrade your skill.
- ☐ Avoid "uh's" and "ah's."
- ☐ Know your audience—their interests, perceptions, expectations, background.
- ☐ Assess and reassess your audience in the course of your presentation, and make adjustments as necessary.
- ☐ Quit on time.
- ☐ Dress properly.
- ☐ Personalize your talk: talk about yourself, your experience, your "goofs."
- ☐ Use a lot of "you's" for audience rapport.
- ☐ Include practical material ("how to") in your talk.
- ☐ Avoid "heavy" statistics; instead, speak generally about quantitative items.

☐ Use everyday language; avoid pomposity.

☐ Try to speak in a conversational tone of voice.

All of this, is useful information—except for one thing: it relates only to how well the person "up front" should and can perform. Unfortunately, the well-intentioned advice has little bearing on *how well the learner will learn.* In other words, the answer to the lecture problem—and anyone who has suffered through lectures in classrooms and training rooms can enumerate scores of such problems without too much prompting—is not just to make better lectures, but to work on ways to involve the group. Certainly, sophisticated trainers would agree that the lecture, at best, is a necessary evil. But on the assumption that the lecture, despite its many demerits, is here to stay, some means of making it more palatable and productive for the participants in your programs are presented.

SECURING PARTICIPATION AT THE OUTSET

Although participative approaches can be used at various stages in a talk or lecture, it's a good idea to get your audience into the act at the outset. This procedure will immediately establish rapport with the group. They will, in effect, say thankfully to themselves: "Hey, this person isn't just going to talk *at us* for the full hour. Sure looks like a lively deal coming up." By putting the group to work, you will also relax yourself and do a better job as a speaker.

Here are some examples of activities to involve the group *before* the lecture is launched.

Pre-work: Reading

Give your conferees an advance reading assignment and have them discuss it in class before the formal presentation.

Audience Answers

Involve your participants on their arrival by having them enter data on flipcharts. Procedurally, post three sheets to the wall or use three separate easels with flipchart pads on them. In the former case, also tape

several marking pens to the wall, one next to each flipchart sheet for ready use.

Assume your session is related to "Delegation and the Manager." You might label your three flipchart sheets as follows:

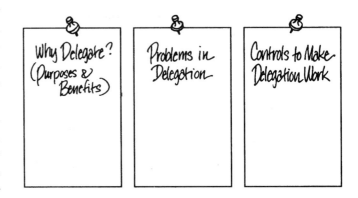

Review the sheets before you start the session and make reference to the data from time to time as you conduct the session.

Note: Since the participants may not be aware that they are to contribute to the flipcharts, you, a colleague, or a participant should call this task to their attention as they arrive.

Pre-work: Case or Problem Analysis

Give participants a short case, incident, or problem in *advance* of the talk. Ask them to come to class with a possible solution. Use the case discussion as an introduction to the formal lecture or talk.

Problem Census

At the outset, elicit from the audience areas of special interest, problems, or concerns that they hope will be covered in the session. Post them on a flipchart and then check off those that will be dealt with in the formal presentation. This procedure will give the audience an assurance that at least some of their problems and interests will be addressed; it will also provide for "instant" participation.

Problem Swap

Assign participants to small groups, have them introduce themselves to one another and then give them this *individualized* assignment to discuss for two minutes: What is the major obstacle you encounter in _____ (introducing change, securing cooperation, selling product X, improving employee safety)? Then have participants put their problems on a 3" × 5" card (each group member puts his/her problem on a card) and share the problems in their groups for five minutes. Hand out a large 5" × 8" card to each group. Have the groups spend five minutes deciding on the one "best" problem in the group and write it on the large card. Collect the big cards and switch them among the groups. Then have the groups take ten minutes to answer the problem on the card they received. Then say "O.K., let's get some reports from several groups. Who wants to start? State the problem you have and your group's answer to it."

Interest Inventory

Ask your audience to respond to questions such as these:

- [ ] What is your interest in this topic?
- [ ] Why are you here?
- [ ] What do you hope to take back?
- [ ] When this session is over, what will have made it successful?

You can ask the participants to respond to questions of this sort on an individual basis or, better still, in pairs or small groups of three to five persons.

Incidents for Involvement

Ask everyone to jot down on a sheet of paper a real-life incident, problem, or event that relates to your topic. Ask several people to share their incident or problem with the total group. A variation is to use small-group work to select the "best" examples before sharing them with the total group.

Problem Probe

Begin things by assigning to small groups a short problem, case, or incident. Secure feedback and discuss it; then begin your talk.

Exercise Excitement

Start things off with a short, simple, exciting, and involving exercise, puzzle, or game. It should be pertinent to the topic and make the point in relatively short order.

Anxiety Reducer

Quiet all concerns about a possible dull lecture by commencing the session with an interest-stimulating instrument or quiz. If appropriate, collect data from the "test" and feed it back to the group. Reference may be made to this data at one or more points in the talk, as appropriate.

Structured Note Taking

Ask the group to draw the tri-column that follows on a sheet of paper.

Talk Monitor Chart

I Accept/Agree	I Reject/Disagree	I Have This Question

Then tell them to use the chart as a guide to note taking and that at a point roughly midway in the session you will have them "process" their notes with a neighbor (or a small group).

Flipchart Fill-up

In advance of the session's start, place a sheet from the flipchart and a felt-tip pen on each table. To start things off, assign a task to the various small groups and then have them post their "products" on the wall. The task may involve a definition, the development of a list, the making of a statement about something by means of a drawing, etc.

Present vs. Preferred States

Start things off by asking your audience to break down into small groups and for 10–12 minutes address themselves to these two questions, applicable to almost any group's concerns:

☐ What is the *current* or present state of affairs?

☐ What do you see to be the preferred or *ideal* state of affairs?

Note: Each small group could address itself to both questions, or, as a variation, one half of the small groups could deal with the first question and the second half with the latter question.

Secure feedback from the small groups and put it on flipcharts. Post the flipcharts on the wall for later reference.

Quiz the Expert

Post on a flipchart three or four major concerns or problem areas with which your talk will deal. Give all group members several 3" × 5" cards and have each of the participants come up with *one* question for each of the problem areas. Retrieve all the cards for topic (problem) one, then for topic two, topic three, and topic four. Return the grouped cards to the small groups for sorting, consolidating, and prioritizing. Then ask for questions from the small groups on all the major areas of concern (for 10–20 minutes). It is not necessary to try to respond to all the questions.

The Two-Step

Give participants a two-stage assignment. For example, to introduce a talk on leadership, have participants list (on the left side of a sheet of paper) three to six individuals, past and present, who might be considered significant leaders or "heroes." Then, on the right side of the paper, list two to four characteristics about these individuals that "justify" the leadership label. Other two-step assignments: cause-effect; risk vs. ways of overcoming the risk; perception: mine vs. theirs.

Thought Stimulator

As soon as people sit down, have them respond in writing to a set of incomplete statements. The questions may be on a prepared form, on the flipchart, or on an overhead projector slide. Examples of such statements for a lecture on time management are:

1. The biggest problem(s) managers have in managing their time is _____.

2. The big time wasters in any organization are _____.

3. If I had total control of my time, I would _____.

When the question sheets are completed, secure random responses to those questions or use small groups to process the data before feedback is secured.

MID-TALK INTERVENTIONS

As the prior section indicated, it is both desirable and practicable to involve participants *before* a formal talk, lecture, or lecturette. It may also be desirable to put the group into action as the formal presentation proceeds. If so, the devices below should prove helpful.

Challenge Rank

Give participants a handout of, or post on a flipchart, a list of "challenges" (or problem areas, difficulties, concerns). Have them rank the challenges as to importance or intensity. Then secure feedback from the group, via a show of hands, concerning the rankings. ("How many ranked 'field relationships' No. 1? No. 2? Why?")

Film Excerpt

Use a brief film vignette either as an opener (thought stimulator) or at a later point in the presentation. Process the data with the aid of small groups.

Defining Dyads (Pairs)

Have participants turn to their neighbor and meet for several minutes to define an issue; to frame a question; to present a reaction, observation, or comment. Remember, in a dyad *everyone* plays!

Buzz Groups

Use small discussion groups at one or more points in the presentation to react, to problem solve, to form questions, to apply learnings to job situations.

Participant Survey

Run a quick survey via slips, questionnaires, or show of hands to produce from the participant group live data pertinent to the topic. Use an associate to tally written data, then feed it back in summary form to the audience.

Participant Assignment

Give the audience (via small groups) a specific task. Example: "Here is a common house brick. Come up with eight ways the brick could be used in your home or office. Be as creative as you can! The sky is the limit! Let your imagination soar." "Think up a number of things you can do to _____" or "Jot down the three most important ways (techniques, methods, procedures) you see to achieve this objective (or end result)."

List Development

Have the group develop a list on a given topic ("Come up with a 'laundry list' on _____").

Structured List

By adding a bit of structure to a list assignment, via a handout such as in Appendix 64, you can encourage participants to "dig in" more.

Test Tease

Give the audience a short quiz, or use an instrument as an attention getter or interest stimulator. Briefly discuss the results.

Listening Teams (with Topic)

Assign participants to listening teams (four to five participants) in *advance* of the presentation. Then assign to the small groups particular issues or questions that they are to reflect on as the talk is given. At mid-point or at talk's end, have the small groups discuss their assigned questions in light of the formal input. Have a spokesperson from each group report back the small group's conclusions to the group at large.

Listening Teams (General)

Provide listening teams with these pre-presentation assignments:

"Group One, you are *the questioners*. You might respond by saying, 'We heard you say _____ and wondered if _____'or 'Your statement on _____ triggered the thought that _____.'

"Group Two, you are *the clarifiers*. You might say, 'We were not clear (or were confused) about _____.'

"Group Three, you are *the disagreers*—not the disagreeables, but the disagreers. Your response might be 'We would question your assertion that _____.'

"Group Four, you are *the agreers*. You might say, 'We were turned on by your statement (or idea) concerning _____.'

"Group Five, you are *the appliers*. Your response might be 'We see an opportunity to put to work your idea concerning _____.'"

As in the previous suggestion, provide opportunities for the teams to respond to their assignments.

Puzzle Fun

Provide participants with puzzles as a stimulator or to make a point. (Puzzle materials may be toothpicks or other physical items such as matches; the puzzle may be written on the board, passed out as a handout, or communicated orally.)

Didactic Enactment

Work into the presentation a demonstration role play. This can be done informally, with the role players working from general role instructions, or more formally with the role players working from a complete dialogue script. Example: How *not* to conduct an appraisal interview. Secure audience comments as to what was done improperly.

Role Play

The ideas in a talk can be made more meaningful by having the entire group act them out. Giving participants "skill practice" is practical in a large as well as in a small group. For example, I was a participant in a lecture-type session on equal employment attended by some 250 people. We were in a hotel ballroom and seated at large round tables, ten to a table. We received this assignment: "Break into trios. One person will assume the role of an applicant applying for a secretarial job. A second will be the boss who is hiring the secretary. The one playing the secretarial role should preferably be someone who has never been in that role in real life. A third person will be an observer." (I assumed the role of the job applicant and acquired considerable insight and empathy about this type of recruiting situation.) The observer provided feedback about the role plays. Our configuration at the tables for the role plays was as shown in Figure 18-1.

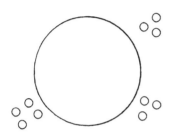

Figure 18-1. Diagram of how role-playing teams could position themselves at a large round table.

Similar role plays could be employed in situations involving prospect-salesperson, police officer-citizen, counselor-counselee, coach-trainee, and boss-subordinate roles.

Voluntary Vignettes

Have participants take a sheet of paper and jot down an incident, instance, or event of which they were a part. A variation is to use a more structured approach by providing them with the handout shown in Figure 18-2.

POINT MADE IN TALK	MY RELEVANT PERSONAL EXPERIENCE
1.	
2.	
3.	
4.	
5.	

Figure 18-2. Example of a handout to aid participants in relating points made in the lecture to their personal experiences.

The personal incidents may be shared in dyads, triads, small groups of four to six persons, or with the group at large.

Feedback Fest

Stop midway in the presentation and ask for feedback or reactions: "Have I said anything that makes sense? How do *you* see what I've been saying?" The response may be obtained on an individual or, preferably, a small group basis for *full* audience involvement. A variation is to do one of the following:

☐ Ask orally: "What points have I made so far that cause you to have some reaction—good-bad? Agree-disagree? Practical-impractical?" Secure responses.

☐ Ask for a response in writing: "Put down the three most important ways, techniques, methods, steps you see as needed to achieve this objective." Then secure feedback.

☐ Ask for a show of hands in response to these kinds of questions: "How many agree? Disagree?" "How many believe it's workable?" "How many have had that experience?" "How many had that kind of supervision?" "How many have tried this procedure at least once?" Ask the hand-raisers to provide a few particulars about the queries posed.

Participant Props

Prior to your presentation, pass out toy whistles, sun glasses, and red clown noses to all participants. Instruct participants on their use as follows:

☐ Don sunglasses if something is unclear.
☐ Don the red clown nose if the group is straying from the subject.
☐ Blow the whistle if you feel the need to add a point, ask a question, or disagree.

Problem Analysis

Assign a problem or case during or after the talk for small-group discussion and resolution.

Definition Dare

Have the group jot down a definition of something: leadership, motivation, time, job enrichment, democracy, communication, coaching, etc. Then have several participants read the definitions back to the group at large for discussion.

Handout Helps

Pass out handouts at critical points in the presentation and discuss them with the group. A handout may be a conceptual model, graph, chart, list of principles, set of concepts, etc. Along with your "straight" handouts, you may wish to pass out a cartoon that makes a relevant point. Prove to the participants that learning need not be dull.

Photo-Object Display

Use photographs and physical objects to illustrate points and excite interest. For example, one speaker used a photo of the Mona Lisa to make an analogy to an effective supervisor. He asked the group: "What is it about this painting that turns people on?" When he elicited the answer of her ambiguous smile, the instructor then made the point that a supervisor can challenge people by presenting an assignment with adequate ambiguity, that is, low structure and few guidelines.

Deep Think

Hold a short meditation period to encourage reflection, spark creativity, relax tensions.

Fanciful Fun

Use fantasy to stimulate interest and ideation. For example: "You are at the bottom of the sea. You notice a large coral-covered cave. You are attracted to the cave. You enter it and you encounter . . ."

Tap Participant Creativity

Ask the group to take a sheet of paper or newsprint and draw a picture (a graphic or illustration) that symbolizes in art form the topic or problem (leadership, the organization, communication). Collect a number of them and share them with the total group, or post all of them on the wall.

Conjecture Challenge

Stimulate audience response and creativity by the "What if . . ." approach. "What if you had a perfect organization (or supervisor)? What might those attributes or characteristics be like?" "If you could set all the goals (or standards) for this project (or program), what would they be?"

Participant Presentation

In advance of the talk or lecture ask one or more audience members to make a short statement or give a brief presentation on the topic. This will provide the audience with a change of pace. However, individual presentations can be "deadly." After all, you may merely be substituting one lecturer for another. So try to give the presenter some advance coaching, if at all possible. This should prevent a dull, rambling, semi-coherent presentation. Some added answers to this problem are to select able presenters only, to keep the reports short (three to five minutes), and if more than one presenter is used, to scatter the presentations throughout the talk.

Movement and Muscles

Assign a task requiring participants to leave their "safe" locations and to stretch a muscle or two in the process. For example, a college statistics instructor asked his students to arrange themselves on the floor on a straight chalk line according to an assigned score [8]. They immediately found themselves in the classic normal or bell-shaped curve. He then asked how they felt and those in the well-populated middle responded "crowded." He then went out to the three standard deviations and the one student there reported her feelings of "loneliness." The result from a learning standpoint: enhanced recall becomes possible, not only because of cognitive images, but with muscles and visual memory of distances.

Chair Fare

Midway in your talk, do what one creative speaker did: ask everyone to stand and lift up their chairs. Several found a dollar bill posted on the bottom of their chairs! The speaker then made his point: "You have to get off your butt to make a buck!"

Pick a Panel

Call on several participants to serve as panel discussants, summarizers, and debaters. Then have the entire group interact with panelists.

Panel Probers

Instead of the audience asking questions of the panel—the usual procedure—have the panel ask questions of the participants. The purpose is to define, clarify, narrow, and/or zero in on issues, concerns, learning, and unresolved questions.

Action Plan

At session's end, provide participants with "A Guide For Action" worksheet which has questions such as these on it:

- ☐ As a result of this session I will _____.
- ☐ The forces favorable to my action plan are _____.
- ☐ The forces unfavorable to my action plan are _____.
- ☐ I can overcome these limiting forces by _____.

Q&A Period

Use an extensive (as opposed to a brief) question and answer period at talk's end, thereby minimizing lecture time considerably.

Question Reversal

Turn a question back to the audience: "I have some ideas on this subject. But I think it would be more useful if we got some *participant* reactions to the question."

Using "Closure" Techniques to Keep Trainees "Tuned In"

You may recall from your Psych 101 course that Gestalt psychology is a school that interprets phenomena as organized wholes, rather than as collections of separate parts. A significant concept from that school is that of "closure," which is the natural tendency of our minds to "fill in" information that's missing. A leading Gestaltist, psychologist Max Wertheimer, coined the term *closure*. He asserted that we have a perceptual *need* to close in or complete apparently incomplete figures.

Trainer Michael J. Zosel quotes Harry Woodward of Wilson Learning, who defines closure as: "the process of mentally adding something that is missing; creating a whole from a series of parts; making a connection between things that may seem unrelated" [9].

Closure, says Zosel, can accomplish the following in the classroom:

- ☐ Maintain participants' curiosity, motivation, and attentiveness.
- ☐ Involve participants in the learning process.
- ☐ Permit learners to discover and solve questions about concepts and methods.
- ☐ Enhance memory capabilities (reinforcement for better retention).
- ☐ Cut down on possible information overload.

Zosel suggests that we consider in our course design the following six major closure techniques, particularly useful in pepping up formal presentations:

1. *Asking questions of participants.* This tool is a great attention getter, for it stimulates curiosity and mental activity. It also challenges participants to draw on their deductive reasoning skills. In ancient times Socrates used it to lead his students to new knowledge. He recognized that asking questions can help people to make connections and do their own problem solving. And by mentally interacting with a concept, one is likely to understand and remember it better.

Note: A full treatment of this technique is given below. See: "Asking Questions of Participants."

2. *Using "embedded messages."* The idea is to create a "subliminal" effect to stimulate greater learning. *Example:* signs on the walls which display key facts to be internalized. Trainees will *naturally* make connections between what is given in the lecture and the embedded messages. To assure trainee-developed closure, the lecturer should *not* point to the signs lest he/she deprive the learner of the opportunity to create his/her own associations.

3. *Employing "analogous" images.* Since pictures are worth a thousand words, images which help participants make connections to what is said can enhance understanding. *Examples:* humorous cartoons; stories such as "The Tortoise and the Hare," which stress the importance of using steady or "tortoise-like" concepts for manufacturing, particularly using "Just in Time" (JIT) manufacturing methods.

4. *Using "word play."* Puns are useful stimulators of attention, curiosity, and amusement. "Twisted" words require more active thinking about the information being presented; they thus enhance learning.

5. *Introducing incongruous surprises.* Again, this is an attention getter and learning enhancer. *Example:* As previously described in "Chair Fare," putting dollar bills under the seat of a chair, which trainees are told to lift and examine, to make the point that "You have to get off your butt to make a buck." *Other devices:* standing on a chair, misstating a clear-cut fact, creating a certain amount of confusion and allowing class members to straighten out the confusion, or using unusual props.

6. *Letting participants fill in the blanks.* The instructor should develop course materials that have sentences with key words missing. As the lecture proceeds, the trainees fill in the blanks. This is essentially akin to note taking during a lecture, which is a form of reinforcement and thus enhances learning.

Key points:

1. Include closure activities when you design your courses to keep your trainees "tuned in."

2. The six closure techniques promote enhanced learning and reinforcement because they augment cognitive activity by tapping several of our senses—auditory, visual, kinesthetic (muscular stimulation in writing while filling in the blanks).

USING THE QUESTION-AND-ANSWER PERIOD EFFECTIVELY

A question-and-answer period has these primary purposes [10]:

- ☐ To check understanding and retention.
- ☐ To correct misunderstandings and misperceptions.
- ☐ To learn of knowledge gaps that require attention.
- ☐ To learn of possible resistances to the learning.
- ☐ To check the extent to which the material presented met needs.
- ☐ To provide a chance to discuss and apply the new learning.
- ☐ To serve as a means of reemphasis or summary.
- ☐ To discuss possible added help the learners may need to be able to apply what was learned.

Note that all of these stated purposes relate to the furthering of genuine learning goals. Conversely, if the question-and-answer period is conducted "Because there's some time left over," or "It's the courteous thing to do," or "The boss expects me to do it," or "It's a good way of cutting down on 'prep time' for the lecture period," then the odds are that the benefits to the group will be minimal.

The question-and-answer period is a traditional way of involving participants. It will not, of course, involve everyone, particularly if a large audience is present and time is limited. But besides the lack of opportunity, many participants hesitate to ask a question for fear of "looking bad" in front of others. In various ways our culture tends to produce a reluctance to ask questions; it stifles natural tendencies toward curiosity. Thus, according to social psychologist Caryl Marsh, children learn very early on the following "don'ts" which are often carried on to adult life [11]:

- ☐ Don't ask questions, especially of strangers. Why not? It's impolite and could be dangerous.

☐ Don't risk asking questions that may embarrass someone or bare his/her ignorance.

☐ Don't ask questions that may challenge someone's authority or may be perceived as belligerent.

☐ Don't show your own ignorance by asking a stupid question.

☐ Don't bother busy people with questions.

Trainers may also have "inner restraints" that subtly inhibit participants from questioning them, says Dr. Marsh. These include:

☐ An actual dislike of being questioned.

☐ A fear of showing one's ignorance or being "bested" by a participant.

☐ A fear of exposing something of which one may be ashamed.

☐ A fear of discussing "painful" subject matter.

☐ A reluctance to share knowledge representing personal or group power or a fear of accidentally revealing something confidential.

☐ A feeling of fatigue, time pressures, and a resentment against those who ask questions that waste time.

These fears were expressed by docents (tour guides in an art museum) who were interviewed for an experiment conducted by Dr. Marsh on the encouragement of visitor questions. Her interviews also revealed the circumstances that encouraged the asking of questions. If an authority figure—parent, aunt, uncle, teacher—served as a role model who exhibited and encouraged curiosity, the willingness to ask questions "rubbed off" on the docents as children.

Marsh's museum experiment on the encouragement of questions required the docents to use two potent techniques in their work with museum visitors: *modeling* and *extended wait-time.* Modeling entailed *asking the visitors questions* that they (the visitors) wanted to pose but felt too constrained to ask. This procedure, it was found, encouraged the visitors to ask more profound, interpretive questions rather than routine, factual ones. The wait-time procedure entailed waiting *six* seconds after a profound question was asked of the visitors. Prior research with elementary school teachers had indicated that

the teachers who used a wait-time of three seconds for the first student to respond to a question produced more interpretive questions and more frequent questions as opposed to those who waited only one second.

The results of Marsh's experiment were dramatic. On tours *before* the experiment, the visitor group asked about seven questions per tour, most of which were "safe" questions such as "Is the artist still alive?" But on the experimental tours, where the docents asked interpretive questions ("Why is this art?"), the visitors in turn asked seven times more interpretive questions per tour.

The research in the elementary school situation and that of Dr. Marsh in the museum indicate clearly that the trainer can hardly treat the question-and-answer period lightly. Certainly the question-and-answer period is an integral part of the learning (and lecturing) process. It, therefore, should be approached properly. Here are some skill pointers to ensure an effective Q&A period:

☐ A good way to communicate effectively that you really want questions is to leave a good block of time for that purpose at lecture's end. For example, if your session is 90 minutes long, leave 30 minutes for questions. Better still, divide the time equally. Nothing is more ineffective and irritating than for the instructor to say: "We've just about used up our time." (Question: Why did you?) "So we'll only be able to take a couple of questions." If you "can only take a couple of questions," you may be saying (or be perceived as saying):

"My material really wasn't that profound or provocative. So why should I expect anyone to want to explore this stuff further?"

"Those clods out there aren't bright enough to have more than a question or two anyhow."

"My anxiety level is such that I don't care for any heckling."

☐ Provide 3" × 5" cards or a question form to participants to encourage the posing of questions. These procedures are ways to overcome the embarrassment of questioning a speaker before others.

☐ Respond to the questioner by name, if at all possible. ("John has an interesting question . . .") The questioner and the audience will appreciate your attempt at personalization.

☐ Anticipate a possible lag in the posing of questions. If you do this, you won't panic over the silence. Instead, you can use the pressure of the silence to elicit a question from the group. The audience will probably be uncomfortable with the silence (unlike yourself!), and this will soon provoke a question. *Skill pointer:* The wait will *appear* longer than it actually is. If the silence won't break after you have given it a fair trial, you have two alternatives:

1. You can ask the audience a question to get things going again.

2. You can call it quits ("Thank you, I enjoyed working with you . . ." or "If there are no more questions, let's move on to . . .").

☐ Avoid "windy" responses. This will give you more time to answer other questions as well as reduce the "yawn factor" by the group.

☐ Don't try to field every question yourself. Instead, toss a question now and then back to the group. Say something along this line: "I've got some ideas on that one. But I think it would be more helpful if we got some other views on this."

☐ Treat irrelevant questions graciously. Invite the questioner to see you at the break or after the talk. ("That's an interesting question, but I'm not sure everyone is interested in that area. See me after the session and we'll talk about it, O.K.?")

☐ Try to defuse hostile questioners. Here are several pointers which should help [12]:

1. Rephrase the question. This will give you time to prepare your response.

2. Use the question to reinforce your views.

3. Don't get defensive. Instead, respond with humor or a short anecdote to lighten the mood.

4. If you can't provide an exact response to the total question, talk about a phase you are sure about.

5. Don't take the "attack" personally. Anticipate that sometimes hostility goes with the territory. Be calm, focused, and courteous to the aggressive questioner.

☐ Don't let any one person monopolize the question period. Instead, try to involve different participants. In a large lecture hall, select questions from different parts of the room.

☐ If you can't answer a question, admit it. Bluffing your way through a phony response won't aid your credibility. You may wish to ask for help from the audience in some circumstances. ("I can't respond to this one. Can anyone help us on this?") Or offer to get the answer later.

☐ If there is a likely possibility that the question was not heard (large or noisy audience, poor acoustics, low voice of questioner) or not understood by the audience, repeat it before responding. Better still, *rephrase* it so that the questioner (and the other participants) will know you understood the question and are interested in it. Your paraphrasing of the question is preferable to asking the participant (or someone else) to restate it. Why? Because if you ask the participant to restate or repeat it, the obvious assumptions are that either you didn't understand it or it was poorly phrased. Of course, if you really didn't understand the question, be candid about it. ("I'm sorry. I failed to catch your question. Could you try me again, please?")

☐ In responding to questions, make certain you show the interrogator that you feel good about his/her query. ("That's a very pertinent question," or "Your question has some profound implications," or "I'm glad you raised that point.") Positive reinforcement is a tremendous way to keep the questions coming to you.

☐ Avoid irritating your questioner with sarcastic responses, putdowns, argumentation, and other attempts at "one-upmanship." The cardinal rule is that you can't win an argument with a participant. The audience will swiftly rally to that person's side (the questioner is "one of them," you know), and the questions from the others will dry up fast.

☐ If possible, secure questions from participants *in advance* of the formal session. This type of prework will not only get people into the act very early on, but will provide a stimulus for others to pose questions in your question period. *A skill point:* Provide the question request form for this, as shown in Appendix 65, as an enticer and encourager.

☐ If time runs out and it appears that there are still a good number of unanswered questions, you may wish to leave the Question Request Form, as shown in Appendix 65, with your name and mailing address on it. This procedure will allow those who are "unsatisfied" to forward the form to you, and you can dictate responses on it later on.

Several added pointers are presented by Steve Gladis, author of *The Manager's Pocket Guide to Public Presentations*, HRD Press, Amherst, Massachusetts, 1999 [13]:

☐ Use your answers to participant questions as an opportunity to stress your main points. Have several theme statements ready to weave into your responses.

☐ Don't select questions from only one section of the room. Vary it by acknowledging questioners from both right- and left-room segments.

☐ Make it your practice to repeat questions. This shows that you are listening and may help others in the audience who may not have heard the question properly.

☐ Reword negative questions. *Example:* You are asked what your outfit is doing about the current totally unfair promotion policy. You try to take the sting out of the question by rephrasing it thusly: "The question presented relates to company promotion policy and what action is being considered about it." A neutral phrasing shifts the discussion to a more objective, professional level.

☐ Keep things on track when asked a tangential question by offering a statement such as this: "That's an interesting (or important, or significant, or profound) question, but I really believe our main issue (or concern, or need, or challenge) is . . ."

Using an Audience Panel

An interesting way to elicit questions from a large audience is to establish a participant question panel. A panel of three to four participants can pose the questions, with one of the panel members acting as moderator. To ensure that the panel works well, they should do enough "homework" so that they can ask questions with both insight and dispatch. In some cases, and if practical, you may wish to meet with the panelists in advance of the session. This will help preparation and ensure a smooth operation in the questioning period.

ASKING QUESTIONS OF PARTICIPANTS

In addition to responding to participants in the Q&A period, consider using some of your lecture time—at lecture's end and during the presentation itself—to pose questions to your training group. This approach will serve to involve participants in the instructional process. It will also help you establish rapport; gauge participant interest, knowledge and outlooks; spot possible blocks to learning; and better adjust your material to the participant group.

Trainer/consultant Dorothy Leeds sees questions as an extremely powerful tool for the trainer. Certainly both Socrates in ancient Greece and game show conductors in modern times have long recognized that people learn from and are fascinated by questions. She states that questions enhance your communication abilities in these powerful ways [14]:

1. *Questions demand answers.* A question provides an electric shock to the mind. When we receive a question, we feel compelled to answer. So it is a great way to get communication started.

2. *Questions allow you to set direction.* As a trainer you have an agenda or, more precisely, a course outline. You know very specifically where you want to take your participants. Questions are a key tool to assist you in that endeavor.

3. *Questions provide information.* You want to know at the outset the state of trainee interest and knowledge, as well as their strengths and weaknesses. Later, you wish to check to see what has been understood and learned, how effective your training has been. Your concern, then, is to get the right information at the right time.

4. *Questions help participants tackle and solve their own problems.* Thoughtful questions can lead trainees to devise their own answers to

their problems, as opposed to adopting "tried and true" solutions offered by the trainer.

5. *Questions provide insight into participants' thinking.* People, as diverse personalities with different life/work experiences, arrive at their conclusions in different ways. Certainly, you, as the trainer, want to know what people think, how they are responding to the training they have experienced.

Leeds also points out that trainers often encounter an "information barrier," that is, getting the right information from one's participants is typically difficult. Responses to trainer questions may not provide the whole story, or even accurate and complete information. So there is a need to probe and clarify to ensure the obtaining of truly useful information. More specifically, trainers are likely to encounter these four communication barriers:

☐ *Participants may be reluctant to volunteer information.* Various fears, real and imagined, enter into this—fear of looking inept by providing inappropriate, off-target, or unwanted information; fear that one has not really understood the question; fear of being regarded as too "avant garde" (too innovative, radical, or forward looking).

☐ *Participants may talk in generalities.* Why? Because they often are too lazy, afraid, or impatient to state their real feelings. They may disagree with the trainer on a point but feel it is "wiser" to soft-pedal their disagreement.

☐ *Participants may make wrong assumptions.* For example, participants with long-time experience as managers may assume that the management course they have been asked to attend has little to offer them. They may consequently enter with a "show-me" attitude. Others may assume that the course or program will answer every back-home problem they have, as opposed to offering general guides and possibly some new tools with which to work on these problems. They may thus be disappointed with the training they receive. Obviously, assumptions, especially if erroneous, are likely to influence the responses that are rendered.

☐ *Participants perceive things differently.* All of us have a "world view" which reflects our experience, education, and values. Our perceptions in particular instances may be out of sync with the perceptions of others. Thus, trainees may feel that the trainer is looking for certain answers, for agreement rather than disagreement, for support rather than criticism of organizational policies and practices, and the like.

Training consultant Rodney P. Beary says that well-crafted questions serve these nine main purposes in a training activity [15]:

1. *To serve as an icebreaker and/or opener.* In our first chapter we discussed the importance of icebreakers, which loosen up the participant group, and openers, which are used to ease into the course's subject matter. A question to participants can serve either or both of these purposes. For example, you can divide your total group into teams (three to four participants) to discuss a pertinent question. This will help people get to know one another, make them more comfortable with the new training experience, and give them an entree into the forthcoming subject matter.

2. *To assess knowledge level.* The comments from the teams will also give you a good fix on how familiar they are with course content. You certainly don't want to either underestimate or overestimate their knowledge/expertise levels. If you can learn early on of their subject matter familiarity, you can (a) better utilize participant talents and (b) make adjustments in your presentation to meet their needs more fully.

3. *To assess attitudes.* Early comments from the group can help you determine interest and enthusiasm levels. You can also determine the presence of any negative attitudes, such as long-held resentments toward bosses or the total organization, possible feelings that bosses "don't walk the talk," feelings of resentment about attending the training program, and so on. You may not be able to work through all these sour attitudes, but you're much better off knowing than not knowing about them. Forewarned is forearmed, as the old saying has it.

4. *To deflect antagonism.* Some participants, for any one of a number of reasons, may feel hostile toward the trainer. Your job at the course's outset is to defuse this anger, if at all possible. A good way to do this is to shift the focus to course subject matter via several well-selected questions such as:

☐ What hopes and fears do you have about this course?

☐ What is the organization's reason for sponsoring this course? Why do they want to take you away from your busy jobs to experience this training? (The objective of questions of this sort is to get participants to verbalize that the organization does have a worthwhile rationale for this training.)

☐ What key issues do you feel should be discussed in this kind of course? (Here you are showing that you want to make the course more participant-oriented.)

☐ What needs to happen, between now and when the course ends on Friday, to make the course successful and worthwhile for you?

5. *To spark discussion.* Well-chosen questions are great thought-stimulators. People may hear a statement and accept it passively, but a question forces people to react, to explore, to imagine, to assess, to express their own view.

6. *To provide "show and tell" opportunities.* If you operate on the assumption that not all of the knowledge and wisdom resides in the front of the room, at the podium, you will want to let your participants "into the act." By giving them a chance to share their expertise, you not only let them learn from one another, but you give them a chance "to shine," to receive recognition for their knowledge and insights.

Assume you are giving a talk on delegation. As an opening question, you might say something like this: "Before I give you all the reasons why delegation is worthwhile and teach you how to make it work better, let me ask you why delegation may not work. In other words, realistically speaking, what are some of the barriers to delegation?"

7. *To link one topic to another.* You can achieve smooth transitions from one subject to another by posing a question which provides a solid connection between the two. Some typical questions are these:

☐ What did you learn about communication that has a bearing on motivation, our next topic?

☐ O.K., we learned a lot about how to deal with absenteeism. But how can we prevent it from happening in the first instance? (Here the switch is from instruction on problem solving to problem prevention.)

8. *To augment/enrich learning.* When presenting data about various studies and surveys, it makes a lot of sense to let the group join in by having them present data about their own experiences or attitudes. You can then use the group-generated data as a basis for increasing their understanding of the "outside" data you are introducing.

9. *To facilitate team development.* You can use the training session as an opportunity for work groups to zero in on problems they encounter frequently in their unit. As an example, assume that your participants are in customer service work and that they regularly encounter hostile customers. You thus might ask: "What can management do to reduce some of the severe reactions which some of our customers project at us?"

Key point: Include the "ask before you tell" technique in your repertoire of instructional techniques. It can provide a variety of solid payoffs for you and your learners.

Characteristics of a Good Question

The above paragraphs have described the psychological dynamics and the purposes of well-crafted questions. However, before you pose a question to your participants, you should have a "good fix" on what constitutes a good question.

Most formal presenters would agree that a good question has these characteristics:

☐ *Brevity.* Long, windy, and wordy questions overload people's intake valves; they are sure-fire ways of creating confusion and thus turning participants off. So keep them "lean" and short.

☐ *Clarity.* Your question should zero in on one point alone. Overly ambitious, multifaceted questions will only produce frustration, not thought.

☐ *Pertinence.* The question should be targeted to the subject being discussed. What constitutes session "enrichment" to the instructor runs the risk of being perceived as "out of the ball park" (out of context) by the participants.

☐ *Challenge.* Worthwhile questions are those that cause thought and provocation and encourage creativity, evaluation, interpretation, comparisons, contrast, synthesis, and reassessment. Accordingly, questions that only tax participants' memory banks are to be avoided.

In respect to questions that "challenge," trainers Patrick Suessmuth and Marit Strengels suggest that there are essentially three types [16]:

☐ *Convergent*—Brings together facts to form another fact or theory. For example: "Based on the behaviors you saw in the film, what principles of motivation can you develop?"

☐ *Divergent*—Evokes interpretation, explanation, and translation. For example: "How would you explain the firm's reluctance to abandon 'yesterday's breadwinners' in its product line?"

☐ *Evaluative*—Requires the making of judgments (via exploration and analysis) about the facts presented. For example: "How would you characterize the company president as a team leader? As a coach? As a communicator?"

Suessmuth and Strengels also make a distinction between *closed* and *open* questions [17]. The former merely seek information, identification, and confirmation; they thus do not really encourage active participation. For example: "What did Peter Drucker say about delegation?" "What are the different types of job evaluation plans now in vogue?" "Would you say job enrichment is preferred to job enlargement?" Conversely, open questions, which cause more active involvement by not "boxing people in," take these forms:

☐ *Subjective question*—What is your thought on the values of the young worker? Can we assume that management was correct in this case? Is

"directive" leadership best in a situation that _____ ?

☐ *Objective question*—What elements make for an effective performance review system? What distinguishes successful employment interviews from unsuccessful ones?

☐ *Problem question*—Given the climate that exists in many organizations today, what are the prospects for a viable organization development program? What is the best way to mount the career ladder in your case, given those difficulties? How would you go about delegating a particular responsibility (for example, P.R.) when you know your boss is vitally concerned about this area?

Another essential form of questioning is that which relates to *follow-up* or *probing*. This type of question enables you and the group to learn what is on the participant's mind. Suessmuth and Strengels offer five reasons to use a probing question [18]:

☐ *To clarify an answer.* At times a participant may offer a response that definitely requires clarification. A good way to do this is to ask another participant to restate what was said. A good, low-key clarifying probe for this is to say: "What did Emma mean by _____?" and sum up what was originally said. The restatement on your part is essential since it is a sure bet that a significant number of the group didn't hear (listening failure) the answer in the first place.

☐ *To justify an answer.* By asking "Why?" or "Why that?" you are augmenting the group's critical awareness.

☐ *To refocus an answer.* This is essential to getting the discussion back on track.

☐ *To expand an answer.* This is easy to do. Merely express puzzlement and wait. Or you can simply ask: "Could someone develop that thought for us?"

☐ *To redirect the answer.* This means involving other participants in addition to the original respondent. There is, of course, a natural temptation to move on to the next question once a response is secured, but we may be overlooking an opportunity to get others into the act. They may have some other insights on the issue which can enrich the discussion.

Paul Mills and Bernard Roberts, partners in a New York City communications skill firm, offer seven types of probes—essentially skill pointers—to encourage a participant to keep talking [19]:

☐ *Nonverbal probes* such as a nod of the head or a smile.

☐ *Short verbal probes* such as "Uh-huh?" "Yes?" "I understand."

☐ *"W" (or journalistic) word probes* (who, where, when, what, why, how) which elicit a great variety of information, for example: "What does that mean?" "Why did it develop as it did?"

☐ *Statement probes* such as "Tell me more" or "I would appreciate it if you could expand on that point."

☐ *Echo probes* which entail a repetition of some of the participant's words.

☐ *Reflective probes* wherein one changes the words but retains the meaning.

☐ *Specialized reflective probes* whereby one implies more than the participant actually intended, for example, "You feel *very uneasy* about taking this up with your boss?"

It should also be mentioned that the basic skills one needs to keep the ball in the participant's court, and thus to learn how the participant sees his/her world, are these: good listening ability, patience, an inviting style, and avoidance of argumentation and one-upmanship. A suggestion: Study the talk show hosts. You'll note that the better ones show a great deal of interest in what the participant has to say. They are enamored with neither their own voice nor their own wisdom. Since they truly want the other person to get into the act and have his/her say, they present an encouraging, low-key questioning style.

How to Elicit a Relevant Response from Every Participant

Savvy instructors know that they must both check for understanding now and then and keep participants thinking, alert, and involved. One good way to do this is to pose questions to the group. All of which is well and good, except for the fact that when one or two hands go up, and the instructor selects one of the eager volunteers to respond, the rest of the group automatically quit thinking about their possible answers and ready themselves to listen to the volunteer.

So by calling on the quickest, the brightest, and/or the most vocal, the instructor has deprived the others of an equal opportunity to learn. He/she has rewarded the speedy hand raisers and cheated their slower classmates by cutting off their need to think anymore.

But all is not lost, for there are techniques to elicit responses from *all* the classmates and thus to keep them all thinking and involved. Longtime trainer/consultant Dr. Scott Parry offers the following arsenal of 16 such techniques [20]:

1. Present a question, pause for ten seconds, look around the room, restate the question, allow everyone to construct an answer, then select a respondent.

2. Use an easy question, one to which everyone can readily respond out loud.

3. If your question only requires a response with a few words or numbers, have your trainees jot down their answers. Walk around the room to read the answers (is everyone correct?) and to help you decide on whom to call.

4. Ask your participants to guess about something which you are about to give them.

5. Pass out a handout having some six questions with space to write in the answers. Secure responses on a one-question-at-a-time basis, that is, learners write an answer and then their responses are discussed.

6. Pass out a preprinted response sheet to complete as the lesson/session proceeds. This might be a flow chart, checklist, schematic diagram, or list of pros and cons on which they must fill in words.

7. Pass out a self-assessment, one that is a self-scoring, quickly administered exercise to let the instructor and the learner know where the learner stands. This might be in respect to attitudes, skills, or knowledge. This device is particularly helpful to ascertain what Parry terms

"entering behavior," or the level of learner skills/knowledge on which the trainer can build.

8. Present a question which is likely to polarize the group, for example, "How many believe money is the most important motivator for secretaries?" Ask for a show of hands.

9. Use dyads (pairs): "Turn to the person on your right and tell him/her how Maslow's ideas might apply in your work." (See in Chapter 4, "Working with the Hierarchy of Needs," which explains Maslow's theory.)

10. With a large group (30 or more), give each person four large cardboard squares, each of a different color. Then present occasional multiple-choice questions with four possible responses, each alternative related to a color. Participant answers are given by raising a colored card. This enables the instructor to know how much learning has taken place.

11. If you are providing training in sales, interviewing, counseling, training, supervision, and/or other dynamic interaction/communication skills, use these procedures for active group involvement:

    a. Develop a script of the interaction.

    b. Give a number to each line in the script.

    c. Pass out copies of the numbered scripts to your participants.

    d. Refer participants to specific lines that demonstrate concepts and/or techniques presented earlier to the class. Have them make responses in a "notes" column as to whether the examples are good ones or otherwise. Be sure to ask why they answered as they did.

12. Tap action plan sheets for class involvement. Do this after each new topic, lesson, or module. *Procedures:*

    a. Ask participants to take out their action plans.

    b. Ask them to indicate what they intend to do to implement their new learnings on the job.

    c. Ask your learners to form triads with their neighbors. The trainees then read one another's plans and provide feedback on them. In effect, each serves as "consultant" to two others.

13. When teaching the learning of an entire job, have your trainees create a job description after a discussion about each task, responsibility, and procedure. Have them include criteria for proper performance. Instruct participants to discuss their job sheets with their bosses to ensure agreement on all job details.

14. Organize and direct "mini"-role plays. Have role players evaluate each other after the action: what went well ("I really liked . . .") and what could be strengthened or done better.

15. Ask questions which require silent decision making as opposed to an immediate response. *Example:* "How would you go about asking for a very well-deserved raise in recessionary times?" Or "When have you last examined your staffers' responsibilities to see if greater delegation is in order?" "What one thing might make your staff meetings more effective?"

16. If responses to a question should be anonymous because of their personal character, have participants respond on small pieces of paper. Fold these pieces up, place them in a box, then withdraw them from the box for posting on a flipchart and discussion. *Examples:* problems with one's boss; difficulties in one's marriage.

Added Skill Points

1. In most cases participants will respond voluntarily or enter into things with a little encouragement. If you do call on someone at the outset ("Can you help us on this, Pat?"), this will break the ice and others will then respond easily. To ensure that others do enter in, simply ask: "Any other thoughts on this?" or "How else might this be done?"

2. Involve the shy participant by occasionally calling on him/her to field an easy question or one in which he/she has special knowledge or experience.

3. If you wish everyone in the group to respond to a given question, use the "circular whip" technique (see Chapter 3).

QUESTIONS THAT CONCERN TRAINERS ABOUT QUESTIONS

In the previous pages we provided a number of skill pointers on the use of the Q&A period and the reverse—asking questions of the participants.

Trainer/consultant Dr. Scott B. Parry finds that in his train-the-trainer workshops on instructional skills, participants have these common questions about questions [21]:

☐ *Should the trainer toss out a question for a voluntary response or call on a trainee by name?* Dr. Parry feels that the better practice is to avoid naming a respondent in advance for these reasons: it may embarrass the participant, who may feel that he/she has been "put on the spot"; another person may be better able to provide an answer for the benefit of the group; it may discourage the rest of the group from thinking through their own answers; it may create a climate which puts the trainer in a parent-to-child relationship with the trainees.

   In some cases, however, it may be desirable to call on a particular participant because of his/her special experience, expertise, or role. *Examples:* "Pat, you have worked in the Far East . . ." "Kim, how would this issue be regarded in a hospital setting?" "Alex, as a law enforcement officer, would it be appropriate for . . .?"

☐ *How do you involve those who never volunteer, the "silent majority"?* Dr. Parry has provided a number of responses to this concern in the preceding section, "How to Elicit a Relevant Response from Every Participant."

☐ *Should the trainer repeat a participant question to be certain that everyone has fully understood it?* Ordinarily it should not be necessary, and to do it for every question would be somewhat boring. So the best practice is to limit your repeat restatement of the question to situations when it is necessary, for example, the question is poorly worded or unusually complex, or the questioner didn't speak up loudly enough for everyone to pick it up.

☐ *What if the respondent gives a wrong answer, particularly if he/she is a high-ranking individual in the group?* Don't worry about rank or status. Everyone in the group can be in error or have misconceptions. But we do want to "save face" for everyone, so broaden your response out along this line: "How does the rest of the class feel about this approach (or answer)?" The merits of this technique are that you're using the

group as a resource and avoiding putting yourself in the correcting role.

   Note: A poor answer from one person may indicate that others are experiencing a like difficulty.

☐ *What if I don't understand a participant's answer?* You have these options:

   a. Frankly state you didn't understand the response and ask for a rewording. (The author uses this technique: "I'm sorry, but I didn't grasp your thought. Could you please try me again?")

   b. Restate what you understood, if your understanding was only partial. Let the trainee supply the needed clarification or amplification.

   c. Ask for help from the group: "I'm not sure that I really caught Charles's thought/response. Can someone help me on this?"

☐ *How do I deal with an extremely slow, rambling, repetitious or disorganized thought?* Consider interrupting the respondent by stating "I think I understand your thought. You're saying (or feel) that . . ." Or consider asking the group to help out: "Can anyone summarize Mary's statement?"

☐ *What if no one responds to my question?* Possible reasons for this are as follows:

   a. The question may have been so simple or obvious that no one wishes to look stupid by responding.

   b. The class may not be "warmed up" yet.

   c. No one may legitimately know the answer, indicating either poor instruction or a question posed prematurely.

   d. Perhaps no one understood it. Consider rephrasing it.

☐ *How do I deal with an irrelevant, possibly distracting question?* If you can provide a short answer, do so to end the "disruptive" behavior. If the questioner is getting you and the group off track, consider saying, "Fred, I'm having trouble tying your question into our discussion of . . . Am I missing something?" This approach gives the participant a chance to (a) rephrase the question or further explain its relevance or (b) simply drop it and admit to the question being "way out in left field."

☐ *What if no one answers the question? Should I, as trainer, answer my own question?* You may wish to wait a bit until someone breaks the silence. Or a rephrasing may be in order. Sometimes you can ask participants to turn to a neighbor and discuss the question in a dyad. If you do this, monitor the dyadic discussions to learn why the group had trouble with your question.

Note: If you answer your own question, you're defeating the purpose of asking a question of the group. Inability to respond to a question may indicate poor question presentation, possible irrelevancy, or actual inability of the group to respond. Your task here is to diagnose the situation since people are ordinarily challenged by a question and eager or willing to respond.

☐ *What do I do if I don't know the answer to a question put to me? Will I lose credibility?* Simply say that you'll try to find out for the next meeting. Bluffing will give you an instant loss of credibility. Also, consider asking group members if they have an answer.

☐ *How do I deal with a question that's really a statement/opinion?* Sometimes trainees want to offer a point and do this by disguising it as a question. A possible response: "That's a good question. What's your own thinking on it?" In effect, you let the participant make his/her point without trying to answer it yourself or passing it on to the group.

☐ *Do I handle a question about something covered ten minutes ago?* If it's a question requiring only a short answer, do so. If it now appears that something was fuzzy rather than clear, possibly for the entire group, respond thusly: "We talked about this a little while ago, but maybe we didn't really button it down properly. Does anyone else have the same question?" If others need more discussion of the question, provide it. If no one else has this need, you may wish to ask the lone questioner to see you at the break or after class "so that we don't take up everyone else's time, O.K.?"

☐ *What if the learners refuse to accept my response, particularly if it deals with corporate policy or procedure?* If the issue involves com-

pany policy or practice, don't take either a defensive or a critical stance. Just say you're merely explaining the policy. If you anticipate some resistance, you may wish to invite a senior official to explain the policy.

If it's not a matter of company policy/procedure, you might ask your group: "What is your experience with this technique? Does it work in whole or in part or not at all?" A good way to defuse possible resentment is to state at the outset that what you're going to present probably won't be acceptable to everyone. The author, in anticipation, uses the metaphor of a cafeteria. "Take only that which makes sense to you or meets your needs. So if the answer I or the course provides isn't relevant, don't act on it."

Involving Individuals

The techniques to secure participation *before* the talk starts, as previously described, relate to the involvement of the *total* audience or group. It may also be desirable to involve actively *one or two* participants in the program for various purposes. Some examples follow:

☐ Appoint various individuals to execute these special roles:

1. Stretch monitor—This participant stands up and calls "stretch" whenever he/she feels it's needed.

2. Handout distributors.

3. Card collectors (the cards have participant-prepared questions or comments on them for response by the speaker).

4. A timer (if needed).

5. Jargon stopper—This assignment entails standing up or raising one's hand when an unexplained or undefined concept, word, or phrase is used by the lecturer or a fellow participant.

6. Card-carrying member—Appoint four or five participants to display large posters bearing key points or topics in large print. The procedure may be used at the outset to indicate overall topic coverage, possibly midway in the lecture to summarize or highlight points already made, or at talk's end as

a summary. As an example of the summary at the end of a talk on persuasive communication and/or selling, the four posters shown in Figure 18-3 might be used.

Figure 18-3. Example of posters displayed by participants to highlight key points made by a presenter.

☐ Conduct a demonstration role play involving yourself and one or two participants (for example, on a sales problem or a disciplinary problem).

☐ Have two participants conduct an impromptu interview that may set the stage for your comments as speaker (for example, the difficulty of introducing change in an organization, or how to deal with a mid-career manager who has "plateaued out").

☐ Have one or more participants present a short report on a previously assigned topic.

WANT TO UPGRADE YOUR QUESTIONING SKILL?

Since you've now read the text on the art of posing questions for your participants, you know the importance of it. You may also have picked up a number of skill pointers to augment your skill as a questioner. But there may still be room for improvement. If so, trainer/consultant Dorothy Leeds, author of *The 7 Powers of Questions* (Perigee, East Rutherford, New Jersey, 2000), offers these six advisories [22]:

☐ *Assessment of your current skill.* Leeds asks: Do you ask questions this year in the same manner

as you did the prior year? Do you ask identical questions of everyone regardless of the personality or situation? If your response to these two questions is "yes," it's probably time for a change. Consider, then, making these adjustments: Turn general questions into more specific ones; e.g., instead of asking "What ideas have we discussed so far?" ask "What are the three most important challenges which lie ahead?" And if you're performing a needs analysis, pose some new questions, for every situation is different. In today's world the scene changes year to year.

☐ *Pinpoint your purpose.* If your question lacks a goal/objective, skip the question. Purposeless questions have no payoff. The best way to overcome purpose-free questions is to prepare (write) them in advance. As you write, ask yourself: "What's my goal?" "What response am I seeking?" "What follow-up questions might be in order?" "Is my goal to have my trainees dig deeper, to reach an agreement, or to empathize?"

☐ *Recognize participant differences.* Since people are different, try to gear your questions to those differences. Recognize, says Leeds, that some trainees are detail people, while others are broad-gauged types. Some are right-brained, while others are left-brained. Also consider such factors as gender, personality, and relationship. In sum, you can't assume that "one size fits all," so take a custom-made approach instead.

☐ *Watch wording.* Besides the use of the journalist's questions—who, what, where, when, why, and how—try more thought-provoking words such as describe, analyze, explain, develop, expand, compare, contrast. Also, use inviting, colorful phrases such as "give me a road map" (or "a ballpark estimate"), "any possible boomerang effect?", "What might lie down the road?", "Can we translate today's pain into tomorrow's promise?" The idea, of course, is to achieve emotional as well as intellectual involvement of your participants.

☐ *Be sensitive to your nonverbal communication.* Recognize that whether we know it or not, or intend it or not, we, as trainers/instructors, are communicating all the time. And your body language is a key part of that communication activity.

It can reveal your level of interest, enthusiasm, concern, support, friendliness, trust, etc. Be aware that your eye contact is a big aspect of your communication modus operandi.

☐ *Listen to responses.* Why ask an important question if you are preoccupied with another thought or bored with it all? And feigning listening is worse than listening half-heartedly or not at all. One way to ensure that you do listen acutely is to paraphrase the responses to some of your questions. Not only will this procedure ensure that you listen, but it will assure the respondents that you really heard what was said and are interested in it. The bottom line, says Dorothy Leeds: "When your questions have a clear and specific purpose, listening is involving and enjoyable."

INFORMATION-CENTERED VS. LEARNER-CENTERED INSTRUCTIONAL STYLES

To put the lecture or "information-centered instruction style" in proper perspective, we should compare it with what longtime trainer/consultant Dr. Scott Parry calls the "learning-centered instructional style." He states that the lecture approach, as an educational model, was appropriate several decades ago when the training goal was only to equip students to become routine, unquestioning employees in offices and industrial plants. But the world has changed. Employees are expected to be active problem solvers and decision makers and to think in terms of improving quality and service.

So these newer skill requirements require a vastly different trainer style. Note, too, that instructors/trainers, intentionally or otherwise, serve as models for their trainees. Learning to listen dutifully is hardly as important as learning dynamic problem-solving skills.

Parry uses 11 factors to clarify the distinction between the two instructional styles [23]:

1. The *objective* in the older, traditional style is to accomplish "coverage," to get a lot of points across while following a detailed lesson plan. Conversely, in the learner-centered approach, the aim is to change behavior or upgrade the learner's performance.

2. A more *basic objective* in the lecture method, not necessarily stated, is often to meet the instructor's need to be recognized as the "authority/expert." In the learner-centered approach the only goal is to meet the learner's needs to perform better.

3. The *instructor's role* in the information-centered approach is merely to disseminate information via lecturing. Conversely, in the newer approach, the trainer is an "arranger of experiences," a facilitator, a catalyst, and a moderator.

4. The *methodology* employed is in clear contrast: talk, show and tell, and consume all or most of the available class time vs. function in a Socratic (question-asking) manner and strictly limit one's talking role.

5. The *questioning* style is also vastly different: "Do you understand?" "Any questions?" vs. "Why do we do it this way?" "Is this the best way?" "What if we . . .?" "What would you do if . . .?"

6. Obviously, the *learner role* is totally dissimilar in the two styles: An information-centered learner is passive, absorbing information and repeating it back to the information disseminator. A learner-centered learner is active; he/she learns by doing and corrects his/her own behavior as a result of experience.

7. *Feedback from the learner* is used differently, too. In the information-centered style, tasks are typically used to assess understanding and retention. In the learner-centered style, feedback functions as a vital check to see if the learner can apply what was learned and whether more practice is essential.

8. *Feedback to the instructor* in the older, traditional method is accomplished by asking the trainees if they have any questions and/or having them repeat what the instructor has presented. In the learner-centered style, the idea is to give the learners tasks/situations to practice and to make learners apply new skills, procedures, and concepts.

9. *Control over the learner* is also accomplished differently: reward and punishment (sanctions, embarrassment) vs. positive and negative reinforcement (praise and constructive criticism).

10. *Qualifications* appropriate to the two styles are these: the information-centered style requires an "expert" who knows it all—procedure, rules, the whole system. The newer instructional style favors a non-directive counselor type who can encourage learning via his/her functioning as a moderator, catalyst, and facilitator.

11. Finally, the *basic philosophy* of the information disseminator, says Parry, is "There's so much our trainees have got to know before they'll ever be able to do the job correctly (before they'll ever know what I know). Much repetition is necessary." The learner-centered instructor sees the instructional world differently: "We learn, not by being told, but by experiencing the consequences of our own actions. Learning is an experiential process. We learn by doing."

PREPARING FOR PERPLEXING PROBLEMS

One might imagine that delivering a presentation is a form of training that should be quite crisis-free. After all, a lecture automatically places you in control of things, right? Well, not exactly. Unfortunately, old Murphy (of Murphy's Law fame) is liable to create (or at least predict) a catastrophe or two for you. Trainer Stephen D. Boyd advises to expect the unexpected. He cites these surprises which any presenter may encounter: mental blocks, emotional upsets, hecklers, somnolent audiences, poor introductions, and electrical disasters. Here are Boyd's suggestions to cope with these humongous headaches [24]:

Mental blocks. All is going well when, in the middle of a presentation, you hit a mental block. What to do? First, don't panic. Instead, pause briefly. This may help to reconstruct your thoughts. If the pause is of no help, just repeat what you were saying. This may get you back on track.

If repetition doesn't work, smile and admit to your audience that you have forgotten what to say next. Your audience will empathize with you and breathe a sigh of relief because of your candor. Actually, they had already sensed that you were "lost at sea."

Now you are free to take appropriate action to return to where you should be. This may mean going to your briefcase, sorting through transparencies, or possibly asking your audience what seems to be a logical statement at this point in your talk.

Audiences are rarely unforgiving, so they will be pulling for you to locate your place and go on.

Uncontrollable weeping or laughter. Anticipate that there may be a highly emotional point in your presentation. So prepare, instead of losing (and having to regain) your composure. First, write out the emotional part so that you can read rather than speak it. Concentrate on your written words, for that will keep you on a logical thinking path in lieu of reacting on an emotional level.

Another procedure is to think of an inanimate object or scene, such as the right rear tire of your car, your concrete (or flagstone) patio, a set of bleachers in the school gymnasium. This logical focus should help you skip the possible emotional reaction and keep you fully on track and in control.

Also consider practicing your presentation with a colleague. This will provide experience in coping with emotional material.

Finally, seek out an inattentive person in your audience. Focus on him/her to give yourself another goal other than the emotional content of your material.

Hecklers. This is any disruption or interruption of your talk, for example, a private conversation between two audience members or an obnoxious disagreer. The best course of action is to ignore the heckler(s). It may only be temporary. Also, peer pressure may take care of your problem child.

Optionally, you may wish to respond actively in this manner: "May I finish my point? Then you may have two minutes to refute my position. This will let me finish my thought and you can have your turn, too. O.K.?" Setting that time limit is paramount.

In extreme cases you may simply have to cut your presentation short. But whatever you do, keep your cool. Don't make the heckler look stupid. You don't want your audience to sympathize with the underdog.

A dozing audience. Your audience begins to nod off, shuffle their feet, or noticeably glance at their watches. What to do to salvage things?

First, change your pace. If you're talking loudly, lower your voice. If you're behind the podium, move into your audience. If you're working from the front of the room, move to the back. Use a visual aid. Any change will be an attention getter and an audience arouser.

If you are using transparencies, toss in one with a relevant cartoon. Or introduce a story. Introduce a question-and-answer period to get involvement. Ask people to volunteer what they have learned up to this point. A stand-up mini-stretch break, in place, may help, too.

Poor introductions. Assume your introducer has loused up his/her introduction of you by providing misinformation or telling an inappropriate joke. How do you react? Above all, neither retaliate in kind by putting down your inept introducer nor refer to the problem in any way. Instead, move right into your prepared material.

If you want your audience to learn something worthwhile about yourself and/or your work, introduce your self as part of your talk—for example, "In my most recent book . . ." or "in my stint at Corporation XYZ . . ."

Electrical failures. You can't get the power back on your own, but you can move closer to the audience so that they can hear you more easily and you can see them better. You can also trot out your funniest and most stimulating stories and examples first. Hopefully, you have mentally arranged your material so that you can do that. It also helps to keep people's attention by moving around the room.

You may also draw on a few one-liners such as "The hotel manager told me that his accountant is a little slow in paying their utility bills." Or "The hotel has a backup electric generator, but no one can find it in the dark." "If you were up late last night, it's O.K. to catch up on your sleep now." "I'd suggest to those of you who are taking notes that it's O.K. to light that candle you brought along."

Strategies for Three Additional Problems

Added problems that may arise during a presentation involve the following [25]:

☐ Unwieldy group size
☐ Group silence
☐ Group-induced tangents

Unwieldy group size

If you are working with a large group of participants, 40 to 75, not everyone will get a chance to be heard. Of course, reliance on extensive small group work is a good answer to the problem. However, if you are mak-

ing a formal presentation, adequate "air time" for all or most participants will be difficult to provide. You can anticipate that the most aggressive and loudest trainees will grab all the opportunities to be heard. These strategies can help to minimize the frustrations of those who can't get a chance to present their ideas:

1. Acknowledge the problem at the outset. If your participants know that you are aware of the problem, they are more likely to be patient and less likely to become frustrated.

2. Advise them that you will try to be fair to everyone by working your way around the room, beginning on one side. This is not only a fair procedure, but it will eliminate the need for trainees to sit frustratingly with their hands in the air. It will also encourage full listening to other people's comments, as opposed to vying to secure the trainer's attention.

3. Procedurally, stand on the opposite side of the room from the trainees when they are speaking. With a large group, it may be difficult for participants to hear other trainees' comments, particularly since trainees tend to present their observations to the trainer. This strategy is designed to get the trainee, as speaker, to talk loudly so all in the room can benefit from what is said.

Group silence

A large group will discourage less verbal and less courageous participants from making inputs. No one wants to risk looking "stupid" before his/her peers. Here are some strategies to get people to open up:

1. Warm up the group before you plunge into your presentation. Use as many icebreakers and/or openers as may be necessary.

2. If the silence is total, address the issue head on. Ask participants why they are reluctant to speak up. Advise them that prior groups have been very vocal about the issues involved, showing no reluctance at all. Also, indicate that people learn by active rather than passive participation. By taking a proactive stance on their silence, you communicate loud and clear to anyone who might wish to speak up that this is a very legitimate expectation of this course/program and one which the trainer supports wholeheartedly.

3. After breaks and lunch, ask: "Would anyone like to share what points came up on that issue in the course of your discussion during the break?"

4. Don't fill the void of silence yourself. Some participants may feel comfortable with the trainer doing all the work for them, but that comfort comes at the expense of their learning. Participants learn best when they are active—questioning, commenting, debating, testing their own ideas—rather than passively holding back.

5. Be sensitive to nonverbal communication. Sudden forward leans, eye rolls, eyes lighting up, etc. may tell you that people are with you. You may wish to process (interpret) these nonverbal signals for the group: "I saw a lot of head nods. Does this mean that this is a serious problem?" Pause and wait for someone to break the silence, even if it seems like an eternity. Your patient silence will put pressure on the group, and someone will respond to fill the uncomfortable void.

6. Render praise to those who provide inputs. This assures the group that it is "safe" to speak up.

7. You may approach someone during the break. Engage him/her in a discussion about the presentation, and then ask if he/she would share his/her comments/reactions with the group.

Group-induced tangents

Inevitably, someone will stray from the issue at hand, either intentionally or unwittingly. Your job is to get the errant ones back on track. These approaches can counteract tendencies to abandon the course's focus:

1. Acknowledge the importance of the comment and assure the group that you will return to that topic/issue. Then ask if anyone has any comments about the actual issue now at hand. Return later to the new topics raised by the participants.

2. If there is a departure from the real or original issue, ask the trainee who raised the *original* issue if the group is addressing it. If not, ask him/her to restate or clarify the issue. Then ask for group comments.

3. You may wish to acknowledge the deviant comment by paraphrasing what was said. Then politely ask the errant one if he/she heard the prior comment and how he/she feels about it.

ACTIVATING ANSWERS

The prior pages have dealt with reluctant participants—those who won't ask questions or answer them—in a number of ways. Trainer Dr. Joel Gendelman uses two "sure shot" devices to get his participants to be active and to set a playful tone as well. His techniques follow [26]:

Money Madness

Advise the participant group that you hope to involve them at various stages of the lecture presentation. Indicate that you will give the first two responders a crisp dollar bill (or a shiny silver dollar). Display the bill or coin. (Affluent stockbrokers may require a larger inducement than one dollar!) After your first rewards, reward participants intermittently. Engage in special efforts to reward shy group members and those who pose particularly profound queries.

Lecture Letup

Before you commence things, assign each class member a number. Set up an electric timer on an interval basis of three to five minutes. When the timer goes off, select a random number. The participant who has that number must do one of three things: ask a question, offer a pertinent comment, or summarize the last segment of the lecture.

Dr. Gendelman promises that these two procedures will keep any audience awake and on their toes.

KEY POINTS

1. Although audience/participant groups respond tepidly to lectures, this method is still widely used by trainers, instructors, and teachers of all sorts.

2. The greatest weaknesses of the lecture method are that lectures are boring and hard to take and retention is low.

3. The strong point of the lecture method is that it is a "quick and dirty" way to impart information to others.

4. The lecture method is something of an anachronism in light of everything we know about adult learning and the communication process.

5. Much advice abounds on how to give a better lecture. However, a lecture is a lecture . . . is a lecture . . . is a lecture.

6. While the idea of improving the techniques of lecturing is O.K., a better approach to meeting a training need is to ask whether another, more dynamic method is available.

7. If one must lecture, one should at least start things off in a participative way.

8. Participative devices used midway in the talk are also helpful.

9. The question-and-answer session, another "must," can be made productive by *modeling* and *extended wait-time.*

10. Asking the participant group questions and involving individual participants in various ways helps, too.

11. Finally, the trainer is well advised to think in terms of lecturettes and short talks if a lecture is really necessary.

REFERENCES

1. McCarthy, Colman, *The Washington Post* (October 31, 1987).

2. Ricks, D. M., "Barriers to Industry—A Successful Trainer Tells Why He Doesn't Hire Academics," *Instructional Innovator* (January 1981), pp. 11–13.

3. Miller, D. B., *Personal Vitality*, Addison-Wesley Publishing Company, Reading, Mass. (1977), p. 129.

4. Bullock, D., "Lecture-Driven Instruction," *National Society for Performance Improvement Journal* (April 1980), p. 15.

5. "How to Moderate a Panel," *Training* (October 1993), pp. 12–17.

6. Watson, Kittie W., and Barker, Larry L., "Eight Dangerous Assumptions about Listening," in "Training 101," *Training and Development* (November 1992), pp. 15–17.

7. Turecamo, Dorrine, "Keeping Audience Attention," *Successful Meetings* (January 1993), p. 106.

8. Hartson, David, "Orchestrating the Teachable Moment," *Training News* (February 1984), pp. 6–7.

9. Zosel, Michael J., "Filling in the Blanks," in "Training 101," *Training and Development Journal* (January 1990), pp. 33–35.

10. Bradford, L. P., "Are There Any Questions?—How to Plan the Question and Answer Period," *Adult Leadership* (July–August 1952), pp. 5–8.

11. Marsh, C., "Opening the Way for Questions," *Northeast Training News* (October 1980), p. 8.

12. Brody, Marjorie, "They Won't Throw Tomatoes . . . But It May Hurt Just as Much," in "Training 101," *Training and Development* (January 1995), pp. 11–12.

13. Allerton, Haidee, "Easy Q & A," in "News You Can Use," *Training and Development* (June 1999), p. 10.

14. Leeds, Dorothy, "The Art of Asking Questions," *Training and Development* (January 1993), pp. 57–62.

15. Beary, Rodney P., "Inquiring Trainers Want to Know," in "Training 101," *Training and Development* (March 1994), pp. 22–25.

16. Suessmuth, P., and Strengels, M., "Training Ideas Found Useful: Questions, Answers and Socrates," *Canadian Training Methods* (March–April 1971), p. 26.

17. Suessmuth, P., and Strengels, M., "Wake Them Up—Ask the Right Questions," *Training in Business and Industry* (May 1972), p. 33.

18. Suessmuth, P., and Strengels, M., "The Follow-Up Question," *Training in Business and Industry* (February 1974), p. 41.

19. Mills, P., and Roberts, B., "Learn to Guide and Control Discussion," *Successful Meetings* (March 1981), pp. 96–97.

20. Parry, Scott, "An Equal Opportunity to Learn," in "Training 101," *Training and Development Journal* (January 1991), pp. 15–18.

21. Parry, Scott B., "Questions About Questions," in "Training 101," *Training and Development Journal* (February 1991), pp. 18–20.

22. Leeds, Dorothy, "Six Techniques to Improve Your Questions," *Performance in Practice, A Supplement to Training and Development Magazine* (Spring 2001), pp. 10–11.

23. Parry, Scott, "The Instructor as Catalyst," in "Training Today," *Training* (August 1993), pp. 56–57.

24. Boyd, Stephen D., "When the Lights Go Out," in "Training 101," *Training and Development* (August 1991), pp. 15–17.

25. DeValk, Steve, "I Can Recite the Program Content in My Sleep. Now What?" in "Training 101," *Training and Development* (March 1994), pp. 19–22.

26. Gendelman, Joel, "Sure Shot Methods for Creating Excitement," *Performance and Instruction* (February 1993), p. 40.

RECOMMENDED READING

Abernathy, Donna J., "Presentation Tips from the Pros," *Training and Development,* October 1999, pp. 19–25.

Seven professional speakers ("show-and-tell masters") present 70-plus tips to help you deliver engaging presentations.

Broadwell, Martin, "In Defense of the Good Old Lecture Method," *Training/HRD,* August 1976, pp. 25–26.

After citing the pros and cons of the lecture method, the author presents a way to overcome its drawbacks; namely, by delivering a "programmed lecture" wherein participants are given problem-solving activities to work on as the lecture proceeds. This procedure keeps learners accountable for results and provides a meaningful goal and a reason to listen.

Brown, David S., "The Lecture . . . and How to Make It More Effective," *Training Director's Journal,* December 1960, pp. 17–22.

This provides pointers to improve the lecture method, particularly when the lecturer is from the "outside." Key points: Help the lecturer understand his/her role and the audience's composition; help him/her in the planning for the lecture; discuss and evaluate the lecturer's contribution.

Feldman, Michael, "Planning for an Indirect Training Style," *Training and Development Journal,* October 1982, pp. 79–81.

To overcome liabilities that accrue from a training style relying on the lecture approach, the trainer can involve participants via use of trainee experiences; use of trainer questions; use of previous trainee statements, positions, and opinions; and use of past, prevailing, and possible future trainee feelings and attitudes.

Kaeter, Margaret, "Perfect Panel Presentations," *Training, A Supplement to July 1994 Issue,* pp. 11–16.

Although panel discussions can be dreary affairs, they don't have to be if attention is paid to pertinent details concerning the *panelists,* the *moderator,* and the *details of the event.* The article discusses all three of these key elements in depth.

Leeds, Dorothy, "The Power of Questions," in "Training 101," *Training and Development,* October 2000, pp. 20–21.

Cites the values of asking questions: stimulate thinking, encourage discovery learning, keep you in control of your agenda, provide information for a needs analysis, bring out quiet participants, encourage thinking for back-home application.

McCarthy, John J., "The Lecture Method," *Sales Training,* June 1976, pp. 22–23, 34–40.

This lists and compares the advantages and disadvantages of the lecture method. The article also provides tips concerning ways to maximize the use of an outside speaker.

Milcal, Paul J., "Socratic Is More Emphatic," *Training/HRD,* March 1981, pp. 58–59.

This recommends the use of the questioning approach to increase learner interest, involvement, rapport with the presenter, and retention of learning.

Tagliere, D. A., "Questions: Use Them to Help Others Discover Ideas," *Sales Meetings,* January 1972, pp. 45, 90–92.

"Inquiry learning" is accomplished via questions on cards given to participants plus encouraging participants to ask questions of their own.

Thiagarajan, Sivasailam, "In Praise of Impromptu Instruction (and Some Practical Tips on How to Do It)," *National Society for Performance and Instruction Journal,* April 1980, pp. 8–9.

Presenters can augment their effectiveness if they know their subject matter, plan and organize the presentation, prepare for adjustments in the plan should this be necessary, conduct a trial run with a member of the target population, avoid note cards to ensure spontaneity, demonstrate ideas by using participants, avoid being trapped by tangential issues.

Vinci, Vince, "Eleven Ways to Hold Your Audience's Attention," *Meetings and Conventions,* May 1974, pp. 83–84, 142–146.

Key points: Zero in on a *universal* interest of your group, think "big" when using visuals and gestures, ask questions, use participants' experiences, try to develop and use a "theatrical" style, relate all activities to your theme, intermittently repeat the main message of your presentation, look for and use new approaches, provide inputs which require the use of more than one sense, use special appeals or motivators, secure participation.

Zenker, Arnold, "Ten Sure Ways to Score with an Audience," in "Training 101," *Training and Development,* April 1992, pp. 19–21.

"Rules" about speaking have changed because of the influence of TV. People's attention spans have diminished, and their expectations have increased. Adjust to this new reality by these guides: limit your objectives; simplify rather than be a technical bore; tell stories and anecdotes; leave your own special world behind and try to relate to the universe; add spice to your talk by varying your techniques; leave the lectern and join the audience; have a good time—communicate energy and enthusiasm; be outrageous, take some risks; don't overstay your welcome; do things your own way if they will make for a successful presentation.

Using Participative Methods to Evaluate Training

Education is what survives when what has been learned has been forgotten

> —B. F Skinner (1904–1990), leading American exponent of behavioral psychology

"Not everything that counts can be counted and not everything that can be counted counts."

> —Albert Einstein (1879–1955), American physicist, German-born formulator of theory of relativity

THE classic model of training evaluation postulates *four* levels of evaluation [1]:

1. Participant reaction level (attitude or feeling regarding satisfaction-dissatisfaction).
2. Learning (observable or measurable behavior change) in the classroom or training situation.
3. New or changed behavior (performance) on the job.

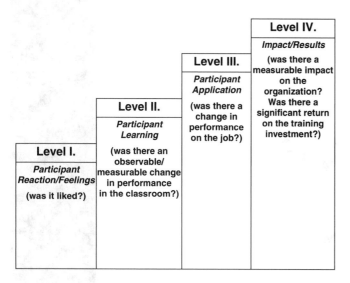

Figure 19-1. Criteria for evaluation of completed training occurring at four levels.

4. Measurable impact of the training on the organization, for example, increases in productivity, sales, quality, and profitability and reductions in cost, waste, scrap, accidents, grievances, absenteeism, and customer complaints.

It will be noted that as we move from Levels 1 to 4, the data become more objective and thus more meaningful (see Figure 19-1). Most training, however, is evaluated only at Level 1 since that information is quite easy to obtain. Conversely, evaluation at Levels 3 and 4 requires much more work and sophistication (ideally, before and after techniques coupled with experimental and control group procedures) and is thus left by the trainers to the researchers and statisticians.

PARTICIPANT REACTION LEVEL

Participant reaction data, which only report attitudes and feelings, are obviously not "hard" data; that is to say, they don't attempt to measure changes in behavior or performance. In fact, research psychologists and others typically use such terms as "happiness data" and "whoopie sheets" to describe the usual self-report feedback rendered by enthusiastic and grateful participants. The enthusiasm, they say, is almost certain, given an adequately interesting and active program, hotel/motel food, a friendly trainer, a chance to get away from the usual office routines (and even the family in some cases), and a chance to have a few drinks with old buddies.

Nevertheless, participant reactions are still useful information for these reasons:

☐ They are easy and economical to gather and certainly better than no data at all.

☐ They do meet the trainer's need to know how well his/her efforts have been perceived. (Trainers have egos that require stroking, too!)

☐ Certainly management also wants to know how well the training is being received by the participants. If the trainees don't like it, there's little point in supporting it.

☐ If the trainees are not satisfied with the training, the likelihood is that it will be ignored in whole or in part. Conversely, if the training is deemed to be worthwhile, there is at least a possibility it will be applied. Thus, it is desirable to know what the satisfaction-dissatisfaction ratio is.

☐ They can be a guide to program improvement.

In the paragraphs that follow, a number of involving, group-in-action methods to collect participant data are described. They are easy to apply and are intended to serve as a supplement, *not* a substitution, for questionnaire-type data. Questionnaires are important, for they permit the garnering of participant reactions in a *systematic* way. The trainer is thus able to learn, for example, that 75% of the trainees felt that learning for them was "high," 15% learned at a "moderate" level, 5% learned in a "minor" way, and the other 5% were "not sure." The trainer may also learn that a majority of the participants favored small-group work over lectures, the day was too long, and the ventilation was poor much of the time.

As to group-in-action methods of evaluation, they serve these useful purposes:

☐ They stimulate trainee thinking about personal learning. Group interaction is an effective means of opening new avenues of thought about the completed training experience and the need for growth or improvement.

☐ The participant's ideas or questions about the program can be "checked out" (reality tested) with others. Conversely, the questionnaire procedure, if used alone, requires preparation of responses in total *isolation* from one's peers.

☐ Aside from personal learning, ideas for program improvement (methods, administration, facilities) can be obtained.

☐ If the training program is a highly participative one, evaluation procedures that involve participants are a logical way to conclude the training effort.

The best evaluation design, then, at the reaction level, involves this *paired* approach:

1. *Begin* with the collection of data via group-in-action methods.

2. *Finish* with the administration of a formal questionnaire. Some trainers may wish to use a "fun type" questionnaire, such as in Appendix 66. (Need training always be grim?)

The following paragraphs offer "how-to-do-it" suggestions for a number of group-in-action evaluation techniques.

Self-Appraisal

Assign participants to dyads, triads, or buzz groups of four to five participants, and have them discuss their learning in one of the following ways:

☐ *Open-ended assignment.* Ask participants to respond to two critical questions such as these: Where do you think you "are" now? Where do you think you "were" when you started?

☐ *Expectations.* Ask participants to respond to these paired questions: What were your expectations for this course? To what degree were they met?

☐ *Course objectives assessment.* Ask participants to assess and discuss their learning in relation to stated course objectives.

☐ *Individual goals assessment.* On the assumption that participants were asked to state specifically their learning goals at the outset (on a sheet of paper, on a form, on a flipchart sheet), have them discuss the degree to which their goals were met. *Note:* In some situations, such as in a time management course, the goals may be both personal and organizational.

☐ *Sentence completion approach.* Provide participants with a sentence completion form, such as the one in Appendix 67, for individual completion and subsequent discussion in small groups.

To maximize the benefits from any one of the five self-appraisal and small group activities just listed, encourage participants (secure volunteers) to share the nature and extent of their new learning with the total group.

Circular Whip

For a quick, easy-to-accomplish assessment about participant learning, form a circle (maximum of 15) and "whip around" it, each participant making a statement concerning the one most significant learning in the course for him/her. This procedure readily generates considerable data about group learning. It is particularly helpful to encourage the "reluctant dragons" to admit that they, too, learned something!

The statements offered by participants may be subject to total group discussion, depending on course objectives and time limits. They may also be used as a "lead-in" to the completion of the formal questionnaire, which elicits more comprehensive and systematic data concerning program reactions.

Note:

1. The statements to which the participants might respond in the whip activity could take one of these forms:

   ☐ The most significant thing to me in this program was _____.
   ☐ What I intend to apply (or do) on the job as a result of this course is _____.
   ☐ I now see (or understand) that _____.
   ☐ I intend to do less of _____.
   ☐ I intend to do more of _____.

2. Following the use of the circular whip to secure statements about individual learnings, the group may be asked (one statement per participant, again) for ideas to strengthen the program.

Using the Fishbowl

With the aid of the fishbowl or group-on-group observation technique, all participants can be involved in a group assessment of the completed training. The procedures are as follows:

1. Decide the evaluation area that is to be discussed. Typical assignments: What did we learn? What did we like about the course and what did we not like (or strengths and weaknesses of the course)? What would have helped to make this course (even) more effective? How can we apply the learning "back home"?

2. Divide the total group into smaller discussion groups of six to eight participants. Two or three fishbowls may be conducted simultaneously.

3. Let the inner group (Group A) discuss the assigned topic for 15–20 minutes with the outer group (Group B) observing.

4. Let Group B switch places and roles and now become the discussant group; Group A is now the observing group. Group B's task is to comment on the observations or critique developed by Group A as well as to respond to the question assigned to Group A.

5. As an optional procedure, repeat Steps 3 and 4 an additional time.

6. Allow time for a final, group-at-large discussion.

Using Movement: Discerning Learning Categories

☐ Ask group members to stand and then position themselves at one of three points in the room representing high learning, moderate learning, and limited or minor learning. In effect, this is a "human continuum." Then ask for volunteers (two or three per location) to explain why they assigned themselves to their particular learning category.

☐ In a highly experiential program, ask everyone to stand up. Then ask *one* group member (a volunteer will do) to "sort" or "assign" the total group into three categories (at three locations in the room): those who learned a great deal, those who learned a moderate amount, and those who learned relatively little. In effect, this is an exer-

cise in giving feedback. Ask group members to be seated at their new locations and to hold a group-at-large discussion on these assignments.

Note:

1. This technique may not be appropriate for the novice trainer, for it entails skill in group process.

2. The assumptions in this activity are that there is a small participant group; that everyone now knows everyone else quite well, including their degree of learning; that giving and receiving feedback is an appropriate part of the learning process.

Using Art

☐ Have group members informally develop a "running mural" (on flipcharts) about the course, starting the first morning and carrying through to the final session. The mural, as an art form, requires that statements be made only in graphic, illustrative, diagrammatic, or pictorial form.

   Note: This may take considerable wall space.

☐ Have group members in an intensive management seminar respond in a graphic or illustrative way to the data requested in the triangle shown in Figure 19-2. The art work is to be completed

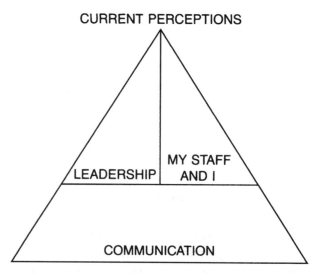

Figure 19-2. Example of a geometrical figure for eliciting data from participants about pre- and post-course perceptions.

twice: at the outset and at program's end. The idea is to have participants note any difference in their perceptions about leadership, communication, etc.

The first completion of the triangle may be treated as a personal thing and simply filed away until program's end. At that time both artistic renditions, pre- and post-course, may be discussed in pairs or trios.

Individual Course Critique

☐ *Posting technique.* Ask participants to take a sheet of paper and jot down their reactions to the course or program in three categories: *content* or subject matter, *methods,* and *administration.* Then have participants post their ideas to three flipchart sheets on the wall that bear those category headings. Lead a general discussion about the total group's posted ideas.

Note: To speed up the posting operation, have two or three separate sets of the three flipcharts available to participants.

☐ *Individual role play.* Toward the end of the program, provide participants with a task assignment sheet such as the one in Appendix 68.

Note:

1. The rationale for this activity is that it forces the participant to think through carefully what the course was trying to accomplish, what was learned, etc. In effect, it provides an opportunity to create a personalized *summation* of the total learning experience.
2. In a small group of 8–12 all participants should be asked to give their presentations. In a larger group ask for six to eight volunteers to do this.
3. Encourage the listening participants to applaud the presenters after their talks.

Small Group Course Critique

☐ At program's end, divide the total group into small-group evaluation or critique teams. Give one or more groups this assignment: What suggestions do you have to improve *course content?*

Give a second group (or set of groups) this assignment: What suggestions for course improvement do you have that relate to *training methods?* Give a third group this assignment: What suggestions do you have to improve this program *other than* in the areas of content and methods? Consider course length, course administration, physical conditions, trainer effectiveness, etc. After the small group work, secure reports orally and post the main ideas on flipcharts.

☐ In an extended (long-term) program, set up evaluation committees at the outset to assess and report back on course effectiveness. The reports should be in writing and summed up orally to the total group. Be sure to provide guidelines to the teams concerning the course elements to consider in the evaluation process.

☐ One way to wrap up a program is to have everyone stand up and form a circle. Ask participants to close their eyes and think of what the experience has meant to them. Allow about a minute or two for this. Now ask participants to "come back" and describe the completed training in *one* word or phrase. (Anticipate words/phrases such as "informative," "eye-opening," "challenging," "not sure.") In an experiential training program the question may be posed as follows: "Using one word, what are you *feeling* now that the training is over?" (Possible responses: "exhilarated," "helped," "fulfilled," "sad.")

Key Points—Recollections

If your course/program has been adequately ramified (a good number of topics were covered), you can be quite certain that a lot of forgetting has taken place. It is thus desirable at course's end to facilitate recall of major learnings and simultaneously to ascertain how much was learned.

One way to do this is to have your participants individually complete the worksheet in Figure 19-3, Worksheet to Recall Major Learning Points in the Course. Then have them meet in small groups to discuss their entries in the worksheet. Point out that they can add their colleagues' ideas to their worksheets. As a wrap-up, hold a general group-at-large discussion about learnings from the activity.

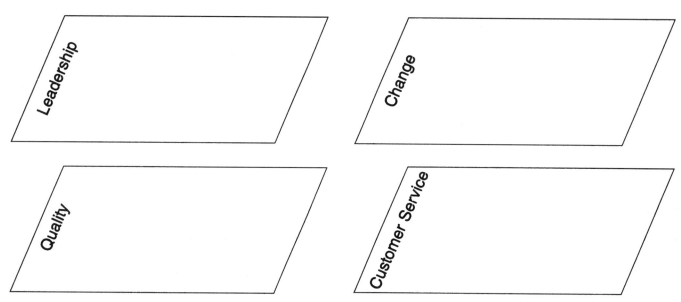

Figure 19-3. Worksheet to recall major training points in the course.

Note: The parallelograms are used to provide a less common geometric than the usual rectangles, triangles, and squares.

Trainees' Testimonials

One way to encourage participants to reflect on their learnings from the completed training course or program is to have them prepare and deliver a short presentation about their experience. The talk should be oriented toward encouraging others to attend. A worksheet for this purpose is given in Figure 19-4.

Presentation Regarding Your Training Experience
You have now completed this workshop. Assume that on your return to your job you are asked by your boss to give a presentation to a group of managers and others about your training experience. Assume further that all those in attendance may wish to attend this program. What might you tell them that would encourage them to attend?

Use the space below to make notes about your presentation. Your presentation should not exceed 3 minutes.

_____

_____

_____

_____

_____

Figure 19-4. A worksheet to prepare for a brief talk promoting program attendance.

Have the participant indicate at the outset to whom the talk is to be delivered. Have him/her deliver the speech as if the class is the audience he/she will address.

LEARNING (CHANGED BEHAVIOR) IN THE CLASSROOM

As previously indicated, participant reactions are always of interest and, given an intelligent and well-organized training effort, generally comforting to the trainer. However, the validity of "happiness ratings" is very much on the low side insofar as real learning is concerned. A better measurement is of the actual learning that has taken place in the classroom. Here we find out not only what participants feel, think, or believe, but what they can now *do* differently as a result of the training. We can accomplish such an assessment in several ways.

☐ *Observation.* It is possible to note differences in performance levels when participants engage in activities such as:

1. *Writing letters*—Samples brought into class at the start of the training can be compared with letters (and reports) produced after the training, or the new letters can be checked against the criteria advocated by the training program.

2. *Delivering talks*—In public speaking training, the before and after performance can be appraised via videotape or by ratings prepared by the participants and/or the trainer.

3. *Role playing*—How one coaches an employee, deals with a reluctant customer, interviews a job applicant, etc., can be appraised, again, on a pre- and post-training basis and/or in relation to course standards. If the role plays have been videotaped, further substantiation is possible.

4. *Case study*—How participants attack (analyze) problems presented in cases, on a before-and-after basis, can provide evidence of change (new learning). The change data may be gathered on an observational basis (somewhat subjective, of course) or via the preparation of pre- and post-course written case analyses.

5. *Field trips*—How well participants collect and analyze data, based on criteria or principles developed in the classroom, is another indicator of actual learning.

A highly sophisticated form of observation of possible changed behavior was used at Hewlett-Packard [2]. Fifteen R&D product managers participated in a technical leadership development program that focused on continuous improvement of project management skills: project planning and schedule management, processes of product definition and product development life cycles, business knowledge, technical knowledge, and interpersonal and leadership skills.

To measure actual performance change, the firm videotaped the participants acting out randomly assigned scenarios two days *before* the training began, for example, initiating a non-negotiable and undesirable change, identifying a technical professional's undeveloped idea and encouraging its development, or delegating an undesirable responsibility. One week after the training, the participants were taped again. To ensure that the trainees' practice in the training situation didn't influence the post-training results, each trainee was assigned a *new* scenario. Note, too, that the trainees were not told to draw on their recent training experience and were not permitted to use any training materials as references. They were merely told to manage the new scenario in the most effective way. The idea, obviously, was to ascertain if the trainees valued the new learning and to judge their competence in applying the newly learned skills.

The videotapings took place in a room with a two-way mirror so that the observers would not affect the comfort level of the participants. For a comparison of the before and after effect, three product managers were chosen as judges. They received the unlabeled tapes in pairs and reviewed them in random order. They made evaluations on a coded rating form.

The results: The judges were able to select with 100% accuracy which tapes were filmed on a pre- and post-training basis. The judges also reported that the new behavior (improvement in skills) was dramatic and clearly visible in the post-training videos.

The judges also rated the program participants on three scales: probability of success, involvement of other parties, and overall effectiveness of approach. The results: Average post-test ratings were significantly higher than pre-test averages on the three scales.

☐ *Action plans.* The nature of action plans or contracts—commitments to engage in a new behavior—can indicate the degree to which the training has been internalized. Of course, pledges and promises are not necessarily the same as on-the-job performance, but they are a hopeful sign. Also, with the right type of follow-up by the trainer and reinforcement by the participant's boss, plans for change are quite likely to be fulfilled.

☐ *Attitude surveys.* Although changes in attitude are obviously not "hard" data as much as changes in performance or behavior, attitude changes do indicate, nevertheless, that a change has taken place. Thus, if a training program is designed to reduce bias or prejudice toward certain groups, before-and-after attitude surveys are helpful to reflect that change. It is hoped that new attitudes will be carried over to the job situation and reflected in new on-the-job behavior. Again, supervisory and/or organizational support for the new attitudes are essential to implement and maintain them.

CHANGE IN ON-THE-JOB BEHAVIOR

Change in observable behavior in the classroom, as previously described, is an indicator that the new learning *may* be carried over to the job. However, this is hardly conclusive evidence. What is needed is "harder" data about actual on-the-job performance such as

- ☐ Implementation of action plans producing measurable/observable change.
- ☐ Supervisor's day-to-day observations concerning changed behavior.
- ☐ Employee reports concerning behavior change in their bosses.

The two sections that follow provide some pointers concerning how supervisors can be encouraged to support and monitor possible behavior change.

Involving Supervisors in the Evaluation Process

Far too many participants attend training programs in which there is little or no involvement by their bosses. That is to say, supervisors may not really know why their subordinates are going to the training, what the specific goals of their courses are, what was actually learned at the courses, and how the new learning may be applied to their jobs. The following procedures are suggested to get supervisors more fully "into the act" and thus to help them overcome their abdication of responsibility.

The form in Figure 19-5 is designed, first, to secure the understanding of both the supervisor and the participant as to the nature and value of the course's major (high-impacting) goals. *Both* parties are thus asked to identify high-impacting goals and to rank and discuss them as to their value or importance *before* the training begins. Secondly, following the completion of the training, the supervisor is expected

Value of Goals—A Pre-Course Assessment

Learning Goals in Customer Relations Course:	Identification of Major or High-Impacting Goals (Use check mark)		Weighted Goal Assessment (Use a % for each goal; total must = 100%)		Weighted Assessment After Joint Discussion (Use % re each goal) (5)	Goal Accomplishment Participant's Post-Course Assessment (Use % re each goal) (6)	Joint Development of an Action Plan (Check when completed) (7)
	Per Participant (1)	Per Participant (2)	Per Participant (3)	Per Participant (4)			
1. Improved product (or service) knowledge		✓		25%	20%	30%	
2. How to deal with frustrations	✓		25%		15%	80%	
3. How to handle difficult customers	✓		60%		20%	95%	
4. How to handle customers to ensure repeat business		✓		40%	30%	50%	
5. How to be a more effective member of the customer relations team		✓		25%	10%	95%	
6. How to keep up enthusiasm (prevent "burnout")	✓	✓	15%	10%	5%	90%	
			100%	100%	100%		

Note
1. Differences in pre-course assessments (columns 1–4) are to be discussed and "negotiated" (column 5).
2. Participant's post-course assessment (column 6) is to be discussed with one's superior and an action plan is to be developed for each goal as may be indicated (column 7).
3. Complete the form in duplicate—one copy is for the participant, one copy is for the superior. (The trainer may also want a copy.)

Figure 19-5. Form for involving supervisors in setting goals for subordinate training and in evaluating the training after it is completed.

to talk to the subordinate about the realization of course goals in the training situation and the development of action plans to implement course learnings. Involving the supervisor in a post-course discussion should be a logical procedure once the supervisor has identified, ranked, and discussed course goals with the participant on a pre-course basis.

Involvement of Supervisors Through Group Audit Sessions

With proper planning and organizing, the key "clients" (participants' superiors) who authorize the training can be fully involved in its evaluation. The following is a system to provide this involvement [3].

Step 1. Invite the clients to a two-session audit (or evaluation) program.

Step 2. At the first session (one hour), explain the overall program. Ask the clients to gather data concerning program results. They, obviously, are best positioned to note and collect data (via discussions with participants, performance observations, etc.) on how the completed training affects their operations. Tell them that they will work in teams at the second session, critically comparing their collected data.

Step 3. At Session Two (about four hours) the clients, in small groups or teams, are asked to do two things (in about one hour):

    a. List (on flipcharts) positive results and prioritize them.

    b. List (on flipcharts) negative or unachieved results and prioritize them.

Note: By keeping program weaknesses separate from its strengths, clients can zero in more readily on program areas requiring improvement.

Step 4. Conduct a general session (three hours) with all client teams who report back on their data. This sharing of data (all flipcharts are posted on the wall) gives the clients a fuller set of data for their subsequent evaluation.

Step 5. A consolidation (in general session) is made of all the teams' lists, one list for strengths and one for weaknesses. Priorities are also established.

Step 6. The trainer who is concerned with the particular program reacts to the lists.

Step 7. The program administrator indicates the nature of and timetable for the necessary follow-up action.

Meetings to evaluate key training programs, as just described, should be conducted at least annually.

MEASURABLE IMPACT OF THE TRAINING ON THE ORGANIZATION

Evaluation of training at this level—the bottom line or payoff level—is not accomplished through group methods such as those suggested for the prior three levels of evaluation. Rather, since "hard" data is desired—increased profitability/productivity; increased sales; better service to customers; reductions in cost, waste, errors, defects, turnover, absenteeism, customer complaints, grievances—pertinent information is obtained from records and reports including those already produced systematically.

NEW APPROACHES TO LEVEL FOUR EVALUATION

Sophisticated trainers know that they should be doing more than evaluation of training on the reaction level (Level One). Yet they don't for reasons of time, cost, and complexity. So if you aren't into Level Four—impact on the organization and ROI (return on the training investment)—consider the following two more trainer-friendly approaches to Level Four–type evaluation:

☐ ROE (Return on Expectations)
☐ Customer satisfaction as a business indicator

ROE (Return on Expectations)

Ideally, we, as trainers, should be able to prove in all our training efforts that we have produced a reasonable return—ROI—on the organization's investments in our training.

We say "ideally" because in the real world it may be neither practical nor possible. The lack of practicality arises because of cost and time factors. If we conduct numerous courses, securing hard data on each course becomes burdensome. The possibility element runs into the problem of proving in quantitative terms that our training in "soft skills"—interpersonal relations, listening, ethics, decision making, etc.—has really paid off.

The senior editor of *Training* magazine, Donna Goldwasser, cites the experience of Toni Hodges, manager of measurements and evaluation for Verizon's Workforce Development Division, Silver Spring, Maryland [4]. Hodges typically spends about. $5,000 for an ROI impact study. Since Verizon's training has to reach a 320,000-employee workforce, it simply is not practical to conduct an ROI study for each and every training effort.

So what to do? Verizon's approach is to limit true ROI studies to situations where it is practical and desirable. Says Hodges, "Gathering ROI data, in addition to being expensive, can be frustrating. Most of our business units don't track the data we need at the individual level, so it's hard to isolate the specific effects of a training program." Verizon thus substitutes "ROE" for ROI. ROE is "return on expectations."

Here's how the ROE approach functions. Before a course starts, a training office staffer conducts a 15–20-minute interview with a key official directly concerned with the learning effort. This is generally a V.P. financially responsible for the project. Based on the V.P.'s expectations, specific learning goals are set up. *Example:* "Waste less time and have fewer meetings." Time management skills would then be taught and the exec is interviewed again after the training has been given.

In the post-training interview Hodges asks for more than a yes/no response as to whether the training met expectations. Rather, the exec in question is asked to quantify the training results, to attach a monetary value to the benefit. Hodges uses that data as "reasonable evidence" in an ROI calculation.

In more specific terms, here's how the ROE system works: Each stakeholder of a training program is asked (a) to place a percentage estimate on the degree to which he/she believes the project has met learning goals, (b) to support that estimate with examples, and (c) to assign a dollar value to the change/improvement.

Additionally, all evaluative information is picked up and stored in a database. It is available on a daily basis with summaries, both monthly and quarterly, to permit alerting managers to likely problem areas. This system saves time, money, and effort because it cuts the assessment wait time to a small portion of what it generally is. Actual problems can be spotted and fixed promptly.

Is the ROE procedure accurate, and if so, to what degree? Hodges has conducted corresponding ROI impact studies, and the results have always supported ROE findings. Hodges concludes, "If I were to conduct an ROI study as the ROE process, the results could be tremendous. The interviews are cheap, and the results I've gotten in every case are very, very valuable."

Note that Hodges still conducts true Level Four ROI impact studies using pre- and post-measurements and experimental and control groups. This is done where hard numbers (e.g., in the sales area) offer the best measurement of success. But where more subjective learning programs are involved, the assessment of expectations might be an adequately worthwhile investment.

The bottom line: Trainers can attach a business value of one type or another to an organizational learning experience. This approach is essential to get the notion of "training for training's sake." It may ensure that the training function in your outfit remains "recession proof." So consider ROE, whose success turns on reasonable evidence, as opposed to hard proof.

Consumer Satisfaction as a Business Indicator

Measuring the precise benefit that a learning activity brings to the organization is very difficult. In fact, according to *The 2000 ASTD State of the Industry Report* only 3% of the respondents try to measure the business results of training programs. This is understandable, say management consultants Peter Bregman and Howie Jacobson, for measuring business results is difficult for the following reasons [5]:

☐ Implementing a precise, quantitative evaluation can be costly and time-demanding.

☐ Determining the impact of training on business results is a tough proposition. Why? Because isolating a direct cause-and-effect relationship, when typically many variables in the system are involved, is very likely to get us into pretty nebulous territory.

☐ Determining the appropriate outcomes to measure is a very complex procedure.

These ideas are discussed more fully below.

What if a training program does succeed in changing behavior of people, for example, to manage "more efficiently"? Are these improvements worthwhile, ask Bregman and Jacobson, if the customer impact is negative, that is, they reduce customer satisfaction? Consider this circumstance: A transportation company reduced its costs by waiting until their trucks were full before sending them out. As expected, in the short term profits were up. But shortly thereafter, customers began to complain about less frequent deliveries. So there may be a boomerang effect—reduced customer satisfaction—if the impact on the total system is ignored.

Here's another illustration. A fast-food chain used, as an efficiency measuring rod, the amount of cooked chicken that was thrown out. Managers met their chicken efficiency quotas simply by not cooking their chickens until ordered. *The result:* high customer dissatisfaction, for they expected their fast food to be just that, fast, rather than having to wait 20 minutes for it. So the managers' desired numbers were achieved, but, sad to relate, store sales soon plummeted [6].

Bregman and Jacobson point out that the biggest problem with assessing training's impact on business results is that organizations are complex systems. So what appears to be an improvement when examined in isolation may prove to be a calamity for the system. *Example:* Suppose we increased efficiency by training our managers to do more themselves and delegate less to staffers. But what if then there is serious resentment over lack of challenge and opportunity, and people start to jump ship? So a focus on discrete results can give us a false impression that our training *is* aiding business results.

So how do we know which results to measure? Possibly financial performance? But ROI is tough to pin down. Why? Because in a complex system the number of variables reaches a level of infinity. *Example:* Sales move up after a big training effort in communication skills. Great! But did training pull off this

coup? We can't be sure, for the competitor may have quit, or the increase may be seasonal, or perhaps there was a big uptick in the economy, and so on.

Can we pin down training results on the enterprise by using the traditional "experimental and control group" approach? Group A gets the training and Group B doesn't. If conditions are similar for both groups, any significant variance in performance will reflect the training input. But Bregman and Jacobson express skepticism about this device—in the real world, most firms don't have the luxury of two identical groups functioning in precisely the same environment. *Example:* The transfer of a staffer from Group A to B will mean a loss of validity in the study. Also, controlled studies of this sort require a lot of time and money.

So what's the best approach—ideally one that's quick and easy—to assess business results accrued from training? Let's use the most important business result—customer satisfaction. Since every organization has customers, both internal and external, the best evaluation is to learn how well their needs are being met by organizational training efforts. Bregman and Jacobson say, "Every business result that matters leads to improved customer satisfaction, either directly or indirectly. An event or process or attitude that does not make customers happy is bad for business, even if it improves efficiency or pads short-term profits. If an organization accepts that premise, the fog lifts and a pathway out of the training evaluation swamp appears."

Fortunately, changes in customer satisfaction in response to training are very measurable. Consider these reasons:

1. Reaction sheets are easy to administer and can measure customer satisfaction reliably and inexpensively. The best procedure, of course is to query the customers before the training and three months thereafter.

2. Reaction sheets produce high response rates. Customers are very willing to give feedback since they are interested in any approaches that will upgrade their service.

3. Making a valid tie between the impact of training on an employee and how customers feel about that person after training is easy. Just use this rule of thumb: A training program pays off when it

alters employees' behavior in ways that are important to customers. *Examples:* (a) sales and customer service reps are trained in active listening, and we then ask customers whether their needs are now met better; (b) managers are taught how to communicate performance feedback, and we ask subordinates whether they now know their job requirements more clearly and how well they're performing; (c) a staffer receives training in better work organization, so we ask her boss and clients, too, if deadlines are being met more consistently and higher-quality work ensues.

To sum up: Per Bregman and Jacobson, consider these added gains by evaluating training along customer satisfaction lines:

1. External customers appreciate being quizzed about their satisfaction with the services rendered. It's solid evidence that the firm seriously wants to improve service and that the customers' patronage is truly valued.

2. It communicates to employees that their outfit takes their development seriously. A message of this sort can ensure the effectiveness of any training endeavor.

3. It also communicates to employees that their most important task is to increase customer satisfaction. So the organization says to the workforce: "The most important job you have is making customers happy. To show you we mean it, we'll measure your success through your customer's eyes."

4. It tells the trainees that their work will be valued to the degree that those trained (the employees) do things differently after training. Your ultimate business test is what your customers think of you.

DAILY PULSE-TAKING

The best training takes place when participants regularly evaluate what they experience. This is desirable from several standpoints:

☐ It forces the participants to think about what they have learned and how it can be applied to their jobs.

☐ It gives the trainer feedback so that he/she knows how well the training is being given and received—what is deemed valuable, what is not—and thereby permits the making of program adjustments to the extent practicable. The alternative is to wait until program's end for the feedback. By then, it is obviously too late to improve things.

Assessment of Participant Learning

To encourage thinking and public statements about what was learned, this procedure may be followed:

1. Ask participants to quickly write ("auto-brainstorm") the ten learning points for you from today's work on a piece of paper.

2. Then conduct a "round robin," asking each of them to select one item from the ten they identified in Step 1 and to report it orally to the total group.

Good assessment procedures also call for participant introspection about what the participant plans to do about training needs uncovered by the program. Accordingly, the Daily Self-Assessment of Learning sheet given in Appendix 69 may be of value. It may be administered in any one of the following ways, depending on your training philosophy:

☐ It may be retained by the participant on a private basis. Although the assurance of privacy may encourage candor in its completion, without the stimulus of at least some discussion with another participant, the likelihood of it being merely tucked into the notebook and forgotten is quite great.

☐ It may be shared in a pair or trio. This procedure should provide some motivation, where needed, to overcome what might just be a paper exercise. The pair or trio approach will provide a good degree of privacy, too.

☐ Upon completion, one writer suggests that the form may be handed in to the trainer [7]. A code number, selected by the participant, is used to ensure both anonymity and candor. The next morning the trainer reports back on the forms before returning them. The idea is to let the total group hear how others intend to use the new learning, thereby expanding and/or reinforcing the interest in self-improvement.

Assessment of Program Effectiveness

At the end of Day 1 of a three- to five-day program, it may be desirable to secure feedback from the participants concerning "how things went." To do this, the trainer can draw a five-point continuum on the flipchart and ask participants to respond to the several points on it by a show of hands. Examples of items for the continuum are given in Figure 19-6.

Another way of using the continuum is to place it on a wall. The five degrees may actually be posted via flipchart sheets at five wall positions or just pointed to in a general way: "'Strongly Agree' is here, 'Agree' is here," etc. Then let participants position themselves *physically* in relation to the five degrees to indicate their reaction or feeling about a given evaluation question.

Another approach to the daily critique is to give participants the guide sheet given in Appendix 70 and follow these procedures:

1. Participants individually complete the form.
2. Small groups consolidate the individual data on flipcharts.
3. The group at large discusses the small group reports.

If it is desired to gather data about the day's work in a more systematic and quantitative way, the participant questionnaire given in Appendix 71 may be of value. The data should be summarized, reported back to the participants the following morning, and discussed with them.

One trainer reports the use of a daily close-of-business evaluation session wherein the trainers meet with trainee representatives for 20 to 30 minutes. The areas of evaluation include pace, problems with materials (too easy? too hard? poorly organized? instructions unclear?), small group interaction problems (nonparticipators, dominators, personality conflicts), problems with the instructions from the trainer, and housekeeping or environmental needs such as temperature and break procedures [8].

Because of its importance, some trainers may prefer to use the last half-hour of class time for this joint critique. In any case, the advantages of the participant-trainer critique are:

☐ Participant input can enrich the critique process. Visualize the trainers discussing an aspect of the day's work that needs strengthening and, after considerable discussion, one of the trainers says: "Let's get a participant view on this issue. I don't think that we, as trainers, have all the answers on this issue by any means."

☐ Participants have the opportunity to observe a democratic model for critique—one that stresses feedback from participants, as opposed to the program conductors only listening to themselves.

☐ Participants are provided with an added opportunity for participation. There is a feeling that they have at least some "ownership" of the training program.

A final procedure: Call attention to a flipchart sheet on the wall entitled "Unfinished Business" and containing three categories: "Want More Of," "Needs Clarification," and "Additions." Advise the group that they may go to the flipchart and enter their ideas on it now, at day's end, or anytime tomorrow.

THE PARTICIPANT GROUP—A SELF-APPRAISAL

A fascinating activity for a participant group is to examine its own culture, that is, the norms that govern

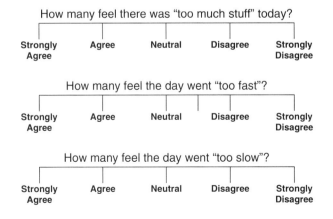

Figure 19-6. Example of scales that can be used in an evaluation procedure involving the flipchart.

NORMS IN OUR CLASSROOM

Helpful to Learning	Not Helpful to Learning	Neutral
O.K. to disagree with trainer.	Everyone takes same seat all week.	Slow return from coffee break and lunch.
Use of first names exclusively.	People who came together stay together.	Profanity is used.
	Holding back of real feelings (by some)	

Figure 19-7. Example of a tri-column used in an exercise on understanding social norms.

its behavior and thus give the group its unique personality and identity. This analysis is particularly helpful and appropriate in an experiential training program, where much of the learning comes from the group's own experience and appraisal of it.

The exercise that follows should be given at the end of a fairly intensive training program, typically of four days or more. If it is done sooner, the group may not have enough data about itself for meaningful analysis.

Understanding Social Norms: An Exercise

Background information for trainer: Every social institution—organizational, family, school, church, recreational—has a system of social norms. Norms, of course, are the *unwritten* rules—the "O.K.'s" and the "no-no's"—that govern the behavior of the members of a social group. For example, executives don't pack a lunch, although it is fine on occasion to eat at the desk; secretaries refer to their bosses as "Mr. _____" rather than by their first name; the lab people, but not the sales personnel, may dress informally.

Norms give an organization order, predictability, stability. On the other hand, norms may not really help productivity or creativity (for example, disagreement with the boss is taboo). They persist nevertheless, because they are seldom questioned [9].

Procedure:

1. Briefly introduce the concept of norms, using the prior information or similar data.
2. Break the total participant group into small groups of three to five persons.
3. Give the following instruction to the small groups: "To help us understand the concept of social norms more fully, let's consider our class as a social system. Let's analyze the norms that

have developed in this classroom. For example, the smokers have been assigned to the right side of the room; neckties are worn only to dinner. So your task in the next 20 minutes is to identify as many norms as you can that influence our behavior in this classroom. O.K.?"

4. The small groups meet for 20 minutes.
5. Secure data from the small groups and enter on flipcharts.
6. Post the flipchart sheets on the wall.
7. Set up a tri-column on a flipchart as in Figure 19-7.
8. Working from the posted data that has been developed by the small groups, ask the group at large to classify the norms into the three groupings. (Sample answers have been provided.)
9. Ask the small groups to meet again for 10–15 minutes, giving them this assignment: "Should *on-the-job* group norms be analyzed? What are the advantages of such an analysis, if any, and the risks, if any?"
10. Secure small group reports and enter on a T-column the advantages and risks discussed.
11. Hold a general discussion of the significance of the exercise.

HOW AND WHEN TO USE FOCUS GROUPS

Focus groups are useful to secure personalized answers to questions you may have about past, current, or future training programs, or about any other concerns. To the extent that you have a "live" audience, something that completed survey forms are not, you can garner a good sense of people's attitudes toward the problems or issues you are facing. That is to say, you can learn not only what people think and feel, but also *why* they do so.

By definition, a focus group is a small group of individuals who are convened to react (present attitudes) to completed, ongoing, or proposed activities, programs, services, or products. They may or may not be "experts" in your area of concern, depending on the type of question about which you need ideas, opinions, attitudes, reactions, or possibly suggestions.

These guidelines should help you to maximize results from your focus groups [10]:

1. *Define the problem narrowly and precisely.* Limit it to one topic or possibly one aspect of the topic. You want tightly focused, "manageable" opinions; you don't want people to develop a detailed manual for you.

2. *Decide on the desired outcome.* Do you want to know how members of recent team-building sessions feel so that you can improve that activity? Do you want to know what topics/skills/concepts should go into next year's introductory course on supervision? Do you want to know how well the training on customer relations has paid off? This is a critical concern, for you'll only get back what you plan for.

3. *Decide who should attend the focus group.* A cross-section of upper-level managers? Graduates of prior courses? Subordinates of the managers who attended the manager development program?

4. *Develop provocative questions.* You certainly don't want "yes" or "no" answers. Questionnaires will give you that. So pose questions which provoke thought, discussion, reaction. *Examples:* "If you were to send your staff members off to training again, what cautions or advice would you give them?" "What did you find to be the most valuable aspect of the writing course you attended? Why?" "What might be done to 'beef up' the public speaking/briefing course?"

5. *Provide a comfortable, professional setting.* Arrange people in a circle or semi-circle so that they can see everyone and readily interact with one another. If written responses are to be secured, provide tables in a squared formation. Consider serving refreshments.

6. *Conduct the session on a facilitated basis.* Your objective is to encourage a free-flowing discussion and to probe people's feelings. So you don't want to behave in a way which might inhibit presentation of ideas.

7. *Add an independent observer(s).* Added observation will help to capture subtle comments, nuances of ideas, recurring themes, and points meriting follow-up. Consider videotaping the session for later review and analysis. Your memory of what was said may let you down.

8. *Recognize the limits of a focus group.* While a focus group can provide many valuable insights, preferences, attitudes, and highlighting of issues, it is not the totality of your research efforts. For example, a focus group can't provide the quantitative data which attitude surveys can. But it is a valuable tool to produce a good many of the answers you may be seeking.

EVALUATION OF PILOT SESSIONS

If you have developed a new course, it makes a lot of sense to evaluate it before you introduce it organization-wide or consider it your best shot. This means (a) conducting a pilot session or trial run and (b) assessing its suitability. Note that Broadway producers send a new play or musical to various cities around the country before they assume it's truly ready for the "big time." In other words, they want to get the bugs out of it before the theater critics descend on it and tear it apart.

Of course, deciding to assess the pilot in a systematic way depends on these factors:

☐ *Resources:* How much time, money, and staff were used to develop the course?

☐ *Attendance:* How many people will attend the course?

☐ *Stakeholders:* What is their interest in the course?

☐ *Restraints:* Are time or other resources to be considered?

☐ *Use of data:* Will the data you collect really be used? Is there a mandate to implement the course "as is"?

In any case, let's assume that this particular pilot course will be subject to evaluation. Are there simple methods that can be used with success? Training evaluation specialist Jan Chernick recommends these two [11]:

☐ A "group debrief" at each day's end
☐ Short surveys administered after certain modules are conducted, and again at course's end

Group debrief. This is a directed group discussion, akin to a focus group, with participants of a short course (three days or less). A group limited to 8 to 15 people is best. The approach is to have participants rate individual modules and then respond to specific questions about the modules. Typical questions to ask are these:

☐ How relevant was the course for your job needs?
☐ How was the pace—too fast or too slow?
☐ Was the sequence O.K.? Did the topics flow easily from one to another?
☐ Were course objectives appropriate and were they met in the course?
☐ Would you recommend the course to others?

Some key skill pointers for the evaluation:

☐ The person who conducts the group debrief should have observed the session. He/she is not likely to understand participant comments and questions if he/she has not attended the course.
☐ The moderator should be an excellent facilitator and should be able to accept feedback in an unbiased way.
☐ The moderator should not be the course designer or instructor. You want someone who can be totally objective.
☐ Prepare carefully. The participants in the pilot group should be members of the audience being targeted in the training course. Stakeholders, who may be course participants, are not to be selected since their perceptions are likely to differ from that of the target audience.
☐ Inform all concerned—instructor, course designer, participants—that an evaluation will take place at the end of each day of the pilot course. Participants will particularly want to know if they will be detained beyond normal work hours. Useful feedback may be jeopardized if participants are "antsy" about getting out late.

☐ Limit the number of modules you will debrief. Five or six per day is enough to prevent overload.
☐ Provide pilot-run evaluation participants with evaluation worksheets to assist in jotting down their thoughts as the course progresses. *Note:* If the group debrief has to be abbreviated or dropped, you will at least have some written worksheets.
☐ If you are the moderator, explain to the evaluation participants what is expected. The aim is to make them feel comfortable about giving feedback. Also explain that a group discussion will be held daily and at course's end. Stress the value of their feedback. Distribute evaluation sheets at the *start* of the course. Stress that they are not to sign these forms.
☐ Advise participants that only they and their moderator will be in the discussion room.
☐ Garner reactions (ratings) via a show of hands. If participants are uncomfortable with this procedure, have them provide ratings privately on the evaluation worksheets.
☐ Typical questions to ask: What worked well? What would you change? Ask added questions as necessary.
☐ Compile average ratings for each module. Consolidate worksheet comments into one composite set.

Survey method. If you don't have the time to do a group debrief, you can use a short, simple survey form (a one-pager) to compile helpful information. Ratings are secured on overall participant impression of the course; the degree to which course objectives were met; degree of skill now possessed on certain course aspects; opinion of the student guide; ratings of various techniques used, such as wall displays, games, and team activities; whether one would recommend the course to others. Open-ended, general comments about the course are also solicited.

GROUP EVALUATION OF TRAINER/FACILITATOR

If you are a trainer/facilitator who is seriously concerned about improving your competency, there are two sources you can tap for reaction and advice about your current prowess:

1. From a co-trainer: see "Co-training: Some ABC's" in Chapter 21, "Ancillary Issues and Techniques"
2. Your participant group, a knowledgeable and observant audience.

Should you decide to check out how your trainees feel about your performance and how it might be upgraded, you may wish to use the procedure outlined in the sample instruction sheet which follows. Provide copies to all participants. *Note:* (1) The procedure is practical, of course, only if your program is long enough for your group to have a good fix on your style and capabilities. (2) Be sure to allow enough time for a good discussion.

KEY POINTS

1. Evaluation of training may be conducted at the (a) reaction level, (b) classroom (change in behavior) level, (c) on-the-job level, and (d) organizational level.
2. While participant reactions are essentially "soft" or subjective data, they do tell us how satisfied participants are with their training, what they feel they learned, how the course might be improved, etc.
3. Participant reactions may be obtained via both group-in-action methods and individually prepared questionnaires.
4. Participant reactions may be obtained via various group-in-action devices including self-appraisal, the circular whip, the fishbowl, movement, art, and individual and group critique.
5. Learning accomplished in the classroom may be ascertained via observation, review of proposed action plans, and attitude surveys.
6. Learning transferred to the job may be ascertained via study of implemented action plans and supervisory and employee reports.
7. Impact of the learning on organizational effectiveness may be measured via "hard" data such as reports on productivity, sales, costs, defects, and turnover.
8. The best evaluation procedures are those that involve "the clients"—that is, managers and

FINAL(!) ACTIVITY: GROUP FEEDBACK TO TRAINER/FACILITATOR

Rationale: Instructors/trainers/facilitators, like managers and supervisors, are hardly perfect performers. All can profit from candid feedback about their performance, behavior, attitudes—how they impact others—as a means of improving their functioning. It thus would seem appropriate for your facilitator, to whom you have been exposed for the period of training, to receive feedback from you as a means of augmenting his effectiveness in future courses.

Procedure:

1. On a sheet of paper write down one or more suggestions which would improve your facilitator's performance.
2. The facilitator will now leave the room.
3. The group will now select a moderator/recorder to:
   a. Record class member ideas on a flipchart(s) sheet.
   b. Lead a discussion concerning member ideas.
   c. Have all class members vote on each suggestion and record the number of members who agree with it.
   d. Prioritize recommendations. (Use a colored marking pen to highlight the priority numbers.)
4. Suggested time: 30 minutes.
5. After all suggestions have been voted on, recorded by number, and prioritized, the moderator will ask the facilitator to return to class.
6. The facilitator will review the recommendations for improvement and discuss them with you.

supervisors at appropriate levels in the organization.
9. Evaluation concerns should extend to daily pulse-taking as well as end-of-course assessments. This procedure will enable changes in the program as may be necessary and practicable.

10. Group feedback to the trainer/facilitator is a worthwhile procedure to ensure one's continuing growth.

REFERENCES

1. Kirkpatrick, D. L., "Techniques for Evaluating Training Programs," a four-part series beginning in the November 1955 issue of the *Training Director's Journal.* (But see the updated Kirkpatrick reference below in "Recommended Reading.")

2. Gunsch, Dawn, "For Your Information: Verify Training Value Through Videotape," *Personnel Journal* (April 1992), pp. 18–19.

3. Coffman, L., "An Easy Way to Effectively Evaluate Program Results," *Training and Development Journal* (August 1979), pp. 28–32, and "Successful Training Program Evaluation," *Training and Development Journal* (October 1980), pp. 84–87.

4. Goldwasser, Donna, "Beyond ROI," *Training* (January 2000), pp.82–90, and Leigh, Pam, "Toni Hodges," in "Training's New Guard 2001," *Training and Development* (May 2001), pp. 48, 63.

5. Bregman, Peter, and Jacobson, Howie, "Yes, You Can Measure the Business Results of Training," *Training* (August 2000), pp. 68–72.

6. Goldwasser, Donna, *op. cit.,* p. 83.

7. Murtha, T. J., "Make Your Course Evaluation Work," *Training and Development Journal* (July 1979), pp. 50–51.

8. Stevenson, G., "Evaluating Training Daily," *Training and Development Journal* (May 1980), pp. 120–122.

9. See Steele, F, and Jenks, S., *The Feel of the Work Place: Understanding and Improving Organization Climate,* "Social Norms and Organizational Climate," Addison-Wesley Publishing Company, Reading, Mass. (1977), Ch. 4, for additional background on norms.

10. Ensman, Richard G., Jr., "Focus Groups: How and When to Use Them," *Successful Meetings* (July 1992), pp. 66–69.

11. Chernick, Jan, "Keeping Your Pilots on Course," *Training and Development* (April 1992), pp. 69–731.

RECOMMENDED READING

Abernathy, Donna J., "Thinking Outside the Evaluation Box," Training and Development, February 1999, pp. 19–23.

Examines additional means of evaluating training, meaning going past the 1959 Kirkpatrick model of training evaluation and taking a balanced view that considers hard- and soft-skill performance gauges, tangible and intangible benefits, and short-and long-term results in training evaluation.

Brinkerhoff, Robert O., "Making Evaluation More Useful," *Training and Development Journal,* December 1981, pp. 66–70.

This is an overall view of evaluation based on the Evaluation Training Consortium project founded by the U.S. Office of Special Education. The author is director of the ETC project.

Harrell, Kathleen D., "Level III Training Evaluation: Considerations for Today's Organizations," *Performance Improvement,* May/June 2001, pp. 24–27.

Presents the case for conducting Level III evaluation (on-the-job behavior), that is, recognizes the significant benefits which can ensue from such assessment.

Kirkpatrick, Donald, *Evaluating Training Programs: The Four Levels,* Berrett-Koehler, San Francisco, 1998, 2nd Edition.

An update of the now classic four-level model to evaluate training. Offers step-by-step guidelines to walk trainers through the four specific areas of measurement: reaction, classroom learning, on-the-job behavior, and organizational results. Has sample survey forms and case studies of evaluation of training in major companies.

Phillips, J. J., *Handbook of Training Evaluation and Measurement Methods,* Gulf Publishing Co., Houston, 1983.

This is a comprehensive source book to aid the trainer in evaluating the training effort. The book shows how to evaluate management and supervisory training (tough areas to assess) in addition to skills areas. Essential statistical approaches are treated in understandable ways.

Phillips, Jack J., *Return Investment in Training and Performance Improvement Programs,* Gulf Publishing Co., Houston, 1997.

A guide to a results-based approach to calculating the ROI (return on investment) on training as a performance improvement.

Pine, Judith, and Tingley, Judith C., "ROI of Soft-Skills Training," *Training,* February 1993, pp. 55–60.

A team-building course, which provided training in the usual leadership skills (communication, problem solving, characteristics of effective work teams, etc.), was subjected to a statistical analysis involving experimental and control groups and before-and-after training measurements. These measures were applied to the classic four levels of evaluation of Donald L. Kirkpatrick (see Reference 1). The trainer used productivity measures (changes in performance) as a basis for determining actual training payoffs.

Purcell, Amy, "20/20 ROI," *Training and Development*, July 2000, pp. 28–33.

An account of how three companies (Lens Crafters, Sears, and Apple) prove a clear link between training and financial results using Jack J. Phillips' Level 5, ROI—the monetary value of training results exceeding the cost of training.

Spitzer, Dean R., "Embracing Evaluation," *Training and Development*, June 1999, pp. 42–47.

Presents six principles to help trainers embrace serious evaluation and thus improve training: (1) Evaluation begins at the beginning. (2) Evaluate based on organization values. (3) "Impact" is not just a synonym for ROI. (4) You need evidence, not proof. (5) Use "causal chains" to trace training's impact. (6) Partner up.

Watson, Scott C., "Five Easy Pieces to Performance Measurement," *Training and Development,* May 1998, pp. 45–48.

A management consultant describes the five principles he has learned in evaluation work at Fortune 500 companies: (1) Focus on the business. (2) Build a bridge between line and training. (3) Track progress, not proof. (4) You're probably already doing measurement. (5) Measurement is simply tracking cause and effect.

20 How to Overcome the Transfer Problem

Nothing is more terrible than activity without insight.

> —Thomas Carlyle (1795–1881),
> Scottish essayist and historian

The art of teaching is the art of assisting discovery.

> —Mark Van Doren (1894–1972),
> American poet, critic, and editor

Up to this point we have been introduced to (or possibly reacquainted with) a broad range of training techniques. All of these devices are designed to facilitate the acquisition of new concepts and skills so that our participants will be more effective when they return to their jobs. As trainers, however, we must ensure that the training really "takes," that it gets "glued in" to the job. Participants thus need meaningful opportunities to apply their learning to work-related problems in the training situation and, more importantly, their work when they return to their jobs.

In the following pages, therefore, we will discuss these pertinent topics:

- ☐ Program design for effective transfer.
- ☐ How to make application activities in the classroom effective.
- ☐ Formats of application activities, such as observation-assessment, practical (hands-on) assignments, role playing, and using worksheets.

☐ Contracting (developing action plans), both pre-session and at program's end.

☐ Skill retention in management training.

☐ Additional ways to aid transfer of training to the job.

☐ Conducting follow-up sessions.

PROGRAM DESIGN FOR EFFECTIVE TRANSFER

Concern with transfer begins *before* the training starts, with design, not after the participants have gone back to their jobs. This means that the trainer must operate so that all parties concerned—management, bosses, trainees, and trainers—are totally clear as to the specific behavioral results that will ensue from the training. Only under these circumstances can we track the application of the new learning to the job. If we are fuzzy about what is to be done on the job at training's end, we can't pinpoint the true success of the new learning.

Trainers/consultants Dana G. and James C. Robinson properly point out that skills are likely to be transferred to the job when both the learning experience and the work environment are in sync about desired end results. They thus suggest that all concerned be aware of and use this formula: L E × W E = Results [1].

"L E" stands for *learning experience* and "W E" refers to *work environment* of the returning learner. The trainer can obviously affect the former, and line management influences the latter. Line management's role is to produce an environment that supports, reinforces, and rewards the learner for applying the newly mastered skill or knowledge provided by the trainer.

To understand the formula in full, note that if either multiplier merits a zero, the final result is also a big goose egg. So how can the trainer ensure that the environment supports the training endeavor? By looking for barriers to transfer in the work environment and then reporting that data back to management, the clients, or the sponsor of the course or program, so that they may take corrective action.

The barriers to skill transfer, according to the Robinsons, fall into three distinct categories:

☐ *The learner.* Because of personal values and concepts about how the job should be performed, he/she might reject the course's values and concepts. Or, alternately, the learner may lack confidence to use/apply the new skills.

☐ *The learner's boss.* The boss may not coach the learner as to how to use the new learning or may not reinforce the learner if he/she applies what was learned. Also, the boss may not serve as a proper model for the learner. In effect, any of those behaviors or attitudes may nullify what was accomplished in the training room.

☐ *The organization.* The learned skills may receive a punishing response when applied in the back-home work environment; for example, if customer relations reps are paid on the basis of the number of orders taken, the skill of dealing with customer concerns/complaints, which may double the time spent with the customer, is not likely to be performed very often. Hence the need for drastic management alteration of its prevailing reward system. Or learners may be inhibited to perform their new learning because of time constraints, inappropriate/incompatible policies or procedures, or lack of authority to act. Or feedback may not be provided about how the application of their new skills actually affects results.

Early Screening of Obstacles to Transfer of Training

To assist in identifying roadblocks to your hopes and efforts to have your training really take, use the checklist which follows.

Identifying Barriers to Training Transfer—A Summary Checklist [2]

Listed below are nine questions managers and their participants have to address if the forthcoming training is likely to stick. A negative response to any statement indicates that the training goal is not understood or supported. Regard any such response as a "red flag" that serious obstacles lie ahead to likely transfer of training.

	YES	NO
1. *Understanding of value.* Do participants and their supervisors know what contribution the training will provide?	❑	❑
2. *Participation.* Were participants and their managers involved in setting training goals?	❑	❑
3. *Practical interest.* Do the participants sincerely wish to experience the training?	❑	❑
4. *Manager interest.* Are managers keen on wanting their staffers to experience the training?	❑	❑
5. *Manager familiarity.* Are managers familiar enough with the training to (a) discuss it with their staffers before the training and (b) to coach them on return to the job?	❑	❑
6. *Support possibilities.* Are there adequate and appropriate/technologies to support the new learning?	❑	❑
7. *Prior support.* Have like training activities been previously supported?	❑	❑
8. *Top management support.* Is there any evidence that senior managers look favorably on the anticipated training outcomes?	❑	❑
9. *Culture.* Does the prevailing culture encourage participant use of the new learning? If not, what are the obstacles?	❑	❑

MAKING CLASSROOM APPLICATION ACTIVITIES EFFECTIVE

In our work on exercises we learned that they may vary greatly as to format, involvement, novelty, time consumption, realism, intensity, and degree of work-relatedness. In the application session (or application activity), however, *all* training work is totally work-related and thus is marked by the highest possible degree of realism. In such sessions, then, participants are presented not only with activities that have "face validity" as to realism, but also with activities that are readily perceived as intrinsically relevant to the work itself. (This does not always mean, unfortunately, that application-type activities are universally applauded by the participants. In fact, they may be resisted because they hit "too close to home." Unfortunately, not everyone wishes to undergo the painful process of introspection that relates to the improvement of one's work.)

In the pages that follow we will suggest a number of application-type activities. They can be worked on by the participants in one of several ways:

❑ *Totally individual work.* This may be desirable when the assignment relates to work that is highly specialized. In such an instance hardly anyone else can offer help or comment constructively on job performance.

❑ *Team assignment.* Certain learnings can best be accomplished via a group or team effort. The assumptions are that several participants, working together, can provide a broader variety of inputs on the task, augment motivation and support, and learn to work well with others.

❑ *Individual work followed by small group work.* This may be accomplished in pairs or in small groups of three to five participants. The assumption in this instance is that one or more persons, as neutral reviewers, can provide certain insights that the preparer cannot. Why not? Because the preparer of the material is often too close to it, too emotionally or ego-involved with his/her own accomplishment. Thus, objective outsiders can aid the preparer of the material by offering helpful feedback or raising questions about the completed assignment: Is it on-target, practical, realistic, cost-effective, complete, policy-based, future-oriented, understandable, likely to meet resistance? A good training design for this type of application assignment is the following:

1. Assign participants to trios. *Note:* The smaller the work team, the greater the likelihood for candid sharing. Hence, I favor work in trios or even pairs as opposed to larger work teams.

2. Tell the participants that they are being assigned to small work teams (trios) to share completed work and to elicit help about the activity from the other team members. Advise

them that the assumption here is that three heads are better than one—that *team* analysis can ensure that proposals are marked by the maximum degree of realism and practicality.

3. Instruct the teams that each participant will present his/her work for review, critique, and assistance by the other two team members. All participants, then, assume the roles of presenter and reviewer (or helper). *Note:* The time for each presentation and receipt of feedback thereon will vary with the complexity of the assignment. If each presenter has 30 minutes, the total critique session will take 90 minutes; if each presenter has 20 minutes, the team's work can be completed in one hour.

4. Remind the participants that in their role of reviewer they are to be as helpful as they possibly can. Similarly, advise the presenters that here is a splendid opportunity to get feedback from two other objective, knowledgeable participants.

5. Assign participants to relatively noise-free locations. If separate training rooms are not available, locate the teams as far as possible from one another in the regular training room.

6. Keep track of the elapsed time. Provide a ten-minute warning as to the imminent close of the application session.

7. Secure small group reports concerning the learning from the activity. This group-at-large sharing should enrich the total experience.

FORMATS OF APPLICATION ACTIVITIES

Application activities in the training situation can assume a variety of formats. Here are several:

Observation-Assessment

Participants and participant teams can be given practical observational assignments, for example, to conduct a safety inspection of a given work area or operation and to prepare a report thereon, to study the operation of the admissions desk at a hospital and to recommend improvements therein, to observe the operation of the complaint desk at a large department store and to write a report thereon.

Note: For true experiential learning, the observers must analyze, suggest improvements, make recommendations, etc. Observation without actual involvement will produce only limited learning.

Practical Assignments

"Learning-by-doing" or "hands on" assignments may include:

☐ Developing a job training plan for a new subordinate.

☐ Developing various checklists, for example, to aid in conducting a safety inspection of one's work area, to help in orienting a new worker, or to assist in dealing with contingencies (unexpected events, emergencies, crises).

☐ Making a critical job inventory for one's area of supervision [3].

☐ Preparing a job safety analysis of one or two jobs that one supervises [4].

☐ Developing a plan to enrich a subordinate's job.

☐ Developing a list of customer objections to certain of our products and coming up with creative ways to deal with the objections.

☐ In a team of management trainees, working for a specified time in a shop or office; selecting a management, administrative, or operational problem for study; and then making recommendations thereon.

☐ Giving oral reports if it is desired to augment skills in talking before groups.

Management training courses typically entail the delivery of considerable conceptual material. Why not, then, redress this imbalance and have the participants also focus on on-going management practices that, for example, influence climate and creativity in the organization? This may include such topics as the career management plan, the suggestion system, the MBO plan, the tuition aid plan, the communication system, and the productivity of staff meetings.

In a training program for logging-camp supervisors of a Canadian lumber company, the trainers took a radically results-oriented approach and decided to abandon "education" for intervention [5]. Although the program was intended to teach the usual management training topics such as planning work, giving directions and feedback, setting short-term goals, and promoting communication and team work, the program they actually built focused on a pressing company problem instead—reduction of hauling costs. All training activities and exercises, management support, and follow-through zeroed in on the cost problem. The results were these:

- [ ] One camp closed three weeks ahead of time.
- [ ] Hauling costs were reduced by 5%.
- [ ] Unit hauling costs decreased by 4%–6%.
- [ ] 20% more wood was stored at the river bank.
- [ ] Task-related radio communications increased from 30% to 90%.

Participants learned the intended managerial skills while engaging in the practical work. As a consequence, the trainer concluded that it is far wiser to concentrate on limited material, practice, and application than on a lot of "standard" concepts and theory. Their program, then, was marked by these principles:

- [ ] Relate the training to organizational goals, priorities, and the system's real performance demands.
- [ ] Focus on short-term productivity improvements, drawing on immediate problems.
- [ ] Gear it to the participants' needs and capabilities.
- [ ] Build in mechanisms to ensure real-world success experiences with the training techniques applied.

Role Plays

Role plays that are job-oriented allow the application of principles and concepts to actual work situations; for example, a customer service representative who has to deal with an irate person; an airline hostess who has to calm down passengers who are anxious, angry, or inebriated; a salesperson who has to deal with certain customer objections; a police officer who has to break up a violent family argument; a supervisor who has to deal with a troubled employee; a supervisor who has to conduct a performance review discussion with a marginal worker.

Using Worksheets

Presented in Appendices 72 through 82 are a number of worksheets (also called guide sheets) for the conduct of application sessions. The structure which the worksheets provide is designed to help participants "zero in" more precisely and quickly on their assignments. An important factor in the psychology of the worksheet is its motivating force; that is to say, to the extent that one is presented with an incomplete form, one is motivated to complete it.

The reader will note that the worksheets exemplify the wide array of formats that may be used. Some of them may be used "as is"; others may be adapted to meet your own training circumstances. The important thing is to develop your thought processes in order to think in "guide sheet terms," thereby creating and providing practical and challenging application assignments to your participants.

INTERIM (POST-SESSION) ACTION PLANS

As we will discuss later, a training program should end with a positive resolve in the form of participant action plans to do something concrete and worthwhile with the training experience upon return to the job. However, it *also* may be desirable to encourage thinking about the application of learnings at the end of particular sessions or possibly at the end of each training day. If so, guide sheets such as the ones in Appendices 83 through 86 may be given to participants for completion.

To increase the likelihood of commitment to action plans, provide five or ten minutes for preparation of the plans in class plus a similar time period for discussion of them in pairs or trios.

Note: End-of-session or daily action plans should help to set the stage for the development of a comprehensive action plan on a major problem at the end of the course or program. If mini-contracts are worked on each day, they should help develop the mindset for the final one.

CONTRACTING AT PROGRAM'S END

On the assumption that the training effort has brought about various changes—acquisitions of new skills and concepts; new ways of looking at bosses, peers, customers, the organization, oneself; and new resolves to perform or manage better—there obviously is a need to help participants convert the new learning and determination into concrete plans for action on the job.

Changing one's behavior in the back-home situation is hardly a simple task. Realistically, there are many forces at work that can undo the best of a participant's good intentions to change. These include a return to the usual job pressures, possible lack of support from superiors, passage of time, the vanishing of support and pressure from the participant group and the trainer, and the absence of opportunities to communicate with others who have shared the training experience. All of these indicate quite clearly that there must be a formal, all-out effort to plan for new behavior on the job. Procedures to accomplish this come under the general heading of "contracting." This entails the development of specific action plans to convert the classroom learning to concrete and realistic job application.

An action plan, then, is a commitment to engage in a new behavior resulting from the impetus of the training experience. It can often be quite simple, entailing no more than a self-pledge such as in Figure 20-1.

The action plan may also have more specifics, such as proposed dates of accomplishments, how the plan will be implemented, who else will have to be involved in the plan (possibly one's boss, subordinates, peers), and criteria to tell whether the plan is working well or not.

MY ACTION PLAN

As a result of the training I plan to:

1. Hold staff meetings regularly (every Wed. at 9:30 A.M.).
2. Appoint an assistant with full authority to act for me while I am away.
3. Use praise more liberally to reward and motivate subordinates.

Figure 20-1. Example of a self-pledge that could be used as an action plan.

Guidelines for an "application session" to accomplish the necessary contracting are given in Appendix 87. Note that the steps that participants are to take in developing their action plans are provided in specific detail. Also, the action plans are submitted to peers for critique and augmented commitment. The trainer may wish to modify the forms given in Appendix 87, to meet the needs of the participant group better.

The contracting idea, although pedagogically sound, is not universally accepted by program participants. Expect resistance in the form of "lip service" to the idea (just going through the motions) or possibly verbal objections: "I could do this better back on the job where I can give it more thought." "Should we be taking up our valuable time in class to do this when we could be learning more of the subject?" "I don't have the information that I need; I've got it back home."

Since the principle of application in the classroom to aid transfer to the job is a sound one, the trainer must insist that practice in the training situation is an integral part of the training process.

How to Help Contracts "Take"

To ensure that participant contracts are carried out as pledged, the observance of these guidelines should be considered:

Early commitment. Secure commitments for goals (action plan) as early as is practicable. In some cases this may be *before* the formal training program begins. Early identification of goals will provide the greatest opportunity to think about them in relation to program inputs. Recognize, however, that in other cases participants may have to acquire "insight" from the program itself before meaningful goal setting is possible. This is particularly true in personal growth programs, leadership development, and the like. Also, with certain participants it may not be desirable to push for action plans until the training is completed. Premature requests for work on action plans may unnecessarily raise anxiety levels and interfere with the hoped-for learning.

Realistic goal setting. Recognize that, as in the case of any goal setting effort, targets (for improvement) must be clearly defined, limited in number, reachable, time-specific, voluntarily arrived at, and organization/boss-supported (as necessary).

Group discussion. Provide opportunities for discussing completed plans with fellow participants. One's colleagues can obviously be useful as helpers, critics, reality-testers, and support-givers. Equally important is the vital role of group discussion as a stimulus to commitment. The reader may be familiar with social psychologist Kurt Lewin's research in World War II which dramatically revealed the impact that discussing a potential course of action may have upon the discussants.

Lewin's research involved the U.S. Department of Agriculture's attempt to convince American housewives to purchase less popular but highly nutritious cuts of meat such as liver, heart, kidneys, and sweetbreads. A change in eating habits was deemed essential by the government since the regular cuts were going to the military in great quantities. Dr. Lewin, then at M.I.T., set up a number of experiments with Iowa housewives that entailed these procedures [6]:

1. Lectures were given to three groups of housewives on the desirability of buying the organ meats. The lectures were accompanied by recipes for their preparation plus patriotic appeals (good nutrition was essential to keep workers productive in the war material industries). There was no group discussion of the information provided.

2. Three other groups received the same information as the first three groups and, in addition, were given an opportunity to discuss the data among themselves.

Lewin's staff followed up on the buying and serving behavior of the housewives. The following shows the results of their research:

Lecture method: 3% acted on the information (served the less-popular cuts)
Lecture plus discussion: 32% served the less popular cuts

Note that the lecture-plus-discussion group was ten times more effective than the lecture-only group. This is not to say that everyone acted as hoped for—only 32% actually did try out the less popular cuts of meat. But the difference in the behavior of the two groups was so large that it has been considered a breakthrough in the social sciences, particularly in the area of group dynamics.

One might ask: Why did group discussion work so dramatically? Peer pressure developed through a feeling of group identification. Visualize the housewives talking about the new information and one of them possibly saying to the others: "If you're willing to try it, so am I." In other words, the group discussion had an encouraging or reinforcing effect on their decision to act. Note that although the decision made was an individual one, that is, it was carried out in the meat market without the presence of the group, it nevertheless represented a commitment to the group which was honored thereafter.

In passing, we might add that savvy politicians understand the power of the group and the importance of *public* commitment. They thus organize neighborhood coffees in people's homes during election campaigns to build up support for and commitment toward their candidates (or candidacy).

Monitoring procedures. Give adequate thought to monitoring or enforcement procedures. From the trainer's standpoint, action plans can be implemented and followed up in different ways and with different degrees of effectiveness:

☐ Provide participants with the necessary forms and procedures and encourage them to develop an action plan when they return to their jobs. This is the "hope and promise" approach, and few will do much about it. Job pressures in the back-home environment will scuttle most good intentions.

☐ A better procedure is to allow time for the preparation of action plans *in the class*. At least a plan will have been developed. Implementation is another matter, of course.

☐ A still more effective procedure is to have the action plans developed in class *and* then have them discussed and critiqued for realism in triads. This will provide some reinforcement for possible back home implementation of the plan.

☐ The best procedures entail some follow-up of action plan commitments. Some possible ways of doing this are as follows:

1. Collect the completed action plans and mail them back to participants, two to four weeks after the training has been completed, with an encouraging letter or memo.

2. Have the action plans prepared in duplicate, collect one copy of them, and mail the plans back to the participants 30 days after the training as a reminder of their commitment in class.

3. Contact participants via questionnaire or interview concerning accomplishment of the action plan.

4. Assemble participants in a group situation 30 days after the training to discuss their progress and problems in implementing their action plans. Pressure by the thrust of the post-training effort, plus that of one's peers, should optimize results.

5. For maximum results, engage the participants' supervisors in the action planning and reviewing process. The theory here is that people are more likely to respond to what is *inspected* rather than merely *expected*. But note: While this procedure may be helpful in many cases, this is not universally so. For example, some participants may have improvement goals that they consider too personal to discuss with their boss. Others may feel that they do not want to "confess" weaknesses to their superior, particularly if the latter is one who is not particularly sensitive to others, or with whom a trusting relationship has not been established.

One way to ensure the full and active involvement of the trainee's supervisor in the action planning is to require him/her to complete the form in Appendix 86 in advance of the training. This form asks the supervisor to indicate what he/she expects the subordinate to learn in the training course in the way of skills, knowledge and/or attitudes.

The completed form, in duplicate, is sent to the trainer, who makes a copy available to the trainee as an aid to completion of his/her action plan. The action plan is prepared in triplicate: one for the trainee, one for the trainee's boss, and one for the trainer, who uses this copy in two ways:

   a. To assess the degree to which the training really "took" (classroom learning).

   b. As a control mechanism to follow up on the intentions stated in the action plan.

☐ At the close-out, one trainer gives each departing participant a postcard and asks them to write on it these four words: start, stop, continue, compliment. He then asks them to write on the card the following in relation to what was learned:

1. One thing they will *start* doing
2. One thing they will *stop* doing
3. One thing they will *continue* doing
4. One *compliment* about themselves

Participants then self-address the postcards and postdate them 90 days. The trainer collects the cards and mails them to the attendees three months later. The objective: to remind people of their commitments and to help "crystallize thought" [7].

Regardless of the particular follow-up procedure employed, the important thing is to keep up the momentum (enthusiasm, commitment) achieved in the training situation.

Peer monitoring/networking. Another approach to monitoring is to ask the participants to pick another person, one with whom they ordinarily do *not* work closely to keep in touch with them on their contract or action plan. The person selected is given a copy of the action plan and agrees to contact its preparer within 30 days or so to ascertain progress.

By committing oneself to another person (and indirectly to the rest of the group and the trainer) to carry through on the action plan, one feels stimulated and enhanced motivation to achieve this goal. In other words, a commitment to someone else is much greater than a promise to one's self. A side benefit of this procedure is that it establishes lines of communication among persons who might not ordinarily be in any direct contact [8].

Networking on purpose. Networking isn't ordinarily a stated end-result of training programs. But it certainly can be—and often is—an unexpected and welcome by-product.

It is to be noted, however, that networking can also become an explicit, primary training goal, one that can dramatically increase effectiveness of communication across organizational lines. Consider the experience of Morgan Guaranty, as expressed by Robert Waterman in *The Renewal Factor: How the Best Get and Keep the Competitive Edge* (Bantam Books, 1987) and quoted by business professors Paul F. Buller and John R. Cragun [9]:

The training program for every new Morgan officer is as much to help classmates establish tight rapport as it is to build their technical banking skills. With their business dependent on rapid communication across time zones, countries, and continents, this rapport means everything. If you know and trust the person on the other end of the telephone, you can put a deal together fast that meets the customer's needs.

With networking as an explicit goal, then, Morgan took these key steps, as described by Buller and Cragun:

☐ Selecting a mix of participants to support the network. Since a goal of the training program was to eliminate cumbersome/ineffective relationships, participants from different departments were grouped together.

☐ Including in the training provisions for trust and relationship building.

☐ Organizing a system to transfer both training and relationships back to the work setup.

☐ Encouraging follow-up and accountability for transfer.

Morgan's training program for managers had three phases:

Phase One, one day in length, provided basic management skills, including specific behavioral guidelines for skill improvement.

Phase Two was a five-day outdoor training program to practice the skills learned in Phase One.

Note:

1. Phases One and Two were particularly designed to build trust. A supportive environment allowed participants to practice skills and to give and receive constructive feedback.

2. At the start of Phase Two each participant selected a fellow attendee to serve as a partner/coach for the total outdoor program.

Phase Three was a one-day follow-up session, held a month after Phase Two. Its purposes: to follow up on participants' action plans, to address possible problems with transferring the training back to the job, and to develop the network further.

Morgan Guaranty worked actively at keeping the training and the spirit of the network alive. Here's what they did:

☐ At the end of Phase Three a banquet was provided, and each grad received a videotape of highlights of the outdoor training.

☐ Each grad also received a special pen and plaque indicating his/her program completion plus a list of all program alumni, their job titles, and their phone numbers.

☐ Most groups initiated work and social get-togethers to sustain their relationships.

☐ Group identity was maintained via special momentos, capturing the unique characteristics of each group's training experience.

A post-training survey (six months after the training) indicated the following on a five-point scale:

☐ Extent to which the training broadened your network of relationships at the firm: rating of 3, 21%; 4, 45%; 5, 34%.

☐ Extent to which the network helped you to get things done more effectively: rating of 3, 30%; 4, 56%; 5, 10%.

☐ Extent to which the training helped you to communicate better with those in other departments: rating of 3, 10%; 4, 56%; 5, 34%.

In addition to ratings, the survey provided an open-ended opportunity to express post-training feelings about the results to date. Here are two particularly powerful quotes:

"Probably on at least a weekly basis, someone who attended training with me will call requesting help in dealing with his or her area of responsibility. The feeling of comradeship that was developed at the training prevails and together we solve the problem."

"I found that the common experience has opened some doors, brought some instant trust and credibility, and generated a growing [network] of enlightened, sensitive leaders."

The bottom line: Networks, developed through a well-planned training program, can help to reduce communication barriers and make for more effective problem solving.

Difficulties questionnaire. Consider conducting a survey of program graduates to ascertain specific difficulties in living up to contracts and to secure suggestions concerning ways to overcome such difficulties.

Note: This procedure would be employed only if overall implementation of action plans was deemed inadequate.

Contracting: Behavior Modification Approach

Another form of the action plan is personal contracting using behavior modification procedures; that is to say, contracting which uses the "baseline" data collection approach (before and after measurement) and positive reinforcement to reward any behavior change. Of course, the reinforcement is self-administered rather than applied by an outside source as in a true "behavior mod" effort.

The change effort may encompass either work-related or personal-type changes, or both. By work-related changes we mean such quantifiable areas as production, downtime, cost, errors, customer complaints, waste, scrap, absenteeism, tardiness, accidents, and grievances. By personal changes we are talking about changing habits of smoking, eating, and/or exercising or improving one's family life (via helping children with home work, doing home chores, reducing nagging behavior, giving one's spouse or children positive reinforcement).

Here is a ten-step procedure given to program participants who wish to participate in the "Behavior Change Project." The system was developed by K. A. Moody, manager, General Management Development of U.S. Steel in Pittsburgh [10]. Basically, the "Behavior Change Project" asks participants to provide data (via a simple form) on these questions or steps:

1. *Targeted or terminal behavior.* Cite specific end results to be achieved—what conditions will exist when the goal is met?

2. *Beginning or entering behavior.* What is the current state of events in respect to the problem or concern? (Cite current weight, number of cigarettes smoked daily, number of times praise is given to spouse each day, cost of production, accident rate.)

3. *Reinforcers for the change.* What are the benefits to you and the person changed? Make separate lists.

4. *Set up a graph or grid to measure the change over time.* On the vertical axis indicate changes in quantity; on the horizontal axis show changes over time. The time measurement can be daily, weekly, monthly. A terminal date should be indicated.

   Note: The starting point or current behavior is referred to by the behavior mod people as "baseline." For example, if one wishes to change a smoking habit, the baseline may be 40 cigarettes smoked per day. The measurement idea, which gives one feedback about progress toward the goal, is basic to the change process.

5. *Consider special reinforcers to reward progress;* for example, special rewards may be given to oneself at the one-fourth, one-half, or three-quarters mark, or at other stages of accomplishment.

6. *Anticipated obstacles to progress.* What factors or events may derail your plan? (List.) How will you meet these impediments to progress?

7. *Securing outside help.* Who can help you meet your goal? In what way? What rewards shall you give them?

8. *Plan maintenance.* How can you prevent fading or slippage of the new behavior, once it is attained? What added reinforcement is essential?

9. *Enter baseline data.* This means recording data on the grid (see Step 4) concerning the point of departure from the baseline. Enter data regularly concerning progress toward terminal behavior.

10. *Evaluation.* Did you succeed? If not, why not? Should the original plan be revised? Are new reinforcers necessary? Any problems in data collection? What was your major learning? How do you feel about your accomplishment?

ENSURING SKILL RETENTION IN MANAGEMENT TRAINING

Management training presents special problems in skill retention for transfer to the job. Relapse rates can be as high as 90%, says Robert Mark, professor of management, University of Massachusetts. A key reason for the fadeout phenomenon, says Dr. Mark, is that many of the complex behaviors taught and learned in management training require numerous *support skills*. Unfortunately, the "trained" manager may lack some of these skills. For example, leadership concepts may be well understood in the classroom, but the manager may not have acquired the time management skills required for their proper execution. Or the manager may learn the "whys" and "hows" of delegation but be uncomfortable with the authority aspects of it, such as giving orders or actually "letting go." Or, to resolve conflicts successfully, the manager may lack the requisite skill of active listening. Other vital support skills are assertiveness and stress management.

A way to help participants understand the vital role of support skills in the retention process is to have them identify the "high-risk" situations back home that may vitiate application of the new learning. If they can become aware of the vulnerability of a new skill to relapse, they can then discover clues to help them diagnose support skill deficits.

To diagnose needed support skills and to develop a modus operandi to increase long-term skill retention, Dr. Mark proposes adoption of the "Relapse Prevention Model" in management training. The RP Model identifies potential causes of training failure by using data from past personal relapses as feedback to make one sensitive to possible future slips back home. Slips are not to be regarded as indicators of inadequacy/incompetence/weak will, but as valuable data for the prevention of future difficulties.

In effect, for the new skills to survive the treacherous work environment, the participants must learn (1) to anticipate job realities, (2) to expect impairing emotional responses to temporary failure, (3) to recognize the need for development of support skills, and (4) to learn to cope with little or no reinforcement from the organization. The RP Model, then, operates on the assumption that retention of learning is aided if the unpredictability of the work environment is reduced and if vital strategies of *self-control* can be provided (by the training) and learned.

In respect to point 4, managers must be trained to realize that skill retention and application is basically a matter of self-management. Even if highly busy bosses up the line are interested and want to be supportive, in the last analysis execution of the new behaviors will be self-motivating, lonely, and private events. For example, no one but the manager can wrestle effectively with all the interpersonal dynamics and nuances of the delegation process.

The key steps in behavioral self-management (relapse prevention strategies) are:

1. *Anticipate and monitor potential difficulties.* Learn to control events via a sensitive early warning system; learn to anticipate harassers, trouble spots, or high risk situations.

2. *Increase rational thinking.* Expect and manage irrational thoughts and emotions which play hob with rational skill building.

3. *Diagnose and practice support skills.* Learn to identify skill shortcomings and acquire and practice appropriate support skills. A review of disruptive patterns is essential, for example, a tendency toward perfectionism.

4. *Provide consequences.* Learn to provide one's own consequences (rewards) for the new behaviors since the environment probably won't (and can't) provide them. Set specific rewards for both short- and long-term accomplishment.

To implement the RP strategies, Dr. Mark states that three steps are required:

1. The manager chooses an appropriate skill he/she wishes to retain, for example, using group decision making.

    Note: It should be described in operational (observable or measurable) terms, so that a slip can be readily noticed. Thus, a goal, in this instance, might be one weekly group decision.

2. The manager applies the above four-step relapse prevention strategies (the RP Model) to his/her on-the-job situation.

3. The manager predicts in detail the circumstances of the first setback. In effect, this is use of "relapse imagery" so that when the predicted negative scenario comes on screen at work, it is no surprise, less disruptive, and much more manageable.

In sum, the RP Model provides a systematic means, a methodology, to identify possible skill-threatening situations and to tie them to possible support skills which can be learned in the training situation [11].

ADDITIONAL WAYS TO AID THE TRAINING TRANSFER

To ensure that the training really "takes," these devices and approaches merit consideration:

Pre-Training

☐ Involve the participant's boss *before* the training begins. Encourage supervisors to nominate their subordinates to training programs based on mutually agreed-upon development needs, to learn as much as possible about the course, and to set goals for learning by the subordinate.

One writer utilizes a two-step program to ensure full supervisory involvement [12]:

1. *The trainer conducts negotiations with the supervisor.* Course or workshop objectives, plus on-the-job expectations after the training is completed, should be discussed with the supervisor for about 20 minutes. It helps if the supervisor is shown a performance or behavior model, that is, what will be done by the participant (subordinate) post-training. Not every supervisor may "buy" all aspects of the model. In such a circumstance, the trainer should promise to mention such objections in the workshop. In any case, a promise should be secured from the supervisor for *active* support/reinforcement of the parts of the model he/she does accept.

2. *A pre-course meeting between the supervisor and the trainee is required.* The meeting must be held to discuss the workshop's performance model, its objectives, and the anticipated benefits from the training. It is desirable to secure some "evidence" that the discussion actually took place. This may take the form of signatures of both parties on the objectives statement or a memo from the supervisor summarizing their discussion of the workshop and his/her expectations of the workshop.

☐ Secure support for the training from participants' superiors via appreciation sessions and help in planning the training or, better still, have the superiors experience the training before their subordinates do.

☐ As appropriate, have an entire unit, section, or department attend the same training. Attendance may be on a joint basis (vertical training) or in separate sessions. The end result should be the acquisition of a common set of concepts, procedures, "language," etc., so that mutual reinforcement of the new learning is an easy and natural thing to do.

☐ Make your training "research-based," that is, collect information via interviews, questionnaires, and operating data and use these inputs (need data) as bases for course design and post-training follow-up.

☐ Have participants identify in *advance* of class one or two problems they will work on in the program. Use pre-work procedures for this purpose.

☐ Use other pre-work assignments such as completing a self-assessment quiz, gathering data for a report to the class, studying an assigned case or problem, interviewing a key figure who is knowledgeable about some aspect of the course, teaming up with another participant to work on an assigned project.

☐ Advise participants in advance of the training session to bring their calendar (desk or wall type) with them, for it will be used in the contracting phase (action planning) of the program. This is not only a practical way to record "good intentions" on a time-frame basis, but it also communicates at the outset that the course has a high expectation that contracting must be taken seriously by the participants.

In the Classroom

☐ Consider the use of "spaced learning," that is, break up the training with one or more opportunities to return to the job to reflect upon and try out the new learning.

☐ In a management training program, introduce live data on managerial practices from the participants' subordinates. This may relate to communication, coaching, team work, rewarding good work, etc. Secure managerial self-assessments on the same behaviors and compare them with the subordinate assessments. Wherever subordinates are more critical of the manager's behavior than the manager is, the latter obviously has a need to study the feedback carefully and possibly to initiate such changes as may be indicated [13].

☐ To overcome possible trainee discouragement upon return from training, ascertain problems and obstacles that might prevent proper performance of the new learning. A fishbowl exercise may be useful for this purpose. Then organize accordingly, based on the data from the participants.

☐ Overlearning (practice beyond the point of mastery) may be helpful to ensure the learning of vital skills, approaches, or concepts, for example, learning a foreign language or, in a restaurant setting, learning how to make special desserts or breads.

☐ Use guided imagery to help the learning really "glue in." Mental rehearsal via vivid mind pictures is very helpful in learning how to close a sale with an undecided customer or how to deal with a highly angry person.

☐ Integrate "assimilation time" into the learning process. People require time to reflect on and apply/practice new behaviors and knowledge applications. This is particularly important with complex subjects before they can perform at expert levels. Recognize that the learning curve continues after the workshop. So everyone— trainees, supervisors, and trainers—must set realistic expectations when a new "grad" will be fully up to speed and, most likely, it won't happen on immediate return to the job [14].

☐ Use "paired sharing" as a device to ensure high retention, says Nancy Maresh, CEO of Brainworks, a Boulder, Colorado, training firm. She pairs participants who then are asked to review the information they have received.

Procedure: One participant shares what he/she has learned. The other partner acts as if he/she is hearing the material for the first time and then asks questions for clarification. The "probing" is a helpful bridge to a more detailed discussion, all of which aids remembering. The pairing may be used at completion of major subject areas or deferred until the start of the class the following day [15].

☐ Train participants to look for cues, signals, or trigger mechanisms that indicate the need for immediate action. Examples: heavy or repeated absences on Monday and Friday over a six-week period indicate the need for a meeting with the employee to review the leave record; in technical areas various sounds, lights, smells, or readings on gauges may serve as action alerts; in a factory setting a particular percentage of rework or customer complaints may evince the need for added quality control measures.

Post-Training

☐ Involve the participant's boss *after* the training. Encourage supervisors to sit down with participants upon their return from the training program to assess what was learned, to discuss how the new learning can be "plowed back" into the on-going operation, and to establish specific goals to capitalize on the new learning.

Data about the results of supervisory follow-ups should be obtained by the trainer via personal visit, written report, or questionnaire. The latter written procedures may be essential if many supervisors are involved or if the supervisors are located at a distance from the trainer's office. Should supervisors be tardy or derelict in submitting their evaluation reports, a tactful phone call along this line should jog the delinquent ones: "We're going through the evaluations for the safety course, and we don't seem to have your report form. Would you care for another copy?"

☐ Where action plans are developed in class, consider structuring them so that the participants' bosses are involved in their review and follow-up.

☐ Encourage participants' supervisors to reward psychologically (positive reinforcement) the new learning upon its performance. ("Charlie, I'm glad to see you're lifting just as they taught you in the training course.")

☐ Provide participants with handy tools or performance aids to facilitate application of the learning, such as checklists, plastic overlay data wheels, flow charts, formulae, tables, guide-sheets, question lists, diagrams, models, reminder cards, and wall charts.

☐ Discuss with the training committee transfer problems, either those anticipated before the training is given and/or those that arise after the training has been completed.

☐ Keep in touch with participants via periodical articles, possibly a newsletter, or occasional questionnaires to produce data that is then shared with all concerned.

☐ If geographically practical, try to bring course graduates together for an "alumni reunion." This might be both a social and a work-oriented activity. Where reunions or class get-togethers take place, the trainer might meet with the group, at least initially, to help in its organization.

☐ As appropriate, team up two course graduates to form a "buddy system." This procedure should provide mutual help, motivation, and support.

☐ Encourage trainees to keep diaries or other records of their experience in applying the training. Then visit with the participants, either on an individual or on a group basis, to ascertain problems, if any, in applying what was learned.

☐ Provide and publicize the availability of follow-up resources such as audio/video cassettes, print materials, visitation services, and assistance to telephone and letter requests.

☐ Use course graduates as instructors/trainers in future courses. This procedure will serve to continue their interest and involvement in their initial learning.

☐ Encourage course graduates to form a network or post-training support group to keep in touch after the formal training is over. Suggest they appoint a secretary-recorder to keep the participant roster current insofar as names, addresses, and phone numbers are concerned.

☐ Think long-term rather than short-term participant involvement. By keeping the participants in a "continuous" state of training, the likelihood of the training becoming part of them and more of a "way of life" is increased. For example, to teach public speaking skills, opt for participation in a Toastmaster's Club rather than attendance at a public speaking course, either in-house or college. Similarly, in time management training, a long-term program (four months),

involving a time-log (pre-work) and three post-workshop follow-ups conducted at monthly intervals, is preferable to a quickie one- or two-day seminar.

In this latter connection, the concept of follow-up training should be considered whenever practical. This topic is covered in more detail in the section "Conducting the Follow-up Session."

☐ Provide participants with pertinent rules to govern their behavior on the job. While many behaviors are subject to contingency shaping, not all are. Hence the need to provide rules for self-monitoring of behavior. For example, the rule "always wear your seat belt" is very much worth learning. Why? Because there's no need to learn to use seat belts by experiencing the result or consequence of *not* having worn them [16].

☐ Consultants may be trained and utilized to follow up and to offer help and encouragement to seminar graduates. A carefully controlled evaluation study (via the use of experimental and control groups) of a seminar for church leaders indicated that the participants who were part of the consultation system improved their attitudes toward transfer of training from the seminar setting. The consultants contacted their "clients" over an eight-week period through personal meetings, phone conversations, and letters. The research also indicated that clients appreciated these consultative contacts and regarded the special attention as helpful, not as an intrusion. The consultants' contact also provided the seminar conductors with information regarding the actual transfer occurring between the seminar and real life applications. In some cases transfer was hindered because of work demands. A salutary byproduct was that the consultants themselves increased their own enthusiasm for and use of the seminar materials [17].

☐ Collect participants' e-mail addresses and key them in as a group on your e-mail browser, advises trainer Jane Bozarth, North Carolina Department of Justice. This procedure permits delivering support messages as a training follow-up. Sending out reminders at regular intervals aids the training to "glue in." *Examples:* Thirty days after a time management class, forward a note concerning creating a daily priority list. Two weeks after that, send pointers to beat procrastination. Two weeks later, e-mail the address of a helpful web site on time management skills. Bozarth states it takes little work to do this and helps her to keep in touch with her former participants. The latter tell her that they appreciate her efforts; some say "it's nice just to know the trainer cares" [18].

☐ Provide managers, whose staffers have had the training, with reinforcement materials. *Purpose:* To give 5–10-minute presentations at staff meetings to remind course grads what was learned and how to apply it. The reinforcement should go on as long as it takes to ensure mastery of the new learning.

   Note: (1) Supervisors should be advised to adapt the materials as they see fit. (2) The supervisors, not the trainers, are to provide the reinforcement. (3) Stress to the supervisors and the trainees that reinforcement is as important as the classroom learning itself to ensure its full transfer to the job [19].

CONDUCTING THE FOLLOW-UP SESSION

The follow-up session is an excellent technique to

☐ *Prevent fadeout.* Time, of course, is a major factor in our forgetting what has been learned. Unless the new learning is regularly practiced on the job, a significant percentage of loss is inevitable. In essence, then, the refresher session is essential to reinforce or help "glue in" what was learned.

☐ *Introduce new, related material.* In this manner, we can build on what has already been learned and experienced. This approach will enrich the participants' initial training experience.

In a given refresher training session, the goal may be to accomplish either or possibly both of these goals.

In the refresher training session the trainer obviously has to decide on "agenda ownership." That is to say, should it be built entirely by the trainer or should it be left to the participants, either in whole or in part? Of course, there is no best answer to this question.

But it is obvious that the greater the extent that we can involve the participants in agenda building, the greater the likelihood of acceptance of the training. Certainly, in the refresher training we are trying to meet participant needs. Also, since the basic program has already been experienced, it would appear adequately logical to expect our participants to be able to decide on agenda items.

The Participant-Developed Agenda

If you decide to secure participant input for the agenda, this can be done in various ways.

☐ A short, pre-session questionnaire, with questions such as the following, might be used:

1. List one or two successes in applying learnings from the course.
2. Cite any difficulties you have encountered in your attempts to implement what you learned in the course.
3. What subjects or topics should we cover in our follow-up session?
4. When the follow-up session is completed, what should have happened to make it a success for you? Answers to these questions can be tallied and analyzed; they can become the building blocks for the agenda. It should be recognized, realistically, that responses to the pre-session questionnaire may well be spotty or even omitted. Hence the need to be prepared to do the agenda-building job as the first order of business in the follow-up session itself.

☐ The agenda in the follow-up session may be developed via small groups or general (group-at-large) inputs. An interesting way to accomplish this with the total group is to ask all participants to take the following "fantasy trip":

   "It is the morning after the follow-up session. A good friend asks you a number of very penetrating questions about it. In discussing it with your friend, you suddenly find yourself saying: 'Gosh, I wish we had covered _____ in our session.'"

   Let's assume that our fantasy procedure, used for a supervisory training course, produced the following nine agenda items:

1. How to handle irrational people
2. Communication problems: up-down, parental approaches, generation-gap aspects
3. How to motivate the person on a "plateau"
4. How to use confrontational skills
5. How to use my acquired skills in a "heated" situation (as opposed to abandoning them under pressure)
6. Group meetings: why hold them, how to conduct them, etc.
7. Mutual expectations, standards setting: how to go about it
8. How to enter into a new supervisory position
9. How to give reinforcement (positive feedback)

☐ Our next procedure is to have our participants rank *in writing* the above nine items in order of priority. Then rankings can be aided by this weighting procedure:

Choice #	Weight (Votes)
1	4
2	3
3	2
4	1

☐ Note that we are asking for only four choices since we can't handle all topics.

You then ask all participants to call out their *votes,* starting with each person's Item 1 on the list. You total the votes for each item aloud. This might give us the following array of scores:

Agenda Item Number	Number of Votes (Weight)
1	8
2	29
3	18
4	9
5	0
6	3
7	3
8	6
9	10

The four agenda items with the highest scores become the agenda. This would be agenda items 2, 3, 9, and 4 in this example.

The Trainer-Developed Agenda

In the preceding paragraphs we discussed participant setting of agendas on the assumption that this was the best way to meet their needs. There may be other circumstances, however, when the trainer necessarily decides upon the agenda. For example, if the program concludes with the development of action plans for back-home implementation, it is essential to check back to see how well and to what extent these plans were carried out. In effect, the action plan reviews automatically become the agenda. In this circumstance it is the trainer's job to structure the agenda to facilitate the action plan discussion/review process.

An example of a trainer-developed agenda is one used in a time management course:

Activity 1: Use fishbowls to allow participants to talk about successes, near successes, problems, etc., in implementing their action plans. The discussion may relate to definition of key responsibilities and setting of priorities, time improvement plans, job improvement plans, delegation, meeting improvement, etc. Note that the discussion/sharing at this point is intended as warm up, "re-entry" motivation, rather than as a means to nail down any specifics of the action plans.

Activity 2: One of the action plans is selected for intensive review/discussion/sharing. This is done as follows:

1. Each person individually reviews his/her action plan for five or ten minutes.
2. Small group work (preferably in pairs) is assigned to allow participants to share and help one another (25–40 minutes).
3. The small groups give reports to the total group on what was learned or accomplished in the small groups.

This activity can be repeated twice again using other topics.

Activity 3: Use the "circular whip" technique— whip around the room, having each participant state the most significant learning from the program *as of now.*

Activity 4: Have participants individually complete the two worksheets given in Appendices 89 and 90. Then process them in trios and secure feedback from the several teams.

Note: The activities proceed from the general to the specific. Also, the last activity, particularly the second worksheet, makes a positive bridge with the back-home situation by asking for further reflection about on-the-job problems.

Key Concepts for Follow-up Sessions

In planning and conducting the follow-up session, these key ideas should be of value:

☐ In planning your session, think in terms of learning *enrichment:* "What can we provide our participants that will augment, upgrade, consolidate, reinforce their skill and/or understanding?" Then ask: "How should I design the program so that learning enrichment will actually take place?"

☐ The training methods used are certainly important. But in another sense *what* is done or *how* it is done is less important than the fact that something is *being done* to keep things alive. The key point of it all is that the organization, through the follow-up session, is saying: "We think the training you have experienced is so important that we want to be certain it is not subject to fade-out. In fact, we're willing to take you away from your very important jobs for so many hours to prevent this."

☐ Give careful thought to the length of the follow-up session. It may be two hours, a half day, or a full day. But the time frame decided upon should be used in a totally productive way. Participants should not leave the follow-up session with the feeling that it was just "busy work."

☐ Any work to be completed by the participants before the follow-up session should be spelled out in precise detail and subject to a written reminder before the session takes place.

☐ Anticipate that in the interval between the regular and follow-up session some participants will forget to bring along their notebooks, workbooks, worksheets, etc. Accordingly, be prepared to provide extra materials as may be needed. If a participant fails to complete or bring an assignment, little can be done about it. One solution is to have that person function as a "consultant" to the other participants in his/her small group.

☐ Don't be surprised if there is a certain amount of fallout insofar as attendance is concerned. Time intervenes, people become involved and busy again with their jobs, and interest may diminish a bit. Thus the forces at work for full attendance are inevitably under attack by these competing counterforces. Some possible solutions to the problem:

1. Involve the participants' bosses in the follow-up session planning, thereby securing their support.

2. Announce the program at the outset as a two-faceted, totally integrated training activity—the initial workshop plus the follow-up session.

3. Stress the importance of action plans in the very first announcement of the program and thereafter whenever practicable. Indicate that the all-important action plans will be reviewed and discussed in the follow-up session. Stating it another way, avoid leaving the impression that the follow-up session is an "add-on," an optional extra, or something that is merely "nice to do."

☐ A simple but effective way to start is with a success story. The objective is to keep things at a high, positive level. The procedure is to whip around the room, each person citing a tangible accomplishment resulting from the course or program.

☐ Be certain to close the session on a high note, too. One way to do this is to ask each participant to "testify" about what has been learned to date or to respond to this question: "My next step in this program is to _____."

Instrumented Follow-up

Follow-up may also be conducted via instrumentation. This approach is useful:

☐ To encourage continuing introspection after program's end. The instrument may be used in conjunction with a follow-up session if one is conducted, or it may be used in lieu of such a session.

☐ When a formal follow-up session may not be practical due to distance (dispersion of participants), time pressures, or other reasons.

A copy of an instrument for follow-up purposes is given in Appendix 91.

KEY POINTS

1. Think of transfer as a key consideration in designing a training program. If transfer becomes a post-course afterthought, the problem is compounded unnecessarily.

2. Application activities that fully involve the learner are essential to ensure transfer of training.

3. Application activities may relate to individual work, small group work, or a combination of these two approaches.

4. Application activities may assume these forms: observation-assessment, practical work, role plays, or worksheets.

5. Action plans (or self-contracting) are essential to ensure that what is learned in the classroom will be applied to the job.

6. Action plans may be developed by participants on either a post-session or a post-course basis, or both.

7. The best contracts entail early commitment, realistic goal setting, small group review and discussion of action plans, monitoring/follow-up procedures, "wiring in" the participants' supervisors to the process, etc.

8. Behavior modification techniques may be employed to ensure that contracts are properly developed and "enforced."

9. Transfer may be aided by numerous techniques including pre-course planning with supervisors, appreciation sessions for management, team or vertical training, pre-work, having participants introduce their own problems into class work, journalizing, post-session meetings with the participants' supervisors and involvement of the training committee, networking, reunions, and expanded rather than compressed time frames for the training.

10. Follow-up sessions are useful to prevent fade-out and to build on initial learnings.

11. Instruments may be used as part of the follow-up process.

12. Gluing in of *management* training can be aided by use of the Relapse Prevention Model.

REFERENCES

1. Robinson, Dana G., and James, C., "Breaking Barriers to Skill Transfer," *Training and Development Journal* (January 1985), pp. 82–83.

2. Rossett, Allison, "That Was a Great Class, but . . . ," *Training and Development* (July 1997), pp. 19–24. The checklist is based on a question list presented in the article.

3. Sources of information are accident reports, maintenance and quality control records, and interviews with employee and other supervisors and various plant engineers.

4. For an excellent article on how to conduct a Job Safety Analysis (JSA) see Smith, L. C., "The J Programs," *National Safety News* (September 1980), pp. 74–75.

5. "Build Better Managers with Short-Term Performance Goals," *Training/HRD* (February 1981), pp. 70, 75.

6. Lewin, K., "Group Decision and Social Change," in Swanson, G., Newcomb, T. M., and Hartley, E. L. (Eds.), *Readings in Social Psychology*, 2nd edition, Holt Publishing Company, New York (1952).

7. Benini, Carla, "In-Room Interaction," *Meetings and Conventions* (May 1995), pp. 125–132.

8. Siegel, S. R., "Improving the Effectiveness of Management Development Programs," *Personnel Journal* (October 1981), pp. 770, 772–773.

9. Buller, Paul F., and Cragun, John R., "Networking: The Overlooked Benefit of Training," *Training and Development* (July 1991), pp. 41–44.

10. "Behavior Change via Personal Contracts," *Bulletin on Training* (November–December 1976), p. 4.

11. Mark, Robert D., "Self-Managed Skill Retention," *Training and Development Journal* (January 1986), pp. 54–57. Note: The self-management strategies presented herein are adapted from Marlatt, G. A., and Gordon, J. R. (Eds.), *Relapse Prevention: Maintenance Strategies in the Treatment of Addictive Behaviors*, Guilford Publications, New York (1985).

12. House, R. S., "Increase Training Benefits," *National Society for Performance Improvement Journal* (June 1982), pp. 14–15.

13. "Training Managers to Rate Their Employees," *Business Week* (March 17, 1980), pp. 178, 183.

14. "What Makes Training Stick?" *Training Directors' Forum Newsletter* (October 1998), p. 5.

15. "How to Make Training Stick," *Successful Meetings* (March 1999), p. 48.

16. Brown, M. G., "Understanding Transfer of Training," *Performance and Instruction Journal* (March 1983), pp. 5–7.

17. Ott, Stanley E., and Russell, James D., "Consultation as a Means of Improving Post-Seminar Performance," *Performance and Instruction Journal* (June–July 1986), pp. 20–21.

18. Bozarth, Jane, "Making Training Stick with E-mail Follow-up," *Creative Training Techniques* (September 1999), p. 3.

19. "What Makes Training Stick?" *Training Directors' Forum Newsletter* (October 1998), p. 5.

RECOMMENDED READING

Baker, Richard A., "In Search of Relevance—Weaving On-The-Job Reality into Supervisory Training," *Training News,* July 1983, pp. 6–7.

This article describes the use of projects selected jointly by participants and their bosses for accomplishment on the job after the completion of training.

Brown, Mark G., "Understanding Transfer of Training," *Performance and Instruction Journal,* March 1983, pp. 5–7.

Since much of our behavior is governed by rules (as opposed to those behaviors that are contingency-shaped), the author advocates that the trainer provide learners with rules so as to maintain the new behavior learned in class. His guidelines: don't teach "false" rules; require participants to repeat rules frequently; teach participants to observe their own behavior and to give themselves positive feedback when rules are followed and negative feedback when rules are ignored.

Feldman, Michael, "Successful Post Training Skill Application," *Training and Development Journal,* September 1981, pp. 72–74.

This article suggests attention be given to needs analysis, full organization support for the training, pre-program activities to motivate trainees, post-program support groups, and contracting as means to ensure transfer.

Ford, Lynda, "Making Training Stick Like Glue," in "Training 101," *Training and Development,* November 2000, pp. 18–19.

Asserts that the key to successful transfer is contained in the acronym PRIORITY, which translates into *P*lan; *R*esearch; *I*nform and communicate expectations; *O*bjectively observe; *R*ole model; *I*nspire, instill, internalize; *T*est techniques; *Y*es attitude.

Garavaglia, Paul L., "How to Ensure Transfer of Training," *Training and Development*, October 1993, pp. 63–68.

This article emphasizes the role of instructional and performance technology techniques to increase transfer. It covers these aspects: why training transfer should be measured; when transfer should be measured; who should measure transfer; how to measure transfer.

Garavaglia, Paul L., "Managers as Transfer Agents," *Performance Improvement,* March 1998, pp. 15–17.

Discusses the manager's role in ensuring transfer of training to the job. Offers 11 actions required to execute the responsibility well, including providing rewards for using the new skills, giving positive reinforcement to encourage trainees to use the new skills, removing obstacles to transfer, and providing necessary tools/equipment for desired performance.

Leifer, Melissa S., and Newstrom, John W., "Solving the Transfer of Training Problems," *Training and Development Journal,* August 1980, pp. 42–46.

The authors discuss contracts, obstacles to successful implementation of the new learning, support groups, delayed evaluation, refresher courses, follow-up handouts, and training incentives as means to aiding transfer.

Mahoney, Francis X., "Targets, Time and Transfer: Keys to Management Impact," *Personnel,* November–December 1980, pp. 25–34.

This article recommends the substitution, at least in part, of "working meetings" in lieu of training sessions. By working on relevant targets or issues, transfer will be facilitated.

McNamara, J. Regis, "Why Aren't They Doing What We Trained Them to Do?" *Training/HRD,* February 1980, pp. 33–36.

This is a uniquely well-thought-out and practical account of the many factors which help/hinder the transfer of training to the job. The article stresses the importance of "consequences" as a factor in anticipating whether the new training will actually take place on the job.

Michalak, Donald F., "The Neglected Half of Training," *Training and Development Journal,* May 1981, pp. 22–28.

This article provides numerous suggestions for "maintenance of behavior" after the training is over including skill practice, letter to self, total department attends, buddy systems, and positive reinforcement by the boss.

Newman, Amy, and Smith, Maureen, "How to Create a Virtual Learning Community," *Training and Development,* July 1999, pp. 44–48.

Tells how to design web-based applications to reinforce learning, facilitate team sharing, and open communication. The authors' thesis: Employees need a place outside the classroom—yet, more interactive than a CBT or CD-ROM—where they can learn from each other and make continuous learning an everyday reality.

Parry, Scott B., "10 Ways to Get Management Buy–in," *Training and Development,* September 1997, pp. 21–22.

A long-time trainer recommends these approaches to the transfer problem: start at the top, conduct a needs analysis, report the results, brief participants' managers, bring the workplace into the workshop, have managers instruct, take the workshop back to the workplace, schedule Alumni Day, write (promote) your success story, and conduct a cost-benefit analysis.

Sedlik, Jay M., Magnus, Arlene K., and Rakow, Joel, "Key Elements to an Effective Training System," *Training and Development Journal,* July 1980, pp. 10–12.

To ensure that training objectives are accomplished in the real world, the authors propose the use of five systems: developmental, internal training, performances installation, and evaluation/modification. The article offers practical tools for successful application including transfer exercises, job performance aids, and the trainee progress record.

Seiler, Clarence J., "Let's Put 'Management' into Management Training," *Training and Development Journal,* September 1981, pp. 68–70.

The author outlines a comprehensive program to ensure that a management training program really pays off back on the job.

Seville, Christine, and Wells, Timothy D., "Contracting to Ensure Training Transfer," in "Training 101," *Training and Development,* June 1998, pp. 10–11.

The authors, information technology experts, pose some questions that can help define the business need for training and outline five steps to ensure training transfer.

Siegel, S. R., "Improving the Effectiveness of Management Development Programs," *Personnel Journal,* October 1981, pp. 770, 772–773.

This article discusses various procedures for and issues in contracting, including motivation, when to request it be done, voluntary vs. involuntary aspects, and success in contracting.

Spitzer, Dean R., "But Will They Use Training on the Job?" *Training/HRD,* September 1982, pp. 48, 105.

To prevent "training entropy," the author suggests 12 approaches: personal action planning, group action planning, multiphase programming (intersperse the training with work), the buddy system, performance aids, recognition systems, training trainees as trainers, use of signed contracts, post-training resource access, follow-up questionnaires, follow-up phone calls and visits, follow-up session.

Tauber, Mark S., "Supervisory Skill Development," *Training and Development Journal,* September 1981, pp. 49–54.

The author's answers to the question: "What happens after they have been trained?" are reunions and supervisory support groups (networks). Procedures to make these activities effective are discussed.

Trost, Arty, "They May Love It, But Will They Use It?" *Training and Development Journal,* January 1985, pp. 78–81.

Involving the learner, trainer, and trainee's boss, before, during, and after the training is essential for effective transfer.

Zemke, Ron, and Gunkler, John, "Twenty-Eight Techniques for Transforming Training into Performance," *Training,* April 1985, pp. 48–63.

This detailed article describes transfer techniques and groups them into five strategies: pre-training, good training, transfer-enhancing, post-training, and finessing.

21 Ancillary Issues and Techniques

Learning without thought is labor lost. Thought without learning is intellectual death.

> —Confucius (551–479 B.C.), Chinese ethical
> philosopher and teacher

A number of added concerns for the trainer are discussed in this chapter. All of them relate to the broad area of participative training. Specifically, we will discuss these topics:

☐ Program design
☐ Need determination
☐ How to deal with inappropriate training requests
☐ Selecting training methods
☐ Climate
☐ The facilitator role
☐ When things go wrong
☐ Guides to managing diversity
☐ Cross-gender leadership training
☐ Training to manage gender differences in communication styles
☐ How to adapt training for other cultures
☐ Augmenting trainer competency
☐ How to become a participative trainer
☐ How to network effectively
☐ Co-training
☐ Broadening the trainer base for management training
☐ Vertical training
☐ How to augment your credibility quotient
☐ Terminology for the training effort

A PARTICIPATIVE APPROACH TO PROGRAM DESIGN

All training programs begin with a determination of need. The more reality-based ones, however, involve as many knowledgeable parties as possible in the need assessment process. This might include the program participants, their bosses, other knowledgeable officials, and, if it is a management or supervisory training program, their subordinates, too. Upper levels of management may also be helpful. In sum, need determination, if conducted in a professional and sophisticated way, is a highly participative process. In fact, it would not be an overstatement to assert that to make the need determination in isolation from the recipients and beneficiaries of the training is to court disaster. Why? Because one runs the risk of providing great training, but on nontargeted subjects or problems.

To the extent practicable, we, as trainers, should convert the identified needs into behavioral or terminal objectives. Thus, if the need is to learn about MBO (Management by Objectives), the behavioral objectives or outcomes may be

□ To identify or establish key responsibilities
□ To set annual targets
□ To develop or identify indicators of accomplishment, so that both the boss and the subordinate have an agreed-upon understanding about what to look for to measure progress toward the accomplishment of each goal
□ To conduct quarterly reviews of progress toward goal accomplishment

Again, these learning outcomes should be set up in conjunction with those who sponsor the course and expect results from it.

If the determination of needs and the setting up of behavioral objectives have been accomplished, evaluation of the completed training will proceed logically. Also, course sponsors will assist in the evaluation process, in the form of postcourse feedback, since the sponsors were in on the training "from the ground floor." The operative maxim is that people support what they help to create. We should also consider the following:

□ Designing the program for small group learning. A program or course for 10–15 participants can achieve the rapport, warmth, intimacy, caring and sharing—all ingredients of a relaxed, participative atmosphere conducive to learning— which a group of 25 or more cannot.

□ Using a design matrix so that we can see at a glance the overall nature and structure of the course and the degree to which participative rather than one-way communication devices have been employed. (A design matrix has the hours of instruction on the left side of the paper in a vertical column; the other related columns, also vertical, show subject or topic, method of instruction, resource person(s), aids or materials used in the session, post-session handouts, if any, etc. An example of a design matrix appears in Figure 21-1.) In respect to the latter point, we, as course designers, must continually ask ourselves: What is an acceptable ratio of lecture/talk/film to bona fide participative techniques for *this* particular program? Can we alter the ratio to favor *involving* activities?

□ The length of the total course. Adults will react negatively to a course that is loaded with filler and thus is too long, or to one that is too hurried and just scratches the surface of the subject.

□ The nature of the training day. Although lunch and breaks are "givens," with a little imagination we may be able to structure a more appealing and invigorating day. For example, in a three- to five-day program, conducted in a "cultural island" setting, we may have a 3:00 P.M. to 5:00 P.M. recreation break and a highly participative session after dinner (from 7:30 P.M. to 9:30 P.M.). Lecture sessions after dinner are a "no-no."

□ Not overlooking the possibilities of designing a pre-work activity into the program.

□ Including icebreakers and/or openers, as appropriate.

□ Considering whether the design includes opportunities for humor and fun via icebreakers, openers, art, music, puzzles, games, exercises, and movement.

Subject: Developing our Listening Skills

Time	Topic	Method	Resource Persons	Aids	Handouts
9:00–9:20	Assignment: What Problems do we have as listeners?	Small group work (10 minutes); general discussion (10 minutes)	Fran & Pat	Flipchart	
9:20–9:30	Results of Poor Listening	Film viewing	Fran & Pat	Film: "Listen, Please"	
9:30–9:45	Assignment: Re Film: What is the main learning from the film?	Pairs to meet	Fran & Pat	Flipchart	
9:45–10:00	Causes for poor listening	Lecturette	Pat	Flipchart	"The Poor Listener—Causes and Cures" (periodical article—15 copies)
10:00–10:15	Your skill as a listener—self-assignment	Quiz—individual work	Fran & Pat	Instrument (15 copies)	
10:15–10:30	BREAK				
10:30–11:00	Learnings from the quiz	Trios to meet	Fran & Pat		
11:00–11:15	ditto	Reports from trios and general discussion	Fran & Pat		
11:15–11:30	Exercise: "Restatement"	Total group in a circle	Fran & Pat		
11:30–11:45	Active listening	Lecturette	Fran	Flipchart	
11:45–12:00	Q & A period summary	Total group discussion	Fran & Pat	Flipchart	"Active Listening—Key To Better Communication" (Staff paper—15 copies)
12:00–1:00	LUNCH				

Figure 21-1. Example of a design matrix.

☐ Examining our completed course design matrix to check whether greater impact may be achieved by switching certain activities. For example, ending the morning session with a potent film/video, game, or exercise may lead to further discussion of the activity at lunch. Or an end-of-day session may serve as a prelude (stage-setter) to a short evening assignment.

☐ Recognizing that the more "threatening" activities (role plays, fishbowls, certain types of movement) should take place later in the program. This caution assumes that we have participants who need to be eased into participative/experiential training.

☐ Including adequate support materials of an interactive sort, as appropriate, for each session, such as worksheets, checksheets, instruments, and quizzes to check for understanding. In this connection, I recall a management seminar at which I used trainer/educator Dr. Malcolm Knowles as a resource person. As we were waiting for the participants to assemble, Dr. Knowles was glancing at my nearby work table, which was completely covered with a variety of support materials. Pointing to the table I said, somewhat self-deprecatingly,

"Lot of paper, eh?" Dr. Knowles looked up and said, "Oh, *no*. Those are all *tools*."

☐ Making provisions for special interest groups to explore certain topics in depth, if appropriate. For example, in a time management course, participants may be grouped around problem areas such as delegation, meetings, telephone use, and use of one's secretary.

☐ Designing the program with opportunities to practice the skills that were introduced. Too many training programs present the skill/concept, but rush on before participants have "buttoned down" what was presented.

☐ Including follow-up sessions in the design to aid in "gluing in" the learning. In some cases the more practical work may be given at this time.

☐ Providing participants with take-home worksheets and other aids to enable them to apply what was learned in the training situation on the job.

☐ Asking: "Is the design cost effective?" Here we are talking about participant time away from the job; the trainer's time; and costs for outside resource people, audio-visual materials, facilities, support materials, off-the-shelf materials, etc.

☐ Getting another professional opinion on the final design, or better still, designing the program with a colleague. "Peer design" should prevent oversights, expose weaknesses and inconsistencies, and generally help to make for a richer, tighter program or course.

To sum up, the design of a training program is basic to program effectiveness. It is analogous to an architect's plan for a physical structure. Hence the need for care in developing the design. A broad, cooperative effort is a key to securing such care.

DETERMINING NEEDS VIA PARTICIPATIVE METHODS

Every trainer knows that the training cycle begins with a determination of training needs. But what is not universally known—or at least not universally observed—is that training programs are more likely to be cost-effective and accepted if *both* the sponsors and recipients of the training participate actively in that need determination. If your philosophy of training is a participative one, here are some ways of ensuring participative need determination.

☐ *Individual interviews.* Participants, their bosses, and other managers may be contacted to learn of *current* problems, difficulties, and deficiencies, as well as of *anticipated* (future) needs. Interviews may be conducted with all program participants, as in the case of team-building sessions, or on a sample basis. Depending on the number of people involved, sampling may be essential since worthwhile interviews run 30 to 60 minutes or more.

☐ *Group interviews.* Small groups of four to ten participants may be interviewed to learn of their problems. This method obviously may lose some of the intimacy of the individual interviewing approach. On the other hand, it is a time saver and the group interaction may trigger added data that the one-on-one method would not. Also, the validity of the data may be verified more readily in the group situation. Finally, by meeting with the participant group before the

program begins, one can begin one's acquaintance with them, and the group itself can begin to develop its identity.

A practical way to help the group zero in on a need is to use the modified critical incident technique developed by David S. Stein of Ohio State University [1]. Stein's procedure is as follows:

1. Provide participants with a stack of 3" × 5" cards.

2. On one set of the cards have participants list incidents/situations where they felt frustrated, underprepared, or ineffective.

3. On another set of cards have them describe the skills and/or knowledge that would have helped them to cope with these incidents.

4. Set up teams of three or four persons and provide them with packets of the two types of cards.

5. Have each small group identify five situations and the corresponding skills necessary for improvement.

6. Secure team reports and screen them to identify bona fide training needs. *Note:* Although problems due to lack of feedback about performance, the work environment, or management shortcomings are important and should be communicated to management, they are *not* training problems and thus cannot be met via training programs.

☐ *Survey procedures.* Data, when large numbers of persons are involved, may also be gathered via various survey forms or questionnaires. The survey approach has the twin advantages of broad or even full coverage of all concerned plus the potential for uniform analysis (standardization) of the data.

If one has a good general feel for the kinds of needs that exist, based on interviews with bosses and various participants, a rating scale may be developed and used to ascertain needs in a more precise way. For example, need data for a proposed communications course may be garnered via the rating scale shown in Appendix 92. Similarly, a rating scale to collect data for a supervisory training course is given in Appendix 93.

A survey form may be used to elicit *written* responses to particular need questions such as current problems, supervisory skills requiring improvement, or information needed to be more effective. A sample form appears in Appendix 94. Written responses, of course, can provide insight as to *why* the survey respondents feel as they do, something which rating forms cannot do for us.

The survey form may also be "open-ended" and ask for a listing and prioritization of needs. This ranking approach is helpful when the trainer has little or no data about existing training needs. A form for this procedure is given in Appendix 95.

A simple way to secure participant input as to need is to forward 5" × 8" cards to the participants and ask them to jot down specific questions that they have about the forthcoming course. Depending on when the cards are received back by the trainer, the data on the cards may be used in actual course design and/or the instruction may be planned around the needs/concerns/expectations of the trainees.

Data Interpretation

Regardless of how the needed data are collected from the participants, the data in summary form should be cleared with the operating officials or supervisors who are sponsoring the training. To avoid this step is a certain means of losing program support, program credibility, and assistance in the evaluation and follow-up phases of the program. One of the reasons post-program or follow-up sessions are often poorly attended by participants is the lack of commitment to the program by the program sponsors. Involving them in need determination is a key strategy to secure that commitment.

Ongoing Adjustments

Another aspect of need determination is the making of adjustments, to the extent practicable, in the ongoing program. Thus it may be desirable to reserve the last half hour or so of each day to meet with participants and learn how well the program is meeting their needs or if new needs have emerged as a result of the training. Not all such needs, obviously, will permit program alteration. But to the extent possible, participant input should be heeded and redesign procedures instituted.

Note: A good way to secure participant input is via a fishbowl approach.

Meeting Individual Needs

The data we have now collected, using the preceding procedures, are concerned with determining and meeting group training needs. On this basis, the trainer would proceed to develop the overall course. It is hoped that this course design would be general and flexible enough so that *individual* needs could also be recognized.

One trainer uses an instrument (or survey form) on site to ascertain from the participants possible alternatives to the previously planned training [2]. In effect, the participant input produces "a contractual agreement" with both parties pledged to work on the meeting of individualized needs. Mutual agreement on intended outcomes should greatly improve the likelihood of successful training. Of course, this procedure will require considerable skill by the trainer to adapt and revise established material and to utilize participant resources/experience for the modified design.

Meeting Special Needs

Most of our training programs operate on the assumption that all participants have the same needs. While this is generally a valid assumption, it may, at times, overlook the principle of individual differences. Obviously not everyone is cast in the same mold and not everyone has identical needs, interests, preferences, or problems.

One way to meet individual or special needs is to organize on a "two-track" system, at least part of the time. For example, let's assume that we are planning a course in leadership for quality circle facilitators and leaders. We thus design the bulk of our sessions around such topics as motivation, team work, power, values, communication, conflict, and stress. However, we may also wish to provide those who are interested with advanced quality circle problem-solving techniques. We can thus run *concurrent* sessions as follows:

- □ *Leadership track:* Small groups conduct "clinics" on leadership problems of quality circles.
- □ *Problem-solving track:* Formal instruction is provided by the seminar leader on advanced quality circle problem-solving techniques (as opposed to concern with leadership).

Multiple special interests can be met by organizing around problem areas identified by the participants. For example, in a time management course participants may have identified their major time management problems as delegation, interruptions, paperwork, meetings, and/or use of the secretary. We can meet these individual needs by establishing "special interest groups," with participants joining a small group of their choice. In these small groups, participants share their concerns and endeavor to help one another resolve their difficulties.

Note: In the two-track system the trainer decides on the optional topic; in the special interest group procedure the participants provide the topics based on their own problems.

Conducting a Quick Needs Assessment

If speed is of the essence because of today's compressed business deadlines, asking the eight questions below may provide enough information to replace an in-depth needs analysis, says Jack Asgar, chairman of Practical Management Inc., Las Vegas [3].

1. Can you tell me what your operating problems are? (Shun the jargonistic "What is the training need?")
2. Are people the factor (cause) in these operating problems? If they are, what is their current behavior and what is your expected performance from them?
3. Could your people do their jobs properly if they had to? Have they done them well lately? ("Yes" answers indicate that training is not the answer to the presumed performance problem.)
4. Is the expected performance now being communicated clearly by the manager to the employee?

If so, explain the way it's done. If not, are you certain that the new behavior will receive the needed reinforcement on the job after we do the training?
5. If present performance is a problem, can you provide us with pertinent evidence? What indicators would you use to satisfy yourself that the problem has been corrected? (Look for needed skills, *not* end results such as added sales.)
6. Are there any other causative factors possibly triggering your operating problem?
7. Does this analysis clearly point up a clear training approach to the problem? If so, what specific skills are to be learned in the training?
8. Assuming training is the way to go, can we anticipate that managers will involve themselves actively in the training endeavor: pre-training, during the training, and post-training?

Asgar finds that these queries frequently discourage unnecessary training or possibly suggest training at variance with that discussed initially. Also, they may point up basic problems in the work environment that interfere with staffers' ability to learn or employ new skills. In general, the eight questions encourage more sophisticated, broader thinking rather than reliance on a surface analysis of what is causing the pain.

HOW TO DEAL WITH INAPPROPRIATE TRAINING REQUESTS

Some trainers may feel that training is not supported by management and that no one seems to want to tap the resources of the training unit. Other trainers may encounter the opposite problem—management may insist on a training program that seems totally inappropriate and is not the likely cure for a performance problem. Management professor Roger Kaufman states that in the latter circumstance you have only two choices:

- □ Respond affirmatively, taking the easy way out.
- □ Work on changing the requestor's mind. *Note:* The requestor may be your boss or another operating official.

Before you make your "train-or-argue" decision, Kaufman suggests you try to answer these seven questions [4]:

1. Assuming training is the best solution, what is the actual problem? Performance? The whole organization? An outside client? Society at large? Some combination of these or none of these?

2. How is the problem defined? Is it defined in terms of *results* and *performance,* or merely in terms of procedures or resources?

3. If it's a performance problem, *who* has the problem, and how many workers are involved?

4. If it's a performance problem, is it only a symptom of a greater problem?

5. What will it cost to resolve the problem? Conversely, what costs will result from ignoring the problem?

6. What are the possible costs if training doesn't provide a solution to the problem?

7. Is there a better way to deal with the performance problem than the requested training? If so, what are the other approaches?

If you have conscientiously responded to these questions and you're still convinced that training is *not* the answer to the performance problem, then confront the requestor directly and attempt to alter his/her mindset.

Rather than run the risk of conducting an unsuccessful training session and possibly being blamed for not solving the problem, use these nine questions to (a) decide if you want to change the requestor's mind and (b) avail yourself of the pertinent talking points to do so successfully:

1. *Costs:* What are current and expected costs if the problem remains as is, that is, without any intervention?

2. *Needs:* What are the gaps in results? Who is sharing them?

3. *Beneficiaries:* If there is an intervention, whom does it benefit? A small group? The total business? Outside clients? Society at large?

4. *The training route:* Can training resolve the problem? What are the risks and benefits of the training approach? Will the problem, if not addressed, solve itself?

5. *A training success:* Would successful training create on-the-job payoffs, organizational gains, external client benefits, societal gains?

6. *Alternatives to training:* What other approaches might better resolve the problem—an organization development (OD) intervention? An organizational change in mission and/or objectives? A workplace layout modification? A Total Quality Management (TQM) program? The use of job aids? A change in the reward system? A restructuring? Personnel shifts or other personnel changes? A new personnel selection system? A change in values or climate?

7. *Costs of alternate interventions:* If another, non-training approach is adopted, what costs might accrue?

8. *Your recommendations:* Are you prepared to propose alternate interventions, and are you sure they will better meet the need than would the traditional training vehicle? Why are you certain of this?

9. *Walk in the requestor's shoes!* What justifications/rationale/argument would be the best evidence to convince the other party of the merit of your alternate approach?

Now that you've done the proper amount of "soul-searching," consider that the person who made the training request wants to be successful and to look good at what he/she undertakes. So think and act on *results,* not means or ends. Amass your data, including needs and costs to meet these needs, plus the costs if the needs are ignored.

Collect the data on your proposed alternate intervention(s). How will your proposed attack on the problem benefit the requestor, the employees, the total firm, the clients, etc., if the performance gaps are closed?

Now make your presentation and recommendation. Be patient, rational, and factual. Don't argue, and don't oversell.

But alas! You gave it your best shot and you couldn't alter the requestor's initial approach. What do you do? You have the following choices:

☐ Provide the training with a smile and a salute. (After all, you can't win 'em all.)

☐ Provide the training, but in a way that you know won't work.

☐ Don't provide the training because it is professionally incorrect or improper from an ethical or safety standpoint.

☐ Don't provide the training because you're stubborn.

☐ Don't provide the training, sharpen up your resume, and start calling on your network for out-placement help.

SELECTING TRAINING METHODS

Many of us, as trainers, have our favorite training methods and thus "know" what works best. However, we might do a better job of methods selection if we considered these principles:

☐ Some methods are more effective and appropriate than others. Two independently conducted studies, both using like criteria employed by an earlier (1972) researcher, are pertinent. Nine training methods were evaluated: case study, conference or discussion method, lecture, business game, film, programmed instruction, role playing, sensitivity training, and TV lecture. These nine methods were evaluated as to effectiveness in relation to six training objectives: knowledge acquisition, changing attitudes, problem-solving skills, interpersonal skills, participant acceptance, and knowledge retention.

The two studies, based on trainers' perceptions as to effectiveness of various methods, were as follows:

1. A study by Dr. John W. Newstrom, University of Minnesota, of 54 training directors working for the largest U.S. firms [5].
2. A study by Linda L. Neider, University of Miami, of 191 A.S.T.D. members [6].

The rankings resulting from the two studies are given in Table 21-1 in a combined table. Note that the responses (rankings) were not overly different. A major difference did occur in results from the *lecture (with questions)* method. Newstrom reported low rather than high knowledge acquisition and low rather

Table 21-1
Perceived Effectiveness (on a Ranking Basis) of Nine Training Methods for Six Objectives as Reported by Newstrom (A) and Neider (B)

Method	Knowledge Acquisition		Changing Attitudes		Problem-Solving Skills		Interpersonal Skills		Participant Acceptance		Knowledge Retention	
	(A)	(B)	(A)	(B)	(A)	(B)	(A)	(B)	(A)	(B)	(A)	(B)
Case study	4	4	5	4	1	1	5	5	1	2	4	4
Conference/ discussion method	1	3	3	3	5	3	4	3	5	1	2	3
Lecture (with questions)	8	2	7	6	7	5	8	6	8	3	3	6
Business games	5	8	4	5	2	2	3	4	2	4	7	5
Movies/films	6	7	6	7	9	8	6	7	4	6	5	7
Programmed instruction	3	1	8	9	6	6	7	9	9	7	1	2
Role playing	2	5	2	1	3	4	1	1	3	5	5	1
Sensitivity training (T group)	7	9	1	2	4	7	2	2	6	9	9	8
TV lecture	9	6	9	8	8	9	9	8	7	8	8	9

than high participant acceptance. Note too, the following trainers' preferences as to methods:

☐ *Case study* was ranked high for problem-solving skills (1,1) and participant acceptance (1,2). *Note:* Numbers in parentheses here and after refer to rankings in the Newstrom and Neider studies.

☐ *Conference/discussion method* was ranked high in both studies for knowledge acquisition (1,3), but only Neider found high participant acceptance (1).

☐ *Lecture (with questions)* received a high ranking for knowledge acquisition by Neider only (2).

☐ *Business games* received a high ranking for problem-solving skills (2,2).

☐ *Films* received mediocre to low rankings on all six objectives.

☐ *Programmed instruction* received high rankings on knowledge acquisition (3,1) and knowledge retention (1,2).

☐ *Role playing* received numerous high rankings on all objectives, although the two studies differed on knowledge retention (5,1).

☐ *Sensitivity training* received high rankings on changing attitudes (1,2) and development of interpersonal skills (2,2), but low rankings on knowledge acquisition (7,9), participant acceptance (6,9), and knowledge retention (9,8).

☐ *TV lecture* garnered low rankings—mostly 8's and 9's—on all six objectives. Since the lecture with questions fared somewhat better in rankings, it may be assumed that its two-way aspects accounted for the difference.

☐ Methods should be related to instructional objectives, such as knowledge acquisition, changing attitudes, developing problem-solving skills, or developing interpersonal skills. However, as we will see later, this "ideal" procedure may not always be practical.

☐ Methods may have to be selected in relation to organizational and/or participant acceptance. For example, many organizations will not permit the use of T-groups even though this technique is recognized in the literature and by many trainers as the best one to use to change

attitudes and to build interpersonal skills. Or a particular participant group may either resist role playing because it may prove embarrassing or object to games as being too frivolous.

☐ A whole host of "environmental constraints" may also influence decisions concerning choice of method or instructional strategy, such as [7]:

1. *Money:* For example, it may be too expensive to "import" a trained facilitator to conduct T-groups or to use a video-telephone hook-up at nine points.

2. *Time:* A ramified business game or three role plays (supervisor, employee, observer, on a rotational basis) may take too long.

3. *Staff:* Expert trainers may not be available to staff a given training program properly; hence, self-teaching methods may have to be utilized.

4. *Trainer philosophy:* A trainer may prefer T-groups, which are based on humanistic psychology, rather than programmed learning, which is underpinned by behaviorist psychology.

5. *Physical space and equipment:* A small room may work against the use of simultaneously enacted mass role plays.

6. *Class size:* One can hardly utilize fishbowls or certain other games and exercises if the participant group has only six people in it.

☐ Certain methods are of minimal effectiveness unless supported by other ones. For example, a film presentation by itself can hardly be effective, hence the need to combine it with one or more methods such as a small group discussion or possibly a role play.

☐ Various methods may be combined to form an "instructional strategy." For example, "behavior modeling" uses a variety of techniques including an introductory talk to explain the skill area to be worked on; a videotape then demonstrates the proper behavior to be learned (modeling). The participants role play the skill in question per the model observed, critique the behavior via feedback after the enactment (positive reinforcement is stressed), and engage in further skill practice through role playing.

Selecting Methods—A Case Example

To help the reader visualize how the trainer might go about selecting methods for a given unit of instruction, my experience in coaching may be useful. I was asked by an organization to conduct a session on "the appraisal interview." By raising many pertinent questions about the real supervisory problems prevalent in the organization, I was able to conclude that the problem was much broader—that supervisors were falling down in their responsibilities as coaches. A session on coaching was thus recommended. The recommendation was accepted, and I "auto-brainstormed" the supervisor's responsibility as a coach. This led to the conclusion that the effective coach had to be concerned, as a minimum, with these skill areas:

☐ Encouraging employee growth and development. *Note:* This skill area was placed on the top of the list to emphasize the idea that this was the most important aspect of the coaching job and that such tasks as assigning and reviewing work were more related to routine supervision than to the broader concept of coaching.

☐ Upgrading performance of employees, that is, bringing about a change in attitude/behavior. The idea was to encourage supervisors to utilize every day events to accomplish this upgrading. For example, a minor accident while backing up a truck could be dismissed with a "let's be more careful next time," or the supervisor could sit down with the careless employee and discuss safety practices in detail as well as the possible consequences of an accident. Similarly, in an office situation a poorly written letter could be returned with the necessary editing, or one could discuss with the writer the "principles" that were overlooked or violated.

☐ Delegating responsibility. This is an area that not only encourages employee growth, but also brings about "invention." As a supervisor, you or I may perform a particular task well, but in all likelihood we will perform it in the same way we always have. If we delegate the task, however, it is likely to be done differently, possibly in a novel and more effective way.

☐ Giving clear, specific, and complete instructions and guidance when assigning work.

☐ Conducting an effective annual performance review.

☐ Introspecting about one's prowess as a coach.

In addition, since all of these activities were *trainer-selected and developed,* it seemed desirable to have a "clinic" where the supervisors could introduce some of their own problems for resolution.

The grid (Table 21-2) was then set up to help design the desired learning sequence on coaching. In general, the approach is to design and provide a set of "stimulus materials" that will zero in on the specific learning objectives that have been pinpointed.

CLIMATE

The "right" climate or atmosphere is essential for high participant learning. While "right" may be subject to a certain amount of debate, most trainers would agree that the following elements are basic ingredients of the climate we require:

☐ Pre-arrival factors
☐ Greeting of participants
☐ The learning facility/environment itself
☐ The trainer's style and behavior

The following sections discuss these elements of climate as well as what to do "when things go wrong."

Setting the Climate Before the Training Session

Ordinarily we think of climate in terms of what participants perceive once the training begins. However, what we as trainers do or fail to do prior to our participants' arrival at the training room door is also an influencing factor. Hence the need to pay attention to such pre-entry elements as:

☐ *Contact.* Do we send participants a letter of welcome briefly explaining the program and its goals; its location and how to get there, if necessary; daily hours; when the program ends; provisions for meals; clothes to wear; recreation possibilities? Remember, the letter, as the first

Table 21-2
Designing a Learning Sequence: Coaching

Skill Area and/or Activity	Rationale	Technique or Method	Specific Task or Assignment	Length of Activity
Encouraging growth	To focus attention on the power all of us, as supervisors, have. We can develop and "turn on" our people *or* discourage them "turn them off," and inhibit their growth and development.	Small group work (trios); data generated by the trios to be posted on a flipchart, compared, and discussed.	1. One set of groups to focus on experiences in career, school, home, etc. that *encouraged* growth. 2. One set of groups to focus on experiences that *discouraged* growth.	Work in trios: 10 minutes Feedback and posting: 15 minutes Discussion: 15 minutes Total time: 40 minutes
Upgrading performance— bringing about a change in attitude or behavior	To provide skill practice in challenging an employee to upgrade his/her performance.	Role play (on a rotational basis so that each participant functions as coach, subordinate, and observer).	Three role plays, each of a different degree of difficulty. Typical cases: A young person with good potential is handicapping himself/herself by poor interpersonal skills; a senior supervisor is a good production person but weak on human relations skills.	*Each* role play runs for 25–30 minutes; feedback and discussion also run for 25–30 minutes.
Delegating responsibility	Delegation is a skill that can be sharpened. It is a skill basic to encouragement of growth and creativity of subordinates.	Exercise: Analysis of one's job with the objective of delegating greater responsibility to subordinates: 1. Individual analysis of responsibility. 2. Sharing in pairs or trios.	Develop a chart listing major and minor responsibilities in Column 1, subordinates to whom responsibilities might be delegated in Column 2, and whether duties are delegatable now or require training in Column 3.	Individual work: 30 minutes Sharing: 30 minutes Total group processing: 20 minutes
Assigning work	In absence of fully helpful instructions, employees may experience frustration, errors, and/or low performance. But with proper guidance by the boss, employees can get the job done more quickly, easily and accurately.	Exercise—Numbers: A Problem Solving Activity (given in *The 1978 Handbook for Group Facilitators*, University Associates, Inc., Publishers, p. 9)	To connect "miscellaneous" numbers on a worksheet. The task is completed five times, with performance going up markedly when full information and assistance are provided.	Individual work: 5 minutes General discussion: 10 minutes
Conducting an annual performance review	Practice via role play can provide confidence and skill in the conduct of the interview.	1. Film or video showing the proper way to conduct the interview. 2. Role play to get skill practice.	Conduct an annual performance review based on data provided by the trainer.	Role play: 20–30 minutes Feedback from observers: 15 minutes General discussion of key points to conduct an effective interview: 15 minutes
Introspection of one's skill as a coach	Supervisors need to look inward to their coaching practices. This is a step toward improved/strengthened coaching ability.	Instrument.	Complete an instrument on coaching to assess one's prowess as a coach.	Individual completion of instrument: 15 minutes Sharing of data: 30 minutes Group discussion: 15 minutes
"Clinic" on coaching skills	This is an opportunity to secure help on a coaching problem one may have.	Small group work (trios).	Come up with one need that you see you have as a coach; discuss it with your team, which will try to provide feedback, advice, and support on the problem. Each member of the trio presents a problem or concern about himself/herself.	Each person presents and discusses his/her problem for 20 minutes. Total time: 60 minutes Group-at-large discussion: 20–30 minutes

contact with the program, immediately begins to set the tone for the program.

☐ *Pre-work.* Do we provide a pre-session assignment (through the mail) to involve participants early on and to indicate that this is a real learning opportunity?

☐ *Pre-session get-together.* Do we try to have a pre-session meeting to pass out a pre-work assignment? For example, in a time management program, distributing a time log and providing instructions concerning how to keep it is a must. Or, in a management training program, do we open with a get-acquainted cocktail party the evening before the first morning session?

☐ *Need determination.* Do we consider the possibility that we can better meet participant needs if we learn of their problems before they arrive at class? In effect, their problems, needs, and ideas can aid us in our work on program design in general and in agenda setting in particular. Certainly, participant input will go a long way in creating high expectations as well as a climate of mutuality.

☐ *Calendar for contracting.* Do we ask our participants to bring along their calendars or appointment books for back-home action planning purposes?

Greeting Your Participants

Although climate is certainly established to some extent before participants arrive at the training room, a key factor in perception of climate is what takes place on arrival. Participants do have questions, even concerns, about what they will experience. ("I wonder what I'm getting into." "Will this be worthwhile?" "What's the trainer like?") By paying attention to the "meeting and greeting" aspects of climate, you can quiet participants' anxieties and facilitate participants' comfortable entry into the program. Some suggestions to do this follow.

First of all, try to provide easy-to-follow instructions concerning the location of the training room. A sign on the door or wall or one standing on the floor will help to eliminate that anxious question: "Is this the place?" (*Note:* Not all groups may have this problem.)

Make it a practice to greet participants when they first arrive. People *do* like to feel welcome. To do this

in a relaxed way, arrive early so that you have completed your preparation chores—checking out the room, setting up A/V equipment, arranging your exercise materials and handouts, completing advance flipcharts, and the like. Try to recall your own feelings about the instructor/trainer who was so busy with setting up that he/she didn't even have time to say hello to anyone. In this connection, it's a good idea to review the roster before participants arrive to get at least some feel for participants' names, titles, locations, etc.

If name cards are to be used, consider making it an informal, "do-it-yourself" procedure. Help people get rid of their anxieties by putting them to work. You may wish to say: "Would you please write your name on this card as you want to be called while you're here? This is your first participative act in our program!" (I prefer this procedure to the formality of preparing cards beforehand, which ordinarily doesn't allow for the use of nicknames. Another undesirable procedure is to have the trainer write the name on the card for the participant. This approach seems to carry an unnecessary tone of: "You look pretty helpless to me; since I'm in charge, *I'll* do it for you.") When the name has been written on the name card it's a good idea to repeat it aloud, both to please the name's owner and to help you to remember it. If the name should have an unusually pleasant ring to it, you may wish to tell the participant about it.

If registration or "signing in" is required, notebooks or learning packets are to be passed out, or a roster of participants is to be distributed, try to make these procedures as painless and expeditious as possible. Use an assistant, if needed.

Suggest the use of the coat rack, as may be appropriate. Be certain of the location of the restrooms, as opposed to "I think it's somewhere downstairs." Avoid inappropriate humor such as: "I'm not sure whether they have one or not."

Consider having a welcoming, early morning (pre-session) coffee service available. This is a natural location, of course, for you to mingle with participants before things get started. Introduce yourself to anyone you don't know.

Create a warm and inviting atmosphere by having some lively music emitting from a table radio or cassette player. (Why let your participants stare uncomfortably at the wall, ceiling, or blank flipchart pad?)

Figure 21-2. An example of how to enliven a blank chart before a session begins.

Also, the flipchart pad can be dressed up a bit with a cheery statement along the lines of Figure 21-2.

Remember, participants are trying to get "a fix" on you as a person. They are asking themselves: "Is he/she approachable or distant? Relaxed or harried? Friendly or aloof? Interested in others or detached? Warm or cold? Human or a machine?" Your behavior is communicating something about you at the very outset. Ask yourself: "Is my communication what I wish it to be?" Are you aware that over 70% of your communication is nonverbal?

Requirements for the Effective Learning Environment/Facility

Changing behavior and/or attitudes or imparting new skill and knowledge is hardly an easy process. Hence conditions for participant learning should be as close to "ideal" as is practicable. One vital condition is the facility. An ideal facility would be chosen based on these concerns:

☐ *Physical appearance.* The physical set-up should help to create an atmosphere that supports the learning process. The ideal facility, then, is attractive, comfortable, bright, relaxing, clean, and generally "easy to take."

☐ *The training area.* The training space should be able to accommodate the nature of the training being offered. Thus, if audio-visual aids are being used, a room with pillars or posts that block visibility is taboo. If a good quantity of flipcharts are to be produced and posted on the wall, the room's wall space must be able to accommodate them. If movement, small group work, and role plays are to be utilized, the room must be large enough to allow for such activity. As necessary, other breakout rooms must be available. If tables are used to form a U, there should be enough room for participants to enter and exit from their chairs easily.

Attention should also be paid to these factors: lighting; dimming or darkening capability for A/V presentations; comfortable chairs; temperature and ventilation; elimination of noise from fans, an adjacent kitchen (if in a motel), the street, competing meetings; the availability of tables if writing is to take place.

Telephones, wall clocks, distracting views from window areas (for example, the swimming pool) are to be shunned. The use of a message board should help avoid telephone and personal interruptions. (Most of such calls can await a response at the break or lunch period.)

☐ *Physical location.* The training facility must be distraction-free. In-house training centers away from the usual location of the learner, out-of-town motels, hotels, or conference facilities, and other cultural island-type facilities are thus preferred. They help participants to forget back-home (job, family) concerns and permit maximum concentration on learning. Conversely, training "in-the-building," all too often, is subject to participants being pulled out for "emergencies" (whatever happened to delegation?), unwanted visitors, phone calls, temptations by participants to return to the office to clean up the in-box at breaks or lunch.

☐ *Participant comfort.* Every training program must provide adequate concern for "creature comforts." In a live-in facility, comfortable beds and good food are a must. In any facility the usual morning and afternoon coffee/refreshments are also essential.

☐ *Accessibility.* Whether in town or away from town, participants should not be burdened with problems of reaching the location or anxieties about "getting home." The great popularity of a conference center—motels near airports—is a confirmation of this principle. Don't overlook providing instructions concerning how to reach the place. Participants also want information about such matters as parking.

☐ *Adequate support.* The facility should be able to provide the lubricants essential to a trouble free training operation—extra tables, flipcharts, A/V equipment, a coat rack, wastebaskets, possibly a photocopy service. Also, cooperation is essential concerning the prompt delivery of coffee and lunch. A cheerful, cooperative contact person representing the facility is certainly desirable.

☐ *Flexibility.* The facility should be amenable to special needs; for example, an evening or early morning session; a change in the lunch period or coffee break; exercises that may deviate from facility norms, such as conducting a trust walk or building towers out of newspaper.

The Trainer as a Climate Setter

As mentioned before, it is important for the trainer to greet and mingle with the group before the program starts. The trainer can also help to set the right climate by concern with these added elements:

Clothing. Encourage the participants to dress informally in the advance notification to them about the program. Also encourage them upon arrival to put their coats on the coat rack or on unused chairs. To the extent that *they* are made comfortable, they will help to make the atmosphere that much "looser." Similarly, you should abandon your academic stance by shedding the traditional suit coat. In fact, in certain situations other informal dress such as a sweater (rather than a coat and tie) may work well.

Personal introduction. If the group doesn't know you, tell them how you want to be called and something about yourself. Don't be a mystery person. But keep the "intro" pertinent, brief, and humble. The participants may be particularly interested in your relationship to this program: did you design it, experience it elsewhere, buy it off the shelf, revise it? Also, have you conducted it before? If so, how often?

Positioning. Where and how you position yourself in the classroom is also significant. Thus, being seated (at least part of the time) is preferable to standing; being seated or standing in front of a table is preferable to being behind it; varying one's positions in the room—to the left or the right side—is preferable to always being up front; letting participants present material "up front" while you are elsewhere is also good; sitting in a circle with the group, if at all practicable, is preferable to always being up front.

Flipcharting. Numerous tear sheets on the walls can help to give the training room a workshop atmosphere. Conversely, the blackboard up front tends to aid the traditional schoolroom look. *Note:* Several flipcharts containing key ideas may be posted on the wall in advance of the session.

Breaks and lunch. Besides the formal morning and afternoon breaks, intermittent one or two minute stretch breaks can help to create a looser, more relaxed feeling. In respect to the lunch period, try to keep the group together so as to develop fuller group cohesion. Also, try to conduct the training away from the building so the lunch period isn't used to check out the in-box.

Using participant names. Try to address participants by their first names or nicknames. Advance study of the roster and the use of name cards and/or tent cards on tables will help you do this. If you are using icebreakers, join in so that you can get acquainted with at least some names and faces from the outset. I like to have people call me by my first name. How do you feel about this? If you like it, it's a safe bet your participants favor it, too.

Group size. Small group situations are basic for achieving high participation, involvement, camaraderie, and learning. While larger groups (20–30 persons) can certainly be broken down into small groups with good results, intimacy and rapport among participants and with the trainer are more readily achieved with the smaller group (8–12 or possibly 15 persons).

Intimacy. The trainer who wishes to create a positive climate will seek out opportunities to get closer to the participants, to become a member of the group. Some suggestions follow:

1. Mingle with participants at the break. Obviously you can't talk with everyone. But the fact that you are talking to one or more group members will be noted and appreciated. In effect, they will identify with the ones you are speaking to.

2. Be certain to join the group at lunch. If it is not an organized group lunch—and it should be, if at all possible—ask two or three participants if you may join them.

3. If it is a "live-in" program, join the group at breakfast, cocktails, and dinner as well.

4. Be particularly understanding and helpful to latecomers. If the late-arriving person has merely missed some introductory material, tell him or her: "Hi, welcome. You haven't really missed anything. We only had a warm-up exercise and the goals for the program are posted on that flipchart sheet." This will help to reduce the latecomer's anxieties and show the group that you do have empathy with *all* participants.

   If the latecomer has missed some significant material, you may wish to make this statement: "We have covered some material which you will want to get checked out on. Would you please see me at the break (or at lunch) and I'm sure that I can fill you in pretty well on what took place. O.K.?"

Trust. Effective learning requires a high degree of trust in the training situation. Participants must feel that they can comment, question, challenge, and disagree without fear of being criticized, attacked, or put down. Certainly, to the extent that the trainer can establish intimacy and rapport with the participants, they will feel free to express their thoughts and feelings.

What about the use of training procedures and techniques that relate to trust building? While such devices will not be a substitute for the trainer's behavior—actions do speak louder than words, and gimmicks, too—they may help if they are in context and perceived as sincere. In any case, here are two such procedures:

1. Conduct a trust walk at the outset to symbolize the importance of building trust (see Chapter 15 on "Movement").

2. Use a message on a flipchart, as in Figure 21-3.

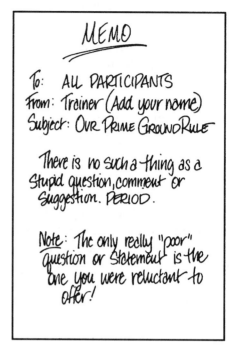

Figure 21-3. An example of a trust-building message.

Style. The most important factor in climate setting is the trainer's style. The following key elements will determine this style:

☐ Using icebreakers and/or openers.

☐ Listening with empathy; don't interrupt.

☐ Accepting an idea you may not agree with.

☐ Credibility—do you communicate frankly what you know and what you do not? Participants appreciate genuineness. Do you practice what you teach, especially if you teach interpersonal skills?

☐ Dealing with "difficult" participants in a respectful way.

☐ Dealing empathically with "slower" participants.

☐ A high energy level—one's energy/electricity, high or low, is very likely to rub off on the participants.

☐ Strong tendencies to utilize positive reinforcement (praise, recognition).

☐ Caring—do we recognize the training situation as an opportunity to make the participants, rather than ourselves, "look good"?

☐ Ability to learn with the group—every training experience is a learning opportunity for the trainer and must be so perceived by the group.

☐ Creating a supportive atmosphere where people feel free to take risks, where they act on the assumption that there are no stupid questions or comments.

☐ Using self-disclosure—become real and human by revealing something personal about yourself. This may be a reference to your spouse, children, parents, hobbies, a recent boo-boo, or a (minor) hang-up.

☐ Being sensitive to the communication process, including participant body language as well as your own.

☐ Organizing the program and behaving in such a way that participants feel that they have "ownership" of the program. Some key questions: Who is spending valuable time away from the job? Who is here to learn? So whose program is it?

☐ Establishing at the outset participant expectations and trainer expectations and the degree to which they coincide.

☐ Establishing in your own mind your own role: catalyst/facilitator vs. lecturer/instructor/expert, and then behaving consistently in that chosen role.

☐ Providing a fun-type atmosphere—need learning be dull, dreary, depressing?

☐ Providing for a change of pace—recreation, a party, field trips, etc.

☐ Stressing opportunities for discovery rather than didactic learning.

☐ Making learning gradual/developmental—no one likes to be "pushed," nor are "uncontracted-for" surprises appreciated.

☐ Securing feedback, to the extent practicable, about your own behavior—for the trainer, a training program should be a growth experience as well as a learning experience.

☐ Making oneself accessible for questioning after the session's or program's end.

Trainer role. We made a previous reference to the need to decide on your own role—catalyst/facilitator vs. lecturer/instructor. Obviously the facilitator role entails high involvement of the participant group. Trainers Betsy Pickren and Roy J. Blitzer point out properly that there may be times when other styles are appropriate or necessary [8]. They cite a study

("Identifying Trainer Styles" by Darlene Russ EFT of Zenger-Miller Inc. and Mary Howard of San Jose State University) which proposes four main trainer styles: Director, Listener, Interpreter, and Coach.

1. **The Director.** This is the "take-charge" type. He/she has detailed outlines and step-by-step lesson plans, provides a lot of lectures, limits group participation, and zeroes in on a specific set of learning points. If time is limited and certain information must be imparted, one may well adopt this style.

2. **The Listener.** This style is the reverse of that of the Director. He/she lets participants take the floor; encourages expression of needs, emotions, and experiences; shows great concern for individual learners; operates in an unhurried way; demonstrates keen interest in what the trainees say; is very empathic; and generally makes certain that participants are noticed and feel important.

3. **The Interpreter.** This type of trainer stresses use of memory to remember terms, stresses mastery of rules, explains events, and shares ideas but not his/her feelings. Methodology-wise, emphasis is on case study, readings, lecture, and disciplined discussion. The stress is on acquisition of facts, terminology, and the logical implications of the subject matter. The task, and not feelings associated with it, is paramount. The Interpreter's assumption is that releasing emotion will undermine the ability or energy of the trainees to apply what is learned.

4. **The Coach.** This style entails high participant involvement in activities and discussion. The Coach encourages experimentation through practical application—trying out new ideas, acquiring new skills, practicing new behaviors. Participants' know-how is tapped extensively so that learning becomes a shared experience. Stress is placed on relevancy and meeting participant needs, plus ensuring that there are full opportunities for everyone to work together. He/she functions as a catalyst rather than as an expert/authority/controller. A clear-cut goal is to ensure transfer of what is learned (skills, knowledge) back to the job.

Key point: While the author obviously favors the style of the coach, there are situations in which the other styles should be implemented. Choice of style depends on the nature of the group, the subject matter, training objectives, the available time, and so on. In a seminar on welding vs. one teaching management ethics, it's quite apparent that the trainer style should hardly be the same.

Gender bias. Watch for possible "gender bias" on your part. Recognize that according to linguistic research, men talk more than women in formal settings. Men volunteer to answer questions more often, and they speak more assertively. So to be an "equal opportunity trainer," use these strategies [9]:

☐ Ensure that your training room is physically comfortable and encourages easy interaction. Use flexible (movable) seating.

☐ Greet all participants warmly; call everyone by his/her name.

☐ Inform participants at the outset that you expect full participation, but no one is to dominate the discussions.

☐ Call on men and women equally. Use their names when you do this and provide praise for contributions on an equal basis.

☐ When asking a question, anticipate women may be slower to raise their hands. So wait an extra five to ten seconds before calling on anyone.

☐ Use eye contact in a way that recognizes everyone. No one wants to be missed.

☐ Encourage participation by asking: "Can you start us off?"

☐ Both sexes are likely to listen more attentively to a man's statements than a woman's, so be ready to listen actively to everyone, regardless of their sex. Head nods, "uh-huhs," and affirming statements will show that you're listening.

☐ Watch your verbal behavior (choice of words and voice tone), for studies show that both male and female teachers tend to express more impatience and condescension to women. Respond in the same way to comments and questions by both women and men.

☐ Use gender-neutral language to avoid stereotypes, for example, making references to CEOs and engineers as "he" but nurses and secretaries as "she."

THE FACILITATOR ROLE

Trainers assume a variety of roles depending on the subject matter, the training techniques used, and the needs and learning styles of the class/participant group. Typical roles are that of instructor, demonstrator, lecturer, and facilitator. Much of the thrust of this book is the importance of facilitation, something that takes place when the trainer is conducting small group discussions, meetings, conferences, and/or workshops.

Facilitation opportunities obviously arise when techniques such as role playing, games, simulations, exercises, etc. are employed. So what competencies (attitudes, behaviors) are essential when the trainer assumes the role of facilitator? Consider the following:

☐ The facilitator regards the class or program as belonging to the participants rather than to him/her. This is because the participants are the ones who are there to learn, and they will learn best if the facilitator helps the learning process rather than dominates it. This means his/her role is to maximize opportunities for participant involvement. He/she is not the "sage on the stage" but the "guide on the side."

☐ Typical facilitator functions are: to clarify group goals, roles, relationships, and problem-solving and decision-making processes; to ask questions to provoke thought; to keep the group on its task; to involve everyone to the extent practical; to mediate disputes but not squelch conflict, for out of debate/disagreement comes ideation and creativity; to focus the attention of the group on issues it may have missed; to encourage the facing up to possible "taboo" topics; to serve as a model for participant behavior, including listening attentively, paraphrasing certain comments, and as needed, summarizing agreement and progress; to encourage group decision making via consensus rather than voting; to help the group to evaluate its own behavior/functioning; to set a tone where people feel relaxed and comfortable rather than being under stress or pressure.

Other facilitator-type roles have been described above under "Style" and "The Coach."

To assist you in assessing your prowess as a facilitator, use the instrument "My Skill as a Facilitator," which follows.

My Skill as a Facilitator—A Self-Quiz

Effective instructors and trainers are those who aspire to and have been able to graduate into the facilitator role, that is, to go from being "the sage on the stage" to becoming the "guide on the side." Are you into facilitation, in whole or in part, and if you are operating as a facilitator, how well do you do it? Your candid response to the following quiz items should give you a good "fix" on your prowess as a facilitator.

For each of the 40 statements below, circle the number which best describes your perception of your skill: 1 = never or almost never; 2 = seldom or rarely; 3 = sometimes or occasionally; 4 = usually or most of the time; 5 = always or almost always. Try to be as candid as you can. In this way you will learn of your true skill and what added work/goals may be needed in order to upgrade your effectiveness as a facilitator.

1. *Entry.* I pay attention to the "meeting and greeting" aspects of participants' arrival and entry into the training room.　　　1 2 3 4 5

2. *Room arrangement.* I try to arrange a room to encourage small group work and to maximize discussion in general, and give it a friendly feel.　　　1 2 3 4 5

3. *Seating.* I prefer sitting in a circle with the participant group as opposed to standing "up front" as "the answer man."　　　1 2 3 4 5

4. *Icebreakers.* I use icebreakers and openers regularly to help set a friendly, anxiety-free tone. I participate in icebreakers when appropriate.　　　1 2 3 4 5

5. *Dress.* I encourage informal/comfortable dress as an adjunct to a free and easy learning environment.　　　1 2 3 4 5

6. *Flipcharting.* I am comfortable and skilled in capturing group ideas and posting them on flipchart sheets.　　　1 2 3 4 5

7. *Agenda.* I am comfortable departing from the announced program or topic if it aids the learning experience overall.　　　1 2 3 4 5

8. *Priorities.* I am willing to let learners set (or reset) priorities to meet their needs better.　　　1 2 3 4 5

9. *Learner interest.* I allow extended discussion in areas of strong learner interest.　　　1 2 3 4 5

10. *Climate: Program ownership.* I try to operate so that participants feel that the program is theirs rather than mine.　　　1 2 3 4 5

11. *Climate: Trust.* I try to establish a supportive, trusting atmosphere where people are free to take risks and express what they feel.　1 2 3 4 5

12. *Climate: Experimentation.* I encourage trying out new ideas, acquiring new skills, practicing new behaviors.　　　1 2 3 4 5

13. *Climate: Fun.* I try to create an easy-to-take, fun, and excitement-filled atmosphere. 1 2 3 4 5

14. *Climate: Conclusions.* I operate so that learners develop their own conclusions rather than automatically adopt mine.　　　1 2 3 4 5

15. *Climate: Controversy.* I try to use disagreements as a basis for increased learning.　　　1 2 3 4 5

16. *Climate: Pace.* I try to vary program activities to adjust to normal highs and lows in people's energy levels.　　　1 2 3 4 5

17. *Communication: General mode.* My programs are dedicated to two-way communication as opposed to one-way transmission of information from on high.　　　1 2 3 4 5

18. *Communication: Nonverbal behavior.* I try to "read" participants' body language and am sensitive to how my body language is constantly communicating to the group.　　　1 2 3 4 5

19. *Communication: Group mood.* I can sense when the group is "turned on" or "turned off," energetic or fatigued, interested or disinterested, friendly or hostile.　　　1 2 3 4 5

20. *Communication: Group mood.* When the group is reacting negatively I "stop the action" to learn what is going on so as to return to a more positive direction.　　　1 2 3 4 5

21. *Communication: Positive reinforcement.* I enjoy giving praise/recognition for comments which are helpful, constructive, incisive, creative, etc.　　　1 2 3 4 5

22. *Communication: Self-disclosure.* I share feelings and personal data about myself so that I am not regarded as a "mystery man" (or "mystery woman").   1 2 3 4 5

23. *Communication: Listening.* I see myself as a person who listens with keen interest in what people say and don't interrupt speakers.   1 2 3 4 5

24. *Communication: Feedback about progress.* When things are not going well, I stop the action to learn what barriers are preventing us from progressing.   1 2 3 4 5

25. *Participation: Risk-taking.* I encourage people to take risks in experiencing new or possibly unpopular ideas.   1 2 3 4 5

26. *Participation: Learner critique.* I encourage participants to freely comment, criticize, question, disagree, without fear of being attacked by me.   1 2 3 4 5

27. *Participation: Sharing.* Participants' know-how is tapped extensively so that learning becomes a shared experience.   1 2 3 4 5

28. *Participation: Slow or shy learners.* I encourage all participants to "get into the act" rather than ignore those who seem to be holding back.   1 2 3 4 5

29. *Style: General.* I am approachable rather than distant, relaxed rather than harried in manner, friendly rather than aloof, and interested in others, not detached.   1 2 3 4 5

30. *Style: Humility.* I admit freely that I have goofed, misunderstood, or have lack of knowledge. I try not to be "the answer man." 1 2 3 4 5

31. *Style: Pace.* I operate in a relaxed, unhurried way to avoid putting undue pressure on my participants.   1 2 3 4 5

32. *Question approach: Self-discovery.* I try to ask trainees questions which help them to self-identify main points.   1 2 3 4 5

33. *Q&A approach.* I often redirect questions addressed to me to other participants. 1 2 3 4 5

34. *Questions and answers.* I try to learn why particular questions are posed to tease out learner concerns, anxieties, and hidden agendas.   1 2 3 4 5

35. *Participant statements.* I use paraphrasing to ensure clarification and understanding. 1 2 3 4 5

36. *Summarization.* I review, when appropriate, (a) group progress/accomplishment and (b) group feelings including agreement/disagreement on particular issues.   1 2 3 4 5

37. *Descriptive behavior.* I try to let the group deal with difficult participants in a respectful way.   1 2 3 4 5

38. *Breaks.* I mingle with participants at our breaks.   1 2 3 4 5

39. *Lunch and/or dinner.* I make it a point to join participants at mealtime and for cocktails.   1 2 3 4 5

40. *Back-home application.* I provide enough time for planning activities to ensure transfer of training to the learners' jobs, e.g., developing contracts regarding future performance.   1 2 3 4 5

Scoring

Scores can range from 200 points (40 × 5 = 200) to zero. If you are very close to 200, you are a top-notch, professional facilitator. Your organization is fortunate to have you on its staff! If you are somewhere in the middle range, you should go over the quiz again and see where you can profit from personal improvement. Should your point score be on the low end, you'll want to do a lot of introspection or soul-searching about your current behavior. Try to bring about some real changes before your bosses have a go at it first!

Note to facilitator in a train-the-trainer program: After the group has processed the data in trios, you may wish to ask participants to call out their scores, enter them on a flipchart, and secure a group average.

WHEN THINGS GO WRONG

Murphy's Law (if anything can possibly go wrong, it will) is a fact of the trainer's life. Thus, we can anticipate that irritations will arise for us and our participants from unanticipated inadequacies in lighting, heating, ventilation, seating, acoustics, equipment, etc.

What do we do? Above all, we should avoid the "ain't it awful" trap. Instead, we should regard these contingencies as a challenge and engage in healthy coping behavior. Thus, if the air conditioning system fails and it is too hot, consider approaches such as these:

☐ Encourage people to adjust their clothing for comfort—remove ties, coats, possibly shoes and shirts, too, in a free-flowing experiential program.

☐ Encourage people to sit on the floor where they can relax and the temperature may be lower.

☐ Relocate to another room or to the outdoors.

☐ Hold frequent stand-up stretches and breaks.

☐ Another possibility is to tell the group: "I'm feeling hot and tired, as I know you are. But maybe we can approach this problem via a contract—if you'll pay attention to (or cooperate with) the program, we'll try to do our best to help you learn from it. OK?"

☐ Suggest to the group this approach: "Let's use our power to cool the room, to produce a breeze. Let's say in unison 'oooo oooo oooo.' Again, louder, 'oooo oooo oooo.' And a final time, much louder, 'oooo oooo oooo.' Now raise your arms over your head and wave them. Feel the breeze?"

☐ If it's really at the impossible stage, defer or cancel the session.

Training Nightmares in Outside Facilities

Unexpected (and unwanted) emergencies in our *own* training facilities can often be handled. After all, we are "at home," aren't we? But surprises/crises/catastrophes in outside facilities, such as a hotel, may be harder to cope with. What to do? Tom Schurr, who operates a hotel training center in San Mateo, California, discusses nine typical disasters and suggests ways they can be prevented [10].

1. *Culinary cacophony.* If you find your training room is next to the hotel kitchen, don't be surprised if you are subject to the deafening din of pots and pans, shouted orders, contentious chefs, and warbling waiters.

   Solutions: Advise the meeting room management that you will be conducting a training session and that student concentration is not possible if there is nearby noise. So at the outset avoid a busy lobby area, entryway, restaurant or pool, and certainly the kitchen.

2. *Disastrous distances.* You don't want your several training sites and eating facilities scattered at the four corners of a resort hotel. Participants who have to gallop from one point to another won't appreciate this unasked-for exercise.

   Solution: Insist on a concentration of the different meeting sites in one main, central area. Time the distances between the several room locations before you sign on the dotted line.

3. *Room switch.* A computer firm had modified tables to meet its special needs. Unfortunately, hotel management switched the meeting to a smaller room. The result: Most of the special tables wouldn't fit into the smaller space. This forced some participants to become intermittent standees, for seating space had to be rotated.

   Solution: Check the night before the event to be certain your training room is being arranged as specified.

4. *Solo staffing.* If you try to run a large-scale program without support staff, you may find to your dismay that you can't really do it all alone. The tasks of greeting people, operating A/V equipment, facilitating sessions, maintaining a liaison with hotel management, etc., may well be more than one very able trainer can manage.

   Solution: Contract out for some of the tasks and check to see whether the hotel can help out on some of them.

5. *Missed messages.* One management trainer arranged for an evening cocktail session after the training session. This was at a hotel he had never used before. The executive VP of the firm was to make a special appearance. But when the group walked over to the party room, they found only chairs stacked against the wall; there was no buffet of delicacies, nor was there a hotel staff awaiting them.

   Solution: To avoid uncaring service, deal only with a hotel with which you have a long-term relationship, one that needs and appreciates your business.

6. *Miscellaneous mishaps.* Mr. Murphy has long advised that if anything can go wrong, it probably will. Heating and cooling systems may go haywire, and construction and remodeling/renovation may harass your training activity.

Solution: You may not be able to predict or control the AC problem, but you can ask the hotel to let you know of their plans for painting, recarpeting, or other heavy physical re-vamping which could create problems for you and your participants. With adequate advance warning, you can make arrangements for other facilities.

7. *Unwanted postings.* A sales organization was all set to deck out its hotel meeting room with banners, charts, graphs, and posters for a high-powered motivational training session. But when the planning team arrived in the morning to decorate the room, they found that management objected to materials being affixed to the walls or ceiling.

   Solution: Learn early on what restrictions may apply to room use.

8. *Vicious victuals.* A health food firm had planned an orientation session for a group of new employees. It ordered bran muffins, fresh fruit, fruit juices, non-fat milk, and herbal tea. But what it found, instead, was a typical breakfast designed to delight a hungry longshoreman: sweet pastries, bagels with cream cheese, and industrial strength coffee.

   Solution: To prevent communication miscues about your special needs, talk directly to the top person in charge of catering. And follow up on your agreement a day or two before the big event.

9. *Out-of-sync site.* A training manager of a growing apparel company bagged a larger budget, which allowed her to take her training group to a plush, full-service resort. Previously, she could only book her sessions at small, non-ostentatious hotels. The result: The new site discouraged bonding and camaraderie crucial to the success of past sessions. Why? Participants used their free time for massages, golf, and trying out the various restaurants.

   Solutions: Know your goals (for example, close interaction), your group, and your facility. A large hotel environment may provide more opportunities for distractions than for building team spirit.

Can You Cope with Training Disasters?

Trainer Terry Chapman presents 11 "challenges," unexpected events or problems which may disrupt your usual training routine [11]. He also provides

techniques to cope with them. We'll describe his 11 challenges first. Write down your responses to them; then check your solutions against the responses which follow the challenges.

Note: Pretend you are the primary trainer/facilitator for a two-day supervisory training program.

1. You learn that your forthcoming program will have a participant in a wheelchair. What do you do?

2. You are advised that a participant will miss the first A.M. session due to an out-of-town field trip. Another will miss all of Day Two. Your possible action?

3. You are told that one participant will attend your program immediately after working a night shift at the plant. Your action?

4. Your boss has learned and informed you that several of the participants who will attend will do so only because of a direct order from their supervisors. What should you do?

5. Your roster of participants indicates that one participant is the boss of another participant. Is this a cause for concern? If so, what do you do?

6. You have been advised that your boss and his immediate supervisor will attend the first A.M. session. Is any special action called for? If so, what?

7. Things get off to a good start. You feel you are establishing rapport with your participant group. A loud lawn mower begins to operate just outside your ground-floor windows. Your course of action?

8. As you begin your class, you suddenly become aware that you've forgotten these items: an extra projector bulb, the end-of-session evaluation forms, the key to open the adjacent breakout rooms for small group work, your flipchart and paper, marking pens. Your actions?

9. The course is ending and all want well. Or so you thought. To your surprise, one participant says, "Very interesting, but I'm not sure I can use this stuff back home." How do you respond?

10. The course has ended. Everyone has gone. Now it's time to . . . ? (To do what and why?)

11. Your supervisor and his boss arrive just as you are ready to leave. What do you say to them about the program's success? (Of the ten written evaluations you received, five gave the program a rating of "Very Useful," two rated it as "Useful," and three rated it as "Not Useful.")

Here are Chapman's suggestions to handle these challenges:

1. Check your training facilities for wheelchair accessibility. If they are not wheelchair accessible, consider possible alterations (accommodations). If there are obstacles which cannot readily be overcome, advise the participant of this and let him/her decide whether he/she wishes to attend.

2. Missing the morning's work on Day One may not be too serious. Be sure to brief the participant about events to the extent practical, and provide him/her with your handout materials. But missing all of Day Two in a two-day course is a bit much. Advise the participant not to attend and to consider, instead, enrollment in a future course.

3. Since a participant should be fully alert, consider arranging his/her attendance at a different session when he/she will be fully rested. If this can't be done, permit his/her attendance. But observe the attendee on Day One, assessing his/her capability to participate.

4. Meet this challenge head on. Say something like this: "I realize that several of you are here only because of your boss's insistence. Nevertheless, I challenge you to take away at least one useful concept or technique. I'll do my best to make certain that everyone will profit from entering into things." (Also, see material in Chapter 2 on "The Unwilling Participant.")

5. This is the traditional problem of vertical training. While it may be useful in a team-building program, it may be problematic in the usual supervisory training course. If the boss does over-shadow the subordinate, at least have them sit apart. Also, you can call on the subordinate first to secure equal participation.

   Author's comment: This type of enrollment should be discouraged when the program is announced. State frankly that many subordi-nates may be reluctant to speak up in their bosses' presence and certainly will not offer comments which are in disagreement with those of their bosses.

6. Depending on your experience, your relationship with your boss, and so on, this may or may not be a problem. If there's no problem with their presence, use it as an opportunity to show how well you conduct the course. if they wish to comment at times, weave their observations into the normal flow of things. You may wish to check with your boss in advance of the course to learn what role will be assumed: observer or participant?

7. Serious noise outside the classroom can be coped with via a break (if the noise is temporary) or by telling the noisemakers that you are conducting a course and asking them to go elsewhere. If the noise will be continuing and you can't move to a quiet location, you may as well stop until the noise ceases. In any case, you can't conduct training if everyone will be subject to a major distraction.

8. On the missing items:

   ☐ The extra bulb: the odds are in your favor that it won't burn out.

   ☐ The evaluation forms: Seek oral evaluations or ask for written responses to questions you provide orally. You can ask for ratings (1–5 point scale) on course interest, course value, course materials, etc.

   ☐ The unavailable break-out rooms: Use the corners of your regular classroom and ask the teams to confer quietly. Some small group work might be deferred until you get a key.

   ☐ Flipchart, paper and pens: There may be a chalkboard to fall back on. If not, you might be able to use notebook paper and highlighters.

9. This should never happen if you build into the course transfer-to-the-job activities such as action plans, role plays, and worksheets for back-home use.

10. Do two things: (a) focus on the course, recording your reactions to it, particularly areas for improvement; (b) review the evaluation forms, looking for items of critique which might be helpful when you revise the course or deliver it again.

11. The stats on the evaluation forms add up to a 70% success rate, which is quite acceptable. (You can't win them all.) So present the data as indicative of a worthwhile experience for the participants. Indicate, too, that the feedback sheets have presented some ideas that you intend to use next time to build on the program's success.

Here's another problem to test your ability to cope with the unforeseen. What if you were to lose your voice just prior to an important training session? How would you cope with what would seem to be a disaster of truly monumental proportions? Well, here's what management trainer Martin Horan did, in respect to a six-hour course on effective speaking, writing, and organizational communication, without speaking a word [12]:

When presented with a question, he looked around the room with an expectant expression and used hand gestures to invite answers from participants. Once an answer was received, he either nodded agreement or disagreement and sometimes gestured for added comments. If he needed to make a point, he wrote on a flipchart or an overhead projector. The overall results: high group satisfaction. He concluded that "instructors could greatly benefit by occasionally enforcing silence on themselves."

To test your coping ability, further, here's a final problem for you: Assume you are invited to conduct an all-day training program for another organization. You neglected to ask about the precise nature of the facilities and as it turns out to your dismay, you have to work in a medium-sized auditorium with fixed seats. You wish to use participative (small group) methods. What can you do to salvage the situation? Some answers follow:

1. Use dyads extensively—simply have people turn to their left or right.

2. Have participants move to the stage, aisles, rear or front of the room for small-group work on a standup basis.

3. If other chairs are available, bring them in for small group work.

4. Form quartets; by having a pair turn around (not comfortable, but workable for a short task).

5. Better still, have everyone stand up for better eye contact.

6. Relocate to the hall outside the auditorium for stand-up, small group work.

GUIDES TO MANAGING DIVERSITY IN THE CLASSROOM

Trainer/consultant Marda N. Steffey advises that sophisticated, insightful, and alert trainers know that there are many types of diversity in the classroom [13]. People with different cultural and ethnic backgrounds represent a form of diversity that is easy to recognize. But there may also be these less obvious differences:

☐ Diverse knowledge levels
☐ Differences in desire/need for detail
☐ Differences in motivation/commitment
☐ Differences in willingness to participate
☐ Conflicting agendas
☐ Varied thinking patterns
☐ Varied preferences for styles of learning
☐ Different levels of responsibility and influence in the organization

A key to managing diversity is a thorough knowledge of the training materials, the learning objectives, and the course outline or agenda, all of which means heavy trainer preparation. Remember the old gag about the professor who came to class very much unprepared and thus announced glibly: "We're all students together!" This makes for a good, funny story, but such an attitude is totally self-defeating in the real world of diversity.

Diverse knowledge/background levels of trainees will require the trainer to work doubly hard to ensure both that everyone is catching on and that the class remains on schedule. Anticipate that diverse groups will require more comprehensive student guides and reference materials than do homogeneous groups. Expect, too, that many learners, due to language or cultural problems or slower learning capabilities, will want to review your written materials at their own pace and on their own time, for example, at breaks.

Rigorous preparation plus full, sincere respect for all participants and their diverse needs are the routes to an enriched classroom environment. It is thus essential to learn of the diverse abilities/interests of one's participants and to incorporate them to the extent practicable into the learning experience.

If you can learn of interest and experience levels early on, you can adapt activities and arrange project sub-groups. Icebreakers and openers can also be adjusted to meet participant needs better. In general, it is a good idea to manage diversity via *instructor pre-work*. Find out who your attendees will be and what differences will most likely be encountered. Written surveys and selected follow-up interviews are tools for this purpose.

One "must" in class is to review prior coverage at the start of each session to ensure that previous learning is properly reinforced. Added advantages: This technique will foster a sense of participant accomplishment and add an opportunity to clarify possible hazy learnings and to remove unwanted misunderstandings. A good way to review earlier modules is via a game or puzzle. Also, start a new session with a preview of learning goals and the course agenda. Advise the level of skill which is expected.

To appeal to a variety of thinking and learning styles, use job aids and varied instructional devices/techniques. Useful learning aids are statistics, checklists, flow charts, examples, analysis trees, demonstrations, hands-on experience, class discussion, brainstorming, group activities, and games.

A good classroom technique to employ is to maintain close physical contact with the group. The group will then feel closer to you both physically and emotionally. It's also a lot easier to detect confusion, disagreement and disinterest from a two-foot distance than from a distant position behind the lectern or the overhead projector.

In the Q&A period, or in other discussion periods, ask participants questions, listen to their answers, and help them listen to one another. Use "redirects" more often than in the typical homogeneous classroom. In the *redirect technique* several participants are asked to respond to each question and to elaborate on each other's answers. This (a) helps (forces) the trainer to learn what others are thinking and (b) helps to expose possible feelings of confusion by participants.

Anticipate that with a diverse group participants' questions are quite likely to veer off in different directions, including those which can put the discussion off the desired track. A good answer to this possibility is to post course objectives prominently. When peripheral issues are brought up, don't hesitate to say, "That's beyond the scope of our learning objectives." And, if practical, suggest other, outside resources which can be tapped to meet those special interests.

Of course, if large numbers of the participants want to go "off-line," you may have to adjust the course outline. Consider, too, that future courses may require you either to establish new or to reinforce existing prerequisites. But be certain to show full respect to everyone, including those with divergent needs and interests.

To tap the richness of trainee diversity, use trainee presentations extensively. Different learners can provide different ideas and possible solutions.

The sensitive trainer who is concerned with his/her learning of possible participant differences should try to spot those who may be shy, insecure or reluctant to participate in ongoing activities. One-on-one consultations, support, encouragement, and praise can help convince those who are holding back that they can safely contribute more. In small group work, watch the twin dangers of teams that are too similar and those that are too diverse. For example, if random structuring of teams produces one or two groups that are totally of one gender, don't hesitate to re-assign them to other teams for greater diversity.

Note: For a unique set of reminders for participants after the diversity training ends, see Chapter 15, "Props for Empathy," which responds to this question: "After our diversity seminars are over, what reminders can we provide the participant managers to be sensitive to the diversity of subordinates, fellow team members, and co-workers?"

CROSS-GENDER LEADERSHIP TRAINING

According to management professors Patricia L. Smith and Stanley J. Smits, organizations are recognizing to a growing degree that "only a diverse leadership team that includes both feminine and masculine strengths is flexible enough to compete in today's highly competitive, global market place. To meet current economic challenges and to prepare for those of the next century, organizations would do well to promote diversity on their leadership teams and to allow women's personal leadership styles to flower" [14].

The latter statement refers to feminine leadership characteristics such as helping subordinates, cooperating with peers, and nurturing a sense of family in the workplace. Women in leadership roles tend to function more as colleagues than as masters, to achieve influence by persuasion rather than position power, to strive for cooperation rather than competition, to encourage collectivism (team effort) rather than individualism (by me, for me), and to use an inclusionary style (power sharing, sense of family) rather than engaging in exclusionary (divide-and-conquer) behaviors.

The above description of the importance of feminine roles and behaviors has leadership training implications. If an organization wishes to balance its "masculine-oriented" leadership traditions with highly desirable "feminine-oriented" strengths, it should devise a synergistic approach to leadership development. It can cross-train leaders in gender-influenced strengths by doing the following, say Smith and Smits:

☐ Being certain that experiential, hands-on learning activities are conducted by gender-balanced teams.

☐ Using male and female professionals to administer the training *jointly.* They should share responsibility equally and model the strengths/skills that come with their differences.

☐ Checking out leadership theories and training materials used in the training (for example, cases, role plays) to ensure that they are free of gender bias and that they encourage diversity.

☐ Training both genders to show their leadership skills, to share responsibilities, and to master leadership training tasks as participants in high-performing, synergistic teams.

In general, the thrust of the gender-balanced leadership training is to encourage male participants to adopt the subtle interpersonal skills used by women participants and to urge women to learn from their competition-oriented male co-workers.

TRAINING TO MANAGE GENDER DIFFERENCES IN COMMUNICATION STYLES

"Why can't a woman be more like a man?"

—The question posed by Professor Henry Higgins in the musical *My Fair Lady* (1956)

Not only are leadership styles different between men and women, but male and female communication styles are also typically quite different.

So if you and your participants encounter difficulty, occasionally or frequently, in communicating with the opposite sex, be assured that you and they are hardly alone. Georgetown University linguistics professor Dr. Deborah Tannen, author of the best seller *You Just Don't Understand: Women and Men in Conversation,* asserts that the difficulty is due to differences in communication style [15]. How different are these styles? Vastly. Women communicate to establish rapport, men to report or to give information. Women talk to develop relationships, men to tell what they know.

To quote Tannen further, men use language to "achieve and maintain the upper hand if they can, and protect themselves from other's attempts to put them down and push them around." Conversely, women typically use language to "seek and give confirmation and support, and to reach consensus."

Tannen's thesis is that men are predominantly concerned with achieving and maintaining *status,* whereas women are primarily concerned with winning and maintaining *intimacy.* The male fixation on status gets translated into lifelong concerns about independence, difference, and rank in the male hierarchy. Men also see life as a series of problems that demand clever solutions. Conversely, the feminine focus is on achieving intimacy and on a lifelong quest for acceptance, understanding, connection, and consensus.

How does all this come about; why the acute difference in communication styles? According to Tannen, men are socialized as small boys to play in groups having a leader and followers: "It is by giving orders and making them stick that high status is negotiated. Another way boys achieve status is to take center stage by telling stories and jokes.

"Girls, on the other hand, play in small groups or in pairs; the center of a girl's social life is a best friend. Within the group, intimacy is key."

An illustration of the consequences of this early development is the way men react to a woman's discussing trouble. The man's immediate reaction: to give a solution. But the woman doesn't want a solution. Says Tannen, "A lot of men go back to saying, 'Well, why does she ask for my advice when she doesn't want it?' It's hard for them to grasp the idea that a woman would want to simply talk—that talking is what she's after."

The result: Women find themselves in a super double bind. To quote Tannen: "Our expectations for how a person in authority should behave are at odds with our expectations for how a woman should behave. Everything she does to enhance her assertiveness risks undercutting her femininity, in the eyes of others. And everything she does to fit expectations of how a woman should talk risks undercutting the impression of competence that she makes."

Tannen, in a more recent book dealing with the corporate world—*Talking from 9 to 5: How Women's and Men Conversational Styles Affect Who Gets Heard, Who Gets Credit, and What Gets Done at Work*—presents the premise that women's socialization makes the climb up the corporate ladder more difficult [16]. Her research in hundreds of workplace conversations found that women engage in these communication behaviors: they apologize more frequently, downplay their accomplishments and ideas, and soften criticisms with compliments. Men, as you would expect, see these traits/behaviors as professional weaknesses.

According to communication research, women may be "verbally disadvantaged" in a male-dominated organizational culture. Thus, in a research study at Hood College, Maryland, personnel officers of 24 companies listened to tapes of a prospective employee [17]. Twelve heard a version containing four characteristically unassertive female speech features (described below), and twelve heard a version that used the same words without those features. As might be expected, the employee who spoke without the "feminine" speech features was rated far more favorably, that is, described as more likely to succeed and more likely to be respected by co-workers.

This study cited four examples of powerless language (also cited in various other studies):

Tag questions. This refers to questions which usually occur at the end of the sentence, asking the listener for confirmation of what is being presented. *Example:* "John is strong in statistics, isn't he?" "We should send this to all field offices, shouldn't we?" Of course, this is polite speech, but it is less direct and powerful. To male managers it may make the speaker appear to be seeking approval or lacking in authority.

Hedges. These are qualifiers which may make the speaker appear indecisive, tentative, and unassertive. *Examples:* "I hope I'm right about this." "I'd kind of like to go." "I guess you could say."

Hesitations. Examples: "uh," "um," "well." Again, these can make the speaker appear submissive, ineffective and unauthoritative.

Intensifiers. These are emphasizing words, usually adverbs. *Examples:* "so," "such," "really," "awfully friendly," "really neat." Again, the speaker may be perceived to lack authority.

Although the above study examined a job applicant interview, there may be a similar carryover to actual on-the-job situations.

As reported by management consultants Arlette C. Ballew and Pamela Adams-Regan, management training groups perceived a number of significant differences between men and women [18]:

☐ *Task orientation.* Men have a strong orientation toward the task. Women have a high orientation toward maintenance of relations with people and environments that impact on the task.

☐ *Competition.* Men, because of early orientations toward team sports, accept or even prefer competition. Women are less comfortable with even friendly competition.

☐ *Kidding/teasing.* Men see and use kidding as a way to develop and maintain relationships. Women take kidding more seriously, especially if it reflects on their job competency.

☐ *Emotion.* Other than showing emotion about sports and other male-oriented topics, men tend to shy away from open displays of emotion. They are likely to be confused when emotion is shown regarding tasks and teamwork.

☐ *People issues.* Women tend to be superior in treating personnel issues because of their high listening skills and attention to maintaining interpersonal relationships.

☐ *Feelings of isolation.* Women may feel isolated from core business concerns because men exclude them from mentoring and bonding activities.

☐ *Rewards.* Women grow up without being rewarded for use of confrontation to resolve a difficulty with another person. Women tend to get their rewards for serving as peacemakers, so they have a need to learn confrontation skills essential to keeping tasks on track.

☐ *Sharing of skills and strategies.* Men can learn to share their more aggressive skills, management strategies, and teamwork capabilities to make a better work environment. Women can learn to share their listening and relationship skills and their detail orientation. Women can learn to express emotion in ways that zero in on task-related issues; men can learn to focus more on implementation, not just the big picture.

Training consultant Judith A. Starkey found in one of her workshops that a group of women defined "women as a cultural group" as "sensitive, adaptable, determined, having fortitude and emotional strength, doers with a high work ethic, nurturing and caring, open, communicative, confrontive in a positive sense, and having integrity [19]."

Men defined "men as a cultural group" as "confident, aggressive, head of the family (including finances), open to change, involved in sports, a hero, we 'fix' things, run the company and the country, are leaders, decision makers, successful and bond with other males."

In a presentation ("Gendertendo—The Games Men and Women Play") before the 1993 National Conference of the American Society for Training and Development, trainer/consultants Karen Grote, Myrna Marofsky, and Kirk Milihone highlighted these ten male/female differences which affect communication style:

☐ *People focus:* Men tend to be self-focused, women other-focused.

☐ *Competition:* Men are likely to be competitive, women cooperative.

☐ *Authority:* Men are apt to be directing, women nurturing.

☐ *Emotions:* Men generally control them, women express them.

☐ *Speaking style:* Men make statements, women ask "why?"

☐ *Action orientation:* Men prefer to act, women prefer to discuss.

☐ *Overall language style:* Men speak and hear a language of status and importance; women speak and hear a language of connection and acceptance.

☐ *Confrontation:* Men enjoy confrontation whereas women tend to avoid it.

It should be obvious from the above comparison of male-female communication styles that these differences can make working together a mine field. But even more importantly, these differences can get translated into workplace tendencies to prefer working within one's comfort zone—men working only with men and women working only with other women.

So unless there is an intervention of some sort, such as training, the gigantic, uncomfortable and less-than-productive communication gap will continue unabated. One company that decided to use training to act on this was the Kinney Shoe Corporation, a 100-year-old, traditionally male-oriented company. Their training had these goals [20]:

☐ To augment awareness/sensitivity to male/female differences in development, communication styles, emotions, and behavior

☐ To learn the values/benefits of the female pattern of behavior

☐ To learn what behavior and communication styles present problems for both genders

☐ To alter the use of any improper language

Note:

1. Preceding the formal training was a survey of Kinney's top 25 officers to learn what the firm's issues were regarding gender-specific perceptions.

2. The training began with the top 25 management people in order to ensure full understanding and support for the training to be given thereafter at the lower organizational levels.

3. The training was not intended to do any finger-pointing or to say that only one style was "right." Rather, the goal was to become aware of both styles and to integrate them into cohesive working relationships.

The Kinney training program ran three full days, used a consultant, and was structured along experiential lines. For example, in an exercise of gender-role expectations, participants were asked to end sentences beginning with:

"Because I am a woman" or "Because I am a man," "I am required to . . . ," or "I am forbidden to . . ."

They were then asked to list five "commandments" their fathers gave them when growing up and five commandments their mothers gave them. Some of the messages which were cited and discussed were these:

☐ The girls were told, "If you can't say anything nice, don't say anything at all" and "Don't get dirty when you go out to play."

☐ The boys were told, "Don't cry" and "If anything happens to your daddy, take care of the family."

At training's end, participants developed action plans for change, both personal and organizational. Plans were then shared with fellow participants.

Adaptive Communication for Trainers

Trainers can be more effective and influential in their communication if they *temporarily* use communication behavior typical of the opposite gender [21]. "Temporarily," says communications authority Dr. Judith C. Tingley, means to consciously choose communication patterns of the other gender during a certain interaction in order to accomplish a particular goal. *Examples:* A man might decide to use a listening approach to problem solving with a female colleague rather than an advice-giving approach. A female trainer might give a talk to a male management group and load her speech with sports metaphors.

Dr. Tingley advises trainers to be aware of communication patterns of the other gender. This means a purposeful adoption of one or more of the characteristics of *content, style,* or *structure* of communication typically associated with the opposite gender. *Note:* When we talk about communication patterns typical of one gender, we are not saying that everyone of that gender communicates in a particular way.

Let's briefly summarize, then, the gender-differentiating characteristics of content, style, and structure in communication.

Content. Women tend to talk about people, feelings, and relationships. Men tend to talk about money,

sports, and business. And even if both genders discuss the same topic, such as restructuring of the organization, male talk generally relates to the bottom line or the productivity angle whereas the female perspective is from a stress response.

Style. Anticipate that men are likely to be competitive communicators, women to be facilitative communicators. Men, then, want to complete the task, fix things, and solve the problem. Women want to understand and be understood. In the training situation, men may *underexplain* issues so as to move on; women may *overexplain* and/or *overquestion* to be certain that understanding has occurred.

Structure. As indicated above, we can expect women to use vague words, disclaimers, exaggerations, qualifiers, and many adjectives. Men are likely to be more concise, precise, and direct when communicating.

The whole thrust of understanding the content, style, and structure of the communication patterns of the other gender is to *customize* your training for your particular audience. The reason? To increase your odds that they will receive, accept, and retain what you have transmitted. The social psychological principle underpinning this concept is that we can more readily influence people if they see us as being like them. So what we should try to do is get on the other gender's wavelength.

For men working with women, then, these adaptations are appropriate:

☐ *Add feelings and relationships to content and topic titles.* Since women's content areas are people, feelings, and relationships, male trainers should provide stories and weave in references to these topics. A certain amount of self-disclosure to humanize yourself would help, too. Even the title of one's presentation might be appropriately customized. *Example*: "The Coaching Relationship in Supervision," not "The Supervisor as Coach."

☐ *Use occasional self-effacing/self-deprecating humor.* Women's humor runs along this line, whereas male humor is more aggressive. So if the male trainer can refer light-heartedly to his inadequacies, women in the class are likely to see him as more human, accessible, and in tune with them.

☐ *Use interactive techniques.* In the training situation, men should limit one-way communication approaches and opt for a lot of discussion, exercises, and participation with the audience.

☐ *Employ a win-win competitive style.* This means putting yourself and the participants "on the same team." In specific terms, you (if you're male) should use a lot of "we's," boost the audience and downplay yourself, provide your participants with a chance to show off their talents and achievements, and use active listening skills (paraphrasing and reflecting feelings, restating and summarizing).

☐ *But keep your precise, concise structure.* This is an asset in training. Using words concisely is likely to endow your statements with accuracy and credibility.

☐ *Use equivalent forms.* This means to use anecdotes that appeal to the gender of your audience. If your participant group is mixed or mostly female and you want to cite an example of a successful business person, consider a reference to Gloria Steinem, founder of *Ms.* magazine, rather than to Lee Iacocca and his achievements at Chrysler Corporation.

For women working with a mixed or a mostly male group, consider these pointers:

☐ *Add business, money, and sports to the content and titles of your presentations.* Men can't get enough of sports stories, references, and metaphors. Stories about families, friends, or colleagues—women's talk—won't be punchy. Dr. Tingley says that the title of her article, "Genderflex: Adaptive Communication for Trainers," was chosen to appeal to both genders. In fact, "Genderflex" sounds like it relates to sports and/or exercise! *Note:* Genderflex is a coined word that means "to temporarily use communication behaviors of the other gender to increase potential for influence."

☐ *Use more humor but not of the self-effacing sort.* Since research shows that women speakers are seen as less credible than their male counterparts, there's little for them to gain in using humor that puts themselves down. Funny stories

to make a point, plus cartoon handouts or cartoons on transparencies, are useful devices.

☐ *Use a win-win competitive style.* To make powerful points, "borrow" power, that is, draw on such sources as *The Wall Street Journal, Forbes,* or *Sports Illustrated.* And being in control of your group is very important. If men are interrupting women, you can stay in firm control by moving into the audience, joking about male interruptions of women and being quiet for a minute before resuming. Then speak more forcefully and continue despite the interruptions.

☐ *Drop disclaimers, apologies, qualifiers, and rambling.* Women tend to do these things because being understood is key to them. But men see these communication gambits as indicators that women are nonassertive and not in control. So with a male or mixed audience, shun these approaches, for they are all too likely to be perceived as communication flaws rather than as communication strengths.

☐ *Add power words.* In lieu of phrases like "really pretty fabulous," add these types of powerful male lingo to your communication style: "that's dynamite," "it's a powerhouse deal," "no doubt," "no way," "knock 'em dead," "hit them between the eyes," "let's not move those goal posts."

Key points:

1. Recognize your own patterns and those of the other gender.

2. Then make appropriate adaptations in your style—"genderflex," as Dr. Tingley terms it.

3. Learn communication techniques that are more akin to the opposite gender, but continue using the ones you're comfortable with.

4. Learn to bridge the male-female communication gap and you will be able to communicate with most people about most things.

HOW TO ADAPT TRAINING FOR OTHER CULTURES

If your organization is operating in the world marketplace, you may be asked to conduct training abroad. You will thus need to adapt your training courses/program to international participant groups. It stands to reason that your out-of-country participants will learn more readily if the training relates more directly to their own experience. This means designing/adapting your training materials and instructional style to what is *culturally relevant.* For example, metaphorical references to baseball and football in countries that are reared on soccer will only garner you an award for cultural illiteracy.

In essence, you want to adapt your training—principles, theory, concepts—so that those in another culture can understand it and implement it. Note that we are not only talking about inappropriate use of words, that is, words which are not translatable into another language, but also about words and concepts which take on an entirely different meaning in another culture. *Example:* In the U.S. an assertive person is a take-charge, dynamic, risk-taking individual. But in Japan one who is assertive is businesslike and isn't readily upset.

For effective cultural adaptation of your training, you must consider these three key components, say trainers Keith Morical and Benhong Tsai: *model, modularized courses,* and a *trainer's manual* [22].

The *model,* or conceptual foundation, on which your course is based is the most critical component of a training program's usefulness. Only if it is culturally adaptable will it be relevant to your special audience. For example, a culture which is not accustomed to icebreakers/openers and feedback, such as are common in many U.S. training programs, will reject training which is conceptually based on these twin methods.

A *modularized course* has components that are interchangeable. With interchangeability, you can exchange specific segments of the course/program without the need to revise the total package. Modularization is a great saver of time and money, but if the course is too segmented, it may be difficult to maintain the flow and its overall integrity.

In the design phase, plan trainee materials, case studies, and role plays so that they can be easily replaced with locally developed activities. Shorter modules are more adjustable to local time constraints.

The *trainer's manual* should provide clear instructions/suggestions about possible local adaptations, but at the same time it should ensure the integrity of the program's objectives. Training of local trainers in the use of the trainer's manual will permit these trainers to adapt the program to local need but will ensure that key models and concepts are adhered to faithfully.

The manual should provide clear-cut objectives for each learning activity. Exercises should be explained in terms of why they are included, what their purposes are, and how they can reach their goals. The manual should also state which activities must be saved and which can be modified or replaced. You should carefully spell out critical vs. non-critical information. Activities requiring modification are typically those that model behavior. Segments requiring replacement are usually case studies. The manual should indicate priorities for the activities. Cite those which are most important so they won't be removed during the local adaptation. Above all, be certain that adaptations don't undermine program integrity.

Morical and Tsai offer 14 pointers to maintain the quality of your training program when you take it abroad:

1. To communicate key concepts, employ a variety of activities.

2. When using visual models, be certain they speak a universal language.

3. Try to stay away from slang, colloquialisms, technical jargon, euphemisms, and words drawn from other languages.

4. Ethnic slurs are taboo.

5. Proceed cautiously with humor. It's hard to translate such material.

6. Anticipate the need to alter references to local culture, pop culture, and nationalistic icons such as those in sports and history.

7. Building a total course around one case study will be self-defeating.

8. Don't overlook the need for a glossary.

9. Plain rather than flowery language is preferred.

10. Employ *generic* locations and backgrounds in video shots.

11. Employ varied actors and props.

12. Strive for "universal" dress in videos. More formal dress is "safer."

13. In your videos, watch nonverbal behavior that may offend or be interpreted in ways you do not intend; avoid cultural-based time references not applicable to non-Western audiences.

14. Use workplace examples and video settings that are both relevant and true to local life.

Added items to think about before you take on an international training class are [23]:

☐ *Starting a session.* Use an icebreaker that's culturally appropriate. *Example:* Company trainers have learned that Russians can become offended if things don't begin with a cocktail hour. Conversely, Germans regard jokes or other attention-getters as a waste of time. They want to get down to business quickly.

☐ *Instructor prestige.* Students in some cultures defer totally to the instructor. *Example:* Asians are not likely to challenge anything their instructor may say. Questions may not be asked, for they imply that the instructor didn't explain his subject well enough.

☐ *Formality.* The training activity may be managed in a more formal manner than in the U.S. or other countries. This is particularly true in Asia. So you must take a long time to do things. Also, if a trainee presentation is required where the boss or peers are present and it is not done well, it may mean loss of face. So let the country manager decide how it will be done.

☐ *Scheduling of classes.* In a Muslim country you must allow extra breaks for prayer. Also, one trainer advises to be sensitive to the fact that the fasting period of Ramadan could make the students tired and irritable during the training day.

☐ *Lunch.* An added cultural booby trap is the luncheon period. One trainer learned during his Paris training session that little could be accomplished after lunch since it was customary to have a dinner-size meal at lunchtime complete with lots of wine. These two-hour (!) lunches meant that the students would not be in the best frame of mind to be bombarded with "heavy" learning on their return to class.

Training Style

As we do our training each day we may not reflect to any degree on our training style. After all, training is what we do, and we undoubtedly do it well. But how well would our training style fly in another culture? Hence the need to reflect on what our style is really like in relation to participant preferences which reside in another culture. Consider these cultural proclivities [24]:

In countries with cultural preferences for hierarchy, such as Japan and France, training that is perceived to have been done well is defined as the transmission/transfer of information and knowledge from the instructor to the students. Response from students is limited. So if you like to deliver lectures and do it well, you're in! These elements are involved in the hierarchical learning situation:

☐ The teacher/trainer in the hierarchical culture is a high-status person and commands high respect, more so than in non-hierarchical (egalitarian) cultures. Participants expect large differences in power and knowledge vis-à-vis themselves and the trainer.

☐ If you are a trainer from an egalitarian country such as the U.S. and you were to try to become close to your trainees, your behavior would be viewed negatively. High informality is neither expected nor appreciated.

☐ In the hierarchical culture, e.g., in Far Eastern nations, participants are not likely to feel comfortable asking any questions. Instructors are to be listened to, not challenged or "heckled."

☐ In collective countries, where people favor acting as a group, participants may not like to be called on in class. Asking someone a direct question to test understanding could produce a "loss of face." The result: the total class is embarrassed. So what to do? You can get around this roadblock by appointing a group spokesperson who collects participants' questions and presents them aloud for them.

☐ Another way to garner participants' feedback and test their knowledge is to allow the group to discuss and report its findings. This is an easy way to blend individual responses with those of the group.

In sum, to succeed in a foreign culture, more has to be observed than how we communicate; whether we do or do not tell jokes; whether we use or avoid colloquial expressions, slang, and technical jargon; and whether we use an interpreter.

Keys to Successful Global Training

The American Society for Training and Development (ASTD) offers these ten added advisories to be a successful global trainer [25]:

☐ *Know thyself.* Insight (self-awareness) into one's values and a keen understanding as to how they influence our attitudes and behavior is basic. It can clue us in as to why we believe as we do and react to other cultures.

☐ *Respect/appreciate other cultures.* This requires us to learn all we can about the salient elements of the culture we operate in. This includes our understanding of the country's religion; family structures and values; educational, political, governmental, and economic systems; plus its demographics, sports, and favored entertainment.

☐ *Cultivate a global outlook.* With a broad perspective and mindset, we can expand our knowledge, be very flexible, be sensitive to cultural diversity, make decisions often with insufficient data, and have a real capacity for reflection.

☐ *Appreciate the values/practices of non-American cultures.* Many of us have grown up believing that our culture is superior to others. If we come across as "ugly Americans," our ability to interact effectively with those in other cultures will be feeble at best. So make certain your mindset favors humility rather than condescension toward others.

☐ *Enter foreign cultures with realistic expectations.* To avoid early frustration, which can readily ensue as we cope in a new and strange environment, we must enter with an added set of values: patience is paramount (make haste slowly); tolerance of differences is essential; and ambiguities are to be regarded as commonplace rather than a cause for surprise.

☐ *Strive for a user-friendly training program.* Your job is to anticipate and thus remove possible barriers to student learning. If you understand the host country's culture, you can achieve an "acculturated" training program. This requires that you adapt everything in the learning endeavor—objectives, content, methods, schedule—to the potentially full understanding by the participant group. In other words, you go to where they are

and not the other way around. This is the only path to their acceptance of your offerings.

☐ *Recognize that sensitive communication is key to your success.* So learn all you can about their listening and speaking behaviors. Brush up on all your communication skills, including sensitivity to nonverbal behavior, asking of open-ended questions, and ability to use silence and active listening (paraphrasing and reflection of feelings).

☐ *Size up the new culture.* This means being in tune with what is going on by observing nonverbal behavior as opposed to posing queries which may be perceived as overly personal, embarrassing, or probing.

☐ *Use patience.* As Americans we wholeheartedly believe we can control time and the future. But other cultures may hold an opposing view. So rather than push for speedy decisions we should necessarily strive for consensus.

☐ *Commit to continuous learning.* Rapid change and explosion of technology and information mean that we have to adjust and adapt to this new dynamic world. The way to do this is to include in our professional self-concept the proposition that "we grow as long as we are green."

Training in a Transition Economy

A country which is moving from a centrally planned economy to the brave new world of global competition is generally referred to as a "transition economy." People in these economies are uniquely naive about what developed countries accept as commonplace. For example, if you were teaching marketing in Uzbekistan, you would learn very quickly that "ring around the collar" is hardly an obsessive concern of the Uzbek citizenry. So if you are to succeed in transition training, pay heed to these key pointers [26]:

☐ *Plan in advance.* It's indispensable to meet with the firm's training coordinators to (a) zero in on the group's specific training needs and (b) verify commitment to the training process.

☐ *Prevent misunderstandings.* It's a good idea to work with the interpreter about your training content before the sessions are launched to ensure that full understanding will take place.

☐ *Use handouts.* For post-session use as reference, provide handouts. One of your handouts should include copies of overhead slides.

☐ *Use videos.* These are essential to show examples of the characteristics/capabilities of the developed countries.

☐ *Relate to their experience.* Employ real-life examples that participants can relate to. Try to draw on their world of experience.

☐ *Respect participant viewpoints.* Present material so as to broaden understandings/insights, not to show that Western ways are superior.

☐ *Learn of training style.* To avoid alienating your participant group, research the training style and methods they're accustomed to.

☐ *Be culturally attentive.* Watch your dress and act in tune with the local culture.

☐ *Avoid the plant site.* If possible, conduct your session away from the plant to avoid interruptions. Also, avoid late-in-the-day training, when your attendees are likely to be fatigued from working.

☐ *Remember Murphy's Law.* Plan for contingencies. "If things can go wrong, they will," says Murphy. If the unexpected and unwanted do arrive, try to be patient, calm, flexible, and innovative.

Note: We would add, in respect to the first point about planning, to do much of your planning *before* you depart the U.S. Contact the embassy or consulate of the country involved to learn of the understanding of certain words in the host country, how to dress, how to address people, important local customs, etc. Other sources of information are the State Department, the World Bank, the American Chamber of Commerce, and the Voice of America. It's also a good idea to arrive early to allow time to solicit reactions of several of the citizenry as to how understandable you are and to get a feel for their accents as well [27].

How to Converse with Non-Native Speakers

Your listener, as a non-native speaker, has a tough task to identify your individual words, translate them into real understanding, group them into meaningful units, and produce a message paralleling the one you intended. And all this has to be done at your normal speaking rate of 220–280 words per minute, too. Obviously, this is a frustrating happening, to experience sounds but to be unable to decipher them. But with a little effort, you can improve your communication effort so that your listener can enter your verbal world, to know whether you are informing, persuading, explaining, complaining, or possibly presenting something else. Here are some basic techniques, then, to upgrade the quality of your interaction, as presented by Patricia Noden, a consultant in business English [28]:

☐ *Speak normally, but slow it down and strive for clarity.* Recognize that unfamiliar words sound like a flowing stream of unintelligible sound. So help the listener to first recognize these strange sounds as a speech unit unrelated to other surrounding sounds.

☐ *Provide pronunciation cues.* Key words require slow delivery plus added emphasis. Avoid blended speech such as "Waddayano?" Say, instead, "What do you know?"

☐ *Use everyday words. Example:* Say "fast" rather than "rapid" or "speedy."

☐ *Be consistent in your choice of words and phrases. Example:* If you use "late," stay with it rather than switching to "tardy."

☐ *Avoid idioms.* These are certain to be major frustrations. Examples: "Drive me up the wall," "ten o'clock scholar," "kick the habit," "welcome to the club."

☐ *Skip those two- and three-word verbs.* Instead use their simpler counterparts. *Examples:* Not "screwed up," but "erred"; not "put up with," but "tolerate."

☐ *Employ simple sentence structure. Example:* Not "the party was perceived by all who attended to be a smashing success," but "everyone enjoyed the party."

O.K., you've tried simple words and sentence structure. But the guy/gal still isn't on your wavelength. So what do you do?

☐ Try other/different words or phrases. *Examples:* If "novel" doesn't clarify, try "new." Or try an opposite: if "clean" doesn't work, try "not dirty."

☐ *Show what you mean with physical objects or gestures. Examples:* If "on time" or "promptly" doesn't work, try pointing to your watch; if "expensive" is unclear, try showing a $20 bill from your wallet.

☐ *Combine techniques. Example:* Point to your watch and present five fingers as you verbalize "five minutes." Or use a series of devices: start with a like word; then try its opposite; and then draw the word or idea, point, or gesture.

☐ *Request clarification when you receive feedback.* This may be verbal or nonverbal. On the verbal side the speaker may say, "too many people," which could imply very crowded or many go there. On the nonverbal side look for a blank stare or obvious confusion about what you said.

☐ *Avoid over-explanation.* If you provide unrelated detail, you'll hinder understanding rather than move it forward. Explain "Congress" by simply saying "It makes the laws for our country" rather than going into such details as there are two bodies, their terms are different, one body is larger in number, much of their work is done in committees, etc.

Key point: Communication is a two-way exchange of information designed to provide *understanding.* If you work toward that end, the other party will appreciate your efforts. Helping someone to understand a new language is a sign of goodwill on your part.

AUGMENTING TRAINER COMPETENCY

On the very valid assumption that the best trainer is one who is either training someone or training himself/ herself, it makes good sense to work actively and systematically at your self-development. One helpful way to start is to list the areas that you might wish to explore and check off those of immediate need or interest. A suggested checklist, emphasizing "newer" subjects, appears in Appendix 96.

The goals of such training could be for

☐ Introduction to the subject, such as for background purposes

☐ Personal development

☐ Development of a new competency so that one can provide the training to others, in-house

Obviously, the intended use of the new skill or knowledge will determine the intensity of the training undertaken (the nature and number of the courses or programs one would take).

It is to be noted that the check list deals with specific *content areas* relating to the training field (for example, TA, MBO, time management). Similar self-development lists could be developed that cover the following:

Trainer skill development, for example, in public speaking (via a Toastmasters Club membership), writing, instrumentation, exercises and games, the systems approach to training, and consultation skills.

Professional growth via participation in training and/or other management associations and societies.

Broadening outlooks and interests via participation in community and civic affairs, college teaching, etc.

HOW TO BECOME A PARTICIPATIVE TRAINER

Working with training groups in a participative way requires three components:

1. A strong philosophy that adults learn best when they are active rather than passive, challenged rather than talked at, involved rather than observing, and committed rather than detached

2. Skill in the use of participative training methods, including a willingness to try out new ways of involving groups

3. Concern with continuing personal and professional growth

Element 1—a sincere belief about the worth of participative training methods—is a "given." We start from this conviction, if it's lacking, the requisite skills cannot be meaningfully learned.

Element 2—ability to use participative training skills—can certainly be acquired. The best prescription for this is to

☐ Attend a basic course in instructional design and methods, paying particular attention to the participative aspects being presented.

☐ Attend courses in both supervision and management development. These are essentially "core" courses and cannot be overlooked.

☐ Seek out additional, more specialized training opportunities in such skill areas as role playing, instrumentation, exercises, games, and team building.

☐ Attend early on a personal growth laboratory. This is a must. This may be the T-group (sensitivity training), an encounter group, or preferably both. Highly experiential activities such as these will acquaint you with the "laboratory method" of training (the group learns from its own behavior); provide you with models of trainers who interact nondirectively but effectively with participants; show you how participative training methods should be properly executed; introduce you to concepts vital in training work such as giving and receiving feedback, introspection, openness, caring, sharing, intimacy, spontaneity, the world of the affect (feelings), and experimentation. Most importantly, the laboratory experience should impact favorably on your growth as a person, for very few of us, especially if we work with adults in the training situation, can assume that we really understand ourselves—our needs, our motivations, our impact on others, our sensitivity to the feelings of others. A good T-group experience should help to clear away some of the psychological impediments all of us carry around with us.

Continuing professional growth (Element 3) can be achieved by

☐ Attending specialized programs to learn such *content* as MBO, transactional analysis, assertiveness training, communication, coaching, counseling, and stress management.

☐ Affiliation with appropriate professional societies that can continue your professional growth and development. Attend their chapter meetings and national conferences and read their journals. The "basic" society to consider is the American Society for Training and Development (ASTD), Alexandria, Virginia. Should your work tend toward the experiential/human growth areas, the Association for Humanistic Psychology, San Francisco, also merits consideration. And if your interests are more oriented toward "hard core," performance-based skills training and you use various educational technologies such as CBI (computer-based instruction) and interactive video discs, consider affiliation with the International Society for Performance Improvement (ISP), Washington, D.C.

☐ Enrollment in appropriate university courses, or even degree-type programs. This might be explored if one lacks adequate grounding in the behavioral sciences/education. Programs that should prove helpful are psychology, organizational behavior, and human resource development.

If all of this seems like a tall order, the answer is that it is. Learning the training job well is not a quickie, overnight proposition. Rather, it takes dedication and continuing application. In fact, one might say that the best trainer is one who is "at it all the time"—either training others or training himself/herself. This follows since the training field is a dynamic one that is constantly expanding, changing, and receiving inputs from the burgeoning behavioral sciences, education, and management fields. This quote from Pope John XXIII is pertinent to one's personal growth: "Always learn something new. This year, I am going to learn Russian."

Experiential training authorities Pfeiffer and Jones provide some added worthwhile advice [29]:

1. Build a repertoire of materials to use in design work, for example, structured experiences, instruments.

2. Work with a variety of other facilitators. There is no substitute for experience with other professionals.

3. Seek out opportunities to work with various client groups.

4. Study other facilitators' designs.

5. Attend professional development workshops.

HOW TO NETWORK EFFECTIVELY

Many of us think of networking as essentially something to fall back on when we find ourselves in a job hunt. You know the old adage, "It's not what you know, but who you know." That purpose is indeed a significant one. But probably more valuable are (a) the outside contacts that can help to keep us alive and growing, (b) the new ideas which external associates can provide us so that we can do our jobs better, (c) the capability of our network to function as a worthwhile part of our overall support system, and (d) in some cases, the professional camaraderie it can bring.

To provide us with some perceptive insights into how to build and maintain a necessary chain of contacts, here are the recommendations of four experienced and successful trainers and trainer-consultants [30]:

Trainer-consultant George M. Smart, Jr., offers these advisories:

☐ Learn how to introduce yourself when making contact with a person for the first time so that you come across well and communicate your job function. First impressions do count, so you don't want to blow your opportunity to create a positive impression in that first, all-important 90 seconds.

☐ Provide responses to these four questions on your initial networking contact:

a. Who are you? (Cite name, job title, and firm.)

b. What product/service do you offer?

c. For whom do you provide the product/ service? (State whether your work is in an in-house or external capacity.)

d. Why is your service worthwhile (or unique, special, better)?

But be certain to let the other party have a chance to answer these same questions for you.

☐ If you seem to have hit it off pretty well, drop the other party a handwritten note indicating that you enjoyed the chit-chat last evening. You may also wish to enclose a brochure about what you do.

☐ Include a follow-up procedure as part of your network development. Contact everyone you know at least every six months via a letter, post-card, phone call, meeting, or lunch. Develop a formal system to keep track of your network contacts. This may involve a card file or, if you have over 100 names, a computer.

☐ Join organizations to make contacts. Don't restrict your memberships to the usual training societies and associations. Consider the local Chamber of Commerce, alumni associations,

trade associations, etc. *Key point:* Don't limit your networking to those who do what you do.

☐ A caution: don't use networking as a sales tool. This will turn most people off. Networking may produce sales, but that should be a natural long-term development.

Trainer/consultant Mary Gail Biebel has these recommendations:

☐ Work on your competency. If you are competent, people will seek you out.

☐ Build your network now. Don't wait until a crisis occurs (for example, a job loss) to jump-start your network. Follow through on all your commitments. Don't make promises you don't intend to keep.

☐ Capitalize on the potential of your professional societies. This means that you not only pay your dues and attend an occasional meeting, but that you also volunteer to work on committees. That's how you get to meet and know people at more than just the surface level.

☐ Don't just focus on what you can get out of networking. Also think in terms of what you can give, how you can help others.

Trainer Susan Fenner advises:

☐ Don't hesitate to seek help and advice. There are more willing people out there than you may imagine. Always give something to the one who gave you something, and the sooner the better. Send thank-you notes to those who did something for you, whether it's an article they sent you, a good speaker they recommended, or another favor. If you want to keep your network working well, think constantly in terms of reciprocity.

☐ Be open to network possibilities from all your daily contacts. They need not be people in your field at all. You have to be open to everyone.

☐ Organize your network, for example, develop a database system for those with whom you want to stay in touch. Consider having a set of mailing labels to send articles of interest to your contacts.

☐ Don't worry about people stealing your ideas. The more you give, the more you'll get back. (Of course, proprietary information can't be shared.)

Frank K. Sonnenberg, a marketing director for a major consulting firm, points out that real networking is something to be worked at. You can't pop into a meeting two minutes before it starts and at meeting's end frantically pass out a ton of business cards. You have to regard networking as a long-term investment if you expect to garner dividends from it. So consider these techniques:

☐ To organize your network, take these three steps:

a. Know and document your network members' strengths. Assess them as to their ability to generate new ideas, advise you of new business possibilities, or give you competitive intelligence.

b. Place your network contacts into helpful categories so that you know easily and quickly whom to contact when a particular need arises. You will know who is a creative person, who is a financial type, who knows non-profit organizations, etc.

c. Recognize your own strengths. Since networking is a two-way street, you want to know yourself well enough so that you know what you can offer others in the way of help.

☐ When asking for help, be reasonable. Consider the time involved in the favors you request. Be sensitive to the fact that contact responses may be limited because of the deadlines they face. Couch your request in a way that won't embarrass either party.

☐ Observe the "Golden Rule of Networking," that is, consider the needs of others as you would your own. More specifically, keep these rules in mind:

a. Promise only what you can realistically deliver.

b. Don't commit information overload. Quality is more useful than quantity.

c. Don't foist your requests on a limited few of your contacts. No one likes someone who's always seeking favors.

d. Consider the timing of your call. You don't want to be an intruder. So considerately ask: "Is this a good time to talk, or would you rather I call back later today or tomorrow?"

e. Avoid asking for or giving away sensitive information.

Follow these rules and you will build and maintain your valuable network.

CO-TRAINING: SOME ABC'S

Just as there is real merit in fully involving participants in the *learning* process, there are also many advantages to making the *training* process a team or co-effort. The ABC's regarding co-training or team training, which are given below, should present the rationale for it.

Anxiety can be significantly reduced. A joint training venture, in which responsibility is shared, has the potential to reduce the assorted stresses and strains entailed in planning and delivering the training. So why go it alone and court fatigue, anxiety, and even "burnout"?

Breaks and breathers become possible in the training situation. Co-training gives the participants a break from the same trainer's face and pace. And with two persons conducting the teaching/facilitating, you get a "breather" in terms of reduced load. You can thus return to the training task recharged and refreshed. Participants are quick to pick up trainer fatigue and may even enter on their evaluation forms such comments as: "The trainer seemed to run out of gas in the afternoon," or "It gets a little tedious working with one training person all day."

Co-presenting can help to share the managing of cognitive tasks—monitoring audience reaction, keeping track of content, and managing time. While one presents, the other can assess the audience or plan modifications in the lesson or session. And should one trainer get off track, the other can help to make the needed correction. A duo also means greater availability for break-time chats with the participants.

Course content can become more varied and more enriched when more than one trainer is making inputs. This follows since the odds are that different trainers will have different competencies, different approaches, different interests, and different emphases. Different material may thus be incorporated into the course at the outset, and in the training situation the trainers may provide different examples or illustrations about the subject matter.

They may also respond to participant questions and comments from different vantage points.

Delivery of material can be more varied, which, as has been indicated, is easier on the participants. Two (or more) trainers are certainly an attention-getting device. Also, if one trainer is more comfortable with a given subject or topic, he/she should obviously handle that area. Two trainers are also useful if two groups have to be formed (for example, in brainstorming, case study, setting up fishbowls) or if you need two trained observers to observe separate group activities.

Evaluation may also be improved with a more-than-one-person effort. This relates to both the planning and the execution of evaluation. Since program assessment is one of the toughest areas of the overall training job, the old adage of "two heads are better than one" merits heeding.

Feedback regarding one's performance, trainee relationships, and so forth is a major route to augmented professional competence. The observations of a colleague, in the form of a professional critique, are invaluable. And if an aspect of program delivery merits rehearsal, feedback from the co-trainer can strengthen such delivery.

Growth, both professional and personal, can be stimulated and enhanced. In the team training situation one certainly learns from the ideas and approaches of the other trainer. Also, one learns how to work cooperatively. Given the fact that both trainers very likely have different backgrounds and personalities, one must learn how to work things out and how to "give and take" with another professional person.

Handouts can be better conceived, developed, and evaluated via the multiple-judgment route.

Interaction with another competent, professional trainer can provide stimulation, confidence, and encouragement to experiment and innovate. The participants also benefit from the opportunity (or even challenge) to interact with another trainer having a different style, personality, pace, and possibly another viewpoint.

Judgments or decisions can be made in a more sophisticated way when more than one resource is employed.

Knuckling down is likely to be facilitated. When one goes it alone, there may be a tendency to defer, postpone, put things "on a back burner." This is understandable since all the motivation to do must come from within. Conversely, in a two-person training effort, one is naturally encouraged to "get with it" by the other's presence. If we may coin a phrase on this problem, we might say: "Pairs prevent pusillanimous procrastination."

Loneliness can be overcome. The best professional effort is one done in concert with a colleague. For this is the way one gets stimulation, encouragement, support, and feedback.

Modeling for participants becomes possible. When two trainers work well together, they establish a model of cooperation for the group. They can demonstrate that two persons with different personalities, styles, and views on various issues can work as a team. They can show how they handle disagreement, which may arise at times, with respect. ("George has worked in both the private and public sectors and thus sees the issue a bit differently than I do. I can respect his view, although my background is such that it's difficult for me to share it totally.")

New ideas, novel approaches are encouraged by the mix of backgrounds. Conversely, with a single background or perspective, plowing new ground is that much harder.

Options can be more readily identified, explored, and exploited by the team approach. The best decisions in any field, training included, come about through consideration of alternative or optional courses of action.

Pedagogical approaches and methods can be subject to greater variety based on dual interests and capabilities.

Questioning of what is planned and designed is facilitated. It's a lot easier to question someone else's ideas than our own. Though it is sad to relate, one's own ideas may be overly revered and thus may tend to become "chiseled in stone."

Reinforcement of certain views or issues may be needed from more than one source should participants resist the program's point of view, If so, the added trainer can help to provide that added reinforcement.

Support can be provided by a colleague at all stages of the program. No person, including the trainer, is an island. A trainer, too, needs praise, encouragement, and support. A "Hey, you really did a good job on that exercise. The group ate it all up," is always welcome. Support also encompasses sharing, caring, intimacy, and camaraderie.

Triumphs are often best when they can be shared: "We really pulled it off. The best first day we ever had."

Unequalness, imbalance, and inconsistency can be detected more readily when two professional minds are at work.

Values which are in sync between the trainers permit the optimum of working well together (as opposed to having to manage conflict which is certain to arise when values differ significantly).

Weaknesses in all aspects of program development, delivery, and evaluation are more likely to be overcome by virtue of a second perspective.

X-cellence is more certain to be stressed when two professional trainers have to be satisfied with their results: "Dave, I don't think this is our best effort. We ought to take another look at the whole thing."

Yesterday is more likely to be abandoned. With time pressures to produce, one critic may well be content to leave things as they are. With the added set of hands and eyes, there should be a greater willingness to question what has been done.

Zest can be augmented when one can profit from the "sparks" which the other produces.

The above ABC's present the rationale for co-training. However, we should recognize that there are circumstances when team training may not be desirable:

☐ When one's boss expects clear-cut, fixed accountability for results and thus is not comfortable with divided or shared responsibility.

☐ When the *skill* levels of the trainers are highly dissimilar. In such a circumstance the more experienced or effective person is likely to have to "carry" the other trainer. And since the weaker person is not really a co-trainer, he/she can only end up looking "weak" in the eyes of the participants. (Of course, a trainer-trainee relationship often exists, but that is not a "co-trainer" relationship.)

☐ When the trainers' *philosophies* are strongly divergent. Although some difference in view-

point has educational or training value, too great or frequent divergencies may confuse and frustrate the participants.

☐ When the *personalities* are quite diverse and thus are likely to produce conflict rather than cooperation.

☐ When the relationship is *not a fully cooperative one.* Hence, one person is forced to carry more than his/her fair share of the workload and do the minor or "dirty" jobs. There may even be quibbling about who "kicks" things off, who wraps it all up, etc.

☐ When there is genuine *rivalry* between the trainers. Visualize, for example, one trainer teasing or putting down the other in front of the participant group.

Organization development consultants Beverly Kaye and Betsy Jackson provide these examples of irritations and frictions which may arise between co-trainers [31]:

"But you said that *you* would bring the overheads."

"He didn't do a fair share of the pre-work detail."

"She tried to take complete control."

"He corrected me in front of the class."

"She used my favorite story."

"He played to the group instead of the learning objectives."

Kaye and Jackson also point out difficulties that may arise due to differences in skill levels of the co-trainers:

"She ignored the agenda."

"He threw us off our time schedule."

"She didn't process the exercises enough."

"He preempted my next lecture."

"She wasn't as prepared as she should have been."

However, there is a bright side to conflict and irritation between co-trainers. Kaye and Jackson state that they "may make us uncomfortable, but they may also keep us on our toes. For example, your feeling of competition with a co-trainer can sometimes heighten your performance level. Confronting control issues with a colleague may give you a chance to practice what you have preached in training sessions."

Recognizing that differences can arise between co-trainers, one trainer suggests that it is very important for the co-trainers to reach agreement on how they will handle these two issues [32]: (1) where the "non-performing" trainer will be physically located (up front, on the side or in the rear) and (2) when and how to intervene during a session.

Note: The author's practice when in the non-performing mode: I take a back seat and try to keep silent unless my colleague calls for my added input.

Co-presentation Formats [33]

The preceding paragraphs have discussed co-presentation in its most common form—one trainer is "on" and the other is "off." Trainer/consultants Robert Garmston and Suzanne Bailey term this style "tag-team." This format is particularly useful for trainers beginning a co-trainer relationship. It is also useful when the material to be delivered is new to one or both parties. Other formats are described in the following.

Speak-and-Add. Both trainers are "on stage" simultaneously. One makes a statement; the other adds to or enriches it. One initiates and leads; the other supports. In general, this format permits the trainers to provide different insights, perspectives, experiences, and examples. However, one trainer is always "in charge," that is, he/she makes the major decisions about content, when to move on, and the like.

Speak-and-Chart. One trainer presents content and elicits ideas from the group; the other records participant responses on the flipchart. The recording chore permits the trainer in the presenter role to devote full attention to his/her work with the participants.

Duet. This format provides the greatest challenge to the trainer pair, for both are operating ensemble. (As metaphors, visualize a ballet duo or a singing pair.) There is a great deal of cooperating, sharing, drawing the other in, deferring to the other, listening, and showing of mutual respect. For the audience, the net effect is the observation of a fascinating, synchronistic style. No competition here, rather, the blending of the work of two individual trainers in a high-level, supportive team effort.

Co-training, or training in tandem, as trainers Glen E. Plutschak and Robert A. Luke, Jr., term it, can be highly useful if these five principles are followed wholeheartedly [34]:

1. *Plan ahead.* Each co-trainer must be totally clear as to who is responsible for what, who will handle which piece of the training operation. In fact, the training vehicle must be so well-integrated that if one trainer can't make it due to illness, heavy traffic, or car trouble, the other trainer must be ready to fill the breech, conducting the entire session or program alone.

   Agreement in the planning must cover a multitude of issues, everything from which training methodologies and visual aids to employ to the type of seating arrangements that are most appropriate.

2. *Know each other's strengths.* Candor is essential to (a) recognize superior strengths in one's partner before the training is launched and (b) provide feedback to one another on a post-training basis.

3. *Stay involved, even when you're not "up front."* Be alert and responsive when your partner calls for inputs to elaborate on or enrich a point at issue. If your partner is the prime actor at a given point, avoid rude behaviors such as leaving the room, nodding off, doodling, or working on something else.

4. *Practice transitions.* This means knowing when to pick up where your partner leaves off. An effective, integrative device is to refer to the prior comments or activities of your partner. Show that you are building on and are in sync with what has preceded your entry into the session. Also watch the clock so you don't steal any of your partner's time. And don't weaken team success by infringing on participants' time for breaks, lunch, and quitting at day's end.

5. *Know when to disagree.* Presenting another view, as opposed to presenting a clear-cut disagreement, is O.K. But frequent reading from two hymn books is taboo, for it will only confuse the participant group and undermine the united image of the team trainers.

BROADENING THE TRAINER BASE FOR MANAGEMENT TRAINING

While training departments routinely use instructors from the organization for professional/technical training, there is a tendency to avoid using line managers for management/supervisory training. The assumption is that teaching management skills and concepts is something that only "training professionals" can do properly. Thus, management/supervisory training becomes the exclusive province of the in-house trainer, possibly supported by outside colleagues, consultants, and academics.

There is no question that a good case can be made to avoid using in-house line managers for management/supervisory training. For one thing, they may not be oriented to participative training methods. For another, they may lack the "necessary" behavioral science background. Then, too, they may have neither the time nor the interest to overcome such shortcomings. Given these circumstances, it is understandable why training staffs decide to "go it alone" in the management/supervisory training area.

On the other hand, the training staff that carves out a monopoly for itself on the delivery of management training runs various risks. These include being insulated from the real problems of managers; an inability to relate well to line people since their "worlds" are so different; a lack of prestige and credibility since the trainers may never have worked on the line; and being perceived as too theoretical, academic, and jargon-prone—visualize trainers bombarding participants with glowing references to Maslow, Skinner, McGregor, Likert, Herzberg, Bennis, and Argyris and such terms and concepts as MBO, TA (transactional analysis), AT (assertiveness training), OD, OJT, TM (transcendental meditation), Johari window, perceptual screen, autotelic behavior, positive reinforcement, and right and left brain thinking.

Weighing the pros and cons of the issue, I feel that line managers *should* be active participants in the conduct of management/supervisory training. My reasoning follows.

Advantages for Participants

☐ Resistance to training can be reduced since the participants understand that it is a *line* product, that managers are involved in its design, delivery and evaluation. The course or program acquires a higher degree of *credibility* for them than does one that was developed in isolation by the training staff.

☐ Participants receive confirmation that the training effort is truly a company-supported one. They are thus more willing to recognize its *relevance*.

☐ Participants are exposed to the values, style, and management philosophy of senior managers. They thus receive a better understanding of the concerns of upper level management and can better see how decisions are made.

☐ Since managers will have worked on the development of training materials such as cases, simulations, and video models, the participants will learn from support materials which reflect corporate cultural realities [35].

Benefits for the Line Manager

☐ Line managers so involved will broaden their perspectives. As long-time practitioners of the management art, they will find that exposure to a certain amount of management science, behavioral science, educational theory, and the classroom itself provides a good complement to that practical, on-the-line experience. As has been stated, "There's nothing so practical as good theory."

☐ For many managers it can serve as a good "shot in the arm." Being tapped to serve as a trainer should establish one as a "special person" and thus augment one's self-esteem. Being stretched to learn new skills and concepts and working with others in the training situation can serve as great motivators/energizers.

☐ It can increase the manager's visibility. He/she is now working on new program areas, focusing on company-wide concerns, and coming in contact with other personnel he/she may have had little to do with previously.

☐ When the manager returns to the job, he/she will be enthusiastic about applying such classroom concepts as management by objectives, Systems 4 management, openness, and job enrichment. In effect, the person will become a more effective, progressive, participative manager. This improvement is likely to occur since the manager has been focusing solely on the management process, management skills, and management concepts for an extended period of time, say during a tour of duty of some three years or so. Teaching others to manage is a spur to better management of one's own functional area.

A firm—Knowledge Plus Training and Development, Carmel, New York—which helps companies prepare subject matter experts (SMEs) to be good occasional trainers, ran a survey on this subject. They asked: Why should SMEs, already with full workloads, take on the task of occasional instructor? Here were the ten most common responses according to company president Peter L. Katz [36]:

1. Increase their value as employees
2. Show their capabilities (skill and knowledge) and garner positive reinforcement for their work
3. Take a breather from their usual chores and have fun and a new experience
4. Augment their stature in the eyes of colleagues
5. Increase their confidence in another work function
6. Acquire a reputation as experts and a special resource
7. Add to their visibility in their outfit
8. Experience the gratification that accrues from helping others learn and grow
9. Improve public speaking skills and gain confidence as presenters
10. Add to their skill bank and thus increase their marketability

Procedures for Success

Of course, the keys to success with such staffing are careful selection of line managers for the training job plus serious attempts at their development. To ignore care in selection is to fall victim to what has been termed the "anyone-can-teach syndrome." Realistically speaking, not everyone can pull it off. While much of the training job is teachable and learnable, the would-be trainer has to bring to the job good interpersonal and communication skills, an openness to new ideas, a strong desire to help others grow, an interest in a broad range of group-in-action training techniques (determined lecturers need not apply), and the like.

As to the training of the line manager in training techniques and concepts, the line manager has to be willing to invest the time and energy needed to begin developing new competencies. This means "going to school" at the outset to learn about the training job in a systematic way plus continuing attendance at workshops and professional training society meetings. The latter is essential to learning the subjects to be taught in the classroom and the training techniques to be used to deliver the content properly.

To ensure that our line managers who link up with the training program are successful, these procedures should be followed:

1. Think in terms of making the line manager an *addition* to the training staff as opposed to his/her becoming an intermittent instructional resource. (Of course, adding other managers to serve as trainers on an "as needed" basis is O.K., too.) *Note:* Adding line managers to the training staff will obviously require full support and approval of upper management as part of the organization's career development and training programs. Once management has given its blessing to the concept, the training staff will play an active role in the selection process, including suggesting standards and procedures for its implementation. Additionally, they can provide inputs (recommendations) to management concerning specific managers they would like to have join the training staff for a significant tour of duty.

2. Select carefully. Those who have reputations as highly competent managers, who are interested in a broad range of management ideas, who feel strongly about helping others to become more effective, and who have a flair for working effectively with others in group situations are to be preferred.

3. Carefully analyze the actual training competencies the new "hire" has. Plan an individualized development program to meet his/her needs.

4. Provide enough training opportunities so that the new trainer will function at a high standard as soon as possible. Provide enough coaching and counseling to provide motivation and to ensure success.

5. Ensure that the line manager's tour of duty in the training unit is long enough—some two and a half to three years—that the job can be learned well and the manager can make a real contribution to it. Those who are merely interested in a "quickie" tour of duty are to be avoided.

6. Secure management support to make this type of assignment a much sought after career opportunity, one having high status, high visibility, and high opportunity to contribute to the success of the organization.

Gains for the Organization

☐ The expanded role of the manager can serve as an organization development intervention, a lever for change. For example, trainers Donna R. Christensen and Dennis C. Kinlaw report that in designing and conducting a performance appraisal workshop, the managers, as trainers, became so aware of the system's weaknesses that a whole new policy and set of guidelines were developed. A massive training effort for all employees was also provided [35].

☐ Since more reality-based training is being provided, the organization's training effort will get more attention, more credibility, greater support at all levels, and thus more return on the training dollar.

☐ Managers so involved profit from an added developmental experience which should augment their managerial capability upon return to line work and thus impact on overall organizational outcomes.

☐ Its image as a career-minded organization is enhanced since it is providing diversified, in-house developmental opportunities, as well as showing strong interest in and support of the training function.

Values for the Training Department

☐ It can augment the credibility of those who deliver the training. Line managers are worthwhile role models in the management training situation. Conversely, when trainers provide management training and have done little or no managing themselves, the training effort may, understandably, be suspect.

☐ It obviously can increase the size of the training staff. Most training units can profit from extra hands.

☐ In planning or designing courses or sessions, the line managers detailed to the staff can serve as an excellent resource to reality test the proposed offerings.

☐ It can provide trainers with increased stimulation and learning by intimate contact with representatives of management.

☐ When the line managers return to their jobs, they are likely to become advocates for the training function. This is one way for the training unit to get the support it always seeks and needs.

In summary, line managers should be involved in training other managers. If the task is approached properly, it can pay dividends to the participants, the managers, the training staff, and the total organization.

As a final point, the organization's culture must recognize the importance of line participation in its training program. A training assignment should be regarded as a prestigious, coveted career opportunity, with appropriate rewards and support provided to program participants.

VERTICAL TRAINING

The trainer who is interested in broad participation is faced from time to time with a request to include a supervisor with his/her subordinates in the same training course. If both parties attend together, we have "vertical training." It is not an overstatement to say flatly that such joint attendance is not a very workable procedure. Why not? For two reasons:

1. The most serious objection is based on the fact that all too many supervisors, wittingly or unwittingly, inhibit the participation of their subordinates. After all, who wants to "look bad" in front of one's supervisor? Or worse still, who wants to disagree openly with one's boss? Disagreement with another participant might not be too threatening, but disagreement with the boss becomes a matter of "high risk."

2. The inhibition to participate also works the other way. Bosses may not feel comfortable discussing their problems as a manager, their shortcomings, or their hang-ups in the presence of subordinates. Nor are they likely to relish any disagreement or feedback from them.

As a trainer, I have been pressured at times to include bosses with their subordinates in the same training activity. Sometimes an assurance is given that "it won't matter." Unfortunately, it does matter. Relatively few bosses can reduce their status enough to allow for full and free communication, either at work or in the training situation.

There are certain situations, of course, where vertical training can work. These are:

☐ In a *technical or skills training course* where everyone is learning new information or new techniques and where problems of varying philosophies or perceptions and giving and receiving feedback are not involved. In fact, it may be desirable or essential that all concerned receive the new learning together since they will be applying it together.

☐ In a *team-building* situation where the boss is *consciously* trying to build a better team, to improve interpersonal communication, and to improve the team's problem-solving capability, it can work. But to be successful in this effort, the boss should be an employee-centered boss and have participated in some kind of feedback program such as an encounter group, the T-group (sensitivity training) or the Managerial Grid®. Also, the team-building sessions should be aided by a trained, outside facilitator-consultant who can referee disagreements and encourage low-key feedback.

☐ There may be some instances wherein a boss is uniquely nondirective, open to new ideas and feedback, and non-status-conscious without any prior training along his line. If so, the boss's presence may not prove to be an inhibitor to full participation by subordinates. (In my experience, however, this happy state is quite rare.) One approach to the problem is to call the high-status person aside, in advance of the program, and level with him/her about the need to "low-key it." Suggest he/she play the role of a devil's advocate rather than an expert, lest overall participation be inhibited. If the problem is presented as a challenge, a few bosses may rise to the challenge and be encouragers rather than smotherers of participation.

HOW TO UPGRADE YOUR CQ (CREDIBILITY QUOTIENT)

Neither trainers nor the training department can function well if their credibility with management at various levels in the organization is low. Training consultants Anthony Nathan and Michael Stanleigh suggest that we, as trainers, engage in sincere introspection to assess our credibility. To do this, they suggest we consider these 32 symptoms of poor credibility [37]:

☐ *Relationship with senior executives.* They are not likely to confide in you. In fact, they exclude you from most high-level meetings.

☐ *Relationship with CEO.* The top exec never calls you in for a chat and does not request your views on key concerns/problems/issues.

☐ *Participation in training department activities by top management.* This is a rare event.

☐ *Evaluation of the training department.* Management's criteria are different from yours.

☐ *Attitudes of middle and upper management.* They do not see you as someone who can assist in solving performance problems.

☐ *Organizational location of training department.* It occupies a low level on the organization chart.

☐ *Reactive/proactive stance.* You only act on what is requested. You are reactive ("firefighting") rather than proactive.

☐ *Your strategic plan.* If you have one, management was not involved in its development. The result: managers don't feel committed to it.

☐ *Communication about your strategic plan.* If asked about it, you can't convincingly describe it.

☐ *Internal consultancy.* Managers rarely use training department staffers as internal consultants to aid in resolving their problems.

☐ *Communication about the training role.* People (managers, employees) are unaware of the training department's functions, its service, or its value to the firm.

☐ *Middle managers' view.* There is the general feeling that the training shop is too theoretical and doesn't understand their needs.

☐ *Use of the training department.* There are frequent requests for outside courses even though similar internal courses are available.

☐ *Involvement in internal training activities.* The various departments don't call on the training department to develop and deliver internal training courses.

□ *Networking.* You have yet to develop a network of organizational contacts to discuss ideas or to secure support.

□ *Perception of the training department.* There is a widespread feeling that the training unit is neither action-oriented nor results-oriented.

□ *Management support.* Money or other resources are not forthcoming when needed.

□ *Training budget.* Does it exist? No one ever indicates what it is.

□ *Spending.* You tend to overspend your budgetary allotments, so you alibi that "It cost more than planned."

□ *The training department in hard times.* Management is likely to cut budget or staff in a recession.

□ *Overall approach.* You tend to offer "quick fixes" to training solutions, and you rarely conduct a needs analysis or offer non-training solutions.

□ *Use of high-paid consultants and packaged programs.* You tend to favor and use these external resources even though they frequently have little or no payoffs.

□ *Nature of workshops.* You tend to stress lectures, information dissemination, and theory at the sacrifice of quality learning and job needs.

□ *Attendance at courses.* "No-shows" and last-minute cancellations are common.

□ *Participant interest in courses.* Trainees interrupt courses often by coming in and out of class.

□ *Transfer of training.* Course grads stop application of the new learning six weeks after the course's end.

□ *Level of evaluation.* Course evaluation is restricted to Level One, securing participant reactions/feelings about the course.

□ *Participant evaluations.* Trainees' assessments of courses are typically average or poor.

□ *Pace.* The training unit often has unplanned breaks in its activity.

□ *Staff morale.* As might be expected, if much of the above occurs, morale is low.

□ *Support from one's boss.* Support from the immediate supervisor is lacking or, worse, he/she may even be quietly undercutting what you try to do.

□ *Comments by other departments.* The staff or the training unit itself is subject to negative comments.

Note:

1. High credibility is the cornerstone of an effective training function.

2. Many factors enter into staff/training unit credibility.

3. No training staff or training department would be subject to all the possible criticisms cited above.

Achieving credibility. If your training department is a new one, you are in a good position to develop a credible image by doing the "right" things at the outset. If your training unit is a well-established one and possesses a poor image, the road back to high credibility is more difficult. In either case, the following 14 practical guidelines presented by trainers Nathan and Stanleigh should help put the training unit on the road to high credibility:

1. *Organizational knowledge.* If you know your organization, you can design/customize training to meet organizational needs and conditions more fully. So learn about organizational goals, problems and priorities, history, culture, competitors, and financial status. Knowing the culture is particularly important, for it will tell you how the outfit reacts to change (resists or supports it).

2. Opt for performance improvement rather than being a peddler of courses.

3. *Design a strategic training plan.* Show (and impress upon) management that you have carefully considered both organizational needs and the training department's capabilities in developing this master plan. Involve management at all levels in your collection of data.

4. *Seek top management support.* Show the top execs that your primary purpose for existence is to help management get its job done better. To do this properly, learn of top management's values, perceptions, and priorities. Recommend the creation of a broadly representative training committee or advisory panel. Show possible outcomes of well-

conducted training: higher productivity, cost control, higher morale, better company image.

5. *Start with a bang.* Get some worthwhile training activities going quickly. You want to show that you are a doer who can achieve significant results. Find a unit or office that wants help and then give them all your support. A significant training effort *now* will make a big splash. Nathan and Stanleigh suggest you start with something that has visible results, for example, an orientation handbook, a newsletter, an incentive program, or a worthwhile skills program (telephone usage, customer service, readable writing).

6. *Build on success.* Start small, achieve A-1 results, and get recognized for them. You don't want any mediocre efforts at your start-up. Work toward reasonable goals. Little "victories" will produce management confidence in your prowess, which may well be translated into greater management support later on—when you want to embark on more top-drawer ventures such as team building or other OD interventions.

7. *Select and use outside resources carefully.* Consultants and packaged, off-the-shelf training programs have their place in any well-thought-out training program. But do a lot of "homework" before you sign on the bottom line for any of it. Probably the only happening worse than a program of yours that backfires is one that you import that bombs!

8. *Design programs which are "lean and mean."* That is to say, stress practical skill development which can easily be transferred to the job. Stress learning, not teaching. Use participative, involving, fun-type training activities. Soft-pedal theory, jargon, and verbosity. Use action plans to monitor skills application and refresher training to ensure transfer of learning to the job.

9. *Assess what you do.* Involve line managers in designing evaluation procedures. Consider skipping course-end evaluation and opting for more meaningful feedback six weeks later. Show impact of your training via before and after training measurements. Be open to constructive criticism.

10. *Learn from non-successes.* Mistakes are inevitable. But don't cover them up. Use them as learning experiences. Correct your miscues or cancel them out promptly.

11. *Manage organizational politics.* This means such things as knowing when to push and when to retreat, compromising when necessary, cultivating key people, networking, forming alliances, and seeking and maintaining your boss's support and counsel. (The author knew one trainer who worked so independently that his boss on one occasion said to him, "You don't really need a boss, do you?")

12. *Respect the bottom line.* Think bottom line, talk to your staff about it constantly, and show top management that you share their concern about it, too. In your reports on training activities, stress how the training has favorably impacted profitability and costs.

13. *Walk the talk.* The training office should be a model of organizational accomplishment, practicing what it preaches. For example, if you expect your operating components to keep themselves actively involved in new learning experiences, the training people can do no less. Try out new programs in the training office before you foist them on anyone else.

14. *Anticipate a slowly developing image of credibility.* You can't expect to achieve high credibility after conducting one good course. Credibility has to be earned; your magic wand won't work for you in this area. It will take time before word gets around that the training folk have a lot to offer. So keep contributing your good works, and your reward in terms of a robust image will materialize in due time.

TERMINOLOGY FOR THE TRAINING EFFORT

Is there any way to distinguish between workshops, seminars, institutes, conferences, symposiums, courses, and programs? And does it matter?

Let's take the second question first: "Does it matter?" Yes, it matters, because participants should know in advance of their attendance how they will learn, how participative it will be, and what the trainers will expect of them before, during, and after the training experience.

To the extent that we use fuzzy language such as "seminars," "institutes," and "courses," and we misuse the language by calling sit-and-listen type programs "workshops," we are not being fair to our potential participants. Remember, more and more people who attend training programs expect to be involved. Our choice of language to describe a training function, which communicates the degree of their potential involvement, should thus be accurate. Of course, the announcement concerning any training effort should state in specific terms the nature and degree of participation that may be encountered.

As to our first question about how to differentiate between the various terms used to describe training efforts, these definitions may help:

Workshop is a term used to describe an intensive training activity in which participants learn primarily by doing. While there may be some formal inputs, these activities are relatively minor. The key idea is heavy participant activity and high interaction, stemming from the use of a good variety of participative training techniques. Typically, the emphasis is on learning new skills as well as new concepts. Application sessions and/or activities are used extensively. Sometimes those who announce or provide this type of training refer to it redundantly as a "hands-on" workshop to communicate that participants will be highly active and involved.

Laboratory describes a training experience in which people learn primarily from their own behavior. Such experiential learning activities as the T-group, the Managerial Grid®, and encounter groups are illustrative of laboratory learning/training. Team building may also be included in this category.

Seminar refers to a learning experience where knowledge rather than skill is to be gained. Thus, there are experts or resource persons (one or more) who provide inputs to stimulate discussion. The learning comes from listening and exchanging views with the experts and other participants. Attendees are expected to have subject-matter background and to be fairly active discussants rather than passive listeners. The group is fairly small (15–20 persons) so that views can be exchanged readily. Other than discussion, participative training devices are not used for the most part.

Conference is a learning experience wherein one or more of the following activities take place:

☐ Current problems may be examined with the idea of producing solutions about them.

☐ There may be some motivational and clarification efforts.

☐ New policies, goals, and products may be presented.

Conferences are designed to accommodate all kinds of groups—sales, management, safety, headquarters-field—and come in all sizes (groups of 20–50, hundreds, or several thousand).

Conferences vary in the degree to which they are participative. The better ones make an effort to secure participant input via small group work plus reports from those groups.

Professional societies and trade groups also hold conferences. Since their audiences are often quite large, the attendees are recipients of lectures, papers, etc. and typically have little opportunity for participation in the proceedings. Occasionally resource people, with imagination and concern for participant involvement, may devise ways "to put participants to work."

Symposium entails a presentation of several points of view by various experts. The audience typically is large and is one that listens primarily, although there may be some opportunity to pose questions to the experts. A moderator is used to introduce the speakers, to summarize, and to guide/control the questioning by the audience. Unlike the panel presentation, there is little or no interchange among the experts.

Forum is a distant cousin to a debate in that different and opposing views are presented to the audience. Typically, however, the presenters do not challenge one another in their views. The audience is encouraged to ask questions after all views have been heard.

Panel is akin to a forum except that there is interchange among the panelists (three to six persons). The audience may also have a chance to comment or to ask questions. The audience may be relatively small (20–25 persons), medium-sized (50–100 persons), or large (200–500 persons).

Institute is a term applied to a meeting of a specialized group. Typically it is a session of limited participation, using assorted lecturers for the most part. In my experience it is a pretentious term that few people really understand.

Courses, programs, sessions, etc. are global terms that tell us very little about the actual nature of the training event insofar as participation is concerned. If one wishes to be vague, for whatever reason, these are excellent terms to use in announcing the training effort.

If these terms appear confusing, it is probably because they are. I prefer to use the term "workshop" when a high degree of participation/interaction is involved. If the training effort is a "sit and listen" affair, conference and course are suitable terms. *Conference* would imply a general presentation of ideas by various experts and a *course* a much more formal and didactic experience.

Note: I prefer these definitions. Others, however, may favor different terminology.

KEY POINTS

1. The design of a training program should involve the participation of colleagues, operating officials, supervisors, and employees as appropriate.

2. Some factors to consider in making the design are the use of behavioral objectives, use of small group learning, course length, the structure of each training day, pre-work, warm-up activities, use of support materials, meeting the needs of special interest groups, aids for back-home application.

3. Need determination should also be approached in a participative way. Individual and group interviews plus survey procedures are basic tools for this purpose.

4. To the extent practicable, the program should seek out individual or special group needs.

5. Attention should be paid to developing strategies to respond to inappropriate training requests.

6. Methods for training should be selected carefully since certain ones are more effective/appropriate than others.

7. Method selection should be based on relationships to instructional objectives, likelihood of acceptance by the participants and/or the organization, environment constraints, and the supporting role of one method in relation to another.

8. Concern with climate is basic to a successful participant learning experience. Factors to consider include pre-arrival concerns, greeting or welcoming procedures, the total training environment including support available to the program, the style of the trainer, and contingency planning.

9. If you wish to improve your prowess as a participative trainer, appropriate training experiences should be undertaken. Laboratory training is one of them.

10. Co-training or joint instruction can enrich the course/program for participants and add to the personal growth of the trainers.

11. Line personnel should be used extensively by the training department, even in programs relating to management development. This procedure benefits both the line and the trainers. Careful selection and considerable training of line trainers are basic to such a training effort.

12. Vertical or team training should be approached with caution. The need for "everyone to know" should be balanced against the problem of status, which the supervisor inevitably brings to the training situation.

13. Trainers should avoid fuzzy language in respect to announcing seminars, institutes, workshops, and the like. The terminology employed should relate to the degree of participation that will actually take place in the training situation.

14. Provide attention to the management of diversity in the classroom. This relates not only to differences in gender, race, ethnicity, age, and physical limitations, but also to difference in knowledge/experience levels and learning styles.

15. Communication with participants in the classroom can be improved if the trainer/facilitator recognizes and respects differences in female vs. male communication needs and styles.

16. If you are required to adapt your training to other cultures, you must consider the cultural relevancy of both your training materials and your instructional style.

17. In today's dynamic training culture, networking (keeping in touch with others in your field) is a must for the trainer/facilitator. It has a number of values, the foremost being its capability to enrich your training offerings.

18. Continuing concern with one's credibility quotient is essential to trainer/facilitator accomplishment and success.

REFERENCES

1. Stein, D. S., "Designing Performance-Oriented Training Programs," *Training and Development Journal* (January 1981), pp. 12–16.

2. Miller, G. V., "Individualizing Learning Objectives," *Training and Development Journal* (July 1979), pp. 40–42.

3. "Speedy Needs Assessment," in "Training Today," *Training* (July 1998), p. 13.

4. Kaufman, Roger, "When Good Bosses Ask for Bad Things," *Training and Development* (May 1991), pp. 29–32.

5. Newstrom, J. W., "Evaluating the Effectiveness of Training Methods," *Personnel Administrator* (January 1980), pp. 55–60.

6. Neider, L. L., "Training Effectiveness: Changing Attitudes," *Training and Development Journal* (December 1981), pp. 24–28.

7. Bell, C. R., "Criteria for Selecting Instructional Strategies," *Training and Development Journal* (October 1977), pp. 3–7.

8. Pickren, Betsy, and Blitzer, Roy J., "How to Escape Your Training Horrors," *Training* (March 1992), pp. 32–35.

9. Ali, Ellen B., "Check Your Gender Bias," in "In Practice," *Training and Development* (April 1994), pp. 11–12.

10. Schurr, Tom, "Training Nighmares and How to Avoid Them," in "Training 101," *Training and Development* (August 1992), pp. 18–19.

11. Chapman, Terry, "What Should You Do?" *Training and Development* (August 1993), pp. 13–15.

12. Horan, Martin, "The Silent Approach," in "In Practice," *Training and Development* (March 1993), pp. 10–11.

13. Steffey, Madra N., "Managing Diversity in the Classroom," in "Training 101," *Training and Development* (April 1993), pp. 22–24.

14. Smith, Patricia L., and Smits, Stanley J., "The Feminization of Leadership?" *Training and Development* (February 1994), pp. 43–46.

15. Tannen, Deborah, *You Just Don't Understand: Women and Men in Conversation*, Morrow, New York (1990).

16. Tannen, Deborah, *Talking from 9 to 5: How Women's and Men's Conversational Styles Affect Who Gets Heard, Who Gets Credit, and What Gets Done at Work*, Morrow, New York (1994).

17. "What's in a Word? A Job, Hood Senior's Study Says," *The Washington Post,* June 6, 1991.

18. Ballew, Arelette C., and Adams-Regan, Pamela, "Sexual Differences in the Workplace: The Need for Training," in *The 1993 Annual—Developing Human Resources*, San Diego, Pfeiffer and Co. (1993).

19. Starkey, Judith A., "Women in Business: A Cultural Change," *Managing Diversity,* newsletter (1995).

20. Laabs, Jennifer J., "Kinney Narrows the Gender Gap," *Personnel Journal* (August 1994), pp. 83–89.

21. Tingley, Judith C., "Genderflex: Adaptive Communication for Trainers," *Performance and Instruction* (April 1993), pp. 12–15.

22. Morical, Keith, and Tsai, Benbong, "Adapting Training for Other Cultures," *Training and Development* (April 1992), pp. 65–68.

23. Rasicot, Julie, "Communication Breakdown?" *Information Technology Recruiter Magazine* (January–February 2000), pp. 190–194.

24. Laroch, Lionel, Bing, John, and Bing, Catherine Mercer, "Beyond Translation," *Training and Development* (December 2000), p. 72.

25. "The Successful Global Trainer," *Member Mailbag*, American Society for Training and Development (ASTD) (August 1999), p. 2.

26. Schrage, Christine R., and Jedlicka, Allen, "Training in Transition Economies," *Training* and *Development* (June 1999), pp. 38–41.

27. Anton, Tom, "There's More Than One Way—How to Anticipate Differences When Presenting Abroad," *Successful Meetings* (October 1999).

28. Noden, Patricia, "Dealing with Diversity: Speaking English They Understand," *The Torch*, newsletter of the Metropolitan Washington, D.C., Chapter of the ASTD (April 1998), p. 9.

29. Pfeiffer, J., and Jones, J. E., "Design Considerations in Laboratory Education," in *The 1973 Annual Handbook for Group Facilitators*, University Associates Publishers, San Diego (1973), pp. 192–193.

30. "Building a Chain of Contacts," in "Four By Four," *Training and Development Journal* (January 1991), pp. 21–27.

31. Kaye, Beverly, and Jacobsen, Betsy, "Tying Ourselves in Knots," *Training and Development Journal* (December 1986), pp. 28–33.

32. Rosenweig, Fred, "Co-Training," *Performance and Instruction Journal* (August 1987), p. 20.

33. Garmston, Robert, and Bailey, Suzanne, "Paddling Together: A Copresenting Primer," *Training and Development Journal* (January 1988), pp. 53–55.

34. Plutschak, Glen E., and Luke, Robert A., Jr., "Training in Tandem," in "Training 101," *Training and Development* (March 1993), pp. 23–24.

35. Christensen, Donna R., and Kinlaw, Dennis C., "Managers Can Do It All—Or Nearly All," *Training and Development Journal* (May 1984), pp. 87–89.

36. Katz, Peter L., Letter to the Editor, *Training* (June 1999), p. 13.

37. Nathan, Anthony, and Stanleigh, Michael, "Is Your Department Credible?" *Training and Development Journal* (January 1991), pp. 41–45.

RECOMMENDED READING

Program Design

Bell, Chip, and Putnam, Tony, "Mastering the Art of Training Design," *Training and Development Journal,* May 1979, pp. 24–27.

This article suggests that "the art of training design requires the logic of people" whereas "the craft of training uses the logic of machines." Attention to both aspects makes for good design, although the people orientation is the primary point of departure.

Darraugh, Barbara, "Course Construction," *Training and Development,* May 1991, pp. 66–71.

On the very valid premise that the most critical part of a training course happens before the trainer enters the training room, the author provides a step-by-step guide to course design and development. Typical coverage: design basics; underlying objectives; elements to be included in course description; learning sequence; learning strategy; course development; evaluation, both formative and summative; course administration; necessary rewards; standards of performance.

Nader, Leonard, *Designing Training Programs: The Critical Events Model,* Addison-Wesley, Reading, Mass., 1982.

The book presents a model for the planning/design of training involving managers and supervisors in all its steps. The CEM covers these steps: identify the needs of the organization, specify job performance, identify learner needs, determine objectives, build curriculum, select instructional strategies, obtain instructional resources, and conduct training. Each step, per the model, is subject to evaluation and feedback.

Putnam, Anthony O., "Designing from the Logic of People," *Training and Development Journal,* May 1981, pp. 125–131.

This article develops the relationship of people orientation to design in more detail (see previous reference); it advises trainers to focus on the person, not the program; pay attention to what causes "movement" for participants, provide the learner with material that is intrinsically interesting, and use "resistance" to facilitate movement.

Rogoff, Rosalind, L., "The Training Wheel: A Simple Model for Instructional Design," *Training,* April 1984, pp. 63–64.

The author suggests a commonsense design model consisting of four steps presented in a circular, sequential format: (1) Find out who, what, and why (a combined needs assessment and audience analysis). (2) Define realistic objectives. (3) Design and implement instruction. (4) Fix what went wrong (evaluation).

Romines, Jack A., and Crump, Bill, "A Self-Examination for Training Developers," *Training and Development Journal,* July 1982, pp. 76–80.

Training program designers should ask themselves these questions: Why is training needed? Who is the training audience? What is the most cost-effective way to reach the training goal? When does the training need to be done? Where will it be given? How will you know if the goal was achieved?

Simpson, Donald T., "Are You an Informed Consumer of Training?" *Training and Development Journal,* December 1981, pp. 34–40.

In this article, which provides guides to purchasing learning packages, the author presents such design principles as examine your philosophy of how people learn, develop a model for the learning and design process, test the model, and compare existing programs against the model. The model, presented in diagrammed format, covers these stages: establish learning objectives, define subject matter, determine learning components of subject matter, determine complexity of subject matter, estimate learner resistance to subject matter, select appropriate methods, develop media to support methods.

Need Determination

Alexander, Anne, "Need Assessment for Planning Training Programs: A Participatory Method," *Canadian Training Methods (CTM): The Human Element,* February 1980, pp. 19–21.

This article describes the use of a participatory method to determine needs. Participants were contacted for help in developing a questionnaire that they subsequently completed. Advantages and limitations of this method are discussed.

Miller, Gerald V., "Individualizing Learning Objectives," *Training and Development Journal,* July 1979, pp. 40–42.

The article raises and answers this question: "How do I, as a trainer, individualize when I have preset learning objectives to meet or a packaged program to present?" The author's answer is to use individualized needs, which become a contractual agreement, and program adjustments to meet these needs.

Nowack, Kenneth M., "A True Training Needs Analysis," *Training and Development Journal,* April 1991, pp. 69–73.

The author presents a nine-step program of needs analysis, distinguishing between training needs and training wants. The nine steps: Conduct a job profile; develop the questionnaire; administer the questionnaire; analyze the questionnaire; interpret results; use small focus groups to clarify results; provide feedback to both respondents and managers; develop training objectives; evaluate training effectiveness.

Stein, David S., "Designing Performance-Oriented Training Programs," *Training and Development Journal,* January 1981, pp. 12–16.

This article describes the use of a modified critical incident technique to uncover learning needs as employees see them. The needs sought for are clear-cut deficiencies in performance rather than "felt learning needs," thus making for cost-effective training.

Walley, John R., "Let Attendees Help Plan Your Meetings," *Successful Meetings,* September 1979, pp. 93–96.

The author explains how you can use agenda questionnaires to design sessions around problems, topics, and program expectations presented by participants prior to the meeting.

Zemke, Ron, "How to Do a Needs Assessment When You Think You Don't Have the Time," *Training,* March 1998, pp. 38–44.

When management wants that training course right now, that isn't a valid reason to accede and deliver lousy training. The author suggests a number of approaches to gaining needed information to permit doing an acceptable training job.

Climate

Bhatti, Tariq, "What to Do in the First Session of a Learning Event," *Canadian Training Methods,* February 1981, p. 19.

The author provides numerous pointers for getting started right, including tips on atmosphere, expectations, greeting participants, introductions, and conducting a needs assessment.

Cook, Jean M., "Psyching Out Offsite," *Training,* Supplement, July 1998, pp. OS60–OS61.

Discusses what happens to employees when they go offsite, both the positive benefits and some negatives, too, since offsite training isn't for everyone. Offers suggestions to make offsite sessions effective.

Finkel, Coleman, "The 'Total Immersion' Meeting Environment," *Training and Development Journal,* September 1980, pp. 32–39.

This article identifies eight separate environments that require attention: the main meeting room, the break area, breakout areas, sleeping rooms, areas for socializing, dining rooms, recreation/exercise areas, and the facility itself.

Garry, William W., "Integrating Wellness into Learning," *Training and Development Journal,* July 1980, pp. 48–53.

The author suggests that appropriate new areas of concern to facilitate the maintenance of learning capability are emotional stress, nutritional imbalances, and the inability to convert oxygen at necessary vitality levels. The latter physical fitness need can be met via vigorous exercise opportunities in the training situation.

Kennedy, William T., "Learning from the Learning Process," *Northeast Training News,* May 1981, pp. 18, 28.

This article stresses the importance of humanistic factors in the training situation, including the trainer as a catalyst and the importance of a caring attitude, trust building, integrating participant needs into the course, and commitment.

Lefton, Robert E., and Buzzota, V. R., "Trainers, Learners, and Training Results," *Training and Development Journal,* November 1980, pp. 12–18.

This paper identifies and explores four major styles of trainer behavior: "tell-and-do," "take-it-or-leave-it," "let-me-entertain-you," "demonstrate-the-payoff." Basically, the styles in the authors' model range from Theory X to Y; this is must reading for the trainer who is particularly interested in assessing and honing his/her interpersonal skills and humanistic approaches.

Potamianos, Pete, and Crilly, Lynn, "Grade 'A' Instructor: How Do You Know One When You See One?" *Performance and Instruction,* June 1980, pp. 24–27.

This article provides criteria, in textual and checklist form, to evaluate an instructor (not a trainer). The article is an interesting counterpoint to the highly humanistic standards for the trainer suggested by Lefton and Buzzota.

Toto, Joseph R., "Credibility—Key to Effectiveness," *Northeast Training News,* February 1981, p. 18.

The author presents keys to trainer credibility that range from learning participant names to dealing with conflict appropriately.

Co-Training

Andie, Lynne M, "How to Train with a Partner (and Not Come to Blows)," *Training and Development,* May 1998, pp. 14–15.

Presents a well-thought-out model for team training considering such make-or-break elements as values, vision, mission, goals, roles, processes, procedures, norms, communication, decision making, relationship, and work environment.

Miller, Gerald V., and Wilson, Patricia G., "Cotraining: A Synergistic Outcome," *Training and Development Journal,* September 1982, pp. 94–100.

> The authors discuss the advantages of co-training, the relationship between co-trainers, and the steps in the development of an effective relationship. They focus on situations where experience levels differ widely, especially where one trainer is a content expert and the other a training expert.

Newstrom, John W., "The Dynamics of Effective Teaching, "*Personnel Administrator,* July 1981, pp. 55–64.

> This article discusses the need for team teaching effort, the various formats for such teaching, potential problems, and the prerequisites for a collaborative effort.

Pfeiffer, J. William, and Jones, John E., "Cofacilitating," in *The 1975 Annual Handbook for Group Facilitators,* University Associates, La Jolla, Calif., 1975, pp. 219–229.

> This paper discusses advantages, disadvantages, and ways to avoid pitfalls in cofacilitating. Also contains an interview guide sheet and a "cofacilitating inventory" to check out mutual compatibility.

Willems, H. A., "Comanagement: An Alternative to the 'Black Hole' of Management Development," *CTM (Canadian Training Methods)*: *The Human Element,* December 1980, pp. 14–16.

> Comanagement of training programs is examined in terms of its assumptions, assessment, and areas requiring attention (for example, selection, relationships, sharing responsibility).

Broadening the Trainer Base for Training

Curry, Theodore H., "Why Not Use Your Line Managers as Management Trainers?" *Training and Development Journal,* November 1977, pp. 43–47.

> Curry cites benefits which accrue to trainers and the organization by using line managers. Conditions for success and potential pitfalls are also presented.

Hilliard, Richard L., "How Travelers Trains Teachers," *Training in Business and Industry,* May 1974, pp. 39–41.

> This article presents details concerning an instructor training program designed to teach subject matter experts good training techniques.

Jackson, Charles W., "Managers as Trainers," *Training News,* May 1983, pp. 18–19.

> This article describes the training and use of line managers in a behavior modeling program for supervisors.

Kozoll, Charles E., "Finding the Trainers Among You," *Training and Development Journal,* July 1975, pp. 12–15.

> This paper cites nine qualities/skills which the potential line trainer should have: empathy, honesty, patience, a controlled pace, democracy, purpose, ability to listen, respect for experience, and prestige. Kozoll also offers ten questions as guides to effective selection.

Sussman, Lyle, Talley, Edwin, and Pattison, Virginia. "Training Nontrainers for Training," *Training and Development Journal,* May 1981, pp. 132–136.

> The authors describe a train-the-trainer training program which used training objectives designed to overcome concerns of the nonprofessional trainer.

Networking

Ghitelman, David, "Networking Life, *Meetings and Conventions,* November 1995, pp. 66–72.

> The author presents ten tips for effective networking: Network with everyone; don't neglect the networks you're already part of; seek out the most useful contacts; join a professional association and devote time and energy to it; be certain it's the right organization for you; network all the time; some places are more conducive to networking than others; you can even network at cocktail parties; follow up!; the heart of network is work.

22 Intelligence and Learning; Principles of Adult, Experiential, and Accelerated Learning

Adults enter their schools with very different feelings from children. . . . They attend . . . from their own desire to learn; they understand the value of the work (study) in which they engage; they keep its end in view. . . . Time to the adult learners is precious. . . . In the instruction of adults, our conduct . . . should demonstrate to them that we are their sincere friends.

—Thomas Pole, *A History of the Origin and Progress of Adult Schools*
(Bristol, England, C. Mcdowall, 1816)

The adult learner of the future will be highly competent in deciding what to learn and planning and arranging his own learning. He will successfully diagnose and solve almost any problem or difficulty that arises. He will obtain appropriate help competently and quickly, but only when necessary.

—Allen Tough, *The Adult's Learning Projects*,
2nd edition
(Austin, Texas, Learning Concepts, 1979)

Life calls not for perfection but for completeness.

—Carl Gustav Jung (1875–1961),
Swiss psychiatrist; first president of the
International Psychoanalytical Association

[The Internet and traditional lecture-based] classroom training is fine for information sharing. But if you have to motivate, change behavior, or revise old habits, experiential training is the way to go. And yes, playing with Tinkertoys can have a positive effect on the bottom line.

—Shari Caudron, "Training and the ROI of
Fun," *Workforce* (December 2000), p. 34

THIS book has provided a large number of techniques/methods to assist you, as a trainer/facilitator, to make your training meaningful and fun to experience. We have also offered ways to help your participants to truly internalize what is learned, to have the training "glue in" for transfer of the training to the job.

Therefore, in the following pages we provide a number of concepts/principles about learning, to ensure that you have a sound understanding of the theory that underpins your practice. For, as has been well stated, to know practice without theory is not to know practice. For this purpose we thus draw on the thinking that various leading training practitioners and educators have passed on to us. Specifically, we cover below:

- ☐ Intelligence and the learner—how our learners process information
- ☐ Principles of adult learning
- ☐ Experiential learning
- ☐ Accelerated learning

INTELLIGENCE AND LEARNING— HOW OUR LEARNERS PROCESS INFORMATION

For much of the prior century, intelligence was perceived as a monolithic whole, something that could be quantified/measured reliably by simple standard testing instruments. But for years we've learned in the workplace that a high IQ is not a sure-fire predictor of success in management situations and high-performance work teams.

In contradiction to the conventional wisdom surrounding the efficacy of the IQ concept, Dr. Howard Gardner, an internationally renowned psychologist/researcher at Harvard and widely acclaimed as one of the most influential theorists since John Dewey, contends that true intelligence resides with all of us in *multiple* forms and styles. In fact, the workplace of today (and tomorrow) requires an amalgam of "smarts."

Dr. Gardner's thesis is that there are at least eight types of human intelligence [1]. This notion has revolutionized ideas about learning and inspired trainers/educators to take a new look at learning and teaching. Nancy Maresh, president of Maresh Brainworks, says, "If people process information in eight different ways, that means we have to apply a wide variety of training strategies to help people learn in the way that they can learn best" [2].

Let's briefly summarize, then, the eight kinds of intelligences Dr. Gardner has identified, and suggest how trainers can help (reach, motivate) learners who are strong in a particular type of intelligence. We'll also recommend how to teach to a participant group that has a wide range of intelligences. The eight intelligences and pertinent training strategies are [3]:

1. *Linguistic intelligence.* This, says Gardner, entails a sensitivity to oral and written language; people having this type of intelligence have the ability to learn languages and the capacity to employ language to reach their objectives. *Typical occupations:* Writers, poets, attorneys, politicians, and TV personalities have a high form of this intelligence. They process information via such diverse verbal methods as

reading, writing, poetry, humor, and metaphor. *Training strategy:* Put information into story or possibly ask them to compose a poem of class terms.

2. *Logical—mathematical intelligence.* This entails the capacity to analyze problems logically, conduct mathematical operations, and study issues in a scientific way. *Typical occupations:* Mathematicians, logicians, scientists, advanced computer folk, and engineers, all people who have the capacity to recognize patterns, employ abstract symbols such as numbers and shapes, and identify connections between separate pieces of data. *Training strategy:* Provide activities that capitalize on participants' strong critical thinking capabilities.

3. *Spatial/visual intelligence* is characterized by the potential to recognize and manipulate patterns of wide space (e.g., used by navigators and pilots) and patterns of confined areas (important to sculptors, surgeons, chess players, graphic artists, architects). *Training strategy:* Since these learners are able to form mental pictures/images in their minds, reach them by using visuals of all sorts, visualization, color, art, and metaphor. *Example:* They might be encouraged to process the ongoing learning by drawing mind maps with colored pens or pencils.

4. *Bodily/kinesthetic intelligence.* Gardner asserts that this taps one's potential to use one's body in whole or in part (e.g., hand or mouth) to solve problems or make products. *Typical occupations:* Obvious individuals are dancers, actors and athletes. But it is also valuable to craftsmen and craftswomen, surgeons, mechanics, bench-top scientists, and other technically oriented professional people. *Training strategy:* Since hands-on activities are important to these people, you should try to figure out devices to incorporate movement in the lessons to be learned. *Example:* A trainer at EDS Corporation [4] plays on trainees' kinesthetic intelligence by having them physically act out the results of a cellular phone customer using his phone outside the range of his home carrier. More specifically, the trainer has four volunteer

participants position themselves at the front of the room. One plays the "server" holding a towel; a second displays a "home sweet home" sign to represent the home carrier; a third holds a cellular phone to be the customer; a fourth volunteer holds an aerial photo of their building to represent EDS. Added volunteers stretch varied colored "slinkies" (candies) between the four representatives to depict the route of communication. This activity provides these kinesthetic learners with concrete concepts that enable them to see the communication process in action.

Another example: For the kinesthetic learner who understands multiple intelligences, he/she might stand up or move about a bit in the rear of the classroom while a lecture is underway.

5. *Musical intelligence.* This entails skill in the performance, composition, and appreciation of musical patterns, according to Gardner. These learners have the capacity to identify and employ rhythmic and tonal patterns. They are highly sensitive to sounds such as people's voices, nature sounds, and musical instruments. *Typical occupations:* singers and musicians of all sorts. *Training strategy:* Use a variety of music to help learners create meaning out of sound. Trainers can help participants come alive by providing background music (especially if people are reading) or putting key learning points into a melodic structure or framework. To learn a sequential task, put the information into rap music.

6. *Interpersonal intelligence.* Gardner states that this signifies one's capacity to recognize/comprehend other people's feelings, motivations, and intentions and thus work effectively with them. They have strong (authentic) communication skills. *Typical occupations:* teachers, trainers, facilitators, sales personnel, psychological clinicians, clergy, political leaders, actors, and athletic coaches. *Training strategy:* Assign participants to small groups for peer sharing, discussion, team/cooperative learning, and role plays. Also, by using a dyad (buddy method), learners can exchange thoughts

and feelings on course content and course progress, and ask for clarification about class material which was not easily grasped by them.

7. *Intrapersonal intelligence.* As Gardner sees it, this entails the capacity for self-understanding (Socrates said, "Know thyself"), which would include, via serious introspection, viewing oneself as one really is—one's motivations, needs, desires, hopes, fears, and capacities (strengths and weaknesses)—and using this self-generated data to order one's life (career, marriage, etc.). These people take responsibility for their own errors or oversights, but still don't blame themselves for every "glitch." *Training strategy:* Reach these people by asking them to recall personal feelings and memories. Allow them a lot of "quiet time" to reflect on their inner selves. *Note:* This is a tough order, for most people rarely allow themselves to look inward.

8. *Naturalist intelligence.* As Gardner's research indicates, people in this category show high skill in recognition and classification of flora and fauna in their environment. In our Western culture we regard a naturalist as one who has extensive knowledge of the living world. They have the capacity to recognize a species, to distinguish among members of a species, to recognize the existence of neighboring species, and to point up relations among the several species. For some with this intelligence type, they are comfortable in the world of organisms and may have the talent to care for, tame, or interact subtly with living creatures (think of Jane Goodall, who is very much at home with apes). *Typical occupations:* biologists, entomologists, ornithologists, environmentalists (e.g., Rachel Carson), hunters, fishermen, gardeners, and cooks. *Training strategy:* Bring nature into the training situation to excite the interest of these types. Use analogies and metaphors to highlight the relationship between nature and a current concern/situation/problem in your outfit

To teach a participant group that possesses a wide range of intelligences, Nancy Maresh suggests follow-ing this procedure [5]: (1) Provide a brief talk on the eight intelligences. (2) Assign participants to groups based on their dominant intelligence. (3) Ask each group to process differently the information that you have provided. For example, ask the visual/spatial group to develop a graphic image/picture of their learning. The interpersonals might be required to produce a role play.

If you can't break your learners into different groups, use a variety of teaching methods to tap into all the intelligences present instead. Maresh states, "Within 20 minutes, if you're mixing things up, you'll be able to sense the dominant intelligences in the crowd, and you can focus on these."

PRINCIPLES OF ADULT LEARNING

Much has been written about the adult as a learner. We thus provide a number of aspects about this important area to trainers, including:

- ☐ The nature of learning
- ☐ The adult learner—needs and characteristics
- ☐ Fundamental principles for meaningful learning
- ☐ Principles/guidelines for the facilitation of adult learning
- ☐ Learner characteristics not to be overlooked
- ☐ Seven laws of learning—applying them to your presentation
- ☐ Myths and misconceptions about adult learning

Nature of Learning

First, let's consider these six observations about learning in general by Robert M. Smith, Professor of Education [6]:

1. *Continuing learning.* Learning carries on throughout life. In fact, to live is to learn. Whether intentional or unintentional, it is a continuing phenomenon. Much of our learning comes from the socializing process, that is, from contacts and influences from family, peers, work, play, the media, and military service. Deliberate efforts at lifelong learning are not

made by everyone because it may be difficult, sometimes painful, although it can be pleasurable at times.

2. *Learning as both a personal and a natural process.* Only you can learn for you. It starts at birth and continues thereafter, a very natural process indeed. Of course, it can be augmented by the learner by adopting a proactive approach to it.

3. *Learning entails change.* Our learning may be added to or removed and it may, at times, involve "unlearning." Also, the learning may be minor or major. Large changes may involve a deep re-orientation in values and/or self-perception. Learning is not always certain, for it may be accompanied by fear, anxiety, or resistance to change.

4. *Learning is integrated with human development.* It influences and is influenced by changes in our personality, values, roles, and tasks we have experienced throughout life. Learning gives meaning to our developmental stages as we experience both stability and transition. Learning helps our movement from one of life's stages to another. At the same time, it helps us to cope with life's crises and inevitable large-scale changes, such as retirement and loss of one's marital partner.

5. *Learning relates to both experience and experiencing.* When we learn we experience, we interact with our environment. Learning occurs through experience and it may, at times, let us learn from it. Adults have had vaster amounts of experience than children. That experience, then, is a rich resource for learning, but also a possible barrier to new learning. Why an obstacle to learning? Because, says Smith, "learning constitutes in part a process of reaffirming, reorganizing, and integrating one's previous experience."

6. *Learning may be intuitive, too.* Important insights may come through a variety of subtle processes—tacit knowing, the subconscious, letting problems/ideas/thoughts simmer, being alert to what seems unrelated, dreams, and certainly meditation as well.

The Adult Learner—Needs and Characteristics

The late, great Malcolm Knowles drew on his extensive experience as an educator, teacher, trainer, and consultant to develop what are regarded by many trainers as the definitive, fundamental concepts of adult learning. Here are his incisive principles about the needs/characteristics of the adult learner [7]:

1. *The learners feel a need to learn.* This principle tells us that adults will be motivated to learn only as their needs and interests are satisfied by their learning. Recall the saying "You can lead a boy to college but you can't make him think." So the role of the trainer/facilitator is to expose the learners to new possibilities/opportunities for self-fulfillment; to assist each learner to clarify his/her aspirations for new, improved behavior; to diagnose/assess the gap between that aspiration and one's current performance level.

2. *The learning environment is marked by mutual trust, mutual helpfulness, freedom of expression, and acceptance of differences. Physical comfort is also essential* (that is, in an informal, comfortable atmosphere). In more specific terms, the trainer/facilitator accepts each learner as a person of worth ("There are no dummies or misfits in my classroom") and respects his/her feelings, perceptions, ideas, and differences. A strong effort is made to build relations of mutual trust and helpfulness by (a) encouraging and providing for cooperative activities; (b) discouraging harmful competition and avoiding being judgmental (putdowns, argumentation, "pulling rank," and the like are not part of the insightful trainer's repertoire); (c) expressing his/her own feelings freely and by offering his/her resources as a "co-learner" (spirit of mutual inquiry).

3. *The goals of the learning experience are perceived by the learners as theirs.* If not, the trainer places himself/herself in the position of "force feeding" the participants. Mutuality becomes lost and everything becomes "uphill." Learning is thus difficult, if not impossible, for the learners' needs are ignored.

4. *Learners and trainer(s) share responsibility for jointly planning the learning experience (or*

possibly a portion of it.) The result: people are committed to the learning effort. The trainer/facilitator provides options and offers his/her feelings about them. But the decisions concerning design of learning experiences, selection of materials, and methods are a joint endeavor. (*Author's comment:* Obviously not all learning experiences readily lend themselves to joint effort, particularly where the learners are introduced to totally new material. But see principle 5, which follows.)

5. *Learners are active participants in the learning effort/process.* The trainer/facilitator's role is to help participants organize themselves into learning activities such as project groups, learning-teaching teams, independent study, and the like, thereby sharing responsibility in the desired process of mutual inquiry.

6. *The learning process relates to and uses the experience of the learners.* This is accomplished by the trainer/facilitator helping learners to tap their own wealth of experience as resources for learning. Group-in-action techniques such as group discussion (both total group and small group), role playing, exercises, games, case method, and so on are used. By helping participants to apply the new learning to their experience, learning becomes more meaningful and integrated. When the trainer presents his/her own resources, it is done in relation to the experience level of the group. *Note:* Knowing the relevance of the material being learned is highly important to adult learners.

7. *Learners have an awareness of how well they are progressing toward their goal.* The trainer involves learners in constructing criteria and methods to measure progression toward learning outcomes. The best assessment procedures are self-evaluation. Why? Because people are more likely to accept/respect what they have discovered for themselves.

Hitch-hiking on Dr. Knowles' incisive principles, we should add the following adult learning fundamentals:

☐ Differences among adult learners increase with factors of age and experience. Therefore, learning activities should take into account their diverse learning styles, the greater amount of time that may be required, the learning locale (in a relaxed, friendly, non-traditional classroom atmosphere), and possibly offering classwork at a somewhat slower pace, too [8].

☐ The trainer should avoid associating the training program with an adult's prior formal educational experience. Why? Many adults carry bad memories and negative attitudes toward traditional classroom learning [9].

☐ Adults are likely to take errors personally. Many adults view training situations as a proving ground where their professional reputation and personal image are on the line [9].

☐ The material most likely to be learned by adult learners is that which is the most relevant. Trainers cite "The Proximity Principle" in this regard: The closer learning behaviors approximate the work behaviors to be learned, the more likely learners will master (learn to perform) the desired work behaviors. Learning situations/experiences should be marked by high realism (high practicality). For example, in an upper-level management development program, participants should work on live problems of the organization—action learning—vs. case study, where they work on "canned" problems relating to other organizations [10].

Adult learning authority Sivasailam Thiagarajan offers the following additional principles [11]:

☐ Learners are more likely to learn more from each other in a diverse group than in a homogeneous group.

☐ Even though a learning experience may be the same for all group members, learners will learn different things from that same experience. Why? Because people's needs, interests, and perceptions are different. As the old saying has it, "They all went to the same school, but they came back with different lessons learned."

☐ Active learning is to be favored over passive learning. Passive learning creates learners who are bored, apathetic, indifferent, and generally p---d off and turned off. *Adults learn best by doing.*

☐ Facilitation is preferable to instruction. (As stated elsewhere, "The guide on the side" mode is favored over "the sage on the stage.")

☐ Learning is essentially a social process. *Significance:* People learn best when they can interact with others. So the sophisticated trainer will think twice before he/she puts the adult learner in an isolated learning situation.

The author would add the following principles:

☐ Since learners learn in different ways (using one or more sensory channels), the learners should experience their learning via different modalities: visual, oral, kinesthetic, print (handouts), discussion, etc.

☐ Depending on the desired "learning outcome," feedback to the learner may be an essential component of his/her assessment of what he/she has learned. Self-assessment may have to be supported by feedback from others for full learning.

Fundamental Principles for Meaningful Learning

Long-time management trainer and organization consultant Bert Juch suggests that we, as trainers/ facilitators, follow these principles to ensure that the learning/development process is enjoyable, ongoing, and self-propagating [12].

1. *The contingency principle.* "It all depends" is what this principle tells us. It all depends on the combination of the learner's needs and talents, the nature of the subject and task, the immediate situation, and the available resources that specify where the focus and emphasis should be at any time. The foregoing requires a frequent check with the learner. Therefore, the sophisticated trainer/facilitator's challenge is: (a) knowing what to apply and when, and (b) flexibly employing all techniques and methods at appropriate times.

2. *The holistic principle.* This concept tell us that we can't think in "either/or" terms—that is, mind or matter, theory or practice, introvert or extrovert, inductive or deductive. The purpose of this principle is to prevent specialization from becoming counterproductive. As educators/trainers we have all-too-natural inclinations to specializing in favorite topics and methods and to lapse into routines. Remember that at certain points in time learners will gain more from a new mode/resource than from relying totally on one already in use. We want our learners to experience/try out new approaches lest their existing skills become too one-sided or irrelevant.

3. *The interactive principle.* This principle postulates that transactions with people and things are basic to personal growth. "Encounter" is the way real learning takes place. When learners shut off their system—when interaction ceases—learning inevitably stops.

4. *The liberating principle.* It makes a world of difference how the learner feels—that is, liberated or restricted, encouraged or oppressed. An apathetic learner may go through all the motions, yet real learning—internalization— may not occur. The adage "You can lead a horse to water, but you can't make it drink" tells us that forced learning will, at best, lead to passive compliance. Yet, if there is no guidance or direction, the learner will be abandoned rather than liberated. The facilitator's job is to always make certain that our learners move solidly in the direction of greater freedom and greater worth. We definitely want our learners to feel empowered and have more rather than fewer options to work with. Our instructional modes should be liberating, thereby augmenting the learner's competence and confidence. Our goal as facilitators is to encourage the learner's independence and to reduce our own inclinations toward control. Bert Juch states that "letting go" of our past isn't easy.

5. *The quality principle.* Quality, per Juch, is a transcending principle. It tells us that the prior principles are inseparable and complementary. If we understand them all, they seem to merge. *Consider:* The positive effect of the contingency principle is that a specialization works best when it's needed; it assists, frees, and strengthens synergistically at the right

moment in a given situation, which is exactly the holistic principle. The positive effect of the interaction principle is that transactions and cross-fertilization ensure keener understanding and diverse ways of accomplishing things, and that is akin to liberating from unhelpful roadblocks, making room for added total development, which is holistic development, and so on. In sum, the principle relates to the human development process which we may call personal growth, actualization, total health, synergy, quality, or any other transcending value.

Principles/Guidelines for the Facilitation of Adult Learning

Educator Dr. Goodwin Watson provides us with the following summary principles of what is known about adult learning [13]:

1. *Rewards*
   a. The learner's behavior that is rewarded is likely to be repeated. *Example:* Joan, a shy learner, offers a comment drawn from her work experience, which elicits this trainer comment: "That's a helpful observation, Joan. The fact that you recalled this incident of some three years ago supports the notion that . . ." Joan thereafter becomes a more active class participant.
   b. Sheer repetition without reward (that is, no new learning) obviously is a poor learning procedure. *Example:* The trainer in a class in supervision provides four brief case studies, all of which provide *similar* learning points. The impact on the participant group: reduced participation.
   c. Negative rewards, such as threats and punishment, are apt to produce variable effects upon the learner and learning. But they do produce "avoidance behavior," because the reward is the reduction of punishment possibilities. *Example:* The supervisory personnel from Division X are sent by their boss to an in-house session on "Valuing Diversity." No preparatory comment (course rationale, values, applications) is presented to them,

nor does the boss herself attend. *The result:* The supervisors attend reluctantly ("Why are we going to hear this stuff when we have so much to do on the job?") and make little effort to involve themselves in class discussion and other activities. The attendees' main accomplishment: avoidance of a confrontation with their supervisor that would have occurred had they resisted attendance.

2. *Readiness.* Being ready for new learning depends upon the coming together of diverse, changing factors such as:
   a. *Prior knowledge and/or experience.* We can only learn in relation to what we now know.
   b. *Adequate significance and relevance.* We can learn only that which relates to our actual needs, goals, motivations, etc.
   c. *Postive outcomes.* We learn best only if there is freedom from discouragement, likelihood of failure, or perceived threats to our physical, emotional, or intellectual well-being.

3. *Unlearnable influences.* We can't learn if we have doubts about our likelihood of learning, what is to be learned seems irrelevant, or the learning situation seems threatening.

4. *Novelty.* Per points 2 and 3 above, novelty of activities is quite certain to be regarded as rewarding. *Example:* In a highly participative training session on creativity, a large number of meaty, incisive flipcharts are developed by group participants. A participant suggests the many helpful ideas be copied on letter-size paper (six sheets) and run off (photocopies) as a group-prepared handout. The handouts are not only returned to all participants but, per the suggestion of a group member, extra copies are made available for distribution elsewhere in the organization. The group is proud of its accomplishment.

5. *Participation.* A strong, positive force for learning is the true (not phony) opportunity to be involved in selecting and planning training activities. Participation must be genuine if it is to intensify motivation, flexibility, and rate of learning.

6. *Atmosphere.* An autocratic climate produces in learners apathy, conformity, even devious kinds of defiance, hostility toward colleagues, and an increasing dependence upon the classroom authority (the instructor). Authoritarian environments condemn most learners to continuing criticism, sarcasm, discouragement, and failure. *The result:* Self-confidence, aspiration (for anything but escape), and a healthy, positive self-concept are destroyed.

Learner Characteristics Not to Be Overlooked

When designing and preparing for a training activity or while delivering it, characteristics or traits of learners should be remembered, says Martin Broadwell, long-time trainer/facilitator, consultant, and author [14]:

☐ *Excitement.* Your participants are not likely to be as excited about the training as you, the course designer/conductor. In other words, your high enthusiasm and motivation may not be shared by your learners. Hence, the following guidelines merit your total observance:

☐ *Need-based training.* If you, as trainer, establish in the learners' minds a clear-cut need for the training (acquisition of a particular skill or knowledge), your learners will tolerate considerable inconvenience to master it. Conversely, if your participants see little point to the training, they will exercise little effort in your class and any inconvenience they may encounter will loom very large to them.

☐ *Learning technology.* When you design and deliver the new learning, the apparatus/technique you employ should not be harder to use than the subject to be learned. Remember, learners hope to encounter turn-ons, not frustration. *Example:* Exercises or games that are too complex for trainees to readily engage themselves in, are to be shunned or simplified.

☐ *Fun and rewards.* The learning you provide should be fun, interesting, or rewarding for your learners. Clearly, the teaching training/techniques you use are basic to these goals. But never forget that your whole endeavor is to ensure *that learning objectives are realized.* You don't want participant comments like this: "It was very interesting, but I'm not sure we learned very much (or anything we can use)."

☐ *Time emphasis.* Your best training design requires that the learners spend the most time doing what they are supposed to learn. Learning by doing is a key principle for learning success. People may (or may not) remember what they heard or saw, but they are certain to remember what they did (experienced).

Seven Laws of Learning—Applying Them to Your Presentation

Long-time trainer/consultant/author Robert N. Pike suggests a number of practical guides (or "laws") to ensure that your presentations—instructional offerings—are effective [15]:

1. *The Law of the TEACHER.* This principle tells us that you, as a trainer/instructor/presenter, must know your subject well. If you haven't learned it well, you can't impart (teach) it effectively to others. The way to learn a subject well is to have experienced it deeply. Your participants expect you to be highly knowledgeable based on your intimate exposure—experience—to the topic you present. So not only must you offer a well-prepared presentation or lesson, you must present from what Pike calls a well-prepared life.

2. *The Law of the LEARNER.* Participants in your class or program will learn well only to the extent that they are interested in and motivated about your subject. They want to know "What's in it for me?" They're looking for benefits, values, applications—clear-cut payoffs. So it's your job not only to present/teach, but to provide the rationale for their spending time in your class or training room. Your job, then, is to ensure that your goals are carried over to your learners.

3. *The Law of the LANGUAGE.* As the trained instructor, it's your job to ensure that the language you employ is common to both the presenter and

the learner. So the challenge is to avoid dumping jargon on the learner. Instead, proceed cautiously from where the learners are and then take them to where you want them to go. Introduce new words/terms carefully. Explain/define them as you proceed, going from the known to the unknown. *Suggestion:* Think of yourself as a teacher of a foreign language (or English for that matter) to people who don't know the language you're presenting. So make your language a stepping stone, not an area to stumble over. Your language is supposed to provide understanding, not confusion.

4. *The Law of the LESSON.* Your effectiveness as a trainer/teacher depends on your recognition of where your learners are. So the wisdom (knowledge, skill) you are imparting must be based on the wisdom your learners already possess. In effect, you build gradually on what your learners already know/understand/have mastered. In dealing with adult learners, who already have considerable knowledge, experience, and insight, you utilize their backgrounds rather than ignore them. To do otherwise is to run the risk of boring and alienating your participant group. In essence, your task is to take your learners from the known to the unknown.

5. *The Law of the TEACHING PROCESS.* Learning will proceed best when you unleash the motivation of your learners. This means that to the extent possible you allow your learners to learn through *self-discovery.* So allow your learners to enter actively into the learning process. Lecturettes, demonstrations, videos, and other one-way communication/training techniques have value. But the most significant and profound learning will ensue from what the learners have discovered on their own. Trainers need to think in terms of providing maximally learning opportunities that are participating, involving, and interacting. When people are ready to leave, you want an "Ah, ha!" rather than a "Ho hum" experience.

6. *The Law of the LEARNING PROCESS.* Real learning takes place only when the learner can apply what has been learned. Pike puts it this way: "The learner must reproduce in his or her own life the content to be learned." The best way to do this is to use as many approaches (techniques) as possible and involve as many of your learners' senses as possible, via visual, aural, verbal, kinesthetic, and print devices. In this manner, you will augment the likelihood that the training/instruction will "glue in." Remember, as a trainer/instructor you must constantly ask yourself: "Do I understand that learning has not occurred until the learners' behavior has changed?"

7. *The Law of REVIEW and APPLICATION.* To confirm the completion of the content taught, Pike says to ask your learners these two questions: "How can you use this in real life?" and "What do you expect if you apply what you've been learning?"

Myths and Misconceptions About Adult Learning

Our culture is replete with fallacies, fables, falsehoods, fact distortions, and half-truths about how people learn. These "old wives' tales" have had a pernicious influence on what trainers and instructors can do to upgrade the capacity of adult learners. We have two types of myths about adult learners to consider: (1) those which emanate primarily from the culture at large and (2) those which have developed within the education/training community itself.

Myths Spawned by the Culture at Large

One of the world's authorities on adult learning, J. R. Kidd, lists these myths which have been impediments to education/training [16]:

1. "You can't change human nature." *The reality:* Actually, human nature changes every day. If human nature were so immutable, we would still be saddled with cannibalism, slavery, duels, lynchings, slums, child labor, and discrimination of all sorts. Our views of human nature have changed drastically in the past century, due in part to the knowledge about different cultures furnished to us by anthropologists, sociologists, psychologists, and others in the behavioral sciences.

2. "You can't teach an old dog new tricks." *The reality:* This hoary chestnut has been thoroughly refuted by research, observation, and everyday experience. People may slow down physically with advancing age, but their capacity to learn and adapt is still a happy reality.

3. The "hole in the head" theory of learning. The assumption here is that the brain is a receptacle into which facts are poured in or stamped in. Those who advocate this funnel theory of learning therefore tell us that children's minds are easier to penetrate because they are less cluttered than those of adults. So the adult as a learner is essentially an unlikely, or at most, a limited possibility. *The reality:* In our everyday experience we find that people at all ages can grow, learn, and develop.

4. The "all-head" notion of learning. This myth operates on the assumption that learning is totally an affair of the mind. Hence it is wholly a rational, intellectual process. Given this premise, learning materials are merely to be presented in a rigorous, rational way. *The reality:* People are much more than mind and intellect. We are also creatures with emotions and feelings that play an important part in our learning. Emotions can facilitate learning or, if they are negative in character, they can block it.

5. The "bitter/sweet" notions. One view is that for learning "to take"—to be mastered—it must always be exciting and exhilarating. These "all fun and games" theorists tell us that if we can make learning delightful, drudgery and effort can be overcome, and rich, insightful learning can be painless. But we know from experience that much of our learning can be difficult, wearing, even repetitive—in short, hard work.

The opposite view is that learning occurs only when it involves harsh unpleasantness. The more stern, disagreeable, and distasteful the learning, the greater its potential for meaningfulness for the learner.

The reality: These views are both fallacious and contradictory. Obviously, both of these learning "schools" are extreme, to say the least. Learning need not be painful to be successful. Nor must it have as its goal the production of totally joyful learning. As we'll see below, there is a valid place for fun in learning.

6. "The mental age of the average adult is 12 years." This myth is based on intelligence scores given to men of limited schooling in World War I. Their scores corresponded to those of school children of 12–14 years of age. Hence the creation of this myth. *The reality:* Obviously, when we look at the number of people who complete high school and college today, this pessimistic view of human intelligence makes little sense.

7. "If you don't have a high I.Q., abandon all hope." *The reality:* Dr. Kidd points out that there is a great part of human life, human achievement, and human dignity that is not at all understood by even the best intellectual standards. In fact, as stated in this chapter, there are a *variety* of intelligences in humans, which means that people have different capacities/talents for learning.

Myths About Adult Learning That Have Arisen in the Education/Training World

Sharon Bowman, a Job Training Partnership Act trainer, suggests that we, as trainers, be conscious of these all-too-pervasive myths about learning [17]:

1. Our anatomy as a learning aid. *The myth:* The more time our bottom is chair-bound, the greater the opportunity for learning. *The reality:* As learners, the greater our sitting time, the more our possibilities for learning decline. As sophisticated trainers put it, "The mind can absorb only as much as the seat can endure." To keep the brain active, we need to keep the body active. Heed the admonition "Bottoms up!" Get your participants out of their chairs and moving frequently, doing something active.

2. The listener as learner. *The myth:* The one who listens the most will learn the most. *The reality:* The one who is the most active in the learning situation—interacting, participating in experiential activities, talking (questioning, debating, opinion giving, etc.), moving, writing—is learning the most. Listening, after all, is a

relatively passive process, with great potential for forgetting and even misperceiving. So when you hear, as I have, a trainer/instructor say, "They're not saying much, but they're listening carefully," you may wish to smile and say politely, "You know, I've had many teachers tell me that they've had silent students nod their heads in agreement, but when I would probe to check for understanding, I would learn the awful truth—little had registered."

3. The "sage on the stage" and the adult learner. *The myth:* A well-planned lecture, delivered from on high by the "sage on the stage," is the best way to provide information to the adult learner. *The reality:* Our capacity to remember is very limited; we remember only 10–20% of what we hear. If *hearing* is our goal, the lecture ("the sage on the stage") approach is appropriate. But if *learning* is our goal, the better strategy is to be the "guide on the side," providing maximum opportunities for participating, involving, and doing.

4. Listening as a memory aid. *The myth:* If we'd listen more, we'd remember more. *The reality:* We tend to remember and learn more—80–90%—of what we say and do. So if our goal is to have our participants learn something well, we should have them discuss it with fellow classmates and perform it (repetition). (The old gag "How do I get to Carnegie Hall?" which has this advisory: "Practice, Practice, Practice," still applies.)

5. "Serious" learning and remembering. *The myth:* The greater the seriousness of the learning, the more we'll remember. *The reality:* The evidence we now have is that we learn more and remember more if we are having fun while the learning takes place. (*Note:* Our high school algebra was pretty serious stuff. So how well do we recollect it?)

6. Fun and learning. *The myth:* Fun has little bearing on learning. *The reality:* Fun (excitement, enjoyment, mirth) is a great aid to learning and memory, and because we're turned on, it can also encourage us to seek out additional (other) challenging learning experiences.

7. Inputs from the expert. *The myth:* The expert or authority in his/her field is *the* individual to be the "sage on the stage." *The reality:* All of us, as participants, are expert at something. Adult learners, as a group, bring numerous skills, insights, and capabilities to the learning situation. They should be tapped fully, not ignored in deference to the expert.

The author wishes to add these myths/misconceptions about the training and learning processes which may affect adult learning.

1. Self-directed learning proceeds best when it functions independently, away from the usual training processes. *The reality:* The trainer, as a facilitator and learning specialist, has several vital roles to play to ensure that the self-directed learner is successful in meeting his/her learning objectives. These roles include: (1) helping the learner to diagnose his/her needs for learning; (2) guiding the learner in setting learning goals that are appropriate, specific, understandable, and attainable; (3) providing the best strategies to meet learning goals, including such help on time management as may be needed; (4) teaching the learner how to learn from others, such as peers, bosses, mentors, various specialists in and out of the organization, those in one's network, customers, suppliers, etc; (5) providing support as needed, including encouragement and praise, and celebrating success; (6) generally serving as a resource on training materials such as multimedia, printed materials, the Internet, possible internal and external courses and workshops, etc.; and (7) collaborating on the development of criteria to assess proper accomplishment.

    In general, self-directed learning should not be equated with learning in isolation. It should be regarded more realistically as an interdependent process.

2. Repetition is to be regarded as a key element in learning. *The reality:* This concept on the surface seems sensible enough. But consider the sage observation of Martin M. Broadwell, a long-time trainer, consultant, and author, on repetition [18]:

☐ Mere repetition without any involvement by the learner is not an efficient way to learn. Retention of learning will be enhanced only to the degree that (a) one is actively involved in the total learning process, (b) the learner receives an explanation of what is happening at every step of the way, and (c) the learner is rewarded for performing properly. *Note:* The emphasis must be on doing, not merely observing or being told what to do.

☐ Repetition will have little payoff if one is repeating a task the wrong way rather than the right way. Practice that includes making errors that go uncorrected is hardly the road to high performance.

☐ Also, repeated practice in learning how to do the wrong things well is hardly a plus. Sure, practice makes perfect, but only if the task is worth doing.

3. Experience is the best teacher. *The reality:* This old saw, if taken literally, is certain to get us into trouble, for experience which is unchanging—that is, the same experience performed over and over again—is hardly anything to admire. (Recall the old anecdote about the plodding, unimaginative employee who asked his boss for a raise on the grounds that he had 14 years of experience with the firm. The boss replied with a smile, "Pat, you haven't really had 14 years' experience. You've merely had one year's experience repeated 13 times!") In other words, experience per se is hardly a criterion for meaningful accomplishment. What is needed, of course, is continuing *growth* experience. Also, the best experience comes from learning properly from other talented people. Consider how well we might do at golf or tennis if we insisted on garnering our experience totally on our own, as opposed to being tutored by a pro at the outset and possibly even at later intervals.

Managers, too, may be proud of their 20–30 years of managerial experience. But if there's been little attempt to evaluate one's prowess via introspection, to get feedback about one's performance from others, and to keep learning/growing in the job, the assumed stellar experience may well be more akin to super-stagnation.

4. Operating officials/line managers are reliable judges of their training needs. *The reality:* Managers may not be expert judges of need, for when a problem/difficulty arises they may resort to the desired training "solution" all too quickly. So what is really needed to determine a training need is a sophisticated *front-end analysis* [19]. This means we, as trainers, must ask managers these questions before we embark on a requested training venture: (1) What are the indicators/symptoms that a problem exists? (2) What are the performance deficiencies pointed up by such data? (3) What is the relative value of solving that problem? These questions are "musts" to be raised, for a performance deficiency may be due to: (a) people who don't know how to do their job—they lack the skill or knowledge; (b) they're prevented from doing the job properly in some manner; or (c) they lack the motivation to do the job.

When we say "prevented from doing their job properly," it may relate to a myriad of factors—faulty equipment, insufficient supplies, inadequate lighting or ventilation, poor policies or procedures, faulty layout, lousy supervising, lack of feedback, illogical time requirements, and so on. In sum, if it's an environmental or a systems problem, let's correct that. If it's a motivational problem, let's look at our incentives and feedback systems and introduce some better ones. And if it's truly a lack of know-how, then and only then do we provide the requested training.

Before we offer the training, we also should ask ourselves whether there are other alternatives, such as *job aids,* re-engineering the work, restructuring the job so it's not an impossible one, and the like. Training is *not* the answer to every performance problem.

Principles of Experiential Learning

When your training activities provide participants with the opportunity to *experience* their learning rather than to be told what they are to learn, you are providing experiential learning. Helpful synonyms for such learning are "discovery learning," "experience-based learning," "action learning" and "interactive learning."

The significant differences between experiential and traditional classroom learning can be summarized with the aid of Table 22-1.

Table 22-1
Traditional Versus Experiential Learning

Element	Traditional Learning	Experiential Learning
Learning unit	The individual	The group and the individual
Learning emphasis	Content	Content and process
Nature of learner involvement	Cognitive (intellectual)	Cognitive and affective (self-knowledge)
Role of participant	Listening, memorizing, passing exams, passive rather than active	Involvement, participation, interaction—highly active
Role of course conductor	Teacher/instructor/lecturer/presenter/evaluator	Resource person/facilitator/trainer; at times a participant too
Responsibility of course conductor	Primarily to provide one-way communication devices (lectures, films, slide talks, panel discussions)	To create conditions for participant experiences from which learning will result
Climate for learning	Formal inhibiting, status-emphasizing	Informal, relaxed encouraging status-reducing
A major concern of course conductor	To come up with better questions to ask the class	To find ways to stimulate group members to think of deeper questions and better approaches to finding answers
Responsibility for learning outcome	Instructor/presenter ("If the student hasn't learned, the teacher hasn't taught")	Participants are responsible for their own learning and behavior
Person whose needs are satisfied most	The presenter	The participant
Possibility of transfer of learning to job	Typically low or uncertain	Moderate to high degree for most participants

We can better understand experiential learning if we look at adult learners and the things that they don't need or want and which, thus, are quite likely to turn them off:

- ☐ Sitting and listening (one-way communication)
- ☐ Note taking
- ☐ High formality
- ☐ Isolation from peers (they want interaction)
- ☐ Tests, grades
- ☐ Overload of theory
- ☐ Homework (unless it contributes to learning goals and could not be structured in any other way)

- ☐ Evening sessions (unless there is a reason for them, as in the T-group or the Managerial Grid®, or unless there is a trade-off for recreation time in the afternoon)
- ☐ Excessive reading
- ☐ Being talked down to
- ☐ Gimmicks (they can very easily sort out the "cutesy" from the vital)

In short, they want a learning experience, not a classroom experience.

Objectives

In more specific terms, experiential learning has these objectives [20]:

Affective objectives—Creating changes in one's feelings, attitudes, or values from an intense or profound training situation/experience/event is a typical goal.

Empathic objectives—Learning how it feels to be in another's shoes is another goal. For example, being pushed in a wheelchair in a crowded shopping center can help one to realize the unconscious cruelty, patronizing attitudes, and even revulsion with which society treats the handicapped.

Interactive objectives—Learning can also take place at the cognitive level to learn cognitive skills such as interviewing, listening, counseling, and debriefing. With proper structuring by the trainer, participants may experience/perceive the interactions from the view of both parties, for example, listener and speaker, coach and subordinate, salesperson and customer. *Note:* These cognitive skills typically require affective learning, too, to support the cognitive.

Higher-level cognitive skills—Evaluation and synthesis skills can also be practiced and learned; feedback to the learner can make certain that the skill will be effective in the real world.

Unlearning objectives—Since many of us carry around such psychological impediments as prejudices, stereotypes, and phobias, it is beneficial if we have the opportunity to "unlearn" them. For example, a good simulation game can help males divest themselves of male chauvinism; or meek persons can have their confidence built via a series of role-playing opportunities involving returning a damaged article to a store and, in time, doing it in a real store.

Forms

Experiential learning assumes a number of forms but can be divided into two major types:

1. Learning primarily from one's experience:

    ☐ T-group
    ☐ Managerial Grid®
    ☐ Team building
    ☐ Encounter groups
    ☐ Instruments
    ☐ Simulations and simulation games
    ☐ Diary or journal keeping
    ☐ Transactional analysis programs
    ☐ Stress management programs
    ☐ Career planning programs
    ☐ Values clarification programs
    ☐ Assertiveness training programs
    ☐ Time management programs (not the lecture-type course)
    ☐ Conflict management programs
    ☐ Role plays (live, real, or current cases)

2. Learning from structured or trainer-prepared experiences:

    ☐ Icebreakers
    ☐ Puzzles
    ☐ Games
    ☐ Exercises
    ☐ Role plays ("canned" or trainer-provided cases)

Obviously, the learning experiences in the first list are likely to be more profound than those in the second. On the other hand, not all trainers may have the skill, inclination, or management support to conduct such training activities, and would probably utilize those in the second list instead.

Although this discussion relates to training events of a formal or planned sort, we know, of course, that participants may also learn from informal or unplanned events. This requires the trainer to be alert for the introduction or highlighting of significant

"live data" should it arise. For example, in a training session I was conducting where several participants knew one another, a group member complimented another participant on her ability to operate her office (a real estate office) on a team basis with high communication, high cooperation, etc. I asked the recipient of the praise how she felt about the compliment. Her enthusiastic response: "It makes me feel good, real good. I'll communicate this feedback to my staff and we'll all work hard to keep things (the team-type operation) that way."

Principles in Regard to Experiential Training and Learning—Assumptions Underlying the Trainer/Facilitator Role

The following assumptions, which underlie experiential training philosophy and the training role, are of critical importance in working with adult learners [21]:

1. *Concern for the individual.* Our training efforts must begin with the assumption that each learner has true worth as a person. In the course of the training experience each person is entitled to maintain his/her self-respect and dignity. People's feelings are of high value and should be fully respected. Critiquing a trainee's behavior as part of the learning process is differentiated from rejecting him/her as a person. (Just as in criticizing a child, the emphasis is on the child's behavior, not on the child's personhood.) *Note:* Argumentation, sarcasm, and one-upmanship are taboos.

2. *Capacity for growth.* Part of our training philosophy is that people have a real capability and capacity to learn and grow. Although people follow their prior learned behaviors and thus act consistently, they also can alter their attitudes/beliefs/assumptions as a result of new, impacting learning experiences.

3. *Group climate.* A key condition for learning is a supportive atmosphere where open discussion and experimentation with new behaviors can take place freely. In a nonjudgmental atmosphere, a trainee will be willing to express himself/herself openly and be receptive to possible feedback from others.

4. *Reflection upon meaningful experiences.* Learning and growth are most likely to occur when (a) people are involved in significant learning experiences; (b) they are encouraged to be highly introspective about their new experiences so that they can better relate them to their own attitudes, beliefs, and behaviors; (c) they have adequate opportunities to reflect on the new learning; and (d) they thus can internalize the new learnings as a result of the twin processes of *introspection* (an inward look at one's perceptions and behaviors) and *reflection* (making meaning out of the material we have developed/discovered via introspection).

5. *Facilitator role.* Obviously the training role assumes that the trainer/facilitator will help participants learn from their experiences. This means developing group climate and conditions to allow maximum learning. The facilitator influences events in the group, and thus his/her behavior is appropriate for assessment by group participants. By exhibiting a willingness to open up his/her own behavior for group scrutiny, he/she establishes a climate which allows appraisal of member (trainee) behavior.

6. *Participant commitment.* To secure commitment to all decisions affecting the group, training activities should be collaboratively planned and evaluated, to the extent that is practical.

7. Since the group is the arena in which learning takes place, it is legitimate, logical, and essential that from time to time the group "stops the clock" and takes a candid look at its "group processes"—"how are we doing as a group?" The "here and now" assessment provides the richest material for learning and improves the group's own functioning and productivity. An important learning from this self-examination is that the concept can be carried back to the workplace. If we can assess how well we are cooperating and communicating here, why can't we do it on the job, where it can have real payoffs in terms of candidly facing up to problems, conflicts, roadblocks, policy and procedural barriers, and less-than-effective teamwork in general?

Teaching Adults Through Inquiry

The inquiry method, also known as the discovery method, self-directed learning, and problem-solving learning, encourages participants to engage in acts of discovery. It is intended to increase intellectual powers, allow for intrinsic (internal) rather than extrinsic (external) rewards, and help to nurture the will to learn. Teachers/trainers/facilitators who are comfortable using the inquiry method engage in these behaviors [22]:

☐ *They rarely tell participants what they think they should know. Their rationale:* Telling deprives learners of the excitement of doing their own finding and of the chance to upgrade their power as learners.

☐ *Their basic mode of communication with participants is Socratic—asking questions.* Questions are seen as instruments to open engaged minds to unsuspected possibilities. Questions are not used to seduce students into parroting the text/syllabus. Also, a single statement as an answer to a question is unacceptable. They have an aversion to any text that provides "The Right Answer." Not that answers and solutions are not wanted, but the right answer serves to shut off further thought/inquiry. So the trainer/facilitator asks for reasons—plural—not for *the* reason. Again, causes and meanings, *not* a single cause and a single meaning, are to be sought. Contingent thinking—"it depends"—is strongly argued.

☐ *They encourage participant-participant interaction rather than trainer-participant interaction. Serving as a judge or mediator of the quality of participant ideas/responses is avoided.* The aim is to encourage the individual learner to depend on himself/herself as a thinker. Trainees/learners are encouraged to develop their own criteria/standards to judge the quality and relevance of ideas. The role of arbiter of participant ideas—what is and isn't acceptable—is minimized.

☐ *They are reluctant to summarize the position taken by participants on learnings.* Why? The act of summary can too readily terminate further thought. Learning is regarded as a process, not a terminal event, so summaries to the learner are presented as hypotheses ("my hypothesis is"), tendencies, and directions. The assumption is that the learner is always acquiring new skills, absorbing new ideas and concepts, and formulating or refining generalizations. Also recognized by the trainer is that learning won't occur with the same intensity in any two individuals. Should a participant arrive at a particular conclusion, little is to be gained by restating it. If the learner has not reached a conclusion, it is both presumptuous and dishonest to claim that he/she has. (The trainer who claims he/she can tell you precisely what was learned by the participants is in a dream world, just blowing smoke!)

☐ *Their lessons develop from the responses of learners, rather than from pre-determined structure.* The most sensible lesson plan or syllabus is one that tries to deal with the actual responses of learners to a particular problem: the types of questions learners may ask, the obstacles to be faced, their attitudes, their possible solutions, etc. So the trainers/facilitators needn't worry about "wrong" answers, inappropriate stats, "off-the-wall" or non-pertinent directions. In fact, these kinds of responses make for the best lessons and learning opportunities. In general, the concern is with processes of thought, not end results of thought ("The Answer," again). Further, there is no compulsion to cover ground or to insist that a particular doctrine is adopted or a trainee's "non-germane" idea must be excluded. Since the trainers/facilitators are exploring *the way* students think, not *what* they should think, they spend much of their time listening to learners rather than talking to or lecturing at them.

☐ *Tasks/assignments serve to present a problem for the learners.* The aim is to have the participants clarify a problem, make relevant observations about possible solutions, and formulate generalizations based on their observations. Key participant activities that stimulate knowledge are these: defining, questioning, observing, classifying, generalizing, verifying, and applying. In essence, the goal is to help the learner become proficient in inductive methods of inquiry.

☐ *Trainers/facilitators measure their accomplishment on the basis of behavioral change in the learners*—specifically, the frequency of their raising questions; the increase in question relevancy and cogency; the frequency of challenges to statements made by the trainer, other learners, or the available reading; how relevant and clear are the standards which underpin these challenges; a willingness to withhold judgment when data is skimpy, squishy, or embryonic; a willingness to alter one's judgment/position as new or opposing data supports such action; an increased tolerance for diverse answers/solutions; an ability to employ generalizations, attitudes, and information to new/different circumstances and situations.

Designing Experiential Learning

To design such activities (programs, courses) properly, the trainer must pay attention to the key parameters, basic principles, and various "do's and don'ts" of the design. The paragraphs that follow develop these points in detail and reflect the perceptive ideas of Dr. John Jones, a leading exponent and practitioner of experiential learning and co-editor of the many books on structured experiences for experiential learning published by University Associates Publishers, San Diego [23].

Major parameters in designing experiential learning. Nine parameters or guidepoints, according to Dr. Jones, are paramount and can be used as a checklist in planning an experiential training program.

☐ *The psychological contract.* What degree of involvement do the participants expect? Ideally, their expectations and those of the trainer should be similar.

☐ *The length and timing of the event.* Is there enough time to work with the group so that the necessary trust will develop?

☐ *The location and physical facilities.* Are facilities flexible enough for the program? Is the trainer flexible enough for the program? Is the trainer flexible enough to adjust to problem-type facilities? Will there be interruptions, spectators, etc., and how are they to be dealt with?

□ *Familiarity of participants with one another.* Should initial tension be expected? Will their past interpersonal history bear on the design or its execution?

□ *Participants' training experience.* Have they engaged in prior interactive learning?

□ *Staff size.* How much interaction do I need in the design, and is the availability of staff a limiting factor?

□ *Size of participant group.* Do I recognize that the larger the group, the more structure I will have to provide? What if a smaller-size group than expected shows up? What logistical contingencies should I anticipate?

□ *Access to materials and other aids.* What A/V and reproduction support do I have?

□ *Follow-through opportunity.* Can participants be brought back? If they are brought back, how will this influence the design?

Basic principles in designing experiential learning. In addition to understanding and utilizing the parameters basic to experiential learning, the trainer must also engage in a variety of mental processes, per Dr. John Jones, to design his/her programs. He provides us with ten principles:

□ *Investment/involvement.* Since in a sense all learning is experiential, it follows that participants should be occupied and challenged all the time.

□ *Sequencing.* Build from prior activities and toward ensuing ones.

□ *Content.* Keep all activities related to the job situation. Participants expect activities marked by realism, credibility, and practicality.

□ *Processing.* Don't generate more data than can be analyzed by the group. Remember, the big payoff is from the "talk-through." So plan carefully for the discussion period.

□ *Pacing.* Keep things lively and moving, but be sensitive to possible fatigue effects. (The afternoon recreation period with an evening session is one way to deal with this concern.) Going too fast will jeopardize learning.

□ *Goals.* Keep things goal-directed throughout the program.

□ *Voluntariness.* Since experiential learning is intended to encourage introspection, it inevitably requires disclosure of one's feelings, attitudes, perceptions, values, etc. Giving and receiving feedback may also be entailed. Yet participation must be voluntary in nature. The trainer's zeal to help should not permit this principle to be abandoned.

□ *Norms (or expectations).* Although it is the trainer's job to encourage sensitivity, participation, experimentation, and openness, this must be done only as the participants' "comfort level" allows.

□ *Data.* Something is always going on, so data is always present. In fact, there may be more data there than one can deal with. So we don't need a lot of gimmicks to manufacture data. Dr. Jones's advice is to publish and focus what is being left unsaid.

□ *Flexibility.* Be prepared to change the basic design as the program evolves.

Points to include. Some "do's" in experiential design, according to Dr. John Jones, are

□ Find out what you have to work with (people, norms, expectations, facilities).

□ Explore what design elements are and are not "negotiable." (The major source or motivator for negotiation about design change is participants' anxiety, says Jones. This includes fear of what could happen or fear of confronting what actually did.) In general, changes in design should be made only if there is group consensus to do so, for different individuals will inevitably hold different views on what should or did take place.

□ Set clear objectives (and "weld them onto your eyeballs").

□ Plan for contingencies. (Murphy's Law has not been repealed.)

□ Build in "maintenance" for the group and for individual participants—people need to talk about what's going on, or anxiety builds up.

□ Establish a home base. (People need a space to go back to, to talk to someone else about what they learned.)

- ☐ Stress application throughout. (Fun and games are great, but only as they direct learning to the back-home situation.)
- ☐ Walk a colleague through your design—if you can't pass this test, you're in trouble.
- ☐ Provide a general road map; for example, tell people the coverage extends to 4 rather than 40 topics.
- ☐ Plan to participate yourself. (In fact, the best trainer is one who can become accepted as a member of the group. This phenomenon will occur if the trainer's behavior indicates that the trainer is there to learn, too.)

Actions to avoid. Some "don'ts" in experiential design, per Dr. John Jones, are these:

- ☐ Don't expect the group to be able to design as a group. (So don't let them plan Wednesday night's work if they have never planned before. *Realism* is the operative word.)
- ☐ Don't overstructure things (for example, providing excessive detail or procedures).
- ☐ Don't cover more than people can absorb.
- ☐ Don't establish participant-trainer distance (for example, by eating separately or conferring with other trainers so frequently that one sets oneself apart from the group).
- ☐ Don't take care of people. (You should let people stand up for themselves, exercise their rights, etc.)
- ☐ Don't use the same design twice. (You should learn from the prior one and revise it accordingly.)
- ☐ Don't overuse favorite techniques. (Don't be "Johnny One-Note.")
- ☐ Don't use non-cumulative units. (Models should correlate with each other.)
- ☐ Don't include material you don't like (for example, don't select non-preferred models which you are then certain to shoot down).
- ☐ Don't short-change time for the vital discussion/ integration phase.

Skill Pointers on Processing

Processing is *the* payoff aspect of experiential learning. Basic pointers relative to this are the need for planning, allotting enough time, and keeping

things job-related. Added key elements for effective processing are as follows:

- ☐ Decide whether activities will be processed by individuals, small groups, the total group, or some combination of these.
- ☐ Tell participants what to zero in on.
- ☐ Decide who collects the data: the trainer, the participants, observers from the group, outside observers, or some combination of these sources.
- ☐ Decide on formats such as video tape; instruments; oral reports (with or without flipcharts), by individuals, small groups, or the total group.
- ☐ Decide on the role of the trainer(s) in the process.
- ☐ Process at appropriate points during an activity as well as at the end.

Typically, we think of our processing/debriefing of the training experience in terms of reporting back solutions, conclusions, learnings, and so on. But other approaches/aids to processing may also be appropriate, according to trainer/consultant Sivasailam Thiagarajan [24]:

- ☐ *Emotional ventilation.* Allow people to let off steam about their experience in the exercise, role play, game, etc. By getting the emotions out, more objective analysis is possible.
- ☐ *Role dropping.* If participants were in particular roles in an exercise or role play, allow time for them to fully discuss their roles as a prelude to the return to the "real world."
- ☐ *Insight sharing.* Have participants exchange perceptions of the experience to serve as the basis for a set of generalizations for discussion.
- ☐ *Hypothesis generating.* Ask participants to focus on cause-effect relationships to provide principles for extended exploration of the topic under review.
- ☐ *Reality check.* Provide a focus as to how closely attuned the experience was to the real world.
- ☐ *Real-world transfer.* To ensure a maximum return from the experience, zero in on how it can be transferred or applied to the workplace.
- ☐ *Second thoughts.* After the experiential activity, ask: Would you do things the same way, given another opportunity?

☐ *What-ifs.* Ask: If we were to change X, Y, or Z, how would that affect your application of the principles involved?

☐ *Formative suggestions.* Secure suggestions to modify (change, improve, expand, reduce) one or more aspects of the training experience. *Note:* A cornerstone of experiential learning is that the lesson plan is in no way engraved in stone. Rather, it should be perceived as a dynamic, flexible, versatile learning device which constantly seeks amendment.

According to Paul Gustavson, manager, organization development, Zilog Inc., these are good questions to ask in processing [23]:

☐ What was the purpose?

☐ How did we do against the objectives?

☐ What did we learn from the activity?

☐ What did we learn about the learning process?

☐ What did we learn about our group process?

☐ What did we learn about others?

☐ What did we do well?

☐ What were our areas for improvement?

☐ What can we apply to the job?

☐ How is this similar to the back-home setting?

☐ How is this different from the back-home setting?

☐ What changes would you suggest as a result of this?

☐ What is your action plan (for example, objectives, specific steps, time frame, social support, plan for evaluation)?

☐ Is this something we can work on? If so, how?

☐ Is this something others can work on? If so, how?

☐ Why did we do what we did?

☐ Why do things seem the way they do?

Ordinarily, we think of the debriefing/processing as something we should do *after* the training experience ends. But as Sivasailam Thiagarajan suggests, it can be helpful at other points, too:

☐ *Before the experiential activity.* Ask participants to think back on their prior experience(s) related to what is about to take place. This affords an opportunity for comparative insight, using the earlier experience as a "baseline."

☐ *During the experience.* With a lengthy activity, it may be helpful to secure mid-point or other interim "readings" or reactions as to what is occurring.

☐ *Emergency debriefing.* If things have gone haywire for one reason or another, stop the action. This may be necessary because instructions were not clear, teams may be getting too hostile, people may feel uncomfortable with the thrust of the action, and so on. By providing a debriefing to learn of the cause for the difficulty, tensions can be reduced and play resumed.

☐ *Delayed briefings.* At times it may be wise to avoid the usual post-activity debriefing. If people need to cool down and return to the real world, a coffee break or lunch preceding the processing may be highly appropriate. Or, in some cases, it may even be desirable to carry it over to the next day to get a more detached view of the experience.

A final point. If you don't formally provide for the processing of the experience, the participants will do it on their own. The obvious likelihood is that it will be done in ways, psychologically speaking, that are not what you, as trainer, would hope for.

PRINCIPLES OF ACCELERATED LEARNING

A form of experiential learning that has been receiving considerable attention of late is "accelerated learning." This technique involves participants in the learning process and stresses collaborative activities and mutual exchange among learners. It relies heavily on action exercises and devices such as metaphors, themes, mnemonics, props, movement, music, poetry, pictures, color, games, exercises, and role plays. It appeals to all senses of the learner including sight, touch, sound, and thought [25].

Trainer Richard Coco of American Express and Dean Robert Preziosi of Nova University report its successful use in skills training. In describing the nature of accelerated learning, they draw on a set of contrasting characteristics, traditional vs. accelerated learning, prepared by the Center for Accelerated Learning, Lake George, Wisconsin, as follows [26]:

Traditional	Accelerated
Data-intense	Process-intense
Information stuffing	Information accessing
Emphasis on data storage	Emphasis on data processing
Rote memorization	Thinking skills
Manpower	Mind power
Emotionless	Expressive
Colorless	Sensory-evocative
Emphasis on correct response	Participants free to "wobble" and grow
Inhibited, guarded	Open, relaxed
Individualistic& judgmental	Collaborative & supportive
Punishing	Empowering
Draining	Energizing
Somber & serious	Playful & enjoyable

Here are several pointers to implement accelerated learning in your classroom training activities [27]:

1. *Watch your methodological mix.* Pay attention to your percentages. Use the 30/70 rule when designing your lesson plan—devote 30% or less of your course time to formal presentations, and the balance of course time (70%) should go to learner practice and integration activities.

2. *Ensure collaboration.* Include a lot of partnered and team-based activities. This will provide learning opportunities with a heavy social, dialogue-type foundation.

3. *Alter pace and add variety.* You can mix things up rotating between physically active vs. physically passive learning activities. *Example:* If you've had a passive activity or session, let learners construct models, manipulate materials, act out a process, or participate in a physically active learning process.

4. *Select your theme judiciously.* Themes serve to make a training session fun and friendly. *Caution:* You don't want to build a session around a theme merely because it's "clever." Ensure that your theme relates to the session so everyone understands its rationale.

5. *Zero in on the complete learner.* Stress not only a trainee's rational and verbal intelligence, but tap their other intelligences as well—emotional, physical, social, creative, and intuitive. *Note:* See

the chapter opener, which summarizes psychologist Howard Gardner's eight intelligences.

6. *Be flexible.* Don't follow your lesson plan rigidly. Design your course in an open-ended format so that it allows for improvement. Look at your course design as a "work in progress," not something that must be adhered to slavishly, minute by minute.

KEY POINTS

1. Intelligence resides with all of us in multiple forms. More specifically, there are at least eight intelligences that have been identified: linguistic, logical/mathematical, spatial/visual, bodily-kinetic, musical, interpersonal, intrapersonal, and naturalist. This is a radical notion that has revolutionized how people think about learning. If our participants process information in a variety of ways, as trainers we have to apply a variety of strategies to help them learn most efficiently. The optimistic concept of multiple intelligences helps to liberate us from thinking about people in traditionally narrow, pessimistic I.Q. terms.

2. Learning starts at birth and continues throughout our lives.

3. Learning is a response to an internal need to know, to become aware, to grow, to accomplish, to create. It is not a form of "forced feeding" which we may do to others.

4. The best learning occurs when it is a shared responsibility between learners and trainers.

5. The best learning takes place when learners are active participants.

6. Adult learners gain most when their learning is relevant to them. Readiness to learn is basic to internalization of new learning.

7. People learn best when they can interact with others.

8. Self-assessment and feedback are key components in the adult learning process.

9. Behavior which is rewarded is likely to be repeated. Negative rewards (punishment, threats) are ineffective ways to train adults.

10. Adults learn best when their learning is marked by novelty, fun, excitement, positive atmosphere, clear-cut goals, doing (as opposed to listening), proceeding from the known to the unknown, an opportunity to engage in self-discovery, and the capability to apply what has been learned.

11. The concept of the "guide on the side" is to be preferred to the "sage on the stage."

12. Experiential learning, which includes learning from unstructured as well as structured experiences, involves the group as well as the individual, stresses process as well as content, reaches both cognitive and affective domains, is active rather than passive, and emphasizes participant rather than instructor responsibility for outcomes.

13. In designing an experiential learning activity, the trainer should consider participant expectations about involvement; length and timing of the experience; adequacy of facilities; participants' prior training experience as well as their familiarity with one another; size of the group and training staff; and use of aids/materials.

14. Design principles for experiential learning include continual participant involvement; keeping things moving; logical sequencing of activities; concern with realism; avoidance of over-generating data; processing what is generated; voluntary participation; and being prepared to redesign things, if indicated.

15. It is a good idea to subject planned experiential learning activities to a discussion with colleagues and, if practicable, to a "dry run."

16. Processing, the payoff phase of experiential learning, requires concern with such issues as deciding what will be processed and who collects the data, formats for data collection, the trainer's role in the process, and relating the data to actual back-home concerns.

REFERENCES

1. Gardner, Howard, *Intelligence Reframed: Multiple Intelligences for the 21st Century*, Basic Books, New York (1999), pp. 41–44, 48–52.

2. Quoted by Melinda Ligus, in "Different Strokes," *Successful Meetings* (June 1998), p. 33.

3. *Ibid.*, p. 33.

4. *Ibid.*, pp. 33–34.

5. *Ibid.*, p. 34.

6. Smith, Robert M., *Learning How to Learn: Applied Theory for Adults*, Follet Publishing Co., Atlanta (1982), pp. 35–37.

7. Knowles, Malcolm, *The Adult Learner: A Neglected Species,* 3rd edition, Gulf Publishing, Houston (1984).

8. Cited by Margolis, Frederic H., and Bell, Chip R., *Managing the Learning Process,* Training Books, Lakewood Publications, Minneapolis (1984).

9. Cited in "Test Your Adult Training Know-How," in an undated promotional brochure for "How to Train Adults," a workshop offered by Padgett-Thompson, a Division of American Management Association, Cleveland Park, Kansas.

10. Ricks, Don M., in "Viewpoint: The Proximity Principle," *Training* (November 1999), p. 148.

11. Thiagarajan, Sivasailam, "Real Interactivity: Connecting People with People," *Performance Improvement* (March 2000), p. 47.

12. Juch, Bert, *Personal Development: Theory and Practice in Management Training,* John Wiley and Sons, New York (1983), pp. 71–74.

13. Watson, Goodwin, "What Do We Know About Learning?," *Teachers College Record* (1960–61), pp. 253–257 (summarized in Malcolm Knowles, *The Adult Learner: A Neglected Species*, 3rd edition, Gulf Publishing, Houston (1984), pp. 79–80).

14. Broadwell, Martin, "Six Fundamentals Worth Remembering About Learners," *Training* (January 2000), p. 18.

15. Pike, Robert W., *Creative Training Techniques Handbook,* 2nd edition, Lakewood Books, Minneapolis (1994), pp. 167–170.

16. Kidd, J. R., *How Adults Learn*, Prentice Hall (1978), pp. 17–21.

17. Bowman, Sharon, "Seven Myths and Three Tips," *Creative Training Techniques* (June 1997), p. 6.

18. Broadwell, Martin M., *The Supervisor as an Instructor*, 3rd edition, Addison-Wesley, Reading, Mass. (1978).

19. "Front-end Analysis," an interview with performance technologist Joe Harless, in *Designing and Delivering Cost-Effective Training—and Measuring the Results,* Lakewood Publications, Minneapolis (1981), p. 29.

20. Thiagarajan, Sivasailam, "Experiential Learning Packages," *National Society for Performance Improvement Journal* (September 1979), p. 14.

21. Nylen, Donald, Mitchell, J. Robert, and Stout, Anthony, *Handbook of Staff Development and Human Relations Training,* NTL Institute for Applied Behavioral Science, Washington, D.C. (1967), pp. 269–270.

22. Postman, N., and Weingarten, C., *Teaching as a Subversive Activity,* Dell, New York (1969), pp. 34–37 (summarized in Malcolm Knowles, *The Adult Learner: A Neglected Species,* 3rd edition, Gulf Publishing, Houston (1984), pp. 89–90).

23. Presented at the 1980 Annual Conference of the American Society for Training and Development, Anaheim, Calif.

24. Thiagarajan, Sivasailam, "Debriefing," *Performance and Instruction* (June/July 1986), p. 45.

25. Zemke, Ron, "Accelerated Learning—Madness with a Method," *Training* (October 1995), pp. 93–100.

26. Coco, Richard, and Preziosi, Robert, in a handout presented at the annual national conference of the American Society for Training and Development, Atlanta (May 1993), entitled "Yes, You Can . . . Successfully Use Accelerated Learning in Skills Training."

27. Ligos, Melinda, "The Accelerated Way," in "Different Strokes," *Successful Meetings* (June 1998), p. 34.

RECOMMENDED READING

Intelligence and Learning

Gardner, Howard, *Intelligence Reframed: Multiple Intelligences for the 21st Century,* Basic Books, New York 1999.

   The learning authority on human intelligence presents his revolutionary optimistic thesis, based on his research at Harvard, that intelligence is not to be understood by the limits of the traditional I.Q. Rather, people may be endowed with one or more of eight intelligences. This means that learners have different intellectual capacities and thus process information in different ways.

Principles of Adult Learning

Knowles, Malcolm, *The Adult Learner: A Neglected Species,* 4th edition, Gulf Publishing, Houston, 1995.

   A definitive work by a leading authority on adult education and training. Explores theories of learning, including a theory of adult learning, theories of teaching, and applying the theories of adult learning and teaching to human resource development (HRD). A splendid source for educators and trainers who wish to cut through the bewildering and often conflicting profusion of learning theories and research findings.

Principles of Experiential Learning

Cooper, Cary L., and Harrison, Kenneth, "Designing and Facilitating Experiential Group Activities: Variables and Issues," in Pfeiffer, J. William, and Jones, John E. (Eds.), *The 1976 Annual Handbook for Group Facilitators,* University Associates, Inc., San Diego, 1976, pp. 157–168.

   To design and implement experiential training, the following variables need to be considered: *initial* variables (learning objectives, learning environment, group structure, training staff); *emergent* variables (management of differences, depth of intervention); and *evaluative* variables (presentation of self, feedback, supportive climate, goal clarity, structure and procedure).

Gibb, Peter, "The Facilitative Trainer," *Training and Development Journal,* July 1982, pp. 14–19.

   This presents a tripartite model for program responsibility: (1) leader (traditional trainer) has authority and responsibility; (2) leader and group share responsibility (facilitative trainer); (3) group has authority and responsibility (facilitator). Shows how the facilitative trainer, combining the styles of the other two, functions. The facilitative trainer utilizes participant expectations, secures participant feedback, uses active listening techniques, and communicates in a congruent way.

Marks, Stephen E., and Davis, William L., "The Experiential Learning Model and Its Application to Large Groups," in Jones, John E., and Pleiffer, J. William (Eds.), *The 1975 Annual Handbook for Group Facilitators,* University Associates, Inc., San Diego, 1975, pp. 161–166.

   This article compares the experiential with the didactic and therapeutic models and presents hazards to be avoided when using the experiential model, the advantages and rationale for use of the model, and the role of facilitator.

Middleman, Ruth R., "The Concept of Structure in Experiential Learning," in Pfeiffer, J. William, and Jones, John E. (Eds.), *The 1972 Annual Handbook for Group Facilitators,* University Associates, Inc., La Jolla, Calif., 1972, pp. 203–210.

   This article discusses the role and importance of structure. For example, certain experiential learning may use very little stucture (the T-group), whereas other forms may have quite a bit (such as The NASA Exercise). It also cites advantages of the structured training experience, for example, the de-emphasis on the personality of the trainer and "psychological safety."

Pfeiffer, J. William, and Jones, John E., "Design Considerations in Laboratory Education," in *The 1973 Annual Handbook for Facilitators*, University Associates, Inc., La Jolla, Calif., 1973, pp. 177–194.

This treats major design parameters to be considered (length of event, number of participants, familiarity of participants with one another); use of particular methods; major considerations in design (sequencing, content, processing); sequencing in personal growth and leadership development programs; acquiring the requisite professional skills to design laboratories.

Pfeiffer, J. William, and Jones, John E., "Introduction to the Structured Experiences Section" in *The 1979 Annual Handbook For Group Facilitators*, University Associates, Inc., San Diego, 1979, pp. 3–6.

This presents a list of do's and don'ts pertinent to the conduct of structured experiences. Some do's: prepare, plan for contingencies, facilitate the process, facilitate learning. Some don'ts: overinstruct, overload, end without closure.

Pfeiffer, J. William, and Jones, John E., "Introduction to the Structured Experiences Section" in *The 1980 Annual Handbook for Facilitators*, University Associates, Inc., San Diego, 1981, pp. 3–8.

The authors present their five-step experiential learning cycle, which includes experiencing, publishing, processing, generalizing, and applying.

Walker, Gordon A., and Marks, Stephen E., *Experiential Learning and Change: Theory, Design and Practice*, John Wiley and Sons, New York, 1981.

The authors' purpose is to provide unity to a field that is currently fragmented. Part One examines the foundations of experiential learning. Part Two emphasizes applications, examining 16 common methods of instruction.

Principles of Accelerated Learning (AL)

Meier, David, *The Accelerated Learning Handbook*, McGraw-Hill, New York, 2000.

The author, founder of the Center for Accelerated Learning, provides a total system for speeding and enhancing both course design and a participant's learning process. Offers a systematic view of the learning process, accelerated learning philosophies and techniques, concrete examples of AL in action, a time-saving rapid design method, and ideas for more technology-driven learning. It offers numerous practical tips and tools for jump-starting and enhancing learning in the workplace. Readers are helped to learn how to use music, technology, natural light, and aromas to speed learning.

23 Distance Learning: Boon or Bane?

Goodbye classes, goodbye books,
Goodbye teacher's dirty looks.

—Old song lyric by the 1970's group
Alice Cooper, quoted in *Training and
Development*, December 2000, p. 26

*We didn't choose e-learning because we are a technology
company or because it's a hot trend or to save money. We
chose e-learning because there is no way to put people in
control of their own learning, 24 hours a day, seven days a
week.*

—John Cone, VP of Dell Learning,
Dell Computer Corporation,
Round Rock, Texas, quoted in *Training*,
November 2000, p. 50

*Classrooms couldn't possibly work today. Centuries
ago, they made sense: one literate person reading to
the illiterate from what might have been the town's
only book. A computer can give you more one-on-one
interaction than a human can when that human has 30
other humans to deal with. In a classroom, people who
are curious, inquisitive and questioning take up too
much time. [Technology has given training] the
possibility of one-on-one for every learner, the ability
to simulate, and the chance to try out stuff and fail in
private without the fear of ridicule from other
students.*

—Roger Schank, director of the Institute for
Learning Sciences at Northwestern
University, quoted in *Training and
Development*, December 2000, p. 26

Despite years of visionary prediction of the inevitable triumph of technology-delivered training, the vast majority of training today is still delivered in the classroom—testament not to "technophobia" but to the enduring human preference for face-to-face, real-time, interactive learning environments.

> —Ruth Colvin Clark and Chopeta Lyons, "Using Web-Based Training Wisely," *Training,* July 1999, p. 52

My biggest disappointment has been the lack of substantial intellectual interaction. Typing messages and waiting constricts the ebb and flow of natural mental play. People tire of the pace of the process. When one's mental pistons are sparking, you need an environment that can keep up.

> —Trainer Joan Mraz, *Training and Development,* January 2000, p. 26

The challenge to live instructors and creators or electronic education is to figure out what is best achieved by a person teaching face-to-face in a classroom and what can best be achieved through distance learning.

> —Ruth Palombo Weiss, "Howard Gardner Talks About Technology," *Training and Development,* September 2000, p. 56

DISTANCE learning is hardly a new way to impart knowledge to learners. In fact, it's been around for as long as there has been snail-mail-delivered correspondence courses. In recent years new formats have become available including the Internet, intranets, extranet, satellite broadcast, audio/video tape, interactive TV, and CD-ROM. The most significant aspect, of course, is the capability of an organization to deliver training on demand to learners, worldwide, via the World Wide Web. As technology advances, most distance learning will be delivered to learners via e-training, either Internet or Intranet.

In the sections which follow we discuss these topics concerning the current state of e-learning:

☐ Distance learning—its advantages and the forces propelling it

☐ What distance learning looks like (formats)

☐ Web-based training—four major formats

☐ If you embark on e-learning, some vital issues to consider

☐ How to maximize your use of online learning

☐ Online learning—problems and challenges

☐ Limitations of e-learning

DISTANCE LEARNING—ITS ADVANTAGES AND THE FORCES PROPELLING IT

Reaching learners at their own work site (or home) has these obvious advantages:

☐ The learning materials can be used by the learner anytime (24/7), anywhere. If the learner is in a remote area or travels a lot, this may be the only way to secure the desired learning.

☐ The learning can proceed at the pace at which the learner is comfortable. Learners can access the learning in digestible chunks and review them (when and as often) as they find it helpful.

☐ Online offerings have the bookmarking capability which permits the learner to stop when necessary and return later to complete the course at his/her own pace.

☐ Expensive costs for out-of-town training classrooms, travel, and hotel facilities are eliminated. Strange hotel beds and high-calorie restaurant fare won't bedevil the learner.

☐ Travel time, meaning loss of on-the-job work time and possibly reduced productivity, can be eliminated.

☐ From an organizational standpoint, masses of employees can be easily trained, overcoming the space limits of the classroom.

☐ Organizations that train globally can eliminate everything from paper-based reproduction of training materials to the need to move instructors and equipment worldwide.

☐ To train people quickly, there is no need to wait until the classroom, with its limited facilities and resources, can respond.

☐ Training material can be made uniform, as opposed to relying on the varying skills of diverse instructors.

☐ If there is a need for a quick updating of course materials, the Internet can meet this need very well. In effect, large masses of learners around the world can be constantly trained.

☐ Some employees are enabled to take the needed training at home, possibly in the evening, rather than take the time at the workplace subject to noise and interruptions. (*But note:* Not all employees may be eager to work at home and may resent such a requirement.)

☐ Students can do their study and classroom work when they are functioning at their highest level. (Some of us are A.M. people and some are P.M. types.)

☐ Classroom-shy students may find it easier to participate via the Net.

☐ It serves well those who can't attend a particular meeting, and it allows a learner/participant to interact before or after a meeting.

☐ Online training provides anonymity. This feature may be desired by executives who (a) don't wish to broadcast the fact that they're adding a skill they're weak in, or (b) don't wish to attend class with learners who may be 20 years their junior or who are immediate subordinates.

Note:

1. Regarding the above-cited anonymity factor favored by some executives, the author's contrary viewpoint is that an executive should be willing (eager) to "advertise" that he/she seeks out training. Everyone in today's dynamic world, regardless of grade or salary level, may well profit from a skill/knowledge update. Also, executives should understand that part of their job is to serve as a positive learning role model, emphasizing the importance of lifelong learning.

2. If the above portrayal of the advantages of online learning sounds too good to be true, we discuss the flip side—limitations and disadvantages—at the chapter's end.

3. The use of learning technologies is advancing slowly. Consider the survey figures below on the state of the training art in 1998 and 1999. Instructor-led classroom training currently accounts for a whopping 79.9% of all learning methods. In fact, states the ASTD report cited below,

The percentage of training delivered via technology in 1999 remains below the highwater mark of 91 percent reported in 1997. This leveling off in the growth of technology as a training tool suggests that organizations are finding the obstacles to implementing technology-based training difficult to overcome. We find this to be especially true among small to mid-size organizations.

Use of Learning Technologies vs. Classroom Training

	1998	1999
Classroom Training, instructor led	78.4%	79.9%
Technology-delivered training	8.5%	8.4%

Source: The State of Industry Report 2000, American Society for Training and Development, Alexandria, Va., 2000, p. 4.

Technological and societal/cultural changes have created a market for distance learning. Consider these influencing elements of both demand and supply [1].

On the *demand* side, these forces/factors are at work:

☐ People's knowledge and training become obsolete at a rapid rate.

☐ Dynamic changes in organizations require the provision of "just-in-time" training.

☐ There is a search for cost-effective approaches to meet a variety of learning needs—new, changed, advanced, refresher, etc. A large return on investment (in e-learning) drives companies to change their behavior and adapt to the new technology.

☐ Lifelong learning, recognized more and more as vital to keep all of us alive and growing, demands flexible access to education/training.

☐ With firms no longer offering lifetime employment, savvy workers are taking career development into their own hands.

☐ New learning models are driven by skills gaps and population changes (a more diverse workforce).

On the *supply* side, consider these helpful drivers:

☐ Access to the Internet is more readily available at both work and home with the widespread availability and use of the computer. (Some learners state their home computers are more useful for online learning than those at work.)

☐ Digital technology, in its various forms, permits building interactive, media-rich content. (*Consider:* Learners could access educators/trainers anywhere, either directly with a next-generation handset or via a wireless modem and laptop.)

☐ E-learning becomes more appealing as bandwidth increases and better delivery platforms are available.

☐ More choice of e-learning products and services is becoming available. (Big customers are fueling demand for Web software.)

☐ As technology standards emerge, compatibility of e-learning products is facilitated.

WHAT DISTANCE LEARNING LOOKS LIKE (FORMATS)

Distance learning takes these formats [2]:

☐ Audio and video tapes
☐ CD-ROM/computer-based
☐ Internet/WWW (World Wide Web)
☐ Intranet (organization's internet network)
☐ Videoconferencing (to group)
☐ Videoconferencing (individual desktop)
☐ Teleconferencing (audio only)
☐ Extranet (an intranet partially accessible to authorized persons outside of a firm or organization)
☐ Satellite/broadcast TV

Most (80%) training is delivered by live instructors, face-to-face, in classrooms. But the trainer may not always be in the same room with the participants. Six percent of courses are conducted by trainers from distant or remote sites via teleconference, videoconference, or more recently, via online programs. Some 13% of all courses are delivered via computer-based training without an in-house instructor at all. CD-ROM is the favored medium of delivery, primarily because of its superior capability to handle video, audio, and complex graphics.

The breakdown of computer-delivered training is as follows: CD-ROM, 40%; online via internal computer network, 31%; online via Internet, 19%; diskette, 7%; other computer means, 4%. Training via internal networks is more common in wholesale/retail firms and least typical in manufacturing, where CD-ROM is heavily favored. *Note:* The most popular subject to teach via computer-delivered modes is, interestingly, computer skills.

What is the nature of online interaction? Of all training delivered in this manner, most (71%) entails interaction of the learner only with his/her computer. Interaction with a live instructor and/or other trainees accounts for only 29%. *Note:* Computer networks may strain under audio/video loads, but they offer an important alternative not available to the learner via CD-ROM—namely, the ability to interact with other learners.

Most online courses adhere to the traditional format of computer-based training (CBT): The trainer functions solo with a pre-programmed tutorial. But almost 30% of online training uses the virtual classroom instead. This connects the trainee with an instructor and/or other learners.

WEB-BASED TRAINING: FOUR MAJOR FORMATS

Web-based training comes in four major formats, varying on the basis of goals, training methodologies, and instructor and learner goals. The four types are discussed below [3]. The first two types are for individual, self-directed learning. The latter two types are for virtual group or classroom learning.

☐ Web computer-based training (WCBT)
☐ Web electronic performance support system (WEPSS)
☐ Web/virtual asynchronous classroom (W/VAC)
☐ Web/virtual synchronous classroom (W/VSC)

1. *Web computer-based training (WCBT).* This is the most common type of WBT. It provides learners with performance-based training with clear-cut, measurable goals. It is similar to the usual computer-based training (CBT) accessed via CD-ROM. It's used to teach relatively simple individual learner skills, that is, those that have clear-cut right and wrong answers (for example, how to prepare a travel expense form). The Web training facilitator, who controls and directs the learning, is available to communicate with the learner, including provision of feedback as necessary. The basic skills that are taught use drill and practice, simulation, reading, and questions and answers. Also relied upon are multimedia, hypertext, hypermedia, simulations, application exercises, e-mail, and bulletin boards.

The training is available on demand on a 24/7 basis. The learner must be self-directed, highly motivated, and at ease with self-paced learning, that is, able to proceed with considerable insight as to his/her capabilities to organize for and absorb new material. Another requirement is to be able to learn in isolation from other learners.

2. *Web electronic performance support system (WEPSS).* Here we have the availability of online job aids, designed to provide practical knowledge and develop problem-solving skills. Employees may learn practical skills such as repairing equipment or resolving (mild, run-of-the-mill as opposed to complex, highly charged) customer complaints. A centralized computer or server can provide updated information economically. The system allows learners to tap the knowledge of experienced, high-performing employee experts, worldwide, via forums, databases, hypertext documents, and Java-based calculators on a just-in-time basis. A benefit of WEPSS is that the delivered training is totally consistent.

Again, as in WCBT, the learner must use his/her own initiative to guide his/her own learning. Determining the degree of detail and assessing one's own progress and success are paramount. At the outset, learners must be taught how to use the system to achieve maximum results.

Note: The next two types of WBT programs are virtual classrooms. They differ from the prior two self-directed programs in their concern with group learning and collaboration.

To understand how W/VAC, described below, functions, you need to be comfortable with two concepts: *asychronous* e-learning and *synchronous* e-learning [4]. (Asychronous means lack of concurrence in time.)

When does asynchronous e-learning take place? When the training occurs in *varied* time frames and the course material is accessed at the individual learner's convenience. *Examples:* CB (self-paced, computer-based training), audio/video cassettes, Internet training delivered via streaming, bulletin boards, e-mail, and snail mail.

Advantages: Convenience, accessibility, self-pacing, and the learner's option to reuse the course materials. *Disadvantages:* No immediate feedback on accomplishment, self-motivation is greatly

needed, and the learner functions in total isolation from other learners ("if it's to be, it's up to me").

Synchronous e-learning operates very differently: Training occurs *at the same time* for a number of learners. The course materials are accessed immediately, and interactivity with the instructor and fellow learners ("classmates") is possible. *Examples:* Audioconferencing, satellite broadcast, videoconferencing, Internet conferencing, chatrooms. *Advantages:* Instant feedback, real-time learning, and adjustability based on feedback. *Disadvantages:* Time zone problems, inconvenience (you can only begin when the program takes place), and lack of self-pacing.

Note: Most WBT is prepared/designed to be asynchronous rather than delivered simultaneously.

3. *Web/virtual asynchronous classroom (W/VAC)* [5]. This type of program permits learners and their instructors to work in union, but without being online simultaneously. Learners work at their convenience. They may brainstorm, offer solutions to case study problems, give presentations, prepare papers, and engage in debates. Learners communicate via e-mail, online forums, and bulletin boards. Skills to be developed are fairly advanced—analysis, synthesis, evaluation. These skills, unlike those to be garnered in WCBT, are not of the simple "right or wrong answer" type. *Examples:* How to close a sale, how to conduct an interview (but not the most complex types such as a career counseling interview or dealing with an upset subordinate), how to evaluate a credit record.

The *advantages* of W/VAC are that the training can be offered to a global audience. Learners are exposed to new viewpoints from their worldwide "classmates," and they can tap the experience of A-1 employees in the outfit. The major *disadvantage* is scheduling, which is quite complex. For example, a one-day class (in a typical live classroom) may require five or more days for completion, so programs may run for weeks. That's the only way everyone will have the opportunity to participate. Another limitation is that collaborative projects, e.g., working on case studies, brainstorming, or developing presentations, must be done independently (on "noncontiguous" time) rather than at the same time. Good writing skills are needed to communicate with the trainer and fellow trainees. And if international learners are involved, other language skills may be required.

4. *Web/virtual synchronous classroom.* This program parallels the traditional instructor/classroom model. These programs bring trainer and learner together, not in the actual classroom, but virtually, electronically, online. They can participate in live dialogue and discussion, debates, brainstorming, role plays, and panel discussions. Various synchronous devices are employed to involve the trainees: Internet chat, application sharing/whiteboards ("application sharing" allows trainees to work together in real time on a software application such as a spreadsheet; whiteboards are like white boards in the classroom, allowing trainees to display their work), audio/videoconferencing. All this activity takes place for all learners on a real-time basis. For example, learners can type questions and answers to one another.

The advantages of this system are group learning, collaborative international groups, and the utilization of the capabilities of all learners. Participants are exposed to a high level of new experiences, ideas, and issues. They can raise issues and achieve consensus in one session. As to difficulties, the major one is the need for strong networks and the availability of powerful computers. International training, different time zones, and language differences obviously create problems. Most important, programs must be interactive and involving. The lecture approach—essentially one-way communication—won't suffice for this medium. Only through heavy, active participation will learners experience the desired community, interactivity, and group learning.

IF YOU EMBARK ON E-LEARNING, SOME VITAL ISSUES TO CONSIDER

For the trainer exploring his/her organization's possible use of e-learning, these vital issues are to be considered:

☐ Is online learning essential for your outfit?

☐ Guides to course/program implementation
☐ Training skills required for in-house preparation of e-learning courses
☐ How to assess an outside vendor's e-learning course
☐ What the learner should ask online learning providers
☐ The challenge for the online instructor
☐ Advice to online presenters
☐ Web-based training (WBT): demands on learners
☐ How best to absorb content delivered online—issues for the e-learner
☐ What we know so far about online training—some do's and don'ts
☐ E-learning: some keys to failure

Is Online Training Essential for Your Outfit?

This question, obviously, is basic to whether your organization should board the e-learning bandwagon. To help you decide whether this approach to training delivery will give your firm the results you require, use the "go/no-go" list of factors provided by a leading authority in the e-learning field, Brandon Hall, in his creative and seminal work *Web-based Training Cookbook* (New York, John Wiley and Sons, 1997) [6]. The Hall factors are:

☐ *Size of the trainee population.* A large group of learners, e.g., 100 or more, indicates that the proposition, cost-wise, merits your consideration.
☐ *Location of trainees.* If the learners are dispersed, say at five or more training sites, this, too, is a supporting factor. In effect, for training purposes think of your organization as "location-independent."
☐ *Learner's distance from current training location.* If your trainees require many overnight stays in relation to your present training site, the online approach provides real convenience and considerable (potential) cost reduction.
☐ *Frequency of course(s)/program offerings.* Frequency of course or program offerings, e.g., 20 or more, is an indicator that online courses are desirable.
☐ *Frequency of major course revisions.* If integrated updates are needed rather infrequently,

say every six months or more, this is an indicator to seriously consider online training. Conversely, too-frequent revisions will make online training a costly, nightmarish investment.

☐ *Available course design time.* If your firm has little time to develop a course/program, online training is a "no-go" proposition. Recognize that development time for online training is hardly a quickie thing. Consider allotting six months or more to develop your online learning endeavor.

☐ *Learning style.* Start with where your learners are. If they can operate on a self-directed basis, consider online. If they prefer a group training experience, e-learning is not the best delivery system for them, Of course, if your training program can blend the two approaches, you should be able to satisfy all learners to a good degree,

☐ *Training schedule.* Online learning is appropriate if your learners can set their own training schedules. Conversely, if you have to set the schedule for them, online learning is not likely to succeed. The best e-learning candidates are self-directed learners.

☐ *Computer know-how.* You can't provide online learning effectively if computer savvy among your potential learners is minimal or absent. Use of a computer on the job indicates adequate computer capability.

☐ *Trainee skill.* If all trainees have the same skill level, online training may not be the best way to go. Conversely, if learners have a range (variety) of skill levels, the online approach, which emphasizes the use of individual learner styles, is appropriate.

☐ *Correction of individualized defects/deficiencies.* If learners require remediation as an individualized need, online training is very much in order.

☐ *Consistency of training material.* If there is a great need (very important) for consistent presentation of subject matter, online learning is a significant means to that end. (Your computer is able to speak with a single voice.)

☐ *Tracking performance.* If your outfit requires performance tracking across multiple courses, online training is recommended.

☐ *Course content.* Hard rather than soft skills are best suited for online learning. *Examples:* Operation of a new piece of simple equipment versus executive team-building, ethics training for managers, or how to deal with an angry person.

☐ *Course material and CBT (computer-based training).* If you can buy suitable (no modification involved) course content already on CBT, you have a green light to go ahead on an online basis. On the other hand, if you have to develop it, time and cost constraints will most likely discourage your use of the online delivery approach.

☐ *Management and CBT.* If your management group has had a highly favorable experience with CBT, online delivery is likely to be accepted by them. But if past experience was unfavorable, don't expect much enthusiasm or support.

☐ *Management and technology.* If your management group relates well to technology, they will probably accept online training enthusiastically. Unfavorable or doubtful views about technology won't get you much support.

☐ *Budgeting and development costs.* When making cost comparisons of online versus traditional training, management's approval is likely if they readily accept the inclusion of your development costs as part of the total delivery system.

☐ *Hardware availability.* If hardware at each learner's site is readily available, online training is feasible. Obviously, if it's not available or requires costly upgrading, you can do little with the online delivery scheme of things.

☐ *Cash flow.* Can your outfit release the needed money now for course development so as to save money in the future? If the money is readily forthcoming, it's a "go" proposition. If not, it's a "no-go."

☐ *Reputation of advocate.* If management regards the person proposing the online training favorably, that is, he/she has an outstanding track record of accomplishment, the new training scheme has a high chance of acceptance. If the track record is poor, don't expect management to jump up and down about it.

☐ *Project management staff.* You can't move into the online training area if you don't have a skilled and available project management staff. If they can manage a CBT project, you have a good chance of getting the green light.

☐ *Production hardware.* This must be available to move ahead on online delivery. If it is not needed at all, you can still move forward. But if it is needed but not available, or it is available but requires upgrading, you're on thin ice.

☐ *Knowledge of CBT design and authoring language.* (Authoring relates to writing a computer software program, especially a hypertext (see Glossary) or multimedia application.) If the training staff is available to design and author CBT, you can move ahead readily. If such knowledge is absent, you may have to buy an off-the-shelf CBT program from an outside vendor.

☐ *Troubleshooters.* If you're into CBT, anticipate various technical problems. So to proceed on a "chaos-free" basis, there must be troubleshooters available to keep your system on track.

☐ *Content experts.* Do you anticipate that content questions will arise requiring answers by subject-matter specialists? If so, your operation must have content experts available. If not, it's a "no go" proposition.

☐ *Current training staff.* Existing trainers will be highly valuable if they can be used on CBT projects. The availability of their skills is a plus. You are less advantaged if they are no longer needed or are to be transferred to new jobs.

Guides to Co.urse/Program Implementation

Key factors to consider in implementing a Web-based training system are these [7]:

☐ *Goals.* Program goals must be business oriented, clear, and realistic to lay a solid foundation for a strong, effective online training plan. (The old saw "If you don't know where you're going, it doesn't matter which road you take" applies here, too.)

☐ *Course content.* How will it be developed? Where will you acquire it? Does your outfit have the resources itself (money, staff, know-how) to do the job, will they have to buy it off the shelf, will it have to be customized by an outside group for you? Or will you combine these diverse approaches? Ideally, if you use an outside vendor, he/she should be an expert in the areas that impact directly on your industry.

☐ *Course design.* Since online learning differs radically from classroom learning, you have to take into account these real differences in your course design. For example, by incorporating interactive experiences to support learning, plus exams to assess knowledge and interaction with other learners and an instructor as appropriate, you can make a significant difference between static Web pages and a dynamic learning operation.

☐ *Technology.* You need to consider the proper technology required to deliver your courses. Your best guide: Use the level of technology to which your learners have access. Keep it simple. Note that audio files will be effective only if your trainees possess sound cards. Similarly, streaming media will only frustrate your learners if they lack fast modems.

☐ *Administration.* Either your inside staff or an outside vendor needs to monitor (track) these program details: student registration and enrollment information; password assignment and management; number of trainee slots for a course and number actually taken; student rosters for all courses and registration (enrollment) dates; registration stats over several months; trainees' activity (course completions) and results (exam responses and scores); maintenance of training records to meet legal requirements such as safety compliance laws.

☐ *Technical support.* A computer-based program obviously requires technical assistance, including the all-important function of troubleshooting.

☐ *Instructor role.* Will your course require one, or is your course/program to be totally a self-directed learning operation?

☐ *Interaction.* Plan for interaction, if you go that route, on two bases: (a) students with instructor and (b) students with one another. Keeping your learners actively engaged in course material will have two worthwhile benefits: (a) greater likelihood of course completion and (b) more certain retention, long-term, of course information.

☐ *Evaluation.* A system of measurement regarding student accomplishment/progress is essential.

☐ *Updating.* Anticipate the need to keep course materials current. Accordingly, develop a plan for this purpose.

☐ *Staffing.* You need to develop a plan which outlines current (and possibly future) staffing requirements.

Training Skills Required for In-House Preparation of E-learning Courses

To bring training content online (e-learning via the Internet or intranet), that is, designing and delivering such programs, highly diverse skills are essential. Pat Galagan, Editor-in-Chief of *Training and Development* magazine, the official journal of the American Society for Training and Development, says that to develop a training program for the Web, there has to be a team effort. Team members include: (1) a content or subject matter person; (2) an instructional designer, who breaks down the content into learning units and designs tests to facilitate and measure the nature of completed learning; (3) the software designer, who determines how the content will operate electronically; and (4) a multimedia expert, who uses audio/video technology to ensure that learners will have a richer learning experience.

In effect, the trainer not only needs A-1 instructional design and presentation skills but also needs to understand the capabilities of the technology and be able to work well in teams. All of which means that instructors thinking of themselves as classroom trainers must have an understanding that they also are responsible for shepherding learning [8].

The author would add that, hopefully, the trainer/ instructional designer would include in his/her design a large number of opportunities for interactive and participative activity to ensure high learner interest so that the training truly "glues in." The section "How to Maximize Your Use of Online Learning" has a number of suggestions for greater participation in e-learning programs.

How to Assess an Outside Vendor's E-learning Course

If your organization has made a commitment to e-learning, including the need to procure courses from outside e-course suppliers, here are some guidelines (questions to ask) to ensure course quality, as offered by management consulting firm Drake Beam Morin [9]:

1. *Goals/objectives.* Is there a description in the course content of learning objectives? If so, are they in sync with your organization's overall business goals?

2. *Design for learning.* Does the course rely upon techniques which recognize the adult as a learner? Is there a solid, self-directed, learn-by-doing design? (If not, anticipate that many of your learners will be bored and drop out rapidly.)

3. *Media.* Is this program only a copy of an established workshop manual? If so, how will learners react to it?

4. *Interactivity.* Does the course/program engage the learner, providing opportunities for participation/ involvement in realistic situations, using a mix of interactive media?

5. *Realism.* Are there realistic examples/situations/ problems so that there is a bridge between learning on the computer and real life?

6. *Flexible navigation.* Will your learners be able to leave the program at their convenience and be able to return, when ready, to the same point?

7. *Skill learning evaluation.* Will the program be able to assess precisely the degree to which trainees will have acquired the hard skills needed to deal with actual life situations?

8. *Overall program assessment.* Will the program have the capability to collect essential data for analysis by the trainee, his/her department, and the total company?

9. *Varied use alternatives.* Can the program deploy these (and possibly other) options: CD-ROM, Internet, and intranet?

If you are interested in accreditation as another means to check the quality of e-learning, here are additional criteria to use [10]:

☐ *Professional status.* Is the program/course one that is recognized in the professional field of your interest?

☐ *Track record.* Does the institution have an established, worthy track record?

☐ *Admission policies.* Are their admitting criteria too easy rather than professionally sound?

☐ *Instructor's credentials.* How qualified are the instructors to teach an e-learning course? (These qualifications should go beyond subject matter expertise.)

☐ *Interaction degree.* Are you satisfied with the level of interaction between students and their instructors?

☐ *Learner services.* Is there a full level of these services offered by the institution?

☐ *Reputation.* What does feedback from other learners (past and present) tell you about the program you're considering?

Note: If you wish to check the accreditation of a particular institution, contact the U.S. Department of Education, the Council for Higher Education Accreditation, and/or the Distance Education and Training Council.

What the Learner Should Ask Online Learning Providers

To avoid possible learner disappointment, he/she should explore online learning opportunities thoroughly by securing specific answers to these questions [11].

☐ *Cost.* Are there added costs above and beyond the figure stated by the provider for the full cost of the course? There may be costs for such items as student materials, software, books, mail and/or phone support, interactive time with the instructor, and possibly access time to the classroom.

☐ *Course length.* Is there a specified limit as to the number of weeks for course completion, or is there some "give" in case other commitments come up?

☐ *Instructor qualifications.* What are the instructor's qualifications, including any certifications he/she possesses? Also, learn of the instructor's length of online teaching time and what other courses he/she has presented.

☐ *Curriculum.* Is a full curriculum offered? If additional courses may be desired, are there special rates/discounts for taking a full curriculum or a follow-up course?

☐ *Schedule match.* Does the learner's schedule fit the interactive sessions offered by the course? Are added sessions available should the learner miss one or more scheduled ones? (If one travels, or has other work or personal problems, this factor should be buttoned down.)

☐ *Software.* Will all software and/or plug-ins be available before the course begins? Also, are there any added requirements/costs as the course moves forward?

☐ *Lab systems.* What hardware may be needed to complete hands-on lab exercises, e.g., a server for specialized computer training. Are multiple systems needed and, if so, does the provider have accessible test systems on the Internet, or does the learner have to provide them?

☐ *Follow-up support.* After the course is completed, is communication via e-mail with the instructor possible? Try to secure answers to these questions: Is there a support mail account for prior learners? May one attend interactive sessions for later questions? Is there any added cost for these activities?

☐ *Reports availability.* Will the learner be able to monitor one's progress and secure course-completion reports?

☐ *Guarantee.* Is there a clear-cut guarantee should the course fail to deliver to the learner as promised?

The Challenge for the Online Instructor

The special needs of students engaged in online learning require instructors to do a lot of mentoring, not just transmitting information. Consider these helpful learning strategies instructors should employ [12]:

☐ *Assessing learning style.* The instructor should be aware of the student as an individual, with particular emphasis on his/her learning style. The aim is to help the learner maximize his/her personal strengths for success.

☐ *Knowing the total student.* The sophisticated instructor will be cognizant of the learner's overall situation—his/her work circumstances, family, career objectives, personality, strengths, limitations, etc. The student obviously has a life outside his/her student status, which must be recognized.

☐ *Communicating/listening sensitively.* In the absence of body language, when one communicates via phone and e-mail, the instructor must use his/her "third ear" to sense what is really being said and what is actually understood. Also, the instructor must be aware of the impact his/her own communication may have on the learner—voice tone, possible perceived negatives, praise, etc.

☐ *Constructing a plan that meets the needs of both the student and the institution.* The instructor must be ever vigilant about a "busy" student who may be falling behind in the absence of the scheduled classes that usually serve as a motivator to keep the learner on top of things.

☐ *Ensuring clarity/comprehensiveness of one's written communication.* The instructor must recognize that the student can't immediately ask follow-up questions when the instructor responds to a written question. So completeness of response is more of an imperative than time-saving brevity. This requires exercise of a special kind of instructional empathy—how will the learner perceive and/or digest my message?

☐ *Responding in timely fashion.* To keep the learner fully engaged, responses to the students' questions must be prompt. A good way to lose a distance learner is to keep him/her waiting unreasonably (several days) for a response. The eager, self-paced student expects high interest from his/her professor in his/her work, response time being a particularly strong indicator of that concern.

Advice to Online Presenters

A trainer who uses distance learning on an online basis has the responsibility to ensure that his/her presenters understand and use the medium (video) properly. Elliot Jaffa, an independent trainer who specializes in distance meetings, offers these pointers which the trainer should pass on to the speakers [13]:

☐ *Audience regard.* Keep your eyes fixed on the lens of the camera. Jaffa says it's the "eye" of your participant group. Even if a participant in the room poses a query, you should respond with your eyes fixed on the camera.

☐ *Advisory to the audience.* To avoid possible misunderstandings about the above, advise your participant group at the outset that you'll be eyeing the camera when you talk to them as a group or to a single participant.

☐ *Establishing rapport.* You must create rapport with your group immediately. So forget about "housekeeping" issues you can attend to later. In fact, it's a good idea to arrive early so you can shake hands with people and learn some of their first names. Ask some of them to repeat their first names. Try to weave those names into your talk (e.g., "Pat and I were comparing notes about . . .")

☐ *Your image.* You want to appear relaxed and friendly rather than the stern lecturer. So forget the slides and Powerpoint and "be your own best visual," says Jaffa. Don't hide behind the lectern; use movement to keep your presentation adequately alive for your listeners.

☐ *Group participation.* Keep your audience involved. For example, ask them to write down two things they hope to learn today or two things they learned today, As a fun thing, ask them to raise their hands if they're hard to work with.

☐ *Fun and humor.* To establish rapport and to keep things on a light, easy-to-take level, introduce fun elements whenever you can.

Web-Based Training (WBT): Demands on Learner

WBT makes these obvious demands of its learners:

☐ Possession of basic computer skills: keyboarding, navigating, and browsing

☐ Access to a computer hooked up to the Internet or intranet (in-house capability), or both

☐ High self-motivation, particularly if one is learning without a live peer group

☐ Willingness to interact with other (distant) learners (in the virtual classroom)

☐ A desire to work synergistically with other learners, even those in other countries and of other cultures

☐ A willingness to forgo the rich benefits of participative classroom training, including opportunities for live networking, organization-paid travel, and an opportunity to get away from the routines of the office, with all its harassing pressures, demands, and interruptions

How Best to Absorb Content Delivered Online—Issues for the E-learner

Most employees are familiar with classroom learning. They know what to expect and readily adjust to it. However, e-learning requires learners to think through carefully these new and radically different issues [14]:

- □ *Course time.* Do I take the material prior to work, after work, weekends, while on field trips, or do I try to squeeze it in on the job?
- □ *Course concentration.* Do I take the learning in small, convenient, digestible chunks, or in one or more long sessions?
- □ *Course locale.* Do I take the learning at my desk or lab or at home? Can I do it away from work and/or on a field trip?
- □ *Course notes.* Do I take notes (after all, in some cases the stuff is always there) and, if so, how?
- □ *Time management.* How do I schedule my time for the course in relation to work, family, travel, etc.?

Of course, a bigger issue for many employees is that they don't know how to use a computer. The rate of computer illiteracy is some 50%. John Moran, President of GPE Learning Technologies, says, "Most employees have poor navigation skills. You need to prepare the workforce through selling, cajoling, and knowledge—or else even a good learning event will fail" [15].

What We Know So Far About Online Training: Some Do's and Don'ts

Kim Kaiser, an associate editor of *Training* magazine, has tapped the experience of corporate trainers, consultants, and university professors to tell us what they have learned so far from putting their courses online. Here are their key findings [16]:

- □ *Don't ignore the MIS (management information systems) folk.* Get the help of the technical people before you buy or develop/design an online course/program. Don't let a vendor tell you that

all that's needed is to install their program and go. Your MIS department can ask the potential vendor technical questions you can't anticipate. This might include everything from which server your program will be on to how to deliver the training to your people in the Philippines who can't access the course over the network because they don't have high-speed phone lines.

- □ *Don't assume you can magically change a classroom program into an online course by transferring available written materials onto a Web site.* You can't expect an upgrade in learners' skill or knowledge merely because they read something on their computer in lieu of a printed page.

  Key point: You have to design your course so that it grabs the learner's attention and holds his/her interest. One commercial course provider, L. Ray Uloth, managing director of DeltaWare Inc., Chicago, found through his research that "when we read something in a hard format, we comprehend about 70% of it; when we read on screen, we comprehend about 25%, even though the words are the same."

- □ *Don't expect the Web to serve totally as a vehicle to deliver "soft" skills.* You can use online courses to teach the structured segment of lessons. *Example:* A four-step model for customer service may be intellectually understood by learners, but it won't work in actual on-the-job action. So virtual role plays have to be provided, giving trainees a chance to select the particular action they would take from among several possible courses of action. Ways have to be devised to allow the practice of what was learned (application phase) without going into the classroom.

  The National Fire Academy has designed a coaching exercise for emergency medical service volunteers wherein they get their basics online followed by a live role play with their supervisor.

  The interaction is picked up on video tape and forwarded to an instructor for critique assessment. In a somewhat similar vein, Harvard Business School Publishing in its online management workshops has participants work with a mentor in their outfit and apply on the job what they have garnered online. Suggestions and guidance then come from their mentor and the online instructor.

☐ *Be realistic. Don't anticipate your employees will perform their training after work or during lunch.* Rather, they will work it into their regular work day. In point of fact, Kim Kaiser cites an American Management Association study of 1000 employees from six Fortune 500 firms who were asked to complete a 30-minute coaching module on their own time. The results? Over 75% of those surveyed accomplished the task *on the job.* The conclusion: People will, indeed, get the training done, but typically not on their own time.

☐ *Assign only "chunks" of training modules to recognize realistically learner needs and capabilities.* Sun Microsystems, Palo Alto, Calif., found that online course takers would stay with the training only up to 45 minutes. Why? Because work demands, including interruptions, allowed only limited attention to the training. So the learning for the company trainers was to provide short modules—5-, 10-, or 15-minute chunks—to accommodate more fully learners' available training time at their desks.

☐ *Recognize limits of your technology.* Trainees on the Internet will wait about two seconds for a page to download. If it takes longer, expect learner frustration to set in. The problem arises particularly when program designers add materials—graphics, photos, videos, animation—that increase download time and may consume too much bandwidth, causing gridlock on the company network. Of course, in time advanced technology may overcome this shortcoming.

☐ *Don't overestimate people's computer know-how.* Learners know their own activities, but they may need prior training, possibly tutorials, to learn computer basics before the online class is launched. Instructors, too, may need help to facilitate their transition from the traditional physical training room to the online classroom.

☐ *Provide your learners with people contacts.* At Sun Microsystems trainees were told to complete a totally self-paced online course. The result? Only a 25% completion rate. But when given access to a tutor via e-mail, phone, or a discussion group, learners achieved a 75% completion rate. "You have to provide people with the ability to ask questions when they run up against something they don't understand," says training manager Jerry Neece.

At the National Fire Academy, which wanted to create a community among their distance learners, they set up a "cyberstation," the electronic equivalent of a coffee room in a fire station. Here learners could introduce themselves to their fellow learners elsewhere in the U.S., ask questions about other departments, and exchange on-the-job experiences. Brandon Hall, a training technology consultant, states that chat rooms don't have as much instructional value as an in-depth discussion on a given topic, but they're tops for socializing. He says, "Chat rooms are like the break time prior to a seminar. Not much happens, but it's part of the glue that holds it together."

☐ *Opt for the blend.* Web-based training can save companies large amounts of money over corporate classrooms. But does this mean classroom training is on the way out? Hardly. For example, IBM, using a combination of online and classroom instruction, starts learners in a supervisory training course with background information about supervision online. Then the trainees engage in live role plays in a classroom to practice the formal, online inputs they've received. Peter Orton, program director of global technology for IBM Management Development, Hillsborough, N.C., says, "One cannot overestimate the power of face-to-face learning for certain people skills, especially teaming, collaboration and leadership."

E-learning: Some Keys to Failure

To stimulate your thinking along this line, recognize that some e-learning courses have an 80% dropout rate. In any case, here are some approaches that will ensure that your e-learning program bombs [17]:

1. *Use a total training approach.* That is to say, think training and forget business. Without a clear business focus, failure is a given. In the absence of a business objective you won't have clear-cut goals to guide your development of course materials. Oh, you want a business goal?

O.K, here are several examples: all ten new store managers are to be fully geared up to go by July 15; customer relations reps are to be able to handle 95% of all calls on their own; all sales personnel are fully checked out on the XR2 unit by November 1, and sales targets are met by 90% of the sales force.

2. *Inflate expectations.* A good recipe for failure is to promise the moon. An example for you: Advise that you now can reduce all training expenditures by 60% and produce no change in learning quality. Not helpful? Of course not. A switch to e-learning means learners will have to learn in a new way and trainers will have to develop courses and teach them in new ways. So, you're realistically dealing with a new challenge: to introduce people to a significant change, something which is never easy, certain, or automatic.

3. *Turn it all over to outsiders.* Total reliance on service providers and consultants is as good a route to failure as you can get. Would you rather avoid failure? Take help from the outsiders, but keep yourself involved at every step of the way. Sophisticatedly examine what the vendors and consultants propose, for they don't know your training history, culture, people's expectations, etc.

4. *Design your course and "let 'er fly."* Offer it and hope for the best, that is, see if people use it. But let's be realistic. A new approach won't gain acceptance merely because it's been announced. Your best (realistic) approach is to start small to get big. So be a change management specialist. Select a few target groups, decide what they should be informed about regarding e-learning, and opt for the best way to tell your story to them. Planned communication is an essential means to avoid very likely resistance/disinterest at the outset.

5. *Push e-learning on the skeptics.* You can't move ahead if you get resistance. So steamroll those who are hindering your forward progress. Not realistic. You're right. So the better approach is to study the reasons for their possible negative response *before* you try to implement anything. Help your people to adjust to e-learning, Accommodate them, possibly, by teaming up

resisters with advocates. Easy does it, but forcing, pushing, or directing won't. *Key point:* People want compelling answers to the question: What's in it for me? If meaningful answers aren't forthcoming, expect a lukewarm or even a negative response.

6. *Skip measurement.* After all, evaluation is hard work. It takes planning and clear thinking. Why not take the easy way out, let learners tell you if e-learning bombed. But you want certainty, truth, validity. Maybe those who complain about failure did, in fact, succeed. So, instead, decide on the fully rigorous approach. Plan for a serious, sophisticated evaluation so you'll know for sure whether you did or did not succeed, including what worked and what didn't. And you can then go on from there to upgrade your program based on fact rather than fantasy.

HOW TO MAXIMIZE YOUR USE OF ONLINE LEARNING

To get the best possible results from online learning, you, as the trainer, should think of using actively these three stages of the learning process:

☐ Pre-work and online learning
☐ During the session
☐ After the session

We discuss below active learning possibilities in all three of the above stages.

Pre-work and Online Learning

Before the session: Provide learners with *pre-work,* that is, tasks to accomplish in advance of their training session. *Rationale:* the more you can get them to start thinking about a topic/problem/subject *before* their formal session, the better they are prepared to enter into the learning event. *Example:* provide an article or two for advance reading on the topic to be presented or discussed. With or without an advance handout, ask your participants to develop questions, concerns, problems, needs to know, etc. which can be brought up in the first (or later) session(s). Provide a brief quiz to test familiarity with a given topic/subject. The students' answers are to be forwarded to the instructor via e-mail or held until Session One for discussion purposes. Actual tasks can be completed before the session. For example, in a leadership training program participants can interview one or more managers on their performance review practices, for later discussion in the class, either actual or virtual.

For course/session development purposes, too, online learners should engage in some type of pre-work—reading an article, completing a self-assessment instrument, taking a content-based quiz, etc. This will permit the facilitator to design and deliver his/her course on the assumption that the trainees have a like fund of knowledge before they enter their virtual classroom. The idea is to allow the trainer to start from a common level of group understanding rather than to have to make adjustments to the needs of "slow" vs. "advanced" learners.

During the Session

Kevin Wheeler, president of Global Learning Resources, Inc., Fremont, Calif., advises trainers to use the Internet to get learners involved with one another. The objective is to establish a network among distant learners taking the same class. A practical way to do this is via instant messaging to pose a question, or there can be a chat room that sits beside the content but with easy accessibility. Recognize that lack of interaction and the ability to share experiences is a major reason for learner dislike of online learning. Wheeler adds that as a minimum there must be a procedure to give and receive feedback from an instructor/trainer/coach. Either synchronous or asynchronous communication might be used, depending on class needs. Of key importance is the involvement of students—passive students should ask questions and be asked to participate by the trainer.

Wheeler offers these examples of ways to engage learners, to have them try out the concepts learned in a manner almost identical to actually executing the task: chemistry classes can build in online labs; similarly, electronic classes can build in circuit simulators; in social studies, such as history, learners can act out a role in a simulated event [18].

Certain types of technical (skills) training work out well on the Internet. For example, Mentor Labs, Annapolis, Md., provides engineers with training to help them reach a higher level of certification. The trainees log onto to a Web site and actually manipulate routers and switches. This training is akin to an aircraft simulator, wherein the "pilot" can "crash" the plane on a virtual basis, with no actual damage occurring, of course. A Mentor trainee may "break" what he/she is working on, but can return to the original setting without any actual harm taking place [19].

Joan Eisenstadt, president of a conference consulting and management company in Washington (Eisenstadt Associates), suggests that distance learning takes place best when the (satellite) broadcast stops regularly for facilitated discussions among participants. She states, "For most people, being part of a group and learning experientially is far better than just talking or listening." She thinks distance learning "can be effective, but I still prefer face-to-face" [20].

Using Web-based training doesn't mean that live, corporate classrooms are abandoned. IBM and other organizations combine the two delivery systems (classroom and online). At IBM, trainees in a supervision program get basic information online about supervising subordinates. They then go to a classroom and role play with others to practice what has been learned. Says Peter Z. Orton, program director of global curriculum technology for IBM Management Development, Hillsborough, N.C., "One cannot overestimate the power of face-to-face learning for certain people skills, especially teaming, collaboration and leadership" [21].

The National Fire Academy, Emmitsburg, Md., uses a coaching exercise for emergency medical service volunteers which has three steps: (1) The participants receive the basics (or content) online. (2) They then do a role play with their supervisors. For example, the supervisor may play a volunteer who consistently arrives late to work or brings family problems to the station. The trainee applies his/her online learning to the problem. (3) The role play is picked up on video tape and sent to the (an) instructor for critique/evaluation [22].

To overcome the lack of the familiar human touch found in regular offline classroom courses, Owens Corning, Toledo, introduced face-to-face components in its online courses. Many of them included real-time assignments such as interviewing managers and encouraging learners to gather offline to discuss such subjects as the new supervisor, management of change, and orienting the new worker [23].

After the Session

For actual transfer of training to the job, you can use e-mail to follow up on what was learned. For example, Jan Bozarth, a staff development coordinator with the North Carolina Department of Justice in Raleigh, collects e-mail addresses of her attendees. She keys them in as a group on her e-mail browser. Her idea is to deliver support messages as a follow-up to the completed training. For example, 30 days after a time management course she may send a note reminding her participants to develop a daily list of priorities (a "to-do list"). Or two weeks later, she might pass along pointers to deal with participants' possible procrastination. And two weeks later, she may e-mail the address of a helpful Web site which has more information on time management skills [24].

Another obvious way to ensure that increased participant understanding (learning) has taken place, is to use pre- and post-session testing procedures. Formal quizzes accomplish two things: They help you quantify a return on your training budget, and they provide documentation that your outfit exercised due diligence should a legal challenge arise questioning whether enough was done to prevent a workplace incident, e.g., regarding sexual harassment [25].

ONLINE LEARNING—PROBLEMS AND CHALLENGES

Several major problems and opportunities for growth exist in the online learning area. We discuss below the following topics:

- ☐ Online learning—the "on whose time?" dilemma
- ☐ The dropout problem in Web-based training courses
- ☐ Universities and online course offerings
- ☐ Online learning—what is the state of the art?

Online Learning—The "On Whose Time?" Dilemma [26]

One of the claimed virtues of online learning is that it can take place "anywhere, anytime." But does anytime mean on the job or at home on employee time? Cost-conscious managers are intrigued by the savings of online training: less travel and hotel costs,

less learning time away from the job, and reduced delivery costs. But Paul Reali, president of Cyber-Skills Computer Training Center, Winston-Salem, N.C., alerts us to this fact: There is no evidence (i.e., a validated study) yet that online delivery significantly reduces learning time—the actual time required to learn a skill, or to amass knowledge—compared with traditional instructor-led training of like quality.

If we accept Reali's logic, why, then, are many managers so enamored with the possibilities of online learning? The answer is one of simple workplace economics. Their thinking is that employees can get their needed training accomplished not in the classroom away from their work site, but on their desktop or laptop. But on whose time? Hopefully, the cost-concerned employers believe, on the employees' own—uncompensated—time.

Of course, nonexempt employees are not the typical target for learning on one's own time, for they are protected by union contracts or labor regulations which require remuneration for training which is overtime based.

So the target for online learning on one's own time is salaried, office-type workers. Certainly some eager careerists may welcome this (or any) type of training opportunity. It may even mean a time saving from not having to travel across town to a company or other training site. Reali doesn't state that asking learners to learn on their own time is necessarily unfair. He believes it becomes a problem when it's the only option the firm offers for needed/wanted learning.

Can reluctant employees be sold on the idea of getting their training after the regular workday? Possibly, by making it part of "the cultural expectation." Of course, the corporate expectation may collide with today's very-much-alive quality-of-life movement. In fact, an American Management study in 1997 found that 1000 people from six Fortune 500 companies were given two after-hours options to access a Web-based training course on coaching skills: before or after work or on their lunch hour. Their choice? Nearly 75% skipped these alternatives and worked the course into their regular work day hours.

But is accessing online learning on the job, to avoid doing it on personal time, the best answer? Probably not, for the work cubicle is a horrific site to have a quality learning experience. After all, it's hard to reserve the necessary time and concentration without actual organizational support, including "time outs" by one's boss. Most learning authorities would agree that the harried, interruption-prone office environment is hardly the optimum locale for focused learning or serious reflection.

The best answer, then? First, assessment is needed to determine the learning needs which must be met by training courses or tutorials and which can be met better by online performance support or electronic job aids. Some authorities advise that changing bigger pieces of training courses into online performance support is step one to solve the off-hours training dilemma. It would reduce requests for "courses," whether accomplished on or off the job. The whole idea per Kevin Kruse, an HR consultant, is to have learning more skill-oriented, presented in smaller chunks, and accessed only when needed. This approach is to be preferred to a one-hour tutorial in a frenzied work cubicle.

Note: If you're curious about where employees actually train, consider these stats (*source:* Frontline Web site, reported in *Training and Development,* January 2001, p. 17):

- ☐ At work (cubicle/office): 39%
- ☐ On own time, at home: 35%
- ☐ No time for training: 13%
- ☐ At off-site programs 9%
- ☐ At organization's learning center: 4%

The Dropout Problem in Web-Based Training Courses [27]

There is considerable anecdotal evidence that trainees drop out of Web-delivered courses. *Examples:* A training manager for an HMO, using an online library and accompanying curriculum, reported that 80% of those who started their training bailed out. Another training supervisor instituted a curriculum on Microsoft products. Employees were given two options: a Web-based course or a two-day classroom course with a live instructor. The result: 90% of the classroom learners completed the course, whereas only 50% of the self-paced Web learners did.

So why do potential learners stay away from e-learning if other opportunities are available, and why do so many quit in midstream? Consider these factors: poor incentives to learn (no carrots, no sticks);

lack of accountability for completing courses (e.g., no testing); technology problems; and poorly designed course materials which don't capture the learner's attention readily. Also some learners may take a chunk of a course to upgrade a skill, or to learn a new one, and then bow out. A physical environment not conducive to learning is another factor.

Elliott Masie, an exponent of high-tech learning, suggests this factor may also be at work: A trainee takes a course online which the boss may not be aware of. Contrast this with a classroom-type course which the supervisor has to formally approve. So if it's not an "observed moment" in the trainee's career, he/she may find little management reinforcement to stay with it.

One way to secure learner commitment to online learning is to use the "hybrid approach" combining group and individual work, which the Global Learning Solutions group of Lucent Technologies (formerly Bell Labs, Englewood Colo.) developed:

1. Start a learning sequence with a group (synchronous or simultaneous mode) kick-off event, e.g., via a two-hour videoconference wherein the instructor establishes rapport with the learners, explains the nature of the total course, and gives the first week's assignment. If the learner needs help, he/she can go to chat rooms or threaded discussion groups to post his/her questions. The trainee can also check in with the instructor using a phone conference or chat room in established "virtual office hours."

2. Learners do their asynchronous (solo), self-paced homework either from an online Web module or an offline CD, workbook, or video. They also complete a quiz in time for the next simultaneous video group session.

3. Before the next synchronous group meeting, the instructor reviews the quiz results to check student group progress, who's "with it" and who's in need of added help. This is a key phase of the course work, for it makes clear that this isn't just busy work, but that the instructor is very much concerned with actual student learning.

4. The testing procedure results in *accountability,* for course credit requires the passing of a series of tests which run throughout the online course of study.

5. Another motivator is built into the curriculum. General managers can garner bonuses if a certain percent of their staffers pass the exams.

Other incentive programs to prevent dropouts are these:

☐ Symbol Technologies, Long Island, N.Y., limits dropouts among sales trainees by having self-paced online courses part of a total curriculum track which must be completed for internal sales certification. Completed course work is essential to continue the education process, which is basic to maintaining a career with the company.

☐ Symbol also keeps "nice-to-have" courses offline. All too often, optional courses are certain recipes for eventual learner abandonment.

☐ A rental car firm awards free use of their cars for prescribed periods to learners who finish online coursework tied to certain skills.

☐ Some companies rely on the virtual university model, granting homespun "degrees"—bachelor's, master's, and even doctorates. The diploma becomes part of the student's personnel file. Business cards are stamped with the internal "degree" earned.

To sum up. Learners exit early from self-paced, computer-delivered training classes for these reasons:

1. *No compelling reason or incentive.* In the absence of money or career advancement possibilities, the motivation to stay with the course is reduced significantly.

2. *Isolation from other learners.* If "connectedness" is not part of the program—people want to feel plugged in and watched over—"jumping ship" is very certain. David Passmore, professor of education, Pennsylvania State University, actively ensures student connectedness by these practices: clear direction, prompt feedback on e-mail assignments, and attempts to communicate with students in some manner each day, Also, he collects information on students' backgrounds and interests and draws on that data when giving feedback.

3. *Delivery mode.* Instructor-led training is favored by learners. One multinational company found in a survey that over 90% of those queried preferred instructor-led as opposed to online modes. This also was true in all foreign countries responding to the survey.

4. *Course attractiveness.* Much of online training, in its design, fails to hook the learners. People expect sophisticated course offerings that will excite them.

5. *Learner selectiveness.* A chunk, rather than the whole ball of wax, is enough to satisfy many online learners. So they take in what it takes to hone a skill and close the door on the rest.

6. *Social interaction.* If the choice is between meeting with colleagues/peers in a friendly hotel/motel, or even in an in-house training site, versus operating alone, punching a keyboard and staring at a computer monitor at your own desk site where telephone and personal interruptions are frequent, the decision is certainly likely to be the former rather than the latter.

Note: No educational/training experience or learning method will fly with everyone. For example, learners who have limited self-motivation most likely will require traditional classroom training with its structure and discipline. At best, they may profit from a blend of self-paced (minimally) and classroom training (mostly) or, as another alternative, some course elements may be online (synchronous variety) and the rest mostly classroom training.

Universities and Online Course Offerings

Many universities have embarked on various online educational ventures. Their conductors generally recognize that a virtual college classroom is not the equivalent of a traditional campus/classroom experience. Nevertheless, they believe that what is offered is still a worthy addition to a person's prior academic experience. Three professors who have taught semester-long online courses in a human resources development program (HRD) at the University of Illinois at Urbana-Champaign have chronicled their online teaching experiences to help others in either the academic or corporate environment [28].

A primary observation of these academics is that designing courses for online instruction is not simply translating course content and the usual lectures, overheads, tests, etc. into online (hypertext) format and posting it on the Web. Since the students in the online (hypertext) program are widely dispersed, face-to-face meetings are impossible. Each course demands weekly study for ten hours. The courses include both asynchronous and synchronous learning. The former comprises lectures, discussions, and assignments accomplished on the students' own time; the latter, conducted weekly, requires all students to log on simultaneously. The instructors are supported by a technical staff proficient in Web design and development and technology, including troubleshooting should problems develop (for learners and instructors) in course delivery. It is important to note that the University of Illinois limits online degree programs to graduate study. Their rationale? Self-motivation and learning skills needed for online learning are less likely to be found among undergraduates, the latter being more likely to succeed with a more traditionally structured classroom environment.

Obviously student participation and involvement in the traditional classroom, particularly if experiential learning is desired, cannot be emulated in online learning. Nevertheless, certain team activities are possible. For example, team discussions in the Illinois program were held on a given topic using Web board conferencing and receiving and providing feedback on peer-assigned work. Rendering feedback to peers counted toward the course participation grade.

Also, a synchronous hour was held weekly. All learners participated, with the instructor leading the discussion. Students received the pertinent agenda in advance by e-mail. It covered general course information, a review of material covered in the prior week, a summary of learner questions and concerns, plus a preview of the next week's work. The instructor used a microphone to talk with the students, while the latter responded by typing and posting replies or questions in real time to an electronic bulletin board.

When students lived near one another they did meet in person to discuss the course and assignments in it. Informal networks, using the phone, were constructed. Personal information was given over the chatboard's "electronic cafe"; support was generously given to each other; and a learning community was created. Support was given on both professional and personal matters.

Compared to traditional instruction, three areas were identified at the Illinois program as requiring special attention:

☐ *Detailing instructions to students.* If you're providing online learning, you must provide greater detail and specificity. Why? Simply because there's no instructor around to clarify things and answer questions about the assigned material.

☐ *Recognizing/establishing the best balance between collaborative and independent assignments.* Online students, like traditional students, have difficulty teaming up with fellow learners to handle group assignments. In the case of the Illinois program, assignments thus took these time frames: one-fourth were collaborative, one-half were independent, and one-fourth combined independent and collaborative work. In the latter case, the majority of the work was done solo and results were then discussed briefly with fellow learners.

☐ *Attending/reporting and communication processes.* In a traditional class learners can give reports to the total group, present data on flipcharts, or present something in other ways which illustrates the work done. This is harder to do online. What can be done, however, is to report via the Web board so that individual and team results can be posted for instructor feedback/critiques. If hard copies of assignments are requested, they are forwarded via computer and feedback is returned electronically.

Here's what the professors learned from their pioneering online graduate-level instruction:

☐ *General instructional principles.* Most classroom instructional principles apply to online instruction as well.

☐ *Information regarding computer literacy.* To avoid unrealistic student expectations, full information must be provided in respect to (a) the computer skill required and (b) hardware/software needs. Full disclosure of these factors can help applicants to decide whether this type of learning setup is suitable for them. The reality is that a good number of students overestimate their computer competency.

☐ *Information regarding learning requirements.* Students should be clearly informed in terms of (a) the high level of motivation required and (b) the learning skills required for success in the distance learning setup.

☐ *Orientation.* Students need fully qualified technical support to mount the usual initial difficulties concerning hardware, software, and technology use. Orientation to provide familiarity with online learning technology is vital. The orientation should take place before the course commences.

Team learning. Whenever possible, collaborative learning opportunities should be provided. This approach will unleash students' know-how and help them to overcome the isolation element of distance learning.

Feedback. Students need to know how well they are doing. Frequent, specific feedback concerning their accomplishments is essential for maintenance of high motivation. (No one wants to feel abandoned!)

Evaluation. A variety of assessment methods should be used. Less reliance on the traditional objective tests is desired.

Bottom line. Distance learning can provide university-level education for those who can't avail themselves of the preferred face-to-face university program. The university's HRD online learning program described here is considered a success by its faculty.

However, discordant notes do arise elsewhere about the alleged virtues of such learning. The American Association of University Professors reports that online courses are more time-intensive than regular classes. Why? Because they require the professors to respond to their students' questions individually, in writing. *The result:* More teachers, and more money to pay them, are needed. Also, the quality of these courses is hard to assess. Instructors can't monitor students taking tests, and it's impossible to be certain that comments and responses made during live online discussions are made by the actual enrollees [29].

Interestingly, online education, as the educational panacea of our time, is not necessarily endorsed by those who have to teach those courses. Consider this professional reaction: A petition was signed recently by several hundred faculty members at the University of Washington opposing state plans for an online university, maintaining they cannot reduce all education to "the passive and solitary activity of staring at a screen" [30].

The experience of one e-learner who sought an MBA degree in international business, cited by HRD writer Shari Caudron, is of interest [31]. Alex Zai, VP of store operations and international development for PAKMAIL Center of America, Inc., enrolled in the University of Phoenix Global MBA program, an entirely online program. He wanted an MBA program that would be friendly to his extensive foreign travel requirements, permit him to study after his kids were bedded down, and allow him to capitalize on his waiting time in airports and while conducting business abroad.

So how did Zai assess the quality of his education? "Mediocre at best," he asserts. He was rarely given feedback on his work, interaction with fellow students was nil, and he frequently felt his writing skills were superior to those of his professors. His benefit from the courses? Only a better understanding and use of the Internet.

If we consider the growing enrollment in university programs, Mr. Zai's experience is not to be assumed to be a universal feeling. Nevertheless, anyone evaluating online degree programs should ask these questions [32]:

1. *Accreditation.* Is the institution accredited? Regional accreditation signifies that a school has been recognized by the U.S. Department of Education, its programs are marked by integrity, and, course units are transferable to other universities.

2. *Reputation.* While we can't assess effectiveness of online programs at this early state of the art, a good caution is to select a university which already has a very good reputation overall. After all, reputable schools have a hard-earned reputation to protect.

3. *Assessment.* What are the demonstrable outcomes the degree-granting school can point to? How does it know whether touted skills/knowledge have been acquired?

4. *Interaction.* This is a key educational item, so it's vital to learn the nature of interaction among students and between faculty and its learners.

5. *Credentials.* Try to learn of faculty degrees, experience in dealing with adult learners, and their comprehension of online learning.

6. *Course currency.* What are the plans and procedures to update course content resources used in the course? How frequently is this done? Is

there access to digitized libraries and global online databases?

7. *Experiential learning.* Is this promoted at all? If so, how, and to what extent? The best online programs require learners to apply what they've learned.

Remember, when all is said and done, says Jeff Creighton, chairman of EduPoint, Inc., who is very much concerned about developing interpersonal and collaborative skills (teamwork), "Measurable skills, such as whether a candidate can read a balance sheet or create a strategic plan, can typically be taught effectively both online and in the classroom. But when it comes to qualitative abilities such as interpersonal skills, leadership qualities, and problem solving, e-learning is not yet delivering because it doesn't provide the immersion and interaction required to change a student's paradigm. Those attributes are still best developed through more traditional classroom-based education" [33].

Online Learning—What Is the State of the Art?

Although e-learning or training on the Web has a certain potential, "it may be years away from living up to its hype," says Kevin Dobbs, Associate Editor of *Training* magazine [34]. He adds, "Like most innovations in their early stages, e-learning is still struggling to define and distinguish itself from what came before. Most of the training curricula you'll find on the Web today amounts to little more than text or video on a computer screen, merely digitized versions of what's already been done."

Dobbs quotes several educators/trainers conversant with today's e-learning as follows:

"Right now, e-learning is a disaster. All you're getting is somebody's classroom notes on the Web. And we call that training. That's frightening to people who know better."—Roger Schank, professor of education and computer science, Northwestern University.

"The fact is people like to be together. We're social. The more you use the latest technology, whatever it is, the more you want to interact with people. We can't ignore that." —Rick Corry, VP of Alliances for Pensare Corporation, an Appleton, Wisc., training company.

"You can't just digitize something and expect it to impress. You have to intrigue people, draw them into activities where they're at the center of everything that's happening. The technology is there for this."—Larraine Segil, instructor, California Institute of Technology.

More optimistically, Dobbs cites two examples of organizations using initiatives aimed at simulating human interaction, one corporate (in-house) and the other a vendor of Internet programming to general audiences.

☐ *Bank of America.* One of its programs, using video and audio, permits a beginning loan officer to interact with a prospective client. The trainee asks a number of questions to check for loan eligibility. If the trainee poses illegal queries, a lawyer enters on video to admonish him for his meandering into the banned areas. The course's direction is determined by the interaction with the virtual client.

☐ *Ninth House Network.* This San Francisco commercial firm combines content from top training/consulting types such as Tom Peters and Peter Senge with the craftsmanship of Hollywood filmmakers. Its offerings are basically interactive sequences of TV-like episodes on topics such as recruiting talent and leadership. The episodes entail trainee dialogue with various professional actors. The plots are directed by the give-and-take with the actors. At episode's end, the user's decisions are evaluated and he/she is advised how the response could be more effective. In effect, the technology is used properly—the training session, online, is changed into a real (true-to-life) problem-solving opportunity determined by the trainee's actual decisions. "Bona fide interaction" is entailed, as the current e-learning jargon would have it.

But note that these episodes are expensive to plan and produce. At Ninth House, a single episode runs to $200,000 and the broad bandwidth and high-speed Web service to transmit them via computer networks are obvious luxuries for most organizations. So Ninth House's clients are only the few big firms who can buy into the scheme.

And a final, pointed observation by editor Kevin Dobbs: "The average worker already spends an increasingly larger chunk of his day staring at a computer monitor. Even if the Web were the universal remedy that the e-learning providers claim, do you think he wants to spend even more time chained to his computer?"

LIMITATIONS OF E-LEARNING

Margaret Driscoll, an authority on distance learning including Web-based training programs, suggests that to understand what Web-based training can and can't do, we must look at learning subject to division into three domains: *cognitive, psychomotor, and affective (emotional)*[35].

The *cognitive* domain is concerned with *thinking* skills. *Examples:* memorizing terms, definitions, and concepts; applying rules and principles; processing information via analysis, synthesis, and evaluation.

The *psychomotor* domain relates to skills involving *physical movement. Examples:* using a power tool, taking a blood sample, batting a baseball.

The *affective* domain relates to teaching learners *new attitudes. Examples:* following a low-calorie diet; involving employees in decisions that affect them or where they can make a significant contribution.

In respect to the cognitive domain, WBT works well. Why? Because numbers, letters, and symbols readily represent the skills/knowledge in this domain. *Examples:* instruction in how to apply for a driver's license or how to plan a wedding.

But skill development in the psychomotor domain doesn't work out well on the Web. Why not? It requires coaching and feedback on the learner's performance to develop total competence and fluidity of performance. *Consider:* Who would want a surgical procedure executed on their brain if the doctor had only learned his/her craft via computer-based observations on the Internet? In other words, certain high-order/complex skills are best acquired only on a hands-on, coach-assisted basis, where the coach is immediately available to answer questions, observe performance closely, and provide such corrective feedback and modeling as may be essential. In the absence of the coach's vital critique, the learner may unknowingly acquire inappropriate behaviors/habits.

Also, we can hardly upgrade people's public speaking skills without a class setting that uses a video camera to provide immediate, unvarnished, visual feedback to the participants. Verbal critiques and positive reinforcement by the fellow participants and the instructor are also indispensable aids for a full and rich learning experience.

In respect to acquisition of skill and knowledge in the affective domain, the Web again falls short. Why? Because to change strongly held attitudes and beliefs, two types of reinforcement are essential: *behavioral modeling* and *behavioral reinforcement.* Reinforcement of this order can't be delivered readily over the Web. *Example:* No one can model for another person how to value diversity. Informal and formal behavior modeling, given the environment of the Web, simply isn't practical. Similarly, we can't use the Web to reward learners (employees, supervisors) who show a shift in attitude. The knowledge aspect of the affective domain may be learned on the Web, but the other, more critical (emotional) aspects can't be internalized on (from) the Web.

Jean Wilkinson, education director for Commonwealth Credit Union, Frankfort, Ky., finds that online learning is not effective for human relations skills (affective domain) such as communication, conflict management, and customer service. In regard to the latter area, she states, "We have found that people can believe, for example, that they are listening and smiling, but unless they are in a learning environment where they have an observer to give feedback, they don't know. The same with tone of voice. It is entirely possible for someone to know all of the facts about customer service and not be able to provide it at all. I am not opposed to online learning. I just found that it has more limitations than I realized" [36].

In respect to leadership training, the consulting firm Development Dimensions International, Bridgeville, Pa., found little preference for electronic delivery among potential leadership candidates [37]. DDI evaluated nine development activities to learn which methods were preferred by leaders. The finding: only moderate enthusiasm about computer-based learning; it received a number six ranking. This ranking was *behind* outside formal training, in-house formal workshops, special projects or assignments, discussion of skills with a mentor/coach, and reading books or other materials. To round out the list: participating in tests, assessment of skills-rating exercises, engaging in community activities, and foreign assignments.

Since people learn in different ways, a reality-based leadership development program should rely on a wide assortment of training/development approaches. Additionally, and most important, managers will develop best from an individually tailored development plan including 360-degree feedback from other managers, suppliers, and possibly others who are familiar with a manager's work.

Another problem with a distance meeting is cultural differences among audience members. Thus Victoria Chorbajion, head of Chorbajion Speaking Enterprises, Paramus, N.J., says, "I don't think it's effective to train employees in Delaware and California and Mexico at the same time" [38].

Additional problems are the following [39]:

1. E-learning applications have improved, reducing the cost of education/training employees online, often below the price for more traditional programs. States Gordon Macomber, CEO and president of NYU (New York University) Online: "Typical instructor-led learning for corporations costs about $300 per hour per student. And that doesn't include travel and other related expenses. Companies can look at significant cost savings and enhanced learning with a well-designed and managed e-learning program."

   The above conclusion may hold for organizations that *outsource* their training/education. But it's less certain for firms that develop proprietary course content for training their workers, business partners, or customers. Why? Because in-house content development can be costly, as can the infrastructure necessary to support the program. States Wayne Hodgins, strategic futurist and director of worldwide learning strategies at Autodesk, Inc., San Rafael, Calif., "The cost of creating content for e-learning is probably higher than it is for the more traditional delivery model, and more of it is required. A live instructor could make up for lack of materials, but you don't have that option online."

2. IBM and others have found that the multimedia need of an in-house learning program can be so large that it can hog network resources and slow down the firm's computer network to a snail's pace. So IBM's managers at Armonk, N.Y. have abandoned video in preparing their online, in-house training materials. Says Nancy Lewis, director of management development for IBM, "We love video as much as the next person. But from a curriculum design point of view, video is sometimes not as effective as other approaches, even though it's very sexy."

3. Lewis finds this added technical problem: video-intensive applications often require "plug-ins," which can turn learners off. She says, "We've determined that users get very frustrated with the need to download software plug-ins required to use video, and if they're frustrated, they won't come back."

4. If management expects its employees to take their training on their own time (remember, online training is available anytime, anywhere), non-management people may expect to be paid overtime for it. So in budgeting for a heavy load of e-training, the finance people should be contacted early on to be certain everyone is on the same wavelength, cost-wise.

Consider, too, one of the biggest challenges of online training. Since the technique/system is self-paced and readily accessed, it lacks a sense of urgency. Siemens Information and Communication Networks, Inc. found that its e-learners simply "don't get around to it." There's no classroom from which the learner can be visibly absent. Also students can all too readily be interrupted by managers who regard training as something less important than "real work" [40].

Finally, there is a limitation or problem for the trainer who, very understandably, has a need to work with people on a fully live basis. Thus Alicia Brown, National Director for Clinical Support, Sunbridge Healthcare Corporation, Albuquerque, N.M., finds a need to combine her online instruction with occasional field training. She states, "The job does become more alive and invigorating for me when I go out and train in person. You also get a better flavor of how a session is received when you're face to face. For me, it would be hard to be completely isolated and not get some chance to have that face-to-face experience" [41].

Is E-learning for All Learners?

Steve Heckler, head of Westlake Internet Training, Arlington, Va., a firm that provides instructor-led training to Web developers, finds these downsides to Web-based training [42]:

□ WBT courses are less likely to be as interactive as instructor-led courses. Without an instructor, most students won't push themselves as hard.

☐ When questions arise, no one is immediately available to respond. Obviously, it's far easier to raise one's hand to get help from a live instructor, than to submit a question to technical support and then wait for a response.

☐ If a student has access to a computer for at least two uninterrupted hours, CBT may be of help. If such time isn't available, an instructor-led class is preferred.

☐ If the learner is distraction-prone and not disciplined enough to finish a CBT course on his/her own, he/she would certainly profit more from the traditional classroom.

☐ Subjects which entail creative tasks, e.g., graphic design, require the aid of a trainer who can assess work quality and give immediate feedback.

☐ Students who require praise from a live instructor will have difficulty learning from CBT.

☐ Detail-oriented learners, those who can catch their own errors, can profit from CBT. Those who aren't so detail oriented need more help than a computer can provide.

So Heckler's conclusion (and remedy) is this: "The best strategy may be to integrate instructor-led training and computer-based training. Let employees choose the mix they want. People spend their lives learning; let them tell you how they prefer to learn. Some of the best designed programs use instructor-led training reinforced with computer-based exercises and reviews."

The bottom line: E-learning certainly can provide convenience and economy. But e-learning has a number of significant disadvantages. For one thing it is subject to technological barriers and breakdowns, Also, some learners may find it awkward to communicate with e-based instructors. And most important, minus the discipline of class attendance and the absence of a live instructor and a peer group for motivational support, it's all too easy to get derailed by at-home demands. So unless one is a supercharged, independent learner, comfortable with having to function solo at the computer without the camaraderie, energy, and rapport with fellow students, e-learning may be a tough venture to buy into.

We should also add that some learners can't absorb information merely by reading it. They, as hands-on learners, learn best by application.

Classroom Setting and Learning Effectiveness

Classroom training has these key advantages over even the best distance-learning offerings:

☐ A high degree of rapport is possible by the learner with the ready availability of the trainer/facilitator/instructor.

☐ It is much easier to exchange ideas in class. The richness of a class discussion is hard to duplicate via phoned-in questions.

☐ Bonding with fellow students is more certain and more satisfying. (But the distance-learning folk will argue that e-mail and chat rooms permit just as easy mingling and brainstorming.)

☐ Communication is richer and more authentic. Online learning can't replace the intimate human interaction which occurs normally in the classroom. If you can't experience (a) the tone and body language of a fellow learner who is making a critical point and (b) the group's reactions—gestures, grimaces, smiles, frowns, grins, blank stares, giggles, head shakes, eye winks, forward body leans, body withdrawals, yawns, doodling, voice tone—you are likely to lose out on the true import and impact of the message. A truism not to be ignored or forgotten: People connect with people (not with a computer screen). In human affairs, substitutes for true people contact are a fruitless search.

☐ The discussion, debate, humor (occasional), questions, agreements, disagreements, supportive comments, interruptions, repetitions, summations, interactions, etc., which arise normally in the classroom, serve as interest inducers and heighteners, and thus as significant motivators to learn in the fullest sense of the term.

☐ The social side of learning is ever present in the form of coffee breaks, lunches, and possibly dinners, too, if the training takes place in a motel, hotel, or off-site corporate training facility. Networking, too, is a natural opportunity in classroom training, and the longer the program the more opportunity there is to accomplish this.

☐ Classroom training also has great potential to build *esprit de corps* of the learner group, a desirable facilitation for group learning.

☐ Experiential learning, in the fullest sense of the term, using dyads, triads, small groups, exercises, games, simulations, and role playing, including the helpful moderating skills and insights of a trained facilitator, can take place successfully only in the live classroom.

Attitude and behavior change for "soft skills" learning can take place only under the ideal conditions/opportunities peculiar to the classroom: experiential learning, a supportive atmosphere, a facilitator who has the skill to build group cohesion, and possibly the conduct of the training in a "cultural island," providing a distraction-free, "total immersion" atmosphere. Another condition for this purpose—attitude and behavior change—is that the training is received in a solid block of time, rather than in limited dribs and drabs, thus increasing possibilities for creating a serious and solid impact on the learner.

☐ Few people will learn new information and soft skills merely by reading. Participation, involvement, and hands-on application opportunities in the classroom are the routes to real learning.

☐ Soft skills, such as interpersonal relations, diversity, communicating, listening, giving and receiving feedback, conflict management, counseling, coaching, motivating, exercising one's creativity, encouraging the creativity of others, team building, managing the boss, managing the organization, conducting sensitive interviews such as for difficult employees, discipline, performance review, career development, selling, customer service, etc. can only be learned well in the classroom.

Question: Is is possible to train a manager (provide skill practice) on how to counsel a burned-out employee via e-learning? Is it possible to provide high-quality team building in a venue other than live, involving group sessions?

The Bottom-Line Question: Can We Increase Learning and Retention by Putting Our Training Program on the Computer?

Here's how Dr. Richard E. Clark, Professor of Educational Psychology and Technology at the Uni-

versity of Southern California and director of a doctoral program on human performance at work, responds to this question [43]. He points out that there are various training developers and contract providers who feel quite strongly that CBT (computer-based training) and WBT (Web-based training) do improve learning. But, states Clark, there's considerable evidence to undermine this contention. But their claim persists, nevertheless.

So if CBT and WBT don't (or can't) improve learning, what can they do? Clark says that they can provide broad *access* to information and learning activities, decrease our cost of the training, improve efficiency of implementation, and often increase opportunities for practice (24/7). But, our choice of *delivery vehicle*— that is, computers—doesn't influence learning.

Let's get down to basics, then. If our aim is to increase learning and retention, we should concentrate on the *learning method.* That is, we should provide clear learning objectives, provide good examples, provide full opportunities for practice, and provide knowledge of results (feedback about performance). *Key point:* It's the *learning method*—how we design learning activities— rather than the *delivery medium* that basically impacts/ influences participant learning.

Clark asks this question: Why should we distinguish between learning methods and delivery medium? His pointed response is that it's difficult enough to construct a successful solution to a knowledge problem (desired learning outcomes) when, as good trainers, we do devote full attention to the various active elements that influence learning processes. But we can only expect mediocre (or worse) outcomes if our focus is on improper elements of the overall training (and learning) process.

KEY POINTS

1. Distance learning, conducted in past decades via snail-mail (correspondence courses), takes a variety of new forms with particular emphasis on computer-based e-learning.

2. E-learning has a number of advantages, the most significant of which is its capability to deliver learning materials anytime, anywhere and at considerable cost reduction compared to classroom training. Also, updating of course materials is

relatively easy, prompt, and inexpensive. E-learning can facilitate just-in-time learning.

3. E-learning is a useful adjunct to traditional classroom learning. It works best to provide information and to develop simple skills. It is a replacement neither for much of traditional face-to-face training nor for experiential learning.

4. To succeed, online learners must take into account such factors as time management, scheduling (when in the day to do it), location (where to do it), and quantity of learning to absorb at one time ("chunks" or long time-frames).

5. Online learners, if operating totally on an independent, self-directed basis, are subject to various challenging demands, including possession of basic computer skills and high motivation to (a) get started, (b) avoid the all-too-easy temptation to defer one's studies (procrastination), (c) work in isolation without colleagues' support and stimulation, and (d) pursue course work to its completion.

6. Online learners may drop out due to factors such as these: lack of learner motivation; absence of strong organizational incentives to learn (both carrots and sticks); lack of accountability for completion of courses (e.g., no testing); technology problems; poorly designed course materials; poor physical environment for learning; lack of supervisory awareness or interest in subordinates' course enrollment; weak instructor involvement in an asynchronous course; slow provision of feedback on learner accomplishment; absence of peer support.

7. E-learning is not the best learning method for all learners. Certain learners may function best if (a) they have immediate access (high availability) to an online instructor, (b) can work well in isolation, (c) are not distraction-prone (home and office may be a poor learning environment), (d) are adequately detail-oriented to catch their own errors or oversights, and (e) can maintain high interest even if course materials are less than exciting.

8. If your organization is considering adopting e-learning in whole or in part, consider the many factors which you must analyze before you decide—everything from the size of your trainee population and their physical location to availabil-

ity of appropriate technology and trainee computer know-how.

9. If your e-learning program is to be launched with the aid of outside sources—particularly vendors of off-the-shelf course materials—consider the cautionary factors cited on pages 562–563.

10. E-learning models that fail consist of course work developed for a live classroom that is just posted on the Internet and expected to work.

11. To maximize participation in your online learning courses/programs, consider a blended approach which combines asynchronous Web courses, synchronous virtual classes, and traditional classroom sessions.

12. To avoid computer-induced boredom, think in terms of frequent opportunities for interaction. Trainers at Aetna U.S. Health Care have a standing policy of allowing no more than 15 minutes to elapse without interaction between instructor and students, in a classroom or over the network (*Training*, Part 2, January 2001, p. 15).

13. To maximize results from e-learning, you must look at the appropriateness of trainee learning via three key domains: *cognitive, psychomotor,* and *affective* (emotional).

14. To maximize results from your synchronous e-learning programs/courses, consider the introduction of interactive activities via pre-work, during the session, and after the session.

15. Successful learning is dependent on the *learning method* (attention to adult learning principles and application of sound learning strategies) to a greater degree than the *delivery vehicle* (i.e., the computer)

REFERENCES

1. Eklund, Bridge, "A Modern Class Struggle," *Red Herring* (October 2000), pp. 330–332.

2. "Industry Report 2000—A Comprehensive Analysis of Employee-Sponsored Training in the United States," *Training* (October 2000), pp. 62–84.

3. Driscoll, Margaret, "Myths and Realities of Using WBT to Deliver Training Worldwide," *Performance Improvement* (March 1999), pp. 37–44.

4. Smith, Reggie, III, "E-learning—It's the New Rage in Distributive Training, but Is There a Downside?" *e-learning* (October 2000), pp. 40–42.

5. Driscoll, Margaret, *op. cit.*

6. These critical factors, which come from the Brandon Hall book, have been taken from a chart based on the Hall book adapted by Steven V. Benson, in "Will CBT Produce the Results You Need?" *Performance Improvement* (February 2000), pp. 27–34.

7. Rosen, Monte, "A Guide to Implementing Web-based Training," *e-learning* (May–June 2000), p. 41.

8. Silver, Sheryl, "e-learning Demands Expanded Skill Set for Trainers," *The Washington Post*, Classified Section (March 8, 2000).

9. Abernathy, Donna J., "E-learning Enchilada to Go— The E List," *Training and Development* (November 2000), p. 21.

10. Abernathy, Donna J., "Accreditation: Who Needs It?" *Training and Development* (January 2001), p. 20.

11. Abernathy, Donna J., "WWW.online Learning: Ten Questions to Ask About Online Learning Sites," *Training and Development* (September 1999), p. 37. The ten questions were adapted by Ms. Abernathy from "Questions to Ask," prepared by the Aris Corporation, aris.com.

12. Ellis, Kristine, "A Model Class," *Training* (December 2000), p. 56.

13. "Pointers to Pass on to Distance-Learning Presenters," *Meeting News* (May 8, 2000), p. 14.

14. Aldrich, Clark, "Customer-focused E-Learning: The Drivers," *Training and Development* (August 2000), p. 38.

15. Moran, John V., "Top Ten Learning Myths," *Training and Development* (September 2000), p. 33.

16. Kiser, Kim, "10 Things We Know So Far About Online Training," *Training* (November 1999), pp. 66–74.

17. Broadbent, Brooke, "How to Fail at e-learning," *e-learning* (January 2001), pp. 36–37.

18. Wheeler, Kevin, "Why People Still Like the Classroom More Than E-learning," *e-learning* (July–August 2000), pp. 46–47.

19. McDonald, Michele, "Debating the Relative Merits of Hi-Tech vs. Human Touch," *Meeting News* (May 8, 2000), p. 12.

20. *Ibid.*, p. 13.

21. Kiser, Kim, *op. cit.*, pp. 72–74.

22. *Ibid.*, p. 70.

23. Frieswick, Kris, "The Online Option," *CFO (Chief Financial Officer) Magazine* (December 1999), p. 91.

24. "Making Training Stick with E-mail Follow Up," *Creative Training Techniques* (September 1999), p. 3.

25. Carey, Robert, "Hazardous Material," *Successful Meetings* (March 1998), p. 46.

26. Zielinski, Dave, "The Lie of Online Learning," *Training* (February 2000), pp. 38–40.

27. Zielinski, Dave, "Can You Keep Learners Online?" *Training* (March 2000), pp. 64–75.

28. Kuchinke, K. Peter, Aragon, Steven R., and Bartlett, Kenneth, "Online Instructional Delivery: Lessons from the Instructor's Perspective," *Performance Improvement* (January 2001), pp. 19–27.

29. Dobbs, Kevin, "Editor's Notebook," *Training* (February 2000), pp. 10–12.

30. *Ibid.*

31. Caudron, Shari, "Evaluating E-Degrees," *Workforce* (February 2001), pp. 44–48.

32. *Ibid.*, p. 46.

33. *Ibid.*, p. 48.

34. Dobbs, Kevin, "What the Online World Needs Now: Quality," *Training* (September 2000), pp. 84–94.

35. Driscoll, Margaret, "Myths and Realities of Using WBT to Deliver Training Worldwide," *Performance Improvement* (March 1999), pp. 37–38.

36. Schaaf, Dick, "The View from the Middle—Special Report: Online Learning," *Training* (September 1999), p. OL12.

37. Wellins, Richard, and Byham, William, "The Leadership Gap," *Training* (March 2001), pp. 98–106.

38. McDonald, Michele, *op. cit.*, pp.13–14.

39. Myers, Randy, "The Absent Professors," CFO (Chief Financial Officer) magazine, Winter 2000, pp. 65–66.

40. Frieswick, Kris, *op. cit.*

41. Brown, Alicia, "Mixing It Up," in "True Confessions," *Training* (March 2001), p. 114.

42. Heckler, Steve, "Viewpoint: Web-Based Delusions," *Training* (December 1999), p. 104.

43. Farrington, Jeanne, and Clark, Richard E., "Snake Oil, Science, and Performance Products," *Performance Improvement* (November 2000), p. 7.

RECOMMENDED READING

Colbrunn, Shonne R., and Van Tiem, Darlene M., "From Binders to Browsers: Converting Classroom Training to the Web," *Performance Improvement,* February 2000, pp. 35–40.

    Discusses organizational readiness to launch WBT (Web-based training), including needed cultural change and technical readiness; course appropriateness for the Web; building the project team; design strategies; project time savers.

e-learning: The Magazine of Distributed Learning.

This monthly journal, started in early 2000, is devoted entirely to e-learning. It is useful as a source for developments/trends, case studies, and commentaries on the state of e-learning in industry, government, and education plus vendor-customer relations/service.

Editorial office: 201 Sand Pointe Ave, Suite 600, Santa Ana, CA 92707 Telephone: 714-513-8400; Fax: 714-513-8611.

Hall, Brandon, *Web-Based Training Cookbook,* New York, John Wiley and Sons, 1997.

A comprehensive text on online training from a leading authority in multimedia. Explains Web-based training principles, introduces the main types of courses, and provides the know-how and tools needed to create the program best for your organization. Tells how to convert existing curricula and design new courses for the Web and evaluate existing Web-based training courses.

Harrison, Nigel, *How to Design Self-Directed and Distance Learning Programs*, McGraw-Hill, New York, 1998.

Presents needed tools to design any type of Web-based, self-directed, or distance learning program to maximize learner participation and retention. The author provides these six steps to achieve your results: Define the problem; select the right format; set measurable, attainable objectives; test and improve your product; put your program into action; assess your success. The author's focus is on the learner, not on the trainer or the technology.

Marquardt, Michael J., and Kearsley, Greg, *Technology-Based Learning: Maximizing Human Performance and Corporate Success,* ASTD Press, Alexandria, Va., 2000.

Explores the interplay and impact on the ways we work and learn. Outlines the principles and practices needed to successfully implement learning technology in the global workplace and illustrates the importance of becoming a learning organization.

Rosenberg, Marc J., *e-learning: Strategies for Delivering Knowledge in the Digital Age,* McGraw-Hill, New York, 2000.

Outlines how to develop an organization-wide learning strategy based on cutting-edge technologies and explains the dramatic strategic, organizational, and technology issues involved. Written for professionals responsible for leading the revolution in workplace learning, *e-learning* takes a broad, strategic perspective on corporate learning. The book discusses the following:

☐ Requirements for building a viable e-learning strategy

☐ How online learning will change the nature of training organizations

☐ Knowledge management and other new forms of e-learning

Smith, Judith M., "How to Teach Online," *e-learning,* August 2001, pp. 22–24, 35.

Discusses the significant differences between traditional and online teaching/training. Thus, presenters need to develop a different skill set and play a new role—one of coach and mentor. Offers pointers on how to bridge the gap between traditional and online instruction skills, particularly regarding communication, classroom management, and technical management. Suggests "self-assessment (is distance learning right for me?) is important for both instructors as well as participants. It is not for everyone."

Zenger, Jack, and Uehlein, Curt, "Why Blended Will Win," *Training and Development,* August 2001, pp. 55–60.

Two long-time training professionals' view on instructor-led training and new technology-driven training is that not only can these two approaches co-exist, but their co-existence is necessary to produce something "better than we've imagined." A blended solution is marked by a completely integrated instructional design, and consistent framework and nomenclature, with each method delivering its best, maximum flexibility, and variety. E-learning seems especially appropriate for transfer of information and cognitive understanding.

Glossary

ABC approach—A checklist which serves as an aid in problem solving. Ideas, as stimuli, are offered in an A to Z format to provoke ideation.

Accelerated learning—A form of experiential or discovery learning which stresses action exercises, games, role plays, metaphors, themes, mnemonics, props, movement, music, poetry, and pictures. The learning appeals to all learner senses—sight, touch, sound, thought. If traditional learning is regarded as somber, stern, and serious, accelerated learning's approach entails freedom, fun, and (even) fantasy.

Action learning—Also known as action-reflection learning (ARL), it is a group-in-action management training technique used to solve actual business/organizational problems. Participants are chosen from different segments of the organization to provide a diverse set of viewpoints when tackling a problem. Participants learn about their own behavior, team functioning, and project management, as well as about problem solving.

Action maze—A highly structured or programmed form of case study. The case includes alternative decisions to resolve the problem presented. Wise decisions will get the team out of its maze; poor ones will mire participants into it more deeply.

Action plan—A specific, concrete "blueprint" to accomplish something on the job as a result of a given training experience. It is also known as a *contract*; the process is called *contracting*.

Active listening—An empathetic form of listening, helpful to establish intimacy and rapport with the speaker, using such techniques as restatement, reflecting feelings, nodding one's head, smiling (as appropriate), maintaining eye contact.

Activity—Generic term for participative training experiences such as exercises, games, role plays, small group experiences, and instrumentation.

Alpha test—An evaluation of a situation in its early stage. Its purpose: to assess the simulation's basic assumptions, overall structure, and logic progression. Problems are to be expected at this stage. See *Beta test*.

American Society for Training and Development (A.S.T.D.)—The professional society of the training occupation, headquartered in Alexandria, Va.

Analogy—In problem solving, the use of a direct comparison of like things, concepts or processes. See also *Metaphor, Direct analogy, Personal analogy,* and *Symbolic analogy*.

Application—Transfer of the classroom training to the job situation.

Application session—A formal (classroom) attempt to aid in transferring the training to the job situation.

Asynchronous—An individualized form of e-learning marked by lack of concurrence in time, that is, the learner accesses the learning materials at his/her convenience (in varied time frames) unrelated to the learning activities of other learners. See *Synchronous*.

Atmosphere—See *Climate*.

Attribute listing—A problem-solving tool that entails identifying or listing all the attributes or characteristics of a problem, product, or process and then systematically examining them.

Authoring—Software device to develop an interactive (learning) program.

Auxiliary—The person, in certain role plays, who functions in the non-leading role. *Example:* The reluctant customer whom the salesperson urges to make a decision. See *Protagonist.*

Bandwidth—Speed with which data is transmitted over a phone line, coaxial cable, by wireless transmission, etc. Larger bandwidth allows information to travel faster.

Behavior modeling—A form of structured role playing wherein participants enact roles as provided by "good" models. Critique is provided by the trainer and the group to ensure proper skill development. Positive reinforcement is stressed throughout.

Behavior modification—A system to influence behavior/performance/learning based on the assumption that behavior is a function of its consequences. In training, the receipt of positive reinforcement is deemed to be a significant consequence for the learner.

"Behind the back" technique—A way of discussing a completed role play. The role player being critiqued turns his/her back to the group, thereby facilitating the giving and receiving of the feedback.

Beta test—A real or "shakedown" test of a simulation in its final or near final stage—when the design is at least provisionally set. See *Alpha test*.

Blend—In distance learning, a combination of online and classroom instruction to overcome the limitations of total (passive) e-learning.

Brainstorming—A basic and highly popular tool for group problem solving. It can be used to identify problems, to suggest causes for problems, and to propose solutions for problems. The technique emphasizes deferred judgment and quantity to get quality.

Browser—Software (application program) used to view Web pages on either the Internet or intranet.

"Butterflying"—In facilitating self-managed teams, the facilitator brings team members together to help one another. (The metaphor draws on butterflies helping flowers to spread their pollen.) In this role the facilitator also tries to "cool" anger and disagreement among team members.

Buzz group—A small group that works on an assigned task; its conversation produces a "buzzing" sound, hence the term.

Buzz words—Generalized words to describe a problem, such as "communication," or "morale," which no one really understands and which inhibit the problem-definition/problem-solving process.

Card posting technique—Although formats may differ, the basic idea is to generate ideas on slips or cards and post them on the wall for better visualization of them. Cards may thus be readily modified, removed, prioritized, or grouped.

Case method—See *Case study*.

Case study—A technique designed to give a group training in solving problems and making decisions. The leader's role is typically catalytic rather than didactic.

CBT—Computer-based training, used primarily for self-instruction.

CD-ROM—A self-learning system using a compact disc capable of storing a large amount of data and providing quick and easy (random accessibility) retrieval of that data in whole or particular portions of it.

Chained or relay technique—A device to involve the low or nonparticipant in discussion. *Procedure:* Ask the same question in sequence of several participants; automatically include the shy person. *Advantage:* It gets the reluctant person into the act without putting him/her on the spot. See *Circular whip*.

Chat room—A branch of a computer system which allows e-learners to engage in live discussions with fellow participants.

Checklist—(1) An aid to memory to ensure that critical factors in either prevention or diagnosis of a problem are not overlooked. (2) Involves the use of "trigger words" to stimulate new thinking about a problem, product, or process.

Check sheet—A simple statistical (tabular) device for gathering data about a problem.

Chunking—The procedure/process of providing integration, structure, or organization to learning material in order to enhance understanding or recall. In other words, chunks (related groupings) of material are more readily assimilated (have greater meaning) than random or isolated bits or pieces.

Circular whip—A participative device wherein the trainer whips quickly around the room to elicit ideas, decisions, and feelings from all participants in the group.

Client-centered approach to problem solving—Utilizes procedures to ensure that processes of idea generation (content) are not inhibited by faulty group process.

Climate—Atmosphere in the training situation that may affect training outcomes in a positive or negative way.

Closure—A term used by Gestalt psychologists to indicate the tendency of our minds to fill in missing information. From a training standpoint it is a significant tool to (1) ensure that participants stay tuned in, particularly in lecture-type presentations and (2) achieve a satisfying training program ending for participants.

Cognitive dissonance—An unsettling condition which arises when the individual is confronted with an apparent inconsistency or imbalance between his/her ongoing beliefs, knowledge, or values and his/her behavior. The individual is thus under psychological pressure to resolve the conflict by changing either his/her attitude or behavior. Defense mechanisms such as rationalizations or denial may be used to resolve the lack of harmony between beliefs and behavior. Experiential training—simulations, role plays, encounter groups, feedbacking—can help to reveal these intrapersonal contradictions.

Conceptual map—Combining the features of a structured overview (outline) with a graphic display, it shows meaningful relationships between learning concepts. By chunking the material, it helps to highlight relationships and enhance meaning/understanding. See *Frames of reference, Graphic display, Structured overview,* and *Chunking.*

Conference—A training session providing the opportunity to receive current information about a problem area or to exchange views on pertinent problems. Its size may vary from a small group to a very large audience.

Continuum—(1) An array of ideas or concepts that, if read from left to right, provide a logical progression. *Example:* styles of leadership, ranging from highly participative to highly autocratic. (2) An array of numerical values, ranging from low to high. *Example:* A rating scale of 1–7 concerning one's ability to listen effectively.

Contract or contracting—See *Action plan.*

Co-training—The use of two or more trainers, also known as team training. This approach has many benefits for both trainers and participants.

Cultural island—A removed or isolated training location in which participants can work and learn better because the distractions of the office or shop situation are absent.

Culturally relevant—Presentation of training concepts and materials adapted to another culture, which permits those in the other culture to learn readily and thus enables them to apply what has been learned.

Debate—A participant-involving technique, structured formally to integrate varying viewpoints on an issue or problem.

Debriefing—Also termed "processing," "sharing," and "reporting," it is the final phase of an experiential activity. At this stage the trainer aids the participants to report back and interpret what was learned from the game, exercise, role play, or other activity.

Delphi technique—In problem solving, a consensus-seeking technique wherein ideas are generated individually and anonymously through the mail and "filtered" a number of times by the same participants. In a more modern version, the group is assembled and polled as to preferences; choices are still accomplished individually and without discussion.

Demonstration role play—An enactment of a problem situation by two or more role players, with the rest of the group functioning as observers who may subsequently critique or discuss the action.

Devil's advocate—A challenging, provocative role assumed by the trainer/facilitator. The idea is to encourage deeper, more original thought and/or to help group participants reconsider assumptions in a problem-solving situation. Also, the aim is to prevent the group from prematurely ending its discussion and/or decision making by encouraging it to consider reasonable objections to its solution. The trainer accomplishes this by suggesting other possible courses of action.

Diary—See *Journal.*

Didactic teaching—Traditional approach to teaching or instructing, entailing the dissemination of facts, knowledge, information, and manual skills. Today, it is contrasted with *experiential* or *discovery learning.*

Direct analogy—In problem solving, entails the comparison of one thing with another. Essentially, it is a search for the similar. See *Personal analogy* and *Symbolic analogy.*

Discovery learning—See *Experiential learning.*

Distance learning—Education and training accomplished on a remote, non-classroom basis, primarily via self-instruction, less commonly on a group basis. Today, it is accomplished primarily electronically (e-learning).

Dramatic skit—A demonstration-type role play presented to the group that closely follows instructions provided by the trainer. Its purpose is didactic as opposed to having an experiential growth orientation. See also *Personal growth enactment.*

Dyad (Pair)—A pair of participants who work together in the training situation. The dyad is a tremendous means of securing involvement, intimacy, rapport, and sharing.

e-mail—A system to transmit messages rapidly, using telecommunications links between computers. Enables the remote e-learner to communicate easily with the instructor and/or fellow trainees.

Embedded message—A subliminal training device to help participants accomplish closure more readily. *Example:* Signs on the wall which bear key words relating to the ideas in a formal presentation have the potential to create vivid and more meaningful connections to presentation of subject matter.

Empty chair technique—A dialogue in a role play with an imagined person in an empty chair; the emotionality and insight is heightened by the single role player switching chairs and thus assuming *both* roles.

Energizers—Activities designed to pep up the group after significant periods of inactivity, fatigue, or plain dullness. See *Movement* and *Standups.*

Entering behavior—The skill, knowledge, or attitude that the learner brings to the training activity; the trainer subsequently builds on this.

Evaluation—(1) The final phase of the training cycle. Its purpose is to assess training outcomes. (2) The last phase in a problem-solving activity such as brainstorming; *ideation* precedes evaluation.

Exercise—A structured training experience marked by a learning goal, high participation, and structure. Its overall purpose is to generate data for participant analysis.

Experiential learning—Method allowing the learner to learn from experience; synonymous with discovery learning. Today, it is contrasted with traditional, didactic methods of instruction.

Extranet—An intranet providing access to authorized users outside the organization. See *Internet* and *Intranet.*

Facilitator—A trainer who functions in a way to allow participants to assume responsibility for their own learning. The term is in contrast to the more didactic instructor, teacher, lecturer, or presenter.

Facing chairs—A device to generate data about opposing positions on a problem, involving physical and verbal reversal of positions on the issue. The idea is to aid participants to see the other side by forcing them to argue for it.

Fade-out—Loss of what was learned, over time, in whole or in part. See *Application.*

Fantasy—Creation of a mind picture by individual participants in response to a *general* (nonspecific) idea/topic provided by the trainer, for example, "What if you were head of the company . . ." See also *Guided fantasy, Mental imagery, Guided imagery,* and *Visualization.*

Feedback—Data received from or given to one or more participants concerning one's behavior, attitudes, and relationships in the training situation.

Field trip—A planned visit to a given area, site, building, or plant to study its operation in depth and to report back thereon. The field trip is typically a team project, although not universally so.

Fishbowl—Also known as clusters, this is a training device entailing a group-on-group activity, the inner group (A) serving as the discussion group and the outer group (B) acting as the observation group. Typically, groups A and B reverse roles.

Five-M (5-M) analysis—A structured format for problem solving (especially identifying causes) using the five factors of manpower, machinery, materials, methods, and money.

Flipcharting—Process of securing participant ideas, recording them on easel paper, and posting the big sheets on the wall; provides reference, recognition, motivation, atmosphere.

Focus group—A group of individuals who are convened to express their opinions, attitudes, or reactions to a particular service, program, activity, or product. They provide "live" data, that is, they explain *why* they feel as they do, information which questionnaires may not elicit. Useful to aid in need determination and evaluation of completed training.

Focused analysis—In case study, discussants are provided specific issues for analysis as opposed to having the case presented to them on an open-ended basis.

Follow-up training—The provision of additional or post-course training to add new material and/or reinforce what was learned in the regular training course. See *Application.*

Forced-choice technique—An instrument that asks the participant to choose between two statements, neither of which may be totally preferred. The choices typically produce a pattern on such things as one's leadership style.

Force field analysis—A training device to assess the forces—favorable and unfavorable—bearing upon a problem.

Forum—Experts present diverse views, but do not challenge one another as they do in a *panel presentation* or a *debate*. Audience participation is limited to posing questions.

Forced relationships technique—A problem-solving device entailing the development of ideas in response to the stimulus of a new unrelated word, concept, or phrase.

Frame game—A type of game that possesses a certain framework or format, only requiring the trainer to "plug in" the *content* to that frame.

Frame of reference—(1) A tool to enhance learning. See *Structured overview, Graphic display,* and *Conceptual map*. (2) Our attitudes, beliefs, and values, which influence our perceptions of a problem, an issue, or our relationships with others. Synonomous with "world view."

Game—An experiential training activity marked by a learning goal, competition, rules, scores or outcomes, and winners and losers. Games may be content-laden or be pure games devoid of content.

Geometrics—An assignment, presented orally or via worksheet, that requests the participant to make an artistic, graphic, or illustrative statement in one or more squares, triangles, rectangles, or other geometric figures. It is intended to encourage introspection.

Gordon technique—A form of problem solving wherein a group of diverse experts are given only a general definition of the problem. The assumption is that a precise definition of the problem will result in premature solutions.

Graphic display—A conceptualization, typically in geometric form—circle, wheel, square, rectangle, triangle, parallelogram—which provides a framework for learning and thus facilitates it.

Group-in-action methods—See *Small group methods*.

Group dynamics—Processes of interaction of a group at work; includes such processes as communication, goal setting, decision making, support giving, and leadership.

Group fantasy—A highly imaginative story development (mind picture) by the total group. The basic,

general input may be provided by the trainer or a participant, the group then embellishes it to form a "far out" mind picture. See also *Guided fantasy, Guided imagery, Mental imagery,* and *Visualization*.

Group role playing—A form of demonstration-type role playing utilizing a group rather than a pair of role players.

Guided fantasy—Creation of a scenario on the basis of a variety of inputs (questioning, channeling, encouraging) provided by the trainer, the latter working jointly with the participants. The initial input by the trainer is general rather than specific. See also *Fantasy, Group fantasy, Guided imagery, Mental imagery,* and *Visualization*.

Guided imagery—On the basis of a specific picture or image provided by the trainer, each participant develops a mind picture; for example, the trainer may offer the image of a waterfall, cave, or old house and ask the participants to go on from there. See also *Fantasy, Group fantasy, Guided fantasy, Mental imagery,* and *Visualization*.

Handouts—Also known as "passouts," "take-homes," and (facetiously) "leave-behinds," they are designed to provide added information, stimulation, and interaction, on either a presession, in-session, or postsession basis. Although they are a form of support material, the latter term has a broader meaning and typically includes participants' and leaders' workbooks and possibly text and film/video materials.

HTTP—Stands for "hypertext transfer protocol." It transfers hypertext documents, the standard protocol for the Web.

Hyperlink—A hypertext link. See *hypertext*.

Hypermedia—A system in which graphics, sound, text, and video are linked by a hypertext program.

Hypertext—Stored data in a computer (text, sound, graphics) that can be accessed randomly (nonsequentially) by the computer operator moving through a link from one document to another.

Icebreaker—Structured, content-free training activity designed to relax participants, get them acquainted with one another, and energize them. See *Opener*.

Idea reinforcement teams—A highly participative form of problem solving wherein each team member is required to listen to the ideas of the other team members and thereby develop the "best" solution to a problem.

Ideation—In problem solving, the process of creating ideas as in a brainstorming session. The ideation phase is kept distinct from the evaluation phase to encourage the free flow of ideas.

Idea writing—Also known as "brainwriting," this entails individual ideation in writing followed by written comments by colleagues in small groups. A total group discussion of all small groups' ideas concludes the operation.

Ideographs—Symbolic pictures used in lieu of written notes, for example, in giving a speech.

Imaging—A tool in problem solving wherein a problem is assumed to be solved and one imagines or visualizes the conditions that existed *before* the solution was created. Also, conditions may be visualized that *will* exist when a problem is solved.

In-basket exercise—A highly structured activity simulating an in-basket. Individual analysis of and decision on the items in the in-basket may be supplemented by group feedback on one's decisions. Learnings from the activity are designed to augment skill in decision making, delegating, coordinating, time management, etc.

Incident process—A variation of case study wherein the discussion group is provided with a brief incident and then must ask the trainer for additional data. When enough facts are garnered, teams are formed to debate a solution to the problem. The aim is to encourage participants to respect the need for thorough fact collecting before making a decision.

Informal role playing—Develops as the need arises in the training situation and is thus unplanned, unstructured, unwritten, and unrehearsed.

Inner advisor—Technique used by a participant in guided imagery to tap his/her wisdom buried below the usual level of awareness.

Institute—A meeting of a specialized group wherein "experts" are the primary sources of information. (The term, generally vague in meaning, is often used interchangeably with forum, symposium, conference, and panel discussion.) Audience participation is typically limited.

Instructor prework—Activities that the instructor conducts in order to learn of the diverse needs of the participant group via assessment of their backgrounds (knowledge, experience levels) and then to organize for these needs (via adapting activities and arranging for project subgroups).

Interaction—Dynamics among participants, including communication patterns, relationships, and role assumptions.

Interactivity—The procedure which permits a learner to be engaged with course content to ensure that the desired learning takes place.

Internet—A major computer network providing a worldwide linkage of smaller computer networks. See *Intranet* and *Extranet*.

Intervention—(1) A conscious decision and action by the trainer to alter what is going on or to introduce a new approach to improve the current situation. *Examples:* A trainee poses a windy, rambling, incoherent question and the trainer interrupts to state it succinctly for the group; in a team-building session the trainer/facilitator confronts the group with the fact that they have been talking *around* an issue for 90 minutes rather than directly confronting it. (2) A trainer proposes to management solving a performance problem(s) with alternate (non-training) approaches such as using job aids, altering the reward system, revamping personnel selection procedures, instituting the use of self-managed teams, reengineering, or Total Quality Management (TQM).

Intranet—An internal computer network having restricted access, i.e., limited to a particular corporation or government agency. See *Internet* and *Extranet*.

Introspection—A looking inward at one's attitudes, beliefs, values, perceptions, and behaviors. See also *Reflection*.

Instruments—Tools used in instrumentation. See *Instrumentation*.

Instrumentation—A technique for experiential learning using various scales, inventories, checklists, questionnaires, and continua designed to elicit data about individuals, teams, groups, or the total organization.

Job aids (procedural tools)—An economical, efficient substitute for training. For example, a trainer may develop a step-by-step checklist of questions or procedures which may then be posted on the wall, kept in a desk drawer, posted on a machine, listed in a computer, etc. The job aid is based on the assumption that memory is too fragile to be relied upon. It might also be used as a reinforcer (memory aid) after the training ends. *Other examples:* flow charts, computation guides/aids, printed instructions on a pay phone, worksheets, models (what a procedure or result should look like), recipes in a cookbook.

Journal or journaling—A device for the capture in writing of one's feelings, attitudes, and values as one undergoes a given set of experiences. It is intended to give one insight or self-awareness about one's values, motivations, and behavior. Also known as a diary.

Journalist's six questions—Entails the use of the questions *who? what? when? where? why?* and *how?* to resolve a problem.

Jury technique—A form of problem solving entailing the search for the real problem and full evidence rather than for villains or scapegoats.

Jury trial—Mock or simulated trial designed to give participants insight into a particular problem area, for example, "trying" a supervisor who avoids conducting annual performance appraisals.

Just-in-time training—(1) Provision of training when it is actually needed, rather than on a deferred basis, so that participants can readily see immediate use for the new skills. This will make them more receptive to the training. (2) Also, in the case of self-managed teams, the facilitator may provide training to a team member(s) when the need is identified as opposed to waiting for a class to become available at an uncertain future date. Today, the Internet is considered to be a highly useful tool for this purpose.

Laboratory training—See *T-group.*

Learner-centered training—A training situation wherein participants are given the opportunity to assume responsibility for their own learning. See *Experiential learning* and *Didactic teaching.*

Learning contract—See *Action plan.*

Learning packet—Materials provided to participants which are essential for the learning experience.

Learning portals—Web sites offering a combination of courses, collaboration, and community.

Learning sequence—A systematic approach to session design entailing a listing in grid or chart fashion of the following elements: skill area/activity to be worked on, training method, specific task or assignment, rationale for the assignment, and time for all tasks.

Lecturette—Short talk designed to prevent boredom from setting in; in experiential learning, trainers/facilitators typically give short inputs rather than full lectures.

Lecture method—A didactic instructional method involving one-way communication from the active presenter to the more or less passive audience or trainee group.

Listening teams—See *Viewing-listening teams.*

Live case—A case or problem of a current nature presented by a manager to a training group; to be distinguished from the usual canned or already-described case.

Managerial Grid®—A structured form of leadership and team training wherein participants give feedback to one another concerning their perceived leadership style.

MBTI—The Myers-Briggs Type Indicator, which is a useful tool to provide participants in experiential-type training programs with a means to understand their personality preferences/styles better. Learning of one's own style and that of others enables one to improve communication and thus working relationships.

Magic wand technique—A form of fantasy in which the participant is given total power to mold, change, or control a given situation, event, or relationship.

Meditation—A silent, relaxing activity designed to encourage psychological regrouping, renewing one's energies, getting in touch with one's feelings, etc.

Mental imagery—Creation of mind pictures by one's self on command, the stimulus being internal rather than external. See also *Guided imagery, Fantasy, Group fantasy, Guided fantasy, Visualization.*

Metaphor—A tool in problem solving in which a word or phrase is used as a reference to suggest a resemblance to something else. *Example:* the ship of state. See *Analogy.*

Mirror technique—In role playing, a procedure wherein either a member of the group or the trainer mirrors the feelings of another role player. It is particularly useful when the original role player is experiencing a block or impasse.

Mirroring—The phenomenon of assuming the behavior of another person on a less than conscious level. *Example:* In a one-on-one interaction, one party modulates his/her voice, leans forward and maintains steady eye contact. The second person gradually responds in kind, that is, mirrors the other person's behavior. So in dealing with a loud, angry person, if we lower our voice to a near whisper, the irate party is likely to reduce his/her volume. *Note:* The behavior emitted and adopted may be pleasant, nasty, or more or less neutral (for example, relaxing noticeably in one's chair).

Mock trial—See *Jury trial.*

Model—A conceptualization designed to present a rather complex body of information or ideas in a relatively easy-to-understand way. *Examples:* The Johari Window; Maslow's Hierarchy of Needs.

Modularized course—One that has interchangeable components. With interchangeability, the training program designer can exchange specific segments of the course without needing to revise the total program.

Monologue—A form of case study, entailing thoughts (in writing) projected by one person.

Morphological analysis—An idea-generating technique in which the learner relates several variables of a problem to aid in finding a new solution.

Mousetrap technique—A form of case study, involving multiple situations designed to reveal that participant thinking may be inconsistent, rationalizing, and tolerant of a double standard.

Movement—An approach to training that departs from the static situation in which participants are typically placed. Its rationale: Movement keeps the group active, alert, energized, loose, creative.

Multiple-case technique—A form of case study involving the analysis of several related cases or incidents.

Multiple-choice instrument—An instrumented format requiring the participant to select the one statement of three to five given statements with which he/she agrees. Typically, the choices produce a pattern, such as of one's managerial style.

Multiple-group role playing—The use of small groups or teams to resolve a problem having multiple characters. In this format, *all* participants "play" regardless of group size.

Multiple role playing—Role playing formats that permit all participants to engage in role plays at the same time. See *Demonstration role play.*

Multiple role taking—The assumption of a single role by two or more participants. The objective is to generate more data about the problem, relationships, or preconceptions.

Need determination—The primary step in the training cycle utilizing available productivity data, interviews, and/or questionnaires.

Networking—A post-program effort by participants to keep in touch so as to lend support to one another and to help learning "glue in." See *Application.*

Nominal group technique—A tool for problem solving entailing individual, silent work. Interaction is purposely limited so that ideation will not suffer due to premature evaluation or social pressure.

Observer—A nonparticipating member of the group who observes and reports back on activity in a role play, game, exercise, small group, or fishbowl. The rationale: An "outsider" can see behavior more objectively than the person engaged in the activity.

Opener—Structured, content-oriented training activity designed to ease participants into the formal program. See *Icebreaker.*

Organization development (OD)—The use of planned interventions to augment organizational effectiveness and health. Typical interventions: team building, data collection, MBO, quality of work life, total quality management (TQM), re-engineering.

Overlearning—Learner practice beyond the point of mastery to ensure that the training "glues in" fully; especially helpful when vital skills or concepts are involved. A key to longer retention.

PCT (purposeful creative thinking) approach—A form of analogy used to solve problems. It entails identifying the paradox or conflict basic to the problem, locating an analogy basic to the paradox, and then producing a new solution or idea based on the equivalent.

Panel presentation—Panelists with diverse positions exchange views; the audience may have an opportunity to pose questions to them.

Pareto's analysis—The 80/20 principle used in problem solving (20% of the effort contributes to 80% of the results). It tells us how to separate the significant few from the trivial many.

Pareto diagram—Bar chart used to show the major problem or major causes for a problem graphically.

Participant-centered learning—See *Learner-centered training.*

Personal analogy—In problem solving, one takes on the identity of an object or person—"gets inside of it"—to understand it better and thus change or improve it. See *Direct analogy* and *Symbolic analogy.*

Personal growth enactment—A demonstration-type role play acted out with few or no guidelines, subject to group critique. See also *Dramatic skit.*

Personal shield—An icebreaker that asks participants to respond in writing to six (self-disclosing) questions that appear on the shield.

Phillips 66 method—A device to enable groups of six participants at a meeting or a training session to produce ideas or solutions relative to a problem. Ideas are generated in the first five minutes and prioritized in the last minute of the six minute time allotment.

Plop—This occurs when a group member makes a statement which is ignored by the group. The comment, in effect, "plops" to the floor, totally unrecognized. Statements which are repeatedly ignored or not commented on indicate that a group (a) is not a very close-knit, sensitive unit and (b) has limited communication skills.

Plug-ins—Software which allows e-learners to increase browser capabilities to play video, audio, or other multimedia files through their Web browser.

Point-of-view team—A small group that is instructed to listen/view from a given frame of reference, for example, that of field as opposed to headquarters personnel. See *Listening/viewing team.*

Portal—A Web site that provides access/entry to the Internet and offers useful content, organizing various sites and features on the Web or other segments of the Internet.

Prediction—By asking participants to predict an outcome in a film/video, how a particular character will behave in it, or the nature of a concept before it is explained, we excite interest and involve participants early on.

Pre-work—An assignment to participants in advance of the training. Its rationale: Advance preparation will facilitate one's easing into the program, stimulate curiosity about it, and augment motivation.

Problem census—In problem solving, a listing of problems by a group. It may be done via brainstorming, the slip method, buzz groups, or general (total group) discussion.

Processing—See *Debriefing.*

Profile—A procedure to show at a glance the significance of data presented on a rating scale. It also permits comparisons between different time frames, individuals, groups, etc.

Projective technique—On the basis of pictures provided by the trainer, the participant projects himself/herself and his/her feelings into the stimulus. It is a means of dredging up or projecting feelings or attitudes that may be difficult to bring forth via more conventional methods.

Prompt—A learning device (stimulus) to trigger or spark thought, insight, understanding, or behavior. *Examples:* A course outline, a check sheet, a job aid, a visual aid, a pre-printed response sheet wherein the learner must fill in missing words or phrases.

Props—Physical objects used in the training situation to augment participant insight into or empathy with the program's content. *Example:* A participant may ride in a wheelchair to appreciate the problems of a handicapped person.

Protagonist—In a role play, the leading player, the one who is refining old roles or learning new ones. *Examples:* A young, bright, well-educated middle manager tries to loosen up the attitude and behaviors of an "old timer," a supervisor who has difficulty adjusting to new organizational demands for acceptance of the diversity concept; or the customer service rep who is learning to deal with an angry customer. See *Auxiliary.*

Protocol—A body of rules defining message format for exchange between computers.

Psychodrama—See *Role playing.*

Pulse taking—Assessment of participant feelings about a given session or a full training day. It is useful for making adjustments in the training program as may be warranted or practicable.

Puzzles—A fun-type form of experiential learning that is designed to stimulate participant curiosity, creativity, and a problem-solving orientation. In some cases puzzles are used just for fun.

Quality circle—An employee group consisting of six to eight volunteers who identify and resolve a problem and recommend a solution to management. Problems may relate to quality, waste, cost, bottlenecks, safety, etc.

Question sheet—By giving participants a list of questions, as opposed to presenting them orally, the trainer can ensure their comprehension to a significant degree. The sheet also simplifies the question assignment process to the participants and can serve as a reference tool.

Rating scale—An instrument, assuming many formats, designed to permit the participant to express degree or strength of feeling about an issue, behavior, attitude, or value.

Recorder—One who records and thereby provides a summary of small group ideas, conclusions, and recommendations to the total group. The recorder may be an active participant as well as a reporter for the small group.

Redirect technique—A helpful trainer device to learn what other participants are thinking and to expose possible feelings of confusion by participants. Procedure: Ask several people to respond to each question and to elaborate on each other's answers.

Reflection—A process, following introspection, wherein we make meaning out of the material we have developed/discovered via introspection. See *Introspection*.

Reinforcement—(1) Praise or encouragement of the learner's performance so as to augment his/her interest, and motivation. (2) Provision of added learning tasks or data so as to aid the comprehension and/or "gluing in" of the training. See also *Application*.

Relaxers—Low-key activities to relax participants or to establish a quiet, serious, pensive mood.

Resource person—A knowledgeable person who provides content for the training effort (session, course).

Responsibility/accountability chart—A control sheet or chart to pinpoint who is responsible for what and when; useful in team building and in implementing an agreed-upon decision or action plan.

Restructuring—A major or strategic change in the way a firm does its business to increase its efficiency and profit and to make it more competitive. *Examples:* Closing or reducing capacity at older plants, consolidating offices or stores, spinning off unprofitable or low-producing units, centralizing planning or other functions, reducing the number of suppliers, adding an overseas production or distribution unit. See *Total Quality Management (TQM)*.

Risk analysis—Using a T-column, the problem-solving group highlights assumed or imagined risks and ways of overcoming them. Typical problems: promoting women and/or minorities to upper-level jobs, delegating, engaging in team building. See *Worst-case scenario*.

ROE (return on expectation)—A quantitative means of measuring training based on the expectations of the operating official who sponsors it. Reasonable evidence rather than hard proof is the standard of measurement. This approach to training evaluation may be used in lieu of ROI (return on investment) when the ROI approach is too costly or of lesser practicality, particularly where evaluation of "soft skills" training is involved.

ROI (return on investment)—The monetary value of training results (e.g., sales, productivity) exceeding the cost of the training provided. A means of meeting Level Four evaluation requirements.

Role clarification—See *Role negotiation.*

Role negotiation—A technique used in team-building programs to clarify and improve work and/or interpersonal relations between two team members. Each party in the negotiation tries to learn what the other expects more of, less of, and what is expected to remain the same.

Role playing—A training technique in which participants act out and thus experience real-life roles and situations. It is both a form of simulation and experiential learning.

Role reversal—A role-playing technique wherein one role player "reverses" and assumes the role of another. The purpose is to acquire empathy and insight concerning the feelings, attitudes, and values of the other person.

Rotational problem-solving technique—Entails the visits of several problem solvers to the stations of several expert advisors, the former gathering ideas from the latter. Each problem solver consolidates the ideas he/she has garnered and reports back to the total group on them.

Scatter diagram—A statistical procedure in problem solving designed to show graphically the relationship between two sets of data.

"Schmoozing"—To further cohesion of self-managed teams, the facilitator will check informally with team members to learn how things are going and if help is needed. Another aspect of schmoozing is "hanging out" and building good will.

Self-directed teams (SDTs)—Work teams which are empowered to produce a whole product or manage a process independently. They set goals, assign and schedule work, and may hire and fire team members. In some cases the team may select its own leader.

Seminar—A training effort dependent primarily on the expertise of knowledgeable resource persons. Participants generally have the opportunity to exchange views with the experts. The participant group is typically limited in size for discussion purposes.

Sensitivity training—See *T-group.*

Sentence-completion instrument—A tool for individual and/or group analysis. It involves using open-ended statements completed by participants to disclose feelings, attitudes, values, perceptions, and behavior.

Server—A computer that makes services, e.g., access to stored data files and programs, available to work stations on a network.

Seven-S (7-S) analysis—A structured format for problem solving (determining causes) using these seven factors: structure, strategy, systems, superordinate goals, skills, style, and staff.

Simulation—A training activity designed to reflect reality. It may range from a role play or in-basket exercise to a mock military invasion.

Simulation-game—A training activity akin to real life marked by such game attributes as competition, scores, outcomes, winners, and losers.

Slip method—A problem-solving tool wherein participants list individually on 3" × 5" slips ideas that relate to problem identification, causes for problems, or solutions to problems.

Small group methods—A term used to describe the use of small groups in identifying and solving problems. These are also known as *group-in-action methods*.

Small group psychological reinforcement—A problem-solving technique designed to secure maximum participation and pinpointed solutions to problems. Several groups are put in competition to produce better ideas.

Sociogram—A diagram which plots interpersonal relations/communication in a group, for example, who talks to whom, how frequently one contributes, how frequently one receives.

Soliloquy—A form of role play in which the single role player talks aloud about his/her problem, role, attitudes, values, relationships.

Spaced learning—By experiencing the training over longer time periods, learners can presumably better "glue in information." See also *Application*.

Spectogram—A "live" continuum to measure where people stand on an issue or belief. Participants physically position themselves on the floor at one extreme or another (left or right) or somewhere between the extremes. *Examples:* to indicate degree of change (or stress) one is experiencing; how satisfied one is with one's career or one's boss; the amount of learning (none, some, a lot) from a just-completed training program.

Spokesperson—A person who presents the ideas of his/her team or small group to the group at large. (The spokesperson may be appointed by the small group, a procedure preferable to appointment by the trainer or to self-appointment.)

Spontaneous role playing—Uses problems or situations that the participants themselves provide; also known as "live" or "hot" role playing. See also *Informal role playing*.

Spread sheet—A chart, on flipchart, used by the trainer to capture data from several role plays. It allows comparison of the results of the several enactments. Also used to display data from exercises, games, and so forth.

Standups—Devices to keep group vitality and creativity from declining. See *Energizers* and *Movement*.

Stop-film technique—A procedure entailing the stopping of a film/video at any one or more points; the group then discusses what took place or possibly predicts the next action or final outcome.

Streaming media—Options such as archived audio and video clips which the e-learner can tap. A downside: A lengthy video (e.g., 90 minutes) or several topics may discourage the viewer not wishing to view it all, who may thus skip the option entirely. (*Note:* Recent product development has made video clips searchable by keyword.)

Structure—Term used to indicate boundaries, guidelines, or limits provided by the trainer. For example, a game is structured; a T-group is basically unstructured.

Structured analysis—Entails the use of a structure or set of guidelines to aid in attacking (determining causes of) a problem. See *Five-M analysis* and *Seven-S (7-S) analysis*.

Structured overview—An outline of course material which provides a prompt or a mental frame of reference.

Structured role play—One that is well planned, typically including the use of written role play instruction sheets, observers, possibly pre– and post–role play guide sheets, etc. The idea is to keep things on track and reduce participant anxieties.

Subgroup—See *Buzz group*.

Support system—A psychological mechanism to help us grow, develop, and cope with life's intermittent frustrations, setbacks, disappointments, even crises. The system may comprise positive elements or *builders* (family, friends, neighbors, hobbies, organizations to which we belong, our network) and negative elements or *harassers* (a bear boss, debts, ill health, an ailing car).

Symbolic analogy—A problem-solving technique using words or phrases that are placed in combat or conflict with one another. A key word from the problem statement triggers the analogy. See *Direct analogy* and *Personal analogy*.

Symposium—Presentation of several points of view by several experts. Since audience participation is minimal, large groups may be accommodated.

Synchronous—A form of e-learning wherein the learning materials are provided to a number of learners at the same time. In effect, a virtual classroom is created. See *Asynchronous*.

Synectics—A theory or system of problem stating and problem solving based on creative thinking. It involves free use of metaphor and analogy, as well as informal interchange within a carefully selected group of individuals of diverse personalities and areas of specialization. See *Client-centered approach to problem solving*.

T-column—A two-column device placed on flipchart/blackboard by the trainer to help participants better see the comparisons and contrasts of issues or problems.

Team building—A training effort designed to augment a work group's effectiveness. The agenda may relate to the work (goals, policies, procedures), group processes, and/or interpersonal relationships.

T-group—A form of unstructured training wherein participants learn about the impact of their own behavior or the behavior of others via feedback from the group. Also known as sensitivity training and laboratory training.

Think sheet—A worksheet assignment to introduce a topic, session, or course. It encourages the participant to reflect on the pertinent subject matter.

Total group role playing—A role play in which everyone has a role at the same time; it thus becomes a simulation, such as role playing a civil defense disaster. See *Simulation*.

Total Quality Management (TQM)—A major improvement program affecting all parts of the organization. Its values relate to A-1 quality and customer service, a systems view (the whole firm is involved), an open system (ideas are welcome from the inside and the outside), teamwork, and continuous, incremental improvement of product and/or service. See *Restructuring*.

Trainer—Term used to describe a learner-centered conductor of a course or program. See also *Facilitator*.

Trainer-centered learning—A training situation in which the trainer assumes responsibility for the learning process. See *Learner-centered training*.

Training cycle—Encompasses the four phases of training: determination of need, design of the program, delivery of the program, and evaluation of results.

Transfer—See *Application*.

Triad (trio)—A group of three participants functioning as a team or small group. Although less intimate than the dyad, it brings more ideas to bear on a task or problem.

Trust walk—Also known as "blind walk," this exercise is designed to loosen up participants and develop trust among them. It may also be used to heighten sensory awareness.

Unstructured training—See *Structure*.

Upside-down problem solving—Unconventional solutions to a problem may be obtained by abandoning common sense and thinking in opposite terms.

Value analysis—A group problem-solving tool to refine, reengineer, and replan a product or service so as to reduce its costs of production.

Vertical training—Involves participants of two or more levels in the same organization. An acceptable procedure if all who work together *must* learn together. More typically, training with one's boss present inhibits participation.

Viewing-listening teams—By giving small groups an assignment in advance of seeing a film/video, the trainer secures their commitment to watch with seriousness and purpose. *Note:* If only a lecture is involved, the teams are called listening teams.

Vignette—A short segment of a film/video used to present a problem or situation for discussion. Quite often the vignette may have considerable impact, particularly if it is well selected, and directed toward a particular problem situation.

Visualization—The participant recalls and interprets actual events, relationships, etc., either past or present. *Example:* an incident involving an early supervisor who influenced one's career for the better. Feelings about the event and/or persons involved are expressed freely. See also *Fantasy, Guided fantasy, Group fantasy, Mental imagery,* and *Guided imagery*.

The Web—Part of the Internet accessed by the learner with browser software that follows the HTTP protocol.

WBT—Web-based training (as opposed to CBT).

WIIFM—An abbreviation of "What's in it for me?," which refers to participants' need to know what benefits they can expect from the training program they are attending, either as a volunteer or because they were sent by the boss.

Warm-up activity—A training procedure, such as an ice-breaker or an opener, designed to start things off and set the proper climate. See *Icebreaker* and *Opener.*

Weather-vane phenomenon—In vertically structured training, lower-level managers (or subordinates) check carefully to see "which way the wind is blowing" before they present their own ideas, opinions, or feelings. They play it safe to avoid running afoul of their bosses' viewpoints.

Whip—See *Circular whip.*

Workshop—A hands-on, highly participative training effort wherein participants learn by doing. Typically the group is small enough to ensure adequate rapport and intimacy.

Worst-case scenario—A form of fantasy used to explore the worst that could happen should a given event occur, as well as one's feelings related to the event. Its purpose is to get out of one's system all the fear and anxieties surrounding a possible happening. See *Risk analysis.*

Writing to Learn (WTL) Method—An easy-to-do, equipment-free, group-in-action technique which stimulates participant thinking, saves time, reduces protectiveness of one's ideas, involves everyone, de-emphasizes facilitator domination, and allows participants to assess their learning by comparing their early written ideas with later ones.

Wrong way–right way—A form of case study, utilizing two cases to illustrate a preferred action, behavior, or decision.

Yes/no instrument—A relatively simple instrument that asks the participant to agree or disagree with the statements or questions included therein. A scoring device generally accompanies the quiz.

Note: Distance Learning definitions have been drawn from (1) *Random House Webster's College Dictionary*, Random House, New York, 2000; and (2) "Get to Know the Technology Buzzwords," *e-learning*, January–March 2000, p. 30.

Appendices

Worksheets and Other Training Tools

The materials in these appendices take the form of worksheets, task assignment sheets, checklists, instruments, note taking sheets, and evaluation forms. They are basic tools for the trainer interested in putting his/her participants to work—a key approach to discovery learning.

Most of these forms may be used in the training situation "as is." Others require a degree of modification to meet the reader's needs better. It is suggested that readers study these forms carefully so as to develop a mind-set toward the regular use and development of such learning tools.

APPENDIX 1

FINDING FELLOW HOBBYISTS

Gardening _____   Skiing _____

Motor boating _____   Bicycling _____

TV watching _____   Swimming _____

Fishing _____   Beer drinking _____

Movies _____   Horseback riding _____

Antique cars _____   Bridge _____

Reading _____   Flower arranging _____

Mountain climbing _____   Meaningful trips _____

Jogging _____   Local sports (pro, college) _____

Waterskiing _____   Tennis _____

Woodworking _____   Sailing _____

Raquetball _____   Motorcycling _____

Crocheting _____   Golf _____

Collecting (coins, stamps, etc.) ____   Gourmet cooking _____

APPENDIX 2

YES, I HAVE PREFERENCES

1. State (in the U.S.) _____
2. City (in the world) _____
3. Soup _____
4. Entree _____
5. Beverage _____
6. Dessert _____
7. Movie _____
8. Book _____
9. Opera _____
10. Symphony _____
11. Athletic team _____
12. Color _____
13. Bird _____
14. TV program _____
15. Vacation, type of _____
16. Movie actor _____
17. Tree _____
18. Flower _____
19. Outdoor activity _____
20. Indoor activity _____

APPENDIX 3

AID FOR DISTRACTION BANISHMENT

When we come to a workshop such as this, it is difficult to leave behind our "real world" concerns—unfinished work or new projects at work, relations with others, family matters, recreational and social interests, financial needs, the car, and so on.

Since reflection on these outside matters won't help our concentration in this workshop, let's see if we can banish them, at least symbolically. A simple way to do this is to list candidly below the major ones:

1.

2.

3.

4.

5.

Now fold this sheet of paper, place it in the envelope provided, seal the envelope, and write on the outside your phone number (or any other number) as an identification code. We'll return the envelope to you at program's end.

APPENDIX 4

PROGRAM HOPES AND PERSONAL CHANGE

1. My hopes and expectations for this seminar are

2. If my superiors could change me, they would

3. If my peers or associates could change me, they would

4. If my subordinates could change me, they would

APPENDIX 5

SESSION OPENER

1. My highest skill as a _____ (manager, trainer, salesperson) is

2. My biggest accomplishment in the last 12 months has been

3. My goal(s) for the next 12 months is (are)

4. My goal(s) for the next 5 years is (are)

APPENDIX 6

SESSION STARTER

1. When I am at my communication best, I

2. When I am at my communication worst, I

APPENDIX 7

INTROSPECTION REGARDING MY MANAGERIAL JOB

Draw anything that comes into your mind in the three boxes below. Let yourself go!

Organization	Leadership

Me and My Job

APPENDIX 8

WHERE DO I GO FROM HERE

My Job Satisfactions	My Job Concerns

A New Job Should Provide	Action Steps for a New Job

APPENDIX 9

HOW I SEE DECISION MAKING

(Check one of the two boxes below)

1 ☐	2 ☐
Managers make the wisest decisions when they • Collect appropriate facts • Assess the facts • Develop alternate solutions • Choose among the alternatives, weighing the pros and cons of each • Clearly communicate the basis for the decision to the staff • Clearly communicate the need for all concerned to support the decision and to implement it fully and promptly	Managers make the wisest decisions when they • Recognize the complexity of a problem • Collect appropriate facts, using group resources as necessary • Work with the staff to discuss facts, develop alternatives, weigh alternatives, and decide on a single course of action • Plan for action with the group

I checked box 1 ☐ 2 ☐ because

APPENDIX 10

PROBLEM CENSUS

What are the major problems (blocks, barriers, obstacles) you see that keep you from doing the quality job you would like to do?

Procedure:

1. We will provide you with several 3″ × 5″ slips.

2. List no more than four or five problems.

3. Write one problem only on each slip. Try to state the problem briefly for ease of tallying.

4. If you do not have any major problems, write "no problems" on one slip.

5. Omit signatures.

6. Meet in small groups to discuss the problems.

7. Collect the slips.

8. We will classify and tally the responses and give you a summary report today or tomorrow.

APPENDIX 11

WORKSHEET: MOTIVATORS

Supervisors have many means of encouraging or unleashing motivation. List some ways you can think of below. Use the reverse side if you need more space.

1. _____

2. _____

3. _____

4. _____

5. _____

6. _____

7. _____

8. _____

9. _____

10. _____

11. _____

12. _____

13. _____

14. _____

15. _____

16. _____

17. _____

18. _____

19. _____

20. _____

APPENDIX 12

HELPED/HINDERED GROWTH INCIDENT

A. Describe a situation or incident wherein your superior, past or present, so behaved as to discourage your growth.

Describe your feelings about the incident at the time.

Describe your feelings about the incident now.

B. Describe a situation or incident wherein your superior, past or present, so behaved as to facilitate your growth.

Describe your feelings about the incident at the time.

Describe your feelings about the incident now.

APPENDIX 13

POST-PROGRAM CONSULTATION

I am currently experiencing this problem and would appreciate your thoughts on it:

Name _____

Title _____

Address _____

My recommendation(s) is (are)

Trainer: _____

APPENDIX 14

GROUP OBSERVATION SHEET

You will shortly be observing the behavior of a group engaging in an assigned fishbowl activity. Here are some things you may wish to look for:

1. Getting started.

   Was the group clear about its task? If not, did the participants attempt to redefine it?

   What method or procedures did they use to attack the problem?

   How was the method adopted? Through the insistence of one dominant person? By group consensus (that is, talking it through without voting)? By voting? By default?

2. Group behavior.

   What was the energy/enthusiasm level of the group?

   Was there high interest in the problem?

   What was the participation pattern? Did some play it safe and hold back? Did all participate with adequate consistency? Was there a dominator? Did people really listen to one another? Did anyone interrupt others consistently?

   What was the trust level in the group? Did members share feelings openly? Were members supportive (did they show concern, caring, etc.) of one another?

   Was the group marked by high esprit de corps, cohesion?

   Was there a leader in the group? If so, did this leader help or hinder progress?

3. Decision making.

   Was a decision reached? If so, how?

   Was the decision arrived at through consensus, bulldozing, voting, bargaining, or what?

   Were members satisfied with the decision?

APPENDIX 15

INDIVIDUAL MEMBER OBSERVATION SHEET

In addition to observing overall group behavior, you may wish to observe the behavior of one or more individuals in the group. If so, here are some things to look for:

Participation (frequency, quality)

Support giving (encouraging, praising, inviting others to comment)

Undesirable behavior (arguing; using sarcasm, putdowns, inappropriate humor)

Assumption of leadership roles (helpful—defining the problem, summarizing, checking for consensus; nonhelpful—dominating, bulldozing, monopolizing the available air time)

Listening (as opposed to interrupting, daydreaming, faking listening)

Sensitivity to other members' views, concerns, feelings, values

Use of nonverbal behavior (body language such as withdrawal, showing interest, smiling, head bobbing, tensing up, flushing, winking at another participant)

APPENDIX 16

Workshop Activities	Course's Stated Learnings (Objectives)	Learnings for Me	Possible Action Plan
A.M.			
1.			
2.			
3.			
4.			
5.			
P.M.			
1.			
2.			
3.			
4.			
5.			

APPENDIX   17

HIERARCHY OF NEEDS

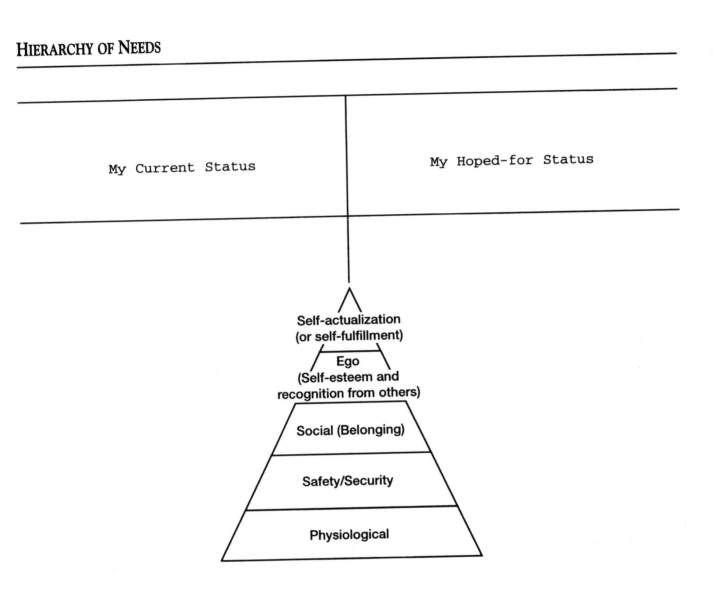

My Current Status   My Hoped-for Status

Self-actualization
(or self-fulfillment)

Ego
(Self-esteem and
recognition from others)

Social (Belonging)

Safety/Security

Physiological

APPENDIX 18

GUIDE SHEET TO PLAN FOR THE INTERVIEW

1. I am about to meet with _____.

2. The main issues or problems to be resolved are

   a.

   b.

   c.

   d.

3. I see _____ as the kind of person who (consider his/her personality, skills, accomplishments, etc.)

4. My past relations with _____ have been

5. My specific goals for the interview are

   a.

   b.

   c.

6. I plan to use the following strategy in the interview:

7. A possible alternate or backup strategy is

APPENDIX   19

GUIDE SHEET FOR THE OBSERVER

1. Strategy used by (cite name) _____.

    Effectiveness of the strategy

1	2	3	4	5	6	7
Lo						Hi

    Basis for my rating:

2. Strategy used by (cite name) _____.

    Effectiveness of the strategy

1	2	3	4	5	6	7
Lo						Hi

    Basis for my rating:

3. Was any agreement reached?   YES_____   NO_____

    Explain your answer:

APPENDIX 19 Continued

4. As I saw the interview

Role Player	Strong Points (Effective Behaviors)	Behaviors That Could Be Strengthened
A.		
B.		

5. Circle the word below that describes the character of the relationships that should exist after the interview:

Worse   Unchanged   Stronger

Explain the basis for your answer:

APPENDIX 20

CHECK SHEET FOR THE OBSERVER

ELEMENT	NO	YES	NOT SURE
1. Did the supervisor attempt to put the subordinate at ease?			
2. Did the supervisor show interest in the subordinate?			
3. Did the supervisor define the problem (objective of the interview)?			
4. Did the supervisor provide specific examples of the problem?			
5. Did the supervisor listen to the subordinate?			
6. Did the supervisor attempt to learn about causes of the problem?			
7. Was there a mutual problem-solving rather than blaming approach?			
8. Did the supervisor use questions rather than rely upon flat assertions?			
9. Did the supervisor propose an action plan?			
10. Was an action plan agreed upon?			
11. Will relations between the two parties be stronger?			

APPENDIX 21

ACTIVE LISTENING—A RATING SCALE

As you watch the role play, rate the customer relations person (or supervisor, teacher, parent, etc.) concerning his/her use of active listening techniques. Note: Active listening is an effective way to help others to clarify their thinking and thus to start them on the road to resolving their own problems, difficulties, and concerns.

1. Use of body posture (for example, leaning forward) and eye contact to show interest.

```
        1      2      3      4      5      6      7
    Ineffective                            Highly effective
```

2. Use of encouraging words (for example, uh huh, yeah or yes) and head nods.

```
        1      2      3      4      5      6      7
    Ineffective                            Highly effective
```

3. Use of inviting, open-ended questions.

```
        1      2      3      4      5      6      7
    Ineffective                            Highly effective
```

4. Restatement of what was said to show real listening and understanding.

```
        1      2      3      4      5      6      7
    Ineffective                            Highly effective
```

5. Checking to clarify what was said.

```
        1      2      3      4      5      6      7
    Ineffective                            Highly effective
```

6. Summing up at appropriate points what was said.

```
        1      2      3      4      5      6      7
    Poorly done                            Skillfully done
```

APPENDIX   22

GUIDE SHEET FOR SELF-CRITIQUE OF THE INTERVIEW

1. My primary objective in the interview was

2. I would characterize the interview as (circle one word or phrase):

   Highly successful   Successful   Partially successful

   Indeterminate   Unsuccessful

   The reasons for this circumstance are

3. The things that I did well in the interview were

   a.

   b.

   c.

   d.

   e.

4. The interview would have been more effective had I

   a.

   b.

   c.

   d.

   e.

5. I anticipate that future relations with the other person, as a result
   of the interview, will be (circle one item):

   Stronger   Weaker   About the same

APPENDIX 23

CONTRACT FOR WORK IMPROVEMENT

My Key Tasks/Responsibilities (List 6-8)	Possible delegation 1. Enter names of staff. 2. Check tasks appropriately.				Comments (for example, training or controls to be provided)
1.					
2.					
3.					
4.					
5.					
6.					
7.					
8.					

APPENDIX 24

MY STYLE AS A MANAGER

Instructions to Trainer

Have participants complete the following quiz and then assign them to groups of three or four to discuss their results.

Most participants will probably recognize that a pattern emerges from the quiz: that is, certain answers define one as "Theory X" and others as "Theory Y." If you wish to provide participants with a score card, you can give them the following data:

Theory X: Items 1a; 2a; 3b; 4a; 5b; 6b; 7a; 8b; 9b; 10b; 11a; 12b; 13a; 14a; 15a; 16a; 17b

Theory Y: The opposite of the above

Rather than cite a numerical score as to what constitutes Theory X or Y, suggest that participants look for tendencies—that is, whether they are mostly X or mostly Y. If someone is in the middle, it would seem to indicate that a clear-cut management philosophy has not as yet developed.

Note: Some individuals may complain about the forced-choice format. All you can do is agree that, yes, it is hard to choose in certain cases. But that is the purpose of this format—to force one to declare oneself by choosing between two possible alternatives.

It may be desirable to make the perhaps obvious point that the quiz indicates one's philosophy of management. It does not necessarily reflect one's on-the-job behavior. In our culture Theory Y behavior is widely espoused; its practice is not as widespread. Hence, considerable self-deception may be at work here.

APPENDIX 24 Continued

MY STYLE AS A MANAGER

Quiz

For each of the 16 paired statements below, select the one item in each pair that best fits with your attitudes and philosophy of management. There are no right or wrong answers, so just choose the ones that make the most sense to you. In some cases it may be a bit difficult to make a choice. If so, just pick the one item of the two that is more acceptable to you.

You will have a chance to discuss your answers with other participants in this program.

1. a. All of us have our limitations due to heredity, background, experience, age.

   b. People are in a constant state of becoming; they are continually growing, learning, adapting.

2. a. For most people the big motivators on the job are money and status.

   b. I see people as motivated by many work satisfactions: pride in accomplishment, a sense of contribution, new challenges, a worthwhile association, and the like.

3. a. It is important to me to supervise my employees so that there is a strong bond of openness and trust among us.

   b. I believe it is essential to supervise my employees so that the usual manager-subordinate relationship is properly maintained.

4. a. I expect people who work for me to exhibit the fullest degree of loyalty. This is something every employee owes his/her employer.

   b. I expect people who work for me to have full opportunities for the exercise of their creativity. If they receive this opportunity, I don't need to worry about their loyalty.

5. a. My job as a manager is to encourage subordinates to develop goals to which they can fully commit themselves.

   b. As a manager, my job is to establish goals that are clear cut so that there are no misunderstandings about what, when, and how much is expected.

6. a. I find that people prefer work assignments that keep them alert, growing, and challenged.

   b. I find that people prefer work assignments that have clear-cut limits and do not make too great demands on their capabilities.

7. a. The job of a manager is to so manage that mistakes and errors are kept to a bare minimum.

   b. The job of a manager is to encourage maximum freedom in the performance of one's tasks.

APPENDIX 24 Continued

8. a. I see employees and managers alike as people who have the potential to create and contribute for the betterment of the organization.

   b. I find that much of the drive and creativity in an organization comes from its managerial group.

9. a. I find that people respond positively to praise and recognition. Hence I am liberal in granting it.

   b. One can go overboard in praising people, for it can all too easily be misunderstood and backfire.

10. a. I find that people in organizations are seeking opportunities for self-direction, prefer limited guidelines, and wish for real opportunities to participate in decisions whenever they can.

    b. I see people in organizations as quite content to follow directions from capable leaders who assume responsibility for results.

11. a. I believe it is important to select capable people, to expect a full day's work for a full day's pay, and to treat your employees in a firm and fair way.

    b. I see myself as a person who is responsible for tapping potential and unleashing creativity in all my subordinates.

12. a. People require the fullest possible communication to carry out their jobs and to feel they are part of the team.

    b. Information is a tool and a resource for the manager. To over-do its dissemination is the mark of a weak manager.

13. a. My job as a manager is to prescribe duties and responsibilities clearly and fully.

    b. I prefer to assign tasks in a general way so that my employees have considerable leeway in carrying out their assignments.

14. a. The best motivators are firm and fair treatment, adequate pay, and clear-cut rules about discipline.

    b. The best motivators are praise, close relationships, and constantly challenging assignments.

15. a. People who work for me know where they stand in the way of assignments, pay, and promotion.

    b. People who work for me expect to be "turned on" by freedom in executing their assignments.

16. a. The job for any manager is to supervise so that employees' natural resistance to change is overcome.

    b. I see employees welcoming change provided that they have been involved in initiating that change.

17. a. I find that it is far more desirable to comment on tasks that are done well than to call attention to mistakes.

    b. I believe that it is essential to call attention to errors, even small ones, lest these mistakes turn into ingrained habits.

APPENDIX 25

CHECK YOUR I.Q. (IMAGINATION QUOTIENT)

Interpret the following:

1. | SAND |

2. MAN
   ‾‾‾‾‾‾
   BOARD

3. STAND
   ‾‾‾‾‾‾
   I

4. | R | E | A | D | I | N | G |

5. WEAR
   ‾‾‾‾‾‾
   LONG

6. R
   ROAD
   A
   D

7. CYCLE
   CYCLE
   CYCLE

8. T
   O
   W
   N

9. LE   VEL

10. KNEE
    LIGHT

11. DEATH/LIFE

12. ECNALG

13. 0
    ‾‾‾‾‾‾
    M.D.
    Ph.D.
    D.D.S.

14. ii   ii
    O   O

15. DICE
    DICE

    CHAIR

16.

17. T
    O
    U
    C
    H

18. GROUND
    ‾‾‾‾‾‾
    FEET
    FEET
    FEET
    FEET
    FEET
    FEET

19. MIND
    ‾‾‾‾‾‾
    MATTER

20. HE'S/HIMSELF

21. GEGS
    GGSE
    EGSG

22. ʞ ı ɔ ʞ

Source: Unknown

APPENDIX 25 Continued

Answer Sheet

1. Sandbox

2. Man overboard

3. I understand

4. Reading between the lines

5. Long underwear

6. Crossroads

7. Tricycle

8. Downtown

9. Split level

10. Neon light

11. Life after death

12. Backward glance

13. Three degrees below zero

14. Circles under the eyes

15. Paradise (pair of dice)

16. High chair

17. Touchdown

18. Six feet underground

19. Mind over matter

20. He's beside himself

21. Scrambled eggs

22. Onside kick (as in football)

APPENDIX 26

ICEBREAKER

Complete the statements below and then discuss them with a partner, preferably someone you do not know very well or at all.

1. My favorite flower is _____.

2. The best movie I've ever seen is _____.

3. My favorite soft drink is _____.

4. My favorite alcoholic beverage is _____.

5. My favorite entree is _____.

6. The sport I like best is _____.

7. The best President we have ever had is _____.

8. The musical instrument I enjoy the most is _____.

9. The TV program I really like is _____.

10. My favorite U.S. corporation is _____.

11. My favorite government agency is _____.

12. For a real vacation, the place to go is _____.

13. The most appealing feminine first name is _____.

14. The masculine first name I most prefer is _____.

15. If I could choose any pet, I would have a _____.

APPENDIX 27

SELLING AN IDEA TO THE BOSS

A Self Test

		YES	NO
1.	I try to prepare the ground in advance of presenting a formal or full-blown proposal.	☐	☐
2.	I do my homework properly—I get the facts, present alternatives, show pros and cons of each alternative, etc.	☐	☐
3.	As part of my preparation I conduct a "dry run" on someone else—a subordinate, a colleague, my spouse—who serves as a tough devil's advocate.	☐	☐
4.	I pay attention to the boss's schedule. I try to see him/her when I know there won't be an obligation to hurry.	☐	☐
5.	I pay attention to timing. I present the idea when it fits in with the concerns of the organization and/or the boss.	☐	☐
6.	I try to involve the boss in the presentation so that there is two-way communication.	☐	☐
7.	I use graphics, visual aids, etc. wherever I can because people respond better to a formal presentation and something they can see.	☐	☐
8.	I consider the boss' view. I know the boss' interests, values, and orientation, and I start from there.	☐	☐
9.	I try to stress "what's in it for him" as opposed to presenting the boss with an idea in the abstract.	☐	☐
10.	I try to tie in my proposal to on-going programs and past successes so that there is a comfortable link with the past.	☐	☐
11.	I try to make clear what the risks and what the chances of success are.	☐	☐
12.	I anticipate possible objections or doubts and am prepared to respond to them.	☐	☐
13.	I am prepared to respond to the possible question of "who else is doing (or using) this?"	☐	☐
14.	I avoid putting my boss on the defensive or making him/her lose face or causing him/her to appear poorly informed, unrealistic, or overly conservative.	☐	☐

APPENDIX 27 Continued

	YES	NO
15. I avoid arguing or debating. I avoid giving the impression that I alone have the right answer or most of the available wisdom.	☐	☐
16. I present realistic end results and avoid exaggeration or overkill.	☐	☐
17. I try to make it clear how we will know if the plan or idea is successful and when we can anticipate results.	☐	☐
18. I increase the possibility of my boss' acceptance of the idea by including a trial or pilot run in the overall proposal.	☐	☐
19. I make sure that the boss, rather than myself, will get the credit for the proposal.	☐	☐
20. I prepare myself for rejection. While I strive for success, I can accept the fact that the boss may defer judgment or give an outright "no."	☐	☐

Scoring

Give yourself 5 points for each "YES" answer.

80 points and above: You go to the top of the class! You are very sensitive to your boss as a person and to his/her needs. You certainly know how to present an idea well.

70–80 points: You have a good working knowledge of what it takes to get an idea across.

60–70 points: You have a fair knowledge and set of skills in selling your boss on an idea.

Below 60 points: Don't be surprised if your efforts at selling an idea frequently backfire. Try to sharpen up your skills before your next proposal up the line.

APPENDIX   28

GIVING EMPLOYEES FEEDBACK

A Self Test

Respond to the items below with a "yes" or "no." Be as frank as you can. The quiz will give you a reading on your skill in and attitudes about one key area of communication—that of giving feedback to your employees.

		YES	NO
1.	Do you avoid giving employees feedback about their performance?	____	____
2.	Do you avoid giving employees negative feedback since employees often do not like to hear this?	____	____
3.	Do you try to give feedback about performance by comparing the employee with other employees?	____	____
4.	Do you avoid giving employees praise, since they are often embarrassed by it?	____	____
5.	Do you criticize the person rather than the action or the behavior?	____	____
6.	Do you give criticism on a number of items at one time?	____	____
7.	In giving feedback, do you ignore the employee's sensitivity or receptivity to it?	____	____
8.	Do you give feedback long after the incident (or behavior) has occurred rather than immediately?	____	____
9.	Do you feel it is more important to communicate your view than to listen to your subordinate's point of view?	____	____
10.	Is your purpose in giving feedback to prove that you are right as opposed to getting at causes for behavior?	____	____
11.	Do you tend to slip in a criticism between two layers of praise?	____	____
12.	Do you give feedback to subordinates when you are angry or upset?	____	____
13.	Does your feedback often involve sarcasm or put downs?	____	____
14.	After you give feedback, do you avoid checking for understanding, since people should get the message easily enough if they really want to?	____	____

APPENDIX 28 Continued

	YES	NO
15. Do you tend to interrupt your subordinates while they are responding to your feedback to them?	____	____
16. Do you give feedback to others without worrying too much about your future relationship with them?	____	____
17. Do you feel that it is more important to point out mistakes than it is to indicate how to correct them?	____	____
18. Do you feel it is more important to give feedback than to receive it?	____	____
19. Do you prefer to give feedback to employees in writing rather than orally?	____	____
20. Do you give criticism to employees in both public and private locations?	____	____

Scoring*

The above test items are designed to stimulate your thinking about this business of giving feedback to others. Now that you have discussed the quiz with your fellow participants, you undoubtedly have a better idea about the topic in general and your own needs for improvement in particular.

The preferred response to all quiz items is "NO." Accordingly, give yourself five points for every "YES" answer. You can use the following table as your guide to your skill as a giver of feedback.

20 points and below: Your understanding of and skill in giving feedback is very good.

20-30 points: You have a satisfactory ability to give feedback.

30-40 points: You have a fair ability to give feedback.

Above 40 points: You are probably in very deep water. Develop some new skills before you go back in.

You may want to give scoring information after participants have discussed the quiz items with their fellow participants.

APPENDIX 29

MY TIME MANAGEMENT PRACTICES

Answer the questions below as candidly as you can. Your responses will give you a profile concerning your use of time.

		YES	NO
1.	I start each day with a daily set of goals.	☐	☐
2.	I set aside a solid block of uninterrupted time each day for accomplishment of tasks.	☐	☐
3.	I regularly review (every three to six months) the authority delegated to my staff.	☐	☐
4.	I rarely take work home evenings or weekends.	☐	☐
5.	I use my secretary fully so that we are a two-person team.	☐	☐
6.	I find it difficult to make the meetings I conduct efficient.	☐	☐
7.	My current telephone habits are a significant cause of wasted time.	☐	☐
8.	I find it somewhat difficult to prevent interruptions from taking place.	☐	☐
9.	I would be a more efficient manager if I learned to say no.	☐	☐
10.	One phrase that describes my work situation is "being on a treadmill."	☐	☐

Scoring

a. Give yourself 2 points for all the answers in the first five   _____
   items you answered with a "NO."

b. Give yourself 2 points for all the answers in the second five   _____
   items you answered with a "YES."

c. Your total point score is   _____

14 points and above: Your time management practices are in need of a major overhaul.

8-12 points: Your management of time is only fair.

Below 8 points: Your time management practices are very good; you should have little difficulty in overcoming the few shortcomings you now have.

APPENDIX 29A

MY CQ (CREATIVITY QUOTIENT)

Please respond ("YES" or "NO") to the 15 self-test items in the "TODAY" (left) columns. Try to be as introspective and candid as you can. You will have a chance to discuss your response with your fellow participants. The second set of yes/no columns is for your review (self-assessment) <u>three months from now</u>.

	TODAY		IN 90 DAYS	
	Yes	No	Yes	No
1. When my staff and I are working on a problem, do we systematically separate <u>idea generation</u> from <u>idea evaluation</u> (deferred judgment)?	☐	☐	☐	☐
2. When working on a problem, do I encourage my staff to seek as many alternative solutions as possible?	☐	☐	☐	☐
3. Do I operate my unit so that fun, playfulness, joy, excitement, free-wheeling are part of what we do?	☐	☐	☐	☐
4. Do I use delegation as a tool to empower my staff, encourage risk taking, and ignite innovative and creative behavior?	☐	☐	☐	☐
5. Do I let my people try things out rather than prescribe detailed procedures to execute the task/job/operation?	☐	☐	☐	☐
6. Do I encourage my staff to present new ideas, even some that may be "off the wall"?	☐	☐	☐	☐
7. When my staffers present "far out" ideas, do I listen to them attentively?	☐	☐	☐	☐
8. Do I encourage my people to short-circuit or modify standards/procedures/rules to help get things done more expeditiously?	☐	☐	☐	☐
9. Do I praise generously those who take risks and perform in creative (non-traditional) ways?	☐	☐	☐	☐
10. Do I encourage disagreements/differences to emerge at our meetings?	☐	☐	☐	☐
11. At the performance review time, do I include risk taking as an element for discussion?	☐	☐	☐	☐
12. Do I take it in stride when a staffer questions or challenges one of my ideas/approaches?	☐	☐	☐	☐
13. Do I use intuition/hunches in problem solving?	☐	☐	☐	☐
14. Do I staff, in part, with those who might be called mavericks/iconoclasts/risk takers/dissenters/free spirits?	☐	☐	☐	☐
15. Do I push for new ideas with my bosses, even at some risk of irritating them?	☐	☐	☐	☐

SCORING PROCEDURE

Your "YES" responses on 12 or more quiz items indicates that you're well in tune with the creative process. You are to be commended. Keep up the creative good work! If you had 11 or fewer "YES" responses, you may wish to re-think your approach to innovation and creativity. You thus may wish to make some changes in your management style. If so, evaluate (rate) yourself again in 90 days, using the second set of "YES" and "NO" responses on this form.

Appendix 30

My Capabilities as a Delegator

A Self Test

This test is designed to help you assess your prowess as a delegator. Simply answer "yes" or "no" to all the questions. Please be as candid as you possibly can be. You will have a chance to discuss your responses with your fellow participants.

1. Do I avoid holding on to the tasks I like to do or feel comfortable with?

2. Do I avoid getting bogged down in "administrivia"?

3. Do I avoid taking work home regularly?

4. Do I so manage that I avoid being constantly on a "treadmill"?

5. Do I avoid falling in the trap of letting my subordinates delegate "in reverse," that is, to me?

6. Do I avoid tendencies to redo my subordinates' work to ensure that it is right?

7. Do I feel it is unimportant to convey the image that I am a hard, tireless worker?

8. Have I ever analyzed my job so that I really know how, where, and on what I am spending my time?

9. Do I really know how I should be spending my time?

10. Am I actually spending my time as I, as a manager, should be?

11. Do I recognize that delegating to others involves my living with uncertainty, even ambiguity?

12. When I delegate, do I specify how much authority the delegate has to do the job?

13. Do I tolerate a certain amount of error in the things my subordinates do as the price I have to pay for delegation?

14. Do my subordinates feel free to act within their delegated authority?

15. Do I see and use my secretary as part of a two-person team in order to get the job done easier?

16. Do I use delegation as a tool to "turn on" my people?

17. Do I see delegation as a means of helping my staff to grow, develop, and achieve higher self-esteem?

APPENDIX 30 Continued

18. Do I see delegation as a tool to force innovation, because if I allow my subordinates to do something, the odds are that they will do it differently than I would have?

19. Do I have a workable or reasonable number of people who report to me, so that I am not suffering from supervisory overload?

20. Do I use controls to monitor delegated authority, that is, to spot problems before they develop?

Scoring

To assess your delegation prowess, give yourself five points for every "yes" response.

Above 80: You are a top-notch delegator. (I and many others would like to work for you!)

70-80: You are now doing an adequate job of delegation. (With a little more thought and effort you could be in Group 1!)

60-70: Your delegation capability is only fair. (Some added work on it is quite desirable.)

Under 60: Look out! Your delegation philosophies and practices have probably caught up with you. (But you now know what is needed to improve.)

APPENDIX 31

MY SKILL AS A LISTENER

A Short Quiz

Listed below are 15 statements that relate to one's ability to listen to others. Rate each item by placing a mark in the appropriate box. Try to be as candid as you can in making your rating.

When you have rated all the items, take a straight edge and draw lines to connect the dots. This will give you a profile of your capabilities as a listener. Obviously the more your profile leans toward the right, the more capable a listener you are.

Element	Never	Seldom	Occasionally	Frequently	Always
1. Do I listen for feelings, attitudes, perceptions, and values as well as for facts?					
2. Do I try to listen for what is not said?					
3. Do I avoid interrupting the person who is speaking to me?					
4. Do I actually pay attention to who is speaking as opposed to faking attention?					
5. Do I refrain from tuning people out because I don't like them, disagree with them, find them dull, etc.?					
6. Do I work hard to avoid being distracted from what is said by the speaker's style, mannerisms, clothing, voice quality, or voice pace?					
7. Do I make certain that a person's status has no bearing on how well I listen to him/her?					
8. Do I avoid letting my expectations—hearing what I want to hear—determine or influence my listening behavior?					

APPENDIX 31 Continued

Element	Never	Seldom	Occasionally	Frequently	Always
9. Do I try to read the "nonverbals" the speaker presents—inflections, gestures, mood, posture, eye contact, and facial expression?					
10. Do I work hard at overcoming distractions (sounds, noises, movement, outside scenes) that may interfere with good listening?					
11. Do I tend to stay with speakers who may be hard to follow—those who are slow in their speech or whose ideas are poorly organized or who tend to repeat themselves?					
12. As a listener do I use nonverbal communication (eye contact, smiles, occasional head nods) to indicate that I wish to hear more?					
13. Do I tend to restate or rephrase the other person's statements when necessary so that he/she will know that I understood?					
14. If I have not understood, do I candidly admit to this and ask for a restatement?					
15. Do I avoid framing my response to what is being said while the other person is still speaking?					

APPENDIX 32

MY C.S.Q. (CUSTOMER SERVICE QUOTIENT)

The 15 statements below relate to working with and providing service to customers. Rate yourself on each item, using the following scale: Often—5; Sometimes—3; Rarely—1; Never—0.

_____ 1. I try to learn all I can about our products (or services) so that I can really help our customers.

_____ 2. I try to size up the customer so that I can get on the customer's wave length.

_____ 3. My philosophy of customer contacts is that the "customer always comes first."

_____ 4. If I can't answer a customer's question, I try to get help from another employee or my supervisor.

_____ 5. I really try to be friendly and courteous toward all customers.

_____ 6. I respect the customer's need to take enough time to make a sound decision.

_____ 7. I am willing to work with a customer past my quitting time, if necessary.

_____ 8. I avoid showing irritation with customers, no matter what.

_____ 9. I work hard at producing repeat business from customers.

_____10. Customers see me as a person with whom they like to do business.

_____11. I always speak highly of our products (or services).

_____12. I avoid saying negative things about our competitors.

_____13. I will refer a customer to a competitor if we don't have the right product.

_____14. I avoid chit-chatting with other employees in the presence of customers.

_____15. I willingly help my fellow employees as may be necessary.

Scoring

Scores can range from 75 points to zero. If you are very close to 75, you are a top-notch, professional, customer-service person. Your organization is fortunate to have you on its staff! If you are somewhere in the middle range, you should go over the quiz again and see where you can profit from personal improvement. Should your point score be on the low end, you'll want to do a lot of introspection or soul-searching about your current behavior. Try to bring about some real changes before your bosses have a go at it first!

Note to trainer: After the group has processed the data in trios, you may wish to ask participants to call out their scores, enter them on a flipchart, and secure a group average.

APPENDIX   33

MY SKILL AS A LISTENER

A Self Test

For each of the 25 statements below, circle the number which best describes your perception of your skill as a listener: 1 = never or almost never; 2 = seldom or rarely; 3 = sometimes or occasionally; 4 = usually or most of the time; 5 = always or almost always. Try to be as candid as you can. In this way you will learn of your true skill and what added work/goals may be needed in order to upgrade your listening effectiveness.

1. I listen for the actual message, not just to the words
    presented to me.   1   2   3   4   5

2. When listening to someone, I try to distinguish between
    facts and judgments, opinions, assumptions, or perceptions. 1 2   3   4   5

3. I try to listen for the feeling which is expressed as well
    as to the message itself.   1   2   3   4   5

4. I listen for the tone of voice as an aid to understanding
    the message more fully.   1   2   3   4   5

5. I observe body language (position, tenseness, facial
    expression, movements) as an aid to understanding the
    sender's message more fully.   1   2   3   4   5

6. When listening to someone, I try to "get into his/her
    shoes" to ensure that I understand his/her frame of
    reference, value or belief system, or world view.   1   2   3   4   5

7. I try to minimize the impact of my own expectations about
    the message; I try to avoid hearing what I expect, need
    or want to hear.   1   2   3   4   5

8. I try to listen with my "third ear"—for example, to what
    is not said as well as to what is said.   1   2   3   4   5

9. When I am in doubt about the significance of a message, I
    restate or summarize it so that both I and the message
    sender can check my understanding of it.   1   2   3   4   5

10. I try to keep in mind that words may have more than one
    meaning; hence the need to check with the sender to ensure
    that I understood what was meant, not just what was said. 1   2   3   4   5

11. When I listen, I may ask relevant questions to aid my
    understanding and/or to show my interest.   1   2   3   4   5

12. When I listen to someone in a location which may have
    distractions (noise, movement of people or objects, low or
    high temperature), I try all the harder to concentrate on
    the speaker's message.   1   2   3   4   5

APPENDIX 33 Continued

13. I try to be an active listener—I use eye contact, head nods, smiles, "uh-huhs," relevant comments or restatements, and positive body posture such as leaning forward.   1 2 3 4 5

14. I recognize that time pressures may limit my listening capability; therefore, I act appropriately to prevent listening distractions.   1 2 3 4 5

15. I listen patiently and empathically to an angry or frustrated person to permit ventilation of feelings. I thus recognize the need to treat the emotion before I can work effectively on the problem.   1 2 3 4 5

16. I recognize that my own values, beliefs, perceptions, and feelings may cloud the message I am trying to receive.   1 2 3 4 5

17. I avoid making judgments about the speaker, particularly when he/she is presenting ideas I may not favor.   1 2 3 4 5

18. When I listen I avoid listening traps such as letting myself be turned off by the speaker's delivery, voice quality, dress, physical appearance, pace or energy level, name, affiliation, skin color, or sex.   1 2 3 4 5

19. I recognize that my receiving rate as listener may be three or four times greater than the rate at which the message is sent. I thus work at overcoming possible tune-out practices such as daydreaming, unrelated thinking, or preparing a response to what is said.   1 2 3 4 5

20. When I listen to someone at my desk, I avoid doodling; signing, reviewing or shuffling papers; making notes on unrelated matters, etc.   1 2 3 4 5

21. I avoid interrupting a speaker at all costs.   1 2 3 4 5

22. I avoid faking interest in or understanding of the other person's message.   1 2 3 4 5

23. I am conscious of and try to minimize the impact of my own emotional state (expectations, needs, attitudes, values, preferences, prejudices, motivations) when I receive messages, for it may influence what I hear.   1 2 3 4 5

24. I recognize that by fully listening to people, I help them meet certain basic needs—namely, to feel important and to feel good about themselves.   1 2 3 4 5

25. When listening to someone, I am aware that my own body language may be communicating messages to the message sender, for example, interest/disinterest, agreement/disagreement, or like/dislike of the other person.   1 2 3 4 5

APPENDIX 33 Continued

Scoring

1. Tally your responses according to the number you assigned to them. Enter your totals below:

```
        1's.... x 1 = ....
        2's.... x 2 = ....
        3's.... x 3 = ....
        4's.... x 4 = ....
        5's.... x 5 = ....
            Grand Total ....
```

2. Multiply each total by the weight provided on each line.

3. Add your scores on each line to arrive at a summary score (grand total).

Your score can range from a high of 125 to a low of 25. If your point total is at or near 125, you probably have the potential to function in an occupation where a high premium is placed on listening—as a counselor, personnel interviewer, social worker, psychiatrist, bartender, etc. If you scored somewhere in the 25 to 75 range, you're probably in trouble in many or most of your interactions with others. A score of around 100 would indicate that you're a pretty good listener.

In any case, you now know where you stand. Use this rating form as a guide to strengthening your listening skills.

Note: As an aid to upgrading your listening skill, you may wish to check your self-ratings with others who know you well—your spouse, boss, colleagues, friends, subordinates. The employee check is a particularly helpful one. However, a trusting relationship must exist before candid feedback will be given to you.

APPENDIX   34

AS I SEE MYSELF

1. When people talk about high achievers, I would say that I

2. What I do best in my work is

3. What I would like to do better in my work is

4. Back home on the job people see me as

5. My greatest skill as a manager (or supervisor) is

6. My greatest need as a manager (or supervisor) is

7. When I get angry I

8. When I make a mistake I

9. I feel most alone when

10. What I expect of other people is that

11. What I feel most disappointed about in life is

APPENDIX 34 Continued

12. What I feel most disappointed about in my job is

13. What I feel most disappointed about in my boss is

14. After an argument with another person I usually

15. In respect to leveling or being candid with others I

16. My reaction to my given name is

17. As a group member I generally

18. At cocktail parties I

19. What bothers me the most about the way the world seems to be going is

20. The feelings (emotions) I can express most easily are

21. The feelings (emotions) I find difficult to express are

22. If I could have anything in the world that I wanted I

APPENDIX 35

MANAGEMENT DEVELOPMENT—OPENERS

A management development seminar causes us to think (or perhaps rethink) about our jobs, our careers, ourselves, our values, our organization. The statements below, which you are to complete, should help you to get started on this. Try to be as candid as you can in making your responses. After you have completed this form, find a partner with whom to share your answers.

1. My biggest achievement in my career has been

2. If I could redo one aspect of my career I would

3. If I had to state what the two most important things about leadership are, I would say

4. My greatest satisfaction in my job is

5. My biggest irritation in my job is

6. If my boss could change me he/she would

7. If my subordinates could change me they would

8. If I could change my organization I would

9. If I had the power to change myself I would

APPENDIX   36

AS I SEE THE COACHING PROCESS

Complete the following statements as you see them. There are obviously no right or wrong answers. You will have an opportunity to discuss your responses with a colleague.

1. What is most important to me about communication is

2. What I find most difficult in the area of motivation is

3. What I find troublesome in the delegation process is

4. What I find most troublesome in the decision-making process is

5. The easiest part of the decision-making process for me is

6. In introducing change I find that

7. My feelings about helping subordinates grow and develop are

8. The best way to unleash creativity in my subordinates is by

9. To have a truly effective management team, one's subordinates must

10. To have a truly effective management team, the team leader must

11. My feelings about loyalty of staff are

12. My feelings about giving praise to subordinates are

13. When I receive praise I generally feel
    and respond by saying

14. My feelings about giving subordinates support are

15. The one thing that separates effective from less-than-effective coaches is

APPENDIX 37

AS I SEE YOU

1. You seem to be the kind of person who

2. When we first met what I liked about you was

3. When we first met what I was unsure of about you was

4. A contribution you have made in this program is

5. I see you as a person who could

6. As a two-person team I could see our strengths as

7. As a two-person team what I would not be sure of is

8. I you were my boss, I

9. If you worked for me, I

10. If you and I were colleagues, we

11. What I am not sure we could talk about freely is

12. On a 100-point scale, I would rate our "simpatico" as _____ because

APPENDIX   38

MY APPROACH TO PROBLEM SOLVING

Ten problems are presented below, each having seven possible solutions. For each problem select the one best solution, as you see it. You will have a chance to discuss your solutions with your fellow participants.

Problem 1.   Tom, a member of your staff, is an average performer. He is neither poor nor outstanding—just adequate. A recent problem with Tom is that he is typically tardy to your Wednesday 11 A.M. staff meetings. Tom is not that big a contributor to these meetings, but his lateness doesn't seem appropriate.

A.   Lay it on the line. Simply remind Tom when he arrives late that these meetings start promptly at 11 A.M.

B.   Treat it as a team problem. Take it up with the total group when other team problems are being discussed. Others may be as annoyed as you are.

C.   Not a big deal. He's probably seeking attention, so why worry about it? In time he'll probably come around.

D.   Change the meeting time to 8:30 A.M. when the workday starts. Since the organization is strict about the morning arrival time, this should force Tom's prompt attendance to the meeting.

E.   While talking to Tom on other business, close the conversation with this statement, "Oh, by the way, Tom, I know you're busy and get wrapped up in things, but could you please try to make our next staff meeting on time? Thanks."

F.   Whenever Tom does arrive on time or close to 11 A.M., compliment him (after the meeting) for his efforts to attend promptly.

G.   Point out to Tom how his lateness hurts group creativity: "Tom, we need your good thinking on our problem solving. If you are late, we are deprived of your helpful input."

Problem 2.   You have seven section supervisors who report to you. Each is in charge of a group of young women who operate sewing machines. One supervisor, Williams, has been having considerable trouble with his people—you are not only getting complaints about his lack of tact, but you find that absenteeism, quits, waste, and rejects are all high in his section. Some of these productivity problems exist in the other sections, too, but to a relatively minor degree. All sections do the same work and have the same layout, except that Williams' area is much more crowded so that Williams doesn't have a separate office as the others do.

APPENDIX 38 Continued

A. Try to counsel your supervisor—ask him to show more consideration to the young women.

B. Invent a reason for a reassignment and move Williams to a staff job where he won't have as much contact with people.

C. Talk to him about his problem and then compliment him whenever you see or learn of his handling someone in the proper way.

D. Tell Williams what you expect in the way of standards. Either he gets his "indicators" (absenteeism, waste, etc.) up, or you will have to take some direct action.

E. Discuss these productivity and human relations problems with all your section chiefs to see if some practical solutions can be arrived at.

F. You decide not to move too precipitously. After all, only one of seven supervisors is a problem, and your outfit overall is doing O.K.

G. You decide to reassign some of Williams' employees to the other sections, take some machines out, and build a small office for Williams on the shop floor.

Problem 3. You are in charge of a factory that assembles electrical appliances for the kitchen. In the last three months there has been a noticeable drop in quality and productivity.

A. Since this is the first bad quarter in the last seven, you decide to take a wait-and-see approach to this.

B. You decide to visit more often with people on the floor and ask them about things they like to be asked about—the kids, the garden, their bowling scores. The friendly touch never hurt anyone.

C. You decide to work on some changes in the system—better lighting, new soldering guns, and giving each worker full responsibility for assembling a given unit of equipment.

D. You decide to set up several quality circles—these are special units of employees to identify productivity and quality problems and to make recommendations to management about them.

E. You meet with your foremen to find out what people-type problems they might be having and what can be done about them. You are afraid that indifferent or overly demanding supervision might not be getting the employee cooperation you need.

F. You tell your foremen very clearly that production and quality are their responsibilities and you expect results—and "no ifs ands or buts about it."

G. You very clearly and fully grant praise to your supervisors and to employees, too, whenever a job is well done, a quota is met, etc.

APPENDIX 38 Continued

Problem 4. You are the supervisor of a large warehouse that has a pipe protruding up from the floor. It's a pretty obvious pipe, although occasionally someone does trip over it. They do this absentmindedly or when they are in a hurry.

A. You give people praise when you see them walk carefully over the pipe.

B. You regularly issue reminders to all concerned about the pipe. The reminders are especially strong after a tripping incident, and you always have several warning signs on the walls nearby.

C. Occasionally someone does complain about the pipe, but you always point out that it is a really big pipe, it is painted bright yellow, and mishaps are minor, few, and far between— really not a big deal.

D. You decide to have the building engineer build a platform, ramp-style, over the pipe.

E. You call your foremen together to discuss what might be done to be sure no serious accidents occur because of the big pipe.

F. You embark on an employee safety program including frequent changes of posters, reminder notices in pay envelopes, movies, etc. The program emphasizes safety in general and the pipe problem is mentioned quite often.

G. You decide to hold an employee safety slogan contest with a really big ceremony and cash prize for the best slogan as decided by the Safety Committee.

Problem 5. Your people leave their lights on in the storage room, tool room, etc. at close of business, despite repeated requests to help save energy.

A. You call everyone together and ask for ideas on saving energy.

B. You give your people strong statements on saving energy. This is done via a pep talk at a special group meeting, a memo, and a notice on the bulletin board.

C. You turn the lights out yourself as necessary; no point in hassling people about everything all the time.

D. You give employees regular feedback, in chart form, on energy use, costs, etc. You also compliment them on any improvement in costs.

E. You install automatic controls that shut off the lights in the rooms in question, five or ten minutes after quitting time.

F. You follow this procedure that you heard worked in another plant: You have your assistant turn out the unwanted lights and then send out "thank you" memos from time to time, praising people for their cooperation.

APPENDIX 38 Continued

G. You politely request cooperation whenever you come across a "guilty" party.

Problem 6. You are the superintendent of the warehouse. Employees from time to time lift improperly and end up with various back and groin injuries. You can't understand why these injuries occur, since all employees were trained in the proper lifting procedure six to eight months ago. You have six foremen who report to you.

A. Train your foremen in positive reinforcement procedures—that is, have them praise a worker anytime he/she lifts properly. But they are not to criticize poor lifting techniques at all.

B. Get an increase in budget for some new equipment to help out on lifting heavy items.

C. Have Personnel put a reminder notice about lifting in everyone's pay envelope every so often.

D. Whenever your foremen see a failure to lift properly, have them tell their employees in no uncertain terms to do it right. You also follow this course of action.

E. Call all your foremen together to discuss the problem and to come up with practical ways of dealing with it.

F. Instruct your foremen to request the cooperation of their employees in lifting properly and to remind workers that they could injure themselves.

G. Show a film on lifting that has some really gruesome scenes in it, showing the results of the failure to follow proper lifting procedures.

Problem 7. One of your subordinate supervisors has expressed concern about lax attention to proper dress standards. This is a large customer service office with regular personal contact between employees and the public.

A. You decide to call everyone concerned to a meeting to get full employee input concerning dress—What are the current standards? Do they best meet the needs of employees and customers? Can we draft a code that everyone will be willing to live with?

B. You believe all standards should be observed; on the other hand, there seem to be only a few of the younger employees who take advantage of the situation now and then. You will probably talk to them when you can get around to it.

C. You ask your assistant to write a memo to all employees on the problem. You ask him to cite a couple of complaints from the public that he presumably received over the phone. The complaints are not real, but they certainly could have occurred and, in any case, will make the office's concern clear.

APPENDIX 38 Continued

D. You ask your supervisors to compliment employees whenever they dress properly.

E. You call all your supervisors together and make it very clear what the dress standards are and what their responsibility is in this regard. You advise them that you expect to make spot inspections on this matter starting Monday.

F. You call a low-key meeting of all employees, give them a gentle reminder of dress standards and the vital reasons for them, and request their fullest cooperation.

G. You decide to inaugurate a program of company-supplied outfits (four in all), all in good taste, really chic-looking, and interchangeable so that considerable variety in dress is possible each day and for each person.

Problem 8. Your boss expects you to deal with a perennial employee relations problem—too much tardiness.

A. You call everyone together and tell them what the problem is, what the rules are, and what disciplinary action you intend to take for offenders.

B. You call everyone together, point out quietly that your boss has called this problem to your attention, and say you would like everyone to please cooperate so that no one will have to be put on the spot about this.

C. You issue the usual annual memo about tardiness, absenteeism, use of public telephones for private business, and the like.

D. You decide to work on the late-comers by complimenting them when they are early, on time, or even a minute or two late. You tell them you appreciate their efforts to get here on time. To those who are late five or ten minutes you express your appreciation for their efforts to get here because "all hands are really needed aboard."

E. You decide to recommend a system of "flex-time" to your boss.

F. You call everyone together to talk about the problem. Your aim is to see if the group can develop standards concerning arrival time that everyone—employees and management—can live with.

G. You decide to rearrange the location of your desk to near the windows so that you will be in a position to see who is coming into the parking lot and when, of course.

APPENDIX 38 Continued

Problem 9. You are the head of an office that has the constant need to protect various documents your employees work with. However, of late there are indications that a worrisome number of people are lax about security matters.

A. You feel breaches of security are too important a matter to be ignored, so you call everyone together and give them a warning—lax security will be a basis for dismissal, with no exceptions and no further warnings.

B. You ask the guard to double check all security safes and file cabinets every night.

C. You adopt a procedure of complimenting people who put classified documents into the safe during lunch and at night, as opposed to leaving them on their desks.

D. You decide to call all employees together to discuss the adequacy of current security procedures and to develop such plans for tighter security as may be indicated.

E. You beef up security by increasing lights outside and inside the building, tightening up procedures on the entry of nonemployees into the building, improving the system for the registration of classified documents, etc.

F. You call a meeting of all employees, compliment them generously on their adherance to all standards and procedures, thank them for their past cooperation on everything, and in the middle of the meeting give everyone a gentle nudge about the importance of security.

G. You call an employee meeting expressly for the purpose of reminding people about security procedures. There is no complaining, no finger-pointing, and no threats, just an appeal to everyone's mature and adult side. A short, friendly, and frank question and answer period is held, too.

Problem 10. You are head of the Operations Branch. You and various members of your staff are having difficulty getting the cooperation you require from the people in Finance. The Finance Branch is located in another building across town.

A. You take the head of the Finance Branch out to lunch with some frequency to really "butter her up."

B. You get the help of the Training Department to hold a confrontation session to help clear the air about difficulties—past and present.

C. Since your boss, a V.P., also supervises Finance, you go to him to get his help in getting Finance in line.

APPENDIX 38 Continued

D.   You call up the head of Finance whenever they do something cooperatively and compliment her and her staff on it.

E.   You let the matter ride, since these things generally right themselves in time.

F.   You work out a move, which is quite possible, to their building, because a lot of misunderstandings and mix-ups are a result of a lack of direct contact and communication.

G.   You start to work actively on improving interpersonal relations with the Finance people and request your staff to do the same.

Note to Trainer

After the participants have completed their individual work on the quiz (about 20–30 minutes) divide them into small groups (3–5) to discuss their solutions. Allow one hour for this. Then pass out the scoring sheet. After they complete the scoring, pass out the "Definition of Problem-Solving Styles" sheet. Then hold a general discussion of the exercise.

APPENDIX 38 Continued

Self-Scoring Sheet

For each of the ten items that composes the quiz, circle the letter that represents your choice as to the best course of action. Then add up the number of responses in each column.

Problem	T	BM	S/S	HR	D/D	M	T/LF
1	B	F	D	E	A	G	C
2	E	C	G	A	D	B	F
3	D	G	C	E	F	B	A
4	E	A	D	F	B	G	C
5	A	D	E	C	B	F	C
6	E	A	B	F	D	G	C
7	A	D	G	F	E	C	B
8	F	D	E	B	A	G	C
9	D	C	E	G	A	F	B
10	B	D	F	G	C	A	E
Column Totals							

After you have tallied each column, read the definitions that follow. They will interpret for you your tendency to choose one or more problem-solving styles in respect to problems involving people.

APPENDIX 38 Continued

Definition of Problem-Solving Styles

T   is your tendency to operate as a Team Leader. Thus, when problems seem to involve the team, you involve your staff in efforts at group problem solving and group decision making.

BM   is your tendency to use Behavior Modification procedures; that is, you provide sincere praise (positive reinforcement) on proper performance. You generally do not comment on below standard performance. Also, wherever possible you use a data collection approach to give people objective feedback on their performance. Talking with people about the problem may precede the giving of praise and/or data about performance.

S/S   is your tendency to approach problems in a Situational/Structural context; that is, you try to change the situation or system as opposed to attempting to influence people's behavior directly (for example, via various lectures, coaching, memos).

HR   is your tendency to use Human Relations approaches, which means you try to elicit cooperation by talking things over, being firm and fair, creating an adult atmosphere of mutual respect, etc. Your concern for people may exceed your concern for production, at times.

D/D   is your tendency to lay it on the line in a Direct/Directive way. No nonsense, no timidity, no hesitation, but "damn the torpedoes, full steam ahead" is your philosophy and way of acting on a problem. Firmness gets both respect and results.

M   is your tendency to get results through Manipulation of people. This is often a less-than-direct approach and at times even a bit less than honest. By outmaneuvering people or finessing the situation, you get results you want and avoid a lot of confrontation and complaints.

T/LF   is your tendency to be Tolerant/Laissez Faire of people and situations. You certainly don't want to confront people, and you believe in "letting sleeping dogs lie," since situations often work themselves out.

APPENDIX 39

FORCE FIELD ANALYSIS

INSTRUCTIONS FOR COMPLETION OF PROBLEM DIAGNOSIS

1. Think of a current problem, phenomenon, or difficulty that you would like to see changed, corrected or improved upon.

2. Enter the problem in the top box on the worksheet (diagnosis sheet).

3. On the right side of the diagnosis sheet, list all the forces at work that are preventing the change you desire from taking place. These are the restraining forces.

4. On the left side of the diagnosis sheet, enter all the forces at work that are pushing for the change you favor. These are the driving forces.

5. After you have completed the Force Field Analysis, assess the driving and restraining forces at work and complete the questions below.

   A. My change strategy is to

      ☐ Increase the driving forces

      ☐ Weaken the restraining forces

      ☐ Do both of the above

   B. Explain the rationale for your strategy.

   C. Explain how you will go about implementing your strategy.

APPENDIX 39 Continued

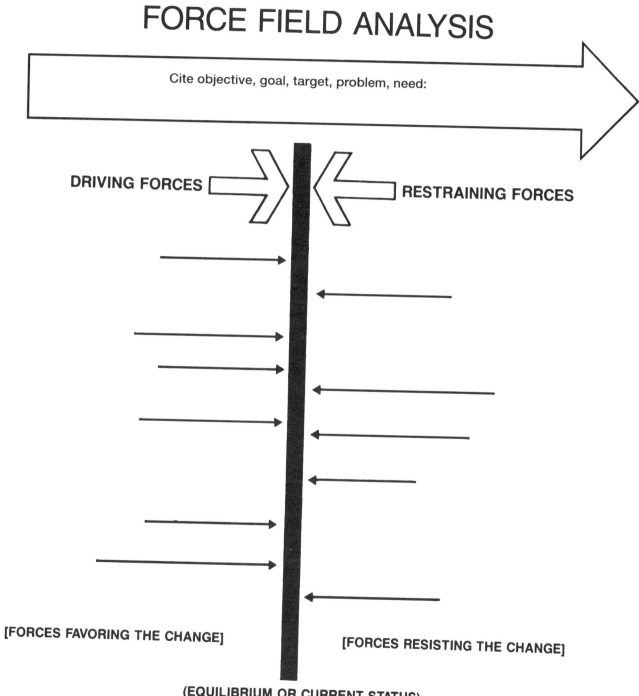

FORCE FIELD ANALYSIS

Cite objective, goal, target, problem, need:

DRIVING FORCES **RESTRAINING FORCES**

[FORCES FAVORING THE CHANGE] [FORCES RESISTING THE CHANGE]

(EQUILIBRIUM OR CURRENT STATUS)

APPENDIX   40

5-M ANALYSIS

Difficulty (problem, obstacle)	Manpower	Machinery	Methods	Materials	Money
1.					
2.					
3.					
4.					
5.					

APPENDIX 41

SOME WAYS OF LOOKING AT LEADERS AND LEADERSHIP

If a leader (or manager) were a

A. Politician, he/she would

B. Gardener, he/she would

C. Athletic coach, he/she would

D. Captain of a ship, he/she would

E. Newspaper publisher, he/she would

APPENDIX   42

ORGANIZATIONS—AN ANALYSIS WITH THE AID OF METAPHOR

Group 1: If an organization were a zoo, it would be like (or have these characteristics or consequences):*

Group 2: Think of an organization as a garden. What would its characteristics or consequences be?

Group 3: Think of an organization as a train. What would its characteristics or consequences be?

Group 4: If an organization were an orchestra, it would

Group 5: If an organization were a human body, it would

Group 6: If an organization were a community, it would

* The assignment could be given with greater specificity by stating the questions this way:
  If an organization were a zoo:
  The managers would _____. The employees would _____.
  The most common problems would probably be described as _____.

APPENDIX 42 Continued

Some Possible Answers to the Metaphor Questions

Zoo Metaphor

Sense of territoriality
Passive behavior
Compartmentalization—
  walls separate everyone
Sexual harrassment (!)
Bosses (the keepers) vs.
  workers (the animals)
Aged animals, past their
  prime, are kept on
No communication between
  groups (of animals)
Tangible rewards alone
  produce results
Short-term perspective

Train Metaphor

Survival problems
Off the track often
Late; slow freight
All going in one direc-
  tion toward a fixed
  goal
In need of modernization

Garden Metaphor

Test soil, prepare soil,
  seed it, nurture it
Get rid of weeds and bad
  plants
Symbiosis
Environment is the key
Seasonal emphasis

Community Metaphor

Gossip abounds
Pride (or conflict)
Order
The other side of the
  tracks
Hard up for cash

Orchestra Metaphor

One-man band
Be in harmony
March to same (or dif-
  ferent) drummer
Off key
Toot own horn
Beat its drum for _____
Out of tune with _____
Hearing the words but
  not the music
Hit a high note (or sour
  note)
Be up-beat

Human Body Metaphor

Eliminate waste
Avoid that tired feeling
  (or have it)
Flex its muscles
Hide its skeletons
Get gray, old, fat, and
  flabby
Keep lean
Be healthy
Need a regular check-up

Appendix 43

My Assessment of Group Functioning

1. My participation thus far has been:

1	2	3	4	5	6	7
(LO)						(HI)

2. The degree to which my ideas have been listened to is:

1	2	3	4	5	6	7
(LO)						(HI)

3. My role in the decisions we have made is:

1	2	3	4	5	6	7
(LO)						(HI)

4. The degree to which members are willing to be open is:

1	2	3	4	5	6	7
(LO)						(HI)

5. The degree to which members listen to one another is:

1	2	3	4	5	6	7
(LO)						(HI)

6. The degree to which the team/group is really working together is:

1	2	3	4	5	6	7
(LO)						(HI)

7. The degree to which we have faced up to our problems is:

1	2	3	4	5	6	7
(LO)						(HI)

8. The degree to which we are reaching our goals (our progress) is:

1	2	3	4	5	6	7
(LO)						(HI)

9. My satisfaction with my membership in this team is:

1	2	3	4	5	6	7
(LO)						(HI)

10. I predict the degree of group functioning as a team six months from now will be:

1	2	3	4	5	6	7
(LO)						(HI)

11. My satisfaction with the role of the facilitator in the group is:

1	2	3	4	5	6	7
(LO)						(HI)

APPENDIX 44

QUESTIONNAIRE—END OF DAY ONE

1. What did I not say today that I should have?

2. What did the group not discuss today that it should have?

APPENDIX 45

FORM FOR ROLE CLARIFICATION/NEGOTIATION

```
To:

From:

I need more of:
```

```
I need less of:
```

```
I need the same of:
```

APPENDIX 46

A RATING SCALE TO ASSESS TEAMNESS

Criteria	Strongly Agree 5	Agree 4	Undecided 3	Disagree 2	Strongly Disagree 1
1. Cooperation: "Team members work well together."					
2. Communication: "Our ability to give and receive necessary information is one of our strengths."					
3. Goals: "Goal setting is truly a team activity."					
4. Creativity: "Innovation is encouraged and rewarded."					
5. Conflict: "Disagreements are faced up to and fully worked through."					
6. Support: "Praise and recognition are given enthusiastically."					
7. Mutual respect: "Team members show appreciation to one another and avoid sarcasm and put-downs."					
8. Commitment: "Everyone is dedicated to furthering team goals."					
9. Atmosphere: "The climate is such that people are willing to put forth their best effort."					
10. Cohesion: "Team members see themselves as a tight-knit group.					
11. Pride: "People feel good about being a team member."					

APPENDIX 46 Continued

Criteria	Strongly Agree 5	Agree 4	Undecided 3	Disagree 2	Strongly Disagree 1
12. Decisions: "Everyone has the fullest opportunity to participate in decisions that affect the group."					
13. Openness: "Everyone is encouraged to say what is on his/her mind without fear of reprisal."					
14. Trust: "Team members feel that no one in the group will take advantage of them in any way."					
15. Assessment: "The team reviews its own functioning regularly on a frank and open basis."					
16. Identification: "I feel that I am treated as a full member of this team and feel very much part of it."					
17. Leadership: "Our team leader is a key to our effectiveness."					
18. Feedback to leader: "The boss is very open to suggestions about the improvement of his/her performance."					

APPENDIX 47

A RATING SCALE TO ASSESS TEAM COMMUNICATION

Criteria	Strongly Agree 5	Agree 4	Undecided 3	Disagree 2	Strongly Disagree 1
1. Team members listen to each other.					
2. The team leader listens to all group members.					
3. Everyone feels free to level and to be candid with everyone else.					
4. All team members check things out with all concerned before action is taken.					
5. Constructive feedback is given freely to group members to improve their functioning.					
6. Broad participation is strongly encouraged at all group meetings.					
7. No one uses a disproportionate amount of the available "air time" at group meetings.					
8. People are available to secure information needed.					
9. Information is shared willingly and no one hoards information.					
10. Information of interest to team members, such as information on new policies, new projects, and pay, is not categorized as secret.					
11. Information about one's performance is communicated regularly and candidly by the team leader so that there are no surprises at performance review time.					
12. Team members are not afraid to give the boss the "bad news."					
13. We communicate well with other groups in the organization.					

APPENDIX 48

A RATING SCALE TO ASSESS TEAM PROBLEM SOLVING/CREATIVITY

Criteria	Strongly Agree 5	Agree 4	Undecided 3	Disagree 2	Strongly Disagree 1
1. Problems are met head on rather than swept under the rug.					
2. Problems are regarded as challenges and opportunities rather than headaches.					
3. A striving for innovation/creativity is a part of the team's way of life.					
4. Broad participation is a basic tool of team problem solving.					
5. The team's climate encourages concern with the big picture rather than with nitpicking new ideas to death.					
6. Conflict/disagreement are utilized for purposes of creativity and ideation.					
7. Delegation is regarded as a tool for innovation.					
8. The team leader regards the team as a constructive problem-solving force.					
9. As appropriate, problems are solved with the total team on a consensus basis.					
10. Group members present and discuss their ideas rather than defend them.					

APPENDIX 49

MY PERCEPTIONS ABOUT MY BOSS

The following 15 statements describe relationships between you and your boss. For each statement, provide a rating, using a 7-point scale: 1 is low or weak; 7 is very high or strong. The scores will be tallied for the total group so that your boss will receive an average score for each item and an indication of the number of low scores (1's or 2's) and high scores (6's or 7's).

 1._____Shares information about goals, policies, procedures, etc.

 2._____Listens to any ideas I may have.

 3._____Delegates fully so that I can get my job done on my own.

 4._____Involves me in decisions which affect me and my work.

 5._____Uses the team to solve problems and make decisions.

 6._____Encourages innovation and creativity.

 7._____Establishes a climate such that our best efforts are put forth.

 8._____Establishes an attitude of trust.

 9._____Provides praise for a job well done.

10._____Provides support so that I feel good about myself.

11._____Shows confidence in my abilities.

12._____Provides opportunities for my growth and development.

13._____Provides regular feedback about my performance so that I know where
        I stand.

14._____Is approachable and friendly.

15._____Seeks and accepts feedback about his/her behavior.

APPENDIX 49A

THE TRUSTING RELATIONSHIP—HOW I SEE IT IN OUR TEAM

Given below are 19 elements/factors which relate to a high-trust relationship between a boss and his/her team members. Rate them as you see the existing trusting relationship in our team. The scores of all team members on each item will be combined to secure an average and used as a basis for discussion of building trust in our team. A rating of 1 is low and 5 is high. Try to be as candid as you can in your ratings to make this discussion a highly worthwhile activity.

ELEMENT	Never	Rarely	Occasionally	Frequently	Always
1. Behavior is consistent and predictable.					
2. The atmosphere/climate is congenial and supportive.					
3. Feelings are encouraged to be expressed openly.					
4. Help is readily available in the form of coaching and counseling.					
5. Ideas/suggestions are listened to.					
6. A questioning attitude by team members is encouraged.					
7. People are respected as individuals—politeness, courtesy, and consideration are the norm.					
8. Experimentation and risk taking are encouraged.					
9. The information we receive is reliable, accurate, and consistent.					
10. Miscues are taken in stride (as opposed to stressing errors or shortcomings).					
11. Problem solving proceeds on a "win-win" basis (as opposed to making points or besting others).					
12. Consensual decision making is the norm (as opposed to reliance on fiat, coercion, railroading, manipulation, emotional appeals).					
13. People are treated fairly. (There is no playing of favorites.)					

APPENDIX 49A Continued

14. Criticism is given fairly and openly. (There is no "back stabbing," blaming, nit-picking.)					
15. The boss readily admits his/her mistakes or when wrong.					
16. Promises/commitments are kept.					
17. Intimacy—a close, open, comfortable relationship exists with the boss.					
18. The boss "goes to bat" for the team with his superior and with other offices.					
19. Expectations are shared and confidences kept.					

SCORING

For each of the 19 elements add the team's individual scores. For example, if the team has eight (8) members, a low score would be 8 (8 × 1 = 8) and a high score would be 40 (8 × 5 = 40).

APPENDIX   50

A Rating Scale to Assess Effectiveness of Goal Setting

Criteria	Strongly Agree 5	Agree 4	Undecided 3	Disagree 2	Strongly Disagree 1
1. Team members work as a group to set goals that pertain to the total group.					
2. Individual goals are worked through on a mutual basis between the team leader and the appropriate team member.					
3. Our goals are marked by clarity.					
4. Our goals are marked by reasonableness.					
5. We try to introduce a "stretch" element into our goals so that we are constantly upgrading our performance.					
6. We set goals for personal growth and development as well as for the work.					
7. Our goals are revised as new circumstances arise, on a joint basis (leader/group; leader/team leader).					
8. Once goals are agreed upon, everyone concerned is given full authority to execute them (deep delegation).					
9. Progress on established goals is reviewed at least quarterly.					
10. Nonaccomplishment of goals is subject to discussion/critique, not punishment.					
11. Goals are assigned and reviewed for results/accomplishment rather than for details of execution.					
12. Goals are reviewed at year's end to plan the next year's work better as well as to learn what was done.					

APPENDIX 51

TEAM MEMBERSHIP—ARE YOU ON TRACK?

The quiz items which follow are designed to give you a reading on your skills, behavior, and attitudes as a member of your work team. Please be as candid as you can in your responses. Simply enter an "x" in the appropriate box for each statement. Do not sign your name to this quiz. The scoring procedure follows the quiz. You will be given the opportunity to discuss your quiz results with your fellow team members.

A. My feelings about our team	Never	Rarely	Occasionally	Frequently	Always
1. I get all the information I need from my teammates.					
2. My teammates listen to what I have to say.					
3. I get a lot of help from team members.					
4. I appreciate my teammates' work styles, contributions, and attitudes.					
5. Cooperation rather than competition/rivalry is the hallmark of our team.					
6. I trust my teammates to always be honest, to do their best work, and to treat me fairly.					
7. No one on the team will take advantage of me or anyone else, for we have a high-trust group.					
8. Team members are very approachable and friendly.					
9. I receive affection, warmth, recognition, and support from team members.					
10. I feel that I am treated as a full member of the group and feel very much a part of it.					
11. I can be myself in our team.					
12. Team members avoid negative, irritating behaviors such as finger pointing, disrespect, nit-picking, bickering, foot dragging or stonewalling.					

APPENDIX 51 Continued

	Never	Rarely	Occasionally	Frequently	Always
13. My teammates demonstrate that they have a high personal opinion of me.					
14. My relations with the team are such that if I were to leave, I believe the team would miss me.					
B. My Role In The Team					
15. I operate to ensure that I don't let anyone on the team down.					
16. I try to help my teammates resolve their problems in any way that I can.					
17. I pitch in to give help as needed, for I see myself as a team player.					
18. My behavior in the group is interdependent, rather than independent or dependent.					
19. I help my teammates work through disagreement/conflicts with others.					
20. I am patient with my team members.					
21. It is more important to me to get good results than to worry about who on the team gets the credit for them.					
22. If we miss a target or a boo-boo occurs, my concern is to find out why rather than to blame anyone for the unwanted result.					
23. I am open to new approaches, procedures, and ideas advanced by my teammates.					
24. I try to consider what other team members have said before I firm up my own opinion and then express it.					
25. I pay close attention to what team members say, for I want to be a good listener.					

APPENDIX 51 Continued

	Never	Rarely	Occasionally	Frequently	Always
26. I do not interrupt when team members speak.					
27. I treat my team members with respect.					
28. I avoid defensiveness when I am subject to negative feedback (constructive criticism) or questioned about a behavior or attitude of mine.					
29. If the facts so warrant, I can alter my opinion/position.					
30. I am willing to tell others how I feel about issues, problems, progress, and policies.					
31. I discuss and give feedback on our group process, that is, how well we are working as a team.					
32. All of us, including myself, can (and do) "tell it like it is."					
33. I give earned praise (compliments, recognition) to my teammates.					
34. At meetings and problem-solving sessions, I feel my influence is high.					

SCORING PROCEDURE

1. Use a straight edge or a ruler to connect the dots in all the boxes. This will give you a profile of your ratings.
2. If your profile primarily encompasses "Frequently" and "Always," you see yourself as a strong, cooperative team member.
3. If your profile primarily encompasses "Never" and "Rarely," you have a lot of doubts about your team, its members, and team operations.
4. If your ratings do not form an obvious pattern, as described in Items 2 and 3 above, your feelings about your team membership are mixed.
5. In your discussion with team members about your ratings and theirs, try to accomplish two things: (a) explore why differences in ratings exist (assuming they do) and (b) discuss what it would take to improve upon any of the ratings.

APPENDIX 52

MEETING MANAGEMENT

(Circle the appropriate degree for each statement as you have experienced it.)

1. Objectives of our meetings are:	Fuzzy	1	2	3	4	5	6	7	Clear
2. Meeting objectives are reduced to writing wherever helpful:	Rarely	1	2	3	4	5	6	7	Regularly
3. Meetings start on time:	Rarely	1	2	3	4	5	6	7	Always
4. Meetings finish on time:	Rarely	1	2	3	4	5	6	7	Always
5. Time at our meetings is used:	Poorly	1	2	3	4	5	6	7	Extremely well
6. Participation at our meetings is:	Narrow	1	2	3	4	5	6	7	Broad
7. The way members listen to one another is:	Casual	1	2	3	4	5	6	7	Intense
8. Plops (ignoring a member's idea, hence it "plops" to the floor) are rare:	Strongly Disagree	1	2	3	4	5	6	7	Strongly Agree
9. The atmosphere, insofar as it encourages creativity, is:	Dull	1	2	3	4	5	6	7	Exciting
10. Support/encouragement/praise recognition of member contributions is:	Miserly	1	2	3	4	5	6	7	Generous
11. In our meetings we search for solutions, not scapegoats:	Rarely	1	2	3	4	5	6	7	Regularly
12. Meetings produce decisions:	Rarely	1	2	3	4	5	6	7	Regularly
13. Decisions made at meetings are subject to follow-up:	Uncertain	1	2	3	4	5	6	7	Rigorous
14. Evaluation (critique) of how we conduct our meetings is undertaken:	Never	1	2	3	4	5	6	7	Frequently

APPENDIX 53

FEEDBACK—MY SKILL/ATTITUDE PROFILE

Place a dot in one of the five boxes for each element stated below. Then connect the dots. This will give you a profile on your prowess as a feedback giver. Elements graded below 4 are those that indicate more work is needed on your part to become a fully effective giver of feedback.

When I give feedback do I consider these elements?	Strength of skill or attitude				
	1 (LO)	2	3	4	5 (HI)
1. The observed behavior—improvability: Do I consider whether it is something over which the recipient has control? Do I have a reasonable expectation that he/she can change his/her behavior as a result of the feedback?					
2. The observed behavior—specificity: Is my feedback to the other person typically specific rather than general? Based entirely on observed/experienced (hence factual) data?					
3. The observed behavior—verifiability: Is my feedback of the sort that I and others can verify its validity?					
4. My motivation: Am I aware why I am doing this? (To help? To support? To ridicule? To punish? To look smart?)					
5. Nature of my feedback: Does it stress the positive side of things as well as the negative?					
6. Volume: Am I careful to avoid feedback overload? (This element relates to zeroing in on a limited number of critical behaviors as opposed to doling it out on many behaviors.)					
7. Style: Does it tend toward the descriptive or nonevaluative rather than the evaluative or judgmental? (Nonevaluative feedback entails the expression or description of one's feelings: "When you behave this way, I feel . . ." or "When you behave this way, I have difficulty meeting my deadline." Evaluative feedback assesses or comments, usually critically, on the other person's behavior: "You argue all the time at our staff meetings" or "You louse up the total operation by ignoring the deadline you agreed to.")					

APPENDIX 53 Continued

	1	2	3	4	5
8. Empathic aspects: Does my feedback tend to be gentle, caring, friendly, considerate, as opposed to hardhitting, crude, rude?					
9. Timing: Do I consider whether the feedback recipient is ready, interested, and receptive to the feedback?					
10. Locale: Do I consider whether it is best given in a private or public setting (that is, in which place will it work best)?					
11. Impact on receiver: Am I aware of how well it will be understood? Do I consider whether it will create defensiveness or that it might create a "get off my back" reaction?					
12. Understanding: Do I assure myself that the feedback I gave has actually been understood by asking the recipient to restate it? Do I recognize that emotional blocks may interfere with understanding?					
13. The relationship: Do I consider whether giving feedback will improve or weaken the relationship or leave it unchanged? (Will it build bridges or walls?)					
14. Two-way flow: Do I try to elicit feedback on my behavior as opposed to solely giving it to others?					

APPENDIX 54

ADVANCE ASSIGNMENT: MY PROBLEMS ON DELEGATION

Worksheet A

As managers we often find that we want to delegate certain tasks to subordinates, but there are barriers to such attempts. In the space below, list as many reasons as you can why delegation is not always practicable. An example is provided.

1. Reluctance by subordinates to assume more responsibility

2.

3.

4.

5.

6.

7.

8.

9.

10.

APPENDIX 54 Continued

                            Worksheet B

For each of the barriers to delegation you listed in Worksheet A, see if
you can provide a solution to the particular dificulty you identified.

   1. Solution a. Fully explore attitudes involved.

              b. Coach and counsel as necessary.

   2. Solution a.

              b.

   3. Solution a.

              b.

   4. Solution a.

              b.

   5. Solution a.

              b.

   6. Solution a.

              b.

   7. Solution a.

              b.

   8. Solution a.

              b.

   9. Solution a.

              b.

  10. Solution a.

              b.

APPENDIX 55

HELP WANTED/HELP OFFERED

Name _____ Title _____

Department _____ Phone number _____

1. I have these skills and will be glad to give help on them:

   a.

   b.

   c.

   d.

   e.

   f.

2. I can use help on:

   a.

   b.

   c.

   d.

   e.

   f.

APPENDIX 56

Significant Ideas in Film/Video	I Question This...	Ambiguities and Omissions

APPENDIX 57

MONITORING ACTIVE LISTENING—A CHECK LIST

Observe the listening skills of _____ in the film/video. Whenever he/she exhibits an aspect of active listening, check the "Yes" column. When a principle of active listening is ignored or violated, check the "No" column. Your checkmarks should provide a comprehensive pattern of _____'s listening.

Element or behavior	No	Yes	Not Sure
1. Used body language to communicate interest (such as leaning forward).			
2. Used body language to show understanding (for example, head nodding).			
3. Used encouraging words/phrases ("I see," "Uh-huh," "Yes") to encourage free flow of conversation.			
4. Maintained eye contact much of the time.			
5. Used open-ended questions to encourage the other person to expand fully on his/her feelings.			
6. Listened quietly, refraining from interrupting or taking over.			
7. Used the restatement technique to encourage communication.			
8. Sought clarification when statements were not totally clear.			
9. Summarized at various points in the conversation.			

Notes:

APPENDIX   58

PERFORMANCE REVIEW INTERVIEW

Guidesheet for Film/Video Observation

Skill pointers to make a performance appraisal interview effective	Behavior shown in film (cite examples)
Friendly opening—puts employees at ease; establishes rapport.	
Explains purpose of interview at outset.	
Quiet, private setting, no interruptions.	
Goals are reviewed.	
Boss gets down to specifics.	
Boss actively listens to employees (paraphrases, nods head, smiles, says "uh-huh").	
Secures agreement as to accomplishment of each goal.	
Boss uses praise (positive reinforcement).	
Goals are developed for the next year.	

APPENDIX 59

FILM/VIDEO—IMPROVING RESULTS THROUGH TIME MANAGEMENT

Post-Film/Video Discussion Questions

The film suggests that time management is basically "work improvement." What is meant by this?

The film stresses that effective time management in an organization requires the total team to work on it. How do you see this issue?

What ideas on time management does the expert (John Humble) present at the end of the film?

Appendix 60

Film/Video—Peter Drucker—Managing Time

Questions to Aid in Film/Video Viewing and Post-Film/Video Discussion

What behaviors did the company president (Lansing) exhibit that indicated an unawareness of how he was managing his time?

What results might we expect from Lansing's time management practices?

What approaches does Drucker offer for better management of one's time?

APPENDIX 61

ADVICE FROM THE PRESIDENT—RATING SCALE

Using the following key, rate each of the statements below as to your agreement-disagreement with them: a = strongly agree; b = agree; c = neutral; d = disagree; e = strongly disagree. Circle your response.

1. The trainees are showing their immaturity by being so impatient.   a   b   c   d   e

2. The trainees are an ungrateful bunch.   a   b   c   d   e

3. The trainees have put their finger on a real weakness in the program.   a   b   c   d   e

4. The president really gave the training director two problems: the one in the letter and what to do with the president's proposal.   a   b   c   d   e

5. The president's proposal missed the boat. The trainees don't want distance-learning (e-learning) they simply don't want to be overlooked. They want more visibility, more of a chance to keep current and stay sharp.   a   b   c   d   e

6. Distance-learning (e-learning) for managers is probably the poorest way to train them.   a   b   c   d   e

7. The training director's two superiors are "yes men."   a   b   c   d   e

8. The management intern training program is not well understood by those above the training director.   a   b   c   d   e

9. The training program is not well supported by top management.   a   b   c   d   e

10. A task force should be set up to study the training program in all its ramifications.   a   b   c   d   e

The discussion leader will assign you to small groups to discuss your responses. This will be followed by a group-at-large discussion.

Appendix 62

Children-at-Work Case

Worksheet

Now that you have listed the risks and benefits, how would you appraise management's decision? Is it a good one? Is it likely to work?

Would you have handled the problem differently? If so, how and why?

APPENDIX 63

THE COUNTY-WIDE ILLNESS

You are the County Health Officer. Several adults and children have requested treatment at various hospitals in the county for an illness marked by these initial symptoms: listlessness, slight fever and influenza-type aches and pains. Typically, by the third or fourth day an eruption appears on the wrists and ankles.

Provide the answers to the following questions:

1. What is the name of this illness?

2. How is this disease acquired?

3. How soon after contact with the source do symptoms occur?

4. What are the preventive measures people should take to avoid becoming victims to this disease?

    a.

    b.

    c.

    d.

5. What is the appropriate treatment for the disease?

6. As County Health Officer, what should you do to help others from succumbing to this disease?

After you have finished answering the above questions, team up with the person next to you to discuss your answers.

APPENDIX 63 Continued

ANSWER SHEET

1. Rocky Mountain Spotted Fever

2. It is transmitted through the bite of ticks. More specifically, Spotted Fever is caused by an organism called rickettsia. Ticks become infected by biting dogs or wild animals which carry this disease agent. If a tick then bites a human (or an animal) it can transmit the disease. The tick bite is painless and thus can escape detection by the victim.

3. Within 3-10 days.

4. a) Learn to recognize ticks

   b) Know how to remove them. (If attached to the skin, remove very slowly with tweezers. Then touch the bitten area with disinfectant or iodine.)

   c) Inspect children and pets daily for bites.

   d) Avoid tick-infested locations. (They usually inhabit woody and bushy areas.)

5. The disease usually responds to antibiotics, if administered early. Vaccine is recommended only for those who must frequent infected areas and are subject to constant exposure to ticks. The vaccine must be repeated annually to be effective.

6. Issue a warning to all rural and suburban residents, vacationers, picnickers, campers, sportsmen, etc. to be on guard against tick bites. Cite the nature of the initial symptoms so that victims will promptly report for treatment.

APPENDIX 64

INCREASED PRODUCTIVITY—HOW CAN IT BE DONE

Organizations (and supervisors) are very much concerned about augmenting productivity. In the space below, list as many methods and techniques as you can to accomplish this. Remember, the only limits are those that you impose upon yourself. So let you imagination soar!

1.	21.
2.	22.
3.	23.
4.	24.
5.	25.
6.	26.
7.	27.
8.	28.
9.	29.
10.	30.
11.	31.
12.	32.
13.	33.
14.	34.
15.	35.
16.	36.
17.	37.
18.	38.
19.	39.
20.	40.

APPENDIX 65

QUESTION REQUEST FORM

For the session on_____to be

held on_____

1. I have the following question:

2. My interest in this question is due to (or based upon):

APPENDIX 66

OPINIONNAIRE—HOW I FEEL ABOUT THIS COURSE

This form is designed to learn about your feelings toward various aspects of the course you have just completed. Check the appropriate picture to indicate the degree of satisfaction you wish to express for each item. Your feedback will help us to develop a more effective course for future participants. Added written comments may be given on the reverse side of the page.

1. Length of course
   Comment:

2. Content (subject matter)
   Comment:

3. Pre-work
   Comment:

4. Talks/lecturette
   Comment:

5. Films and discussion
   Comment:

6. Small group work
   Comment:

7. Exercises/games
   Comment:

APPENDIX 66 Continued

8. Handouts
    Comment:

9. Evening sessions
    Comment:

10. Outside resource people
    Comment:

11. Training staff
    Comment:

12. Organization of course
    Comment:

13. Physical facilities
    Comment:

14. Overall benefit from course
    Comment:

15. How other participants might react
    to this course
    Comment:

16. Additional comments:

APPENDIX 67

END-OF-COURSE REACTIONNAIRE

What I learned most in the course was

What I still need to learn more of is

What I will have difficulty in applying is

My overall feelings about the course are

If I were asked by a close friend how I saw this course, I would say

APPENDIX 68

Communicating the Program to Others

You now have been through most (or all) of the program. You should have a pretty good idea of its major components and possible benefits to participants. Assume that you wish to explain the program to your colleagues (or to field personnel or to the key personnel of another plant or office) so that they, too, will be motivated to attend. Jot down several key reasons why their attendance might be beneficial to them. You will have a chance to present your talk containing those ideas to the total group (three minutes).

APPENDIX 69

DAILY SELF-ASSESSMENT OF LEARNING

1. As a result of today's training, I now realize that I have a need for

   A.

   B.

   C.

2. I see meeting these needs by taking these action steps:

   For Need A I will

   For Need B I will

   For need C I will

APPENDIX   70

What Might Have Made the
Session More Effective?
(Please Be Specific)

1.

2.

3.

What Concerns Do You
Have About the Session?
(Please Be Specific)

1.

2.

3.

What Did You Like
About Today's Session?
(Please Be Specific)

1.

2.

3.

APPENDIX 71

DAILY END-OF-SESSION QUESTIONNAIRE

1. Please rate today's activities on the scales below. The data will be summarized and reported back to you at tomorrow's meeting.

Activity:

1. Talk on_____

1	2	3	4	5	6	7	8	9	10
LO									HI

2. Small group work on_____

1	2	3	4	5	6	7	8	9	10
LO									HI

3. Exercise on_____

1	2	3	4	5	6	7	8	9	10
LO									HI

4. Film on_____

1	2	3	4	5	6	7	8	9	10
LO									HI

5. Role play on_____

1	2	3	4	5	6	7	8	9	10
LO									HI

6. Simulation on_____

1	2	3	4	5	6	7	8	9	10
LO									HI

2. My overall reaction to the day's training is

3. The training could be made more effective by

APPENDIX   72

SUPERVISOR-SUBORDINATE PERCEPTIONS

A. List the areas or ways in which your subordinates could improve or
   strengthen their communication with you:

   1.

   2.

   3.

   4.

B. List the ways your subordinates might feel you could improve your communication with them:

   1.

   2.

   3.

   4.

C. List actions you can take to overcome the communication deficits you
   listed in A above:

   1.

   2.

   3.

   4.

D. List actions you can take to overcome the communication deficits you
   listed in B above:

   1.

   2.

   3.

   4.

(Note to trainer: Similar lists could be developed on other subjects: for
example, delegation practices—what I delegate well vs. what subordinates
might expect of me in the way of delegation; motivation—what turns me on
vs. what motivates my subordinates; performance appraisal—the problems I
see in it vs. the problems my employees may see.)

APPENDIX 73

PROBLEM SOLVING AND DECISION MAKING

Step 1. Problem definiton:

Step 2. Main facts bearing on problem resolution:

Step 3. Possible solutions (options) to problem resolution:

     A.

     B.

     C.

     D.

Step 4. Evaluation of alternatives:

     Solution A:

     Pros:

     Cons:

     (Continue this process—pros and cons—for each possible solution.)

Step 5. Selection of solution (also explain why this one was chosen):

Step 6. Implementation (planning for action):

     Who is to be notified of the decision?

     What are the action steps for implementation?

     1.

     2.

     3.

     4.

     Who is to assume responsibility for

     Action Step 1?

     Action Step 2?

     Action Step 3?

     Action Step 4?

Step 7. How will this plan, when completed, be evaluated? (How will we know when the need has been met?)

APPENDIX   74

PROBLEMS AND ACTION PLANS

Form A—Overcoming Communication Problems

Problem	Action Plan

Form B—Overcoming Communication Problems

Problem	Causative Factors	Action Plan

APPENDIX 74 Continued

Form C—Overcoming Communication Problems				
Problem	Causative Factors	Action Plan	Forces Favorable to Action Plan	Possible Resistance Points

APPENDIX 75

PERFORMANCE IMPROVEMENT ANALYSIS

Name of Employee_____

Part A

Analysis of Current Performance

Employee Exceeds Standards in These Duties	Employee Meets Standards in These Duties	Employee Is Below Standards in These Duties
1.	1.	1.
2.	2.	2.
3.	3.	3.
4.	4.	4.

Part B

Employee Performs These Duties Below Standard	Agreed-Upon Plan to Help Employee Meet Standard
1.	1.
2.	2.
3.	3.
4.	4.

APPENDIX 76

TIME WASTERS

Part I

Time Wasters I Encounter in My Work	Frequency (Infrequently-I; Often-O; Regularly-R)	Severity (Low, Medium, or High)	Degree Controllable (None-N; Some-what-S; Consider-able-C; Total-T)

Part II

List Time Wasters You Rated C or T	Action to Be Taken to Correct Condition

APPENDIX 76 Continued

Part III

Candidly list the things you may do that waste the time of others; then
indicate necessary corrective action.

Using the Time of Others

Ways in Which I Waste Time of Others	Procedure to Overcome Such Activities
1.	1.
2.	2.
3.	3.
4.	4.
5.	5.

APPENDIX 77

TIME AND YOUR SUBORDINATES

Bosses often get trapped into doing their subordinates' work for them. Check the rating form below to indicate the way you deal with such efforts by staff members. Enter dots in the boxes on the left side if you rarely engage in the practices cited and on the right side if you typically perform them. Then connect the dots for a profile on your skill in securing completed staff work.

Practice	1 (Rarely)	2	3	4	5 (Typically)
1. When subordinates ask: "What do I do on this?" I reply: "What do you recommend?" rather than tell them what to do.					
2. When memos, reports, or letters prepared for my signature require editing, I return such items for rewriting rather than try to clean them up myself.					
3. I encourage submission of final copy rather than rough drafts.					
4. I insist that subordinates meet deadlines on reports and projects so that I don't get caught up in a crisis situation and have to pick up the pieces.					
5. I insist that my subordinates present their proposals in complete form so that all I need do is indicate approval or disapproval.					

APPENDIX 78

TIME AND YOUR MEETINGS

Meetings are notorious for their tendency to waste participants' time. Please complete the three columns below. They should help you to deal with problems at meetings.

Meetings I have attended in the last 60 days (Consider staff meetings, your own, your boss' committee meetings, special meetings, task forces)	Two of the Most Severe Problems I Noted at These Meetings	Action I Can Take to Overcome or Reduce the Frequency or Severity of the Problems
1.	a. b.	
2.	a. b.	
3.	a. b.	
4.	a. b.	
5.	a. b.	
6.	a. b.	
7.	a. b.	

APPENDIX 79

TIME AND YOUR BOSS

If I were to ask my boss: "What do I now do that uses your time unnecessarily?" he/she would probably reply

1.

2.

3.

4.

5.

If I were to ask my boss: "What extra things might I do to conserve your time?" he/she would say

1.

2.

3.

4.

5.

Note to participants: Consider discussing this guidesheet with your boss after you return to the job.

APPENDIX 80

TIME AND YOUR SECRETARY

A versatile and competent secretary is a key to the effective use of managerial time. List below the ways in which he/she can help you to save time. (Some examples: fielding of phone calls; following up on work assignments to staff; arranging meetings.)

Note: Secretarial dissatisfaction and turnover are often related to the fact that their bosses do not give them adequate responsibility.

1.

2.

3.

4.

5.

6.

7.

8.

9.

10.

11.

12.

13.

14.

15.

16.

17.

18.

19.

20.

APPENDIX 81

DELEGATION PLANNING GUIDE

Major Responsibilities	Not Delegable at All (State why)	Delegable Now (Check)	Delegable with Added Training of Staff (Check)
1.			
2.			
3.			
4.			
5.			
6.			
7.			

Minor Responsibilities			
1.			
2.			
3.			
4.			
5.			
6.			
7.			

APPENDIX   82

HAZARD IDENTIFICATION AND CONTROL

Now that you have completed the course on safety, here is a practical assignment to help you apply what you have learned.

I. Individual work

Analyze two jobs in your unit as to (1) hazards that may exist in them and (2) appropriate safety procedures essential to controlling these hazards. (30 minutes)

Hazard Potential and Control			
Job A	Principal Tasks	Possible Hazards	Accident Control Measures
1.			
2.			
3.			
4.			
Job B	Principal Tasks	Possible Hazards	Accident Control Measures
1.			
2.			
3.			
4.			
5.			

II. Small group work

In teams of three, review and discuss each job analysis, offering suggestions to one another to strengthen the proposed accident control procedures. Each presenter will have 20 minutes to present his/her plan and to receive feedback and help on it from the other two team members.

III. Group-at-large-discussion

After your trio has completed its work, your trainer will hold a general discussion about it: What was learned? How helpful were the helpers? Is it easy to help others on their plans?

APPENDIX 83

COMMITMENT TO MYSELF

End of Session Plan for Action

Based on the learnings from the session (or training day) just completed, I intend to do more of the following:

I intend to do less of the following:

I intend to continue doing the following:

APPENDIX 84

POST SESSION ACTION PLAN

Key Points of Session	Key Points Applicable to My Development Needs (Check)	Action I Intend to Take
1.	1.	1.
2.	2.	2.
3.	3.	3.
4.	4.	4.
5.	5.	5.
6.	6.	6.
7.	7.	7.

APPENDIX 85

ACTION PLAN

My Needs for Improvement	My Plans for Improvement	Quarterly Follow-up (Add comments)	
		First Quarter	Second Quarter
1.			
2.			
3.			

APPENDIX 86

CONTRACT WITH MYSELF

My major area (opportunity or need) for growth is

My action plan related to the above is

APPENDIX 87

APPLICATION SESSION
RELATING COURSE LEARNINGS TO ON-THE-JOB PROBLEMS

I. Purpose

The final phase of this program is designed to give you an opportunity to apply the concepts and skills that you have learned to an actual on-the-job problem of your choice. This should provide real and lasting meaning to your training experience. It will also provide you with a maximum return from your investment of time and effort in the class-room.

II. Procedure

A. Select a topic about which you have genuine concern, that is, a problem area that requires some worthwhile improvement or remedial action. The problem may relate to a management concern, an operational matter, an administrative change, a plan for self-improvement, an improvement in relations with others (boss, subordinates, peers), etc. It may involve overcoming a deficiency or meeting a new challenge or opportunity. You alone know where a real need for change or betterment exists.

B. Individual work (60 minutes): Use the three-part Application Worksheet to help you work through the details of your problem-solving activity.

C. Small group work (60 minutes): You will be assigned to a team of three (two other participants and yourself). Each of you will have the opportunity to present your problem and plan for action to the other two members for review, critique, feedback, and counsel. Each presenter will have 20 minutes to secure help from the other two participants. Remember that although this is your problem, objective "outsiders" can be of real help, because they may see things that you, because of your immediate involvement, have overlooked. As a minimum, they will help sharpen the issues for you and make you more fully think through the realism of your action plan.

APPENDIX 87 Continued

<pre>
                    Application Worksheet

I. Defining my problem

    1. I have carefully reviewed my "back-home" situation, and the problem
       area I would like to see improved relates to

    2. I am concerned about the above stated problem because

    3. The major facts that relate to my problem are these:

II. Seeking a solution

    1. The elements of my problem most amenable to change are

    2. The elements of my problem least amenable to change are

    3. I would use these indicators to consider the problem satisfactorily
       resolved:
</pre>

APPENDIX 87 Continued

4. The forces that I see as unfavorable to (blocking) the hoped-for change are

5. The forces I see as favoring (supporting) the change are

6. The solution I see to my problem is

III. An action plan to implement my solution

1. I see the time frame for the plan to be operative as follows:

2. I will need the assistance of these individuals to implement the plan:

   Name_____ Task_____

   Name_____ Task_____

   Name_____ Task_____

   Name_____ Task_____

3. I will need to communicate the plan to

   Name_____ About_____

   Name_____ About_____

   Name_____ About_____

   Name_____ About_____

4. I intend to follow up and evaluate the success of the plan by doing the following:

APPENDIX   88

SUPERVISORY EXPECTATIONS OF RESULTS/OUTCOMES OF A TRAINING COURSE TAKEN BY A SUBORDINATE

NAME OF TRAINEE: _____

TITLE OF COURSE: _____

DATE(S) OF COURSE: _____

I. My expectations, as to results/outcomes of the above-referenced training

   for trainee _____, are as follows:

   A. SKILL: _____

   _____

   _____

   B. KNOWLEDGE: _____

   _____

   _____

   C. ATTITUDES: _____

   _____

   _____

II. ACTION PLAN: Please provide this form to trainee as an aid to developing
    his/her action plan. A copy of the completed action plan should be
    returned to me for my follow-up.

Signature: _____ Title:_____

Date: _____

APPENDIX 89

TIME SAVINGS

As a result of my participation in the training program, I estimate my weekly time savings to be _____ hours per week.

This time saving has principally come from

The time I have saved has enabled me to

APPENDIX 90

TIME-THIEF ANALYSIS

Based on all the work I have done on time management, both in and out of class, I would say my most serious time robber right now is

Time-wise I would say this time theft adds up to_____hours_____ minutes per week.

Two possible ways to cut down on that time loss are

1.

2.

APPENDIX 91

MY COMMUNICATION SKILL

A Self Appraisal

Use the following rating scale to rate your communication attitudes/behaviors at various time intervals in relation to this training program: 1-rarely; 2-occasionally; 3-somewhat frequently; 4-frequently; 5-regularly or usually.

Element	Prior to Training Session	At End of Training Session	60-Day Follow-Up	120-Day Follow-Up
1. I understand that my frame of reference is not necessarily that of the receiver of my message.				
2. I recognize that the receiver may interpret a message differently because of his/her attitudes, values, experience, or needs.				
3. I recognize that the meaning of a message is in the receiver, not in the message.				
4. To ensure that my message is fully understood, I ask the receiver to restate it (elicit feedback).				
5. I restate things to the other person so he/she knows that I understood what was said to me("You are saying that...").				
6. I accept responsibility for a message of mine that is misinterpreted by the receiver.				
7. When listening to someone else I try to "tune in" for feelings as well as facts.				
8. I try to avoid the use of emotional words, those that may irritate or inflame the other person.				

APPENDIX 91 Continued

Element	Prior to Training Session	At End of Training Session	60-Day Follow-Up	120-Day Follow-Up
9. I recognize when others are communicating a fact, an assumption, or a value judgment.				
10. I recognize when I am communicating a fact, an assumption, or a value judgment.				
11. I try to state things in a tentative way so that others are drawn into the communication effort.				
12. I pay attention to the body language of those communicating to me.				
13. I am aware of the congruency between my nonverbal behavior and my verbal communication.				
14. I use full eye contact when communicating with others.				
15. I maintain warm, friendly relations with others to aid communication with them.				
16. I use praise freely so as to get closer to people, thereby aiding communication with them.				
17. I try to level with others so as to ensure authentic communication.				
18. My employees are willing to speak freely to me, to question my decisions, to give me bad news, to debate an issue fully, etc.				
19. I recognize that my status as a supervisor/manager may inhibit communication with me.				

APPENDIX 92

SURVEY OF NEEDS FOR PROPOSED COMMUNICATIONS, COACHING, COUNSELING COURSE

For each topic below, please circle the number that best expresses your need for it. (Number 1 is low and 5 is high.)

Improving communication with subordinates	1	2	3	4	5
Improving communication with peers	1	2	3	4	5
Improving communication with the boss	1	2	3	4	5
Conducting the appraisal interview	1	2	3	4	5
Counseling a problem employee	1	2	3	4	5
Counseling for career development and planning	1	2	3	4	5
Improving assertiveness skills	1	2	3	4	5
Coaching for improved performance	1	2	3	4	5
Improving listening skills	1	2	3	4	5
Dealing with my anger	1	2	3	4	5
Improving effectiveness of group meetings	1	2	3	4	5

Note to trainer: The items in the above list could merely be checked off by participants. However, this procedure would not provide us with data on strength or depth of need.

APPENDIX 93

QUESTIONNAIRE REGARDING SUPERVISORY TRAINING NEEDS

Rate each item below as to its potential to strengthen your skill as a supervisor.

Skill Area	1 (least)	2	3	4	5 (most)
COMMUNICATION					
Listening					
Interpreting nonverbal messages					
Persuading others					
Delivering talks					
Negotiating agreements in conflict situations					
Leading meetings					
Getting my message across					
Selling my boss on a idea					
MOTIVATION					
Helping people to be more creative					
Creating more cooperative attitudes					
Encouraging more self-starting					
Giving praise/recognition					
PLANNING AND ORGANIZING					
Time management					
Delegation					
Setting/revising priorities					
Assigning work					
Dealing with the unexpected (crisis management)					
ADMINISTRATION					
Budget preparation					
Report preparation					
Records management					
Accounting					
Cost control					
Procurement procedures					
PERSONNEL MANAGEMENT					
EEO					
Writing job descriptions					
Interviewing job applicants					
Appraising performance					
Disciplinary procedures					
Orienting a new worker					

APPENDIX 94

MEMORANDUM

August 8

TO: All Supervisors, BWPSC
FROM: HRD Office
SUBJECT: Organization-Wide Supervisory Training Program
Response due: Aug. 30

As you know, the Best Widget Products and Services Corp. is about to launch a supervisory training program. Its purpose is to assist you to do your job, as a supervisor, more effectively. Your ideas as to your developmental needs will ensure that the training program is of maximum benefit to you. Please complete the form below.

It is not necessary to sign your name on the form since we are endeavoring to learn of group needs, in general, which can be used to plan the overall training course.

1. The most pressing/difficult problems I face today are

2. My skill as a supervisor could be helped by training in

3. I could become more effective as a supervisor if I received information/knowledge about

4. What would really make the supervisory training course effective/helpful to me is (are)

APPENDIX 95

SURVEY OF NEEDS

Please list below the topics you wish to have covered in the course. Your number one listing is the most important to you. Your number ten is the least important to you.

1.

2.

3.

4.

5.

6.

6.

7.

8.

9.

10.

APPENDIX 96

SELF-DEVELOPMENT—A CHECK LIST FOR TRAINERS

Course or program	For my background or orientation (to keep up with my field)	For my personal growth (self-development)	To develop expertise to introduce the program into my organization
Assertiveness training			
Assessment center			
Behavior modeling			
Behavior objectives			
Behavior modifi-cation			
Career planning			
Change (introducing it, managing it)			
Communication			
Coaching			
Competency-based education			
Conflict management (intergroup relations)			
Counseling			
Creativity			
Cross-cultural training			
Diversity training			
Experiential learning			
Equal Employment Opportunity			
Group dynamics			
Guided Imagery			
Internal consultant			
Interpersonal skills			

APPENDIX 96 Continued

Course or program	For my background or orientation (to keep up with my field)	For my personal growth (self-development)	To develop expertise to introduce the program into my organization
Life planning			
Management by objectives			
Managerial grid			
Matrix management			
Models for management			
Negotiation skills			
Neuro-linguistic programming			
Nonverbal communication			
Organization development			
Problem solving			
Quality circles			
Quality of work life			
Stress management			
Systems theory			
T-group (sensitivity training)			
Team building			
Time management			
Transactional analysis (TA)			
Values clarification			
Women in management			
Other_____			
Other_____			

APPENDIX 97

UTILIZING INSTRUMENT LEARNINGS FOR CHANGE—MY ACTION PLAN

Now that you have completed your discussion of the data you produced on the instrument (self-quiz), you will wish to capitalize on your learnings from it. You can do this by carefully completing the action plan below.

1. My principal learnings from the instrument are the following:

a.

b.

c.

2. In light of the above (item 1), I plan to do the following more often:

a.

b.

c.

3. In light of the above, I intend to do the following less often:

a.

b.

c.

4. I see these possible roadblocks to accomplishing these changes:

a.

b.

c.

5. I can overcome these barriers to change by doing the following:

a.

b.

c.

Index